AUDITING

AUDITING

THEORY AND PRACTICE

C. William Thomas
Hankamer School of Business
Baylor University

Emerson O. Henke
J. E. Bush Distinguished Professor of Accounting
Hankamer School of Business
Baylor University

KENT PUBLISHING COMPANY
A Division of Wadsworth, Inc.
Boston, Massachusetts

KENT PUBLISHING COMPANY
A Division of Wadsworth, Inc.

Senior Editor: David S. McEttrick
Production Editor: Sarah Evans
Interior Designer: Carol Rose
Cover Designer: Carol Rose
Production Coordinator: Linda Siegrist

Printed in the United States of America

1 2 3 4 5 6 7 8 9—87 86 85 84 83

LIBRARY OF CONGRESS CATALOGING IN PUBLICATION DATA

Thomas, C. William.
Auditing: theory and practice.

Includes index.
1. Auditing. I. Henke, Emerson O. II. Title.
HF5667.T45 1983 657'.45 82-21262
ISBN 0-534-01388-0

PREFACE

General Overview

Auditing: Theory and Practice is designed primarily for use in an introductory undergraduate auditing course. This text covers the subject of auditing with an optimum blend of theory and application. It is divided into four logically sequenced parts.

Part One introduces the student to the services provided by the accounting profession, including tax and management advisory services, and to the discipline of auditing. This includes a discussion of the requirements that must be met to comply with the three general standards of generally accepted auditing standards (GAAS).

Part Two ("Audit Field Work") develops the auditor's general approach to complying with the three standards of field work and introduces computer audit and statistical sampling tools. Part Three ("Development of Audit Procedures") explains how the internal control and evidence standards are met as the auditor verifies the accounting procedures followed and the account balances included in each of the accounting subsystems. This part follows a transaction cycle approach. Each chapter in this part presents an overview of the cycle, the audit objectives, the compliance and substantive tests, and the use of electronic data processing (EDP).

Part Four ("Reporting the Results of the Audit") explains how the auditor meets the requirements of the reporting standards and describes the ethical and legal responsibilities of the accountant engaged in public accounting work.

Auditing: Theory and Practice is organized to deal in a comprehensive manner with what the auditor has to do to comply with generally accepted auditing standards. Each chapter is supplemented with extensive questions, cases, and problems (including multiple choice questions from past AICPA examinations) that can be used to enlarge the student's understanding of the chapter. Many appendixes, including illustrative working papers from an actual audit, are also included for use as reference materials.

Specific Features

- The text provides comprehensive coverage of the independent audit with an effective blending of theory and practice. Governmental auditing and internal auditing are also discussed and compared with the independent audit.
- Ethics and legal liability are introduced briefly in Chapter 2, where the importance of these issues is highlighted, and are reinforced in Parts Two and Three. Detailed coverage of ethics and legal liability is then presented and summarized in Chapters 20 and 21, respectively.
- Chapter 5 ("Study and Evaluation of Internal Control") introduces the student to the procedures followed in evaluating internal control, with particular emphasis on the SEADOC (Systems Evaluation Approach: Documentation of Controls) approach developed and used by Peat, Marwick, Mitchell & Co.
- Chapter 7 ("The Computer as an Audit Tool") introduces the student to the use of the computer in performing an audit. It includes an illustration of the ways in which the Arthur Andersen and Company AUDEX software package is used by that firm in the performance of an audit.
- EDP auditing and statistical sampling are introduced in Part Two as *general* audit field work tools, and are then used as appropriate in the discussion of audit procedures throughout Part Three.
- Part Three takes a transaction cycle approach and covers both compliance and substantive tests, as well as EDP ramifications for each of the subsystems. The organization ensures a clear, complete presentation.
- A uniform set of audit working papers is presented in appendixes to Chapters 10–16. These were adapted in simplified form from an actual audit, and make it easier for the instructor to illustrate (and for the student to understand) how the various working papers form an integrated body of evidence.
- Auditing of nonprofit organizations (Chapter 17) receives unique, full-chapter coverage in light of the increased attention this little-known area is getting in AACSB Accounting Accreditation guidelines and in actual practice.
- A large number of multiple choice questions adapted from professional certification examinations have been included with most chapters. These questions are particularly useful in assuring comprehensive coverage and for exam preparation. When used with the diagnostic comments included in the *Solutions Manual*, these questions can be particularly effective for use in classroom discussion.

Acknowledgments

We are indebted to a number of organizations, several of the major accounting firms, and a number of people for their assistance in producing this text. More specifically, we acknowledge the American Institute of Certified Public Accountants for permission to quote extensively from Statements on Auditing Standards, the Code of Professional Ethics, Uniform CPA Examinations, and other publications. We are also indebted to the Institute of Internal Auditors for permitting us to use certain of their materials, including problems from past CIA Examinations. The U.S. General Accounting Office has permitted us to quote from the publication that sets out generally accepted auditing standards for that organization. We also wish to acknowledge the significant contributions of Peat, Marwick, Mitchell & Co., Arthur Andersen and Company, Deloitte Haskins & Sells, Ernst & Whinney, and Touche Ross & Co., who allowed us to use certain materials from firm publications.

We wish to express our appreciation to Mrs. Evelyn Hupp and Peggy A. Curry for their untiring work in typing and retyping the manuscript as the book was being produced.

We are also greatly indebted to the following reviewers for their helpful criticisms and suggestions:

John A. Beegle
Western Carolina University

William Felix
University of Washington, Seattle

William K. Grollman
Seidman and Seidman, New York

John Y. Lee
California State University

William J. Morris
North Texas State University

William E. Perry
William E. Perry Enterprises, Inc.

Gerald Smith
University of Nebraska at Omaha

John A. Tracy
University of Colorado

Finally, the encouragement and support of our wives, Mary Ann and Be, are gratefully and lovingly acknowledged.

CONTENTS

PART ONE
Introduction

PART TWO

Audit Field Work

5 Study and Evaluation of Internal Control 158

6 Electronic Data Processing and Internal Controls 208

7 The Computer as an Audit Tool 274

PART THREE

Development of Audit Procedures

AUDITING

PART ONE

INTRODUCTION

CHAPTER

1

THE ACCOUNTING PROFESSION

We live in a society characterized by large and complex corporate entities whose resources depend to a large extent on public investments in stocks and bonds. In such a setting, it is necessary to report the results of economic activities to interested parties; ***accounting*** is the language used in this reporting process. In this book we are primarily concerned with the work of the ***auditor*** — a specific kind of accountant who examines and verifies reports of economic activities to determine whether those reports conform to the generally accepted guidelines for their presentation.

A ***profession*** is generally defined as an occupation that requires formal education and training and that involves public trust. Accounting has long been recognized as meeting those criteria. Professional accountants are employed both by entities reporting economic activities and by various investigative governmental agencies. They may also offer their services to the general public; in this case, they are appropriately called "public accountants." Our discussion in this chapter covers the following aspects of professional accounting:

1. The audit — its general nature and definition.
2. Audit services performed by internal auditors.
3. Audit services performed by Government Accounting Office (GAO) auditors.
4. Nonaudit services performed by certified public accountants.
5. Independent audits, the most important service provided by certified public accountants.
6. Professional organizations that influence the work of accountants.

We also include, as appendixes to this chapter, summaries of the general provisions included in the standards for the practice of internal auditing, General Accounting Office audit standards, AICPA tax practice standards, management advisory services standards, and accounting and review standards.

THE NATURE OF AN AUDIT

Auditing is a process in which one person verifies the assertions of another. To be effective, an audit must be based on a sound and logical conceptual foundation, which must entail a thorough understanding of what the term means and the circumstances in which the audit process is applied.

A committee of the American Accounting Association (AAA) has broadly defined auditing as

> a systematic process of objectively obtaining and evaluating evidence regarding assertions about economic actions and events to ascertain the degree of correspondence between those assertions and established criteria and communicating the results to interested users.[1]

This definition is broad enough to encompass all the different types of auditing — such as internal audits performed by the employees of business entities, governmental audits performed by employees of the general accounting office, and independent audits performed by public accounting firms. The first two of these are described in the following pages. The third, the independent audit, is the primary concern of this text. It is introduced in this chapter and described and illustrated throughout the remainder of the text.

The AAA definition describes the audit as a systematic process. Therefore, it is made up of a series of well-planned procedures based on a sound conceptual framework, and will include appropriate audit standards and objectives. We describe the standards and objectives associated with internal auditing and governmental auditing later in this chapter, while those associated with an independent audit are discussed in Chapter 2.

The phrase "objectively obtaining and evaluating evidence" explains the very nature of the auditing process. The evidence-gathering process should be, above all else, objective — that is, not subject to the biases of the observer. The evidence itself may possess varying degrees of objectivity, but the auditor must retain an objective mental attitude throughout the evidence-gathering and evaluating stages of the audit.

Another phrase, "assertions about economic actions and events," suggests that the audit can involve an examination not only of the information presented in financial statements, but also of the information system and the accounting process from which the financial data were derived. This includes the system of internal control. The word *economic* may be interpreted to include any situation in which a choice must be made involving the allocation of scarce resources. For example, internal auditors will be concerned with economic assertions relating to the internal activities of the enterprise, whereas governmental auditors will be concerned with whether a government agency has operated within the regulations under which it was created or whether a private concern has complied with terms of a government contract.

The "established criteria" against which economic assertions are evaluated must be, to a large degree, uniform and mutually understandable by both preparer and user groups. For independent audits and external reporting, established criteria are commonly referred to as ***generally accepted accounting principles*** (GAAP). The conceptual basis underlying these principles is discussed in Chapter 2. There are also well-defined bases of accounting other than GAAP that may serve as acceptable criteria against which assertions can be evaluated. For the governmental audit, established criteria may consist of rules and regulations within which the entity operates. For internal audits, the criteria may be budgets or other standards of efficiency and effectiveness established by managerial policy of the company.

"Communicating the results to interested users" involves the preparation of the audit report. The audit report is the device used to communicate the results of the auditor's examination. Format and content of audit reports vary with the type of audit involved and the circumstances under which the report is issued. In this text we are primarily concerned with the independent auditor's report described briefly in this chapter and discussed more completely in Part Four of the text.

THE INTERNAL AUDIT

Within an economic entity, management is always concerned with the extent to which employees are adhering to its policies and directives and with the efficiency of operations and effectiveness of the recordkeeping system. Accountants employed for the purpose of evaluating internal operations and recordkeeping activities are called ***internal auditors.*** Such people are, in effect, extensions of the arm of management employed for the purpose of verifying what other key employees are doing and evaluating the efficiency and effectiveness of their work.

Internal auditors are employees of the company being audited. To be effective, however, they should be members of an autonomous group that answers directly to an upper level officer or authoritative group of the company. They are expected to evaluate performance, effectiveness, and compliance of various activities and departments against prescribed managerial policies.

The ***operational audit*** is generally an element of the internal audit function that can apply to almost any aspect of a company's operations. Such audits may also occasionally be performed by independent accountants. Its primary objective is to improve operations by suggesting more efficient operating procedures and by forcing compliance with managerial directives. The operational audit should help the company to achieve the following benefits:

- More accurate and timely operating information.
- Compliance with stated policies, plans, procedures, laws, and regulations.
- The security of having its assets safeguarded against misuse.
- More economic and efficient use of resources.
- More effectiveness in accomplishing its established objectives and goals.

This type of audit includes an appraisal of the efficiency with which both human and physical resources have been used: the findings are reported in the form of evaluations of present practices and recommendations of changes in those practices.

The Institute of Internal Auditors (IIA) makes it possible for an auditor to be licensed as a certified internal auditor (CIA) if she or he passes a qualifying examination. Although this is a desired credential for internal auditors, it is not a prerequisite for performing the internal audit function. In addition, the IIA has developed standards for the practice of internal auditing. These are summarized in Appendix 1–A at the end of this chapter.

THE GENERAL ACCOUNTING OFFICE (GAO) AUDIT

The General Accounting Office is the accounting, auditing, and investigating entity of the U.S. Congress. It is this agency's job to conduct audits of financial reports and activities of other governmental agencies as well as to review their compliance with applicable laws and regulations. Efficiency and economy of operation and effectiveness in achieving desired results from particular governmental programs are also evaluated.

The GAO has used the term ***comprehensive auditing*** to describe its audit process. A GAO auditor is charged with the responsibility of ascertaining that financial reports are fairly stated, but he or she has these duties in addition:

- The auditor must be sure that the entity has complied with applicable laws and regulations.
- The auditor must determine that the entity is managing or utilizing its resources (including budgeted financial resources, space, personnel, supplies, etc.) in an economical and efficient manner and that causes of inefficiencies or uneconomical practices are promptly reported.
- The auditor must find out whether the desired results or benefits of the governmental program are being achieved, and whether the intended legislative purpose of the program has been considered.

Standards for audits of governmental agencies have evolved over the past fifty years. They reflect a desire of the United States Congress to have a periodic, comprehensive evaluation of the operations of these entities. The GAO audit standards are summarized and discussed in Appendix 1–B.

NONAUDIT PROFESSIONAL SERVICES PROVIDED BY THE CPA

There are approximately 20,000 firms of certified public accountants operating within the United States. Of these, there are eight firms, commonly known as the Big Eight, which as a group bill the majority of professional fees. These firms have offices in all the major cities across the country and in many foreign countries. The size of an individual office may range from less than twenty to more than 1,000 professional accountants. There are also other multiple office firms refered to as international firms, because they, like the Big Eight, have offices throughout the world. In addition there are a few hundred large local and regional firms with professional staffs in excess of fifty people. However, that still leaves more than 95 percent of all CPA firms in the United States having single offices with fewer than twenty-five professional staff members. All these firms provide a variety of services in addition to auditing. These include the following:

- Tax services.
- Management advisory services.
- Small business services.

Tax Services

Because income taxes are so directly related to the accounting data, tax services constitute an important part of the total services performed by CPA firms. These range from the preparation of tax returns of all types to providing tax advice and tax planning services. Some firms and individual CPAs may specialize in tax services to the extent that these services compose the majority of the firm's billings. The AICPA (the American Institute of Certified Public Accountants) has established the Committee on Responsibilities and Tax Practice, as well as the Federal Taxation Executive Committee, to monitor the tax practice of certified public accountants. These bodies have issued statements defining the accountant's responsibilities in tax practice, which serve as qualitative guidelines for rendering tax services. These statements are summarized in Appendix 1–C.

Management Advisory Services

The CPA, because of her or his professional exposure to the operations of many different types of clients and because of professional expertise in designing accounting systems and interpreting financial data, is especially well equipped to provide management advisory services (MAS). Indeed, this is a very rapidly expanding area of practice for most CPA firms. Such services can include systems analysis, advice on improvements of existing systems, the installation of accounting systems, and in some instances assistance to clients in finding qualified management personnel.

Management advisory services are sanctioned and encouraged by the AICPA as long as they are consistent with the professional competence, ethical standards, and responsibilities of accountants. Although an accountant is expected to be professionally competent to perform such services, he or she is not expected to have technical training as a management consultant. Management advisory services staffs are typically found only within the organizations of larger CPA firms and may well consist of people trained in nonaccounting fields, such as computer applications or management. Because the nature of some management advisory services is so different from pure auditing and accounting, MAS staffs often have little or no contact with the audit, tax, or other nonaudit service staffs of the same firm.

The AICPA has established a Management Advisory Services Executive Committee to provide technical support and guidance to practitioners in this area of practice. This committee has issued a series of statements on management advisory services that constitute the standards against which such services are to be measured. These statements are summarized in Appendix 1–D.

Small Business Nonaudit Accounting Services

Nonaudit services to small companies is another growing element of public accounting practice. These services may even be a major part of the practice of many small local firms. Some large firms have established separate small business divisions to provide these services to their clients. The services may range from bookkeeping to the preparation and filing of governmental regulatory and tax return forms. In performing these services, the accountant can simultaneously function as financial advisor, tax consultant, and bookkeeper. In some cases, there may also be a need for the CPA to prepare the client's financial statements for presentation to management, creditors, or investors.

In 1977, the Accounting and Review Services Committee was established by the AICPA to monitor nonaudit services of public accounting firms. This committee was formed in response to external criticism alleging that too little attention had been given to setting standards in the area of nonaudit services. From its inception until this writing, the Committee for Accounting and Review Services has issued four Statements on Standards for Accounting and Review Services (SSARS). The first two of these standards are summarized in Appendix 1–E.

THE INDEPENDENT AUDIT

The independent audit is the most important service rendered by the public accounting profession.[2] Audit fees account for the majority of professional fees billed by CPA firms each year. More importantly, however, the independent CPA firm is uniquely qualified to perform this highly specialized accounting service. In the following sections, we shall see how the economic environment creates a need for the independent audit, as well as the ways in which the public accounting profession meets this need.

The Economic Environment and the Need for an Independent Audit

The environment in which modern economic activities are conducted is extremely complex. In the private sector, which is composed of all sorts of businesses ranging from small single-owner entities to large corporations, management decisions must be made daily. These decisions concern the internal affairs of an enterprise as well as lending and investment decisions of creditors and investors. In the public sector (government), interested parties must decide whether managers are complying with the controls placed on them and whether the entity is operating efficiently and effectively. In both the private and public sectors, it can often happen that the personal interests of managers may conflict with those of the entity's owners or constituents. It is necessary, therefore, for managers to collect and report information about the entity which satisfies the needs of externally interested decision makers. In determining how those needs should be met, we must consider the nature of the data to be communicated, the nature of user needs, and the natural inclinations of those providing the information. All these factors contribute to the need for independent verification of the data in order to assure fairness of presentation.

Communicating Economic Data. To assist investors, creditors, and other individuals in making informed decisions, financial managers provide information about the entity's economic resources and obligations at specified points in time; they also report on changes in those resources and obligations over periods of time. These types of economic assertions are called ***financial statements.*** Such financial statements may be prepared for any of the various types of enterprises such as corporate and noncorporate entities, consolidated groups of corporations, and nonprofit organizations (including governmental units). Economic assertions, however, are not limited to financial statements: they can also include statistical data, charts, tables, and related narrative information. We often use the term ***financial data*** to describe the financial statements and the comments, charts, and other material relating to those statements.

The Needs of Users. The users of financial data have various needs. For example, investors, creditors, and others are interested in reported earnings and balance sheet data to allow them to estimate the future earnings potential or probable debt-paying ability of a business. Investors are also interested in relating the reported earnings of the entity to the market prices of its securities. Managers of profit-seeking enterprises desire accurate and timely operating information so they can assess their own efficiency and effectiveness, and thereby more effectively manage the resources of the entity.

The constituents of nonprofit organizations desire timely reported financial information to help them judge the ***fiscal accountability*** of the managers. Such information will disclose the extent to which managers are adhering to the restrictions placed on the uses of resources. It will also help to show whether the goals of the organization are being met and whether the resources provided by taxpayers and voluntary contributors are being used effectively and efficiently. Internal financial information is as important to the managers of these enterprises as it is to the constituents and outside interested parties. Although this book gives some attention to the communication of internal information, we are primarily concerned with communicating the information required by externally interested groups.

The Need for Unbiased Data. Preparers of financial information include the financial managers of enterprises and persons at various levels of responsibility within those enterprises. Like the user groups mentioned in the previous section, preparers of financial information have their own operating goals. However, since it may be assumed that each of us places primary importance on maximizing her or his own welfare, the goals of the persons preparing the information will often be different from those of the persons using it. For example, while the users of financial information of business entities seek data that will aid them in making wealth maximization decisions, the providers of the information want to maximize the image and remuneration associated with their work. Such motivations can cause the preparers of financial information to incorporate personal biases into those data.

Because of the complex nature of the business and regulatory environment within which financial information is reported, and because of the large number of transactions processed, there is always the possibility that financial information will be recorded erroneously. In isolated cases, financial data may even be intentionally misrepresented by preparers. Since the measured performance of managers — and in some instances their immediate incomes (bonuses, incentives, etc.) — may be directly affected by the reported operating results of the entity, it is easy to see why unverified financial information from preparers is potentially unreliable.

The Need for Independent Verification of Reported Data. We can summarize our observations to this point by concluding that there may be a conflict of interests between the providers of financial information and the externally interested parties using that information. In order for the external users to have assurance that the financial data they receive is complete, consistent, and fairly presented, that information must be verified. To meet this need, each user might attempt personally to verify the information, but in most cases, this would be impracticable because the typical investor or creditor has neither the time nor the skills required. Therefore it generally becomes cost effective and desirable to hire independent and technically competent individuals to examine the externally reported financial information and to provide an opinion as to its creditability.

Meeting the Need for Independent Verification

The public accounting profession has responded to the need for independent verification of financial data by providing an independent audit service to both profit and nonprofit enterprises. In providing this service, the public accountant, operating as an objective independent party, examines the financial statements and renders an opinion (audit report) as to the fairness of their presentation when evaluated against generally accepted accounting principles or other applicable criteria. (See Figure 1–1.) This text is devoted to an explanation of the various aspects of the independent audit. In the remainder of this chapter we briefly summarize the ways in which independent auditors report the results of their examinations.

In Figure 1–2, we see the standard short-form unqualified report recommended for use by the AICPA when the audit evidence justifies its issuance.[3] The report is addressed to the group who engaged the auditor. For corporate clients, this group may be the company's board of directors, stockholders, or both. However, the report may also be addressed to the audit committee of the board of directors. The ***audit committee*** is a separate, autonomous group of directors that acts in a liaison capacity between the board of directors and the auditor. It has charge of engaging the auditor and of receiving the audit report and other communications (such as suggestions for improvements in the system of internal control) from the auditor.

An audit report may also in some instances be addressed to third parties who have engaged the auditor to conduct an examination in their behalf. For example, Corporation X may engage an auditor to conduct an examination of the financial statements of Corporation Y, in connection with a proposed merger or acquisition. The audit report would in that case be addressed to the board of directors of Corporation X.

Observe that the audit report is typically divided into two paragraphs. The first, or ***scope paragraph***, contains a statement describing what has been done. The second is the ***auditors's opinion paragraph;*** in this paragraph, the auditor states his or her view of the fairness and consistency of data included in the financial statements.

The audit report also bears a signature and a date. The signature is usually placed on

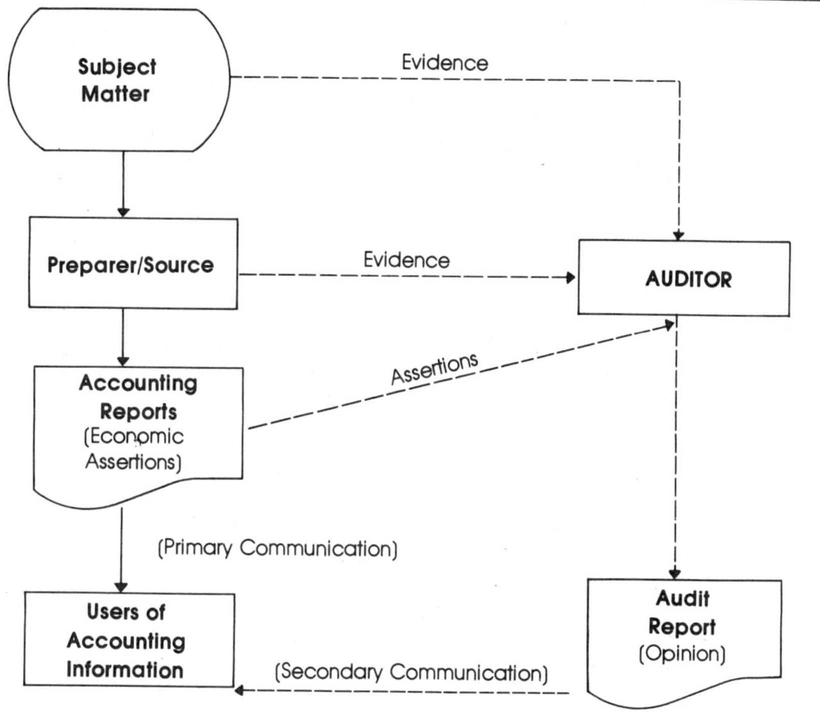

Source: "Report of the Committee to Prepare a Statement of Basic Auditing Concepts," *Accounting Review*, Supplement (1972): 27.

FIGURE 1–1. The Communication Process for Audit Reports

the report on behalf of the auditing firm by the auditor with final responsibility for the engagement. This is usually the engagement partner. The date of the audit report is always the day on which all audit procedures have been completed. We will look further into the meaning of this report, as well as something of its history and evolution, in Chapter 2.

There are basically six situations that call for the auditor to depart from the standard unqualified type of audit report shown in Figure 1–2.[4] These situations are as follows:

1. The scope of the auditor's examination is affected by conditions that preclude the performance of some of the generally accepted auditing standards necessary (as the auditor sees it) for expressing an opinion.
2. The auditor's report is based in part on the report of another auditor.
3. The financial statements are materially affected by a departure from GAAP.
4. The client has not applied GAAP in a consistent manner (that is, certain accounting changes have been made).
5. The financial statement presentations are affected by material uncertainties concerning future events, the outcome of which cannot be evaluated by the client or other experts as of the date of the audit report.

rectors of ABC Company, Inc.:

mined the balance sheets of ABC Company, Inc., as of
X2 and 19X1, and the related statements of income, retained
and changes in financial position for the years then ended. Our
minations were made in accordance with generally accepted auditing
standards and, accordingly, included such tests of the accounting records
and such other tests as we considered necessary in the circumstances.

In our opinion, the financial statements referred to above present fairly the financial position of ABC Company, Inc., as of December 31, 19X2 and 19X1, and the results of its operations and the changes in its financial position for the years then ended, in conformity with generally accepted accounting principles applied on a consistent basis.

Best & Company
Certified Public Accountants
March 21, 19X3

FIGURE 1–2. Short-Form Audit Report

6. The auditor wishes to emphasize matters regarding certain disclosures in the financial statements.

All these nonstandard reports are discussed at length in Chapter 18.

A variety of other reports may be issued by independent auditors. These include reports on internal control, reports on limited reviews of interim financial information, a variety of special reports, and nonstandardized reports on the operational and managerial effectiveness of the entity.

Internal auditors and governmental auditors also issue audit reports that are not standardized insofar as contents and format are concerned. These are discussed further in Chapter 19.

ORGANIZATIONS DIRECTLY INFLUENCING THE PROFESSION

The most prominent professional organization for the certified public accountant is the *American Institute of Certified Public Accountants* (AICPA). Membership in the AICPA is voluntary. However, about three-fourths of the approximately 200,000 certified public accountants in the United States are members. Members of the AICPA generally are also voluntary members of state societies or associations of CPAs. State societies are usually divided into local chapters, which hold periodic meetings featuring topics of interest to practitioners in a particular locale.

One of the most important objectives of the AICPA is to promote and maintain high standards of professional conduct, both technically and ethically. Four divisions have been established to facilitate the achievement of that goal. They are:

1. The Auditing Standards Division.
2. The Division for CPA Firms.

3. The Quality Control Review Division.
4. The Professional Ethics Division.

The last three of these divisions are discussed in a later chapter.

The Auditing Standards Division consists of the Auditing Standards Board (formerly the Auditing Standards Executive Committee), plus an advisory council that monitors the Board's activities, along with various task forces and administrative staff. The primary function of the Auditing Standards Board is to issue authoritative pronouncements, each of which is a ***Statement on Auditing Standards*** (SAS). These standards provide guidelines for developing and applying audit procedures, and for reporting the findings of the audit. We will refer to these statements throughout this text. Statements on Auditing Standards are interpretations of the ten basic ***generally accepted auditing standards*** (GAAS), which will be taken up in Chapter 2. Departures from these standards must be justified by the auditor. Penalty for failure to do so can include disciplinary action by the AICPA. Periodically, individual statements are codified into a single volume entitled *Codification of Statements on Auditing Standards*. In addition to Statements on Auditing Standards, the Auditing Standards Division also issues interpretations of SASs (which explain their applicability to certain circumstances) and Industry Audit Guides (which contain auditing and reporting requirements for various industries).

The Auditing Standards Board is composed of fifteen members, all of whom must have had extensive audit experience. It includes persons from public accounting, business, government, and academia. Approval of a publication requires nine affirmative votes from the Board. The Financial Accounting Standards Board (FASB), consisting of seven members chosen from the business and academic environments, is an independent body whose major responsibility is the development and interpretation of the generally accepted accounting principles (GAAP). The FASB was established in 1973, after a lengthy study by members of the accounting profession concerning the objectives of financial reporting. The FASB superseded the Accounting Principles Board (APB) of the AICPA (which, until 1973, was responsible for issuing statements defining accounting principles). Statements and interpretations issued by the FASB and opinions issued by the Accounting Principles Board, all recognized as elements of GAAP, are discussed more thoroughly in Chapter 2.

In addition to national and state organizations and rule-making bodies, each state has its own Board of Public Accountancy. The primary responsibility of these boards usually is to administer the state laws governing the practice of public accountancy within the states. Those laws relate to certification, licensing, professional conduct, and (in some cases) continuing professional education of public accountants. Although state boards are not affiliated directly with the AICPA or state societies of CPAs, they work with those organizations in monitoring the professional conduct of public accountants.

The Securities and Exchange Commission is a governmental body created by the Securities and Exchange Act of 1934. It has the authority to issue technical standards governing the presentation of financial reports for companies whose securities are offered for public sale or are subsequently traded on the stock exchanges or on over-the-counter markets. We call these companies "public entities." In effect, the

SEC has been granted the authority to establish GAAP for such companies. They have traditionally delegated this authority to the AICPA, and more recently to the FASB. In some instances, however, SEC disclosure requirements extend beyond those required by GAAP. The SEC requirements are issued in the form of ***Accounting Series Releases*** (ASR).

The SEC also requires that audits of financial statements of publicly owned companies be in accordance with generally accepted auditing standards. While the responsibility for determining audit standards for these companies has been delegated to the AICPA, the SEC has the right to interpret an audit rule (such as the ethics rule on independence) more strictly than does the AICPA.

The Institute of Internal Auditors (IIA), mentioned earlier in this chapter, is a national organization with chapters throughout the United States. Its purpose is to encourage exchanges of ideas among internal auditors, adherence to standards of the internal auditing profession, and expansion of services of internal auditors into phases of business beyond the financial realm. The IIA publishes a bimonthly journal, *The Internal Auditor;* it also sponsors the publication of several books on internal auditing. Administration of the certification examination and establishment of rules governing the actions of Certified Internal Auditors (CIA) are other important functions of this group.

SUMMARY

In this chapter we have looked at the services provided by the accounting profession. We began by defining and briefly describing audit services. Then we explained how those services are provided within enterprise units by internal audits and within the federal government by the General Accounting Office.

Next we turned our attention to nonaudit services provided by public accountants — such as tax services, management advisory services, and small business accounting services. We observed that the profession has established standards for these services and noted that summaries of those standards are provided as appendixes at the end of this chapter.

In the last part of the chapter we briefly explained what independent audit services involve and why they are needed in today's world. Then we listed some of the professional organizations that influence the work of accountants and explained how that influence is exerted.

APPENDIX 1–A: Summary of General and Specific Standards for the Professional Practice of Internal Auditing

100 *INDEPENDENCE* — Internal auditors should be independent of the activities they audit.

110 *Organizational Status* — The organizational status of the internal auditing department should be sufficient to permit the accomplishment of its audit responsibilities.

120 *Objectivity* — Internal auditors should be objective in performing audits.

200 *PROFESSIONAL PROFICIENCY* — Internal audits should be performed with proficiency and due professional care.

The Internal Auditing Department

210 *Staffing* — The internal auditing department should provide assurance that the technical proficiency and educational background of internal auditors are appropriate for the audits to be performed.

220 *Knowledge, Skills, and Disciplines* — The internal auditing department should possess or should obtain the knowledge, skills, and disciplines needed to carry out its audit responsibilities.

230 *Supervision* — The internal auditing department should provide assurance that internal audits are properly supervised.

The Internal Auditor

240 *Compliance with Standards of Conduct* — Internal auditors should comply with professional standards of conduct.

250 *Knowledge, Skills, and Disciplines* — Internal auditors should possess the knowledge, skills, and disciplines essential to the performance of internal audits.

260 *Human Relations and Communications* — Internal auditors should be skilled in dealing with people and in communicating effectively.

270 *Continuing Education* — Internal auditors should maintain their technical competence through continuing education.

280 *Due Professional Care* — Internal auditors should exercise due professional care in performing internal audits.

STATEMENT OF RESPONSIBILITIES

OF INTERNAL AUDITING

The purpose of this statement is to provide in summary form a general understanding of the role and responsibilities of internal auditing. For more specific guidance, readers should refer to the *Standards for the Professional Practice of Internal Auditing*.

NATURE

Internal auditing is an independent appraisal activity established within an organization as a service to the organization. It is a control which functions by examining and evaluating the adequacy and effectiveness of other controls.

OBJECTIVE AND SCOPE

The objective of internal auditing is to assist members of the organization in the effective discharge of their responsibilities. To this end, internal auditing furnishes them with analyses, appraisals, recommendations, counsel, and information concerning the activities reviewed. The audit objective includes promoting effective control at reasonable cost.

The scope of internal auditing encompasses the examination and evaluation of the adequacy and effectiveness of the organization's system of internal control and the quality of performance in carrying out assigned responsibilities. The scope of internal auditing includes:

- Reviewing the reliability and integrity of financial and operating information and the means used to identify, measure, classify, and report such information.
- Reviewing the systems established to ensure compliance with those policies, plans, procedures, laws, and regulations which could have a significant impact on operations and reports, and determining whether the organization is in compliance.
- Reviewing the means of safeguarding assets and, as appropriate, verifying the existence of such assets.
- Appraising the economy and efficiency with which resources are employed.
- Reviewing operations or programs to ascertain whether results are consistent with established objectives and goals and whether the operations or programs are being carried out as planned.

RESPONSIBILITY AND AUTHORITY

Internal auditing functions under the policies established by management and the board. The purpose, authority and responsibility of the internal auditing department should be defined in a formal written document (charter), approved by management, and accepted by the board. The charter should make clear the purposes of the internal auditing department, specify the unrestricted scope of its work, and declare that auditors are to have no authority or responsibility for the activities they audit.

The responsibility of internal auditing is to serve the organization in a manner that is consistent with the *Standards for the Professional Practice of Internal Auditing* and with professional standards of conduct such as the *Code of Ethics* of The Institute of Internal Auditors, Inc. This responsibility includes coordinating internal audit activities with others so as to best achieve the audit objectives and the objectives of the organization.

INDEPENDENCE

Internal auditors should be independent of the activities they audit. Internal auditors are independent when they can carry out their work freely and objectively. Independence permits internal auditors to render the impartial and unbiased judgments essential to the proper conduct of audits. It is achieved through organizational status and objectivity.

Organizational status should be sufficient to assure a broad range of audit coverage, and adequate consideration of and effective action on audit findings and recommendations.

Objectivity requires that internal auditors have an independent mental attitude, and an honest belief in their work product. Drafting procedures, designing, installing, and operating systems, are not audit functions. Performing such activities is presumed to impair audit objectivity.

The *Statement of Responsibilities of Internal Auditors* was originally issued by The Institute of Internal Auditors in 1947. The current *Statement*, revised in 1981, embodies the concepts previously established and includes such changes as are deemed advisable in light of the present status of the profession.

300 *SCOPE OF WORK* — The scope of the internal audit should encompass the examination and evaluation of the adequacy and effectiveness of the organization's system of internal control and the quality of performance in carrying out assigned responsibilities.

310 *Reliability and Integrity of Information* — Internal auditors should review the reliability and integrity of financial and operating information and the means used to identify, measure, classify, and report such information.

320 *Compliance with Policies, Plans, Procedures, Laws, and Regulations* — Internal auditors should review the systems established to ensure compliance with those policies, plans, procedures, laws, and regulations which could have significant impact on operations and reports and should determine whether the organization is in compliance.

330 *Safeguarding of Assets* — Internal auditors should review the means of safeguarding assets and, as appropriate, verify the existence of such assets.

340 *Economical and Efficient Use of Resources* — Internal auditors should appraise the economy and efficiency with which resources are employed.

350 *Accomplishment of Established Objectives and Goals for Operations or Programs* — Internal auditors should review operations or programs to ascertain whether results are consistent with established objectives and goals and whether the operations or programs are being carried out as planned.

400 *PERFORMANCE OF AUDIT WORK* — Audit work should include planning the audit, examining and evaluating information, communicating results, and following up.

410 *Planning the Audit* — Internal auditors should plan each audit.

420 *Examining and Evaluating Information* — Internal auditors should collect, analyze, interpret, and document information to support audit results.

430 *Communicating Results* — Internal auditors should report the results of their audit work.

440 *Following up* — Internal auditors should follow up to ascertain that appropriate action is taken on reported audit findings.

500 *MANAGEMENT OF THE INTERNAL AUDITING DEPARTMENT* — The director of internal auditing should properly manage the internal auditing department.

510 *Purpose, Authority, and Responsibility* — The director of internal auditing should have a statement of purpose, authority, and responsibility for the internal auditing department.

520 *Planning* — The director of internal auditing should establish plans to carry out the responsibilities of the internal auditing department.

530 *Policies and Procedures* — The director of internal auditing should provide written policies and procedures to guide the audit staff.

540 *Personnel Management and Development* — The director of internal auditing should establish a program for selecting and developing the human resources of the internal auditing department.

550 *External Auditors* — The director of internal auditing should coordinate internal and external audit efforts.

560 *Quality Assurance* — The director of internal auditing should establish and maintain a quality assurance program to evaluate the operations of the internal auditing department.

APPENDIX 1–B: General Accounting Office (GAO) Audit Standards

Scope of Audit Work

The expanded scope of auditing a government organization, a program, an activity, or a function should include:

1. *Financial and compliance* — determines (a) whether the financial statements of an audited entity present fairly the financial position and the results of financial operations in accordance with generally accepted accounting principles and (b) whether the entity has complied with laws and regulations that may have a material effect upon the financial statements.
2. *Economy and efficiency* — determines (a) whether the entity is managing and utilizing its resources (such as personnel, property, space) economically and efficiently, (b) the causes of inefficiencies or uneconomical practices, and (c) whether the entity has complied with laws and regulations concerning matters of economy and efficiency.
3. *Program results* — determines (a) whether the desired results or benefits established by the legislature or other authorizing body are being achieved and (b) whether the agency has considered alternatives that might yield desired results at a lower cost.

In determining the scope for a particular audit, responsible audit and entity officials should consider the needs of the potential users of audit findings.

General Standards

1. Qualifications: The auditors assigned to perform the audit must collectively possess adequate professional proficiency for the tasks required.
2. Independence: In all matters relating to the audit work, the audit organization and the individual auditors, whether government or public, must be free from personal or external impairments to independence, must be organizationally independent, and shall maintain an independent attitude and appearance.
3. Due professional care: Due professional care is to be used in conducting the audit and in preparing related reports.
4. Scope impairments: When factors external to the audit organization and the auditor restrict the audit or interfere with the auditor's ability to form objective opinions and conclusions, the auditor should attempt to remove the limitation or, failing that, report the limitation.

Appendix 1–B has been summarized from *Standards for Audit of Governmental Organizations, Programs, Activities, and Functions* (Washington, D.C.: General Accounting Office, 1981). Reprinted with permission.

Examination and Evaluation (Field Work) and Reporting Standards for Financial and Compliance Audits

1. AICPA Statements on Auditing Standards for field work and reporting are adopted and incorporated in this statement for government financial and compliance audits. Future statements should be adopted and incorporated, unless GAO excludes them by formal announcement.
2. Additional standards and requirements for government financial and compliance audits.
   a. Standards on examination and evaluation:
      (1) Planning shall include consideration of the requirements of all levels of government.
      (2) A review is to be made of compliance with applicable laws and regulations.
      (3) A written record of the auditors' work shall be retained in the form of working papers.
      (4) Auditors shall be alert to situations or transactions that could be indicative of fraud, abuse, and illegal expenditures and acts and, if such evidence exists, extend audit steps and procedures to identify the effect on the entity's financial statements.
   b. Standards on reporting:
      (1) Written audit reports are to be submitted to the appropriate officials of the organization audited and to the appropriate officials of the organizations requiring or arranging for the audits unless legal restrictions or ethical considerations prevent it. Copies of the reports should also be sent to other officials who may be responsible for taking action and to others authorized to receive such reports. Unless restricted by law or regulation, copies should be made available for public inspection.
      (2) A statement in the auditors' report that the examination was made in accordance with generally accepted government auditing standards for financial and compliance audits will be acceptable language to indicate that the audit was made in accordance with these standards. (See ch. V, par. 2b for AICPA-suggested language.)
      (3) Either the auditors' report on the entity's financial statements or a separate report shall contain a statement of positive assurance on those items of compliance tested and negative assurance on those items not tested. It shall also include material instances of noncompliance and instances or indications of fraud, abuse, or illegal acts found during or in connection with the audit.
      (4) The auditors shall report on their study and evaluation of internal accounting controls made as part of the financial and compliance audit. They shall identify as a minimum: (a) the entity's significant internal accounting controls, (b) the controls identified that were evaluated, (c) the controls identified that were not evaluated (the auditor may satisfy this requirement by identifying any significant classes of transactions and related assets not included in the study and evaluation), and (d) the material weaknesses identified as a result of the evaluation.
      (5) Either the auditors' report on the entity's financial statements or a separate report shall contain any other material deficiency findings identified during the audit not covered in (3) above.
      (6) If certain information is prohibited from general disclosure, the report shall state the nature of the information omitted and the requirement that makes the omission necessary.

Examination and Evaluation Standards for Economy and Efficiency Audits and Program Results Audits

1. Work is to be adequately planned.
2. Assistants are to be properly supervised.

3. A review is to be made of compliance with applicable laws and regulations.
4. During the audit a study and evaluation shall be made of the internal control system (administrative controls) applicable to the organization, program, activity, or function under audit.
5. When audits involve computer-based systems, the auditors shall:
   a. Review general controls in data processing systems to determine whether (1) the controls have been designed according to management direction and known legal requirements and (2) the controls are operating effectively to provide reliability of, and security over, the data being processed.
   b. Review application controls of installed data processing applications upon which the auditor is relying to assess their reliability in processing data in a timely, accurate, and complete manner.
6. Sufficient, competent, and relevant evidence is to be obtained to afford a reasonable basis for the auditors' judgments and conclusions regarding the organization, program, activity, or function under audit. A written record of the auditors' work shall be retained in the form of working papers.
7. The auditors shall:
   a. Be alert to situations or transactions that could be indicative of fraud, abuse, and illegal acts.
   b. If such evidence exists, extend audit steps and procedures to identify the effect on the entity's operations and programs.

Reporting Standards for Economy and Efficiency Audits and Program Results Audits

1. Written audit reports are to be prepared giving the results of each government audit.
2. Written audit reports are to be submitted to the appropriate officials of the organization audited and to the appropriate officials of the organizations requiring or arranging for the audits unless legal restrictions or ethical considerations prevent it. Copies of the reports should also be sent to other officials who may be responsible for taking action on audit findings and recommendations and to others authorized to receive such reports. Unless restricted by law or regulation, copies should be made available for public inspection.
3. Reports are to be issued on or before the dates specified by law, regulation, or other special arrangement. Reports are to be issued promptly so as to make the information available for timely use by management and by legislative officials.
4. The report shall include:
   a. A description of the scope and objectives of the audit.
   b. A statement that the audit (economy and efficiency or program results) was made in accordance with generally accepted government auditing standards.
   c. A description of material weaknesses found in the internal control system (administrative controls).
   d. A statement of positive assurance on those items of compliance tested and negative assurance on those items not tested. This should include significant instances of noncompliance and instances of or indications of fraud, abuse, or illegal acts found during or in connection with the audit. However, fraud, abuse, or illegal acts normally should be covered in a separate report, thus permitting the overall report to be released to the public.
   e. Recommendations for actions to improve problem areas noted in the audit and to improve operations. The underlying causes of problems reported should be included to assist in implementing corrective actions.

f. Pertinent views of responsible officials of the organization, program, activity, or function audited concerning the auditors' findings, conclusions, and recommendations. When possible their views should be obtained in writing.
g. A description of noteworthy accomplishments, particularly when management improvements in one area may be applicable elsewhere.
h. A listing of any issues and questions needing further study and consideration.
i. A statement as to whether any pertinent information has been omitted because it is deemed privileged or confidential. The nature of such information should be described, and the law or other basis under which it is withheld should be stated. If a separate report was issued containing this information it should be indicated in the report.

5. The report shall:
   a. Present factual data accurately and fairly. Include only information, findings, and conclusions that are adequately supported by sufficient evidence in the auditors' working papers to demonstrate or prove the bases for the matters reported and their correctness and reasonableness.
   b. Present findings and conclusions in a convincing manner.
   c. Be objective.
   d. Be written in language as clear and simple as the subject matter permits.
   e. Be concise but, at the same time, clear enough to be understood by users.
   f. Present factual data completely to fully inform the users.
   g. Place primary emphasis on improvement rather than on criticism of the past; critical comments should be presented in a balanced perspective considering any unusual difficulties or circumstances faced by the operating officials concerned.

APPENDIX 1–C: Tax Practice Standards

The practice of public accounting related to taxation in the United States is regulated by the U.S. Treasury Department and the AICPA Code of Professional Ethics, as interpreted by the Committee on Responsibilities in Tax Practice. This committee, through the authority of the AICPA's Division of Federal Taxation, has issued standards of responsibilities in tax practice for members of the AICPA which are more restrictive in some respects than those established by the Treasury Department or by the Code of Professional Ethics. These standards are actually a body of advisory opinions as to what constitutes good tax practice; to the extent that they are more restrictive than the Code of Professional Ethics or Treasury Department rules, their authority depends on the general acceptability of the opinions expressed on the statements. Hence, they do not have the force of authority that the Treasury Department rules have. Nevertheless, they do carry the weight of general acceptability for what are considered to be appropriate responsibilities of the CPA engaged in tax practice.

As of April 1982, ten Statements on Responsibilities in Tax Practice had been issued. These statements are summarized briefly in the following paragraphs.

Signature of Preparer

A CPA should sign as preparer any federal tax return that requires the signature of a preparer if it is prepared for and transmitted to the taxpayer or another, whether or not the return is prepared for compensation. This rule goes beyond Treasury Regulation 1.6065-1 (b) (1), which requires the preparer to sign the return only if he or she has prepared it in exchange for compensation.

Signature of Reviewer

If the CPA is not the preparer of a federal tax return, he or she is not required to sign the preparer's declaration. However, the CPA may sign the declaration if he or she reviews the return and acquires knowledge of the matters therein that is substantially equivalent to that which would have been acquired had the CPA been the preparer. Unless at least such a review is made, the CPA should not sign the tax return as preparer.

Answers to Questions on Returns

A CPA should sign the preparer's declaration on a federal tax return only if the taxpayer has made a reasonable effort to provide all the answers to applicable questions on the return. Whenever a question is left unanswered by the taxpayer, the reason for the omission should be stated. The possibility that an answer to a question might prove disadvantageous to the taxpayer does not justify omitting an answer or a statement of the reason for such an omission.

Recognition of Administrative Proceedings of Prior Year

An "administrative proceeding" can be an examination (audit) by an internal revenue agent, a district conference, or an appellate conference relating to a taxpayer's return on a claim for refund. A "waiver" can be a waiver of restrictions upon the Internal Revenue Service (IRS) of a deficiency on tax; the acceptance of the IRS's findings by a partnership, fiduciary, or Subchapter S corporation; or the acceptance of an overassessment.

The selection of the treatment of an item (income, deduction, credit, etc.) in a tax return should be based on the facts and rules as of the time the return is prepared. Normally, the disposition of an item in a later year as part of an administrative proceeding by the execution of a waiver from a prior year does not govern that item's treatment in a later year's return, unless the taxpayer is bound by agreement with the IRS to a certain treatment. A CPA may therefore sign a return as preparer in a later year if the return contains a departure from the prior year's treatment. He may do this without disclosing the departure.

Use of Estimates

A CPA may prepare tax returns involving estimates if the use of such estimates is generally acceptable or if it is impracticable, under the circumstances, to obtain exact data. When estimates are used, the CPA should present them in such a manner that greater accuracy than exists is not implied. The CPA should be satisfied with the reasonableness of all estimates used in a taxpayer's return before signing the return as preparer.

Knowledge of Error

A CPA is required to advise the tax client promptly when errors or omissions are discovered in a previously filed return, or when it is learned that a client has failed to file a required return. The CPA's advice should include a recommendation of the measures to be taken (usually, an amended return for the prior year is advisable). The CPA is not obligated to inform the IRS of the error and, in fact, may not do so without the client's permission.

If the CPA has knowledge of an uncorrected error in a client's prior year return which results in an understatement of tax liability, he or she should consider this fact in deciding whether to proceed with preparation of any subsequent returns. If such returns are prepared, steps should be taken by the CPA to ensure that the error is not repeated.

Knowledge of Error: Administrative Proceedings

When a CPA is representing a client in an administrative proceeding concerning a return in which the CPA is aware of an error resulting in a material understatement of tax liability, she or he should request that the client agree to disclose the error to the IRS. If the client refuses to agree to disclose the error, the CPA's recourse may be withdrawal from the engagement.

Advice to Clients

In providing advice to a client, the CPA must use judgment to ensure that such advice reflects adequately informed professional competence and that it suits the client's needs. When subsequent developments (such as changes in the law) affect advice previously provided to a client, the CPA is not obligated to inform the client of such developments unless: (1) the CPA is assisting the client in implementing plans associated with the advice previously provided, or (2) a specific agreement exists to inform the client of new developments.

Certain Procedural Aspects of Preparing Returns

A CPA is normally allowed to rely on information provided by the client without examining or reviewing any documents or other supporting evidence. However, the client should be encouraged to provide supporting data where appropriate.

The CPA should make use of prior year's returns of the client whenever feasible. Whenever information provided by the client appears to be incorrect or incomplete, the CPA should make enough inquiries to resolve doubts and take measures to correct the information, before signing the return as preparer.

If a CPA prepares a federal tax return, he or she should always sign it without modifying the preparer's declaration.

Positions Contrary to the Government

A CPA may take positions contrary to the Internal Revenue Code or Treasury Regulations in the preparation of a federal tax return — if there is reasonable support for this position. Reasonable support might exist, for example, when two internal revenue code provisions conflict, or when the Internal Revenue Code and Treasury Regulations are silent on a matter. When a position taken is contrary to the Internal Revenue Code, (expected to be a rare circumstance), the CPA should disclose the treatment in the tax return. Positions contrary to Treasury Regulations or IRS interpretations may be taken without disclosure in the return. In no event may a CPA take a position that lacks reasonable support.

APPENDIX 1–D: Management Advisory Services Standards

Some of the most important nonaudit services a CPA can perform for a client are management advisory services consistent with the accountant's professional competence, ethical standards, and responsibilities.

Management advisory services (MAS) are defined by the AICPA as professional consulting, the primary purpose of which is to improve the efficiency and effectiveness with which clients use their capabilities and resources to achieve the objectives of their organizations. Typically these services relate to such areas as the following:

- Counseling management with regard to its analysis, planning, organizing, operating, and controlling functions.
- Conducting special studies (such as studies of the system of internal accounting and administrative controls), preparing recommendations, proposing plans and programs, and providing advice and technical assistance in their implementation.
- Reviewing the suggested improvement of policies, procedures, systems, methods, and organizational relationships.
- Introducing new ideas, concepts, and methods of management.

Because the nature of management advisory services places the accountant in an advocacy role with clients, there exists a potential for sacrifice of the objectiveness needed by an accountant who also performs audit services for the same clients. The accounting profession has come under criticism in recent years by certain members of Congress and others who feel it is impossible to perform management advisory services for clients and at the same time maintain audit independence. For this and other reasons, the Management Advisory Services Executive Committee has begun an effort to more clearly define the role of accountants engaged in management advisory services. Part of this effort is issuance of a new series of statements on standards for management advisory services; these statements provide guidance for adhering to the general and technical standards of the accounting profession's Code of Professional

Appendix 1–D has been summarized from *Statements on Management Advisory Services* (New York: AICPA, 1981).

Conduct. To date, only one such statement has been issued. In addition, a series of statements on management advisory services were issued in 1974, which, while not enforceable under the AICPA Rules of Conduct, provide practical guidance and advice on MAS.

The purpose of MAS Statement 1 is to set forth basic definitions and standards for MAS practice. In addition to providing the definition of MAS discussed above, the statement defines the MAS practitioner as any Institute member in the practice of public accounting who carries out MAS for a client either on his or her own behalf or on the behalf of any other Institute member. The statement then differentiates between an MAS engagement and an MAS consultation. An ***MAS engagement*** is that form of MAS in which an analytical approach, such as the one outlined below, is applied in a study or project. It typically involves more than just an informal or incidental effort devoted to some combination of activities (including audit and tax services). In contrast, an ***MAS consultation*** is a more informally structured form of MAS, often referred to as informal advice. MAS consultation is incidental to other services performed and rendered within a relatively short time and does not usually entail an analytical approach.

The analytical approach the accountant uses in performing an MAS engagement typically involves these steps:

1. Ascertaining facts and circumstances pertinent to the engagement.
2. Seeking and identifying the objectives of the engagement.
3. Defining the client's problem or opportunity regarding improvement of systems and procedures.
4. Determining and evaluating possible solutions to client problems.
5. Presenting findings and recommendations.

The MAS services of the CPA may cease with step 5. However, in some instances, the client may decide to proceed in implementing one of the solutions the CPA has recommended. In that case, a CPA may then undertake these steps:

6. Planning and scheduling the actions to achieve the desired results.
7. Advising and providing technical assistance in implementing the suggestions in order to produce useful solutions to the client's problems.

The Management Advisory Services Executive Committee has published nine standards for MAS practice. We shall consider these standards in two groups: general standards and technical standards. *General standards* apply to both MAS engagements and MAS consultations. By and large, they follow Rule 201 of the AICPA Rules of Conduct, which specifies general standards for the practice of public accounting as a whole. The general standards for MAS are as follows:

1. *Professional competence.* Engagements are to be performed by practitioners having competence in the analytical approach and methods. Both engagements and consultations are to be performed by persons having adequate training in the subject matter.
2. *Due professional care.* The practitioner should exercise due professional care in the performance of the engagement.
3. *Adequate planning and supervision.* The engagement should be adequately planned, and assistants should be adequately supervised.

4. *Sufficient relevant data.* The practitioner should gather sufficient relevant data on the engagement to afford a reasonable basis for his or her report.
5. *Forecasts.* A member of AICPA should not allow his or her name to be used with any forecast of future transactions in a manner that might lead to the belief that he or she vouches for the reliability of the forecast.

Technical Standards apply to MAS engagements but not to consultations. They are established under Rule 204 of AICPA Rules of Conduct, which governs technical standards for all aspects of the public accounting profession. A brief summary of the technical standards follows:

1. *The role of the MAS practitioner.* In all phases of the MAS engagement, the practitioner should refrain from assuming the role of management and from taking any position that might have an adverse effect on his or her objectivity. This rule has been a cornerstone of MAS practice, and, if followed strictly, allows the practitioner to render concurrent MAS and audit services.
2. *Understanding with the client.* The practitioner should have an oral or written understanding with the client concerning the nature, scope, and limitations of the MAS engagement to be performed.
3. *Client benefit.* Potential benefit to the client is a major consideration in giving MAS advice through a full-scope engagement. Therefore, before an engagement is undertaken, the CPA should try to assess the potential benefit to the client of the results of the engagement, and the client should be informed of any reservations the CPA might have. In addition, results should not be explicitly or implicitly guaranteed by the practitioner. When estimates of quantifiable results are presented by the practitioner, they should be clearly identified as estimates. Support for all such estimates should be disclosed.
4. *Communication of results.* Significant information pertinent to the results of the MAS engagement, together with any limitations, qualifications, or reservations needed to assist the client in making a decision, should be communicated to the client either orally or in writing.

It is important to remember that even though the CPA is providing technical advice to a client (and may even assist in the implementation of suggestions), he or she is still a professional. This means that the CPA must maintain integrity and objectivity and must exercise due professional care in handling the engagement. In the practice of MAS, the CPA should be careful not to shed the role of advisor and assume the role of manager or employee on any task that is performed on behalf of the client. Similarly, the CPA should possess the same competence and exercise the same care as any other adequately trained professional in the engagement. Although the same degree of objectivity is not required for MAS or tax services as for audit services, it is advisable for the CPA to maintain audit independence in all aspects of professional practice. The Code of Professional Ethics of the AICPA does not allow a member or a firm in which the member is a partner or shareholder to express an opinion on the financial statements of an enterprise that the firm is serving in the capacity of manager or employee. When the CPA is rendering concurrent MAS and audit services, as is often the case, this ethical rule is paramount in importance.

With respect to the understanding with the client, one of the most important things to keep in perspective throughout the entire engagement is the role the CPA is allowed to assume. Specifically, the CPA should not assume either a subservient or a dominant position with respect to the client, but should act in the capacity of an advisor. The ultimate decision maker should be the client. This and other understandings with the client should be made clear at the outset of the engagement, preferably in writing in an engagement letter. Other items that should be made clear in the engagement letter include (1) the exact nature of the work to be performed on the engagement; (2) the work that the auditor does not expect to perform (particularly if an audit is not to be performed concurrently); (3) the type of communication or report the client may expect; (4) the appropriate time frame of the engagement; (5) whether the CPA will attend meetings of the board of directors to communicate his findings verbally; and (6) the fee structure of the engagement. With respect to communication of the results of the engagement, no specific report format is emphasized for MAS engagements, as it is for audit engagements. Rather, the report is expected to be a tailored, concise statement of the consultant's conclusions, recommendations, accomplishments, and the major assumptions relied upon; it must also declare any limitations, reservations, or qualifications. The report may be either written or oral, but in most cases it is written. Whenever an oral report is rendered, the practitioner should prepare a memorandum for the files documenting recommendations and other information discussed with the client.

Although no report content is specified for MAS engagements, the recommendations given by the practitioner may resemble those specified for governmental audits by GAO audit standards. The GAO reporting standards, referred to in Appendix 1–B, might be a useful point of departure for inclusions in a report for an MAS engagement.

APPENDIX 1–E: Accounting and Review Standards

Not all the work that CPA firms do consists of audit, management advisory services, and tax work for large, sophisticated corporations. Another rapidly growing segment of public accounting practice is accounting and review services. Nonpublic entities may need the services of a certified public accountant for anything from business advice to systems analysis to bookkeeping, but often they do not need audits of financial statements.

Statements on standards for accounting and review services (SSARS) are issued by the AICPA's Accounting and Review Services Committee; they pertain to an accountant's ***association*** with the unaudited financial statements of nonpublic entities. For purposes of these statements, a nonpublic entity is defined as any entity other than (1) one whose securities are traded in a public market (including local exchanges); (2) a company that makes a filing with a regulatory agency in preparation to "go public"; or (3) a subsidiary, corporate joint venture, or other entity controlled by an entity mentioned in (1) or (2).

Appendix 1–E has been summarized from Statement on Standards for Accounting and Review Services (SSARS) 1 (New York: AICPA, 1978).

The CPA may have two levels of association with respect to unaudited financial statements of a nonpublic entity. The lower level is that of ***compilation.*** A compilation is limited to developing financial statements from client records. A higher level of association (but a lower level than an audit) is the ***review,*** which consists of performing inquiry and analytical review procedures on either client-prepared or accountant-prepared financial statements.

The fourth audit standard of reporting requiring an expression of opinion regarding the financial statements taken as a whole or an assertion to the effect that an opinion cannot be expressed, applies anytime a CPA is associated with a set of financial statements. It also requires the accountant to indicate in a written report (1) the nature of the work performed on the financial statements, and (2) the degree of responsibility taken with respect to the financial statements. Standards for accounting and review services provide guidance for the nonauditor CPA performing such services.

Compilation procedures are usually limited to obtaining an understanding of the client's industry and business practices, preparation of the financial statements, and reading them afterward to ascertain that they are free from obvious material errors. No opinion or any other form of assurance is expressed by the CPA in a compilation. However, as in any association with financial statements, the CPA is responsible for correcting or disclosing all departures from GAAP that are brought to her or his attention. He or she must also disclaim an opinion on such statements.

Review procedures consist of inquiry of management and other knowledgeable individuals concerning the accounting principles used and the procedures followed in preparing the financial statements. In addition, the CPA applies analytical procedures, which consist of ratio and trend analyses showing the relationships among data in the financial statements. Also, the CPA performs certain other limited procedures that are not extensive enough to allow expression of an audit opinion of the financial statements. Therefore, the CPA expresses ***limited assurance,*** which is an opinion of whether material modifications should be made to the financial statements in order for them to conform to GAAP (or another comprehensive basis of accounting). Compilation and review procedures and related reports are discussed in Chapter 19.

NOTES

1. "Report of the Committee to Prepare a Statement of Basic Auditing Concepts," *Accounting Review,* Supplement (1972): 18.

2. Information in this section is based upon R. K. Mautz and H. A. Sharaf, *The Philosophy of Auditing* (Sarasota, Fla.: American Accounting Association, 1961); and upon Michael C. Jensen and W. H. Meckling, "Theory of the Firm: Managerial Behavior, Agency Costs and Ownership Structure," *Journal of Financial Economics* 3 (1976): 305–60.

3. Statement on Auditing Standards (SAS) 15, paragraph .03 (New York: AICPA, 1976).

4. SAS 2, paragraph .09 (New York: AICPA, 1974). This standard lists seven circumstances requiring a departure from the standard wording of an unqualified audit report. Items (c) and (d) of that list are combined in the third item of our list for the sake of conciseness.

QUESTIONS FOR CLASS DISCUSSION

Q1–1 What is the relationship between the complexity of business organizations and the need for accounting services?

Q1–2 What justification is there for the recognition of accounting as a profession?

Q1–3 What is the difference between the public accounting and private accounting segments of the accounting profession?

Q1–4 Are all public accountants certified public accountants? Explain.

Q1–5 What is meant by the term auditing?

Q1–6 What is the difference between an internal audit and an independent audit?

Q1–7 What is the primary objective of an operational audit?

Q1–8 What is the relationship of the General Accounting Office to the elements of the United States Government? Describe the work done by this agency.

Q1–9 What nonaudit services are provided by public accountants?

Q1–10 Why is the public accountant particularly well suited to provide clients with management advisory services?

Q1–11 What are the services typically provided in management advisory services engagements?

Q1–12 Why are independent audits required in our present-day economic environment?

Q1–13 What, in general, does the public accountant do in performing an independent audit?

Q1–14 What device does the public accountant use in communicating to the public his or her findings after completing an independent audit of a company's financial statements?

Q1–15 What is the most important professional organization for practicing certified public accountants?

Q1–16 What is the relationship of the American Institute of Certified Public Accountants to the auditing profession?

Q1–17 What is the relationship of the Financial Accounting Standards Board to the accounting profession?

Q1–18 What is the relationship of the Securities and Exchange Commission to published financial statements?

SHORT CASES

C1–1 Jaime Gomez is president of the Gomez Manufacturing Company, a small corporation manufacturing air-conditioning units. Until recently the company has had no need for credit other than open account obligations associated with the purchases of raw materials. However, the volume of business has grown significantly during the last year, and as a result, Mr. Gomez is seeking to establish a line of credit with a local bank. The bank has asked Mr. Gomez for audited financial statements for the company covering its most recent fiscal period. Mr. Gomez states that he sees no reason for such a request because the company has an excellent internal auditing staff that monitors all accounting activities. For that reason, he feels certain that his financial statements are fairly presented.

Required:

Explain to Mr. Gomez why the bank insists on independently audited financial statements.

C1–2 Your public accounting firm has just completed an audit of the financial statements of the Swanson Corporation and has delivered an unqualified audit report to the company's board of directors. Julia Burnett, the president of the company, states that she considers the independent audit to be a nonproductive activity because it has produced no significant changes in the financial statements. She therefore concludes that the fees paid for the audit constitute a waste of the company's resources.

Required:

Respond to the position taken by Ms. Burnett.

C1–3 The president of the Leander Corporation is seeking advice relating to the operating activities of the firm. The public accounting firm currently providing audit services for the company has indicated that it also provides management advisory services for many of its clients. President Eric Leander asks the representative of public accounting firm whether the persons providing those services have had technical recognition as management consultants. When the accountant answers in the negative, Leander asks how public accountants can be qualified to provide management advisory services if they are not recognized as management consultants.

Required:

Respond to the comments of the president of the company.

C1–4 Your friend Stephen Cho is a business executive who resides in a state that requires public accountants to be certified (CPAs) before they can be licensed to practice public accounting. Cho expresses the feeling that such a requirement is unnecessary and that anyone wishing to practice public accounting should be given the opportunity to do so. He states that in his business, competition determines which firms will succeed and which ones shall fail. He maintains that the same competitive arrangement should be allowed to operate in the public accounting industry.

Required:

Respond to your friend's comments.

C1–5 A disgruntled taxpayer has just learned that large federal expenditures are incurred to maintain the operations of the General Accounting Office (GAO). He concludes that the GAO is just another unnecessary bureaucratic element of an overexpanded federal government and suggests that it should be abolished along with certain other agencies so that the federal "tax bite" can be reduced.

Required:

Respond to the disgruntled taxpayer.

C1–6 Nancy Packard operates a small business. She feels that the volume of business activities does not presently justify her hiring an accountant to maintain her accounting records, but realizes that she must have accounting data to properly manage her business and to help her determine the tax obligations of the business.

Required:

Suggest possible solutions for Ms. Packard's problem.

C1–7 Your father recently purchased one hundred shares of Nelco Corporation stock. As a stockholder he has just received the company's annual report. He observes that the public accounting firm of Alfred Ciri and Company has audited the financial statements and presented an unqualified opinion regarding the fairness of the financial statements. In discussing the annual report with you, he states that he presumes that the public accounting firm has prepared the financial statements and that since they have rendered an unqualified opinion on those statements, his investment is a good one.

Required:

Respond to your father's observations.

C1–8 The operations of the Zero Company have expanded so much that top management feels the company should employ an internal auditing staff. In discussing this move, the chief accountant suggests that the internal auditing staff be placed under his supervision — because much of the work the internal audit staff would be doing would be accounting oriented.

Required:

Advise the firm management regarding their need for an internal auditing staff and the way it should be fitted into the company organization.

C1–9 Aaron Wluka is a businessman not familiar with the accounting profession; he has just learned that the American Institute of Certified Public Accountants is the principal organization of CPAs. He has also learned that this organization has established the generally accepted auditing standards referred to in the standard short-form audit report that he has just finished reading. In discussing the report with you, Wluka states that he assumes that the AICPA also establishes generally accepted accounting practices, another term included in the short-form report. He says that if that is the case, he questions the desirability of CPAs' establishing their own auditing standards and generally accepted accounting practices without other elements of the business world having input into the establishment of those standards and practices.

Required:

Respond to Wluka's concerns.

PROBLEMS

P1–1 Select the best answer for each of the following questions.

a. The independent audit is important to readers of financial statements because it
   (1) Determines the future stewardship of the management of the company whose financial statements are audited.
   (2) Measures and communicates financial and business data included in financial statements.
   (3) Involves the objective examination of and reporting on management-prepared statements.
   (4) Reports on the accuracy of all information in the financial statements.

b. Which of the following *best* describes the reason why an independent auditor reports on financial statements?
   (1) A management fraud may exist and it is more likely to be detected by independent auditors.
   (2) Different interests may exist between the company preparing the statements and the persons using the statements.
   (3) A misstatement of account balances may exist and is generally corrected as the result of the independent auditor's work.
   (4) A poorly designed internal control system may be in existence.

c. An independent audit aids in the communication of economic data because the audit
   (1) Confirms the accuracy of management's financial representations.
   (2) Lends credibility to the financial statements.
   (3) Guarantees that financial data are fairly presented.
   (4) Assures the readers of financial statements that any fraudulent activity has been corrected.

d. Operational audits generally have been conducted by internal auditors and governmental audit agencies but may be performed by certified public accountants. A primary purpose of an operational audit is to provide
   (1) A means of assurance that internal accounting controls are functioning as planned.
   (2) Aid to the independent auditor, who is conducting the examination of the financial statements.
   (3) The results of internal examinations of financial and accounting matters to a company's top level management.
   (4) A measure of management performance in meeting organizational goals.

e. Which of the following is a Management Advisory Service Engagement Practice Standard only?
   (1) In performing management advisory service, a practitioner must act with integrity and objectivity and be independent in mental attitude.
   (2) The management advisory services engagement is to be performed by a person or persons having adequate technical training as a management consultant.
   (3) Management advisory service engagements are to be performed by practitioners having competence in the analytical approach and process, and in the technical subject matter under consideration.

(4) Before undertaking a management advisory service engagement, a practitioner is to notify the client of any reservations regarding anticipated benefits.

f. Which of the following *best* describes why publicly traded corporations follow the practice of having the outside auditor appointed by the board of directors or elected by the stockholders?
   (1) To comply with the regulations of the Financial Accounting Standards Board.
   (2) To emphasize auditor independence from the management of the corporation.
   (3) To encourage a policy of rotation of the independent auditors.
   (4) To provide the corporate owners with an opportunity to voice their opinion concerning the quality of the auditing firm selected by the directors.

g. Which of the following *best* describes the operational audit?
   (1) It requires the constant review by internal auditors of the administrative controls as they relate to the operations of the company.
   (2) It concentrates on implementing financial and accounting control in a newly organized company.
   (3) It attempts and is designed to verify the fair presentation of a company's results of operations.
   (4) It concentrates on seeking out aspects of operations in which waste would be reduced by the introduction of controls.

h. Auditing interpretations, which are issued by the staff of the AICPA Auditing Standards Division in order to provide timely guidance on the application of pronouncements of the Auditing Standards Board, are
   (1) Less authoritative than a pronouncement of the Auditing Standards Board.
   (2) Equally authoritative as a pronouncement of the Auditing Standards Board.
   (3) More authoritative than a pronouncement of the Auditing Standards Board.
   (4) Nonauthoritative opinions which are issued without consulting members of the Auditing Standards Board.

i. Which of the following *best* describes why an independent auditor is asked to express an opinion on the fair presentation of financial statements?
   (1) It is difficult to prepare financial statements that fairly present a company's financial position and changes in financial position and operations without the expertise of an independent auditor.
   (2) It is management's responsibility to seek available independent aid in the appraisal of the financial information shown in its financial statements.
   (3) The opinion of an independent party is needed because a company may *not* be objective with respect to its own financial statements.
   (4) It is a customary courtesy that all stockholders of a company receive an independent report on management's stewardship in managing the affairs of the business.

j. In connection with an audit of financial statements by an independent CPA, the client suggests that members of the internal audit staff be utilized to minimize external audit costs. It would be *inappropriate* for the CPA to delegate which of the following tasks to the internal audit staff?
   (1) Selection of accounts receivable for confirmation, based upon decision rules established by the independent CPA and with appropriate supervision by the CPA.
   (2) Investigation of negative accounts receivable responses, for later review by the independent CPA.

(3) Preparation of an accounts receivable aging schedule.
(4) Determination of the adequacy of the allowance for uncollectible accounts.

k. In comparison to the external auditor, an internal auditor is more likely to be concerned with
(1) Internal administrative control.
(2) Cost accounting procedures.
(3) Operational auditing.
(4) Internal accounting control.

l. During the course of an audit engagement an auditor prepares and accumulates audit working papers. The primary purpose of the audit working papers is to
(1) Aid the auditor in adequately planning his work.
(2) Provide a point of reference for future audit engagements.
(3) Support the underlying concepts included in the preparation of the basic financial statements.
(4) Support the auditor's opinion.

m. Operational audits generally have been conducted by internal auditors and governmental audit agencies but may be performed by certified public accountants. A primary purpose of an operational audit is to provide
(1) A means of assurance that internal accounting controls are functioning as planned.
(2) A measure of management performance in meeting organizational goals.
(3) The results of internal examinations of financial and accounting matters to a company's top level management.
(4) Aid to the independent auditor, who is conducting the examination of the financial statements.

n. The independent auditor lends credibility to client financial statements by
(1) Stating in the auditor's management letter that the examination was made in accordance with generally accepted auditing standards.
(2) Maintaining a clear-cut distinction between management's representations and the auditor's representations.
(3) Attaching an auditor's opinion to the client's financial statements.
(4) Testifying under oath about client financial information.

(AICPA adapted)

P1–2 Select the best answer for each of the following questions. (Refer to the appendixes.)

a. As part of your annual audit of a client, you prepare the federal income tax return. What modifications, if any, should you make to the preparer's declaration when signing the return?
(1) You should make no modification.
(2) You should modify the declaration to conform with the wording of your audit report.
(3) You should add a sentence to the declaration that the information contained herein was taken from audited financial statements covered by your report dated ____________.
(4) You should add a sentence to the declaration that some of the information contained herein was furnished by the client without audit.

b. A CPA firm's primary purpose for performing management advisory services is to
(1) Prepare the CPA firm for the changing needs and requirements of the business community.

(2) Establish the CPA firm as a consultant, which will enable the CPA firm to ensure future viability and growth.
(3) Provide advice and technical assistance that will enable a client to conduct its business more effectively.
(4) Enable staff members of the CPA firm to acquire the necessary continuing education in all areas of business.

c. The AICPA Committee on Management Services has stated its belief that a CPA should *not* undertake a management advisory service engagement for implementation of the CPA's recommendations unless
(1) The client does not understand the nature and implications of the recommended course of action.
(2) The client has made a firm decision to proceed with implementation based on his complete understanding and consideration of alternatives.
(3) The client does not have sufficient expertise within his organization to comprehend the significance of the changes being made.
(4) The CPA withdraws as independent auditor for the client.

d. In tax practice, which of the following would *not* be considered reasonable support for taking a position contrary to the Internal Revenue Code?
(1) Proposed regulations advocated by the IRS.
(2) Legal opinions as to the constitutionality of a specific provision.
(3) Possible conflicts between two sections of the Internal Revenue Code.
(4) Tax court decisions *not* acquiesced to by the IRS.

e. Juanita Adams, CPA, is preparing a federal tax return for Ralph Evans. In an interview to gather the necessary data, Evans stated he had given about $100 to charitable organizations soliciting at the door such as the local volunteer fire department and March of Dimes. What should Adams do with this information when preparing the tax return?
(1) She should ignore it because Statements on Responsibility in Tax Practice issued by the AICPA prohibit the use of estimates.
(2) She should identify $100 as "Other miscellaneous contributions."
(3) She should identify as contributions "volunteer fire department — $50; and March of Dimes — $50."
(4) She should increase one of Evans's other specifically named contributions by $100.

f. Tim Cortney has moved to a distant city but desires to continue to retain Hugo Blake, CPA, to prepare his personal federal tax return. Blake telephones Cortney after receiving his written list of information to be used in the preparation of the tax return because it appears to contain an understatement of interest expense. From the conversation Blake learns that the interest expense should be double the amount indicated on the written list. Blake, who asked Cortney to send a photocopy of the supporting evidence indicating the correct amount of the interest expense, has not received the correspondence and the filing deadline is five days away. Under the circumstances Blake should
(1) Prepare the return based on the written information received and *not* sign the preparer's declaration.
(2) Prepare the return based on the written information received, clearly indicating that an amended return will follow.
(3) Prepare the return based on the written and oral information received.
(4) Send Cortney a telegram indicating that no tax return will be prepared until all requested data are received.

g. When a CPA prepares a federal income tax return for an audit client, one would expect
(1) The CPA to take a position of client advocacy.
(2) The CPA to take a position of independent neutrality.
(3) The taxable net income in the audited financial statements to agree with taxable net income in the federal income tax return.
(4) The expenses in the audited financial statements to agree with the deductions in the federal income tax return.

h. In accordance with the AICPA Statements on Responsibilities in Tax Practice, if after having provided tax advice to a client there are legislative changes that affect the advice provided, the CPA
(1) Is obligated to notify the client of the change and the effect thereof.
(2) Is obligated to notify the client of the change and the effect thereof if the client was not advised that the advice was based on existing laws which are subject to change.
(3) Can *not* be expected to notify the client of the change unless the obligation is specifically undertaken by agreement.
(4) Can *not* be expected to have knowledge of the change.

i. In accordance with the AICPA Statements on Responsibilities in Tax Practice, where a question on a federal income tax return has not been answered, the CPA should sign the preparer's declaration only if
(1) The CPA can provide reasonable support for this omission upon examination by IRS.
(2) The information requested is *not* available.
(3) The question is *not* applicable to the taxpayer.
(4) An explanation of the reason for the omission is provided.

j. While performing tax services for a client, a CPA may learn of a material error in a previously filed tax return. In such an instance the CPA should
(1) Prepare an affidavit with respect to the error.
(2) Recommend compensating for the prior year's error in the current year's tax return where such action will mitigate the client's cost and inconvenience.
(3) Advise the client to file a corrected return regardless of whether or not the error resulted in an overstatement or understatement of tax.
(4) Inform the IRS of the error.

(AICPA adapted)

P1–3 Judd Hanlon, CPA, was engaged to prepare the federal income tax return for the Guild Corporation for the year ended December 31, 19X2. This is Mr. Hanlon's first engagement of any kind for the Guild Corporation.

In preparing the 19X2 return, Mr. Hanlon finds an error on the 19X1 return. The 19X1 depreciation deduction was overstated significantly — accumulated depreciation brought forward from 19X0 to 19X1 was understated, and thus the 19X1 base for declining balance depreciation was overstated.

Mr. Hanlon reported the error to Guild's controller, the officer responsible for tax returns. The controller stated: "Let the revenue agent find the error." He further instructed Mr. Hanlon to carry forward the material overstatement of the depreciable base to the 19X2 depreciation computation. The controller noted that this error also had been made in the financial records for 19X1 and 19X2 and offered to furnish Mr. Hanlon with a letter assuming full responsibility for this treatment.

Required:

a. Evaluate Mr. Hanlon's handling of this situation.
b. Discuss the additional action that Mr. Hanlon should now undertake.

(AICPA adapted)

P1–4 The CPA firm of Blank, Miller & Tage prepares a significant number of individual and corporate income tax returns. G. DeFilippo is a newly hired junior accountant. This is DeFilippo's first job since graduation from school. His initial assignment is to work with the tax department in the preparation of clients' 19X2 income tax returns. DeFilippo was instructed that he was not required to examine supporting data and that he could use the 19X1 returns of all clients in preparing the 19X2 returns. Further, he was instructed to sign all returns he prepared.

Required:

Answer the following, setting forth reasons for any conclusions stated.

a. What is the professional responsibility of the CPA firm and DeFilippo to clients in connection with the preparation of income tax returns, examining supporting data, and signing the return?
b. Give some examples of performance that would result in violation of these responsibilities.
c. If client X brings his already prepared return to DeFilippo and requests him to review the return, should DeFilippo sign the return as preparer? If so, should the preparer's declaration be modified to indicate that DeFilippo *reviewed* and did not prepare the return?

(AICPA adapted)

P1–5 Jones and Todd, a local CPA firm, responded to an invitation to bid for the audit of a local federally assisted program. The audit was to be conducted in accordance with the audit standards published by the General Accounting Office (GAO). Jones and Todd have become familiar with the GAO standards and recognize that the GAO standards are not consistent with generally accepted auditing standards (GAAS). They found that the GAO standards, unlike GAAS, are concerned with more than the financial aspects of an entity's operations.

Jones and Todd are engaged to perform the audit of the program, and the audit is to encompass all three elements that constitute the full scope of a GAO audit.

Required:

a. Jones and Todd should perform sufficient audit work to satisfy the financial compliance element of the GAO standards. What should such audit work determine?
b. After appropriate review and inquiries are covered, what uneconomical practices or inefficiencies should Jones and Todd be alert to as they work to satisfy the efficiency and economy element of the GAO standards?
c. After making appropriate review and inquiries, what should Jones and Todd consider to satisfy the program results element of the GAO standards?

(AICPA adapted)

P1–6 Marco Savage, CPA, has been requested by an audit client to perform a nonrecurring engagement involving the implementation of an EDP information and control system. The client requests that in setting up the new system and during the period prior to conversion to the new system, Savage undertake the following tasks:

a. Counsel on potential expansion of business activity plans.
b. Search for and interview new personnel.
c. Hire new personnel.
d. Train personnel.

In addition, the client requests that during the three months subsequent to the conversion Savage perform these services:

a. Supervise the operation of the new system.
b. Monitor client-prepared source documents and make change in basic EDP-generated data as Savage may deem necessary without concurrence of the client. Savage responds that he may perform some of the services requested, but not all of them.

Required:

a. Which of these services may Savage perform and which of these services may Savage not perform?
b. Before undertaking this engagement, Savage should inform the client of all significant matters related to the engagement. What are these significant matters?
c. If Savage adds to his staff an individual who specializes in developing computer systems, what degree of knowledge must Savage possess in order to supervise the specialist's activities?

(AICPA adapted)

P1–7 Your client, The Altamonte Corporation, has been experiencing a gradual but steady decline in profits and cash flow over the past five years. Mr. Eugene O'Flaherty, president of the company, has been very concerned with the situation. He feels that the decline in profits may be at least partially related to operational inefficiencies and to uneconomical and inefficient use of resources by certain departments. He calls you, a CPA, and asks if you have the knowledge and expertise to perform an intensive study and detailed report of the operational efficiency of the departments of purchasing and receiving, inventory stores, and production.

Required:

a. How would you respond to Mr. O'Flaherty's question as to whether you, a CPA, have the knowledge and expertise to perform such an examination?
b. How does the type of examination called for in this case differ from the type of audit CPAs usually do? Who normally performs these types of services?
c. What are some of the problems that you as an independent auditor might encounter on such an engagement?

P1–8 Your CPA firm has been approached by Lazy Acres, a small local real estate operation in Butte, Montana, about the possibility of performing auditing or some other type of service for them. You have determined that the company is in need of the following:

a. Monthly assistance in posting entries from the cash receipts and disbursements records to their general ledger.
b. Preparation of monthly cash basis financial statements to submit to the First State Bank of Helena, an institution that has extended the real estate firm a $200,000 line of credit.
c. Preparation of quarterly payroll tax returns.
d. Preparation of the company's annual partnership tax return.

The president of the company, J. R. Thomas, is not certain as to the types of services he needs you to perform. He asks your advice as to the kinds of services you are qualified to perform.

Required:

a. Of each of the services listed above, discuss the ones you feel qualified to perform.
b. What additional information, if any, might you want to obtain before advising Mr. Thomas?
c. On the basis of the facts listed above, what services would you recommend?

CHAPTER

2

CONCEPTUAL FRAMEWORK UNDERLYING THE INDEPENDENT AUDIT

In Chapter 1 we explained why the independent audit of financial statements is needed, and we described the report used to communicate the results of the audit to external users of those statements. We now turn our attention to the theoretical structure underlying the independent audit. Our discussion covers the following topics:

1. The attest function.
2. The responsibilities relating to errors and irregularities in financial statements that the auditor assumes as the audit report is signed.
3. The structure of audit theory.
4. The auditing standards the profession has adopted to control the quality of the independent audit.

We also include an appendix summarizing the conclusions and recommendations of the Commission on Auditors' Responsibilities regarding the independent audit.

THE ATTEST FUNCTION: A PRIMARY RESPONSIBILITY OF THE AUDITOR

The primary responsibility of the independent auditor is to assure the investing and lending public that the financial statements are objectively and fairly presented. As you saw in Chapter 1, that is accomplished by including an audit report attesting to fairness of presentation of the audited financial statements. In this section we further develop the responsibilities of the auditor associated with the attest function by these steps:

- Examining the key elements of the short-form audit report.
- Relating the historical development of the attest function to the evolution of the independent audit.
- Showing the importance of verifying fairness of presentation.
- Explaining how the principle of materiality and the concept of relative risk enter into the expression of an audit opinion.
- Noting briefly the kinds of decisions that the auditor must make as he or she performs the attest function.

Elements of the Short-Form Audit Report

The auditor performs the attest function by issuing an audit report (illustrated in Chapter 1) after completing an audit examination. The report is typically made up of two paragraphs. We saw that the first of these, characterized as a scope paragraph, explains what the auditor did in the process of examining the financial statements and that the second, described as the opinion paragraph, relates what the auditor found as a result of the work described in the scope paragraph. The auditor's signature at the bottom of the conventional unqualified audit report means that after the examination has been completed, the financial statements are judged to be materially correct (i.e., free from material errors) when measured against the criteria of generally accepted accounting principles (GAAP). If the auditor finds the statements not to be so presented, that fact must be appropriately indicated in the opinion paragraph before the report is signed.

A closer examination of the standard short-form audit report reveals three phrases vital to the performance of the attest function. The first of these, found in the scope paragraph, is *generally accepted auditing standards* (GAAS). These are standards of performance that must be met as the financial statements are examined, before an opinion can be expressed on them. There are ten such standards. They cover (a) the general implementation of the audit, (b) the field work to be done in connection with an audit, and (c) the report that must be rendered on the audited financial statements. These standards constitute the basic foundation from which the audit performance portions of this book are developed. They are discussed at some length later in this chapter.

The second important phrase in the short-form audit report is *fairly presented in accordance with generally accepted accounting principles*. The "fairly presented" portion of this phrase is discussed later in this section of the chapter. At this point, however, let's consider the standard against which fairness of presentation is measured, namely, *generally accepted accounting principles* (GAAP). Although the accounting profession has not seen fit to develop a thoroughly concise and uniform statement summarizing those principles, they have been defined in Statement 4 of the Accounting Principles Board (APB) as follows:

> Generally accepted accounting principles encompass the conventions, rules, and procedures necessary to define accepted accounting practice at a particular time. The standard of generally accepted accounting principles includes not only broad guidelines of general application but also detailed practices and procedures.[1]

These guidelines, practices, and procedures have evolved over the life of the accounting profession and are therefore reflected in accounting textbooks and official pronouncements coming from the Committee on Accounting Procedures, the Accounting Principles Board (APB) of the AICPA, and the Financial Accounting Standards Board (FASB). You have studied these principles, practices, and procedures in your financial accounting courses. The FASB is currently the authoritative body charged with resolving questions relating to GAAP. For example, an audit client that disagrees with the auditor on a significant matter affecting its financial statements may appeal its case to the FASB. Under the AICPA Code of Professional Ethics, the APB opinions and the accounting research bulletins issued by the AICPA, as well as FASB statements and interpretations, qualify as elements of GAAP. However, accounting interpretations issued by the AICPA *do not qualify* as elements of generally accepted accounting principles.

Although the accounting profession has not officially spelled out the elements of generally accepted accounting principles in a concise manner, practicing accountants, in the work they do, seem implicitly to operate within a framework of qualitative characteristics, principles, and conventions — similar to those shown in Figure 2–1.

We can observe from this illustration that a conceptually sound way of handling financial transactions is based fundamentally on the two qualitative requirements of ***relevance*** and ***reliability.*** The meaning of each of these requirements should, in turn, be interpreted by reference to the qualitative characteristics and concepts shown in the middle column of Figure 2–1. Ultimately the implementation of the accounting process, within the basic framework prescribed by the qualitative characteristics and principles, is accomplished through application of the four basic conventions shown to the right. It is important to observe again that fairness of presentation is measured against the accountant's interpretation of what constitutes generally accepted accounting principles for the enterprise unit being audited. That interpretation must, in turn, be based on the accounting literature, including the official pronouncements of the profession (far right column).

Development of the Attest Function and the Independent Audit

Throughout the early history of the auditing profession, there was little need for the attest function as it is performed today. There were no laws requiring an opinion on the financial statements and there was little reliance on public investors for funds. During those times, audits were performed primarily for managers who were also owners. They were therefore directed primarily toward discovering bookkeeping irregularities and fraudulent activities on the part of employees. For example, an early auditing text written by Lawrence R. Dicksee indicated that auditing had a threefold objective — including the detection of fraud, the detection of technical errors, and the detection of errors of principle.[2] Auditors during that period placed relatively greater emphasis on the examination of documentary support than they do now.

Audits during that period also centered on the examination of the balance sheet, which was often the only published financial statement. In view of the objective of discovering bookkeeping irregularities and internal fraud, the examination typically

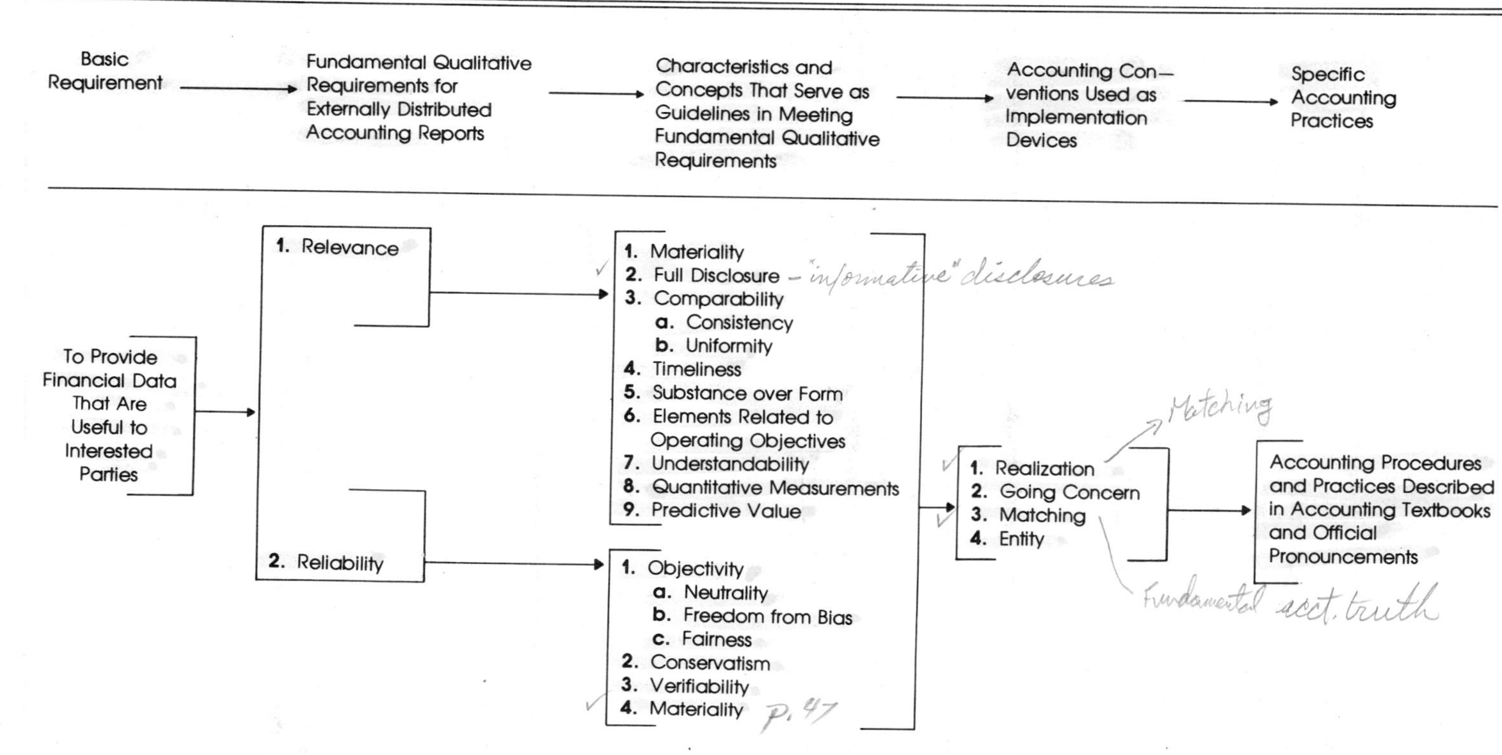

FIGURE 2–1. A Conceptual Framework for Determining Generally Accepted Auditing Practices

included a rather complete verification of transactions against supporting documents. In many instances this was interpreted to require a detailed check of all transactions. These audits relied almost completely on internal evidence, which meant that the "certified" statements were simply proved to be consistent with the account balances on the books. The following audit report, typical of those used during the early years of the profession, can be compared to the short-form report presented in Chapter 1 to show the difference between the type of work done by the auditor prior to 1920 and that done today:

> We have audited the books and accounts of the ABC Company for the year ended December 31, 1915, and we certify that, in our opinion, the above balance sheet sets forth its position as at the termination of that year and that the company profit and loss account is correct.[3]

Perhaps the most authoritative publication on auditing during the period from 1912 to 1957 was the Montgomery auditing text. The changes in auditing objectives are clearly reflected in the various editions of this text. In the earlier editions, Montgomery stated that the detection or prevention of fraud and the detection or prevention of errors were the primary objectives of the audit. He gave less and less emphasis to the fraud objective in subsequent editions and finally in his 1957 edition stated that it was a "responsibility not assumed." At that time he emphasized the attest function as the primary responsibility of the auditor.

The changes reflected in the Montgomery text were associated with changes in the business environment. Beginning in the 1920s, firms began to rely more heavily on capital from public investors. This generally took the form of stock being sold to third-party investors not affiliated with the firm in a managerial capacity. As a result of this change in the environment, auditors also began to be the target of litigation. They began to substitute the determination of fair presentation for the detection of bookkeeping errors and fraud in the performance of independent audits.

The legal responsibility of the auditor for meeting third-party needs for fairly presented financial information was first emphasized by the courts in the *Ultramares v. Touche* case.[4] In this case, a third-party creditor sued the auditors for negligence and fraud in the performance of the audit because of a loss suffered on a loan made to Fred Stern and Company. This legal case is important because it established a basis for third-party action against an auditor for serious negligence in the proof of account balances. It led to a greater emphasis on the development of external support for such things as accounts receivable through confirmation procedures.

Another milestone in the movement toward emphasizing the attest function occurred in 1933. During that year the Securities Act was passed by Congress. This act further increased the auditor's potential liability to third parties. A year later Congress passed the Securities Exchange Act, which was designed to regulate public security trading. It created the Securities and Exchange Commission as an agency to regulate those activities.

In the late 1930s, the *McKesson & Robbins* case further emphasized the need for objectively developed financial statements for which selected account balances are verified against external evidence. Largely as a result of this case, the AICPA issued a pronouncement requiring auditors to gather independent and external evidence regarding the existence of accounts receivable and inventory when those accounts were material. This case led to the establishment of ten generally accepted auditing standards (GAAS), which are still the foundation of the present-day auditing process. As a result of this case, the SEC, in addition to recommending the gathering of external evidence, also stated that (1) the stockholders should hire the auditor, (2) the audit report should be addressed to the stockholders, and (3) the auditors should attend stockholders meetings for the purpose of answering questions posed by that group.

Over the years since 1940 (and particularly during the 1960s and 1970s), various public accounting firms have been involved in lawsuits initiated by third parties who had relied on audit opinions rendered with financial statements of businesses in which the third parties had creditor or investor interests. These events have had their influence on the development of generally accepted auditing standards (GAAS) and statements on auditing standards (SAS), which accountants use as guidelines for determining the tests of the accounting records and the auditing procedures that are "considered necessary in the circumstances." Statements on auditing standards are interpretations of the ten basic generally accepted auditing standards, and are discussed at various points throughout this book.

The United States Congress has also become involved with the accounting profession because of its concern for improving the accountability of publicly owned corporations. During the 1970s the Metcalf Committee[5] of the U.S. Senate and the Moss Committee[6] from the U.S. House of Representatives gave considerable attention to the auditing and reporting practices followed by independent auditors in servicing firms. The Metcalf Report made several recommendations including one of establishing a self-regulatory organization with disciplinary powers similar to those of the New York Stock Exchange and the National Association of Security Dealers. Although no organization of this type has been established, this action has obviously influenced the accounting profession toward programs of self-investigation and self-discipline.

Primarily in response to those congressional committee actions, we have seen a strong emphasis placed on *peer review practices* for firms involved in work monitored by the SEC. This involves having a firm's practices reviewed and evaluated by another public accounting firm. The SEC Practice Section of the AICPA has created a Public Oversight Board charged with the following responsibilities:

- Monitoring and evaluating the regulatory and sanction activities of the peer review and executive committees to ensure their effectiveness.
- Determining that the peer review committee is ascertaining that firms are taking appropriate action as a result of peer reviews.
- Conducting continuing oversight of all other activities of the section.
- Making recommendations to the executive committee for improvements in the operations of the section.
- Publishing an annual report and such other reports as may be deemed necessary with respect to its activities.
- Engaging staff to assist in carrying out its functions.
- Having the right for any or all of its members to attend any meetings of the executive committee.[7]

Emphasis on Fairness of Presentation

As we examine the short-form audit report currently used by auditors, it is important to recognize that the terms *true* and *correct*, historically used by auditors to express their finding relating to the financial statements, have been replaced by the phrase *fairly presented.* This change in terminology has occurred as the profession has recognized that there is no such thing as a completely correct set of financial statements. The meaning of *fairly presented* is partially clarified by Statement on Auditing Standards (SAS) 5. It requires that before signing an opinion stating that the statements are fairly presented, the auditor must judge whether each of the following criteria has been met:

- Accounting principles selected and applied have general acceptance.
- Accounting principles are appropriate in the circumstances.
- Financial statements including related notes are appropriately informative.
- Information presented in the financial statements is classified and summarized in a reasonable manner.
- Financial statements appropriately reflect the underlying events and transactions within a range of acceptable limits that are reasonable and practical to attain.[8]

This standard emphasizes the importance of the judgments to be made by the auditor as the audit is being performed and the audit report is being written.

The sources of established accounting principles include

1. Pronouncements of authoritative bodies designated by the AICPA under its Code of Professional Conduct. These include FASB Statements and Interpretations, APB Opinions, and AICPA Accounting Research Bulletins.
2. Pronouncements of bodies composed of expert accountants that follow an approval procedure similar to that of the FASB for their professional pronouncements. Such pronouncements include AICPA Industry Audit Guides and Statements of Position.
3. Practices of pronouncements other than (1) or (2) that are widely recognized as being prevalent practice in a particular industry. Such pronouncements include FASB Technical Bulletins and AICPA Accounting Interpretations, as well as recognized industry practices.
4. Other authoritative literature such as APB Statements, AICPA Issues Papers, FASB Statements of Financial Accounting Concepts, and accounting textbooks and articles. The appropriateness of literature in this category as a source of established accounting principles depends on its relevance to particular circumstances, specificity of the guidance, and general recognition of the issuer or author as authority.

Materiality and Relative Risk

Figure 2–1 showed us that the qualitative requirement of relevance is interpreted to require the application of the concept of materiality. It is impractical to expect the accountant to present precisely correct financial statements. In the process of recording, classifying, and summarizing the financial data, many judgments have to be made which could cause the specific data presented in the financial statements to differ according to the judgments that might be made. Furthermore, there is, realistically, little to be gained by pursuing a goal of precise correctness. Instead, the accounting profession has adopted the ***principle of materiality,*** which, in effect, says that the accountant, in making decisions relating to the accounting process, should be concerned only with those things that have a significant effect on the financial statement data. As a result, the auditor must judge whether or not reported results are within a *range of acceptable limits.*[9] Here again, however, the accounting profession has failed to develop specific criteria for determining the meaning of materiality in specific decision situations.

As a general rule, the accountant considers an item to be material if an error in, or an omission of, it *would cause a prudent individual, who can use financial statements intelligently, to change a decision that might be made on the basis of those statements.* Sometimes percentages relating the individual item to the balance in an account, to total assets, or to net income may be established by an auditor or an auditing firm as a basis for judging materiality. In the use of such guidelines, however, it is important to realize that specific percentage relationships should be evaluated in the light of the way the item being considered affects all other items relating to it. For example, an error in inventory that is insignificant in relationship to total inventory may be significant if net income will be misstated by the amount of the inventory error. Another important factor to consider is the effect that an error may have on trends and on the relative change in an item.

As we shall explain later, one of the ten generally accepted auditing standards relates directly to the principle of ***full disclosure*** in the presentation of financial data. Basically, that standard allows the users of financial statements to conclude that all significant financial facts have been disclosed, either in the financial statements or in the footnotes relating to those statements, unless an exception is reflected in the audit report.

A reference to ***consistency*** is included in the last sentence of the opinion paragraph of the short-form audit report. The inclusion of this principle points up the importance of the technique of comparison in the use of financial data. Therefore consistency in the application of generally accepted accounting principles helps users make appropriate judgments regarding the changes observed between the two or more years' data included in the annual report.

The ***relative risk*** associated with a possible error must also be considered in judging whether or not it would be significant to the audit opinion. In this context, relative risk can refer to the possibility of the item in question being misappropriated. For example, a small error in cash, because of the susceptibility of this account to fraud, may be significant even though it represents only a small percentage of the total cash on hand or of the total assets of the firm. In contrast, the same dollar error in property and equipment may not be significant, because property and equipment is not as susceptible to misappropriation as is cash.

Decisions Relating to the Attest Function

Our discussion to this point has emphasized the content of the typical short-form audit report and the way in which it assures the users of the financial statements that those statements are objectively and fairly presented. Obviously the findings of the audit may cause the auditor to conclude that the financial statements are not (within the range of acceptable limits) fairly presented. When such situations arise, the auditor must make the decision as to whether a qualified or an adverse opinion should be expressed. If the departure from generally accepted accounting principles is not significant enough to cause an unfair presentation but still provides a significant deviation from fairness, the report should be qualified by citing the deviation and explaining the significance of it. On the other hand, if the deviation is significant enough to cause an unfair presentation of the financial statements, the auditor must express an adverse opinion. The considerations involved in these decisions are discussed in the chapters on reporting.

As observed earlier, some audits are performed for the purpose of attesting to the fairness of statement presentation measured against something other than GAAP. In those situations the report can reflect attestation to the fairness of the information in relation to some other comprehensive basis of accounting. The specific wording of such reports is discussed in Chapter 18.

RESPONSIBILITIES RELATING TO ERRORS AND IRREGULARITIES

In the preceding section we noted that, prior to 1920, independent auditors were primarily concerned with the detection of fraud and the discovery of bookkeeping errors. We also observed a shift away from those objectives as the need for the attest function developed during the 1920s and in subsequent years. Beginning in the early 1960s a large number of lawsuits were filed against members of the profession, contending that fraud should have been discovered in the performance of the audit and seeking damages from the auditor for failure to discover the irregularities. These actions have led the profession back toward requiring the independent auditor to accept more responsibility for the detection of errors and irregularities.

In this section we examine the auditor's current responsibilities for discovering errors and irregularities and for reacting to those discoveries. We do that in the following ways:

- Observing the effects that such errors may have on the fairness of statement presentation.
- Describing the accounting profession's current position regarding the discovery of fraud.
- Briefly summarizing interested parties' apparent expectations regarding the discovery of fraud.

The Effects of Errors and Irregularities on the Fairness of Statement Presentation

The audit report discussed earlier in this chapter includes an expression of opinion regarding the fairness of the financial statements. To meet the auditor's responsibilities insofar as the attest function is concerned, he or she must clearly take the responsibility for actively searching for both errors and irregularities that would materially affect the fairness of the data included in the financial statements. Furthermore, if an examination leads an auditor to suspect fraud, even though it may not be material enough to effect the audit opinion, he or she should refer the matter to appropriate representatives of management with the suggestion that it be pursued to a conclusion.

Historically the official pronouncements of the American Institute of Certified Public Accountants, prior to 1960, tended to stress the fact that the independent auditor was, within the framework of an ordinary audit, severely limited insofar as his or her capability of discovering "defalcations and other similar irregularities." The codification of auditing pronouncements issued in 1951 included the following statements relating to the auditor's responsibility for discovering irregularities:

> The ordinary examination incident to the issuance of an opinion respecting financial statements is not designed and cannot be relied upon to disclose defalcations and other similar irregularities although their discovery frequently results. In a well-organized concern reliance for the detection of such irregularities is placed principally upon the maintenance of an adequate system of accounting records with appropriate internal control.[10]

This document also states that, if the auditor were to direct her or his work toward the discovery of all defalcations, the audit work would have to be extended to the point where the cost to the client would be prohibitive. It indicates further that the auditor relies on the integrity of the client's organization — unless circumstances are such that suspicion may be aroused. In those instances auditing procedures are expected to be extended to determine whether or not such suspicions are justified.

As noted before, the attitude expressed in the preceding paragraph began to change in the early 1960s and the official pronouncements issued since that time have reflected that change in attitude. However, even within the pre–1960 official attitude, the auditor had a responsibility for discovering any errors or irregularities that would have a significant influence on the fairness of the data included in the financial statements because of the responsibilities associated with the attest function.

Responsibilities Relating to the Discovery of Fraud

Fraud often involves the intentional introduction of errors into the accounting data for the purpose either of concealing the theft of assets or of deliberately misrepresenting a firm's financial position or results of operations. Statement on Auditing Standards (SAS) 16 characterizes such intentional errors as irregularities. The frauds associated with such irregularities are divided into two categories — namely, employee fraud and management fraud.[11]

Employee fraud generally involves the theft of resources from the firm, with intentional errors introduced into the accounting records to conceal the theft. Businesses rely on their systems of internal control to reduce the probability of this occurring without the collusion of two or more employees. Therefore, as the auditor evaluates a firm's system of control, it is especially important for her or him to identify the points of weakness and call them to the attention of management. Furthermore, the auditor should be expected to detect those employee frauds that the exercise of professional skill and care would normally uncover. This calls for awareness of the ways in which such frauds could be perpetrated and the maintenance of an attitude of professional skepticism as elements of the accounting system subject to the possibility of fraud are examined.

Management fraud generally involves an intentional introduction of error into the accounting records by upper level management for the purpose of deliberately misrepresenting the firm's financial position or results of operations. This type of fraud can occur even with a sound system of internal control because the control procedures can be overidden by management directive. As a result of that fact this type of fraud, which can most directly affect the fairness of presentation of the financial statements, is especially difficult to discover.

The negative and defensive tone of the official position on fraud detection, evident in the 1951 codification, began to change after 1960. To some extent this change in attitude can be traced to user expectations and the various lawsuits against members of the profession since 1960. Statement on Auditing Standards (SAS) 1, issued in November 1972, contains the following statement, which reflects the official position on the detection of fraud at that time:

> In making the ordinary examination the independent auditor is aware of the possibility that fraud may exist . . . The auditor recognizes that fraud, if sufficiently material, may affect his opinion on the financial statements and his examination, made in accordance with generally accepted auditing standards, gives consideration to this possibility. However, the ordinary examination directed to the expression of an opinion on financial statements is not primarily or specifically designed and cannot be relied upon to disclose defalcations and other similar irregularities although their discovery may result. Similarly, although the discovery of deliberate misrepresentation by management is usually more closely associated with the objective of the ordinary examination, such examination cannot be relied upon to assure its discovery. The responsibility of the independent auditor for failure to detect fraud arises only when such failure clearly results from the failure to comply with generally accepted auditing standards.[12]

The tone of this statement clearly shows a greater concern for management fraud than that exhibited in the 1951 codification, but it is still hedged by negative language. However, this statement does specifically state that the independent auditor has a responsibility for detecting any fraud that would cause the financial statements to fail to fairly present the financial position or the results of operations for the period.

The movement toward acceptance of greater responsibility for the discovery of the management type of fraud is also reflected in Statement on Auditing Standards (SAS) 6[13] issued in 1975 and in SAS 16[14] issued in January 1977. The first of these deals with ***related party transactions*** and calls for the auditor to give special attention to the examination of material transactions between the firm and related parties. That statement includes a list of procedures that are designed to help determine the existence and identification of related party transactions. Furthermore, it requires the auditor to disclose with the financial statements the fact that the reporting entity participated in related party transactions — if they are material.

SAS 16 draws a careful distinction between unintentional and intentional distortions of the financial statements.[15] It emphasizes the fact that the auditor has a responsibility, within the inherent limitations of the auditing process, to search for errors or irregularities that would have a material effect on the financial statements and to exercise due skill and care in the conduct of that examination. Furthermore the examination is expected to be approached with an attitude of professional skepticism that recognizes the possibilities of errors or irregularities. This statement also points out that the auditor cannot depend on the normal system of control to prevent management fraud since the system can be overridden by management directive. However, it also says that the auditor is justified, unless there is evidential matter to the contrary, in relying on the truthfulness of certain representations and on the genuineness of records and documents obtained during the examination. Nevertheless if the auditor's examination suggests that material errors or irregularities may exist, the auditor should consider their implications. The matter and extent of further investigation should be discussed with the appropriate level of management that is at least one level above those thought to be involved in the fraud. Beyond that, the statement suggests that if the auditor is still uncertain about whether errors or possible irregularities materially affect the financial statements, the opinion should be qualified or disclaimed. If the auditor concludes that the financial statements contain material undisclosed errors and irregularities, he or she should either express a qualified or adverse opinion or possibly withdraw from the engagement.[16]

Illegal acts by clients may be characterized as another type of management fraud. These occur when an employee of the client commits an act for the firm that is in violation of the law. The auditor's responsibilities relating to such acts are described in SAS 17. This statement states that the typical audit examination cannot be relied upon for the detection of client illegal acts.[17] It recognizes that the auditor is neither an attorney nor a detective. The statement therefore cautions the auditor to be alert to the possibility of client illegal acts and indicates what should be done if such acts are suspected.

If procedures performed for the purpose of expressing an opinion on the financial statements bring possible illegal acts of the client to the auditor's attention, SAS 17 requires that the auditor inquire of the client's management and consult with the client's legal counsel or other specialists as is necessary.[18] Illegal acts generally involve unauthorized transactions, transactions improperly recorded, or transactions not recorded in a complete or timely manner. The discovery of any of these characteristics should raise questions about the possible existence of an illegal act. If the auditor determines that an illegal act has occurred, its implications, insofar as disclosure in the financial statements is concerned must be considered. The circumstances should also be reported to personnel within the client's organization at a level of authority at least one level above that at which the illegal act occurred so that appropriate action may be taken by the client.[19] This could involve remedial action, adjustments or disclosures in financial statements, or disclosures in other documents. The auditor may find it necessary to inform the client's board of directors or audit committee of the findings if management refuses to act. If these bodies fail to give proper consideration to an illegal act that has been discovered, the auditor should consider withdrawing from the engagement or refraining from any future association with the financial statements of the client.[20] If the auditor decides to remain associated with the financial statements of the client, steps should be taken to see that undisclosed illegal acts including their financial statement implications are disclosed in the audit report, and either a qualified or adverse opinion should be expressed.

Expectations of Interested Parties

The product that the auditor sells is a professional opinion on financial statements. Therefore, just as is the case with the producers of other products, the profession must attempt to meet the expectations of the users of those statements. In responding to those expectations, the auditor seeks to provide as much of what the users want as is possible within the constraints of the auditing environment. In some instances the cost of providing what users want may exceed the benefits which they would derive from that information. In other instances, however, the auditor can and should respond completely to the expectations of parties interested in the audited financial statements.

The expectations of the users are, in many instances, reflected through the medium of regulatory agencies and other groups created to protect statement users and to serve as intermediaries in the interpretation of financial statements. For example, as early as 1940, Accounting Series Release (ASR) 19 stated that even in balance sheet examinations for corporations whose securities are held by the public, accountants can be expected to detect gross overstatements of assets and profits whether these overstatements result from collusive fraud or otherwise.[21] That position was reiterated in 1974 in ASR 153.[22]

A survey conducted for Arthur Andersen and Company in 1974 indicated that 66 percent of the investing public believed that the most important function of the public accounting firm's audit of a corporation is to detect fraud. The general viewpoint of various groups of users and regulatory agencies was expressed well in an article published in *Accountancy* in 1971. This article states that "the first object of an audit is to say that the accounts can be relied upon and that they are right; it is absurd to say that they are all right subject, of course, to the possibility that undetected fraud may have made them all wrong."[23]

If these observations represent the expectations of users, we can expect the auditing profession to move in the direction of accepting more responsibility for the detection of fraud. As the preceding pages have shown, this is at least partially evident in the issuance of SAS 6, SAS 16, and SAS 17. The current attitudes of the profession in this matter are also reflected in the report of the Commission on Auditors' Responsibilities, which is summarized in Appendix 2–A.

THE STRUCTURE OF AUDIT THEORY

Theory provides a foundation or basis for organizing one's thoughts and carrying out subsequent actions. Auditing theory helps describe, explain, and identify the decisions the auditor must make in performing an audit. The auditor relies on auditing theory in making the decisions associated with each step of an audit. That theory comprises a series of postulates, concepts, standards (or precepts), objectives, and procedures. These elements of the theory relate to each other as shown in Figure 2–2. In this illustration, the arrows pointing toward the right signify that each successive element is developed as a logical consequence of the preceding element.

FIGURE 2–2. The Elements of Audit Theory

Auditing Postulates

Postulates are defined as prerequisite, fundamental beliefs upon which other ideas, propositions, beliefs, or rules can be based. The following basic postulates are fundamental to auditing theory:

- No potential conflict of interest exists between the auditors and the preparers of financial information.
- The auditor acts exclusively as an auditor.
- The auditor adheres to identifiable professional obligations.
- Economic assertions can be verified.
- Strong internal control implies greater reliability of financial information.
- In the absence of known conditions to the contrary, what has held true in the past for the enterprise will hold true for the future.
- "Fair presentation" implies use of GAAP or other stated criteria.

Auditing Concepts

Concepts imply mental generalizations, central ideas, or foundations for thought. In auditing they represent broad generalizations inferred from the postulates previously mentioned. The concepts, in turn, underlie the standards and procedures. In auditing, at least five basic concepts can be identified:

- Ethical conduct.
- Independence.
- Due care.
- Evidence.
- Fair presentation.

Auditing Standards

Standards are criteria that the auditor must meet in performing an audit. They proceed logically from the postulates and concepts that support them. All of the professional literature of the AICPA, the GAO, and the IIA, which set forth the rules of practice for all types of auditors, begin with standards. Later in this chapter, we list and briefly explain the standards established for independent audits.

Auditing Objectives

Objectives are goals to be achieved in carrying out an activity. The main goal for the independent auditor is the expression of an opinion on the financial statements.

However, this opinion is the culmination of a long process of inductive and deductive reasoning and rational argument. In the process of forming an opinion, the auditor must meet the following six audit objectives in verifying financial statement account balances. These objectives serve as intermediate goals and guides to the practical application of audit standards. They call for the verification of these elements:

- Statement presentation.
- Transaction validity.
- Ownership.
- Periodicity (cutoff).
- Valuation.
- Existence.

These objectives are discussed in Chapter 3. We list them here only to show their position within the framework of auditing theory. Audit objectives serve as a connecting link between auditing standards and auditing procedures. They are the medium by which audit standards are translated into and fullfilled by audit procedures.

Auditing Procedures

Procedures reflect specific acts to be performed in carrying out an activity. They are different from auditing standards in that they relate to acts to be performed whereas the standards are qualitative goals to be met. Audit procedures are summarized in the audit program, and are the steps by which audit objectives are operationalized. Figure 2–3 explains diagrammatically the relationship among postulates, concepts, standards, and objectives. As we shall explain later, auditing procedures are developed to meet the audit objectives identified for each segment of the audit.

AUDITING STANDARDS

We now identify and briefly discuss the standards that have been established for the independent audit. These standards have been established by the AICPA and approved by its membership. They are probably the most widely recognized of the various sets of audit standards and should be complied with on every audit engagement. The standards for an independent audit are divided into three broad groups: general standards, field work standards, and reporting standards.

General Standards

General standards relate to the personal qualifications and attributes of the auditor and to the quality of audit work performed. The auditor must in effect decide whether these standards can be met in performing an audit engagement before he or she can accept the engagement. The AICPA has adopted three general audit standards:

1. The examination is to be performed by a person or persons having adequate technical training and proficiency as an auditor.
2. In all matters relating to the assignment, an independence in mental attitude is to be maintained by the auditor or auditors.

Postulates	Concepts	Auditing Standards	Auditing Objectives
1. No potential conflict of interest	1. Ethical conduct	Adequate training	
2. Auditor acts exclusively as auditor	2. Independence	(AICPA, GAO)	
3. Professional obligations	3. Due audit care	Independent attitude (AICPA, GAO) Due professional care (AICPA, GAO) Scope of audit (GAO) Needs of users (GAO)	
4. Verifiability	4. Evidence	Planning and supervision (AICPA, GAO)	
5. Strong internal control provides more reliable financial information		Study and evaluation of internal control (AICPA, GAO) Sufficient, competent evidential matter (AICPA, GAO)	Transaction validity Ownership Periodicity Valuation Existence
6. Past holds true for the future		Compliance review (GAO)	
7. Fair presentation implies GAAP	5. Fair presentation	Statements conforming to GAAP (AICPA, GAO) Other specified accounting principles (AICPA, GAO) Consistency (AICPA, GAO) Adequate information disclosure (AICPA, GAO) Compliance violations (GAO) Expression of opinion or disclaimer (AICPA, GAO) Distribution and timing (GAO) Detail report content (GAO)	Statement presentation

FIGURE 2–3. The Relationship Among the Elements of Audit Theory

3. Due professional care is to be exercised in performance of the examination and the preparation of the report.

Technical Training and Proficiency. This standard recognizes that in order to adequately conduct an audit examination, the auditor must possess both education and experience. The education which the auditor acquires should begin with a solid formal education in both accounting and auditing. Because accounting principles are the criteria that the auditor must apply in determining whether the financial statements of the client are fairly presented, it is not possible to be a proficient auditor without first becoming a proficient accountant. Furthermore, since the disciplines of accounting and auditing are continually changing, it is essential that an auditor's formal education be periodically updated through continuing professional education courses beyond the college level. For this reason many CPA firms have established quality control policies and procedures relating to the professional development of staff accountants.

The foundation for the application of all audit procedures is ***seasoned audit judgment.*** No matter how much formal education the auditor possesses, that alone is not sufficient to afford the auditor a basis for an opinion. Formal education must therefore be supplemented by extensive experience to enable the supervising auditor to make the judgments required in a typical audit engagement. Auditors at every subordinate level must spend much time in on-the-job training and in being supervised and reviewed regularly by more experienced auditors. The auditor with final responsibility for the engagement (usually a partner or shareholder of the audit firm who signs the audit report) must exercise the greatest degree of seasoned judgment, because he or she is ultimately responsible for the firm's position with respect to a client's financial data. These stringent requirements for extensive education and experience for auditors are based upon the postulate of ***professional obligations:*** along with the status of "professional" comes the responsibility of the auditor to society, to the client, and to fellow auditors to do the best job possible in the light of one's background and expertise. If an auditor is not technically or experientially competent to handle an audit problem, he or she should (1) obtain the necessary expertise if time permits; (2) refer the audit work to another more experienced professional; or (3) decline the engagement.

Independent Mental Attitude. The second general audit standard requires that the auditor maintain an independent mental attitude so that she or he can act with integrity and objectivity in all matters relating to the assignment. Independence is the keystone of the auditing profession. It is therefore emphasized in staff training programs and in supervision and review of audit work. The very justification for the social and economic value of the audit report (the primary tangible product of the audit) is that it provides an unbiased opinion of an informed observer as to the propriety of accounting information. The auditor's opinion would be of no social or economic value if the auditor were not independent of the client.

Independence is of such primary importance to the auditing profession that it is one of the concepts upon which auditing theory is founded. It follows logically from two auditing postulates: (1) no potential conflict of interest exists between the auditor and management of the client; and (2) *the auditor acts exclusively as an auditor*. The first of these postulates means that, since there may be a conflict of interest between management and appropriately prepared financial statements, it is essential that the person who examines the statements have no relationship with management or the audited entity which could cause that person to gain from improprieties in the financial statements. The second of these postulates means that, although auditing is a service-oriented profession, the nonaudit services (management advisory services, tax services, etc.) when performed for an audit client, must take a role of secondary importance to the audit responsibility. The auditor must, both in actions and appearances, be a person who exercises sole independent judgment and responsibility over the following steps in the audit:

1. Writing the audit program.
2. Gathering the audit evidence.
3. Writing the audit report.

Although client employees (including internal auditors) may assist the auditor in gathering evidence, any area of the audit that requires the exercise of professional judgment must not be relinquished to others.

Independence, from a conceptual standpoint, is a two-pronged issue. The auditor must be independent both *in fact* and *in appearance*. Independence in fact is an intellectually honest state of mind. The auditor may, in some situations, be the only person capable of assessing this facet of independence. Beyond *being* independent, however, the auditor must appear to others to be independent. Therefore he or she is required to be free from any obligation to or interest in the client, its management, or its owners. For example, even though an auditor might be intellectually unbiased with respect to a client, it is unlikely that the general public would believe that fact if the auditor owned stock in the client company. Independence is of such importance to maintaining public confidence in the auditing profession that precepts to guard against the presumption (or appearance) of loss of independence have been written into the AICPA's Code of Professional Conduct. Also, as part of its Statement on Quality Controls Standards No. 1 ("System of Quality Control for a CPA firm"), the AICPA has set up guidelines to assist the CPA firm in pursuing the goal of maintaining the appearance of independence.

Due Professional Care. The third general audit standard requires the auditor to exercise due professional care in the conduct of the audit examination. Based on the postulate of professional obligations to the general public and others, the concept of due professional care concerns what the auditor does and how well it is done. Every person who offers services to the general public assumes the responsibility of performing as a professional with the degree of skill commonly possessed by others in the field. The concept of due care imposes a level of performance responsibility that must be met by all persons involved in meeting the field work and reporting standards. For example, the auditor must exercise due care in judging whether the evidence is both sufficient and competent enough to provide support for the audit report.

The due care concept recognizes, however, that auditors, like all other human beings, are subject to mistakes in judgment. These types of errors occur in every profession, and allowances must be provided for them. The auditor undertakes a service in good faith and integrity, but is not infallible. He or she is liable to the client and, as has been shown in the courts many times, to third parties, for negligence, bad faith, or dishonesty.

Field Work Standards

The field work standards set forth the guidelines for the actual evidence-gathering segment of the audit. There are three standards governing the field work of independent auditors:

1. The work is to be *adequately planned*, and assistants, if any, are to be *properly supervised*.
2. There is to be a proper *study and evaluation of the existing system of internal control* as a basis for reliance thereon and for the determination of the resultant extent of the tests to which auditing procedures are to be restricted.
3. *Sufficient competent evidential matter* is to be obtained through inspection, observation, inquiries, and confirmation to afford a reasonable basis for an opinion regarding the financial statements under examination.

Adequate Planning and Supervision. Underlying the adequate planning and supervision standard is the due professional care concept. In order to exercise proper care on an audit engagement, attention should be given to the timing factors involved in acceptance of the engagement, to adequate planning of the actual procedures, and to appropriately appointing and supervising assistants on the engagement.

With respect to acceptance of the engagement, it is desirable that the auditor be appointed at an early date, before the end of the client's fiscal year. This is true because important elements of the audit field work can be done at ***interim dates*** (during the client's fiscal year), thus allowing the auditor to be more efficient. Planning may include preliminary *analytical review procedures* to assist in identifying potential problem areas which require a heavier-than-usual concentration of effort during final audit work, performed on or after the end of the fiscal year. The auditor's preliminary study and evaluation of internal controls can also be beneficially performed at interim dates. This procedure can help identify potential material weaknesses in the system of controls, which will necessitate more extensive tests of the balances produced by the system than would otherwise be necessary.

Planning of the audit involves developing an overall strategy for the expected conduct and scope of the examination. Supervision involves directing the work of assistants who are involved in accomplishing the objectives of the examination and in determining whether those objectives have been accomplished at the end of field work.

Evaluating the System of Internal Control. The second field work standard involves the auditor's study and evaluation of the client's system of internal control. This standard helps the auditor in determining the nature, timing, and extent of audit tests of the financial statement balances. The postulate that explains this reasoning is that strong internal control provides reliable financial information. Since most financial statement balances of large audit clients are the result of thousands of transactions, it is impossible to audit 100 percent of the transactions comprised by a particular account on a cost effective basis. Therefore, as observed earlier, the auditor must rely on sampling techniques. When sampling techniques are used, there is always an inherent risk that misstatements in the financial statements will go undetected by the auditor. SAS 1 describes audit risk in the following way:

> It should be understood that the ultimate risk against which the auditor and those who rely on his opinion require reasonable protection is a combination of two separate risks. The first of these is that material errors will occur in the accounting process by which the financial statements are developed. The second is that any material errors that occur will not be detected by the auditor's examination.[24]

The auditor relies on internal controls to reduce the first of the two risks mentioned above. We can conclude that an inverse relationship exists between the quality of the internal control system and the amount of material error being emitted from the system. A material error is defined by SAS No. 1 as

> a condition in which the auditor believes (1) the prescribed procedures or (2) the degree of compliance with them does not reduce to a relatively low level the risk that errors or irregularities which are material in the financial statements being audited would be detected within a timely period by employees in the normal course of performing their assigned functions.[25]

Sufficient Competent Evidence. The third standard of field work requires the auditor to gather sufficient competent evidential matter to afford a reasonable basis for an opinion regarding the financial statements. The concept of ***evidence*** is basic to the audit process and supports all of the field work standards. All of the decisions the auditor reaches become justifiable only if they are adequately supported by evidence. Evidence provides a rational basis for forming judgments about the fairness of financial information. The auditor uses her or his findings regarding the system of internal control to determine how much other evidence must be gathered to support the balances on the financial statements.

The concept of evidence is based on the postulate of ***verifiability.*** Unless the financial data are verifiable, auditing has no meaning or reason for existence. Therefore the propositions or hypotheses which the auditor is trying to test must be supported by "sufficient competent evidential matter."

Audit evidence can take many forms, such as *physical observation, mathematical computations, statements by third parties, documents, statements by officers and employees of the company,* and *satisfactory internal control procedures.* These types of evidence may range from compelling to only mildly persuasive. As we explain below, the auditor must evaluate the quality as well as the quantity of evidence. Both of these characteristics help evidence to be ***persuasive.*** Various types of evidence are discussed more fully as we explain the implementation of audit procedures later in the text.

As observed above, the persuasiveness of evidence depends on both its quantity and its quality. First, it should be ***sufficient.*** Sufficiency implies that a reasonable quantity of evidence should be available to support an opinion. Since sampling techniques are often employed in developing evidence, samples must be large enough to afford the auditor a reasonable basis for an opinion. On the other hand, the auditor can also obtain samples larger than required to afford a reasonable audit conclusion. The concept of ***reasonable assurance*** states that the cost of the audit effort should not exceed the expected benefits. If the sample size is too large, the auditor is "overauditing," and the audit cost will be high in relation to that of the auditor's competitors in the marketplace. Clients who must absorb the fees for overauditing may become dissatisfied with the auditor's services, and seek a more efficient competitor auditing firm. Auditors who continue this practice may eventually drive themselves out of business. On the other hand, if the sample size is too small to support an opinion, the auditor may be expressing an unqualified opinion when it is not justified. The costs associated with this error are potential litigation involving the auditor's negligence.

The second broad characteristic that evidence should possess is ***competency,*** a qualitative characteristic. For evidence to be of high quality (competent), it should be both *relevant* and *valid.* Validity of evidence often depends on its objectivity, freedom from personal bias, and preferably, quantifiability. When evidence has these characteristics, it provides much of what the auditor needs to make informed judgments about the fairness of the financial data. Thus a small quantity of high quality evidence may be more persuasive than a large quantity of poor quality evidence.

Another postulate related to the evidence-gathering process is that, barring clear evidence to the contrary, *that which held true in the past will hold in the future.* This postulate simply means that the auditor takes his experience with the company into account during the verification process. This postulate depends to some extent on the going concern convention, mentioned earlier in this chapter. Therefore, the auditor uses the past experience of the company in evaluating disclosures, such as the allowance for doubtful accounts, obsolete inventories, and the estimated useful lives of assets. Additionally, if the system of internal control was found to contain no material weaknesses in the preceding three years, and if there is no indication that the system or operating personnel have changed in the current period, the auditor may reasonably begin by expecting that good internal control is still in effect. Of course, her or his expectations may be changed by tests performed in the current period. Under no circumstances can the auditor allow presumptions based on the past to substitute for readily apparent current evidence.

Reporting Standards

The audit report is the primary tangible product of the audit. It is the only communication that most users receive from the auditor. It is very important, therefore, that this report be as informative as possible. However, it must also be clear and concise; in addition it must conform to a style that is uniform throughout the auditing profession. The following AICPA reporting standards, which govern independent audits, are intended to provide audit reports that meet these objectives:

1. The report shall state whether the financial statements are presented in *accordance with generally accepted accounting principles.*
2. The report shall state whether such principles have been *consistently observed* in the current period in relation to the preceding period.
3. Informative *disclosures* in the financial statements are to be regarded as reasonably adequate unless otherwise stated in the report.
4. The report shall either contain an *expression of opinion* regarding the financial statements, taken as a whole, or an assertion to the effect that an opinion cannot be expressed. When an overall opinion cannot be expressed, the reasons therefor should be stated. In all cases where

> an auditor's name is associated with financial statements, the report should contain a clear-cut indication of the character of the auditor's examination, if any, and the degree of responsibility he is taking.

These reporting standards are applicable anytime a CPA is associated with a financial statement.[26]

The postulate underlying the reporting standards is that *"fair presentation implies use of generally accepted accounting principles."* Embodied in the concept of ***fair presentation*** are the concepts of accounting propriety, adequate disclosure, and audit obligation. ***Accounting propriety*** and ***adequate disclosure*** pertain to the faithfulness with which reported financial data portray the realities of an enterprise's financial resources and obligations at one point in time and changes in those resources and obligations over a period of time. ***Audit obligation*** pertains to the faithfulness (or due care) with which the auditor discharges his or her responsibility to judge propriety and adequate disclosure of the financial data.

The phrase applied to reflect correspondence of reported economic data to economic reality is "present fairly." Past research has revealed that members of the investing public do not understand this phrase.[27] They tend to infer that "present fairly" is the auditor's seal of approval that the statements are free from all error and are a 100 percent accurate portrayal of economic reality. In truth, however, about all the phrase actually means, as pointed out earlier, is that the most applicable generally accepted accounting principles have been used and that, in the auditor's judgment, economic reality (within the constraint imposed by GAAP) has been reasonably approximated. Because the phrase "present fairly" is so often misunderstood by investors, the Commission on Auditors' Responsibilities has recommended that it be dropped from the standard audit report at some time in the future.[28] In the meantime, however, we must recognize that the objective of clarity in reporting has not been fully realized in the standard audit report.

Statements in Accord with GAAP. In the first reporting standard, the requirement that the report shall state whether the financial statements are presented in accordance with GAAP implies that GAAP is the usual criterion against which fairness of presentation is judged. This is true anytime the financial statements purport to present financial position and results of operations. In some cases financial statements may present other widely accepted and understood information such as cash flow and assets and liabilities resulting from cash transactions. In these circumstances, there are four acceptable comprehensive bases of accounting other than GAAP which the auditor may use as criteria for judging fairness of presentation. These bases of accounting are discussed in SAS 14, and are included in the discussion of auditor's special reports in Chapter 19 of this book. Unless either GAAP or one of the other comprehensive bases of accounting are used, the statements will be deemed "not presented fairly" — unless, as is rarely the case, the auditor can show that adherence to one of these bases of accounting would have caused the information to be misleading.

Consistent Observation of GAAP. The second reporting standard requires the audit report to state whether GAAP have been consistently applied. The reference to consistency in the audit report is intended (a) to provide assurance that comparability between financial statements of succeeding years has not been materially affected by changes in accounting principles or the methods of applying them,[29] or (b), if comparability has been materially affected by such changes, to require appropriate modification of the audit report.

Adequate Disclosure Presumed. The third reporting standard requires the auditor to disclose in the audit report any financial data considered necessary for fair presentation, if those data are omitted from the bodies or footnotes of the financial statements by preparers of the information. Stated in another way, adequate disclosure is *presumed* unless the audit report states that necessary disclosures are lacking. Therefore, when the readers of financial statements see an unqualified audit report, they may properly infer that the auditor has reached the conclusion that no further disclosures are necessary for fair presentation.

It is important again to recall that the financial statements, including related footnotes, are the property of the client. Although the auditor can recommend that the changes be made in those statements, the ultimate decision about which information will or will not be included in them rests with the client. Therefore, if the auditor judges that disclosures in those statements are inadequate or not in conformity with GAAP, he or she has no authority to force the client to amend the statements to include such disclosures. However, the auditor controls the *content* of the audit report and consequently has a responsibility to include necessary disclosures in it anytime the client's financial statements omit disclosures or contain inaccurate disclosures.

Expression of Opinion. The fourth standard is the most complicated of all the reporting standards. Its application is also more far-reaching than any of the others. It contains three important statements, for each of which we will analyze and discuss the implications.

> The report shall either contain an expression of opinion regarding the financial statements, taken as a whole, or an assertion to the effect that an opinion cannot be expressed.

When a CPA is associated with a set of financial statements, he or she must always either express one type of opinion (unqualified, qualified, or adverse) or disclaim an opinion (state that no opinion can be expressed) with regard to the financial statements taken as a whole. According to SAS 15, the term "financial statements, taken as a whole" applies to the financial statements for the current period as well as those of one or more previous periods that are presented for comparative purposes.[30]

> When an overall opinion cannot be expressed, the reasons therefore should be stated.

When an opinion on financial statements is disclaimed, the accountant has a reporting obligation to explain the reason for the disclaimer. Among the possible reasons are:

- A scope limitation that materially affects the extent of an auditor's examination. (If that limitation is significant enough, the auditor may conclude that no opinion can be expressed because sufficient verification work has not been performed.)
- An uncertainty or combination of uncertainties that materially affect the financial statements

taken as a whole. (This situation could cause the auditor to conclude that an opinion qualified for reason of the uncertainty is not appropriate.)

- Unaudited financial statements. (The accountant has not attempted to gather evidence necessary to support an opinion, so he or she can offer none.)
- Nonindependence with respect to the client. (Clearly, no opinion can have credibility under these circumstances.)

In each of the situations just cited, the accountant must clearly state the reason for the disclaimer of opinion. In the first two cases, a middle paragraph stating the reasons for the disclaimer should be included in the report. In the last two cases, the accountant may state the reasons for the disclaimer in a single-paragraph report. All these reports are discussed further and illustrated in Chapter 18.

> In all cases where an auditor's name is associated with financial statements, the report should contain a clear-cut indication of the character of the auditor's examination, if any, and the degree of responsibility he is taking.

"Association" is defined by SAS 26 as either: (1) consent by the accountant to the use of her or his name in a report, document, or written communication containing the financial statements, or (2) submission by the accountant to a client of financial statements which the accountant has prepared or assisted in preparing, whether or not the accountant's name is appended to the statements.[31]

Notice that the accountant may be associated with either audited or unaudited financial statements. The financial statements are regarded as audited if the accountant has applied auditing procedures sufficient to allow the issuance of an audit report. Otherwise the statements are regarded as unaudited. In either case, the fourth reporting standard requires a clear statement of the work the accountant did and the responsibility taken with regard to the financial statements. If the statements are unaudited, the accountant must state that fact, and disclaim an opinion as to fairness of presentation. If the statements are audited, the accountant must state that fact and express an audit opinion. The nature of the opinion given will depend on the scope of the audit work performed and the results of the audit examination.

SUMMARY

In this chapter we have shown how auditors' responsibilities have been shaped by the perceived requirements of the users of financial information. We began by describing the attest function associated with the auditor's short-form report and by showing how the need for that service has developed as public ownership of corporate securities has increased.

Next we examined the responsibilities of the auditor for the discovery of errors and irregularities. We again observed how statement user expectations have recently caused the profession to assume more responsibility for the detection of errors and irregularities as financial statements are being audited.

We then turned our attention to the basic elements composing the underlying framework of auditing. This framework includes postulates, concepts, standards, and objectives that lead to logically derived audit procedures. After defining these elements of the conceptual framework and showing how they relate to each other, we focused our presentation upon auditing standards adopted by the AICPA.

APPENDIX 2–A: Conclusions and Recommendations of the Commission on Auditors' Responsibilities

In 1974 the accounting profession established a Commission on Auditors' Responsibilities. The Commission was asked to

> develop conclusions and recommendations regarding the appropriate responsibilities of independent auditors. The original charge further stated that the commission should consider whether a gap may exist between what the public expects or needs and what the auditors can and should reasonably expect to accomplish. Furthermore if such a gap was found to exist it should be explored to determine how the disparity can be resolved.[32]

The Commission reported its findings in its *Report, Conclusions, and Recommendations*, published in 1978.

Throughout its study the Commission was concerned with the issues relating to auditing as an element of the discipline of accounting. The following quotations and interpretations from the Report reflect the Commission's conclusions regarding the independent auditor's role in society:

1. Users of financial statements expect auditors to penetrate into company affairs, to exert surveillance over management and to take an active part in improving the quality and extent of financial disclosure.
2. Users expect the auditor to be concerned with the possibilities of both fraud and illegal behavior by management.
3. An independent audit is necessary because of the inherent potential conflict between an entity's management and the users of its financial information. Users of financial statements need assurance that management has fulfilled its stewardship responsibility by establishing and supervising a system that adequately protects corporate assets and permits the presentation of financial information in accordance with standards. An audit provides reasonable assurance that management has fulfilled that responsibility.
4. Audited financial statements provide a means of confirming or correcting the information received earlier by the market. They help assure the efficiency of the market by limiting the life of inaccurate information or by deterring its dissemination.
5. Since management and employees know the financial statements will be audited, the anticipation of the audit may influence their conduct and lead to more acceptable behavior than otherwise might have occurred.

Appendix 2–A summarizes *The Commission on Auditors' Responsibilities: Report, Conclusions, and Recommendations* (New York: AICPA, 1978), and is printed with permission.

6. If accepted accounting principles have limitations, audited financial statements remain constrained by those limitations.
7. The traditional division of responsibility places direct responsibility for financial statements on management. The auditor's responsibility is to audit the information and express an opinion on it. This division of responsibility has been challenged recently and suggestions have been made that all or a substantial portion of the responsibility for determining financial representations about the entity should be charged to the independent auditor. However, the rationale of the present relationship is sound and it should remain in its present form.
8. Insofar as the responsibility for detection of fraud is concerned, the commission has stated that the auditor should be concerned with the adequacy of controls and other measures designed to prevent fraud. It concluded that the auditor has a duty to search for fraud and should be expected to detect those frauds that the exercise of professional skill and care would normally uncover.[33]

In addition to the professional skill and care position relating to fraud detection expressed in item 8, the following recommendations are suggested as a means of improving the effectiveness of independent auditors in the detection of fraud. These recommendations require the auditor to maintain an *attitude of professional skepticism* and to recognize the implications of certain of his or her relationships with the management personnel of the client.

- The auditor should establish an effective client investigation program. This requires the auditor to carefully evaluate each potential client before accepting an engagement. The rationale for this requirement rests on the premise that the reputation and integrity of a company and its management are critical in determining whether an opinion can be expressed on the company's financial statements.
- The auditor is expected to take immediate responsive action to relationships that could logically encourage management to commit fraud. Such things as, for example: economic conditions that would logically lead to the desire to overstate earning power or solvency; the existence of insufficient working capital; the existence of securities subject to restrictive convenants; heavy dependence on a relatively few products, customers, or transactions; or the lack of effective internal audit functions — all may represent conditions that would encourage management fraud.
- The auditor should observe conditions suggesting predisposition to management fraud.
- The auditor is expected to maintain an understanding of a client's business and industry. Such understanding should include knowledge about economic conditions, inherent control problems, and other peculiarities of the industry.
- The auditor should extend his or her study of controls relating to the prevention of fraud and report any material weaknesses in the system of internal control to management. The auditor should follow up to determine whether the weaknesses have been subsequently eliminated.
- The profession should aggressively pursue the development and dissemination of information on frauds and methods of detecting them.
- The auditor should strive to be aware of the possible deficiencies in the individual audit techniques employed. Constant attention should be given to improving those techniques.
- Both auditors and clients should be made aware of the limitations associated with any engagement not constituting an ordinary audit.[34]

NOTES

1. American Institute of Certified Public Accountants, *APB Statement 4, Basic Concepts and Accounting Principles Underlying Financial Statement of Business Enterprise* (New York: AICPA, 1970), pp. 54–55.

2. Lawrence R. Dicksee, *Auditing* (New York: Ronald Press, 1905), p. 54.

3. George Cochraue, "The Auditor's Report: Its Evolution in the U.S.A.," *Accountant* (November 1950): 448–60.

4. *Ultramares Corporation* v. *Touche* (255 N.Y. 170, 174 N.E. 441, 1931).

5. Floyd W. Windal and Robert N. Corley, *The Accounting Professional* (Englewood Cliffs, N.J.: Prentice-Hall, 1980), p. 16.

6. Ibid., p. 103.

7. AICPA Division for CPA firms, *SEC Practice Section Peer Review Manual* (New York: AICPA, 1978), pp. 1-5 to 1-8.

8. Statement on Auditing Standards (SAS) 5, paragraphs 4–8 (New York: AICPA, 1975), as amended by SAS 43 (New York: AICPA, 1982).

9. Ibid.

10. *Codification of Statements on Auditing Procedures* (New York: AICPA, 1951), p. 12.

11. SAS 16, paragraph 3 (New York: AICPA, 1977).

12. SAS 1, paragraph 110.05 (New York: AICPA, 1973), pp. 2–3.

13. SAS 6, "Related Party Transactions" (New York: AICPA, 1975).

14. SAS 16, "The Independent Auditor's Responsibility for Detection of Errors or Irregularities."

15. Ibid., paragraphs 2 and 3.

16. Ibid., paragraph 14.

17. SAS 17, paragraph 3 (New York: AICPA, 1977).

18. Ibid., paragraph 4.

19. Ibid., paragraph 13.

20. Ibid., paragraph 18.

21. Accounting Series Release 19, "In the Matter of McKesson & Robbins, Inc.," 1940, pp. 34–35.

22. Accounting Series Release 153.

23. A. M. C. Morison, "The Role of the Reporting Accountant Today," *Accountancy* (March 1971): 122.

24. SAS 1, Section 320A.14.

25. Ibid., Section 320.68.

26. SAS 26 (New York: AICPA, 1979).

27. Lee J. Seidler, *Symbolism and Communication in the Auditor's Report*, 1976, and M. J. Epstein, *The Corporate Shareholder's View of the Auditor's Report: Conclusions and Recommendations*, research projects of the AICPA, results of which are published in *The Commission on Auditors' Responsibilities: Report, Conclusions, and Recommendations* (New York: AICPA, 1978), pp. 164 and 74, respectively.

28. *Commission on Auditors' Responsibilities*, pp. 74–78.
29. SAS 1, Section 420.02.
30. SAS 15, paragraph .02 (New York: AICPA, 1976).
31. SAS 26, paragraph .03.
32. *Commission on Auditors' Responsibilities*, p. xi.
33. Ibid., summarized from pp. xvii, xix, and xx.
34. Ibid., summarized from pp. 37–40.

QUESTIONS FOR CLASS DISCUSSION

Q2–1 What is meant by the term *generally accepted auditing standards?* How is it used in the short-form audit report?

Q2–2 How do the statements on auditing standards relate to generally accepted auditing standards?

Q2–3 What is meant by the term *generally accepted accounting principles?* How is that term used in the short-form audit report?

Q2–4 Have auditors always assumed a responsibility for expressing an opinion regarding fairness of statement presentation? Discuss.

Q2–5 What is the significance of the *Ultramares* v. *Touche* case in the development of auditing practices?

Q2–6 What, in general, has been the effect of the *McKesson & Robbins* case on auditing practice?

Q2–7 Has the federal government shown any interest in the way accountants perform the auditing function? Explain.

Q2–8 What is meant by the term *peer review?* Why have peer review practices become a part of the public accounting profession?

Q2–9 Does the fact that an auditor expresses an opinion that the financial statements of a client are fairly presented mean that they are free from error? Explain.

Q2–10 What is the historical development of the responsibilities accepted by auditors relating to the discovery of errors and irregularities?

Q2–11 How do errors and irregularities relate to fairness of presentation?

Q2–12 What is the independent auditor's responsibility under generally accepted auditing standards for the discovery of fraud?

Q2–13 What is meant by the term *illegal acts by clients?* What is the auditor's responsibility in connection with such acts?

Q2–14 What are the relationships between auditing postulates, concepts, standards, objectives, and procedures?

Q2–15 What distinguishes auditing procedures from auditing standards?

Q2–16 What are the objectives associated with the three general standards of auditing? Describe them.

Q2–17 How does a public accounting firm meet the general standard requiring that the examination be performed by persons having adequate technical training and proficiency as auditors?

Q2–18 Why is independence such an important standard for the auditor?

Q2–19 What is meant by the term *due professional care?*

Q2–20 What are *field work standards?* Explain their objectives.

Q2–21 What is the relationship between general auditing standards and field work standards?

Q2–22 Why is it important for the auditor to be independent both in fact and in appearance?

Q2–23 Why does the independent auditor evaluate the client's system of internal control? Explain.

Q2–24 How does the auditor determine when he or she has gathered sufficient competent evidential matter? Explain.

Q2–25 Does the auditor insist on evidence that proves beyond a shadow of a doubt that the financial statements are fairly presented? Explain.

Q2–26 What are reporting standards? Explain their objectives.

Q2–27 Under what circumstances may an accountant be associated with financial statements and not express either an opinion or a disclaimer of opinion regarding those statements? Explain.

Q2–28 Who accepts the primary responsibility for the data included in financial statements? Can the auditor force the client to change an item in the financial statements? Explain.

Q2–29 How should the audit report be modified when a client refuses to make the change in the financial statements that the auditor feels is significant enough to interfere with their fair presentation?

SHORT CASES

C2–1 A local certified public accountant has expressed opposition to the requirement established by his state society that he participate in at least forty hours of continuing professional education each year. He states that he has a college degree and has passed the CPA examination and therefore sees no need for additional professional education.

Required:

Respond to the local certified public accountant.

C2–2 The Able Corporation has been asked by its bank to present statements audited by a certified public accountant in connection with a loan application. A local CPA, who owns stock in the company, would like to perform the audit. He states that he knows that he can be independent in performing the audit in spite of the fact that he owns stock in the company. Another CPA claims that the first one does not meet the standard of independence and therefore cannot accept the engagement.

Required:

Explain the justification for the position expressed by the second CPA.

C2–3 A certified public accountant has been doing write-up work for one of his clients. The client has just asked him to prepare financial statements from the accounting records on the client's stationery. The CPA tells the client that he will have to include a disclaimer of opinion with the statements. The client does not understand why the accountant insists on including the disclaimer, because the accountant's name will not be included anywhere in the financial statement document.

Required:

Explain to the client why the profession insists on a disclaimer of opinion with such statements.

C2–4 An accounting firm has been told that it should subject itself to peer review. A partner in the firm objects to this practice and observes that other business enterprises are not subject to such reviews. He maintains that the way his firm conducts its activities should not be of interest to anyone else because the competitive market for accountants' services will cause the more efficient firms to prosper and the less efficient ones not to prosper.

Required:

Explain to the partner why the operations of his firm should be subject to peer review.

C2–5 A certified public accountant has just completed an audit of the Beta Corporation. A short time later, the client discovers that an employee has embezzled funds during the audit period. The company president has asked the CPA to explain how the embezzlement could have escaped discovery during the audit.

Required:

Respond to the client's request.

C2–6 An auditor asked the president of Gama Company to identify related party transactions occurring during the year. The president responds by saying that he sees no reason for the auditor to be concerned with such transactions. Furthermore, he states that if such transactions are important to the auditor he should be expected to discover them during the normal course of conducting the audit.

Required:

Respond to the president.

C2–7 James Ball, a friend of yours, is interested in the stock of Rich Corporation. He has observed the "fairly presented" phrase in the independent auditor's report and states that he interprets this to mean that the assets and liabilities shown in the balance sheet have a current value equal to the amounts shown for them.

Required:

Explain to James what the "fairly presented" phrase means in the audit report.

C2–8 An auditor requests a client to disclose information relating to legal actions against the company. The client refuses to include the disclosure.

Required:

What action should the auditor take in this situation?

C2–9 Your friend, Judy Heinz, a finance student, has been examining audited financial statements of a number of companies in connection with a course she is taking in investment analysis. She complains that even though the financial statements are audited, she finds that the capital sections of the balance sheets do not come close to showing the real values of the stock. Judy asks you why the auditor does not adjust each stockholder's equity section to agree with the market price of the company's stock as of the date of the financial statements.

Required:

Respond to your friend.

C2–10 A fellow accounting student has been studying various court cases in which auditors have been held legally liable to third parties in connection with audits they have performed. He contends that the laws should be changed to eliminate any responsibility that the auditor has to third parties because the audit is being performed for the client.

Required:

Respond to the accounting student's contention.

C2–11 Matthew Goulding, a local certified public accountant, is disturbed by the fact that his congressman has initiated a study of the ways in which certified public accountants conduct their audits of financial statements. He contends that such activities are the concern of the auditor and the client and, therefore, he sees no reasons why the U.S. Congress should be interested in such matters.

Required:

Respond to Matthew.

C2–12 The auditors have just finished their annual audit of the Delta Corporation. Your father, who is president of that company, complains to you, a university accounting major, that the auditors in performing their work seemed to be skeptical about everything they examined. He contends that this attitude of skepticism is not consistent with the requirement that the accountant be objective.

Required:

Respond to your father's contentions.

C2–13 Margot Strone is the president of Aero Corporation, an audit client of your firm. She does not want you to contact her company's legal counsel, and states that she has told you about all of the legal problems in which the corporation is currently involved. She feels that should be sufficient for you as the auditor and, therefore, requests that you not disturb the lawyer handling those matters.

Required:

Respond to Ms. Strone.

C2–14 Your audit client feels that your auditing procedures should be confined to an examination of the internal records and actions taken by the company. He sees no reason for you to make external verifications in the process of developing sufficient and competent evidential matter for an audit opinion.

Required:

Respond to your client.

C2–15 Shady Graves, the president of Shady Corporation, is widely suspected of having connections with personalities whose integrity is questionable. He recently asked a local certified public accountant to audit the Shady Corporation. The local CPA refused to accept the engagement. Shady says he does not understand why the CPA has rejected the opportunity to perform the audit.

Required:

Discuss the probable justification of the certified public accountant's action in this case.

PROBLEMS

P2–1 Select the best answer to each of the following questions relating to auditor independence.

a. A firm of CPAs may use policies and procedures such as notifying professional personnel as to the names of audit clients having publicly held securities and confirming periodically with such personnel that prohibited relations do *not* exist. This is done to achieve effective quality control in which of the following areas?
   (1) Acceptance and continuance of clients.
   (2) Assigning personnel to engagements.
   (3) Independence.
   (4) Inspection.

b. An independent auditor must be without bias with respect to the financial statements of a client in order to
   (1) Comply with the laws established by governmental agencies.
   (2) Maintain the appearance of separate interests on the part of the auditor and the client.
   (3) Protect against criticism and possible litigation from stockholders and creditors.
   (4) Insure the impartiality necessary for an expression of the auditor's opinion.

c. Which of the following *most* completely describes how independence has been defined by the CPA profession?
   (1) Performing an audit from the viewpoint of the public.
   (2) Avoiding the appearance of significant interests in the affairs of an audit client.
   (3) Possessing the ability to act with integrity and objectivity.
   (4) Accepting responsibility to act professionally and in accordance with a professional code of ethics.

d. In pursuing its quality control objectives with respect to independence, a CPA firm may use policies and procedures such as
   (1) Emphasizing independence of mental attitude in firm training programs and in supervision and review of work.
   (2) Prohibiting employees from owning shares of the stock of publicly traded companies.
   (3) Suggesting that employees conduct their banking transactions with banks that do *not* maintain accounts with client firms.
   (4) Assigning employees who may lack independence to research positions that do *not* require participation in field audit work.

e. A CPA, while performing an audit, strives to achieve independence in appearance in order to
   (1) Reduce risk and liability.
   (2) Maintain public confidence in the profession.
   (3) Become independent in fact.
   (4) Comply with the generally accepted standards of field work.

f. What is the meaning of the generally accepted auditing standard which requires that the auditor be independent?
   (1) The auditor must be without bias with respect to the client under audit.
   (2) The auditor must adopt a critical attitude during the audit.
   (3) The auditor's sole obligation is to third parties.
   (4) The auditor may have a direct ownership interest in his client's business if it is not material.

(AICPA adapted)

P2–2 Select the best answer to each of the following questions relating to generally accepted auditing standards.

a. Which of the following underlies the application of generally accepted auditing standards, particularly the standards of field work and reporting?
   (1) The elements of materiality and relative risk.
   (2) The element of internal control.
   (3) The element of corroborating evidence.
   (4) The element of reasonable assurance.

b. The third general standard states that due care is to be exercised in the performance of the examination. This standard should be interpreted to mean that a CPA who undertakes an engagement assumes a duty to perform
   (1) With reasonable diligence and without fault or error.
   (2) As a professional who will assume responsibility for losses consequent upon error of judgment.
   (3) To the satisfaction of the client and third parties who may rely upon it.
   (4) As a professional possessing the degree of skill commonly possessed by others in the field.

c. According to court decisions, the generally accepted auditing standards established by the AICPA apply
   (1) Only to the AICPA membership.
   (2) To all CPAs.
   (3) Only to those who choose to follow them.
   (4) Only when conducting audits subject to AICPA jurisdiction.

d. Auditing standards differ from auditing procedures in that procedures relate to
   (1) Measures of performance.
   (2) Audit principles.
   (3) Acts to be performed.
   (4) Audit judgments.

e. Statements on Auditing Standards issued by the AICPA's Auditing Standards Executive Committee are
   (1) Part of the generally accepted auditing standards under the AICPA Code of Professional Ethics.
   (2) Interpretations of generally accepted auditing standards under the AICPA Code of Professional Ethics, and departures from such statements must be justified.
   (3) Interpretations of generally accepted auditing standards under the AICPA Code of Professional Ethics, and such statements must be followed in every engagement.
   (4) Generally accepted auditing procedures that are not covered by the AICPA Code of Professional Ethics.

f. A CPA is most likely to refer to one or more of the three general auditing standards in determining
   (1) The nature of the CPA's report qualification.
   (2) The scope of the CPA's auditing procedures.
   (3) Requirements for the review of internal control.
   (4) Whether the CPA should undertake an audit engagement.

g. The primary reason why a CPA firm establishes quality control policies and procedures for professional development of staff accountants is to
   (1) Comply with the continuing educational requirements imposed by various states for all staff accountants in CPA firms.
   (2) Establish, in fact as well as in appearance, that staff accountants are increasing their knowledge of accounting and auditing matters.
   (3) Provide a forum for staff accountants to exchange their experiences and views concerning firm policies and procedures.
   (4) Provide reasonable assurance that staff personnel will have the knowledge required to enable them to fulfill responsibilities.

h. The first general standard of generally accepted auditing standards, which states in part that the examination is to be performed by a person or persons having adequate technical training, requires that an auditor have
   (1) Education and experience in the field of auditing.
   (2) Ability in the planning and supervision of the audit work.
   (3) Proficiency in business and financial matters.
   (4) Knowledge in the areas of financial accounting.

i. Which of the following is mandatory if the auditor is to comply with generally accepted auditing standards?
   (1) Possession by the auditor of adequate technical training.
   (2) Use of analytical review on audit engagements.

(3) Use of statistical sampling whenever feasible on an audit engagement.
(4) Confirmation by the auditor of material accounts receivable balances.

j. The third general auditing standard requires that due professional care be exercised in the performance of the examination and the preparation of the report. The matter of due professional care deals with what is done by the independent auditor and how well it is done. For example, due care in the matter of working papers *requires* that working paper
(1) Format be neat and orderly and include both a permanent file and a general file.
(2) Content be sufficient to provide support for the auditor's report, including the auditor's representation as to compliance with auditing standards.
(3) Ownership be determined by the legal statutes of the state where the auditor practices.
(4) Preparation be the responsibility of assistant accountants whose work is reviewed by senior accountants, managers, and partners.

k. Which of the following *best* describes what is meant by generally accepted auditing standards?
(1) Acts to be performed by the auditor.
(2) Measures of the quality of the auditor's performance.
(3) Procedures to be used to gather evidence to support financial statements.
(4) Audit objectives generally determined on audit engagements.

l. The objective of quality control mandates that a public accounting firm should establish policies and procedures for professional development which provide reasonable assurance that all entry-level personnel
(1) Prepare working papers which are standardized in form and content.
(2) Have the knowledge required to enable them to fulfill responsibilities assigned.
(3) Will advance within the organization.
(4) Develop specialties in specific areas of public accounting.

m. The "generally accepted auditing standards" are standards that
(1) Are sufficiently established so that independent auditors generally agree on their existence.
(2) Are generally accepted based upon a pronouncement of the Financial Accounting Standards Board.
(3) Are generally accepted in response to the changing needs of the business community.
(4) Are generally accepted as a consequence of approval of the AICPA membership.

n. A CPA should comply with applicable generally accepted auditing standards on every engagement
(1) Without exception.
(2) Except in examinations that result in a qualified report.
(3) Except in engagements where the CPA is associated with unaudited financial statements.
(4) Except in examinations of interim financial statements.

(AICPA adapted)

P2–3 Select the best answer for each of the following questions relating to errors and irregularities.

a. When is the auditor responsible for detecting fraud?
   (1) When the fraud did not result from collusion.
   (2) When third parties are likely to rely on the client's financial statements.
   (3) When the client's system of internal control is judged by the auditor to be inadequate.
   (4) When the application of generally accepted auditing standards would have uncovered the fraud.

b. When the auditor's regular examination leading to an opinion on financial statements discloses specific circumstances that make him suspect that fraud may exist and he concludes that the results of such fraud, if any, could *not* be so material as to affect his opinion, he should
   (1) Make a note in his working papers of the possibility of a fraud of immaterial amount so as to pursue the matter next year.
   (2) Reach an understanding with the client as to whether the auditor or the client, subject to the auditor's review, is to make the investigation necessary to determine whether fraud has occurred and, if so, the amount thereof.
   (3) Refer the matter to the appropriate representatives of the client with the recommendation that it be pursued to a conclusion.
   (4) Immediately extend his audit procedures to determine if fraud has occurred and, if so, the amount thereof.

c. When conducting an audit, errors that arouse suspicion of fraud should be given greater attention than other errors. This is an example of applying the criterion of
   (1) Reliability of evidence.
   (2) Materiality.
   (3) Relative risk.
   (4) Dual-purpose testing.

d. When an independent auditor's examination of financial statements discloses special circumstances that make the auditor suspect that fraud may exist, the auditor's *initial* course of action should be to
   (1) Recommend that the client pursue the suspected fraud to a conclusion that is agreeable to the auditor.
   (2) Extend normal audit procedures in an attempt to detect the full extent of the suspected fraud.
   (3) Reach an understanding with the proper client representative as to whether the auditor or the client is to make the investigation necessary to determine if a fraud has in fact occurred.
   (4) Decide whether the fraud, if in fact it should exist, might be of such a magnitude as to affect the auditor's report on the financial statements.

e. An auditor should recognize that the application of auditing procedures may produce evidential matter indicating the possibility of errors or irregularities and therefore should
   (1) Design audit tests to detect unrecorded transactions.
   (2) Extend the work to audit most recorded transactions and records of an entity.
   (3) Plan and perform the engagement with an attitude of professional skepticism.
   (4) *Not* depend on internal accounting control features that are designed to prevent or detect errors or irregularities.

f. In connection with the examination of financial statements, an independent auditor could be responsible for failure to detect a material fraud if
   (1) Statistical sampling techniques were *not* used on the audit engagement.
   (2) The auditor planned the work in a hasty and inefficient manner.

(3) Accountants performing important parts of the work failed to discover a close relationship between the treasurer and the cashier.
(4) The fraud was perpetrated by one client employee, who circumvented the existing internal controls.

g. If as a result of auditing procedures an auditor believes that the client may have committed illegal acts, which of the following actions should be taken immediately by the auditor?
(1) Consult with the client's counsel and the auditor's counsel to determine how the suspected illegal acts will be communicated to the stockholders.
(2) Extend normal auditing procedures to ascertain whether the suspected illegal acts may have a material effect on the financial statements.
(3) Inquire of the client's management and consult with the client's legal counsel or other specialists, as necessary, to obtain an understanding of the nature of the acts and their possible effects on the financial statements.
(4) Notify each member of the audit committee of the board of directors of the nature of the acts and request that they give guidance with respect to the approach to be taken by the auditor.

h. An auditor's examination performed in accordance with generally accepted auditing standards generally should
(1) Be expected to provide assurance that illegal acts will be detected where internal control is effective.
(2) Be relied upon to disclose violations of truth in lending laws.
(3) Encompass a plan to actively search for illegalities which relate to operating aspects.
(4) *Not* be relied upon to provide assurance that illegal acts will be detected.

i. Which of the following statements *best* describes the auditor's responsibility regarding the detection of fraud?
(1) The auditor is responsible for the failure to detect fraud only when such failure clearly results from nonperformance of audit procedures specifically described in the engagement letter.
(2) The auditor must extend auditing procedures to actively search for evidence of fraud in all situations.
(3) The auditor must extend auditing procedures to actively search for evidence of fraud where the examination indicates that fraud may exist.
(4) The auditor is responsible for the failure to detect fraud only when an unqualified opinion is issued.

j. Which of the audit procedures listed below would be *least* likely to disclose the existence of related party transactions of a client during the period under audit?
(1) Reading "conflict-of-interest" statements obtained by the client from its management.
(2) Scanning accounting records for large transactions at or just prior to the end of the period under audit.
(3) Inspecting invoices from law firms.
(4) Confirming large purchase and sales transactions with the vendors and/or customers involved.

k. Which of the following statements best describes the auditor's responsibility with respect to illegal acts that do *not* have a material effect on the client's financial statements?
(1) Generally, the auditor is under no obligation to notify parties other than personnel within the client's organization.

(2) Generally, the auditor is under an obligation to see that stockholders are notified.
(3) Generally, the auditor is obligated to disclose the relevant facts in the auditor's report.
(4) Generally, the auditor is expected to compel the client to adhere to requirements of the Foreign Corrupt Practices Act.

(AICPA adapted)

P2–4 Select the best answer to each of the following items.

a. Which of the following publications does *not* qualify as a statement of generally accepted accounting principles under the AICPA Code of Professional Ethics?
(1) AICPA Accounting Research Bulletins and APB Opinions.
(2) Accounting interpretations issued by the AICPA.
(3) Statements of Financial Standards issued by the FASB.
(4) Accounting interpretations issued by the FASB.

b. The auditor's judgment concerning the overall fairness of the presentation of financial position, results of operations, and changes in financial position is applied within the framework of
(1) Quality control.
(2) Generally accepted auditing standards which include the concept of materiality.
(3) The auditor's evaluation of the audited company's internal control.
(4) Generally accepted accounting principles.

c. Which one of the following statements is correct concerning the concept of materiality?
(1) Materiality is determined by reference to guidelines established by the AICPA.
(2) Materiality depends only on the dollar amount of an item relative to other items in the financial statements.
(3) Materiality depends on the nature of an item rather than the dollar amount.
(4) Materiality is a matter of professional judgment.

d. The independent auditor's plan for an examination in accordance with generally accepted auditing standards is influenced by the possibility of material errors. The auditor will therefore conduct the examination with an attitude of
(1) Professional skepticism.
(2) Subjective mistrust.
(3) Objective indifference.
(4) Professional responsiveness.

e. Independent auditing can *best* be described as
(1) A branch of accounting.
(2) A discipline which attests to the results of accounting and other functional operations and data.
(3) A professional activity that measures and communicates financial and business data.
(4) A regulatory function that prevents the issuance of improper financial information.

f. The auditor's opinion makes reference to generally accepted accounting principles (GAAP). Which of the following *best* describes GAAP?

(1) The interpretations of accounting rules and procedures by certified public accountants on audit engagements.
(2) The pronouncements made by the Financial Accounting Standards Board and its predecessor, the Accounting Principles Board.
(3) The guidelines set forth by various governmental agencies that derive their authority from Congress.
(4) The conventions, rules, and procedures which are necessary to define the accepted accounting practices at a particular time.

g. A publicly held company that disagrees with the independent auditor on a significant matter affecting its financial statements has several courses of action. Which of the following courses of action would be *inappropriate?*
(1) Appeal to the Financial Accounting Standards Board to review the significant matter.
(2) Modify the financial statements by expressing in the footnotes its viewpoint with regard to the significant matter.
(3) Ask the auditor to refer in the auditor's opinion to a client footnote which discusses the client point of view with regard to the significant matter.
(4) Engage another independent auditor.

h. The concept of materiality would be *least* important to an auditor in determining the
(1) Transactions that should be reviewed.
(2) Need for disclosure of a particular fact or transaction.
(3) Scope of the CPA's audit program relating to various accounts.
(4) Effects of direct financial interest in the client upon the CPA's independence.

i. When compared to the auditor of fifty years ago, today's auditor places less relative emphasis upon
(1) Confirmation.
(2) Examination of documentary support.
(3) Overall tests of ratios and trends.
(4) Physical observation.

j. Which of the following is a conclusion reached by the Commission on Auditors' Responsibilities, the independent commission established by the American Institute of Certified Public Accountants to study the role and responsibilities of independent auditors?
(1) Different auditing standards should apply to audits of publicly owned and private entities.
(2) The AICPA Auditing Standards Executive Committee should be replaced by a larger, part-time group.
(3) The oversight of professional practice should remain with the accounting profession.
(4) "Safe Harbors" should be made available for all work done by an auditor.

k. It would *not* be appropriate for the auditor to initiate discussion with the audit committee concerning
(1) The extent to which the work of internal auditors will influence the scope of the examination.
(2) Details of the procedures which the auditor intends to apply.
(3) The extent to which change in the company's organization will influence the scope of the examination.

(4) Details of potential problems which the auditor believes might cause a qualified opinion.

(AICPA adapted)

P2–5 Jennifer Ray, the owner of a small company, asked Thorvald Holm, CPA, to conduct an audit of the company's records. Ray told Holm that an audit had to be completed in time to submit audited financial statements to a bank as part of a loan application. Holm immediately accepted the engagement and agreed to provide an auditor's report within three weeks. Ray agreed to pay Holm a fixed fee plus a bonus if the loan was granted.

Holm hired two accounting students to conduct the audit and spent several hours telling them exactly what to do. Holm told the students not to spend time reviewing the controls but instead to concentrate on proving the mathematical accuracy of the ledger accounts, and summarizing the data in the accounting records that support Ray's financial statements. The students followed Holm's instructions and after two weeks gave Holm the financial statements, which did not include footnotes. Holm reviewed the statements and prepared an unqualified auditor's report. His report, however, did not refer to generally accepted accounting principles nor to the year-to-year application of such principles.

Required:

Briefly describe each of the generally accepted auditing standards and indicate how the action(s) of Holm resulted in a failure to comply with *each* standard.

Organize your answer as follows:

Brief Description of Generally Accepted Auditing Standards	Holm's Actions Resulting in Failure to Comply with Generally Accepted Auditing Standards

(AICPA adapted)

P2–6 For many years the financial and accounting community has recognized the importance of the use of audit committees and has endorsed their formation.

At this time the use of audit committees has become widespread. Independent auditors have become increasingly involved with audit committees and consequently have become familiar with their nature and function.

Required:

a. Describe what an audit committee is.
b. Identify the reasons why audit committees have been formed and are currently in operation.
c. What are the functions of an audit committee?

(AICPA adapted)

P2–7 You have accepted the engagement of examining the financial statements of the Thorne Company, a small manufacturing firm that has been your client for several years. Because you were busy writing the report for another engagement, you sent an assistant accountant to begin the audit with the suggestion that she start with the accounts receivable. Using the prior year's working papers as a guide, the assistant prepared a trial balance of the accounts, aged them, prepared and mailed positive confirmation requests, examined underlying support for charges and credits, and performed such other work as she deemed necessary to obtain reasonable assurance about the validity and collectibility of the receivables. At the conclusion of her work, you reviewed the working papers that she prepared and found that she had carefully followed the prior year's working papers.

Required:

The opinion rendered by a CPA states: "Our examination was made in accordance with generally accepted auditing standards. . . ."

List the three generally accepted standards of field work. Relate them to the illustration in this case by indicating how they were fulfilled or, if appropriate, how they were not fulfilled.

(AICPA adapted)

P2–8 Lief Erickson, CPA, has completed the audit examination of the financial statements of Lexington Products, Inc., upon which he plans to express an unqualified audit opinion.

Required:

a. What assurances are provided to the public when the auditor states that the financial statements present the data "fairly . . . in conformity with generally accepted accounting principles applied on a consistent basis"?
b. What are Erickson's responsibilities for the detection of: (1) errors or irregularities, and (2) illegal acts of personnel of Lexington Products, Inc.? What should Erickson have done if the examination had aroused his suspicions of errors or irregularities or of illegal acts?
c. Given that Erickson is expressing an unqualified audit opinion, what are the possible consequences to him should there be discovery in the future of: (1) errors or irregularities or (2) illegal acts?
d. In light of the recent recommendations of the Commission on Auditors' Responsibilities, how might the CPA's responsibilities be expanded, if at all, in future years with respect to the responsibility for detection of fraud?

P2–9 Lane McWhorter, CPA, was engaged to audit the financial statements of Rudder Construction Co., Inc., a closely held corporation engaged in the construction and operation of car wash and self-storage operations. The percentage-of-completion method was used by Rudder to account for all construction projects. Usually, as Rudder completed a construction project, the building and property were sold to an operator who made a 20 percent down payment and gave an installment note for the balance. Rudder then discounted the note with the Central National Bank and received the proceeds minus the bank discount. Rudder remained contingently liable on all the notes discounted. Economic hard times have fallen upon the construction business, and 60 percent of the discounted notes are now in default. In addition, Rudder's own business has fallen off to virtually nothing in the past eight months.

When McWhorter arrived to discuss the 19X3–X4 audit, he noticed that activity had slowed somewhat: the company's parking lot, usually a beehive of activity, was only half full. The controller, David McNeese, assured McWhorter that the slowdown was only temporary, and that the company was getting more new contracts in every day. In fact, according to McNeese, new crews were being hired to begin five new projects next week.

As the audit progressed, McWhorter noticed a number of things that disturbed him:

- **a.** The company's system of internal control, which had been represented to McWhorter to be excellent, showed a number of compliance deviations.
- **b.** The company's property and equipment ledgers and records for depreciation could not be reconciled to the general ledger.
- **c.** Of the 300 requests for confirmations of accounts receivable that were mailed, only 75 were returned after two mailings.
- **d.** A number of transactions appeared in the general ledger but lacked documentary support.

Required:

- **a.** Define the terms *error* and *irregularity* as used in generally accepted auditing standards. Does it appear that errors may exist in the Rudder Construction Company's financial statements? Does it appear that irregularities may exist?
- **b.** Discuss the responsibility McWhorter has with respect to errors and irregularities in conducting an examination in accordance with generally accepted auditing standards.
- **c.** Discuss the effect that the following factors have on the scope of McWhorter's audit examination:
  - (1) The integrity of Rudder Construction and its management.
  - (2) The quality of Rudder's system of internal control.
  - (3) The other circumstances previously noted.
- **d.** What are the inherent limitations of an audit examination with respect to the detection of errors and irregularities?
- **e.** What should McWhorter do if the procedures he performs indicate that errors or irregularities exist?

PART TWO

AUDIT FIELD WORK

CHAPTER 3

AUDIT EVIDENCE

As we observed in Chapter 2, auditing involves a systematic process of gathering and evaluating evidence relating to economic assertions, which are generally in the form of financial statements. In this chapter, we discuss the evidence-gathering process. Evidential matter supporting the financial statements consists of the underlying accounting data and all corroborating information available to the auditor. We divide our discussion of evidence in this chapter into the following topics:

1. The nature of evidence.
2. The relationship of materiality and relative risk to evidence.
3. Audit tests and evidence.
4. Procedures followed in the evidence-gathering process.
5. The timing of audit tests.

THE NATURE OF EVIDENCE

Evidence is the data on which a judgment or a conclusion can be based, or by which proof or probability may be established.[1] Audit evidence includes all things that influence the auditor's judgment regarding the conformity of financial presentations to economic reality. Most of the independent auditor's work in forming an opinion on financial statements consists of obtaining and evaluating evidence. In the case of the independent audit, the auditor must gather evidence that allows her or him to judge whether the financial statements have been presented in accordance with generally accepted accounting principles. To make such judgments, the auditor must meet the third standard of field work, which requires that

> sufficient, competent, evidential matter is to be obtained through inspection, observation, inquiries and confirmations to afford a reasonable basis for an opinion regarding the financial statements under examination.[2]

Observe from this statement that evidence is expected to possess the broad qualities of *sufficiency* and *competency*. Furthermore, it states that the procedures for gathering evidence include *inspection, observation, inquiry,* and *confirmation*. Finally, audit evidence is supposed to provide the auditor with a *reasonable basis* for an audit opinion. This means that the evaluation of evidence in terms of its sufficiency and competency is a judgment-based decision, influenced by such factors as cost – benefit relationships, materiality, and relative risk.

Evidential matter supporting financial statements can generally be classified into two broad categories: (1) *underlying accounting data;* and (2) all other *corroborating information*. Included in underlying accounting data are the client's journals, general and subsidiary ledgers, related accounting manuals, and various informal records (such as worksheets which support cost allocations and bank reconciliations). All these records directly support the financial statements and make up a valuable part of the audit. However, by themselves, accounting data are not considered sufficient support for the financial statements. They must be further supported by corroborating evidence, gathered by the application of audit procedures. Corroborating evidence consists of documentary materials such as checks, invoices, contracts, confirmations, and other written representations. It also includes information obtained by the auditor's inquiry, observation, physical examination, and analytical review techniques. These underlying parts of the audit permit the auditor to reach valid conclusions about the propriety of accounting (recorded) information.

The auditor generally tests underlying accounting information by analysis and review, by retracing procedural steps followed in the accounting process, by recalculation of client numbers, and by reconciling recorded amounts to other independently derived information. Testing of corroborating information is typically performed by inspection of documents and physical facilities, observation of client procedures, inquiry of knowledgeable client personnel, and confirmation of certain information with persons who are outside of (and therefore independent of) the client's organization.

The auditor gathers evidence by performing audit tests. These include tests of internal controls (compliance tests) and tests relating to financial statement balances (substantive tests). We will be referring to these tests again at various points throughout this chapter and the remainder of the book.

Sufficiency of Evidence

In general, sufficiency relates to the *amount* or *extent* of evidence necessary to support an informed audit opinion. Since a financial audit is often based on tests (or samples) of the data that underlie the various systems and balances reflected in the financial statements, the pertinent questions to be answered relating to sufficiency of evidence are: How much evidence is enough? And how big does a sample have to be to adequately support an audit opinion?

Audit standards do not provide exact guidelines for judging sufficiency of evidence. On the contrary, the decision of sample size is largely dependent on the auditor's judgment after consideration of the facts associated with the situation. Several factors should be considered by the auditor in making these judgments:

- The nature of the item under examination.
- The materiality of possible errors and irregularities associated with the item under examination.
- The degree of relative risk associated with the item under examination.
- The kinds and competence of evidential matter that are available to the auditor.

Although auditing standards do not require the use of statistical sampling methods for all samples, statistical literature does give us quantitative determinants of sample size. These include the size of the universe being examined, level of precision required for the universe value, the degree of confidence that we need to have regarding the relationship between the true value of the universe and the value suggested by the audit sample, and the variability of the audit universe. All of these terms and their effects on sample sizes are discussed in Chapters 8 and 9.

The process of drawing and auditing a sample of universe elements is often expensive. It requires a significant amount of time on the part of audit firm personnel and client employees who assist on the audit. Therefore, the auditor should always consider ***cost–benefit factors*** when gathering evidence. To be useful, the cost of audit evidence should not exceed its expected benefits. As we learned in Chapter 2, auditors must operate within a very competitive environment. Partly for that reason, the auditor will often use less costly audit procedures that produce persuasive evidence rather than the more costly procedures that might be required to secure absolutely convincing evidence. Excessive audit sample sizes can result in inefficient work and excessive fees, which in turn may eventually result in the loss of clients. On the other hand, there are also costs associated with inadequate evidence. Specifically, audit conclusions based on inadequate evidence are considered negligent conduct and could result in adverse legal exposure. In summary, we may conclude that ***sufficiency of evidence*** means "enough to provide the benefits of adequate support of an audit opinion without being excessively expensive or producing legal repercussions." Therefore, auditors often rely on evidence that is persuasive rather than totally convincing.

Competency of Audit Evidence

To be competent, evidence must be both *valid* and *relevant*. ***Validity*** refers to qualities that will enable the auditor to derive logical conclusions. It may consist of *natural or observable objects*,[3] which the auditor may see and touch. Examples of such evidence include the observation of the client's physical inventories or plant and equipment to ascertain that they actually exist. Evidence may also be *created*.[4] As an example, the confirmation of the client's accounts receivable and accounts payable or certain types of inventory represents evidence created by the auditor. Finally, evidence may be *developed logically or mathematically*.[5] For example, logically derived evidence includes the development of conclusions regarding the truth of verbal evidence presented to the auditor by the client. It may also include value judgments concerning the quality of the client's system of internal control. Mathematical evidence can range from recalculations of numbers included in the client's financial statements to more sophisticated analyses, such as linear bivariate or multiple regression used by some firms in their analytical review programs.[6]

Professional standards provide for judging validity of evidence. Generally the following presumptions apply:

- Evidence that originates outside the business generally is more reliable than evidence that originates inside the business. We shall explore this later in the chapter when we discuss the levels of competence of documentary evidence (Figure 3–3).
- Evidence developed under satisfactory conditions of internal control generally is more reliable than evidence developed under poor conditions of internal control.
- Direct personal knowledge obtained by the auditor through inspection, observation, confirmation, and physical examination is generally more persuasive than information obtained through hearsay (i.e., verbally, from the client).

To be competent, evidence must have ***relevance***; it must be related to the audit objective at hand. For example, in order to satisfy the audit objective to verify the existence for accounts receivable, we generally use direct confirmation with the customers because it provides the most relevant or persuasive evidence. On the other hand, if the auditor wishes to ascertain the proper valuation or statement presentation of accounts receivable, he or she would find that the addition of the individual accounts, analysis of accounts for probable collectibility, and review of client disclosure policies for receivables would provide the most relevant evidence to satisfy those objectives.

Still another desirable characteristic for competent audit evidence is ***objectivity***, or freedom from bias. These terms refer to the ability of two or more independent parties to examine the evidence and draw the same audit conclusions. For example, if the auditor desires to ascertain that equipment was owned by the client, vendor's invoices and supporting papers showing that the equipment was purchased, received, and paid for should be examined. Such documents have a high degree of objectivity, because, from examining them, two or more auditors may draw the same independent conclusion regarding ownership. If evidence is highly objective, it reduces the likelihood of personal bias in judging the audit results. That in turn reduces the uncertainty as to the audit conclusion reached.

RELATIONSHIP OF MATERIALITY AND RELATIVE RISK TO EVIDENCE

The factors of *materiality* and *relative risk* play an important role in judging the quantity and quality of evidence required to provide a reasonable basis for an opinion regarding a particular accounting system or account balance.

Materiality

The term *material* is used throughout accounting and auditing literature. Unfortunately the auditing profession has failed to establish an operationally useful definition of the term. Nevertheless, materiality is an important factor in determining such audit evidence decisions as the following:

- The dollar amount constituting a "significant deviation from anticipated results," which must be investigated during the analytical review phase of the audit.

- Determining whether the probable results of weaknesses in a system of internal control are significant enough to warrant extension of substantive tests or a report of the weaknesses to management.
- Determining whether errors and irregularities are material (significant) enough to require some special treatment by the auditor.
- An evaluation of "departures from GAAP" to determine whether they are significant enough to merit special consideration by the auditor.
- Evaluation of the significance of financial and other uncertainties facing the client and determination of whether they require disclosure in the financial statements or a modification of the audit report.[7]

The preceding list is by no means exhaustive. However, the list is sufficient to illustrate that ***materiality*** in auditing involves issues related to accounting procedures and disclosures by the client as well as issues relating purely to the auditor's judgment.

The measurement of materiality in an accounting sense often involves a decision regarding the relative size of a financial statement item compared to total assets, total sales, working capital, or net income. However, judgments regarding materiality can also have a qualitative as well as a quantitative dimension. That is to say, an item can be important (thus requiring elaborate client disclosure and a lot of audit evidence) without being large. In 1975, the Financial Accounting Standards Board issued a discussion memorandum entitled *An Analysis of the Issues Related to Critieria for Determining Materiality*. This document lists the factors that should be considered by auditors and others in making materiality judgments:

- Environmental factors: state of the economy, business practices, and political climate.
- Enterprise-related factors: management characteristics of the enterprise, and nature and characteristics of its operations.
- Accounting policies of the enterprise.
- Uncertainty with respect to future effects of matters not currently resolved.
- Circumstances surrounding a matter and its characteristics: relationship of an item to normal operations, unusual expectations as to timing or amount, liquidity, and business purpose.
- Magnitude and financial effect of an item.
- Cumulative financial effect of an item.[8]

Another vital aspect of the materiality issue for the auditors to consider in gathering evidence is what is important for the primary users of audited information to know. Recent research into the theory of capital markets has led to the ***efficient markets hypothesis:*** this hypothesis states that markets for securities react rapidly and unbiasedly to new information that becomes public and that these markets fully reflect this information through changes in security prices.[9] If we accept this hypothesis, the relevant question to ask in judging the materiality of an item is how large an item has to be to affect investors' decisions. It is that threshhold which the auditor should consider in developing her or his own concept of materiality. To date, no research has identified any definitive materiality threshholds with respect to investment decisions. Nevertheless, when making judgments regarding materiality, the auditor should always give attention to the probable reaction of users to individual items and conditions discovered during the audit. Such judgments then will affect the quantity and quality of evidence that must be gathered before an opinion should be expressed on the financial statements. In order to properly plan an audit, it is essential that, early in the engagement, the auditor develop preliminary materiality threshholds for fairness, both for the financial statements taken as a whole and for individual account balances. We will discuss how this is done during the planning phase of the audit (Chapter 4).

Relative Risk

Closely related to materiality is the factor of relative risk. This term is defined as the susceptibility of a financial statement item to misappropriation.[10] In the last section, we observed that the term *material* does not merely mean large or relatively large. The very nature of an item, in terms of its susceptibility to errors and irregularities, may make the item important even if the balance on the financial statement is relatively small. For example, cash is subject to greater risk of misstatement through irregularities than are fixed assets. Actually, most items in the current section of the balance sheet are more susceptible to irregularities than are noncurrent items. Therefore, a good deal of the auditor's time may be spent gathering evidence on these items even though their amounts may be small in relation to noncurrent items. Generally, there is a direct relationship between the relative risk associated with a financial statement item and the quantity and quality of evidence that are necessary to verify the item.

It is important to point out here that materiality and relative risk are interrelated and must be considered together when an auditor is deciding on the quantity and quality of evidence necessary to support an audit opinion. For example, an auditor's judgment regarding the amount shown for cash usually requires a considerable amount of high quality audit evidence, regardless of the size of the cash amount, because cash is the asset with the highest risk of misstatement through irregularities. On the other hand, property and equipment (often the largest single asset on the balance sheet) might also require considerable evidence because of its size. Accounts receivable may also require a substantial amount of high quality evidence because it is often both material and characterized by a high degree of relative risk. Ultimately the decision regarding sufficiency and competency of evidential matter must be based on the somewhat subjective judgments of the auditor.

RELATING AUDIT TESTS TO EVIDENCE

Since audit evidence is most often obtained through tests, it is important to understand the relationship between the audit objectives, audit procedures, and the evidence produced by those tests. As we have stated earlier, the performance of the audit requires many decisions. The ultimate decision the auditor makes is whether the financial statements are free from material misstatements. However, this final decision cannot be made without testing evidence of many different types from many different sources. In order for the ultimate decision to be made on consistent and logical grounds, the evidence-gathering process should be systematic and coordinated. It is therefore necessary that, for each audit problem addressed, the auditor go through the following steps:

1. Identify the audit objectives.
2. Design the nature, timing, and extent of audit procedures to obtain the evidence required to meet the objectives. Design of these procedures involves consideration of:
   a. the financial statement assertions to be tested;
   b. the type of tests desired; and
   c. the direction of tests desired (if appropriate).
3. Gather the evidence.
4. Audit the evidence.
5. Evaluate the evidence obtained in terms of its sufficiency and competence.
6. Develop a logical conclusion about the audited system or balance, in view of the evidence obtained.

Audit Objectives and Audit Procedures

One element of the evidence-gathering process involves determining the audit procedures that are to be followed in verifying a particular part of an accounting system or a specific account balance. Audit procedures are set forth in a document called the ***audit program.*** But how does the auditor select the appropriate procedures to demonstrate that the audit has been performed in accordance with generally accepted auditing standards? As stated in Chapter 2, audit objectives bridge the gap between generally accepted auditing standards and the procedures that are performed to satisfy those standards. The pertinent objectives must first be identified in order to determine the evidence-gathering procedures that must be performed. There are normally six audit objectives, some or all of which must be met in verifying each of the balances shown in the financial statements:

- Statement presentation (disclosure).
- Transaction validity (completeness).
- Ownership (rights and obligations).
- Cutoff (proper allocation of transactions between periods).
- Valuation.
- Existence (occurrence).

Notice that these audit objectives are actually developed or based on the *client's assertions regarding the elements of the financial statements.*[11]

Statement Presentation (Disclosure). In meeting the ***statement presentation (disclosure)*** objective, the auditor is concerned with whether particular components of the financial statements are properly classified, described, and disclosed in accordance with generally accepted accounting principles. For example, management in showing accounts receivable on its balance sheet is asserting that they are entirely from trade creditors and that a proper allowance has been provided for doubtful accounts. Similarly, management asserts that obligations classified as short-term liabilities in the balance sheet will mature within one year. The auditor must then carry out procedures designed to verify those assertions. Disclosures may be included either in the body of the financial statements or in the footnotes, as appropriate. The statement presentation objective must be met for all material elements of the financial statements.

Transaction Validity (Completeness). The ***transaction validity*** objective requires the auditor to verify the client's assertion that all transactions recorded during the period are valid reflections of the changes in the company's resources and obligations during the period. Verification of transaction validity includes two subordinate objectives. First, to help assure validity, the transactions should be supported by a proper system of *internal control*. It is therefore the auditor's responsibility to study and evaluate the system of internal control underlying each of the various types of transactions recorded during the period. The study and evaluation of internal control helps the auditor to decide the nature, timing, and extent of substantive tests that must be performed in relation to the various account balances in order to express an opinion as to their fairness. If the client has a strong system of internal control, there is a higher probability that the transactions creating the account balances will be reliable than would be the case if the controls are weak. The second subobjective requires the auditor to ascertain that *proper documentary support* exists to validate the transactions creating the various account balances. The extent of documentary support required varies with the nature of the client and the transaction; but it is appropriate to observe at this point that some documentary support should exist for all transactions, in order to enhance their validity. This audit objective applies to all elements of the account balances arising as the result of business transactions.

Ownership (Rights and Obligations). ***Ownership*** must be verified for many *assets*. Although possession may be accepted as evidence of ownership of some assets, the auditor must take further steps in ascertaining that many of the recorded assets are in fact owned by the client. The procedure most often used for satisfying this objective is examination of documents evidencing the transfer of title or the current holding of title. For example, deeds can be examined to verify the ownership of real property. Sales contracts, on the other hand, will typically be examined to verify the ownership of inventory. Lease contracts provide the best verification of ownership in the case of assets secured through financing leases. For property belonging to others and leased by the client, the auditor should ascertain that payments for the use of property belonging to others are properly expensed rather than capitalized. For example, payment for the use of noncapitalized (operating) lease property should be properly reflected in the accounts as periodic charges to income.

With respect to *liabilities*, the ownership objective may be interpreted as establishing that a *bona fide obligation* exists for all recorded liabilities. For example, the auditor should perform tests to ascertain that recorded notes payable represent claims of bona fide creditors. This is normally accomplished by the confirmation of all pertinent details of such obligations with those creditors.

Cutoff. The ***cutoff*** objective involves verifying the client's assertion that revenues and costs have been properly allocated among the appropriate accounting periods. This requires the auditor to verify that all transactions occurring before the end of an accounting period have been recorded as part of that period's activity. Similarly, the auditor must verify that transactions belonging to the next accounting period have not been included in the activity of the period under audit. This objective is often met by examining serially numbered documents around the year end and tracing those documents to the records of the appropriate period. Recalculations of amounts such as depreciation, amortization, and various accruals of income and expenses are also procedures performed in fulfilling the cutoff objective. This audit objective must be met for all elements of the financial statements but is much more important for some items than it is for others.

Valuation. Ascertaining appropriate ***valuation*** is a particularly important audit objective for noncash accounts. Typically, assets are valued at unamortized cost, historical cost, or the lower of historical cost or market value to meet the requirements of GAAP. Recent pronouncements have also mandated the disclosure of price-level – adjusted historical costs, as well as current costs for inventories, property, and equipment of large companies. Historical costs may be verified by examining documentary evidence, such as contracts and vendor's invoices. Market values for marketable securities can be verified by reference to daily prices published in the financial press. Market values of assets such as obsolete inventory, on the other hand, can best be verified by independent appraisals. At the present time, client disclosures of price-level – adjusted and current value data are not required to be audited, but the auditor still has some responsibility for them. Specific responsibilities and procedures relating to these disclosures are discussed in Chapters 11 and 13. For the most part, liabilities should be valued at the number of dollars required to liquidate them at the balance sheet date. This audit objective must be met for all noncash items.

Existence (Occurrence). Verification of ***existence*** is an audit objective for all asset, liability, and owners' equity accounts. The auditor's primary responsibility with respect to asset and equity accounts is to ascertain that the recorded assets and equity capital claims actually exist. With respect to liability accounts, on the other hand, the auditor has the responsibility of verifying that all existing liabilities are, in fact, recorded. Procedures to verify existence depend on the nature of the item and the cost effectiveness of obtaining the evidence.

Audit Tests and Audit Evidence

In connection with the audit of each subsystem producing financial statement balances, the auditor begins by *identifying the objectives* to be met. Next, he or she must *identify the evidence-gathering procedures* necessary to meet those objectives. Most audit procedures are then carried out in the form of *audit tests*. Finally, there must be *an evaluation of the evidence gathered* before a conclusion may be reached and an opinion expressed regarding fairness of presentation.

The procedures followed during the audit and the evidence gathered in applying them are summarized in the ***audit working papers***: these documents are retained by the auditor as support for the audit opinion and to show that the auditor has met generally accepted auditing standards. They should be retained by the auditing firm for the full statutory period within which legal action might be brought against the auditor. The primary purpose of audit working papers is to support the auditor's opinion.

The normal sequence of steps in gathering evidence involves first a review of internal control followed by compliance tests of the system and substantive tests of account balances. During the (1) *initial study and evaluation of internal controls,* the auditor's objective is to find out if the client has prescribed adequate internal controls. During this phase of the audit, compliance with those policies is assumed to exist. (2) *Compliance tests* are performed in the next phase of the audit, and they provide evidence that the client is actually adhering to the controls that were said to exist. If weak or inadequate controls were prescribed by the client, there is generally no need to perform compliance tests. It is only when the client prescribes potentially strong internal accounting controls, ones that the auditor wishes to rely upon, that compliance tests need to be performed. After the initial study and review of the internal control system and compliance tests, if any, have been completed, the auditor is in a position to decide the extent and nature of (3) the *substantive tests* to be performed. ***Substantive tests*** are direct tests of transactions that produce the financial statement balances, or direct tests of the balances themselves.

The specific types of tests to be performed depend on the audit objectives that must be met. For example, if the audit objective is to verify the existence of inventories, the auditor will want to perform substantive tests of these account balances. On the other hand, the transaction validity audit objective, as it relates to internal control, should be verified through compliance testing. Sometimes audit tests can produce evidence relating to both transaction validity (internal control) and another audit objective — such as existence, valuation, or statement presentation. These tests are called ***dual-purpose tests.***[12]

When substantive tests are used, it is important to define the ***direction*** toward which tests should be oriented. We may, for example, test financial statement balances for both overstatement and understatement. Directly testing every balance for both possibilities, however, is inefficient and unnecessary. By deciding in advance the audit objective to be accomplished, we can establish a testing direction of *primary concern* — overstatement or understatement. For example, the audit objectives of existence and occurrence require a test for overstatement. Because of the self-balancing feature of the financial statements, a direct test of selected entries in one account results in an indirect (corollary) test of the offsetting entries in one or more other accounts.

Accounts, to be overstated, must include either fictitious amounts or overstatement of accounts that actually exist. If, for example, accounts receivable are overstated, some individual customer account(s) may include amounts that do not represent valid claims against them. To test for such an overstatement, it is generally best to begin with the recorded balance and obtain evidence in support of the recorded amounts. This can be done by: (a) direct confirmation of amounts owed by individual customers; (b) examining collections in the client's cash receipts records of the period following the balance sheet date; or (c) inspecting underlying documents, such as sales invoices and shipping tickets, to ascertain that the original sales were properly recorded. The important thing to note here is that the direction of the tests for overstatement is typically *from the recorded amount back to the supporting evidence.* When documents are involved, we call this process ***vouching.***

On the other hand, tests for understatement cannot begin with the recorded amount because the objective in this case is to see that all existing items were actually recorded in the accounting records. For example, if accounts payable are understated, confirmation of recorded payables will not generally reveal the understatment. Therefore, we should begin with the *source documents supporting payables*, such as vendor invoices and receiving reports, and *follow them through to ascertain that they were properly recorded.* We call this process ***retracing*** *(or tracing).*

In Figure 3–1 we show how various tests for overstatement and understatement errors in each of four types of accounts (assets, liabilities, revenues, expenses) are related to offsetting tests for errors in one of the other accounts. Primary (direct) tests that are designed primarily to detect errors in audit populations shown in the left-hand column should also indirectly discover the related offsetting errors shown in the audit populations in the other four columns. These and other predictable relationships associated with the double-entry system make the performance of an audit somewhat like putting together a jigsaw puzzle. In both instances, all the pieces must fit together.

The following example illustrates how the analysis shown in Figure 3–1 can be used. Assume we suspect that accounts receivable may be overstated because of fictitious or erroneous charges. By reference to the analysis, we can conclude that the offsetting credits will cause one of four other errors:

1. An understatement of another asset account (such as cash).
2. An overstatement of a liability account (such as customer deposits).
3. An overstatement of a revenue account (such as sales).
4. An understatement of an expense account (such as bad debts expense).

By confirming individual accounts receivable and by vouching items from the accounts receivable accounts to source documents, we should simultaneously discover both the error in the accounts receivable and the offsetting error in the other accounts.

PRIMARY (DIRECT) TEST		**RESULTING (COROLLARY) TEST**			
(Audit Population)		**Assets =**	**Liabilities +**	**Revenue −**	**Expense**
Assets	O	U	O	O	U
Liabilities	U	U	O	O	U
Revenue	U	U	O	O	U
Expense	O	U	O	O	U

Note: O = overstatement; U = understatement.

Source: Adapted from Deloitte Haskins & Sells, "Audit Scope" program. Printed with permission.

FIGURE 3–1. Audit Test Matrix

THE EVIDENCE-GATHERING PROCESS

The relationship between audit objectives, types of tests, and evidence-gathering procedures is shown in Figure 3–2. The third standard of audit field work lists four basic procedures by which evidence is gathered. They include the following:

1. Inspection.
2. Observation.
3. Confirmation.
4. Inquiry.

The auditor also uses other procedures to supplement those listed in the field work standard. These may be viewed as subdivisions of the inspection procedure. However, because of their distinctive natures, we describe them separately. They are:

- Recomputation.
- Reconciliation.
- Scanning and analytical review.

Procedures are always shown in written form in the audit program and their results are documented in the audit working papers.

In gathering evidence, we must always be concerned with two questions: (1) What things need to be investigated? (2) Which procedures produce the most competent evidence? The answer to both of these questions depends on two things: (1) the auditor's objective; and (2) whether the tests are meant to verify a particular systems control practice (compliance test), a monetary transaction or balance (substantive test), or a combination of those two types of tests (a dual-purpose test). In this section, we explain the evidence-gathering procedures just listed and relate them to the questions raised in this paragraph.

Inspection

Like other evidence-gathering techniques, ***inspection*** can take various forms. For example, facilities of the client can be inspected in order to determine that they exist. Inventories can be inspected for physical condition to help determine their proper valuation. However, inspection is most often used in connection with documentary evidence.

The competency or persuasiveness of ***documentary evidence*** is largely dependent upon (1) where the document originates and (2) whether the document is directly transmitted to the auditor. Documents that originate outside the client's organization generally provide more persuasive evidence than those which originate inside the organization. Also documents transmitted directly to the auditor from outside parties generally provide more persuasive evidence than documents that first pass through the hands of client employees (thus risking alteration) before reaching the auditor. More specifically, documentary evidence may be classified in descending order of competence as follows:

1. Documents originating outside the client organization and transmitted directly to the auditor.

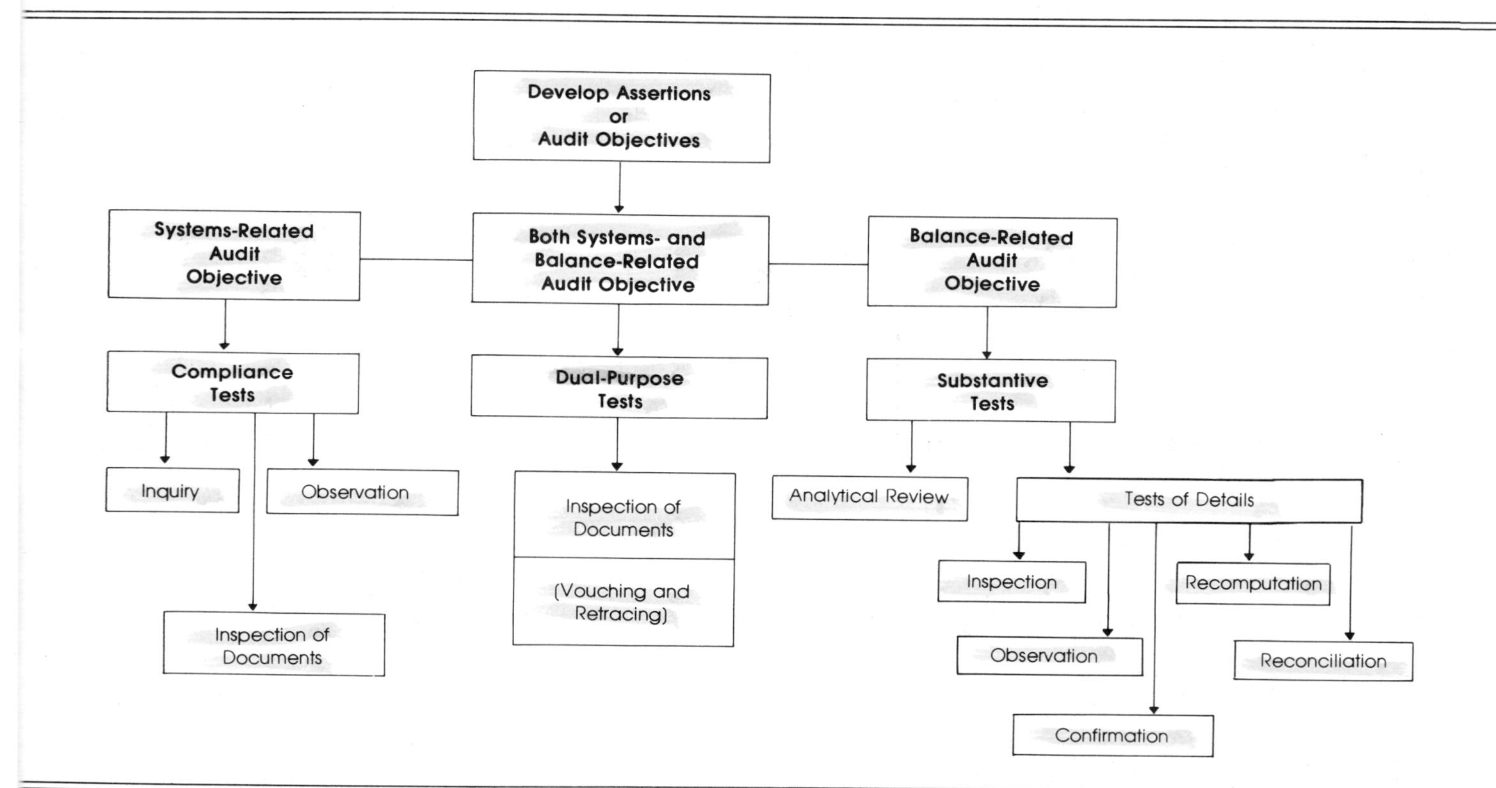

Source: Adapted from Deloitte Haskins & Sells, "Audit Scope" program. Printed with permission.

FIGURE 3–2. Relating Audit Objectives to Audit Procedures by Type of Evidence

2. Documents originating outside the client's organization and held by the client.
3. Documents originating inside the client's organization but circulated outside before being returned directly to the auditor.
4. Documents originating inside the client's organization but circulated outside before being returned to the client.
5. Documents originating inside the client's organization, then transmitted to the auditor.
6. Documents originating inside the client's organization and held by the client.

Examples of documentary evidence falling into each of these six categories are shown in Figure 3–3.

As a general observation, we can conclude that the competence of documentary evidence declines in direct relationship to the opportunity that the client's personnel may have to change the document.

The auditor may use documentary evidence in one of two ways:

- He or she may, in verifying a financial statement balance, progress backward in the accounting system, from *the statement* item through the *underlying accounting data* (general and subsidiary ledgers and books of original entry) to *source documents or corroborating information.* We call this process vouching. We refer to the chain of evidence (ledgers, journals, and supporting documents) as the ***audit trail.*** As observed earlier in this chapter vouching is a technique that is often used to detect overstatement of balances.
- He or she may locate corroborating supporting documents in the system and attempt to ascertain that these documents were properly recorded in the records and therefore appear either in the financial statement balances or footnotes. This process of working forward through the audit trail is called retracing. Again, because of the direction of the test, retracing is often used to detect understatement of balances.

LEVEL OF COMPETENCE		
Where Originated	**Where Transmitted**	**Examples**
(1) Outside	Auditor	Cutoff bank statements Audit confirmations
(2) Outside	Client	Client's monthly bank statements Vendor invoices
(3) Inside	Outside, auditor	Cancelled checks in cutoff bank statement
(4) Inside	Outside, client	Cancelled checks in monthly bank statements
(5) Inside	Auditor	Client representation letter
(6) Inside	Client	Sales invoices Sales summaries Cost distribution reports Shipping documents Receiving reports Purchase orders

FIGURE 3–3. Documentary Evidence Classified by Level of Competence

The relationship between vouching and retracing is shown in Figure 3–4, which depicts the audit trail.

Observation

Observation is probably the most direct way of obtaining audit evidence. Almost any tangible phenomenon pertaining to the client may be observed. This audit procedure is most often used in meeting the audit objectives of transaction validity (internal control) and existence. Observations are made from the perspective of the correspondence of the observed phenomena with the client's records of them. For example, in compliance testing for transaction validity, the auditor observes whether the client's established and documented control procedures are actually being implemented. In substantive testing, the auditor observes many of the client's tangible assets to ascertain whether they exist and whether they correspond with the records of them. Similarly, cash and marketable securities are counted and compared with client detail records. The auditor observes the client's physical count of inventories and compares selected counts with client detail. The existence of land, buildings, machinery, and equipment can be corroborated through the auditor's observations. If, for example, as

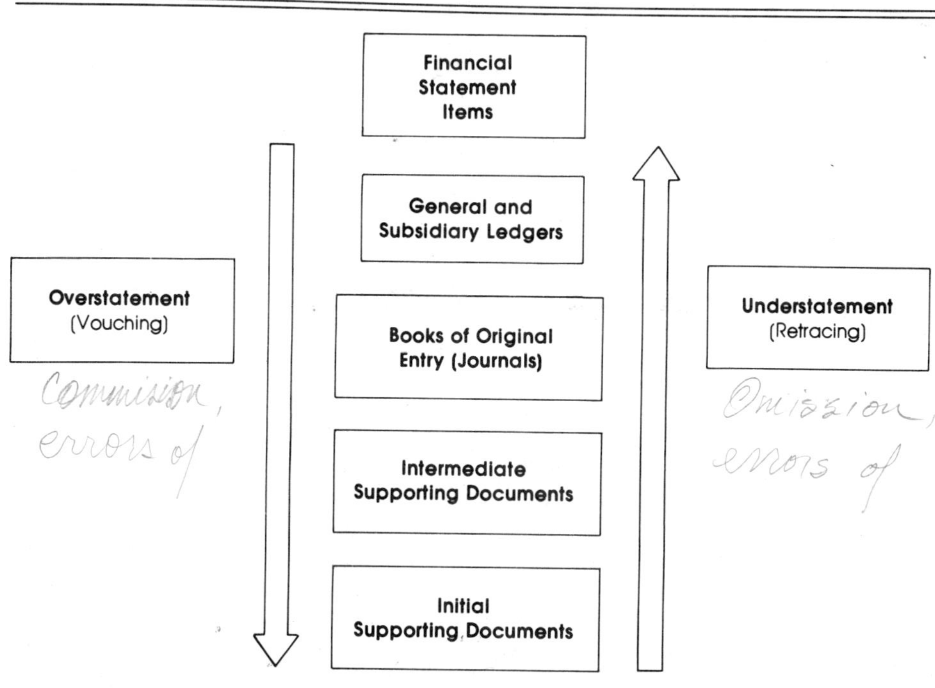

Source: Adapted from Deloitte Haskins & Sells, "Audit Scope" program. Printed with permission.

FIGURE 3–4. The Audit Trail, Showing the Relationship Between Vouching and Retracing

part of the preliminary tour of the client's premises, the auditor observes that certain new machinery and equipment is being used, he or she should ascertain that the equipment has been recorded on the books as purchased or leased. If it has been purchased, then the client's records should reflect proper charges to depreciation expense.

It should be noted that even though observation of tangible assets might provide valuable evidence that the assets exist, it will generally be of little or no usefulness in verifying the validity of other client assertions — such as proper valuation, proper cutoff, or validity of the transaction by which the asset was recorded on the books of the company. Other procedures such as inspection of documents, recalculation of amounts, and inquiry of client personnel are more useful to verify those assertions. All important audit objectives must be satisfied, of course, before an opinion can be expressed regarding fairness of presentations of an account balance. Rarely, if ever, can the auditor reach a conclusion regarding fairness of a balance after only one audit objective has been met.

Confirmation

As shown in Figure 3–3, one of the most competent types of documentary evidence is provided by the audit ***confirmation:*** typically, the auditor uses the confirmation procedure to verify the existence of certain assets, liabilities, and capital stock. Confirmations are used most commonly to ascertain the existence of cash, accounts or notes receivable, accounts or notes payable, inventories, marketable securities, and capital stock issued and outstanding. Such confirmations provide reliable elements of evidence because they are supplied from outside the client's organization and are transmitted directly to the auditor without the risk of alteration by the client.

Confirmations vary in format and style according to the type of information needed. Generally, there are two types of audit confirmation requests:

- ***Positive requests***, in which the confirming party is requested to communicate with the auditor regardless of whether the confirming party agrees that the information on the confirmation request is correct; and
- ***Negative requests***, in which the confirming party is requested to communicate with the auditor only if the information supplied in the confirmation request is incorrect.

Typical positive and negative accounts receivable confirmation requests are shown in Figures 3–5 and 3–6, respectively.

Because of the nature of the negative confirmation request, the auditor assumes that an unanswered confirmation is an indication that the item is correctly stated. This is a tenuous assumption considering the fact that many confirming parties may simply ignore the confirmation request and therefore never actually compare the information on it with their records. For that reason, negative confirmations are generally used when the auditor is seeking to confirm relatively small items from a relatively large audit population or when internal controls of the client are so good that there is very little risk of errors or irregularities in the balances being confirmed. For example, negative confirmation requests are often used to confirm small customer demand deposit balances with banks or savings institutions or small customer accounts receivable, which individually are immaterial.

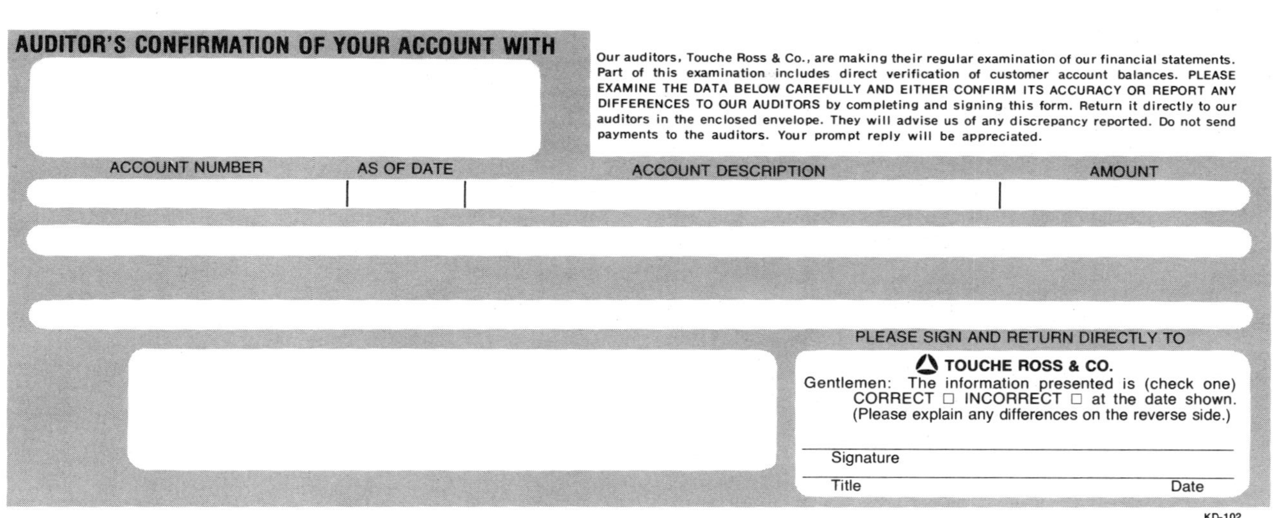

AUDITOR'S CONFIRMATION OF YOUR ACCOUNT WITH

Our auditors, Touche Ross & Co., are making their regular examination of our financial statements. Part of this examination includes direct verification of customer account balances. PLEASE EXAMINE THE DATA BELOW CAREFULLY AND EITHER CONFIRM ITS ACCURACY OR REPORT ANY DIFFERENCES TO OUR AUDITORS by completing and signing this form. Return it directly to our auditors in the enclosed envelope. They will advise us of any discrepancy reported. Do not send payments to the auditors. Your prompt reply will be appreciated.

ACCOUNT NUMBER	AS OF DATE	ACCOUNT DESCRIPTION	AMOUNT

PLEASE SIGN AND RETURN DIRECTLY TO

TOUCHE ROSS & CO.

Gentlemen: The information presented is (check one) CORRECT ☐ INCORRECT ☐ at the date shown. (Please explain any differences on the reverse side.)

Signature

Title Date

KD-102

THIS IS NOT A REQUEST FOR PAYMENT

Source: Touche Ross & Co. Used with permission.

FIGURE 3–5. Positive Accounts Receivable Confirmation Request

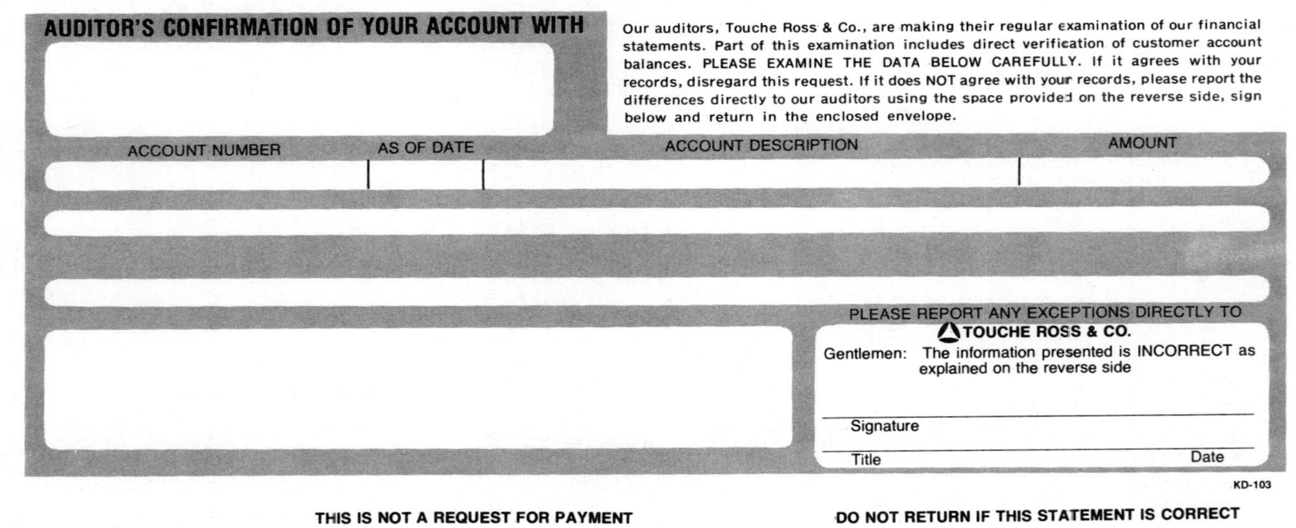

AUDITOR'S CONFIRMATION OF YOUR ACCOUNT WITH

Our auditors, Touche Ross & Co., are making their regular examination of our financial statements. Part of this examination includes direct verification of customer account balances. PLEASE EXAMINE THE DATA BELOW CAREFULLY. If it agrees with your records, disregard this request. If it does NOT agree with your records, please report the differences directly to our auditors using the space provided on the reverse side, sign below and return in the enclosed envelope.

ACCOUNT NUMBER	AS OF DATE	ACCOUNT DESCRIPTION	AMOUNT

PLEASE REPORT ANY EXCEPTIONS DIRECTLY TO

TOUCHE ROSS & CO.

Gentlemen: The information presented is INCORRECT as explained on the reverse side

Signature

Title Date

KD-103

THIS IS NOT A REQUEST FOR PAYMENT

DO NOT RETURN IF THIS STATEMENT IS CORRECT

Source: Touche Ross & Co. Used with permission.

FIGURE 3–6. Negative Accounts Receivable Confirmation Request

Because of the nature of the positive confirmation request, the auditor must follow up on all positive requests not returned. In using a positive request, the auditor expects to get some response from the confirming party regardless of whether the party agrees with the information on the request. These requests are generally used when the auditor is seeking to confirm relatively large or otherwise material items from a relatively small audit population or when the study and evaluation of the system of internal control reveals that there is a relatively high risk that errors or irregularities may exist in the balances being confirmed. Positive confirmation requests are typically used for such things as these:

- The verification of bank balances.
- The verification of marketable securities held by lenders.
- The verification of large, questionable, or past due accounts receivable.
- The verification of inventories in public warehouses.
- Clearing matters of importance with the client's attorneys.
- Verification of long- and short-term notes receivable and notes payable.
- The verification of capital stock outstanding.

Confirmation is particularly useful in satisfying the audit objective of existence of key asset and liability accounts. Nevertheless, we should remember that it will not provide complete evidence as to valuation, cutoff, or transaction validity of accounts in many cases. For example, a positive account receivable request returned by a client customer and stating that the customer agrees with the client's balance constitutes evidence as to existence of the account receivable, but does not constitute evidence as to its valuation (collectibility). For satisfaction of the valuation objective, the auditor must rely on recalculation and analysis of the allowance for doubtful accounts, as well as on discussions with the client regarding past due accounts. Again we must observe that all pertinent audit objectives must be satisified with respect to an account balance before an unqualified audit opinion is justified.

Inquiry

An ***inquiry*** is a set of questions directed to persons having knowledge about a particular phase of the client's operations. It is generally directed to client employees and may be raised during virtually every phase of the audit, from preliminary planning to the final tests of account balances. Oral evidence produced by such inquiries is less competent than that produced by inspection, observation, or confirmations. However, the auditor does rely to some extent on it. Ultimately, even though these oral responses are incorporated into ***representation letters*** (letters signed by managers and containing selected representations by them), the only real support for oral evidence is the integrity and reputation of the client. Since auditors, as a matter of policy, are strongly urged to avoid association with clients who lack integrity, they logically have some right to rely on the assertions made to them by their clients.

While professional standards for independent auditors (SAS 19) recognize the validity of oral evidence, they warn that the procurement of oral evidence should not be regarded as a substitute for other techniques which provide more direct and more competent forms of evidence. In addition, SAS 19 requires that all oral representations of management should be followed up by having them included in a representation letter to the auditor.[13] Written representations from management thus confirm oral representations made by the client during the course of the engagement. In that way they serve to reduce the possibility of misunderstandings concerning the matters that are the subject of the representation. Furthermore, they also emphasize the client's primary responsibility for the data included in the financial statements. Representation letters should be dated as of the last day of audit field work and therefore represent one of the last tasks which the auditor performs on the audit engagement. Such letters are addressed to the auditor and are signed by the appropriate official(s) of the company.

A variety of client assertions covering all aspects of financial statement disclosures appear in a representation letter. Among the assertions are such statements as these:

- Management is responsible for fairness of presentation in the financial statements.
- All financial records and related data have been made available to the auditor.
- To the extent of management's knowledge, no material erorrs or irregularities are contained in the financial statements.
- To the extent of management's knowledge, the company has complied with pertinent contractual arrangements.
- All information concerning related party transactions has been disclosed.
- All contingencies (liabilities, losses, illegal acts, unasserted claims, etc.) of which management has knowledge have been revealed to the auditor and adequately disclosed.
- All material events subsequent to the balance sheet date relating to the financial statements under audit have been properly disclosed.

We must realize that the preceding list is simply representative and does not include all items that may be covered in such a letter. Realistically, management and the auditor may agree on any item they feel is appropriate for disclosure in the representation letter. Those representations should generally be limited to the items considered either individually or collectively to be material. Such materiality limitations do not apply, however, to disclosures of illegal acts or irregularities. Neither do they apply to management's assertions regarding completeness of accounting records.

Although representation letters are not considered to be highly competent evidence, they are often so important in corroborating oral evidence that management's refusal to furnish such a letter may preclude the auditor from providing an unqualified audit opinion. In such cases, the auditor would typically render a scope-qualified audit report or a disclaimer, whichever is more appropriate. Client representation letters are obtained as part of completion of the audit engagement. They are discussed further in Chapter 16.

Recomputation

The procedure of ***recomputation*** is used to provide evidence when we are verifying account balances determined by calculations. This evidence, sometimes called mathematical evidence, can provide proof toward fulfilling both the valuation and transaction validity audit objectives. Recomputations are performed throughout the audit as we test the details of account balances for such items as depreciation, bad debts, and accruals. When the auditor uses a client-prepared working paper of any kind, one of the first procedures she or he will perform on it will be ***footing and cross-footing*** (readdition) to ascertain that the totals agree with the details included in it. Recomputation often accompanies other evidence-gathering techniques, such as inspection of documents and confirmation.

Reconciliation

We have already observed the importance of evidence provided by parties outside the client organization. The specific amounts included in such information may often differ from the client's record of those data because of timing differences associated with increases or decreases to the item being proven. Because of these differences, the auditor must frequently perform reconciliations to explain the differences between the balance of the item shown in the client's records and that provided by the outside party. The reconciliation procedure is always used when the auditor is comparing the cash balance reported by the client's bank with the amount shown in the cash ledger account. Also, reconciliations are frequently necessary in comparing confirmed balances of individual accounts receivable with the balances shown for those accounts in the client's subsidiary ledger.

Scanning and Analytical Review

Scanning and analytical review techniques are often used jointly to help detect unusual events or unusual relationships among recorded data. ***Scanning*** is also called *scrutinizing* in some audit programs. For example, a typical element of an audit program may require the auditor to "scrutinize the accounts receivable subsidiary ledger for unusually large credit balances and trace those balances to source documents." Scanning, while often providing direct evidence itself, frequently draws the auditor's attention to unusual matters which require other audit procedures, such as inquiry or vouching to source documents. Most larger audit firms have computer software package programs that allow the scanning process (and other audit techniques) to be performed by the computer when client data files are in machine readable form. These programs are discussed in Chapter 7.

Analytical review also provides evidence of unusual relationships among client data; like scanning, its purpose is to draw the auditor's attention to unusual matters that might require further evidence, such as additional documentary support for those items. Analytical review techniques are used in the planning stages of the audit to identify unusual items that might require the auditor's special attention during the evidence-gathering process. However, analytical review is also used as a substantive test during the field work, and at the end of the evidence-gathering phase of the audit, to provide corroborative support for statement balances.

Because of the double-entry accounting system, paired interrelationships exist among the client's recorded data. Therefore, a misstatement in one account will always cause a misstatement in some other account. For example, an overstatement of end of period inventories will cause an understatement of cost of goods sold and an overstatement of net income. Other items will have a logical cause and effect relationship. During analytical review, the auditor should recognize that these relationships exist and be alert to them when unusual balances are discovered. Some of the most obvious interrelationships among recorded data include the following:

- Sales — accounts receivable.
- Cash — accounts receivable.
- Notes receivable — interest income.
- Accounts receivable — bad debts.
- Investments — investment income.
- Inventories — cost of sales.
- Fixed assets — depreciation.
- Accounts payable — inventories and purchases.
- Accrued interest payable — interest expense.
- Net income — net income tax expense and income taxes payable.

Logic also suggests relationships between insurance expense and fixed assets, legal fees expense and contingent liabilities, and notes payable and interest expense.

TIMING OF AUDIT TESTS

In general, audit tests are performed during the *interim* and *final* field work stages of the audit. Decisions about timing of audit tests should be based partly on the audit objective and partly on other factors.

For example, if the audit objective is systems-related, as is the internal control element of transaction validity, it is desirable to perform the inquiry, observation, and inspection of documents necessary for the preliminary evaluation of the system at an interim date. In general, *tests should be performed as soon as practicable after audit objectives have been identified*, thus preventing rush and overtime during the final field work stages.

Other factors that should influence the auditor's judgment include (1) whether adverse business conditions increase the risk of applying tests of details at interim dates; (2) whether the client's accounting system has the attributes necessary to process accurate information at interim as well as final field work dates; (3) whether sufficient evidential matter will be available at both the interim date and the balance sheet date concerning transactions between those dates; and (4) whether effective substantive tests can be designed in the absence of internal accounting controls.

SUMMARY

In this chapter, we have explained what is meant by audit evidence and have shown how such evidence may be gathered by applying the auditing procedures listed in the third standard of field work. We have shown, in a general way, how these auditing procedures are related to the audit objectives discussed earlier in the text.

We began by describing the nature of evidence and showing how materiality and relative risk affect the evidence-gathering process. We then showed the relationship between audit tests and the evidence-gathering process by describing the procedures followed in the evidence-gathering process.

Finally, we turned our attention to the timing of audit tests. In that portion of the chapter, we observed that certain audit tests can be performed prior to the end of the period under audit (interim tests) while others should be performed either at the end of the period or after the end of the period.

NOTES

1. *The American Heritage Dictionary*, New College Edition (Boston: Houghton Mifflin, 1978), p. 455.

2. Statement on Auditing Standards (SAS) 1, Section 330.01 (New York: AICPA, 1973).

3. R. K. Mautz and H. A. Sharaf, *The Philosophy of Auditing* (Sarasota, Fla.: American Accounting Association, 1961), Chap. 5.

4. Ibid.

5. Ibid.

6. For example, Deloitte, Haskins & Sells uses a statistical approach to analytical review procedures that incorporates these methods to estimate financial statement amounts from various financial and nonfinancial variables.

7. For a more thorough discussion of issues related to materiality in auditing, see C. W. Thomas and Jack L. Krogstad, "Materiality Guidance for Auditors, *Journal of Accountancy* (February 1979): 74–77.

8. "An Analysis of the Issues Related to Criteria for Determining Materiality," Financial Accounting Standards Board, March 21, 1975.

9. For a review of this literature, see Eugene F. Fama, "Efficient Capital Markets: A Review of Theory and Empirical Work," *Journal of Finance* 25 (May 1970): 383–417.

10. SAS 1, Section 150.05.

11. See SAS 31, paragraphs 3–8 (New York: AICPA, 1980).

12. See SAS 1, Section 320 B. 37.

13. SAS 19, paragraph .01 (New York: AICPA, 1977).

QUESTIONS FOR CLASS DISCUSSION

Q3–1 What is audit evidence?

Q3–2 What is meant by *sufficient, competent, evidential matter?*

Q3–3 How can the nature of an item under examination influence the auditor's judgment regarding sufficiency of evidence?

Q3–4 How does the quality (competence) of evidence influence the amount of evidence required in support of the audit opinion?

Q3–5 Why is an auditor often willing to accept evidence that is persuasive even though it is not absolutely convincing?

Q3–6 What are the costs of overauditing (obtaining excessive evidence) and underauditing (expressing an opinion based on inadequate evidence)?

Q3–7 What criteria can the auditor apply in determining whether or not sufficient evidence has been gathered during the audit process?

Q3–8 What is meant by *validity* and *relevance* in determining whether evidence is competent?

Q3–9 What does the term *objectivity* mean when applied to audit evidence?

Q3–10 What is the relationship of materiality and relative risk to the evidence required to support the auditor's judgment regarding fairness of presentation?

Q3–11 Can you list at least five factors that should be considered by auditors in making judgments regarding materiality?

Q3–12 What is the relationship between users of financial data and the auditor's judgment as to the materiality of an error in the financial data?

Q3–13 Why is the time given to the audit of cash and other current assets typically so much larger in proportion to the sizes of those account balances than is the time given to the verification of fixed assets?

Q3–14 Why does the auditor rely on testing procedures in gathering audit evidence? Explain.

Q3–15 What is meant by the *transactions validity audit objective?*

Q3–16 How does the auditor preserve the audit evidence gathered through the performance of auditing procedures?

Q3–17 What is meant by these terms: *Compliance test? Substantive test? Dual-purpose test?*

Q3–18 Why do auditors generally vouch elements of the account balances for assets to their underlying documentary support and trace such support to the account balances for liabilities? Explain.

Q3–19 The auditor discovers an overstatement of an asset; where should he or she logically look for the compensating error? Explain.

Q3–20 Can you list and briefly describe the four auditing procedures specifically mentioned in the third standard of field work? Are all of these procedures used in verifying each statement item? Explain.

Q3–21 Can you list and briefly describe four specific procedures that represent different ways of applying the inspection procedure?

Q3–22 Why is externally originated documentary evidence more competent than similar internally originated documentary evidence? Explain.

Q3–23 What is meant by the *audit trail?* List the formal records and documents normally appearing on the audit trail for accounts receivable, sequencing them in the order in which they are normally encountered in the vouching and tracing processes.

Q3–24 What is the difference between a positive and a negative confirmation request? When would each be likely to be used?

Q3–25 How are the results of oral inquiries preserved as evidence in an audit?

Q3–26 What is meant by *scanning and analytical review procedures?* How are they used?

Q3–27 Should any audit tests be performed before the end of the period under audit? Explain.

SHORT CASES

C3–1 A staff accountant, working under your supervision, is concerned because he feels that the audit evidence being gathered does not establish beyond the shadow of a doubt that the financial statements are fairly presented. He expresses the feeling that the audit team is, therefore, not appropriately meeting its responsibilities.

Required:

Respond to your staff accountant.

C3–2 During an in-house professional training seminar, a newly employed staff accountant expresses the feeling that the accounting profession should establish specific criteria defining the amount of evidence that should be gathered prior to expressing an opinion as to the fairness of the financial statements. He states that, without such criteria, no two auditing firms would be likely to insist on the same amount of evidence in the same audit engagement.

Required:

As discussion leader, respond to the staff accountant's comments.

C3–3 James Manzi, a newly employed staff accountant, is working under your direction on an audit engagement. He has observed from the audit program that the evidence gathered in examining purchase invoices is looked upon as being more competent than the evidence produced by examining sales invoices. He maintains that since each of these documents reflects quantities of goods, prices, and dollar amounts, they should be equally competent.

Required:

Explain to your staff accountant why the auditor places greater confidence in the purchase invoice evidence than in the sales invoice evidence.

C3–4 At the beginning of an audit engagement, Alice Robinson, the senior in charge of the audit, takes Bryan Rosenberger, a staff accountant, to tour the client's plant; they observe the general condition of the equipment and specifically identify the new pieces of equipment acquired by the client during the year. After the tour, Alice asks Bryan to examine the documentary evidence in support of the new equipment observed during the plant tour. Bryan questions the wisdom of that assignment, suggesting that Alice is overauditing those items because they have already been observed during the plant tour.

Required:

Tell how the senior accountant should respond to the staff accountant.

C3–5 During the course of an audit, a valuation error in the amount of $10,000 is discovered during the audit of inventory. Total inventory is valued at approximately

$1,000,000. The staff accountant discovering the error suggests that since the error amounts to only 1% of total inventory it can be ignored as being immaterial.

Required:

Evaluate the position taken by the staff accountant.

C3–6 Beverly Grillo, a staff accountant working under your supervision, has been charged with the responsibility of reconciling the balance in the cash ledger account with the bank balance. After working with the data for some time, she reports that she is unable to completely reconcile the two balances, but that the difference is small and therefore in her judgment not material to the audit.

Required:

What position would you take in responding to the staff accountant?

C3–7 In conferring with your audit staff prior to an audit engagement, you explain that the primary concern of the audit team will be the discovery of overstatements of assets and understatements of liabilities. A newly employed staff accountant states that he does not understand why the audit team is not equally concerned with both overstatements and understatements of assets and liabilities.

Required:

Justify the position taken by the audit team.

C3–8 Joanna Grove, a newly employed staff accountant, has observed from an auditing text that there are normally six audit objectives to be met in performing the audit procedures; she knows the procedures exist for the purpose of gathering sufficient competent evidential matter relating to the fairness of the financial statements. Joanna states that she presumes that all these objectives will have to be met in verifying all the account balances appearing in each of the accounting subsystems.

Required:

Evaluate the position Joanna has taken.

C3–9 A staff accountant working under your supervision is vouching cash transactions to cancelled checks and cash receipt vouchers. He states that he presumes that the cancelled checks and cash receipt vouchers each constitute equally persuasive documentary evidence in support of cash disbursements and cash receipts respectively.

Required:

Comment on the staff accountant's assumption.

C3–10 You, as the senior in charge of an audit engagement, have instructed Emilia Ciri, a staff accountant, to vouch, on a test basis, the debits in accounts receivable to the sales invoices. After she completed that task, you asked her to trace the purchase invoices to credits in the accounts payable ledger accounts. She asked you why she was required to work from the account balances back to the underlying documents in connection with accounts receivable and then was requested to work from the documents to the entries in the accounts in verifying items in the accounts payable accounts.

Required:

Justify your instructions.

C3–11 Nino Parmakian, a staff accountant, observes that the audit program calls for a member of the audit team to inspect the cash receipts and cash payments journals for the months of January and February following the end of the audit period. The audit team has been cautioned against overauditing and he therefore questions the wisdom of examining accounting records for those months because they are outside the period under audit. Nino feels that by eliminating those procedures the audit team could reduce the amount of time spent on the engagement and in that way reduce the likelihood of overauditing.

Required:

Respond to the staff accountant's concerns.

C3–12 Russell Green, a staff accountant serving as a member of your audit team, observes that the audit program calls for the system of internal control to be reviewed and for the application of extensive compliance tests to verify that the system is functioning as designed. He observes that the audit program also calls for substantive tests of account balances and transactions. Russell asks you, as the senior in charge, why the audit team has to perform the substantive tests if they are going to place reliance on the system of internal control to be sure that all transactions are valid and properly recorded.

Required:

Respond to the staff accountant.

C3–13 In August you are visiting with a prospective client regarding the possible performance of an audit for the calendar year ending December 31. The prospective client states that he presumes that he can make his decision at the end of the year, since the audit will be performed after that date.

Required:

Respond to the prospective client.

C3–14 You are the senior in charge of auditing a client whose management refuses to provide you with a client representation letter. The president states that he sees no reason for such a letter — since the audit team has the responsibility of discovering departures from generally accepted accounting principles, errors, and irregularities. Besides, he says, his firm has employed the auditors for those purposes.

Required:

Explain to the client why the representation letter must be provided and the action that you will have to take in the event that he continues to refuse to provide the document. Justify your position.

PROBLEMS

P3–1 Select the best answer for each of the following items.

a. The sequence of steps in gathering evidence as the basis of the auditor's opinion is
   (1) Substantive tests, internal control review, and compliance tests.
   (2) Internal control review, substantive tests, and compliance tests.
   (3) Internal control review, compliance tests, and substantive tests.
   (4) Compliance tests, internal control review, and substantive tests.

b. During the course of an audit, an auditor required additional research and consultation with others. This additional research and consultation is considered to be
   (1) An appropriate part of the professional conduct of the engagement.
   (2) A responsibility of the management, *not* the auditor.
   (3) A failure on the part of the CPA to comply with generally accepted auditing standards because of a lack of competence.
   (4) An unusual practice which indicates that the CPA should *not* have accepted the engagement.

c. Before expressing an opinion concerning the results of operations, the auditor would best proceed with the examination of the income statement by
   (1) Applying a rigid measurement standard designed to test for understatement of net income.
   (2) Analyzing the beginning and ending balance sheet inventory amounts.
   (3) Making net income comparisons to published industry trends and ratios.
   (4) Examining income statement accounts concurrently with the related balance sheet accounts.

d. What is the general character of the three generally accepted auditing standards classified as standards of field work?
   (1) The competence, independence, and professional care of persons performing the audit
   (2) Criteria for the content of the auditor's report on financial statements and related footnote disclosures.
   (3) The criteria of audit planning and evidence gathering.
   (4) The need to maintain an independence in mental attitude in all matters relating to the audit.

e. In connection with the third generally accepted auditing standard of field work, an auditor examines corroborating evidential matter which includes all of the following *except*
   (1) Client accounting manuals.
   (2) Written client representations.
   (3) Vendor invoices.
   (4) Minutes of board meetings.

f. When an examination is made in accordance with generally accepted auditing standards, the independent auditor must
   (1) Utilize statistical sampling.
   (2) Employ analytical review procedures.
   (3) Obtain certain written representations from management.
   (4) Observe the taking of physical inventory on the balance sheet date.

g. Evidential matter supporting the financial statements consists of the underlying

accounting data and all corroborating information available to the auditor. Which of the following is an example of corroborating information?
(1) Minutes of meetings.
(2) General and subsidiary ledgers.
(3) Accounting manuals.
(4) Worksheets supporting cost allocations.

(AICPA adapted)

P3–2 Select the best answer for each of the following items.

a. Which of the following types of documentary evidence should the auditor consider to be the most reliable?
(1) A sales invoice issued by the client and supported by a delivery receipt from an outside trucker.
(2) Confirmation of an account-payable balance mailed by and returned directly to the auditor.
(3) A check issued by the company and bearing the payee's endorsement, which is included with the bank statement mailed directly to the auditor.
(4) A working paper prepared by the client's controller and reviewed by the client's treasurer.

b. The sufficiency and competency of evidential matter ultimately is based on the
(1) Availability of corroborating data.
(2) Generally accepted auditing standards.
(3) Pertinence of the evidence.
(4) Judgment of the auditor.

c. To be competent, evidence must be both
(1) Timely and substantial.
(2) Reliable and documented.
(3) Valid and relevant.
(4) Useful and objective.

d. Audit evidence can come in different forms with different degrees of persuasiveness. Which of the following is the *least* persuasive type of evidence?
(1) Documents mailed by outsiders to the auditor.
(2) Correspondence between auditor and vendors.
(3) Sales invoices inspected by the auditor.
(4) Computations made by the auditor.

e. Which of the following ultimately determines the specific audit procedures necessary to provide an independent auditor with a reasonable basis for the expression of an opinion?
(1) The audit program.
(2) The auditor's judgment.
(3) Generally accepted auditing standards.
(4) The auditor's working papers.

f. Most of the independent auditor's work in formulating an opinion on financial statements consists of
(1) Studying and evaluating internal control.
(2) Obtaining and examining evidential matter.
(3) Examining cash transactions.
(4) Comparing recorded accountability with assets.

g. Although the validity of evidential matter is dependent on the circumstances under which it is obtained, there are three general presumptions having some usefulness. The situations given below indicate the relative reliability a CPA has placed on two types of evidence obtained in different situations. Which of these is an *exception* to one of the general presumptions?

(1) The CPA places more reliance on the balance in the scrap sales account at plant A where the CPA has made limited tests of transactions because of good internal control than at plant B where the CPA has made extensive tests of transactions because of poor internal control.
(2) The CPA places more reliance on the CPA's computation of interest payable on outstanding bonds than on the amount confirmed by the trustee.
(3) The CPA places more reliance on the report of an expert on an inventory of precious gems than on the CPA's physical observation of the gems.
(4) The CPA places more reliance on a schedule of insurance coverage obtained from the company's insurance agent than on one prepared by the internal audit staff.

h. Failure to detect material dollar errors in the financial statements is a risk the auditor primarily mitigates by
(1) Performing substantive tests.
(2) Performing compliance tests.
(3) Evaluating internal control.
(4) Obtaining a client representation letter.

i. Audit programs generally include procedures necessary to test actual transactions and resulting balances. These procedures are primarily designed to
(1) Detect irregularities that result in misstated financial statements.
(2) Test the adequacy of internal control.
(3) Gather corroborative evidence.
(4) Obtain information for informative disclosures.

j. The following statements were made in a discussion of audit evidence between two CPAs. Which statement is not valid concerning evidential matter?
(1) "I am seldom convinced beyond all doubt with respect to all aspects of the statements being examined."
(2) "I would not undertake that procedure because at best the results would only be persuasive and I'm looking for convincing evidence."
(3) "I evaluate the degree of risk involved in deciding the kind of evidence I will gather."
(4) "I evaluate the usefulness of the evidence I can obtain against the cost to obtain it."

(AICPA adapted)

P3–3 Auditors frequently use the terms *standards*, *procedures*, and *objectives*.

Required:

a. Define *standards* as generally contemplated in the auditing literature. For each standard, discuss the foundational postulates and concepts upon which the standard is based.
b. Define the term *procedure* as generally contemplated in the auditing literature. List at least eight different types of procedures that an auditor would use during an audit examination.
c. List the six audit objectives discussed in this chapter. How do these objectives relate to the assertions that are made in the financial statements of audit clients?

What is the function of audit objectives when compared to both standards and procedures?

(AICPA adapted)

P3–4 A CPA accumulates various kinds of evidence upon which he will base his auditor's opinion as to the fairness of financial statements he examines. Among this evidence are confirmations from third parties.

Required:

a. What is an audit confirmation?
b. What characteristics should an audit confirmation possess if a CPA is to consider it as valid evidence?

(AICPA adapted)

P3–5 The types of documentary evidence typically obtained by auditors are

a. Bank statements.
b. Confirmation of accounts receivable.
c. Subsidiary accounts receivable ledgers.
d. Minutes of board meetings of directors and stockholders.
e. Shipping documents (bills of lading).
f. Cancelled checks.
g. Documents of title for building, land, other assets.
h. Attorney's letter.
i. Client representation letter.
j. Employment contracts for key executives.
k. Signed W-4 copies from employees.
l. Signed lease agreements.
m. Purchase orders.
n. Payroll time cards.
o. Receiving reports for goods received.
p. Notes payable confirmation.
q. Insurance policies, in force.
r. Remittance advices.
s. Payroll records for gross pay, withholding, etc.

Required:

a. List each of the preceding documents according to
   (1) Point of origination.
   (2) Where transmitted (to auditor, to client) or held.
b. Classify each of the documents in order of competence. Use the following ordering system:
   (1) Very competent (V).
   (2) Somewhat competent (SC).
   (3) Less competent (L).
c. What criteria should be used for classifying documentary evidence in order of its competence?

P3–6 The third generally accepted auditing standard of field work requires that the auditor obtain sufficient competent evidential matter to afford a reasonable basis for an opinion regarding the financial statements under examination. In considering what constitutes sufficient competent evidential matter, a distinction should be made between underlying accounting data and all other corroborating information available.

Required:

a. Discuss what is generally meant by *underlying accounting data*. Give examples.
b. Discuss what is generally meant by *corroborating information*. Give examples.
c. Discuss procedures the CPA uses to examine (1) underlying accounting data and (2) corroborating information.

(AICPA adapted)

P3–7 As auditor of Texstar Manufacturing Company, you have obtained an unadjusted trial balance from the books of the company for the year ended February 28, 19X1. The following accounts are included on the trial balance.

	Dr. (Cr.)
Cash in bank, unrestricted	$ 37,245
Cash in bank, restricted	45,000
Marketable securities (at lower of cost or market)	58,600
Accounts receivable, trade	86,295
Trade notes receivable	55,000
Inventories	220,000
Land	500,000
Building, less accumulated depreciation	595,000
Furniture and fixtures, net of accumulated depreciation	247,620
Patents, net of amortization	46,250
Trade accounts payable	(60,250)
Notes payable to banks, short term	(76,480)
Mortgage payable	(795,000)
Capital stock	(250,000)
Retained earnings	(425,000)
Sales	(1,250,000)
Cost of sales	844,000
General and administrative expenses	162,000
Legal and professional fees	16,480
Interest expense	123,000

Additional information:

(1) All trade notes receivable are held by Texstar.
(2) Marketable securities are held in the company's safe deposit box at Texas National Bank.
(3) The company has $72,000 of inventory stored in a public warehouse in Houston.

Required:

a. In order to fulfill the *existence* audit objective, which of the accounts on the trial balance should you confirm from outside sources? Briefly explain from whom they should be confirmed and the information that should be confirmed. Organize your answer as follows:

Account Name	From Whom Confirmed	Information to Be Confirmed

b. For the items that cannot be confirmed to determine existence, describe briefly the procedure that should be performed to satisfy this objective.

(AICPA adapted)

P3–8 For each of the items in the following list, describe (1) the auditor's primary audit objectives in examining them; (2) one audit procedure that will satisfy each objective; and (3) when these procedures should be performed (i.e., at interim or during final audit field work).

a. Recorded entries in the cash receipts journal.
b. Property plant and equipment.
c. Trademarks.
d. Accrued wages payable.
e. Investment in subsidiary company.
f. Notes payable.
g. Retained earnings.
h. Miscellaneous expense.

P3–9 The types of tests that auditors perform can be subdivided into categories as (1) compliance tests, (2) substantive tests, and (3) dual-purpose tests. For each of the audit objectives in the following list, state whether a (1) compliance test, (2) substantive test, or (3) dual-purpose test would be most appropriate.

The audit objective is

a. To ascertain whether the credit department is approving all sales before goods are shipped.
b. To ascertain that all items shipped have been recorded properly in the sales journal.
c. To ascertain the proper valuation of recorded obsolete raw materials inventory.
d. To ascertain whether all cash disbursements are made by serially numbered checks.
e. To ascertain that all major additions to property and equipment were approved by the board of directors.
f. To test pricing (valuation) of finished goods inventory.
g. To ascertain that proper rates were used for hourly employees in figuring payroll expense.
h. To determine that petty cash exists.
i. To determine whether all existing trade accounts payable are recorded.
j. To determine if mathematical checks were performed on sales invoices by departmental supervisors.

P3–10 In examining documentary support during substantive tests of balances, the direction of the audit test to be performed is quite important. In turn, the direction of test to be performed often depends on whether there is greater potential for client overstatement or understatement. On the other hand, for some audit tests, direction of test is less important because the audit objective may not be to detect client overstatements and understatements.

Required:

a. Explain the terms *vouch* and *trace* in the context of the preceding statement.
b. For each of the following audit objectives, state whether the test is for overstatement or understatement, and whether either direction might be inferred. Also, state whether you would select vouching or tracing as the required audit procedure. Then determine the client data file from which it would be most appropriate to select a sample; also, name the client data file to which the sample should be vouched or traced. Possible client data files for this problem include the following:
   (1) Sales invoice file.
   (2) Bill-of-lading file.
   (3) Credit files.
   (4) Purchase order file.
   (5) Accounts-receivable subsidiary ledger.
   (6) General ledger postings.
   (7) Receiving report file.
   (8) Purchase journal entries.
   (9) Vendor invoice file.
   (10) Sales journal entries.
   (11) Sales journal totals.
   (12) Materials requisition file.
   (13) Cost of production reports.
   (14) Perpetual inventory files.

Arrange your answer as follows (the first objective has been done for you as an example):

Audit Objective	Overstatement, Understatement, or Either	Vouch or Trace	From (Data file)	To (Data file)
(a)	Overstatement	Vouch	Sales journal entries	Sales invoice file, bill of lading file

The audit objectives are

a. To ascertain that recorded sales were actually made.
b. To ascertain that all purchases that were made were recorded.
c. To ascertain that sales invoices were recorded properly in the sales journal.
d. To ascertain that sales invoices were posted to the appropriate customer accounts receivable.
e. To ascertain that requisitions of raw materials inventory were recorded correctly as used in manufacturing work-in-process.
f. To ascertain that raw materials used were removed from perpetual inventory records.

g. To ascertain that general ledger postings for sales are adequately supported by a detailed summary of transactions.

h. To ascertain that sales journal entries were posted correctly in the company's general ledger.

P3–11 For each of the following situations assume that the auditor's preliminary tests indicate that there may be an error in a particular account; the error of primary concern is identified as either overstated (O) or understated (U). For each case presented, list one possible offsetting error of secondary concern — that is, the account that may be misstated and whether it would be overstated (O) or understated (U); also name the substantive tests that may detect both the primary and secondary errors. The first case has been done for you as an example.

Case	Error of Primary Concern	Error of Secondary Concern	Substantive Tests to Detect
(1)	Accounts receivable (O)	Sales (O)	Confirmation of accounts receivable Vouching sales invoices to shipping documents
(2)	Inventories (O)		
(3)	Accounts receivable (O)		
(4)	Accounts payable (U)		
(5)	Sales (U)		
(6)	Notes payable (U)		
(7)	Property and equipment (U)		
(8)	Cash (O)		
(9)	Cost of goods sold (O)		
(10)	Depreciation expense (U)		

CHAPTER

PLANNING AND SUPERVISING THE AUDIT

Adequate planning and supervision are vital prerequisites to a timely and successful completion of any complex audit engagement. For this reason, the first standard of audit field work requires that "the work is to be adequately planned and assistants, if any, are to be properly supervised."[1]

In this chapter we discuss the elements involved in the general planning and supervision of an audit. Our discussion covers the following topics:

1. Elements of the audit process.
2. Meeting the planning portion of the first standard of field work.
3. Meeting the supervision portion of the first standard of field work.
4. Relating the audit working papers to the planning and supervision standard.
5. Using the client's internal auditors in an independent audit.

ELEMENTS OF THE AUDIT PROCESS

We show the chronological order of the various events associated with audit field work in Figure 4–1 to help you understand how they relate to each other as they are discussed in this and later chapters.

The numbered elements in the figure indicate the following events:

(1) The accountant is approached by a prospective client.
(2) The accountant spends time obtaining knowledge about the business reputation and

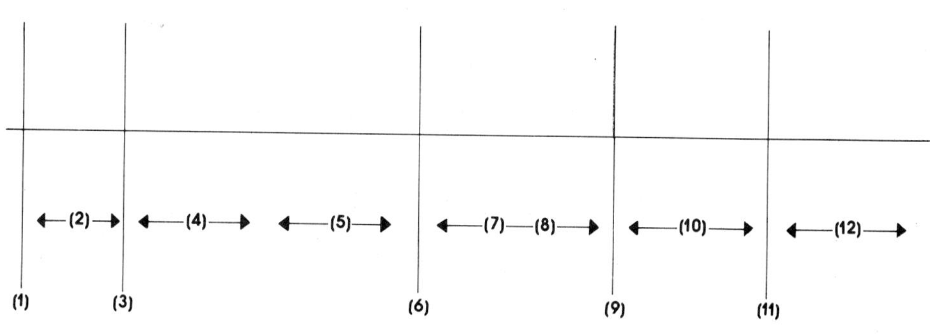

FIGURE 4–1. Chronological Order of the Elements of the Audit

integrity of the prospective client, as well as the quality and completeness of the client's records.

(3) An engagement conference with the potential client takes place. Agreement is reached that if records are complete enough to permit it, an audit will be performed.

(4) The engagement is planned; there is a preliminary review of the system of internal control, and interim tests of internal controls over transactions (compliance tests) are also performed.

(5) Interim tests of transactions creating financial statement balances (substantive tests) are performed.

(6) The fiscal year ends.

(7) There is a final evaluation of internal control.

(8) A program for the audit of financial statement balances (substantive tests) is developed and implemented.

(9) The audit report date (last day of audit field work) occurs.

(10) Financial statements are drafted; there is an office review of audit workpapers, and the audit report is drafted.

(11) Financial statements and the audit report are delivered to the client.

(12) A follow-up takes place.

Items (1) and (2)

Under optimal conditions, the prospective client should contact the accountant well in advance of the end of the fiscal year to be audited so that the accountant may have time to decide whether to accept the engagement, and to plan the engagement adequately. The first standard of field work recognizes that early appointment of the auditor benefits both auditor and client. Early appointment enables the auditor to do much of his audit work before the balance sheet date, (that is, at interim dates) and thus allows the field work to be done in a more efficient manner.

An auditor who has been asked to examine the financial statements of a company whose fiscal year has *already ended* may, under appropriate circumstances, still be able to perform an adequate examination and issue an unqualified audit report.

However, if inventories and other assets that require physical observation by the auditor are material income-producing factors, this may be difficult. The auditor must in this case assess the circumstances, such as the quality of the client's perpetual inventory system, to determine if the scope of the examination can be expanded to allow the expression of an unqualified opinion. This situation is discussed more thoroughly in Chapter 11.

Quality control standards of the AICPA for an independent audit include standards for acceptance and continuance of clients; these standards exist to help auditors avoid association with clients who lack integrity. An auditor may investigate the past history, integrity, and reputation of prospective clients by any of these means:

1. Reading past periods' financial statements.
2. Contacting present and former business associates, bank, and attorneys as well as various credit agencies.
3. Discussing with the potential client the need for an audit.
4. Contacting the potential client's predecessor auditor.

SAS 7 governs communications between predecessor and successor auditors. Because of the ethical rule regarding confidential client information, the successor auditor may contact the predecessor only with the client's permission. Once permission is granted, the successor's inquiry of the predecessor should include questions bearing on the integrity of the potential client, disagreements that may have arisen because of application of GAAP or GAAS, and, in general, the reason why the predecessor auditor is no longer engaged. The predecessor should respond promptly and fully to all of the successor's inquiries, and indicate areas of limited response. The successor should take all this information into account in deciding whether to accept an engagement. If the results of this communication, communications with other parties, and discussions with the client do not raise serious doubts as to the prospective client's integrity and reputation, the accountant may be reasonably assured that the engagement may be accepted without undue risk.[2]

Item (3)

It is extremely important that the accountant and the client reach preliminary agreement concerning the work to be done and the responsibilities to be assumed by each. This agreement between the accountant and the client is often documented through the issuance of an engagement letter. A typical engagement letter is illustrated in Figure 4–2. Although the accountant may include any information that has bearing on the engagement, the letter typically includes these elements:

- The nature of the work to be performed (audit, MAS, tax, write-up or any combination of those services).
- The period of time over which the engagement is expected to be performed.
- Limitations of the engagement regarding the CPA's responsibility with respect to detection of errors and irregularities.
- In the case of exclusively nonaudit services, a statement that the engagement is not to be construed as an audit.
- Time to be spent on the audit engagement and fee arrangements.[3]

BEST & COMPANY
Certified Public Accounts

June 15, 19X3

Mr. Lane G. Collins, Chairman
JEP Manufacturing Co., Inc.
2140 Bryan Tower
Dallas, Texas

Dear Mr. Collins:

This letter will confirm our understanding of the arrangements concerning our audit examination of the balance sheets of JEP Manufacturing Co., Inc., at December 31, 19X2 and X1, and the related statements of income, retained earnings, and changes in financial position for the years then ended.

Our examination will be made in accordance with generally accepted auditing standards. Accordingly, it is expected to include the tests and procedures that are necessary to express an opinion concerning the conformity of the financial statements with generally accepted accounting principles.

Generally accepted auditing standards require us to search for errors and irregularities that would have a significant impact upon the financial statements. However, since our examination is based on selected tests of the accounting records, it cannot provide absolute assurance that such errors and irregularities will be detected. Additionally, the audit examination should not be relied upon for detection of illegal acts that may have occurred. Should errors, irregularities, or illegal acts that affect financial statements come to light during our examination, we will promptly bring them to your attention. Our findings regarding your system of internal control, including information about material weaknesses, will be communicated to you in a separate letter after the completion of our audit work.

At your request, we will perform the following nonaudit services: (1) timely preparation of all federal income tax returns; (2) review and analysis of your compliance with certain contractual loan arrangements with banks.

Our fees for the above work will be based on our regular rates for such services, plus actual out-of-pocket expenses. A billing will be rendered upon completion of our services, payable within 30 days from receipt. We will immediately notify you of any circumstances that could significantly affect our initial fee estimate in the amount of $54,000.

We expect to begin our preliminary field work on September 1, 19X2. The preliminary work should continue until approximately October 1, 19X2. Final field work should begin on February 20, 19X3, immediately after your expected year-end closing of February 15, 19X3.

Final field work should be complete by March 15, 19X3 and you should receive the audit report and report on internal control no later than March 31, 19X3.

If the foregoing is in accordance with your understanding, please sign below and return the duplicate copy of this letter to us. If you have further questions, please feel free to call me.

Very truly yours,

Robert C. Best, Partner

Accepted: ______________

By: ______________

Date: ______________

FIGURE 4–2. Typical Engagement Letter

Item (4)

Once the auditor and the client have reached an agreement, planning of the engagement can begin. In planning an audit engagement, the auditor should develop an appropriate overall ***audit strategy.*** This requires identification of areas of potential audit risk and the establishment of preliminary materiality thresholds for errors. In doing those things, the auditor relies on discussions with the client, preliminary analytical review of the client's records, and preliminary study and evaluation of the client's internal control system — among other things. Interim tests of transactions will also typically be performed during this period in order to ascertain whether the system is operating as it was designed.

Item (5)

In many cases, the auditor may reach an early conclusion regarding the adequacy of the system of internal control and may thus begin performing substantive tests of transactions and balances at an interim date.

Item (6)

Planning and preliminary work can continue through the client's fiscal year end, but ideally it should end some time before that date, because the auditor must then be concerned with completing the audit on a timely basis. Adequate planning enables the auditor to schedule preliminary work so that it provides adequate time to decide on the nature, timing, and extent of final substantive tests of balances and other disclosures during final audit field work — when time deadlines for completing the audit are often critical. Properly timed communication of approximate audit time frames to the client's personnel will enable them to prepare physical facilities to accommodate the audit and to provide any client-prepared working papers that the auditor might be able to use in completing the examination on a timely basis. Client inventory counts should be observed and cash funds on hand should be counted at the end of the period.

Items (7), (8), and (9)

Final audit field work usually begins immediately after the clients' books have been closed for the fiscal year. This will generally be approximately three to four weeks after the end of the fiscal year. It is during this time that a final evaluation is made of the client's internal control system, in order to determine the nature, timing, and extent of final substantive tests to be performed. The auditor may decide at this time that tests of internal controls, begun during interim work, should be extended to cover the time periods at or near the fiscal year end. This would occur, for example, when circumstances surrounding the client's system of internal controls have changed substantially since interim tests of transactions were performed.

Substantive tests include both a final analytical review of the financial statement data and detailed tests of balances. The time period to which substantive tests apply includes both the period under audit and the period after the balance sheet date, up to and including the last day of field work (the date of the audit report). As part of the audit program the auditor must review the events and transactions of the client between the close of the year being audited and the date of completion of the audit field work. These events and transactions, better known as *subsequent events*, are examined to provide the advantage of hindsight in evaluating the disclosures of various elements in the body of the financial statements and to determine whether disclosures relating to the activities of the subsequent period should be included in the footnotes to the financial statements. Subsequent events are discussed at length in Chapter 16.

Item (10)

After the audit staff leaves the client's office, the working papers for the engagement are typically subjected to several reviews by supervisory audit personnel and finally by the partner in charge of the engagement. During this time, recommended audit adjustments and supplementary disclosures will be discussed with the client. As we have previously observed, management is primarily responsible for the financial statements, including footnote disclosures. Therefore the auditor has no authority to change them without the permission of client management.

After completion of the final review, the auditor is ready to write the audit report. The nature of the report will depend on the nature and extent of audit evidence gathered and on the attitude of management toward accepting any proposed corrections to the financial statements. After that, the financial statements are proofread.

Item (11)

The audited financial statements and the audit report are delivered to the client. In addition, the auditor may have decided that material weaknesses exist in the client's system of internal control. If so, the auditor should communicate these weaknesses to the client at this time. A management letter, in which the auditor may communicate suggestions for improvements in operating efficiency as well as internal controls may also be provided for the client at this time.

Item (12)

The auditor's responsibility does not end with the issuance of the audit report and the related report on internal control. However, the responsibility of the auditor shifts at this time from an active to a passive one. More specifically, after the issuance of the audit report, the auditor may discover facts that existed at the report date but were unknown to him or her at the time. If knowledge of those previously undisclosed facts renders the previously issued financial statements and audit report misleading, the auditor is required to take appropriate action to see that the newly discovered facts are made known as soon as possible. Specific responsibilities relating to the subsequent discovery of such facts are covered in SAS 1, Section 561; we discuss them at length in this book in Chapter 16.

PLANNING THE AUDIT

The general objectives of planning an audit are to develop an overall strategy for the audit and to facilitate its timely and successful completion.[4] During the planning phase of an audit, the auditor should decide in general the nature, timing, and extent of all audit tests as well as the number and quality of audit personnel required to perform those tests. The extent of planning necessary for an audit examination varies with the complexity of the engagement and the extent of the auditor's experience and knowledge of the client's affairs. During this period the auditor should develop an overall familiarity and expertise with respect to the client's industry, accounting policies, internal controls, and reporting structure. Potential problem areas in the audit should be identified, including financial statement items likely to require adjustment.

Developing Preliminary Materiality Thresholds

It is during the planning stages of the audit that the need for developing materiality thresholds first appears. In Chapter 2, we defined a material financial statement item as a disclosure (or lack of disclosure) that affects the decision of an informed user of the financial statements. In that sense, materiality relates to financial statement disclosure. It is the primary responsibility of the client's financial management to determine whether something is material enough (individually or collectively) to disclose or immaterial enough to omit from disclosure. For example the client may decide to disclose contingent liabilities arising from pending litigation because of the potentially material effect on the financial statements. On the other hand, the client may decide not to disclose separately the deferred interest charges from capitalized leases, because in this case the effect on the financial statements is judged to be immaterial. The deferred interest charges might instead be aggregated with other items under the heading "other assets" on the balance sheet.

Materiality has a slightly different meaning for the auditor examining the financial statements and reporting on them. The auditor must determine whether the financial statements are free from *material errors and irregularities*. In this sense the auditor must decide, in advance, a "range of acceptable limits" within which it is appropriate to conclude that the client's disclosures are fair representations of accounting reality. That in turn requires the auditor to decide which areas of the financial statements are most important so that more conclusive evidence may be gathered relating to those areas. For this purpose, the most important financial statement areas are those that contain the highest potential for material errors or irregularities.

It is essential that the auditor develop a clear perception of what is material for at least two reasons. First, early establishment of materiality guidelines provides a threshold for errors and irregularities beyond which the auditor is unwilling to accept misstatements. It serves as evidence that the auditor is concerned about material errors from the very outset. Furthermore, and perhaps more importantly, once those guidelines have been set they also define items and amounts that are *immaterial*. Thus, the auditor is able to focus on the important aspects of the job and to perform a more efficient audit; that is, to attain a maximum level of assurance at a minimum level of cost. This is one of the key advantages of audit planning, and a vital element of the long-range benefits of both the individual auditor and the audit firm.

Two proper qualifying questions may be asked regarding materiality. They are: "Material with respect to whom?" and "Material with respect to what?" Therefore, the auditor should be concerned with (1) the intended users of the financial statements and

(2) the resultant financial statement variables that most affect those users' decisions. With respect to the first question, the auditor should try to identify the intended financial statement user groups during the preliminary discussions with the client. The primary purpose for the engagement should be identified as part of audit planning. If the purpose of the audit, for example, is to obtain a bank loan, bank creditors may be logically assumed to be the primary user group. On the other hand, if the purpose of the audit is to satisfy annual reporting requirements under the rules of the SEC for publicly traded companies, the primary user groups may be presumed to be investors and prospective investors.

After primary and other user groups are identified, the auditor should consider those elements of the financial statement having the most significant impact on decisions to be made by the identified user group(s). Creditors, for example, might be greatly concerned with the financial statement variables that show the company's ability to repay debts (such as current assets, current liabilities, total assets, total debt, total capital, and the various ratios that are derived from those items). Investors, on the other hand, will be more interested in those financial statement variables that would most directly influence their judgments regarding the company's short- or long-range profitability (such as sales, net income, net worth, total assets, and the related ratios developed from those items).

Although we can cite some general guidelines for establishing materiality thresholds, we must remember that there are no uniform standards for judging audit materiality. The common standard which has evolved through practice is that a 10 percent error in a financial statement item such as total assets or net income is generally considered material. An error less than 5 percent is generally considered immaterial, unless there are extenuating circumstances. Errors in relative magnitude between 5 and 10 percent must be weighed according to the circumstances and the needs of the intended user groups. However, when any question arises, it is probably better to presume that an item is material and therefore perform more audit tests than to presume that the item is immaterial and make no further investigation, thus risking failure to detect material misstatements. In any case, the costs of both overauditing and underauditing must be weighed carefully.

Applications of the guidelines described in the preceding paragraph may be useful in setting a ***materiality threshold*** for error based on an aggregate financial statement base, such as 5 percent of total assets or 10 percent of net income before taxes. Once this decision is reached, however, the auditor must make an effort to judgmentally allocate the materiality threshold among the various financial statement items comprising the aggregate base financial statement variable. For example, assume that the recorded value of assets in a client's financial statements is $10,000,000. If the auditor selects a 5 percent materiality threshold for overstatement errors, he or she will accept a total of $500,000 overstatement of total assets and still express an unqualified audit opinion. Once this threshold is set, the auditor must then allocate the $500,000 among receivables, inventories, property and equipment, and the other asset accounts. The nature of the asset account should be considered to determine the portion of the $500,000 allocated to it. For example, if certain accounts possess higher risk-of-error characteristics (such as related party transactions, known irregularities, or known errors), the materiality threshold for error would be narrower (smaller) for those financial statement items than for other accounts not having those characteristics.

Preliminary audit materiality guidelines may be set only after the auditor has sufficient knowledge about the client to permit an ***assessment of risk of error***. This requires the in-charge auditor to perform several tasks: identify users of financial statements; analytically review current versus prior years' financial statements and the relevant audit working papers; tour the client's premises; conduct preliminary discussions with client personnel; and conduct preliminary discussions with other accounting firm personnel, such as the audit engagement partner. All those procedures are performed to help identify potential high risk-of-error areas. Once these areas have been identified, overall audit materiality may be allocated among the areas on the basis of such factors as relative risk of misstatement and overall desired confidence in the audit result.[5]

Procedures Associated with the Planning Phase of the Audit

One of the most important tools used by the auditors to identify material potential problem areas is a ***preliminary analytical review***. As defined in SAS 23, analytical review is the study and comparison of relationships among recorded data.[6] The data may be in the form of absolute dollars, physical quantities, ratios, or percentages. Analytical review may be performed by these means:

- Comparing the company's financial information with comparable information from prior periods (horizontal analysis).
- Comparing the financial information with anticipated results (budgets).
- Comparing the company's financial information with comparable industry averages.
- Studying relationships of elements of the financial data to relevant nonfinancial information.

The overall objective of analytical review is to analyze relationships among financial statement data and to recognize the relationships that would be expected to conform to a reasonable pattern. During the planning phase of the audit, when these relationships do not conform to expectations, the auditor is alerted to potential problem areas in the financial statements that merit special attention.

Analytical review can also reveal a significant trend over several years — such as deteriorating cash flows, uncollectible receivables, obsolete inventories, and other characteristics of the entity that are important to the auditor. If the client's financial data are recorded correctly, such trends could point to *upcoming financial difficulty* or the possible *inability to remain solvent*. On the other hand, the *figures might contain errors*. Either way, if significant deviations from expectations are noted during the planning stage of the audit, the auditor should investigate them and should normally plan to perform more extensive audit tests relating to the affected balances than would ordinarily be required.

To be useful as a planning tool, preliminary analytical review must be conducted during the year under audit (on unaudited interim data or audited data from the previous year). A final analytical review will also be performed when the auditor returns to complete the audit field work.

One of the first things the auditor should do in an initial audit engagement is to tour the client's facilities. During the ***plant tour*** the auditor should learn more about the client's business and industry, and the physical condition of inventories and plant assets. In addition, observations made during the plant tour can be useful later, during substantive test work, to refresh the auditor's memory about such things as obsolete inventory, extraordinary or routine maintenance and repairs, and fully depreciated assets.

Other procedures normally performed during the planning phase of the audit include a ***review of past records*** of the client, and ***discussions with other personnel of the accounting firm*** who are (or have been) involved in work for the client. These persons may include members of the firm's MAS, tax, or accounting and review staffs. Client records for review include past correspondence with the client, prior years' working papers, if any, and prior audit reports.

If the audit engagement of the previous year was performed by other independent auditors, the CPA may seek permission of the client to request a ***review of the predecessor auditor's working papers.*** This type of communication with predecessor auditors, like that discussed earlier in this chapter (before the engagement is accepted), is governed by SAS 7. Review of the predecessor auditor's working papers is useful and sometimes necessary for the current auditor to express an opinion on the financial statements of the current year, as well as to assess the consistency of application of GAAP between the current and preceding years. Remember that audit evidence concerning the current year's beginning balance sheet accounts was obtained in previous years. A CPA auditing financial statements for the first time must obtain evidence regarding the fairness of presentation of beginning balances — such as inventories, property and equipment, accrued liabilities, capital stock, and retained earnings. The auditor may substantially reduce the audit effort in verifying these accounts and others by reviewing the working papers of the predecessor auditor.

The predecessor auditor should be available to the successor auditor for consultation and should make certain working papers available for the successor's review. The predecessor's working papers most often needed by the successor are those which will provide the successor with general information about the client's business and those which provide information of continuing accounting significance relating to the client. These typically include the corporate charter and bylaws, previous planning memoranda, and minutes of board of directors meetings. Information of continuing accounting significance may be obtained from analyses of both current and noncurrent balance sheet accounts, analytical review summaries of past years, and analysis of contingencies.

The predecessor auditor may decide for valid business reasons (such as pending or threatened litigation) not to allow the successor auditor access to certain working papers. In such cases, the predecessor should provide the successor with an appropriate explanation of the circumstances.

The logistics of the audit work should be discussed with the client's management, board of directors, or audit committee during the planning phase of the audit. This helps prevent misunderstandings and inefficient use of client personnel. Current-year interim financial statements should be read for information which could be helpful in planning the engagement. New accounting or auditing pronouncements should be considered to determine how they will affect the scope of the audit. The senior or supervising auditor should also estimate the number of audit staff members and the number of client firm personnel that will be required for the engagement.

After these actions have been completed, the auditor is ready to finalize the plans with the client for completing the audit.

Knowledge of the client's industry, business, and organization can be obtained primarily by experience in the industry, as well as by discussions with client personnel. The auditor should also examine prior years' working papers, and read AICPA industry audit guides, industry publications, financial statements of other businesses in the industry, textbooks, and periodicals to enlarge the auditing firm's knowledge of the client's business and operating practices.

The Audit Program: Relating Audit Objectives to Procedures

A vital part in planning an audit engagement should be an advance listing of expected procedures to be performed. This normally takes the form of a written ***audit program,*** in which the outlined procedures are designed primarily to direct the evidence-gathering process. The audit program aids in instructing assistants because it states in reasonable detail how audit objectives can be achieved.[7] The form of the audit program and the details included in it will vary, depending on the complexity of the engagement. Figure 4–3 illustrates a partial audit program for the preliminary planning phase of an audit. The complete and final audit program for a particular segment of the engagement should be developed after the auditor has finished the preliminary evaluation of the system of internal controls over that segment. The audit program for a particular segment of the audit will typically include all the procedures to be followed in that segment of the audit, including the examination and the verification of the system of internal controls as well as each account affected by that system.

The Planning Memorandum

After the preliminary work has been completed, the accountant in charge of the field work typically summarizes in written form the results of the planning procedures. This summary is called the ***audit planning memorandum.*** It includes sections summarizing the auditor's preliminary orientation to the client's business; the discussions with principal officers concerning significant matters; the results of the preliminary evaluation of internal controls; preliminary materiality estimates; the extent of dependence on client staff, including internal auditors; a time budget and staff assignments for the audit. Figure 4–4 illustrates a typical planning memorandum for a manufacturing audit client.

SUPERVISING THE AUDIT

Supervision involves directing the work of assistants in accomplishing audit objectives.[8] We have observed that the auditor must evaluate her or his technical competence to handle particular audit tasks. In a similar manner, supervisors are responsible for determining that specific audit tasks are assigned only to persons who have the technical capability required to complete them. Other elements of supervision include (1) instructing assistants, (2) keeping informed about significant problems encountered on the engagement, (3) reviewing completed work, and (4) resolving differences of

	PROCEDURES	PROCEDURES PERFORMED BY	COMMENTS OR REFERENCES
	1–PRELIMINARY ORIENTATION		
1-1	Coordinate with the Supervising Partner and Manager concerning which preliminary orientation procedures and which preliminary discussions with principal officers will be performed by whom. Discuss any information based on their knowledge of or contacts with the client's operations that is pertinent to this program. If it is necessary to start audit tests concurrently with the performance of this program, establish tentative monetary precision and reliability factors for such purpose after consultation with the Supervising Partner and Manager.	WLB	See Memo
1-2	Read the following:		
	(a) The financial statements for the preceding year and the auditors' report thereon.	WLB	
	(b) The commentary report for the preceding year.	WLB	
	(c) Any reports issued since our last examination in connection with a transfer of interests, security registration, financing, or MAS engagement.	WLB	
	(d) The Federal income tax returns for the preceding year, with particular emphasis on "Schedule M" items.	WLB	
	(e) Any memorandums relating to unusual or complex tax matters, current or pending revenue agent's examinations, or significant changes in the tax law, regulations and decisions. (If the client is not subject to income taxes, or has special status for income tax purposes, this procedure should include familiarization with the applicable criteria for continuing such nontaxable or special status.)	WLB	See Memo
	(f) Material in the correspondence file of current interest, including the engagement memorandum and supplements.	WLB	
	(g) Any recent reports on the client or its industry distributed by a financial reporting service, such as Standard & Poor's or Value Line, or by a brokerage firm. (Such reports generally are obtainable from the client, a brokerage firm, or Executive Office.)	WLB	See Memo
	(h) Any analyses prepared by the client comparing its operations with selected competitors or with industry statistics. (Statistics prepared by the trade association serving the client's industry generally are obtainable from the client, our Subject File Binder, or Executive Office.)	WLB	None prepared
	(i) The most recent interim financial statements and internal reports for management. For later discussion (and for a more detailed investigation under the program for analytical review), note unusual or questionable items or trends and any significant changes in financial position or results of operations as compared with the same period for the preceding year and, if available, with the budget for the current year-to-date period (including any internal narrative reports relating to variances from budget). If the client does not prepare interim financial statements, scan the general ledger accounts to determine whether the amounts and relationships appear reasonable in comparison with the preceding year.	WLB	Through 6/30/X7
	(j) Any quarterly reports to shareholders, current reports on Form 10-Q to the Securities and Exchange Commission, and periodic financial reports to any governmental agency having regulatory authority over the client's accounting. Note any unusual matters disclosed in such reports for later discussion.	WLB	No unusual items noted

Source: Deloitte Haskins & Sells, *Control Set* (December 1977). Used with permission.

FIGURE 4–3. Partial Audit Program

JEP Manufacturing Co. and Subsidiaries
PLANNING MEMORANDUM
3-31-X1

JEP Manufacturing Company is a small specialty manufacturing company located in Greensboro, Texas. The company's common stock is approximately 90 percent owned by J. E. Coletrain, JEP's president and chairman; 9.9 percent of the remaining shares are owned by other members of the family.

JEP manufactures transformers, load break oil switches, vacuum interruptors, and substations for the electric utility industry, oil industry, and other users of heavy electrical equipment. Transformers and switches compose the majority of JEP's sales volume and are sold primarily to Tarsit Co. and Indiana Electric. In the Switch Division, their primary competitors include Neverblow Electric, Sunpower Industries, and Light Equipment Company. The Transformer Division competes primarily with General Electric and Westinghouse. In order to remain competitive with mass producers such as G. E. and Westinghouse, JEP specializes in made-to-order products, as opposed to standard models.

A five-year summary of earnings follows:

March 31,	19X6	19X7	19X8	19X9	19X0
Revenues	$4,809,744	$4,558,083	$5,126,796	$6,269,841	$6,600,945
Expenses	4,440,841	4,517,082	5,068,786	5,690,732	5,992,253
	92.3%	99.1%	98.9%	90.8%	90.8%
Net earnings before taxes	368,903	41,001	58,010	579,109	608,692
Taxes	166,479	8,179	16,375	240,603	260,592
Net Earnings	202,424	32,822	41,135	338,506	348,100
Earnings per share	1.69	.19	.30	3.05	3.17

Planning Meeting

On March 30, 19X1, prior to commencement of field work on April 27, Mitchell Cloud, engagement manager, and John Hulme, in-charge accountant, met to discuss our audit and approach. On March 26, 19X1, the overall audit approach was discussed by Robert Best, engagement partner, and Mitchell Cloud, engagement manager.

Significant Audit Areas

Inventory is considered a critical audit area because of its material effect on the balance sheet. Also critical is management's estimation of percentage complete and the resulting completion of work-in-process and impact on earnings. The client will take a physical inventory at year end, which will be observed and test counted by MMP & Co. (auditors). Percentage-of-completion estimates will be tested as to propriety, price allocations, and firm purchase commitments. A review of obsolete inventory will also be performed.

Other Audit Areas

Accounts Receivable: standard procedures will be performed, including confirmation, aging analysis, and vouching subsequent collections.

The ratio of gross sales to expenses will be tested in sales and cash disbursements test work.

Analytical review procedures will also be performed at year end on material income statement accounts.

Other Matters

The engagement is budgeted at approximately 300 hours with final field work beginning April 27. Completion of field work is scheduled for approximately May 29.

The audit staff will consist of the following individuals:

			Hours
In-Charge	John Hulme	Sr.	190
Staff	Steve Golding	Ass't.	120
			310

Per discussion with client, final deadline is tentatively scheduled for conclusion of field work May 29 and final reports June 5.

The client has agreed to prepare working papers in the following areas:

- Percentage completion of work-in-process inventories.
- Federal income tax accruals.
- Year end accruals.
- Management bonus plan.
- Pension and profit-sharing plan.

FIGURE 4–4. Planning Memorandum

opinion among firm personnel. The extent of supervision required depends on the expertise of the audit personnel involved, as well as on the complexity of the audit task.

As a means of formalizing authority–responsibility relationships within a public accounting firm, individual accountants are designated as *partners, managers, seniors* (in-charge auditors), or *staff members*. The highest level of authority (and therefore the one having ultimate authority and supervisory responsibilities) is the partner. The next level is made up of managers who typically have supervisory responsibilities for a designated group of in-charge auditors, or seniors. Staff members have no supervisory responsibilities. They are supervised by seniors assigned to specific audit engagements. Most large firms also have managers and partners who specialize in the audits of specific industries. In that capacity these persons are expected to help in resolving questions associated with the audits of clients in their fields of specialization.

Supervision involves day-by-day analysis of the work being done by those being supervised to judge whether they are meeting overall audit objectives. It is important that communications between the supervisor and assistants go two ways. Assistants should be expected to communicate technical and other problems upward within the firm until those problems are effectively resolved. This communication is consistent with the consultation standard for quality control within a firm. On the other hand, overall audit objectives and progress should be continually communicated from the supervisor downward through the ranks to staff personnel. This will help all persons involved in the engagement to feel that they have an important part in the overall audit effort. It also allows all persons involved to keep abreast of the pertinent activities as they happen.

One element of supervision that requires special consideration is that of resolving differences of opinion among firm personnel. On rare occasions, a staff member may feel, after appropriate consultation, that he or she disagrees with a conclusion reached by supervisors regarding a technical accounting or auditing issue. The CPA firm should establish procedures that will encourage the staff member to document her or his disagreement in such a situation. Only by doing so may staff members be encouraged to think for themselves as they will have to do in their move up the authority–responsibility ladder.

AUDIT WORKING PAPERS

Working papers are the records brought together by the auditor to document the nature, timing, and extent of the testing carried out during the audit process. They show the procedures followed, the compliance and substantive tests performed, the information obtained, and the audit conclusions reached for each subsystem and for each account balance shown in the financial statements. The chief objectives of working papers are to *aid the auditor in conducting the examination* and to *provide evidence in support of the audit opinion.*[9] It is important that the auditor plan the form and content of working papers at the beginning of the audit. Such an arrangement leads to the most effective use of audit staff in the engagement, as well as of client personnel who might assist in working paper preparation.

In this section we first examine the guidelines for preparing audit working papers. Then we discuss their organization and content. After that, we consider the ownership and custody rights to working papers and relate their preparation to the planning phase of the audit.

Guidelines for Audit Working Papers

Generally accepted auditing standards do not contain specific guidelines for preparing working papers. They do, however, state that the form and content of working papers should fit the needs and circumstances of the engagement to which they apply. Indeed, the guidelines set forth in those standards are so broad that they apply to engagements for nonaudit (tax, MAS, and write-up) services as well as to those for audits. Factors that determine the desired quantity, type, and content of audit working papers for a particular engagement include the nature of the audit report expected to be rendered; the nature of the financial statements, schedules, or other information upon which the auditor is reporting; the condition of the client's records and internal controls; and the amount of supervision and review required for the assistants' work on a particular engagement.

Audit standards specify six broad guidelines for the organization and content of working papers:

1. The working papers must contain sufficient information to show that the audited information (financial statements or otherwise) agrees with the client's records.
2. The working papers must be organized to show that the engagement has been adequately planned and that the work of assistants has been supervised, in accordance with the first standard of audit field work.
3. The working papers must also show that the client's system of internal control has been reviewed and evaluated, in accordance with the second standard of audit field work.
4. The audit procedures followed and the tests performed in gathering sufficient competent evidential matter must be shown to meet the third standard of audit field work.
5. There must be evidence that the exceptions and unusual matters disclosed by audit procedures were appropriately resolved or treated.
6. The working papers must also demonstrate that the conclusions reached by the auditor concerning significant aspects of the engagement (including client's compliance with internal controls and conformity of financial presentations with generally accepted accounting principles) are supported by the findings of the audit.[10]

Content of Audit Working Papers

Audit working papers are generally divided into two parts: permanent files and current files. Permanent files are intended to show the history of the company and contain data which are of continuing interest to each succeeding examination. Current files, on the other hand, usually contain data that are pertinent only to the current year's examination.

The Permanent File. The ***permanent file*** serves several purposes. First, it contains certain historical data of the company which are used to reacquaint continuing auditors with the client from year to year, and to provide new audit staff with an initial understanding of the client's affairs. Sometimes when one auditor succeeds another auditor on an engagement, the permanent file of the client can assist the successor in planning the engagement. Finally, many of the records in the permanent file do not change, or require only minor change, from year to year. Placing such papers in one location for easy reference eliminates the necessity for duplicating the repetitive (but necessary) information year after year.

The auditor constructs a permanent file for the client on the first audit engagement. As the years pass, elements are added, deleted, or modified as necessary. Contents of the permanent file include copies of the following items:

- The company charter, if applicable.
- The articles of incorporation and bylaws or partnership agreement.
- Organization charts and other data pertaining to internal control — such as flowcharts; questionnaires; narrative descriptions of pertinent systems; and observations concerning strengths, weaknesses, and actions taken by the company to eliminate weaknesses.
- Permanent financing arrangements of the company, such as bond indentures and stock issue agreements.
- Contracts with key employees, such as the company president; and other agreements — such as leases, stock options, pension plans, and contracts with major suppliers or customers which have continuing significance over the years.

- Analyses of key balance sheet accounts that have continuing significance. These include such accounts as capital stock, retained earnings, long-term debt, property and equipment, and intangible assets. These analyses provide vital information about the company history, which can be used in planning each successive engagement. Typically they require only yearly update to remain current.
- The results of analytical review procedures. These data include year-to-year changes in key operating and financing ratios — such as gross profit, current ratio, and rate of return on stockholder's equity. As pointed out earlier, year-to-year fluctuations in these accounts can assist the auditor in planning the audit by pinpointing areas in the financial statements requiring special attention. (Some CPA firms include analytical review results in the current file rather than in the permanent file.)
- Revised and updated minutes of board of directors meetings, which serve as the auditor's permanent evidence that the client's major transactions over the years have been approved by appropriate company officials.
- Time budgets, which contain columns for estimated and total time spent on each of the various balance sheet and income statement categories. The time budget is a key factor in scheduling work to be done and in controlling the progress of the engagement (including supervision of assistants' work).

The Current File. The ***current file,*** as mentioned previously, contains descriptions of audit procedures performed on various accounting subsystems and account balances of the current period, plus audit adjustments to those accounts. These working papers in the current file help to document the evidence-gathering concepts. (These concepts are covered in Chapters 10 – 16; appendixes to Chapters 10 – 16 contain segments of audit working papers for a typical manufacturing concern.)

Figure 4–5 shows how parts of a typical current file of working papers relate to each other. The results of findings flow from supporting schedules to the working trial balance. These papers contain the auditor's record of all evidence-gathering procedures followed, tests performed, results of tests, and conclusions reached during the current audit. Since these papers are the only evidence that generally accepted auditing standards were followed and that conclusions reached were consistent with the evidence available, it is important that they be: clearly and concisely written; complete enough to assure the validity of the audit conclusions reached (such as degree of client's compliance with internal controls); informative of material matters concerning the financial presentations (such as adequacy of disclosures, etc.); and cross-referenced in such a way as to facilitate greater understanding during the review process.

In accordance with the third standard of audit fieldwork, sufficient competent evidential matter should be gathered by the auditor to support each material financial statement assertion. In terms of working papers, this means that each material account (and the systems supporting that account) in the financial statements should be supported by its own series of working papers. To ensure ease of understanding by reviewers, *each series of working papers should be treated as a unit*, showing the following:

- Book balances.
- Adjusting and reclassifying entries recommended.
- Pertinent audit objectives (discussed earlier in this chapter).

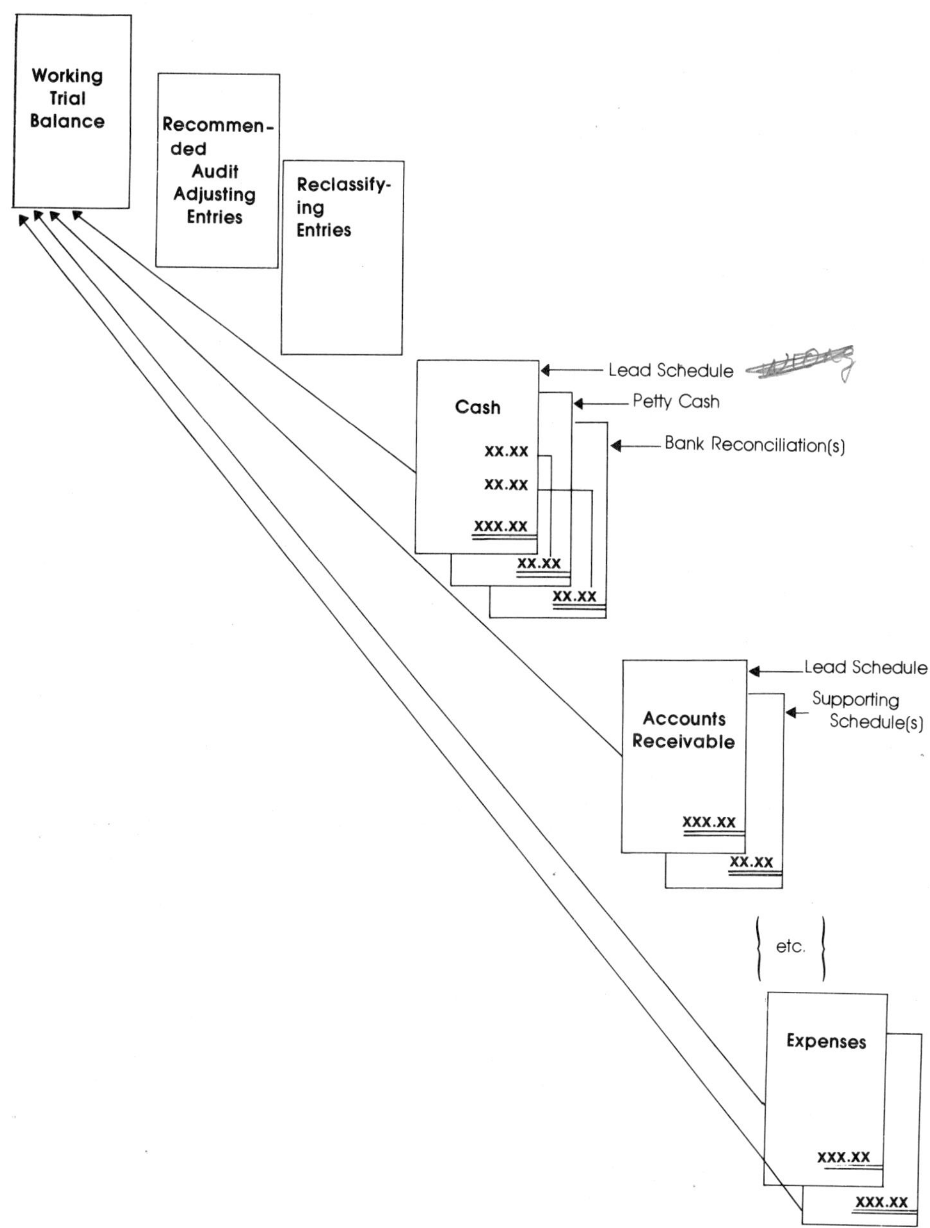

FIGURE 4–5. Current Working Paper File

- Systems and balances to be audited, and samples drawn.
- Evidence gathered to support or reject each assertion tested.
- Conclusions reached.

Because of the double-entry system of recordkeeping, financial statement accounts are interrelated. Because of these interrelationships, misstatements in one account are always offset by corresponding misstatements in other accounts. Therefore, each segment of the working papers and the conclusions related to them should be adequately cross-referenced to other financial statement segments that are interrelated so that reviewers can ascertain whether proper attention was given to all interrelated information.

As Figure 4–5 shows, the current file working papers are usually arranged in the following order:

Working trial balance. These show all financial statement account balances before adjustments, as well as recommended audit adjustment and reclassification entries, relating those balances to the audited financial statements. Each account on the working trial balance should be cross-referenced to the appropriate lead schedule in the various segments of the working papers.

Recommended audit adjusting entries. These are entries the auditor has ascertained should be made by the client in order to make the financial statements conform to generally accepted accounting principles. Audit adjustments typically affect income, either individually or collectively, in a material way. They should be written neatly and concisely, and should contain appropriate explanations and appropriate working paper cross-references.

Reclassifying entries. In contrast to adjusting entries, reclassifying entries are made in the audit working papers and financial statements only. Since they typically do not affect income, there is usually no need for the client to incorporate them into company records. Reclassifications are often needed, however, for adequate informative financial statement disclosures. These entries should also be cross-referenced to appropriate segments of the working papers.

Financial statement segments. As discussed earlier, each important segment of the financial statements should have its own series of working papers, capable of showing individually the audit evidence gathered and the conclusions reached. Each segment should contain the following:

- *A lead schedule,* showing pertinent information about account balances before adjustment, plus recommended audit adjustment and reclassification entries, and the final balance. The final balance should be cross-referenced directly to the working trial balance.
- *Supporting schedules,* showing audit evidence gathered and conclusions reached with regard to individual account balances and systems. These conclusions include those regarding propriety of client disclosures in conformity with generally accepted accounting principles and the extent of the client's adherence to prescribed internal controls.

Typically the lead schedules and related supporting schedules are grouped by segments of the financial statement (current assets, noncurrent assets, liabilities, equities, revenues, and expenses). As shown in Figure 4–5, they will generally follow the adjusting and reclassifying entries segments of the work papers. Figure 4–6 illustrates the format of a typical audit working paper lead schedule for cash. (The actual audit work performed with respect to cash, and reasons pertaining to it, are discussed in Chapter 12 and would be shown in the related supporting schedules.)

The current files may also contain a ***general section***, which includes, among other things, the audit program. As stated earlier, the audit program contains a detailed listing of the audit procedures to be performed. The results of those procedures are then documented on the various lead schedules and supporting schedules. The client representation letter, the attorney's confirmation letter(s), other confirmation letters, and other documentary evidence of general importance to the current year audit is also included in the general section of the audit working papers. Each audit firm will have its own specific guidelines for working paper format. However, every working paper should include the following elements:

- Indexing numbers, so that it can be located, removed, replaced, and used efficiently by reviewers.
- Cross-referencing numbers showing all important interrelated information found in other segments of the working papers.
- Heading, showing name of the client, title of the working paper, and date or period of time to which the audited information pertains.
- Signatures and initials of preparers so that persons responsible for performing the audit work can be easily identified if reviewers later question the evidence gathered or conclusions reached.
- Dates of the audit work, including interim field work, and initial and later review by supervisory personnel.
- Tick marks and legend. Audit ***tick marks*** are symbols placed on the working papers that explain the auditor's evidence-gathering procedures. Many firms have standard tick marks that are used uniformly throughout the firm for various procedures (footings, cross-footings, vouching, etc.). Other audit firms do not have such a policy. In the latter instances, it is necessary that a legend be placed on each working paper, explaining the meaning of the tick marks to the reviewer.

Audited financial information relating to individual account balances is generally presented within one of two formats within the working papers:

The ***analysis format*** is organized along the lines of a four-element equation showing the beginning balance, additions, removals, and the ending balance. This format is used when the auditor needs to retain all that information. Figure 4–7 shows a typical analysis type of working paper. The analysis format is generally used for notes receivable, notes payable, accrued receivables, accrued payables, property and equipment, accumulated depreciation, prepaid expenses and other assets, retained earnings, and capital stock.

The ***summary format*** is used when the auditor determines that details of the ending balance in the accounts are more important than the elements associated with the accumulation of the account balance. Figure 4–5, the cash lead schedule, is an example

JEP Manufacturing Co.
Cash
Dec. 31, 19X1

W. P. No.	A
ACCOUNTANT	CWT
DATE	2-1-X2

	W/P #	12/31/X1 Per Books	Adjustments & Reclassification DR <CR>	Final
Regular Account	B-1	101616 32		
Payroll Account	B-2	10000 00		
Special Account	B-3	315873 16		
Petty Cash	B-4	300 00		
Total Cash		427789 48		

FIGURE 4–6. Summary Audit Working Paper (Cash Lead Schedule)

of a summary type of working paper. The summary format is typically used for cash balances, accounts receivable, accounts payable, revenue and expense accounts.

These types of working papers are illustrated more completely in the appendixes to Chapters 10 through 16.

Ownership and Custody of Working Papers

Working papers are the property of the auditor or, more accurately, of the firm for whom the auditor works.[11] However, an audit firm's ownership rights to working papers are subject to certain ethical limitations. For example, when working papers are needed as an integral part of the client's records to make them complete, the auditor is required, under Rule 501 of the Code of Professional Ethics, to make copies available to the client. Audit standards contain the warning that an auditor's working papers should not substitute for client records. Furthermore, information in the working papers is considered confidential under Rule 301 of the Code of Professional Ethics.

There are no explicit rules relating to the retention of working papers. In deciding on an appropriate records retention policy, the accountant should be aware of pertinent legal requirements for records retention, such as the statute of limitations for examination of the client's tax returns, which is three years in most cases. Beyond that, the general guidelines require that the accounting firm should retain records for a period of time sufficient for the firm's needs. Most firms have adopted their own records retention policies for working papers supporting the financial statements, and for permanent file papers. Use of modern techniques, such as microfilming, makes storage easier and allows for extensive record retention when it is needed.

Planning and the Preparation of Working Papers

As mentioned previously in this chapter, it is advantageous for the auditor to be appointed as early during the client's fiscal year as possible. For one thing, such action will permit more complete documentation of audit work. Initial permanent file construction will begin and will continue through the planning phase of the audit because it is part of the work that needs to be done in order to acquaint the auditor with the client and the industry in which the client operates. Preliminary analytical review should also begin during the planning phase of the audit and be documented in the permanent file.

Early appointment of the auditor also permits an early decision about the extent to which client employees, including internal auditors, may be used by the independent auditor. Often, client employees can be used to prepare ***pro forma working papers***, which include detailed analyses or summaries of accounts in the general ledger. These working papers can be included in the auditor's current file as part of the total evidence of audit work done. By using client employees to prepare some of these working papers, the amount of time the independent auditor spends can be reduced. This, in turn, results in lower fees and greater satisfaction for the client.

J E P Manufacturing Co.
Notes Payable and Accrued Interest Principal
12-31-X6

W. P. No. M-1
Accountant JJ
Date 1-22-X7

Bank	Date Issued	Date Due	Balance 12-31-X5	Principal Additions	Principal Payments	Balance 12-31-X6
Fidelity Union Trust:						
	10-31-X5	1-31-X6	100000 – z	–	100000 – ų	–
	12-31-X5	4-30-X6	200000 – z	–	200000 – ų	–
	4-30-X6	8-31-X6	–	70000 – √ ¥	70000 – ų	–
	8-31-X6	1-31-X7	–	150000 – √ ¥	–	150000 –
			300000 – z	220000 –	370000 –	150000 – C
President Trust Company:						
	11-30-X5	2-28-X7	25000 – z	–	25000 – ų	–
	2-28-X6	5-31-X7	–	75000 – √ ¥	75000 – ų	–
			25000 – z	75000 –	100000 –	– C₄
Total			325000 – z	295000 –	470000 –	150000 –
			To A-2			To A-2

√ – Examined Bank advice for proceeds of the note

¥ – Examined copy of note, noting interest rate, principal amt., and Due date

ų – Examined cancelled note and paid notice from bank

C – Agrees with Bank confirmation on B-2-1

C₄ – Agrees with Bank confirmation on B-3-1

z – Per prior year's working paper

ø – Traced to cash disbursement journal

∠ – Verified Computation

FIGURE 4–7. Analysis Type of Working Paper

Int. Rate	Collateral		Accrued 12-31-X5	Interest Expense 19X6		Payments		Accrued 12-31-X6	
8	None		1333 33 ƶ	666 67	∠	2000 00	ɸ	—	
8			—	5332 80	∠	5332 80	ɸ	—	
8¼			—	1924 81	∠	1924 81	ɸ	—	
8½			—	4250 00	∠	—	C	4250 00	∠
			1333 33 ƶ	12174 28		9257 61		4250 00	
8	None		166 67 ƶ	333 33	∠	500 00	ɸ	—	
8¼			—	1443 75	∠	1443 75	ɸ	—	
			166 67 ƶ	1777 08		1943 75		—	
			1500 00 ƶ	13951 36		11201 36		4250 00	
			To O	To A-3				To O	

gD

RELIANCE ON THE WORK OF INTERNAL AUDITORS

In addition to providing assistance in preparing pro forma working papers, the client's internal auditors may be used to actually affect the nature, timing, and extent of necessary compliance tests and substantive tests that the independent auditor will perform. SAS 9 discusses the extent to which the independent auditor can rely on the work of internal auditors.[12]

As explained in Chapter 1, the objective of the internal audit differs significantly from that of the independent audit. Internal auditors perform a number of *high-level monitoring services* for top management, including a continuing study and evaluation of internal control. Beyond that, they typically *review operating practices* of the client in order to promote increased efficiency and economy, and make inquiries of operating departments at management's direction. The effect of the internal audit function on the quality of the internal control system is discussed further in Chapter 5.

Although the client's internal audit staff may have complete organizational autonomy, it must be remembered that they are still client employees. Therefore, they do not have the level of independence required by generally accepted auditing standards to render an audit opinion on the client's financial statements. In some parts of the audit, however, internal auditors possess adequate objectivity, training, experience, and expertise to assist the independent auditor in the evidence-gathering process.

According to SAS 9, the auditor should evaluate the following attributes of the client's internal audit staff in deciding the extent to which their work can be relied upon:

- *The purpose served by the internal audit function.* If the internal audit function is truly an autonomous internal control-monitoring arm of top management, the internal audit staff may be used much more heavily than if the internal audit department is merely an element of the accounting department.
- *The competency of the internal audit staff.* Competency may be investigated by evaluating the professional credentials of the internal audit staff, their prior experience, and the client's practices for hiring, training, and supervising internal audit staff.
- *The objectivity of the internal audit staff.* In evaluating objectivity, the independent auditor should consider the organizational level to which the internal audit staff reports. This may be done by referring to the client's organization chart, and by examining the internal auditor's recommendations in previously issued reports.
- *The work of the internal audit staff.* The independent auditor should examine, on a test basis, working papers that have been prepared by the internal audit staff in the past. In addition, the independent auditor should examine samples of the internal auditor's work and follow through the logic used by the internal audit staff in reaching conclusions.

If it is decided that the work of the internal audit staff can be relied upon, the independent auditor's activities may be affected in either or both of the following ways:

- Because the internal audit staff's work overlaps certain work of the independent auditor and improves the client's system of internal control, the nature and extent of the independent auditor's tests may be reduced.

- The independent auditor may actually use the client's internal audit staff to perform certain compliance and substantive tests. If this alternative is selected, it must be remembered that although the internal auditor may perform the actual tests, the independent auditor is the only one qualified to make the final audit judgments about adequacy of internal control and fairness of presentation of financial statement balances.

SUMMARY

In this chapter, we have discussed the planning and supervision phases of the audit. After defining the terms *planning* and *supervision*, we discussed the various implications of each of these parts of the first audit field work standard. We looked at the time sequence of the elements of the audit and briefly discussed important procedures to be performed during each phase of the examination.

We then turned our attention to the audit working papers. We discussed them and described the permanent file, which is either constructed or updated during the planning phase of the audit engagement. We also described the basic contents of the current file and the relationships among the elements of that file.

Finally, we explained how the independent auditor may rely on the work of client employees, with particular emphasis on use of the work of internal auditors.

NOTES

1. Statement on Auditing Standards (SAS) 1 Section 310.01 (New York: AICPA, 1973).

2. SAS 7, "Communication Between Predecessor and Successor Auditors," paragraph .04 (New York: AICPA, October 1975).

3. For more detailed coverage of the contents of audit engagement letters, see *AICPA Professional Standards*, vol. 1, Section 8002 (New York: AICPA, June 1980).

4. SAS 22, "Planning and Supervision," paragraph .01 (New York: AICPA, 1978).

5. Theoretical approaches to this problem are beyond the scope of this book. See Barry E. Cushing, G. Gerald Searfass, and Reed H. Randall, "Materiality Allocation in Audit Planning: A Feasibility Study," *Journal of Accounting Research* 17, Supplement (1979): 172–216.

6. SAS 23, "Analytical Review Procedures" (New York: AICPA, 1978).

7. SAS 22, paragraph .05.

8. Ibid., paragraph. .09.

9. SAS 41, paragraph 2 (New York: AICPA, 1982).

10. Ibid., paragraph .05.

11. Ibid., paragraph .06.

12. SAS 9, "The Effect of an Internal Audit Function on the Scope of the Independent Auditor's Examination" (New York: AICPA, 1975).

QUESTIONS FOR CLASS DISCUSSION

Q4–1 What does the term *planning* mean as it is used in generally accepted auditing standards?

Q4–2 What does the term *supervision* mean as it is used in generally accepted auditing standards?

Q4–3 What are the elements of a typical audit engagement, in chronological sequence?

Q4–4 Can you explain the concept of materiality as applied to auditing? Why is this concept important to the auditor during the planning stages of the audit?

Q4–5 What are the contents of a typical engagement letter? Explain why this document is important.

Q4–6 Why is it important to have communications between predecessor and successor auditors?

Q4–7 What are at least four things an auditor should do to determine whether a prospective client should be accepted?

Q4–8 What standards has the AICPA established to guide the CPA in deciding whether to accept a client? Why were those standards established?

Q4–9 What steps may an auditor take to identify areas of potentially high risk in an audit? Why should this be done? When should it be done?

Q4–10 What types of information would an auditor expect to secure by examining a client's charter and bylaws? Contrast the procedures followed in examining those documents during a first year engagement with the procedures followed in subsequent years.

Q4–11 What is the meaning of the term *analytical review* as it is used in an independent audit? During which stages of a typical audit engagement are analytical review procedures performed? How are the findings used in each of these stages?

Q4–12 What is an *audit program?* Describe its purposes. During which phase(s) of the audit examination should the audit programs be written?

Q4–13 Why is the supervision of assistants such a vital part of a typical audit engagement? What activities are included in the supervision process?

Q4–14 What are *audit working papers?* Why are they important? Who owns them? Explain.

Q4–15 What are the guidelines provided by the AICPA relating to the organization and content of working papers? Discuss them.

Q4–16 What is the meaning and purpose of audit *tick marks?*

Q4–17 What is the difference between analysis-type working papers and summary-type working papers? In what circumstances would each be used?

Q4–18 What function(s) are typically performed by the client's internal audit department? To what extent can the work done by this department be (1) relied upon and (2) used by the independent auditor?

SHORT CASES

C4–1 A CPA has been asked to audit the financial statements of a publicly held company for the first time. All preliminary verbal discussions and inquiries have been completed between the CPA, the company, the predecessor auditor, and all other necessary parties. The CPA is now preparing an engagement letter.

Required:

List the items that should be included in the typical engagement letter in these circumstances and describe the benefits derived from preparing an engagement letter.

(AICPA adapted)

C4–2 The auditor should obtain a level of knowledge of the entity's business — including events, transactions, and practices — that will permit the planning and performance of an examination in accordance with generally accepted auditing standards. Adhering to these standards enables the auditor's report to lend credibility to financial statements by providing the public with certain assurances.

Required:

a. How does knowledge of the entity's business help the auditor in the planning and performance of an examination in accordance with generally accepted auditing standards?

b. What assurances are provided to the public when the auditor states that the financial statements "present fairly . . . in conformity with generally accepted accounting principles applied on a consistent basis"?

(AICPA adapted)

C4–3 An important part of every examination of financial statements is the preparation of audit working papers. You are instructing an inexperienced staff member on his first auditing assignment. He is to examine an account. An analysis of the account has been prepared by the client for inclusion in the audit working papers.

Required:

a. Discuss the relationship of audit working papers to each of the standards of field work.

b. Prepare a list of the comments, commentaries, and notations that the staff member should make or have made on the account analysis to provide an adequate working paper as evidence of his examination. (Do not include a description of auditing procedures applicable to the account.)

(AICPA adapted)

C4–4 In the middle summer of 19X1 you are given the in-charge responsibility for the Shop-Rite Corporation, a company that has been a client of your firm for six years. You have met the engagement partner, Richard Hamilton, who has advised you that you are to be in charge of planning and supervising the audit field work. The corporation has a fiscal year end of October 31.

Required:

Discuss the necessary preparation and planning for the Shop-Rite Corporation annual audit before beginning audit field work at the client's office. Include in your discussion the sources of possible information you would consult, the kind of information you would seek, and the preliminary plans you would make for client assistance and staffing requirements. *Do not write an audit program.*

(AICPA adapted)

C4–5 During the course of an audit examination, an independent auditor gives serious consideration to the concept of materiality. This concept is inherent in the work of the independent auditor and is important for planning, preparing, and modifying audit programs. The concept of materiality underlies the application of all the generally accepted auditing standards, particularly the standards of field work and reporting.

Required:

a. Briefly describe what is meant by the independent auditor's concept of *materiality*.
b. What are some common relationships and other considerations used by the auditor in judging materiality?
c. Identify how the planning and execution of an audit program might be affected by the independent auditor's concept of materiality.

(AICPA adapted)

C4–6 An auditor knows that analytical review procedures are substantive tests that are extremely useful in the initial planning stages of the audit.

Required:

a. Explain why analytical review procedures are called substantive tests.
b. Explain how analytical review procedures may be useful to the auditor in the initial planning stages of the audit.
c. Identify the analytical review procedures that a CPA would probably utilize during an examination performed in accordance with generally accepted auditing standards.

C4–7 When a CPA has accepted an engagement from a new client who is a manufacturer, one of the first things he or she may do is to tour the client's facilities.

Required:

a. Name at least five things a CPA may observe during a plant tour.
b. Discuss the ways in which these observations will be of help to the CPA in planning and conducting the audit.

(AICPA adapted)

C4–8 Betsy Klima, CPA, is approached by a prospective client who desires to engage her to perform an audit which in prior years was performed by another CPA.

Required:

Identify the procedures Betsy should follow in accepting the engagement.

(AICPA adapted)

C4–9 Jimmarc, Inc., a closely held company, wishes to engage Carlos Noro, CPA, to examine its annual financial statements. Although Jimmarc was in general satisfied with the services provided by its prior auditor, Delbert Killington, it thought the audit work that Killington performed was too detailed and interfered excessively with normal office routines. Noro has asked Jimmarc to inform Killington of the decision to change auditors, but Jimmarc does not wish to do so.

Required:

a. List and discuss the steps Noro should follow before accepting the engagement.
b. What additional procedures should Noro perform on this first-time engagement over and beyond those Noro would perform on the Jimmarc engagement of the following year.

C4–10 Joan Pimentel is a CPA who is conducting preliminary analytical review tests for the Broadaxe Manufacturing Company during the planning stages of the 19X3–X4 audit. During her review, Joan notices the following changes in relationships over the past three years. (You may assume that Joan is the continuing auditor for the years 19X0–X4.) Inventory turnover declined steadily over three years, from 18.3 times per year to 14.2 times per year. Average receivable collection period was twenty-three days in 19X1; and based on analysis of unadjusted financial statements, that comparative number was twenty-eight days in 19X4.

Required:

Tell what each of these changes shows Joan. How can she use them in planning the 19X3–X4 audit examination?

C4–11 Ben Talbert, CPA, has been engaged to perform the audit examination of the Huaco Resort Inn, the largest motor hotel in Arizona. The grounds of the hotel cover approximately forty acres and include swimming, tennis, golf, and racquetball facilities. There are 540 guest rooms, which have an average occupancy rate of 80 percent. The hotel also does extensive convention business through its convention center.

There are a total of fifteen members on the inn's accounting staff, which is headed by Mr. Mike Lively. Lively's official title is internal auditor, and his duties include supervision of the billing, cash receipts, and cash disbursements functions, as well as analysis of uncollectible accounts. Lively's staff performs all the major bookkeeping functions, which have included excellent internal controls in the past. Lively and his staff are very cooperative and have set aside 200 manhours to assist Talbert in the audit.

Required:

a. Discuss the description and function of the internal auditor in terms of generally accepted auditing standards.
b. On the basis of your description in (a), does Lively fit the description of an internal auditor in terms of generally accepted auditing standards?
c. What audit work may Talbert use Lively and his staff to perform? For what audit work may they not be used?
d. How would Lively's duties need to be realigned, if at all, to permit Talbert to use him more extensively? What audit work may be performed by Lively and his staff in this case?

C4–12 You are the senior auditor on the audit engagement of Mixit Plastics, Inc., a large manufacturer of prefabricated plastic products. Your assistant on the job is Sue Smart, a recent honors graduate of So Hi University who has never before worked on an audit. The areas of the audit examination that you have assigned to her are

a. Accounts receivable, sales, and the allowance for doubtful accounts.
b. Raw materials, work-in-process, and finished goods inventories and cost of goods sold.
c. Contingent liabilities.

Since you were deeply involved in completing another engagement when you learned you were to be in charge of the Mixit audit, you neglected to call Sue until two days before the audit was to begin. Feeling pinched for time, you told Sue to go to the file room, request the prior year's working papers, and begin her planning by reading them. You also told her to prepare pro forma current-year working papers using last year's papers as a model for her assigned areas. Since you followed prior year's working papers last year and had no problems when you audited these same areas, you feel that Sue can do the same this year. Besides, since she made an A in auditing, you feel that she should have a firm grasp of what she should be doing without much help from you.

Required:

a. What problems might there be in your actions — on the basis of generally accepted auditing standards?
b. Should Sue be performing the audit of these financial statement areas? Why or why not?
c. List the six audit objectives that were discussed in Chapter 3. How would you use these audit objectives in instructing Sue with respect to the audit of
   (1) Accounts receivables, sales, and the allowance for doubtful accounts?
   (2) Raw materials, work-in-process, and finished goods inventories and cost of goods sold?
   (3) Contingent liabilities?

PROBLEMS

P4–1 The following items pertain to planning the typical audit examination. Choose the best response for each item.

a. Preliminary arrangements agreed to by the auditor and the client should be reduced to writing by the auditor. The best place to set forth these arrangements is in

(1) A memorandum to be placed in the permanent section of the auditing working papers.
(2) An engagement letter.
(3) A client representation letter.
(4) A confirmation letter attached to the constructive services letter.

b. Which of the following is an effective audit planning and control procedure that helps prevent misunderstandings and inefficient use of audit personnel?

(1) Arrange to make copies, for inclusion in the working papers, of those client supporting documents examined by the auditor.
(2) Arrange to provide the client with copies of the audit programs to be used during the audit.
(3) Arrange a preliminary conference with the client to discuss audit objectives, fees, timing, and other information.
(4) Arrange to have the auditor prepare and post any necessary adjusting or reclassification entries prior to final closing.

c. Which of the following is the most likely first step an auditor would perform at the beginning of an initial audit engagement?

(1) Prepare a rough draft of the financial statements and of the auditor's report.
(2) Study and evaluate the system of internal administrative control.
(3) Tour the client's facilities and review the general records.
(4) Consult with and review the work of the predecessor auditor prior to discussing the engagement with the client management.

d. As generally conceived, the audit committee of a publicly held company should be made up of

(1) Representatives from the client's management, investors, suppliers, and customers.
(2) The audit partner, the chief financial officer, the legal counsel, and at least one outsider.
(3) Representatives of the major equity interests (bonds, preferred stock, common stock).
(4) Members of the board of directors who are not officers or employees.

e. The concept of materiality would be *least* important to an auditor in determining the

(1) Transactions that should be reviewed.
(2) Need for disclosure of a particular fact or transaction.
(3) Scope of the CPA's audit program relating to various accounts.
(4) Effects of direct financial interest in the client upon the CPA's independence.

f. The first standard of field work recognizes that early appointment of the independent auditor has many advantages to the auditor and the client. Which of the following advantages is *least* likely to occur as a result of early appointment of the auditor?

(1) The auditor will be able to plan the audit work so that it may be done expeditiously.
(2) The auditor will be able to complete the audit work in less time.
(3) The auditor will be able to plan better for the observation of the physical inventories.
(4) The auditor will be able to perform the examination more efficiently and will be finished at an early date after the year end.

g. The first standard of field work — which states that the work is to be adequately planned, and assistants, if any, are to be properly supervised — recognizes that
   (1) Early appointment of the auditor is advantageous to the auditor and the client.
   (2) Acceptance of an audit engagement after the close of the client's fiscal year is generally not permissible.
   (3) Appointment of the auditor subsequent to the physical count of inventories requires a disclaimer of opinion.
   (4) Performance of substantial parts of the examination is necessary at interim dates.
h. An auditor is planning an audit engagement for a new client in a business that is unfamiliar to the auditor. Which of the following would be the most useful source of information for the auditor during the preliminary planning stage, when the auditor is trying to obtain a general understanding of audit problems that might be encountered?
   (1) Client manuals of accounts and charts of accounts.
   (2) AICPA Industry Audit Guides.
   (3) Prior-year working papers of the predecessor auditor.
   (4) Latest annual and interim financial statements issued by the client.
i. Which of the following actions should be taken by a CPA who has been asked to examine the financial statements of a company whose fiscal year has ended?
   (1) Discuss with the client the possibility of an adverse opinion because of the late engagement date.
   (2) Ascertain whether circumstances are likely to permit an adequate examination and expression of an unqualified opinion.
   (3) Inform the client of the need to issue a qualified opinion if the physical inventory has already been taken.
   (4) Ascertain whether a proper study and evaluation of internal control can be conducted after completion of the field work.
j. An auditor who accepts an audit engagement and does *not* possess the industry expertise of the business entity, should
   (1) Engage financial experts familiar with the nature of the business entity.
   (2) Obtain a knowledge of matters that relate to the nature of the entity's business.
   (3) Refer a substantial portion of the audit to another CPA who will act as the principal auditor.
   (4) First inform management that an unqualified opinion can *not* be issued.
k. Early appointment of the independent auditor will permit
   (1) A more thorough examination to be performed.
   (2) A proper study and evaluation of internal control to be performed.
   (3) Sufficient competent evidential matter to be obtained.
   (4) A more efficient examination to be planned.
l. Engagement letters are widely used in practice for professional engagements of all types. The primary purpose of the engagement letter is to
   (1) Remind management that the primary responsibility for the financial statements rests with management.
   (2) Satisfy the requirements of the CPA's liability insurance policy.
   (3) Provide a starting point for the auditor's preparation of the preliminary audit program.
   (4) Provide a written record of the agreement with the client as to the services to be provided.

m. After preliminary audit arrangements have been made, an engagement confirmation letter should be sent to the client. The letter usually would *not* include
   (1) A reference to the auditor's responsibility for the detection of errors or irregularities.
   (2) An estimate of the time to be spent on the audit work by audit staff and management.
   (3) A statement that management advisory services would be made available upon request.
   (4) A statement that a management letter will be issued outlining comments and suggestions as to any procedures requiring the client's attention.

(AICPA adapted)

P4–2 The following items pertain to communication between prodecessor and successor auditors. Choose the best response for each item.

a. When a CPA is approached to perform an audit for the first time, the CPA should make inquiries of the predecessor auditor. This is a necessary procedure because the predecessor may be able to provide the successor with information that will assist the successor in determining
   (1) Whether the predecessor's work should be utilized.
   (2) Whether the company follows the policy of rotating its auditors.
   (3) Whether in the predecessor's opinion internal control of the company has been satisfactory.
   (4) Whether the engagement should be accepted.

b. A CPA may reduce the audit work on a first-time audit by reviewing the working papers of the predecessor auditor. The predecessor should permit the successor to review working papers relating to matters of continuing accounting significance such as those that relate to
   (1) Extent of reliance on the work of specialists.
   (2) Fee arrangements and summaries of payments.
   (3) Analysis of contingencies.
   (4) Staff hours required to complete the engagement.

c. If, during an audit examination, the successor auditor becomes aware of information that may indicate that financial statements reported on by the predecessor auditor may require revision, the successor auditor should
   (1) Ask the client to arrange a meeting among the three parties to discuss the information and attempt to resolve the matter.
   (2) Notify the client and the predecessor auditor of the matter and ask them to attempt to resolve it.
   (3) Notify the predecessor auditor who may be required to revise the previously issued financial statements and auditor's report.
   (4) Ask the predecessor auditor to arrange a meeting with the client to discuss and resolve the matter.

d. Which of the following analyses appearing in a predecessor's working papers is the successor auditor *least* likely to be interested in reviewing?
   (1) Analysis of noncurrent balance sheet accounts.
   (2) Analysis of current balance sheet accounts.
   (3) Analysis of contingencies.
   (4) Analysis of income statement accounts.

(AICPA adapted)

P4–3 The following items pertain to the meaning and use of audit working papers. Choose the best response for each item.

a. Audit working papers are used to record the results of the auditor's evidence-gathering procedures. When preparing working papers the auditor should remember that
   (1) Working papers should be kept on the client's premises so that the client can have access to them for reference purposes.
   (2) Working papers should be the primary support for the financial statements being examined.
   (3) Working papers should be considered as a substitute for the client's accounting records.
   (4) Working papers should be designed to meet the circumstances and the auditor's needs on each engagement.

b. Although the quantity, type, and content of working papers will vary with the circumstances, the working papers generally would include
   (1) The copies of those client records examined by the auditor during the course of the engagement.
   (2) The evaluation of the efficiency and competence of the audit staff assistants by the partner responsible for the audit.
   (3) The auditor's comments concerning the efficiency and competence of client management personnel.
   (4) The auditing procedures followed, and the testing performed, in obtaining evidential matter.

c. Audit programs are modified to suit the circumstances on particular engagements. A complete audit program for an engagement generally should be developed
   (1) Before beginning the actual audit work.
   (2) After the auditor has completed an evaluation of the existing internal accounting control.
   (3) After reviewing the client's accounting records and procedures.
   (4) When the audit engagement letter is prepared.

d. Which of the following is generally included or shown in the auditor's working papers?
   (1) The procedures used by the auditor to verify the personal financial status of members of the client's management team.
   (2) Analyses that are designed to be a part of, or a substitute for, the client's accounting records.
   (3) Excerpts from authoritative pronouncements that support the underlying generally accepted accounting principles used in preparing the financial statements.
   (4) The manner in which exceptions and unusual matters disclosed by the auditor's procedures were resolved or treated.

e. Which of the following eliminates voluminous details from the auditor's working trial balance by classifying and summarizing similar or related items?
   (1) Account analyses.
   (2) Supporting schedules.
   (3) Control accounts.
   (4) Lead schedules.

f. The permanent section of the auditor's working papers generally should include
   (1) Time and expense reports.

(2) Names and addresses of all audit staff personnel on the engagement.
(3) A copy of key customer confirmations.
(4) A copy of the engagement letter.

g. Which of the following is *not* a factor that affects the independent auditor's judgment as to the quantity, type, and content of working papers?
(1) The timing and the number of personnel to be assigned to the engagement.
(2) The nature of the financial statements, schedules, or other information upon which the auditor is reporting.
(3) The need for supervision of the engagement.
(4) The nature of the auditor's report.

h. For what minimum period should audit working papers be retained by the independent CPA?
(1) For the period during which the entity remains a client of the independent CPA.
(2) For the period during which an auditor – client relationship exists but not more than six years.
(3) For the statutory period within which legal action may be brought against the independent CPA.
(4) For as long as the CPA is in public practice.

i. Which of the following is *not* a factor affecting the independent auditor's judgment as to the quantity, type, and content of audit working papers?
(1) The needs in the particular circumstances for supervision and review of the work performed by any assistants.
(2) The nature and condition of the client's records and internal controls.
(3) The expertise of client personnel and their expected audit participation.
(4) The type of the financial statements, schedules, or other information upon which the auditor is reporting.

j. During an audit engagement pertinent data are compiled and included in the audit workpapers. The workpapers primarily are considered to be
(1) A client-owned record of conclusions reached by the auditors who performed the engagement.
(2) Evidence supporting financial statements.
(3) Support for the auditor's representations as to compliance with generally accepted auditing standards.
(4) A record to be used as a basis for the following year's engagement.

(AICPA adapted)

P4–4 The following items pertain to the meaning and use of the audit program. Choose the best response for each item.

a. Which of the following is a basic tool used by the auditor to control the audit work and review the progress of the audit?
(1) Time and expense summary.
(2) Engagement letter.
(3) Progress flowchart.
(4) Audit program.

b. An audit program provides proof that
(1) Sufficient competent evidential matter was obtained.
(2) The work was adequately planned.

(3) There was compliance with generally accepted standards of reporting.
(4) There was a proper study and evaluation of internal control.

c. Audit programs are modified to suit the circumstances on particular engagements. A complete audit program for an engagement generally should be developed
(1) Prior to beginning the actual audit work.
(2) After the auditor has completed an evaluation of the existing internal accounting control.
(3) After reviewing the client's accounting records and procedures.
(4) When the audit engagement letter is prepared.

d. Which of the following is an aspect of scheduling and controlling the audit engagement?
(1) Include in the audit program a column for estimated and actual time.
(2) Perform audit work only after the client's books of account have been closed for the period under examination.
(3) Write a conclusion on individual working papers indicating how the results thereon will affect the auditor's report.
(4) Include in the engagement letter an estimate of the minimum and maximum audit fee.

(AICPA adapted)

P4–5 The following items pertain to analytical review procedures in the audit examination. Choose the best response for each item.

a. Significant unexpected fluctuations identified by analytical review procedures will usually necessitate
(1) Consistency qualification.
(2) Review of internal control.
(3) Explanation in the representation letter.
(4) Auditor investigation.

b. Which of the following is *not* a typical analytical review procedure?
(1) Study of relationships of the financial information with relevant nonfinancial information.
(2) Comparison of the financial information with similar information regarding the industry in which the entity operates.
(3) Comparison of recorded amounts of major disbursements with appropriate invoices.
(4) Comparison of the financial information with budgeted amounts.

c. Which of the following analytical review procedures should be applied to the income statement?
(1) Select sales and expense items and trace amounts to related supporting documents.
(2) Ascertain that the net income amount in the statement of changes in financial position agrees with the net income amount in the income statement.
(3) Obtain from the proper client representatives, the beginning and ending inventory amounts that were used to determine costs of sales.
(4) Compare the actual revenues and expenses with the corresponding figures of the previous year and investigate significant differences.

(AICAP adapted)

P4–6 Discuss the information you would expect to find in the permanent file section of a client's audit working papers. What *information relevant to the audit* would you expect to find in the following permanent file documents?

a. Minutes of board of directors and audit committee meetings.
b. Corporate charter and bylaws.
c. Organization charts.
d. Permanent financing arrangements such as mortgage loan agreements, bond indentures, stock issue agreements.
e. Employment contracts with key employees.
f. Time budget from previous year.

(AICPA adapted)

CHAPTER

5

STUDY AND EVALUATION OF INTERNAL CONTROL

The second standard of audit field work requires a "proper study and evaluation of the existing internal control as a basis for reliance thereon and for the determination of the resultant extent of the tests to which [substantive] auditing procedures are to be restricted."[1] In this chapter we focus our attention on the general meaning of that standard as it relates to the auditing process. Our discussion includes the following:

1. An examination of the general relationship of the system of internal control to the performance of an audit.
2. Identification of the elements of the system of internal control that are of direct interest to the auditor.
3. Demonstration of how the characteristics of an effective system of internal control can be derived from the objectives of the internal control process.
4. Identification of some of the special internal control problems that occur in small businesses.
5. An explanation of how we study and evaluate the system of internal control during the audit process.
6. A description of the Systems Evaluation Approach: Documentation of Controls (SEADOC), a procedure for evaluating a system of internal control used by one national public accounting firm.

RELATIONSHIP OF THE INTERNAL CONTROL SYSTEM TO THE AUDIT

Internal control is defined in SAS 1 as "a plan of organization and all of the coordinate methods and measures adopted within a business to safeguard its assets, check the accuracy and reliability of its accounting data, promote operational efficiency and encourage adherence to prescribed managerial policies."[2] Auditors are particularly concerned with the extent to which the client's operating procedures safeguard the assets and provide accurate, reliable accounting data. They want to know whether they can be reasonably assured that the system of internal control will prevent or detect material errors or irregularities in the financial statements. Auditors accept *reasonable assurance* here because they recognize that the cost of operating the internal control system cannot be expected to exceed the benefits derived from it.

Because it is not cost feasible to test substantively each transaction occurring during the audit period, auditors often depend heavily on the client's system of internal control plus tests of compliance over those controls to provide reasonable assurance that financial statement balances and other disclosures are fairly presented in accordance with GAAP.

Because of the auditor's dependence on the system of internal control, the study and evaluation of that system is an important part of each audit. In this section we shall do the following:

- Explain how the study and evaluation of internal control affects the other parts of the audit process.
- Observe how the risks associated with the audit are related to the study and evaluation of internal control.
- Identify the objectives of a system of internal control.

Internal Control and the Audit Process

In Chapter 4, we listed the elements of the audit process in chronological order. Generally, four of those elements call for some consideration of the system of internal control:

- The preliminary phase of the review of internal controls is designated to give the auditor an understanding of the *control environment* and the *flows of transactions* through the *accounting system.* For this purpose, an accounting system is distinguished from an internal control system. An accounting system comprises the coordinate functions by which *exchanges*, transfers, or uses of assets and services take place between the entity and outside parties. Data representing such exchanges, or ***exchange documents,*** are assembled, processed, analyzed, and reported in the accounting system. An understanding of the control environment should acquaint the auditor with the client's organizational structure, methods of communicating responsibility and authority, and methods of supervising the system, including the internal audit function, if any. An understanding of the flows of transactions should familiarize the auditor with the various classes of transactions and the means by which they are authorized, executed, recorded, and processed. This includes an understanding of the client's methods of data processing.
- After completing the preliminary phase of the review, the auditor may conclude (1) that further study and evaluation are unlikely to justify *any* restriction of substantive tests, or (2) that the cost of further study and evaluation, including compliance tests, exceeds the benefits. If either of these conclusions is reached, the auditor will discontinue further study and evaluation of internal accounting control and will design a substantive audit program that does not contemplate reliance on accounting control procedures. In such a case, the auditor's documentation of the study and evaluation of the internal control may be limited to a record

of the reasons for deciding not to extend the review. There is no need in this case to document the auditor's understanding of the internal control system.

- If, after completion of the preliminary phase of the review, *the auditor plans to rely on the system* of internal control, he or she should complete the review of the system to determine whether adequate controls are prescribed to provide reasonable assurance against material errors or irregularities. The review should *concentrate on specific controls designed to detect specific errors and irregularities* and should include inquiries of client personnel, inspection of written documentation (tests of compliance), and observation of the processing of transactions and handling of related assets.[3]
- On the basis of the preliminary evaluation and tests of compliance, the auditor makes a final evaluation of the system of internal control. As a result of that evaluation, he or she is also ready to make two additional judgments relating to the audit. The first and more important of these is a judgment as to the amount of detailed evidence concerning the financial statement balances that should be accumulated. The second, a byproduct of the examination, involves a judgment as to whether the system has significant weaknesses that must be communicated to the client (see SAS 20). If significant weaknesses are discovered, the auditor is required to communicate those weaknesses to the client, usually in the form of a letter. In addition, although not specifically required by generally accepted auditing standards, the internal control letter may contain the auditor's recommendations for improvements in the system.

Risks Associated with the Audit

In evaluating the system of internal control and while planning means of gathering evidence, the auditor is attempting to achieve some assurance regarding two risks associated with the expression of an audit opinion:

- Material errors may exist in the accounting records.
- The examination may be inadequate to detect those errors.

The auditor depends very heavily on the system of internal control to prevent material errors and irregularities from being included in the accounting records. If the various elements of the system are adequate to produce reliable accounting data, the likelihood of material errors and irregularities existing in the accounting records is minimized. On the other hand, the risk that the examination may be inadequate to detect such errors is directly related to the degree of professional care with which the auditor conducts the examination. The auditor, in meeting this risk, must adjust the nature, timing, and extent of tests of transactions and financial statement balances to compensate for material weaknesses discovered in the system of control.

Objectives of the System of Internal Control

The client's primary objective in establishing a system of internal control is to *synchronize employee actions and behavior patterns with the operating objectives of owners.* In small businesses, this can be accomplished by oral instructions and direct day-by-day supervision by owners. However, in large businesses, it is necessary to formalize authority – responsibility relationships and to specifically assign the tasks to be performed to various employees throughout the organization. The organization chart and procedures manual are devices used in implementing such a formalized system of operations.

The client's *primary objective*, described in the preceding paragraph, can be interpreted into more specific, subordinate *operating objectives* and ultimately into *underlying characteristics* for a sound system of internal control. Figure 5–1 shows that the basic synchronization of employee actions with owner objectives requires the implementation of *accounting controls* and *administrative controls*.

Administrative Controls. In this context, administrative controls are defined to include the managerial policies, plan of organization, specifically assigned tasks, and records that are concerned with the decision process leading to management's authorizations of transactions.[4] They are designed, among other things, to promote operating efficiency, to encourage adherence to prescribed managerial policies, and to reduce the probability of violating laws imposed upon the client organization. This portion of the system goes beyond those matters that relate directly to the functions of the accounting and financial departments to include such things as time and motion studies, the budgetary system, and employee training programs.

Accounting Controls. Accounting controls are concerned with assuring reliable accounting data and with safeguarding the assets and accounting records. The study and evaluation of internal control contemplated by GAAS require particular consideration of these controls. They should provide reasonable assurance that transactions are executed in accordance with management's general policy or specific directive; they should also make certain that transactions are recorded as necessary to permit preparation of financial statements in conformity with generally accepted accounting principles or other criteria applicable to such statements.[5] In addition, they should include provisions for maintaining assets and for restricting access to assets within the limits of management's authorizations. Furthermore, the recorded accountability for assets should be compared with the existing assets periodically and appropriate actions should be taken to reconcile any differences.

You should recognize that the interpreted operating objectives listed in Figure 5–1 imply an automatic synchronization assumption of manager and owner interests that may not be appropriate for "hired managers." Such managers may act according to their own self-interests as hired employees rather than in the interest of owners. In some cases they may even try to circumvent established policies for their own benefit.

The interpreted operating objectives are implemented by organizational relationships and procedures that we can characterize as underlying characteristics required for a sound system of internal control. Therefore, in evaluating a system of internal control, the auditor should begin by determining the extent to which those characteristics are present within the system being evaluated. We discuss each of these characteristics in detail later in the chapter.

Limitations. Certain limitations are associated with the auditor's dependence on the system of internal control. For example, errors may arise from an employee's misunderstanding of instructions. Mistakes may also be caused by poor judgment, personal carelessness, distractions, and fatigue. Furthermore, the system depends heavily on the underlying assumption *that two or more employees will not work together in perpetrating an error in the accounting records.* If such collusion occurs, we cannot

Primary Objective of System	Interpreted Operating Objectives	Underlying Characteristics Required for System to Achieve Operating Objectives
To synchronize employee actions and behavioral patterns with owner operating objectives	*Accounting Controls*	Appropriate segregation of individual employee responsibilities
	Safeguarding of assets	Clearly defined lines of authority that assign specific responsibilities to specific people
	Safeguarding of records	Personnel appropriately qualified for tasks assigned to them
	Assurance of reliable financial data	Appropriate records, authorization, and approval procedures, including vouchers documenting them
	Administrative Controls	Appropriate provisions for physical storage and care of assets and records
	Promotion of operating efficiency	Provisions for monitoring compliance with provisions of organization chart and procedures manuals
	Encouragement of adherence to managerial policies and directives	
	Reduction of probability of violating laws imposed on organization	

FIGURE 5–1. System of Internal Control Objectives Related to Underlying Characteristics

depend on the system of control to ensure either the absence of fraud or the fair presentation of items in the financial statements. Perhaps an even more significant limitation exists because *top level managers, by virtue of the authority granted them, can circumvent the provisions of the system of control and perpetrate and conceal errors and irregularities.* The auditor must recognize these limitations as the auditing process unfolds and as the audit report is written.

ELEMENTS OF THE CONTROL SYSTEM IMPORTANT TO THE AUDIT

In Figure 5–1, as we developed operating objectives from the primary objective of a system of internal control, we found three accounting controls directly related to the performance of the audit. These include safeguarding the assets, safeguarding the records of the company, and assuring reliable financial data. We also found three objectives which, although general enough to include some elements of accounting control, are more directly related to the administration of the business. They include promotion of operating efficiency, encouragement of adherence to managerial policies and directives, and compliance with laws imposed on the company.

Because of the need for expressing an opinion on the fairness of presentation of the financial statements, the auditor is primarily concerned with the accounting controls; but he or she must also be concerned with the last two administrative controls. A system of control is of no real value unless it is adhered to by the management and employees of the company. Furthermore, the auditor also needs to be concerned about the possibility of the client having violated legal regulations such as the Foreign Corrupt Practices Act. We may therefore conclude that the auditor is particularly concerned with all pure accounting controls but has a vital interest in at least two of the administrative-type controls.

CHARACTERISTICS OF AN EFFECTIVE SYSTEM OF INTERNAL CONTROL

We now turn our attention to the practices a firm should follow in establishing a sound system of internal control. We describe them as the *underlying characteristics* of a sound system of control. The inclusion of all, or some combination, of these characteristics in an internal control system suggests control strengths in the system. The auditor who finds that such strengths exist may rely on them, thereby reducing the number of required tests of transactions and financial statement balances. If any of these characteristics are missing from the controls of any subsystem, there is probably a control weakness in that subsystem. The auditor must recognize such weaknesses and compensate for them by expanding the nature and extent of transactions and account balance tests verified in the area. We now examine each of these characteristics for a sound system of internal control.

Appropriate Segregation of Responsibilities

A firm should follow a practice of segregating responsibilities to reduce the probability of fraud and to reduce the likelihood of unintentional errors in the accounting data. Both of these anticipated results depend on the basic assumption that two or more employees will not work in collusion to perpetrate a fraud or to cover up an unintentional error.

The separation of *custodial, recordkeeping,* and *authorization responsibilities* is one of the fundamental requirements in appropriately segregating employee responsibilities. An employee who has access to an asset, such as the cashier receiving cash receipts, is characterized as having custodial responsibilities. However, those responsibilities also extend to persons charged with originating documents required for the acquisition or disposal of assets as well as for actually handling and holding assets. Within this definition, custodial employees include the treasurer of an organization and many of those who work under her or his jurisdiction — such as cashiers, cash disbursements personnel, and credit management personnel. They also include many employees involved in the manufacturing and payroll functions — such as persons charged with shipping, receiving, and storing inventories and with the payment of employees.

Recordkeeping personnel include the controller and those working under her or his jurisdiction — including all accounting and bookkeeping employees. If custodial and recordkeeping responsibilities are appropriately segregated, a recordkeeper and a custodial employee will have to collude for an intentional error to be committed and still have the physical asset agree with the recordkeeper's record of it. Stated in another way, the recordkeeper shows what the custodial employee is charged with. This arrangement reduces the probability that the custodial employee will deliberately misappropriate assets unless there is collusion with the recordkeeper to cover the misappropriation. On the other hand, if these two functions are assigned to the same person, it would be relatively easy for that person to change the records to hide the theft of an asset.

Authorization personnel include those persons at every level of activity whose duty is to authorize transactions. The board of directors is usually charged with the ultimate authority in a corporation. They should approve most major transactions — such as major asset acquisitions, financing or borrowing arrangements, employment agreements with key officers, and purchase agreements with major suppliers. Other types of authority may be delegated by the board of directors to various organization personnel. For example, authority to purchase inventory will typically be vested in the purchasing agent; authority to sign checks may be assigned to the treasurer; authority to employ personnel may be delegated to the personnel department; and authority to approve write-offs of uncollectible accounts may be vested in the credit manager.

Within the custodial, recordkeeping, and authorization areas, the system should also provide for separation of responsibilities so as to allow one employee to check on the work of another employee. The client should try to do this with a minimum duplication of effort. For example, in the custodial area, those persons authorized to acquire and dispose of assets should be separated from those having control over the assets. Such an arrangement involves at least two people in the acquisition or disposal of an asset; in that way, it reduces the probability that improper actions will be taken. Similarly, the same person should not authorize the payment of a vendor invoice and also sign the check paying the invoice. Neither should the authority for adding new employees or terminating existing employees be performed by the person distributing payroll checks.

In the recordkeeping area, it is always desirable to have subsidiary ledgers maintained by someone other than the person recording the transactions in the related control accounts to avoid the tendency to cover an error by changing one of the records. It is also desirable to assign transaction approval responsibilities to someone other than the person responsible for recording them.

Another device used to encourage employees in custodial, recordkeeping, and authorizing positions to perform their tasks responsibly is a mandatory vacation policy. If all employees are required to take vacations, they know that their normal duties will be performed by someone else while they are away from the firm. The probability of thefts or bookkeeping errors occurring, for example, will be reduced by knowledge of the fact that such errors are likely to be discovered by the person temporarily handling the duties of the vacationing employee.

The effectiveness of segregating employee responsibilities depends on the basic assumption that two or more employees are unlikely to work in collusion to perpetrate a fraud or to cover up an unintentional error. Personnel who are related to each other or employees having personal dealings with a client's customers are examples of situations that might promote collusion both within the firm and between an employee and a customer. Therefore, it is desirable for a firm to follow a practice of not employing related personnel in positions vulnerable to collusion. It is also important to establish a policy relating to conflicts of interest to reduce the probability of an employee colluding with customers or other outside parties to the detriment of the firm.

Clearly Defined Lines of Authority and Responsibility

The activities of a firm are carried out by individual employees. If operations are to be appropriately controlled, each individual employee must be held accountable for specific assets, liabilities, or activities. Such accountability can be accomplished only by assigning specific responsibilities to specific people. The primary document in establishing the overall authority – responsibility relationships is an ***organization chart*** similar to the one shown in Figure 5–2. As you examine the organization chart, you will observe that the controllership function is carefully separated from the responsibilities of the treasurer and the vice-president in charge of manufacturing. Note also that authority runs from the top down, while responsibility runs from the bottom up. That means that all the accounting functions, for example, are performed by persons responsible to the controller. The custodial functions are performed by persons responsible to the treasurer or the vice-president of manufacturing.

A ***procedures manual*** should be used to specifically identify and describe the tasks assigned to the persons holding the various positions shown in the organization chart. The list of tasks assigned to a person holding a particular position is often called a job description. In Figure 5–3, we illustrate a page from a procedures manual listing the specific tasks to be performed by a cashier.

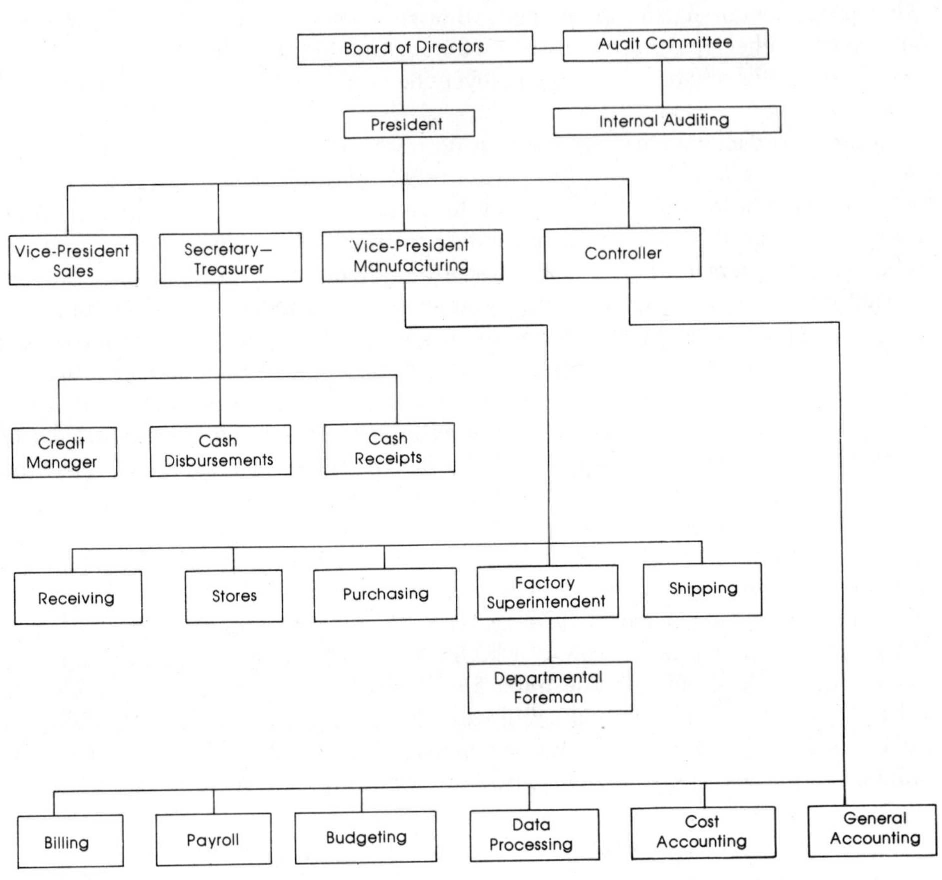

FIGURE 5–2. Organization Chart

Appropriately Qualified Personnel

As we have seen, an adequate system of internal control ultimately depends on the people involved in implementing it. A system may have discrete responsibilities and defined lines of authority and still be completely inadequate if the personnel of the company are not appropriately qualified to carry out their assigned tasks and responsibilities. On the other hand, honest and properly qualified people can provide a good system of control even without the formal documents suggested by those characteristics. It is important, therefore, that the hiring and promotion practices of the firm give appropriate consideration to the qualifications required in each position as people are hired or promoted into those positions. In determining whether the qualified personnel characteristic is being met, the auditor will be concerned with evaluating those practices and with evaluating the capabilities of key recordkeeping personnel as the audit progresses.

Job Title: Cashier

Responsible to: Treasurer

Summary of Responsibilities: Responsible for receiving and depositing all cash (checks and currency) received by the company and for handling petty cash fund.

Detailed Responsibilities

1. The cashier shall receive all checks delivered by mail from mail clerk each day.
2. The cashier shall receive all cash (checks and currency) delivered to the cashier's window.
3. The cashier shall prepare a cash receipts voucher (Form C–1) in duplicate for each payment made through cashier's window. One copy of the voucher shall be delivered to the person making the cash payment. The other shall be kept for use by the cashier.
4. At the end of each day the cashier shall prepare a list in triplicate of all cash received (checks and currency) on Form C–2. One copy of this list shall be sent to the bookkeeper, another shall be attached to the deposit slip. The third copy shall be filed in chronological order in the cashier's office.
5. Cash received each day shall be deposited intact in the bank. A deposit form (Form C–3) shall be prepared in duplicate and reconciled with the list of cash receipts (Form C–2) as the deposit is made. One copy shall be included with the deposit. The other shall be filed with the office copy of Form C–2.
6. The cashier shall be responsible for the company's imprest petty cash fund in the amount of $500.
7. Payments shall be made from the petty cash fund on presentation of a validated voucher amounting to less than $10. Vouchers in excess of that amount should be routed to the Accounts Payable Department.
8. Any person receiving payment from the petty cash fund shall be expected to sign a petty cash voucher (Form C–4) for the amount of the payment.
9. At the end of each day, the cashier shall reconcile the petty cash fund (cash + petty cash vouchers) with the imprest balance. Any shortages shall be reported to the Treasurer on the Petty Cash Reconciliation form (Form C–5).
10. When the cash in the petty cash fund declines to $75, the cashier shall initiate a reimbursement request (Form C–6) in duplicate. One copy with attached supporting petty cash vouchers shall be sent to the controller for recording and approval. The approved voucher shall then be sent to the Treasurer for reimbursement. The other shall be filed chronologically in the cashier's office.

FIGURE 5–3. Job Description in a Procedures Manual

The use of appropriately qualified personnel also implies a need for the bonding of custodial employees who are in positions of trust. Such an arrangement should serve as a deterrent to fraud and also provide for recovery of losses in the event that fraud occurs. For example, persons holding positions of treasurer or cashier should always be bonded. On the other hand, there is no necessity for bonding recordkeeping personnel because they should have no access to assets likely to be stolen.

Appropriate Records, Authorization, and Approval Procedures

Records provide information about past achievements and establish responsibilities of custodial and operating employees. To be most useful, they should be organized along authority – responsibility lines. We frequently use the term ***responsibility accounting*** to describe recordkeeping and reporting procedures organized to show the extent to which assigned responsibilities have been achieved. The income statement, for example, reflects the operational accountability of top level managers, and the balance sheet shows the net resources available to them. Operational accountability reports for departmental supervisors are reflected in departmental expense reports.

Budgets are also used as devices for controlling segments of operations and for measuring the extent to which the segments have achieved or have failed to achieve the goals planned for them. Flexible budgets, for example, can be used as devices both to measure the extent to which departmental operating objectives have been achieved and to identify the reasons for failures to achieve those goals.

Authorization and approval procedures are important to the division of the responsibilities associated with a particular transaction sequence among two or more persons; these procedures also bring together the judgment of several persons in connection with decisions. For example, an authorization requirement can reduce the probability of inappropriate acquisitions or disposals of assets by employees charged with custodial responsibilities for those assets. Individual responsibilities associated with authorization and approval procedures should be spelled out in the procedures manual. Appropriately organized documents, which must bear signatures or initials indicating authorizations and approvals, should be required in the implementation of those processes.

In addition to the development and use of appropriate records, another important consideration is appropriate record retention policies. In determining how long various records should be preserved, the firm should consider federal and state laws relating to particular types of records.

Protection of Assets and Records

Appropriate facilities must be provided to safeguard both assets and records from unnecessary deterioration, destruction, or misplacement. Perishable foods, for example, require appropriately refrigerated storage facilities to prevent them from deteriorating unnecessarily. Also, appropriate maintenance policies should be followed for fixed assets to prevent premature loss of usefulness. Materials and supplies should be stored in appropriately organized storage areas so that they are less likely to be misused or lost.

Records should be stored in facilities that reduce probability of their alteration or destruction. Manually maintained accounts receivable records, for example, should be stored in a fireproof vault at the end of each day. Magnetic tape records should be stored in an area where an appropriate temperature is maintained. They should also be carefully checked in and out of the storage area. As a further precaution, backup tapes should be maintained so that in the event a record is destroyed, it can be reproduced.

Monitoring of Compliance

All the characteristics just cited are of little use unless they are actually being carried through in practice. Therefore, each firm should establish procedures to check employee compliance with the provisions of the system. In small businesses the owner – manager may do this personally. In larger businesses, however, the responsibility for monitoring compliance may be delegated through separation of duties to supervisory personnel. These persons, independent of both the recordkeeping and custodial functions, will compare the recorded accountability over assets (performed by the recordkeeping personnel) with the existing assets themselves, at intervals, and will take remedial action when necessary. For example, a supervisory person in the accounting department, one independent of both the cash-handling function and the function of posting cash receipts to individual customer accounts, may prepare the monthly bank reconciliation. This provides an independent check of both the custodial responsibilities of the people handling cash and the recordkeeping associated with that asset.

In very large businesses, effective monitoring of compliance with company policies may mandate the establishment and use of a separate internal auditing department. The internal auditing department should be independent of the elements of the internal control system. Observe, in the organization chart shown in Figure 5–2, that the internal auditing department reports directly to the audit committee of the board of directors. Such an arrangement is designed to give that department a degree of independence that allows critical evaluation of the activities of both custodial and recordkeeping personnel within the organization. For example, if the internal auditing department reported to the controller, it would not be appropriately independent in evaluating the effectiveness of recordkeeping activities.

The internal auditor operates by examining various phases of operations and reporting on them. Because of that method of operation, the internal auditing function is frequently referred to as the *arm of management.* It is designed to encourage adherence to management policy and directives and to improve the efficiency of operations.

In other instances, verification may be accomplished by duplication of effort. For example, when a physical inventory is taken, the count should be provided by one inventory team, with another team used to check the count.

SPECIAL INTERNAL CONTROL PROBLEMS IN SMALL BUSINESSES

Some of the control characteristics described in the preceding section are difficult to implement in a business with a small number of employees. For example, it is often difficult to have an appropriate segregation of recordkeeping, custodial, and authorization responsibilities because the company may have only two employees. Also, it may be difficult to find a person appropriately qualified for the tasks that have to be performed. It is often difficult to work out appropriate authorization and approval procedures in small firms. Where these limiting conditions exist, the system of internal control has to depend largely on the owner-manager exercising direct day-today supervision over the employees and retaining some of the key custodial and recordkeeping functions. For example, in a small business, the owner-manager may sign checks, handle cash receipts, examine accounts receivable statements sent to customers, approve credit, and approve bad debt write-offs.

INTERNAL CONTROLS AND THE AUDIT PROCESS

Internal Control Systems

To fully understand how internal control affects the audit process, the auditor must divide the entire internal control system into segments or subsystems for detailed study and evaluation. By doing this, he or she can devise a comprehensive set of audit procedures for each system. In this text we consider six major subsystems applicable to a typical commercial audit client engaged in manufacturing. However, this approach can also be adapted to the audit of service-oriented businesses — such as banks, savings and loan institutions, insurance companies, hospitals, and governmental units. The six subsystems we consider are as follows:

- The revenue system — sales, receivables, cash collections, and related balances.
- The cost of sales system — purchases, inventories, cash disbursements, and cost of sales.
- The payroll system.
- The investments system — the investment accounts, intangible asset accounts, and related income and expense accounts.
- The operating assets system — acquisition, retirement, and depreciation of fixed assets.
- The capital acquisition and repayment system — debt and equity financing transactions for the business.

Figure 5–4 shows how these systems are interconnected.

A business usually begins with infusions of cash through the capital acquisition system (either equity or debt financing). Cash, which is labeled "the eye of the needle," is probably the most important single account on the financial statements — not only because of its high relative risk but also because almost every other system's transactions eventually culminate in the disbursement or receipt of cash. Cash is used to purchase operating assets, to pay personnel, and to purchase raw materials inventories. These inputs are then used to manufacture the company's finished product. The finished product is stored briefly until sold, when an appropriate cost of sales record must be made. Once sold, the product is exchanged for a receivable, which is held briefly until converted back to cash. If the process generates excess cash, it can either be paid out in dividends or invested in such things as income-earning securities or other near-cash assets that can be easily converted back to cash as needed. If the amount of cash generated is insufficient to meet the entity's operating and financing needs, additional funds must be obtained through borrowing.

The auditor typically studies and evaluates internal control in each of these systems separately, because each can easily be regarded as a relatively independent segment of the overall business activity. A preliminary review is made of each system to determine whether the client has prescribed internal controls that are reliable. If the auditor

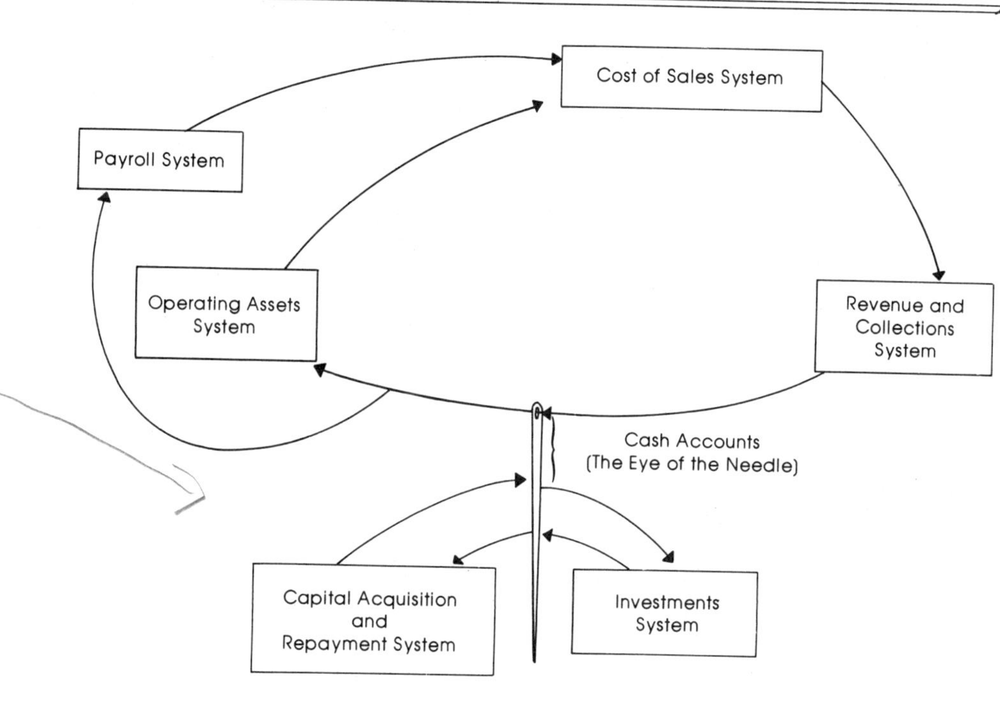

FIGURE 5–4. The Subsystems of a Business

determines that the client has prescribed adequate controls, he or she must then perform compliance tests to determine if the prescribed internal controls are actually in effect. After the compliance tests, the auditor makes a decision as to the nature, timing, and extent of tests that must be performed on transactions and the financial statement balances that the system has produced. The details of this process are described in the sections which follow.

A Comprehensive Approach to the Study and Evaluation of Internal Control

A comprehensive approach to the study and evaluation of a system of internal controls involves both of the following:

- A thorough understanding of the six underlying characteristics of good internal control and how those characteristics are implemented.
- A thorough understanding of the client's systems and operating procedures.

By understanding the characteristics of good internal control as applied to a particular system, such as revenue and collections, the auditor establishes a standard of *how a good system is supposed to operate.* Then, by gaining a thorough understanding of the particular client's system, the auditor has a basis for evaluating that system.

A conceptually logical approach to evaluating an internal control subsystem requires the auditor to begin by recognizing that the purpose of the system is *to prevent material errors and irregularities*. The auditor can then follow this logical progression:

1. Consider the types of errors and irregularities that could occur.
2. Consider whether these errors and irregularities could cause a material misstatement in the financial statements; if so, consider which accounts in the financial statements would be affected and in which direction (overstatement or understatement).
3. Determine the accounting control procedures that should prevent or detect such errors and irregularities.
4. Determine whether the necessary procedures are being prescribed by the client.
5. Determine whether prescribed procedures are being followed by the client (compliance tests).
6. Based on the results of steps 1 through 5, determine the nature, timing, and extent of audit tests of transactions and balances emerging from the systems (substantive tests).

At least seven general types of material errors and irregularities may occur in any system. We will list and discuss each type, along with the controls that are generally designed to prevent or detect them.

Erroneously Recorded Transactions. Transactions may contain material errors of overstatement or understatement. These errors may arise from mathematical miscalculations, insertions of fictitious transactions, or omissions. A possible major cause of error is that duties of personnel working on various aspects of the transaction are not appropriately segregated. To prevent or detect such errors, responsible supervisory personnel should review all transactions for reasonableness and accuracy before they are processed. In addition, care should be taken to segregate the custodial, record-keeping, and approval functions for each system.

Invalidly Recorded Transactions. Transactions may possess inadequate documentary support. Alternatively, transactions may not have been subjected to the proper approvals process before being recorded. To prevent or detect these errors, management should require adequate documentary support for all transactions and submit all transactions to appropriate approval procedures.

Unrecorded Transactions. This error is particularly important for liabilities. Transactions may have occurred, which, by error or intent, have been omitted from the records. To prevent this error, the client must have adequate controls to search out unrecorded transactions and to make sure they are recorded.

Improperly Valued Transactions. Whenever transactions occur (e.g., sales, purchases, payrolls), they typically are supported by information indicating quantities and unit costs or prices. In the case of improperly valued transactions, either quantities or prices may have been misstated, so that the extended value of the recorded transaction is erroneous. The client should submit each transaction to supervisory personnel for review of number of units, prices, and extensions calculations.

Improperly Classified Transactions. Errors of this type could result in misclassifications of amounts in balance sheet or income statement accounts (e.g., fixed assets vs. investments, or selling expense vs. general and administrative expenses). A more serious misclassification might be between balance sheet and income statement accounts, an error that affects net income. An example of such error might be misclassification of labor charges as inventory (an asset) rather than as expense. The client, once again, should submit transactions to a review process to ensure that they are appropriately classified.

Transactions Recorded in the Wrong Period. This type of error could result in overstatement or understatement of an account because of violation of the periodicity (cutoff) objective (see Chapter 4). To prevent or detect these errors, the client should use adequate, prenumbered documents in all systems such as sales, purchases, cash receipts, and cash disbursements. In addition, an end-of-period review should be made to ensure that proper cutoff of transactions has been achieved for all systems.

Improperly Summarized Transactions. Transactions may have been posted to the correct accounts, but a corresponding entry may not have been entered into the subsidiary records. As a result, the detail of an account fails to agree with the control account. Potential errors of this type are particularly applicable to sales and receivables, purchases and accounts payable, and property and equipment additions and retirements. The client's procedures should provide controls to ensure that account postings are checked for accuracy and completeness. In addition, there should be a periodic reconciliation of each subsidiary ledger total with its control account total.

Notice that the recommended controls for errors and irregularities can be accomplished only by incorporating the six characteristics of effective internal control. You should also notice that these errors and irregularities are common to all the systems listed above. Thus, we shall apply this comprehensive approach to the study and evaluation of internal controls in each of the major subsystems used to record and summarize accounting data.

We now turn our attention to the means by which the auditor can obtain an understanding of the client's system of internal controls. This is done through a preliminary review and evaluation of the system and by performing tests of compliance (steps 4 and 5 of the comprehensive review approach).

Preliminary Evaluation of the System of Internal Control

To obtain an understanding of the client's control environment and flow of transactions, the auditor may rely on previous experience with the entity, inquiry, observation, and reference to prior years' working papers. In addition, he or she may refer to the client's organization chart and procedures manual.

The firm should have an organization chart showing the relationships among various supervisory personnel. This document is important in determining whether there is a proper control environment relating to segregation of responsibilities. For example, the organization chart in Figure 5–2 shows the responsibilities of the controller completely separated from those of the treasurer. This is an appropriate segregation of supervisory recordkeeping responsibilities. Operations responsibilities have also been segregated under the jurisdiction of the vice-president in charge of manufacturing. Therefore, the auditor would be justified in concluding that the system provides for proper segregation of top level management responsibilities.

The procedures manual may be examined to determine the flow of transactions and responsibilities delegated to various custodial, operating, and recordkeeping personnel. The page from the procedures manual shown in Figure 5–3 shows the responsibilities assigned to the cashier. It is important to observe that all the appropriate tasks assigned to the person in this position are custodial in nature.

Detailed Study and Evaluation of the System of Internal Control

If on completion of the preliminary review the auditor plans to rely on the system of internal accounting control, he or she continues the study and evaluation by considering specific controls designed to prevent, detect, or correct errors or irregularities. Documentation of this phase of the study might include internal control questionnaires and flowcharts, as discussed below.

Internal Control Questionnaire. You should observe that all the data gathered in this stage of the study of internal control are based on documents or inquiry. They tell the auditor the way things are supposed to be done. The auditor will generally use an internal control questionnaire (see Figure 5–5) to document initial client responses to his or her questions. The questionnaire should be organized so that "yes" answers

INSTRUCTIONS: These questions are based on the provisions of the procedures manual. Check "yes" or "no" for each of the following questions.

	Yes	No
1. Does a person handling cash receipts have access to the accounting records for cash receipts?	____	____
2. Are receipts deposited intact daily?	____	____
3. Is a list of cash remittances prepared each day?	____	____
4. Does the accounting department use the list of cash receipts as a basis for the cash receipts entry?	____	____
5. Are validated deposit slips returned to someone other than the cashier?	____	____
6. Is the bank statement and cancelled checks package returned to someone other than the cashier?	____	____
7. Are the daily remittance lists used as the sources of credits to customer accounts in the accounts receivable subsidiary ledger?	____	____
8. Is immediate control established over mail receipts?	____	____
9. Are cash discounts periodically reviewed by a person independent of the Treasurer's staff?	____	____
10. Are cash receipts entries reconciled with deposit slips?	____	____

FIGURE 5–5. Internal Control Questionnaire Relating to Cash Receipts

indicate system strengths and "no " answers indicate system weaknesses. Such an arrangement allows the auditor to isolate the weaknesses by simply looking at the "no" items. Client responses to the questionnaire are usually documented further by a narrative description of the system, a decision table, or a systems flowchart.

Flowchart. Flowcharts are particularly helpful in understanding the sequences of relationships among activities involving documents associated with the system of internal control. They are symbolic representations of a system or series of sequential processes and are designed to describe the flow of work in relationship to a system of related activities. The auditor, while tracing the flow of work and documents, should be able to obtain a thorough understanding of the system. Once he or she achieves this understanding, the auditor can recognize strengths or weaknesses in the system by considering the types of material errors that could occur, and by determining whether the controls necessary to prevent or detect those errors are prescribed by the client.

The preliminary review of a system of internal control is initially a time-consuming and therefore a costly process. However, once a system's weaknesses and strengths have been documented, they normally need only to be reviewed and updated on a year-by-year basis. The steps in preparing a systems flowchart are as follows:

1. Obtain a thorough understanding of the duties performed, the documents handled, and the ways the documents flow as they are processed. This often will involve much time and conversation with client personnel as well as the completion of the internal control questionnaire.
2. Write a preliminary description of the system as it is understood to operate at this stage. Some auditors use a "play script" such as the one illustrated in Figure 5–6 to initially

Actors	Functions Performed
Mail clerk	1. Receives and opens all mail not marked "confidential." 2. Distributes mail to appropriate persons. Prepares cash receipts list. Distributes checks from customers, plus list of checks received to cashier.
Cashier	1. Receives customer checks and list of checks from mailroom. 2. Prepares deposit slip in duplicate. 3. Reconciles deposit slip with cash receipts list. 4. Deposits cash receipts intact, each day. 5. Files copy of cash receipts list.
General ledger bookkeeper	1. Records cash receipts each day from cash receipts list. 2. Files copy of cash receipts list.
Accounts receivable subsidiary ledger bookkeeper	1. Records credits to individual accounts receivable subsidiary ledger accounts from cash receipts list. 2. Files copy of cash receipts list.

FIGURE 5–6. Play Script of the System

document the description. Notice that the play script working paper is organized in two columns. The one on the left is for the actors, showing the persons who perform each of the various tasks. The right-hand column shows the tasks performed and the documents prepared by each person.

3. Draw the flowchart, basing it on the knowledge obtained from the play script and from the client's answers to inquiries about the system. The play script described above is thus used as a tool in preparing the flowchart. Actors in the system are depicted (by department) as column headings in the flowchart. Actions taken by the various actors, documents generated, and direction of flow of those documents are shown by symbols on the flowchart. Figure 5–7 shows a few of the standard symbols, which will be used throughout this text and in problem solutions to depict processing functions, documents, and communication links. Standardization of symbols within a firm is important so that each flowchart can be readily understood by all persons reviewing it.

The following rules should be observed when drawing a system flowchart:

1. Each chart should be properly labeled as to working paper reference numbers, company name, and type of system (cash receipts, inventory, purchases, etc.)

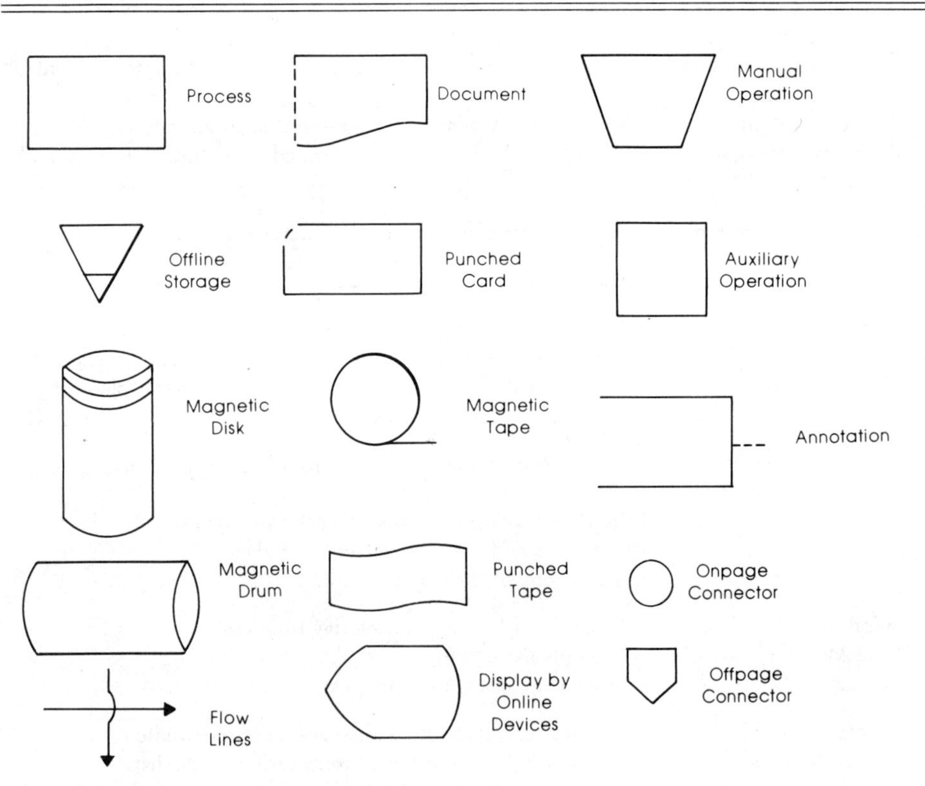

FIGURE 5–7. Standard Flowcharting Symbols

2. Departments and actors within the departments should be shown in column headings across the top of the chart.
3. Actions taken within a department, and documents generated by those actions, should appear in the columns. The general flow of documents as they are handled by actors within a department should be depicted in a top-to-bottom of the page sequence. Therefore, the document flow on the chart should be from left to right (by department), and from top to bottom within departments. Figure 5–8 depicts a flowchart for the mail cash receipts system; it was derived from the play script appearing in Figure 5–6.
4. Always use a flowchart template and ruler. A messy flowchart is difficult to read.
5. Narrative explanations should appear on the face of the chart in the form of annotations, or at the bottom of the chart in a reference key.

The flowchart should communicate all relevant internal control actions in the system, as well as show which persons perform those actions. The review of the system of internal control is not complete until the auditor analyzes the system, as depicted by the flowchart, in terms of its relative strengths and weaknesses. The auditor's finding and preliminary conclusions are then written up in the working paper files.

One very important purpose of the preliminary study and evaluation of internal control is to pinpoint isolated conditions in the system that could allow an employee to either perpetrate or conceal a material misstatement of the data in the financial statements. Such conditions constitute material weaknesses in the system. When they are present, there is little point in testing compliance with the controls reflected for the system. However, an unqualified report might still be rendered by introducing extensive substantive tests to compensate for the control weaknesses.

For example, in the hypothetical mail cash receipts system described in Figures 5–5 and 5–8, it appears that, as the mail is opened, the mail clerk does not stamp checks received with a restrictive endorsement for deposit to the account of the company. Good internal control normally requires this procedure. After determining that the procedure is missing, the auditor should determine whether its absence could lead to a material misstatement in the client's financial statements. If the auditor concludes that it could, he or she should expand the substantive tests of cash receipts transactions. In this case, a compliance test of that element of the cash receipts procedures would be useless because the preliminary review of internal control has revealed that the appropriate control practice is not included in the prescribed procedures. However, if the results of the preliminary review of internal control are acceptable to the auditor, the next step in the auditing process calls for the system to be tested for compliance.

Another very important purpose of the preliminary study and evaluation phase is to identify possible strengths in the system, which serve as the basis for reduction of further substantive audit tests and therefore increased audit efficiency. Potential strengths that are pinpointed at this stage, however, cannot be relied upon until they are tested for compliance, as discussed in the next section.

Audit Tests

As we have previously observed, an important part of the audit consists of audit tests involving the examination of samples of the evidence supporting various types of

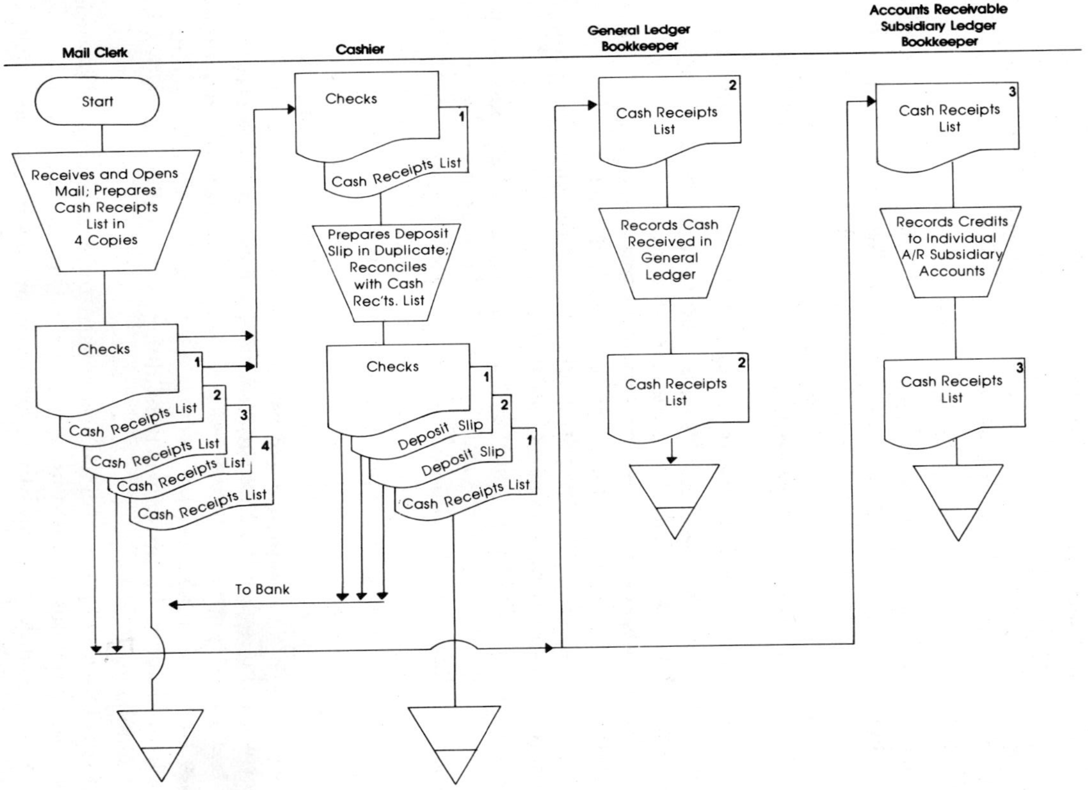

FIGURE 5–8. Flowchart for the Mail Cash Receipts System

transactions and the account balances appearing in the financial statements. These tests are of two types: *compliance tests* and *substantive tests.* In Figure 5–9 we show the relationship between the preliminary work described in the preceding paragraphs and those tests. This figure also shows the chronological relationship of these tests to each other and the effects that the results of compliance tests have on the nature, timing, and extent of substantive tests.

Compliance Tests. Compliance tests are conducted after the auditor has completed the preliminary study, evaluation, and documentation of internal controls and concluded that the system includes strengths that can be relied upon. Compliance tests are designed to provide assurance that the strengths prescribed by the client actually exist and that the system of internal control is functioning in accordance with the provisions set out in the procedures manual or identified through inquiry of client personnel. These tests help the auditor decide ultimately how much reliance can be placed on the system of control.

Compliance testing of some controls can be merely *observing* client activities to see that prescribed controls exist. An example of controls that can be tested by observation is segregation of the duties of authorization, recordkeeping, and custody of related assets. Transactions that leave an audit trail of documentary evidence can be compliance tested by *drawing samples* of each of the various types of transactions and following them through the system to determine whether the company is complying with the provisions of the system of control as documented in the organization chart and procedures manual. As shown in Figure 5–9, the outcome of the preliminary review and compliance testing phases of the audit can produce three possible conclusions:

1. The system as represented to the auditor is both adequately prescribed and is operating as it should. In such a situation, the auditor would need to perform only limited substantive tests on the transactions and financial statement balances to justify the expression of an opinion on the statements.
2. Although the system seems, after the preliminary review, to be satisfactory, the client is not complying with the established procedures. This causes the auditor to ask a further question: Could the observed lack of compliance result in material errors in the financial statements? If not, we may disregard the lack of compliance and still not expand our substantive tests. On the other hand, if the failure to comply can cause a material misstatement, but the system is not totally devoid of controls, the auditor should extend the substantive tests to compensate for the observed weaknesses.
3. If the review indicates a reasonably satisfactory system, but the compliance tests indicate no compliance, it might be necessary in extreme cases either to withdraw from the audit or to issue a disclaimer of opinion.

Many of the internal control evaluation procedures just mentioned can be completed as part of interim work. However, even if the control procedures are found to be effective at that time, they should be tested again at year end to determine that they are still effective. This is particularly true if inquiries and observations at year end cause the auditor to suspect that conditions may have changed.

The relationship between compliance tests and substantive tests can be illustrated by the following example. Suppose that you are examining the client's system of sales,

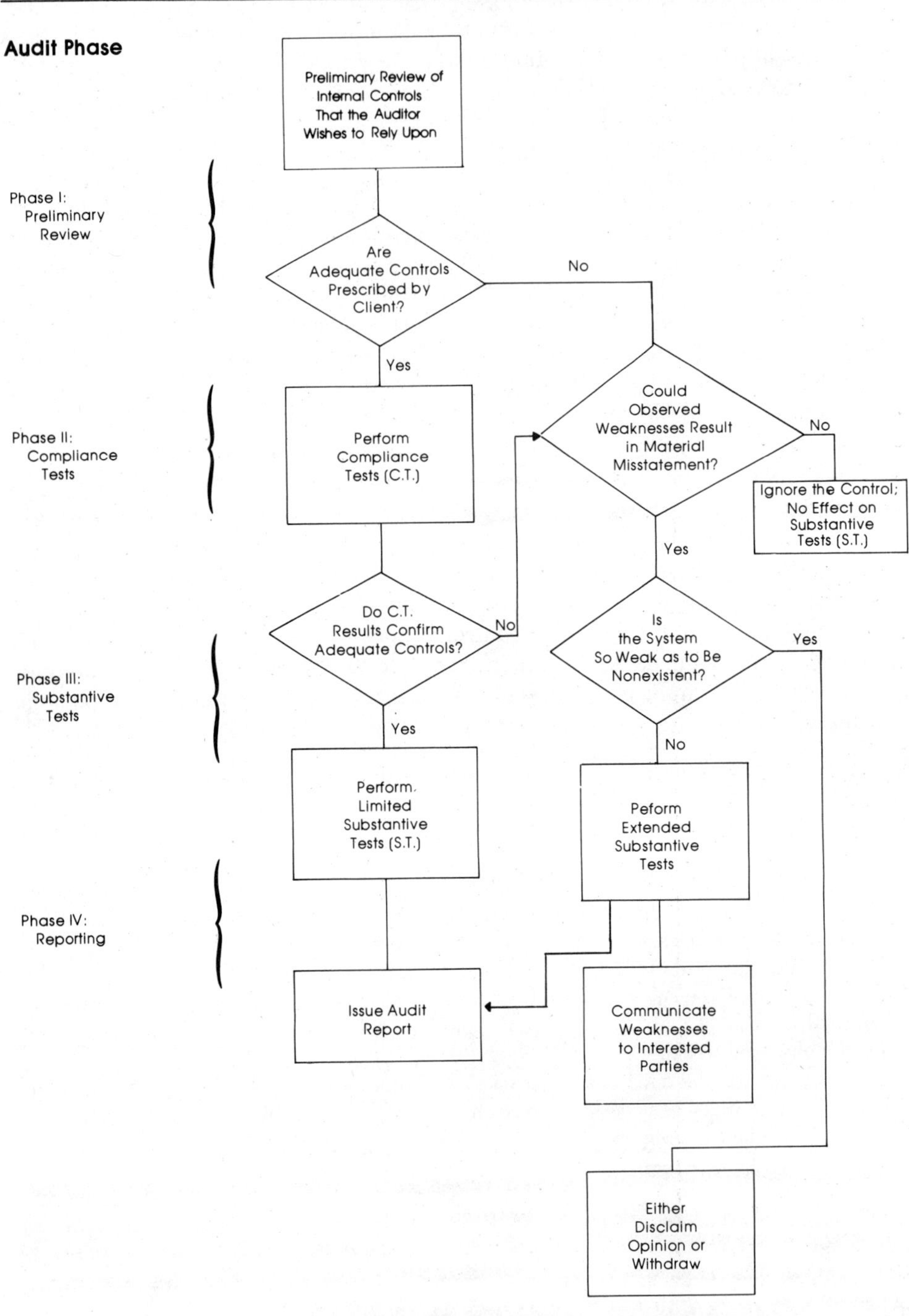

FIGURE 5–9. Internal Controls Reliance: Effect on the Audit

accounts receivable, and cash receipts. On the basis of your preliminary review of internal control, you conclude that the client has prescribed the following internal control strengths that you wish to rely upon:

1. There is adequate separation of duties between persons recording sales, persons authorizing sales, and persons handling cash collections.
2. All sales invoices are prepared on the basis of written customer orders.
3. All sales are approved by the credit manager before they are shipped.
4. Sales invoices are posted to individual customer accounts in the accounts receivable subsidiary ledger.

The next step in the evaluation of the system is to determine whether the controls prescribed by the client actually exist. To obtain this assurance, it is necessary to perform compliance tests of the system. The following tests might be conducted on controls 1 through 4, respectively:

1. Observe employees in their duties to ascertain that the segregation of duties found in the job descriptions are actually being observed.
2. Select a sample of sales invoices and vouch the invoices to customer order files. This means that for each sales invoice, a customer purchase order must be located in the customer order files.
3. Examine the sales invoice included in compliance test 2 for the initials of credit manager.
4. Trace the sample of sales invoices in test 2 to postings in individual customer accounts in the accounts receivable subsidiary ledger.

The results of these tests should then be translated into the needs for substantive tests by following the pattern of reasoning shown in Figure 5–9.

It is important to observe that the auditor's study and evaluation of the system of internal control is carried out for each of the separate subsystems being audited. This involves evaluating the practices found in each subsystem against the characteristics of a sound system of internal control, described earlier in the chapter. We begin by identifying the ways in which each of those characteristics applies to each of the subsystems. Therefore, in later chapters, as we describe the auditing procedures to be followed in gathering sufficient evidential matter, we also describe the characteristics that should be present in a sound system of control for each of the individual subsystems.

Substantive Tests. These tests involve the verification of financial assertions made by the client in transactions and in individual account balances appearing in the financial statements. We verify the client's assertions by gathering, on a test basis, evidence in support of those items. As indicated in the third standard of field work, this is accomplished by applying such auditing procedures as inspection, observation, inquiry, and confirmation to secure evidence that will either support the balances shown in the accounts or show them to be incorrect. Furthermore, in the substantive testing phase we will verify the existence of documentary support for transactions resulting in these account balances. All these tests are developed further in Chapters 10 through 17.

The Reporting Phase

As we have previously noted, the final phase of the audit involving an association with internal control concerns the possible issuance of a report on the control system. Reports on internal control are governed by SAS 30. That statement discusses specifically the procedures that should be applied and the form of the report that should be used when an auditor has been engaged to do the following:

1. Express an opinion on the entity's system of internal accounting control in effect as of a specified date or over a specific period of time.
2. Report (without an opinion) on the entity's control system. In this case, the report on internal control is based solely on the study and evaluation made as a part of a financial statement audit. This type of report is a byproduct of an audit of the financial statements.
3. Report (without an opinion) on all or part of an entity's system, basing the report on the preestablished criteria of a governmental or other regulatory agency.
4. Other special-purpose reports on an entity's system of control.

We will now explain the auditor's involvement with the second type of report listed above. Others will be discussed in Chapter 19.

When an auditor is engaged to examine a client's financial statements, the procedures she or he applies to the study and evaluation of the company's system of internal control are restricted to those which will enable the auditor to *meet the second standard of fieldwork*. The auditor needs only to perform enough inquiries, inspections, and observations to determine the extent of the reliability of the client's system. The auditor's perceived reliability of the system then determines the nature, timing, and extent of substantive tests. Such procedures, however, are not considered adequate for expressing an opinion on the entity's system of control.

A written report provided for the client relating to the company's system of control is not specifically a part of the auditor's reporting responsibility under generally accepted auditing standards. However, such a report can be an important byproduct of the audit examination. Partly in recognition of that fact, Statement on Auditing Standards (SAS) 20 requires the auditor to communicate to senior management and the client's board of directors or its audit committee "material weaknesses in internal control" that have come to her or his attention during the audit. This communication is required even though the auditor was not specifically engaged to study and report on internal control. A material weakness in internal control is defined as

> a condition in which the auditor believes the prescribed procedures or the degree of compliance with them does not reduce to a relatively low level the risk that errors or irregularities in amounts that would be material in relation to the financial statements being audited may occur and not be detected within a timely period by employees in the normal course of performing their assigned functions.[6]

Although such weaknesses may be discovered during various phases of the audit, breakdowns in prescribed procedures are usually brought to the auditor's attention either during the preliminary review and evaluation of internal control or during the compliance testing phase of the audit. It is important to observe at this point that the auditor is responsible for judging whether the weaknesses discovered could result in material errors or irregularities in the financial statements. If the auditor judges such to be the case, the weaknesses must be communicated to management. Although these communications may be oral, it is strongly recommended that they be in the form of a letter or report, preferably rendered after the substantive testing phase of the audit has been completed.

Although the auditor is not required to communicate recommendations for improvements in the client's system of internal control, he or she generally includes them as a service to clients. A letter similar to the one shown in Figure 5–10 can be used for the purpose of communicating material internal control weaknesses to management. Such a letter should state the purpose of evaluating the system of internal control and should always cite the limitations associated with such an evaluation as part of an audit engagement. This is designed to prevent a misunderstanding as to what the normal audit is expected to accomplish in evaluating the system of control. The auditor should retain a copy of the letter and follow up on it in subsequent audits, to ascertain whether the weaknesses observed in the preceding audit have been corrected.

SYSTEMS EVALUATION APPROACH: DOCUMENTATION OF CONTROLS

Peat, Marwick, Mitchell & Co. has developed an innovative approach to the study and evaluation of internal control. It is known as SEADOC, short for Systems Evaluation Approach: Documentation of Controls.[7] Conceptually, it fits into the planning, interim, and final phases of the audit as shown in Figure 5–11.

In the process of identifying, evaluating, and testing internal control characteristics, the SEADOC system begins by evaluating the control environment. This includes the overall control consciousness of an organization's management and staff. Consideration is also given to the possibility of management override in this phase of the evaluation. The general impressions gained from such observations help shape not only the rest of the internal control evaluations but also the level of skepticism to be associated with all phases of the audit.

Specific controls are divided into the following three categories for the purpose of evaluating the control system:

- Boundary controls.
- Processing controls.
- Safeguard controls.

Boundary controls include the operating and documentation procedures associated with capturing the economic effects of exchanges. These include the documents and control procedures associated with the transfers of goods, services, money, promises, or releases from promises. In evaluating these controls, the auditor begins by determining which boundary controls are supposed to be in operation and whether or not they would be effective if properly performed. After those controls have been identified, they are compliance tested to determine that the system is functioning as designed. These control procedures are expected to provide reasonable assurance of

BROWN AND SMITH
Certified Public Accountants

February 20, 19X2

Board of Directors
Client Company
Address

Gentlemen:

We have examined the financial statements of XYZ Company for the year ended December 31, 19X1, and have issued our report thereon dated February 15, 19X2. As part of our examination, we made a study and evaluation of the company's system of internal accounting control to the extent we considered necessary to evaluate the system as required by generally accepted auditing standards. The purpose of our study and evaluation was to determine the nature, timing, and extent of the auditing procedures necessary for expressing an opinion on the company's financial statements. Our study and evaluation was more limited than would be necessary to express an opinion on the company's system of internal accounting control taken as a whole.

The management of XYZ Company is responsible for establishing and maintaining a system of internal accounting control. In fulfilling this responsibility, management must assess the expected benefits and related costs of control procedures. The objectives of a system are to provide management with reasonable, but not absolute, assurance that assets are safeguarded against loss from unauthorized use or disposition, and that transactions are executed in accordance with management's authorization and recorded properly to permit the preparation of financial statements in accordance with generally accepted accounting principles.

Because of inherent limitations in any system of internal accounting control, errors or irregularities may nevertheless occur and not be detected. Also, projection of any evaluation of the system to future periods is subject to the risk that procedures may become inadequate because of changes in conditions or that the degree of compliance with the procedures may deteriorate.

Our study and evaluation made for the limited purpose described in the first paragraph would not necessarily disclose all material weaknesses in the system. Accordingly, we do not express an opinion on the system of internal control of XYZ Company taken as a whole.

However, our study and evaluation disclosed the following conditions that we believe result in more than a relatively low risk that errors or irregularities in amounts that would be material in relation to the financial statements of XYZ Company may occur and not be detected within a timely period:

1. Purchase invoices are paid without an independent verification of the receipt of materials included on the invoices.

2. Purchase invoices are not stamped "paid" when checks are issued in payment of them.

These conditions were considered in determining the nature, timing, and extent of the audit tests to be applied in our examination of the 19X1 financial statements, and this report does not affect our report on these financial statements dated February 15, 19X2.

Sincerely yours,

BROWN AND SMITH, CPAs

FIGURE 5–10. Sample Auditor's Letter Citing Weaknesses in Internal Control

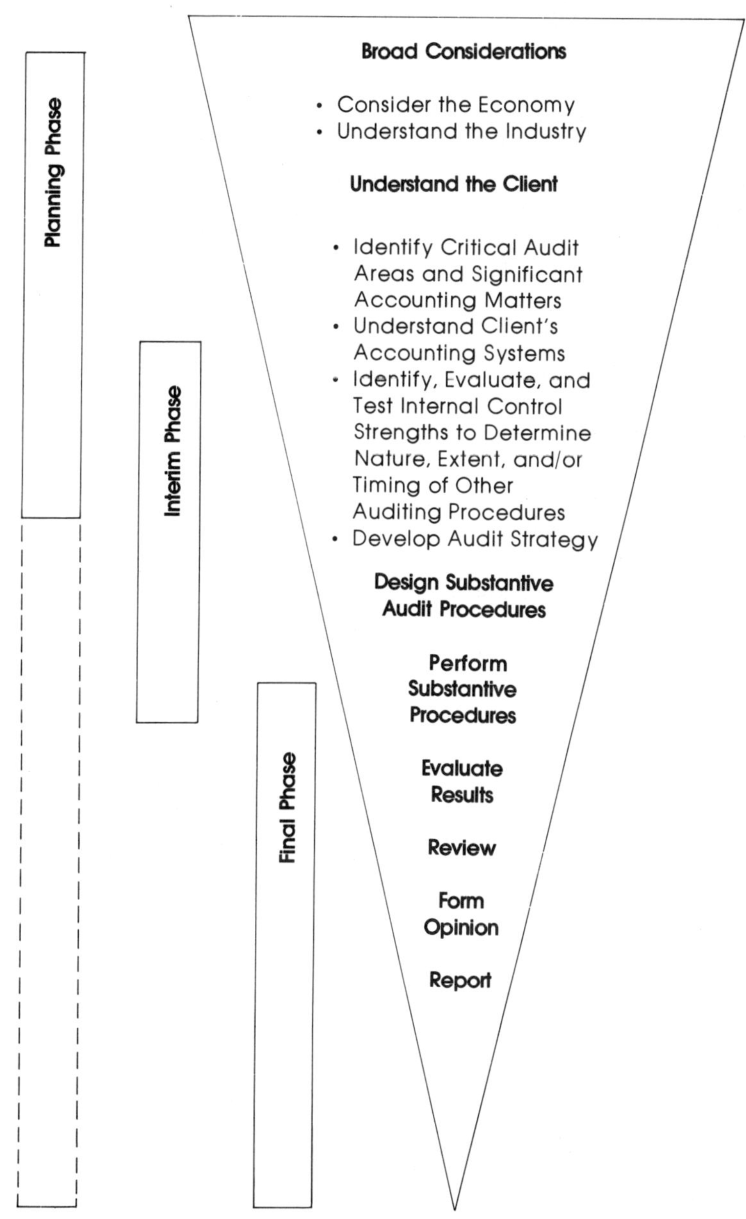

Source: Accounting Faculty Seminar—Systems Evaluation Approach: Documentation of Controls (SEADOC), prepared by Peat, Marwick, Mitchell & Co., 1981. Used with permission.

FIGURE 5–11 SEADOC: Its Phases and Activities

exchange transaction validity. As we discuss controls of this type later in the text, we shall refer to them as *exchange controls*.

Controls over processing exchange data, allocations, and valuations are referred to as ***processing controls***. The auditor seeks to understand the processing system by appropriate walk-through, inquiry, or observation procedures. In this phase of the evaluation, the auditor determines which controls exist and whether or not they would be effective if properly performed. These controls are also compliance tested to determine that they are functioning appropriately.

Controls over valuable movable assets are called ***safeguard controls***. They ensure that such assets are not lost, stolen, or allowed to deteriorate unnecessarily and that accountability is appropriately maintained for them. The auditor also seeks to understand a client's safeguard control procedures by appropriate walk-through, inquiry or observation procedures. On the basis of such evaluations, the auditor makes a preliminary judgment as to whether or not appropriate safeguard controls are present and reliable. Next, those control procedures are compliance tested, largely by observation and inquiry designed to test the functioning of the specific controls ostensibly in operation.

As Figure 5–12 shows, worksheets document the status of each of the three types of controls. As part of the evaluation process, Peat, Marwick, Mitchell & Co. classifies all possible errors into one of two categories — population errors and accuracy errors. ***Population errors*** are violations of the integrity of the number of items of data. If an item of data, for example, is lost during processing or is not captured at the time goods or services are exchanged, a population error has occurred. And, conversely, if an item of data is captured when it should *not* be recognized, a population error has occurred. ***Accuracy errors*** are discrepancies between items of information captured or processed and the economic events they represent. For example, if data about an exchange do not correctly reflect an element of an exchange in terms of quantities, prices, etc., an accuracy error has occurred.

As stated earlier, this approach to the study, evaluation, and documentation of internal control represents a change from the conventional practices followed in meeting the second standard of field work. It appears to have the advantage of directing the auditor's attention to the *crucial activities in the control process*. It should also be less expensive to implement and easier for staff personnel to understand.

SUMMARY

In this chapter we have defined an internal control system and explained how the auditor studies and evaluates that system in performing an audit engagement. The objectives of such a system are to safeguard the assets and records, assure reliable financial data, promote operating efficiency, and encourage adherence to managerial policies and directives.

The audit process includes four elements relating to internal control. Initially, the auditor studies the system to determine whether or not an opinion audit can be performed and then to evaluate the quality of the control system that is supposed to be in operation. Next, the actual operations of the system are compliance tested to see

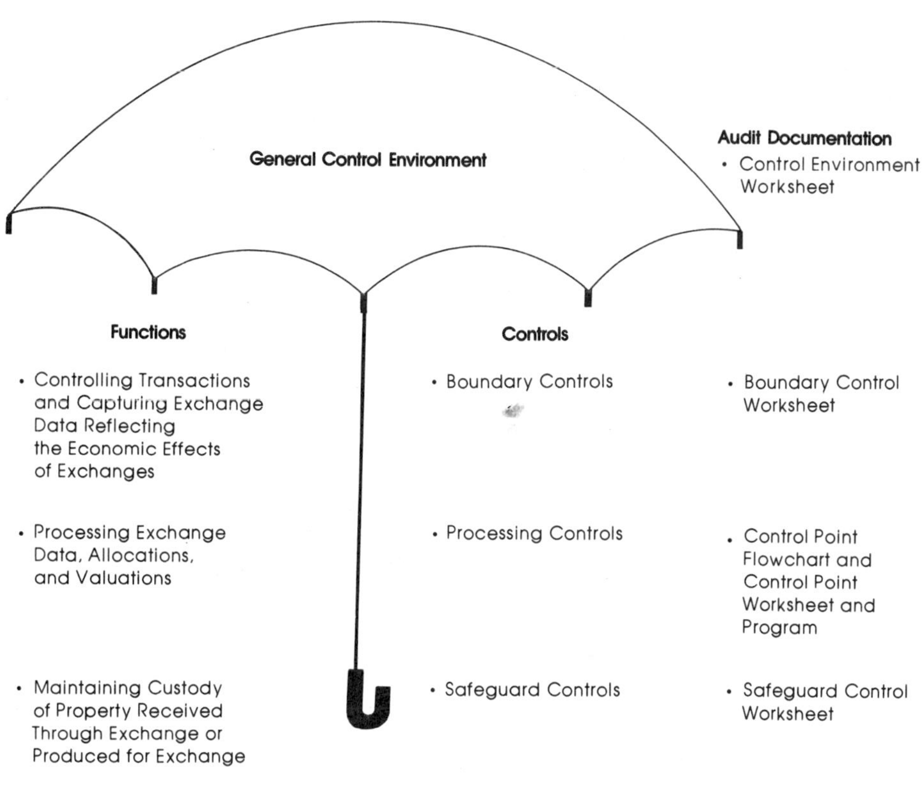

Source: Accounting Faculty Seminar—Systems Evaluation Approach: Documentation of Controls (SEA-DOC), prepared by Peat, Marwick, Mitchell & Co., 1981. Used with permission.

FIGURE 5–12. Documentation of the Internal Control System

whether the employees are adhering to the prescribed controls in the system. Then, on the basis of findings in the first two steps, the auditor develops detailed plans for the substantive testing phase of the audit. Finally, the auditor is required to communicate any significant weaknesses in the system of internal control to the client.

We observed that the system of control relating to each accounting subsystem is evaluated as the elements of that subsystem are verified in the audit process. The evaluation process requires the auditor to compare the actual operations of each subsystem with the practices dictated by the characteristics of an ideal system. Those characteristics include appropriate segregation of responsibilities, clearly defined lines of authority and responsibility, the use of appropriately qualified personnel, proper provision for the protection of assets and records, and provisions for checking compliance with the procedures prescribed by the system. We also noted that the evidence relating to internal control findings is generally reflected in internal control questionnaires, narrative descriptions of the system, or flowcharts. We noted that SAS 20 requires the auditor to communicate "material weaknesses in internal control" to the client. That report is normally communicated to management through the medium of an internal control letter.

The last section of the chapter was devoted to a brief discussion of the SEADOC program used by Peat, Marwick, Mitchell & Co. to evaluate systems of internal control during audit engagements.

NOTES

1. Statement on Accounting (SAS) 1, Section 320.01 (New York: AICPA, 1973).
2. Ibid., Section 320.09.
3. Ibid., Section 320.52, as amended by SAS 45 (New York: AICPA, 1982).
4. Floyd W. Windal and Robert N. Corley, *The Accounting Professional* (Englewood Cliffs, N.J.: Prentice-Hall, 1980), p. 98.
5. Ibid.
6. SAS 1, Section 320.68.
7. Materials in this section are taken from Accounting Faculty Seminar — Systems Evaluation Approach: Documentation of Controls (SEADOC) prepared by Peat, Marwick, Mitchell & Co., 1981. Used with permission.

QUESTIONS FOR CLASS DISCUSSION

Q5–1 What is the relationship between a client's system of internal control and the substantive tests to be performed by the independent auditor?

Q5–2 What is the primary objective of a system of internal control? Discuss.

Q5–3 Why is the auditor willing to express an opinion on the financial statements if he or she is *reasonably sure* rather than absolutely certain that the data included within the financial statement are fairly presented?

Q5–4 Is it possible for a client's system of internal control to be so weak that the auditor would have to disclaim an opinion on the financial statements? Explain.

Q5–5 What are the two basic risks always associated with the expression of an opinion on the financial statements?

Q5–6 From what sources does the auditor obtain the information to support his or her preliminary evaluation of a client's system of internal control?

Q5–7 What is the difference between accounting controls and administrative controls?

Q5–8 What are the six characteristics that should underlie an effective system of internal control? Discuss.

Q5–9 Which types of responsibilities should be separated in an effective system of internal control? Explain.

Q5–10 How can a mandatory vacation policy improve the reliability of a system of internal control?

Q5–11 Why is it important for a firm to have clearly defined lines of authority and responsibility? What are the media through which this is achieved?

Q5–12 How can an auditor judge whether or not a client has appropriately qualified personnel assigned to the various tasks to be performed?

Q5–13 What is the relationship between responsibility accounting and the lines of authority and responsibility?

Q5–14 Why is it important to have appropriate authorization and approval procedures associated with the various transactions carried out by the client?

Q5–15 What is the relationship between a client's internal auditing staff and the system of internal control?

Q5–16 What are some of the special problems associated with the establishment of a system of internal control for a small client?

Q5–17 What actions does the auditor take to ascertain that a client's system of internal control is operating in accordance with the provisions contained in the organization chart and procedures manual? Explain.

Q5–18 Does the fact that the client has a good system of internal control for handling cash receipts mean that the auditor can be reasonably assured that the cash balance is correct? Explain.

Q5–19 What are the seven general types of material errors and irregularities that could occur because of a weak system of internal control? Discuss.

Q5–20 The auditing process typically concerns itself with the verification of account balances produced by each of the client's accounting subsystems. How does the auditor's evaluation of the client's system of internal control relate to each of these subsystems?

Q5–21 What is the purpose of an internal control questionnaire? How does it fit into the overall evaluation of internal control? Discuss.

Q5–22 How are flowcharts used in the evaluation of the internal control procedures for an accounting subsystem?

Q5–23 What is the relationship between compliance tests and substantive tests? Discuss this relationship.

Q5–24 What are the various types of reports an auditor may render on a client's system of internal control? In what situation would each be used?

Q5–25 How may the Systems Evaluation Approach be used in meeting the field work auditing standard relating to internal control?

Q5–26 What is meant by *boundary controls?* Give two examples of such controls.

Q5–27 What is meant by *processing controls?* Provide two examples of such controls.

SHORT CASES

C5–1 The town of Commuter Park operates a private parking lot near the railroad station for the benefit of town residents. The guard on duty issues annual prenumbered parking stickers to residents who submit an application form and show evidence of residency. The sticker is affixed to the auto and allows the resident to park anywhere in the lot for twelve (12) hours if four quarters are placed in the parking meter. Applications are maintained in the guard office at the lot. The guard checks to see that only residents are using the lot and than no resident has parked without paying the required meter fee.

Once a week the guard on duty, who has a master key for all meters, takes the coins from the meters and places them in a locked steel box. The guard delivers the box to the town storage building where it is opened, and the coins are manually counted by a storage department clerk who records the total cash counted on a "Weekly Cash Report." This report is sent to the town accounting department. The storage department clerk puts the cash in a safe and on the following day the cash is picked up by the town's treasurer who manually recounts the cash, prepares the bank deposit slip, and delivers the deposit to the bank. The deposit slip, authenticated by the bank teller, is sent to the accounting department where it is filed with the "Weekly Cash Report."

Required:

Describe weaknesses in the existing system and recommend one or more improvements for each of the weaknesses to strengthen the internal control over the parking lot cash receipts.

Organize your answer sheet as follows:

Weakness	Recommended Improvement(s)

(AICPA adapted)

C5–2 Jordan Finance Company opened four personal loan offices in neighboring cities on January 2, 19X0. Small cash loans are made to borrowers who repay the principal with interest in monthly installments over a period not exceeding two years. Ralph Jordan, president of the company, uses one of the offices as a central office and visits the other offices periodically for supervision and internal auditing purposes.

Mr. Jordon is concerned about the honesty of his employees. He came to your office in December 19X0 and stated, "I want to engage you to install a system to prohibit employees from embezzling cash." He also stated, "Until I went into business for myself I worked for a nationwide loan company with 500 offices and I'm familiar with that company's system of accounting and internal control. I want to describe that system so you can install it for me because it will absolutely prevent fraud."

Required:

a. How would you advise Mr. Jordan on his request that you install the large company's system of accounting and internal control for his firm? Discuss.

b. How would you respond to the suggestion that the new system would prevent embezzlement? Discuss.

c. Assume that in addition to undertaking the system's engagement in 19X1, you agreed to examine Jordan Finance Company's financial statements for the year ended December 31, 19X0. No scope limitations were imposed.
   (1) How would you determine the scope necessary to satisfactorily complete your examination? Discuss.
   (2) Would you be responsible for the discovery of fraud in this examination? Discuss.

(AICPA adapted)

C5–3 You were recently appointed the auditor for a private college. Your first assignment is to appraise the adequacy and effectiveness of the student registration procedures. You have completed your preliminary study. On the basis of your interviews and a walk-through of the student registration operation, you prepared the play script shown on page 192.

Required:

a. Prepare a formal systems flowchart based on the play script, using appropriate symbols and techniques.

b. Examine the flowchart and list five internal control weaknesses (such as omissions of certain steps or measures) in the student registration procedures. Use the six characteristics of internal control discussed in this chapter as guidelines for your evaluation.

(CIA Examination adapted)

C5–4 Theresa Crane, administrator of Departure Haven Nursing Home, seeks your advice on a problem. Departure Haven employs three clerical employees who, among them, must perform the following functions. Mrs. Crane requests your advice as to how to assign the functions among the employees so as to achieve the highest degree of internal control.

a. Maintains disbursements (payments) journal.
b. Reconciles bank account.
c. Prepares checks for signature.
d. Opens mail and lists receipts.
e. Deposits cash receipts.
f. Maintains accounts receivable records.
g. Determines when accounts receivable are uncollectible.
h. Is responsible for petty cash fund.

Required:

a. How would you distribute the various functions among clerks X, Y, and Z? Assume that all functions require approximately the same amount of time.

b. List at least three unsatisfactory combinations of the functions.

(AICPA adapted)

ADMISSION — PROCESSING OF REGISTRATIONS

1 Mail Room

- Opens all mail, prepares remittance advices, and remittance listings
- Sends copies of advices and listings to:
  - A. Cashier (with cash and cheques)
  - B. Accounts receivable clerk
  - C. General bookkeeper
- Destroys other copies of advices and listings

2 Registration Clerk

- Receives three copies of completed registration forms from students
- Checks for counselor's or similar approval
- Records appropriate fee from official class catalog
- If completed properly, approves forms and sends students with registration forms to cashier
- If not completed properly, returns forms to student for follow-up and reapplication

3 Cashier

- Collects funds or forwards two copies of registration forms to billing clerk
- Records cash receipts in daily receipts record
- Prepares and makes daily deposits
- Forwards duplicate receipted deposit slips and daily receipts records to general bookkeeper
- Destroys copies of daily receipts records

4 Billing Clerk

- Receives two copies of registration form, prepares bill, and makes entries in registration (sales) journal
- Forwards copies of billings and registration forms to accounts receivable clerk and forwards copies of bill to general bookkeeper

5 Accounts Receivable Clerk

- Posts accounts receivable subsidiary ledger detailed accounts from remittance listings
- Matches billings and registration forms and posts accounts receivable subsidiary ledger detailed accounts

6 General Bookkeeper

- Journalizes and posts cash receipts and applicable registrations to general ledger
- Enters registration (sales) journal data in general ledger

C5–5 The following cases describe systems of internal control for different companies.

a. When Sharon Fisher, purchasing agent for Cooper Cosmetics, orders materials, she sends a duplicate copy of the purchase order to the receiving department. When materials are received, Joe Ferguson, receiving clerk, records the date of receipt on the copy of the purchase order but does not count the goods received. The same copy of the purchase order is sent to accounting, where Lyle Brown uses it to support the purchase entry in the voucher register. The copy is then sent to raw materials stores, where William Potter uses it to update the perpetual inventory cards.

b. At Halfiva Manufacturing Company, time cards of 450 employees are collected weekly by the foreman and delivered to the data processing department. There the cards are sorted and the hours worked are entered on Cathode Ray Tube Devices into the computer. These records are used to prepare individual payroll records, pay checks, and labor cost distribution records. The payroll checks are compared with individual payroll records and signed by the treasurer, who returns them to the data processing supervisor for distribution.

c. A sales branch of Rocklin Manufacturing Company has an office force consisting of the branch manager, I.C. Parma, and two assistants, Truett Beard and Jerry Martinetz. The branch has a local bank account in which it deposits cash receipts. Checks drawn on the bank account require Parma's signature or the signature of R.C. Timball, treasurer of the company. Bank statements and paid checks are returned by the bank to Parma who retains them in his files after preparing the monthly bank reconciliation. Reports of disbursements are also prepared by Parma and submitted to Timball at the home office on scheduled dates.

Required:

For each of the internal control systems described, point out

a. The weaknesses, if any, that exist.
b. The material errors or irregularities, if any, that might occur because of those weaknesses.
c. Your recommendations for improvement in the system.

(AICPA adapted)

C5–6 In early September the Sharp Corporation retained you to make an examination of its financial statements for the current year ending December 31. Your appointment occurred shortly after the death of the CPA who had audited the company in prior years. Assume that you have completed your examination during the following February and have prepared a draft of your audit report containing an unqualified opinion on the financial statements. Your report, as required by your engagement letter, was addressed to the board of directors. You have also drafted a special report describing weaknesses in the system of internal control observed during your examination and setting forth your recommendations for the correction of these weaknesses.

During your review of the drafts of these reports with the president of Sharp Corporation, he expressed his satisfaction with the unqualified report on the financial statements but indicated that the report on internal control was unnecessary. The president stated that he was aware of the weaknesses in internal control and that he would personally take steps to remedy them. Finally, the president instructed you not to render the internal control report. He explained that he felt the board of directors should deal with major policy decisions and not be burdened with day-to-day management problems.

Required:

a. Enumerate at least five separate factors which should be considered before reaching a decision whether to render the internal control report.

b. In the event that you decide to render the internal control report to Sharp Corporation, would you render it to the board of directors or to the president? Explain fully.

(AICPA adapted)

PROBLEMS

P5–1 Select the best answer to each of the following items relating to the benefits and limitations associated with a system of internal control.

a. In general, material irregularities perpetrated by which of the following are *most* difficult to detect?
(1) Cashier.
(2) Controller.
(3) Internal auditor.
(4) Key-punch operator.

b. The auditor faces a risk that the examination will not detect material errors that occur in the accounting process. In regard to minimizing this risk, the auditor primarily relies on
(1) Substantive tests.
(2) Compliance tests.
(3) Internal control.
(4) Statistical analysis.

c. When considering the effectiveness of a system of internal accounting control, the auditor should recognize that inherent limitations do exist. Which of the following is an example of an inherent limitation in a system of internal accounting control?
(1) The effectiveness of procedures depends on the segregation of employee duties.
(2) Procedures are designed to assure the execution and recording of transactions in accordance with management's authorization.
(3) In the performance of most control procedures, there are possibilities of errors arising from mistakes in judgment.
(4) Procedures for handling large numbers of transactions are processed by electronic data processing equipment.

d. Internal administrative control includes the overall plan of organization and the procedures that are concerned with
(1) Safeguarding the assets and providing reliable financial records.
(2) The decision process leading to management's authorization of transactions.
(3) The execution of transactions in accordance with special or general authorization.
(4) Providing reasonable assurance that access to assets is permitted only in accordance with management authorization.

e. Internal control can generally be subdivided into administrative controls and accounting controls. The scope of study and evaluation of internal control contemplated by generally accepted auditing standards requires the consideration of
(1) Both administrative controls and accounting controls.
(2) Administrative controls.
(3) Accounting controls.

(4) Accounting controls in an audit engagement and administrative controls in a management advisory service engagement.

f. The auditor recognizes that a "system" of internal control extends beyond those matters which relate directly to the functions of the accounting and financial departments. Which one of the following would the auditor generally consider least a part of a manufacturing company's "system" of internal control?
   (1) Time and motion studies that are of an engineering nature.
   (2) Quarterly audits by an insurance company to determine the premium for workmen's compensation insurance.
   (3) A budgetary system installed by a consulting firm other than a CPA firm.
   (4) A training program designed to aid personnel in meeting their job responsibilities.

g. In internal accounting control, the basic concept recognizing that the cost of internal control should *not* exceed the benefits expected to be derived is known as
   (1) Reasonable assurance.
   (2) Management responsibility.
   (3) Limited liability.
   (4) Management by exception.

h. A well-designed system of internal control that is functioning effectively is most likely to detect an irregularity arising from
   (1) The fraudulent action of several employees.
   (2) The fraudulent action of an individual employee.
   (3) Informal deviations from the official organization chart.
   (4) Management fraud.

i. Which of the following is an invalid concept of internal control?
   (1) In cases where a person is responsible for all phases of a transaction there should be a clear designation of that person's responsibility.
   (2) The recorded accountability for assets should be compared with the existing assets at reasonable intervals and appropriate action should be taken if there are differences.
   (3) Accounting control procedures may appropriately be applied on a test basis in some circumstances.
   (4) Procedures designed to detect errors and irregularities should be performed by persons other than those who are in a position to perpetrate them.

(AICPA adapted)

P5–2 Select the best answer for each of the following items relating to the characteristics of an internal control system.

a. Which of the following activities would be *least* likely to strengthen a company's internal control?
   (1) Separating accounting from other financial operations.
   (2) Maintaining insurance for fire and theft.
   (3) Fixing responsibility for the performance of employee duties.
   (4) Carefully selecting and training employees.

b. Transaction authorization within an organization may be either specific or general. An example of specific transaction authorization is the
   (1) Establishment of requirements to be met in determining a customer's credit limits.

(2) Setting of automatic reorder points for material or merchandise.
(3) Approval of a detailed construction budget for a warehouse.
(4) Establishment of sales prices for products to be sold to any customer.

c. Effective internal control in a small company that has an insufficient number of employees to permit proper division of responsibilities can *best* be enhanced by
(1) Employment of temporary personnel to aid in the separation of duties.
(2) Direct participation by the owner of the business in the recordkeeping activities of the business.
(3) Engaging a CPA to perform monthly write-up work.
(4) Delegation of full, clear-cut responsibility to each employee for the functions assigned to each.

d. The independent auditor should acquire an understanding of a client's internal audit function to determine whether the work of internal auditors will be a factor in determining the nature, timing, and extent of the independent auditor's procedures. The work performed by internal auditors might be such a factor when the internal auditor's work includes
(1) Verification of the mathematical accuracy of invoices.
(2) Review of administrative practices to improve efficiency and achieve management objectives.
(3) Study and evaluation of internal accounting control.
(4) Preparation of internal financial reports for management purposes.

e. Internal control is a function of management, and effective control is based upon the concept of charge and discharge of responsibility and duty. Which of the following is one of the overriding principles of internal control?
(1) Responsibility for accounting and financial duties should be assigned to one responsible officer.
(2) Responsibility for the performance of each duty must be fixed.
(3) Responsibility for the accounting duties must be borne by the auditing committee of the company.
(4) Responsibility for accounting activities and duties must be assigned only to employees who are bonded.

f. Effective internal control requires organizational independence of departments. Organizational independence would be impaired in which of the following situations?
(1) The internal auditors report to the audit committee of the board of directors.
(2) The controller reports to the vice-president of production.
(3) The payroll accounting department reports to the chief accountant.
(4) The cashier reports to the treasurer.

g. Proper segregation of functional responsibilities calls for separation of the
(1) Authorization, approval, and execution functions.
(2) Authorization, execution, and payment functions.
(3) Receiving, shipping, and custodial functions.
(4) Authorization, recording, and custodial functions.

h. It is important for the CPA to consider the competence of the audit client's employees because their competence bears directly and importantly upon the
(1) Cost/benefit relationship of the system of internal control.
(2) Achievement of the objectives of the system of internal control.
(3) Comparison of recorded accountability with assets.
(4) Timing of the tests to be performed.

i. Internal accounting control comprises the plan of organization and the procedures and records that are concerned with the safeguarding of assets and the
   (1) Decision processes of management.
   (2) Reliability of financial records.
   (3) Authorization of transactions.
   (4) Achievement of administrative objectives.

j. Which of the following *best* describes the inherent limitations that should be recognized by an auditor when considering the potential effectiveness of a system of internal accounting control?
   (1) Procedures whose effectiveness depends on segregation of duties can be circumvented by collusion.
   (2) The competence and integrity of client personnel provides an environment conducive to accounting control and provides assurance that effective control will be achieved.
   (3) Procedures designed to assure the execution and recording of transactions in accordance with proper authorizations are effective against irregularities perpetrated by management.
   (4) The benefits expected to be derived from effective internal accounting control usually do *not* exceed the costs of such control.

k. A system of internal accounting control normally would include procedures that are designed to provide reasonable assurance that
   (1) Employees act with integrity when performing their assigned tasks.
   (2) Transactions are executed in accordance with management's general or specific authorization.
   (3) Decision processes leading to management's authorization of transactions are sound.
   (4) Collusive activities would be detected by segregation of employee duties.

l. The independent auditor should acquire an understanding of the internal audit function as it relates to the independent auditor's study and evaluation of internal accounting control because
   (1) The audit programs, working papers, and reports of internal auditors can often be used as a substitute for the work of the independent auditor's staff.
   (2) The procedures performed by the internal audit staff may eliminate the independent auditor's need for an extensive study and evaluation of internal control.
   (3) The work performed by internal auditors may be a factor in determining the nature, timing, and extent of the independent auditor's procedures.
   (4) The understanding of the internal audit function is an important substantive test to be performed by the independent auditor.

(AICPA adapted)

P5–3 Select the best answer for each of the following items relating to the use of flowcharts in evaluating a client's system of control.

a. Which of the following best describes the principal advantage of the use of flowcharts in reviewing internal control?
   (1) Standard flowcharts are available and can be effectively used for describing most company internal operations.

(2) Flowcharts aid in the understanding of the sequence and relationships of activities and documents.
(3) Working papers are not complete unless they include flowcharts as well as memoranda on internal control.
(4) Flowcharting is the most efficient means available for summarizing internal control.

b. The normal sequence of documents and operations on a well-prepared systems flowchart is
(1) Top to bottom and left to right.
(2) Bottom to top and left to right.
(3) Top to bottom and right to left.
(4) Bottom to top and right to left.

c. One important reason why a CPA, during the course of an audit engagement, prepares systems flowcharts is to
(1) Reduce the need for inquiries of client personnel concerning the operations of the system of internal accounting control.
(2) Depict the organizational structure and document flow in a single chart for review and reference purposes.
(3) Assemble the internal control findings into a comprehensible format suitable for analysis.
(4) Prepare documentation that would be useful in the event of a future consulting engagement.

d. In connection with the study of internal control, an auditor encounters the following flowcharting symbols:

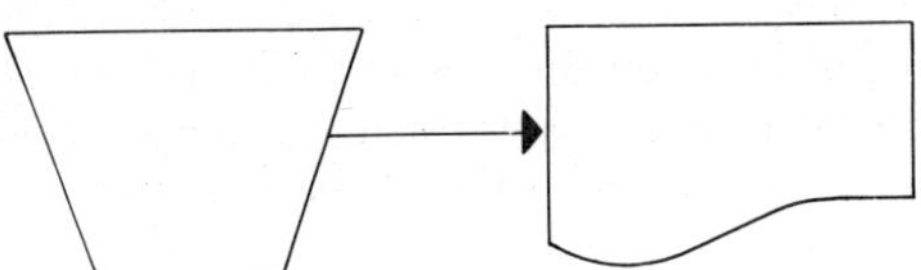

The auditor would conclude that
(1) A document has been generated by a manual operation.
(2) A master file has been created by a computer operation.
(3) A document has been generated by a computer operation.
(4) A master file has been created by a manual operation.

e. During which phase of an audit examination is the preparation of flowcharts *most* appropriate?
(1) Review of the system of internal accounting control.
(2) Tests of compliance with internal accounting control procedures.
(3) Evaluation of the system of internal administrative control.
(4) Analytic review of operations.

f. When preparing a record of a client's system of internal accounting control, the independent auditor sometimes uses a systems flowchart, which can *best* be described as a
(1) Pictorial presentation of the flow of instructions in a client's internal computer system.
(2) Diagram that clearly indicates an organization's internal reporting structure.

(3) Graphic illustration of the flow of operations, used to replace the auditor's internal control questionnaire.
(4) Symbolic representation of a system or series of sequential processes.

g. One reason why an auditor uses a flowchart is to aid in the
(1) Evaluation of a series of sequential processes.
(2) Study of the system of responsibility accounting.
(3) Performance of important, required, dual-purpose tests.
(4) Understanding of a client's organizational structure.

h. Which of the following *best* describes the primary reason for the auditor's use of flowcharts during an audit engagement?
(1) To comply with the requirements of generally accepted auditing standards.
(2) To classify the client's documents and transactions by major operating functions, e.g., cash receipts, cash disbursements, etc.
(3) To record the auditor's understanding of the client's system of internal accounting control.
(4) To interpret the operational effectiveness of the client's existing organizational structure.

i. Which of the following is *not* a medium that can normally be used by an auditor to record information concerning a client's system of internal accounting control?
(1) Narrative memorandum.
(2) Procedures manual.
(3) Flowchart.
(4) Decision table.

j. An auditor's flowchart of a client's internal control system is a diagrammatic representation depicting the auditor's
(1) Understanding of the system.
(2) Program for compliance tests.
(3) Documentation of the study and evaluation of the system.
(4) Understanding of the types of irregularities probable, given the present system.

k. The program flowcharting symbol representing a decision is a
(1) Triangle.
(2) Circle.
(3) Rectangle.
(4) Diamond.

(AICPA adapted)

P5–4 Select the best answer to each of the following items relating to compliance testing.

a. Before relying on the system of internal control, the auditor obtains a reasonable degree of assurance that the internal control procedures are in use and operating as planned. The auditor obtains this assurance by performing
(1) Substantive tests.
(2) Transaction tests.
(3) Compliance tests.
(4) Tests of trends and ratios.

b. Which of the following statements relating to compliance tests is most accurate?
(1) Auditing procedures can not concurrently provide both evidence of com-

pliance with accounting control procedures and evidence required for substantive tests.
(2) Compliance tests include physical observations of the proper segregation of duties which ordinarily may be limited to the normal audit period.
(3) Compliance tests should be based on proper application of an appropriate statistical sampling plan.
(4) Compliance tests ordinarily should be performed as of the balance sheet date or during the period subsequent to that date.

c. Which of the following would be *least* likely to be included in an auditor's tests of compliance?
(1) Inspection.
(2) Observation.
(3) Inquiry.
(4) Confirmation.

d. The two phases of the auditor's study of internal accounting control are referred to as *review of the system* and *tests of compliance*. In the tests of compliance phase the auditor attempts to
(1) Obtain a reasonable degree of assurance that the client's system of controls is in use and is operating as planned.
(2) Obtain sufficient, competent evidential matter to afford a reasonable basis for the auditor's opinion.
(3) Obtain assurances that informative disclosures in the financial statements are reasonably adequate.
(4) Obtain knowledge and understanding of the client's prescribed procedures and methods.

e. Which of the following audit tests would be regarded as a test of *compliance*?
(1) Tests of the specific items making up the balance in a given general ledger account.
(2) Tests of the inventory pricing to vendors' invoices.
(3) Tests of the signatures on cancelled checks to board of director's authorizations.
(4) Tests of the additions to property, plant, and equipment by physical inspections.

f. Tests of compliance are concerned primarily with each of the following questions *except*
(1) How were the procedures performed?
(2) Why were the procedures performed?
(3) Were the necessary procedures performed?
(4) By whom were the procedures performed?

g. The primary purpose of performing compliance tests is to provide reasonable assurance that
(1) Accounting control procedures are being applied as prescribed.
(2) The flow of transactions through the accounting system is understood.
(3) Transactions are recorded at the amounts executed.
(4) All accounting control procedures leave visible evidence.

h. Which of the following is essential to determine whether the necessary internal control procedures were prescribed and are being followed?
(1) Developing questionnaires and checklists.
(2) Studying and evaluating administrative control policies.

(3) Reviewing the system and testing compliance.
(4) Observing employee functions and making inquiries.

(AICPA adapted)

P5–5 Select the best answer to each of the following items relating to the auditor's evaluation of a client's system of internal control.

a. On the basis of tests he made during the year, an independent auditor has found that internal control in the client company was effective; he concludes that the client's records, procedures, and representations can be relied upon. The auditor should test the records, procedures, and representations again at year end if
   (1) Inquiries and observations lead the auditor to believe that conditions have changed significantly.
   (2) Comparisons of year-end balances with like balances at prior dates revealed significant fluctuations.
   (3) Unusual transactions occurred subsequent to the completion of the interim audit work.
   (4) Client records are in a condition that facilitate effective and efficient testing.

b. A secondary objective of the auditor's study and evaluation of internal control is that the study and evaluation provide
   (1) A basis for constructive suggestions concerning improvements in internal control.
   (2) A basis for reliance on the system of internal accounting control.
   (3) An assurance that the records and documents have been maintained in accordance with existing company policies and procedures.
   (4) A basis for the determination of the resultant extent of the tests to which auditing procedures are to be restricted.

c. If, during the course of an annual audit of a publicly held manufacturing company, an independent auditor becomes aware of a material weakness in the company's internal accounting control, the auditor is required to communicate the material weakness to
   (1) The senior management and the board of directors of the company.
   (2) The senior management of the company.
   (3) The board of directors of the company.
   (4) The audit committee of the board of directors.

d. The primary purpose of the auditor's study and evaluation of internal control is to provide a basis for
   (1) Determining whether procedures and records that are concerned with the safeguarding of assets are reliable.
   (2) Constructive suggestions to clients concerning improvements in internal control.
   (3) Determining the nature, extent, and timing of audit tests to be applied.
   (4) The expression of an opinion.

e. An auditor evaluates the existing system of internal control in order to
   (1) Determine the extent of compliance tests which must be performed.
   (2) Determine the extent of substantive tests which must be performed.
   (3) Ascertain whether irregularities are probable.
   (4) Ascertain whether any employees have incompatible functions.

f. In general, a material internal control weakness may be defined as a condition in which material errors or irregularities would ordinarily *not* be detected within a timely period by
   (1) An auditor during the normal study and evaluation of the system of internal control.
   (2) A controller when reconciling accounts in the general ledger.
   (3) Employees in the normal course of performing their assigned functions.
   (4) The chief financial officer when reviewing interim financial statements.

g. How does the extent of substantive tests required to constitute sufficient evidential matter vary with the auditor's reliance on internal control?
   (1) Randomly.
   (2) Disproportionately.
   (3) Directly.
   (4) Inversely.

h. The auditor's review of the client's system of internal control is documented in order to substantiate
   (1) Conformity of the accounting records with generally accepted accounting principles.
   (2) Representation as to adherence to requirements of management.
   (3) Representation as to compliance with generally accepted auditing standards.
   (4) The fairness of the financial statement presentation.

i. When considering internal control, an auditor must be aware of the concept of reasonable assurance, which recognizes that
   (1) The employment of competent personnel provides assurance that the objectives of internal control will be achieved.
   (2) The establishment and maintenance of a system of internal control is an important responsibility of the management and *not of* the auditor.
   (3) The cost of internal control should *not* exceed the benefits expected to be derived from internal control.
   (4) The segregation of incompatible functions is necessary to obtain assurance that the internal control is effective.

j. At interim dates an auditor evaluates a client's internal accounting control procedures and finds them to be effective. The auditor then performs a substantial part of the audit engagement on a continuous basis throughout the year. At a minimum, the auditor's year-end audit procedures must include
   (1) Determination that the client's internal accounting control procedures are still effective at year end.
   (2) Confirmation of those year-end accounts that were examined at interim dates.
   (3) Tests of compliance with internal control in the same manner as those tests made at the interim dates.
   (4) Comparison of the responses to the auditor's internal control questionnaire with a detailed flowchart at year end.

k. Which of the following *best* describes how an auditor, when evaluating internal accounting control, considers the types of errors and irregularities that could occur and determines those control procedures that should prevent or detect such errors or irregularities?
   (1) Discussions with management with respect to the system of internal accounting control and how management determines that the system is functioning properly.

(2) Review of questionnaires, flowcharts, checklists, instructions, or similar generalized materials used by the auditor.
(3) Exercise of professional judgment in evaluating the reliability of supporting documentation.
(4) Use of attribute sampling techniques to gather information for tests of compliance.

l. In connection with the study and evaluation of internal control during an examination of financial statements, the independent auditor
(1) Gives equal weight to internal accounting and administrative control.
(2) Emphasizes internal administrative control.
(3) Emphasizes the separation of duties of client personnel.
(4) Emphasizes internal accounting control.

m. Which of the following is the *least* likely reason for the auditor's study and evaluation of internal control?
(1) To determine the extent of audit testing.
(2) To serve as a basis for reliance on the controls.
(3) To determine the nature of transactions.
(4) To serve as a basis for constructive service suggestions.

n. That segment of an auditor's internal control work which focuses directly on the purpose of preventing or detecting material errors or irregularities in financial statements is known as
(1) Compliance with the existing system of internal control.
(2) Review of the existing system of internal control.
(3) Evaluation of the existing system of internal control.
(4) Study of the existing system of internal control.

(AICPA adapted)

P5–6 Internal control comprises the plan of organization and all of the coordinate methods and measures adopted within a business to safeguard its assets, check the accuracy and reliability of its accounting data, promote operational efficiency, and encourage adherence to prescribed managerial policies.

Required:

a. What is the purpose of the auditor's study and evaluation of internal control?
b. What are the objectives of a preliminary evaluation of internal control?
c. How is the auditor's understanding of the system of internal control documented?
d. What is the purpose of tests of compliance?

(AICPA adapted)

P5–7 As a CPA, you have been engaged to audit the financial statements of University Books, Incorporated. University Books maintains a large revolving cash fund exclusively for the purpose of buying used books from students for cash. The cash fund is active all year because the nearby university offers a large variety of courses with varying starting and completion dates throughout the year.

Receipts are prepared for each purchase and reimbursement vouchers are periodically submitted.

Required:

Construct an internal control questionnaire to be used in the evaluation of the system of internal control of University Books's buying segments revolving cash fund. The internal control questionnaire should elicit a yes or no response. *Do not discuss the internal controls over books that are purchased.*

(AICPA adapted)

P5–8 The partially completed charge sales systems flowchart on the facing page depicts the charge sales activities of the Bottom Manufacturing Corporation.

A customer's purchase order is received and a six-part sales order is prepared therefrom. The six copies are initially distributed as follows:

Copy No. 1 — Billing copy, to billing department.
Copy No. 2 — Shipping copy, to shipping department.
Copy No. 3 — Credit copy, to credit department.
Copy No. 4 — Stock request copy, to credit department.
Copy No. 5 — Customer copy, to customer.
Copy No. 6 — Sales order copy, to a file in sales order department.

When each copy of the sales order reaches the applicable department or destination, it calls for specific internal control procedures and related documents. Some of the procedures and related documents are indicated on the flowchart. Other procedures and documents on the flowchart are merely labeled with letters *a* to *r*.

Required:

List the procedures or the internal documents that are labeled with letters *c* to *r* in the flowchart of Bottom Manufacturing Corporation's charge sales system.

Organize your answer as follows (note that an explanation of the letters *a* and *b* which appear in the flowchart are entered as examples):

Flowchart Symbol Letter	Procedures or Internal Document
a	Prepare six-part sales order
b	File by order number
c	

(AICPA adapted)

P5–9 Internal auditing is an important part of an organization's system of internal control.

Required:

a. List six major objectives of internal control.
b. For each of the objectives listed, tell whether fulfillment of the objective is of primary concern for the internal auditor, the independent auditor, or both.

(CIA Examination, adapted)

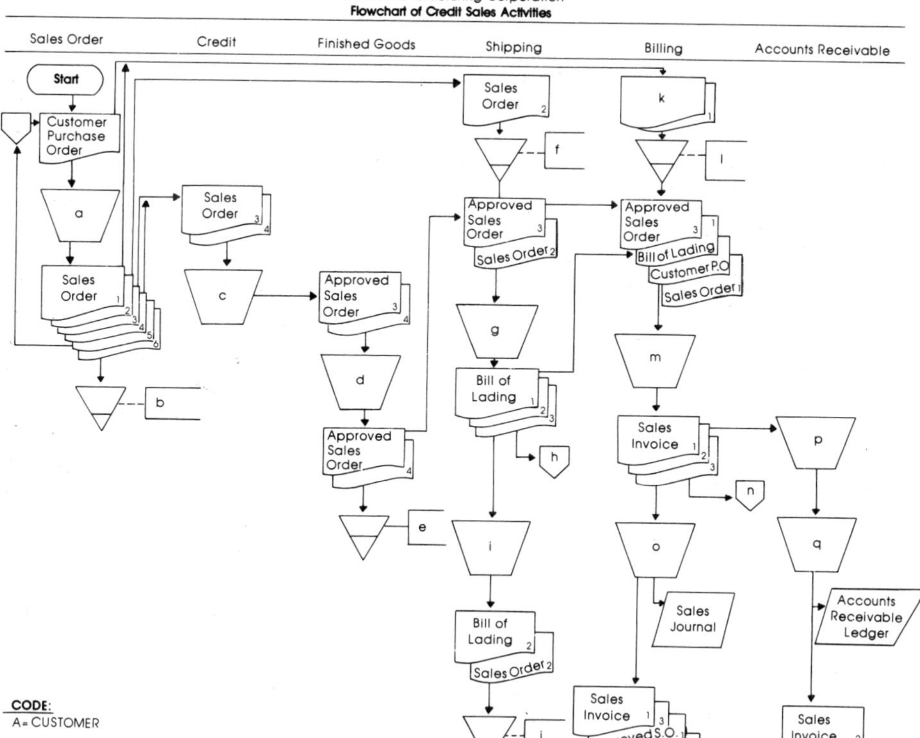

P5–10 Each of the following situations describes a problem in internal control.

a. The accounts receivable bookkeeper, who was also the cashier, misappropriated a \$1,000 check from a customer (A); the next day, when \$1,000 was received on another customer's account (B), the bookkeeper credited customer (A)'s account instead.

b. Incorrect quantities are being used on receiving reports for goods received from vendors.

c. Goods are not being counted as they are received. Instead, receiving department personnel are using the quantities on a copy of the purchase order sent from the purchasing agent as the correct quantities received.

d. The purchasing agent has a brother-in-law who is the salesman-owner of a supplier of the company. The purchasing agent places orders with his brother-in-law but pays double the price that the brother-in-law normally charges. When payment is received by the brother-in-law, he splits the excess with the purchasing agent.

e. The factory foreman, who hires new employees, inserted a fictitious employee in the payroll records and has been submitting an extra time card for twenty-four months for the fictitious employee.

Required:

Discuss each of the errors or irregularities described in the case situations in terms of

a. An internal control procedure that, if in operation, would have prevented the error or irregularity from occurring.
b. A compliance test to ascertain if the control procedure was in place.
c. A substantive test that, depending on the strengths or weaknesses of the particular control procedure, would have to be expanded or limited.

P5–11 The division of the following duties should provide the best possible controls for Lazy J Enterprises, a small wholesale store.

*a. Assemble supporting documents for disbursements and prepare checks for signature.
*b. Sign general disbursement checks.
*c. Record checks written in the cash disbursements and payroll journal.
d. Mail disbursement checks to suppliers.
e. Cancel supporting documents to prevent their reuse.
*f. Approve credit for customers.
*g. Bill customers and record the invoices in the sales journal and subsidiary ledger.
*h. Open the mail and prepare a prelisting of cash receipts.
*i. Record cash receipts in the cash journal and subsidiary ledger.
*j. Prepare daily cash deposits.
*k. Deliver daily cash deposits to the bank.
*l. Assemble the payroll time cards and prepare the payroll checks.
*m. Sign payroll checks.
n. Post the journals to the general ledger.
o. Reconcile the accounts receivable subsidiary account with the control account.
p. Prepare monthly statements for customers by copying the subsidiary ledger account.
q. Reconcile the monthly statements from vendors with the subsidiary accounts payable account.
r. Reconcile the bank account.

Required:

You are to divide the accounting-related duties *a* through *r* among Jill Thomas, Todd Robison, Lena Pini, and Bill Merck. Thomas, who is president of the company, is not willing to perform any functions designated by an asterisk and will do a maximum of two of the other functions. All the responsibilities marked with an asterisk are assumed to take about the same amount of time and must be divided equally between the two employees, Robison and Pini, who are equally competent.

(AICPA adapted)

P5–12 Adherence to generally accepted auditing standards requires, among other things, a proper study and evaluation of the existing internal control. The most common approaches to reviewing the system of internal control include the use of a questionnaire, preparation of a memorandum, preparation of a flowchart, and combinations of these methods.

Required:

a. What is a CPA's objective in reviewing internal control for an opinion audit?
b. Discuss the advantages to a CPA of reviewing internal control by using an internal control questionnaire and by using a flowchart.
c. If, after completing her or his evaluation of internal control for an opinion audit, the CPA is satisfied that no material weaknesses in the client's internal control system exist, is it necessary for him or her to test transactions? Explain.

(AICPA adapted)

CHAPTER

6

ELECTRONIC DATA PROCESSING AND INTERNAL CONTROLS

As we discussed the study and evaluation of internal control in Chapter 5, we were, by implication, assuming an operating environment depending largely on manually maintained accounting records. After identifying the objectives of internal control in that environment, we examined six characteristics that should be present in an effective system of internal control. Because of the increased volume of transactions and the concurrent development of the computer, we have seen a significant change in the data-processing environment over the last twenty-five years: because of its accuracy and speed and its adaptability to data-processing activities, the computer is now used to maintain most business accounting records.

In this chapter we explain how the use of electronic data processing (EDP) affects the auditor's study and evaluation of internal control.[1] Our discussion covers the following:

1. The effect that the use of the computer has had on the elements of the control system.
2. Classification and analysis of the types of controls that should be provided in an accounting system using EDP equipment.
3. Development of the procedures that the auditor should follow in studying and evaluating the system of internal control when the computer is used to process accounting data. These procedures include the use of a specific application questionnaire similar to that shown in Appendix 6–A.

We also include, as Appendix 6–B, a glossary of computer terms.

IMPACT OF THE COMPUTER ON THE INTERNAL CONTROL SYSTEM

Use of the computer does not in any way change the basic objectives of a sound system of internal control. However, the organization and procedures employed by the entity to implement those objectives *do* change. When the computer is used in significant accounting applications, the auditor must assess its impact and consider the EDP activity in his or her study and evaluation of internal control. In addition, the auditor must obtain a sufficient understanding of the computer system to be able to identify and evaluate its essential control features. To help you understand the impact of electronic data processing on internal controls, we now examine the general environmental characteristics associated with computerized accounting records, as well as the component elements of an electronic data-processing system. We also briefly consider the vulnerability of computerized accounting systems to fraud.

Environmental Characteristics Associated with Using the Computer

The special internal control problems caused by the use of electronic data-processing equipment are officially recognized in Statement on Auditing Standards (SAS) 3 entitled "The Effect of EDP on the Auditor's Study and Evaluation of Internal Control." The discussion throughout the remainder of this chapter describes and expands on the problems and procedures discussed in that statement.

The rapidly expanding use of the computer has revolutionized financial data classification, accumulation, and reporting procedures. It has also brought with it a new universe of terminology that must be understood as we examine computerized recordkeeping systems. A glossary of those terms is provided in Appendix 6–B. You should refer to it as you encounter computer-related terms that are unfamiliar to you.

To operate effectively, a computerized accounting system must combine certain logically related elements of a particular series of tasks in one department, namely the data-processing center. As an illustration, the various steps associated with processing a customer's order from the point of receipt through collection of the sales price — such as credit analysis, production scheduling, billing, sales analysis, and the recording of accounts receivable and cash collections — will typically be concentrated in the data-processing center. Thus, the need for combining many processing steps in one department *eliminates the traditional internal control provided by separating those duties* among various people in different departments. In an interrelated system, for example, a single input record describing a transaction can be used to update all files associated with the transaction. Also, the data-gathering, analysis, and reporting functions are often integrated into a management information system designed to provide management with all the information needed to carry out its functions. While this method of processing is very efficient, it eliminates the traditional separation of the authorization, custodianship of assets, and recordkeeping duties that are vital for traditional internal control purposes.

Insofar as the system of records is concerned, computerized applications have *eliminated many of the elements of the visible audit trail* that could normally be used to trace an item from the transaction document to an account balance or from an account balance back to the original transaction document. A majority of the accounting data are typically maintained in machine-readable files (such as magnetic tapes or disks), thus eliminating certain typical historical accounting records. Therefore, anyone seeking such data in person-readable form must request computer printouts that can be used as transactions registers.

Partially compensating for the problems mentioned in the preceding paragraphs is this fact: systems analysts who write computer programs typically include certain processing controls within the program itself. In addition, certain controls are built into the computer machinery. This tends to shift the review of transactions processed from people to the computer. Typical computer edit routines include various programmed checks (discussed later) to determine the validity and completeness of processed transactions and the reasonableness of such transactions as they flow through the system.

Component Elements of an Electronic Data-Processing System

The components of an electronic data-processing system are shown in Figure 6–1. As you can see from that figure, the system includes software in the form of a computer program, plus input devices, processing equipment, and output devices. Such a system requires that the documents supporting various accounting-related actions be converted from person-readable form to machine-readable form to be accepted by the input devices. Those data, along with a machine-readable program telling the computer what to do, are then transmitted by means of one or more input devices to the processing unit. A compiler program (not shown in Figure 6–1) often is used to convert person-readable data and programmed instructions to machine-readable form. After processing, the central processing unit in turn transmits the processed data, again according to program instructions, to one of the output devices shown in Figure 6–1.

If the accounting system simply calls for the accounting data (such as accounts receivable related transactions) to be processed by the computer and conveyed back to the accountant through the medium of printed copy, the computer is basically being used as a sophisticated bookkeeping machine. In such a situation, the internal control problems, except for those relating to the computer software (programs), are little different from the ones described in Chapter 5 for a manually maintained accounting system. Such a system also can normally be audited without examining or directly testing the computer programs used in the system.

In most instances, however, the use of the computer for accounting purposes involves much more than simply processing a series of transactions through to a printed document. Most EDP recordkeeping systems are more advanced and call for the storage of accounting data in machine-readable form and the actual issuance of company documents, such as invoices and checks, by the computer. For example, the record of accounts receivable will generally be accumulated and stored on either magnetic tape or magnetic disks, with balances being updated each day, as shown in Figure 6–2. Such a system will generally be programmed to have the computer print invoices and statements going out to customers. It may also be programmed to check

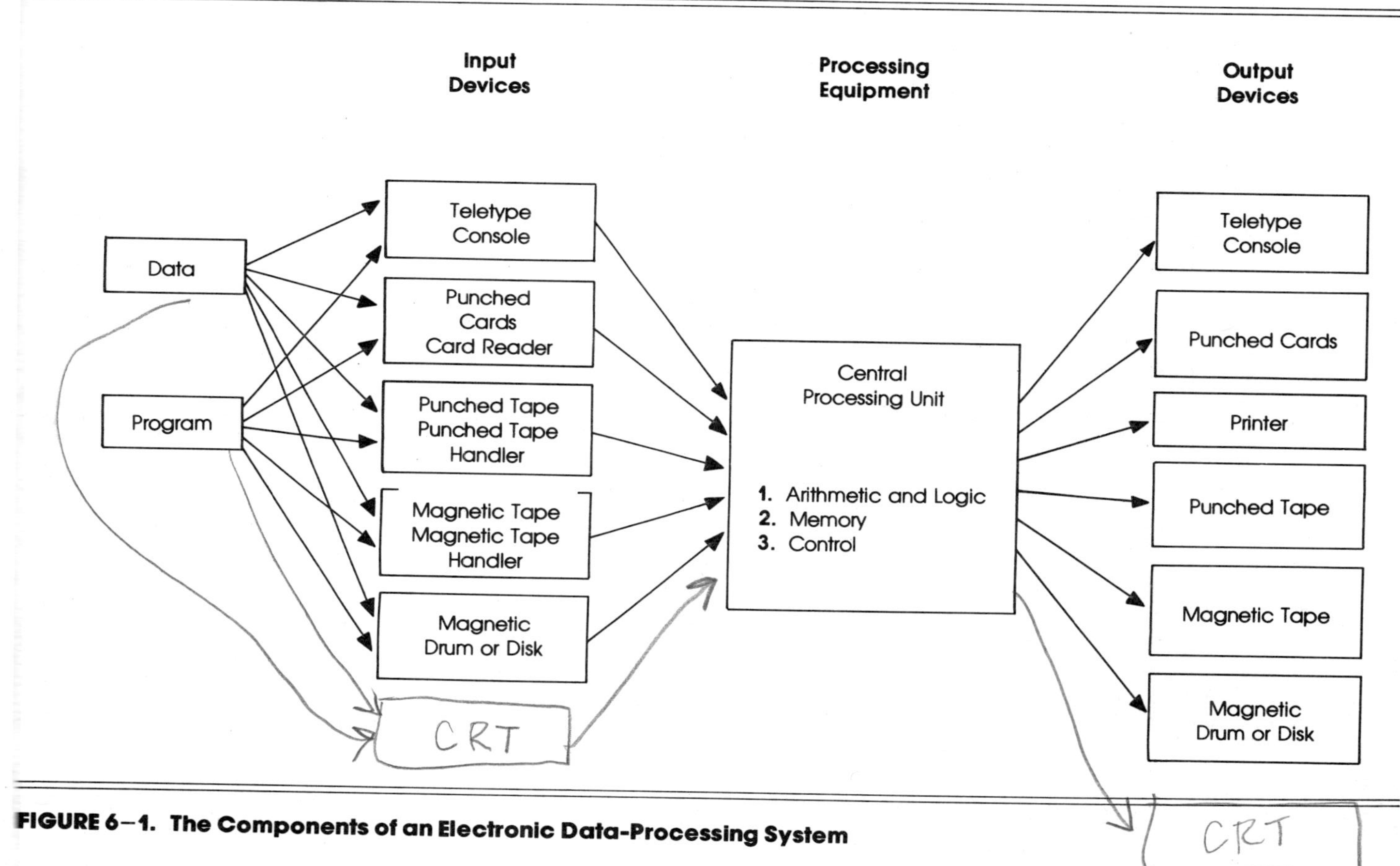

FIGURE 6–1. The Components of an Electronic Data-Processing System

discount computations and even to age the accounts so as to provide a listing of past due account balances.

When the computer is used as described above, the person-readable audit trail often ceases at the point where the original documents are converted to machine-readable form and does not appear again until the final account balances are printed by the computer in the preparation of financial statements. Furthermore, in processing collections on account, the computer is performing both recordkeeping and custodial duties. Such a comprehensive computer installation creates special problems in implementing some of the internal control objectives — such as appropriate separation of responsibilities and appropriate authorization procedures required for a sound system of internal control.

Fraud and the Computer

Fraud has frequently been associated with computerized accounting systems. It is evident from our preceding observations that the use of EDP equipment requires elements of the systems of internal controls to be restructured to meet changes in the operating environment. This has often created control gaps, causing new risks for the auditor — such as increased possibilities of theft, distortion of records, and espionage.

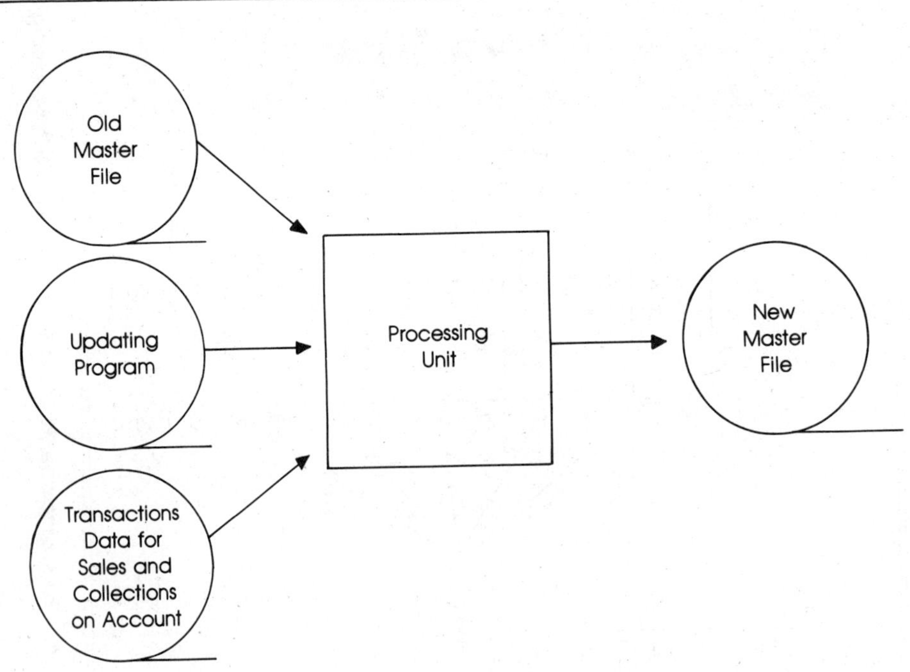

FIGURE 6–2. Systems Flowchart Showing the Updating of the Accounts Receivable Master File

These are sometimes described as *crime by computer*. The Equity Funding Corporation fraud case (described in Chapter 21) is but one example of such computer crime cases. Literally hundreds of other cases have been reported, and one can only wonder how many crimes have been perpetrated without having been discovered. The advantages of using the computer for maintaining accounting records and for related activities, however, cause the usage of this equipment to continue to grow. In the meantime, computer technicians and systems designers continue to wrestle with the problem of potential fraud associated with the use of the computer.

ANALYSIS OF ELECTRONIC DATA-PROCESSING CONTROLS

In Chapter 5 we divided the organizational and procedural elements of internal control into two categories characterized as *administrative controls* and *accounting controls*. Administrative controls for firms using electronic data-processing systems are much the same as they are for firms maintaining their records manually. They are implemented through the company organization chart, procedures manuals, job descriptions, and organizational policies. Those documents, in effect, provide the framework within which the business of the organization is conducted.

EDP accounting control, however, differs significantly from manual accounting control. A firm using a computerized accounting system has two control systems at work: general controls and application controls.[2] The relationships among these controls are illustrated in Figure 6–3.

General Controls

General controls provide the standards and guidelines within which employees associated with the information-gathering, classifying, and summarizing activities carry out their responsibilities. They relate to all EDP activities and can be viewed as the *administrative controls* over the *electronic data-processing department*. Weaknesses in the general controls are regarded as serious, because they may affect all phases of the client's processing. General controls include (1) organization controls within the department; (2) designated procedures for documenting, testing, and approving systems and changes thereto; (3) hardware controls; and (4) controls over access to equipment and data files.

Organization Controls. These controls in the EDP department are important because they must be relied upon to compensate for an operating arrangement that eliminates many of the control effects of the traditional segregation of duties. In the interest of appropriate independence for the department, it is important for it to have a high level of *organizational autonomy* within the firm. In particular, the EDP department should be separated organizationally from the accounting department.

The client should also have an appropriate *segregation of responsibilities within the EDP department*. This requires that the responsibilities for various tasks within the EDP department be separated. These functions are defined briefly as follows.

- ***System analysts*** are the persons who evaluate systems, analyze requirements for information, and design the systems for handling the data-processing needs of the company. They provide the system specifications that serve as guides for the programmers to follow in developing computer programs.
- ***Programmers*** prepare the computer programs to meet the specifications of systems analysts. They are responsible for coding the program logic to meet the requirements of specific processing problems and for documenting the programs in the form of flowcharts.
- ***Computer operators*** are the persons who operate the EDP equipment. They work from a set of operating procedures prepared by the systems analysts. Instructions for operations are documented in the *run manual.*
- ***Data conversion operators*** are equipment operators who convert person-readable documentary data into machine-readable form. They prepare the data for machine processing.
- ***Librarians*** in the electronic data-processing department are in charge of maintaining physi-

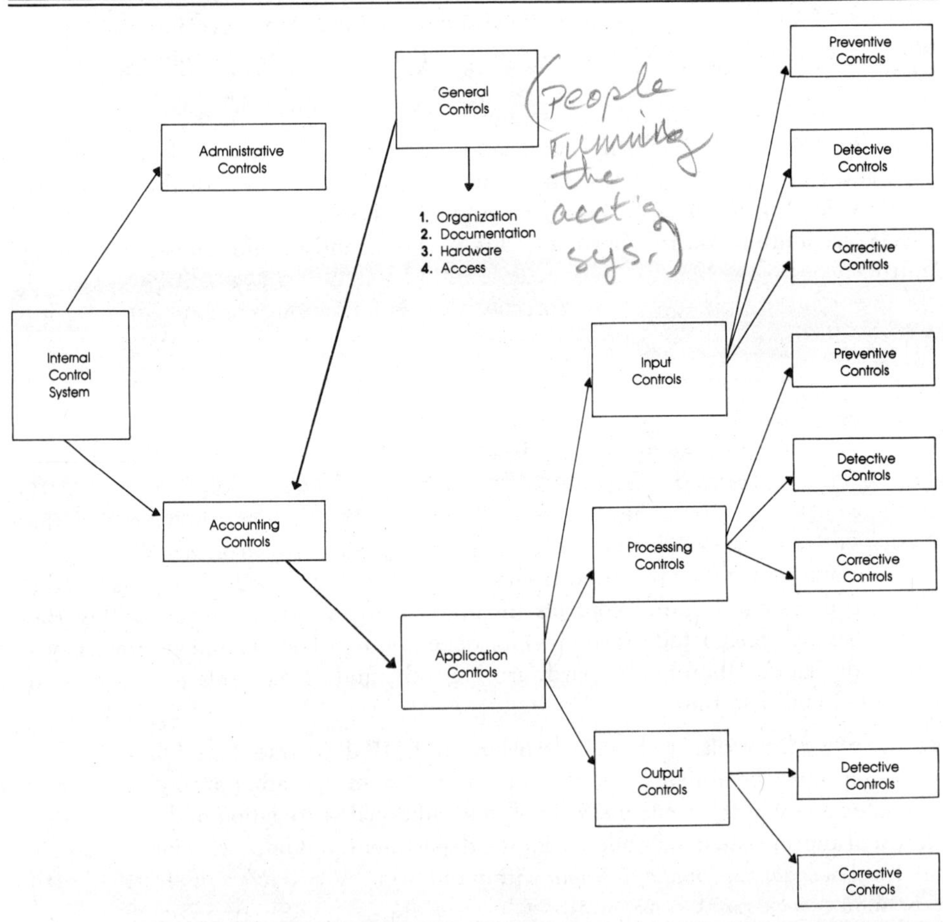

FIGURE 6–3. Flowchart Showing Relationships Among Elements of the Control System

cal safeguards over the systems files (program files, data files, and program documentation). Such protection is necessary to provide adequate controls in design and redesign of systems as well as to maintain controls over data files and programs used in every-day processing.

- The ***quality control group*** acts as liaison between the data-processing center and the various user departments (such as accounting, production, etc.). They perform a function similar to that of internal auditors because they continually test the processing accuracy of both hardware and software. They also review and follow up error messages from the computer, compare control totals to EDP output, review document numbers, and distribute output to various user departments.

If the client has a comprehensive electronic data-processing system, the EDP department may well be organized along the lines shown in Figure 6–4. As you can see from the organization chart, the systems and programming responsibilities of the data-processing system are completely segregated from the information-processing facility (IPF). This should mean that analysts and programmers are precluded from carrying out computer operations and that computer operators are precluded from changing the computer programs in any way. This segregation of responsibilities should be maintained, even with a very small electronic data-processing facility. In sophisticated data-processing systems, it is also desirable to have the library, data conversion, and quality controls functions separated as shown in the organization chart. Such a separation of responsibilities has several benefits:

- It provides an effective check on the accuracy and propriety of changes introduced into the system.
- It prevents operating personnel from implementing revisions without prior approval.
- It eliminates access to the equipment by nonoperating personnel and other people who have knowledge of the system.
- It improves efficiency because the capabilities, training, and skills required in carrying out each of these activities differ significantly.

Another provision that can help compensate for the lack of proper segregation of responsibilities is *required job rotation* among computer operators. All operators should also be *required to take vacations.*

As a means of checking on the separation of duties and on the existence of other organizational control characteristics in an electronic data-processing department, the auditor should ask questions like those shown in Figure 6–5. These questions suggest organizational characteristics that can help compensate for the lack of segregation of custodial, authorization, and recordkeeping responsibilities that is found in electronic data-processing systems.

Documentation Controls. Procedures for documenting, testing, and approving systems and changes thereto should be formalized in *EDP procedures manuals.* Those manuals should describe the procedures to be followed in establishing new EDP systems, testing computer programs, and changing computer programs. They should also carefully describe the documentation required as support for those actions. Ideally such documentation should include information relating to the study of the data system, flowcharts, and computer operating instructions. Many firms develop a ***documentation standards manual*** for the purpose of setting out more specifically the documentation required in support of all programs and program changes. Once a

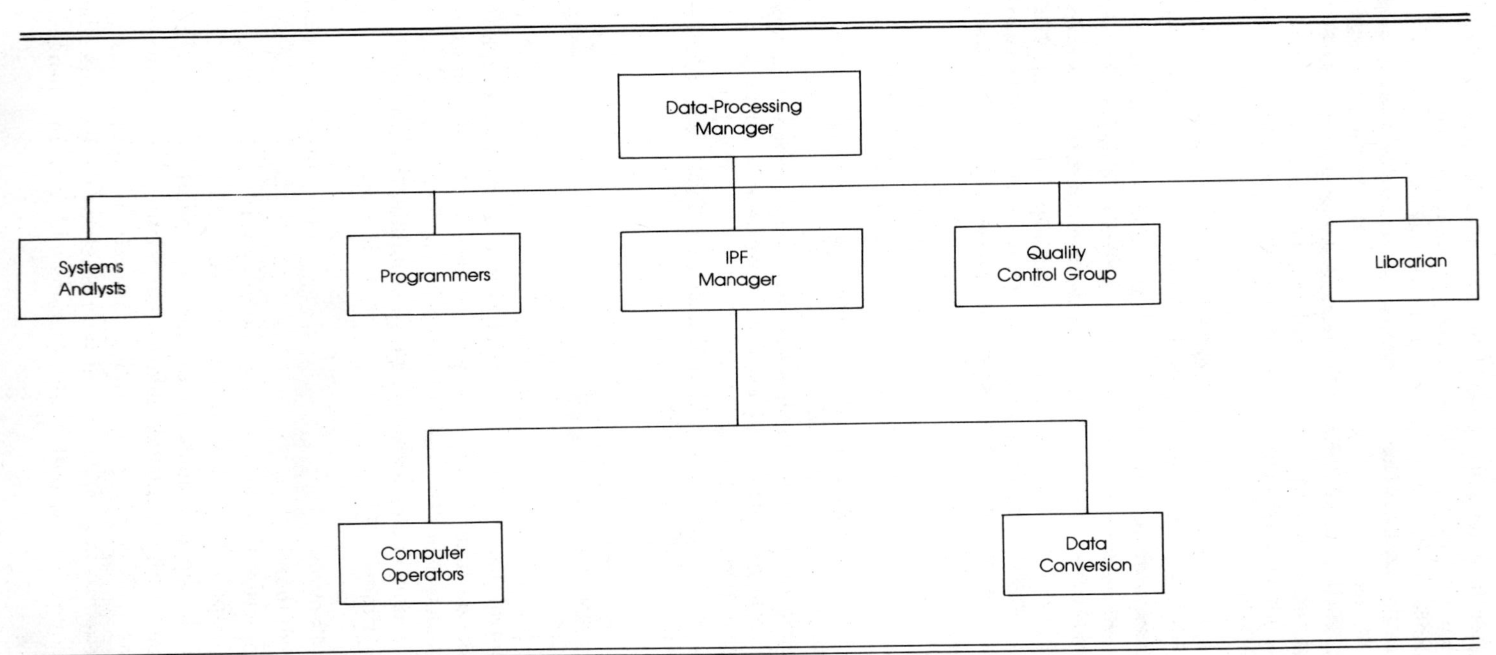

FIGURE 6–4. Organization Chart for an Electronic Data-Processing Department

1. Does the internal auditor's program include a review of the arrangement of duties and responsibilities in the data-processing department?
2. Have procedures been established by which the qualifications of the data-processing employees to perform their functions can be determined?
3. Are proof and control functions performed by personnel other than machine operators and programmers?
4. Are the functions and duties of computer operators and programmers separate and distinct?
5. Are the operators assigned particular jobs or applications subject to periodic rotation?
6. Are operators required to take vacations?
7. Are operators in data processing separated from all duties relating to the initiation of transactions and master file changes?
8. Are departments that initiate changes in master files or program data factors furnished with notices or a register showing changes actually made?
9. Is control being effectively exercised to verify operators' adherence to prescribed operating procedures?
10. Have formal program-testing procedures been established to check the functioning of new applications and revisions to existing programs?
11. Are security provisions in effect at all times to restrict unauthorized access to the data processing department?

Source: Adapted from W. Thomas Porter and William E. Perry, *EDP Controls and Auditing*, 3rd ed. (Boston: Kent, 1981), pp. 256–58.

FIGURE 6–5. Internal Control Questions Relating to Organizational Controls

program has been developed, it should be documented through preparation of a ***run manual***, which generally contains the following sections:

- Problem definition. This section contains a statement of the problem that requires an EDP solution. Examples could include the processing of cash receipts, accounts receivable, and sales.
- System description. This section provides a statement of how the system was designed. It should also include flowcharts, decision tables, and records of data format. For this reason, it is of particular benefit to the auditor.
- Program description and logic. This section explains details of the program. It includes program flowcharts, decision tables, storage locations, console switch settings, program modifications, and program listings, all of which help the auditor to understand how the system was designed to operate.
- Computer operator instructions. This section repeats the instructions found in the program description section for computer operators. It includes instructions for switch settings, the file header and trailer labels, and the proper tape and disk drives to use.
- Listing of controls. This section includes a description of the program controls built into the client's program — controls over input, processing, and output.
- Testing records. This section includes records of debugging procedures performed by systems analysts before the system was placed in operation. All test data used by the client (error messages and other validity tests) in this process should be fully documented. Any recommendations by systems analysts for modifications in the program should be documented in this section.

As you can see from its contents, the run manual can be of much help to the auditor in understanding the client's overall system of EDP controls. The auditor should conduct a thorough review of this documentation as part of the preliminary review of the client's system.

Hardware Controls. These are general controls built into the equipment to detect erroneous internal handling of data and to ensure the equipment's processing accuracy and reliability. *Parity check,* a term explained in Appendix 6–B, is an example of such a hardware control. Other such controls are *dual circuitry* and *auxiliary power supplies,* which can help provide protection against errors that might otherwise occur as a result of a machine malfunction during power surges and outages. Although an auditor is not expected to be an engineering expert, he or she should at least be familiar with the basic controls built into the equipment. In evaluating the operating capabilities of a computer system, the auditor must always consider "downtime" caused by malfunctioning equipment. One way to be sure that the likelihood of errors from malfunctioning equipment is minimal is to examine the client's maintenance contract with the computer supplier. If scheduled maintenance is being performed, the auditor can be reasonably confident that hardware controls are working as they were designed to work. Other general evidence of hardware controls may be obtained by reviewing the client's computer downtime logs.

Access Controls. Access to equipment and data files should be carefully controlled. Operating procedures should be adopted to protect files and programs from possible loss, destruction, or unauthorized use. Those practices should include the following:

- Provisions limiting access to the computer room.
- Controls over the use of library files.
- Qualitative standards to be met in the data conversion phase of operations.
- Operational control procedures for scheduling use of the equipment and for controlling the use of files.
- Physical security for files and equipment. This should include provisions for backup facilities and plans for reconstruction of data that might inadvertently be destroyed.[3]

File security, which relates to measures taken to safeguard files from total loss, is enhanced by such operating practices as the storage of backup files in fireproof vaults and in printed or microfilm form. *File retention policies* are related to file security and pertain to practices that protect against damage or minor loss to data files. One of the most important functions of a file retention policy is to provide for adequate reconstruction of data files if they are lost or destroyed. One of the most popular methods of providing for magnetic tape file reconstruction is the *grandfather, father, son* arrangement.[4] In essence, this is a practice of retaining two generations of both master and transaction file data until a new master file is produced; thus, the current period's master file could be reconstructed if the original copy of that file were lost or destroyed.

When master files are maintained on magnetic disks rather than magnetic tape, updating files usually results in destruction of the previous generation's master file. The most efficient and least costly method of retaining the data in such a situation is to "dump" the file onto tape periodically (weekly or daily). In other instances the data on the disks may be printed out periodically. Either of those files can then be used along with the proper period transaction files in reconstructing the data in the same manner as are the backup tapes in the grandfather, father, son technique mentioned above.

Application Controls

The auditor is always concerned with the accuracy and reliability of the accounting records. If those records are computerized, the specific tasks to be performed by the EDP department must be carefully monitored and controlled to make the records reliable. The practices followed in controlling these tasks are called application controls. They are traditionally subdivided into three categories (listed in chronological order): input controls, processing controls, and output controls.

Input controls are of vital importance in an EDP system because this is the stage in the recordkeeping process at which most errors occur. These controls are designed to provide reasonable assurance that the data received by the EDP department for processing have been (1) properly authorized, (2) properly converted to machine-readable form, and (3) properly accounted for subsequent to submission. Input controls also include controls associated with the rejection, correction, and resubmission of initially incorrect data.

Processing controls are designed to provide reasonable assurance that the computer has processed the data as it was intended to be processed in each individual application. By that we mean that all transactions are processed as authorized, that no authorized transactions are omitted, and that no unauthorized transactions are added.

Output controls are designed to ensure the accuracy of the processing result and to ensure that only authorized personnel receive the output.[5]

Included in each of the previously cited categories of application controls are specific controls designed for specific functions:

- To prevent errors from occurring. These are characterized as *preventive controls.*
- To detect errors. These are characterized as *detective controls.*
- To correct errors. These are characterized as *corrective controls.*

The relationships among the various types of application controls are shown in Figure 6–3. Certain preventive, detective, and corrective controls are implemented during all three stages of processing. We therefore divide our discussion of the various application controls into preventive, detective, and corrective control categories. These controls are described in Figure 6–6.

Preventive Controls.

Preventive controls are designed to detect mistakes that could occur in handling computerized accounting data — before they occur. They are located at various stages in the EDP system but relate primarily to either the input or processing functions. The following preventive controls should be *associated with the input function:*

1. ***Source data authorization.*** All transactions should be processed in accordance with management's general or specific authorization. This normally calls for a visual audit of

INPUT CONTROLS

Preventive

1. Source data authorization
2. Data conversion controls
   a. Keypunch verification
   b. CRT verification
   c. Creation of machine-readable source documents
   d. Turnaround documents
3. Use of sequentially prenumbered forms
4. Programmed checks
   a. Validity tests
   b. Completeness checks
   c. Logic checks
   d. Limit tests
   e. Self-checking digits

Detective

1. Batch control totals
   a. Record counts
   b. Control totals
   c. Hash totals
2. Data conversion controls (same as preventive controls)
3. Machine-readable labels
   a. Header labels
   b. Trailer labels
4. Programmed checks (same as preventive controls)

Corrective

1. Error log
2. Error input record

PROCESSING CONTROLS

Preventive

1. External identification labels
2. Programmed checks (same as for input controls)

Detective

1. Batch control totals
2. Machine-readable labels (same as for input controls)
3. Programmed checks (same as for input controls)

Corrective

1. Error log

OUTPUT CONTROLS

Detective

1. Reconciliations of output data with controls totals
2. Review of output data

Corrective

1. Use of control group
2. Error log
3. Resubmission of erroneous transactions through identical process

FIGURE 6–6. Applications Controls

transactions (cash receipts, cash disbursements, sales, payrolls, etc.) by knowledgeable people in the various departments. Evidence of this review should be provided by notation (signature, initials, or stamped approval on the source document). When like transactions are assembled into batches for processing, the appropriate supervisory personnel in the various departments should indicate their approval by attaching their signature, initials, or stamped approval to each batch. Visual audit at the departmental level can detect misspellings, invalid codes, unreasonable amounts, and other improper conditions to promote accuracy of input data.

2. ***Data conversion controls.*** These controls include such things as keypunch or cathode ray tube (CRT) verification of data, the creation of machine-readable source documents as a byproduct of the manual recording of operations, and the use of turnaround documents. Keypunch or cathode ray tube verification is designed to make sure that the transactions data have been appropriately transferred from person-readable documents to machine-readable media. To ensure agreement between actual transaction data and input data, machine-readable source documents are often created as a byproduct of a manual recording operation. For example, sales data, as it is recorded in the cash register, can be simultaneously recorded in punched tape or entered directly onto magnetic tape for purposes of providing machine-readable data for sales and removals from inventory. Turnaround documents are often used in billing for services such as those provided by a public utility. The billing may be in the form of a punched card which includes a prepunched segment to be returned with the payment of the utility bill. The return segment is thus machine-readable to the same account, etc., contained in the original billing. Such procedures help to reduce the likelihood of erroneous input data.
3. ***Use of sequentially prenumbered forms.*** Use of such forms with full accountability established for all numbers is a traditional control technique, not only for computerized systems but also in manually maintained accounting systems. That practice helps prevent data from being omitted from computer inputs and also reduces the probability of unauthorized data being used.
4. ***Use of the editing capability of the computer.*** This capability can be used to validate input data after it has been converted to machine-readable form. The process requires that the computer be programmed to inspect and accept or reject transactions according to certain *validity or reasonable-limit tests* applied to quantities, amounts, codes, and other data contained in the input records. These often are referred to as ***programmed checks*** or programmed controls. They include:
   a. ***Validity tests***, designed to ensure that the transactions reflect transaction codes and valid characters and fit within a valid field size.
   b. ***Completeness tests***, made to ensure that the input has the prescribed amount of data in all data fields.
   c. ***Logic checks***, used when certain portions or fields of the record bear logical relationships to each other. The computer can be programmed to check for these relationships and to reject illogical combinations.
   d. ***Limit tests***, designed to prevent amounts in excess of certain predetermined limits from being accepted by the computer. For example, a program for payroll can include a provision causing it to reject payroll rate changes greater than a specified percentage of the presently existing rate.
   e. ***Self-checking digits***, used to ensure accuracy of identification numbers such as account numbers. To do this, the computer is programmed to perform an arithmetic operation in such a way that typical errors encountered in transcribing numbers can be detected.[6]

Preventive controls *for the processing function* include external file identification labels and various programming checks:

1. ***External identification labels*** allow operators to visibly identify the type of data included on a magnetic tape. This helps ensure that the proper master files and data will be used by operators in processing transactions. By doing that, they also minimize the possibility that data or program files will be destroyed through operator error.
2. ***Programmed checks*** include such things as checks for validity, for completeness and for logic. These are accomplished by applying limit and reasonableness tests to the data during the processing function. These tests are designed to ensure that the program logic is consistent and that preprogrammed limits are not exceeded during processing.

Detective Controls. Detective controls are designed to alert EDP personnel that a problem exists. They simply point out a problem once it has occurred. The problem must then be corrected to allow the production of correctly processed data. Detective controls *applied to the input and processing functions* often involve use of these elements:

1. ***Batch control totals.*** Batching involves the grouping of a specified number of transactions that are to be processed sequentially. *Control totals* should be established for each block of transactions. These should then be used to make certain that all transactions in the block are being processed. They may relate to *record counts* (the number of records included in each batch) or to *control totals* (the sum of a particular quantitative field of data, such as total sales or total net pay). *Hash totals* are another type of control total. They involve determining the sum of a series of numbers in the data file that would not ordinarily be added, such as account numbers in the accounts receivable file or social security numbers in the payroll file: as each batch of similar transactions is finished, control data for the input, processing, and output stages are compared; if the control total numbers for each of these stages agree, we are justified in assuming that the complete batch of transactions was processed.
2. ***Data conversion controls.*** Data conversion to machine-readable media, performed during the input stage, takes the form of keypunch verification or, more often, cathode ray tube (CRT) verification. As explained earlier, this technique is designed to detect errors that may have occurred in transcribing the data from the original documents to machine-readable media. It should be performed on separate equipment and by operators other than the ones who created the original input media.
3. ***Machine-readable labels.*** The use of machine-readable labels on data recording media during the input and processing stages involves the use of computer program logic to help detect the use of improper file data. *Header labels* include such things as volume, file, and table of contents data. *Trailer labels,* typically containing one or more control totals that can be checked against the total accumulated when the file is read, are used to guard against failure to process any records in the file.
4. ***Programmed checks.*** Validity and reasonableness tests, discussed in the previous section, can be described as detective as well as preventive in nature. The presence of these controls in the client's programs alert operating personnel when a problem occurs or as soon as a programmed limit is exceeded or a validity test is violated. Errors in processing should be recorded in an error log and should be handled by the EDP control group.

Detective controls *for the output function* include such things as these:

1. ***Reconciliations of output data.*** These reconciliations, particularly control totals, should agree with previously established control totals developed in the input phase or in the processing cycle.

2. ***Review of output data.*** This review looks for reasonableness and proper format. Basically, the functions of detective output controls are to determine that the processing does not include unauthorized alterations by the computer operation section and that the data are substantially correct and reasonable.

Corrective Controls. Corrective controls are designed to assist individuals in investigating and correcting the causes of errors that have been detected as data were being processed. Like many of the preventive and detective controls previously discussed, corrective controls can be performed during the input, processing, or output stages of operations. Once errors have been detected, control techniques should be established to be sure that corrections are made to the transactions that are in error and to reenter the corrected transactions into the system. This is normally accomplished in three steps:

1. The ***control group*** should be required to enter all data rejected from the processing cycle in an *error log*. As the erroneous transactions are corrected and reentered, they should be checked off in the error log. The open (unresolved) items appearing in the log should be investigated periodically.
2. An ***error input record*** or ***error log*** (a report explaining the reason for each rejected item) should be prepared. Typically, each error should be returned to the department originating the data for correction and resubmission. The EDP department should provide the source department with instructions for handling any such errors.
3. There should be a ***resubmission of corrected transactions*** to the error detection and input validation processes that were applied to the original transactions.

STUDY AND EVALUATION OF INTERNAL CONTROLS

The general relationship between the study and evaluation of internal controls and the nature, timing, and extent of further audit evidence was developed in Chapter 5. We have seen in this chapter that the objectives of internal control do not vary because of the method of data processing used. Similarly, the generally accepted auditing standards are the same for the auditor, whether or not EDP is used by the client. However, because the environment of an EDP system is significantly different from that of a non-EDP system, the procedures the auditor follows are somewhat different.

In this section, we examine the ways that certain generally accepted auditing standards are interpreted in the EDP environment. After that we see how the general controls and applications controls of the EDP system are reviewed and how they are tested for compliance. Finally, we look at some of the unique features associated with the evaluation of controls for online realtime systems and at the audit of data accumulated by independent service centers.

Generally Accepted Auditing Standards in an EDP Environment

Certain generally accepted auditing standards are interpreted and complied with differently in an EDP environment than in a non-EDP environment. The auditor should recognize those differences as they relate to three of the generally accepted auditing standards.

The *first general standard* requires the auditor to possess adequate technical training and proficiency. In a non-EDP environment, the training and proficiency related to the processing of accounting data can be met by understanding the general manually oriented recordkeeping process. In contrast, the auditor working in an EDP environment must have some training and proficiency in computer operations. This does not mean that he or she must be a computer systems analyst, a programmer, or an engineer to be sufficiently competent to evaluate the internal control system associated with computerized operations. However, the auditor must have sufficient technical training and proficiency to understand the client's full system of internal control, including EDP activities. This understanding should be sufficient to allow an evaluation of the system's essential accounting control features. A special task force of the AICPA has recommended that the staff members of an auditing firm possess at least this knowledge:

- A basic knowledge of the computer systems, parts, functions, and processing capabilities.
- The ability to design and construct a typical systems flowchart of modest complexity and to analyze it for its relative strengths and weaknesses.
- A general expertise in programming languages sufficient to permit the programming of a simple problem.
- An understanding of audit methodology which utilizes the computer.[7]

The *second standard of field work* requires a study and evaluation of internal control. The *third standard of field work* requires that sufficient, competent, evidential matter be gathered to support assertions in the financial statements. Because of the differences in control practices, the auditor will need to apply different auditing procedures when an EDP system is used than she or he would need if the accounting system were maintained manually. The main reasons for these differences in auditing may be summarized as follows:

- Some control procedures in EDP systems have no person-readable documentary evidence showing that they were performed. This requires the auditor to use different methods in compliance testing when a firm uses an electronic data processing system.
- Files and records maintained by EDP systems are most often in machine-readable form and therefore cannot be read without using the computer. This situation generally requires the auditor to use the computer in the evidence-gathering process.
- Since significantly fewer persons are involved in the operation of EDP systems, there is a much higher probability of errors being obscured in an EDP system than in a manually oriented system. Therefore the quality of application controls becomes especially important in judging the reliability of audit evidence.
- Computer processing is much faster and much more accurate than manual processing. Therefore, there is a lower probability of errors due to carelessness, distraction, or fatigue in EDP systems than would be the case in manually maintained systems.[8]

In the following paragraphs, all these differences are related to the auditor's study and evaluation of internal control.

Review of the System

As we have seen, the overall review and evaluation of internal control is conducted at various stages of the audit, occurring chronologically as follows:

1. Preliminary review of internal controls.
2. Preliminary evaluation of internal controls.
3. Final review of internal controls.
4. Final evaluation before compliance testing.
5. Compliance testing of the system.

The first stage of the auditor's overall review and evaluation provides an understanding of these elements:

- The flow of transactions through the accounting system.
- The extent to which EDP is used in each significant accounting application.
- The basic structure of internal accounting controls within the organization.[9]

The auditor's *preliminary review* of a client's EDP system is obtained primarily by inquiry. In conjunction with that inquiry, the auditor may use an internal control questionnaire. The EDP internal control questionnaire is typically divided into two parts — a general part and an applications part. Illustrative questions for the *general part of the questionnaire* can beneficially be divided into four categories: organization controls (see Figure 6–5), documentation controls (see Figure 6–7), file protection controls (see Figure 6–8), and other general controls (see Figure 6–9).

---

1. Does the internal auditor's program include a review of programs supplied by the data-processing department, a review used to prepare audit data?
2. Are blank checks and other negotiable papers used by the data-processing department controlled by someone independent of the machine operators?
3. Have documentation procedures standards been established?
4. Is there supervisory review of documentation for adequacy, completeness, and current status?
5. Are adequate machine operations logs being maintained?
6. Is a schedule kept of reports and documents to be produced by the EDP department?
7. Are output reports and documents reviewed before distribution to ascertain the reasonableness of output?
8. Are there adequate procedures for control over the distribution of reports?
9. Are standardized operator instructions and run descriptions prepared and made available to computer operators?
10. Do the run books contain the following information:
    a. Explanation of the purpose and character of each run?
    b. Identification of all machine system components used and the purpose thereof?
    c. Identification of all input and output forms and media?
    d. Detailed set-up and end-of-run operator instructions including all manual switch settings required?
    e. Identification of all possible programmed and machine halts and specifically prescribed restart instructions for each?

Source: Adapted from W. Thomas Porter and William E. Perry, *EDP Controls and Auditing*, 3rd ed. (Boston: Kent, 1981), pp. 256–58.

FIGURE 6–7. Internal Control Questions Relating to Documentation

1. Have standardized programming techniques and procedures been compiled in a programming manual, and is the manual current?
2. Is a file of test data prepared and maintained for each new or revised program?
3. Are there adequate procedures for authorization, approval, and testing of program revisions?
4. Are reasonable precautions in force to prevent access of operators and unauthorized personnel to program details that are not necessary to their function and that could help them perpetrate deliberate irregularities?
5. Are procedures for issuing and storing magnetic tapes, disk packs, and program documentation formally defined, and are such responsibilities assigned to a librarian as either a full-time or a part-time duty?
6. Are copies of all important master files and programs stored in a fireproof off-premises storage location?
7. Does insurance coverage include the cost of recreating lost files, rewriting destroyed programs, and payments for the use of alternate equipment?

Source: Adapted from W. Thomas Porter and William E. Perry, *EDP Controls and Auditing,* 3rd. ed. (Boston: Kent, 1981), pp. 256–58.

FIGURE 6–8. Internal Control Questions Relating to File Protection

Questions for the *applications part of the questionnaire* cover the client's procedures for controlling the use of the computer in the accounting process. As we have observed earlier, these controls should be designed to prevent, detect, and correct errors and irregularities in the input, processing, and output stages of the EDP data accumulation process. An illustrative application controls questionnaire is included in Appendix 6–A.

The auditor's preliminary review of the system of internal control should begin with the completion of the two questionnaires. The review can also be enhanced by observing client personnel and by reading client documents, such as procedures manuals and run manuals.

After completing the questionnaires, the auditor should be in a position to make a

1. Does the internal auditor's program include a review of the controls of serviced departments over the processing performed by the data-processing department?
2. Have arrangements been made for alternate processing at some other location in the event of breakdown?
3. Is there written procedure for utilizing back-up facilities?
4. Have the back-up facilities been used or tested?
5. Are preventive maintenance procedures in effect to minimize potential equipment failure?

Source: Adapted from W. Thomas Porter and William E. Perry, *EDP Controls and Auditing,* 3rd ed. (Boston: Kent, 1981), pp. 256–58.

FIGURE 6–9. Internal Control Questions Relating to Other General Controls

preliminary evaluation (second stage) of the significance of the accounting controls; this, in turn, should permit him or her to determine the extent to which EDP accounting controls should be further reviewed. Generally, one of four decisions will be reached at this stage in the evaluation process:

1. EDP accounting controls appear to be strong enough to provide a basis for reliance on them. The logical result of this decision would be to complete the review as discussed in the next section before proceeding to test the system for compliance.
2. EDP accounting controls contain a sufficient number of significant weaknesses to preclude reliance on them. In this event, the auditor would discontinue the review of EDP accounting control procedures. Any further audit objectives (beyond transaction validity and internal controls) would have to be met by extensive substantive tests.
3. EDP accounting controls appear adequate, but the auditor will not perform a further review of those controls because of the high costs of such a review in relation to the benefits to be derived from the review. Again, any further audit objectives would have to be met by extensive substantive tests.
4. EDP accounting controls appear adequate, but the auditor will not perform further review of them or rely on them because they are redundant. In this case, the auditor is, in effect, relying on non-EDP controls to assure transaction validity.[10]

As suggested in the preceding paragraphs, final review of EDP accounting controls occurs only when there are significant EDP applications and when EDP controls are judged, as a result of the auditor's preliminary assessment, to be strong enough to rely on them.

In the *final review* stage, the auditor must obtain a more thorough knowledge of the entire system and all its significant accounting applications. This is done by making additional inquiries and observations, by reviewing program and systems documentation, by preparing systems and program flowcharts, and by walk-through reviews of selected transactions. In this stage of the review, the auditor asks questions of the client to ascertain two things:

- The adequacy of general EDP controls pertaining to each significant accounting function.
- The adequacy of prescribed EDP accounting controls over the input, processing, and output functions.[11]

After the auditor has completed the final review of the EDP accounting system, he or she can make a *final assessment* as to (1) the types of errors or irregularities that could occur; (2) the accounting control procedures that should be incorporated into the system to prevent or detect them; and (3) whether the necessary procedures are prescribed in the system. These are determinations that the auditor must make in reviewing a manual processing system as well as an EDP processing system. In this respect, only the procedures to accomplish the objective are changed to accommodate the EDP environment.

Tests of Compliance

When businesses first started using computers, two terms were used to describe the auditor's involvement with computer-generated records. These terms were "auditing around the computer" and "auditing through the computer." *Auditing around the computer* basically calls for the auditors to perform audit procedures (vouching, retracing, scanning, etc.) on the input and output data without regard for the controls built into the computer programs. This attitude toward the audit of computerized records developed largely because most auditors, at that time, had virtually no technical training in computer operations. Auditing around the computer can still be a satisfactory method of auditing computerized records if the computer is simply used as a highspeed calculator and bookkeeping machine. In that situation, it simply performs clerical activities; as long as source documents, ledgers, and journals take the familiar hard copy (printout) form, those data can be verified in essentially the same manner as are manually maintained records. As we have observed throughout this chapter, however, modern computers are more generally used in systems applications that are far more sophisticated than that.

Computers are often directly involved in handling approval and recording of transactions without leaving documentary evidence of programs controls built into the system. When such controls are performed, *leaving no visible evidence*, it becomes necessary to employ a technique to verify them. When we do this, we are *auditing through the computer*.

In recent years, most audit firms have also achieved the capability of *auditing with the computer:* essentially, this involves using the computer to perform audit procedures on computerized records, a topic we take up in Chapter 7.

In the paragraphs that follow, our discussion will focus on auditing through the computer — by the performance of compliance tests designed to determine whether an EDP system has properly utilized both the visible and nonvisible controls assumed, after the preliminary review, to be in existence.

We know that the purpose of tests of compliance is to provide reasonable assurance that the accounting controls prescribed by the client are actually being applied. In these tests, we are concerned with three basic questions:

- Were the necessary procedures performed?
- How were the procedures performed?
- By whom were the procedures performed?

Some EDP accounting controls leave *visible evidence* of having been performed. Some examples of such controls are these:

- Files documenting program changes for each EDP application, along with approvals of those changes.
- EDP-generated error listings and exception reports.

The typical approach used in verifying compliance with these controls is to examine the documentation and all necessary corroborating evidence. For example, for the controls listed above, the auditor would first vouch program changes to approval signatures of appropriate personnel; then the auditor would ascertain that the control group followed up error listing by returning the erroneous transactions to the proper personnel for corrections and resubmission.

Compliance testing for *nonvisible program controls* has to rely on the development of machine-readable evidence. This is especially the case with the *programmed checks* discussed earlier (i.e., validity tests, limit and reasonable tests, etc.). Because of the critical importance of these controls to the presentation of the financial statements, the auditor should perform audit tests to be sure that transactions having unacceptable conditions will be rejected by the computer and followed up for correction. The most widely accepted procedures for this type of compliance testing involve the use of test data, parallel simulation, and integrated test facility approaches.

In the ***test data approach*** (sometimes referred to as the use of ***test decks***), the auditor first obtains duplicate copies of the client's master programs (usually on magnetic tape). The object of the test data is to test the controls included in each program (as shown in Figure 6–10). This is done by preparing a series of hypothetical transactions to be processed with the duplicate copy of the client's master program. Some of the transactions will be valid (i.e., no program checks, limits, or control amounts violated). Other transactions will violate the controls supposedly incorporated into the program. Thus, as the hypothetical transactions are run, the program checks should identify the invalid transactions and print them on an error listing or exception report. For example, suppose that the client's payroll master program prescribed a limit test of 60

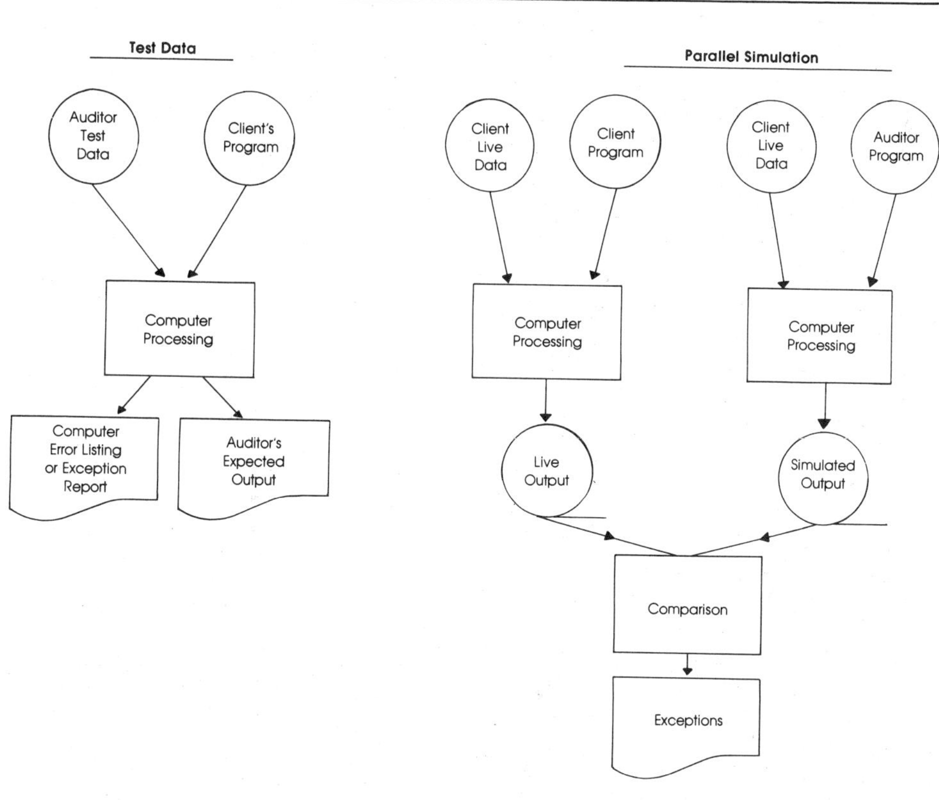

FIGURE 6–10. Comparison of Test Data and Parallel Simulation Approaches for Tests of Compliance

hours a week. To test this program control, the auditor might insert in the test data a transaction that contains 60.5 hours in a pay period. If the control is performing as prescribed, the program should pinpoint the exception and include it in an error list or exception report. The use of test data is a relatively simple, fast, and inexpensive way to test programmed controls. However, this approach has the following weaknesses:

- Since the program tested is usually a duplicate program supplied by the client, the auditor has no assurance that he or she is testing the program actually used by the client, unless the program is intercepted immediately after processing and duplicated at that point.
- Controls tested with test data are those that exist only at a point in time (i.e., when the test data is being processed). There is no provision for testing controls over the entire audit period unless repetitive tests are made.
- With test data, there is no opportunity to examine the documentation actually processed by the system.
- The scope of the test data approach is limited to the auditor's imagination. It is important, therefore, to be very careful in developing erroneous hypothetical transactions that would reveal material weaknesses in internal control.

Parallel simulation (sometimes called ***controlled reprocessing***) utilizes "live" client data that is reprocessed with an auditor-controlled program (Figure 6–10). Usually the software used in parallel simulation is a generalized audit program, prepared by the auditor. It consists of a series of specialized computer subroutines designed to perform the same process and produce the same result as the client's programs. The output of this system is then compared with the client's output from the same processing operation. Exception reports can then be prepared and investigated by the auditor.

Parallel simulation may be performed at various interim dates during the audit period. It may also be applied to the reprocessing of historical data. Parallel simulation has several advantages over the test data approach. For one thing, the auditor is using duplicate files of real client data, which can be verified by vouching transactions to source documents and approvals. Additionally, since the auditor's simulated system is separate from the client's, the simulated data can be processed at an independent facility. Furthermore, sample sizes in this approach can be greatly expanded at relatively small costs.

The major disadvantage of parallel simulation is the time, effort, and expense of producing the program. Both the initial cost and the cost of the yearly update to keep the program current can be significant. Since the client will ultimately be billed for this cost, the auditor will have to convince the client that the program's ultimate benefits exceed those costs.

The ***integrated test facility (ITF)*** approach involves the creation of a "dummy" or fictitious subsystem (or ***minicompany***) within the client's EDP system. The auditor then processes fictitious data for the minicompany simultaneously with the client's live data and appends those records to the client's regular system. Test data specially coded to correspond with the "dummy" master files should contain all kinds of errors and exceptions (similar to the test data approach described earlier).

The advantage of the ITF approach is that it *provides assurance that the test data are subjected to the same programs controls as the client's live data.* The disadvantage of this approach is that it risks exposure and contamination of the client's master files and financial statements with the "dummy" file data.

Still other accounting controls in the EDP activity leave *neither visible nor machine-readable evidence* of having been performed. An example of these controls is segregation of duties within the EDP department. Evidence of such controls, in this case, can only be obtained by *observing client personnel* and *making corroborative inquiries*.

Special Considerations Concerning Online Realtime Systems

Online realtime systems are considered the most advanced EDP systems in use. ***Online*** refers to equipment or devices that are in direct communication with a computer's central processing unit. ***Realtime*** pertains to the mode of operation allowing input functions to be performed simultaneously with the processing function. As a result, output is made immediately available to the user. Online devices consist of remote terminals, connected to a central processing unit by means of telephone or other direct communication lines. The reservations systems used by major airlines, sales terminals used by major department store chains, and terminals used in certain types of transactions at major banks and savings and loan institutions — all are examples of online realtime installations.

The major advantage of online realtime systems over alternate batch-processing systems is their processing speed and instantly available output. Potential disadvantages, which can be prevented through proper controls, are chiefly these: (1) the danger of *unauthorized access* to sensitive or confidential client files (including unauthorized access to assets such as cash); and (2) risk of *loss of the audit trail* by an inadvertent or careless mistake or by intentional concealment of irregularities by client personnel.

The same general controls and application controls common to all EDP systems also apply to systems that utilize online realtime processing. However, the way these controls are implemented differs somewhat from the typical EDP controls for batch-processing systems. Specifically, controls must be instituted to help prevent the occurrence of the two major potential weaknesses. We now examine each of those weaknesses more completely for the purpose of identifying the controls that should be in place to reduce the probability of their occurrence.

- *Unauthorized access to assets* may occur because, in an online realtime system, many persons (including, potentially, some who are unauthorized) have access to the central processing unit through the terminals. To provide necessary controls, each authorized user should have a *code or other identification* number that must be used to secure access to the files he or she is to work with. Files with greater levels of sensitivity should be protected through multiple layers of protective codes. Internal controls associated with the system can be strengthened by requiring a validity check of identification numbers before they can be used to obtain assess to computer files.
- *The loss of the audit trail* may occur in an online realtime system during the instantaneous updating of files. In this process, old master files recorded on master tapes or disks are continuously updated by writing over them. Unless the computer is programmed to save detail from a file, it will not do so. Therefore, details needed for the audit trail may be lost. Controls in this area include *logging input* at the terminal level or the central processing unit level to identify the terminal from which a transaction was entered. Also, although it is expensive to do so, the daily *dumping of input* from various input terminals onto hard copy

can provide appropriate documentation of the audit trail. The audit trail can best be maintained by programming the computer to *save the files needed for the audit trail* and to print them on command.

Compliance testing in an online realtime system can involve the use of test data. However, this is potentially dangerous because it can contaminate the client's master files. To avoid such contamination, the computer must be programmed to reverse the "dummy" test transactions, which is often difficult. Usefulness of parallel simulation is also limited because of the great difficulty involved in simulating an online realtime system.

Continuous monitoring is a technique that is often used in testing transactions entered into an online realtime system. With this method, an audit routine is added to the client's master program. Transactions are sampled at random intervals and output from the audit routine is used to test controls. To provide for such monitoring, ***audit modules*** or ***audit hooks*** must be built into the client's operating and applications programs. These modules provide a means for the auditor to select a transaction that exceeds certain limits (e.g., a dollar amount) for testing. Once the audit hook has identified the transaction, the computer can be programmed to *tag the transaction and to trace it through the system as it is processed*. The computer can then be programmed to provide a hard copy printout of the paths followed by the transaction as well as the data with which the transaction interacts in processing. An alternative method to tagging is the use of an ***audit log***, which records transactions selected for audit in a special file made available only to the auditor for the purpose of making further audit tests.

Audits of Time-Sharing Systems Administered by Independent Service Centers

Some clients have a large volume of transactions but still find it impractical or impossible to own their own computer. These clients often utilize ***computer service centers.*** Such centers employ large computers and process data on a contractual basis. Each of the many users might have one or more remote terminals for entering input data, such as payrolls, sales, receivables, and cash receipts. The service center, which maintains the client's master files and programs, processes the client's data and returns the output in usable form to the client.

The major concerns for the auditor examining records produced by computer service centers are the accounting controls exercised during processing of the data at the service center, along with the controls over input and output of data. Of course, computer service centers are almost always independent (i.e., not connected through ownership or joint interests) with respect to clients. However, the mere independence of the service center does not provide conclusive evidence as to controls exercised over data. If the service center processes a significant portion of the client's financial data, the auditor should consider the possible need to study and evaluate the service center's system of control over those data.

The criteria for an auditor's study and evaluation of internal processing controls at the service center are the same as the criteria for evaluating a client's EDP system.

These factors generally determine the extent of auditor involvement with controls at the service center:

- The significance of the data processed by the service center to the overall financial statements.
- The complexity of the data-processing system used by the service center.
- The extent to which the auditor desires to rely on controls over such a system to reduce substantive tests on financial statement balances emerging from the system.

On the basis of these factors, the auditor may decide to perform an extensive study and evaluation of service center controls utilizing test data and other compliance tests. In addition to evaluating the client's controls over input and programs, the auditor in this case should also obtain satisfaction on these points:

- That boundary protection for files within the computer is adequate to prevent unauthorized access to client master files.
- That proper identification and password numbers are required for all users before sensitive client data files can be accessed.
- That file reconstruction capability of the service center is adequate.

When a service center facility processes data for numerous clients, there would be massive confusion and interruption to service center operations if each user's auditor were to ask to perform tests of the service center's controls. Therefore, in many cases, service centers employ their own independent auditors to study and evaluate the system of controls at the center and to issue a special report on the adequacy and effectiveness of those controls. Then, the user's auditor may decide the extent to which he or she will rely on the report of the service center's auditor regarding controls at the service center.

SUMMARY

In this chapter we have been concerned with the general problem of evaluating systems of internal control for firms having computerized accounting records. We began by recognizing that such systems should still have the same six basic characteristics identified and discussed in Chapter 5. But a number of functions normally segregated when accounting records are maintained manually must be combined to allow the electronic data-processing system to operate effectively. Therefore the practical *inability to appropriately separate responsibilities* must be compensated for by other control practices when a firm uses a computerized accounting system. Also specialized checking procedures must be used to verify the *reliability of accounting data*.

We began by identifying the organizational structure that should be established for an electronic data-processing department when it is used to accumulate accounting data. We characterized that structure, including the job descriptions and various other documents defining the responsibilities of computer department personnel, as *general controls*. We explained how those controls can compensate for violations of some of the six basic internal control characteristics and how they should be evaluated by use of a general internal control questionnaire covering the organizational controls, the documentation controls, and the file protection controls within the EDP department.

Next, we considered *application controls* that should be in place for data input, data processing, and data output. These were characterized as *preventive controls*, designed to prevent errors from being incorporated into the computerized accounting records; *detective controls*, designed to detect errors in the input, processing, or output activities; and *corrective controls*, constituting the follow-up on errors detected in any of the three phases of computer operations. We include Appendix 6–A to show an internal control questionnaire that can be used in evaluating application controls.

In the last part of the chapter, we observed that if the auditor is going to rely on the prescribed controls, he or she must test those to see whether employees are actually following them. We characterized this as *compliance testing* and observed that its objective is the same with both manual and computerized accounting records. Controls in an EDP system include those leaving visible evidence or machine-readable evidence, as well as those leaving neither visible nor machine-readable evidence. We concentrated our discussion on the evaluation of controls leaving machine-readable evidence. These controls can be tested by using the test data, parallel simulation, or integrated test facility (ITF, minicompany) approaches. Finally, we discussed the special control problems associated with online realtime systems as well as records processed at independent service centers and the procedures that may be followed to compensate for those problems.

APPENDIX 6–A: Specific Application Questionnaire

PART II – SPECIFIC APPLICATION QUESTIONNAIRE

Accountant

Date ________

Company ____________________ Period ended ____________________

Branch, division, or subsidiary ________________________________

SYSTEMS QUESTIONNAIRE

GENERAL

This questionnaire must be completed for each major accounting application where a computer is used to process financial data. This intensive review should be planned so that all the client's major accounting applications will be covered over a period of years and that the audit papers will contain a reasonably current description of all the clients major computerized accounting applications. Completed questionnaires not revised in a particular year should be reviewed to determine if they basically reflect the client's current systems and procedures. If they do not, changes should be recorded on the questionnaire.

The answers to the questions are designed so that:

1. A "no" answer indicates less than the minimum control required. The reason for the "no" must be explained. As a "no" answer may have an impact on the audit, the audit program should be revised where applicable. The attached audit program guide lists audit steps to be considered when "no" answers are received to selected questions.

2. A "N/A" answer (not applicable) means a particular question is not a factor in the client's system. All "N/A's" must be accompanied by a brief explanation.

Appendix 6–A is from W. Thomas Porter and William E. Perry, *EDP Controls and Auditing*, 3rd ed. (Boston: Kent, 1981), pp. 259–67.

INSTRUCTIONS

Review the list of applications prepared in Part I, Section C. Determine those applications which have an audit impact and decide which are major applications from an audit standpoint. For the applications selected, perform the following:

1. Ask the client to provide system flowcharts. If the client does not have system flowcharts, it may be necessary to prepare them in order to complete the review of internal control. Since this may involve a large amount of time, consult with the partner or manager on the engagement before undertaking any large flowcharting effort. Lack of such documentation is a weakness in management control and should be an item in our letter to management.

2. Complete the specific application questionnaire.

3. Review the flowcharts and the questionnaire and verify their accuracy by testing them against the documentation, output, and other hard copy which can be used to determine that the controls operate as described. These tests *do not* have to be extensive since they are only concerned with systems verification.

4. Obtain a set of control reports for a test period. Review for evidence that controls are being utilized and enforced in accordance with the system design.

5. Examine controls over error correction procedures, paying particular attention to those controlling corrections to master file records.

6. Analyze the completed questionnaire(s):

   a. Evaluate the effect of internal control deficiencies and prepare a list of comments with recommendations for improvement. Wherever possible, an explanation of the possible consequences resulting from inadequate controls should be included.

   b. Review your findings and conclusions with the audit management on the engagement.

   c. Prepare comments to be included in a letter to management.

PART II – SPECIFIC APPLICATION QUESTIONNAIRE

Accountant

Date

Company ______________________ Period ended ______________________

Branch, division, or subsidiary ______________________

At the completion of the review of a particular application, the following information should be considered for inclusion in the workpapers as deemed necessary to adequately describe the system and the work performed.

1. System flowchart.
2. Written description of the system with copies of input and output layouts and sample printouts.
3. A brief description of the file control procedures.
4. Notes regarding the procedural tests performed to verify the existence and satisfactory operation of controls.
5. Application questionnaire.
6. Notes concerning control weaknesses, if any, in the system.

Note: Identify any gaps which exist in the audit trail associated with this system and consider possible solutions such as a special printout of the file used, a special computer program for audit purposes, alternative audit procedures, etc. Discuss your conclusions with the audit management on the engagement.

Accountant

Date

PART II – SPECIFIC APPLICATION QUESTIONNAIRE

Company ______________________ Period ended ______________________

Branch, division, or subsidiary ______________________

The following audit steps are to be used as a guide in response to "no" answers to selected questions on the Data Processing Internal Control Questionnaire Part II - Specific Applications. These suggested audit steps relate only to the more significant questions and are to be used as a guide in developing an audit program for a specific engagement. Additional or alternative auditing procedures, considered necessary or desirable should be adopted. For "yes" answers, the related audit step should be marked "N/A" (not applicable).

B. Input Controls

Question 1

1. Transactions may be lost before they enter the system and are recorded for data processing. Make a reasonably comprehensive test of current or historical records to insure that basic source transactions are being entered in the system. Determine the initial document which triggers an entry to the system and trace a test group to insure they were recorded.

Question 2

2. Transactions may be improperly entered in the system. Follow the basic procedure outlined in Item 1 to verify if data is being correctly recorded.

Question 3

3. Data may be lost during the conversion process. Obtain, for a current date, a printout of the original data and the data after conversion. On a test basis, verify that the conversion is complete and correct. This can be done by tracing items from one file to another in both directions.

Question 4

4. As in Question 1, transactions may be lost. On a test basis, communicate directly with other locations and obtain copies of the data they submitted as input to the system. Trace this input to the related files.

Question 5

5. Obtain several examples of errors and trace through to correct processing.

C. Program and Processing Controls

Question 2

6. Improper or erroneous data may be entering the system. Obtain, on a test basis, a printout of the input data and manually perform the tests outlined in the Questionnaire.

D. Output Control

Questions 2 and 3

7. Control totals may not be correctly verified. On a test basis, review the reconciliation and vertification of control totals.

Questions 4 and 5

8. Error corrections may be improperly entered. On a test basis, review error listings and trace corrections into the related files.

E. File Control

Question 4

9. Errors may have gotten into master file records. On a test basis, obtain a printout of the master file and trace selected items to their underlying support.

PART II – SPECIFIC APPLICATION QUESTIONNAIRE

Accountant

Date

Company ________ Period ended ________

Branch, division, or subsidiary ________

Question	Yes	No	Answer Remarks *
A. Documentation			
General			
Documentation consists of workpapers and records which describe the system and procedures for performing a data processing task. It is the basic means of communicating the essential elements of the data processing system and the logic followed by the computer programs. Preparing adequate documentation is a necessary, though frequently neglected, phase of computer data processing. A lack of documentation is an indication of a serious weakness within the management control over a data processing installation.			
Is the program or programs supported by an adequate documentation file?			
A minimum acceptable level of documentation should include: 1. Problem statement 2. System Flowchart 3. Transaction and activity codes 4. Record layouts 5. Operator's instructions 6. Program flowchart 7. Program listing 8. Approval and change sheet 9. Description of input and output forms			
B. Input Controls			
General			
Input controls are designed to authenticate the contents of source documents and to check the conversion of this information into machine readable formats or media. Normally these controls will not be designed to detect 100% of all input errors since such an effort would be either too costly or physically impractical. Therefore, an economic balance must be maintained between the cost of error detection and the economic impact of an undetected error. This should be considered when evaluating input control. Judgment must be used when identifying "essential information," the accuracy of which *must* be verified. The following questions can also be used to evaluate internal control practices used in master file conversions.			
1. Are procedures adequate to verify that all transactions are being received for processing?			
(To accomplish this, there must be some systematic procedure to insure all batches that enter the machine room for processing or conversion are returned from the machine room. Basic control requirements are being met if the answer to *one* of the following questions is "yes.")			
a. Are batch controls (at least an item count) being established *before* source documents are sent to the machine room for keypunching or processing?			

*NOTE — In the case of a "No" answer, the "Remarks" column should (1) cross-reference either to the audit program step (or steps) which recognizes the weakness or to the supporting permanent file memorandum on accounting procedures which explains the mitigating circumstances or lack of importance of the item, and (2) indicate whether the item is to be included in the draft of the letter to management on internal control.

PART II – SPECIFIC APPLICATION QUESTIONNAIRE

Accountant ____

Date ____

Company ____ Period ended ____

Branch, division, or subsidiary ____

Question	Answer Yes	No	Remarks *
b. If batch controls are established *in* the machine room, is there some other form of effective control (such as prenumbered documents) which provides assurance that all documents have been received?			
c. If no batch control is used, is there some other means of checking the receipt of all transactions? If yes, describe. (For example, in a payroll operation, the computer may match attendance time cards and corresponding job tickets for each employee as the master file is updated.)			
2. Are procedures adequate to verify the recording of input data on cards, magnetic tape or disk?			
(Control is being maintained if the answer to *one* of the following questions is "yes.") a. Are important data fields subject to machine verification?			
b. If only some (or none) of the important data fields are verified, is an alternate checking technique employed?			
Some acceptable alternate techiniques are: 1) Self checking digits 2) Control totals 3) Hash totals 4) Editing for reasonableness			
3. If input data is converted from one form to another (card to tape, cards to disk) prior to processing on the computer system, are controls adequate to verify the conversion?			
Normal conversion controls include: a. Record Counts b. Hash totals c. Control totals			
4. If data transmission is used to move data between geographic locations, are controls adequate to determine transmission is correct and no messages are lost? Controls would normally include one or more of the following:			
a. Message counts b. Character counts c. Dual transmission			
5. Is the error correction process and the re-entry of the corrected data subject to the same control as is applied to original data?			
(If control over corrections is lax, the correction process may be the largest source of error in the system.) 6. Are source documents retained for an adequate period of time in a manner which allows identification with related output records and documents?			
(Failure to maintain documents may make it impossible to recreate files in the event they are damaged or destroyed.)			

*NOTE — In the case of a "No" answer, the "Remarks" column should (1) cross-reference either to the audit program step (or steps) which recognizes the weakness or to the supporting permanent file memorandum on accounting procedures which explains the mitigating circumstances or lack of importance of the item, and (2) indicate whether the item is to be included in the draft of the letter to management on internal control.

PART II – SPECIFIC APPLICATION QUESTIONNAIRE

Accountant

Date

Company ____________________ Period ended ____________________

Branch, division, or subsidiary ____________________

Question	Answer Yes	Answer No	Remarks *
C. Program and Processing Controls			
General			
Programs should be written to take the maximum advantage of the computer's ability to perform logical testing operations. In many cases, tests which could be employed are not used because the programmer does not know the logical limits of the data to be processed. Since the auditor will usually have a good knowledge of the proper limits of the data, he is in a position to detect weakness in program controls.			
1. Is adequate control exercised to insure that all transactions received are processed by the computer?			
(Note: The answer to one of the following two questions should be "yes.")			
a. If predetermined batch control techniques are being used, does the computer accumulate matching batch totals in each run wherein the corresponding transactions are processed, and is there adequate provision for systematic comparison of computer totals with predetermined totals?			
(Note: Having the computer internally match totals is more accurate than external visual matching. In addition, it should be noted that very often original batch totals are internally combined into pyramid summary totals as different types of input transactions are merged during progressive stages. This is acceptable if it does not create a serious problem in attempting to locate errors when the overall totals are compared.)			
b. If no batch total process is in use, is there an effective substitute method to verify that all transactions are processed? (Example: Any application where source documents are serially numbered and the computer system checks for missing numbers.)			
2. Is adequate use being made of the computer's ability to make logical data validity tests on important fields of information?			
These tests may include:			
a. Checking code or account numbers against a master file or table.			
b. Use of self-checking numbers.			
c. Specific amount or account tests.			
d. Limit tests.			
e. Testing for alpha or blanks in a numeric field.			
f. Comparison of different fields within a record to see if they represent a valid combination of data.			
g. Check for missing data.			

*NOTE — In the case of a "No" answer, the "Remarks" column should (1) cross-reference either to the audit program step (or steps) which recognizes the weakness or to the supporting permanent file memorandum on accounting procedures which explains the mitigating circumstances or lack of importance of the item, and (2) indicate whether the item is to be included in the draft of the letter to management on internal control.

PART II – SPECIFIC APPLICATION QUESTIONNAIRE

Accountant

Date

Company ______________________ Period ended ______________________

Branch, division, or subsidiary ______________________

Question	Yes	No	Remarks *
3. Is sequence checking employed to verify sorting accuracy of *each* of the following:			
a. Transactions which were presorted before entry into the computer (sequence check on first input run)?			
b. Sequenced files (sequence check incorporated within processing logic that detects out–of–sequence condition when files are updated or otherwise processed)?			
4. Are internal header and trailer labels on magnetic media files (i.e., tape, disk, data cell) tested by the program?			
Such tests should include: a. Input 1) Correct file identification 2) Proper date 3) Correct sequence of files 4) Record count check 5) Control and hash total check b. Output Retention date has passed. 5. If processing requires more than 30 minutes of computer time for any one program, are there adequate provisions for restarting the program if processing is interrupted?			
D. **Output Control** **General** Output control is generally a process of checking if the operation of input control and program and processing controls has produced the proper result. The following controls should be in effect in most data processing operations: 1. Are internal header and trailer labels written on all magnetic media files created as output?			
Header labels consist of an identification record which is written as the first record on each file. The labels normally contain: a. File identification (usually a code number) b. Date created c. File sequence number (for multiple reel or volume files) d. Retention date or period (used to determine the earliest date on which a file may be released for reuse) Trailer labels consist of a control record which is written as the last record on each file. These labels normally contain: a. Record count b. Control or hash totals for one or more fields c. End-of-file or end-of-reel code			

*NOTE — In the case of a "No" answer, the "Remarks" column should (1) cross-reference either to the audit program step (or steps) which recognizes the weakness or to the supporting permanent file memorandum on accounting procedures which explains the mitigating circumstances or lack of importance of the item, and (2) indicate whether the item is to be included in the draft of the letter to management on internal control.

Accountant

Date

PART II – SPECIFIC APPLICATION QUESTIONNAIRE

Company ______________________ Period ended ______________________

Branch, division, or subsidiary ______________________

Question	Answer Yes	No	Remarks *
2. Are all control totals produced by the computer reconciled with predetermined totals? (Basically, control totals on input plus control totals on files to be updated should equal the control totals generated by the output.)			
3. Are control total reconciliations performed by persons independent of the department originating the information and the data processing department?			
4. Are error corrections and adjustments to the master file:			
a. Prepared by the serviced departments' personnel and			
b. Reviewed and approved by a responsible official who is independent of the data processing department?			
5. Are procedures adequate to insure that all authorized corrections are promptly and properly processed and that the corrections result in a file that matches the control totals?			
E. File Control			
General			
As data processing files (cards, tape, disk) can be destroyed by careless handling or improper processing, proper file control is vital in all data processing installations.			
1. Are control totals maintained on all files and are such totals verified each time the file is processed?			
2. Are all files supported by enough backup to permit the file to be recreated if it is destroyed during processing?			
(The kind of support required depends upon the type of the file. The most common types of backup are outlined below. In each case minimum control is being maintained if any of the support described is being provided.			
a. Card files			
Since each card in the file is an independent physical unit, processing damage will usually only effect a few cards which can be repunched. However, one safeguard should be employed. The retention period on source documents should be adequate to permit repunching of card files.			
b. Tape files			
Are all tape files subject to a minimum of son, father, grandfather support? (For example, if an updated accounts receivable tape is written every day, today's tape (son) should be supported by yesterday's tape (father), the day-before-yesterday's tape (grandfather), and all the transaction records which were used to update the files. Should today's tape be destroyed, the father tape and the transactions could be processed to recreate today's tape.)			

*NOTE — In the case of a "No" answer, the "Remarks" column should (1) cross-reference either to the audit program step (or steps) which recognizes the weakness or to the supporting permanent file memorandum on accounting procedures which explains the mitigating circumstances or lack of importance of the item, and (2) indicate whether the item is to be included in the draft of the letter to management on internal control.

Accountant

Date

PART II – SPECIFIC APPLICATION QUESTIONNAIRE

Company ______________________ Period ended ______________________

Branch, division, or subsidiary ______________________

Question	Answer		
	Yes	No	Remarks *
c. Disk files and mass storage files File support can take many different forms. The following are typical of controls employed:			
1) Is the file periodically dumped to magnetic tape and are all transaction records retained between dumps so files may be reconstructed?			
2) If disk packs are used, are the disks supported on a son, father basis?			
3) Is the file periodically dumped to cards or to the printer and are all transaction records retained between dumps so files may be reconstructed?			
4) Are two copies of the file maintained on the disk with only one file being updated until the processing has been verified?			
3. Are all files physically protected against damage by fire or other accidental damage?			
This question may be answered "yes" if the following provisions have been made: a. All files, supporting transaction files and programs should be stored in temperature and humidity controlled fireproof storage areas.			
b. All important master files should be reproduced periodically and the duplicate copy should be stored off-premises. If this technique is not employed, some alternate form of master file protection should be employed.			
4. Are there adequate provisions for periodic checking of the contents of master files by printout and review, checking against physical counts, comparison to underlying data, or other procedures?			

*NOTE — In the case of a "No" answer, the "Remarks" column should (1) cross-reference either to the audit program step (or steps) which recognizes the weakness or to the supporting permanent file memorandum on accounting procedures which explains the mitigating circumstances or lack of importance of the item, and (2) indicate whether the item is to be included in the draft of the letter to management on internal control.

APPENDIX 6–B: Glossary of Computer Terms

This glossary contains selected terms used in computer auditing, only some of which are used in the text. They will all, however, be useful to you in practice.

Several different types of cross-references are used. Their meanings are as follows:

1. *Same as:* The referenced term has the same meaning as the term containing the reference and the referenced term is the preferred one.
2. *Synonymous with:* The referenced term has the same meaning as the term containing the reference and the term containing the reference is the preferred one.
3. *Contrast with:* The referenced term is a related term that has a meaning significantly different from that of the term containing the reference.
4. *See also:* The referenced term is a related term whose definition provides additional background or clarification.
5. *See:* The referenced term is an alternative or qualified form of the term containing the reference.

Access Time. The time interval between the instant when a computer or control unit calls for a transfer of data to or from a storage device and the instant when this operation is completed. Thus, access time is the sum of the waiting time and transfer time. Note: In some types of storage, such as disk and drum storage, the access time depends upon the location specified and/or upon preceding events; in other types, such as the core storage, the access time is essentially constant.

Accounting Control. The plan of organization and the procedures and records that are concerned with the safeguarding of assets and the reliability of financial records. See also *control.*

Audit Software. A collection of programs and routines associated with a computer that facilitates the programming and operation of the computer and the evaluation of machine-readable records for audit purposes. See also *computer-audit program.*

Audit Trail. A means for systematically tracing the progress of specific items of data through the steps of a process (particularly from a machine-generated report or other output back to the original source document) in order to verify the validity and accuracy of the process.

Auditape. An audit software package developed by Haskins & Sells. Probably the first one developed for audit purposes. Most of the major accounting firms have now developed audit software packages, some of which are available to interested parties. In addition, several commercial software companies have developed audit software packages.

Auditing. The examination of information by a third party other than the preparer or the user with the intent of establishing its reliability and the reporting of the results of this examination with the expectation of increasing the usefulness of the information to the user. Specific purpose audits are conducted by specific types of auditors. See also *external auditor, internal auditor.*

This glossary is from W. Thomas Porter and William E. Perry, *EDP Controls and Auditing,* 2nd ed. (Boston: Kent, 1977), pp. 252–62. Almost 85 percent of the entries included here are taken or adapted from, with permission, the glossary contained in *AUERBACH Computer Technology Reports,* published by AUERBACH Publishers Inc. The definitions of *data base, dump, emulator, high order, record layout, storage protection,* and *utility program* are taken from, with permission, William C. Mair, Donald R. Wood, and Keagle W. Davis, *Computer Control & Audit* (Institute of Internal Auditors, 1976, copyright © 1976 by Touche Ross & Co.).

Auxiliary Storage. Storage that supplements a computer's *working storage*. Note: In general, the auxiliary storage has a much larger capacity but a longer *access time* than the working storage. Usually, the computer cannot access auxiliary storage directly for instructions or instruction operands.

Back-up. Pertaining to equipment or procedures that are available for use in the event of failure or overloading of the normally used equipment or procedures. Note: The provision of adequate back-up facilities is an important factor in the design of every data-processing system and is especially vital in the design of *realtime* systems, where a system failure may bring the total operations of a business to a virtual standstill.

Batch Processing. A technique in which items to be processed are collected into groups (i.e., batched) to permit convenient and efficient processing. Note: Most business applications are of the batch-processing type; the records of all transactions affecting a particular master file are accumulated over a period of time (e.g., one day) and are then arranged in sequence and processed against the master file.

Batch Total. A sum of a set of items which is used to check the accuracy of operations on a particular batch of records.

Batching. The process of grouping a large number of transactions into small groups usually for control purposes. See also *batch total.*

Card. Usually same as punched card; see also *edge-notched card, edge-punched card, magnetic card.*

Card Field. In a punched card, a group of columns (or parts of columns) whose punchings represent one item. For example, a three-column field might hold an item representing order quantity, whose value ranges from 000 to 999.

Central Processor. The unit of a *computer* system that includes the circuits which control the interpretation and execution of *instructions*. Synonymous with *CPU* (central processing unit) and *main frame*.

Change Register. Printout of the results of testing changes to a program. This register acts as a document for management review and approval of the change and as a permanent record of all changes to a program.

Character. A member of a set of mutually distinct marks or signals used to represent *data*.

Check Bit. A binary *check digit*. Note: A *parity check* usually involves appending a check bit of the appropriate value to an array of bits.

Check Digit. A *digit* associated with a *word* or part of a word for the purpose of checking for the absence of certain classes of *errors*.

COBOL (COmmon Business Oriented Language). A *process-oriented language* developed to facilitate the preparation and interchange of programs to perform business *data-processing* functions. Every COBOL *source program* has four divisions, whose names and functions are as follows: (1) identification division identifies the source program and the output of a compilation; (2) environment division specifies those aspects of a data processing problem that are dependent upon the physical characteristics of a particular computer; (3) data division describes the data that the *object program* is to accept as input, manipulate, create, or produce as output; (4) procedure division specifies the procedures to be performed by the object program, by means of English-like statements such as SUBTRACT TAX FROM GROSS-PAY GIVING NET-PAY. PERFORM PROC-A THRU PROC-B UNTIL X IS GREATER THAN Y.

Coding. (1) An ordered list or lists of the successive *instructions* which will cause a computer to perform a particular *process*.

Communication. The transfer of information from one person, place, or device to another. See also *data communications.*

Compiler. A computer program that *compiles.* Note: Compilers are an important part of the basic *software* for most computers; they permit the use of *process-oriented languages* that can greatly reduce the human effort required to prepare computer programs. However, the computer time required to perform the compilation process may be excessive, and the *object programs* produced by the compiler usually require more execution time and more storage space than programs written in *machine language* or *symbolic coding.*

Completeness Tests. A type of *program check* designed to test input for the prescribed amount of data in the input fields.

Computer. A device capable of solving problems by accepting *data,* performing prescribed *operations* on the data, and supplying the results of these operations, all without intervention by a human operator.

Computer-Audit Program. A computer program written for a specific audit purpose or procedure. A computer-audit program can be written by or under the supervision of the auditor for a specialized audit application (i.e., brokerage house auditing) or can be developed by adapting *audit software* routines for specific audit purposes.

Computer Operations. A function within an EDP department primarily concerned with the production of computer-processed information. With the computer at the hub, computer operations are primarily concerned with bringing data into the computer center, getting it to the computer, and delivering results to users at minimum costs.

Computer Operator Instructions. A set of instructions prepared by a programmer, as part of program *documentation,* for specific use by computer operators when operating programs. Synonymous with *console run book.* See also *operating system.*

Configuration. A specific set of equipment units which are interconnected and (in the case of a computer) programmed to operate as a system. Thus, a computer configuration consists of one or more *storage* devices and one or more *input-output* devices. Synonymous with *system configuration.*

Console. A portion of a *computer* that is used for communication between operators or maintenance engineers and the computer, usually by means of displays and manual controls.

Console Log. See *log.*

Console Run Book. A book containing computer operator instructions for a run. Same as *computer operator instructions.*

Console Switch. See *switch.*

Control. The plan of organization and all the coordinate methods and procedures adopted within a business to safeguard its assets, check the accuracy and reliability of its accounting data, promote operational efficiency, and encourage adherence to prescribed managerial policies (AICPA definition). See also *accounting control.*

Control Log. A record of *control totals* used by the control function in an *EDP department* to enable the reconciliation of control totals generated in related computer processing runs.

Control Totals. Totals developed on important data fields in input records and on number of records processed to ensure that data have been transmitted, converted, and processed correctly. See also *batch total, hash total, record count.*

Control Unit. (1) A section of a *computer* that effects the retrieval of instructions in the proper sequence, interprets each instruction, and stimulates the proper circuits to execute each instruction. (2) A device that controls the operation of one or more units of peripheral equipment under the overall direction of the *central processor*.

CPU. Same as *central processor*.

Cross-footing Check. A *program check* in computer processing in which individual items used in arriving at result items are totaled and the total is compared to an independently derived result total; for example, a total net pay figure reached by subtracting a deduction item total from a gross pay total can be compared with a total net pay figure developed by other program steps.

Data. Any representation of a fact or idea in a form capable of being communicated or manipulated by some *process*. The representation may be more suitable for interpretation either by human beings (e.g., printed text) or by equipment (e.g., punched cards or electrical signals). Note: *Information*, a closely related term, is the meaning that human beings assign to data by means of the known conventions used in its representation.

Data Base. An integrated file containing multiple record types or segments that may be accessed in a nonsequential manner.

Data Communications. The transmission of data from one point to another.

Data Processing. A systematic sequence of *operations* performed upon *data;* e.g., handling, computing, merging, sorting, or any other transformation or rearrangement whose object is to extract information, revise the data, or alter their representation.

Data Transcription. Conversion of *data* from one *medium* to *another* without alteration of their information content. Note: The conversion may be performed by a manual keystroke operation, by a computer system, or by a specialized converter, and may or may not involve changes in the format of the data.

Data Transfer. The movement of *data* from a source to a destination (e.g., from one storage location or device to another).

Data Transmission. See *data communications*.

Decision Table. A table that lists all the contingencies to be considered in the description of a problem, together with the corresponding actions to be taken. Note: Decision tables permit complex decision-making criteria to be expressed in a concise and logical format. They are sometimes used in place of *flowcharts* for problem definition and documentation. Moreover, *compilers* have been written to convert decision tables into programs that can be executed by computers.

Detail File. A *file* containing information that is relatively transient, such as records of individual transactions that occurred during a particular period of time. Synonymous with *transaction file*. Contrast with *master file*.

Direct Access. Same as *random access*.

Disk Storage. A type of *magnetic storage* that uses one or more rotating flat circular plates with a magnetic surface on which data can be stored by selective magnetization of portions of the surface.

Document. (1) A *medium* and the *data* recorded on it for use (e.g., a check, report sheet, book). (2) By extension, any record that has permanence and can be read by man and/or machine.

Documentation. The collecting, organizing, storing, citing, and disseminating of *documents* or the *information* recorded in documents. Note: Complete, up-to-date documentation of all *programs* and their associated operating procedures is a necessity for efficient operation of a computer installation and maintenance of its program.

Drum Storage. A type of *magnetic storage* that uses a rotating cylinder with a magnetic surface on which data can be stored by selective magnetization of portions of the surface.

Dump. A printed record of the contents of computer storage usually produced for diagnostic purposes.

EAM (Electrical Accounting Machine). Pertaining to *data-processing* equipment that is predominantly electromechanical such as *keypunches, collators,* mechanical *sorters,* and *tabulators.* Note: EAM equipment is still widely used in lieu of, or in support of, electronic digital computers. (The computers themselves are classified as *EDP* equipment rather than EAM equipment.)

Edge-Notched Card. A card of any size provided with a series of holes near one or more of its edges for use in coding information for a simple mechanical search technique. By notching away the edge of the card into a particular hole, the card can be coded to represent a particular item. Cards containing desired information can be selected from a deck by inserting a long needle into the appropriate hole position and lifting the deck, allowing notched cards to fall from the deck while unnotched cards remain.

Edge-Punched Card. A card in which data can be recorded by punching holes, in patterns and codes similar to those used for *punched tape,* near one edge. Note: Many punched-tape readers and punches can be equipped to utilize edge-punched cards as well. *Unit records* can be stored and selectively retrieved more conveniently on edge-punched cards than on punched tape.

Edit. (1) To modify the form or *format* of data. Editing may involve the rearrangement of data, the addition of data (e.g., insertion of dollar signs and decimal points), the deletion of data (e.g., suppression of leading zeros), *code translation,* and the control of layouts for printing (e.g., provision of headings and page numbers). (2) An input control technique used to detect input data that are incomplete, invalid, unreasonable, etc. Editing can be performed manually or by computer. See also *edit run.*

Edit Run. A separate computer process to edit input data before regular processing of *detail files* and *master files* takes place.

EDP (Electronic Data Processing). *Data processing* performed largely by electronic equipment, such as electronic digital *computers.*

EDP Department. This department is responsible for *systems analysis, program development,* and *computer operations.*

Electrical Accounting Machine. See *EAM.*

Emulator. A hardware device that enables a computer to execute object language programs written for a different computer design.

Error. A discrepancy between a computed, measured, or observed quantity and the true, specified, or theoretically correct value or condition. Note: An error may result from an equipment fault or a human mistake, but errors also arise from insufficient precision which is foreseen and accepted.

Error Listing. *Hard copy* of errors detected in the processing of data by *program checks* in *edit runs* or in regular processing.

Execute. To carry out an *instruction* or an *operation,* or to run a *program.*

External Auditor. Usually a CPA, typically involved in rendering an independent opinion on the reasonableness of an organization's financial representations.

External Label. A specialized record used to identify an assorted collection of data, such as a paper label attached to a reel of magnetic tape to identify its contents. Contrast with *internal label.*

Field. (1) In a *punched card,* a group of columns whose punchings represent one *item.* (2) A subdivision of a computer *word* or *instruction,* e.g., a group of bit positions within an instruction that hold an address. (3) A subdivision of a *record.*

File. A collection of related records, usually (but not necessarily) arranged in sequence according to a *key* contained in each record. Note: A *record,* in turn, is a collection of related items, while an *item* is an arbitrary quantity of data that are treated as a unit. Thus, in payroll processing, an employee's payrate forms an item, all the items relating to one employee form a record, and the complete set of employee records forms a file.

File Maintenance. The updating of a *file* to reflect the effects of nonperiodic changes by adding, altering, or deleting data, e.g., the addition of new programs to a *program library* on magnetic tape.

File Processing. The periodic updating of a *master file* to reflect the effects of current data, often transaction data contained in a *detail file,* e.g., a weekly payroll run.

File-Protection Ring. A removable plastic or metal ring the presence or absence of which prevents an employee from writing on a magnetic tape and thereby prevents the accidental destruction of a magnetic tape file. Note: The most common method involves the insertion of the ring to allow writing and the removal of the ring to prevent writing.

Fixed-Length Record. A *record* that always contains the same number of characters. The restriction to a fixed length may be deliberate, in order to simplify and speed processing, or it may be dictated by the characteristics of the equipment used. Contrast with *variable length record.*

Flowchart. A diagram that shows the structure and general sequence of operations of a *program* or *process* by means of symbols and interconnecting lines which represent operations, data, flow, and equipment.

Format. A predetermined arrangement of *data* (e.g., characters, items, lines), usually on a form or in a file.

FORTRAN (FORmula TRANslating System). A *process-oriented language* designed to facilitate the preparation of computer programs to perform mathematical computations. The essential element of the FORTRAN language is the assignment statement; for example, $Z = X + Y$ causes the current values of the variables X and Y to be added together and causes their sum to replace the previous value of the variable Z.

Hard Copy. Pertaining to *documents* containing data printed by data-processing equipment in a form suitable for permanent retention (e.g., printed reports, listings, and logs), as contrasted with "volatile" output such as data displayed on the screen of a cathode-ray tube.

Hardware. Physical equipment, such as mechanical, magnetic, electrical, and electronic devices. Contrast with *software.*

Hash Total. A *control total* which can be used to establish the accuracy of processing whereby a total of data is made by adding values which would not normally be added together, e.g., the sum of a list of customer numbers.

Header Label. A machine-readable record at the beginning of a file containing data identifying the file and data used in file control.

High Order. The left-most digit within a number representing the highest order of magnitude in the number.

IDP (Integrated Data Processing). Data processing by a system that coordinates a number of previously unconnected processes in order to improve overall efficiency by reducing or eliminating redundant data-entry or -processing operations. An example of IDP is a system in which data describing orders, production, and purchases are entered into a single processing scheme that combines the functions of scheduling, invoicing, inventory control, etc.

Index. (1) An ordered list of the contents of a *document, file,* or *storage* device, together with keys that can be used to locate or identify those contents. (2) To modify an *address* by adding or subtracting the contents of an *index register.*

Index Register. A *register* whose contents can be added to or subtracted from an *address* prior to or during the execution of an *instruction.* Note: Indexing (i.e., the use of index registers) is the most common form of *address modification* used in stored-program computers. Indexing can greatly simplify programming by facilitating the handling of *loops, arrays,* and other repetitive processes. Some computers have many index registers, some have only one, and others have none.

Input. (1) The process of transferring *data* from *external storage* or *peripheral equipment* to *internal storage* (e.g., from punched cards or magnetic tape to core storage). (2) Data that are transferred by an input process. (3) Pertaining to an input process (e.g., input *channel,* input *medium*). (4) To perform an input process. (5) A signal received by a device or component. Note: As the above definitions indicate, *input* is the general term applied to any technique, device, or medium used to enter data into data-processing equipment, and also to the data so entered.

Input-Output. A general term for the techniques, devices, and media used to communicate with data-processing equipment and for the data involved in these communications. Depending upon the context, the term may mean either input *and* output or input *or* output. Synonymous with *I/O.*

Input-Output Channel. A *channel* that transmits *input* data to, or *output* data from, a *computer.* Note: Usually a given channel can transmit data to or from only one peripheral device at a time. However, some current computers have *multiplexor channels,* each of which can service a number of simultaneously operating peripheral devices.

Internal Auditor. An auditor who is typically involved in appraising the accounting, financial, and operating controls within an organization in which he is employed and who renders the results of his appraisal to management.

Internal Label. A record magnetically recorded on tape to identify its contents as an integral part of the program function. Contrast with *external label.* See also *header label.*

Interrecord Gap. Same as *interblock gap.*

I/O. Same as *input-output.*

Keypunch. A keyboard-actuated card punch. The punching in each column is determined by the key depressed by the operator.

Library. An organized collection of information for study and reference purposes. See also *program library.*

Log. A record of the operations of data-processing equipment, which lists each job or run, the time it required, operator actions, and other pertinent data.

Loop. A sequence of *instructions* that can be executed repetitively, usually with modified addresses or modified data values. Each repetition is called a cycle.

Machine Language. A *language* that is used directly by a computer. Thus, a machine-language program is a set of instructions that a computer can directly recognize and execute, and that will cause it to perform a particular process.

Machine-Readable. Pertaining to *data* represented in a form that can be sensed by a data-processing machine (e.g., by a card reader, magnetic tape unit, or optical character reader).

Magnetic Card. A thin, flexible card with a magnetic surface upon which *data* can be stored. Note: Some large-capacity *auxiliary storage* devices use a large number of magnetic cards, contained in interchangeable cartridges. One card at a time is extracted from the cartridge, transported to a read/write station where data are read and/or recorded and then returned to the cartridge.

Magnetic Tape. A tape with a magnetic surface on which *data* can be stored by selective polarization of portions of the surface.

Main Frame. (1) Same as *central processor*. (2) That portion of a computer system which is not considered *peripheral equipment*.

Master File. A *file* containing relatively permanent information which is used as a source of reference and (usually) is periodically updated. Contrast with *detail file*.

Medium. Any agency or means for representing data; usually, a material on which data are recorded. Note: Among the most widely used media are *punched cards*, *punched tape*, *magnetic tape*, and printed forms.

Memory. Same as *store* (i.e., a device into which data can be inserted and retained, and from which the data can be obtained at a later time).

Multiplexor. A device that makes it possible to transmit two or more messages simultaneously over a single *channel* or other transmission facility.

Multiprocessing. The simultaneous execution of two or more sequences of *instructions* in a single computer system. This may be accomplished through the use of either two or more *central processors* (i.e., a *multiprocessor* system) or a single *central processor* with several *instruction registers* and several sequence counters.

Multiprogramming. A technique for handling two or more independent *programs* simultaneously by overlapping or interleaving of the execution of the various programs; usually controlled by an *operating system* that attempts to optimize the overall performance of the computer system in accordance with the priority requirements of the various jobs.

Object Language. A *language* that is an output from a *translation* process. Contrast with *source language*.

Object Program. A *program* expressed in an *object language* (e.g., a machine-language program that can be directly executed by a particular computer).

Offline. Pertaining to equipment or devices that are not in direct communication with the *central processor* of a computer system. Contrast with *online*. Note: Offline devices cannot be controlled by a computer except through human intervention.

Online. Pertaining to equipment or devices that are in direct communication with the *central processor* of a computer system. Contrast with *offline*. Note: Online devices are usually under the direct control of the computer with which they are in communication.

Operating System. An organized collection of routines and procedures for operating a computer. These routines and procedures will normally perform some or all of the following functions: (1) Scheduling, loading, initiating, and supervising the execution of *programs*. (2) Allocating storage, input-output units, and other facilities of the computer system. (3) Initiating and controlling input-output operations. (4) Handling *errors* and *restarts*. (5) Coordinating communications between the human operator and the computer system. (6) Maintaining a log of system operations. (7) Controlling operations in a *multiprogramming*, *multiprocessing*, or *time-sharing* mode.

Operation. (1) A general term for any well-defined action. (2) The derivation of a unit of *data* (the "result") from one or more given units of data (the "operands") according to rules that completely specify the result for any permissible combination of values of the operands. (3) A *program* step undertaken or executed by a *computer* (e.g., addition, multiplication, comparison, shift, transfer).

Output. (1) The process of transferring *data* from internal storage to external storage or to peripheral equipment (e.g., from core storage to magnetic tape or a printer). (2) Data that are transferred by an output process. (3) Pertaining to an output process (e.g., output *channel*, output *medium*). (4) To perform an output process. (5) A signal transmitted from a device or component. Note: As the above definitions indicate, *output* is the general term applied to any device or medium used to take data out of data processing equipment, and also to the data so transferred.

Parallel Processing. Same as *multiprocessing.*

Parity Bit. A *bit* (binary digit) that is appended to an array of bits to make the sum of all the 1-bits in the array either always even (even parity) or always odd (odd parity). For example, see the following table:

	Even Parity	Odd Parity
Data bits	0 1 1	0 1 1
	0 1 0	0 1 0
	0 1 0	0 1 0
	0 1 1	0 1 1
	0 1 1	0 1 1
	1 1 0	1 1 0
Parity bit	1 0 1	0 1 0

Parity Check. A *check* that tests whether the number of 1-bits in an array is either even (even parity check) or odd (odd parity check).

Peripheral Equipment. All the *input-output* units and *auxiliary storage* units of a computer system. Note: The *central processor* and its associated *working storage* and *control units* are the only parts of a computer system that are *not* considered peripheral equipment.

Process. A system of *operations* designed to solve a problem or lead to a particular result.

Process-Oriented Language. A *language* designed to permit convenient specification, in terms of procedural or algorithmic steps, of data processing, or of computational *processes.* Examples include *ALGOL, COBOL,* and *FORTRAN.*

Program. (1) A plan for solving a problem. (2) To devise a plan for solving a problem. (3) A computer routine, i.e., a set of *instructions* arranged in proper sequence to cause a *computer* to perform a particular *process.* (4) To write a computer routine.

Program Check. Tests in the program to determine the absence of certain classes of errors in input or for the correct performance of processing steps. The tests are carried out by a series of *instructions* in a *program.*

Program Flowchart. A flowchart diagramming the processing steps and logic of a computer program; contrast with *systems flowchart.*

Program Library. An organized collection of tested *programs,* together with sufficient *documentation* to permit their use by users other than their authors.

Program Run Manual. See *run manual.*

Program Segment. See *segment.*

Programmer. A person who devises *programs.* Note: The term *programmer* is most suitably applied to a person who is mainly involved in formulating programs, particularly at the level of *flowchart* preparation. A person mainly involved in the definition of problems is called an *analyst,* while a person mainly involved in converting programs into coding suitable for entry into a computer system is called a *coder.* In many organizations, all three of these functions are performed by programmers.

Programming Language. An unambiguous language used to express *programs* for a computer.

Random Access. Pertaining to a *storage* device in which the access *time* is not significantly affected by the location of the data to be accessed; thus, any item of data that is stored online can be accessed within a relatively short time (usually less than one second). Synonymous with *direct access.* Contrast with *serial access.*

Read-after-Write Check (Dual Read/Write). A second read or write station that compares input from a first input station for accuracy. This control is used with input/output equipment such as card readers and punches.

Read/Write Head. A head used to read or write data on a storage medium.

Realtime. (1) Pertaining to the actual time during which a physical process takes place. (2) Pertaining to a mode of operation in which the instants of occurrence of certain events in the system must satisfy restrictions determined by the occurrence of events in some other independent system. For example, realtime operation is essential in computers associated with process control systems, message switching systems, and reservation systems.

Record. A collection of related items of data. Note: A *file,* in turn, is a collection of related records. Thus, in payroll processing, an employee's payrate forms an item, all the items relating to one employee form a record, and the complete set of employee records forms a file. See also *fixed-length record* and *variable-length record.*

Record Count. A count of the number of records in a file or the number of records processed by a program.

Record Layout. A diagram showing the nature, location, size, and format of fields within a record.

Record Mark. A *special character* used in some computers either to limit the number of characters in a data *transfer* operation or to separate blocked *records* on tape.

Reproducer. A *punched card* machine that has two separate card-feed paths, one equipped with a sensing station and the other with a punching station. Its basic function is to *copy* data from one *deck* of cards into another deck of cards in card-by-card fashion.

Rerun. To make another attempt to complete a job by executing all or part of the process again with the same or corrected inputs.

Rerun Point. A place in a *program* where its execution can be reestablished after an equipment failure or some other interruption. Note: At a rerun point, sufficient data have been recorded to permit a *restart* from that point in the event of a subsequent interruption. Thus the provision of rerun points at reasonable intervals can save computer time by making it unnecessary to rerun a program from the beginning whenever a run is interrupted.

Restart. To reestablish the execution of a *program* whose execution has been interrupted, using the data recorded at a *rerun point.*

Run. A performance of a specific *process* by a *computer* on a given set of *data,* i.e., the execution of one routine or of several routines that are linked to form one operating unit, during which little or no human intervention is required.

Run Manual. A manual documenting the processing system, program logic, controls, program changes, and operating instructions associated with a computer run.

Segment. One of the parts into which a program is divided by a *segmentation* process.

Segmentation. The division of a *program* into parts so that each part can be stored within a computer's *working storage* and contains the necessary linkages to other parts. Each part thus formed is called a *segment*. Note: Segmentation makes it possible to execute programs that exceed the capacity of a computer's working storage; it is performed automatically by some *compilers*.

Self-Checking Number. A numeral that contains redundant information (such as an appended check digit) which permits the numeral to be checked for accuracy after it has been transferred from one medium or device to another.

Sequence. To arrange items so that they are in the order defined by some criterion of their keys. Note: Often the keys are groups of numbers or letters, and the items are arranged so that the keys of successive items are in numerical or alphabetical order.

Sequential Processing. Same as *batch processing*.

Serial Access. Pertaining to a *storage* device in which there is a sequential relationship between the *access times* to successive locations, as in the case of *magnetic tape*. Contrast with *random access*.

Software. The collection of *programs* and routines associated with a *computer* (*compilers* and *operating systems*) that facilitates the programming and operation of the computer. Contrast with *hardware*.

Source Document. A document from which data are extracted, e.g., a document that contains typed or handwritten data to be keypunched.

Source Language. A *language* that is an input to a *translation* process. Contrast with *object language*.

Source Program. A *program* written in a *source language* (e.g., written in *COBOL*, *FORTRAN*, or *symbolic coding* for *input* to a *compiler* or assembler).

Storage Protection. A provision by the software to protect against unauthorized reading or writing between portions of storage.

Store. (1) A device into which *data* can be inserted and retained, and from which the data can be obtained at a later time. (2) To insert or retain data in a storage device.

Stored-Program Computer. A *computer* that, under control of *instructions* held in an internal *store*, can synthesize, alter, and store instructions as if they were data and can subsequently execute these new instructions. Thus a stored-program computer is capable of modifying its own *programs*, a feature that permits great flexibility and responsiveness to changing problem conditions.

Switch. (1) In a *program*, an *instruction* or parameter that causes selection of one of two or more alternative paths (i.e., sequences of instructions). The selection, once made, persists until it is altered. (2) In *hardware*, a device that can be placed in one of two or more distinct settings by a human operator or an instruction.

Symbolic Coding. *Coding* that uses *machine instructions* with *symbolic addresses*. Note: The input to most *assemblers* is expressed in symbolic coding. Mnemonic *operation codes* are usually employed along with the symbolic addresses to further simplify the coding process. For example, a two-address instruction that subtracts an employee's taxes from his gross pay might be written SUB TAX GPAY.

Systems Analysis. The examination of an activity, procedure, method, technique, or business to determine what needs to be done and how it can best be accomplished.

System Configuration. (1) Same as *configuration*. (2) The rules for interconnecting the available equipment units that collectively define the range of possible *configurations* for a particular computer system.

Systems Flowchart. A flowchart diagramming the flow of work, documents, and operations in a data-processing application.

Telecommunications. The transmission of signals over long distances, such as by radio or telegraph. See also *data communications*.

Temporary Storage. Storage locations used by a *program* to store intermediate results that are generated and must be temporarily retained.

Terminal. A point or device in a system or communications network at which data can either enter or leave.

Test Data. See *tests*.

Tests. Predetermined data used to run a complete system or program to establish its adequacy and reliability.

Time Sharing. (1) The use of a given device by a number of other devices, programs, or human users, one at a time and in rapid succession. (2) A technique or system for furnishing computing services to multiple users simultaneously, while providing rapid responses to each of the users. Note: Time-sharing computer systems usually employ *multiprogramming* and/or *multiprocessing* techniques, and they are often capable of serving users at remote locations via a *data communications* network.

Trailer Record. A *record* that follows another record or group of records and contains pertinent data related to that record or group of records.

Transaction File. Same as *detail file*.

Utility Program. A standard routine that performs a frequently required process, such as sorting, merging, data transcription, printing, etc.

Variable-Length Record. A *record* that may contain a variable number of characters. Contrast with *fixed-length record*.

Voice-Response Unit. A device that accepts digitally coded input (usually from a computer) and converts it into machine-generated human-voice messages that can be transmitted over telephone lines. Usually the human-voice messages are replies to digital inquiries entered via push button telephones.

Working Storage. The storage locations in a computer that can be accessed directly for instructions used in arithmetic and logical operations. Synonymous with *main storage*.

NOTES

1. In writing this chapter, the authors have relied extensively on the materials in W. Thomas Porter and William E. Perry, *EDP Controls and Auditing*, 3rd ed. (Boston: Kent, 1981).
2. Ibid., pp. 96–116.

3. Ibid., p. 85.
4. Ibid., p. 88.
5. Statement on Auditing Standards (SAS) 3, Section 320.08 (New York: AICPA, 1974).
6. Porter and Perry, *EDP Controls and Auditing,* p. 98.
7. Adapted from *Information for CPA Candidates* (New York: AICPA, 1975), p. 7.
8. Computer Services Executive Committee, AICPA, *The Auditor's Study and Evaluation of Internal Control in EDP Systems,* (New York: AICPA, 1977), p. 30.
9. SAS 3, Section 320.25.
10. SAS 3, Section 320.26.
11. Computer Services Executive Committee, AICPA, *Internal Control in EDP Systems,* p. 16.

QUESTIONS FOR CLASS DISCUSSION

Q6–1 What are the special internal control problems that must be recognized in auditing computerized accounting records?

Q6–2 Historically, in expressing an opinion on financial statements, the auditor has depended on the examination of documents supporting various items in the account balances for verification of account balances. How has the use of computerized accounting records affected this portion of the audit? Explain.

Q6–3 Why is the auditor so concerned with the organizational structure of the electronic data-processing department?

Q6–4 Are you confident of the meaning of the following terms? Define.

a. *Computer software.*
b. *Input media.*
c. *Central processing unit.*
d. *Output devices.*
e. *Systems analyst.*
f. *Programmer.*
g. *Computer operator.*
h. *Hardware controls.*
i. *Parity check.*
j. *Validity check.*
k. *Completeness check.*
l. *Logic test.*
m. *Limit test.*
n. *Self-checking digits.*
o. *Batch processing.*
p. *Machine-readable labels.*
q. *Validity and reasonableness test.*

Q6–5 What is meant by the phrase *crime by computer?* Explain.

Q6–6 Can you distinguish between *general controls* and *application controls* as those terms are used in auditing a computerized accounting system?

Q6–7 What functions within the electronic data-processing department should be separated in achieving appropriate internal control over the EDP process?

Q6–8 Can you list and describe the hardware controls that may be incorporated into electronic data-processing equipment?

Q6–9 How does the grandfather, father, son arrangement for handling, processing, and storing computerized data help in protecting against the loss of data contained in computerized records?

Q6–10 What are: Input controls? Processing controls? Output controls? Briefly describe each.

Q6–11 What is the difference between preventive controls and detective controls?

Q6–12 Can you describe four preventive controls associated with the input function?

Q6–13 What are two types of preventive controls associated with the processing function?

Q6–14 How are batch controls used as a detective control device?

Q6–15 How are machine-readable labels useful in exercising control over the input and processing functions?

Q6–16 What is meant by *corrective controls?* Explain.

Q6–17 How does the first general standard of GAAS relate to the auditors responsibility in the audit of financial statements developed from computerized accounting data?

Q6–18 What are the four possible conclusions that an auditor may arrive at during the preliminary evaluation of a system of controls associated with an electronic data-processing system?

Q6–19 What is meant by the following terms: *Auditing around the computer? Auditing through the computer?* Under what circumstances might each of those auditing processes be followed? Explain.

Q6–20 What is the test data approach to the verification of computerized accounting data? Explain how that approach is carried out by the auditor. What is meant by the term *parallel simulation?* Explain.

Q6–21 What are some of the special control problems associated with use of an online realtime system for recording accounting data? Describe.

Q6–22 What are the special considerations associated with the audit of data maintained on a time-sharing basis by independent service centers?

SHORT CASES

C6–1 The McMillan Pharmaceutical Company's system for billing and recording accounts receivable is as follows:

a. An incoming customer's purchase order is received in the order department by a clerk who prepares a prenumbered company sales order form in which is inserted the pertinent information, such as the customer's name and address, customer's account number, quantity, and items ordered. After the sales order has been prepared, the customer's purchase order is stapled to it.

b. The sales order form is then passed to the credit department for credit approval. Rough approximations of the billing values of the orders are made in the credit department for those accounts on which credit limitations are imposed. After investigation, approval of credit is noted on the form.

c. Next the sales order form is passed to the billing department, where a clerk types the customer's invoice on a billing machine that cross-multiplies the number of items and the unit price, then adds the automatically extended amounts for the total amount of the invoice. The billing clerk determines the unit prices for the items from a list of billing prices.

The billing machine has registers that automatically accumulate daily totals of customer account numbers and invoice amounts to provide "hash" totals and control amounts. These totals, which are inserted in a daily record book, serve as predetermined batch totals for verification of computer inputs.

The billing is done on prenumbered, continuous, carbon-interleaved forms having the following designations:

(1) "Customer's copy."
(2) "Sales department copy," for information purposes.
(3) "File copy."
(4) "Shipping department copy," which serves as a shipping order. Bills of lading are also prepared as carbon copy byproducts of the invoicing procedure.

d. The shipping department copy of the invoice and the bills of lading are then sent to the shipping department. After the order has been shipped, copies of the bill of lading are returned to the billing department. The shipping department copy of the invoice is filed in the shipping department.

e. In the billing department, one copy of the bill of lading is attached to the customer's copy of the invoice and both are mailed to the customer. The other copy of the bill of lading, together with the sales order form, is then stapled to the invoice file copy and filed in invoice numerical order.

f. A keypunch machine is connected to the billing machine so that punched cards are created during the preparation of the invoices. The punched cards then become the means by which the sales data are transmitted to a computer.

The punched cards are fed to the computer in batches. One day's accumulation of cards comprises a batch. After the punched cards have been processed by the computer, they are placed in files and held for about two years.

Required:

List the procedures that a CPA would employ in his examination of his selected audit samples of the company's:

a. Typed invoices, including the source documents.
b. Punched cards.

(The listed procedures should be limited to the verification of the sales data being fed into the computer. Do not carry the procedures beyond the point at which the cards are ready to be fed to the computer.)

(AICPA adapted)

C6–2 You will be examining for the first time the financial statements of Central Savings and Loan Association for the year ending December 31. The CPA firm which examined the association's financial statements for the prior year issued an unqualified audit report.

During the current year, the association installed an online, realtime computer system. Each teller in the association's main office and seven branch offices has an online input/output terminal. Customers' mortgage payments and savings account deposits and withdrawals are recorded in the accounts by the computer from data input by the teller at the time of the transaction. The teller keys the proper account by account number and enters the information in the terminal keyboard to record the transaction. The accounting department at the main office has both punched card and typewriter input/output devices. The computer is housed at the main office.

Required:

You would expect the association to have certain internal controls in effect because an online realtime computer system is employed. List the internal controls that should be in effect solely because this system is employed, classifying them as:

a. Those controls pertaining to input of information.
b. All other types of computer controls.

(AICPA adapted)

C6–3 Ted Leonardi, CPA, is examining the financial statements of the Georgetown Sales Corporation, which recently installed an offline electronic computer. The following comments have been extracted from Ted's notes on computer operations and the processing and control of shipping notices and customer invoices.

> To minimize inconvenience Georgetown converted without change its existing data-processing system, which utilized tabulating equipment. The computer company supervised the conversion and has provided training to all computer department employees (except keypunch operators) in systems design, operations, and programming.
>
> Each computer run is assigned to a specific employee, who is responsible for making program changes, running the program, and answering questions. This procedure has the advantage of eliminating the need for records of computer operations because each employee is responsible for his own computer runs.
>
> At least one computer department employee remains in the computer room during office hours, and only computer department employees have keys to the computer room.
>
> System documentation consists of those materials furnished by the computer company — a set of record formats and program listings. These and the tape library are kept in a corner of the computer department.
>
> The corporation considered the desirability of program controls but decided to retain the manual controls from its existing system.
>
> Company products are shipped directly from public warehouses which forward shipping notices to general accounting. There a billing clerk enters the price of the item and accounts for the numerical sequence of shipping notices from each warehouse. The billing clerk also prepares daily adding machine tapes ("control tapes") of the units shipped and the unit prices.
>
> Shipping notices and control tapes are forwarded to the computer department for keypunching and processing. Extensions are made on the computer.

Output consists of invoices (in six copies) and a daily sales register. The daily sales register shows the aggregate totals of units shipped and unit prices which the computer operator compares to the control tapes.

All copies of the invoice are returned to the billing clerk. The clerk mails three copies to the customer, forwards one copy to the warehouse, maintains one copy in a numerical file, and retains one copy in an open invoice file that serves as a detailed accounts receivable record.

Required:

Suppose that, as Ted's business partner, you are required to carry out this audit for him because Ted has been appointed to a government position, effective immediately. Referring to Ted's notes, describe weaknesses in internal control over information and data flows and in the procedures for processing shipping notices and customer invoices. Recommend improvements in these controls and processing procedures. Organize your worksheet as follows:

Weakness	Recommended Improvement

(AICPA adapted)

C6–4 The following paragraphs are quoted from an article describing defects in the system of internal controls of Equity Funding Life Insurance Company, defects that resulted in one of the largest cases of computer fraud in history.

> The EDP function ran in a mode that courted disaster but left the EDP staff apparently isolated from knowledge of the fraud. An open shop functioned where a central staff developed and ran the primary programs for the business, but programmers in other departments such as actuarial could also write and run their own programs that had access to the live data base of insurance policies. The special processing required to carry out the fraud could have been done, and, it is claimed, was done by the programmers outside of the central EDP staff. . . .
>
> It is also claimed that EDP management had proposed on numerous occasions the establishment of an internal audit group for the EDP environment, but it was always rejected by top management. . . .
>
> The EDP staff also observed the external auditors from a revealing point of view. The auditors were apparently handed EDP listings of policy records printed from the master files and accepted them as documents of record since they had no capability or skills to directly access the master files in the system themselves. When the auditors happened to select a fake policy for confirmation, they were told that policy folder was in use by somebody in the company and would be available the next day. . . .

The way it worked was that Equity's head, Stanley Goldblum, set standards for growth in income, assets, and earnings. The desired quarterly and annual profits were relayed to Alan Green through Lewis and another executive. . . . Green would then go on the computer and crank out the necessary fictitious policies.*

Required:

a. What EDP controls were violated in this case?
b. As auditor of Equity Funding Life Insurance Company, how would you have reacted to these facts?

C6–5 Karen Hernandez, CPA, was engaged to examine the financial statements of Horizon Incorporated which has its own computer installation. During the preliminary review, Karen found that Horizon lacked proper segregation of the programming and operating functions. As a result, she intensified the study and evaluation of the system of internal control surrounding the computer and concluded that the existing compensating general controls provided reasonable assurance that the objectives of the system of internal control were being met.

Required:

a. In a properly functioning EDP environment, how is the separation of the programming and operating functions achieved?
b. What are the compensating general controls that Karen most likely found? *Do not discuss hardware and application controls.*

(AICPA adapted)

C6–6 Rip van Longsleeper, a public accountant, has just emerged from a thirty-year siesta and is attempting to reactivate his public accounting practice. On his first audit engagement, he finds that his client's records are maintained on reels of magnetic tape. He examines one reel and even by using a magnifying glass is unable to read anything on it. He does not understand how he can audit financial data that he cannot see.

Required:

Explain to Mr. Longsleeper how he should proceed with the audit of computerized accounting records.

PROBLEMS

P6–1 Select the best answer for each of the following items relating to computerized accounting records.

a. An electronic data processing technique that collects data into groups to permit convenient and efficient processing is known as
   (1) Document-count processing.

*Donn B. Parker, "Further Comment on the Equity Funding Insurance Fraud Case," *EDPACS* (January 1975): 16. Used with permission of *EDPACS, The EDP Audit, Control, and Security Newsletter*, 11250 Roger Bacon Drive, Suite 17, Reston, Va. 22090.

(2) Multiprogramming.
(3) Batch processing.
(4) Generalized-audit processing.

b. So that the essential accounting control features of a client's electronic data-processing system can be identified and evaluated, the auditor must, at a minimum, have
(1) A basic familiarity with the computer's internal supervisory system.
(2) A sufficient understanding of the entire computer system.
(3) An expertise in computer systems analysis.
(4) A background in programming procedures.

c. Which of the following employees in a company's electronic data-processing department should be responsible for designing new or improved data processing procedures?
(1) Flowchart editor.
(2) Programmer.
(3) Systems analyst.
(4) Control group supervisor.

d. An auditor should be familiar with a client's electronic data-processing hardware and software. An important element of the client's software is the program. Another element of software is the
(1) Cathode ray tube (CRT).
(2) Central processing unit (CPU).
(3) Magnetic tape drive.
(4) Compiler.

e. Which of the following client electronic data-processing (EDP) systems generally can be audited without examining or directly testing the EDP computer programs of the system?
(1) A system that performs relatively uncomplicated processes and produces detailed output.
(2) A system that affects a number of essential master files and produces a limited output.
(3) A system that updates a few essential master files and produces *no* printed output other than final balances.
(4) A system that performs relatively complicated processing and produces very little detailed output.

f. The most efficient and *least* costly method of dumping information for purposes of maintaining a back-up file is from disk to
(1) Dump.
(2) Printout.
(3) Cards.
(4) Tape.

g. Any assessment of the operational capabilities of a computer system must consider down time. Even in a fully protected system, down time will exist because of
(1) Electrical power losses.
(2) Unscheduled maintenance.
(3) Unauthorized entry.
(4) Keypunching errors.

(AICPA adapted)

P6–2 Select the best answer to each of the following items relating to general controls over electronic data processing.

a. Which of the following *best* describes a fundamental control weakness often associated with electronic data-processing systems?
   (1) Electronic data-processing equipment is more subject to systems error than manual processing is subject to human error.
   (2) Electronic data-processing equipment processes and records similar transactions in a similar manner.
   (3) Electronic data-processing procedures for detection of invalid and unusual transactions are less effective than manual control procedures.
   (4) Functions that would normally be separated in a manual system are combined in the electronic data-processing system.

b. An auditor's investigation of a company's electronic data-processing control procedures has disclosed the following four circumstances. Indicate which circumstance constitutes a weakness in internal control.
   (1) Machine operators do not have access to the complete run manual.
   (2) Machine operators are closely supervised by programmers.
   (3) Programmers do not have the authorization to operate equipment.
   (4) Only one generation of back-up files is stored in an off-premises location.

c. Some electronic data-processing accounting control procedures relate to all electronic data-processing activities (general controls) and some relate to specific tasks (application controls). General controls include
   (1) Controls designed to ascertain that all data submitted to electronic data processing for processing have been properly authorized.
   (2) Controls that relate to the correction and resubmission of data that was initially incorrect.
   (3) Controls for documenting and approving programs and changes to programs.
   (4) Controls designed to assure the accuracy of the processing results.

d. Where computers are used, the effectiveness of internal accounting control depends, in part, upon whether the organizational structure includes any incompatible combinations. Such a combination would exist when there is *no* separation of the duties between
   (1) Documentation librarian and manager of programming.
   (2) Programmer and console operator.
   (3) Systems analyst and programmer.
   (4) Processing control clerk and keypunch supervisor.

e. Accounting functions that are normally considered incompatible in a manual system are often combined in an electronic data-processing system by using an electronic data-processing program, or a series of programs. This necessitates an accounting control that prevents unapproved
   (1) Access to the magnetic tape library.
   (2) Revisions to existing computer programs.
   (3) Usage of computer program tapes.
   (4) Testing of modified computer programs.

f. When erroneous data are detected by computer program controls, such data may be excluded from processing and printed on an error report. The error report should most probably be reviewed and followed up by the
   (1) Supervisor of computer operations.
   (2) Systems analyst.

(3) EDP control group.
(4) Computer programmer.

g. Which of the following would *lessen* internal control in an electronic data-processing system?
   (1) The computer librarian maintains custody of computer program instructions and detailed listings.
   (2) Computer operators have access to operator instructions and detailed program listings.
   (3) The control group is solely responsible for the distribution of all computer output.
   (4) Computer programmers write and debug programs that perform routines designed by the systems analyst.

h. The auditor's preliminary understanding of the client's EDP system is primarily obtained by
   (1) Inspection.
   (2) Observation.
   (3) Inquiry.
   (4) Evaluation.

(AICPA adapted)

P6–3 Select the best answer for each of the following items relating to application controls within an EDP system.

a. A procedural control used in the management of a computer center to minimize the possibility of data or program file destruction through operator error includes
   (1) Control figures.
   (2) Cross-footing tests.
   (3) Limit checks.
   (4) External labels.

b. A customer inadvertently ordered part number 12368 rather than part number 12638. In processing this order, the error would be detected by the vendor with which of the following controls?
   (1) Batch total.
   (2) Key verifying.
   (3) Self-checking digit.
   (4) An internal consistency check.

c. An advantage of manual processing is that human processors may note data errors and irregularities. To replace the human element of error detection associated with manual processing, a well-designed electronic data-processing system should introduce
   (1) Programmed limits.
   (2) Dual circuitry.
   (3) Echo checks.
   (4) Read after write.

d. Which of the following is an example of application controls in electronic data-processing systems?
   (1) Input controls.
   (2) Hardware controls.

(3) Documentation procedures.
(4) Controls over access to equipment and data files.

e. The grandfather, father, son approach to providing protection for important computer files is a concept that is most often found in
(1) Online realtime systems.
(2) Punched-card systems.
(3) Magnetic tape systems.
(4) Magnetic drum systems.

f. In its electronic data-processing system a company might use self-checking numbers (check digits) to permit detection of which of the following errors?
(1) Assigning a valid identification code to the wrong customer.
(2) Recording an invalid customer's identification charge account number.
(3) Losing data between processing functions.
(4) Processing data arranged in the wrong sequence.

g. Program controls, in an electronic data-processing system, are used as substitutes for human controls in a manual system. Which of the following is an example of a program control?
(1) Dual read.
(2) Echo check.
(3) Validity check.
(4) Limit and reasonableness test.

h. Parity checks, read-after-write checks, and duplicate circuitry are electronic data-processing controls that are designed to detect
(1) Erroneous internal handling of data.
(2) Lack of sufficient documentation for computer processes.
(3) Illogical programming commands.
(4) Illogical uses of hardware.

i. Automated equipment controls in an electronic data-processing system are designed to detect errors arising from
(1) Operation of the electronic data-processing equipment.
(2) Lack of human alertness.
(3) Incorrect input and output data.
(4) Poor management of the electronic data-processing installation.

j. A control feature in an electronic data-processing system requires the central processing unit (CPU) to send signals to the printer to activate the print mechanism for each character. The print mechanism, just prior to printing, sends a signal back to the CPU verifying that the proper print position has been activated. This type of hardware control is referred to as
(1) Echo control.
(2) Validity control.
(3) Signal control.
(4) Check digit control.

k. In an electronic data-processing system, automated equipment controls or hardware controls are designed to
(1) Arrange data in a logical sequential manner for processing purposes.
(2) Correct errors in the computer programs.
(3) Monitor and detect errors in source documents.
(4) Detect and control errors arising from use of equipment.

l. Totals of amounts in computer-record data fields, which are *not* usually added but are used only for data-processing control purposes, are called

(1) Record totals.
(2) Hash totals.
(3) Processing data totals.
(4) Field totals.

m. Which of the following is a computer test made to ascertain whether a given characteristic belongs to the group?
(1) Parity check.
(2) Validity check.
(3) Echo check.
(4) Limit check.

n. In updating a computerized accounts receivable file, which one of the following would be used as a batch control to verify the accuracy of the posting of cash receipts remittances?
(1) The sum of the cash deposits plus the discounts less the sales returns.
(2) The sum of the cash deposits.
(3) The sum of the cash deposits less the discounts taken by customers.
(4) The sum of the cash deposits plus the discounts taken by customers.

o. In the study and review of a client's EDP internal control system, the auditor will encounter general controls and application controls. Which of the following is an application control?
(1) Dual read.
(2) Hash total.
(3) Systems flowchart.
(4) Control over program changes.

p. The use of a header label in conjunction with magnetic tape is *most* likely to prevent errors by the
(1) Computer operator.
(2) Keypunch operator.
(3) Computer programmer.
(4) Maintenance technician.

(AICPA adapted)

P6–4 Select the best answer for each of the following items relating to compliance testing of controls in EDP system.

a. The auditor looks for an indication on punched cards to see if the cards have been verified. This is an example of a
(1) Substantive test.
(2) Compliance test.
(3) Transactions test.
(4) Dual-purpose test.

b. An independent auditor studies and evaluates a client's electronic data-processing system. The auditor's study portion includes two phases: (1) a review or investigation of the system and (2) tests of compliance. The latter phase might include which of the following?
(1) Examination of systems flowcharts to determine whether they reflect the current status of the system.
(2) Examination of the systems manuals to determine whether existing procedures are satisfactory.

(3) Examination of the machine room log book to determine whether control information is properly recorded.
(4) Examination of organization charts to determine whether electronic data-processing department responsibilities are properly separated to afford effective control.

c. Accounting control procedures within the EDP activity may leave *no* visible evidence indicating that the procedures were performed. In such instances, the auditor should test these accounting controls by
(1) Making corroborative inquiries.
(2) Observing the separation of duties of personnel.
(3) Reviewing transactions submitted for processing and comparing them to related output.
(4) Reviewing the run manual.

d. Compliance testing of an advanced EDP system
(1) Can be performed using only actual transactions since testing of simulated transactions is of no consequence.
(2) Can be performed using actual transactions or simulated transactions.
(3) Is impractical since many procedures within the EDP activity leave no visible evidence of having been performed.
(4) Is inadvisable because it may distort the evidence in master files.

e. In a daily computer run to update checking account balances and print out basic details on any customer's account that was overdrawn, the overdrawn account of the computer programmer was never printed. Which of the following control procedures would have been *most* effective in detecting this irregularity?
(1) Use of the test deck approach by the auditor in testing the client's program and verification of the subsidiary file.
(2) Use of a running control total for the master file of checking account balances and comparison with the printout.
(3) A program check for valid customer code.
(4) Periodic recompiling of programs from documented source decks, and comparison with programs currently in use.

f. After a preliminary phase of the review of a client's EDP controls, an auditor may decide not to perform compliance tests related to the control procedures within the EDP portion of the client's internal control system. Which of the following would *not* be a valid reason for choosing to omit compliance tests?
(1) The controls appear adequate.
(2) The controls duplicate operative controls existing elsewhere in the system.
(3) There appear to be major weaknesses that would preclude reliance on the stated procedure.
(4) The time and dollar costs of testing exceed the time and dollar savings in substantive testing if the compliance tests show the controls to be operative.

g. An auditor will use the EDP test data method in order to gain certain assurances with respect to the
(1) Input data.
(2) Machine capacity.
(3) Procedures contained within the program.
(4) Degree of keypunching accuracy.

h. Which of the following is *not* a problem associated with the use of test decks for computer audit purposes?

(1) Auditing through the computer is more difficult than auditing around the computer.
(2) It is difficult to design test decks that incorporate all potential variations in transactions.
(3) Test data may be commingled with live data causing operating problems for the client.
(4) The program with which the test data are processed may differ from the one used in actual operations.

(AICPA adapted)

P6–5 Select the best answer for each of the following items relating to more sophisticated computer systems.

a. What is the computer process called when data processing is performed concurrently with a particular activity and the results are available soon enough to influence the particular course of action being taken or the decision being made?
   (1) Realtime processing.
   (2) Batch processing.
   (3) Random access processing.
   (4) Integrated data processing.

b. Which of the following is a characteristic of an integrated system for data processing?
   (1) An integrated system is a realtime system where files for different functions with similar information are separated.
   (2) A single input record describing a transaction initiates the updating of all files associated with the transaction.
   (3) Parallel operations strengthen internal control over the computer processing function.
   (4) Files are maintained according to organizational functions such as purchasing, accounts payable, sales, etc.

c. When an online, realtime (OLRT) electronic data-processing system is in use, internal control can be strengthened by
   (1) Providing for the separation of duties between keypunching and other listing operations.
   (2) Attaching plastic file-protection rings to reels of magnetic tape before new data can be entered on the file.
   (3) Preparing batch totals to provide assurance that file updates are made for the entire input.
   (4) Making a validity check of an identification number before a user can obtain access to the computer files.

d. A management information system is designed to ensure that management possesses the information it needs to carry out its functions through the integrated actions of
   (1) Data-gathering, analysis, and reporting functions.
   (2) A computerized information retrieval and decision-making system.
   (3) Statistical and analytical review functions.
   (4) Production-budgeting and sales-forecasting activities.

e. Which of the following is necessary to audit balances in an online EDP system in an environment of destructive updating?

(1) Periodic dumping of transaction files.
(2) Year-end utilization of audit hooks.
(3) An integrated test facility.
(4) A well-documented audit trail.

(AICPA adapted)

P6–6 When auditing an electronic data-processing (EDP) accounting system, the independent auditor should have a general familiarity with the effects of the use of EDP on the various characteristics of accounting control and on the auditor's study and evaluation of such control. The independent auditor must be aware of those control procedures commonly referred to as "general" controls and those commonly referred to as "application" controls. General controls relate to all EDP activities and application controls relate to specific accounting tasks.

Required:

a. What are the general controls that should exist in EDP-based accounting systems?
b. What are the purposes of each of the following categories of application controls?
   (1) Input controls.
   (2) Processing controls.
   (3) Output controls.

(AICPA adapted)

P6–7 The following topics are part of the relevant body of knowledge for CPAs having field work or immediate supervisory responsibility in audits involving a computer.

a. Electronic data-processing (EDP) equipment and its capabilities.
b. Organization and management of the data-processing function.
c. Characteristics of computer-based systems.
d. Fundamentals of computer programming.
e. Computer center operations.

CPAs who are responsible for computer audits should possess certain general knowledge with respect to each of these five topics. For example, on the subject of EDP equipment and its capabilities, the auditor should have a general understanding of computer equipment and should be familiar with the uses and capabilities of the central processor and the peripheral equipment.

Required:

For each of topics b–e above, describe the general knowledge that should be possessed by those CPA's responsible for computer audits.

(AICPA adapted)

P6–8 When auditing the financial statements of a client who utilizes electronic data processing, it is important for the CPA to understand the essential characteristics of the client's system and the controls that are built into it.

Required:

a. Describe how the client's EDP department should be organized to maximize internal control over processing activities. Include in your description how the EDP department should relate to the rest of the client's organization.
b. An effective system of internal control also requires effective controls over source data as they flow into and out of the computer. These controls include input controls, processing controls, and output controls. List the characteristics of an effective system of input, processing, and output controls in a batch-controlled system.

(AICPA adapted)

P6–9 An extract from the problem statement section of the run manual for the pension fund accounting program of the Riley Insurance Company reads as follows:

> Persons who are 60 years of age or over when commencing employment are not eligible for the pension plan. All other employees automatically become members during the 37th month of continuous employment, and each employee's pension fund contribution will be deducted on the employee's payroll check each month thereafter.

Block Flowchart

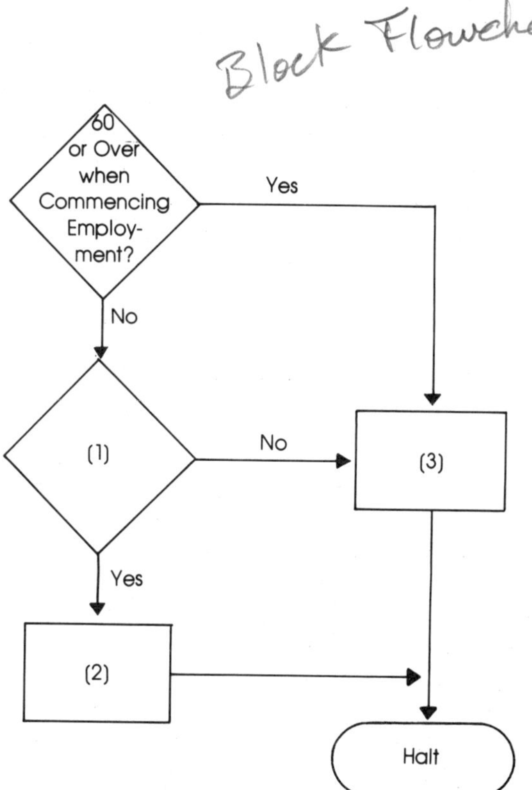

Required:

a. Numbered symbol (1) in the above flowchart should be replaced by which of the following statements?
   (1) Deduct pension fund contribution.
   (2) Print ineligibility list.
   (3) Employed more than 36 months?
   (4) Employed more than 37 months?
b. Numbered symbol (2) should be replaced by which of the following statements?
   (1) Deduct pension fund contribution.
   (2) Print ineligibility list.
   (3) Employed more than 36 months?
   (4) Employed more than 37 months?
c. Numbered symbol (3) should be replaced by which of the following statements?
   (1) Deduct pension fund contribution.
   (2) Print ineligibility list.
   (3) Employed more than 36 months?
   (4) Employed more than 37 months?

(AICPA adapted)

P6–10 CPAs may audit *around* the computer, but when the computer is used extensively in all processing applications, most CPAs prefer to audit *through* the computer. In still other applications it is possible to audit *with* the computer.

Required:

a. Describe the auditing approach referred to as auditing around the computer. Why do auditors generally *not* use that approach?
b. Under what circumstances would the CPA decide to audit through the computer instead of around it? What are some ways to audit through the computer?
c. In auditing through the computer, the CPA may use a variety of methods.
   (1) What are test data? Why does the CPA use the test data approach? What are some of its disadvantages? How might those disadvantages be alleviated with proper planning?
   (2) What is the parallel simulation approach? What are some of its advantages and disadvantages?
   (3) What is the minicompany approach? What are some of the advantages of this method over other methods?

(AICPA adapted)

P6–11 Auditing standards require that the auditor study and evaluate a client's system of internal control; this requirement does not change when clients use EDP systems. However, the CPA must adapt her or his methods to the EDP environment.

Required:

a. Describe the two phases of the review and evaluation process for a system of internal control that utilizes EDP to accumulate financial data.
b. What conclusions can the auditor reach after evaluating the system? What is the resultant effect on the nature, timing, and extent of further tests to be performed?
c. How does the processing environment change when clients, instead of purchas-

ing or leasing their own computer systems, lease time from independent computer service centers?

d. Explain how the CPA's review and evaluation of internal controls would change if a service center instead of the client's computer were used to process accounting data.

P6–12 You are reviewing audit work papers containing a narrative description of the Tenney Corporation's factory payroll system. A portion of that narrative is as follows:

> Factory employees punch timeclock cards each day when entering or leaving the shop. At the end of each week the timekeeping department collects the time cards and prepares duplicate batch-control slips by department showing total hours and number of employees. The time cards and original batch-control slips are sent to the payroll accounting section. The second copies of the batch-control slips are filed by date.
>
> In the payroll accounting section payroll transaction cards are keypunched from the information on the time cards, and a batch total card for each batch is keypunched from the batch-control slip. The time cards and batch-control slips are then filed by batch for possible reference. The payroll transaction cards and batch total card are sent to data processing where they are sorted by employee number within batch. Each batch is edited by a computer program which checks the validity of employee number against a master employee tape

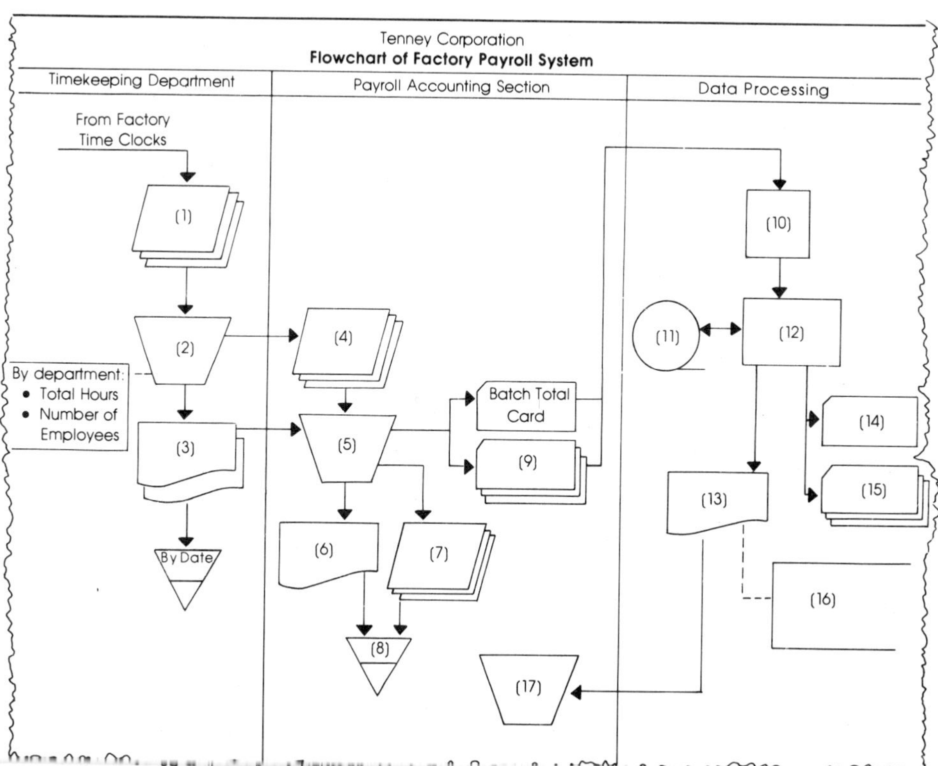

file and the total hours and number of employees against the batch total card. A detailed printout by batch and employee number is produced, which indicates batches that do not balance and invalid employee numbers. This printout is returned to payroll accounting to resolve all differences.

In searching for documentation you found a flowchart of the payroll system which included all appropriate symbols (American National Standards Institute, Inc.) but was only partially labeled. The portion of this flowchart described by the preceding narrative appears on page 271.

Required:

a. Number your answer 1 through 17. Next to the corresponding number of your answer, supply the appropriate labeling (document name, process description, or file order) applicable to each numbered symbol on the flowchart.
b. Flowcharts are one of the aids an auditor may use to determine and evaluate a client's internal control system. List advantages of using flowcharts in this context.

(AICPA adapted)

P6–13 You are assigned to review the documentation of a data-processing function.

Required:

a. List three advantages of adequate documentation for a data-processing function.
b. Below are two columns of information. The left column lists 6 categories of documentation, and the right column lists 18 elements of documentation related to the categories. Match each of the elements of documentation with the category in which it should be found. List letters A through F on your answer sheet. After each letter, list the numbers of the elements that best apply to that category. Use every element, but none more than once.

Categories

A. Systems documentation.
B. Program documentation.
C. Operations documentation.
D. User documentation.
E. Library documentation.
F. Data entry documentation.

Elements

1. Flowcharts showing the flow of information.
2. Procedures needed to balance, reconcile, and maintain overall control.
3. Storage instructions.
4. Contents and format of data to be captured.
5. Constants, codes, and tables.
6. Verification procedures.
7. Logic diagrams and/or decision tables.
8. Report distribution instructions.
9. Messages and programmed halts.
10. Procedures for back-up files.
11. Retention cycle.
12. Source statement listings.
13. Instructions to show proper use of each transaction.
14. A complete history from planning through installation.
15. Restart and recovery procedures.

16. Rules for handling blank spaces.
17. Instructions to insure the proper completion of all input forms.
18. List of programs in a system.

(CIA Examination adapted)

CHAPTER

7

THE COMPUTER AS AN AUDIT TOOL

The third standard of field work requires that sufficient, competent, evidential matter be gathered to support the auditor's opinion about a client's financial statements. When accounting records are maintained manually, the auditor performs the auditing procedures manually — using electronic calculators and adding machines to perform simple calculations. In such a situation, the auditor is always working with person-readable data. Therefore the audit trail from original documents to financial statement balances, or from the statement balances back to source documents, can be visibly traced.

In this chapter, we examine the ways in which the auditor uses the computer in gathering evidence from computerized accounting records.[1] In doing that, we discuss the following topics:

1. The audit capabilities of the computer.
2. The problems of developing programs for use with the computer in the evidence-gathering process.
3. The steps associated with developing and using a generalized computer audit software package.
4. The use of a typical audit software package.

We also include, as an appendix to this chapter, a listing of the general software packages used by various public accounting firms and other entities in auditing computerized accounting data.

COMPUTER AUDIT CAPABILITIES

With the advent of the computer, two significant changes complicated the evidence gathering process. First and most significant was the *maintenance of accounting records on machine-readable media* — such as punched cards, magnetic tape, or magnetic disks. The second change involved *an ever-increasing volume of data* to be verified. Faced with these problems, the auditor must choose from the following practices in implementing the evidence-gathering process:

1. ***Audit around the computer*** by performing tests on samples from original source documents and recalculating various items appearing on the financial statements. Those data could then be compared with the data included in the statements to determine whether they had been recorded correctly.
2. Evaluate internal controls included in the client's computer programs by means of test data, parallel simulation, or other methods (discussed in Chapter 6), and require a printout of selected elements of the audit trail. That arrangement, often referred to as ***auditing through the computer***, would then permit performance of the evidence-gathering procedures in much the same manner as they have historically been performed in auditing person-readable records.
3. After evaluating the system of controls, use the computer to read, select, and process sample data from the machine-readable records. Within this arrangement, many of the tedious audit procedures historically performed manually are performed by the computer. Since this method goes beyond merely auditing the controls included in client programs to the actual performance of audit procedures, we refer to the evidence-gathering process as ***auditing with the computer***, or using the computer as an audit tool.

The first of these options is often inefficient because it ignores the effects of the quality of the system of internal controls on the nature and extent of substantive tests necessary to verify financial statement balances. The second option, while desirable, can produce only incomplete results, because it can reach a conclusion only as to the adequacy of the system of internal controls, leaving the major task of verification of financial statement balances yet undone. The auditing profession, over a period of years, has therefore developed the capability of using the computer as an auditing tool. By using the computer to perform audit work, the auditor often maximizes audit efficiency, taking advantage of the computer's speed and accuracy to perform tedious (and expensive) audit procedures that would otherwise have to be performed manually.

We have seen that the central processing unit of a computer, properly programmed, can read data from cards, tapes, or disks. It can also perform arithmetic calculations and make certain logic choices among those data. The performance of audit evidence-gathering procedures requires a program that will tell the computer specifically (1) what is to be done in gathering the data to be analyzed, (2) the work to be performed on the data to produce the evidence required in support of the financial statement data, and (3) instructions to print out certain findings from steps (1) and (2). Such a program causes the computer to read the machine-readable files for data to be verified, to select samples of those data, and to perform the appropriate evidence-gathering procedures. The computer can also be programmed to print out the results of those procedures. The auditor thus uses the computer's arithmetic, logic, and printing capabilities to carry out certain steps in the performance of auditing procedures.

By being aware of the basic functions and capabilities of the computer, and by applying the principles of auditing with regard to evidence, the auditor can achieve the following objectives:

- Use the computer's arithmetic capability to *verify the client's calculations* — such as depreciation charges; extensions (multiplication); and footings (addition) of sales invoices, inventory, accounts receivable, and property and equipment files. Because of the computer's great speed and accuracy, most of these calculations can be 100 percent verified, often at lower cost than would result from auditing merely a sample of them manually.
- Use the computer's logic capability to *sort various data files and select samples* of individual items directly from the machine-readable records for verification. Such samples might include individual accounts receivable for confirmation or individual items of inventory for observation.
- Use the computer's reading and printing capabilities to *print out all the details of confirmation letters* for accounts receivable, inventories, or any other accounts where confirmation is appropriate.
- Use the computer's logic and memory capability to *perform mathematical analyses directly from machine-readable records*. It can, for example, be programmed to compute and compare various balance sheet and operating ratios over a period of time. It can also examine documents such as invoices for completeness, consistency between different items, valid conditions, and reasonable amounts.
- Use the editing capability of the computer to *scan the accounting records for unusual items*, such as credit balances in accounts receivable or obsolete or slow-moving inventory items. These exceptional items can then be printed out on hard copy for the auditor's further investigation.
- Use the computer's mathematical capabilities to *calculate and provide lists* of audit samples and the results of audit procedures performed in person-readable form for inclusion in the audit work papers. All of the statistical calculations illustrated in Chapters 8 and 9 for both sample size and evaluation of sampling results can be done by the computer with appropriate programming.[2]

For example, the AUDEX 100 software package, which is described in detail later in this chapter, includes these ten capabilities:

- *Selecting* data for testing against source documents.
- *Comparing* audited source data to data recorded in computerized records.
- *Recomputing* computer-manipulated data.
- *Testing* computer processing logic by simulating the processing of computer programs.
- *Examining* entire populations for certain criteria to compare with tests of the population.
- *Changing the sequence* of data extracted from the client's data files for audit purposes.
- *Preparing confirmations*, statements, and special reports.
- *Preparing audit lead schedules* from computerized general ledger files.
- *Analyzing* accounts and variations and identifying items for investigation.
- *Testing account distribution* of transactions through EDP systems.[3]

DEVELOPMENT OF COMPUTER AUDIT PROGRAMS

After recognizing what the computer is capable of doing in implementing the evidence-gathering process, we must, of course, also be aware that those functions can be performed only with appropriate programming. We now turn our attention to the problem of developing computer software programs that will allow the auditor to use the computer as an audit tool.

Basically, there are three sources from which computer audit programs for a specific audit engagement can be secured. In some instances, the auditor may be able to use programs written by the client. Another possibility is for the audit firm to write its own program for each audit. A third possibility is for the auditing firm to develop a generalized audit program that can be used on many different audits by introducing supplementing adaptations for each specific audit.

Programs Written by the Client

Some of the analyses normally performed during an audit, such as the aging of accounts receivable and the analysis of various financial ratios, are often useful to the client in managing day-to-day activities of the enterprise unit. Because of that fact, the client may already have programs available to provide the data for internal use, programs that could be adapted for the auditor's use. In other situations, the auditor may be able to persuade the client to write such programs by citing future cost savings and other benefits as incentives. When these situations exist, the auditor may advantageously use client-prepared programs. However, if the programs are written by the client, there is a risk that *the auditor's independence may be compromised*. Therefore, if a client-prepared computer audit program is used, it will be necessary for the auditor to test the program thoroughly to determine whether it can be relied upon to produce the desired results. The extent of program verification will depend to some extent on the results of the study of controls over programs and operations. As a minimum, the auditor will need to review the client's program documentation and run book. It is generally also important for the auditor to perform tests to demonstrate that the program actually performs the required functions. Preferably, these tests should be performed at an independent data-processing facility.

In summary, use of clients' prepared programs require auditors to evaluate and test the programs before they are used. Such procedures are often complex and certainly time consuming. Furthermore, use of such programs often *requires an expertise in programming* beyond the level normally achieved by many auditors.

Programs Written by the Auditor

The auditor can avoid the testing required in the use of client-prepared programs by having experts at her or his firm write the program. The procedures for doing this are the same as those required for the development of any other computer program. In general, this involves the following five steps, *for each application:*

1. Determination of the audit objectives and procedures to be met by use of the program.
2. Preparation of a statement that defines in detail the processing required to meet those audit objectives and to perform the required auditing procedures.
3. Development of a systems flowchart showing all inputs, outputs, and processing steps.
4. Development of the audit program from the system flowchart, written in a language compatible with the equipment on which the program is to be used.
5. Debugging and testing the program to see that it meets the audit objectives and procedures set out for it.[4]

After a program has been developed through the steps just suggested, the auditor is ready to use it to perform the procedures necessary to achieve the audit objectives of step 1. Most of the accounting firms have in-house personnel capable of preparing EDP programs. This approach has the advantages of independent preparation and a tailoring of the system to the audit being performed and to the audit objectives established for it. It is nevertheless a *time-consuming and expensive process*, particularly when we consider that the *program's use will be limited to a specific client* and that the audit program must be continuously monitored and revised for client program changes. As a result of these disadvantages, a third approach involving the development of generalized audit programs has been followed by most large public accounting firms.

Generalized Audit Programs

It should be apparent that many audit functions change very little from client to client. Therefore many of the larger public accounting firms have dealt with the problem of using the computer as an audit tool by developing generalized programs that perform a wide range of computer audit functions and can be used with a minimum of user training and expertise. They can also be used for audits of clients with different types of EDP equipment.

One approach to the generalized audit program is to develop a series of programs, each of which may be applicable to clients in a particular industry. With this type of program, the client's files are read, duplicated, and converted to a standard format on magnetic tape, after which the data are processed by a generalized audit program. There is an important observation to make at this point: even though two computers' systems may not be program compatible, they may be data compatible if records are put on magnetic tapes in standardized format. The tapes produced in such operations are often referred to as ***audit work files.***

Another approach has been to develop an ***audit software package*** that can be used with limited adaptations for different types of clients. These packages are designed to be used by nonprogrammers and can perform a wide range of general data-gathering and processing functions — such as reading files; selecting and preparing work files of data fields from certain records; processing, sorting, and summarizing records; performing auditor-specified calculations, and printing auditor specified reports. A number of the larger public accounting firms have developed such programs, each of which carries a distinctive name. For example, AUDEX and AUDEX 100 are software packages used by Arthur Andersen and Company. Auditape is the package used by Deloitte Haskins & Sells. Auditpack II is the program used by Coopers and Lybrand.

Strata is the name given to the software package used by Touche Ross & Co. Peat, Marwick, Mitchell & Co. uses a software package called S/2190. Price Waterhouse and Company uses a software package simply entitled Computer File Analyzer. All of these packages operate in a similar manner, which is perhaps best described by the name of the Price Waterhouse package. The software packages used by the larger public accounting firms and selected corporations and agencies are listed in Appendix 7–B.

The audit software packages listed in the preceding paragraph are written to perform the basic functions identified earlier in this chapter. They typically have these capabilities:

- *Comparing data* on different computer records or files and printing a list of irregularities as defined by the program.
- *Selecting samples* of various types from computerized records and printing them out.
- *Preparing analyses and listings* such as aged accounts receivable.
- *Checking computations* and printing out those found to be incorrect.
- *Scanning computerized records* for unusual items and communicating those items to the auditor through the medium of a printed list.

As observed above, generalized computer audit programs are designed to perform a wide range of audit functions on computerized records. Therefore, the auditor must *add specifications to adapt the generalized software to the specific application requirements* of each individual audit. However, this coding requires only a small fraction of the amount of time and expertise typically required to accomplish the same task using a program developed from scratch. Generally, these adapting specifications are keypunched and read into computer memory, where they are used to sequence and further define the routines performed by the software package. The specific adapting specifications required for the various generalized software packages differ significantly. However, all of them require a consideration of the following:

- The characteristics of the computer system being audited, including its input/output devices.
- The format desired for the work file produced by the software.
- Characteristics of the client's file.
- The functions required to be performed.
- The calculations required.
- The characteristics of the required reports.[5]

The relationships between the client's files, the auditor's specifications, the generalized audit program, and the work record produced by those inputs are illustrated in Figure 7–1.

STEPS IN DEVELOPING AND USING GENERALIZED AUDIT SOFTWARE

We find at least four distinct steps followed by the auditor in developing and using generalized computer audit software packages. These include the following:

- A study and planning phase.
- Development of an overall flowchart and other documentary support for the audit software.
- Coding and testing the software package.
- Use of the software package in an actual audit situation.[6]

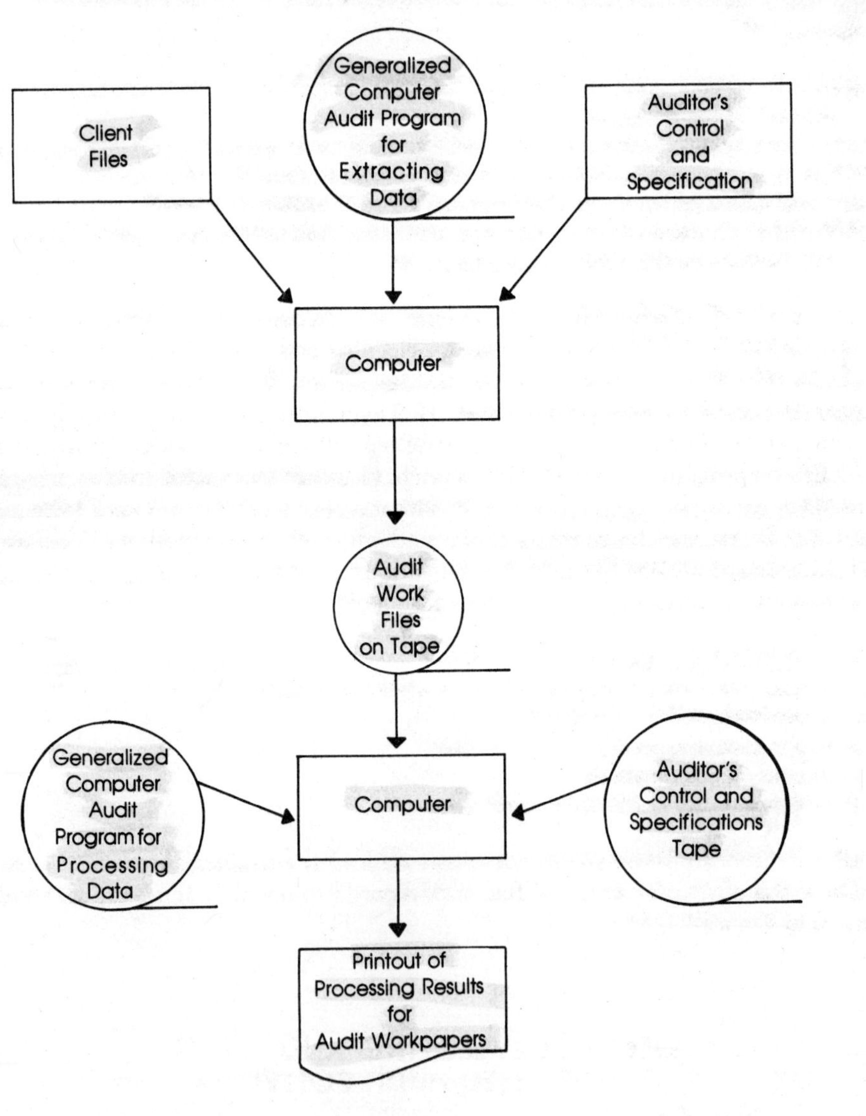

FIGURE 7–1. Use of Generalized Audit Software

Planning the Software Package

The first portion of the planning phase calls for a definition of the audit objective to be achieved by the software package. The computer is expected to do certain functions that assist the auditor in performing auditing procedures. That in turn requires the auditor to define the audit objectives by using a preliminary audit program including as much detail as possible. The objectives in using the computerized program should then be consistent with the elements of that audit program.

Next, the auditor should obtain information from clients about their computer and file characteristics, record layouts, and the availability of files. These data must then be evaluated to determine if they are compatible with the proposed audit software package. If so, the generalized audit procedures can be finalized, and a working plan can be developed for the other steps described below.

Development of Underlying Documentary Support

At this point, an overall flowchart should be developed, laying out the planned audit software applications. The audit software application requirements — including logic, calculations, format of reports, and procedures for controlling its application — should be appropriately defined. All these data should then be drawn together into appropriate documentary support in the form of a flowchart for the actual audit software application.

Coding and Testing the Software Package

The auditor is now ready to code the specification forms required to adapt the general software package to a specific application. Those specifications will be keypunched into cards or placed on magnetic tape to provide computer readability. After that, the full package — including the generalized audit software and the specification cards or tape — should be applied to a test file or to a portion of the client's file to prove that the auditor has correctly interpreted the client's file content and has specified the generalized software logic that creates the information necessary to achieve her or his audit objective.

Using the Computer Audit Package on an Element of the Audit

After coding and testing, the auditor is ready to use the generalized audit software in combination with the specifications adapting it to the client's computer and records files in the performance of an element of the audit program. Such a software package is typically adaptable to a large number of functions in the actual performance of the audit. The package may be used, for example, to *create a work file* by having the computer read records from a client master file being audited and then create a new file consisting of selected data fields from the master file. The information on the work file may then be subjected to the various auditing procedures without risk of contamination of client master files. After processing, audited information from the work file may be printed out and actually become a part of the audit workpapers.

The computer may also be used to *sort records* into a new sequence required for calculations, report printing, or other processing. For example, it may be used to resequence the work file into an ascending or descending sequence based on values in auditor-specified sort control fields.

The program can also call for the computer to *calculate certain additional values or to test existing file values.* In performing this function, the computer can, in effect, duplicate the procedures typically performed by the auditor working on person-readable records in verifying client calculations previously incorporated into the accounting records.

The program can also be used to *generate new files* within formats specified by the auditor. In a similar manner, the program can call for the *selection of certain records* or special processing of randomly selected test data from either the client or work records. For example, items recorded showing a value greater than a specified amount can be extracted from the client or work records and either processed in accordance with program specifications or printed out for manual use and for inclusion in the audit workpapers.

Obviously, the results of the audit procedures performed by the computer must, with our present level of audit expertise, ultimately be made available in person-readable form. At some stage the data being processed by the computer or specified segments of it must be printed out to provide the auditor with visible proof of the results of the computerized audit procedures.

Recently in an article entitled "A Case for Automated Workpapers," David N. Ricchiute suggested that in the future we may find automated workpapers taking the place of manually prepared ones. He suggested that the wave of the future may find "workpapers stored on space-saving cassette tapes much as record albums are today."[7] Such an arrangement would eliminate the need for printouts except where the auditor or others needed to visually inspect some specific sequence of the workpaper file.

THE AUDEX SOFTWARE PACKAGE

We have discussed in general how the auditing profession has responded to the problem of auditing computerized records by developing general software packages that allow the computer to extract and process financial data directly from machine-readable records. Most large public accounting firms have software packages of this type (see Appendix 7–B). As a means of acquainting you more specifically with the ways these packages are used, we now examine the organization, content and use of AUDEX 100, the generalized audit software system used by Arthur Andersen and Company.[8] We begin our discussion with a brief consideration of the historical background from which the software package was developed. Then we list its capabilities and show how it is actually used in performing an audit. In the last part of this section we make some concluding remarks about the use of the computer as an audit tool.

Background of the Program

Throughout the decade of the 1960s, the use of the computer in recording financial operations increased significantly. During that period most of the accounting firms, including Arthur Andersen, determined that the extensive application of computers offered an excellent opportunity for introducing automation into audit procedures. As a result, Arthur Andersen developed and put into use in 1969 the generalized computer package called AUDEX. It was designed to provide the auditor with a tool to meet the computer challenge.

During the early 1970s, computers became more sophisticated, with larger memory capacities and more complex file structures. To meet that challenge, Arthur Andersen developed AUDEX 100 in 1975. This presently used software package has two advantages: it meets the challenge of being adaptable to more sophisticated computers, and it allows the auditor to perform audit functions that could not be performed with the original AUDEX package.

Performance Capabilities

As we begin to consider what this software package will do, it is helpful to note that the name AUDEX is an acronym for AUDit EXtract, which describes the program's fundamental function — namely, the extraction of data from a variety of computer files. This program goes beyond that, however, because it has the capability of processing the extracted data into formats best suited to the need of each audit. The functional capabilities of AUDEX 100 include *select, extract, sort, merge, match, accumulate, summarize, sample, format, calculate, sequence check, and print.* These functional capabilities allow the auditor to use the computer to carry out the general audit procedures listed on page 276.

The functions just listed may be performed by AUDEX 100 on an IBM System 350, 370, 303X, and 430D series of computers, as well as on plug-compatible machines such as Amdahl and ITEL. For those computers, there are certain memory and other requirements. The software package will accept tape and card data files created on such hardware as the Univac-9000 Series computers. Also, data that can be converted to large computer tape or card format from other manufacturers' equipment can also be processed by AUDEX 100. A file conversion program must be run before using AUDEX 100 in processing such data.

The use of AUDEX 100 does not require the auditor to have programming capability. He or she must, however, be familiar with the information contained within the computer files and must understand the AUDEX 100 functions to be applied to the data to accomplish the desired audit objectives. The system is basically designed to allow the auditor to accomplish the desired audit procedures in a more effective and efficient manner, to reduce the clerical effort involved in the examination, and to provide a more practical way to gain access to computer-maintained data.

Using the Program in the Performance of an Audit

AUDEX may be described as a *library of computer routines* that can be combined to perform desired audit procedures. By applying various combinations of the routines in the package, the auditor is able to tailor it to accomplish the desired procedures on a wide range of audit assignments. The auditor may, for example, simply use the functions of extracting, adding, and printing to foot a data file and to print out control totals. On the other hand, he or she may use many of the functions to review an inventory data file for slow-moving inventory and to print out a report of all inventory meeting the criteria established for slow-moving inventory.

The AUDEX 100 system is divided into two main programs or phases called AUDEX I and AUDEX II. AUDEX I is designed to *extract data from computer files and to perform certain functions* the user selects. Its output is a new file of data called the "AA Record File." You can see this illustratated in the flowchart of Figure 7–2.

AUDEX II has been designed to *process the files created by AUDEX I and to print the desired reports* or confirmations from the data contained in the AA Record File. One example of the processing flow for this program is shown in Figure 7–3.

Another AUDEX program in the AUDEX 100 system is called AUDEX III. It is a *utility print program,* used to print additional reports from an edited report file created by the AUDEX II program. The processing flow for this program is shown in Figure 7–4. It is important to recognize that in some situations a number of AUDEX I passes may have to be performed before AUDEX II or AUDEX III is run.

The functions of the programs just described are controlled through use of the AUDEX specification sheets. The user selects and links together the individual routines contained in the AUDEX program by inserting, on the AUDEX specification coding sheets, the answers to the AUDEX processing specifications. These are a series of narrative instructions, each of which requires a predefined type-coded answer. These specifications are completed only after the user has determined the input needed for the application and the form of output desired from it. Punched cards are then prepared from the specification coding sheets and are used in connection with the AUDEX programs and data files (see Figures 7–2, 7–3 and 7–4) in order to make the generalized routines achieve a specific purpose with the data available. The letters *JCL* (in Figure 7–4) are an abbreviation for "job control language."

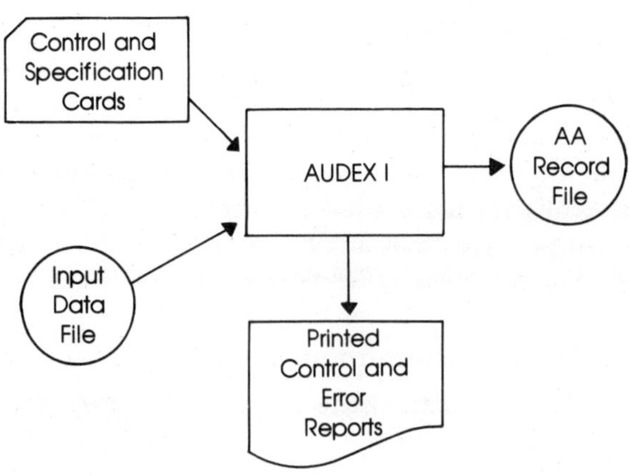

FIGURE 7–2. The AUDEX I Program

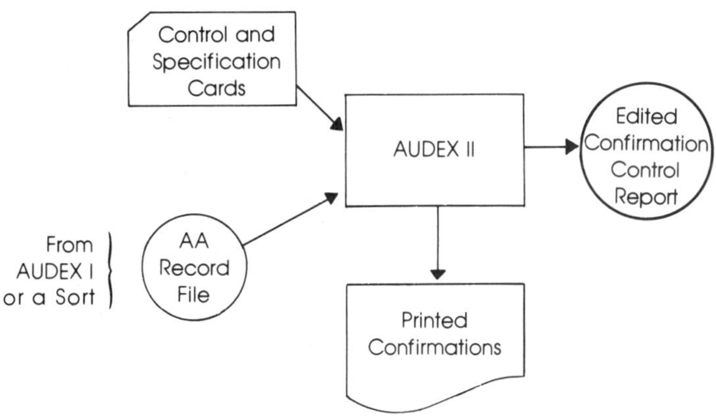

FIGURE 7–3. The AUDEX II Program

AUDEX I. As we observed, the principal function of AUDEX I is to extract data from input files and to reformat the extracted data in a consistent manner into special records characterized as the AA Record File. This file is then used with the report generation program (AUDEX II) to provide a report that can be incorporated into the working papers. In addition to extraction and reformatting, AUDEX I can, at the user's option, do the following:

1. Check input fields for proper sequence or order.
2. Perform mathematical calculations — such as addition, subtraction, multiplication, and division — on extracted fields.
3. Accumulate extracted fields.

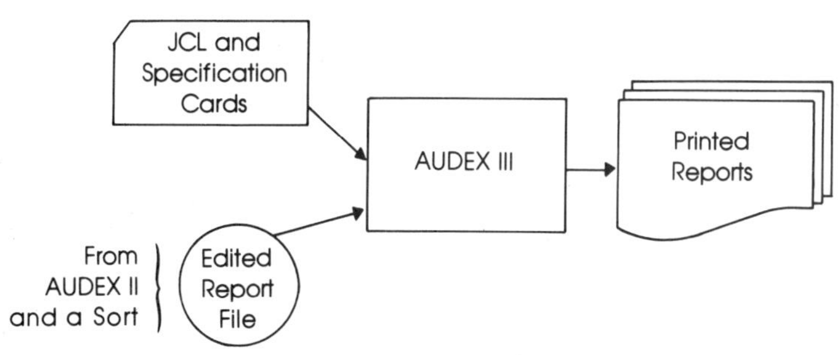

FIGURE 7–4. The AUDEX III Program

4. On the basis of specific characteristics or sampling criteria, choose data to be passed on to AUDEX II.

This program will process input data from card, tape, and disk files.

AUDEX II. The principal function of AUDEX II, we said, is to format the printed reports or confirmations from data contained in the AA Record File. The user need only describe the format of the output report for AUDEX II through specification cards. Before editing and printing reports, AUDEX II can, at the user's option, be used to do these tasks:

1. Analyze a field and sort it into one of several categories, such as stratification of an accounts receivable master file by dollar amount.
2. Summarize records with similar characteristics, such as inventories with very slow turnover.
3. Accumulate data for control and grand totals, such as payrolls, cash receipts, or cash disbursements.
4. Select or reject records with specific characteristics, such as credit balances in accounts receivable.
5. Sample input records on a random, systematic, or block basis.

Additional Capabilities of AUDEX 100. In addition to the basic functions discussed in the preceding paragraphs, AUDEX 100 contains certain features, uses of which are optional. These include four distinct abilities:

1. To process two data files simultaneously as input to AUDEX I.
2. To sort the AA Record File before printing in AUDEX I.
3. To produce additional output files during the running of AUDEX II that can be used to print specific reports or for additional processing.

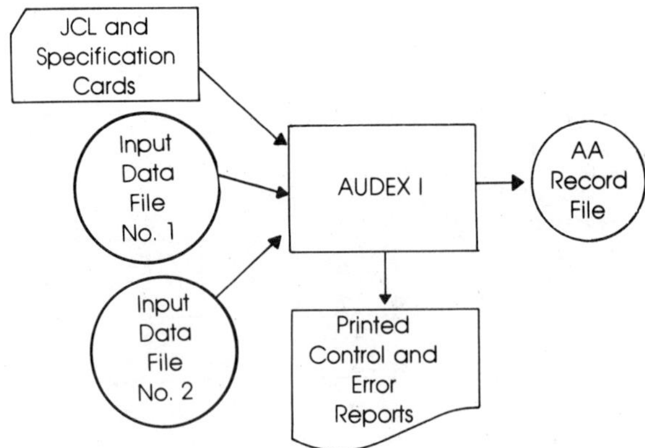

FIGURE 7–5. Simultaneous Processing of Two Files

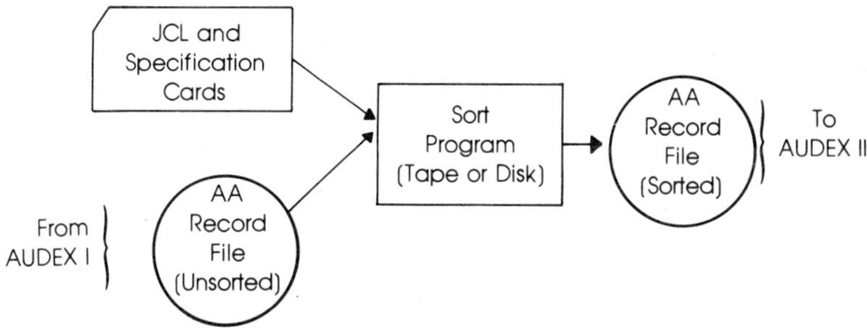

FIGURE 7–6. Sorting of Record Files

4. To print an edited report file containing the data written temporarily on tape or disk during the running of AUDEX II by using AUDEX III.

The processing flows associated with the uses of these options are shown in Figures 7–5, 7–6, 7–7, and 7–8.

Concluding Remarks

As we have observed, an auditor can use AUDEX 100 without having computer programming capability. Arthur Andersen does, however, provide an AUDEX training school to equip the auditor to design, specify, and implement AUDEX specifications, all of which can be done without having to know or apply programming

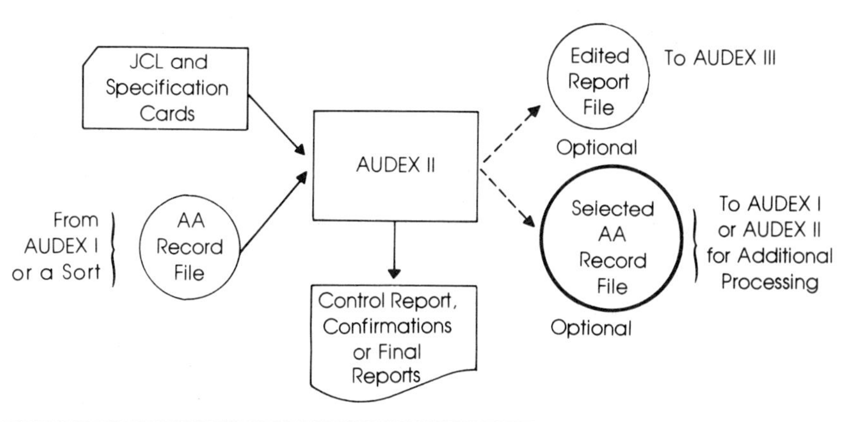

FIGURE 7–7. Production of Additional Output Files

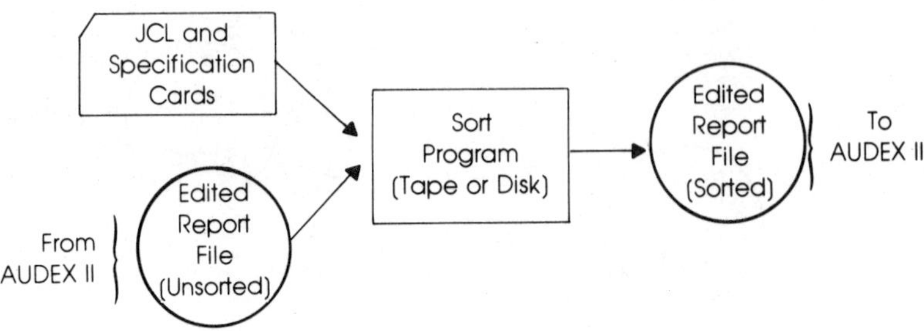

FIGURE 7–8. Printout of Edited Report File

language skills. The firm has a policy of having all its auditors receive a certain amount of training in auditing in a computer environment: it appears that such an education and training program would be necessary to implement effectively the use of the AUDEX 100 software package.

AUDEX 100 provides the auditor with the tool to meet the computer challenge but it is important that we recognize that it is only a tool. Its use does not affect the auditor's basic objectives. Furthermore, AUDEX 100 alone cannot do auditing. Computer programs can be prepared to instruct the computer to perform some of the tasks that auditors have historically done manually. However, in the final analysis, *the auditor must still apply judgment* as to how those programs will be used, provide the detailed instructions of the procedures they are to perform, and evaluate the results produced by them.

Appendix 7–A more specifically illustrates how this general purpose audit software package can be used in verifying computerized records of inventory and accounts receivable.

SUMMARY

Computerized accounting records have provided a challenge to an auditing profession accustomed to following a person-readable audit trail in accumulating audit evidence. In this chapter we have seen how that challenge could be met by (1) auditing around the computer, (2) auditing through the computer by use of extensive printouts, or (3) using the computer to directly extract and process data from the machine-readable records. The third option is the most effective and is the one followed by larger auditing firms today.

We pointed out that the third option could be accomplished by using client-developed programs, specific firm-developed programs, or a generalized computer software package that could be adapted to a wide variety of situations. Larger auditing firms have for the most part elected to implement the last of these choices.

In the concluding part of the chapter we elaborated on the development and use of generalized computer software packages, with particular emphasis on the AUDEX 100 package used by Arthur Andersen.

APPENDIX 7–A: Uses of General Purpose Computer Audit Software

A general purpose computer audit software package will include computer programs that allow the auditor to perform a number of functions on a variety of file media and record formats. Such a package can be used to do the following:

1. Perform or verify mathematical calculations.
2. Include, exclude, or summarize items having specified characteristics.
3. Provide subtotals and final totals.
4. Compute, select, and evaluate statistical samples for audit tests.
5. Print results in a form specified by the auditor.
6. Arrange detailed items in a format or sequence that will facilitate an audit step.
7. Compare, merge, or match the contents of two or more files.
8. Provide machine-readable files in a format specified by the auditor.

However, as we saw in the chapter, appropriate control and specification cards must be meshed with the general purpose computer program to achieve these goals. In this appendix, we explain in more detail how that meshing is accomplished in two functions: verifying computerized inventory and accounts receivable records.

Use of General Purpose Software in the Verification of Inventory

In situations where, for example, the client has prepunched inventory count cards identifying individual inventory items, specification cards can be introduced along with the general purpose audit program to cause the computer to carry out any of the following auditing procedures:

1. Comparison of the data on a CPA's set of prepunched inventory count cards secured from test counts of inventory items, with the data included on the disk or tape containing the client's inventory. The output from the computer in this situation would be a printout that lists all differences by inventory items.
2. Selection and printout of a random sample of items from the client's inventory file, based on such things as unit cost or total value. The printout can then be compared with the test counts and independently determined values for those inventory items.
3. Test of the inventory file for items or parts on which the client has had no recent transaction. A printout of those items can then be used in identifying slow-moving and obsolete inventory items.

4. Examination of the inventory file for items or parts for which the quantity on hand is excessive in relation to either a maximum quantity listed or the quantity used or sold during the year. The printout of that list can then be used in determining overstocked or slow-moving items.
5. Keypunching of auditor's test counts of quantities into cards and introduction of specification cards that will cause the computer to match those cards against the client's master file of quantities for the parts shown on those cards. The output would then be a printout of differences between the recorded amounts and the auditor's count of those items.
6. Introduction of specification cards to cause the computer to extend the values on the auditor's test count cards on the basis of the unit costs found in the client's master inventory file. The printout of those items can then be compared with market in verifying the valuation of inventory.

Use of General Purpose Software in the Verification of Accounts Receivable

1. Specification cards can be introduced to require the computer to stratify the individual accounts in the accounts receivable master file according to specified dollar ranges and to print out accounts to be verified on the basis of specified test parameters.
2. The computer can be directed to select individual accounts receivable from the client's master file if those accounts meet specified characteristics for confirmation. The computer will generally also be directed to print out the confirmation requests for the selected accounts. Information from confirmation requests can then be converted to machine-readable form so that the computer can compare the confirmation data with the client's file for the confirmed accounts.
3. Specification cards can be introduced to cause the computer to identify and print out all accounts receivable, with certain characteristics — for example, accounts showing credit balances. Those accounts can then be verified against underlying documents.
4. The computer can be directed to examine the client's master file of accounts receivable for the purpose of identifying and listing the individual account balances that are past due in terms of the credit arrangement in effect with the individual customers.
5. Specification cards can be introduced to cause the computer to test the extensions and footings of elements of the accounts receivable ledger and to print out a list of errors found in that process.
6. The computer can be directed to test the accounts receivable file for completeness — for example, locating accounts with no credit limits.
7. Specification cards can be used to cause the computer to scan the accounts and print out a list of accounts that have balances in excess of credit limits.

APPENDIX 7–B: Computer Software Packages Used by Various Firms

Firm	Software	Firm	Software
Whinney Murray 57 Chiswell Street London, EC1 4SY, England	ASK-360	Price Waterhouse & Co. 1251 Avenue of the Americas New York, N.Y. 10020	Computer File Analyzer
Alexander Grant & Co. One First National Plaza Chicago, Ill. 60670	AUDASSIST	Dylakor Software Systems, Inc. 16255 Ventura Boulevard Encino, Calif. 91436	DYL-250 DYL-260

Firm	Software	Firm	Software
Arthur Andersen & Co. 69 West Washington Street Chicago, Ill. 60602	AUDEX AUDEX 100	Cullinane Corporation Wellesley Office Park 20 William Street Wellesley, Mass. 02181	EDP-Auditor
U.S. Department of Commerce Springfield, Va. 22151	AUDIT		
Seymour Schneidman & Associates 405 Park Avenue New York, N.Y. 10022	AUDITAID	Department of Health, Education and Welfare Audit Agency Office of the Assistant Secretary, Comptroller 330 Independence Avenue, S.W. Washington, D.C. 20201	HEWCAS
Deloitte, Haskins & Sells 1114 Avenue of the Americas New York, N.Y. 10036	AUDITAPE		
Dataskil Reading Bridge House Reading, England	AUDITFIND	Informatics, Inc. 21050 Vanowen Street Canoga Park, Calif. 91303	MARK IV AUDIT
Coopers & Lybrand 1251 Avenue of the Americas New York, N.Y. 10020	AUDITPAK II	Computer Resources Corp. 23 Leroy Avenue Darien, Conn. 06820	PROBE
Program Products, Inc. 95 Chestnut Ridge Road Montvale, N.J. 07645	AUDIT ANALYZER	Programming Methods, Inc. 1301 Avenue of the Americas New York, N.Y. 10019	SCORE-AUDIT
Ernst & Whinney 1300 Union Commerce Building Cleveland, Ohio 44115	AUTRONIC-16 AUTRONIC-32	Touche Ross & Co. 1633 Broadway New York, N.Y. 10019	STRATA
John Cullinane Corporation 20 Williams Street Wellesley, Mass. 02181	CARS EDP AUDITOR	Peat, Marwick, Mitchell & Co. 345 Park Avenue New York, N.Y. 10022	S/2190

Source: W. Thomas Porter and William E. Perry, *EDP Controls and Auditing*, 3rd. ed. (Boston: Kent, 1981), p. 271.

NOTES

1. In writing the first pages of this chapter, the authors have relied extensively on materials from W. Thomas Porter and William E. Perry, *EDP Controls and Auditing*, 3rd ed. (Boston: Kent, 1981).

2. Ibid., pp. 152–53.

3. Robert S. Roussey, "Audex 100 — A Compiler Audit Program for Larger Memory Systems," *Arthur Andersen Chronicle* (July 1975): 17.

4. Porter and Perry, *EDP Controls and Auditing*, pp. 153–54.

5. Ibid., p. 161.

6. Ibid., pp. 157–61.

7. David N. Ricchiute, "A Case for Automated Workpapers," *Journal of Accountancy* (January 1981): 71–75.

8. This section of the chapter is a summarization of the following publications by Arthur

Andersen and Company: Milton H. Fortsons and Eugene L. Delves, "AUDEX — Computer AUDit EXtract System," *Arthur Andersen Chronicle* (December 1969); Robert S. Roussey, "Audex 100 — A Compiler Audit Program for Larger Memory Systems," *Arthur Andersen Chronicle* (July 1975): 10–18; Arthur Andersen and Company, *AUDEX 100 — Computer AUDit EXtract System User's Manual* (September 1975).

QUESTIONS FOR CLASS DISCUSSION

Q7–1 What is the relationship between the development of computerized accounting records and the use of the computer as an audit tool?

Q7–2 Has the use of the computer as an audit tool increased the cost of performing audits? Explain.

Q7–3 Can you name at least ten procedures that a typical computer software package can be expected to perform during the course of an audit?

Q7–4 What are the sources from which the auditor might be able to secure a computer program that will allow use of the computer in the performance of an audit?

Q7–5 What are the advantages and disadvantages of using an audit program prepared by a client in performing an audit? If such a program is used, what must the auditor do before accepting the computer output produced by the program?

Q7–6 Is it practical for the auditing firm to prepare a separate computer program to be used in the performance of the audit for each client? Explain.

Q7–7 What are the five steps the auditor must carry out in the development of a computer audit program?

Q7–8 How can generalized audit programs overcome the disadvantages associated with the use of client-prepared programs and with the use of programs prepared by the auditor for each individual audit?

Q7–9 What is meant by *audit work files*? How are they created?

Q7–10 What are five functions that generalized audit software programs typically have the capability of performing?

Q7–11 What are four distinct steps normally followed by an auditor in developing and using a generalized computer audit software package?

Q7–12 How is a generalized computer software package typically adapted to the specific audit tasks to be performed during the audit of a client's financial statements?

Q7–13 Will computer printouts be included as part of the audit workpapers when the computer is used as a tool in performing the audit? Explain.

Q7–14 What is meant by *automated workpapers*?

Q7–15 What are the functional capabilities of the AUDEX 100 software package?

Q7–16 What is the function of control and specification cards in using the AUDEX 100 computer software package?

Q7–17 What relationship exists between the AUDEX I and AUDEX II elements of the AUDEX 100 computer software package?

Q7–18 Can you name at least five inventory audit procedures that can be performed by the computer using a generalized computer audit program supplemented by appropriate job control language and specification cards?

Q7–19 What are at least five accounts receivable audit procedures that the computer can perform using a generalized computer audit program and appropriate job classification language specification cards?

SHORT CASES

C7–1 A CPA's client, Boos & Baumkirchner, Inc., is a medium-sized manufacturer of products for the leisure time activities market (camping equipment, scuba gear, bows and arrows, etc.). During the past year, a computer system was installed, and inventory records of finished goods and parts were converted to computer processing. The inventory master file is maintained on a disk. Each record of the file contains the

a. Item or part number.
b. Description.
c. Size.
d. Unit of measure code.
e. Quantity on hand.
f. Cost per unit.
g. Total value of inventory on hand at cost.
h. Date of last sale or usage.
i. Quantity used or sold this year.
j. Economic order quantity.
k. Code number of major vendor.
l. Code number of secondary vendor.

In preparation for year-end inventory, the client produces two identical sets of preprinted inventory count cards. One set is for the client's inventory counts and the other is for the CPA's use to make audit test counts. Keypunched into the cards and interpreted on their face are the

(1) Item or part number.
(2) Description.
(3) Size.
(4) Unit of measure code.

In taking the year-end inventory, the client's personnel will write the actual counted quantity on the face of each card. When all counts are complete, the counted quantity will be keypunched into the cards. The cards will be processed against the disk file, and quantity-on-hand figures will be adjusted to show the actual count. A computer listing will be prepared to show any missing inventory count cards and all quantity adjustments of more than $100 in value. These items will be investigated by client personnel, and all required adjustments will be made. When adjustments have been completed, the final year-end balances will be computed and posted to the general ledger.

The CPA has available a general purpose computer audit software package that will run on the client's computer and can process both card and disk files.

Required:

a. In general and without regard to the preceding facts, discuss the nature of general purpose computer audit software packages and list the various types and uses of such packages.

b. List and describe at least five ways a general purpose computer audit software package can be used to assist in all aspects of the audit of the inventory of Boos & Baumkirchner, Inc. (For example, the package can be used to read the disk inventory master file and list items and parts with a high unit cost or total value. Such items can be included in the test counts to increase the dollar coverage of the audit verification.)

(AICPA adapted)

C7–2 In the past, the records to be evaluated in an audit have been printed reports, listings, documents, and written papers — all of which are visible output. However, in fully computerized systems employing daily updating of transaction files, output and files are frequently in machine-readable forms such as cards, tapes, or disks. Thus, they often present the auditor with an opportunity to use the computer in performing an audit.

Required:

Discuss how the computer can be used to aid the auditor in examining accounts receivable in such a fully computerized system.

(AICPA adapted)

C7–3 Regina Peters, CPA, has examined the financial statements of the Solt Manufacturing Company for several years and is making preliminary plans for the audit for the year ended June 30, 19X2. During this examination, Peters plans to use a set of generalized computer audit programs. Solt's EDP manager has agreed to prepare special tapes of data from company records for the CPA's use with the generalized programs.

The following information is applicable to Peters's examination of Solt's accounts payable and related procedures:

a. The formats of pertinent tapes (see the accompanying four file formats).

b. The following monthly runs are prepared:

(1) Cash disbursements by check number.

(2) Outstanding payables.

(3) Purchase journals arranged by account charged and by vendor.

c. Vouchers and supporting invoices, receiving reports and purchase order copies are filed by vendor code. Purchase orders and checks are filed numerically.

d. Company records are maintained on magnetic tapes. All tapes are stored in a restricted area within the computer room. A grandfather, father, son policy is followed for retaining and safeguarding tape files.

Required:

a. Explain the grandfather, father, son policy. Describe how files could be reconstructed when this policy is used.

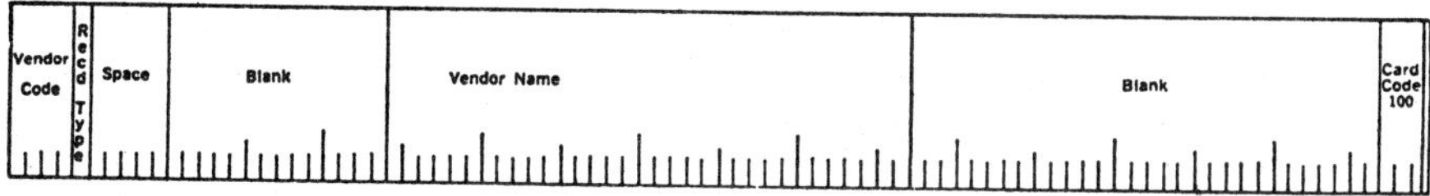

Master File—Vendor Address

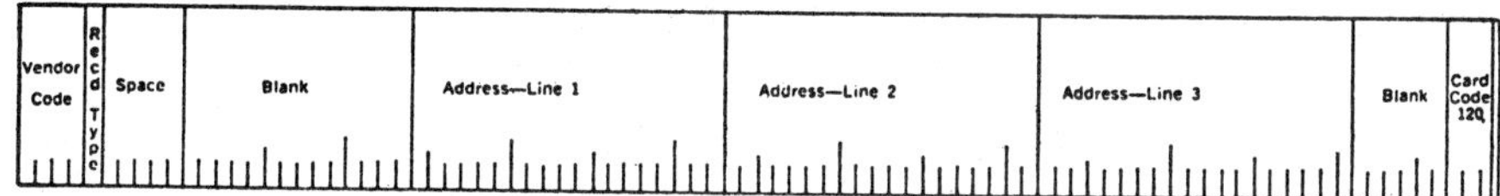

Transaction File—Expense Detail

Vendor Code | Record Type | Voucher Number | Blank | Batch | Voucher Number | Voucher Date | Vendor Code | Invoice Date | Due Date | Invoice Number | Purchase Order Number | Debit Account | Prod Type | Product Code | Blank | Amount | Quantity | Card Code 160

Transaction File—Payment Detail

Vendor Code | Record Type | Voucher Number | Blank | Batch | Voucher Number | Voucher Date | Vendor Code | Invoice Date | Due Date | Invoice Number | Purchase Order Number | Check Number | Check Date | Blank | Amount | Blank | Card Code 170

b. Discuss whether company policies for retaining and safeguarding the tape files provide adequate protection against losses of data.

c. Describe the controls that the CPA should maintain over
   (1) Preparing the special tape.
   (2) Processing the special tape with the generalized computer audit programs.

d. Prepare a schedule for the EDP manager outlining the data that should be included on the special tape for the CPA's examination of accounts payable and related procedures. This schedule should show the
   (1) Client tape from which the item should be extracted.
   (2) Name of the item of data.

(AICPA adapted)

C7–4 Rip van Longsleeper, CPA, introduced to you in the Short Cases section of Chapter 6, has just completed his evaluation of the computerized accounting system in accordance with your earlier recommendations. He now needs to confirm a sample of his client's accounts receivable. He asks you to explain how he can select that sample and then best proceed with the confirmation of accounts receivable. He again complains that he cannot find the individual accounts on the reel of magnetic tape containing the accounts receivable balances.

Required:

Explain to Mr. Longsleeper how he should proceed with the confirmation of accounts receivable.

PROBLEMS

P7–1 Select the best answer for each of the following items.

a. Data Corporation has just completely computerized its billing and accounts receivable recordkeeping. You want to make maximum use of the new computer in your audit of Data Corporation. Which of the following audit techniques could *not* be performed through a computer program?
   (1) Tracing audited cash receipts to accounts receivable credits.
   (2) Selecting on a random number basis accounts to be confirmed.
   (3) Examining sales invoices for completeness, consistency between different items, valid conditions, and reasonable amounts.
   (4) Resolving differences reported by customers on confirmation requests.

b. An auditor would be *least* likely to use a generalized computer audit program for which of the following tasks?
   (1) Selecting and printing accounts receivable confirmations.
   (2) Listing accounts receivable confirmation exceptions for examination.
   (3) Comparing accounts receivable subsidiary files to the general ledger.
   (4) Investigating exceptions to accounts receivable confirmations.

c. The primary purpose of a generalized computer audit program is to allow the auditor to
   (1) Use the client's employees to perform routine audit checks of the electronic data-processing records that otherwise would be done by the auditor's staff accountants.
   (2) Test the logic of computer programs used in the client's electronic data-processing systems.
   (3) Select larger samples from the client's electronic data-processing records than would otherwise be selected without the generalized program.
   (4) Independently process client electronic data-processing records.

d. An auditor can use a generalized computer audit program to verify the accuracy of
   (1) Data-processing controls.
   (2) Accounting estimates.
   (3) Totals and subtotals.
   (4) Account classifications.

e. Auditors often make use of computer programs that perform routine processing functions such as sorting and merging. These programs are made available by electronic data-processing companies and others and are specifically referred to as
   (1) User programs.
   (2) Compiler programs.
   (3) Supervisory programs.
   (4) Utility programs.

f. The purpose of using generalized computer programs is to test and analyze a client's computer

(1) Systems.
(2) Equipment.
(3) Records.
(4) Processing logic.

g. A primary advantage of using generalized audit packages in the audit of an advanced EDP system is that it enables the auditor to
(1) Substantiate the accuracy of data through self-checking digits and hash totals.
(2) Utilize the speed and accuracy of the computer.
(3) Verify the performance of machine operations that leave visible evidence of occurrence.
(4) Gather and store large quantities of supportive evidential matter in machine-readable form.

h. Which of the following is an advantage of generalized computer audit packages?
(1) They are all written in one identical computer language.
(2) They can be used for audits of clients that use differing EDP equipment and file formats.
(3) They have reduced the need for the auditor to study input controls for EDP-related procedures.
(4) Their use can be substituted for a relatively large part of the required compliance testing.

(AICPA adapted)

P7–2 An auditor is conducting an examination of the financial statements of a wholesale cosmetics distributor with an inventory consisting of thousands of individual items. The distributor keeps its inventory in its own distribution center and in two public warehouses. An inventory computer file is maintained on a computer disk, and at the end of each business day the file is updated. Each record of the inventory file contains the

a. Item number.
b. Location of item.
c. Description of item.
d. Quantity on hand.
e. Cost per item.
f. Date of last purchase.
g. Date of last sale.
h. Quantity sold during year.

The auditor is planning to observe the distributor's physical count of inventories as of a given time. The auditor will have available a computer tape of the data on the inventory file on the date of the physical count and a general purpose computer software package.

Required:

The auditor is planning to perform basic inventory auditing procedures. Identify the basic inventory auditing procedures and describe how the use of the general purpose software package and the tape of the inventory file data might be helpful to the auditor in performing such auditing procedures.

Organize your answer as follows:

Basic Inventory Auditing Procedure	How General Purpose Computer Software Package and Tape of the Inventory File Data Might Be Helpful
1. Observe the physical count, making and recording test counts where applicable.	Determining which items are to be test counted by selecting a random sample of a representative number of items from the inventory file as of the date of the physical count.

(AICPA adapted)

CHAPTER

SAMPLING TECHNIQUES AND INTERNAL CONTROL EVALUATION

Sampling is the technique used to gather most documentary audit evidence. Historically, individual items included in audit samples were selected on a purely judgmental basis. However, in recent years auditors have, to an increasing degree, used statistical sampling techniques in selecting the elements of various audit samples.

In this chapter, we deal with the problem of selecting and using audit samples, with primary emphasis on statistical sampling techniques. Our discussion covers the following topics:

1. The need for audit sampling.
2. Statistical terminology relevant to the use of statistical sampling in auditing.
3. The relationship between generally accepted auditing standards and statistical sampling techniques.
4. The relationship between the objectives of statistical sampling and various statistical sampling techniques.
5. Attribute sampling.
6. Discovery sampling.

We also include appendixes consisting of tables for determining sample sizes and evaluating sample results at 90, 95, and 99 percent reliability levels.

THE NEED FOR SAMPLING IN AUDITING

In their examinations of financial statements, auditors often encounter balances resulting from many small repetitive transactions. These transactions are evidenced by many documents, all possessing somewhat similar characteristics. Clearly, it is not cost effective to inspect every transaction or document for a particular characteristic. Furthermore, when the audit population is somewhat homogeneous, we are justified in concluding that such an inspection is not necessary — that we can *reasonably infer* whether a particular control or account balance was treated appropriately as all the documents were processed. In such situations, auditors typically select a sample of transactions and examine those items for the desired characteristic. Then, on the basis of the findings in the sample, they make inferences about the true (but unknown) occurrence of the characteristic in the audit population. Actual occurrence is unknown because they have checked only a sample rather than all transactions.

To use sampling techniques effectively, the auditor must be fully aware of the risks associated with their use. He or she must also understand the differences between purely judgmental and statistical sampling procedures.

Risks Associated with Sampling in Auditing

When less than 100 percent of the items in a population are examined, the conclusions drawn therefrom about the audit population are subject to risk of error. That is to say, there is always some risk that the auditor inferred a certain characteristic about the population that is not, in fact, present. ***Ultimate risk*** is approximately the mathematical product of two separate risks: (1) the risk that *material errors or irregularities have occurred* in the process used to develop the financial statements, and (2) the risk that the audit *sample was inadequate* to detect those errors and irregularities. The auditor relies on the system of *internal control* to reduce the first risk, and on *substantive tests* (analytical review and tests of details) to reduce the second risk. The relationship between these types of risks is shown mathematically later in this chapter.

The errors associated with each of these types of risk can advantageously be classified into two general categories: sampling errors and nonsampling errors. A ***sampling error*** occurs when the auditor draws a sample that does not contain the same characteristics as those possessed by the population as a whole. When that happens, the auditor may make improper inferences because the sample was not representative of the population with respect to the characteristic being tested. Such sampling errors can be classified into two subcategories:

- ***Alpha (α) risk,*** or Type I error: The risk of rejecting a hypothesis (a statement to be tested) which in fact is true.
- ***Beta (β) risk,*** or Type II error: The risk of accepting a hypothesis which in fact is false.

A ***nonsampling error,*** on the other hand, is the result of errors made in auditing the sample. Examples of nonsampling errors include use of inadequate or irrelevant supporting documents, misunderstanding the inferences drawn from various types of evidence, and mistaken judgments based on that evidence.

The audit should be directed toward adequately controlling both sampling and nonsampling errors. *The risk of sampling error* can be reduced in both nonstatistical and statistical applications by increasing sample size. However, *the probability of sampling error* can be measured only when statistical sampling techniques are employed. Nonsampling errors, on the other hand, must be controlled by adherence to the general and fieldwork portions of GAAS, as well as quality control standards for the conduct of an audit practice.

Comparison of Statistical Sampling with Judgmental Sampling

We have observed that the auditor may rely either on judgment or statistical techniques in drawing an audit sample. Each of these methods is appropriate in one or more phases of most audit engagements.

Strict ***judgmental sampling*** relies purely on *the auditor's seasoned experience* in drawing an appropriate sample. This technique is used primarily when audit populations consist of either a small number of high-dollar-value items or items with an immaterial aggregate amount. For example, judgmental sampling typically would be used in selecting twenty additions to property and equipment, worth $100,000, for vouching when total additions consist of forty items aggregating $150,000.

Statistical sampling, in contrast to strict judgmental sampling, relies on *the laws of probability* in selecting sample data. In evaluating sample data, then, the discipline of statistics allows the auditor to quantitatively measure (and therefore control) the risk of sampling error that results from examining only part of the data. Statistical sampling is used primarily when making judgments about an audit population consisting of a large number of homogeneous items. For example, an auditor may use this sampling technique to estimate the percentage of deviation from an established internal control procedure relating to sales, when 75,000 sales transactions have been processed during the year.

In contrasting statistical sampling with judgmental sampling, you should remember that *all sampling requires the exercise of judgment* by the auditor. Sampling results are not ends in themselves. They merely provide evidence which, when taken with other information collected by the auditor, provides the basis for making sound judgment-based audit decisions. It is not possible, or even desirable, to eliminate judgment from any sampling plan. GAAS do not require statistically valid sampling plans. However, *GAAS do require that samples upon which conclusions regarding the entire audit population are based be selected from the entire audit population* under examination. Statistically valid sampling plans have an advantage over strictly judgmental plans because of their unique ability to provide a mathematical measure of uncertainty (risk) that results from examining a sample rather than an entire population of data. Statistical plans also eliminate personal biases in choosing the elements of the sample and in establishing the sample size. Since mathematical laws are used to determine the size of the statistical sample, it is possible for the auditor to specify and control the extent of both α (Type I) and β (Type II) risks that he or she is willing to take. Generally, such sampling risks are controlled by varying the size of the sample. There is always an inverse relationship between sampling risk and sample size. (For example, the sampling risk could be reduced to zero by taking a 100 percent census of each population. As stated previously, however, because of cost factors, we rarely evaluate 100 percent of the population.)

STATISTICAL TERMINOLOGY RELEVANT TO AUDITING

To apply statistical sampling appropriately in conducting an audit, the auditor must understand statistical terminology and be able to relate those terms to the audit process. In this section we discuss the statistical terms most relevant to auditing.

Probability

Statistical sampling relies on the laws of probability for its validity. In auditing, we are concerned with two interpretations of probability. One, ***relative frequency***, is an objective interpretation, based purely on the laws of chance: each item in the population is seen to have a known probability of being selected. This interpretation allows the auditor to make statistical calculations based on sample results and to make probabilistic statements about the entire population based on the sample results. For example, if the probability of a specific item being chosen is .02 (2 chances in 100), then *repeated choices* made under the same circumstances would produce that item about two percent of the time. As is illustrated later, the relative frequency interpretation of probability is utilized in making *statistical inferences* about population characteristics.

A second interpretation, ***subjective probability***, considers probability to be a measure of the auditor's judgment. Subjective probability judgments, although made quite frequently by auditors, have been given minimal attention in the practical auditing literature. As an example of a subjective probability, an auditor may state: "The probability that analytical review will detect a material misstatement is .60." In other words, the auditor is giving .60/.40 odds in favor of the procedure detecting a misstatement.

Successful usage of statistical sampling in auditing requires integration of both the objective and subjective interpretations of probability. We will elaborate further on both interpretations as we continue our discussion of the sampling process. The relative frequency interpretation of probability requires the auditor to specify ***parameters*** — such as population, sampling unit, frame, characteristic, and selection method. On the other hand, he or she is always, either by implication or by specific statement, making subjective probability judgments.

Terms Associated with Sample Selections

A ***population*** (universe, field) is a well-defined collection of objects or events. The auditor may specify any audit population that gives the highest probability of fulfilling the audit objective. Audit populations may consist of all entries in an account, or a collection of customer accounts, or even the total number of dollars in a financial statement balance.

Sampling units are the individual members of the population. For example, the sampling units for the populations described in the preceding paragraph, would be the individual entries in an account, the individual customer accounts, or the individual dollars in a dollar population, respectively.

The ***frame*** is the physical representation of the sampling units. For example, each individual credit entry in a sales account would be represented by a sales invoice; each customer account would be supported by a ledger record (visible or machine readable).

The purpose of sampling is to enable the auditor to draw conclusions about a particular ***characteristic*** of the population. For example, the auditor may wish to draw a conclusion about the existence of an attribute or a variable within a population. An ***attribute*** *is a qualitative characteristic* that occurs with a certain frequency within a population. An example of such a characteristic is deviation from an established internal control procedure. A ***variable*** *is a quantitative characteristic*, such as the total audited dollar amount, the recorded dollar amount, or the difference between the audited amount and the recorded amount. To make an inference about a specified population characteristic, a corresponding characteristic for each sampling unit should be defined. In ***attribute sampling,*** which is the method most often used for compliance tests, specified deviations from established internal control procedures are the characteristics of interest to the auditor. Attributes of the sample are measured by the *number of occurrences* of deviations in the sample, and the corresponding population characteristic inferred is the ***frequency*** *(percentage)* of the population units that contain deviations. In ***variables sampling,*** which is the method most often used for substantive tests, the auditor may, for example, define as the characteristic either an audited amount or a difference between audited and book values for each sample item. This, in turn, will lead to an inference of either an amount for the population from which the sample was selected or a total amount of dollar error in the population, respectively.

The validity of inferences based on any sampling plan depends on the ***selection method*** chosen by the auditor. The selection method often used in the days before statistical sampling was ***block sampling.*** Block sampling is the selection of several sample items in sequence. By specifying a certain item to be included in a transaction, the auditor automatically will choose the remainder of that block of transactions for examination. An example of block sampling that is no longer permitted under generally accepted auditing standards is the ***test month*** selection method. In this method, a test month was selected arbitrarily by the auditor and all tests of transactions were performed using only that month's transactions as sample items. This method is no longer used because generally accepted auditing standards require sample items to be representative of the entire population from which they are drawn. Other block sample selection methods may produce representative samples and therefore be used under generally accepted auditing standards. This technique is acceptable only *if a sufficiently large number of blocks are used to produce a representative sample.* If the blocks of data chosen are monthly data, there should probably be data chosen from all months of the year in order to meet this criterion.

The method chosen for statistically selecting items should result in a known probability of selecting each item in the population. ***Random selection*** thus becomes an important element of each statistical sampling plan. While random selection cannot guarantee an audit sample that possesses characteristics representative of the population, it *allows use of probability laws to estimate the probability of selecting an unrepresentative sample.* The most common ways of selecting random samples are unrestricted sampling, systematic sampling, and stratified sampling.

Unrestricted random sampling without replacement of the sample items selected (the selection method most often used by auditors) relies on two basic underlying properties for its usefulness: (1) each unit in the population has an equal chance of being selected, and (2) each possible group of n items has an equal chance of being selected. To use unrestricted random selection, the auditor must first be able to identify each item in the population with a specific number. ***Random number tables*** or computer programs with *random number generators* can then be used to select items by number to be included in the sample. Selection of sample items can be made *either with or without replacement*, although sampling without replacement is usually more appropriate for audit populations. Figure 8–1 illustrates a partial random number table. In using the table, the auditor begins by selecting a random starting number. This can be done by making a "blind stab" at a certain point on the table or by using some other arbitrary method to select the first number. Next, the auditor must decide the interval between items and the direction to proceed (top to bottom, left to right, etc.). The sample can then be selected by following that plan until items equaling the desired sample size have been selected.

Let's look closer at the use of a random number table; suppose we want to select 360 sales invoices without replacement from a population of 25,000 items, numbered consecutively from 00001 to 25,000. We would first select an arbitrary starting point by making a "blind stab" with a pencil at the random number table. Assume that the point of the pencil falls on column (B), group 1, row 5 in Figure 8–1. We would then select invoice number 16856 as the first sample item. If we decide to proceed from that point down the columns of the random number table, selecting every tenth item, and from left to right by columns, the next sales invoice selected would be number 3651. We then continue that process until all 360 sample sales invoices have been selected. If duplicate numbers arise in the random number table, they are disregarded because we are sampling without replacement.

Systematic sampling is another means of obtaining a randomly selected sample if the population units are already in random order. Once the sample size (n) is determined by the auditor, the interval k is calculated as follows:

$$k = N/n,$$

where N = the number of items in the population. Using a random start as explained above, the auditor then selects every kth item for the audit sample. As an example, assume that we have decided on a sample size of 200 from an audit population containing 2,200 items. The interval $k = (2{,}200/200) = 11$. Using a random number table we will then obtain a random start from within the first eleven items in the population. We will then choose every eleventh item from the random starting point until a total of 200 sampling units have been drawn.

A major advantage of systematic selection is that it can be used without numbers being assigned to the units in the population. Therefore it may require less time than other random selection methods. However, the auditor should not assume that

	A	B	C	D	E	F	G
1	835431	206253	467521	029822	700399	554652	450184
	512651	743206	118787	587401	921517	015407	206860
	376187	189133	154812	828785	667020	998697	579598
	092530	869028	483691	165063	847894	041617	762973
	238036	016856	290105	538530	079931	412195	838814
	308168	717698	919814	092230	215657	469994	805803
2	773429	915639	900911	276895	149505	540379	224349
	171626	601259	009905	572567	441960	299704	313987
	180570	665625	424048	713009	830314	664642	521021
	558715	965963	494210	875287	488595	898691	713010
	345067	361180	989224	138905	355519	045847	746266
	583819	310956	174728	099164	118461	758000	496302
3	615026	599459	722322	555090	572720	826686	456517
	812358	389535	166779	441968	105639	632418	340890
	784592	003651	279275	055646	341897	510689	026160
	094619	636747	934082	787345	772825	603866	565688
	450908	919891	157771	114333	710179	062848	615156
	593546	728768	984323	290410	970562	906724	315005
4	873778	491131	209695	604075	783895	862911	772026
	965705	317845	169619	921361	315606	990029	745251
	311163	943589	540958	556212	760508	129963	236556
	454554	284761	269019	924179	670780	389869	519229
	124330	819763	596075	064570	495169	030185	866211
	920765	122124	423205	596357	469969	072245	359269
5	183002	540547	312909	389818	464023	768381	377241
	600135	865974	929756	162716	415598	878513	994633
	235787	023117	895285	027055	943962	381112	530492
	953379	655834	283102	836259	437761	391976	940853
	009658	521970	537626	806052	715247	808585	252503
	176570	849057	387097	311529	893745	450267	182626
6	747456	304530	931013	678688	270736	355032	400713
	486876	631985	368395	154273	959983	672523	210456
	987193	268135	867829	025419	301168	409545	131960
	358155	950977	170562	246987	884126	785621	467942
	021394	182615	049084	942153	278313	872709	693590
	735047	428941	630704	893281	716045	267529	427605

Source: Abridged with the permission of the author and publisher from H. N. Broom, "New Random Sampling Numbers," *Baylor Business Studies* No. 1 (Waco, Tex.: Hankamer School of Business, Baylor University, 1949).

FIGURE 8–1. Selected Random Digits

because the population is not sequentially ordered, it must be randomly ordered. When the auditor is unsure as to exactly how the population is ordered, he or she can beneficially use several random starts instead of one. For example in applying this method to the preceding example (seeking k), the auditor might plan to use 10 random starts and a sampling interval of 110. That would produce 10 subsamples of 20 items each (200 items in all).

Stratified sampling can be used in combination with either unrestricted random sampling or systematic sampling. The main advantage of stratified sampling is that it allows the auditor to adjust his or her sampling criteria for different segments of a ***heterogeneous population.*** Unrestricted random selection and systematic selection, when used without stratification, are most useful when populations are *homogeneous as to the characteristic which the auditor is examining.*

The primary objective of using stratification in audit samples is to decrease the effect of population variance on sample sizes. When the population is relatively homogeneous, variance (or average difference of items from the population mean) is relatively small, causing sample sizes to be small. Audit populations, however, are often heterogeneous, particularly when the characteristic being audited is the dollar amount. Many audit populations will, for example, contain numerous items with small dollar amounts, a few items with relatively large dollar amounts, and many items between the two extremes. This causes the population variance to increase substantially, which in turn may cause unstratified samples to be unreasonably large and costly to use. Stratified sampling has the advantage of dividing the heterogeneous audit population into a number of subpopulations, each of which has a much smaller variance than that of the unstratified population. The auditor may then apply different sampling criteria to each stratum in the population. Typically this would manifest itself by having the sample include a larger percentage of high-value stratum items than small-value stratum items. Stratification has the advantage of optimizing total sample size (i.e., making it as small, efficient, and cost effective as possible), while still providing a desired level of precision and confidence for the sampling results.

Precision and Reliability

All statistically valid statements include estimates of *precision* (accuracy) and *reliability* (risk). GAAS describes these terms as follows:

> Statistical samples are evaluated in terms of "precision," which is expressed as a range of values, plus and minus, around the sample result, and "reliability" (or confidence), which is expressed as the proportion of such ranges from all possible similar samples of the same size that would include the actual population value.[1]

Precision reflects the extent to which the characteristic found in the sample can be expected to correspond to the true (but unknown) characteristic of the population being tested. For example, assume that an auditor is examining a sample of sales invoices for proper approval by supervisory personnel and finds that the sample shows that 2 percent of the sample items deviate from this established internal control procedure. What may the auditor infer about the rate of deviation for the population as a whole? It is unlikely that the population occurrence rate will be exactly equal to the sample occurrence rate of 2 percent. However, he or she may statistically establish an interval (or range), say ±1 percent, around the sample occurrence rate, within which the true population characteristic is expected to fall. Precision ranges are stated in percentages for attribute samples and in dollar amounts for variables sampling.

There is an *inverse relationship between the absolute size of the precision interval and the preciseness of inference for the population.* In the example just cited, a precision interval of ±2 percent allows us to be only half as precise in our inference for the population as would a precision interval of ±1 percent. Therefore if all other factors remain the same, increasing the desired level of precision requires us to increase the size of the audit sample. The upper and lower boundaries of the precision interval are called the ***precision limits.*** In attribute sampling, we are more concerned with upper precision limits because these limits express the maximum (most conservative) estimate of possible deviations from the internal control attribute being tested. In variable sampling, we may be more concerned with either the lower precision limits or the upper limits, *depending on whether the major risk of misstatement is understatement or overstatement,* respectively. However, in all our variables estimation examples, we will establish both upper and lower precision limits.

Materiality is directly related to the statistical term "precision." The materiality of an allowable margin of error that the auditor is willing to accept determines the level of precision required in establishing a statistical sampling plan. Precision measures the maximum range of tolerable deviation from the true population characteristic; when the precision level is established we can decide whether to accept a sample result as being representative of the audit population. In attribute sampling, for example, a maximum acceptable upper precision limit of 5 percent means that the auditor is willing to accept as much as 5 percent deviation from a certain attribute in the population and still say that the client has substantially complied with the control procedure being tested. In variables sampling, a precision limit of ±$25,000 means that the auditor will accept a population as being *free from material error* if the value of the true population is within ±$25,000 of the value estimated from the sample.

Reliability, or confidence, is the mathematical probability that the true characteristic of the population will fall somewhere within the precision range described above. In this case, the relative frequency definition of probability is used. It is based on a hypothetical case involving an infinite number of random samples being drawn from the population, each with a stated precision range. The phrase "the proportion of such ranges" may be stated as "the number of times out of every 100 samples" that the true population characteristic would be included within the precision range. For example, if we have 90 percent confidence in our attribute sample cited above, we are willing to conclude that, if repeated random samples were drawn from the audit population, 90 out of every 100 samples would contain no more than 5 percent procedural deviations. With this degree of confidence, we are also projecting that in 10 of every 100 samples, the true population rate will be outside the 5 percent level and in that way could cause our conclusion about the population as a whole to be wrong.

Other things being the same, greater confidence can be achieved by increasing the size of the sample. In attribute sampling, the auditor often specifies a desired reliability (confidence) level of at least 90 percent. Also, with other factors being held constant, broadening the precision range will increase the level of confidence.

STATISTICAL SAMPLING AND GENERALLY ACCEPTED AUDITING STANDARDS

Statistical sampling techniques can beneficially be used in meeting the second and third standards of field work. The second standard requires that there be a proper study and evaluation of internal control. Statistical sampling can be used beneficially in selecting and evaluating items as the *auditor tests elements of the internal control system for compliance.* The client's key internal control procedures may be tested, for example, through the use of attribute sampling. The third standard of field work requires that sufficient, competent evidential matter be obtained (through the procedures of observation, inspection, confirmation, and inquiry) which will either support or refute the client's financial assertions. After the auditor has established the level of reliance that can be placed on the system of internal controls, he or she can use statistical sampling techniques in selecting and evaluating the individual elements of certain financial statement account balances — such as accounts receivable inventories, sales, and any other account balances that are derived from a large number of transactions.

The results of compliance tests of the system of control directly *affect the design of the audit program.* They help the auditor determine the nature, timing and, particularly the extent of substantive tests to be performed on account balances. Let us recall that the evidence-gathering phase of the typical audit examination can be divided into three distinct phases:

1. The preliminary review of the system of internal controls.
2. Tests for compliance with established control procedures.
3. Substantive tests of elements of the account balances.

During the preliminary review of internal controls, the auditor determines what control procedures are ostensibly included in the system. In this phase, compliance with those controls is assumed. During the compliance testing phase, on the other hand, the auditor tries to ascertain whether that assumption is warranted. Only after that has been done can the specific elements of the audit program relating to substantive tests be established.

There is always a possibility that the auditor's compliance tests (which may include both statistically selected samples and samples selected on the basis of the auditor's judgment) may lead to the conclusion that the system is reliable when, in fact, it is not. We can characterize this as the ***risk of unwarranted reliance.*** Specifically, the auditor might conclude that the system of internal control is reliable (and thus reduce substantive tests of balances produced by that system) when, in fact, the internal control system is unreliable. As we have observed, this risk can be traced to both sampling and nonsampling components.

On the other hand, the auditor must at the same time be concerned about the ***risk of overauditing.*** For example, he or she might conclude, after performing tests of compliance, that the system is unreliable and therefore might extend the substantive tests of balances produced by the system. Of course, such extended work could lead to the conclusion that the system was reliable after all, but only after unnecessary additional tests have been performed. Such errors can also be traced to both sampling and nonsampling components. They can lead to excessive fees and possible loss of clients.

While we need to control sampling risks in compliance tests by increasing sample sizes to appropriate levels, this should be accomplished within the broader context of controlling the ***total risk of unwarranted reliance*** — both the sampling and nonsampling portions. This means not only that the sample size must be sufficiently large, but also that the auditor must follow through with a careful analysis of the nature and causes of errors for the purpose of controlling nonsampling risks.

In substantive testing, the primary objective is to obtain evidence supporting the conformity of transactions, balances, and disclosures with GAAP or, stated another way, the *absence of material errors and irregularities* in their presentation. The auditor is confronted with the risk of concluding that the elements of the financial statements are presented in accordance with GAAP when in fact they are not. This risk can be subdivided into sampling and nonsampling components. Conversely, the auditor must consider the risk of concluding that the elements of financial statements are not presented in accordance with GAAP when in fact they are. This risk, too, may be subdivided into both sampling and nonsampling components.

Since the audit risk associated with either compliance or substantive tests can be subdivided into sampling and nonsampling components, it is desirable to consider each of those components separately for the purpose of controlling them. The format provided in auditing assumes that, *of the sampling risk components, the risk of accepting a hypothesis that is in fact false (β risk) is the most important to control.* This is logical, since the consequences of unwarranted reliance on internal control and unwarranted inference of fair presentation generally lead to unwarranted unqualified audit opinions. That can, in turn, result in legal repercussions for the auditor. However, remember that the result of the other (α risk) component can be loss of clients. Therefore, controlling that risk is also important. The following formula can be used to relate the ultimate risk associated with the entire audit *(R)* to the risk of unwarranted reliance on internal control *(IC)* and to the risk of unwarranted inference of fairness from substantive tests (*AR* and *TD*):

$$R = IC \times AR \times TD$$

where

R = *allowable ultimate risk* that monetary errors equal to a maximum tolerable (material) amount might remain undetected in the account or class of accounts after the auditor has completed all tests including compliance tests and substantive tests and analytical review procedures.

IC = assessment of risk that, if material errors have occurred in the financial statements, the system of *internal control* is inadequate to detect them. This risk is assigned after completion of both the preliminary review of internal control and compliance tests. It consists of both sampling and nonsampling components.

AR = assessment of the risk that *analytical review* and other relevant procedures would fail to detect material errors that may have occurred and were not detected by the system of internal control. This risk consists of sampling as well as nonsampling components.

TD = the allowable risk of incorrect acceptance of statement data based on *test data* from substantive tests of details of account balances. This risk also consists of both sampling and nonsampling components.

It is important, during the planning phase of the audit, to establish a maximum acceptable rate for *R*. Often, this risk will be subjectively set quite low, perhaps at .01. This means that the auditor is willing to accept a mathematical probability of 1 chance in 100 of material monetary errors going undetected because of the combined failure of the system of internal controls, the auditor's analytical review, and tests of financial statement details.

The risk of failure of the internal control system to detect material misstatements if they exist (*IC*) is usually a number assigned (between zero and one) *after the completion of the auditor's study and evaluation of the system of internal control.* It is composed of the β sampling risk element of *IC*, which is a function of the sample size, and the nonsampling risk element, which is a function of the judgment of the auditor. For example, suppose that the auditor's tests of compliance reveal a .05 chance that the compliance tests sample was unrepresentative of the true population characteristic. In addition, assume that the auditor subjectively determines that there is a .35 chance that the compliance tests produced mistaken inferences by the auditor which were related to inadequate audit procedures and mistakes in judgment. Total *IC* risk, therefore, would be .40 (.05 + .35).

The auditor must also subjectively judge the probability that analytical review (*AR*) will not detect a material misstatement. This probability is also set at some number between zero and one. In that way, judgments regarding the maximum allowable risk for (*R*) and (*AR*), plus maximum assessed risks for (*IC*), allow the calculation of (*TD*). For example, if *R* = .01, *IC* = .40, and *AR* = .50, it follows that

$$
\begin{aligned}
TD &= R \,/\, (IC \times AR) \\
&= .01 \,/\, .40 \times .50 \\
&= .05.
\end{aligned}
$$

This risk consists of both sampling (β) and nonsampling components. As we shall see in the next chapter, the risk for *TD* obtained by the preceding formula is instrumental in helping determine the sample size for substantive tests in statistical sampling.

STATISTICAL SAMPLING OBJECTIVES

There are several possible objectives of testing in auditing. For example, we may test for the purpose of estimating a characteristic of the population, protecting against large errors, discovering whether a specific characteristic exists in a population, or correcting a population balance. It is essential that the auditor establish the objective of the particular test to be performed before selecting a sampling plan because each of them typically calls for its own unique approach.

Estimation sampling is designed to project a characteristic of the audit population, such as the total dollar amount, or the occurrence rate of a particular internal control attribute. We were implicitly using the *estimation objective* in earlier sections of this chapter as we described sampling for variables and for attributes, respectively. Estimation is often the primary sampling objective of the independent auditor.

In implementing ***protective sampling***, the auditor uses random selection techniques to obtain the greatest coverage of population dollar amount. This technique provides assurance that large-dollar-value items, which could lead to large-dollar errors, will not be overlooked. The protection concept underlies the use of stratified sampling techniques discussed earlier in the chapter.

Discovery sampling is designed to ascertain whether a specifically defined characteristic falls within a predetermined critical minimum frequency. The sample size selected must be large enough to provide a specified *probability of finding at least one occurrence* of the characteristic in the population if that characteristic occurs with a certain frequency. The characteristic might, for example, be the occurrence of some type of irregularity, such as a fictitious account in accounts receivable. Discovery sampling is often used by the auditor in cases when there is reason to believe that some type of defalcation has occurred. In such cases the auditor must have reasonable assurance that a specific sample size would include at least one instance of such an occurrence if it exists with certain regularity within the population being examined.

The objective of ***corrective sampling*** is to find whether enough errors exist to cause the auditor to propose an audit adjustment. Corrective sampling is generally used when the auditor suspects in advance the probable nature or location of errors in the population, for special purpose examinations (such as when fraud has occurred and the auditor is engaged to determine its extent), or as an extension of auditing procedures after errors found in a sample have been analyzed.

Samples should be designed to prevent client employees from knowing which items are to be selected for testing by the independent auditor. This can be done by adding a few judgmentally selected items to a previously selected random sample, to ensure that certain types of transactions do not escape audit. When this is done, the auditor should be careful not to add the judgmentally selected items to his statistically selected random sample when evaluating the results of that sample. Instead, she or he should evaluate the judgmentally selected items separately.

COMPLIANCE TESTS: SAMPLING FOR ATTRIBUTES

Estimation sampling for attributes (or attribute sampling) is the method most often used by auditors to perform tests of compliance over internal controls. The population characteristic being estimated is usually deviation from established internal controls, *expressed as percentages*. For example, an auditor may wish to estimate the frequency of errors in sales invoice preparation or in posting to individual customer accounts receivable. Attribute sampling is not, however, limited to compliance tests in its application. It can also be used in substantive tests of account balances, in estimating, for example, the percentage of overdue accounts receivable or the percentage of raw materials inventory that is obsolete.

All statistical sampling processes, including attribute sampling, are accomplished through the following steps, listed in chronological order:

1. Identify the audit problem or objective.
2. Formulate a testable hypothesis statement from the identified audit objective.
3. Gather the audit evidence (the sampling process).
4. Examine the evidence gathered.
5. Evaluate the evidence.
6. Develop a logical conclusion based on the evidence.

We now show how these steps are followed in tests of compliance.

Identifying the Audit Problem

The ***basic audit problem*** in testing for compliance is to verify compliance with established control procedures. That involves dividing the system into its various control attributes (segments) so that the occurrence of each attribute can be considered as a separate audit problem. For example, there may be several critical control attributes included in the system of internal control over sales. Some of them are listed in Figure 8–2. To improve efficiency in sampling for attributes, the ***sampling frame*** can often be defined in such a way that several different attributes can be tested by use of the same sample of items. The auditor must determine how this can be done as the first step in designing the overall sampling plan and in evaluating the results.

As part of identifying the audit problem, we must define (1) the audit population, (2) the sampling unit, (3) the sampling frame, and (4) the attribute to be tested. For example, in tests of compliance with control procedures in the sales system, the audit population may be defined as all sales transactions. The ***sampling unit*** would then be

---

1. Prenumbered sales orders are prepared and controlled numerically for each sale.
2. Each sales order must be approved by a supervisor in the credit department before the sales transaction may be completed.
3. Prenumbered shipping tickets should be originated when sales orders have been approved.
4. Sales invoices are prepared only after a properly approved sales order is received by the sales department.
5. Supervisors in the sales department should review each sales invoice for pricing and mathematical accuracy and indicate that fact by initialing the sales documents.
6. The shipping department should receive a copy of each approved shipping ticket as authority to release goods.
7. The billing department should check each sales invoice for correct prices, quantities, and extensions before the invoice is mailed to the customer.
8. The accounts receivable department should prepare a daily sales summary and a control total from the approved sales invoices issued each day.
9. A copy of the prenumbered shipping ticket and one copy of each sales invoice should accompany all merchandise shipped to customers.

FIGURE 8–2. Attributes of Internal Control over Sales

each entry in the sales journal. The sampling frame or physical representation of those sampling units, would be the sales invoice package, containing copies of the sales order and sales invoice. The attribute to be tested could be approval of the sales order by a supervisor (as in attribute 2 of Figure 8–2).

Formulating a Testable Hypothesis

The *attribute to be tested* must be selected and a *hypothesis* must be developed for it. The control attributes of a system can be identified from a list of procedures such as those shown in Figure 8–2, from a flowchart, or from a narrative description of the system prepared during the review phase of the audit. It is important to select for compliance testing only those internal control attributes which the auditor wishes to rely upon and which, if missing, could result in material misstatements of financial statements. Recall from our earlier discussion of internal control that a *material weakness* is described as a condition in which the specific control procedures or the degree of compliance with them do not reduce to a relatively low level the risk that material errors or irregularities may occur and remain undetected. If these controls are found to be weak, the auditor must expand substantive tests over related financial statement balances in order to be able to express an unqualified audit opinion on the financial statements. Of the material attributes, some will be more important than others. For example, in Figure 8–2 the auditor may determine that the absence of prenumbered sales orders (control attribute 1) is more critical than the failure to have prenumbered shipping documents and sales invoices accompanying each order (attribute 9). More stringent requirements (precision and confidence levels) should be specified for samples testing the more material internal control attributes.

Once the attributes to be tested have been identified, we are ready to develop a testable hypothesis for each attribute. This testable statement is usually put in terms of the ***maximum acceptable deviation*** from the attribute that will be accepted. For example, if we want to test control attribute 1 in Figure 8–2, we might establish the following testable hypothesis for it:

> The rate of deviation for preparation of prenumbered sales orders does not exceed 5 percent.

Notice that this hypothesis is *specific.* It deals with a particular attribute — the preparation of prenumbered sales orders. If tests support the hypothesis, we can conclude that the client is complying with this internal control attribute. Compliance with this particular internal control procedure provides some evidence that financial statement balances associated with the control are materially correct. As a result, substantive tests over those balances may be reduced. If compliance tests lead to rejection of the hypothesis, we can conclude that the client is not complying with this control attribute. In the absence of mitigating strengths in other related controls, that finding would logically lead to the inference that financial statement balances associated with the control have a relatively high risk of error. Therefore, the auditor would probably extend the substantive tests of balances associated with this control.

Notice also that the hypothesis is *quantifiable.* That is, a maximum rate of acceptable deviation is stated which, if exceeded, affects the auditor's decision. For example, if the maximum rate of population deviation inferred from the audit sample exceeded our hypothesized 5 percent, we will make a different audit decision (i.e., extend substantive tests of associated financial statement balances) from the one we would make if the inferred population rate did not exceed 5 percent.

Gathering the Audit Evidence

The evidence-gathering process involves two steps:

1. Determining an appropriate sample size.
2. Selecting representative items of evidence (the sample).

Sample Size. Although population size may be important in developing the overall sampling plan, it becomes less important in attribute sampling when the population exceeds 1,000 items. With populations of this size, changes in the size of the population have only a minimal effect on sample size for a stated range of precision and level of confidence. The sample size is determined primarily by (1) desired level of precision; (2) desired reliability (confidence) in the sample result; and (3) expected population occurrence rate.

As stated previously, the *desired upper precision limit* (DUPL) is in a sense a specification of what constitutes a material deviation. The auditor is, through this device, expressing the maximum acceptable deviation from the established control procedure that is possible while asserting the conclusion that substantial compliance exists. *Desired reliability* expresses the auditor's judgment as to the mathematical probability that the upper precision limit will not exceed the prespecified level. *Expected population occurrence rate* is the auditor's "best guess" judgment as to the deviation rate expected to be found in the population. To determine this rate in practice, the auditor generally begins with the rate of occurrence found in the previous year. This rate may then be adjusted judgmentally, upward or downward, based on current-year improvement (or deterioration) in controls observed during the preliminary review of internal control. In a new engagement, the auditor may take a preliminary sample of transactions, examine them, and use that error occurrence rate as the expected occurrence rate.

Once the desired upper precision limit, the desired confidence, and the expected occurrence rate have been prespecified, tables such as those in Appendixes 8–A, 8–B, and 8–C may be consulted to determine sample size. Notice that these are separate tables for various levels of desired reliability — 90 percent, 95 percent, and 99 percent. Various desired upper precision limits appear in the column headings across the top of the table. Expected occurrence rates appear in the far left column. The following example should help illustrate how the table is used.

Assume that the auditor desired a maximum error occurrence rate of 5 percent at a 95 percent level of confidence. If the expected population occurrence rate were 2.5 percent, Appendix 8–B shows that the auditor should select a sample of 240 items. A computer audit program can be used to provide sample sizes if it is programmed to react to inputs of data included in these tables. When this is the case, computer files generally also contain a random number generator to select a representative sample in a random fashion.

Figure 8–3 describes the effect on sample size of changes in various inputs regarding population size, desired level of precision, desired confidence, and expected occurrence rate relating to a specific attribute. Although sample size does vary slightly with the size of the population, when we are sampling large populations (generally, those in excess of 1,000), changes in the size of the population have only a very small effect on sample size. However, changes in the desired level of precision, desired confidence, and expected error occurrence rate will have a significant effect on sample size. For example, if we specify a 95 percent confidence level and have a 2.5 percent expected error occurrence rate, and the desired upper precision limit is decreased from 5 percent to 4 percent, the sample size would increase from 240 to 550 items, an increase of 120 percent (see Appendix 8–B).

If the desired confidence level in the example above was decreased from 95 percent to 90 percent, with a 2.5 percent expected error rate and a desired upper precision limit of 5 percent, the sample size would be reduced from 240 to 160, or 33⅓ percent. Finally, if the expected error occurrence rate increased from 2.5 to 3.5 percent, at a 95 percent desired level of confidence and a 5 percent desired upper precision limit, sample size would increase from 240 to 650, or 171 percent. Figure 8–4 illustrates the process of sample selection for each control attribute in our hypothetical example, using the tables provided in Appendixes 8–A, 8–B, and 8–C.

Sample Items. After sample sizes have been determined, the auditor should next *select representative sample items.* The items selected depend on the population, the sampling unit, and the sampling frame. Because several (and, in some cases, all) critical control attributes may appear on documents supporting all transactions in the population, it is probable that the sampling frame and sampling unit will not change over the entire system. Therefore, *the auditor may test several attributes using the same sample*

Factor (Other Factors Constant)	Sample Size
1. Population size	
a. Increase	a. Increase
b. Decrease	b. Decrease
2. Desired upper precision limit	
a. Decrease (smaller absolute number, more precision)	a. Increase
b. Increase (larger absolute number, less precision)	b. Decrease
3. Desired confidence	
a. Increase	a. Increase
b. Decrease	b. Decrease
4. Expected occurrence rate	
a. Increase	a. Increase
b. Decrease	b. Decrease

FIGURE 8–3. Effect of Changes in Parameters on Sample Size

Attribute of Interest	Reliability	Expected Exception Proportion	Desired Upper Precision Limit	Sample
1. Prenumbered written sales order prepared	.95	2.5%	5%	240
2. All sales orders approved for credit	.99	1.0%	4%	260
3. Prenumbered shipping tickets should be originated when sales orders have been approved	.95	2.5%	5%	240
4. Sales invoices prepared for each sales order	.95	2.5%	5%	240
5. Review of sales orders by supervisors	.99	1.5%	4%	360
6. Shipping department receives copy of shipping ticket as authority to release goods	.99	2.0%	5%	300
7. Billing department checks each sales invoice	.99	1.5%	4%	360
8. Accounts receivable daily control total agrees with sales summary	.99	0	0	260*
9. Prenumbered shipping tickets accompany all sales invoices	.90	2.5%	5%	160

Note: Whenever zero precision is specified, knowledge is required for the entire population. In this case, 260 control totals from the entire population (of days of the year) must be examined.

FIGURE 8–4. Sample Sizes for Compliance Tests

items. When this can be done, it improves audit efficiency and therefore reduces audit cost. However, different sample sizes may still be required for each attribute since the inputs for the desired precision limit and the desired confidence level may vary with the materiality of the control attributes being tested. Generally the more critical (material) the internal control attribute, the more likely the auditor is to increase the sample size by specifying greater desired confidence or a higher level of precision from the sample result.

As stated previously, the auditor must use a random selection technique in selecting the items to obtain a representative sample. The most appropriate technique for a particular test depends on the homogeneity of the audit population and on whether the sampling units or frames of the audit population are sequentially numbered.

Homogeneity refers to the relative similarity of units included in the population insofar as the characteristic under consideration is concerned. For example, the client's audit population may be homogeneous with respect to control attribute 1 in Figure 8–2 if it is company policy to prepare written sales orders for all sales, regardless of individual amounts. On the other hand, the client's population of sales transactions may not be homogeneous with respect to control attribute 7 in Figure 8–2 if the billing department is expected to check prices, quantities, and extensions only on sales invoices in excess of a specified amount, such as $100. As we observed earlier, unrestricted random sampling is designed for use with populations that are homogeneous with respect to the characteristic being tested. *Heterogeneous populations should be stratified,* after which random sampling techniques can be applied within each of the various strata.

If the audit population is numerically sequenced, we can use a random number table and manual sample selection or a computer audit program with a random number generator to help assure proper selection of a random sample. If the audit population is randomly ordered, a random sample can be selected by systematic sampling.

Examining the Evidence

After choosing a representative sample, the auditor must next examine the elements of the sample. In attribute sampling, this means that each unit in the sample must be examined for the presence or absence of the desired attribute. The auditor should be careful to note the number of sample units containing deviations from established controls. For example, assume that the auditor is examining a sample of 240 invoices selected from an audit population of sales invoices for compliance with control attribute 1 in Figure 8–2. Assume further that the auditor discovers one sales invoice in the sample not supported by a written sales order. This deviation from established internal control is regarded as a procedural error, and may be expressed in terms of a percentage: 1/240 or .42 percent.

Evaluating the Evidence

Once the results of the sample have been obtained, the auditor must evaluate the evidence. This requires a judgment as to the sufficiency and competency of the evidence obtained. ***Sufficiency*** of evidence is directly related to sampling risk, which is then expressed through the desired precision limits and level of confidence. For example, by specifying desired confidence of .95 in the sampling plan outlined above, the auditor implicitly expressed willingness to accept a sampling error of .05. If this level of risk coupled with the pertinent precision limits is acceptable to the auditor, the 240-unit sample is large enough to meet the sufficiency test.

Competency of evidence is a qualitative decision: The auditor must decide whether the evidence obtained is, within the constraint of cost effectiveness, the *best obtainable in support of the conclusion* regarding the attribute being tested. In our example, the most competent evidence available in support of the audit conclusion as to whether the client is preparing prenumbered sales orders for each sale would be a sample of sales invoices, which can be vouched to written sales orders.

Developing a Logical Conclusion

The final step in the sampling process requires the auditor to make an audit conclusion regarding the item under investigation. In attribute sampling, the audit conclusion has to be stated in terms of judgment as to whether the client has complied with the control attribute. There are tables available to assist the auditor in evaluating the sample result and in making such judgments. Appendix 8–E can be used to illustrate how this audit decision is made with respect to our example. Observe that Appendixes 8–D, 8–E, and 8–F consist of three tables for confidence levels of 90 percent, 95 percent, and 99 percent, respectively. Sample sizes, selected by the process described earlier, are listed in the extreme left-hand column. The numbers in the body of each table represent the number of deviations found in testing the attribute. Numbers across the top of the table represent the calculated upper precision limits (CUPL): they show the *maximum inferred population error rates,* based on our findings as we examined the items in the sample. Recall that the results for our example, with respect to control attribute 1, revealed one deviation in a sample of 240 items. Appendix 8–E shows that, with this result from the sample, the auditor may infer with 95 percent confidence, that the error rate for attribute 1 in the entire population does not exceed 2 percent. The auditor can then compare the CUPL (maximum inferred upper error limit) for attribute 1 with DUPL (desired upper precision limit). If CUPL is equal to or less than DUPL, the auditor may conclude, with measured confidence, that the client is, within specified limits, complying with the established control attribute.

The existence of a company policy requiring this control attribute, coupled with actual compliance on the part of the client, supports the auditor's hypothesis that this element of the system of internal control is in place and is functioning as it should. If other attributes, considered important in the control system, also are functioning as they should, the second standard of field work then justifies limited substantive tests of details of balances produced by this particular control attribute.

On the other hand, if CUPL is greater than DUPL, the auditor must conclude that the client is not complying with established controls. In this case, even though the company policy for a particular control attribute may exist, noncompliance on the client's part indicates a weakness in internal control; depending on the relative importance of the control attribute to financial statement presentations, such noncompliance may lead to an extension of substantive tests of details. In our example, CUPL of 2 percent is less than DUPL of 5 percent. The auditor may therefore conclude that controls over attribute 1 are in place and functioning as they should. This evidence, if consistent with results of compliance tests over all other attributes in the system, will allow the auditor to conclude that the control system over sales can be relied upon. Substantive tests of details of sales system account balances, then, may be limited.

Recall that a full evaluation of the internal control procedures for a particular subsystem requires the auditor to follow a logical progression with respect to each material financial statement balance in the system:

1. Consider the errors and irregularities that could occur in those balances. For this purpose, transactions may
   a. Be erroneously recorded.
   b. Possess inadequate or invalid support.
   c. Be unrecorded.
   d. Be improperly valued.
   e. Be improperly classified.

   f. Be recorded in the wrong period.
   g. Be improperly summarized.
2. Consider whether those errors and irregularities could cause a material misstatement.
3. Determine the accounting control procedures that should prevent or detect such errors and irregularities.
4. Determine whether the necessary procedures are being prescribed by the client.
5. Determine whether the prescribed procedures are being followed by the client (compliance tests).
6. On the basis of steps 1 through 5, determine the nature, timing, and extent of audit tests on transactions and on balances emerging from the system (substantive tests).

The procedures in the paragraphs that follow are based on the study and evaluation of internal controls over the sales and accounts receivable system. It is presumed that the auditor has already considered possible errors and irregularities in the system as well as the controls that should prevent or detect those errors. It is also presumed that the auditor has determined by studying the client's system that the appropriate controls are prescribed by the client. The following discussion is concerned with compliance tests (step 5).

All significant control attributes pertaining to a particular financial statement account should be evaluated before proceeding to substantive tests of those account balances. For example, in Figure 8–2, assume that attributes 1 through 9 have been prescribed by the client as part of the system that created debits to accounts receivable, for both the control account and the subsidiary accounts, along with corresponding credits to the sales account.

It is important for each control attribute to be evaluated in terms of the financial statement error or irregularity it was designed to detect or prevent in the system. To illustrate this point, we note that control attributes 1, 4, and 5 are designed to prevent inaccurate and incomplete recording of sales invoices in the sales journal. Compliance failures in these controls could result in a misstatement of the sales account through omission or duplicate recording of sales invoices, or in mathematical mistakes in arriving at individual sales amounts. In Figure 8–5, we see that compliance tests reveal acceptable compliance with control attributes 1 and 4. Therefore the auditor can infer that the system was operating effectively to ensure that all orders received were properly recorded on sales invoices. Substantive tests of details, such as recalculations of footings and extensions of sales invoices, and tracing of invoice postings to journals and ledgers, may then be limited or curtailed, if there are no offsetting weaknesses in other controls in the process.

Tests over control attribute 5, a related control, reveal an unacceptably high rate of failure to have supervision approval over mathematical accuracy of sales invoices. The lack of supervisor initials on a sales document, however, does not necessarily mean that the control procedure was not done. The supervisor may have merely forgotten to initial documents after they were reviewed. Neither does the lack of supervisor initials mean that an equivalent percentage of sales invoices were inaccurately prepared and, therefore, have caused a misstatement in the sales account balances. Nevertheless, due to the lack of acceptable compliance in this area, there is a higher probability of sales misstatement than if the compliance rate had been acceptable. In this situation, the auditor may choose from these alternative courses of action:

(1) Attributes of Interest	(2) Sample Size	(3) Exceptions Noted	(4) Error Rate in Sample [(3) and (2)]	(5) Statistical Confidence	(6) EVALUATION CUPL	(7) DUPL	(8) Conclusion[a]
1. Prenumbered written sales orders prepared	240	1	.4%	.95	2%	5%	S
2. All sales orders approved for credit	260	5	.8%	.99	5%	4%	N
3. Prenumbered shipping tickets should be originated when sales orders have been approved	240	1	.4%	.95	2%	5%	S
4. Sales invoices prepared for each sales order	240	2	.8%	.95	3%	5%	S
5. Review of sales order by supervisor	360	8	2.2%	.99	5%	4%	N
6. Shipping department receives copy of shipping ticket as authority to release goods	300	3	1%	.99	4%[b]	5%	S
7. Billing department checks each sales invoice	360	3	.8%	.99	3%	4%	S
8. Accounts receivable daily control total agrees with sales summary	260	0	0	.99	0	0	S
9. Prenumbered shipping tickets accompany all sales invoices	160	1	.6%	.90	3%	5%	S

[a]S = supports reliance; N = does not support reliance.
[b]Rounded to next most conservative estimate per table.

FIGURE 8–5. Results of Compliance Tests over Sales System

- Look for a mitigating control that offsets the weakness; or
- Extend substantive tests over the account balance(s) likely to be misstated because of the weakness.

In our example, control attribute 7 calls for the billing department to check the mathematical accuracy of sales invoices. Figure 8–5 reveals the CUPL was acceptably low in the billing department. This may convince the auditor that there is sufficient mitigation over the weakness in control attribute 5 in the sales department to prevent the necessity for extension of tests of mathematical details over the sales account.

If the second alternative is elected, substantive tests of the elements of the accounts receivable and sales balances should be expanded. In this case, a larger sample of sales invoices than otherwise necessary would be selected. Each sales invoice would then be extended and footed. Prices would be traced to applicable price lists and quantities would be vouched to appropriate shipping documents.

In any event, a ***thorough error analysis*** should be performed on each observed compliance deviation. This should give the auditor insight as to the underlying reasons for the errors and in that way help in formulating a judgment as to the quality of the system. In the end, *the auditor's judgment must still prevail* in determining the effects of the system of internal control upon the extent, timing, and nature of the substantive audit tests.

DISCOVERY SAMPLING

Although it is in some ways a form of attribute sampling, discovery sampling has a *different audit objective* from that of attribute sampling. The objective of discovery sampling is to select a sample (n) which has a specified probability (x) of yielding at least one occurrence of an attribute within a given population size (P) with a critical rate of occurrence (p). The attribute sought in this case is usually the ***existence of an irregularity.***

Discovery sampling is most useful in any of these situations:

- When the auditor suspects that a particular kind of critical irregularity or fraud has occurred, and would like to determine if it is an isolated case.
- When it is possible to estimate a critical rate of occurrence of an irregularity that would cause a material misstatement in the financial statements if not disclosed.
- When an audit population of high relative risk (such as cash or accounts receivable) reveals a breakdown in the segregation of duties (recordkeeping and cash handling, for example) after the preliminary evaluation of internal control.

Figure 8–6 illustrates a discovery sampling table. With discovery sampling, the *population size should be specified as a parameter*. Therefore we will have different tables for populations of different sizes. The table illustrated is for population sizes of 5,000 to 10,000. Sample sizes increase from top to bottom in the first column of the table. Critical rates of occurrence appear across the top of the table, rising from left to right. Probabilities of occurrence appear in the body of the table.

To illustrate the technique of discovery sampling, assume that the auditor suspects fraud may be occurring in the handling of cash receipts and the posting of credits to

Sample Size	Upper Precision Limit: Critical Rate of Occurrence							
	.1%	.2%	.3%	.4%	.5%	.75%	1%	2%
50	5%	10%	14%	18%	22%	31%	40%	64%
60	6	11	17	21	26	36	45	70
70	7	13	19	25	30	41	51	76
80	8	15	21	28	33	45	55	80
90	9	17	24	30	36	49	60	84
100	10	18	26	33	40	53	64	87
120	11	21	30	38	45	60	70	91
140	13	25	35	43	51	65	76	94
160	15	28	38	48	55	70	80	96
200	18	33	45	56	64	78	87	98
240	22	39	52	62	70	84	91	99
300	26	46	60	70	78	90	95	99+
340	29	50	65	75	82	93	97	99+
400	34	56	71	81	87	95	98	99+
460	38	61	76	85	91	97	99	99+
500	40	64	79	87	92	98	99	99+
600	46	71	84	92	96	99	99+	99+
700	52	77	89	95	97	99+	99+	99+
800	57	81	92	96	98	99+	99+	99+
900	61	85	94	98	99	99+	99+	99+
1,000	65	88	96	99	99	99+	99+	99+
1,500	80	96	99	99+	99+	99+	99+	99+
2,000	89	99	99+	99+	99+	99+	99+	99+

Source: Audit Sampling Reference Manual, © Ernst & Whinney, 1977. Used with permission.

FIGURE 8–6. Discovery Sampling Table: Probability of Including at Least One Occurrence in a Sample for Populations Between 5,000 and 10,000

accounts receivable, both of which are done by the same client employee. Assume further that the audit population contains 10,000 credit postings to accounts receivable, and that the auditor estimates that a material misstatement may result if as many as 100 transactions (1 percent) are improperly posted. The auditor therefore desires to know how large a sample would have to be drawn to be 99 percent confident of uncovering at least one occurrence of such a fraud. Using the table in Figure 8–6, we find that the auditor would have to examine a sample of 460 transactions.

As you can see in Figure 8–6, discovery sampling requires inordinately large sample sizes when critical rates of occurrence in a population are less than .5 percent and the required confidence is high. This sampling procedure is designed to uncover only those irregularities that occur with some degree of frequency. Therefore it cannot be expected to uncover rare occurrences of irregularities. Although discovery sampling has its place in the audit process, it is used much less frequently than pure attribute sampling.

SUMMARY

In this chapter we have introduced the concept of sampling as it relates to the performance of auditing procedures. We began by explaining that the auditor must, because of cost considerations associated with the performance of auditing procedures, rely on the verification of samples of the documents, transactions, and account elements being examined rather than verifying all elements of those populations. We also observed that the samples may be selected either on the basis of the auditor's judgment or by the use of statistical techniques.

We then defined some of the statistical terminology especially relevant to statistical sampling in auditing. The relationship between generally accepted auditing standards and statistical sampling techniques was then explained. Next, we demonstrated how a random sample of an audit population is selected and briefly discussed the characteristics of a population, which would be considered in determining the sample size.

In the last part of the chapter, the objectives of statistical sampling were related to various statistical sampling techniques, with particular emphasis on attribute sampling and discovery sampling. Attribute sampling was defined as a technique used to determine the existence of particular attributes within a specified audit population. We also explained how the auditor develops logical conclusions from attribute sampling data. Discovery sampling was described as a special form of attribute sampling designed to discover the existence of a particular attribute, such as an irregularity in handling and processing a specified type of transaction.

APPENDIX 8–A: Determination of Sample Size; Reliability = 90 Percent

Expected Percent Rate of Occurrence	Upper Precision Limit: Percent Rate of Occurrence																				
	1	2	3	4	5	6	7	8	9	10	12	14	16	18	20	25	30	35	40	45	50
.25	400	200	140	100	80	70	60	50	50	40	40	30	30	20	20	20	20	10	10	10	10
.5	800	200	140	100	80	70	60	50	50	40	40	30	30	30	20	20	20	10	10	10	10
1.0		400	180	100	80	70	60	50	50	40	40	30	30	30	20	20	20	10	10	10	10
1.5			320	180	120	90	60	50	50	40	40	30	30	30	20	20	20	10	10	10	10
2.0		*	600	200	140	90	80	50	50	40	40	30	30	30	20	20	20	10	10	10	10
2.5			*	360	160	120	80	70	60	40	40	30	30	30	20	20	20	10	10	10	10
3.0				800	260	160	100	90	60	60	50	30	30	30	20	20	20	10	10	10	10
3.5				*	400	200	140	100	80	70	50	40	40	30	20	20	20	10	10	10	10
4.0					900	300	200	100	90	70	50	40	40	30	20	20	20	10	10	10	10
4.5					*	550	220	160	120	80	60	40	40	30	20	20	20	10	10	10	10
5.0						*	320	160	120	80	60	40	40	30	20	20	20	10	10	10	10
5.5						*	600	280	160	120	70	50	40	30	30	20	20	10	10	10	10
6.0							*	380	200	160	80	50	40	30	30	20	20	10	10	10	10
6.5							*	600	260	180	90	60	40	30	30	20	20	10	10	10	10
7.0								*	400	200	100	70	40	40	40	20	20	10	10	10	10
7.5								*	800	290	120	80	40	40	40	20	20	10	10	10	10
8.0									*	460	160	100	50	50	40	20	20	10	10	10	10
8.5									*	800	200	100	70	50	40	20	20	10	10	10	10
9.0										*	260	100	80	50	40	20	20	10	10	10	10
9.5										*	380	160	80	50	40	20	20	10	10	10	10
10.0											500	160	80	50	40	20	20	10	10	10	10
11.0											*	280	140	70	60	30	30	20	20	10	10
12.0												550	180	90	70	30	30	20	20	10	10
13.0												*	300	160	90	30	30	20	20	10	10
14.0													600	200	100	40	30	20	20	10	10
15.0													*	300	140	40	30	20	20	10	10
16.0														650	200	50	30	30	20	10	10
17.0														*	340	70	40	30	20	20	10
18.0															700	100	50	30	20	10	10
19.0															*	100	50	30	20	10	10
20.0																160	50	30	20	10	10
22.0																400	80	40	30	20	20
24.0																*	120	50	30	20	20
26.0																	260	80	30	30	20
28.0																	1000	100	50	30	20
30.0																		180	50	30	20
33.0																		1000	100	50	30
36.0																			280	80	40
39.0																			*	160	60
42.0																				500	90
46.0																					300

Note: * = more than 1000.

Source: Audit Sampling Reference Manual, © Ernst & Whinney, 1977. Used with permission.

APPENDIX 8–B: Determination of Sample Size; Reliability = 95 Percent

Expected Percent Rate of Occurrence	Upper Precision Limit: Percent Rate of Occurrence																				
	1	2	3	4	5	6	7	8	9	10	12	14	16	18	20	25	30	35	40	45	50
.25	650	240	160	120	100	80	70	60	60	50	40	40	30	30	30	20	20	20	10	10	10
.5	*	320	160	120	100	80	70	60	60	50	40	40	30	30	30	20	20	20	10	10	10
1.0		600	260	160	100	80	70	60	60	50	40	40	30	30	30	20	20	20	10	10	10
1.5		*	400	200	160	120	90	60	60	50	40	40	30	30	30	20	20	20	10	10	10
2.0			900	300	200	140	90	80	70	50	40	40	30	30	30	20	20	20	10	10	10
2.5			*	550	240	160	120	80	70	70	40	40	30	30	30	20	20	20	10	10	10
3.0				*	400	200	160	100	90	80	60	50	30	30	30	20	20	20	10	10	10
3.5				*	650	280	200	140	100	80	70	50	40	40	30	20	20	20	10	10	10
4.0					*	500	240	180	100	90	70	50	40	40	30	20	20	20	10	10	10
4.5					*	800	360	200	160	120	80	60	40	40	30	20	20	20	10	10	10
5.0						*	500	240	160	120	80	60	40	40	30	20	20	20	10	10	10
5.5						*	900	360	200	160	90	70	50	50	30	30	20	20	10	10	10
6.0							*	550	280	180	100	80	50	50	30	30	20	20	10	10	10
6.5							*	1000	400	240	120	90	60	50	30	30	20	20	10	10	10
7.0								*	600	300	140	100	70	50	40	30	20	20	10	10	10
7.5								*	*	460	160	100	80	50	40	30	20	20	10	10	10
8.0									*	650	200	100	80	50	50	30	20	20	10	10	10
8.5									*	*	280	140	80	70	50	30	20	20	10	10	10
9.0										*	400	180	100	70	50	30	20	20	10	10	10
9.5										*	550	200	120	70	50	30	20	20	10	10	10
10.0											800	220	120	70	50	30	20	20	10	10	10
11.0											*	400	180	100	70	40	30	20	20	20	20
12.0												900	280	140	90	40	30	20	20	20	20
13.0												*	460	200	100	50	30	20	20	20	20
14.0													1000	300	160	50	40	20	20	20	20
15.0													*	500	200	60	40	20	20	20	20
16.0														*	300	80	50	30	30	20	20
17.0														*	550	100	50	40	30	20	20
18.0															*	140	50	40	30	20	20
19.0															*	180	70	40	30	20	20
20.0																220	70	40	30	20	20
22.0																600	100	50	30	30	20
24.0																*	200	70	40	30	20
26.0																	400	100	50	30	30
28.0																	*	160	60	40	30
30.0																		280	80	40	30
33.0																		*	160	60	30
36.0																			460	100	50
39.0																			*	220	80
42.0																				800	140
46.0																					550

Note: * = more than 1000.

Source: Audit Sampling Reference Manual, © Ernst & Whinney, 1977. Used with permission.

APPENDIX 8–C: Determination of Sample Size; Reliability = 99 Percent

Expected Percent Rate of Occurrence	Upper Precision Limit: Percent Rate of Occurrence																				
	1	2	3	4	5	6	7	8	9	10	12	14	16	18	20	25	30	35	40	45	50
.25	*	340	240	180	140	120	100	90	80	70	60	50	40	40	40	30	20	20	20	20	20
.5	*	500	280	180	140	120	100	90	80	70	60	50	40	40	40	30	20	20	20	20	20
1.0		*	400	260	180	140	100	90	80	70	60	50	40	40	40	30	20	20	20	20	20
1.5		*	800	360	200	180	120	120	100	90	60	50	40	40	40	30	20	20	20	20	20
2.0			*	500	300	200	140	140	100	90	70	50	40	40	40	30	20	20	20	20	20
2.5			*	1000	400	240	200	160	120	100	70	60	40	40	40	30	20	20	20	20	20
3.0				*	700	360	260	160	160	100	90	60	50	50	40	30	20	20	20	20	20
3.5				*	*	550	340	200	160	140	100	70	50	50	40	40	20	20	20	20	20
4.0					*	800	400	280	200	160	100	70	50	50	40	40	20	20	20	20	20
4.5					*	*	600	380	220	200	120	80	60	60	40	40	20	20	20	20	20
5.0						*	900	460	280	200	120	80	60	60	40	40	20	20	20	20	20
5.5						*	*	650	380	280	160	90	70	70	50	40	30	30	20	20	20
6.0							*	1000	500	300	180	100	80	70	50	40	30	30	20	20	20
6.5							*	*	800	400	200	120	90	70	60	40	30	30	20	20	20
7.0								*	*	600	240	140	100	70	70	40	30	30	20	20	20
7.5									*	800	280	160	120	80	70	40	30	30	20	20	20
8.0									*	*	400	200	140	100	70	50	30	30	20	20	20
8.5									*	*	500	240	140	100	70	50	30	30	20	20	20
9.0										*	700	300	180	100	90	50	30	30	20	20	20
9.5										*	1000	360	200	140	90	50	30	30	20	20	20
10.0											*	420	220	140	90	50	30	30	20	20	20
11.0											*	800	300	180	140	60	40	30	30	20	20
12.0												*	500	240	160	70	40	30	30	20	20
13.0												*	600	360	200	90	50	30	30	20	20
14.0													*	500	280	100	50	40	30	20	20
15.0													*	900	360	120	60	40	30	20	20
16.0														*	550	160	80	40	30	30	20
17.0														*	1000	180	80	40	40	30	20
18.0															*	240	100	50	40	30	20
19.0															*	300	100	60	40	30	20
20.0																420	120	60	40	30	20
22.0																*	200	90	50	40	30
24.0																*	340	120	70	40	30
26.0																	800	180	80	50	30
28.0																	*	280	100	60	40
30.0																		550	140	70	40
33.0																		*	300	100	60
36.0																			900	180	80
39.0																			*	400	140
42.0																				*	240
46.0																					900

Note: * = more than 1000.

Source: Audit Sampling Reference Manual, © Ernst & Whinney, 1977. Used with permission.

APPENDIX 8–D: Evaluation of Results; Reliability = 90 Percent

Sample Size	Upper Precision Limit: Percent Rate of Occurrence																				
	1	2	3	4	5	6	7	8	9	10	12	14	16	18	20	25	30	35	40	45	50
10																0		1		2	
20											0				1	2		3	4	5	6
30								0				1		2		4	5	6	8	9	10
40						0				1		2	3		4	6	7	9	11	13	15
50					0			1			2	3	4	5		8	10	12	15	17	19
60				0			1		2		3	4	5	6	7	10	13	15	18	21	24
70				0		1		2		3	4	5	6	8	9	12	15	18	22	25	29
80			0		1		2		3	4	5	6	8	9	10	14	18	22	25	29	33
90			0		1	2		3	4		6	7	9	11	12	16	20	25	29	33	38
100			0	1		2	3	4		5	7	9	10	12	14	19	23	28	33	38	43
120		0		1	2	3	4	5	6	7	9	11	13	15	17	23	29	34	40	46	52
140		0	1	2	3	4	5	6	7	9	11	13	16	18	21	27	34	41	48	54	61
160		0	1	2	4	5	6	8	9	10	13	16	19	22	25	32	40	47	55	63	71
180		0	2	3	4	6	7	9	10	12	15	18	22	25	28	37	45	54	63	71	80
200		1	2	4	5	7	8	10	12	14	17	21	24	28	32	41	51	60	70	80	90
220		1	2	4	6	8	10	12	13	15	19	23	27	31	35	46	56	67	78	89	99
240	0	1	3	5	7	9	11	13	15	17	21	26	30	35	39	50	62	74	85	97	109
260	0	1	3	5	8	10	12	14	17	19	24	28	33	38	43	55	68	80	93	106	119
280	0	2	4	6	8	11	13	16	18	21	26	31	36	41	46	60	73	87	101	114	128
300	0	2	4	7	9	12	14	17	20	22	28	33	39	45	50	64	79	93	108	123	138
320	0	2	5	7	10	13	16	18	21	24	30	36	42	48	54	69	85	100	116	132	148
340	0	3	5	8	11	14	17	20	23	26	32	38	45	51	58	74	90	107	123	140	157
360	0	3	6	9	12	15	18	21	25	28	34	41	48	55	61	79	96	113	131	149	167
380	0	3	6	9	13	16	19	23	26	30	37	44	51	58	65	83	102	120	139	158	177
400	1	4	7	10	14	17	21	24	28	31	39	46	54	61	69	88	107	127	146	166	186
420	1	4	7	11	14	18	22	26	29	33	41	49	57	65	73	93	113	134	154	175	196
460	1	4	8	12	16	20	24	28	33	37	45	54	63	71	80	102	124	147	170	192	215
500	1	5	9	13	18	22	27	31	36	40	50	59	69	78	88	112	136	160	185	210	235
550	2	6	10	15	20	25	30	35	40	45	55	66	76	87	97	124	150	177	204	232	259
600	2	7	12	17	22	28	33	39	44	50	61	72	84	95	107	135	165	194	224	253	283
650	2	8	13	19	24	30	36	42	48	54	66	79	91	104	116	147	179	211	243	275	308
700	3	8	14	20	27	33	39	46	52	59	72	85	99	112	126	159	194	228	262	297	332
800	4	10	17	24	31	38	46	53	61	68	83	99	114	129	145	183	222	262	301	341	381
900	4	12	20	28	36	44	52	61	69	78	95	112	129	146	164	207	251	296	340	385	430
1000	5	13	22	31	40	49	59	68	77	87	106	125	144	164	183	232	280	330	379	429	479

Note: The number of observed occurrences are shown in the body of the table.

Source: Audit Sampling Reference Manual, © Ernst & Whinney, 1977. Used with permission.

APPENDIX 8–E: Evaluation of Results; Reliability = 95 Percent

Sample Size	Upper Precision Limit: Percent Rate of Occurrence																				
	1	2	3	4	5	6	7	8	9	10	12	14	16	18	20	25	30	35	40	45	50
10																	0		1		
20												0				1	2	3		4	5
30										0			1		2	3	4	5	7	8	10
40								0			1		2		3	5	6	8	10	12	14
50						0				1		2	3	4	5	7	9	11	13	16	18
60					0			1			2	3	4	5	6	9	11	14	17	20	23
70					0		1		2		3	4	5	7	8	11	14	17	20	24	27
80				0		1		2		3	4	5	7	8	9	13	16	20	24	28	32
90				0		1	2		3	4	5	6	8	9	11	15	19	23	27	32	36
100			0		1		2	3	4		6	8	9	11	13	17	22	26	31	36	41
120			0	1		2	3	4	5	6	8	10	12	14	16	21	27	33	38	44	50
140			0	1	2	3	4	5	6	7	10	12	14	17	19	26	32	39	46	52	59
160		0	1	2	3	4	5	6	8	9	12	14	17	20	23	30	38	45	53	61	69
180		0	1	2	3	5	6	8	9	11	14	17	20	23	26	35	43	52	60	69	78
200		0	1	3	4	6	7	9	11	12	16	19	23	26	30	39	48	58	68	77	87
220		0	2	3	5	7	8	10	12	14	18	22	25	29	33	44	54	64	75	86	97
240		1	2	4	6	8	10	12	14	16	20	24	28	33	37	48	59	71	83	94	106
260		1	3	4	7	9	11	13	15	17	22	26	31	36	41	53	65	77	90	103	116
280		1	3	5	7	10	12	14	17	19	24	29	34	39	44	57	71	84	98	111	125
300	0	1	3	6	8	11	13	16	18	21	26	31	37	42	48	62	76	91	105	120	135
320	0	2	4	6	9	11	14	17	20	22	28	34	40	45	51	66	82	97	113	128	144
340	0	2	4	7	10	12	15	18	21	24	30	36	42	49	55	71	87	104	120	137	154
360	0	2	5	8	10	13	17	20	23	26	32	39	45	52	59	76	93	110	128	146	163
380	0	2	5	8	11	14	18	21	24	28	34	41	48	55	62	80	98	117	135	154	173
400	0	3	6	9	12	15	19	22	26	29	37	44	51	59	66	85	104	123	143	163	183
420	0	3	6	9	13	16	20	24	27	31	39	46	54	62	70	90	110	130	151	171	192
460	0	4	7	11	15	18	22	26	31	35	43	51	60	68	77	99	121	143	166	188	211
500	1	4	8	12	16	21	25	29	34	38	47	56	66	75	84	108	132	157	181	197	221
550	1	5	9	14	18	23	28	33	38	43	53	63	73	83	94	120	146	173	200	227	255
600	1	6	10	15	20	26	31	36	42	47	58	69	80	92	103	132	161	190	219	249	279
650	2	6	12	17	23	28	34	40	46	52	64	76	88	100	112	143	175	207	239	271	303
700	2	7	13	19	25	31	37	43	50	56	69	82	95	108	122	155	189	223	258	292	327
800	3	9	15	22	29	36	43	51	58	65	80	95	110	125	141	179	218	257	296	336	376
900	4	10	18	26	34	42	50	58	66	74	91	108	125	142	159	203	247	291	335	379	424
1000	4	12	20	29	38	47	56	65	74	84	102	121	140	159	178	227	275	324	374	423	473

Note: The number of observed occurrences are shown in the body of the table.

Source: Audit Sampling Reference Manual, © Ernst & Whinney, 1977. Used with permission.

APPENDIX 8–F: Evaluation of Results; Reliability = 99 Percent

Sample	Upper Precision Limit: Percent Rate of Occurrence																				
Size	1	2	3	4	5	6	7	8	9	10	12	14	16	18	20	25	30	35	40	45	50
10																			0		
20																0	1		2	3	4
30													0			1	3	4	5	6	8
40											0		1		2	3	5	7	8	10	12
50									0			1	2		3	5	7	9	11	13	16
60								0			1	2	3		4	7	9	12	14	17	20
70							0			1	2	3	4	5	6	9	11	14	18	21	24
80						0			1		2	4	5	6	7	10	14	17	21	25	29
90					0			1		2	3	5	6	7	9	12	16	20	24	29	33
100					0		1		2	3	4	6	7	9	10	14	19	23	28	33	37
120				0		1	2		3	4	6	8	9	11	13	18	24	29	35	40	46
140				0	1	2	3		4	5	7	10	12	14	16	22	29	35	42	48	55
160			0		1	2	3	5	6	7	9	12	14	17	20	27	34	41	49	56	64
180			0	1	2	3	4	6	7	8	11	14	17	20	23	31	39	47	56	65	73
200			0	1	3	4	5	7	8	10	13	16	19	23	26	35	44	54	63	73	83
220			0	2	3	5	6	8	10	11	15	18	22	26	30	39	50	60	70	81	92
240		0	1	2	4	6	7	9	11	13	17	21	25	29	33	44	55	66	78	89	101
260		0	1	3	5	6	8	10	12	14	19	23	27	32	36	48	60	72	85	97	110
280		0	2	3	4	7	9	12	14	16	21	25	30	35	40	53	65	79	92	106	120
300		0	2	4	6	8	10	13	15	18	23	28	33	38	43	57	71	85	99	114	129
320		0	2	4	7	9	11	14	17	19	24	30	35	41	47	61	76	91	107	122	138
340		1	3	5	7	10	13	15	18	21	26	32	38	44	50	66	82	98	114	131	148
360		1	3	6	8	11	14	16	19	22	28	35	41	47	54	70	87	104	122	139	157
380		1	3	6	9	12	15	18	21	24	30	37	44	50	57	75	93	111	129	148	166
400		1	4	7	10	13	16	19	22	26	32	39	46	54	61	79	98	117	136	156	176
420		2	4	7	10	14	17	20	24	27	35	42	49	57	64	84	103	124	144	164	185
460	0	2	5	8	12	15	19	23	27	31	39	47	55	63	72	93	114	136	159	181	204
500	0	3	6	10	13	17	21	26	30	34	43	52	60	70	79	102	125	149	174	198	223
550	0	3	7	11	15	20	24	29	34	38	48	58	68	78	88	113	139	166	192	219	247
600	0	4	8	13	17	22	27	32	37	43	53	64	78	86	97	125	153	182	211	241	271
650	0	4	9	14	19	25	30	36	41	47	58	70	82	94	106	136	167	198	230	262	294
700	1	5	10	16	21	27	33	39	45	51	64	76	89	102	115	148	181	215	249	283	319
800	1	7	13	19	25	32	39	46	53	60	74	89	103	118	133	171	209	248	287	326	366
900	2	8	15	22	29	37	45	53	61	69	85	101	118	135	152	194	237	281	325	369	414
1000	2	9	17	25	34	42	51	60	69	78	96	114	133	151	170	218	266	314	363	412	462

Note: The number of observed occurrences are shown in the body of the table.

Source: Audit Sampling Reference Manual, © Ernst & Whinney, 1977. Used with permission.

NOTE

1. Statement on Auditing Standards (SAS) 1, Section 320A.03 (New York: AICPA, 1973).

QUESTIONS FOR CLASS DISCUSSION

Q8–1 Why do auditors use samples of the various universes of data in carrying out their audit procedures rather than all elements of the universe? Explain.

Q8–2 Does the auditor accept any risks in using the sampling technique in performing an audit? Discuss.

Q8–3 What is meant by a *sampling error?*

Q8–4 What is meant by a *nonsampling error?*

Q8–5 What is the difference between statistical and judgmental sampling? Discuss.

Q8–6 What are the advantages associated with using statistical sampling rather than judgmental sampling? Do those differences mean that the auditor should use statistical sampling techniques in performing all phases of the audit? Explain.

Q8–7 Because statistical sampling relies on the laws of probability in selecting sample data, the auditor is relieved from judgment decisions. Is the preceding statement true or false? Explain.

Q8–8 What is the meaning of the terms *relative frequency* and *subjective probability* as they relate to the use of statistical sampling techniques in the performance of an audit. Discuss.

Q8–9 What do the following terms mean?

a. *Probability.*
b. *Population.*
c. *Sampling unit.*
d. *Unrestricted random sample.*
e. *Systematic sampling.*

Q8–10 How would an auditor select an unrestricted random sample without replacement from a data universe he or she is auditing?

Q8–11 Under what circumstances might it be preferable to use a systematic rather than an unrestricted random sampling technique in selecting a sample of universe data for verification?

Q8–12 What is the relationship between precision and reliability in the selection and use of a statistically valid sample?

Q8–13 What statistical sampling term is most closely related to the concept of materiality? Explain.

Q8–14 Other things being equal, the reliability of a statistical sample increases as the size of the sample increases; therefore, auditors, to minimize their risks of being wrong in expressing an opinion on the financial statements, will always use exceptionally large samples. Is the preceding statement true or false?

Q8–15 How can the auditor quantify the ultimate risk associated with the performance of an audit by evaluating the risks judged to be taken in relying on internal control, analytical review, and substantive tests of account balances?

Q8–16 How may attribute sampling be used in compliance tests of elements of a system of internal control?

Q8–17 What is the difference between discovery sampling and pure attribute sampling? Explain.

Q8–18 What functions are performed by the auditor after the elements of a sample have been selected?

Q8–19 What is meant by *estimation sampling?*

Q8–20 What is the relationship between precision and reliability in selecting and using the items included in a statistically valid sample?

Q8–21 The precision limits established for a particular attribute sample are stated at plus or minus 2 percent. What is meant by those figures?

Q8–22 A particular sample has been selected to produce a desired reliability of 95 percent. What is meant by that statement?

Q8–23 What relationship exists between homogeneity of data in a universe and the use of stratified sampling techniques?

Q8–24 In working with statistically valid samples, can we have both stratified and random sampling techniques used in verifying the same universe? Explain.

Q8–25 An attribute sample indicates that a client has failed in some instances to implement a particular control procedure. Does that automatically mean that the substantive tests of those items must be expanded? Explain.

Q8–26 In what type of situations would an auditor be likely to use discovery sampling?

SHORT CASES

C8–1 Joe Caplin, CPA, is conducting the annual audit of the financial statements of the Monarch Corporation for the year ended December 31, 19X4. Mr. Caplin has decided to employ statistical sampling techniques in testing the effectiveness of internal control procedures over cash disbursements. All cash disbursements for Monarch Corporation are evidenced by sequentially numbered checks. In the three prior years, Monarch was audited by Schnook & Co., CPAs, who did not employ statistical techniques. When reviewing the previous year's working papers of Monarch, Caplin noticed that Schnook's audit program for cash disbursements controls (written twenty years ago) called for selection of February as a test month. All material controls were tested for February's transactions, and all errors found were resolved to Schnook's satisfaction.

Required:

a. Did Schnook and Company follow generally accepted auditing standards on the previous year's audit? Explain.

b. Explain the logical progression of steps that Caplin should follow in evaluating internal controls over the cash disbursements system of the Monarch Corporation.

c. Explain how statistical sampling fits into the logical progression of steps as described in requirement b above.

d. Given his stated audit objective, which type of sampling methodology (i.e., attributes, discovery, variables) would Caplin be most likely to follow?

e. Explain how the items in the sample Caplin derives would be selected. Explain how the method used here is preferable to that used in prior years.

C8–2 You want to select a sample of 100 paid vouchers to be examined for appropriate supporting documents (invoices, purchase orders, receiving reports, and purchase requisitions). The paid vouchers range from numbers 1 to 10,000 for the period June 1, 19X2 to May 31, 19X3. The vouchers are listed on 400 pages of the client's voucher register, numbered from page 1 to page 400. Each page of the voucher register contains 25 items.

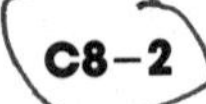

Required:

a. Describe three ways that a random sample of vouchers might be selected from the population of vouchers payable.

b. How could the computer be used in performing this task?

C8–3 In each of the following independent situations, design an unrestricted random sampling plan using the random number table in Figure 8–1. The plan should include identification of

a. The audit problem.
b. The audit population.
c. The sampling unit.
d. The sampling frame.
e. The attribute to be tested.

For each independent situation, after a sampling plan has been designed, select the first five items to be included in the sample from the table in Figure 8–1. Use a starting point of item 0925, Column A, for each situation. Read down the table and from left to right by column, using the left-most digits in the columns.

Required:

a. Assume that you are examining sales invoices for approval signatures of departmental supervisors. Sales invoices for the audit period are consecutively numbered from 5,924 to 10,242.

b. Assume that you are examining cash disbursements for proper supporting documents. Cash disbursements for the audit period are all made by check sequentially numbered from 32,115 to 46,851.

c. Assume that you are examining insurance claim forms to ascertain that proper supporting documents were filed for each claim and that those supporting documents were examined before the claim was paid. Insurance claims are recorded in a claims register by policyholder. The register contains 160 pages for the audit period with 40 claims recorded on each page, except for the last page, which has only 24 claims on it.

d. Assume that you are examining prenumbered receiving reports in a receiving report register to ascertain whether the goods listed thereon were recorded in the perpetual inventory records as received during the audit period. The numbering of these receiving reports starts over at 1 each month. Each month's receiving reports are prefixed with a number 1 through 12 to designate the month of the year. There are 400 pages for the year, and a maximum of 40 pages per month. All pages have 30 entries, except for the last page for each month.

C8–4 Mavis Stores had two billing clerks during the year. Snow worked three months and White worked nine months. As the auditor for Mavis Stores, Darren Lowe, CPA, uses attribute sampling to test clerical accuracy for the entire year. Because of the lack of internal verification, the system depends heavily upon the competence of the billing clerks. The quantity of bills per month is constant.

Required:

a. Lowe decided to treat the billing by Snow and White as two separate populations. Discuss the advisability of this approach, considering the circumstances.

b. Lowe decided to use the same confidence level, expected error rate, and desired upper precision limit for each population. Assuming he decided to select a sample of 200 to test Snow's work, approximately how large a sample is necessary to test White's?

(AICPA adapted)

C8–5 The Whitehall Company's principal activity is buying milk from dairy farmers, processing the milk, and delivering the milk to retail customers. You are engaged in auditing the sales transactions of the company and determine that

a. The company has 50 retail routes; each route consists of 100 to 200 accounts, the number that can be serviced by a driver in a day.

b. The driver enters cash collections from the day's deliveries to each customer directly on a statement form in record books maintained for each route. Mail remittances are posted in the route record books by office personnel. At the end of the month the statements are priced, extended, and footed. Photocopies of the statements are prepared and left in the customers' milk boxes with the next milk delivery.

c. The statements are reviewed by the office manager, who prepares a monthly list for each route of accounts with 90-day balances or older. The list is used for intensive collection action.

d. The audit program used in prior audits for the selection of sales transactions for compliance tests stated: "Select two accounts from each route, one to be chosen by opening the route book at random and the other as the third account on each list of 90-day or older accounts. For each account selected, choose the latest transaction for testing."

Your review of sales transactions leads you to conclude that statistical sampling techniques may be applied to their examination.

Required:

a. Since statistical sampling techniques do not relieve the CPA of his responsibilities in the exercise of his professional judgment, of what benefit are they to the CPA? Discuss.

b. Give the reasons why the audit procedure previously used for selection of sales transactions (as given in d above) would not produce a valid statistical sample.
c. Suggest two ways to select a valid statistical sample.
d. Assume that the company has 10,000 sales transactions and that your statistical sampling disclosed 6 errors in a sample of 200 transactions. Is it reasonable to assume that 300 transactions in the entire population are in error? Explain.

(AICPA adapted)

C8–6 You are now conducting your third annual audit of the financial statement of Elite Corporation for the year ended December 31, 19X1. You decide to employ unrestricted random number statistical sampling techniques in testing the effectiveness of the company's internal control procedures relating to sales invoices, which are all serially numbered. In prior years, after selecting one representative two-week period during the year, you tested all invoices issued during that period and resolved all of the errors to your satisfaction.

Required:

a. Explain the statistical procedure you would use to determine the size of the sample of sales invoices to be examined.
b. Once the sample size has been determined, how would you select the individual invoices to be included in the sample. Explain.
c. Would the use of statistical sampling procedures improve the examination of sales invoices as compared with the selection procedures used in prior years? Discuss.
d. Assume that the company issued 50,000 sales invoices during the year, and, as auditor, you had to meet a specified confidence level of 95 percent with a precision range of plus or minus 2 percent.
   (1) Does this mean that you would be willing to accept the reliability of the sales invoice data if errors are found on no more than four sales invoices out of every 95 invoices examined?
   (2) If there is a specified precision range of plus or minus 1 percent, would the confidence level be higher or lower than 95 percent, assuming that the size of the sample remains constant? Why?

(AICPA adapted)

PROBLEMS

P8–1 Select the best answer for each of the following items.

a. What is the primary objective of using stratification as a sampling method in auditing?
   (1) To increase the confidence level at which a decision will be reached from the results of the sample selected.
   (2) To determine the occurrence rate for a given characteristic in the population being studied.
   (3) To decrease the effect of variance in the total population.
   (4) To determine the precision range of the sample selected.

b. For a large population of cash disbursement transactions, Arno Malchevsky, CPA, is testing compliance with internal control by using attribute sampling techniques. Anticipating an occurrence rate of 3 percent, he found from a table that the required sample size is 400 with a desired upper precision limit of 5 percent and reliability of 95 percent. If Malchevsky anticipated an occurrence rate of only 2 percent but wanted to maintain the same desired upper precision limit and reliability, the sample size would be closest to
(1) 200.
(2) 400.
(3) 533.
(4) 800.

c. To satisfy the auditing standard to make a proper study and evaluation of internal control, Tanya Jewett, CPA, uses statistical sampling to test compliance with internal control procedures. Why does Jewett use this statistical sampling technique?
(1) It provides a means of measuring mathematically the degree of reliability that results from examining only a part of the data.
(2) It reduces the use of judgment required of Jewett because the AICPA has established numerical criteria for this type of testing.
(3) It increases Jewett's knowledge of the client's prescribed procedures and their limitations.
(4) It is specified by generally accepted auditing standards.

d. How should an auditor determine the precision required in establishing a statistical sampling plan?
(1) By the materiality of an allowable margin of error the auditor is willing to accept.
(2) By the amount of reliance the auditor will place on the results of the sample.
(3) By reliance on a table of random numbers.
(4) By the amount of risk the auditor is willing to take that material errors will occur in the accounting process.

e. Which of the following is an advantage of systematic sampling over random number sampling?
(1) It provides a stronger basis for statistical conclusions.
(2) It enables the auditor to use the more efficient "sampling with replacement" tables.
(3) There may be correlation between the location of items in the population, the feature of sampling interest, and the sampling interval.
(4) It does not require establishment of correspondence between random numbers and items in the population.

f. An auditor makes separate compliance and substantive tests in the accounts payable area (which has good internal control). If the auditor uses statistical sampling for both of these tests, the confidence level established for the substantive test is normally
(1) The same as that for tests of compliance.
(2) Greater than that for tests of compliance.
(3) Less than that for tests of compliance.
(4) Totally independent of that for tests of compliance.

g. An example of sampling for attributes would be estimating the
(1) Quantity of specific inventory items.
(2) Probability of losing a patent infringement case.

(3) Percentage of overdue accounts receivable.
(4) Dollar value of accounts receivable.

h. The purpose of tests for compliance is to provide reasonable assurance that the accounting control procedures are being applied as prescribed. The sampling method that is *most* useful when testing for compliance is
(1) Judgment sampling.
(2) Attribute sampling.
(3) Unrestricted random sampling with replacement.
(4) Stratified random sampling.

i. Precision is a statistical measure of the maximum likely difference between the sample estimate and the true but unknown population total, and is directly related to
(1) Reliability of evidence.
(2) Relative risk.
(3) Materiality.
(4) Cost benefit analysis.

j. Statement on Auditing Standards 39 suggests a formula for determining the reliability level for substantive tests of details (TD) based upon the risk assigned to internal accounting control (IC) and analytical review (AR) and the combined reliability level desired from both internal control and the substantive tests (R). This formula is
(1) $TD = 1 - R/IC \times AR$.
(2) $TD = R - IC - AR$.
(3) $TD = R/(IC \times AR)$.
(4) $TD = R - 1/IC \times AR$.

k. An important statistic to consider when using a statistical sampling audit plan is the population variability. The population variability is measured by the
(1) Sample mean.
(2) Standard deviation.
(3) Standard error of the sample mean.
(4) Estimated population total minus the actual population total.

l. The ultimate risk against which the auditor requires reasonable protection is a combination of two separate risks. The first of these is that material errors will occur in the accounting process by which the financial statements are developed, and the second is that
(1) A company's system of internal control is *not* adequate to detect errors and irregularities.
(2) Those errors that occur will *not* be detected in the auditor's examination.
(3) Management may possess an attitude that lacks integrity.
(4) Evidential matter is *not* competent enough for the auditor to form an opinion based on reasonable assurance.

m. Statistical sampling generally may be applied to test compliance with internal accounting control when the client's internal accounting control procedures
(1) Depend primarily on appropriate segregation of duties.
(2) Are carefully reduced to writing and are included in client accounting manuals.
(3) Leave an audit trail in the form of documentary evidence of compliance.
(4) Permit the detection of material irregularities in the accounting records.

n. Which of the following *best* describes what the auditor means by the rate of occurrence in an attribute sampling plan?

(1) The number of errors that can reasonably be expected to be found in a population.
(2) The frequency with which a certain characteristic occurs within a population.
(3) The degree of confidence that the sample is representative of the population.
(4) The dollar range within which the true population total can be expected to fall.

o. Which of the following *best* describes the distinguishing feature of statistical sampling?
(1) It requires the examination of a smaller number of supporting documents.
(2) It provides a means for measuring mathematically the degree of uncertainty that results from examining only part of a population.
(3) It reduces the problems associated with the auditor's judgment concerning materiality.
(4) It is evaluated in terms of two parameters: statistical mean and random selection.

p. When using statistical sampling for tests of compliance an auditor's evaluation of compliance would include a statistical conclusion concerning whether
(1) Procedural deviations in the population were within an acceptable range.
(2) Monetary precision is in excess of a certain predetermined amount.
(3) The population total is not in error by more than a fixed amount.
(4) Population characteristics occur at least once in the population.

q. Which of the following *best* describes the distinguishing feature of statistical sampling?
(1) It provides for measuring mathematically the degree of uncertainty that results from examining only a part of the data.
(2) It allows the auditor to have the same degree of confidence as with judgment sampling but with substantially less work.
(3) It allows the auditor to substitute sampling techniques for audit judgment.
(4) It provides for measuring the actual misstatements in financial statements in terms of reliability and precision.

r. If an auditor, planning to use statistical sampling, is concerned with the number of a client's sales invoices that contain mathematical errors, the auditor would *most* likely utilize
(1) Random sampling with replacement.
(2) Sampling for attributes.
(3) Sampling for variables.
(4) Stratified random sampling.

s. Auditors who prefer statistical to judgmental sampling believe that the principal advantage of statistical sampling flows from its unique ability to
(1) Define the precision required to provide audit satisfaction.
(2) Provide a mathematical measurement of uncertainty.
(3) Establish conclusive audit evidence with decreased audit effort.
(4) Promote a more legally defensible procedural approach.

t. The objective of precision in sampling for compliance testing on an internal control system is to
(1) Determine the probability of the auditor's conclusion based upon reliance factors.
(2) Determine that financial statements taken as a whole are *not* materially in error.
(3) Estimate the reliability of substantive tests.
(4) Estimate the range of procedural deviations in the population.

u. When using a statistical sampling plan, the auditor would probably require a smaller sample if the
   (1) Population increases.
   (2) Desired precision interval narrows.
   (3) Desired reliability decreases.
   (4) Expected error occurrence rate increases.

v. If certain forms are *not* consecutively numbered
   (1) Selection of a random sample probably is *not* possible.
   (2) Systematic sampling may be appropriate.
   (3) Stratified sampling should be used.
   (4) Random number tables can *not* be used.

w. Tim McCann, CPA, believes the industry-wide occurrence rate of client billing errors is 3% and has established a maximum acceptable occurrence rate of 5%. In the review of client invoices McCann should use
   (1) Discovery sampling.
   (2) Attribute sampling.
   (3) Stratified sampling.
   (4) Variable sampling.

x. An advantage of using statistical sampling techniques is that such techniques
   (1) Mathematically measure risk.
   (2) Eliminate the need for judgmental decisions.
   (3) Define the values of precision and reliability required to provide audit satisfaction.
   (4) Have been established in the courts to be superior to judgmental sampling.

y. The objective of precision in sampling for compliance testing on an internal control system is to
   (1) Determine the probability of the auditor's conclusion on the basis of reliance factors.
   (2) Determine that financial statements taken as a whole are not materially in error.
   (3) Estimate the reliability of substantive tests.
   (4) Estimate the range of procedural deviations in the population.

z. In estimation sampling for attributes, which one of the following must be known in order to appraise the results of the auditor's sample?
   (1) Estimated dollar value of the population.
   (2) Standard deviation of the values in the population.
   (3) Actual occurrence rate of the attribute in the population.
   (4) Sample size.

(AICPA adapted)

P8–2 Select the best answer for each of the following items.

a. An accounts receivable aging schedule was prepared on 300 pages, with each page containing the aging data for 50 accounts. The pages were numbered from 1 to 300 and the accounts listed on each were numbered from 1 to 50.

   Gunther Godla, an auditor, selected accounts receivable for confirmation using a table of numbers as illustrated:

PROCEDURES PERFORMED BY GODLA

Select Number from Table of Numbers	Separate 5 digits: 3 for Page 2 for Account
02011	020—11 *x*
85393	853—93 *
97265	972—65 *
61680	616—80 *
16656	166—56 *
42751	427—51 *
69994	699—94 *
07942	079—42 *y*
10231	102—31 *z*
53988	539—88 *

x Mailed confirmation to account 11 listed on page 20.
y Mailed confirmation to account 42 listed on page 79.
z Mailed confirmation to account 31 listed on page 102.
* Rejected.

This is an example of which of the following sampling methods?
(1) Acceptance sampling.
(2) Systematic sampling.
(3) Sequential sampling.
(4) Random sampling.

b. A CPA examining inventory may appropriately apply sampling for attributes in order to estimate the
(1) Average price of inventory items.
(2) Percentage of slow-moving inventory items.
(3) Dollar value of inventory.
(4) Physical quantity of inventory items.

c. An advantage of using statistical sampling techniques is that such techniques
(1) Mathematically measure risk.
(2) Eliminate the need for judgmental decisions.
(3) Define the values of precision and reliability required to provide audit satisfaction.
(4) Have been established in the courts to be superior to judgmental sampling.

d. In estimation sampling for attributes, which one of the following must be known in order to appraise the results of the auditor's sample?
(1) Estimated dollar value of the population.
(2) Standard deviation of the values in the population.
(3) Actual occurrence rate of the attribute in the population.
(4) Sample size.

e. If the size of the sample to be used in a particular test of attributes has *not* been determined by utilizing statistical concepts, but the sample has been chosen in accordance with random selection procedures, then

(1) No inferences can be drawn from the sample.
(2) The auditor has committed a nonsampling error.
(3) The auditor may or may *not* achieve desired precision at the desired level of confidence.
(4) The auditor will have to evaluate the results by reference to the principles of discovery sampling.

f. Assume that an auditor estimates that 10,000 checks were issued during the accounting period. If an EDP application control which performs a limit check for each check request is to be subjected to the auditor's test data approach, the sample should include
(1) Approximately 1,000 test items.
(2) A number of test items determined by the auditor to be sufficient under the circumstances.
(3) A number of test items determined by the auditor's reference to the appropriate sampling tables.
(4) One transaction.

(AICPA adapted)

P8–3 Evidential matter supporting the financial statements consists of the underlying accounting data (ledgers, journals, etc.) and all corroborating (documentary and other) information available to the auditor. In the course of performing an independent audit, the CPA is faced with the problems of deciding how to go about gathering this evidence, and how much evidence to accumulate.

Required:

a. When is sampling an appropriate procedure for the auditor to use in the evidence-gathering process?
b. Describe strict judgmental sampling and explain when it would be more appropriate than using a more sophisticated statistical approach.
c. Describe statistical sampling and explain its advantages over strict judgmental sampling.
d. Do auditing standards require the use of statistical sampling? If not, what do they require?
e. List four sampling objectives that can be accomplished with the use of various statistical sampling techniques. Which of the four is the most common objective of the independent auditor?

P8–4 James Wilson, CPA, is planning the audit of Art Products Supply Company, a very large manufacturing corporation. Wilson is technically well trained and understands how to apply statistical sampling procedures in gathering audit evidence. He wants to use statistical sampling in the audit of Art Products Supply Company, particularly in the study and evaluation of the company's system of internal control.

Required:

a. Although statistical sampling during an audit allows for greater objectivity than purely judgmental sampling, there will be four areas where Wilson must still exercise audit judgment in planning his statistical tests. Identify them, and explain.
b. Assume that Wilson's sample of internal controls over inventory pricing for Art

Products shows an unacceptable error rate. Describe the various actions that Wilson might take.

c. A nonstratified sample of 120 accounts payable vouchers is to be selected from a population of 3,200. The vouchers are numbered consecutively from 1 to 3,200 and are listed, forty to a page, in the computer printout of the voucher register. Describe two different techniques that Wilson may use to select a random sample of vouchers for review. Which of these techniques seems more appropriate? Why?

d. Describe in general how computer audit software can be used to assist Wilson in this portion of the audit.

(AICPA adapted)

P8–5 Levelland, Inc., a client of your firm for several years, uses a voucher system for processing all cash disbursements (about 500 each month). After carefully reviewing the company's internal controls, your firm decided to statistically sample the vouchers for eleven specific characteristics to test operating compliance of the voucher system against the client's representations as to the system's operation. Nine of these characteristics are to be evaluated using attributes sampling and two are to be evaluated using discovery sampling. The characteristics to be evaluated are listed on the voucher test worksheet (see page 342).

Pertinent client representations about the system are as follows:

a. Purchase orders are issued for all goods and services except for recurring services such as utilities, taxes, etc. The controller issues a check request for the latter authorizing payment. Receiving reports are prepared for all goods received. Department heads prepare a services-rendered report for services covered by purchase orders. (Services-rendered reports are subsequently considered receiving reports.)

b. Copies of purchase orders, receiving reports, check requests, and original invoices are forwarded to accounting. Invoices are assigned a consecutive voucher number immediately upon receipt by accounting. Each voucher is rubber stamped to provide spaces for accounting personnel to initial when (1) matching invoice with purchase order or check request, (2) matching invoice with receiving report, and (3) verifying mathematical accuracy of the invoice.

c. In processing each voucher for payment, accounting personnel match each invoice with the related purchase order and receiving report or check request. Invoice extensions and footings are verified. Debit distribution is recorded on the face of each invoice.

d. Each voucher is recorded in the voucher register in numerical sequence after which a check is prepared. The voucher packets and checks are forwarded to the treasurer for signing and mailing the checks and canceling each voucher packet.

e. Canceled packets are returned to accounting. Payment is recorded in the voucher register, and the voucher packets are filed numerically.

Following are characteristics of the voucher population already determined by preliminary statistical testing. Assume that each characteristic is randomly distributed throughout the voucher population.

(1) Of the vouchers, 80 percent are for purchase orders; 20 percent are for check requests.

(2) The average number of lines per invoice is four.

Levelland, Inc.
VOUCHER TEST WORKSHEET
Years Ended December 31, 19X2

Characteristics	YEAR 1	YEAR 2						
	Column A	Column B	Column C	Column D	Column E	Column F	Column G	Column H
	Sample Size	Estimated Error Rate	Specified Upper Precision Limit	Reliability (Confidence Level)	Required Sample Size	Assumed Sample Size	Number of Errors Found	Upper Precision Limit
For Attribute Sampling								
1. Invoice in agreement with purchase order or check request.		1.1%	3	95%		460	4	
2. Invoice in agreement with receiving report.		.4%	2	95%		340	2	
3. Invoice mathematically accurate.								
a. Extensions		1.4%	3	95%		1,000	22	
b. Footings		1.0%	3	95%		460	10	
4. Account distributions correct.		.3%	2	95%		340	2	
5. Voucher correctly entered in voucher register.		.5%	2	95%		340	1	
6. Evidence of accounting department checks.								
a. Comparison of invoice with purchase order or check request.		2.0%	4	95%		240	2	
b. Comparison of invoice with receiving report.		1.3%	4	95%		160	2	
c. Proving mathematical accuracy of invoice.		1.5%	3	95%		340	10	
For Discovery Sampling								
7. Voucher and related documents cancelled.		At or near 0	.75%	95%		600	5	
8. Vendor and amount on invoice in agreement with payee and amount on check.		At or near 0	.4%	95%		800	0	

(3) The average number of accounts debited per invoice is two.

Appropriate statistical sampling tables appear in Appendixes 8–A, 8–B, and 8–C and in Figure 8–6. For values not provided in the tables, use the next value in the table which will yield the most conservative result.

Required:

a. An unrestricted random sample of 300 vouchers is to be drawn. Enter in Column A of the worksheet the sample size of each characteristic to be evaluated in the sample.

b. Given the estimated error rates, specified upper precision limits, and required reliability (confidence level) in columns B, C, and D, respectively, enter in column E the required sample size to evaluate each characteristic.

c. Disregarding your answers in column E and considering the assumed sample size and numbers of errors found in each sample as listed for each characteristic in columns F and G, respectively, enter in column H the upper precision limit for each characteristic.

d. On a separate sheet, identify each characteristic for which the sampling objective was not met and explain what steps the auditor might take to meet his or her sampling or auditing objectives.

(AICPA adapted)

P8–6 Rebecca Resnik, an audit partner, is developing a staff training program to familiarize her professional staff with statistical decision models applicable to the audit of internal controls. She wishes to demonstrate the relationship of sample sizes to various statistical parameters. To do this, Resnik has prepared the following table using comparative statistics drawn from two separate audit populations.

	POPULATION 1 RELATIVE TO POPULATION 2		SAMPLE FROM POPULATION 1 RELATIVE TO SAMPLE FROM POPULATION 1	
	Size	**Expected Error Rate**	**AUPL**	**Required Reliability**
Case 1	Larger	Equal	Lower	Equal
Case 2	Equal	Equal	Higher	Equal
Case 3	Equal	Smaller	Equal	Equal
Case 4	Smaller	Equal	Lower	Lower
Case 5	Equal	Smaller	Higher	Higher

Required:

Given the characteristics of two separate populations and two samples (one drawn from population 1 and one from population 2), state whether, for each of the independent cases in the table, the sample size from population 1 would be

a. Equal to the required sample size from population 2.
b. Smaller than the required sample size from population 2.
c. Greater than the required sample size from population 2.
d. Indeterminate relative to the sample size from population 2.

(1) The required sample size from population 1 in case 1 is ______.
(2) The required sample size from population 1 in case 2 is ______.
(3) The required sample size from population 1 in case 3 is ______
(4) The required sample size from population 1 in case 4 is ______.
(5) The required sample size from population 1 in case 5 is ______.

(AICPA adapted)

P8–7 In the development of an audit program it is determined that to achieve specified precision and confidence a sample of 254 items from a population of 5,000 is adequate on a statistical basis.

Required:

a. Briefly define each of the following terms used in the above statement:
   (1) Population.
   (2) Sample.
   (3) Precision.
   (4) Confidence.
b. If the population is 50,000 and the specifications for precision and confidence are unchanged from the situation above for a population of 5,000, which of the following sample sizes could be expected to be statistically correct for the larger population: 254, 260, 1,200, or 2,540? Justify your answer. (Your answer should be based on judgment and reasoning, rather than actual calculation.)
c. Statistical sampling techniques are being used in auditing. A sample is taken and analyzed to draw an inference or reach a conclusion about a population, but there is always a risk that the inference or conclusion may be incorrect. What value, then, is there in using statistical sampling techniques?

(AICPA adapted)

P8–8 As the auditor for the Gabbert Company, you have elected to use statistical sampling in performing compliance tests for the purchases and cost of sales systems. You have already studied and made a preliminary evaluation of the control attributes that the client has said are prescribed to accomplish the objectives shown on page 345.

Required:

a. Prepare a sampling plan worksheet similar to that shown in Figure 8–4 which determines sample sizes for compliance tests.
b. For each of the samples in step a, state the
   (1) Population from which you would draw the sample.
   (2) The sampling unit.
   (3) The sampling frame.
   (4) The type of audit procedure (vouching, tracing, recalculation, comparison, inspection, etc.).
   (5) If vouching or tracing, to which file the vouching or tracing would be done.
c. Assume that your sample results in step b yielded, respectively, 1, 2, 1, 2, and 3 deviations from established internal control procedures. Prepare a sample evaluation worksheet similar to that shown in Figure 8–5. Statistically interpret the results of these samples. Which of the tests support reliability of internal control (S) and which of the tests do not (N)?

d. What action do you recommend for the compliance tests that do not support reliance on internal control? If the action includes expansion of substantive tests, which of those tests would you expand?

Objectives	Control Attribute	Desired Upper Precision Limit (%)	Reliability (%)	Estimated Population Occurrence Rate (%)
1. Only materials needed are ordered	Require prenumbered written purchase requisitions	5.0	90	1.0
2. Complete records of all goods ordered	Require prenumbered written purchase orders	5.0	95	1.0
3. Ordering at most economical prices	Require approval of prices by responsible officer	6.0	95	1.0
4. All goods paid for were, in fact, record	Require written receiving reports to be matched with all vendor invoices	4.0	99	.5
5. Accurate recording of all purchases	Require supporting documents comparison of quantities, prices and recalculation of extended prices for all approved purchases invoices	4.0	99	1.0

CHAPTER

9

VARIABLES SAMPLING TECHNIQUES

In Chapter 8 we discussed statistical sampling, its relationship to generally accepted auditing standards, and the objectives of statistical sampling that are applicable to auditing. We concluded that chapter with an illustration of attribute sampling applied to auditors' tests of compliance with internal control procedures. In this chapter we extend our discussion to variables sampling techniques. Our discussion covers the following topics:

1. The audit objectives of variables sampling as compared with those of attribute sampling.
2. Statistical terminology and relationships associated with variables sampling.
3. Audit risk and variables sampling.
4. A description and illustration of difference estimation.
5. A description and illustration of mean-per-unit estimation.
6. A description and illustration of dollar unit estimation.

VARIABLES VERSUS ATTRIBUTE SAMPLING TECHNIQUES

It is important to recognize the differences between the objectives of variables sampling and those of attribute sampling. We have seen that the overall audit objective of sampling is to provide an estimation of some population characteristic.

Let us recall that for attribute sampling, the audit objective is to *estimate the rates of deviation* from established internal control procedures. In developing that idea in the last chapter, we considered a situation in which the auditor found transactions for which the client had failed to prepare a written sales order. The auditor was able to conclude that there was a 95 percent probability that the client's error rate in preparing written sales orders was between 0 and 2 percent (computed upper precision limit). Thus, the auditor's best estimate of error frequency in that case was .4 percent, and the precision interval was 1.6 percent (2.0 percent − .4 percent).

The extent of deviation from established internal controls does not bear a one-to-one relationship with possible misstatements in account balances. Therefore attribute sampling, in itself, fails to meet the auditor's ultimate objective, which is estimation of material correctness of financial statement balances. For example, the client's omission of one written sales order from a sample of 240 (an error rate of .4 percent) does not allow the auditor to infer that the sales account is misstated by as much as 2 percent in dollar amount. Instead, when a client is not complying with certain internal control procedures, the *noncompliance results in a higher probability of misstatement* of related account balances than if the client were in complete compliance.

The audit objective for *variables sampling*, on the other hand, is to estimate the *true amount* of some audit population characteristic. That characteristic may be either *total error* or *total amount*, usually expressed in terms of dollars. For example, the auditor's ultimate objective may be to estimate, with 95 percent confidence, that the sales account is not misstated by more than $50,000. Variables sampling techniques allow the auditor to make such an estimate, based on sample results, and to measure objectively the probable sampling error in doing so. The auditor must utilize her or his knowledge about internal control (which may include compliance tests) in deciding on sample sizes that will allow estimation of population dollar characteristics, such as total error or total amount. Compliance tests are not, however, a prerequisite for variables sampling. The auditor may decide, for example, to proceed directly from the preliminary evaluation of internal control to tests of dollar amounts of balances, because the cost of conducting compliance tests is judged to exceed the benefits derived therefrom. Thus, attribute sampling, utilized in compliance tests, is an optional but often useful preliminary step in determining the nature, timing, and extent of substantive tests. Variables sampling, on the other hand, includes useful statistical estimation techniques for substantive tests, which are essential in order to allow the auditor to attest to the material correctness of financial statement balances.

STATISTICAL RELATIONSHIPS AND VARIABLES SAMPLING

Although the objectives of variables sampling differ from those of attribute sampling, the statistical terminology is similar. Precision and reliability are defined the same way as before, although they are applied to *absolute amounts for variables sampling*, as opposed to percentages for attribute sampling.

For example, ***precision*** in variables sampling may be expressed as a *plus or minus dollar range* around the result developed from the sample. In this case, the auditor may be interested in both an upper and a lower precision limit, because the amount for an account may be understated or overstated. This contrasts with attribute sampling plans, where the concern is chiefly for the upper precision limit for errors, expressed as a percentage. In both attribute and variables sampling, the auditor specifies the desired level of precision and then designs the sample to meet that specification.

Reliability (confidence) for variables sampling may be explained as the percentage of times that the population value may be expected to fall within the precision limits. Stated another way, reliability is the mathematical probability that the true but unknown population value will fall within the specified range around the sample result. Typically, the auditor also specifies an acceptable reliability level to use in selecting the sample and in evaluating its results. In the following pages, we further develop some of the *statistical parameters* as these parameters apply to variables sampling techniques.

Population Distributions

In applying variables sampling methods, it is essential for the auditor to know or to estimate two very important parameters: (1) the shape of the population distribution with respect to the characteristic the auditor desires to measure; and (2) the population standard deviation. Knowledge of these two parameters is essential because of their impact on sample size and the generalizations that may be inferred from the sampling process.

The statistical distribution most often utilized in statistical sampling is the ***normal distribution,*** illustrated in Figure 9–1. As you can see from that illustration, the normal distribution possesses two distinguishing characteristics. First, it is *symmetrical,* meaning that exactly 50 percent of the population items fall on either side of the sample mean. Statistical inferences made by auditors typically are based on the *assumption of a normally distributed population* with respect to its mean. As we shall see, these

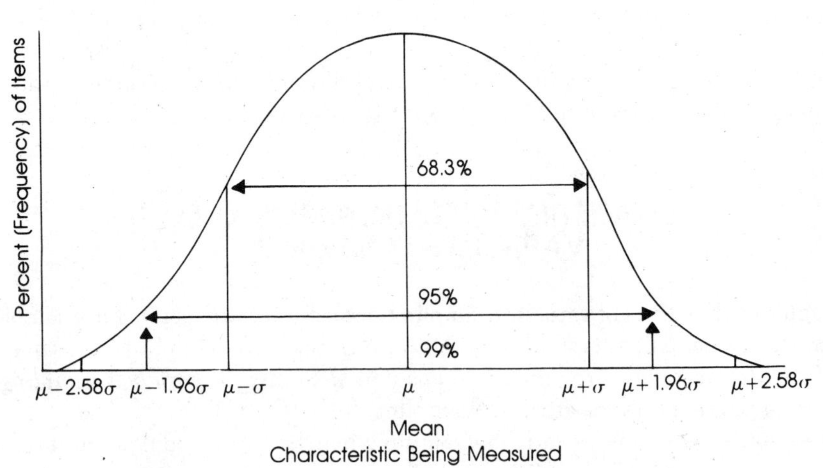

Note: σ = standard deviation of the population.

FIGURE 9–1. The Normal Distribution

inferences for audit populations create some problems that the auditor must deal with in applying variables sampling techniques.

The second characteristic of the normal distribution illustrated in Figure 9–1 is that the population items tend to congregate around the mean in such a way that 68.3 percent of them fall within plus or minus 1 standard deviation from the mean. Furthermore, 95 percent and 99 percent of the items fall within plus or minus 1.96 and 2.58 standard deviations from the mean, respectively. The ***standard deviation*** is the *measure of dispersion* of the population, stated in terms of the average difference of any one individual item from the population mean. It is calculated as follows:

$$\text{Standard deviation } (\sigma) = \sqrt{\frac{\sum_{j=1}^{N} (x_j - \mu)^2}{N-1}},$$

where

x_j = the value of an individual item in the population from $j=1$ to $j=N$;
N = the number of items in the population;
μ = the true population mean.

In applying variables sampling techniques, the auditor typically faces two problems:

1. The exact shape of the audit population distribution is unknown.
2. The exact mean of the population is almost always unknown.

With respect to the first problem, recent research has shown that audit population distributions, with respect to *individual dollar amounts*, are often ***positively skewed***, as shown in Figure 9–2.[1]

Figure 9–2 illustrates that there are a large number of accounts with relatively small dollar-value balances; we know this because the mode (most frequently occurring

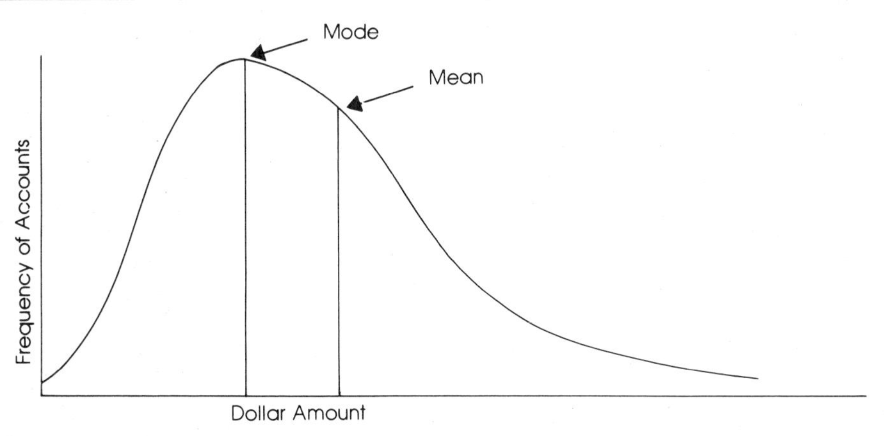

FIGURE 9–2 Positively Skewed Audit Population Distribution

item) is of lower dollar value than the mean (average dollar amount). Also, we can see that there are a few accounts with relatively large dollar-value balances, as indicated by the slope of the curve downward and to the right. Such is the case, for example, with many client accounts receivable populations.

With respect to the ***absolute value of errors,*** many audit populations are shaped as shown in Figures 9–3 and 9–4. In Figure 9–3 we see that some populations possess a high frequency of zero dollar errors and of very small dollar errors and a low frequency of very large dollar errors. Still other populations may possess both a very high frequency of zero or small dollar errors and a relatively high frequency of large dollar errors, as shown in Figure 9–4.

Unless the true mean of the population is known, the true standard deviation of the population cannot be calculated. Most often, the true population mean for the desired characteristic is not known because it is the very parameter the auditor desires to estimate. This problem is generally solved by drawing a preliminary sample from the audit population, auditing the sample for the desired population characteristic (such as dollar amount or dollar error) and calculating a ***sample mean.*** The sample standard deviation can then be derived from the following formula:

$$S_x = \sqrt{\frac{\sum_{j=1}^{n} (x_j - \bar{x})^2}{n - 1}},$$

where

S_x = the estimated population standard deviation;
x_j = value of the individual items in the sample, from $j=1$ to $j=n$;
$\bar{x}$ = the mean of the preliminary sample;
n = the number of items in the sample.

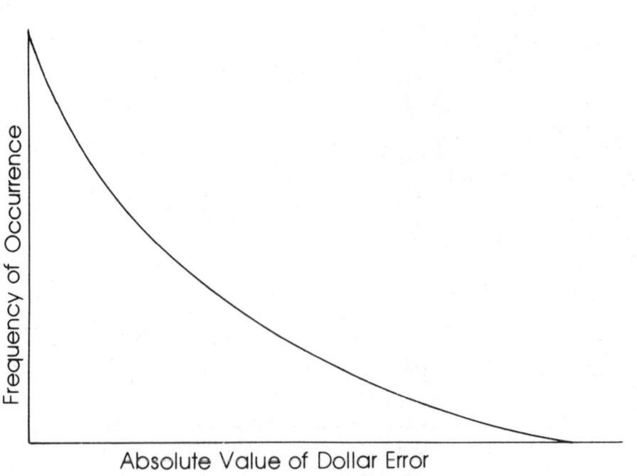

FIGURE 9–3. A Typical Shape for an Audit Population

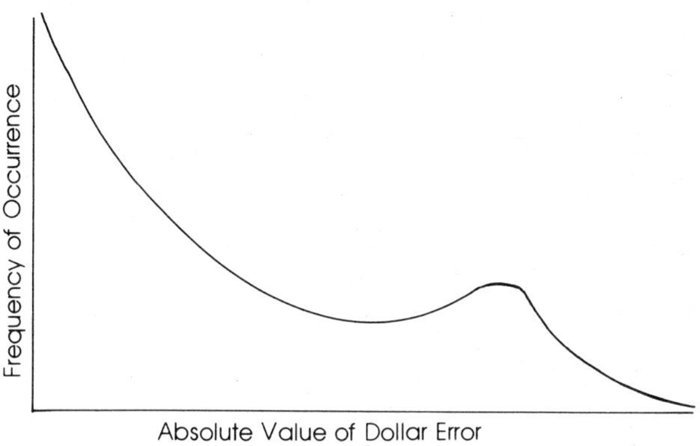

FIGURE 9–4. Another Typical Shape for an Audit Population

The estimated standard deviation (S_x) is then used in the auditor's subsequent calculations, as illustrated later in this chapter.

To solve the problem of ***nonnormality of the audit population,*** the auditor relies on the theory of ***sampling distributions.*** Samples, we recall, are representative subsets of populations. Whereas *parameters* describe the features of populations, *statistics* describe the features of samples. Figure 9–5 shows the relationship between the population parameters of mean and standard deviation and their sample statistics. Since population values are unknown to the auditor, and since their determination may be the very objective of the sampling process, it is appropriate for the auditor to *use related sample statistics as* estimations of population parameters. For example, when estimating the mean of the population characteristic (μ), the auditor's "best estimate" or "point estimate" is the mean of an audited sample drawn from the population ($\bar{x}$). The same applies to estimation of σ by calculation of S_x, as described in the preceding paragraph.

The auditor also seeks help with the nonnormal population from the ***central limit theorem:*** if the population of items (X) consists of random variables with finite mean and variance, then, *irrespective of the form of the distribution of* X, the sampling distribution of sample means $\bar{x}$ approaches a normal distribution as the sample sizes increase.[2] This means that, since the auditor's work involves taking samples, auditing

	Population Parameter	Sample Statistic
Mean	μ	$\bar{x}$
Standard Deviation	σ	S_x

FIGURE 9–5. Relationship Between Population Parameters and Sample Statistics

them, and calculating means of certain sample characteristics (such as dollar amount or dollar error), the auditor can make statistical inferences based on the central limit theorem.

Suppose, for example, that the auditor desired to estimate the dollar amount of an audit population whose individual items were distributed as shown in Figure 9–2. Regardless of the positively skewed shape of that distribution, the auditor can rely on the central limit theorem, applied as follows. If the auditor, as an experiment, took an infinite number of random samples from the distribution, and for each sample (n) calculated a mean ($\bar{x}$), then the shape of the frequency distribution of the sample means about the population mean is normal, for large samples (thirty or more).[3] The frequency distribution of the sample means would then appear as shown in Figure 9–2. In this figure, the *mean of the sample means* (midpoint of the distribution) would equal the population mean. The standard deviation of the sample means, known as the ***standard error of the means,*** expresses the average *deviation of a sample mean from the true (but unknown) population mean.* The standard error of the mean (SE) is expressed by the following formula:

$$SE = \frac{S_x}{\sqrt{n}},$$

where

S_x = the estimated population standard deviation;
n = the sample size.

To illustrate numerically the estimation of a population amount, suppose the auditor desired to estimate the average dollar amount of a client's raw materials inventory. From a random sample of 400 items, he or she estimates S_x as \$50. The mean ($\bar{x}$) of the sample is calculated to be \$100. The value of each SE is then calculated as

$$\frac{\$50}{\sqrt{400}} = \frac{\$50}{20} = \$2.50.$$

Because of the central limit theorem, the auditor's range of inferences about the true (but unknown) population mean (μ) for raw materials inventory may be as shown in Figure 9–6.

By using illustrated data, the auditor can, without knowing the true population parameters, state that there is a 95 percent probability that the true value of the population mean (μ) is somewhere between \$95.10 and \$104.90. Similarly, there is a 68.3 percent probability that the true mean of the populations is between \$97.50 and \$102.50, and a 99 percent probability that the true mean is between \$93.55 and \$106.45.

Efficiency and Reliability of Estimation Methods

There are several statistical estimation methods that can be applied in the auditing process: difference estimation, mean-per-unit estimation, and dollar unit sampling. The most appropriate method to use depends on the situation and the audit objective. In deciding which method to apply, the auditor must consider two factors: efficiency and reliability.

(1) Number of Standard Errors of the Mean (Confidence Coefficient)	(2) Value of Range [(1) × \$2.50]	(3) Range Around $\bar{x}$ [\$100 ± (2)]	(4) Percent of Sample Means Included in Range (Confidence Level)
1	2.50	97.50 – 102.50	68.3
1.96	4.90	95.10 – 104.90	95
2.58	6.45	93.55 – 106.45	99

FIGURE 9–6. Sampling Distribution from Populations with Known Mean and Standard Deviation

A specific estimation method is generally considered to be characterized by ***efficiency*** if the desired results are obtainable using a smaller sample size than would be required by another method. For example, assume an auditor wants to be satisfied that inventory is not overstated by more than \$50,000. If an unstratified difference estimation technique is expected to produce the desired information with a sample size of 250 and a stratified difference estimation technique can achieve the same result with a sample size of 175, the stratified technique would produce a more efficient sample.

The efficiency of a particular sampling process is affected by the *population standard deviation* because this parameter has a significant effect on the sample size required to meet specified precision and confidence goals. By stratifying, the auditor in effect breaks the population down into several subpopulations, each of which will have a smaller standard deviation than that of the population taken as a whole. Because of that fact, the combined samples from the various strata required to produce the desired statistical conclusions will be smaller than the size of one large sample taken from the population. Therefore, the technique of stratification often results in greater sampling efficiency.

Reliability of an estimating device pertains to how closely the computed confidence limits conform to the results than can be expected from a normal distribution. In calculating initial sample size, the auditor must prespecify a desired precision range within which he or she expects the true population value to fall, with a desired confidence level. On the other hand, after the sampling process is completed, the auditor is in position to measure an actual (achieved) precision range. The statistical estimator is *reliable only if the actual result falls within the confidence limits approximately the same percentage of the time as that stated in the desired confidence level.* For example, suppose that an auditor is examining a population with a known mean of \$4,000 and a population standard deviation of \$200. The auditor knows that if repeated samples of, say, 100 items, were taken, 95 out of every 100 samples would include means of amounts within the interval from 3,960.80 to 4,039.20; that is, 4,000 ± $[1.96(200/\sqrt{100})]$. If the researcher takes 100 samples and finds that 99 of them produce means within this interval, his estimator would be unreliable. The same would be true if only 80 of such samples produced means within the stated interval.

The *estimate would be reliable only if approximately 95 of such samples produced means with values within the predetermined interval.*

Assessing the reliability of estimators is important because this is the means by which sampling risk is controlled. The auditor could, for example, make a costly mistake in judgment if he or she concludes with 95 percent confidence that the value of a population is between \$500,000 and \$600,000, when, in fact, a reliable estimator would have caused a conclusion that the population value is between \$450,000 and \$650,000 (or between \$525,000 and \$575,000).

The example just described was based on the hypothetical assumption that the auditor *continues to take random samples* from a population. *In reality, however, only one sample is generally drawn* for any single audit test. Assessing the reliability of the estimator is therefore difficult in practice. The effects of unreliable estimators are usually most dangerous to auditors when they lead to unduly high acceptance of a false hypothesis (β risk). To reduce the effects of unreliable estimators, auditors often take larger-than-necessary sample sizes. This, of course, increases the cost of the audit — a problem that may have to be resolved with the client.

AUDIT RISK AND VARIABLES SAMPLING

As discussed in the last chapter, overall audit risk (R) can be viewed as the mathematical product of the risk that the internal control system will not detect misstatements (IC) and the risk that the auditor's substantive tests (ST) will not detect misstatements. The substantive tests risk (ST) itself can be thought of as the product of the risks associated with the analytical review phase of the audit (AR) and the tests-of-details phase of the audit (TD). Hence,

$$\begin{aligned} R &= IC \times ST \\ &= IC \times AR \times TD. \end{aligned}$$

IC, AR, and TD risks each possess the approximately additive components of *sampling risk* and *nonsampling risk*. Therefore, for purposes of visualizing the total risk associated with the audit,

$$R = IC(S + N) \times AR(S + N) \times TD(S + N),$$

where

S = the sampling component of each class of risk;
N = the nonsampling component of each class of risk.

Nonsampling risk is controlled by adhering to quality control standards and to the general and field work audit standards. Such risk will always be present in an audit environment, and cannot be controlled by increasing sample size, as can sampling risk. The auditor should, however, be continually aware that nonsampling risk exists and should attempt to control it by proper planning, due audit care, and adherence to quality control standards. The sampling component of IC was discussed earlier. We therefore confine our discussion in this chapter to the ***sampling risk component of ST*** ($AR \times TD$), which may be controlled by varying the sample sizes.

Sampling risk for both *AR* and *TD* consists of both α (Type I) and β (Type II) statistical errors, where α is the risk of rejecting a hypothesis that, in fact, is true, and β is the risk of accepting a hypothesis that, in fact, is false. In using variables sampling for substantive tests of details or during analytical review, the hypothesis tested (H_o) is usually some variant of the following:[4]

H_o: The client's recorded book value (*BV*) is equal to the GAAP value of the audit population.

The alternative hypothesis (H_a) is then stated as follows:

H_a: The client's recorded book value (*BV*) is materially different from the GAAP population value.

These hypotheses in effect confine the auditor to a finite *two-state world*, one of which describes the financial statement item being audited as materially misstated. The range of audit decisions available to the auditor is depicted by the matrix in Figure 9–7. If *after sampling*, the auditor infers that the book value of the client is materially correct when in fact it is materially correct, he or she has made a correct audit decision. On the other hand, the auditor who infers that the book value is materially correct, when in fact it is materially misstated, commits a Type II (β) sampling error.

If the auditor infers after sampling that the book value of the client is materially in error when in fact it is materially in error, he or she has made a correct audit decision. On the other hand, the auditor who infers that a book value is materially misstated, when in fact it is materially correct, commits a Type I (α) sampling error.

β risk is usually of serious concern to auditors because the cost associated with acceptance of a materially incorrect balance is *potential legal liability*. An account balance, once accepted as correct, may be either materially understated or materially overstated, but not both. As shown in Figure 9–8, therefore, the measure of β risk is a ***one-tailed statistical test.***

In Figure 9–8, assume that the auditor has accepted a range of values around the mean $\bar{x}$ as a materially correct estimation of the true (but unknown) mean of the population. Assume that, in fact, the population has a mean $\bar{x}'$, which is materially less than $\bar{x}$. Thus, $\bar{x}$ represents a material overstatement of the true dollar amount. β risk represents the area of curve centered around $\bar{x}'$, which overlaps the accepted curve

SAMPLE-INFERRED STATE OF THE AUDIT POPULATION	TRUE STATE OF THE AUDIT POPULATION	
	(1) Materially Correct	(2) Materially misstated
(1) Materially correct	Correct decision	Type II (β) risk
(2) Materially misstated	Type I (α) risk	Correct decision

FIGURE 9–7. Audit Decision Matrix

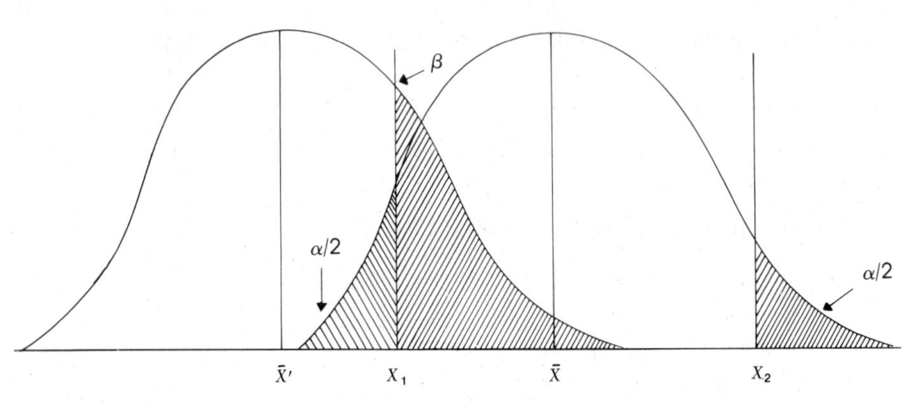

FIGURE 9–8. α and β Risks as Areas of Normal Distribution

centered around $\bar{x}$. Alternatively, the auditor may have accepted the range of values around $\bar{x}'$ when, in fact, it represents a material understatement of the true value. In this case, the true mean would lie somewhere to the right of the interval around $\bar{x}$ in Figure 9–8. Whether the auditor is more concerned with *overstatement* or *understatement* depends on the account being estimated. If the amount being estimated is associated with an ***asset account*** (the offsetting credit to a revenue account), the auditor's primary concern for purposes of certain audit objectives may be for overstatement. Conversely, if the amount being estimated is associated with a ***liability account*** (the offsetting charge to an expense account), the auditor's primary concern may be for understatement.

Before the auditor selects a variable sample for tests of details (TD), the planned β risk should be prespecified. In doing this, the audit risk formula cited earlier should be used:

$$R = IC \times AR \times TD.$$

We stated earlier that the nonsampling risk component of IC, AR, and TD could not be controlled by varying the sample size. In this chapter we concentrate on sampling risk and its effect on sample size. In addition, if we want to control the β sampling risk component of R, we may hold constant the α sampling risk component of IC, AR and TD at some level (say .05). Then IC may be defined as the β risk that internal control errors have occurred and gone undetected by the system of internal control. And AR becomes the β risk that analytical review procedures will not produce samples that result in detection of errors. Thus, TD is the β risk that the sample selected will not be representative of the population and that, as a result, a material error will not be detected by tests of details. In Chapter 8, we stated that the auditor must reach a subjective conclusion regarding the failure of (1) the system of internal control (IC) and (2) the auditor's analytical review procedures (AR) to detect material weaknesses after each of these stages of the audit has been completed. In practice, some firms set IC at

10 percent or 20 percent if controls are excellent and 70 percent or higher when controls are weak. The auditor seldom sets AR above 50 percent because of the inexact nature of analytical review procedures. Although there is no set standard for R, much of the theoretical literature mentions a 5 percent overall risk. As we saw earlier, we can calculate the planned β risk for TD by rearranging the risk formula as follows:

$$TD = R/(IC \times AR).$$

We also illustrated that, with $R = .01$, $IC = .40$, and with $AR = .50$, we would obtain TD of .05. This means that the auditor is willing to accept an overall risk of misstatement from tests of details of .05. This overall risk consists of both a sampling and a nonsampling component. To isolate the sampling component, therefore, it is necessary to estimate subjectively the nonsampling component and subtract it from total TD. For example, if the auditor in the above example had desired nonsampling risk to be no more than .01 for TD, the planned β sampling risk would be .04 (.05 − .01). As planned risk decreases, the sample size necessary for substantive tests of details increases. As planned β risk decreases, the sample size necessary for substantive tests of details increases.

In controlling sampling efficiency, α risk, known as the risk of overauditing, is an important consideration. By definition, α risk can only occur when the auditor rejects a population as being fairly stated. In Figure 9–8, α risk is illustrated graphically as the area outside the acceptance limits (x_1 to x_2) of the hypothetical sampling distribution. If an audit sample yields a sample mean that is outside x_1 to x_2, leading to rejection of $\bar{x}$ as the true population mean, when in fact that range truly represents the population, the auditor commits an α error.

The best way to understand α risk is to conceptualize what happens when an auditor, on the basis of a sample, rejects a client's book balance as being fairly stated. In most cases, further audit work will be performed to understand the full impact of the perceived error on the financial statements. Usually this extended audit work will lead to the conclusion that the balance was fairly stated after all. Unfortunately, by the time the correct conclusion is reached, additional costs will have been incurred and passed on to the client. When marginal costs of increased sample sizes are high, auditors who continually make α errors may lose the confidence and, ultimately, the business of their clients because of unjustifiably high fees. As shown in Figure 9–8, α risk is usually regarded as two-tailed statistical risk.

Figure 9–9 shows confidence coefficients ($1 - \beta$ and $1 - \alpha/2$) for various levels of β and α risk. The figure demonstrates that confidence coefficients become larger as confidence levels become larger and, conversely, as β and α risks become smaller. As we will show later, increased confidence coefficients from smaller desired β and α have the effect of increasing the required sample size for substantive tests.

DIFFERENCE ESTIMATION

Description

Difference estimation is used by the auditor to estimate the ***total dollar error*** in an audit population. In this case, a point estimate of error is calculated for the population

Confidence Level (%)	β Risk (%)	α Risk (%)	Confidence Coefficient
99	.5	1	2.58
95	2.5	5	1.96
90	5.0	10	1.64
80	10.0	20	1.28
75	12.5	25	1.15
70	15	30	1.04
60	20	40	.84
50	25	50	.67
40	30	60	.52
30	35	70	.39
20	40	80	.25
10	45	90	.13
0	50	100	0

FIGURE 9–9. Confidence Coefficients for Various Degrees of β and α Risks

by multiplying the average difference between a sample of recorded client book values and audited amounts for those same recorded book values by the number of items in the population. A precision range is calculated around that point estimate of error. If the auditor's predetermined materiality threshhold for error includes the precision range, the population is accepted as fairly stated. If the auditor's materiality threshhold for error is less than the precision range, the population value is rejected. For example, suppose that an auditor were making tests to determine that the client had applied the correct unit cost to a raw materials inventory. The auditor using difference estimation would take a sample of items from raw materials inventory, each of which had a recorded unit cost. Each item in the sample would then be vouched to vendor's invoices to determine the audited value of each sample item. Then differences between book values and audited values would be obtained for each item in the sample. The differences would then be added together and divided by the sample size to arrive at an ***average difference.*** The auditor then estimates the total population error inferred by this average by multiplying that figure by the number of items in the population. The estimate of population dollar error is then expressed in terms of a precision range and a stated level of confidence (reliability). The results are compared with the auditor's predetermined specification of materiality. If the auditor finds that the precision range of error is within the specified limits of materiality, he or she will conclude that the book balance is free from material error. On the other hand, if the precision range of error is greater than the specified limits of materiality, the auditor will reject the book value in favor of the proposition that it contains material error.

There are several advantages in using difference estimates rather than estimates of balances in auditing. For one thing, the technique produces a direct estimate of total dollar error, which is what the auditor wants to know. A second advantage of the technique is that, because estimates are based on differences that are often quite small, sample sizes necessary to make inferences are smaller than with other estimation techniques. For these reasons the method is more efficient than others, particularly if the size of individual errors is independent of recorded values. Furthermore, the difference estimation technique is also reasonably easy to use.

The disadvantages of difference estimation are a result of its unreliability in certain situations. Specifically, when the population error rate is small, many sample observations will show zero errors. This can result in inappropriate conclusions about total population error. At least fifteen to twenty differences should be noted between book values and sample values for the method to produce unbiased results. Also, difference estimation is an unreliable estimator when most errors in the population are in the same direction. If 75 percent or more of the errors noted are in one direction (overstatement or understatement), and if the population error rate is less than 10 percent, there is a risk that the difference technique will result in an unreliable estimate.

A variant of the difference estimation technique is the ***ratio estimation technique:*** ratio estimation calculates the proportion (ratio) of the sample dollars in error to the total dollar value of the sample items, and multiplies that proportion by the recorded book value of the population to determine the auditor's estimate of total population error. Ratio estimation is a *more efficient estimator than difference estimation when the sizes of individual errors are proportional to the recorded value of population items* (i.e., when there are large errors in large population values and small errors in small population items). Due to its similarity to the difference estimation technique, the ratio estimation technique is subject to the same limitations. It should therefore not be applied in situations in which the error rate in the population is less than 10 percent and in which errors are predominantly in one direction.

In using difference estimation, the auditor's goal is to *ascertain whether the client's recorded balance is materially correct.* The hypothesis tested in this case is that the client's book value is correct as recorded, within an allowable error rate that is defined as not material. If the auditor's tests allow acceptance of this hypothesis, the recorded amount will be accepted as materially correct. If the hypothesis is rejected, some other course of action, such as extension of the nature and extent of audit tests or an audit adjustment of the recorded value, must be followed.

An Illustration

Suppose that you have completed the study of internal accounting control over sales and receivables as described in Chapter 8. Your client, Huaco Business Forms, Inc., has an aged trial balance of 5,000 customer accounts receivable having a recorded book value of $6,000,000. Total assets of Huaco are $75,000,000, and net earnings before tax are $5,000,000. The next phase of the audit calls for you to perform substantive tests of details on the accounts receivable balances to determine that they do exist and that they are stated in a materially correct manner. The recommended substantive test of details in order to determine that accounts receivable exist and are stated correctly is ***confirmation of accounts receivable.*** The calculations illustrated in this section demonstrate the decision process involved with the question of how large a sample to take from the client's aged accounts receivable trial balance for the purpose of confirmation by direct correspondence with the client's trade customers. Suppose further that, because of material weaknesses discovered in internal controls (which affect the accounts receivable balances), you have judgmentally determined that reliance on these internal controls is only .80. For example, you may have discovered numerous errors in posting both sales and cash collections to individual customer accounts during the compliance testing phase. This low reliance on related internal controls is coupled with the results of preliminary analytical review tests on accounts receivable (*AR*), which in turn have a fifty-fifty chance of detecting a material misstatement in the account balance. In the following pages, we illustrate the phases of hypothesis formulation, evidence gathering, evidence evaluation, and audit conclusion of difference estimation applied to this audit problem.

The Hypothesis. As stated previously, the two hypotheses in difference estimation may be stated in terms of the value for accounts receivable either being materially correct or materially misstated. The hypothesis tested in this case is that the statement amount is materially correct.

Gathering the Evidence. Before a representative sample can be selected, for example, to verify existence by confirmation, the auditor must decide on the *size of the sample* necessary for *TD*. Determinants of sample size include:

1. β risk.
2. α risk.
3. Maximum acceptable dollar materiality threshold for error (M).
4. Population size (N).
5. Expected point estimate of dollar error in the population (E').
6. The estimated standard deviation of the population (SD).

In predetermining β risk, recall that the auditor has subjectively determined that reliance on key internal controls affecting the balances was only .80. Risk of incorrect acceptance of internal control (*IC*) is then 1 − .80, or .20. If the auditor has devised analytical review procedures (*AR*) that have a 50 percent chance of detection of material misstatements, the risk of incorrect acceptance from *AR* is 1 − .50, or .50. Then, assuming overall audit risk of incorrect acceptance (*R*) is .01, the desired β risk for test of details (*TD*) is calculated as follows:

$$\begin{aligned} TD &= R/(IC \times AR) \\ &= .01/(.20 \times .50) \\ &= .01/.10 \\ &= .10. \end{aligned}$$

The auditor may then conclude that the total risk of failure of tests of details to detect a material misstatement is .10. Remembering from our previous discussion that *TD* includes both a sampling and a nonsampling component and that these components are additive, we may substract from total *TD* nonsampling component to determine that portion of *TD* duc to sampling error. For example, if the nonsampling component of *TD* were assessed subjectively at .05, then sampling risk for *TD* would be equal to .05

(.10 − .05). The corresponding confidence coefficient for purposes of determining sample size, according to Figure 9–9, is then 1.64.

In predeterming α risk, the auditor must consider the *cost of resampling* should the population be rejected. If marginal cost is high, a low level of α risk should be prespecified, necessitating higher confidence levels and resultant larger original sample sizes. The procedure involved in additional sampling in our problem would be mailing second confirmation requests and vouching subsequent collections. The marginal cost of these procedures is high. Therefore, risk should be set low in the initial sample size. Presume that a .05 level of α has been selected as appropriate in this case. According to Figure 9–9, the confidence coefficient for α risk of 5 percent is 1.96.

The *maximum acceptable dollar error* can be influenced by both qualitative and quantitative factors. Qualitative factors include the nature of the item. For example, if the auditor suspects the existence of an irregularity in a population, he or she would do well to specify a lower threshold of materiality for that population than for others where only a few scattered inadvertant errors are anticipated. Quantitative variables playing a part in the materiality decision include the relative effect of the item on total assets and the relative effect of the item on reported net earnings.

Suppose now that you have discussed the situation of Huaco, Inc., with your superiors with regard to deciding on the maximum error you could accept and still reach a positive conclusion regarding material correctness of the balance: you decide it can be \$30,000. This means you can accept as much as a \$30,000 overstatement or understatement of accounts receivable (a total materiality range of \$60,000) and still say that the balance is fairly stated.

Population size is determined by count. In this illustration it consists of 5,000 customer accounts receivable. The sampling unit in this case is each account in the accounts receivable subsidiary ledger. The sampling frame, or physical representation of these units, might be ledger cards in a manual system, or individual records on an accounts receivable master file stored on magnetic tape in an EDP system.

An *expected point estimate* of the population's dollar error (E') must be prespecified by the auditor when using difference estimation. This expected dollar error estimate is similar to the expected occurrence rate for error in compliance tests. The auditor may use experience gained from prior years in setting E'. Assume now that the previous year's audit of accounts receivable for Huaco Corporation revealed an estimated *overstatement* of accounts receivable in the amount of \$3,000.

The estimated *standard deviation* (SD) of a population was described in an earlier part of this chapter. In this case, it is the auditor's estimate of the variability of the population error, or the dispersion of errors about the average population error rate.

For example, suppose that we took a preliminary sample of 30 accounts from the accounts receivable population mentioned above. We should audit the accounts in this preliminary sample and compare the audited value of each account with the client's book value to obtain a difference (x). Since we are only trying to get a preliminary estimate of SD, confirmation will probably not be a necessary audit procedure for this purpose. Instead, the alternative procedures of vouching subsequent collections and vouching charges in accounts to supporting documents will probably be sufficient. Suppose these procedures yielded the results shown in Figure 9–10.

(1) Sampling Unit (Account)	(2) Audited Value	(3) Book Value	(4) Difference (x_j) [(3)−(2)]	(5) $(x_j - \bar{x}_D)$	(6) $(x_j - \bar{x}_D)^2$
1	$ 500	$ 470	−$30	−65	4225
2	370	400	+ 30	− 5	25
3	200	280	+ 80	+45	2025
4	360	390	+ 20	−15	225
5	480	560	+ 80	+45	2025
6	2640	2720	+ 60	+25	625
•	•	•	•	•	•
•	•	•	•	•	•
•	•	•	•	•	•
30	3820	3825	+ 5	−30	900
			+$1,050		26,100

$\bar{x}_D$ = average difference between audited and book value = $1050/30 = $35.

FIGURE 9–10. Procedure for Estimated Standard Deviation of Errors

We can calculate the estimated standard deviation of error as follows:

$$SD = \sqrt{\frac{\sum_{j=1}^{n} (x_j - \bar{x}_D)^2}{n-1}} = \sqrt{\frac{26{,}100}{29}} = 30,$$

where

x_j = the jth difference between audited and book values for sample items $j=1$ through $j=n$.

On the basis of all these statistical determinants, *sample size* can be calculated using the following formula:[5]

$$n = \left[\frac{N(Z_\beta + Z_\alpha)SD}{M - E'}\right]^2,$$

where

n = sample size;
N = population size;
Z_β = confidence coefficient for β risk;
Z_α = confidence coefficient for α risk;
SD = estimated standard deviation error of the audit population;
M = materiality threshold;
E' = expected point estimate for error.

This formula yields a sample size of 400 for the Huaco Corporation:

$$n = \left[\frac{5{,}000(1.64 + 1.96)30}{30{,}000 - 3{,}000}\right]^2 = 400.$$

An examination of the formula reveals the effects on sample size of changing the various factors in the formula. Figure 9–11 summarizes those effects. These changes are the same as those observed when varying the determinants of sample size for attribute sampling.

After the sample size (n) has been determined, the auditor will select the sample on a random basis from the population of 5,000 accounts. Next he or she will prepare and mail 400 positive accounts receivable confirmation requests.

The next part of the evidence-gathering process calls for an *audit* of the confirmation requests, which includes these steps:

1. Receiving the confirmation replies and following up on those requests for which no replies were received. This generally involves sending second (and possibly third) requests.
2. Performing alternative procedures (such as vouching subsequent collections to the cash receipts journal, vouching sales entries to invoices, shipping documents, etc.) for non-responses.
3. Reconciling differences between customer replies and the receivable amounts shown in the client's records.

After these procedures have been completed, the auditor will *determine the amounts* of all *errors* in the sample. Errors in this case are defined as the unreconciled differences between the verified balances and the balances shown on the client's records. An error value is then determined for each of the 400 units in the sample. When audited (customer-derived) values equal recorded values, the differences (error value) will be zero. Figure 9–12, step 2(d), shows the assumed findings of eighty unreconciled differences. The net *sum* of these differences (E) was $925 in the direction of overstatement.

Evaluating the Evidence. Evaluating the evidence requires several steps, shown in Figure 9–12. These evaluative steps include the following:

(a) Calculation of the point estimate of average dollar error ($\bar{e}$) and total dollar error ($\hat{E}$).
(b) Computation of the estimated population standard deviation of errors (SDE).

Nature of Change in Parameters	Effect on Sample Size
Increased confidence level (decreased β or α)	Increase
Increased precision (decreased M)	Increase
Increased standard deviation (SD)	Increase
Increased population size (N)	Increase

FIGURE 9–11. Effects of Changes in Population Parameters on Sample Size

Steps	Statistical Formulas	Illustration for Huaco, Inc.
1. Develop a testable hypothesis		H_o: The recorded value of accounts receivable ($6,000,000) materially correct as stated
2. Gather the evidence by (a) specifying β, α, SD, M, N, and E' (b) drawing a random sample (c) auditing the sample	$n = \left[\frac{N(Z_\beta + Z_\alpha)\ SD}{M - E'}\right]^2$	n = 400 customer accounts drawn at random from the population of 5,000 customers accounts and audited by noting unreconciled differences between audited amounts and book value for those amounts
(d) determining the value of each unrecorded error in the sample and summing the errors	$E = \sum_{i=1}^{n} e$, where e = individual unreconciled error	330 accounts confirmed by customers, and 70 accounts audited by alternative procedures, with a total of 80 customers reporting differences that could not be reconciled; algebraic sum of these differences = $925 overstatement
3. Evaluate the evidence by (a) calculating the point estimate of the average dollar error ($\bar{e}$) and the projected population error ($\hat{E}$)	$\bar{e} = \frac{E}{n}$ $\hat{E} = N \cdot \bar{e}$	$\bar{e}$ = $925/400 = $2.31 $\hat{E}$ = 5000 × 2.31 = $11,550
(b) computing SDE	$SDE = \sqrt{\frac{\Sigma(e_j)^2 - n(\bar{e})^2}{n-1}}$, where e_j = error for jth item and $\bar{e}$ and n are defined as before	Assume $\Sigma(e_j)^2$ = $60,095 $SDE = \sqrt{\frac{\$60{,}095 - 400(\$2.31)^2}{399}}$ = $12.05
(c) calculating the precision interval (P)	$P = N\left[Z_\beta \cdot \frac{SDE}{\sqrt{n}} \cdot \sqrt{\frac{N-n}{N-1}}\right]$, where N, Z_β, SDE, and n are defined as before $\sqrt{\frac{N-n}{N-1}}$ = finite correction factor (assuming a confidence level of .95 for β risk)	$P = 5000\left[1.64 \cdot \frac{12.05}{\sqrt{400}} \cdot \sqrt{\frac{4600}{4999}}\right]$ = [5000 • 1.64 • .6025 • .9593] = 4739
(d) computing the precision limits: upper precision limit (UPL); lower precision limit (LPL)	$UPL = \hat{E} + P$ $LPL = \hat{E} - P$, where E and P are defined as before	UPL = $11,550 + $4739 = $16,289 LPL = $11,550 − $4739 = $6811

FIGURE 9–12. Summary of the Difference Estimation Technique

(c) Calculation of the precision interval for errors (P).
(d) Computation of the precision limits (UPL and LPL).

The ***point estimate*** of average dollar error per account ($\bar{e}$) is obtained by dividing the algebraic sum of all errors by the number of sampling units (accounts). The auditor then can project a point estimate of the dollar error in the population ($\hat{E}$) by multiplying ($\bar{e}$) by the number of items in the population (N). In our example, $\bar{e}$ is \$2.31 (\$925/400). Then $\hat{E}$ is calculated as \$11,550 (\$2.31 × 5000).

Since no statistical statement can be made merely on the basis of a point estimate applied to the population, the auditor's next step is to construct a ***precision interval*** (P) around $\hat{E}$. This is done by statistical formulas in a series of steps. First, the standard deviation for error (SDE) must be estimated. This is the expected variability of dollar error around the true mean of the population. The distribution of errors is centered around a mean of \$2.31 ($\bar{e}$), the estimated average error in the population.

The ***variability of errors*** in the population will generally be much less than the variability of values of the population items. This explains in large part why sample sizes for difference estimation are usually more efficient than those for unstratified mean-per-unit estimation. For example, suppose that our population of accounts receivable had a mean of \$500, including equal numbers of items valued at \$100, \$400, and \$1000. That population would have a much larger standard deviation than would a population of errors (differences between audited and book values in accounts receivable), the average of which is \$2.31, and individual differences of which were \$12.00, (9.40), and 4.33, respectively. The smaller the variability of the error in population, as measured by the standard deviation, the more precise will be the estimate of the population error rate, and the smaller (more efficient) will be the sample size required to make the estimate. In our example, SDE is calculated to be \$12.05.

The next step in the evaluation process requires computation of the precision interval (P) around $\hat{E}$ as shown in Figure 9–12, step 3(c). P represents the range of values around the sample result $\hat{E}$ within which the true population error (expressed in dollars) is expected to fall. P is measured by multiplying the confidence coefficient for the desired level of β risk by a standard error factor ($SDE/\sqrt{n}$). Close examination of the formula for P reveals that it is derived from the formula for n: P is the *after-sampling equivalent of* ($M - E'$) in the sample size formula (step 2 of Figure 9–12).

Both P and ($M - E'$) measure precision. However, there are some important differences: P is ***achieved precision,*** whereas ($M - E'$) is ***desired precision.*** These factors correspond to the calculated upper precision limit ($CUPL$) and desired upper precision limit ($DUPL$) for attribute sampling. It is achieved precision (P) which must ultimately be the basis for making statistical inferences from the samples. In addition, β is the only relevant risk coefficient for estimating P, whereas both β and α were used to estimate sample size. This is because, after sampling has been done, the auditor desires to know whether the population is acceptable. β risk is the only relevant risk to consider when one accepts a population.

Once P has been estimated, the auditor uses it to estimate a ***precision interval*** around $\hat{E}$. This interval consists of $\hat{E} \pm P$, as shown in Figure 9–12, step 3(d). In our illustration of Huaco, Inc., the upper precision limit (UPL) is \$16,289 and the lower precision limit (*LPL*) is \$6,811. This means that, given the auditor's acceptance of the population book value, there is a 5 percent sampling risk that the population is overstated by as much as \$16,289 or overstated by as little as \$6,811.

Developing the Conclusion. After applying the process described above, the auditor is now ready to test the original hypothesis that the client's book value for accounts receivable is not misstated by a material amount. For this test, the auditor must ***apply a decision rule.*** That rule assumes an equal concern for overstatement and understatement and requires that the auditor return to the original estimate of materiality (M) as a criterion for determining whether a material error exists. The decision rule is stated as follows:

> If the precision interval (*UPL* to *LPL*) for total population error falls completely within the range formed by the original estimate of M, accept the hypothesis (H_o) that the book value is not misstated by a material amount. Otherwise, reject that hypothesis and accept the alternate hypothesis (H_a) that the book value is misstated.

Of course, that decision rule can be applied only if the auditor is reasonably assured that nonsampling errors and other subjectively obtained evidence regarding the year-end balances of accounts receivable also point to fairness of presentation of those balances. In the case of Huaco, Inc., M was originally estimated at ±30,000. As a result of the sampling process, P was estimated at +\$6,811 to +\$16,289, a range completely within M. If P had fallen out of the range set by M (either on the understatement or overstatement side), H_o would have been rejected in favor of H_a.

When an auditor rejects H_o and concludes on the basis of sample results that an account balance is materially misstated, she or he must follow one of the following courses of action available to the auditor:

1. *If the error is isolated* to a particular type, such as sales cutoff, it may be desirable to expand audit work in the problem area. For example, extended tests may be performed on sales cutoff to determine more exactly the causes and extent of the error.
2. *The account balance may be adjusted* to an amount within the auditor's threshold of materiality. For example, if P had been \$20,000, *UPL* would have been \$31,550 and *LPL* would have been (\$9,500). Assuming M of \$30,000, a minimum credit adjustment of \$1,550 $[(11{,}550 + 20{,}000) - 30{,}000]$ would bring *UPL* within the bounds of M, and the auditor could then accept the population. If the client is unwilling to adjust the population on the basis of a sample, the auditor may have to develop more evidence to convince the client that this action is desirable. Also if the computed precision interval (P) is greater than M, it is impossible for the book value to be adjusted to be within M. This would have been the case for Huaco, Inc., if P had exceeded \$30,000.
3. *Sample size could be increased.* When this happens, E and *SDE* remain the same if the number of errors and their amount is essentially the same in the expanded sample as in the original sample. However, referring to the formula in Figure 9–12, step 3(c), we see that P gets smaller as sample size increases. This, in turn, may cause the inteval (*UCL* – *LCL*) to be narrower, to the point at which it is within the auditor's materiality range (M). The formula stated in Figure 9–10 may be used for the revised sample size (n), but the actual estimates for error (E) and standard deviation of error (*SDE*) from Figure 9–12 should be used in place of their presampling counterparts (E' and *SD*, respectively) in the sample size formula stated

earlier. The chief disadvantage of this approach is that it is often *costly*, and offers no guarantee of a satisfactory result.

Regardless of which course of action is chosen, the auditor must realize satisfactory results, (either acceptance of the hypothesis or adjustment of the account balance) before he or she can issue an unqualified audit opinion. If such results cannot be achieved, a qualified or adverse opinion will be necessary, since the account is presumed to contain a material misstatement.

MEAN-PER-UNIT ESTIMATION

Description

The objective of mean-per-unit estimation is *to estimate the total value* of an audit population. This estimate is based on a precision range of values around a point estimate of the population total. That point estimate is the product of the mean of an audited sample and the number of items in the population to arrive at an estimate of total value. The precision range is calculated in a manner similar to that illustrated for difference estimation. Once the precision range around the point estimate is calculated for the desired confidence level, a decision may be made regarding the fairness of presentation of the population by comparing the accounts within the calculated precision range with the recorded book values.

The mean-per-unit estimation process can provide a highly reliable estimate of the population total, as long as the population values are not extremely skewed. Furthermore, mean-per-unit estimation is useful when the client does not have recorded book values for all items in the population. For example, suppose that the client has not taken a yearly physical count of inventory, but instead has used a statistical technique to estimate, within specified precision limits, the value of inventory. The auditor could, after drawing a representative sample of inventory items, compute his or her own point estimate of inventory and construct a precision range (P) around that point estimate. If the client's recorded book value (BV) fell within P, the auditor would accept the book value as a fair statement of inventory. If, on the other hand, the recorded value fell outside P, the auditor would reject the book value as being fairly stated. Difference or ratio estimation could not be used in such a situation because both of those methods require a recorded book value for each item in the population.

The chief disadvantages of the mean-per-unit approach are its failure to yield a dollar estimate of error (which is often the desired audit objective) and the fact that unstratified mean-per-unit estimation techniques are inefficient, especially in populations with large standard deviations.

An Illustration

Assume that Huaco, Inc., your client, had statistically estimated a value of $6,000,000 for its 50,000-item work-in-process inventory. Suppose further that a preliminary sample of the work-in-process inventory showed a standard deviation of $20, and that a material misstatement of value for the population (M) has been determined to be

±\$300,000. Finally, assume that, based on attributes sampling, you have found internal control of inventory to be 80 percent reliable and you have concluded that analytical review techniques have a 50 percent chance of detecting material misstatements. Using the formula for β risk stated earlier, and an assumed 1 percent overall risk from the audit, β risk is calculated at .10 $[.01/(.20 \times .50)]$. Using the same reasoning as explained in the difference estimation technique, assume that nonsampling risk has been calculated at .05, leaving the sampling component of risk equal to .05. You may also assume that because of the high cost of additional sampling, you have set α risk at .05 as well. Figure 9–13 contains a step-by-step summary of the results from the mean-per-unit estimation technique. Notice that the initial hypothesis is the same as that stated under the difference estimation technique. The sample size formula for the mean-per-unit technique differs from that of the difference technique only by the item being estimated. That is, for the mean-per-unit technique, it is the *actual value* of the population being estimated, whereas the difference technique estimates the total error in the population. Notice further that, in the unstratified mean-per-unit technique, the standard deviation has the potential to be very large, causing this technique to be potentially less efficient than a stratified sampling technique.

After the sample has been selected and audited, a mean ($\bar{x}$) is calculated for the sample. This value becomes the auditor's point estimate of the true population mean. The point estimate (V) of the total value of the population can then be calculated by $N \cdot x$, which, in the case of Huaco, Inc., is \$5,900,000.

Since a statistical conclusion cannot be made on the basis of a point estimate, a precision range (P) must be constructed on either side of V. This is done in three steps:

1. Calculating an actual standard deviation (SD) of the sample.
2. Calculating a standard error of the mean ($SD/\sqrt{n}$).
3. Multiplying the standard error by the desired confidence coefficient (Z_α) and the population size. Notice that, in contrast with the difference estimation technique, Z_α (and not Z_β) is used as the appropriate confidence coefficient. This is because in mean-per-unit estimation, the objective, after sampling, is to *estimate the amount of, not the accountability of,* a population. It is based upon the hypothesis that the client's recorded amount is true, which leaves open the possibility of rejecting that hypothesis, and thus incurring α risk.

For Huaco, Inc., P = \$294,000. The upper and lower precision limits (UPL and LPL) can then be computed as \$6,194,000 and \$5,606,000, respectively.

The auditor must now *adopt a decision rule,* which can be stated as follows: Compare the recorded book value (BV) with the precision limits (UPL and LPL). If BV falls within those limits, it will be accepted as a fair presentation of the true value of the population. If BV falls outside those limits, the auditor will reject it.

If the auditor accepts BV as fairly presented, he or she incurs β risk (risk of acceptance of a false hypothesis). In the case of Huaco, Inc., the auditor has accepted \$5,900,000 as the true population value, and \$118 as the true mean of that population. Suppose that the true mean of the population of Huaco's inventory is not \$118, but \$114 (a value materially different from the hypothesized mean of \$120, according to the original hypothesis).[6] The auditor can calculate the β risk associated with the decision to accept \$118 as the true value of the mean of the population. The formula is stated as follows:

Steps	Statistical Formulas	Illustration for Huaco, Inc.
1. Develop a testable hypothesis		H_o: The recorded value of inventory ($6,000,000) is materially correct as stated
2. Gather the evidence by (a) specifying Z_α, Z_β, SD, M, and N	$n = \left[\frac{N(Z_\alpha + Z_\beta)\ SD}{M}\right]^2$	$= \left[\frac{50{,}000(1.96 + 1.64)20}{300{,}000}\right]^2$
(b) drawing a random sample		= 144 items drawn at random
(c) auditing the sample		Perform counts of merchandise and vouch to client listing to verify quantities Vouch price figures to vendors' invoices, labor reports, overhead summaries to verify unit pricing Recalculate inventory extensions (number of units × unit price = extended price)
3. Evaluate the evidence by (a) determining the average audited value of an item in the sample ($\bar{x}$) and calculating a point estimate of the population total therefrom (V)	$\bar{x} = \frac{\sum_{i=1}^{n} x_i}{n}$, where x_i = value of each item in sample and n = number of sampling units $V = N \cdot \bar{x}$	Assume $\bar{x} = 118$ $V = 50{,}000 \cdot 118 = \$5{,}900{,}000$
(b) computing the actual standard deviation of the sample (SD)	$SD = \sqrt{\frac{\Sigma(x)^2 - n(\bar{x})^2}{n - 1}}$	Assume $SD = 36$
(c) calculating the precision interval	$P = N\left(Z_\alpha \cdot \frac{SD}{\sqrt{n}}\right)^\dagger$	$= 50{,}000\left(1.96 \cdot \frac{36}{12}\right)$ $= 294{,}000$
(d) computing the precision limits: upper precision limit (UPL); lower precision limit (LPL)	$UPL = V + P$ $LPL = V - P$	$UPL = 5{,}900{,}000 + 294{,}000 = 6{,}194{,}000$ $LPL = 5{,}900{,}000 - 294{,}000 = 5{,}606{,}000$

†As in Figure 9–12, a finite population correction factor would be appropriately multiplied by the other factors in the formula if the sample size (n) relative to the population size (N) were greater than 10 percent.

FIGURE 9–13. Summary of the Mean-Per-Unit Estimation Technique

$$Z_\beta = \frac{\bar{x} - \mu}{SE},$$

where

Z_β = confidence coefficient for β risk;
$\bar{x}$ = the mean that was accepted;
μ = the hypothetical true mean;
SE = the standard error = $SD/\sqrt{n}$.

Substituting the assumed data in the formula, we find that the confidence coefficient for β risk is 1.33, as shown below:

$$Z_\beta = \frac{\$118 - \$114}{\$3} = \frac{\$4}{\$3} = 1.33.$$

We see that Z_β of 1.33 yields a β risk of 9.2 percent (see Appendix 9–B). Thus, the auditor is assuming a sampling risk of 9.2 percent that the mean of the population was, in fact, \$114 rather than the accepted figure of \$118.

If the auditor rejects the book value as a fair presentation of the item, he or she incurs α risk. In our illustration, for example, suppose that the auditor had calculated a sample mean ($\bar{x}$) of \$113, which was less than the amount considered as the lowest precision limit from the \$120 *BV* mean of the population. If, in fact, \$120 was the true mean, the auditor would have committed a Type I (α) statistical error. The calculation of the probability of this occurrence is

$$Z_\alpha = \frac{\mu - \bar{x}}{SE},$$

where

Z_α = confidence coefficient for α risk;
μ = hypothesized true mean;
$\bar{x}$ = sample mean that was accepted as the true mean;
SE = standard error of the mean = $SD/\sqrt{n}$.

Using the assumed data in the formula, we arrive at a Z value of 2.33 as shown below:

$$Z_\alpha = \frac{\$120 - \$113}{\$3} = \frac{\$7}{\$3} = 2.33.$$

Z_α of 2.33 translates into an α sampling risk of 1.98 percent (see Appendix 9–A). Thus there is a 1.98 percent chance that the auditor has decided that the book value is materially misstated when in fact the true population value is equal to the book value (\$6,000,000).

DOLLAR UNIT ESTIMATION

Dollar unit sampling is a technique developed in recent years, combining certain features of attributes and variables estimation. It is unique in that it allows the auditor to make inferences regarding the dollar error in a population by using an attributes sampling evaluation table. Dollar unit sampling is also characterized as *cumulative monetary sampling* and *sampling with probability proportional to size,* which are actually two separate but closely related methods. The dollar unit sampling technique has been researched and used extensively by Canadian authorities[7] and is gaining acceptance among auditors in the United States. The technique underlies the cumulative monetary amount (CMA) sampling approach, which was first developed by Kenneth Stringer of the firm of Deloitte, Haskins and Sells; CMA sampling has been a significant part of that firm's sampling approach for several years.

The basic feature of dollar unit sampling is that it defines the population in terms of *number of dollars* instead of number of items. The sampling unit thus becomes a dollar rather than an account, transaction, or document. Whereas in the difference estimation technique, the accounts receivable population for Huaco, Inc., was defined as 5,000 accounts, with dollar unit estimation the accounts receivable population is defined as 6,000,000 dollar units. If the auditor takes a random sample of the population of $6,000,000, confirms the account balances included in the sample, and calculates the error in those balances, he or she can make statistical inferences about the *dollar error of the population* in much the same way as was done for percentage deviation from established attributes of internal control in Chapter 8.

The dollar unit sampling technique has the following advantages over other techniques:

- It allows a direct estimation of *maximum dollar error* in an audit population. This contrasts with the end result of attribute sampling, in which the auditor estimates the maximum percentage deviation from established internal control attributes. Thus dollar unit sampling is more suited to the auditor's ultimate objective than is pure attribute sampling.
- It includes *automatic stratification* of the population, which makes the sampling process more efficient. For example, if 500 of the dollars in a $6,000,000 population were selected systematically for examination, every 12,000th dollar (6,000,000/500) would be selected. This means that, if systematic selection were used, every account with an amount of $12,000 or more would be selected. Similarly, a $12,000 account would have twice the probability of being selected as a $6,000 account and three times the probability as a $4,000 account.
- It does not suffer the same problems of reliability as do the ratio and difference techniques, because it does not require specified differences between audited and book values in order to be useful.
- It provides a self-contained, quantitative model of the *linkage* between attribute sampling methods (used to judge the reliability of internal controls) and variables sampling methods (used to reach a conclusion about the fairness of presentation of account balances). Thus, with the same tests, it is possible to judge both the adequacy of internal controls and the fairness of balances that have emerged from the system. Thus, a high degree of audit efficiency is achieved.

The dollar unit sampling technique also has some disadvantages, especially when applied to certain types of populations. *Specifically when a large number of errors exist* in an audit population, the sample size needed to satisfy most auditors' materiality standards for maximum allowable error is much higher for dollar unit sampling than would be required with other variables sampling techniques. Furthermore, it is often difficult to obtain a random sample of the dollars in a population, without the use of a computer.

A discussion of dollar unit sampling is not complete without a brief discussion of the selection methods used to draw a dollar unit sample. Two basic selection methods are used: random selection based on random number tables; and systematic selection, based on a recurring pattern. Both of these selection techniques utilize *probability proportional to size* (PPS) *sampling*. In the interest of brevity, we will look only at the systematic selection technique.[8] This selection technique entails the following five steps:

1. Calculate the reported dollar value (X) of the population:

$$\sum_{i=1}^{N} x_i = X.$$

2. Cumulate the reported account values such that there are as many accumulations as there are number of accounts (N).
3. For a specified sample size n, compute a *sampling interval* k according to the following formula:

$$\sum_{i=1}^{N} x_i/n = k.$$

4. Select a random number between 1 and k; denote it by g.
5. Select the first account such that it contains the gth dollar, the second account such that it contains the ($g \pm k$)th dollar, the third account such that it contains the ($g \pm k \pm k$)th, or the ($2k \pm g$)th dollar, and so forth, until fewer than k dollars of cumulated population remain.

Consider the example in Figure 9–14. The reported dollar value of the population (X) is \$6,000,000, consisting of 5000 accounts (N). The sample size (n) of 138 accounts (discussed later) is divided into the population value (X) of \$6,000,000 to obtain the internal (k) of \$43,470. A random number (g) between 1 and 43,470 is selected. Say this number is 22,416. The population, cumulated from 1 to 5000 accounts, is then entered for the 22,416th dollar. The first account selected would be the first account which contains the 22,416th dollar. The second account selected would contain the 65,886th cumulative dollar (43,470 + 22,416). The third account would contain the 109,356th dollar [2(43,470)+ 22,416] and so forth until 138 accounts are selected, at which time fewer than 43,470 population dollars would be found in k.

It should be easy to see from the preceding example that the probability that any account of k or more dollars (43,470 in our example) will be included in the sample is 1.0. If an account is *larger* than k dollars in size, it may be included in the sample more than once. To handle this duplication, auditors often stratify the population into accounts of k or more dollars. These strata are then 100 percent audited. The statistical analysis described in the paragraphs that follow is then applied only to accounts of fewer than k dollars. The results of the 100 percent audited items and sampled items are then aggregated, and appropriate inferences are made.

In Figure 9–14 we assume the same facts as those illustrated previously for Huaco, Inc., for the difference estimation technique, except that the auditor's preliminary materiality threshold for error (M) is $\pm$\$300,000. Notice that the hypothesis tested in this technique is the same as for the difference technique and the mean-per-unit

Steps	Statistical Formulas	Illustration for Huaco, Inc.
1. Develop a testable hypothesis		H_0: The recorded value of inventory (6,000,000) is materially correct as stated
2. Gather the evidence by (a) specifying β and M	$n = \frac{RF \times BV}{M}$, where RF = β risk factor (see Figure 9–15) and BV and M are defined as before	$n = \frac{3.0 \times 6{,}000{,}000}{300{,}000} = 138$
(b) drawing a random sample		A random sample of the accounts included in every 43,470th population dollar (\$6,000,000/138) would be drawn
(c) auditing the sample		Sample audited by noting unreconciled differences between audited amounts and book values for those amounts
(d) determining the value of each error in the sample and the percentage error to book value		One account with 10% overstatement; one account with 25% overstatement
3. Evaluate the evidence by (a) using attribute sampling table		See Figure 9–16
(b) obtaining net upper error percentage limit		See Figure 9–16
(c) converting percentage error limit to dollar limit		
(d) comparing dollar error limit with M		

FIGURE 9–14. Summary of the Dollar Unit Sampling Technique

technique. The sample size calculation, however, is different for the dollar unit technique than for the others. Specifically, the difference and mean-per-unit techniques require an estimate of population standard deviation for error or absolute amount, respectively, in order to calculate sample size. The dollar unit sample size *requires only an estimate of β risk and preliminary materiality threshold.* β risk factors are established on the basis of the auditor's evaluation of internal control. A range of these factors is shown in Figure 9–15.[9] These factors assume all zero errors in the population. The β risk factor is then multiplied by the book value of the population (BV). The result is then divided by the maximum amount considered material (M) to

Maximum Acceptable β Risk β (%)	Risk Factor (RF)
20	1.61
15	1.90
10	2.30
5	3.00
2.5	3.69
1	4.61

FIGURE 9–15. Risk Factors for Maximum Acceptable Beta Risk

obtain a sample size (n). In our illustration, β = 5 percent, and so RF = 3.00. This calculation produces a sample of $138 from the population of $6,000,000. The auditor then *audits the accounts* included in every 43,470th population dollar (6,000,000 ÷ 138). As pointed out above, this means that, assuming systematic selection, every account with a balance of at least $43,470 would have a 100 percent probability of selection in the sample. The individual accounts in the sample are audited in the same way as was previously illustrated. Errors are defined as ***unreconciled differences*** between audited amounts and book balances for these amounts. Assume for purposes of our illustration that an audited sample produced one account with a 10 percent overstatement and another account with a 25 percent overstatement. We show in Figure 9–16 how these results would be interpreted in the most conservative way.

Column (1) lists the "dollars sampled." In reality, these are the individual accounts that encompass the 138 "dollars" in the dollar unit sample, assuming no duplication of items selected. Column (2) lists the errors that were found. Notice that no errors were

(1) Dollars Sampled	(2) Errors Found	(3) Tainting Percentage	(4) Worst Allocation of Total Upper Error Limit Frequency (%)	(5) Net Upper Error Limit by Value (%) [(3) × (4)]
136	0	100	2.16	2.16
1	1	25	1.26	.32
1	1	10	1.16	.12
138	2			2.60

Source: Adapted from R. Anderson and A.D. Tietlebaum, "Dollar Unit Sampling," *Canadian Chartered Accountant* (April 1973): 30–39.

FIGURE 9–16. Calculation of Net Upper Error Limit for Dollar Unit Sampling

(1) Errors Found in Sample, Ranked in Declining Percentages	(2) Upper Error Limit Incremental Factor [a]	(3) 1/Sample Size	(4) Worst Allocation of Total Upper Error Limit Frequency [(2) × (3)] [b]
0	3.0	1/138 = .0072	2.16%
1	1.75	1/138 = .0072	1.26%
2	1.55	1/138 = .0072	1.16%
3	1.45	1/138 = .0072	1.04%
4	1.40	1/138 = .0072	1.01%

[a] Based on the Poisson probability distribution at the 95 percent level of confidence.
[b] This table yields approximately the same results as those used to evaluate attribute samples (see Appendixes 8–D, 8–E, and 8–F).

FIGURE 9–17. Derivation of Worst Allocation of Total Upper Error Limit Frequency

found in 136 of the dollars sampled. Using tables based on the binomial distribution (or the Poisson approximation of the binomial) at 95 percent confidence as shown in Figure 9–17, we may infer that there is, *at worst,* a 2.16 percent probability of these items being misstated by 100 percent (the ***tainting percentage*** referred to in column [3] of Figure 9–16). This probability, in turn, is the product of the Poisson upper error limit incremental factor times 1/sample size (column [3]). A similar calculation is made for the first and second errors found. In each case, the net upper error limit by value, shown in column (5) in Figure 9–16, is the product of the tainting percentage (3) times the worst allocation of total upper error limit frequency (4) from Figure 9–17.

The results of the example (Figure 9–16) show a total net upper error limit of 2.60 percent. The auditor may therefore conclude with 95 percent probability that Huaco, Inc.'s accounts receivable may be overstated by as much as $156,000 (2.6 percent × $6,000,000). If, as explained previously, the sample had included duplicated accounts, requiring the auditor to stratify the audit population and to select items in excess of the kth dollar for 100 percent audit, the amount of error from the 100 percent audited stratum would be added to the inferred error resulting from the sampling process at this point. The auditor must then compare this amount of error with the preliminary estimate of materiality (M). In this case, since M = $300,000, the auditor may conclude that the balance of accounts receivable is materially correct as stated.

SUMMARY

In Chapters 8 and 9, we have explained some of the statistical techniques used in auditing. We began in Chapter 8 by developing the general concepts underlying the use of statistical sampling in auditing. We then described how the sampling technique is used in attribute sampling. In Chapter 9, we began by observing the differences between the audit objectives for variables and attribute sampling. Then we reviewed the statistical terminology associated with the variables sampling techniques. We also identified and discussed the nonsampling and sampling risks inherent in variables sampling and the means of controlling them. In the last part of this chapter, we described and illustrated the application and usage of three variables sampling techniques: difference estimation, mean-per-unit estimation, and dollar unit estimation.

APPENDIX 9–A: Areas in Two Tails of the Normal Curve at Selected Values of Z_α from the Arithmetic Mean

This table shows the black areas:

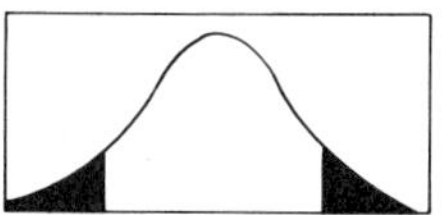

Z_α	.00	.01	.02	.03	.04	.05	.06	.07	.08	.09
0.0	1.0000	.9920	.9840	.9761	.9681	.9601	.9522	.9442	.9362	.9283
0.1	.9203	.9124	.9045	.8966	.8887	.8808	.8729	.8650	.8572	.8493
0.2	.8415	.8337	.8259	.8181	.8103	.8026	.7949	.7872	.7795	.7718
0.3	.7642	.7566	.7490	.7414	.7339	.7263	.7188	.7114	.7039	.6965
0.4	.6892	.6818	.6745	.6672	.6599	.6527	.6455	.6384	.0312	.6241
0.5	.6171	.6101	.6031	.5961	.5892	.5823	.5755	.5687	.5619	.5552
0.6	.5485	.5419	.5353	.5287	.5222	.5157	.5093	.5029	.4965	.4902
0.7	.4839	.4777	.4715	.4654	.4593	.4533	.4473	.4413	.4354	.4295
0.8	.4237	.4179	.4122	.4065	.4009	.3953	.3898	.3843	.3789	.3735
0.9	.3681	.3628	.3576	.3524	.3472	.3421	.3371	.3320	.3271	.3222
1.0	.3173	.3125	.3077	.3030	.2983	.2937	.2801	.2846	.2801	.2757
1.1	.2713	.2670	.2627	.2585	.2543	.2501	.2460	.2420	.2380	.2340
1.2	.2301	.2263	.2225	.2187	.2150	.2113	.2077	.2041	.2005	.1971
1.3	.1936	.1902	.1868	.1835	.1802	.1770	.1738	.1707	.1676	.1645
1.4	.1615	.1585	.1556	.1527	.1499	.1471	.1443	.1416	.1389	.1362
1.5	.1336	.1310	.1285	.1260	.1236	.1211	.1188	.1164	.1141	.1118
1.6	.1096	.1074	.1052	.1031	.1010	.0989	.0969	.0949	.0930	.0910
1.7	.0891	.0873	.0854	.0836	.0819	.0801	.0784	.0767	.0751	.0735
1.8	.0719	.0703	.0688	.0672	.0658	.0643	.0629	.0615	.0601	.0588
1.9	.0574	.0561	.0549	.0536	.0524	.0512	.0500	.0488	.0477	.0466
2.0	.0455	.0444	.0434	.0424	.0414	.0404	.0394	.0385	.0375	.0366
2.1	.0357	.0349	.0340	.0332	.0324	.0316	.0308	.0300	.0293	.0285
2.2	.0278	.0271	.0264	.0257	.0251	.0238	.0288	.0232	.0226	.0220
2.3	.0214	.0209	.0203	.0198	.0193	.0188	.0183	.0178	.0173	.0168
2.4	.0164	.0160	.0155	.0151	.0147	.0143	.0139	.0135	.0131	.0128
2.5	.0124	.0121	.0117	.0114	.0111	.0108	.0105	.0102	.00988	.00960
2.6	.00932	.00905	.00879	.00854	.00829	.00805	.00781	.00759	.00736	.00715
2.7	.00693	.00673	.00653	.00633	.00614	.00596	.00578	.00561	.00544	.00527
2.8	.00511	.00495	.00480	.00465	.00451	.00437	.00424	.00410	.00398	.00385
2.9	.00373	.00361	.00350	.00339	.00328	.00318	.00308	.00298	.00288	.00279

Z_α	.0	.1	.2	.3	.4	.5	.6	.7	.8	.9
3	.00270	.00194	.00137	$.0^3967$	$.0^3674$	$.0^3465$	$.0^3318$	$.0^3216$	$.0^3145$	$.0^4962$
4	$.0^4413$	$.0^4413$	$.0^4267$	$.0^4171$	$.0^4108$	$.0^5680$	$.0^5422$	$.0^5260$	$.0^6159$	$.0^6958$
5	$.0^6573$	$.0^4340$	$.0^6199$	$.0^6116$	$.0^7666$	$.0^7380$	$.0^7214$	$.0^7120$	$.0^8663$	$.0^8364$
6	$.0^8197$	$.0^8106$	$.0^9565$	$.0^9298$	$.0^9155$	$.0^{10}803$	$.0^{10}411$	$.0^{10}208$	$.0^{10}105$	$.0^{11}520$

Source: From *Tables of Areas in Two Tails and in One Tail of the Normal Curve*, by Frederick E. Croxton.

APPENDIX 9–B: Cumulative Standardized Normal Distribution

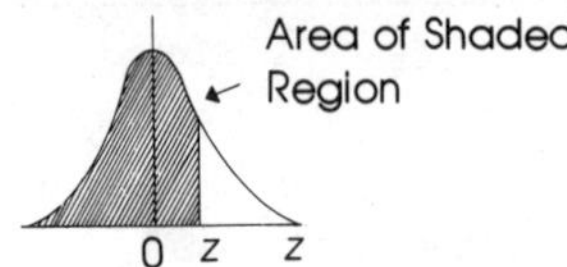

x	.00	.01	.02	.03	.04	.05	.06	.07	.08	.09
.0	.5000	.5040	.5080	.5120	.5160	.5199	.5239	.5279	.5319	.5359
.1	.5398	.5438	.5478	.5517	.5557	.5596	.5636	.5675	.5714	.5753
.2	.5793	.5832	.5871	.5910	.5948	.5987	.6026	.6064	.6103	.6141
.3	.6179	.6217	.6255	.6293	.6331	.6368	.6406	.6443	.6480	.6517
.4	.6554	.6591	.6628	.6664	.6700	.6736	.6772	.6808	.6844	.6879
.5	.6915	.6950	.6985	.7019	.7054	.7088	.7123	.7157	.7190	.7224
.6	.7257	.7291	.7324	.7357	.7389	.7422	.7454	.7486	.7517	.7549
.7	.7580	.7611	.7642	.7673	.7704	.7734	.7764	.7794	.7823	.7852
.8	.7881	.7910	.7939	.7967	.7995	.8023	.8051	.8078	.8106	.8133
.9	.8159	.8186	.8212	.8238	.8264	.8289	.8315	.8340	.8365	.8389
1.0	.8413	.8438	.8461	.8485	.8508	.8531	.8554	.8577	.8599	.8621
1.1	.8643	.8665	.8686	.8708	.8729	.8749	.8770	.8790	.8810	.8830
1.2	.8849	.8869	.8888	.8907	.8925	.8944	.8962	.8930	.8997	.9015
1.3	.9032	.9049	.9066	.9082	.9099	.9115	.9131	.9147	.9162	.9177
1.4	.9192	.9207	.9222	.9236	.9251	.9265	.9279	.9292	.9306	.9319
1.5	.9332	.9345	.9357	.9370	.9382	.9394	.9406	.9418	.9429	.9441
1.6	.9452	.9463	.9474	.9484	.9495	.9505	.9515	.9525	.9535	.9545
1.7	.9554	.9564	.9573	.9582	.9591	.9599	.9608	.9616	.9625	.9633
1.8	.9641	.9649	.9656	.9664	.9671	.9678	.9686	.9693	.9699	.9706
1.9	.9713	.9719	.9726	.9732	.9738	.9744	.9750	.9756	.9761	.9767
2.0	.9772	.9778	.9783	.9788	.9793	.9798	.9803	.9808	.9812	.9817
2.1	.9821	.9286	.9830	.9834	.9838	.9842	.9846	.9850	.9854	.9857
2.2	.9861	.9864	.9868	.9871	.9875	.9878	.9881	.9884	.9887	.9890
2.3	.9893	.9896	.9898	.9901	.9904	.9906	.9909	.9911	.9913	.9916
2.4	.9918	.9920	.9922	.9925	.9927	.9929	.9931	.9932	.9934	.9936
2.5	.9938	.9940	.9941	.9943	.9945	.9946	.9948	.9949	.9951	.9952
2.6	.9953	.9955	.9956	.9957	.9959	.9960	.9961	.9962	.9963	.9964
2.7	.9965	.9966	.9967	.9968	.9969	.9970	.9971	.9972	.9973	.9974
2.8	.9974	.9975	.9976	.9977	.9977	.9978	.9979	.9979	.9980	.9981
2.9	.9981	.9982	.9982	.9983	.9984	.9984	.9985	.9985	.9986	.9986
3.0	.9987	.9987	.9987	.9988	.9988	.9989	.9989	.9989	.9990	.9990
3.1	.9990	.9991	.9991	.9991	.9992	.9992	.9992	.9992	.9993	.9993
3.2	.9993	.9993	.9994	.9994	.9994	.9994	.9994	.9995	.9995	.9995
3.3	.9995	.9995	.9995	.9996	.9996	.9996	.9996	.9996	.9996	.9997
3.4	.9997	.9997	.9997	.9997	.9997	.9997	.9997	.9997	.9997	.9998

Nóte: β *risk* = (1 − table value for Z_β coefficient).
All entries from 3.49 to 3.61 equal .9998. All entries from 3.62 to 3.89 equal 9999. All entries from 3.90 and up equal 1.0000.

Source: From *Introduction to the Theory of Statistics* by Alexander M. Mood et al. Copyright © 1950, McGraw-Hill Book Company. Used with the permission of McGraw-Hill Book Company.

NOTES

1. J. Neter and J.K. Loebbecke, *Behavior of Major Statistical Estimators in Sampling Accounting Populations*, Auditing Research Monograph No. 2 (New York: AICPA, 1975).
2. Charles T. Clark and Lawrence L. Schkade, *Statistical Analysis for Administrative Decisions*, 2nd ed. (Cincinnati: Southwestern, 1974), p. 240. Most authors agree that $n = 30$ constitutes a sufficiently large sample to make valid inferences using the central limit theorem.
3. Ibid.
4. We usually express the recorded value as a mean (BV/N, where BV = book value and N = the number of items in the population). Alternatively, we may use as our statistic the mean (average) difference between audited and book values. In this case, the null hypothesis for the mean difference would be

$$H_o : \bar{D} = 0.$$

That is, the average difference between the audited and book values is zero. The alternative hypothesis would be

$$H_a : \bar{D} \neq 0.$$

That is, the average difference between the audited and book values is an amount materially different from zero. Another way of stating H_o and H_a in this instance is that

H_o: The book balance is not materially misstated.
H_a: The book balance is materially misstated.

5. This formula is usually adjusted by the small (finite) population correction factor whenever the sample size is more than 10 percent of the population size. The factor may be stated as follows:

$$\sqrt{\frac{N - n}{N - 1}}.$$

Correction for small relative population sizes should also be made for estimated standard deviation and for precision range intervals whenever the population (relative to the sample size) is small (that is, when the sample size approaches 10 percent of the population size).

In addition, whenever SD is large, indicating a diverse population with accounts ranging from very large to very small, the population should be stratified to permit a more efficient sample size. In effect, stratification divides the audit population into several subpopulations, each of which has an SD smaller than that of the population taken as a whole. Larger samples are taken for higher dollar amounts, ensuring that the material individual accounts in the population will be examined.

6. The original analysis hypothesized that BV = the true value of the population. That implies that the mean formed by BV/N is hypothesized as the true mean ($6,000,000/50,000, or $120). If M were originally set at ±$300,000, on a per item ($M/N$) basis, materiality would be 300,000/50,000, or $6. Thus, on a per item basis, a value materially different from $120 would be any value less than $114 or more than $126.
7. R. Anderson and A.D. Tietlebaum, "Dollar Unit Sampling," *Canadian Chartered Accountant* (April 1973): 30–39.

8. For a more thorough presentation of this technique, see A. D. Bailey, Jr., *Statistical Auditing* (New York: Harcourt Brace Jovanovich, 1981), pp. 177–201.
9. See R.J. Anderson, *The External Audit 1* (Toronto: Pittman, 1977), p. 624.

QUESTIONS FOR CLASS DISCUSSION

Q9–1 What is the difference between attribute and variables sampling techniques?

Q9–2 Is the completion of compliance testing an essential prerequisite for variables sampling? Explain.

Q9–3 What is the relationship between variables sampling and substantive testing?

Q9–4 Are the terms "precision" and "reliability" defined and applied in the same manner for variables sampling as for attribute sampling? Explain.

Q9–5 What is meant by the term "normal distribution"? How is it related to the application of variables sampling procedures?

Q9–6 What is meant by the term "standard deviation"? How is the term related to the application of variables sampling techniques?

Q9–7 What is meant by a "skewed population distribution"? Give an example of a skewed audit population.

Q9–8 Can the true standard deviation of a population be calculated when one does not know the true mean of the population? Explain. How does the auditor cope with this situation?

Q9–9 What procedures would an auditor follow in developing a statistically valid estimate of the value of inventory by using variables sampling techniques?

Q9–10 What is the relationship between the standard deviation of a population and the sample size required to meet specified precision and reliability goals?

Q9–11 An auditor specifies a desired precision range within which the true population value is expected to fall with a specific desired confidence level. How will the size of the sample be changed if the auditor changes his or her mind and desires to achieve a higher level of reliability?

Q9–12 What is the relationship between the desired precision range in estimating the value for a population and the concept of materiality as it is applied in the audit process?

Q9–13 An auditor uses a variables sampling technique to estimate the value of an asset such as inventory. How does the auditor express statistically the risk that she or he takes in expressing an opinion on that element of the financial statements?

Q9–14 What are the risks the auditor takes in relying on the estimated value of an audit population, a value that has been determined by applying variables sampling techniques?

Q9–15 Why doesn't the auditor always use extremely large samples to minimize the risk of being wrong in his or her opinion relating to the financial statements? Explain.

Q9–16 What is meant by estimation sampling?

Q9–17 What is meant by difference estimation sampling? Explain how this type of sampling is used.

Q9–18 What options are open to the auditor in the event that a variables sample shows either an estimated total or an estimated difference that is outside the auditor's range of acceptability? Explain.

Q9–19 What are the four steps an auditor follows in evaluating evidence included in a variables sample? Explain.

Q9–20 What is the mean-per-unit estimation technique? How is the technique used?

Q9–21 What is meant by dollar unit estimation? How is that technique used in the development of audit evidence?

Q9–22 What is meant by the term "tainting percentage"? How is the percentage used in the calculation of the net upper error limit for dollar unit sampling?

SHORT CASES

C9–1 You have been engaged to perform the annual examination of the financial statements of The Mountainview Corporation, a wholesale office supply business, for the year ended September 30, 19X4. You are currently in the process of auditing the client's inventory account, the largest current asset on the balance sheet, which has a book value of $5,560,000. The inventory consists of 5,000 individual stock items, which are kept in perpetual inventory files maintained by the company's computer. The file for each item of inventory consists of the following information:

a. Item number.
b. Description.
c. Number of units on hand at year end.
d. Unit cost.
e. Extended cost (number of units × unit cost).
f. Location.
g. Vendor code.
h. Date of most recent purchase.
i. Date of most recent sale.

You decide that you would like to determine if the client's recorded book value of $5,560,000 is materially correct as of September 30. Your audit procedures will include these steps:

(1) Observation of client inventory counts and the taking of test counts to determine if client counts are materially correct.
(2) Inventory pricing tests to determine if the client's unit cost is supported by adequate documentation.
(3) Recalculation of extensions and footings to ascertain that they are mathematically correct.

Your preliminary analytical review work and the results of your study and evaluation of internal controls revealed the following:

a. Numerous weaknesses existed in the client's inventory taking procedures. You have concluded that controls in the area of quantities are only 60 percent reliable, although controls over pricing appeared to be good. Since all inventory records are kept by computer, all calculations are done internally by the computer.
b. Your preliminary analytical review procedures, while they are valuable in highlighting obvious mistakes, have only a 50 percent chance of detecting a single material misstatement.
c. You desire that total audit risk be no more than .01, and that nonsampling risk for tests of details be no more than .02.
d. You have decided, on the basis of the nature of this account, that your materiality threshold for error is $50,000. You are more concerned that the client might be trying to *overstate* inventories than understate them. Last year your tests revealed a $20,000 overstatement error in inventory quantities.
e. A preliminary sample revealed an estimated standard deviation of the error rate in the population of $15.
f. Because of the high costs of additional sampling, you have set α risk at .05.

Required:

a. Calculate the required *sample size* for difference estimation, basing it on the above assumptions. (Use the formula in Figure 9–12.)
b. Why is the difference estimation technique well suited to this type of audit problem?
c. What are some of the practical limitations for use of the difference (or ratio) estimation technique?
d. How can computer audit software be used to perform audit procedures a, b, and c? (You may want to refer back to Chapter 7 before answering this question.)
e. Why might application of the difference estimation technique result in a *more efficient* sample than the mean-per-unit estimation technique?

C9–2 Assume the same facts as stated in Case 9–1 and the following additional facts:

a. Your audited sample resulted in 70 differences between your test count and client-recorded count, for a net overstatement error of $500 in the sample.
b. Your revised estimate of the standard deviation of error (*SDE*) in the population, based on your audited sample, is now $12.

Required:

a. What is your point estimate ($\hat{E}$) of the dollar overstatement in the inventory population due to client errors in physical counts?
b. On the basis of your original expectations and preliminary estimate of materiality, do you think the client's inventory is materially overstated?
c. Redo the problem assuming a net $700 sample overstatement. What are your alternative courses of action based on this result?

C9–3 In auditing the financial statements of Textron Plastics, Inc., you are currently in the process of confirming accounts receivable. At a recent staff training school, you learned of the advantages of dollar unit sampling and have decided to apply the technique to Textron's accounts receivable population. You have gathered the following information:

a. Since you are dealing with an accounts receivable population, you are more concerned with errors of *overstatement* than of understatement. You are making the assumption that the maximum amount of overstatement is the complete amount of each account, but no more than the reported account value.

b. The company's accounts receivable population consists of 1,250 individual accounts, which total $1,350,000.

c. You have decided to accept a maximum risk of acceptance of a materially overstated balance (β) of .05, and a maximum error in the population (M) of $40,500.

Required:

a. What features of dollar unit sampling make it desirable for use in an audit setting?

b. Discuss the relative benefits of the use of dollar unit sampling (DUS) as opposed to the more traditional mean-per-unit and difference estimation techniques.

c. Given the facts of the problem, calculate a sample size for the dollar unit sample. Also, define the sampling unit and sampling frame for this technique.

d. Describe how you would go about selecting a random sample using the DUS approach.

C9–4 Refer to Case 9–3. Suppose your sample results show 97 accounts without error and 3 accounts overstated as follows:

Account Name	Reported	Audited
Short Supply Co.	$500	$450
Small Circuit Co.	50	30
Rough Rider Co.	800	760

Required:

a. On the basis of the above findings, what would you conclude about the maximum dollar error in the population of accounts receivable for Textron Plastics, Inc.?

b. What further alternative courses of action would you take, considering the conclusion you reached in step a above?

C9–5 John Valle, president of Data Base, Inc., learns that Eileen Farley has verified the overall balance in the inventory account of his company by using an estimation sampling technique. He is surprised that an accountant would rely on estimates but at the same time insist that all accounting records be appropriately balanced out at the end of the period. Furthermore, he says he doubts that he can be sure that the inventory balance is correctly stated if the auditor only estimates what it should be. Ms. Farley explains that the estimate that she has derived using the estimation sampling technique shows an inventory balance of $865,000 plus or minus $12,000.

Required:

Respond to Mr. Valle's concerns. Include an explanation of what the plus or minus $12,000 means.

PROBLEMS

P9–1 Select the best answer for each of the following items.

a. There are many kinds of statistical estimates an auditor may find useful, but

basically every accounting estimate is either of a quantity or of an error rate. The statistical terms that roughly correspond to "quantities" and "error rate," respectively, are
(1) Attributes and variables.
(2) Variables and attributes.
(3) Constants and attributes.
(4) Constants and variables.

b. An auditor selects a preliminary sample of 100 items out of a population of 1,000 items. The sample statistics generate an arithmetic mean of $120, a standard deviation of $12 and a standard error of the mean of $1.20. If the sample was adequate for the auditor's purposes and the auditor's desired precision was plus or minus $2,000, the *minimum* acceptable dollar value of the population would be
(1) $122,000.
(2) $120,000.
(3) $118,000.
(4) $117,600.

c. In estimation sampling for variables, which of the following must be known in order to estimate the appropriate sample size required to meet the auditor's needs in a given situation?
(1) The total amount of the population.
(2) The desired standard deviation.
(3) The desired confidence level.
(4) The estimated rate of error in the population.

d. Which of the following sampling plans would be designed to estimate a numerical measurement of a population, such as a dollar value?
(1) Numerical sampling.
(2) Discovery sampling.
(3) Sampling for attributes.
(4) Sampling for variables.

e. Use of the ratio estimation sampling technique to estimated dollar amounts is *inappropriate* when
(1) The total book value is known and corresponds to the sum of all the individual book values.
(2) A book value for each sample item is unknown.
(3) There are some observed differences between audited values and book values.
(4) The audited values are nearly proportional to the book values.

f. An important statistic to consider when using a statistical sampling audit plan is the population variability. The population variability is measured by the
(1) Sample mean.
(2) Standard deviation.
(3) Standard error of the sample mean.
(4) Estimated population total minus the actual population total.

g. An auditor selects a preliminary sample of 100 items out of a population of 1,000 items. The sample statistics generate an arithmetic mean of $60, a standard deviation of $6 and a standard error of the mean of $.60. If the sample was adequate for the auditor's purposes and the auditor's desired precision was plus or minus $1,000, the *minimum* acceptable dollar value of the population would be
(1) $61,000

(2) $60,000
(3) $59,000
(4) $58,800

h. The major reason that the difference and ratio estimation methods would be expected to produce audit efficiency is that the
   (1) Number of members of the populations of differences or ratios is smaller than the number of members of the population of book values.
   (2) Beta risk may be completely ignored.
   (3) Calculations required in using difference or ratio estimation are less arduous and fewer than those required when using direct estimation.
   (4) Variability of the populations of differences or ratios is less than that of the populations of book values or audited values.

i. The auditor's failure to recognize an error in compliance with internal controls or a misstated account balance is described as
   (1) A standard deviation.
   (2) A standard error of the mean.
   (3) A nonsampling error.
   (4) A sampling error.

j. As the auditor for Miller Rubber Co. you have made separate statistical tests of compliance and substantive tests of details for accounts payable. The system of internal control for Miller was found to be excellent. The confidence level established for substantive tests in this case will be
   (1) Greater than that for tests of compliance.
   (2) Less than that for tests of compliance.
   (3) Equal to that for tests of compliance.
   (4) Unrelated to that for tests of compliance.

k. How should an auditor establish her or his desired precision in a statistical sampling plan that has as its objective the estimation of dollar amounts (dollar error)?
   (1) By reliance on a computer program.
   (2) By reliance on internal controls.
   (3) By the amount of risk the auditor is willing to take that the client's accounting system contains a material error.
   (4) By the materiality of the amount of dollar error the auditor is willing to accept and still allow an unqualified audit opinion.

(AICPA adapted)

P9–2 The following statements refer to the use of stratified sampling in auditing. For each one, select the best response.

a. Mr. Murray decides to use stratified sampling. The basic reason for using stratified sampling rather than unrestricted random sampling is to
   (1) Reduce as much as possible the degree of variability in the overall population.
   (2) Give every element in the population an equal chance of being included in the sample.
   (3) Allow the person selecting the sample to use his own judgment in deciding which elements to include in the sample.
   (4) Reduce the required sample size from a nonhomogeneous population.

b. In an examination of financial statements, a CPA will generally find stratified sampling techniques to be most applicable to
   (1) Recomputing net wage and salary payments to employees.
   (2) Tracing hours worked from the payroll summary back to the individual time cards.
   (3) Confirming accounts receivable for residential customers at a large electric utility.
   (4) Reviewing supporting documentation for additions to plant and equipment.

c. From prior experience, a CPA is aware that cash disbursements contain a few unusually large disbursements. In using statistical sampling, the CPA's best course of action is to
   (1) Eliminate any unusually large disbursements that appear in the sample.
   (2) Continue to draw new samples until no unusually large disbursements appear in the sample.
   (3) Stratify the cash disbursements population so that the unusually large disbursements are reviewed separately.
   (4) Increase the sample size to lessen the effect of the unusually large disbursements.

(AICPA adapted)

P9–3 During the course of an audit engagement, any CPA attempts to obtain satisfaction that there are no material misstatements in the accounts receivable of a client. Statistical sampling is a tool the auditor often uses to obtain representative evidence to achieve the desired satisfaction. On a particular engagement an auditor determined that a material misstatement in a population of accounts would be \$35,000. To obtain satisfaction the auditor had to be 95 percent confident that the population of accounts was not in error by \$35,000. The auditor decided to use unrestricted random sampling with replacement and took a preliminary random sample of 100 items (n) from a population of 1,000 items (N). The sample produced the following data:

Arithmetic mean of sample items ($\bar{x}$) = \$4,000.
Standard deviation of sample items (SD) = \$200.

The auditor also has available the following information:

PARTIAL LIST OF RELIABILITY COEFFICIENTS

If Reliability Coefficient (R) Is	Then Reliability Is
1.70	91.086%
1.75	91.988
1.80	92.814
1.85	93.568
1.90	94.256
1.95	94.882
1.96	95.000
2.00	95.450
2.05	95.964
2.10	96.428
2.15	96.844

Standard error of the mean $(SE) = SD \div \sqrt{n}$.
Population precision $(P) = N \times R \times SE$.

Required:

a. Define the statistical terms *reliability* and *precision* as applied to auditing.
b. If all necessary audit work is performed on the preliminary sample items and no errors are detected,
   (1) What can the auditor say about the total amount of accounts receivable at the 95 percent reliability level?
   (2) At what confidence level can the auditor say that the population is not in error by $35,000?
c. Assume that the preliminary sample was sufficient;
   (1) Compute the auditor's estimate of the population total.
   (2) Indicate how the auditor should relate this estimate to the client's recorded amount.

(AICPA adapted)

P9–4 Acme Corporation does not conduct a complete annual physical count of purchased parts and supplies in its principal warehouse but uses statistical sampling instead to estimate the year-end inventory. Acme maintains a perpetual inventory record of parts and supplies; management believes that mean-per-unit statistical sampling is highly effective in determining inventory values and is sufficiently reliable to make a physical count of each item of inventory unnecessary.

Required:

a. Identify the audit evidence-gathering procedures used by the auditor that *change* or are *in addition to* normal required audit procedures for inventories when a client utilizes statistical sampling to determine inventory value and does not conduct a 100 percent annual physical count of inventory items.
b. Explain why mean-per-unit sampling is uniquely suited to this type of audit problem.
c. Assume that you evaluated internal controls over physical counts of inventory and assessed the risk of overreliance on internal controls (IC) at 10 percent. In addition, assume that your analytical review procedures in this area yielded a 40 percent chance of letting a material error pass undetected. Assuming that you desire an overall sampling risk of .01, and that you desire to hold the nonsampling risk component for tests of details to .15, compute the β risk for tests of details.
d. Using the β risk factor calculated in c, calculate a sample size for the mean-per-unit sample (n) using the following additional assumptions:

   Population size $(N) = 5{,}000$.
   Estimated standard deviation $(SD) = \$30$.
   α sampling risk $= .05$.
   Preliminary materiality threshold $= \pm 30{,}000$.

   Use the formula in Figure 9–13 for your calculation.
e. Assume the same facts as above, except that after your study and evaluation of internal controls, you assessed the risk of overreliance on internal controls (IC) to be .25 instead of .10. Calculate the effect that this finding has on sample size.

What does it show about the relationship of the quality of the client's internal controls to the auditor's substantive tests of details (TD)?

P9–5 Assume the same facts as are established in Problem 9–4, through part d. Suppose that you audited a sample of Acme Corporation's inventories and calculated the following:

Mean of the audited sample ($\bar{x}$) = \$110.
Standard deviation of the audited sample (SD) = \$25.

Required:

a. What is your point estimate of the client's inventory based on these findings?
b. What may your statistical conclusion be regarding the true value of your client's inventory of purchased parts and supplies at the 95 percent confidence level?
c. Suppose your client has a recorded value for inventories of purchased parts and supplies of \$540,000. How will you relate this fact to your findings above? What type of sampling risk are you incurring in this decision?
d. If the true value of your client's inventories were \$500,000 and not the amount recorded on the books, what is the probability of your reaching the conclusion you reached in parts a through c above?

P9–6 You want to evaluate the reasonableness of the book value of the inventory of your client, Draper, Inc. You satisfied yourself earlier as to inventory quantities. During the examination of the pricing and extension of the inventory, the following data were gathered using appropriate unrestricted random sampling with replacement procedures.

Total items in the inventory (N)	12,700
Total items in the sample (n)	400
Total audited value of items in the sample	\$38,400
$\sum_{j=1}^{j=400} (x_j - \bar{x})^2$	312,816

Formula for estimated population standard deviation

$$S_{X_j} = \sqrt{\frac{\sum_{j=1}^{j=n} (x_j - \bar{x})^2}{n = 1}}$$

Formula for estimated standard error of the mean

$$SE = \frac{S_{X_j}}{\sqrt{n}}$$

Confidence level coefficient of the standard error of the mean at a 95% confidence (reliability) level

$$Z_\alpha = \pm 1.96$$

Required:

a. On the basis of the sample results, what estimate can you make of the total value of the inventory? Show computations in good form where appropriate.
b. What statistical conclusion can be reached regarding the estimated total inventory value calculated above at the confidence level of 95 percent? Present computations in good form where appropriate.

c. Independent of your answers to a and b, assume that the book value of Draper's inventory is $1,700,000, and based on the sample results the estimated total value of the inventory is $1,690,000. As auditor, you desire a confidence (reliability) level of 95 percent. Discuss the audit and statistical considerations you must evaluate before deciding whether the sampling results support acceptance of the book value as a fair presentation of Draper's inventory.

(AICPA adapted)

P9–7 An audit partner is developing an office training program to familiarize his professional staff with statistical decision models applicable to the audit of dollar value balances. He wishes to demonstrate the relationship of sample sizes to population size and variability and the auditor's specifications as to precision and confidence level. The partner prepared the following table to show comparative population characteristics and audit specifications of two populations.

	CHARACTERISTICS OF POPULATION 1 RELATIVE TO POPULATION 2		AUDIT SPECIFICATIONS AS TO A SAMPLE FROM POPULATION 1 RELATIVE TO A SAMPLE FROM POPULATION 2	
Case	**Size**	**Variability**	**Specified Precision**	**Specified Confidence Level**
1	Equal	Equal	Equal	Higher
2	Equal	Larger	Wider	Equal
3	Larger	Equal	Tighter	Lower
4	Smaller	Smaller	Equal	Lower
5	Larger	Equal	Equal	Higher

Required:

In each item (1) through (5) you are to indicate for the specified case from the above table the required sample size to be selected from population 1 relative to the sample from population 2. Your answer choice should be selected from the following responses.

a. Larger than the required sample size from population 2.
b. Equal to the required sample size from population 2.
c. Smaller than the required sample size from population 2.
d. Indeterminate relative to the required sample size from population 2.
   (1) In case 1 the required sample size from population 1 is ________.
   (2) In case 2 the required sample size from population 1 is ________.
   (3) In case 3 the required sample size from population 1 is ________.
   (4) In case 4 the required sample size from population 1 is ________.
   (5) In case 5 the required sample size from population 1 is ________.

(AICPA adapted)

P9–8 As auditor for the Roberts Publishing Company, you are auditing the balances of the work-in-process inventory account as of June 30. 19X2. The following information has been made available to you by the client, based on their estimates and records:

> Number of items in work-in-process inventory (N) = 5,000.
> Book value of work-in-process inventory (X) = \$1,500,000.
> Mean of the population (μ_x) = \$300 = (X/N).
> Standard deviation of the population (σ_x) = \$75.

You selected a sample of 30 item numbers from the inventory, as shown in column (1) of the table on page 391. Also shown in the table are the client's reported values (x_i) and the corresponding audited values (y_i) for each item examined in the inventory columns (3) and (4), respectively.

Required:

a. Complete columns (5) through (7) of the table. This will provide you with the needed information to compute the revised estimated standard deviation of the population (SD), the average difference between book values and audited values ($\bar{d}$), and the estimated standard deviation of differences (SDE) as shown by the following formulas:

$$SD = \sqrt{\frac{\Sigma(y_i - \bar{y})^2}{n - 1}}$$

$$\bar{d} = \frac{\sum_{i=1}^{n} (y_i - x_i)}{n}$$

$$SDE = \sqrt{\frac{\Sigma(d_i - \bar{d})^2}{n - 1}}$$

Compute $\bar{x}$, $\bar{y}$, SD, $\bar{d}$, and SDE.

b. Construct the appropriate confidence interval using the mean-per-unit estimation technique assuming (1) 90 percent confidence, and (2) 95 percent confidence. In each case, indicate what action you would take based on your sample results and the client's recorded amount.

c. Independent of your answers to step b above, compute the necessary sample size for the population based on the mean-per-unit formula in Figure 9–13 for the following two independent cases:

	α Risk	β Risk	Precision (Materiality)
(1)	.20	.25	\$135,000
(2)	.10	.05	\$100,000

d. Construct the appropriate confidence interval using the *difference* estimation technique, assuming (1) 90 percent confidence, and (2) 95 percent confidence. In each case, as in step b above, indicate what action you would take, on the basis of your sample results and the client's recorded amounts. Compare these results with those of step b.

e. Independent of your answers to step d above, compute the necessary sample size for this population based on the difference estimation formula in Figure 9–12, for the following two independent cases:

	α Risk	β Risk	Precision (M − E′)
(1)	.20	.25	\$ 25,000
(2)	.10	.05	\$100,000

Compare these results with those of step c. *Note:* You must compute $\bar{x}$; $\bar{y}$; $\Sigma(y_i - \bar{y})^2$; $\bar{d}$; and $\Sigma\ (d_i - \bar{d})^2$ in order to solve the problem.

(1) Sample Item No. n_i	(2) Part No. #	(3) Reported Value x_i	(4) Audited Value y_i	(5) $(y_i - \bar{y})^2$	(6) Audit Differences $d_i = y_i - x_i$	(7) $(d_i - \bar{d})^2$
1	1786	\$ 342.04	\$ 325.93			
2	2714	210.53	236.77			
3	4870	259.62	321.13			
4	655	278.44	307.95			
5	2297	376.31	359.27			
6	1797	169.89	201.81			
7	3676	293.76	330.21			
8	2978	158.93	196.84			
9	4156	341.39	379.07			
10	3423	408.80	408.78			
11	3980	320.11	325.20			
12	4990	426.51	414.93			
13	381	368.26	373.79			
14	3713	336.98	344.33			
15	1937	291.82	321.19			
16	1630	233.46	272.90			
17	4653	353.86	367.36			
18	499	290.31	275.35			
19	1521	262.64	388.51			
20	380	312.47	377.30			
21	105	231.80	259.92			
22	612	257.39	271.58			
23	32	357.80	352.53			
24	3416	196.53	233.31			
25	4956	228.99	274.90			
26	118	303.16	323.49			
27	4927	228.16	271.07			
28	978	195.66	229.54			
29	1029	324.92	319.11			
30	3707	247.34	268.79			
		\$8,607.88	\$9,332.86			

Source: From *Statistical Auditing: Review, Concepts and Problems* by Andrew D. Bailey, Jr. Copyright © 1981 by Harcourt Brace Jovanovich, Inc. Reprinted by permission of the publisher.

PART THREE

DEVELOPMENT OF AUDIT PROCEDURES

CHAPTER

10

THE REVENUE SYSTEM AND RELATED ACCOUNT BALANCES

As we observed earlier, the primary audit objective is to verify the data in financial statements for the purpose of expressing an opinion as to whether those data conform to GAAP. This objective is achieved in part by meeting the three standards of field work. We also noted that performing an audit is somewhat like fitting the pieces of a jigsaw puzzle together. Various elements of the financial statements, because they are derived from the double-entry system of accounting, are closely related and must fit together. Thus we can beneficially subdivide the overall audit of the client's financial statements into the verification of the component subsystems that contain directly related accounts.

In this chapter we develop the procedures normally followed in meeting the planning, internal control, and evidence standards for the account balances found in the client's revenue system. Our discussion covers the following topics:

1. The audit objectives to be met in verifying the elements of the client's revenue system.
2. Verification of the validity of revenue system transactions.
3. The auditing procedures followed in performing the substantive tests of receivables and other related account balances.
4. Using the computer in auditing the revenue system.

Appendixes to the chapter illustrate audit working papers for accounts receivable and sales balances.

AUDIT OBJECTIVES

The account data in the revenue system include sales or other trade revenues, sales returns and allowances, sales discounts, the allowance for doubtful accounts, bad debts expense, notes receivable, and cash receipts from cash sales and collections on account. Figure 10–1 illustrates diagrammatically the typical flow of transactions through the system. Because the planning standard is met through the development of an audit program for the subsystem (as discussed in Chapter 4), we now concern ourselves primarily with meeting the internal control and evidence standards.

In Chapters 2 and 3 we described audit objectives as connecting links that bridge the gap between auditing standards and audit procedures. At that time we listed the verification of transaction validity, existence, ownership, cutoff, valuation, and appropriate statement presentation as objectives of an independent audit. We now give attention to the ways those objectives are achieved for the revenue system and related account balances. As we examine the objectives, it will be helpful for you to visualize them as client assertions that must be verified if the various account balances associated with the revenue system are to be presented in accordance with GAAP. Because of the perceived inclination of management to overstate assets, the auditor is often concerned with verifying that the receivables element of the system and the offsetting credits to sales are *not overstated.* Therefore many but not all of our substantive tests in this area are directed toward detection of overstatement of these items.

Verification of Transaction Validity

If the auditor could be certain that all transactions associated with the revenue system have been recorded, classified, and summarized in a manner which minimizes the risk of material misstatement, he or she could, on the basis of that evidence, conclude that the account balances in that system are fairly presented. In judging whether or not such a conclusion is justified, auditors depend on the reliability of the system of internal control. Therefore in meeting the objective of verifying transaction validity, the auditor must evaluate the system of controls under which the various revenue-related transactions were recorded. As we shall see shortly, this includes two phases:

1. Analyzing and evaluating the system that is supposed to be in operation.
2. Making compliance tests to see that the control procedures are actually being implemented.

Other Audit Objectives

Conceptually, at least, if the auditor felt that the system of internal control associated with the revenue system were so strong that all transactions would have been appropriately recorded, classified, and summarized, and if the auditor judged the system to preclude the possibility of fraud, there would be no need to perform other auditing procedures. A more practical point of view, however, recognizes that it is unlikely any system can provide that kind of assurance. For that reason, the auditor always performs some substantive tests of the balances shown in the material balance sheet accounts. In auditing the revenue system, for example, this calls for audit tests of sales, accounts

Cash

Beginning bal. xxx	
Receipts xxx (2)	

Sales

	xxxx (1)

Sales Discounts

xxxx (2)	

Accounts Receivable

Beginning bal. xxxx	
xxxx (1)	xxxx (2)
	xxxx (3)
	xxx (5)
Ending bal. xxxx	

Sales Returns and Allowances

xxxx (3)	

Allowance for Doubtful Accounts

	Beginning bal. xxx
xxx (5)	xxxx (4)
	Ending bal. xxx

Bad Debts Expense

xxxx (4)	

(1) Sales; (2) Cash receipts and sales discounts; (3) Sales returns and allowances; (4) Adjustment of allowance for doubtful accounts; (5) Write-offs of uncollectible accounts.

FIGURE 10–1. Flow of Transactions Through Revenue System

receivable, and cash collections transactions as well as tests of the related account balances. While performing tests of transactions creating debits and credits to accounts receivable, the auditor is also verifying credits to revenue accounts and debits to the cash account arising from the collections of receivables. We depend on the verification of the validity of sales transactions and the audit of the cash balance in verifying cash receipts from cash sales.

In identifying the other audit objectives applicable to the revenue system and related balance sheet accounts, we begin by asking ourselves *what could cause those account balances to contain amounts materially different from the actual amounts receivable and the actual inflows of cash associated with the revenue system.* One possible source of error is the inclusion of receivables that do not really exist. This can occur through the introduction of fictitious receivables or the failure to reduce valid receivables for amounts that have been collected. The audit objective in proving or disproving that point can be characterized as the ***verification of existence (or validity).***

Still another possible source of error can arise from the client's continuing to account for factored or pledged receivables as if full ownership rights still existed in those receivables. Certain audit procedures discussed later in the chapter are designed to verify that the client has full ownership rights to all recorded accounts and notes receivable. The audit objective that is fulfilled by these procedures can be characterized as ***verification of ownership***.

The going concern convention (discussed in Chapter 2) requires that trade receivables be valued at their net realizable value. A failure to do so is another source of error in the financial statements. Therefore the auditor is concerned with verifying that appropriate provision has been made for anticipated losses from uncollectible receivables. We characterize this audit objective as the ***verification of valuation.***

Increases in receivables (sales) or collections on account (or cash inflows resulting from those collections) and cash sales that occur near the end or beginning of a fiscal period can be recorded in the wrong period. This type of error would be a violation of the matching concept discussed in Chapter 2. The auditor therefore must be concerned with the audit objective of ***verifying cutoff*** (the proper cutoff of sales and collections on account near the end of the period being audited).

Receivables must also be properly *disclosed* in the financial statements. That includes proper classification, proper labeling, and appropriate parenthetical and footnote disclosures. Therefore, a distinction should be made between: (1) notes and accounts receivable, (2) trade and nontrade receivables, and (3) current and noncurrent receivables. In addition, once a proper net realizable value of receivables (gross amount less allowance for doubtful accounts) is determined, that value should be the amount disclosed in the financial statements. Furthermore, the statements must properly disclose any information relating to the assignment or pledging of accounts receivable. The audit objective in this case can be characterized as the ***verification of appropriate statement presentation.***

VERIFICATION OF TRANSACTION VALIDITY

As we have observed, the auditor depends primarily on the reliability of the system of internal control in judging whether or not revenue system transactions have been appropriately recorded, classified, and accumulated in the accounting records. In the case of manually maintained records or where the computer is used only as a sophisticated bookkeeping machine, the reliability of the system of internal control is evaluated by verifying the extent to which it includes the desirable internal control characteristics, which were listed in Figure 5–1. This involves a review and evaluation phase based on an analysis of the organization chart and procedures manual or an inquiry of appropriate client personnel; it also entails compliance tests, to see whether the prescribed provisions of those internal control documents are actually being followed.

In auditing a computerized revenue system, we will be concerned with the internal organization of the electronic data-processing department and with the existence and documentation of appropriate application controls in the processing of revenue system data.

Review and Evaluation of the Control System

The purpose of the auditor's preliminary evaluation of internal control is twofold: to identify controls that can be relied on in each system (so that the auditor can determine the nature, timing, and extent of necessary substantive tests of the transactions and account balances found within that system) and to pinpoint areas of material weakness that must be communicated to the client. In meeting those objectives, the auditor should undertake these steps for the controls upon which he or she wishes to rely:

1. Consider the types of errors and irregularities that could occur.
2. Determine the accounting control procedures that should prevent or detect such errors and irregularities.
3. Determine whether the necessary procedures are prescribed by the client.

While communication of internal control weaknesses is important, the primary objective of the independent audit is to issue an opinion regarding the fairness of presentation of the financial statements. All audit procedures, including the study and evaluation of internal accounting controls, should be performed with this objective in mind. As the auditor conducts the study, he or she should concentrate on discovering only the ***material internal control weaknesses*** in the system. Auditing standards define a material internal control weakness as *a condition within the system* or *lack of compliance with established internal controls* which has a relatively high risk of causing a material misstatement in the financial statements. Therefore, the independent auditor should be concerned only with studying and testing controls which, if missing, could result in materially misstated balances. Although the client may have many accounting controls built into a system, not all of them would be material in this respect. For example, a breakdown in segregation of the duties of cash handling and recordkeeping for accounts receivable would certainly be a control weakness that results in a high risk of materially misstated balances. On the other hand, failure of certain supervisory personnel to initial documents that pass through their hands, while still a weakness, may not be as material as the lack of proper segregation of duties.

Deciding on the controls that are material is often a complex task, requiring the exercise of seasoned judgment. For controls evidenced by documentation, the auditor may apply the following reasoning process:

- Consider the financial statement balances generated by the system.
- Working backward through the audit trail from the financial statement balances, identify documents which evidence the *point of exchange* between the client and outside entities. We call these ***boundary documents.***
- For each boundary document identified above, consider *supporting documents* which provide evidence of transaction validity through approvals, cross checks, recalculations, follow-up, etc.

It is the accounting controls over these boundary transactions and the approvals and records associated with those transactions which are material internal controls. In the revenue, receivables, and cash receipts systems, the primary balances generated are accounts receivable, sales, and cash. The primary exchange transactions involved are sales of goods and services for cash or on account, and the collection of customer accounts or notes. Figure 10-2 illustrates exchange transactions, as well as boundary

Exchange Transaction	Boundary Document	Supporting Document(s)
Sales for cash	Sales ticket or sales invoice	Cash register tape or duplicate sales ticket
Sales on account	Sales invoices	Shipping document Bill of lading
Collection of cash	Customer remittance advice	Remittance lists Validated bank deposit slips

FIGURE 10–2. Exchange Transactions and Supporting Documents

documents and supporting documents, which are associated with sales and cash collections.

The *functions* performed within the revenue, receivables, and cash receipts systems in order to process exchange transactions from the boundary point of the entity to ultimate recording in the client's financial statements may be classified into three categories. Since controls over these functions are material, they must be documented in the working papers if the auditor wishes to rely upon them.

- **Exchange functions** requiring specific controls (see Figure 10–3), which are designed to protect resources and encourage efficiency of operations. These embrace the following: processing customer orders, including the evaluation of credit risk; shipping goods; billing customers; processing cash receipts; processing sales returns and allowances.
- **Processing functions** (see Figure 10–4), requiring controls designed to establish accountability and provide reliable financial data. This category comprises the following: recording sales; recording cash receipts; recording sales returns and allowances; establishing an appropriate provision for uncollectible accounts.
- **Safeguard functions,** which require custodial controls for assets and records associated with the system (see Figure 10–5).

As we analyze the functions in the preceding list, we can recognize that the objectives of internal control can be achieved within the system by appropriate execution of the exchange functions, by appropriate handling of the recording or processing functions, and by establishing appropriate safeguard (custodial) controls over the assets and records associated with the system.

Errors and Irregularities. In Figures 10–3, 10–4, and 10–5, we show by examples some of the errors and irregularities that can be introduced if exchange, processing, and safeguard functions are not properly controlled. Then we cite possible results of such irregularities and certain procedures that would prevent, detect, or correct them. A system properly performing these functions must include the control characteristics, discussed in Chapter 5. The auditor must then examine the system to determine whether those characteristics are being appropriately implemented in the handling of revenue system transactions. He or she typically uses an internal control questionnaire (such as the one shown in Figure 10–6) and a systems flowchart (such as the ones in

Figures 10–7, 10–8, and 10–9 depicting customer order processing, sales recording, and cash receipts processing, respectively) in that examination.

After flowcharts are completed, it is common practice to walk through, or trace, one or two source documents through the system just to see if the flowcharts properly depict what actually occurs in the system.

Appropriate Separation of Responsibilities. The appropriate separation of responsibilities requires that elements of many of the functions of internal control be assigned to different employees to protect resources and provide reliable financial data.

In *processing customer orders,* the credit function should be separated from the handling of cash receipts and from the recordkeeping function and the sales function. This segregation of critical duties reduces the likelihood that the system will contain errors or irregularities. If, for example, the credit function was performed by the same person handling cash receipts, that person could take cash paid by a customer and initiate an authorization to write the customer's account off as a bad debt to cover the defalcation. If the credit and bookkeeping functions were performed by the same person, it would be possible for that person to cover up mistakes in granting credit to customers by improperly recording the write-off of uncollectible accounts as sales returns and allowances. The primary reason for separating the credit function from the sales function is to reduce the probability of the firm accepting undesirable credit risks to improve sales volume. The sales manager, for example, is unlikely to be as concerned with the collectibility of accounts as he or she would be with showing a larger volume of sales.

In *processing and recording cash receipts,* it is important that the person handling cash receipts not have access to the accounts receivable records. This arrangement is designed to prevent the person receiving cash from taking cash and introducing changes into the accounting records to cover the defalcation.

The *billing function* should be separated from the handling of cash receipts. It is important to observe that any system of internal control relies on the assumption that the parties to a transaction will always act in their own self-interest. Therefore, we count on customers objecting to receiving bills for amounts already paid as part of our control system. If the person handling cash receipts also bills customers, cash could be taken and discovery of the defalcation could temporarily be prevented by not billing the customer whose payment was taken.

Any *special discount concessions* to customers should be approved by a responsible supervisor. Without this provision, it would be possible for a person handling cash receipts to remove cash equal to the discount associated with an account paid after the discount period and cover the defalcation by showing a debit to sales discounts rather than to cash.

The *accounts receivable ledger clerk recording sales and cash collections* should be someone other than the general ledger bookkeeper. This separation of responsibilities is designed to force two individuals to check their records with each other in recording the sales and cash receipts transactions. The general ledger bookkeeper will have a control account balance that should equal the sum of the subsidiary ledger account

Functions	Possible Errors or Irregularities	Results of Undetected Errors	Control Attributes to Prevent, Detect, or Correct Errors or Irregularities
Processing customers' orders Evaluation of credit risk	Invalid transactions: Sales to customers who will be unable to pay for merchandise	Excessive losses from bad debts Inadequate provisions for bad debts	Proper evaluation of credit risk before approval of shipment (evidenced by approval signature)
General Processing	Erroneous transactions: Orders lost and therefore not shipped Shipment that is duplicated	Loss of revenue Customer dissatisfaction Errors in sales and receivables	Prenumbered written sales orders to be originated from customer orders Accounting for all sales orders
Shipping	Transactions recorded in wrong period: Items recorded as sold not shipped Items shipped but not recorded as sold	Sales and receivables overstated Unrecorded sales and receivables Loss of inventory Cost of sales understated	Proper approval and matching of prenumbered shipping documents with sales orders and sales invoices
Billing customers	Erroneous transactions: Customers billed for unordered merchandise Customers not billed for merchandise shipped	Receivables and sales improperly stated Failure to collect for goods shipped	Matching of approved sales orders with shipping tickets for all billings Use of prenumbered sales invoices and accounting for all numbers Matching of sales invoices with shipping tickets

Processing cash receipts Cash sales receipts	Unrecorded transactions: Misappropriation of cash Unrecorded sales	Loss of cash Sales and cost of sales understated	Use of cash registers with daily reconciliation by supervisors
Mail receipts	Invalid transactions: Misappropriation of cash Improperly recorded collections on account	Loss of cash Delay in receiving cash Cash or accounts receivable misstated	Prelisting of all cash received Proper segregation of responsibilities Periodic reconciliation of cash bank accounts
Processing sales returns and allowances	Improperly classified transactions: Improper credits to receivables Returned merchandise improperly recorded	Loss of merchandise Misappropriation of cash Receivables or sales returns and allowances misstated	Prenumbered and properly controlled credit memos Receiving report for goods returned in support of credit memo Approval of all returns

FIGURE 10–3. Exchange Functions Requiring Specific Controls

Functions	Possible Errors and Irregularities	Possible Results of Undetected Errors and Irregularities	Control Attributes to Prevent, Detect, or Correct Errors or Irregularities
Recording sales Accuracy of journalizing and posting	Unrecorded or improperly recorded transactions: Unrecorded sales Improperly recorded sales	Sales and receivables misstated	Use of prenumbered sales invoices and accounting for all numbers Periodic mathematical proof of invoices against records by the supervisor or someone designated by the supervisor
Proper updating of subsidiary ledger accounts	Improperly summarized transactions: Inaccurate balances in customer accounts	Receivables control not in agreement with subsidiary ledger	Review of postings Periodic reconciliation of control account with subsidiary ledger
Recording cash receipts	Unrecorded or improperly valued transactions: Unrecorded cash receipts Inaccurate recording of cash receipts	Lack of accountability: Misappropriation of cash and receivables or sales misstated	Use of clearly defined procedures for accounting for cash receipts from specifically identified and controlled documents Periodic and continuing reconciliation of inflows of cash with cash receipts records
Recording sales returns and allowances	Improperly recorded transactions: Improperly recorded sales returns and allowances	Lack of accountability: Loss of merchandise Sales returns and allowances and receivables misstated	Use of clearly defined procedures for accounting for sales returns and allowances from specifically identified and controlled documents
Recording allowances for bad debts and write-off of bad accounts	Improperly valued transactions: Improper provision for bad debts Improper charge-offs of receivables	Possible defalcation: Receivables improperly valued Bad debt expense misstated	Use of clearly defined procedures for providing for bad debts Use of clearly defined procedures for determining when receivables should be written off, including appropriate approval procedures Periodic aging of receivables

FIGURE 10–4. Processing Functions

Functions	Possible Errors and Irregularities	Possible Results of Undetected Errors and Irregularities*	Control Attributes to Prevent, Detect, or Correct Errors or Irregularities
Custodial care of cash receipts	Failure to maintain appropriate custodial care over cash received	Loss of cash Theft of cash	Custodial accountability for cash at point of receipt All receipts deposited intact each day Safe storage facilities for undeposited cash
Storage and care of records	Failure to maintain appropriate custodial care over accounting records	Loss of records Alteration of accounting data	Custodial responsibility for accounting records Appropriately protected storage areas for records when not being used Back-up capability to allow records to be reconstructed if lost or damaged

*Errors and irregularities in safeguarding functions can lead to any of the seven general types of material errors or irregularities involving transactions (listed in Chapter 5).

FIGURE 10–5. Safeguarding Functions Requiring Specific Controls

1. Are all credit sales approved by the Credit Department prior to shipment?
2. Is the Credit Department independent of the Sales Department?
3. Are sales priced on the basis of approved price lists?
4. Are prenumbered sales invoice forms used?
5. Are all sales invoice forms properly controlled?
6. Are prenumbered shipping orders used to authorize shipments to customers?
7. Are prenumbered shipping order forms properly controlled?
8. Is a prenumbered bill of lading prepared in the Shipping Department prior to release of goods to the common carrier?
9. Are prenumbered bill-of-lading forms properly controlled?
10. Are shipping orders, bills of lading, and invoices properly matched before sales are recorded in the accounting records?
11. Are sales invoices properly checked for mathematical and billing accuracy?
12. Are sales data reported independently to the general ledger bookkeeper and the accounts receivable bookkeeper?
13. Are sales returns, sales credits, and other credits properly supported by prenumbered documentation forms?
14. Are all sales returns, sales credits, and other credits approved by a responsible officer?
15. Is the mail opened by someone other than the cashier or bookkeeper?
16. Are daily remittance lists prepared by the person opening the mail?
17. Is the daily remittance list reconciled with the daily deposit of cash?
18. Are the daily remittance lists and deposit slips regularly compared to the cash debits and accounts receivable credit entries?
19. Are prelists of receipts on account reported independently to the general ledger bookkeeper and the accounts receivable bookkeeper?
20. Is the subsidiary accounts receivable ledger reconciled regularly with the accounts receivable control account balance?

FIGURE 10–6. Internal Control Questionnaire

balances. If each of these records is maintained by a separate person, it will be necessary for the two persons to periodically check their records against each other.

Persons having the *authority to originate noncash credits* to receivables should not have access to cash. Failure to separate these responsibilities could allow the theft of cash to be covered by the origination of a noncash debit (sales return, sales discount, etc.) to balance the credit to receivables. Similarly, the authority to initiate write-offs of uncollectible accounts should be vested in an independent person, subject to the approval of a responsible official.

As we examine the internal control questionnaire in Figure 10–6 and the flowcharts in Figures 10–7 through 10–9, we can observe that they are *designed to disclose failures to meet the separation of responsibilities criteria* just described.

Specific Responsibilities for Specific Personnel. It is important that the responsibilities associated with all elements of the revenue system should be identified with particular persons within the organization. This requirement has three especially significant aspects:

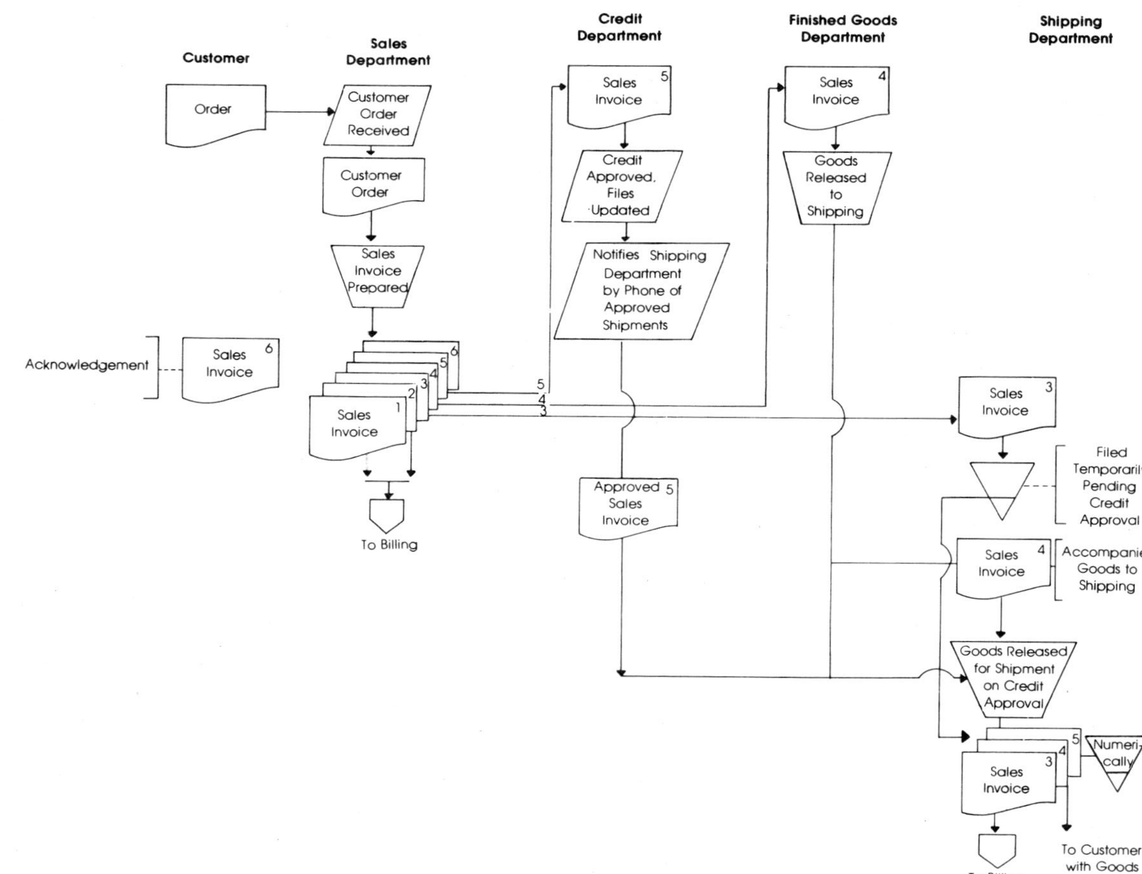

FIGURE 10–7. Flowchart for Processing Customer Orders and Shipping

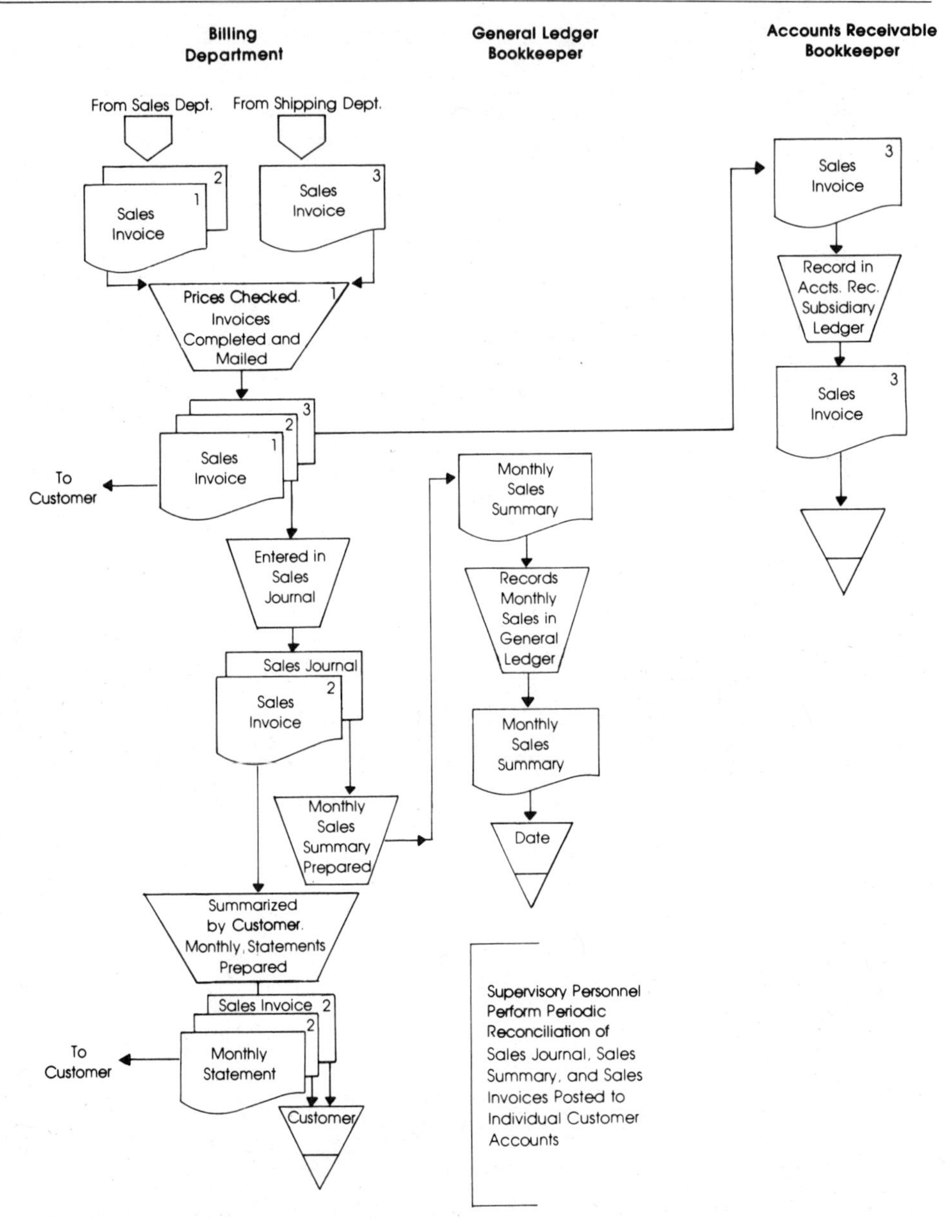

FIGURE 10–8. Flowchart for Recording Sales and Accounts Receivable

The person handling cash receipts should be held accountable for those funds from the point where they are received until they are deposited in the bank. Thus, the cashier's job description should require the preparation of a list of cash receipts at the time they are received. This list should become the basis for the cash receipts entry in

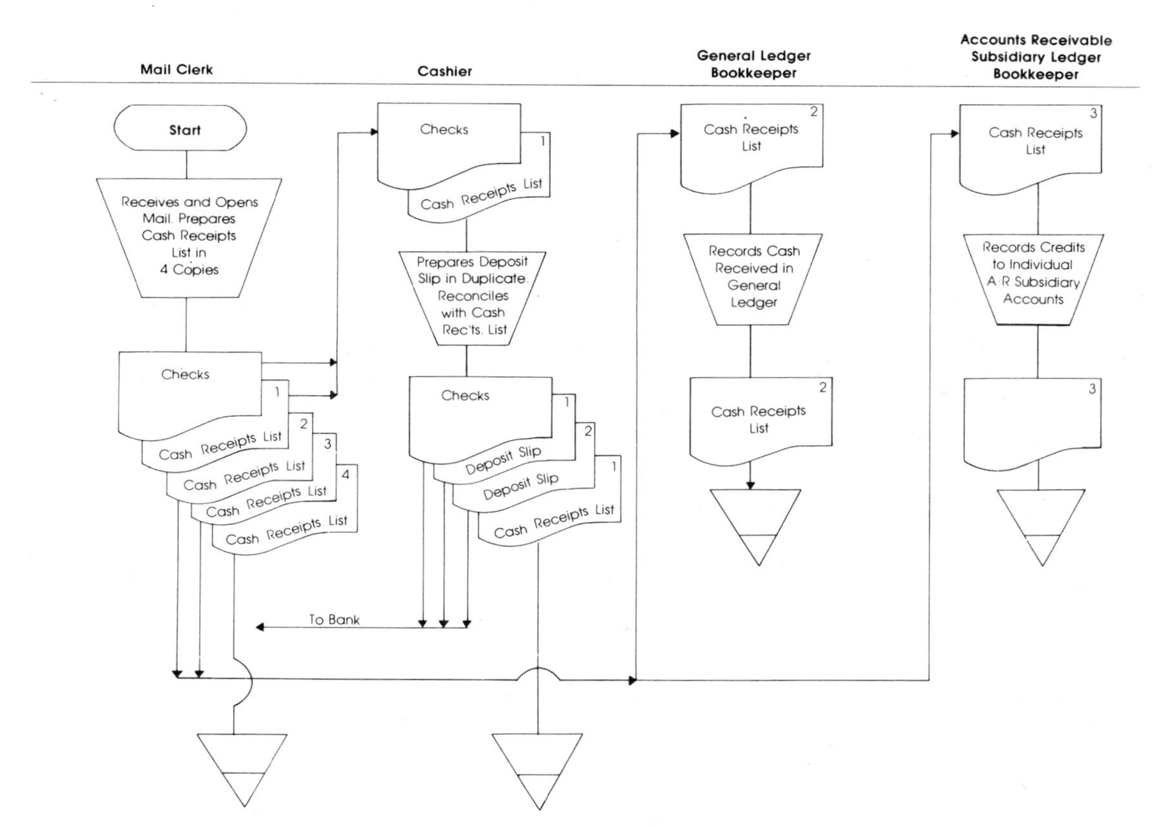

FIGURE 10–9. Flowchart for Mail Cash Receipts System

the receivables records. That receipts record should also be reconciled with cash deposited in the bank. By implication, this also requires that no payments should be made from receipts before they are deposited in the bank.

Accounts receivable charged off as uncollectible should be properly controlled by a specifically identified employee having no connection with the handling of cash receipts.

All the other functions performed within the sales system — such as origination and authorization actions — should be assigned to specific individuals. For example, a specific person should be charged with the evaluation of credit risks and his or her initialed approval should be required before a sales transaction can be consummated. Also, all goods shipped should be cleared through a shipping clerk and any merchandise returned by customers should be delivered to the receiving clerk.

The Necessary Documents. All activities within the sales system should be documented by an adequate system of records, forms, and authorizations. The documents typically associated with the revenue system are these:

- The customer order.
- The customer order approval form. One copy of the sales invoice may serve this purpose (see Figure 10–7).
- The sales invoice.
- A shipping ticket authorizing the shipment of merchandise. One copy of the sales invoice may serve this purpose (see Figure 10–7).
- A document, generally in the form of a bill of lading, showing the goods transferred to the common carrier when such a shipping medium is used. One copy of the sales invoice may also serve that purpose (Figure 10–7).
- The credit memo.
- Cash remittance advice form or turnaround document.
- A form to be used in authorizing the write-off of an account receivable as uncollectible. This form should require approval by a responsible official.
- A form to be used in authorizing and approving the acceptance of notes receivable.
- Monthly statement to be sent to each customer.
- A separate ledger maintained for accounts written off.

The results of the sales system activities are typically recorded in a sales journal, a sales returns and allowances journal, and a cash receipts journal. In analyzing the flowcharts in Figures 10–7 through 10–9, you should notice that the system depicted therein contains most of the preceding documents.

The documents and records listed will provide an adequate system of records if they are *organized and processed* as follows:

- Proper credit investigation and approval procedures should be performed and documented on the customer order approval form.
- Sales invoices should be sequentially numbered and a procedure should be established to account for the use of each of the invoice forms.
- Credit memos should also be sequentially numbered and controlled in the same manner as are sales invoices. Appropriate authorization and approval procedures should be performed and documented in connection with the issuance of each credit memo.

- Sequentially numbered remittance advice forms should be prepared at the point where cash is received by the company.
- Authorization and approval procedures, including the approval by a responsible official within the company, should be performed and documented before an account receivable is allowed to be written off as uncollectible. Formal procedures should be established for a continuing review of accounts written off for possible collections of them. Failure to establish such procedures would make cash receipts from such accounts especially vulnerable to defalcation.
- Formal procedures should be established for carrying out the billing function.
- Properly controlled sequentially prenumbered shipping tickets may be used to authorize shipments. The tickets used should be appropriately accounted for and reconciled with customer orders and sales invoices. In this way a firm makes sure that all goods or services are billed as they are delivered.
- Accounts receivable records should include both an accounts receivable control account and a subsidiary ledger.
- Formal procedures should be established for the authorization and approval of the acceptance of notes receivable.

Qualified Personnel. The qualified personnel characteristic requires that special attention be given to the skills of persons assigned to perform the various functional responsibilities within the revenue system. This means that the company should follow hiring and promotion practices designed to assign people to tasks they are capable of performing. For example, the recordkeeping function should be performed by a person having appropriate recordkeeping skills. Cash receipts should be handled by a person showing evidence of trustworthiness; that person should also be bonded. The credit investigation function should be performed by a person having appropriate training in credit and collection practices.

Protection of Assets and Records. All assets and records associated with the revenue system should be appropriately protected from physical loss or alteration:

- The company should provide appropriately protected storage facilities for undeposited cash receipts.
- All cash receipts should be deposited intact daily.
- The accounts receivable records should be stored in a safe or vault designed to protect those records from damage or alteration when they are not being used.

Evaluation of Computerized Records Controls. When the accounting records for the revenue system are computerized to the extent that the system's data are maintained on machine-readable media, many of the functions normally assigned to separate employees will be performed within the electronic data-processing department. The evaluation of internal control requires an analysis of the organizational structure of the electronic data-processing department to determine the adequacy of the general controls over those operations. The auditor next turns to an evaluation of the application controls. This evaluation requires the auditor to consider the adequacy of input, processing, output and file controls relating to the accumulation of revenue system data. In general terms, this control requirement means that the data-processing procedures should include the following practices:

Input Controls

- The system should include provisions designed to account for and control all revenue systems transactions data from their origin to the time they are submitted to the EDP department. These procedures should be directed toward assuring that all transactions reach that department.
- Within the electronic data-processing department, the company should have an appropriate verification process designed to make sure that the revenue system input data are correctly converted to machine-readable media.
- The error correction and resubmission process for revenue system data should be properly controlled within the EDP department.

Processing Controls

- After the revenue system's transactions have been converted to machine-readable media, the EDP department should provide controls that will assure that all transactions are processed. Control totals over sales, sales returns, and cash collections should be developed at the point where transaction data are received. These should subsequently be reconciled with totals placed in process.
- The computer should be programmed to make logical validity tests on the important fields of information transmitted to the computer's processing unit. These might include, for example, field validity tests to ensure that numerical information is in the proper fields and the use of check digits to see that transactions are posted to the proper individual customer accounts.
- Provisions should be made for sequence checking of revenue system input data by accounting for all invoice or other document numbers.
- Header and trailer labels should be included on magnetic media files and should be tested as those files are used.

Output Controls

- Header and trailer labels should be placed on all media files created as output to reduce the probability of those files being misused.
- Control totals for output should be produced by the computer and should be reconciled with predetermined totals for various revenue system data by someone independent of the department originating the information.
- Error corrections and adjustments to master files should be properly reviewed and approved prior to being incorporated in those files.
- Authorized and approved corrections to master files should be followed up to see that they are promptly and properly incorporated in those files.

File Controls

- Control totals should be maintained on all files and should be verified each time a file is processed.
- All files containing revenue system data should be adequately supported by back-up data that will allow the files to be reproduced if they are damaged or destroyed. The grandfather, father, son technique is an example of this capability.
- The files containing revenue system account data should be physically protected against damage from fire or other accidental damage.
- The electronic data-processing department should make adequate provisions for periodically checking the contents of master files by having them printed out and reviewed against underlying data.

The auditor typically determines whether these application controls are in place by using an applications controls questionnaire similar to the one that is shown in Appendix 6–A.

Testing the System for Compliance

During the preliminary study of controls, the auditor obtains an understanding of the client's control environment and flow of transactions by referring to the organization chart and procedures manual and by inquiry of client personnel. This is done to identify the controls, if any, that the auditor wishes to rely upon. Those controls are then studied in detail by using the procedures described in the preceding pages.

If the auditor is satisfied that the prescribed controls can reasonably be expected to prevent or detect serious errors or irregularities, he or she must then determine the *extent of employee compliance* with those controls. Management should, as one element of the company's control system, establish operating practices designed to promote compliance with the established practices. This should include adequate orientation and training with respect to each employee's assigned duties, so that each will fully understand his or her responsibilities and how they fit in the overall system. That orientation should be followed up from time to time with periodic checks by either management personnel or internal auditors to see that employees both understand and comply with the responsibilities assigned to them.

Even though the client's system includes compliance-oriented operating practices, the independent auditor must still perform tests of the various controls to be relied upon to ascertain whether the controls are working as planned. Such compliance tests focus on the following questions:

- Were the necessary procedures performed?
- Were they performed as prescribed in the procedures manual?
- By whom were they performed?

Some control provisions, such as adequate segregation of duties, may not be susceptible to testing by sampling because they are not supported by documentary evidence. These controls are tested chiefly by inquiry and by observing the functions being performed.

Other controls are evidenced by data appearing on documents and are therefore susceptible to *testing for compliance by sampling*. We shall concentrate the remainder of our discussion on these tests of compliance.

Compliance testing for documented internal controls is performed by selecting a representative sample of documents from the appropriate accounting population. The sample size may be determined on a purely judgmental basis or on a more scientific basis by using the statistical techniques discussed in Chapter 8. Either way, the overall methodology is the same. It includes the following steps:

1. Define the audit objective of the tests.
2. Establish an appropriate hypothesis for each internal control attribute.
3. Draw a representative sample.
4. Examine the sample.

5. Interpret the results of examining the sample.
6. Make the audit decision.

Figures 10–10 and 10–11 illustrate audit programs for selected tests of sales and cash receipts transactions. The audit objective for each test is to ascertain compliance with internal control attributes previously identified in the review and evaluation phase of the audit. The procedures listed in Figures 10–12 and 10–13 are designed to test the internal control attributes of items selected in the audit programs. They illustrate the transactions-testing procedures for these various attributes by defining the data field (audit population), hypothetical sample size, audit evidence-gathering procedure, and description (or direction) of each test. These cover the first four steps just listed.

Notice that samples are drawn from data files located in each major department shown in the systems flowchart in Figures 10–7 through 10–9. Also observe that the procedures performed on each sample consist of one or more of the evidence-gathering techniques discussed in Chapter 3. In each case, the technique selected is the one that best meets the objective of ascertaining compliance with the appropriate internal

AUDIT PROGRAM FOR SALES AND ACCOUNTS RECEIVABLE TRANSACTIONS

1. Select a sample from the sales order file.
   a. Account for numerical sequence of sales orders.
   b. Trace sales orders to matching sales invoices, shipping documents, and entries into sales journal.
   c. Review sales orders and matching invoices for approval of credit department supervisor noting that prices, quantities, extensions and footings were checked, and that credit was properly approved before sale.
2. Select a sample of shipping documents from shipping department files.
   a. Account for numerical sequence of shipping documents.
   b. Vouch shipping documents to sales invoice files.
3. Select a sample from sales invoice file.
   a. Account for numerical sequence of sales invoices.
   b. Inspect invoices for stamp indicating that inventory was relieved.
   c. Vouch invoices to shipping department files and sales order file.
4. Select a sample of individual entries to sales journal.
   a. Vouch entries to supporting documents (sales invoice, sales order, shipping documents).
   b. Trace entries to postings in accounts receivable subsidiary ledgers.
5. Select a sample of sales journal monthly totals. Compare totals to postings in general ledger for sales and accounts receivable for agreement.
6. Select a sample of general ledger postings to sales and accounts receivable. Compare debit and credit postings to sales journal monthly totals for agreement.
7. Select a sample of postings to accounts receivable subsidiary ledger accounts. Vouch postings to individual entries in sales journal.

FIGURE 10–10. Selected Audit Program Procedures for Transactions Testing: Sales and Accounts Receivable Charges

AUDIT PROGRAM FOR CASH RECEIPTS TRANSACTIONS

1. Select a sample of cash sales slips or register tapes.
   a. Reconcile register readings with recorded sales and trace to sales journal postings.
   b. Reconcile register readings with cash deposit and vouch to deposit slip.
   c. Account for numerical sequence of cash sales tickets, if applicable.
2. Select a sample of credit postings to the accounts receivable subsidiary ledger.
   a. Vouch the credits to remittance advice file.
   b. Vouch noncash credits to credit memo file or write-off file in credit manager's department. Note any undocumented credits.
3. Reconcile total credit postings per subsidiary ledger with total credit to accounts receivable control account for selected months.
4. Select a sample from the credit memo file.
   a. Account for numerical sequence of credit memos.
   b. Trace postings of credit memos to individual and control accounts.
   c. Recalculate sales discounts and verify sales returns to receiving reports.
5. Select a sample of daily remittance lists.
   a. Vouch entries to remittance advices.
   b. Trace individual postings by date to specific subsidiary ledger accounts. Trace total posting to general ledger account entries (cash debit, accounts receivable credit).
   c. Reconcile total of remittance list to daily cash deposit. Vouch to bank validated deposit slip by date.
6. Select a sample of cash receipts journal postings.
   a. Vouch to cash sales tickets or remittance advices.
   b. Trace credit postings to individual accounts receivable and total posting to accounts receivable and cash control.
   c. Agree daily cash summaries to daily deposit slips validated by bank.
7. Select a sample of deposits per bank statement. Vouch to remittance list totals and cash receipts journal totals.
8. Select a sample of postings to cash, accounts receivable, and sales in the general ledger. Vouch to bank deposits.

FIGURE 10–11. Selected Audit Program Procedures for Transactions Testing: Cash Receipts and Accounts Receivable Credits

control attribute. A careful analysis of Figures 10–12 and 10–13 will reveal that *necessary audit procedures are performed for each important data population.* Where vouching and tracing are involved, both vouching and tracing are performed on each important data population in the system.

As evidence regarding internal control is gathered, the auditor should note the frequency and causes of deviations (errors) with respect to each internal control attribute. As the frequency of error increases, the findings should be interpreted as evidence of decreased reliability of internal control within the system. Therefore, there is a higher probability that undetected errors will result in misstated financial data than if a low frequency of errors had been found. The auditor's resulting decision will usually be to *extend the substantive tests of transactions within the system and of*

Attribute of Interest	Data Field (Population)	Sample Size[a]
Sales orders are:		
Numerically controlled	Sales order file	240
Recorded on sales invoices, shipping documents, sales journals	Sales order file	240
Reviewed for approvals of prices, extensions, footings, credit check	Sales order file	240
Shipping documents are:		
Numerically controlled	Shipping document files	Judgmental
Required for all sales	Shipping document files	Judgmental
Sales invoices are:		
Numerically controlled	Sales invoice files	Judgmental
Received by inventory control as authority to release goods	Sales invoice files (copy # ____)	300
Supported by shipping reports and sales orders	Sales invoice files	160
Sales Journal entries are:		
Supported by documentation	Sales journal entries	240
Entered properly in subsidiary ledgers	Sales journal entries	240
Entered properly in general ledger	Summary postings in sales journal	Judgmental
General ledger entries are supported by monthly journal totals	General ledger debit and credit postings	Judgmental
Subsidiary ledger postings agree with entries in sales journal	Subsidiary ledger debit postings	Judgmental

[a] Sample sizes in these examples were selected using the attribute sampling methodology discussed in this chapter. The following parameters were prespecified for applicable cases, for simplicity: Desired confidence = 95%; expected exception proportion = 2.5%; desired upper precision limit = 5%. In practice, each sample size must differ, depending on the precision and reliability the auditor is seeking.

FIGURE 10–12. Transactions Testing Methodology: Sales and Accounts Receivable

elements of the account balances affected by weak controls (Figure 10–13) to include a greater number of items than would have been examined if controls had been satisfactory. Conversely, if the auditor finds few deviations from established controls, he or she may infer a lower probability of error and as a result perform fewer substantive

Audit Procedure	Description of Test	
	From	To
Inspect numerical sequences	N/A	
Trace	Sales order file	Sales invoice file
Recompute extensions	N/A	
Vouch	Sales order file	Price lists Credit files
Inspect numerical sequences	N/A	
Vouch	Shipping files	Sales invoice file
Inspect numerical sequences	N/A	
Inspect for approval: Stamp of inventory Control supervision	N/A	
Vouch	Sales invoice file	Shipping document file Sales order files
Vouch	Sales journal	Sales orders, sales invoices, shipping documents
Trace	Sales journal	Accounts receivable ledger
Reconcile	Sales journal	General ledger account
Reconcile	General ledger	Sales journal
Reconcile	Subsidiary ledger	Sales journal entries

FIGURE 10–12 (continued)

tests on those transactions and account balances. Also, in such situations more audit procedures, such as confirmation of receivables, can be performed at interim dates. The relationship between the outcome of compliance tests and the extent of substantive tests is discussed further in the next section.

SUBSTANTIVE TESTS OF ACCOUNT BALANCES

We have stated that, theoretically, the auditor could depend on a sound system of internal control, compliance therewith having been proven through transaction valid-

Attribute of Interest	Data Field (Population)	Sample Size[a]
Cash sales slips/register tapes are:		
Controlled numerically	Cash sales slips/register tapes	Judgmental
Used as posting medium for cash sales	Cash sales slips/register tapes	240
Balanced daily to cash received and deposited	Cash sales slips/register tapes	Judgmental
Subsidiary ledger credit postings:		
For cash, are supported by remittance advices	Credit postings to subsidiary ledger	240
For noncash credits, are supported by credit memoranda	Credit postings to subsidiary ledger	240
Write-off memoranda properly approved by credit manager		
Total credits posted to subsidiary ledgers agree with credits posted to control accounts	Credit postings to subsidiary ledger	Judgmental
Credit memoranda are:		
Accounted for numerically	Credit memoranda file	Judgmental
Posted properly to accounts	Credit memoranda file	240
Reviewed for calculations	Credit memoranda file	240
Daily remittance lists are:		
Supported by remittance advices	Remittance list file	Judgmental
Properly posted to individual accounts and control accounts	Remittance list file	160
Reconciled to daily deposit	Remittance list file	160
Cash receipts journal postings are:		
For cash sales, supported by sales	Cash receipts journal entries	160
Posted properly to individual and control accounts	Cash receipts journal entries	160
Supported by validated deposit slips	Cash receipts journal entries	160
Daily deposits are supported by remittance lists	Deposit slip file	Judgmental
General ledger cash account debits are supported by validated deposit slips	Cash account postings	Judgmental

[a]Sample sizes in these examples were selected using the attribute sampling methodology discussed in this chapter. The following parameters were prespecified for applicable cases, for simplicity: Desired confidence = 95%; expected exception proportion = 2.5%; desired upper precision limit = 5%. In practice, each sample size must differ, depending on the precision and reliability the auditor is seeking.

FIGURE 10–13. Transactions Testing Methodology: Cash Receipts

Audit Procedure	Description of Test	
	From	To
Inspect numerical sequence	N/A	
Trace	Sales slips/register tapes	Sales journal
Reconcile	Sales slips/register tapes	Cash summary and deposit slips
Vouch	Ledger entries	Remittance advices
Vouch	Ledger entries	Credit memoranda and write-off memoranda
Reconcile	Subsidiary ledgers	General ledger
Inspect numerical sequence	N/A	
Trace	Credit memoranda file	Subsidiary ledger postings
Recompute discounts, etc.	N/A	
Vouch	Remittance list	Remittance advices
Trace	Remittance list	Subsidiary ledger credit postings
Reconcile	Remittance list	General ledger postings deposit slips
Vouch	Journal postings	Sales tickets/receipts tapes
Trace	Journal postings	Subsidiary and control accounts
Vouch	Journal postings	Validated deposit slips
Vouch	Deposit slips	Remittance lists
Vouch	Postings	Validated deposit slips

FIGURE 10–13 (continued)

ity tests, as a basis for an opinion on the financial statements. However, reality takes account of the uncertainties associated with the testing process; so some substantive tests of material account balances will always be performed. These tests are designed to determine whether the asset and liability accounts associated with each subsystem are stated in accordance with GAAP. The results of these tests, as well as of those designed to verify transaction validity, are accumulated as evidence in working papers similar to those shown in the appendixes at the end of the chapter.

Reliance on the verification of balance sheet accounts in the substantive testing phase of the audit *depends on two basic relationships inherent in the double-entry system of accounting*. The first of these recognizes that except for reclassification entries, all debits and credits to nominal (income statement) accounts will carry related and balancing debits or credits to real (balance sheet) accounts. The second characteristic recognizes that the nominal (income statement) accounts simply reflect elements of the changes in owners' equity associated with operations occurring during the accounting period. Since owners' equity at any particular point in time can be calculated by subtracting liabilities from assets, the verification of the assets and liabilities at the end of each fiscal period in effect provides evidence as to the validity of recorded changes in owners' equity during the period. That figure can be adjusted for nonoperating changes in owners' equity to provide verification of the net income or net loss figure shown in the income statement. Thus the beginning and end of period balance sheet figures can be visualized as *fences* within which the net result of the nominal account data must fit. Therefore, if the auditor has verified the asset and liability account balances at both ends of the period being audited, the net result of nominal account data has in effect (because of the first relationship observed above) also been verified. Because of the second relationship, the substantive tests performed on the asset and liability accounts also provide additional evidence as to whether the net income or net loss is stated in accordance with GAAP.

As we deal with the substantive tests of account balances phase of the audit in this chapter and in the chapters to follow, we will be developing the auditing procedures normally followed in verifying the balance sheet and income statement accounts most directly associated with each subsystem being evaluated. For the revenue subsystem, that includes accounts and notes receivable, allowance for doubtful accounts, sales, and cash account balances. In this chapter, we limit our discussion to the substantive tests performed on accounts and notes receivable, the allowance for doubtful accounts, and sales. The substantive tests performed to verify the cash balance reflecting the results of recording cash receipts and cash disbursements are discussed in Chapter 12.

The audit procedures associated with the substantive tests performed on receivables and their related accounts are designed to include verification of existence, ownership, cutoff, valuation, and appropriate statement presentation. Appendixes 10–A through 10–F illustrate some of the audit procedures that satisfy these objectives.

Reconciliation of Account Balances with Underlying Accounting Records

As shown in Figure 10–14 we begin our verification of receivables and their related valuation accounts by tracing the statement amount to the general ledger accounts for accounts receivable and notes receivable. It is also important to balance the accounts and notes receivable subsidiary ledgers against their control accounts. During the reconciliation process, we also recompute ledger and special journal column totals by footing and crossfooting those records. If the underlying records support the statement

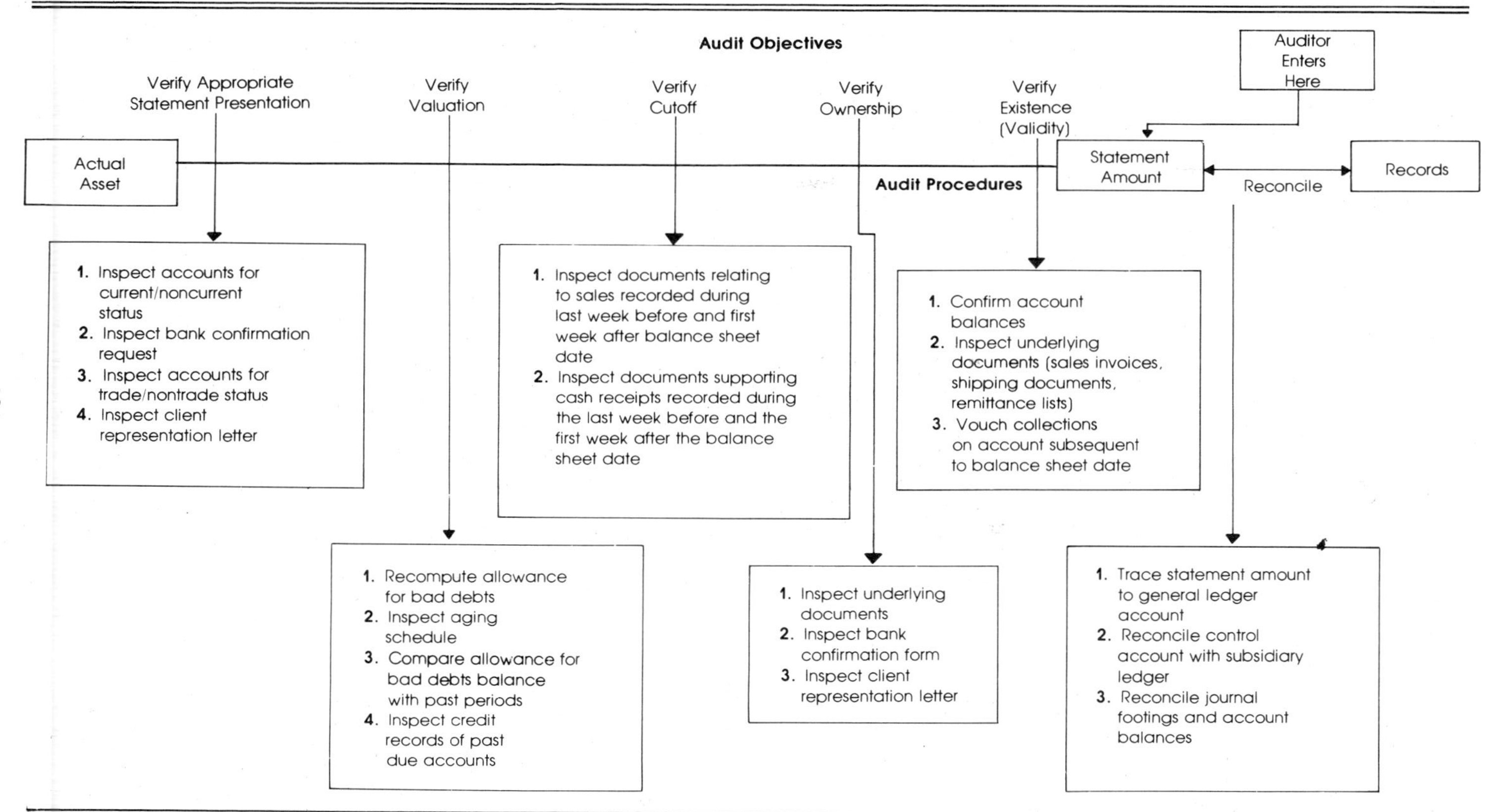

FIGURE 10–14. Flowchart for Substantive Tests of Accounts Receivable

balance, the auditor is ready to carry out the procedures necessary to meet the audit objectives cited earlier in the chapter. The reconciliation, footing, and crossfooting procedures are illustrated on working paper E, Appendix 10–A.

Verification of Existence

The actual existence of a receivable as an asset depends on the client having a valid claim for the amount shown in the account.

Confirmation. Confirmation, on a test basis, of amounts shown to be receivable from various customers is the primary auditing procedure used in verifying existence. This procedure is judged to be so important that it is required by generally accepted auditing standards, unless confirmation is impossible or impractical to perform. Chapter 3 included illustrations of both the negative and positive type of account receivable confirmation requests. As a means of improving the dependability of these requests, their mailing should be carefully supervised by the auditor, and all responses to confirmation requests should come directly to the auditor. Appendixes 10–A and 10–D illustrate the statistics kept regarding both the number and percentage of confirmation requests sent and received with no exceptions, as well as those received with exceptions. All confirmations returned with exceptions noted by customers require follow-up procedures by the auditor to ascertain whether the client or the customer has recorded the proper amount receivable. If the client has recorded an erroneous amount receivable, an adjusting journal entry may be required. An example of a confirmation request returned by the customer with no exceptions noted is shown in Appendix 10–C.

The confirmation of notes receivable often takes the form of a letter to the maker of the note, confirming such details as the original balance, unpaid balance as of the balance sheet date, interest rate, accrued interest receivable as of the balance sheet date, and any collateral held by the client as security for the note. When the signed notes themselves are available for the auditor's examination, there would logically be less need for confirming them than for confirming accounts receivable. Nevertheless, these, too, are often confirmed in the same manner as accounts receivable. Because of their negotiability, they should be inspected at the time cash is counted and should be controlled until the cash count has been completed. Notes owned but not on hand for inspection should always be confirmed with the parties holding them.

The accounts and notes to be confirmed will be chosen either by using judgment or by statistical sampling techniques. Because material errors are more likely to occur in recording large receivables, we will generally use a stratified sample. That requires the auditor to divide the receivables into two or more groups or strata on the basis of amounts shown in the accounts. The sample is then drawn to include a larger percentage of accounts with large balances and a lower percentage of the smaller ones.

The replies to confirmation requests should be appropriately processed by the auditor. This requires a careful investigation of all replies that suggest balances different from the ones shown on the client's books. As we have observed, *negative confirmation requests* are typically used in confirming small account balances; and the presumption is that an unanswered confirmation request validates the account balance. In the case of *positive confirmation requests,* however, the auditor must follow up on all unanswered confirmation requests until satisfied that the balance shown on the client's books is correct or that it needs to be adjusted to make it correct.

Differences between the account balances shown on the client's books and the balances reported in the confirmation requests can often be explained by shipment of goods or by collections in transit. In these instances, the auditor should be particularly concerned with delays in recording credits resulting from customer payments on account. Significant delays of this type suggest possible ***lapping*** of the accounts. Lapping occurs when the person receiving cash temporarily takes cash and covers that act by delaying the credit to the receivable account. Later, when payment is received from another customer, a credit is entered to the account that should have been credited for the cash that was stolen rather than the account that was actually being paid. The person committing such an act generally intends to reimburse the company for the cash temporarily stolen but often may be unable to do so. One way of protecting against lapping is to have customer payments sent directly to the company's bank, where they can be picked up by persons who have no recordkeeping responsibilities for cash collections.

In other instances, the differences between the book and confirmation balances may bring to light *disputed account balances or client errors* in recording sales. In such instances, appropriate audit adjustments must be made to allow the receivables, sales or sales return and allowances balances to be fairly presented in the financial statements.

Alternative Procedures. In some cases, it may be impractical or impossible to confirm accounts receivable as of the balance sheet date. For example, some of the client's customers may have voucher systems for payment of accounts incompatible with the client's receivables system. The federal government is another example of a customer with which accounts receivable confirmation is virtually impossible. In the event that it is impractical or impossible to confirm the accounts receivable, the auditor may rely on alternative procedures in rendering an opinion on the financial statements. These include the following:

1. Vouching subsequent collections of accounts receivable.
2. Inspection of underlying documentation for charges and credits to accounts receivable.

Vouching of collections on account subsequent to the balance sheet date is probably the most useful procedure as an alternate to confirmation because it allows the auditor the benefit of hindsight in the verification of receivables. Keep in mind that the audit field work will be performed after the close of the period being audited. That allows the auditor to apply this procedure for verifying the validity of receivables by inspecting the cash receipts journal for a period of time following the end of the fiscal period under audit. The collection of a receivable following the end of the period provides strong evidence in support of the existence and validity of the receivable as of the end of that period. In vouching subsequent collections, however, the auditor must be sure that the collections being vouched pertain to sales and their related receivables that actually occurred before the balance sheet date, and not in the intervening period between the balance sheet date and collection date.

For this reason, the auditor should also inspect on a test basis the documents underlying the entries to the accounts receivable subsidiary ledger accounts: the sales invoices, shipping tickets, bills of lading, credit memos, and the documents supporting receipts from customers. As these documents are inspected, they should be properly *matched* to individual transactions and *traced* through the accounting records to the appropriate receivable account, noting the dates of the transactions. If the auditor is concerned with the possible overstatement of sales and receivables, the appropriate audit procedure is generally *vouching* the debit entries to customer accounts receivable back to the sales invoices. This procedure shows that the debit entries are properly supported by sales invoices. On the other hand, if we were concerned with a possible understatement of these items, we would trace the invoices to the debits in customer accounts receivable. Alternative procedures performed on accounts receivable are illustrated in Appendix 10–B.

It is important to observe that if receivables are material and the auditor can perform neither confirmation nor alternative procedures, a limitation is considered imposed on the scope of the audit which will *usually preclude the expression of an unqualified audit opinion*. Furthermore, a client-imposed restriction on such procedures is usually regarded as a more serious matter than a restriction attributed solely to the auditor in an unrestricted client environment. In cases of client-imposed restrictions, the auditor might contemplate more seriously a disclaimer of opinion, depending on the amount of receivables to which the scope limitation pertains. However, if the auditor can satisfactorily verify the existence of the receivables balances by expanding the alternate procedures, an unqualified opinion may still be rendered on the financial statements.

Verification of Ownership

In the case of receivables, the existence of the typical documentary support in the form of sales invoices, shipping documents, notes, etc., provides evidence of ownership. However, the auditor is always concerned with contingencies that may cloud the ownership rights of a client. For example, accounts receivable are sometimes assigned or pledged for the purpose of securing cash during the time they would normally be outstanding and awaiting collection. Quite logically, the primary source of funds in such a situation would be the client's banker. Therefore, as we shall see in Chapter 12, the *bank confirmation request* used in verifying cash also requests the banker to indicate whether or not the bank has any contingent claims against the client's receivables, either as a result of pledged receivables or discounted notes receivable. The auditor will also typically request a *representation letter* from the client stating that all such contingent claims against receivables have been disclosed in the financial statements. Shipment of goods on consignment, for example, is sometimes incorrectly recorded as a sale; the auditor must be concerned with discovering such errors. This type of error is often suggested by unusually large periodic debits and credits to accounts receivable.

Verification of Cutoff

Because of the matching convention associated with the financial reporting process, it is important for the auditor to verify that transactions have been appropriately cut off at the end of each period. The point at which revenues should be recognized is determined by reference to the ***realization convention***, which was described in Chapter 2. In the case of sales, the earning process is generally presumed to have been completed and a legal claim against the purchaser established at the point where title passes. *Title passage,* in turn, is generally determined by the *FOB point.* For example, merchandise sold FOB shipping point should be recognized as a sale on the date of shipment. On the other hand, merchandise sold *FOB destination* should be recognized as a sale only when it reaches its destination. Therefore, in verifying the cutoff of sales transactions, it is important for the auditor to inspect the shipping documents associated with merchandise shipped around the end of the fiscal period to determine whether those sales have been recorded in the proper period.

The auditor is often more concerned with overstatement than with understatement of the client's sales. Thus, he or she should be particularly sensitive to *sales recorded before the cutoff date but not shipped until after the cutoff date.* The most appropriate test for this kind of overstatement, therefore, is vouching the last several entries in the client's sales journal to shipping documents. Assuming the client's shipping terms are FOB shipping point, sales entries dated before the cutoff date accompanied by shipping documents dated after the cutoff date generally indicate sales overstatements, except in unusual circumstances such as the sale of custom-made goods.

In the case of *income from services,* the earning process is presumed to have been completed as services are performed. Therefore, the auditor should examine the documents supporting the service efforts rendered near the end of the period to appropriately verify the cutoff of that type of income. *In the nonprofit area,* taxes and contributions received as revenues are generally designated for use over specific periods of time. It is important for the auditor to identify those designations and to verify that revenues have been recognized in the reporting period during which the resources provided by them are expected to be used.

In connection with the collection of accounts receivable, it is important for the auditor to inspect the documents associated with cash receipts near the end of the period to determine that they have been recorded as credits to accounts receivable in *the appropriate fiscal period.* The client, in an effort to improve the firm's current ratio, may keep the cash record open and record both cash received after the end of the fiscal period and payments on account after the end of the period as though they occurred at the end of the period under audit. If the client holds only the cash receipts book open, cash will be overstated and accounts receivable will be understated. This obviously will have no effect on the current ratio. On the other hand, if the cash disbursements book is also held open and if current assets are in excess of current liabilities, the current ratio will be overstated. There is usually a higher risk of this type of cutoff error when the client has long-term debt with a restrictive current ratio covenant. Therefore the auditor must give particular attention to such possibilities if he or she discovers such convenants during the planning phase of the audit.

We have observed the effect of an improper cash cutoff in the preceding paragraph. If sales are improperly cut off, both the net income and accounts receivable balances will be incorrect. The extent of the error, however, depends on whether or not the sales cutoff error is consistent or *inconsistent with the cost of sales cutoff.* If, for example, a sale properly associated with the period following the one being audited is improperly recorded in the period under audit, both sales and accounts receivable will be overstated. Net income will therefore be overstated by the amount of the sales price of the goods. However, if at the same time, the cost of the goods associated with the sale is also inappropriately recorded as cost of sales for the period under audit, the distortion in net income and retained earnings will be equal to the gross margin on the sale of the goods. For that reason it is extremely important for the auditor to be sure that not only are the sales and cost of sales cutoffs individually proper, but that they are consistent with each other.

Verification of Valuation

Under generally accepted accounting principles, short-term receivables are reported at net realizable value. Accordingly, it is necessary to establish a proper allowance for uncollectible accounts and notes receivable. Audit procedures in this area are directed toward evaluating the adequacy of the client's provision for uncollectible accounts and notes. In accounting theory courses, one learns that the provision for bad debts is generally determined on the basis of past experience and is calculated either as a percentage of sales or as a percentage of receivables. The auditor typically ***recomputes*** the client's allowance for uncollectible accounts, based on whichever of these procedures has been followed by the client. In addition, he or she may compute either or both of the following key analytical ratios over several years:

- Accounts receivable turnover (sales ÷ average accounts receivable).
- Days' sales to collection (365 ÷ accounts receivable turnover).

Examining these trends over time gives the auditor an idea of the success of the client's continuing collection efforts for accounts and notes receivable.

For the purpose of more precisely evaluating the adequacy of the allowance for uncollectible accounts, the auditor will generally ***age the accounts receivable.*** That procedure involves listing the individual amounts receivable as current or, if past due, by the number of days they are past due as is illustrated in the working paper aging schedule shown in Appendix 10–A. This schedule allows the auditor to give special attention to the past due accounts in evaluating the adequacy of the allowance for uncollectible accounts. In doing that the auditor will typically inspect the records of past due accounts and correspondence developed in attempts to collect them. Another procedure for verifying the adequacy of the allowance account includes a comparison of the allowance provision in the current period with those of prior periods. Just as in the case of the procedures discussed earlier, this evaluation may show that an audit adjustment should be made to establish an appropriate provision for estimated losses in the collection of receivables. If accounts receivable have increased due to slow collection, the tests of collectibility should be expanded. Sometimes a client will hold securities as collateral for certain receivables. When that is the case, the auditor should examine the securities to ascertain their value in judging any possible loss in collecting the receivables.

Accrued interest on notes receivable should be recomputed. It is also necessary to recompute the unearned discount on noninterest-bearing or low-interest–bearing notes to be sure that those items are appropriately valued in the financial statements. Proper valuation for sales revenue accounts is often verified by *analytical review*. More specifically, the auditor might perform comparisons of year-to-year totals in sales accounts by category (see Appendix 10–E) or by month (see Appendix 10–F). If unusual fluctuations are noted in these accounts, the auditor will need to obtain explanations from the client and to corroborate the client's explanations by further inspection of documentary support. Unusual fluctuations in sales may be explained by any one or a combination of the following factors:

- Unusual changes in operations caused by such external factors as strikes, recessions, increased competition, and so on.
- Exceptional circumstances that greatly increase or decrease demand for the client's product.
- Accounting changes in method of accounting for sales.
- Cutoff errors for sales and shipments.

If sales fluctuations are caused by either of the first two factors and corroborative audit tests support the client's explanations, no further audit tests usually need to be performed. On the other hand, major sales fluctuations caused by accounting changes generally need to be disclosed by the client. Material cutoff errors need to be corrected by means of an adjusting journal entry.

Ascertaining Appropriate Statement Presentation

The procedures just discussed are primarily concerned with verifying the balances that should be shown for receivables and their related valuation accounts. In presenting those receivables in the balance sheet, it is important that the auditor verify that an appropriate distinction has been made between current and noncurrent receivables and that appropriate disclosures have been made relating to any contingent claims against the receivables. In distinguishing between current and noncurrent receivables, we should recall that a current receivable should, in the normal course of business operations, be expected to be collected within one year or the operating cycle; whichever is longer. The operating cycle provision, for example, allows installment accounts receivable, due within the normal collection period, even though longer than twelve months, to be classified as current receivables.

To meet the requirement of full disclosure, accounts receivable assigned to a financing agency should be so labeled. It is also important to disclose parenthetically or in a footnote information relating to pledged accounts receivable. In making judgments regarding these disclosures, the auditor relies on the findings from procedures followed in the verification of ownership as discussed earlier in this section. It is also important to distinguish between trade and nontrade receivables. Receivables from officers and employees, for example, should be presented in a separate account in the balance sheet. Notes receivable should be separated from accounts receivable in the balance sheet.

Supplemental Audit Procedures for an Initial Audit

Because the substantive tests rely on the double-entry accounting relationships between the balance sheet and income statement accounts, the auditor must perform supplemental auditing procedures during an initial audit engagement to express an opinion on the operating statements, (income statement, statement of changes in financial position, and statement of retained earnings). Those procedures are designed to satisfy the auditor that the beginning of the period balance sheet account balances were fairly presented. Again the auditor relies heavily on the proof of transaction validity in expressing an opinion on the income statement in an initial audit. Beyond that, however, the auditor must reconcile individual beginning-of-the-period balance sheet account balances with their end-of-the-period audited balances by *analyzing the increases and decreases to the accounts during the year* and fitting them into a basic four-element equation, stated as follows:

Beginning-of-the-period balance + increases to the account during the period – decreases in the account during the period = ending balance in the account.

This equation reflects the basic format for the analysis type of work paper typically prepared as evidence in support of long-term asset balances. If the supplemental procedures show that the beginning-of-the-period account balance fits into the four-element equation for that account, the auditor can express an opinion on the financial statements in an initial audit through the medium of a normal unqualified audit report. However, the auditor can, in an initial audit, express an opinion on the *end-of-the-period balance sheet only,* without performing the supplemental procedures described in this paragraph. If such procedures cannot practicably be performed, the auditor must disclaim an opinion on the operating statement and statement of changes in financial position for the period.

USING THE COMPUTER IN AUDITING THE REVENUE SYSTEM

As we observed in Chapters 6 and 7, electronic data-processing equipment is quite generally used today in the maintenance of revenue system records. When a completely computerized system involving the maintenance of accounts receivable and sales data in machine readable form is used, the auditor can advantageously use the computer to select the various sample data required for the performance of audit tests. For example, the computer can be programmed to *calculate an appropriate sample size* and to *select the accounts to be confirmed.* Furthermore, it can be programmed to *print out all pertinent details on each of the confirmation requests.*

The computer can also be programmed to scan the accounts receivable records for the purpose of *testing the aging of those accounts.* The scanning capability of the computer can also be used to identify unusual conditions in the files, such as credit balances in accounts receivable created by improper recording practices. The computer's mathematical capability can be used to *recalculate* such important numerical fields as the totals of all categories in the client's aged accounts receivable listing. In order to test appropriate sales cutoff, the computer can be programmed to *extract and print out* the sales and cash collection transactions for the last few days of the period under audit and the first few days of the next period. The printout can then be checked against the documentary support for those transactions to verify the appropriateness of cutoff in connection with both types of transactions. Test transactions to be verified against documentary support can also be selected from the machine-readable records by the computer. The printout of those transactions can then be verified against the documents from which they have been originated. These are cited as examples rather than as a complete list of the ways in which the computer can be used as an audit tool in the audit of computerized records for revenues, receivables, and cash receipts.

SUMMARY

In this chapter we have developed the audit procedures to be followed in verifying the various account balances associated with a client's primary revenue system. We began by observing that the auditor typically verifies the accounts associated with each of the different subsystems as individual segments of the overall audit because of their direct relationships to each other.

We then observed that the verification of transaction validity, existence, ownership, cutoff, valuation, and appropriate statement presentation are the audit objectives to be met in auditing the revenue system. We explained the importance of the study and evaluation of the internal control system in verifying transaction validity. We also made this observation: If the auditor could have complete confidence in the control system, the transaction validity audit objective would be the only one that would have to be met prior to the expression of an opinion on the fairness of presentation of the accounts related to the revenue system. From a practical point of view, however, the limitations associated with the testing process require the auditor to meet the other objectives through substantive tests of the related balance sheet accounts.

In the process of evaluating the system of internal control, we identified the various functions performed within the revenue system. Then we recalled that the system must possess the following basic characteristics:

- Appropriate separation of responsibilities.
- Specific placement of responsibilities.
- Use of appropriate authorization and approval forms and procedures.
- Use of appropriately qualified personnel.
- Proper protection of assets and records associated with the system.

We then explained the operating practices required within the revenue system to meet those five characteristics.

In the last part of the chapter, we described the audit procedures that must be performed to verify existence, ownership, cutoff, valuation, and appropriate statement presentation of accounts receivable and sales balances. These are characterized as the substantive tests of account balances, which the auditor performs to supplement the transaction validity tests. Finally, we described briefly how the computer can be used to perform some of the substantive tests.

APPENDIX 10–A: Accounts Receivable Aged Trial Balance

JEP Manufacturing Co.	W. P. No.	E
Accounts Receivable	ACCOUNTANT	SMG
Aged Trial Balance 3/31/X1	DATE	5/8/X1

Confirmation Number	Customer	Current	30-60 Days	60-90 Days	Over 90 Days
	Amco Production	562 30			
	Am East Well and Pump	1012 23			
①	Alabama Power	105 46			
	Aaco Services Co.		5731 87	989 94	
	City of Federal Heights		300 47		
	City Public Service Board		613 30		
	Cabrillo Services		566 22		
②	Consolidated Edison	30120 00	232 52	E-1-1	
	D&L Tool, Inc.		407 07		
	Dallas Power Co.	21525 00	1 05		
	Duke Powell	7364 00			
	Elliott Central	14499 25			
	Florida Power & Light	62752 00			2450 00
	Florida Power Corporation	14200 00			
	Other (Details Omitted)	640865 66	207706 49	⟨346 17⟩	⟨3588 19⟩
	Totals 3-31-X1	793005 90	215558 98	643 77	⟨1138 19⟩
		∧	∧	∧	∧
	Percentage of total	78.6	21.4	0.1	⟨0.1⟩
	Totals 3-31-X0	327268 ꝟ	176305 ꝟ	16592 ꝟ	15727 ꝟ
	Percentage of total	61.1	32.9	3.1	2.9

C, Ⓒ Confirmation sent; received
∧ ⩚ Footed, Cross-footed
Ⓒ No reply received to confirmation, or customer not able to reply. See alternative procedures performed on E-1 and E-1-1
ꝟ Per prior year working papers
✓ Agreed to 3-31-X1 general ledger
* Tested Aging to accounts receivable billings. No exceptions noted.

This is a P.B.C.

	Total *	
	562 30	
	1012 23	
	105 46	ҁ
	6721 81	
	300 47	
	613 30	
	566 22	
E-1	303524 52	©
	407 07	
	215260 05	ҁ
	7364 00	
	14499 25	
E-1	652020 00	©
	14200 00	
	844637 79	
	1 008070 47	* ✓
	A-1	
	100.0	
	535887	✓
	100.0	

Note: The large increase in the total accounts receivable balance over prior years (primarily in the over-30 days category) is due largely to end-of-year sales in 19X1 to many customers, including [details deleted]. Considering these increases in individual receivables accounts as well as the large increase in the over-30 day category and subsequent collections by JEP of these balances, the increase in accounts receivable at 3-31-X1 appears reasonable.

Note: No allowance for doubtful accounts is used by JEP since their business is strictly a special order-type operation and all their customers are reliable. Past collection experience indicates that this is reasonable.

Conclusion: Based on the audit work performed as documented in the E-series working papers, which was considered adequate to meet the objectives of the audit for receivables, accounts receivable appear to be fairly stated at 3-31-X1, in accordance with generally accepted accounting principles.

SMS

APPENDIX 10–B: Alternative Procedures Performed on Accounts Receivable

JEP Mfg. Co.
Alternative Procedures Performed on A/R
3-31-X1

W. P. No.	E-1
ACCOUNTANT	Smb
DATE	5/8/X1

SEE TICK LEGEND ON E-1-2

	Invoice #	Amount		
Consolidated Edison			E	
Receivable @ 3-31-X1			30402 52	E-2-1 ②
Cash rec'd subsequent to 3-31-X1	19084	30120 00 ✓		
Unpaid invoice	18972	282 52 ✗	30402 52	
Amount unconfirmed			-0-	
Florida Power & Light				
Receivable @ 3-31-X1			65202 00	E-2-1 ④
Cash rec'd subsequent to 3-31-X1	19059	14400 00 ✓		
↓	19090	4388 00 ✓		
	19091	7200 00 ✓		
	19119	13164 00 ✓		
	19120	7200 00 ✓		
	19058	16400 00 ✓		
Unpaid invoice	18560	2450 00 ⊗	65202 00	
Amount unconfirmed			-0-	
Houston Lighting & Power			E	
Receivable @ 3-31-X1			89730 00	E-2-1 ⑤
Cash rec'd subsequent to 3-31-X1	18970	49850 00 ✓		
Unpaid invoice	19093	39880 00 #	89730 00	
Amount unconfirmed			-0-	
Texaco			E	
Receivable @ 3-31-X1			26337 00	E-2-1
Unpaid invoice	19092	26337 00 ✗		
Amount unconfirmed			-0-	

W. P. No.	E-1-2
ACCOUNTANT	Sms
DATE	5/11/X1

JEP Mfg. Co.
Alternate Procedures performed on A/R
3-31-X1

	Invoice #	Amount		
Westinghouse Electric-Houston			E	
Receivable @ 3-31-X1			29424 46	E-2-1 (13)
Cash rec'd subsequent to 3-31-X1	19029	29424 46 ✓		
Amount unconfirmed			-0-	

✓ Agreed amount of payment and invoice # to appropriate invoice, noting that invoice date was prior to 4-1-X1 and therefore appropriately classified as a receivable @ 3-31-X1. Traced receipt of this payment to validated daily deposit slip subsequent to 3-31-X1. Amounts do appear to be receivables @ 3-31-X1.

Agreed amount to invoice #18972 dated 2-13-X1. Noted that goods were shipped 2-13-X1 per shipping order. Agreed description of goods shipped to customer's P.O. # 1650324 dated 1-5-X1. Amount appears to be a receivable @ 3-31-X1.

Agreed amount to invoice #19092 dated 3-20-X1. Agreed description of goods per invoice to customer's P.O # HO-167247-JM and to shipping documents dated prior to 3-31-X1 and signed as rec'd by Texaco personnel. Amounts appear to be properly classified as a receivable @ 3-31-X1. 1 month lag appears reasonable considering client.

(X) Agreed amount to invoice #18560 dated 9-25-X0. Agreed description of goods per invoice to customer's P.O.# 27956-14475 and to shipping documents due 9-25-X0. Amount appears to be properly classified as a receivable @ 3-31-X1. Receivable still has yet to be collected because of a rework performed on the goods that were still in transport at this date.

⌗ Agreed amount to invoice # 19093 dated 3-20-X1. Agreed description of goods per invoice to customer's P.O. # M-46477 dated 7-31-X0. Goods were shipped 3-20-X1. Amount does appear to be a receivable @ 3-31-X1.

APPENDIX 10–C: Accounts Receivable Confirmation

JEP MANUFACTURING COMPANY
P.O. Box 1000
Greensboro, Texas 75401

E-2-1
SMG
5/11/X1

April 10, 19X1

Dallas Power Co.
15 Providence
Dallas, Tx. 75201

Gentlemen:

Best and Company, Suite 4500, Byron Building, Dallas, Texas 75201 are making their usual examination of our accounts; therefore, would you confirm directly to them the amount of your indebtedness to us as of the close of business on March 31, 19X1.

According to our records, you were indebted to us as follows: $21,526.05.
E

Yours truly,

L. Philip Neeson

L. Philip Neeson
Financial Vice-President

LN:gr

The above information is correct, except as noted:

____

____

____

J. F. Wagner 5/01/X1
Signature

Supervisor, Accounts Payable
Title

APPENDIX 10–D: Accounts Receivable Confirmation Statistics

JEP Mfg. Co.
A/R Confirmation Stats
3-31-X1

W. P. No.	E-3
ACCOUNTANT	Sms
DATE	5/11/X1

	Number 19X0 △	Number 19X1	Amount 19X0 △	Amount 19X1
Year-End Balance	31	34	535887 19	E 1008070 47
Confirmations Requested	11	13 E0	513695 34	E-2-1 921605 37
% of Total	35%	38%	96%	91%
Confirmations Received				
w/o exception	6	4	314189 46	E-2 435344 65
w/ exception-cleared	0	0	–	–
	6	4	314189 46	435344 65
% of Total	36.4%	30.1%	61.2%	47.2%
Alternate Procedures				
Nonresponding A/C's	5	6	101905 46	E-2-1 333250 88
Unable to Confirm	2	3	97600 42	E-2 153009 84
	7	9	199505 88	486260 72
% of Total	63.6%		38.8%	
Total Verified	11	13	513695 34	921605 37
% of amt. mailed	100%	100%	100%	100%

△ Per prior year's w/p's.

APPENDIX 10–E: Sales

JEP Mfg. Co.	W. P. No.	X
Sales	ACCOUNTANT	SmG
3-31-X1	DATE	5/21/X1

A/C #	Description	Year Ended 3-31-X0	Year Ended 3-31-X1	
302	Liquid Dist. Transformers through 100 KVA	779,849.05	3,874,548.73	①
304	Liquid Dist. Transformers above 100 KVA	1,870,680.40	252,364.00	②
307	Potheads / Parts	6,790.22	113,600.80	③
306, 308, 309	Oil Fuel Circuits, Disconnect Assemblies	113,866.25	-0-	④
310	Purchased Parts	50,394.51	1,576.62	③
311	Manufactured Parts	104,108.81	220.50	③
312	Repair Sales	38,150.56	13,767.89	
315	Cancellation Sales	1,015.00	3,685.00	
316-324	Load Break Switches	3,451,410.76	3,908,748.53	⑤
325	Adjustments & Allowances	<19,938.60>	<19,769.30>	
330	Freight	<164,669.49>	<182,811.36>	
350-360	Other (Compensators, Motor Controls)	42,273.49	67,148.95	⑥
		6,273,930.96	8,033,080.36	
	AJE <1> To reverse prior year % completion		<1,158,377.00>	
	AJE <2> To record current year % completion.		964,886.05	
		6,273,930.36	7,839,589.41	
			A-3	

Explanation of Significant Fluctuations

Conclusion: Based on the audit work performed, which was considered adequate to meet the objectives per the audit program (APG), it appears that sales for 19X1 are fairly stated.

① Sales are up in the A/C due to increased orders from REDA for this type of transformer. REDA is developing large oil field in Saudi Arabia and in China, therefore the large increase in this particular pump. When REDA develops a field in this way, they require many of these transformers because of the tremendous expense of the undertaking. Fluctuation appears reasonable.

② Sales here are down because a competitor, Southwest Transformer, is currently offering a product in this class that is much less expensive.

③ Sales formerly charged to Accounts 310 + 311 are now being charged to A/C 307, now entitled "Parts", explaining the significant increase in this account and the decreases in the other two. Overall decrease appears reasonable as JEP now concentrates in completed units.

④ Sales formerly charged to 306, 308, + 309 are now being spread to other, more appropriate sales A/C's, especially "Load Break Switches."

⑤ Most significant customer of Load Break Switches from JEP is So. California Edison. Sales this year have remained relatively constant while JEP has been able to increase its margin from 24% to 29%.

⑥ Motor controls sales have shown an increase in both gross sales and margin, although it is difficult to allocate the costs of this category, since is so closely associated with the activity in R&D. Increase does appear reasonable.

APPENDIX 10–F: Analysis of Sales

JEP Manufacturing Corporation
Analysis of Sales
12-31-X6

W. P. No.	X-1
ACCOUNTANT	Client / CMT
DATE	2-20-X7

	19X6 ø		19X5 ø		Increase ⟨Decrease⟩
January	188390	✓ ⱳ	206720		⟨18330⟩
February	126240		110460		15780
March	280530		290520		⟨9990⟩
April	452410	✓ ⱳ	450690		1720
May	774890		829460		⟨54570⟩
June	1057410		957670		99740
July	923890	✓ ⱳ	964290		⟨40400⟩
August	544580		763240		⟨218660⟩
September	311620		401240		⟨89620⟩
October	433050	✓ ⱳ	384290		48760
November	313720		247360		66360
December	234970	—	214170	—	20800
Total	5641700 ʌ		5820110 ʌ		⟨178410⟩ ʌ
	T/B-2				

ʌ Footings checked.
ø Agreed to general ledger. No exceptions noted.
✓ Priced, extended, and totaled 240 invoices. No exceptions noted
— Compared invoices and shipping records for last 10 days of period. Cutoff proper at 12-31.
ⱳ Tested postings to customer accounts. No exceptions noted.

Note: Decline in sales for 19X6 due largely to labor strike in July, August and September 19X6. Examined union correspondence to corroborate work stoppages. Explanation agrees to details in inventory and labor statistics.

QUESTIONS FOR CLASS DISCUSSION

Q10–1 What is meant by the term *audit objectives?*

Q10–2 What audit objectives should be achieved in verifying the account balances included in the revenue system?

Q10–3 What does the auditor depend on as the primary evidence in verifying transaction validity?

Q10–4 Is it conceptually possible for an auditor to express an opinion on the financial statements without performing substantive tests? Explain.

Q10–5 What is meant by *boundary documents?*

Q10–6 What are the boundary documents that support revenue system transactions?

Q10–7 What is meant by *exchange functions? Processing functions? Safeguard functions?*

Q10–8 What tasks, typically performed in handling revenue system activities, should be separated from each other? Cite the reasons for each of those separations.

Q10–9 Why is it inappropriate to have the billing function performed by the cashier?

Q10–10 Why is it important to have special discount concessions approved by responsible supervisors?

Q10–11 Why is it important to have specific responsibilities associated with the operations of the revenue system assigned to specific persons?

Q10–12 Why is it important to use sequentially numbered invoices and shipping tickets? Explain how these documents are used as control devices.

Q10–13 What problems are associated with the identification and handling of uncollectible accounts?

Q10–14 How does the auditor evaluate the system of internal control for a revenue system that is computerized?

Q10–15 What are the audit objectives typically met by substantive testing procedures in the audit of revenue system accounts?

Q10–16 How does the auditor rely on the double-entry system and beginning-and-end-of-period asset balances in the verification of revenue account balances?

Q10–17 How does the auditor verify the existence (validity) of accounts receivable? Explain.

Q10–18 What does the auditor do when it is impractical or impossible to confirm accounts receivable as of the balance sheet date? Explain.

Q10–19 What evidence does an auditor gather in verifying the ownership of receivables?

Q10–20 Why is it important for the auditor to verify the cutoff of sales and cash receipts transactions? What procedures are used in verifying the cutoff of those transactions?

Q10–21 How does the auditor verify the valuation of accounts receivable? Explain.

Q10–22 What are the primary concerns of the auditor in verifying the appropriate statement presentation of receivables?

Q10–23 What supplemental procedures must the auditor perform in an initial audit to express an opinion on all the financial statements for the period under audit? Explain why those procedures must be performed.

Q10–24 Is it possible for an auditor to express an opinion on the end-of-period balance sheet only in an initial audit, without performing the supplemental procedures discussed in the preceding question? Explain.

Q10–25 What (briefly) are the ways in which the computer can be used in performing the audit of revenue system transactions and account balances?

SHORT CASES

C10–1 Darlene Dodge, CPA, is examining the financial statements of a manufacturing company with a significant amount of trade accounts receivable. Dodge is satisfied that the accounts are properly summarized and classified and that allocations, reclassifications, and valuations are made in accordance with generally accepted accounting principles. Dodge is planning to use accounts-receivable confirmation requests to satisfy the third standard of field work as to trade accounts receivable.

Required:

a. Identify and describe the two forms of accounts-receivable confirmation requests and indicate what factors Dodge will consider in determining when to use each.

b. Assume Dodge has received a satisfactory response to the confirmation requests. Describe how Dodge could evaluate collectibility of the trade accounts receivable.

(AICPA adapted)

C10–2 After determining that computer controls are valid, Janis Hastings is reviewing the sales system of Rosco Corporation in order to determine how a computerized audit program may be used to assist in performing tests of Rosco's sales records.

Rosco sells crude oil from one central location. All orders are received by mail and indicate the preassigned customer identification number, desired quantity, proposed delivery date, method of payment, and shipping terms. Since price fluctuates daily, orders do not indicate a price. Price sheets are printed daily and details are stored in a permanent disk file. The details of orders are also maintained in a permanent disk file.

Each morning the shipping clerk receives a computer printout which indicates details of customers' orders to be shipped that day. After the orders have been shipped, the shipping details are inputted in the computer, which simultaneously updates the sales journal, perpetual inventory records, accounts receivable, and sales accounts.

The details of all transactions, as well as daily updates, are maintained on disks which are available for use by Hastings in the performance of the audit.

Required:

a. How may a computerized audit program be used by Hastings to perform substantive tests of Rosco's sales records in their machine readable form? *(Do not discuss accounts receivable and inventory.)*

b. After having performed these tests with the assistance of the computer, what other auditing procedures should Hastings perform in order to complete the examination of Rosco's sales records?

(AICPA adapted)

C10–3 The Art Appreciation Society operates a museum for the benefit and enjoyment of the community. During hours when the museum is open to the public, two clerks positioned at the entrance collect a five-dollar admission fee from each nonmember patron. Members of the Art Appreciation Society are permitted to enter free of charge upon presentation of their membership cards.

At the end of each day, one of the clerks delivers the proceeds to the treasurer. The treasurer counts the cash in the presence of the clerk and places it in a safe. Each Friday afternoon the treasurer and one of the clerks deliver all cash held in the safe to the bank, and receive an authenticated deposit slip which provides the basis for the weekly entry in the cash receipts journal.

The board of directors of the Art Appreciation Society has identified a need to improve their system of internal control over cash admission fees. The board has determined that the cost of installing turnstiles, sales booths, or otherwise altering the physical layout of the museum will greatly exceed any benefits which may be derived. However, the board has agreed that the sale of admission tickets must be an integral part of its improvement efforts.

Hubert Smith has been asked by the board of directors of the Art Appreciation Society to review the internal control over cash admission fees and provide suggestions for improvement.

Required:

Indicate weaknesses Smith should find in the existing system of internal control over cash admission fees and recommend one improvement for each of the weaknesses identified.

Organize the answer as indicated in the following illustrative example:

Weakness	Recommendation
1. There is no basis for establishing the documentation of the number of paying patrons.	1. Prenumbered admission tickets should be issued upon payment of the admission fee.

(AICPA adapted)

C10–4 Your client is the Spring Valley Shopping Center, Inc., a shopping center with thirty store tenants. All leases with the store tenants provide for a fixed rent plus a percentage of sales, net of sales taxes, in excess of a fixed-dollar amount computed on an annual basis. Each lease also provides that the landlord may engage a CPA to audit all records of the tenant for assurance that sales are being properly reported to the landlord.

You have been requested by your client to audit the records of the Bali Pearl Restaurant to determine that the sales totaling $390,000 for the year ended December 31, 19X1, have been properly reported to the landlord. The restaurant and the shopping center entered into a five-year lease on January 1, 19X1. The Bali Pearl Restaurant offers only table service. No liquor is served. During meal times there are four or five waitresses in attendance who prepare handwritten prenumbered restaurant checks for the customers. Payment is made at a cash register, manned by the proprietor, as the customer leaves. All sales are for cash. The proprietor also is the bookkeeper. Complete files are kept of restaurant checks and cash register tapes. A daily sales book and general ledger are also maintained.

Required:

a. List the audit objectives that would be of primary concern to you in auditing the sales system of Bali Pearl Restaurant.

b. List the auditing procedures you would employ to verify the total annual sales of the Bali Pearl Restaurant. (Disregard vending machines and sales and counter sales of chewing gum, candy, etc.)

(AICPA adapted)

C10–5 You are auditing the Alaska Branch of Far Distributing Co. This branch has substantial annual sales, which are billed and collected locally. As a part of your audit you find that the procedures for handling cash receipts are as follows:

Cash collections on over-the-counter sales and COD sales are received from the customer or delivery service by the cashier. Upon receipt of cash, the cashier stamps the sales ticket "paid" and files a copy for future reference. The only record of COD sales is a copy of the sales ticket given to the cashier to hold until the cash is received from the delivery service.

Mail is opened by the secretary to the credit manager, and remittances are given to the credit manager for his review. The credit manager then places the remittances in a tray on the cashier's desk. At the daily deposit cutoff time, the cashier delivers the checks and cash on hand to the assistant credit manager, who also takes them to the bank. The assistant credit manager also posts remittances to the accounts receivable ledger cards and verifies the cash discount allowable.

You ascertain that the credit manager obtains approval from the executive office of Far Distributing Co., located in Chicago, to write off uncollectible accounts. You also learn that he has retained in his custody as of the end of the fiscal year some remittances that were received on various days during the last month.

Required:

a. From the narrative above, construct a systems flowchart for the cash receipts system of the Alaska Branch.

b. Describe the material internal control weaknesses under the procedures now in effect for handling cash collections and remittances.

c. Give procedures that you would recommend to strengthen internal control over cash collections and remittances.

(AICPA adapted)

C10–6 You have been asked by the board of trustees of a local church to review its accounting procedures. As a part of this review you have prepared the following comments relating to the collections made at weekly services and recordkeeping for members' pledges and contributions:

a. The church's board of trustees has delegated responsibility for financial management and audit of the financial records to the finance committee. This group prepares the annual budget and approves major disbursements but is not involved in collections or recordkeeping. No audit has been considered necessary in recent years because the same trusted employee has kept church records and served as financial secretary for fifteen years.

b. The collection at the weekly service is taken by a team of ushers. The head usher counts the collection in the church office following each service. He then places the collection and a notation of the amount counted in the church safe. Next morning the financial secretary opens the safe and recounts the collection. He withholds about $100 to meet cash expenditures during the coming week and deposits the remainder of the collection intact. In order to facilitate the deposit, members who contribute by check are asked to draw their checks to "cash."

c. At their request, a few members are furnished prenumbered predated envelopes in which to insert their weekly contributions. The head usher removes the cash from the envelopes to be counted with the loose cash included in the collection and discards the envelopes. No record is maintained of issuance or return of the envelopes, and the envelope system is not encouraged.

d. Each member is asked to prepare a contribution pledge card annually. The pledge is regarded as a moral commitment by the member to contribute a stated weekly amount. On the basis of the amounts shown on the pledge cards, the financial secretary furnishes a letter to members who request it to support the tax deductibility of their contributions.

Required:

a. Ben Grim, former CPA for the church, told you, "I never bothered to study and evaluate internal controls for the church since: (1) they are not a profit-making entity, and (2) I was a member of the church at the time and knew the procedures." Evaluate Grim's comments.

b. Describe the weaknesses and recommend improvements in procedures for:
   (1) Collections made at weekly services.
   (2) Recordkeeping for members' pledges and contributions.

Organize your answer sheets as follows:

Weakness	Recommended Improvement

(AICPA adapted)

C10–7 You have been engaged by Gibraltar Savings and Loan Association to audit its financial statements for the year ended December 31, 19X2. The CPA who audited last year's financial statements rendered an unqualified opinion.

In addition to servicing its own mortgage loans, the association acts as a mortgage-servicing agency for three life insurance companies. In this later activity, the association maintains mortgage records and services as the collection and escrow agent for the mortgagees (the insurance companies) who pay a fee to the association for these services.

Cash collections (all by mail) on the serviced mortgages are batched daily and entered in an EDP system through an input terminal located in the association's main office. The operator keys the proper mortgage number and enters the receipt information on the terminal keyboard. (This information is obtained from a remittance advice enclosed with the payment.) By this operation, magnetic master files are updated, the transaction data is stored on a random-access disk; once each month a hard-copy transcript of the account is printed out as a report to the mortgagee. Cash disbursements from the escrow accounts are keypunched on cards, merged monthly with the magnetic master file, also stored on disk, and printed out on the monthly hard-copy report. All disk-stored records are erased after the monthly report is printed. The remittance advices and disbursement authorization documents are filed by mortgage account number.

Required:

You would expect the association to have certain internal controls in effect in the EDP system with respect to input controls, processing controls, and output controls. What controls unique to the EDP system described above should be in effect? You may classify controls as:

a. Those controls pertaining to input of information.
b. All other types of computer controls.

(AICPA adapted)

C10–8 The customer billing and collection functions of the Nash-Robinson Company, a small paint manufacturer, are attended to by a receptionist, an accounts receivable clerk, and a cashier who also serves as a secretary. The company's paint products are sold to wholesalers and retail stores.

The following describes all the procedures performed by the employees of the Nash-Robinson Company pertaining to customer billings and collections:

a. The mail is opened by the receptionist, who gives the customers' purchase orders to the accounts receivable clerk. Fifteen to twenty orders are received each day. Under instructions to expedite the shipment of orders, the accounts-receivable clerk at once prepares a five-copy sales invoice form which is distributed as follows:

(1) Copy 1 is the customer billing copy and is held by the accounts-receivable clerk until notice of shipment is received.
(2) Copy 2 is the accounts-receivable department copy and is held for ultimate posting of the accounts-receivable records.
(3) Copies 3 and 4 are sent to the shipping department.
(4) Copy 5 is sent to the storeroom as authority for release of the goods to the shipping department.

b. After the paid order has been moved from the storeroom to the shipping department, the shipping department prepares the bills of lading, then labels the cartons. Sales invoice copy 4 is inserted in a carton as a packing slip. After the trucker has picked up the shipment, the customer's copy of the bill of lading and copy 3, on which are noted any undershipments, are returned to the accounts-receivable clerk. The company does not back-order in the event of undershipments; customers are expected to reorder the merchandise. The Nash-Robinson Company's copy of the bill of lading is filed by the shipping department.

c. When copy 3 and the customer's copy of the bill of lading are received by the accounts-receivable clerk, copies 1 and 2 are completed by numbering them and inserting quantities shipped, unit prices, extensions, discounts, and totals. The accounts receivable clerk then mails copy 1 and the copy of the bill of lading to the customer. Copies 2 and 3 are stapled together.

d. The individual accounts-receivable ledger cards are posted by the accounts-receivable clerk by a bookkeeping machine procedure whereby the sales register is prepared as a carbon copy of the postings. Postings are made from copy 2, which is then filed, along with staple-attached copy 3, in numerical order. Every month, the general ledger clerk summarizes the sales register for posting to the general ledger accounts.

e. Since the Nash-Robinson Company is short of cash, the deposit of receipts is also expedited. The receptionist turns over all mail receipts and related correspondence to the accounts-receivable clerk who examines the checks and determines that the accompanying vouchers or correspondence contain enough detail to permit posting of the accounts. The accounts-receivable clerk then endorses the checks and gives them to the cashier who prepares the daily deposit. No currency is received in the mail, and no paint is sold over the counter at the factory.

f. The accounts-receivable clerk uses the vouchers or correspondence that accompanied the checks to post the accounts-receivable ledger cards. The bookkeeping machine prepares a cash receipts register as a carbon copy of the postings. Monthly the general ledger clerk summarizes the cash receipts register for posting to the general ledger accounts. The accounts-receivable clerk also corresponds with customers about unauthorized deductions for discounts, freight or advertising allowances, returns, etc., and prepares the appropriate credit memos. Disputed items of large amount are turned over to the sales manager for settlement. Each month the accounts-receivable clerk prepares a trial balance of the open accounts receivable for the accounts-receivable listing.

Required:

a. Discuss the internal control weaknesses in the Nash-Robinson Company's procedures related to customer billings and remittances and the accounting for these transactions. In your discussion, in addition to identifying the weaknesses, explain what could happen as a result of each weakness.

b. For each weakness, list one substantive audit procedure for testing the significance of the potential error.

(AICPA adapted)

C10–9 The Mocik Pharmaceutical Company, a drug manufacturer, has the following system for billing and recording accounts receivable:

a. An incoming customer's purchase order is received in the order department by a clerk who prepares a prenumbered company sales order form in which is inserted the pertinent information — such as the customer's name and address, customer's account number, quantity and description of items ordered. After the sales order form has been prepared, the customer's purchase order is stapled to it.

b. The sales order form is then passed to the credit department for credit approval.

Rough approximations of the billing values of the orders are made in the credit department for those accounts on which credit limitations are imposed. After investigation, approval of credit is noted on the form.

c. Next, the sales order form is passed to the billing department, where a clerk types the customer's invoice on a billing machine that crossmultiplies the number of items and the unit price, then adds the automatically extended amounts for the total amount of the invoice. The billing clerk determines the unit prices for the items from a list of billing prices.

The billing machine has registers that automatically accumulate daily totals of customer account numbers and invoice amounts to provide "hash" totals and control amounts. These totals, which are inserted in a daily record book, serve as predetermined batch totals for verification of computer inputs.

The billing is done on prenumbered, continuous, carbon-interleaved forms having the following designations:

(1) "Customer's copy."

(2) "Sales department copy," for information purposes.

(3) "File copy."

(4) "Shipping department copy." This form serves as a shipping order. Bills of lading are also prepared as carbon copy byproducts of the invoicing procedure.

d. The shipping department copy of the invoice and the bills of lading are then sent to the shipping department. After the order has been shipped, copies of the bill of lading are returned to the billing department. The shipping department copy of the invoice is filed in the shipping department.

e. In the billing department one copy of the bill of lading is attached to the customer's copy of the invoice; both are mailed to the customer. The other copy of the bill of lading, together with the sales order form, is then stapled to the invoice file copy and filed in invoice numerical order.

f. A keypunch machine is connected to the billing machine so that punched cards are created during the preparation of the invoices. The punched cards then become the means by which the sales data are transmitted to a computer for preparation of the sales journal, subsidiary ledger, and perpetual inventory records.

The punched cards are fed to the computer in batches. One day's accumulation of cards comprises a batch. After the punched cards have been processed by the computer, they are placed in files and held for about two years.

Required:

a. Prepare a flowchart to document your understanding of the Mocik Company's system of internal controls over billing.

b. Identify (1) the internal control strengths and (2) the internal control weaknesses in the system.

c. For each internal control strength identified in **b** that you feel can be relied upon, describe a compliance test for that control.

d. For each internal control weakness identified in **b**, describe a substantive audit procedure that would need to be expanded in order to obtain satisfaction that account balances produced therefrom are fairly stated.

For parts **c** and **d**, organize your answer as follows:

Internal Control Strength	Description of Compliance Test	Internal Control Weakness	Description of Substantive Test

(AICPA adapted)

C10–10 You are auditing the accounts receivable account of Rob Roy Plastics, Inc. As part of that examination you mailed 280 positive accounts-receivable requests to confirm trade receivables directly with Rob Roy's customers. Several accounts receivable confirmations have been returned with the notation that "verification of vendors' statements is no longer possible because our data-processing system does not accumulate each vendor's invoices."

Required:

Tell what alternative auditing procedures could be used to audit these accounts receivable.

(AICPA adapted)

C10–11 Jerome Paper Company engaged you to review its internal control system. Jerome does not pre-list cash receipts before they are recorded and has other weaknesses in processing collections of trade receivables, the company's largest asset. In discussing the matter with the controller, you find he is chiefly interested in economy when he assigns duties to the 15 office personnel. He feels the main considerations are that the work should be done by people who are most familiar with it, capable of doing it, and available when it has to be done.

The controller says he has excellent control over trade receivables because receivables are pledged as security for a continually renewable bank loan and the bank sends out positive confirmation requests occasionally, based on a list of pledged receivables furnished by the company each week.

Required:

a. Explain how pre-listing of cash receipts strengthens internal control over cash.
b. Assume that an employee handles cash receipts from trade customers before they are recorded. List the duties that employee should not do to withhold from him the opportunity to conceal embezzlement of the receipts.

(AICPA adapted)

C10–12 Charting, Inc., a new audit client of yours, processes its sales and cash receipts documents in the following manner:

a. *Payment on account.* The mail is opened each morning by a mail clerk in the sales department. The mail clerk prepares a remittance advice (showing customer and amount paid) if one is not received. The checks and remittance advices are then forwarded to the sales department supervisor who reviews each check and forwards the checks and remittance advices to the accounting department supervisor.

The accounting department supervisor, who also functions as credit manager in approving new credit and all credit limits, reviews all checks for payments on past due accounts and then forwards the checks and remittance advices to the accounts-receivable clerk who arranges the advices in alphabetical order. The remittance advices are posted directly to the accounts-receivable ledger cards. The checks are endorsed by stamp and totaled. The total is posted to the cash receipts journal. The remittance advices are filed chronologically.

After receiving the cash from the previous day's cash sales, the accounts-receivable clerk prepares the daily deposit slip in triplicate. The third copy of the deposit slip is filed by date, and the second copy and the original accompany the bank deposit.

b. *Sales.* Salesclerks prepare sales invoices in triplicate. The original and second copy are presented to the cashier. The third copy is retained by the salesclerk in the sales book. When the sale is for cash, the customer pays the salesclerk who presents the money to the cashier with the invoice copies.

A credit sale is approved by the cashier from an approved credit list after the salesclerk prepares the three-part invoice. After receiving the cash or approving the invoice, the cashier validates the original copy of the sales invoice and gives it to the customer. At the end of each day the cashier recaps the sales and cash received and forwards the cash and the second copy of all sales invoices to the accounts-receivable clerk.

The accounts-receivable clerk balances the cash received with cash sales invoices and prepares a daily sales summary. The credit sales invoices are posted to the accounts-receivable ledger and then all invoices are sent to the inventory control clerk in the sales department for posting to the inventory control cards. After posting, the inventory control clerk files all invoices numerically. The accounts-receivable clerk posts the daily sales summary to the cash receipts journal and sales journal and files the sales summaries by date.

The cash from cash sales is combined with the cash received on account to comprise the daily bank deposit.

c. *Bank deposits.* The bank validates the deposit slip and returns the second copy to the accounting department where it is filed by date by the accounts-receivable clerk.

Monthly bank statements are reconciled promptly by the accounting department supervisor and filed by date.

Required:

a. Prepare a systems flowchart to assist in your understanding of the sales and cash receipts system of Charting, Inc.
b. On the basis of your understanding of the system, identify its potential material weaknesses.
c. For each identified weakness in the preceding requirement, presuming there are not mitigating controls, identify the substantive test(s) of transactions or account balances it would be necessary to expand in order to obtain assurance as to the fairness of their presentation.

(AICPA adapted)

C10–13 You are in charge of your second yearly examination of the financial statements of Toledo Equipment Corporation, a distributor of construction equipment. Toledo's equipment sales are either outright cash sales or a combination of a substantial cash payment and one or two 60- or 90-day nonrenewable interest-bearing notes for the balance. Title to the equipment passes to the customer when the initial cash payment is made. The notes, some of which are secured by the customer, are dated when the cash payment is made (the day the equipment is delivered). If the customer prefers to purchase the equipment under an installment payment plan, Toledo arranges for the customer to obtain such financing from a local bank.

You begin your field work to examine the December 31 financial statements on January 5, knowing that you must leave temporarily for another engagement on January 7 after outlining the audit program for your assistant. Before leaving, you inquire about the assistant's progress in the examination of notes receivable. Among other things, the assistant shows you a working paper listing the makers' names, the due dates, the interest rates, and amounts of 17 outstanding notes receivable totaling $100,000. The working paper contains the following notations:

a. Reviewed system of internal accounting control and found it to be satisfactory.
b. Total of $100,000 agrees with general ledger control account.
c. Traced listing of notes to sales journal.

You are informed by the assistant that positive confirmation will be requested of the amounts of all outstanding notes receivable and that no other audit work has been performed in the examination of notes receivable and interest arising from equipment sales. There were no outstanding accounts receivable for equipment sales at the end of the year.

Required:

a. List the audit objectives for the audit of notes receivable and briefly explain each.
b. List the additional audit procedures the assistant should apply in the audit of the account for notes receivable arising from equipment sales (Toledo has no other notes). No subsidiary ledger is maintained. (You may want to refer to the notes receivable working paper in the appendixes to the chapter.)
c. You ask your assistant to examine all notes receivable on hand before you leave. The assistant returns in 30 minutes from the office safe where the notes are kept and reports that notes on hand total only $75,000.

   List the possible explanations that you would expect from the client for the $25,000 difference. (For our purposes, eliminate fraud or misappropriation from your consideration.) Indicate beside each explanation the audit procedures you would apply to determine if each explanation is correct.

(AICPA adapted)

PROBLEMS

P10–1 Select the best answer for each of the following items relating to internal control within the revenue system.

a. A company policy should clearly indicate that defective merchandise returned by customers is to be delivered to the
   (1) Salesclerk.
   (2) Receiving clerk.
   (3) Inventory control clerk.
   (4) Accounts receivable clerk.

b. When scheduling the audit work to be performed on an engagement, the auditor should consider confirming accounts receivable balances at an interim date if
   (1) Subsequent collections are to be reviewed.
   (2) Internal control over receivables is good.
   (3) Negative confirmations are to be used.
   (4) There is a simultaneous examination of cash and accounts receivable.
c. Which of the following is an effective internal accounting control over accounts receivable?
   (1) Only persons who handle cash receipts should be responsible for the preparation of documents that reduce accounts receivable balances.
   (2) Responsibility for approval of the write-off of uncollectible accounts receivable should be assigned to the cashier.
   (3) Balances in the subsidiary accounts receivable ledger should be reconciled to the general ledger control account once a year, preferably at year end.
   (4) The billing function should be assigned to persons other than those responsible for maintaining accounts receivable subsidiary records.
d. Which of the following internal control procedures will *most* likely prevent the concealment of a cash shortage resulting from the improper write-off of a trade account receivable?
   (1) Write-offs must be approved by a responsible officer after review of credit department recommendations and supporting evidence.
   (2) Write-offs must be supported by an aging schedule showing that only receivables overdue several months have been written off.
   (3) Write-offs must be approved by the cashier who is in a position to know if the receivables have, in fact, been collected.
   (4) Write-offs must be authorized by company field sales employees who are in a position to determine the financial standing of the customers.
e. Which of the following is *not* a primary objective of the auditor in the examination of accounts receivable?
   (1) Determine the approximate realizable value.
   (2) Determine the adequacy of internal controls.
   (3) Establish validity of the receivables.
   (4) Determine the approximate time of collectibility of the receivables.
f. Which of the following would be the *best* protection for a company that wishes to prevent the "lapping" of trade accounts receivable?
   (1) Segregate duties so that the bookkeeper in charge of the general ledger has *no* access to incoming mail.
   (2) Segregate duties so that *no* employee has access to both checks from customers and currency from daily cash receipts.
   (3) Have customers send payments directly to the company's depository bank.
   (4) Request that customers' payment checks be made payable to the company and addressed to the treasurer.
g. An accountant examines a sample of copies of December and January sales invoices for the initials of the person who verified the quantitative data. This is an example of a
   (1) Compliance test.
   (2) Substantive test.
   (3) Cutoff test.
   (4) Statistical test.

h. To conceal defalcations involving receivables, the experienced bookkeeper would probably charge which of the following accounts?
   (1) Miscellaneous income.
   (2) Petty cash.
   (3) Miscellaneous expense.
   (4) Sales returns.

i. In order to safeguard the assets through proper internal control, accounts receivable that are written off are transferred to a(n)
   (1) Separate ledger.
   (2) Attorney for evidence in collection proceedings.
   (3) Tax deductions file.
   (4) Credit manager since customers may seek to reestablish credit by paying.

j. In the examination of which of the following general ledger accounts will tests of procedures be particularly appropriate?
   (1) Equipment.
   (2) Bonds payable.
   (3) Bank charges.
   (4) Sales.

(AICPA adapted)

P10–2 Select the best answer to each of the following items relating to the confirmation of receivables.

a. The auditor obtains corroborating evidential matter for accounts receivable by using positive or negative confirmation requests. Under which of the following circumstances might the negative form of the accounts receivable confirmation be useful?
   (1) A substantial number of accounts are in dispute.
   (2) Internal control over accounts receivable is ineffective.
   (3) Client records include a large number of relatively small balances.
   (4) The auditor believes that recipients of the requests are unlikely to give them consideration.

b. In determining validity of accounts receivable, which of the following would the auditor consider *most* reliable?
   (1) Documentary evidence that supports the accounts receivable balance.
   (2) Credits to accounts receivable from the cash receipts book after the close of business at year end.
   (3) Direct telephone communication between auditor and debtor.
   (4) Confirmation replies received directly from customers.

c. The confirmation of the client's trade accounts receivable is a means of obtaining evidential matter and is specifically considered to be a generally accepted auditing
   (1) Principle.
   (2) Standard.
   (3) Procedure.
   (4) Practice.

d. It is sometimes impracticable or impossible for an auditor to use normal accounts receivable confirmation procedures. In such situations the *best* alternative procedure the auditor might resort to would be

(1) Examining subsequent receipts of year-end accounts receivable.
(2) Reviewing accounts receivable aging schedules prepared at the balance sheet date and at a subsequent date.
(3) Requesting that management increase the allowance for uncollectible accounts by an amount equal to some percentage of the balance in those accounts that *cannot* be confirmed.
(4) Performing an overall analytic review of accounts receivable and sales on a year-to-year basis.

e. Confirmation of individual accounts receivable balances directly with debtors will, of itself, normally provide evidence concerning the
(1) Collectibility of the balances confirmed.
(2) Ownership of the balances confirmed.
(3) Validity of the balances confirmed.
(4) Internal control over balances confirmed.

f. Jacob Hirsch is engaged in the audit of a utility that supplies power to a residential community. All accounts receivable balances are small and internal control is effective. Customers are billed bi-monthly. In order to determine the validity of the accounts receivable balances at the balance sheet date, Hirsch would most likely
(1) Examine evidence of subsequent cash receipts instead of sending confirmation requests.
(2) Send positive confirmation requests.
(3) Send negative confirmation requests.
(4) Use statistical sampling instead of sending confirmation requests.

g. During the first part of the current fiscal year, the client company began dealing with certain customers on a consignment basis. Which of the following audit procedures is *least* likely to bring this new fact to the auditor's attention?
(1) Tracing of shipping documents to the sales journal.
(2) Test of cash receipts transactions.
(3) Confirmation of accounts receivable.
(4) Observation of physical inventory.

(AICPA adapted)

P10–3 Select the best answer to each of the following items relating to the verification of cutoff of sales.

a. A sales cutoff test of billings complements the verification of
(1) Sales returns.
(2) Cash.
(3) Accounts receivable.
(4) Sales allowances.

b. To determine that sales transactions have been recorded in the proper accounting period, the auditor performs a cutoff review. Which of the following *best* describes the overall approach used when performing a cutoff review?
(1) Ascertain that management has included in the representation letter a statement that transactions have been accounted for in the proper accounting period.
(2) Confirm year-end transactions with regular customers.
(3) Examine cash receipts in the subsequent period.
(4) Analyze transactions occurring within a few days before and after year end.

c. A CPA is engaged in the annual audit of a client for the year ended December 31, 19X1. The client took a complete physical inventory under the CPA's observation on December 15 and adjusted its inventory control account and detailed perpetual inventory records to agree with the physical inventory. The client considers a sale to be made in the period that goods are shipped. Listed below are four items taken from the CPA's sales cutoff test worksheet. Which item does *not* require an adjusting entry on the client's books?

	DATE (MONTH/DAY)		
	Shipped	**Recorded as Sale**	**Credited to Inventory Control**
(1)	12/10	12/19	12/12
(2)	12/14	12/16	12/16
(3)	12/31	1/2	12/31
(4)	1/2	12/31	12/31

d. Which of the following might be detected by an auditor's cutoff review and examination of sales journal entries for several days prior to and subsequent to the balance sheet date?
(1) Lapping year-end accounts receivable.
(2) Inflating sales for the year.
(3) Kiting bank balances.
(4) Misappropriating merchandise.

e. An auditor is reviewing sales cutoff as of March 31, 19X0. All sales are shipped FOB destination, and the company records sales three days after shipment. The auditor notes the following items:

		(Amounts in Thousands)	
Date Shipped	**Month Recorded**	**Selling Price**	**Cost**
March 28	March	$192	$200
March 29	March	44	40
March 30	April	77	81
April 2	March	208	220
April 5	April	92	84

If the client records the required adjustment, the net effect on income in thousands of dollars for the period ended March 31, 19X0 is:
(1) An increase of 12.
(2) An increase of 8.
(3) A decrease of 12.
(4) A decrease of 8.

(AICPA adapted)

P10–4 Select the best answer to each of the following items relating to the valuation of receivables.

a. The audit working papers often include a client-prepared, aged trial balance of

accounts receivable as of the balance sheet date. This aging is *best* used by the auditor to
(1) Evaluate internal control over credit sales.
(2) Test the accuracy of recorded charge sales.
(3) Estimate credit losses.
(4) Verify the validity of the recorded receivables.

b. Once a CPA has determined that accounts receivable have increased due to slow collections in a "tight money" environment, the CPA would be likely to
(1) Increase the balance in the allowance for bad debts account.
(2) Review the going concern ramifications.
(3) Review the credit and collection policy.
(4) Expand tests of collectibility.

c. In determining the adequacy of the allowance for uncollectible accounts, the *least* reliance should be placed on which of the following?
(1) The credit manager's opinion.
(2) An aging schedule of past due accounts.
(3) Collection experience of the client's collection agency.
(4) Ratios calculated showing the past relationship of the valuation allowance to net credit sales.

d. Some firms that dispose of only a small part of their total output by consignment shipments fail to make any distinction between consignment shipments and regular sales. Which of the following would suggest that goods have been shipped on consignment?
(1) Numerous shipments of small quantities.
(2) Numerous shipments of large quantities and few returns.
(3) Large debits to accounts receivable and small periodic credits.
(4) Large debits to accounts receivable and large periodic credits.

(AICPA adapted)

P10–5 Select the best answer to each of the following items.

a. Madison Corporation has a few large accounts receivable that total $1,000,000. Nassau Corporation has a great number of small accounts receivable that also total $1,000,000. The importance of an error in any one account is, therefore, greater for Madison than for Nassau. This is an example of the auditor's concept of
(1) Materiality.
(2) Comparative analysis.
(3) Reasonable assurance.
(4) Relative risk.

b. A CPA auditing an electric utility wishes to determine whether all customers are being billed. The CPA's best direction of test is from the
(1) Meter department records to the billing (sales) register.
(2) Billing (sales) register to the meter department records.
(3) Accounts-receivable ledger to the billing (sales) register.
(4) Billing (sales) register to the accounts-receivable ledger.

c. Which of the following audit procedures is most effective in testing credit sales for understatement?
(1) Age accounts receivable.
(2) Confirm accounts receivable.

(3) Trace sample of initial sales slips through summaries to recorded general ledger sales.
(4) Trace sample of recorded sales, from general ledger to initial sales slip.

d. An auditor is testing sales transactions. One step is to trace a sample of debit entries from the accounts-receivable subsidiary ledger back to the supporting sales invoices. What would the auditor intend to establish by this step?
(1) All sales have been recorded.
(2) Debit entries in the accounts-receivable subsidiary ledger are properly supported by sales invoices.
(3) All sales invoices have been properly posted to customer accounts.
(4) Sales invoices represent bona fide sales.

e. An auditor is testing sales transactions. One step is to trace a sample of debit entries from the accounts-receivable subsidiary ledger back to the supporting sales invoices. What would the auditor intend to establish by this step?
(1) Sales invoices represent bona fide sales.
(2) All sales have been recorded.
(3) All sales invoices have been properly posted to customer accounts.
(4) Debit entries in the accounts-receivable subsidiary ledger are properly supported by sales invoices.

f. A corporation is holding securities as collateral for an outstanding account receivable. During the course of the audit engagement the CPA should
(1) Verify that title to the securities rests with the corporation.
(2) Ascertain that the amount recorded in the investment account is equal to the fair market value of the securities at the date of receipt.
(3) Examine the securities and ascertain their value.
(4) Refer to independent sources to determine that recorded dividend income is proper.

(AICPA adapted)

P10–6 Items **a** through **i** below are questions excerpted from a typical internal control questionnaire for the purpose of evaluating internal accounting controls over processing of customer orders and shipping. As explained in the text, a "yes" response to such a question indicates a potential strength in the system while a "no" response indicates a potential weakness.

a. Are all credit sales approved by the credit department prior to shipment?
b. Is the credit department independent of the sales department?
c. Are sales prices based on approved price lists?
d. Are prenumbered sales invoice forms used?
e. Are all sales invoice forms numerically controlled?
f. Are prenumbered shipping orders used to authorize shipments to customers?
g. Are shipping orders used to authorize shipments to customers?
h. Are prenumbered bills of lading prepared in the shipping department prior to release of goods to the common carrier?
i. Are bills of lading numerically controlled?

Required:

For each question above, list

a. The error or irregularity that item was designed to detect.

b. The effect that the absence of the control would have on the financial statements.
c. The compliance test that would be necessary in order to ascertain whether the control were actually being implemented if the answer to the internal control question were "yes." When sampling of documents is involved, indicate the data file from which a sample would be chosen and the appropriate audit procedure (e.g., vouching, tracing, recalculation, etc.). You may want to refer to Figure 10–12.
d. The substantive test (see Figure 10–14) that would have to be extended, if any, if that control were missing or if the client demonstrated a low level of compliance.

Organize your answer according to the following format. The first question has been answered as an example.

Item	Error or Irregularity	Effect on Financial Statements	Compliance Test	Substantive Test
(a)	Invalid transaction	Excessive losses from bad debts	Vouch from sales invoice files to credit files	Inspect credit records for past due accounts

P10–7 Items **a** through **k** below are questions excerpted from a typical internal control questionnaire for the purpose of evaluating internal accounting controls over the billing, sales returns and allowances, and cash receipts systems. As explained in the text, a "yes" response to such a question indicates a potential strength in the system while a "no" response indicates a potential weakness.

a. Are shipping orders, bills of lading, and invoices properly matched before sales are recorded in the accounting records?
b. Are sales invoices properly checked for mathematical and billing accuracy?
c. Are sales data reported independently to the general ledger bookkeeper and the accounts-receivable bookkeeper?
d. Are sales returns, sales credits, and other credits properly supported by prenumbered documentation forms?
e. Are all sales returns, sales credits, and other credits approved by a responsible officer?
f. Is the mail opened by someone other than the cashier or bookkeeper?
g. Are daily remittance lists prepared by the persons opening the mail?
h. Is the daily remittance list reconciled with the daily deposit of cash?
i. Are the daily remittance lists and deposit slips compared to the cash debits and accounts-receivable credit entries regularly?
j. Are pre-lists of receipts on account reported independently to the general ledger bookkeeper and the accounts-receivable bookkeeper?
k. Is the subsidiary accounts-receivable ledger reconciled regularly with the accounts-receivable control account balance?

Required:

For each question above, list:

a. The error or irregularity which that control attribute was designed to detect.
b. The effect that the absence of the control would have on the financial statements.

c. The compliance test that would be necessary to ascertain whether the control was actually being implemented if the answer to the internal control question were "yes." When sampling of documents is involved, indicate the data file from which a sample would be selected and the audit procedure (e.g., vouching, tracing, recalculation, etc.) most appropriate for the sample (see Figures 10–12 and 10–13).

d. The substantive test (see Figure 10–14) that would have to be extended, if any, if that control were missing or if tests indicated inadequate compliance.

Organize your answer in the same format as that shown above for Problem 10–6.

P10–8 Items a through **i** below list procedures typically performed by the auditor as part of the audit of the revenue and accounts receivable system.

a. Trace a sample of sales orders to the sales invoice file.
b. Reconcile the total amount of accounts receivable per the general ledger account with the total of the accounts-receivable subsidiary ledger.
c. Vouch totals from the daily deposit slips to daily remittance lists.
d. Recompute extensions and footings on a sample of sales invoices.
e. Trace a sample of sales invoices or cash register tapes to entries in the sales journal.
f. Inspect a sample of sales invoices for evidence of credit approval.
g. Trace entries in sales journal to corresponding entries in accounts-receivable subsidiary ledger (individual customer accounts).
h. Vouch entries in general ledger for write-offs of accounts receivable to credit memoranda and write-off memoranda.
i. Confirm individual accounts receivable directly with customers.

Required:

For each item above, state

a. Whether the test is a compliance test, a substantive test, or possibly both (a dual-purpose test).
b. The audit objective(s) being fulfilled by the test: statement presentation, transactions validity, ownership, periodicity, valuation, or existence. *Note:* A particular procedure may satisfy one or more audit objectives simultaneously.

CHAPTER

11

THE COST OF SALES SYSTEM AND RELATED ACCOUNTS

In this chapter we turn our attention to the procedures followed in gathering audit evidence about the system and various account balances associated with inventory, purchases, cost of sales, and cash disbursements. As with revenues and cash receipts, the best way to deal with the inventory, cost of sales, and cash disbursements system and related account balances is to consider them as a group because the elements within them are directly related to each other.

In auditing this subsystem, we follow the same general format established in Chapter 10. That means that our discussion will include the following topics:

1. Identification of the audit objectives associated with the system.
2. Verification of transaction validity for purchases, cost of sales, and cash disbursements.
3. Development of procedures for performing the substantive tests relating to inventories and cost of sales.
4. Development of procedures for performing the substantive tests relating to trade payables.
5. Use of the computer in this portion of the audit.

We also include, as appendixes to this chapter, illustrated working papers for the cost of sales system. The accounts included in this subsystem are inventories of raw materials, work in process, and finished goods; cost of goods sold; purchase discounts; purchases returns and allowances; accounts payable; and credits to the cash account associated with cash purchases and payments on account.

AUDIT OBJECTIVES

Figure 11–1 presents diagrammatically the typical flow of transactions through the cost of sales system. In auditing the purchases, cost of sales, and cash disbursements system and related balances, the auditor must be concerned with verification of these aspects: transaction validity, existence, ownership, cutoff, valuation, and appropriate statement presentation. The primary asset accounts associated with the cost of sales system are inventories. The primary liability accounts are trade accounts payable or vouchers payable. Inventories are often the largest and most important of current assets on the

Raw Materials Inventory

Beginning bal. xxx xxx (1)	xxx (2)
Ending bal. xxx	

Accounts Payable

xxx (7)	Beginning bal. xxx xxx (1)
	Ending bal. xxx

Work-in-Process Inventory

Beginning bal. xxx xxx (2) xxx (3) xxx (4)	xxx (5)
Ending bal. xxx	

Cash

	xxx (7)

Finished Goods Inventory

Beginning bal. xxx xxx (5)	xxx (6)
Ending bal. xxx	

Direct Labor

	xxx (3)

Cost of Goods Sold

xxx (6)	

Manufacturing Overhead

	xxx (4)

(1) Raw material purchases; (2) Raw material used in production; (3) Direct labor used in production; (4) Manufacturing overhead allocation; (5) Transfer of completed goods; (6) Cost of sales; (7) Payment of trade payables.

FIGURE 11–1. Flow of Transactions Through the Cost of Sales System

balance sheets of manufacturing or commercial business enterprises. As such, they are vulnerable to errors of many types that may well have the potential for being material. In addition, because of the many different (and sometimes unique) methods used to account for inventories, the audit of these areas can be quite complex. Errors in inventories often have pervasive effects because they may affect income statement as well as balance sheet accounts. It is important, therefore, that the auditor become thoroughly familiar with controls in the cost accounting, cost of sales, and cash disbursements subsystems before performing substantive tests of inventory, cost of sales, and trade payables balances.

Just as with receivables, the auditor is likely to be inclined to believe that, if an intentional misstatement in inventories were to occur, the client would be more likely to ***overstate inventories*** than to understate them. Consequently, many of the procedures used to meet the audit objectives for inventory balances are designed to verify recorded amounts. However, when we shift our attention from inventories to trade liabilities, the greatest risk is that a client will ***understate liabilities.*** Therefore the procedures used to accomplish the audit objectives for payables change from those designed to verify recorded amounts to those designed to detect unrecorded amounts. This is illustrated more specifically as we discuss those procedures.

Verification of Transaction Validity

As we observed earlier, if the auditor could be certain that all transactions affecting balances in the cost of sales system have been recorded, classified and summarized in the accounting records so as to minimize the risk of material misstatement, he or she could, on the basis of that evidence, conclude that the account balances in the system would be fairly presented. *Evaluation of the system of accounting controls* within which the various purchases, cost of sales, and cash disbursements transactions have been recorded is an important element of the auditing process directed toward verifying transaction validity. This procedure has two phases:

1. Review and evaluation of accounting system to find what controls the client says are in operation.
2. Compliance tests to see that the stated control procedures are actually being implemented.

Other Audit Objectives

In establishing the other audit objectives that must be met in gathering audit evidence for the purchases, cost of sales, and cash disbursements system and related accounts, we begin by identifying what could cause those account balances to contain amounts materially different from the actual amount of inventory, the actual amounts owed in the form of payables, and the actual outflows of cash associated with the system, respectively. For example, one possible source of error is the inclusion of inventory items that do not really exist. The audit objective in proving or disproving that point can be characterized as the verification of ***existence***. The auditor's concern in that phase of the verification process is directed primarily toward being sure that the inventory account is not overstated to include nonexistent inventory. Because of the transactional relationships that exist between inventory and cost of sales balances, overstatement errors in inventory produce understatement errors in cost of sales. By way of contrast, the verification of existence for payables is primarily concerned with seeing that payables are not understated — that is, that there are no payables unrecorded. Understatement errors in payables often cause understatement errors in cost of sales or expense accounts related to the particular payables.

Possession is ordinarily considered to be evidence of ***ownership***. However, some attention must be given to the inspection of underlying documents and to management representations in validating this audit objective.

The auditor is also concerned with verifying the ***valuations*** of inventory, payables, and cost of sales. The going concern convention logically requires two things: (1) that inventory and cost of sales be valued at cost, and (2) that payables be valued at the amount at which they could be settled in the normal course of business operations as of the balance sheet date. Although cost is theoretically the most acceptable basis for valuing inventory, the ***principle of conservatism*** has caused accountants to also accept the *lower of cost or market value* as a generally accepted basis of valuation for inventories.

Increases and decreases in inventories, payables, and cash outflows resulting from purchases or payments on account that occur near the end or beginning of a fiscal period are susceptible to being recorded in the wrong period. Such errors constitute violations of the matching concept. Because of the possibility of such errors, the auditor is concerned with the audit objective of verifying the ***cutoff*** of inventory, purchases, cost of sales, and payments on account transactions near the end of the period.

Inventories, payables, and cost of sales must also be ***properly presented*** *in the financial statements.* For example, the concept of full disclosure requires that the financial statements include information about the valuation methods for inventories. The statements should also disclose information relating to the pledging of inventory and to collateral pledged as security for payables. Accounts or vouchers payable and notes payable must be appropriately classified as current or noncurrent and an appropriate distinction must be made between trade and nontrade payables.

VERIFICATION OF TRANSACTION VALIDITY

The auditor depends primarily on the reliability of the system of internal control in judging whether inventory, cost of sales, and cash disbursements transactions have been appropriately recorded, classified, and accumulated in the accounting records. If those data are processed manually or through a computer used primarily as a sophisticated bookkeeping machine, the reliability of the system of internal control can be evaluated by verifying the extent to which it includes the desirable internal control characteristics (listed in Figure 5–1). This check on reliability has, as we saw, three phases: (1) a preliminary review and evaluation phase, based on an analysis of the organization chart and procedures manual or on an inquiry of appropriate client personnel; (2) a detailed review and evaluation phase, consisting of documentation of controls upon which the auditor wishes to rely; and (3) compliance tests designed to test whether prescribed controls are actually being followed.

In auditing a computerized system, the auditor will be concerned with the internal organization of the electronic data-processing department and the existence and documentation of appropriate application controls for processing inventory, cost of sales, and cash disbursements systems data. These are the controls discussed at some length in Chapter 6.

Review and Evaluation of the Control System

The purpose of the preliminary and detailed evaluation stages of internal control and the procedures followed in achieving that goal for the cost of sales system are:

1. To identify controls that can be relied on in determining the nature, timing, and extent of substantive tests.
2. To pinpoint areas of material weakness that must be communicated to the client.

Just as we have discussed earlier, it is important for the independent auditor to remember that the primary objective of the financial statement audit is to issue an opinion about the fairness of presentation of the financial statements. All audit procedures, including the study and evaluation of internal control, should be performed with this objective in mind. Although many controls go into each accounting system, *not all controls affect financial statement balances in a material way.* As the auditor studies internal control, therefore, he or she need give attention only to those controls which are material; that is, those controls which, if missing, could result in material misstatement of account balances.

Material controls can be identified most readily by considering the *exchange transactions* and related documents which produce the inventory, cost of sales, and cash balances in the financial statements. Figure 11–2 lists the major exchange transactions resulting in purchases of inventory, sales of inventory, and payment of trade accounts payable. For each of these types of exchanges, the documents generated at the point of exchange (boundary documents) are listed. For example, the boundary document representing an exchange transaction between the client and another entity for the purchase of inventories is the vendor's invoice. For sales, the boundary document is the sales invoice. For payment of trade payables, it is the

Exchange Transaction	Boundary Document	Supporting Document(s)
Purchase of inventory	Vendor's invoice	Purchase requisition Purchase order Receiving report
Sale of inventory	Sales invoice	Shipping documents
Payment of trade accounts payable	Check Vendor's invoice	Accounts payable voucher Purchase requisition Purchase order Receiving report

FIGURE 11–2. Exchange Transactions and Documents

client's prenumbered check. A series of supporting documents provide evidence that the exchange transactions were subjected to proper approvals and controls to ensure their validity and accuracy; these are shown for each boundary document.

In the purchases of goods and services, supporting documents for each vendor's invoice should include a purchase requisition, a purchase order, and a receiving report. These documents should be sequentially numbered and controlled. The purchasing department is primarily responsible for the acquisition of goods by the issuance of purchase orders. Poor internal control over these documents can open the way for improper acquisitions or possible collusion of the purchasing agent with parties outside the firm. Prenumbering of purchase orders and other controls over purchase orders also help prevent unauthorized purchases. Overall, the auditor's primary responsibility in reviewing the purchasing cycle is to evaluate the reliability of information generated by the purchasing process. This involves seeing that goods recognized as purchases have been received, counted, and checked against purchase orders and invoices.

Accounting control functions that should be performed in a system of inventory purchases, cost of sales, and cash disbursements can be classified into three categories. Although the categories are the same as those discussed in Chapter 10 for revenues and cash receipts, the components of each of these categories are different.

1. ***Exchange functions*** require specific controls (see Figure 11–3) designed to prevent the recognition and payment of incorrect or fictitious payables. These include controls over:
   a. Processing purchase orders;
   b. Receipt of goods and services;
   c. Recording acquisitions of goods and services;
   d. Payments on account;
   e. Storage, processing, and recordkeeping of inventory;
   f. Shipment of merchandise.
2. ***Processing functions*** require controls (see Figure 11–4) designed to establish accountability and provide reliable financial data. These include controls over:
   a. Recording acquisitions of goods and services;
   b. Recording payments on account;
   c. Recording purchase returns and allowances;
   d. Recording the transfer and processing of raw materials.
3. ***Safeguard functions*** require controls (see Figure 11–5) to ensure proper custody of assets and records within the inventory and cost of sales systems.

Figures 11–3, 11–4, and 11–5 show examples of some of the errors and irregularities that can occur if controls over exchange, processing, and safeguard functions are not performed adequately. After observing the problems created by such errors and irregularities, we shall look at control attributes that would prevent, detect, or correct them. While this does not represent a complete list of possible errors or irregularities or of results they could bring, it does illustrate the thought process the auditor should follow in the study and evaluation of controls. A system properly performing these functions must include all the internal control characteristics discussed in Chapter 5.

Examining the Functions. The auditor should examine the functions to determine whether the control characteristics are being appropriately implemented in handling

FIGURE 11–3. Exchange Functions and Specific Controls

Functions	Possible Errors or Irregularities	Results of Undetected Errors	Control Attributes to Prevent, Detect, or Correct Errors or Irregularities
Processing purchase orders: Requisitions of goods, services	Invalid transactions: Ordering material not needed; duplicate purchase	Oversupplies or short supplies; work inefficiencies	Require the use of Economic Order Quantity (EOQ) calculations for all significant orders purchased Require prenumbered written requisitions from stores department personnel for all goods ordered Receiving department should accept merchandise only if a purchase order or other approval has been issued by the purchasing department Systematic reporting of product changes which affect raw materials needs
Ordering of goods or services	Invalid transactions: Incomplete records of goods ordered	Understatement of accounts payable and cost of sales	Require prenumbered written purchase orders for all goods ordered
	Ordering at uneconomical prices	Inefficient usage of funds; possible illegal kickbacks for employees from suppliers	Require all purchases to be made by competitive bids in order to get the most economical prices Require approval of prices by responsible officer
Receipt of goods and services	Invalid transactions: Paying for goods not received Unauthorized delivery of goods to other employee-controlled locations	Overstatement of accounts payable	Require prenumbered receiving reports for all purchases approved Separation of purchasing and receiving functions Require employee purchases to be made through regular purchasing channels
	Unrecorded transactions: Transactions recorded in the wrong period	Understatement of accounts payable and cost of sales	Require follow-up on receiving reports, purchase orders, or vendor invoices for which there is no support

	Invalid transactions: Receiving inferior quality or inaccurate quantity of goods	Loss of production time; reorders of merchandise	Require receiving personnel to count all quantities of goods received; send one copy of receiving report to purchasing department Require purchasing department to review all major purchases for quality and quantity, then recalculate footing and extensions on vendor invoices and other supporting papers
Payments on account	Improperly valued transactions: Inaccuracies in recording amounts payable, and payments thereon	Overstatement or understatement of payables	Require verification of recorded amounts, such as account distributions and extended amounts on vouchers, etc.
		Discrepancies between subsidiary ledger total and control accounts	Use of control totals in posting routines, periodic reconciliation of general and subsidiary ledger totals
	Invalid transactions: Misappropriation of cash payments by employees	Misstatements in cash or accounts payable balances	Separation of accounting, check preparation, and check signing functions Require checks to be signed by responsible official with no recordkeeping or preparation responsibilities; dual signatures on checks; check protector devices, etc. Require checks to be mailed under supervision of the signer without being returned to preparer Checks should be sequentially numbered and should be accounted for by person preparing bank reconciliation Check preparation should be based on properly authorized and approved vouchers that are mutilated (stamped paid) when check is signed

FIGURE 11–3 (continued)

Functions	Possible Errors or Irregularities	Results of Undetected Errors	Control Attributes to Prevent, Detect, or Correct Errors or Irregularities
Payments on account (*continued*)	Invalid transactions: Resubmission of supporting documents for payment a second time	Overstatement of accounts payable	Require cancellation of all supporting papers (invoices, purchase orders, receiving reports, requisitions) as checks are signed
Storage processing and recordkeeping of inventory	Improperly valued transactions: Incomplete or inaccurate records of movement of goods	Discrepancies between control accounts and subsidiary ledgers	Require documentation of receipts (receiving reports) and issues (bills of materials, issue slips)
	Thefts of merchandise	Discrepancies between physical counts and amounts per books	
	Ineffective control of inventory on consignment out or in:	Discrepancies in records; overstatement or understatement of inventory, cost of sales	Require documentation of inventory on consignment out or consignment in
	Ineffective control of inventory in public warehouses		Require proper controls over inventory stored in public warehouses
	Inaccurate records of obsolete, overstocked, slow-moving inventory	Overstatement of inventory	Require periodic review by responsible officials for obsolete, overstocked, or slow-moving inventory
Shipment of merchandise	See Figure 10–1		

FIGURE 11–4. Processing Functions and Related Controls

Functions	Possible Errors or Irregularities	Results of Undetected Errors	Control Attributes to Prevent, Detect, or Correct Errors or Irregularities
Recording acquisitions of goods and services	Improperly valued, classified, summarized transactions: Transactions recorded in the wrong period Inaccurate or incomplete accounting for goods requisitioned, ordered, or received	Understatement of accounts payable and cost of sales	Require prenumbered purchase requisitions, purchase orders, and receiving reports; require accounting department to receive copies of all of these before purchase is recorded or voucher is prepared Require all purchases to be routed through accounts payable and not directly through cash disbursements Require checking of all vendors' invoices for mathematical accuracy, quantity, prices, and terms Require reconciliation of invoices with supporting documents Require use of accounting manuals and employee approval for determining distribution of invoice charge to general ledger Require double-check of distribution of charges on vouchers payable Require periodic balancing of accounts payable subsidiary ledger or open voucher register items with the general ledger control account Require follow-up on receiving report purchase orders or vendors' invoices for which there is no support
	Erroneous transactions: Recording purchases of goods and services not requisitioned, purchased, or received	Overstatement of accounts payable; paying for goods not received	Separation of accounting function from purchasing and receiving Require proper documentation for all approved purchases: purchase

FIGURE 11–4 (continued)

Functions	Possible Errors or Irregularities	Results of Undetected Errors	Control Attributes to Prevent, Detect, or Correct Errors or Irregularities
			requisitions, purchase orders, receiving reports, vendor invoices Copy of purchase orders going to receiving department should omit quantities to force receiving clerk to count goods
	Unrecorded or improperly valued transactions: Unrecorded or inaccurate recording of goods purchased	Overstatement or understatement of accounts payable, inventories	Require verification of recorded amounts, such as account distributions and extended amounts on vouchers, etc. Use of control totals in posting routines, periodic reconciliation of general and subsidiary ledger totals
Recording payments on account	Erroneous transactions: Inaccurate record of payment	Misstatements of cash, accounts payable	Require use of prenumbered checks Require prenumbered vouchers to support each check written Require all disbursements to be made by check Require checking of the numerical sequence of cancelled checks during the reconciliation process
	Invalid or unrecorded transactions: Incomplete record of payments	Misstatements of cash, accounts payable	Require voided checks to be mutilated and retained for inspection Require monthly reconciliation of bank accounts by person independent of cash custody or recordkeeping functions Require that checks be examined and compared to cash disbursements records in the bank reconciliation process

			Require check signee to examine all supporting documents Require effective accounting control over interbank transfers to prevent or detect kiting
Recording purchase returns and allowances	Erroneous or invalid transactions: Failure to record items returned Failure to accurately record items returned	Misstatements of book inventories and accounts payable	Require approval by responsible official of purchase returns and allowances Require purchase returns to be cleared through proper receiving department procedures Require the accounts payable department to be notified of all goods returned
Recording the transfers and processing of raw materials	Invalid transactions or Improperly valued, classified, summarized transactions: Failure to record items purchased or used Inaccurate recording of items purchased or used	Misstatements of inventories, cost of sales	Require separate inventory accounting procedures, including documentation of materials received (receiving reports) and used (bill of materials and issue slip) Require posting to perpetual records from prenumbered receiving reports and raw materials issue slips Require accounting of numerical sequence of documents by inventory Require periodic spot checks of inventory quantities and comparison with perpetual records

Functions	Possible Errors or Irregularities	Results of Undetected Errors	Control Attributes to Prevent, Detect, or Correct Errors or Irregularities
Custody of inventory	Mishandling of physical inventories; waste and pilferage	Deterioration of inventory	Require storage facilities that protect goods from physical deterioration
		Wastage and pilferage of inventory	Require designated inventory custodians who are held responsible for physical control over various categories of inventories
		Errors in physical counts	Require periodic counts by teams with one person counting and one person recording counts; persons counting should be independent of inventory custodians Require tagging or other identification system that adequately identifies goods counted Require spot checks by supervisory personnel of goods counted
		Discrepancies between physical counts and records	Require perpetual records of inventories Require reconciliation or adjustment of perpetual inventories to physical counts

Note: Errors and irregularities in custody of inventory can lead to any one of the general types of errors and irregularities associated with erroneous, invalid, unrecorded, improperly valued, or improperly summarized transactions (see Chapter 5).

FIGURE 11–5. Safeguard Functions and Related Controls

inventory, cost of sales, and cash disbursements system transactions. In doing that, he or she may use an internal control questionnaire such as the one shown in Figure 11–6 or flowcharts similar to the ones shown in Figures 11–7, 11–8, and 11–9. These are developed from the organization chart, the procedures manual, and/or inquiry of client personnel. As explained earlier, "yes" answers to questions in the internal control questionnaire indicate that potential strengths exist in the system. If the auditor decides to rely on these potential strengths, compliance tests must be performed on the control procedures before the auditor decides the extent to which related substantive tests of transactions and balances may be limited. On the other hand, inquiries answered with a "no" indicate potential weaknesses in the system. Once the auditor has determined that these weaknesses are material (i.e., that they can cause material financial misstatements), she or he must undertake related substantive tests of transactions and balances; these tests may have to be more extensive than if adequate controls had been prescribed and found to be working as planned.

Checking Separation of Responsibilities. The appropriate separation of responsibilities should be checked by making inquiries, observing procedures, and examining policy and procedures manuals. This characteristic requires that many of the functions be assigned to different employees to protect resources and provide reliable financial data:

- In processing purchase orders and the vouchers authorizing the payment of payables, the persons preparing and approving the vouchers for payment should have no other responsibilities relating to cash payments.
- The person authorized to sign checks should have no responsibilities relating to the preparation of vouchers and should have no access to cash receipts or the cash records.
- The authority to borrow should be separated from the cash-handling transactions. Normally, this authority would be vested in the treasurer or a special committee of the client's board of directors.
- In connection with the handling and storage of inventory, the stores ledger clerk should not have access to the storeroom or to the handling of inventory items.
- The various authorization and approval functions associated with payments of accounts should be divided among a number of different persons.
- Persons having a responsibility for the purchase of goods or services should have no access to cash.

As we examine the internal control questionnaire in Figure 11–6 and the flowcharts in Figures 11–7, 11–8, and 11–9, we can observe that they are designed to disclose failures to meet the separation of responsibilities criteria we have just described.

Identifying Specific Responsibilities with Specific Persons. It is also important that the responsibilities associated with all elements of the systems should be identified with specific persons within the organization. More specifically, this requirement entails the following:

- The person signing checks in payment of payables should be held accountable for verifying the validity and completeness of all documents originated in support of payment requests.
- The receiving clerk should be held responsible for checking both the quantity and quality of goods received from vendors.

Processing of Purchase Orders	Yes	No	Comments
1. Are purchases of goods and services so authorized that persons who approve and execute transactions can determine whether the authorization was issued by persons acting within the scope of their authority?	____	____	
2. Are prenumbered purchase orders prepared and approved for conformity with general or specific authorization as to vendor, goods or services ordered, prices, and other elements?	____	____	
3. Are all major purchases made on the basis of competitive bids or some other scheme to ensure that the company obtains the most economical price?	____	____	
Receipt of Goods and Services			
4. Are prenumbered receiving reports prepared for all receipts of goods or services?	____	____	
5. Are vendor invoices and purchase orders compared with receiving records for quantity, prices, amounts back-ordered, etc.?	____	____	
Recording Acquisitions of Goods and Services			
6. Is the preparation of initial purchase records performed by persons who do not also:			
a. Prepare supporting documents required for payment?	____	____	
b. Sign checks?	____	____	
c. Handle signed checks?	____	____	
d. Handle cash receipts after initial recording?	____	____	
7. Is proper documentation (purchase orders, receiving reports, purchase requisitions, vendor invoices) required before any purchase is recorded?	____	____	
8. Are supporting records (purchase orders, receiving reports, etc.) compared to vendor invoice for prices, quantities, terms, etc.?	____	____	
Payments on Account			
9. Are subsidiary records maintained of trade payables by persons who do not also:			
a. Prepare supporting documents required for payment of vouchers?	____	____	
b. Issue checks?	____	____	
c. Handle cash receipts after initial recording?	____	____	
10. Are recorded disbursements matched individually or adequately tested with initial credits in the subsidiary records, and are the balances of individual vendor accounts computed or adequately tested by persons who do not also:			
a. Prepare supporting documents required for payment of vendors?	____	____	
b. Issue checks?	____	____	
c. Handle signed checks?	____	____	
d. Handle cash receipts after initial recording?	____	____	

FIGURE 11–6. Selected Internal Control Questionnaire Items

Storage Processing and Recordkeeping of Inventory	Yes	No	Comments
11. Are inventories physically safeguarded (e.g., by using fenced compounds and similar areas with restricted access)?	____	____	
12. Are the following duties regarding inventories separate?			
a. Receiving?	____	____	
b. Handling and storing?	____	____	
c. Shipping?	____	____	
d. Perpetual recordkeeping?	____	____	
13. Is the following documentation required for entries to perpetual records?			
a. Materials issues (issue slip)?	____	____	
b. Materials purchases (receiving reports)?	____	____	
14. Is some form of perpetual record keeping employed over:			
a. Quantities?	____	____	
b. Unit prices?	____	____	
15. Are perpetual records of inventories reconciled periodically to physical counts?	____	____	
16. Are perpetual records of inventories reconciled periodically to general ledger accounts?	____	____	
17. As to counting of inventory quantities:			
a. Are all participants given proper written instructions and adequately supervised during the making of counts?	____	____	
b. Are there procedures ensuring that all goods are counted and that none is double-counted?	____	____	
c. Are there procedures to ensure an adequate cutoff of			
(i) Sales?	____	____	
(ii) Purchases?	____	____	
(iii) Movement of inventories between areas?	____	____	
d. Are differences between counts and records of inventory quantities investigated and recorded immediately upon discovery?	____	____	
e. Is work-in-process inventory inspected and adequate effort made to ascertain stage of completion?	____	____	
f. Are slow-moving, obsolete, or damaged inventories appropriately identified?	____	____	
g. Are goods on consignment-in or consignment-out appropriately identified?	____	____	
h. Are there procedures for preventing alteration, omission, or duplication of inventory counts?	____	____	

FIGURE 11–6 (continued)

- The stores keeper, defined as "the person in charge of the storeroom," should be held responsible for all stock delivered to the storage area. This means that he or she should check the quantities of goods received into the storeroom against receiving reports and release goods only on the basis of properly executed and approved requisitions.
- The shipping clerk should be held responsible for releasing shipments only in accordance with shipping authorization procedures.

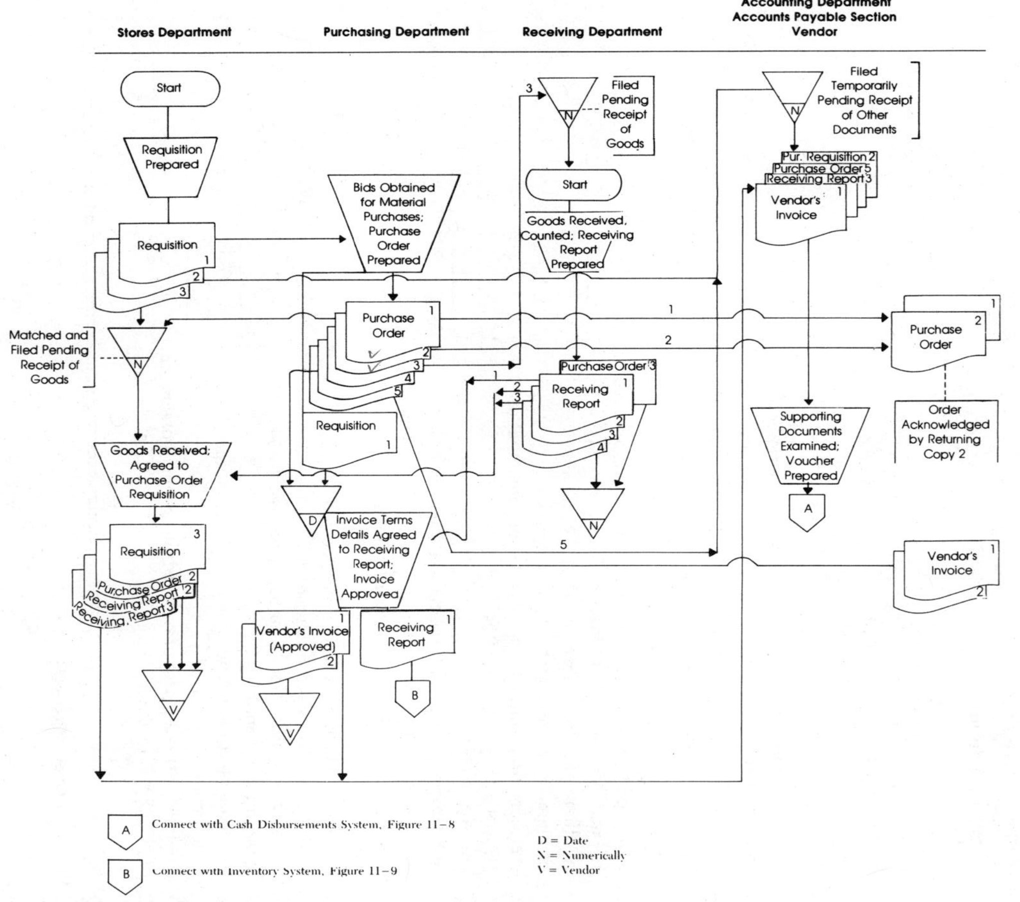

FIGURE 11–7. Inventory Purchasing, Receiving, and Vouchers Preparation

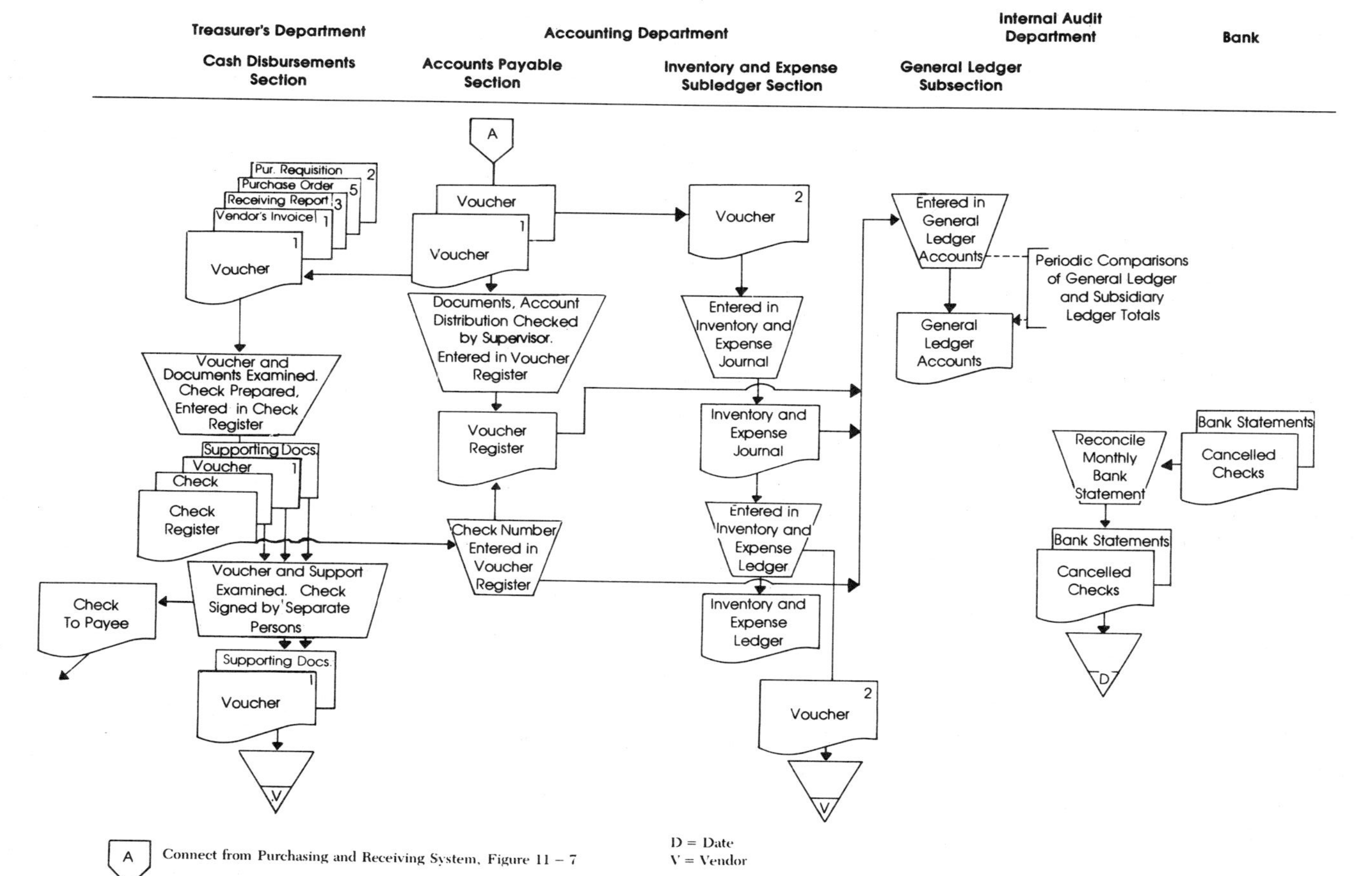

Treasurer's Department
Cash Disbursements Section
Accounting Department
Accounts Payable Section
Inventory and Expense Subledger Section
General Ledger Subsection
Internal Audit Department
Bank
A
Pur. Requisition 2
Purchase Order 5
Receiving Report 3
Vendor's Invoice 1
Voucher 1
Voucher
Voucher 1
Voucher 2
Voucher and Documents Examined. Check Prepared, Entered in Check Register
Documents, Account Distribution Checked by Supervisor. Entered in Voucher Register
Entered in Inventory and Expense Journal
Entered in General Ledger Accounts
General Ledger Accounts
Periodic Comparisons of General Ledger and Subsidiary Ledger Totals
Supporting Docs.
Voucher 1
Check
Check Register
Voucher Register
Inventory and Expense Journal
Reconcile Monthly Bank Statement
Bank Statements
Cancelled Checks
Check Number Entered in Voucher Register
Entered in Inventory and Expense Ledger
Voucher and Support Examined. Check Signed by Separate Persons
Check To Payee
Inventory and Expense Ledger
Supporting Docs.
Voucher 1
V
Voucher 2
V
D
A Connect from Purchasing and Receiving System, Figure 11 – 7
D = Date
V = Vendor

FIGURE 11–8. Cash Disbursements System

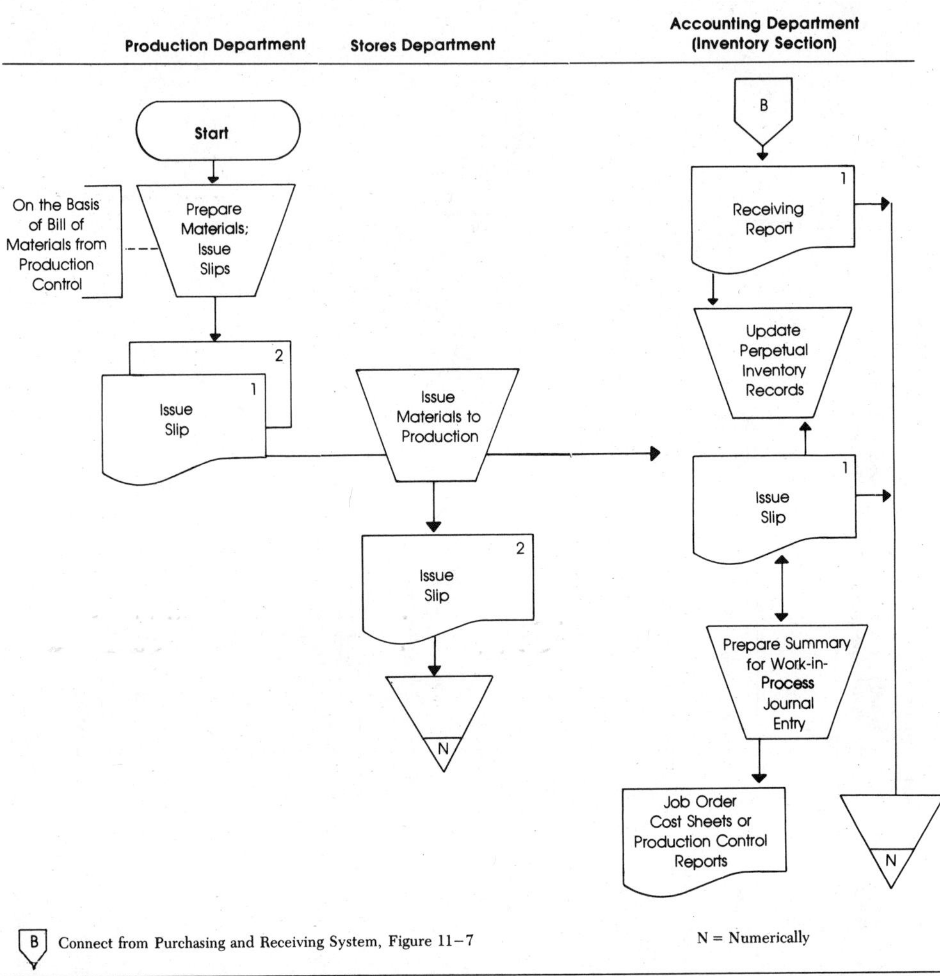

FIGURE 11–9. Inventory Accounting System

Checking Documentation. All activities within the system should be documented by adequate systems of records, forms, and authorizations. The documents typically associated with the cost of sales system include the following:

- Purchase requisitions.
- Purchase orders.
- Receiving reports.
- Vendor invoices.
- Voucher forms originated to initiate payment on account.
- Checks.
- Materials issued requisitions.
- Job order sheets or cost of productions reports.
- Perpetual inventory records.
- Bills of materials.

As we analyze the flowcharts in Figures 11–7 through 11–9, we notice that the system depicted therein contains all the documents just listed. The acquisitions of goods and services (including purchase returns and allowances) associated with the cost of sales system are typically recorded in a voucher register, an inventory and expense journal, and a check register or cash payments journal.

The documents and records in the preceding list can provide an adequate system of records if they are appropriately organized and processed. An adequate system of control requires that

- A properly approved ***purchase requisition*** be originated as the first document in support of materials acquisitions.
- ***Purchase orders,*** originated in response to properly approved purchase requisitions, be sequentially numbered and a procedure should be established to account for the use of each of the purchase order forms. Those forms should require a validating signature by the purchasing agent before it becomes an authentic order for goods or services.
- ***Debit memos,*** issued in connection with purchase returns and allowances, be sequentially numbered and controlled in the same manner as are purchase orders. Appropriate authorization and approval procedures should be performed and documented in connection with the issuance of each debit memo.
- ***Sequentially numbered vouchers*** be prepared and properly approved in support of all cash disbursements. Procedures should be established to account for all voucher forms. When a ***check*** is issued against a properly approved voucher, the voucher should be cancelled by being stamped "paid" and should be initialed by the person signing the check in payment of it.
- A ***voucher register*** be maintained to record all approved vouchers; payments should be matched against those vouchers to allow an appropriate determination of the balance in the vouchers payable control account.
- Properly controlled, sequentially numbered ***receiving report forms*** be used to acknowledge receipt of goods from vendors. One copy of the receiving report should go to the stores keeper while another should go to the accounting department to be matched against the vendor's invoice in support of the voucher to be originated for payment of the obligation.
- ***Job order cost sheets*** or ***cost of production reports*** be used to account for goods in the process of being manufactured.
- Subsidiary ***perpetual inventory records*** be maintained for raw materials and finished goods.

Determining Qualifications of Personnel. The qualified personnel characteristic requires that special attention be given to the skills of persons assigned to the various functional responsibilities within the systems. Thus, the company must follow hiring and promotion practices designed to assign people to tasks they are capable of performing:

- The recordkeeping functions should be performed by people having appropriate recordkeeping skills.
- Cash disbursements should be handled by persons showing evidence of trustworthiness.
- Persons receiving and handling inventory should have an adequate knowledge of the special characteristics associated with the goods being handled.
- The purchasing agent should be properly trained for his or her responsibilities in the acquisitions of goods.

Ensuring the Physical Safety of Assets and Records. All assets and records associated with the cost of sales system should be appropriately protected from physical loss or alteration. This requires that all payments be made either directly or indirectly by use of prenumbered checks. Also, the firm should provide appropriate protection for any mechanical check-signing equipment. The inventory storage areas should be fitted to the goods stored in them, so as to minimize deterioration; and storage facilities should be properly organized, with good housekeeping practices followed in the stores area. Finally, the vouchers payable and inventory records should be stored so as to protect them from damage or alteration when they are not being used.

Checking Controls Over Computer Operations. When the cost of sales system records are computerized, the auditor must evaluate the general controls over EDP operations and the application controls relating to the processing and accumulation of cost of sales system data. The auditor should expect to find the same types of input, processing, output, and file control procedures applied to these data as are listed in Chapter 10 for the revenue system data. Again, an application controls questionnaire would be used in evaluating those controls for the cost of sales system.

Testing the System for Compliance

All the procedures described in the preceding pages will have been identified, reviewed, and evaluated during the preliminary and detailed review phases of the audit by reference to the organization chart and procedures manual and by inquiry of client personnel. Controls upon which the auditor wishes to rely will have been documented by internal control questionnaires, system flowcharts, and narrative descriptions.

If the auditor is satisfied that the prescribed controls can reasonably be expected to prevent or detect serious errors or irregularities, he or she must then determine the extent of employee compliance with those controls. The control system should contain, as one of its elements, operating policies designed to promote compliance with the established practices. This should include adequate orientation and training of employees as well as periodic checks by management or the internal auditors to see that employees both understand and comply with their assigned responsibilities.

Even though the control system includes compliance-oriented operating practices, the independent auditor must still perform tests on controls to be relied upon to ascertain whether the controls are working as planned. Some control provisions such as the segregation of duties will not necessarily be supported by documentary evidence. These controls must be tested chiefly by inquiry and by observing the functions being performed. Other controls that leave documentary evidence of having been performed are testable by sampling. The sampling methodology used for the inventory, cost of sales, and cash disbursements systems is the same as that described in Chapter 10 for sales receivables and cash receipts.

Figure 11–10 illustrates selected audit program procedures for testing transactions of the inventory, cost of sales, and cash disbursements system. Figure 11–11 is presented to show how selected tests of the cost of sales and cash disbursements system transactions are performed. Both of these figures are designed to test the various control attributes categorized as boundary and processing controls in Figures 11–3 and 11–4. Notice that the procedures listed in Figure 11–11 are designed to test the existence of the control attributes that would prevent, detect, or correct possible errors and irregularities (Figures 11–3 through 11–5). Notice also that samples in

Figure 11–11 are drawn from data files located in each major department shown in the system flowcharts (Figures 11–7 through 11–9). In each case where sampling is appropriate, the auditor selects from the evidence-gathering techniques — inspection, vouching, tracing, reconciling, etc. — the one that best meets the objective of ascertaining compliance with the appropriate internal control attribute. A study of Figure 11–11 will reveal that where vouching and tracing procedures are involved, both vouching and tracing are performed for each important data population.

The auditor should note both the frequency and causes of deviations from each internal control attribute. High frequency of deviation in critical control attributes may cause the auditor to conclude that the system is unreliable. That in turn would cause an extension of the substantive tests of balances affected by those controls. Conversely, low frequency of deviation for critical control attributes may lead the auditor to rely heavily on the internal accounting control system, so that perhaps he or she will perform only limited substantive tests of account balances.

SUBSTANTIVE TESTS OF INVENTORY AND COST OF SALES ACCOUNT BALANCES

Substantive tests are designed to determine whether the financial statement accounts associated with the inventory, cost of sales, and cash disbursements systems are stated in accordance with GAAP. As we apply the various substantive testing procedures to the verification of inventories and cost of sales, we will be primarily concerned with errors that tend to overstate inventories or understate cost of sales. As we seek to verify the trade payables balances, we will be focusing attention primarily on determining whether all the client's obligations are included in the account balances. Working papers that illustrate the audit procedures that we will discuss appear in Appendixes 11–A through 11–K.

Interrelationship of Inventory and Cost of Sales Balances

The cost of sales figure can be approximated by use of the following familiar four-element equation (See Figure 11–1):

> Beginning-of-period finished goods inventory + additions in the form of cost of goods manufactured – end-of-period inventory of finished goods = cost of sales.

Cost of goods manufactured can also be approximated by using the following equation (See Figure 11–1):

> Beginning-of-period work-in-process inventory + additions in the form of materials, direct labor, and manufacturing overhead – end-of-period work-in-process inventory = cost of goods manufactured.

The cost of raw materials used in the manufacturing process in turn can be approximated with the following equation:

> Beginning-of-period materials inventory + purchases of materials – end-of-period inventory = materials issued into process.

1. a. Inspect a series of purchase requisitions and account for proper numerical sequence.
   Select a sample from the purchase requisition file.
   b. Trace the sample through the system to its posting in the general ledger, and match with purchase orders, receiving reports, and vendor invoices.
   c. Inspect for proper approval signatures of store's supervisors.

2. a. Account for the numerical sequence of a series of purchase orders.
   Select a sample of purchase orders.
   b. Vouch quantities to purchase requisitions from stores department.
   c. Inspect for approval signatures of purchasing agent.

3. a. Account for the numerical sequence of a series of receiving reports.
   Select a sample of receiving reports.
   b. Vouch to purchase orders and requisitions, agreeing quantities received and placed in stores to quantities requisitioned and ordered. Trace to vendor invoices and to posting to vouchers payable. For sales returns and allowances, ascertain proper recording.
   c. Trace quantities to postings in perpetual inventory records.

4. Select a sample of vendor invoices from the vouchers payable file.
   a. Inspect for approval signatures of purchasing agent.
   b. Recalculate extensions, footings.
   c. Trace prices to vendor price lists or catalogs. Compare quantities with receiving reports, purchase orders.

5. Select a sample of entries to the purchases and expense journal.
   a. Vouch to purchase requisitions, purchase orders, receiving reports, vendor invoices.
   b. Trace postings to inventory and accounts payable ledgers, if available.
   c. Reconcile summary postings to general ledger accounts for inventories, accounts payable, and expenses.

Note: Audit procedures in this program are numbered to correspond with the procedures outlined in Figure 11–11.

FIGURE 11–10. Selected Audit Program Procedures for Transactions Testing

As you can see from these equations, *the various inventory accounts are the fences* at both ends of the fiscal period defining the cost of sales figure. Therefore, in ascertaining the reasonableness of cost of sales data, it is important to verify the various inventory balances.

We have already observed the audit objectives (things to be proven) in connection with the verification of the inventory accounts. The relationships between these objectives and the auditing procedures followed in verifying them are shown in Figure 11–12. The auditor begins the inventory substantive testing phase of the audit by ***reconciling*** the amounts shown in the balance sheet for various inventory items with the underlying accounting records. The first step in this reconciliation process involves vouching the statement amounts back to the respective ledger account balances. Those balances should in turn be reconciled with the subsidiary ledgers (perpetual inventory records) for merchandise inventory, raw materials, work in process, or finished goods. This procedure is illustrated in Appendix 11–A (working paper F), the lead schedule for inventories.

6. Select a sample of vouchers payable.
   a. Inspect for approval signatures indicating verification of amounts, account distribution, etc. Recalculate extensions, footings.
   b. Vouch to supporting documents.
   c. Trace entries in voucher register.
   d. For paid vouchers, agree check numbers to voucher register and check register. Examine documents for cancellation.

7. Select a sample of entries from the voucher register.
   a. Vouch entries for paid vouchers to check register and cancelled checks.
   b. Foot voucher register for one or more periods and trace postings to general ledger and subsidiary ledgers, if appropriate.

8. Select a sample of entries to the check register.
   a. Vouch to cancelled checks, paid vouchers, and related supporting documents.
   b. Select a sample of paid vouchers. Inspect the documents included in the vouchers for proper cancellation.
   c. Foot and cross-foot the check register for one or more periods and trace postings to general ledger.

9. Select a sample of sales invoices. Relate to finished goods credits.

10. Select a sample of postings to perpetual inventory records. Vouch debit postings to receiving reports; vouch credit postings to materials issue slips.

11. Select a series of postings to inventory, payables, cost of sales, and cash disbursements. Vouch to appropriate journals.

12. Select a series of postings to subsidiary ledger accounts. Vouch to appropriate journals for inventory, purchases, cash disbursements, etc.

FIGURE 11–10 (continued)

In a merchandising firm, selected debits to the perpetual inventory records can also be traced to purchase invoices. Receiving reports may also be tested to verify the accuracy of additions to inventory. The totals in the voucher register, inventory and expense journal, purchases and returns and allowances journal, and cash disbursements journal should also be ***recomputed*** and be balanced in the reconciliation process. The pertinent items should be traced to their respective ledger accounts. Some of these procedures were covered during the discussion of tests of compliance (as illustrated in steps 10 and 11 of Figure 11–11). These are examples of *dual-purpose tests*, designed to verify both compliance with internal controls and details of balances.

Verification of Existence

The verification of existence of inventories involves gathering evidence regarding the quantity of inventory on hand as of the balance sheet date. Although it is the client, not the auditor, who is responsible for determining inventory quantities, usually by physical count, the auditor is responsible for ascertaining that client counts were made effectively and that they accurately reflect quantities on hand as of the balance sheet

Attributes of Interest	Data Field (Population)	Sample Size[a]	Audit Procedure	From	To
1. Purchase requisitions are:					
a. Numerically controlled	Purchase requisition file	Judgmental	Inspect num. sequence		N/A
b. Followed up with proper procedures	Purchase requisition file	240	Trace	Purchase requisition file	Purchase orders, receiving reports, vendor invoices, vouchers payable, posting
c. Approved by supervisory personnel	Purchase requisition file	240	Inspect for approval signature or initials		N/A
2. Purchase orders are:					
a. Numerically controlled	Purchase order file	Judgmental	Inspect num. sequence		N/A
b. Supported by purchase requisitions, competitive bids	Purchase order file	240	Vouch	Purchase order file	Purchase requisition file, vendor files
c. Approved properly	Purchase order file	240	Inspect for approval signatures or initials		N/A
3. Receiving reports are:					
a. Numerically controlled	Receiving report file	Judgmental	Inspect num. sequence		N/A
b. Matched with other papers supporting purchases as to quantity, quality of goods	Receiving report file	240	Vouch	Receiving report file	Purchase orders, requisition file, vendor files
c. Posted accurately to perpetual inventory records	Receiving report file	240	Agree quantities; check for verification of goods received in saleable condition; trace	Receiving report file	Entries in perpetual inventory records
4. Vendor invoices are:					
a. Reviewed and approved by purchasing agent	Vendor invoice, vouchers payable files	240	Inspect for purchasing agent signature		N/A
b. Recalculated and prices checked	Vendor invoice, vouchers payable files	240	Recalculate, vouch	Vendor invoice	Recent vendor catalog price list
c. Compared to receiving reports for quantity	Vendor invoice, vouchers payable files	240	Compare quantities	Invoice	Receiving report
5. Purchase and expense journal entries are:					
a. Supported by documentation	Purchase and expense journal entries	240	Vouch	Purchase and expense journal entries	Purchase requisitions, purchase orders, receiving reports, vendor invoices
b. Entered properly in subsidiary ledgers	Purchase and expense journal entries	240	Trace	Purchase and expense journal entries	Accounts payable and inventory ledgers

c. Entered properly in general ledger	Purchase and expense journal entries	Judgmental	Reconcile	Purchase and expense journal entries	General ledger accounts
6. Vouchers payable are:					
a. Checked by accounts payable personnel for proper amounts, account distributions	Vouchers payable file (unpaid and paid)	240	Recalculate extensions, verify accuracy of account distribution		N/A
b. Supported by adequate documentation	Vouchers payable file (unpaid and paid)	240	Vouch	Vouchers	Supporting documents
c. Posted accurately to accounts when prepared	Vouchers payable file (unpaid and paid)	240	Trace	Vouchers	Entries in voucher register, general ledger, subsidiary ledgers
d. Recorded properly as paid	Paid vouchers	240	Agree check numbers	Voucher register	Check register
7. Payments on account are:					
a. All supported by prenumbered checks	Voucher register entries	240	Vouch	Voucher register	Check register and cancelled checks
b. Supported by adequate documentation	Check register	240	Vouch	Check register	Vouchers, invoices, receiving reports, purchase orders, purchase requisitions
c. Accompanied by cancellation of supporting documents	Paid vouchers (see 6(d))	240 (see 6(d))	Inspect for cancellation of documents		
d. Posted to proper accounts in general and subsidiary ledgers	Check register (see 7(b))	240 (see 7(b))	Trace	Check register	Postings to general ledger accounts
8. Shipment of merchandise and cost of sales entries	See Figure 10–12 steps 2 and 3				
9. Perpetual inventory records are updated correctly for purchases and issues	Perpetual inventory records	240	Vouch	Perpetual inventory records	Receiving reports and materials issue slips
10. General ledger entries are supported by monthly journal totals	General ledger account postings (inventory, cost of sales, cash disbursements)	Judgmental	Reconcile	General ledger	Appropriate journals
11. Subsidiary ledger postings agree with entries in journals	Subsidiary ledger account postings	Judgmental	Reconcile	Subsidiary ledger	Appropriate journals

[a] Sample sizes in these examples were selected using the attribute sampling methodology discussed in Chapter 8. The following parameters were prespecified for applicable cases, for simplicity: Desired confidence = 95%; expected exception proportion = 2.5%; desired upper precision limit = 5%. In practice, each sample size must differ, depending on the precision and reliability the auditor is seeking.

FIGURE 11–11. Transactions Testing Methodology: Inventories, Cost of Sales, Cash Disbursements

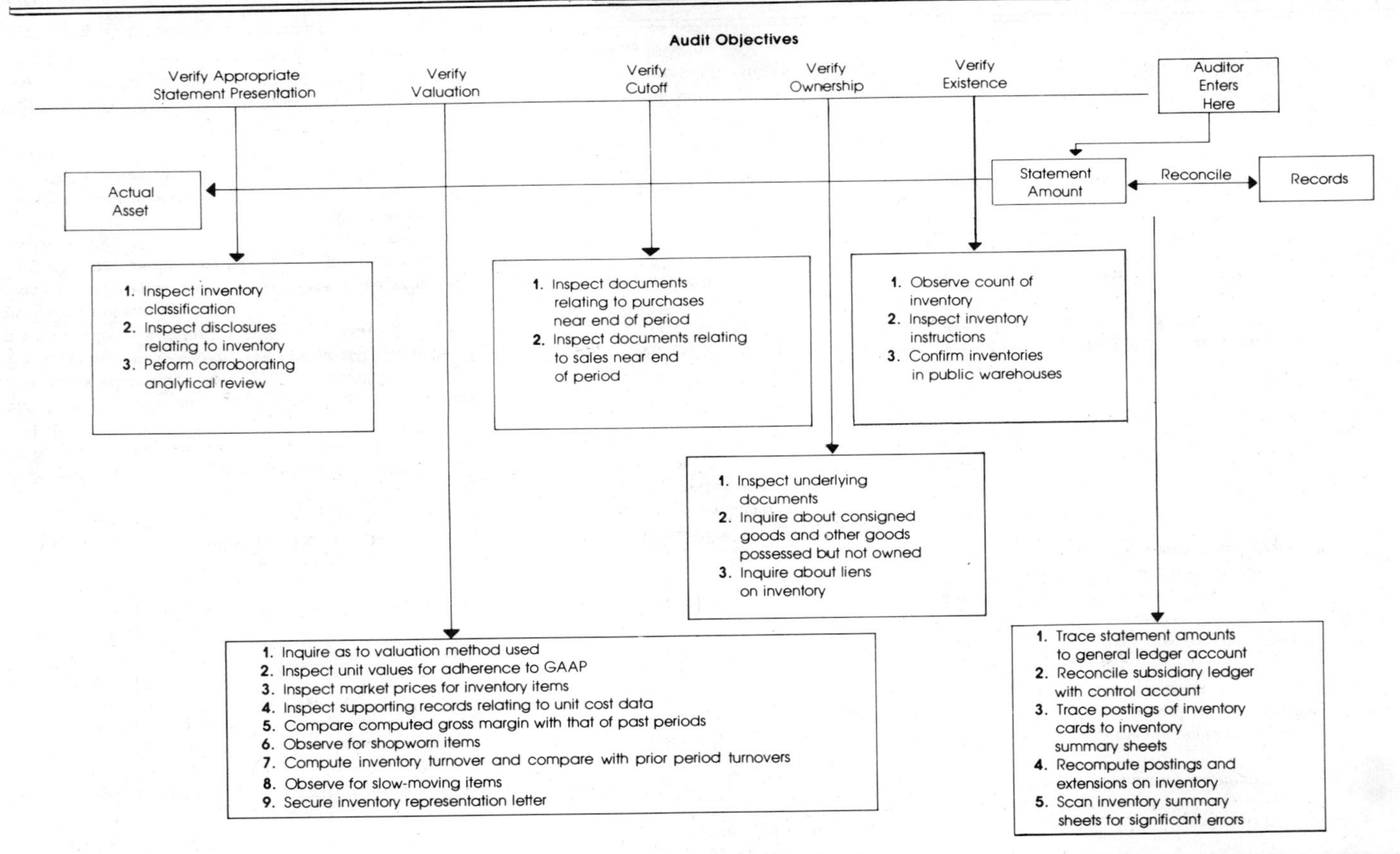

FIGURE 11–12. Flowchart for Substantive Tests of Inventory

date. The predominant audit procedure used to satisfy the existence objective is ***observation of client inventories.***

Observation. It is important to remember that, whenever inventories exist and are material to the financial statements taken as a whole, the auditor must generally be present to observe and to take some test counts when the client physically counts the inventory in order to justify the issuance of an unqualified audit opinion. The auditor usually traces the details of test counts to the final inventory schedule to be sure the items observed are included in that schedule. The extent of observation and test counting necessarily varies with the design and quality of the client's system of internal accounting control, as well as external circumstances facing the client. Figure 11–13 summarizes some of these variables and the resultant procedures necessary to verify the existence of inventories. Appendix 11–B illustrates the inventory observation memorandum that is typically required in order to explain the results of the inventory observation procedure. Appendix 11–C illustrates the inventory observation questionnaire that often serves as a checklist to make sure that counts were properly taken by the client. It also may serve as the basis for writing the observation memorandum.

Observation of inventory ordinarily begins with an inspection of the client's physical inventory instructions. In making this inspection, the auditor should be alert for weaknesses in those instructions that could allow particular elements of the inventory to be counted twice, or possibly omitted during the inventory-taking process. One of the procedures the auditor would expect to find incorporated in the instructions to prevent such errors is the use of *prenumbered inventory tags* with detachable segments. The instructions should include a provision requiring that all inventory tags be accounted for both at the point of issuance to the inventory counting teams and when the detachable segments are returned and listed on the inventory summary sheets.

The auditor should observe the client's inventory-taking process for the purpose of determining adherence to the inventory instructions and for evaluating the competency of the inventory teams. He or she should then *test count* certain items and *reconcile* those counts with the amounts shown on the inventory summary sheets. This has the effect of also verifying the clerical accuracy of transferring amounts from individual inventory tags to the inventory summary sheets. The physical count of inventory should be compared with the perpetual inventory. If the physical count is higher than the perpetual inventory, the auditor should be concerned with the possibility that credit memos may not have been prepared for items returned by customers. A variance in the opposite direction could be caused by unrecorded cost of sales or thefts of inventories. Test counts of raw materials and finished goods inventories are illustrated in Appendixes 11–D and 11–E.

Some clients may maintain such excellent controls over perpetual inventories that they do not take physical counts of all goods. Instead they may take only periodic rotational spot checks of quantities at selected storage locations at interim dates. In such cases, the auditor should be on hand to observe the interim counts and take such test counts as he or she deems necessary.

In other cases, the client may estimate year-end inventories by means of statistical sampling, as illustrated in Chapter 9. In such cases, the auditor should always, among

Situation	Audit Procedure to Verify Existence
Inventories determined periodically by physical count	Observation imperative: extensive test counts
Perpetual records kept, adjusted periodically for physical counts	Observation imperative: test counts may be limited if client internal controls are good
Extremely good client internal control rotational counts made at interim periods or client uses statistical sampling method to estimate year-end inventories	Perform limited observation procedures at interim dates when counts are made and ascertain validity of sampling plan if that method of estimation is used
Impossible or impracticable for auditor to observe year-end counts because not engaged until after client's fiscal year end	Perform alternative procedures; however, must still make such test counts as deemed necessary
Client requests auditor not to observe inventories	Qualify or disclaim audit opinion and state reason
Goods stored in public warehouses; amount not material to financial statements	Confirm amounts with warehouseman
Goods stored in public warehouses; amount material to financial statements	Confirmation and supplemental procedures (including test counts)
First year of audit, so auditor unable to obtain satisfaction with respect to opening inventories	Perform alternative procedures; if not possible, disclaim an opinion on the income statement, retained earnings statement, and statement of changes in financial position along with unqualified opinion on balance sheet

FIGURE 11–13. Circumstances Affecting Inventory Audit Procedures to Verify Existence

other procedures, ascertain the validity of the statistical sampling plan and the representativeness of the sample used to estimate the inventory balance.

Alternative Procedures. In some situations, it may be impossible or impracticable for the auditor to observe and test count inventories at the balance sheet date. This may be the case, for example, when the auditor has not been engaged until after the balance sheet date. In these situations, if the client has maintained proper perpetual records, the auditor may still be able to verify the existence of year-end inventories by the use of alternative procedures. These procedures are performed as soon as possible after the balance sheet date and include the following:

1. Review of client inventory instructions.
2. Inquiry of the client as to how counts were made.
3. Inspection of physical inventory records, noting that the proper procedures were performed and adjustments were made where necessary.
4. Test counting of selected items, then tracing the movement of inventories back through the perpetual records by use of issue slips and receiving reports, then reconciling the resultant calculations with amounts shown on the perpetual records as of the balance sheet date.

You should notice that alternative procedures usually require more audit effort than ordinary observation of the inventory-taking process, and that they still require such test counts as the auditor deems necessary to verify goods on hand as of the balance sheet date. Furthermore, the longer the time span between the balance sheet date and the date the tests counts are actually made, the more cumbersome and therefore costly these procedures become. When the auditor concludes that performing such procedures is too costly to justify them, a scope-qualified audit report is appropriate.

There may also be circumstances in which the client specifically requests the auditor not to observe the counts of inventories. Such client-imposed scope restrictions on the audit are usually sufficient to preclude the expression of an unqualified opinion, especially when inventories are material. In most cases, the auditor should evaluate the client's reasoning carefully, and issue either a scope-qualified audit report or a disclaimer of opinion, depending on the materiality of inventories to the financial statements taken as a whole.

Working papers have been provided in the appendixes of this chapter to illustrate inventory observation questionnaires and memoranda that are written as a part of a typical inventory observation. In addition, inventory test count sheets are illustrated, showing auditor test counts vouched to client final inventory listings. All these procedures are performed to ascertain that inventory exists and that it is being accounted for properly.

When *inventories are held in public warehouses and are not material* to the financial statements, the physical observation requirement does not apply. Instead, the auditor is expected to confirm with the independent custodians the amounts of such inventory items. This procedure, however, cannot be substituted for the observation of inventories *held in company-operated warehouses located away from the client's main office* because of the lack of independence of the warehouse operator. In those situations the auditor must either visit the warehouses or engage a public accounting firm in that locality to perform the observation procedure. Additionally, when goods stored in independent warehouses are material to the financial statements, the auditor should perform supplemental procedures on the inventory, which include such test counts as the auditor deems necessary.

If the auditor is engaged in an *initial audit* for a client, and inventories have not been observed in previous years, the auditor may not be able to obtain satisfaction with regard to opening inventory quantities. Since opening inventories affect the income statement and statement of changes in financial position, the auditor may issue a disclaimer of opinion for those statements while expressing an unqualified opinion on the end-of-period balance sheet, for which inventory quantities have been verified by observation. However, if the client has maintained perpetual inventory records with appropriate controls, the auditor may still be able to express an opinion on all statements.

Valuation

The verification of inventory valuation generally begins when the auditor *investigates the valuation method* used by the client. The auditor must then determine whether that method produces, within the limits of materiality, a valuation that is in accordance either with one of the generally accepted cost flow assumptions or with the lower of cost or market valuation procedures. The second method (valuation at the lower of cost or market value) is the more conservative method and is therefore generally preferred by accountants.

Inspection and Vouching. Having ascertained that the valuation method in use is in accordance with GAAP, the auditor will then, on a test basis, *inspect the values assigned* to various inventory items to determine whether the valuation method ostensibly being used by the client has been followed. The costs assigned to inventory should be the invoice cost less cash discounts taken. Discounts taken can be verified by comparing on a test basis cash disbursements with their respective purchase invoices. The auditor verifies that proper costing has been used by the client by vouching raw material prices to vendor invoices, as shown in the working papers in Appendixes 11–F and 11–G.

In addition to ascertaining that proper historical costing has been used, the principle of conservatism requires the auditor to *compare the values assigned to inventory with replacement cost,* for the purpose of determining whether they are significantly lower than cost. If that has occurred, the auditor will have to calculate lower-of-cost-or-market values for inventories. This also involves obtaining selling price and selling cost data, as well as costs to complete work in process and normal profit margin. These data would then be used to calculate the cost-or-market ceiling and floor limitations.

In verifying the valuation of work-in-process and finished goods inventories, it is important for the auditor to *inspect the supporting records* found within the cost accounting subsystem. This will include job order sheets (if the firm is using a job order cost system), cost-of-production reports (when a process cost system is being used), and standard cost cards (where inventories are valued at standard costs). The inspection of such cost data should include tests of the procedures for allocating material, labor, and overhead costs to the individual units of the product where historical costs are used. When standard costs are used, the auditor should *analyze and recompute variance account balances* on a test basis. The auditor is primarily interested in determining that costs have been properly assigned to finished goods, work in process, and cost of goods sold. It is important to recognize that these inventories should be valued at amounts not significantly different from those derived from generally accepted full absorption cost accounting procedures.

If the client is a retail store, valuation of inventories involves vouching not only the unit cost of goods but also the retail price. In this case, the best evidence to support retail price would be current client catalogs or price lists. Markups and markdowns would be vouched to appropriate documents indicating management approval. Finally, the retail estimation method used by the client would be recalculated by the auditor.

During the observation of inventory, it is important for the auditor to give special attention to *inventory items that may be damaged, shopworn, or obsolete.* Slow-moving (obsolete) items are most likely to be discovered by examining the perpetual inventory records. Attribute sampling may appropriately be used in estimating the percentage of slow-moving inventory items. The valuation of such items should be reduced to provide for probable losses in the disposal of them.

Some General Checks. There are some overall checks that are important in helping the auditor determine whether or not inventory and cost of sales have been valued in accordance with GAAP. The first of these general checks requires computation of the *gross margin percentage* realized during the audit period and a comparison of that percentage with the percentages realized historically. It is also important for the auditor to compute the *turnover of inventory* for the purpose of helping determine whether the inventory includes obsolete or slow-moving items that may be improperly valued. A significant decline in turnover, one that is not appropriately accounted for by changes in operating practices, would suggest the possibility of obsolete or slow-moving items being included in inventory. Appendix 11–H illustrates the computation and comparison of historical trends in inventory turnover.

It is also desirable for the auditor to secure an *inventory representation letter* from the client stating that a particular generally accepted method of inventory valuation has been followed and that appropriate provision has been made for obsolete and slow-moving inventory items. This representation letter should also include a statement to the effect that inventory held on a consignment has been excluded from the inventory balance.

In verifying the valuation of inventories, it is also important to *recompute the footings and extensions* on the physical inventory summary sheets and to *scan* those sheets for unusual amounts. Entries required to adjust the perpetual inventory account balances to amounts shown on the inventory sheets summarizing the results of the physical inventory should be traced to the inventory accounts.

Ownership

The verification of ownership requires the auditor to *inspect*, on a test basis, the documents underlying the acquisitions of individual inventory items. These include purchase orders, receiving reports, and vendor invoices. If these documents are in order and can be properly related to inventory possessed by the client, the auditor has good evidence in support of client ownership of inventory. Notice that vouching of documents was also the recommended procedure for verification of valuation. The same procedure used to achieve that objective can be used to ascertain ownership. The price-testing working papers, which appear as Appendixes 11–F and 11–G, illustrate the vouching process.

With respect to consigned goods, the auditor should inquire about them and secure an inventory representation letter stating that such goods have been excluded from the inventory accounts. He or she can then examine the final inventory listing to verify that such goods have, in fact, been excluded from inventories.

Cutoff

Cutoff (periodicity) errors occur near the beginning or end of the audit period when entries involving the acquisitions or disposals of merchandise are improperly included as transactions in the wrong period. In verifying proper cutoff, the auditor must *inspect the underlying documents relating to both purchases and sales* made near the end of the period under audit and during the first few days of the succeeding period. This procedure is performed to determine that the documents have been recorded in the proper period and that the client held legal title to the goods as of the balance sheet date. Ordinarily, merchandise acquisitions should be recorded as of the date the title to the goods passes to the purchaser. Generally this is the FOB point, but there are some exceptions. For example, the title to custom-made merchandise passes to the purchaser when the production process has been completed. From a practical point of view, a firm may follow a practice of recognizing all merchandise acquisitions as additions to inventory when they are received at the client's receiving dock. If this practice is followed consistently, and does not have a material effect on the financial statements from period to period, such an arrangement would be considered acceptable.

As we observed in Chapter 10, it is also important to verify the cutoff of shipments for the purpose of seeing that inventory going out to customers is transferred to cost of sales in the appropriate period. Again the auditor will inspect the documents underlying the sales transactions occurring near the end of the period under audit and during the first few days of the next period, giving particular attention to the dates of the shipping tickets and the terms of sale to determine when each shipment should have been transferred from inventory to cost of sales. Entries from the sales journal should be selected for dates up to and including the balance sheet date. Each entry should be vouched to shipping documents indicating that the goods were, in fact, shipped and not on hand (and counted) at the balance sheet date.

Sometimes *inventory in transit* will exist at the balance sheet date. In these cases, the auditor must ascertain that inventory has been properly recorded as purchased at that date if the goods were shipped FOB shipping point. The working paper in Appendix 11–I illustrates the audit work typically performed on in-transit inventory.

Statement Presentation

The verification of appropriate statement presentation primarily involves seeing that the disclosure requirements relating to inventory have been met. The auditor must inquire of the client as to *whether any part of the inventory has been pledged* as security against creditor claims. If so, the auditor must ascertain that the amount of the pledged inventory has been appropriately disclosed in the balance sheet. It is also necessary for the financial statements to disclose *the method used in valuing the inventory*. Furthermore, in the case of a manufacturing firm, appropriate distinction should be made between inventories of raw materials, work in process, and finished goods. The client representation letter mentioned earlier in this section should include information regarding any amount of inventory pledged and the valuation practices followed by the client.

In cost of sales systems which utilize perpetual inventories, clients will usually make individual *entries to cost of goods sold* as each sale is made. To verify these amounts, the auditor should select samples of sales invoices, recompute the cost of sales on each invoice, and trace those amounts to the amounts recorded in the books. The auditor would also match the amount of cost of goods sold on each invoice with the sales amount, and ascertain that the two amounts were both recorded in the same accounting period. In situations where cost of goods sold is not recorded in individual transactions, the auditor would verify the various elements of the cost of goods sold formula stated earlier in this section. Beginning inventories would be traced to the prior year's audit workpapers, and appropriate audit procedures would be performed on purchases and ending inventories. Cost of goods sold would then be verified as the mathematical result of the formula.

Often as a final overall check of the reasonableness of the inventory, the auditor will perform *analytical review of key financial statement ratios regarding inventory.* After ratios have been calculated, explanations should be obtained from the client for material fluctuations in them, and should be followed up with further documentation when the auditor considers it necessary. Relationships shown between inventory turnover, ending inventory levels, and sales volume, for example, should all corroborate the results of the tests of details we have discussed in this section. The working paper in Appendix 11–H illustrates some of the analytical review procedures that can assist the auditor in deciding whether the pieces of the puzzle actually fit together to form a coherent and consistent picture concerning the presentation of inventories.

SUBSTANTIVE TESTS OF TRADE PAYABLES

The verification of trade payables is important in helping the auditor decide whether inventory acquisitions and payments on accounts and notes payable have been appropriately recorded. They fit into the four-element equation as follows:

> Beginning-of-period trade payables + purchases of goods on account − payments of trade payables = end-of-period trade payables.

Therefore, if the auditor has verified the trade payables balance at the end of the preceding period (beginning of the current period) and is able, as a result of transactions validity tests and substantive tests of the cash balance to rely on the cash disbursements data, he or she can develop significant evidence in support of inventory purchases by verifying the trade payables balances at the end of the period under audit. Thus the jigsaw puzzle relationships are especially evident in the verification of cost of sales system data. In effect, we rely on verification of the validity of transactions in the system plus verification through substantive *tests of the balances for the fences* (inventories, payables, and cash) within the confines of which the system's data are accumulated. The relationships between the audit objectives for payables and the procedures used to meet those objectives are shown in Figure 11–14. The audit procedures explained below are illustrated in part in Appendixes 11–J and 11–K.

As the auditor begins to verify the payable accounts, it is important to recognize that the primary effort will be directed toward *discovering understatements* rather than overstatements of these items. Because of that fact, the audit procedures followed in verifying liability balances will be directed primarily toward verifying liabilities that may have been omitted or that may have been understated.

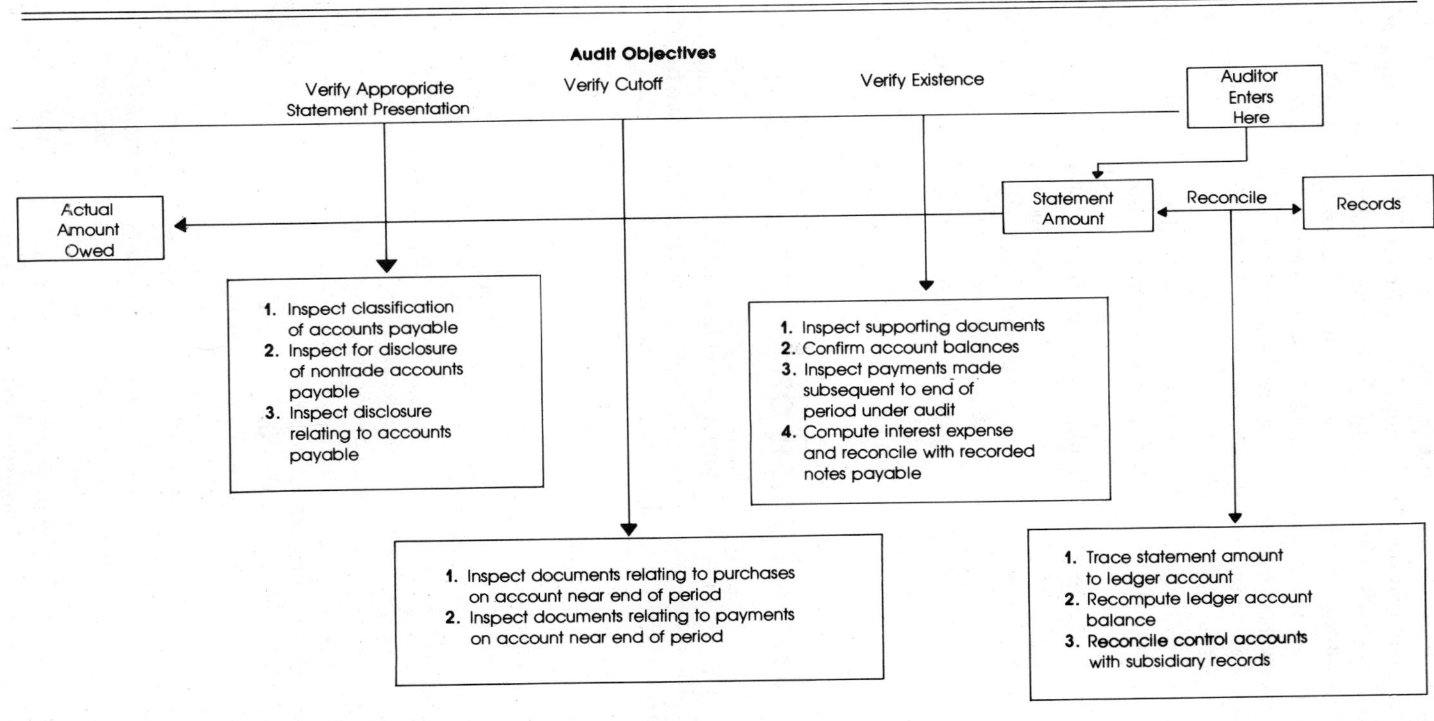
Recopy this
Audit Objectives
Verify Appropriate Statement Presentation
Verify Cutoff
Verify Existence
Auditor Enters Here
Actual Amount Owed
Statement Amount
Reconcile
Records
1. Inspect classification of accounts payable
2. Inspect for disclosure of nontrade accounts payable
3. Inspect disclosure relating to accounts payable
1. Inspect supporting documents
2. Confirm account balances
3. Inspect payments made subsequent to end of period under audit
4. Compute interest expense and reconcile with recorded notes payable
1. Inspect documents relating to purchases on account near end of period
2. Inspect documents relating to payments on account near end of period
1. Trace statement amount to ledger account
2. Recompute ledger account balance
3. Reconcile control accounts with subsidiary records

FIGURE 11–14. Flowchart for Substantive Tests of Accounts Payable

We begin our verification of payables by reconciling the statement balances with the underlying accounting records. This involves tracing the financial statement amount to the ledger accounts, recomputing purchase and expense and cash disbursements journal totals, recomputing ledger account balances, and reconciling control accounts with the appropriate subsidiary records. A schedule of unpaid vouchers may often be secured by listing the open vouchers in the voucher register. However, if a client expects to make partial payments to vendors, it is desirable to have a subsidiary ledger for vouchers payable. When the reconciliation procedures have been completed, the auditor is ready to give attention to verifying that the account balances show the actual obligations outstanding. That requires the performance of procedures to meet the audit objectives (things to be proven) cited earlier in the chapter.

The *verification of existence of liabilities* generally takes the form of ascertaining that individual balances shown in the accounts are actually obligations of the client and that they include all of those obligations. Because most liability balances such as accounts payable, notes payable, etc., can be directly related to externally related documents, one of the very important auditing procedures involves the inspection of those documents. In verifying accounts payable, those documents include vendors' invoices and internally originated receiving reports. Although the legally enforceable note payable will normally be held by the person to whom the obligation is to be paid, the client will often have *a copy of the note payable* which can be inspected. In all cases the auditor in inspecting documentary support will be concerned with verifying both the terms and the amounts reflected in those documents. In view of the fact that the auditor is often primarily concerned with understatements rather than overstatements, he or she will generally trace, on a test basis, various documents to the liability accounts.

In some instances, it may be desirable for the auditor to confirm liabilities for accounts payable and notes payable. Here again, however, because we are often looking for understated or omitted items rather than overstated balances, the items selected for confirmation should include vendors and note holders with small or even zero account balances as well as some accounts showing large payable balances. You should recognize that the *confirmation of payables* is not considered as effective or as important an audit procedure as the confirmation of receivables, because of the emphasis on discovering understated payables and because we have externally originated documentary evidence in support of recorded payables.

One of the most effective procedures for discovering unrecorded or understated payables is the inspection of payments made subsequent to the end of the period under audit. This process is often called the *search for unrecorded liabilities.* It allows the auditor the benefit of hindsight in identifying the liabilities outstanding at the end of the period. It is also helpful in the verification of cutoff. If the auditor discovers a payment that has been made subsequent to the end of the period under audit which cannot be related to a liability shown in the end of the period balance sheet, he or she should search out the underlying documents and determine whether it should have been included as a liability in that statement. Furthermore, in searching for unrecorded notes payables, the auditor would analyze the interest expense account for the period under audit and vouch each entry in the account to the underlying note documents. Charges to interest expense not supported by underlying notes payable signal an unrecorded note payable. The cutoff of credits to trade payables will have been verified when the acquisition element of the cutoff of inventories was verified. As we noted in the preceding paragraph, the cutoff of debits is verified by inspecting documents relating to payments made around the end of the audit period and the beginning of the next period.

Verification of *appropriate statement presentation* requires the auditor to inspect the classifications of payables in the balance sheet to see that a proper distinction has been made between trade and nontrade payables and between current and noncurrent items. Disclosures relating to trade payables should also be inspected.

A letter of representation, including client assertions relating to inventories and payables, is secured by the auditor to remind management that the primary responsibility for overall fairness of presentation of these items rests with management rather than the auditor.

USING THE COMPUTER IN AUDITING THE INVENTORY, COST OF SALES, AND CASH DISBURSEMENTS SYSTEM

The computer is used extensively in many inventory, cost of sales, and cash disbursements systems. Applications include maintenance of perpetual inventory files, cost accounting systems, and the related subsidiary ledgers and journals. In such cases the auditor can, with appropriate computer audit software, use the computer in both the compliance and substantive testing phases of the audit.

In the compliance testing phase, for example, the auditor might apply the test data approach to ascertain whether certain control attributes (listed in Figure 11–11) were, in fact, being applied to transactions processed. Alternatively, the auditor might use parallel simulation or other approaches to reprocess live client data and compare results with those obtained by the client.

In the substantive testing phase of the audit, the computer can be used extensively to verify inventory, cost of sales, and trade payables balances. For example, the computer can be used *in the initial reconciliation of accounting records* by comparing totals of general and subsidiary ledger accounts. *In verifying the* existence of inventories, the computer can stratify master files of inventory, contained on magnetic tape, by dollar amount; then select a sample for inventory observation; and print the sample items, including listings of locations, to facilitate the test counting process. Auditor test counts may then be recorded on computer input documents. The computer can be used to compare test counts with client perpetual inventories and print out an exceptions report. *In verifying the existence of trade accounts payable,* the computer can select and print out a sample of accounts payable items for confirmation.

In verifying valuation, the auditor can utilize the computer audit software to foot and extend all master files of inventory and trade payables. The computer can also be used *to compute ratios such as inventory turnover, by item.* Alternatively, the sorting capability of the computer can be used *to identify inventory by date of last sale* or shipment to help determine if certain items are slow-moving or obsolete.

To help verify proper cutoff of inventory and trade payables, the computer can be used to print lists of the last shipping documents or receiving reports processed during the period. The auditor can then vouch or trace the items to the appropriate accounting records. These are examples rather than a complete list of ways in which the computer can be used in this part of the audit. You should remember that the computer with proper software, in general, can be used to perform the mechanical, repetitive procedures of the audit, and has the capability of performing these tasks in a fraction of the time required to perform them manually.

SUMMARY

In this chapter we have developed the audit objectives and the procedures to be performed in the examination of the inventory, cost of sales, and cash disbursements system. We have dealt with that system and its related account balances as a unit because of the direct relationships among those accounts. We began by identifying the applicable audit objectives. These include verification of transaction validity, existence, ownership, cutoff, valuation, and appropriate statement presentation. We then identified and explained in detail the transaction validity phase of the audit, including compliance tests of critical internal controls over the boundary, processing, and safeguarding of assets functions. In the process of explaining the controls associated with these functions and the tests to evaluate the extent to which they were being followed, we showed how the five basic characteristics of internal control relate to the system and account balances.

In the last part of the chapter, we described the audit procedures followed in verifying existence, ownership, cutoff, valuation, and proper statement presentation of inventories, cost of sales, and trade payables accounts. We also included a brief discussion regarding ways in which the computer can be used to perform selected procedures when the underlying records are maintained on machine readable media.

APPENDIX 11–A: Inventory Summary

JEP Manufacturing Co. / Inventory Summary / 3-31-X1	W. P. No.	F
	ACCOUNTANT	JB
	DATE	5-5-X1

		Adjusted Balance 3-31-X0 ✓	Balance Per Books 3-31-X1 Δ
Costs + Estimated Earnings on Income Contracts	A-1	1104937 12	
#130 Obsolete	A-1	—	55798 89
#125 Raw Materials		5915169 6	4064686 83
#127 Work-in-Process		1114219 0	927741 61
#129 Inventory in Transit		24300 77	31306 01
		7272396 3	5079533 34

Note: See F-50 Raw materials bulk file.

Conclusion: Based upon the work performed which was adequate to acheive the audit objectives as stated in the APG; it appears that inventories & estimated costs and earnings on incomplete contracts are fairly stated @ 3-31-X1 and on a basis consistent with prior years.

✓: Per prior years workpapers.

Δ: Per 3-31-X1 general ledger

Adjustments DR	Adjustments CR	Adjusted Balance 3-31-X1	Final Adjustments DR	Final Adjustments CR	Final Balance 3-31-X1
			<2> 904138 95		904138 95 A-1
F-50 <104> 34288 63	<104> 55798 89	F-50 34288 63		<3> 34288 63	-0-
<103> 647417 23	<105> 4054765 70 <102> 9921 13	F-50 647417 23			
<103> 900577 33	<103> 927741 61	F-1 900577 33		<2> 706082 52	194494 81 A-1
		F-6 31306 31			31306 01 A-1
		1613589 20 F-a			873218 05 F-a

APPENDIX 11–B: Observation of Inventory

JEP Manufacturing Co. Inventory Observation 3-31-X1	W. P. No.	F-21
	ACCOUNTANT	TB
	DATE	3-31-X1

Our representative, Todd Burnett, arrived at JEP Mfg. Co. Greensboro, Texas at approx. 8:30 a.m. on 3-31-X1 to observe client's physical inventory. We accompanied inventory control mgr., Elvis Rizor (who had all responsibility for physical inventory), on a tour of the warehouse & premises. The warehouse was well arranged and in good order; it appeared that all goods were being tagged & counted. Scrap & obsolete material appeared to be properly identified (which was immaterial to total inventory).

After a tour of the plant facilities, we made several test counts of raw materials, work-in-process, & a small amt. of finished goods in the various depts. See work paper F-24 → F-26.

Subsequently, we went to East Texas Distributors, a wholly owned subsidiary of JEP Mfg. Co. We toured the facility with Burt Andrews, President, who had overall responsibility for the count of both East Texas Distributors inventory and the JEP Mfg. inventory located

W. P. No.
ACCOUNTANT
DATE

there. The plant appeared in good order and JEP Mfg. Co. inventory was appropriately segregated.

We made several test counts as documented on East Texas F-11 & F-24-6 (JEP Mfg. Co. Inventory held @ E. Texas).

We supervised the pulling of tags and it appeared that the East Texas Dist. Client was following prescribed inventory procedures.

Upon returning to JEP Mfg. Co., we commenced our test counts of work-in-process, going through all depts. and stages of completion, including finished goods.

After sufficient test counts were made, we supervised the pulling of tags and accounted for all tags issued, used, & voided. See F-23. Based on the above, the physical inventory performed by the client & under our observation, appeared adequate @ 3-31-X1 to properly reflect inventory quantities.

APPENDIX 11–C: Inventory Observation Questionnaire

F-20
JB
3-31-X1

JEP MANUFACTURING COMPANY
INVENTORY OBSERVATION QUESTIONNAIRE
3-31-X1

CLIENT JEP Manufacturing Co.

LOCATION Greensboro, Texas

INVENTORY OBSERVATION as of 3-31-X1

QUESTION	ANSWER
1. Did the company issue printed inventory instructions?	Yes
2. If so, have we obtained a copy for our files?	Yes see F-22
3. Was the plant shut down for inventory taking?	Yes
4. If plant was not shut down, how was proper control exercised over quantities?	N/A
5. State the following dates and hours that the inventory:	
Was started	3/31/X1 7 30 AM
Was completed	3/31/X1 — PM
6. Who was in overall charge of the inventory taking (give name and title)?	Elvis Reisor Mgr. - INVENTORY CONTROL
7. Was he present during the entire time?	Yes
8. State the date and time that auditors' representatives were present.	9:00 AM PM
9. Were all items actually counted, weighed or measured?	Yes
10. Perpetual inventory records:	
(a) Have been or will they be adjusted to the physical count?	yes
(b) If required, have you checked your test count to perpetual inventor records?	N/A
(c) Are adjustments to count material?	NO
11. How is merchandise not belonging to the company shown on the inventory?	None
12. How were the following classes of items indicated so as to be properly priced:	
Obsolete Discontinued	} Counted & Identified by Elvis Reisor, Inv. Mgr.

Damaged
Overstocked

} with 20 yrs. Experience
} & Excluded from Inventory
see final Inventory
listing Bulk F-50

13. Were all physical counts:

    (a) Subject to adequate supervision? — Yes

    (b) Subject to dual control in which at least one person is independent of the regular storekeeper? — Yes

    (c) Based on numbered tag (or other controllable system). If not, explain. — Yes

    (d) If numbered tags were used, did you account for all numbers used, voided and not used? — Yes see F-23

    (e) Subject to clerical checking where necessary? — Yes

14. Were there any machinery or materials charged to property accounts included in the inventory count? — No

15. How was merchandise in "cars on track" accounted for? — N/A

16. Was warehouse or storeroom orderly and the stock adequately protected against the weather or other losses? — Yes

17. In your opinion have all merchandise and supplies been properly inventoried, and if not, why? — Yes

18. Are we to receive a complete copy of the company's inventory; if so, is it attached? — Yes

19. Obtain last receiving record number(s) **for checking** cutoff. (If not numbered, **list last few receivers.**) — see F-25 series

20. Obtain last shipping or sales record number(s) for checking cut-off. (If not numbered, list last few shippers and sales invoices.) — L

21. If the inventory observation is on the balance sheet date the following procedures should be followed:

    (a) List the number of the last check(s) issued. — NCN

    (b) Count cash on hand including undeposited receipts. — NCN

    (c) Examine securities. — NCN

    (d) Mail all possible confirmations. — NCN

22. Consider confirmation or observation of the company's inventories located to suppliers or with others. — Immaterial NCN

23. Other comments: (Reverse side if necessary).

APPENDIX 11–D: Test Count of Raw Materials

JEP Manufacturing Co.
Test Counts – Raw Materials
3-31-X1

W. P. No.	F-24
ACCOUNTANT	FB
DATE	3-31-X1

#	Description	Item #	Count	Unit of Measure
505	100X160 Copper		1170 ✓	LBS
509	Copper 9 sq. HF		201 ✓	LBS
514	Copper 182 X 325		59 ✓	LBS
602	Copper 10HF		518 ✓	LBS
736	Core Steel		98030 ✓	LBS
743	Core Steel		8720 ✓	LBS
710	Core		40 ✓	EA

✓ Agreed to final inventory listing F-50 (not reproduced)

APPENDIX 11–E: Test Count of Finished Goods

JEP Manufacturing Co.
Test Counts – Finished Goods
3-31-X1

W. P. No.	F-26
ACCOUNTANT	JB
DATE	3-31-X1

	#	Description	Work Order #	Count	Unit of Measure
Golden	198	Transformer	80-01-065	6 ✓	each
Golden	196	Switches	80-10-025	2 ✓	each

✓ Agreed to final inventory listing F-3 (not reproduced)

APPENDIX 11–F: Inventory Price Testing

JEP Manufacturing Co. Memo Re: Inventory Price Testing 3-31-X1	W. P. No.	F-4-0
	ACCOUNTANT	JB
	DATE	5-4-X1

We examined several items for inventory costing (pricing) on F-4-1 & F-4-2 based on a sample selection determined in compliance with our firm's sampling policy. The FIFO quantity layers were obtained for each item selected from the clients perpetual inventory systems. The related supporting documents (purch. order, paid invoice) were examined, the calculated FIFO price per layer determined, & inventory values extended. Small immaterial differences were noted attributable mainly to rounding error.

In addition, we noted invoice date relating to the inventory layers to determine the presence of slow-moving or obsolete items. None of a significant nature were noted on items price tested. See raw materials BUIK F-50, where we reviewed for obsolescence and amounts adjusted.

APPENDIX 11–G: Raw Materials Price Testing

JEP Manufacturing Co.
Raw Materials – Pricing Testwork
3-31-X1

W. P. No.	F-4-1
ACCOUNTANT	PBC/LB
DATE	4-30-X1

	Inventory Page No.	Description	Quantity	Unit Cost	(A) Extended Value	Supplier
1	24	#9F524 Fuse	147	4 75	698 25	General Elec. Co.
2	26	#7200-66 Bushings	38	41 66	1583 08	Central Maloney
3	26	#600-54 Bushings	79	24 65	1947 35	Elastimold Spec.
4	28	#3009-1 Bushing Assembly	73	30 16	2201 68	Warco Co.
5	32	#662 Core	40	131 33	5253 20	S&M Mfg.
6	66	1007 x 3/4" Cotton Tape	543.5	2 82	1532 27	Hisco Co.
7	94	#KU-4814 Relay	124	4 75 Ea.	589 00	Potter & Brumfield
8	105	#1925 Thermometer with Brass Wheel	189	18 51 Ea.	3498 39	Rochester Guages
9	105	Type T-2 Thermometer Spec.	19	122 23 Ea.	2322 37	Marshalltown Mfg.
10	144	#164 Pivot Arm Aux. Switch	123	7 50 Ea.	741 69	Lindale Precision
11	164	#41268 Body J2CX	42	36 84 Ea.	1547 28	ETD Machinery
12	164	#443 Stud. Bushing Comp.	22	36 58 Ea.	804 76	Midland Casting

Note ① Item selected per work paper F-4 judgementally in compliance with SAS 39.

Note ② Inventory is priced at lower of cost or market. Cost is determined on FIFO Basis and replacement cost is market. Methods are consistant with prior years.

Note ③ $167583.81 price tested which is approximately 24% of total inventory.

∨ – Agreed to paid invoice for applicable FIFO layer quantity and/or recalculated based on paid invoice and freight charges.

⚹ – Per final inventory listing F-50 for items judgementally selected.

∠ – Per client maintained perpetual records.

Conclusion – Based upon the audit work performed which was considered adequate to obtain the audit objectives as stated in the audit programs, raw materials inventory appears to be fairly valued at 3-31-X1. /LB

Quantity Per Layer	Purchase Order	Invoice Date	FIFO Price Per Layer	(B) Extended FIFO Value	(A) - (B) Difference
125	39745	12/12/X9	4 74 ✓	696 78	1 47
205	41676	3/3/X1	41 26 ✓	1567 85	15 20
112	39923	1/24/X0	24 65 ✓	1947 38	-0-
13	39378	2/26/X0	30 16 ✓	2201 68	-0-
6	39977	2/5/X0	131 50 ✓	5260 00	<6 80>
500	40498	10/7/X0	2 78 ✓	1510 93	21 34
150	28649	7/24/X4	4 75 ✓	589 00	-0-
36	41580	2/16/X1	18 51 ✓	3498 39	-0-
2	41414	1/27/X1	122 23 ✓	2322 37	-0-
194	39490	2/25/X0	6 23 ✓	741 69	-0-
48	18880	3/31/X6	36 84 ✓	1547 28	-0-
48	1498	3/5/X1	36 58 ✓	804 76	-0-
					31 21

Pass – Due Mainly to Rounding and minor Clerical Inaccuracy.

APPENDIX 11–H: Inventory Turnover

JEP Manufacturing Co.	W. P. No.	F-A
Inventory Turnover	ACCOUNTANT	JB
3-31-X1	DATE	5-4-X1

	✓ 3-31-X9		✓ 3-31-X0	
Cost of Sales	4767149		~~4814446~~ 4939060	~~Before adjustment~~ After adjustment
(%)	80.1%		82.7%	after adjustment
Before work-in-process adj.				
Beg. Inventory	976972		1322969	
End. Inventory	1322969		1563873 Ⓐ	
Total	2299941		2886842	
Divide by 2	÷ 2		÷ 2	
Average	1149971		1443421	
Related Turnover	4.15		3.34	
(%)				
After work-in-process adj.				
Beg. Inventory	658148		610950	
End. Inventory	610950		727240 Ⓑ	
Total	1269098		1338190	
Divide by 2	÷ 2		÷ 2	
Average	634549		669095	
Related Turnover	7.51		7.38	

✓ Per prior year work papers

Note: Per discussion with Phil Neeson, V.P. of Finance, slight decrease in turnover is attributable to increase in production and size of backlog. Inspected production & backlog reports and noted that these explanations reflected actual facts.

3-31-X1		Adjusted & Reclassified Balance 3-31-X1
5717336 Before adjustment		
5596840 after adjustment		5579933
81.4% after adjustment		
Ⓐ 1563873		
1613589		
3177462		
÷ 2		
1588731		
3.60		
Ⓑ 727240		727240
F 907507		F 873218
1634747		1600458
÷ 2		÷ 2
817374		800729
6.85		6.97

APPENDIX 11–1: In-Transit Inventory

JEP Manufacturing Co.
In-Transit Inventory
3-31-X1

W. P. No.	F-6
ACCOUNTANT	JB
DATE	5-12-X1

Company		Invoice #		Amount
Ayar Mach. Production		207		1125.70
Boyle's Galvanizing		7717		308.92
Delair Investment		4314	✓	2445.57
"		4315		1054.26
"		4321	✓	1285.00
Detroit Coil Co.		3-1203		894.31
"		3-1204		900.20
Electromagnetic Ind.		88-1094	✓	82.48
"	F-25-3	35-8934		108.07
General Electric		086-11209-3	✓	1400.10
Gould-Brown		46-00167		617.76
"		46-92870		31.19
Hisco Corp.		5-2453		651.00
Murray Industrial	F-25-3	1-397214		116.60
Newark Electronics		142574		85.23
Parmeli Inc.		81-361	✓	2135.00
Potter & Brumfield		F-47932		379.33
Qualitex Corp.		00897	✓	2087.67
S & M Manufacturing		0215	✓	9620.64
L. V. Weatherford		529143		8.12
Texas Precision Investment		1829		5968.96
Note: Per JEP Mfg. Co. purchase journal				31306.11

✓ Vouched to invoice & receiver indicating goods rec'd after 3-31-X1 but should have been included in inventory.

APPENDIX 11–J: Trade Accounts Payable

JEP Manufacturing Co.
Trade Accounts Payable
3-31-X1

W. P. No.	N-1
ACCOUNTANT	PBC/Smd
DATE	5/11/X1

Name	Amount	
Allegheny Ludow	30421 20	
Alter Corporation	75 55	
American Packing	2709 00	
Amco, Inc.	26093 48	
Arrow Electronics	5 88	
Austin Hardware	991 37	
B & G Supply	339 72	
Centaur Metals Supply	2297 24	C
Clemtex, Ltd.	258 37	
Colt Industries	867 00	Ⓒ ✓
Dal Air Investment	16055 02	C
Decco, Inc.	594 00	
East Texas Distributors	262406 43	
Elastimold Division	3789 70	Ⓒ ✓
Ex-Cel Steel	19030 86	Ⓒ ✓
Exxon Co.	16953 22	
General Electric Co.	3691 29	
Other [Details Omitted]	115336 50	
Total	501915 83 ^	✓
Less: RJE ⟨B⟩ To reclassify payable to East Texas Distributors as intercompany (payable to wholly-owned subsidiary)	⟨262406 43⟩	
	239409 40	
	A-2	

^ Footed
C Confirmations sent, received on N-2 (not shown)
Ⓒ No reply. Alternative procedures performed. See ✓ below
✓ Examined copy of check dated subsequent to 3-31-X1 with supporting invoices attached. Noted that amount was properly included as account payable at 3-31-X1.
✓ Agreed to 3-31-X1 general ledger

Conclusion: Based on audit work performed which was considered adequate to meet the audit objectives, accounts payable is fairly stated at 3-31-X1. Smd

APPENDIX 11–K: Search for Unrecorded Liabilities

JEP Mfg. Co.
Search for Unrecorded Liabilities
3-31-X1

W. P. No.	N-3
Accountant	Smg
Date	5/12/X1

SCOPE > #1000

Check # ✓	Payee	Amount	Applicable to 19X1	Properly Recorded in A/P or Accrued in 19X1	Applicable to 19X2
6941	Wyoming Valley Machinery	4950 00			✓
6995	Gen'l Life Ins. Co.	8249 81			✓
7033	X Systems	4175 08	4175 08	✓	
7037	J C Ross Truck Line	1482 56			✓
7231	X Systems	2527 08	2527 08	✓	
7251	Gen'l Life Ins. Co.	10257 11			✓
7264	ABC	1256 90			✓
7280	J. Hughes Co.	2522 53			✓
7286	PZN	5000 00	5000 00	✓	
	Total applicable to 19X1		11702 16	Immaterial. Pass further investigation. Smg	

✓ Per check register for the period beginning 4-1-X1, through 5-12-X1 (end of audit field work).
✓ Applies to column heading.

Note: This search for unrecorded liabilities was conducted through 5/12/X1 and check #7291 with a scope of #1000. No unrecorded liabilities were noted. In consideration of the above results, continuation of the search past 5/12/X1 is not considered necessary.

Note: The above search included payments to East Texas Dist. as well.

QUESTIONS FOR CLASS DISCUSSION

Q11–1 How does the auditor's attitude when verifying inventory differ from his or her attitude when verifying accounts payable? Explain.

Q11–2 What relationship exists between the verification of inventory and the verification of cost of sales?

Q11–3 What are the boundary documents typically found in the cost of sales system? Relate each to a specific exchange transaction.

Q11–4 Which exchange functions are typically found in the cost of sales system?

Q11–5 Why is it important to have sequentially numbered purchase orders and to control the use of those documents? Explain.

Q11–6 What elements of the control system are designed to protect a firm from paying for merchandise it did not receive?

Q11–7 What elements of a control system are designed to provide assurance that all merchandise shipped is billed to the customers?

Q11–8 What responsibilities should be segregated in the purchasing and cash payments elements of the cost of sales system? Explain.

Q11–9 What documents are typically associated with the cost of sales system? What function is each document expected to perform?

Q11–10 How does the auditor verify compliance in evaluating the internal controls found within the cost of sales system?

Q11–11 What auditing procedures are performed to verify the existence of inventory?

Q11–12 How does the auditor verify the valuation of inventory? Explain.

Q11–13 How does the auditor react to significant differences between physical and perpetual inventory balances?

Q11–14 What differences are there between the procedures followed in verifying the existence of inventory stored in a public warehouse in another city and inventory stored in a company warehouse in another city? Justify those differences.

Q11–15 Why is the auditor concerned with calculating the gross margin percentage and inventory turnover in the verification of inventory? Discuss fully.

Q11–16 Why does the auditor secure an inventory representation letter from the client? Explain.

Q11–17 What are the effects on the net income of the client of an improper cutoff of inventory at the end of the audit period?

Q11–18 Why is the confirmation of accounts receivable a more generally followed audit procedure than is the confirmation of accounts payable? Explain.

Q11–19 What procedures does the auditor follow in his or her search for unrecorded liabilities? Explain.

Q11–20 What are some of the ways in which the computer may be used in auditing elements of the inventory and cost of sales system when the inventory data are maintained on computer readable media?

SHORT CASES

C11–1 Alicia Decker, CPA, is performing an examination of the financial statements of Allright Wholesale Sales, Inc., for the year ended December 31, 19X0. Allright has been in business for many years and has never had its financial statements audited. Decker has gained satisfaction with respect to the ending inventory and is considering alternative audit procedures to gain satisfaction with respect to management's representations concerning the beginning inventory, which was not observed.

Allright sells only one product (bottled Brand X beer), and maintains perpetual inventory records. In addition, Allright takes physical inventory counts monthly. Decker has already confirmed purchases with the manufacturer and has decided to concentrate on evaluating the reliability of perpetual inventory records and performing analytical review procedures to the extent that prior years' unaudited records will enable such procedures to be performed.

Required:

What are the audit tests, including analytical review procedures, which Decker should apply in evaluating the reliability of perpetual inventory records and gaining satisfaction with respect to the January 1, 19X0, inventory?

(AICPA adapted)

C11–2 Henri Mincin, CPA, is the auditor of the Raleigh Corporation. Mincin is considering the audit work to be performed in the accounts payable area for the current year's engagement.

The prior year's working papers show that confirmation requests were mailed to 100 of Raleigh's 1,000 suppliers. The selected suppliers were based on Mincin's sample that was designed to select accounts with large-dollar balances. A substantial number of hours were spent by Raleigh and Mincin resolving relatively minor differences between the confirmation replies and Raleigh's accounting records. Alternate audit procedures were used for those suppliers who did not respond to the confirmation requests.

Required:

a. Identify the accounts payable audit objectives that Mincin must consider in determining the audit procedures to be followed.
b. Identify situations when Mincin should use accounts payable confirmations and discuss whether Mincin is required to use them.
c. Discuss why the use of large-dollar balances as the basis for selecting accounts payable for confirmation might not be the most efficient approach; indicate what

more efficient procedures could be followed when selecting accounts payable for confirmation.

(AICPA adapted)

C11–3 Retail Corporation, a ten-store men's haberdashery chain, has a written company policy stating that company buyers may not have an investment in nor borrow money from an existing or potential supplier. Robert Chan, the independent auditor, learns from a Retail employee that Ira Williams, a buyer, is indebted to Hubert Park, a supplier, for a substantial amount of money. Retail's volume of business with Park increased significantly during the year. Chan believes the debtor – creditor relationship of Williams and Park constitutes a conflict of interest that might lead Williams to perpetrate a material fraud.

Required:

a. Discuss what immediate actions Chan should take upon discovery of the above facts.
b. Discuss what additional actions Chan should take to be satisfied that Retail has no significant inventory or cost of sales problems as a result of the weakness in internal control posed by the apparent conflict of interest. Identify and discuss in your answer the specific problems, such as overstocking, which Chan should consider.

(AICPA adapted)

C11–4 Ace Corporation does not conduct a complete annual physical count of purchased parts and supplies in its principal warehouse but uses statistical sampling instead to estimate the year-end inventory. Ace maintains a perpetual inventory record of parts and supplies and believes that statistical sampling is highly effective in determining inventory values and is sufficiently reliable to make a physical count of each item of inventory unnecessary.

Required:

a. When a client utilizes statistical sampling to determine inventory value and does not conduct a 100 percent annual physical count of inventory items, the auditor must proceed differently. Identify the audit procedures the independent auditor will be using that change or are in addition to normal required audit procedures.
b. List at least ten normal audit procedures that should be performed to verify physical quantities whenever a client conducts a periodic physical count of all or part of its inventory.

(AICPA adapted)

C11–5 Katharine Long, CPA, has been engaged to examine and report on the financial statements of Maylou Corporation. During the review phase of the study of Maylou's system of internal accounting control over purchases, Long was given the following document flowchart for purchases:

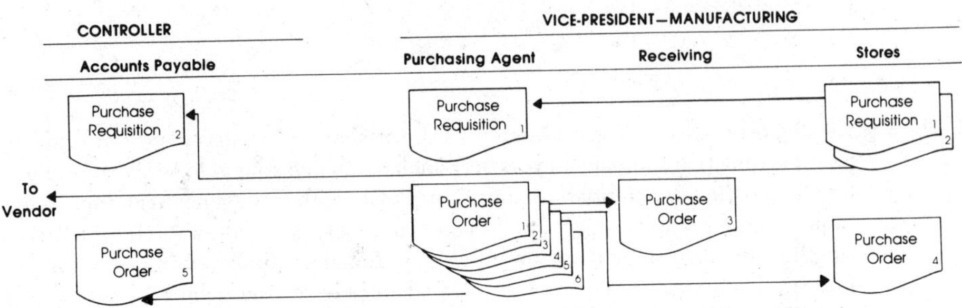

Required:

a. Identify the procedures, relating to purchase requisitions and purchase orders, that Long would expect to find if Maylou's system of internal accounting control over purchases is effective. For example, purchase orders are prepared only after giving proper consideration to the time to order, and quantity to order. *Do not comment on the effectiveness of the flow of documents as presented in the flowchart or on separation of duties.*

b. What are the factors to consider in determining the time to order? What factors affect the quantity to order?

(AICPA adapted)

C11–6 An auditor is conducting an examination of the financial statements of a wholesale cosmetics distributor with an inventory consisting of thousands of individual items. The distributor keeps its inventory in its own distribution center and in two public warehouses. An inventory computer file is maintained on a computer disk; and at the end of each business day the file is updated. Each record of the inventory file contains the following data:

a. Item number.
b. Location of item.
c. Description of item.
d. Quantity on hand.
e. Cost per item.
f. Date of last purchase.
g. Date of last sale.
h. Quantity sold during year.

The auditor is planning to observe the distributor's physical count of inventories as of a given date. The auditor will have available a computer tape of the data on the inventory file on the date of the physical count and a general purpose computer software package.

Required:

The auditor is planning to perform basic inventory auditing procedures. Identify the basic inventory auditing procedures and describe how the use of the general purpose software package and the tape of the inventory file data might be helpful to the auditor in performing such auditing procedures.

Organize your answer as follows:

Basic inventory auditing procedure	How general purpose computer software package and tape of the inventory file data might be helpful
1. *Observe the physical count, making and recording test counts where applicable*	*Determining which items are to be test counted by selecting a random sample of a representative number of items from the inventory file as of the date of the physical count*

(AICPA adapted)

C11–7 You have been engaged by the management of Alden, Inc., to review its internal control over the purchase, receipt, storage, and issue of raw materials. You have prepared the following notes to describe Alden's procedures:

> Raw materials, which consist mainly of high-cost electronic components, are kept in a locked storeroom. Storeroom personnel include a supervisor and four clerks. All are well trained, competent, and adequately bonded. Raw materials are removed from the storeroom only upon written or oral authorization of one of the production foremen.
>
> There are no perpetual inventory records; hence, the storeroom clerks do not keep records of goods received or issued. To compensate for the lack of perpetual records, a physical inventory count is taken monthly by the storeroom clerks who are well supervised. Appropriate procedures are followed in making the inventory count.
>
> After the physical count, the storeroom supervisor matches quantities counted against a predetermined reorder level. If the count for a given part is below the reorder level, the supervisor enters the part number on a materials-requisition list and sends this list to the accounts-payable clerk. The accounts-payable clerk prepares a purchase order for a predetermined reorder quantity for each part and mails the purchase order to the vendor from whom the part was last purchased.
>
> When ordered materials arrive at Alden, they are received by the storeroom clerks. The clerks count the merchandise and agree the counts to the shipper's bill of lading. All vendor's bills of lading are initialed, dated, and filed in the storeroom to serve as receiving reports.

Required:

a. Describe the weaknesses in internal control and recommend improvements of Alden's procedures for the purchase, receipt, storage, and issue of raw materials. Organize your answer sheet as follows:

Weaknesses	Recommended Improvements

b. For each weakness noted in the system, discuss what its impact, if any, would be on the financial statements of Alden, Inc., and thus whether you feel that the weakness is material.
c. For each material weakness noted in **b**, discuss the substantive audit procedures (tests of transactions, tests of balances) that you would *extend* (given that no mitigating strengths exist in other components of the system) in order to permit the expression of an unqualified audit opinion on the raw materials inventories of Alden, Inc.

(AICPA adapted)

C11–8 Dunbar Camera Manufacturing, Inc., is a manufacturer of high-priced precision motion picture cameras in which the specifications of component parts are vital to the manufacturing process. Dunbar buys valuable camera lenses and large quantities of sheetmetal and screws. Screws and lenses are ordered by Dunbar and are billed by the vendors on a unit basis. Sheetmetal is ordered by Dunbar and is billed by the vendors on the basis of weight. The receiving clerk is responsible for documenting the quality and quantity of merchandise received.

A preliminary review of the system of internal control indicates that the following procedures are in effect:

Receiving report. Properly approved purchase orders, which are prenumbered, are filed numerically. The copy sent to the receiving clerk is an exact duplicate of the copy sent to the vendor. Receipts of merchandise are recorded on the duplicate copy by the receiving clerk.

Sheetmetal. The company receives sheetmetal by railroad. The railroad independently weighs the sheetmetal and reports the weight and date of receipt on a bill of lading (waybill), which accompanies all deliveries. The receiving clerk merely checks the weight on the waybill to the purchase order.

Screws. The receiving clerk opens cartons containing screws, then inspects and weighs the contents. The weight is converted to number of units by means of conversion charts. The receiving clerk then checks the computed quantity to the purchase order.

Camera lenses. Each camera lens is delivered in a separate corrugated carton. Cartons are counted as they are received by the receiving clerk and the number of cartons is checked to purchase orders.

Required:

a. List the attributes of strength, if any, that exist in the system of internal control for Dunbar Camera Manufacturing, Inc., as described above.
b. For each control attribute listed, describe a compliance test that should be performed to ascertain whether the control strength is actually being implemented by the company.

c. List the material control weaknesses, if any, that exist in the system as described above, along with your recommended improvements. Use the following format:

Control Weakness	Effect on Financial Statements	Recommended Improvements

d. For each material control weakness listed in part **c**, describe the substantive test of transactions or balance that you should *extend* (given that no mitigating strengths exist elsewhere in the system) in order to permit the expression of an unqualified audit opinion on inventories of Dunbar Camera Manufacturing, Inc.

(AICPA adapted)

PROBLEMS

P11–1 Select the best answer for each of the following items relating to internal control within the cost of sales system.

a. Sandra Jackson, the purchasing agent of Judd Hardware Wholesalers, has a relative who owns a retail hardware store. Jackson arranged for hardware to be delivered by manufacturers to the retail store on a COD basis, thereby enabling her relative to buy at Judd's wholesale prices. Jackson was probably able to accomplish this because of Judd's poor internal control over
   (1) Purchase orders.
   (2) Purchase requisitions.
   (3) Cash receipts.
   (4) Perpetual inventory records.

b. Which of the following is a primary function of the purchasing department?
   (1) Authorizing the acquisition of goods.
   (2) Ensuring the acquisition of goods of a specified quality.
   (3) Verifying the propriety of goods acquired.
   (4) Reducing expenditures for goods acquired.

c. Which of the following procedures would *best* detect the theft of valuable items from an inventory that consists of hundreds of different items selling for $1 to $10 and a few items selling for hundreds of dollars?
   (1) Maintain a perpetual inventory of only the more valuable items with frequent periodic verification of the validity of the perpetual inventory record.
   (2) Have an independent CPA firm prepare an internal control report on the effectiveness of the administrative and accounting controls over inventory.
   (3) Have separate warehouse space for the more valuable items with sequentially numbered tags.

(4) Require an authorized officer's signature on all requisitions for the more valuable items.

d. Effective internal control over the purchasing of raw materials should usually include all the following procedures *except*
(1) Systematic reporting of product changes that will affect raw materials.
(2) Determining the need for the raw materials prior to preparing the purchase order.
(3) Obtaining third-party written quality and quantity reports prior to payment for the raw materials.
(4) Obtaining financial approval prior to making a commitment.

e. Which of the following is an internal control weakness for a company whose inventory of supplies consists of a large number of individual items?
(1) Supplies of relatively little value are expensed when purchased.
(2) The cycle basis is used for physical counts.
(3) The storekeeper is responsible for maintenance of perpetual inventory records.
(4) Perpetual inventory records are maintained only for items of significant value.

f. An effective internal accounting control measure that protects against the preparation of improper or inaccurate disbursements would be to require that all checks be
(1) Signed by an officer after necessary supporting evidence has been examined.
(2) Reviewed by the treasurer before mailing.
(3) Sequentially numbered and accounted for by internal auditors.
(4) Perforated or otherwise effectively cancelled when they are returned with the bank statement.

g. Sanbor Corporation has an inventory of parts consisting of thousands of different items of small value individually, but significant in total. Sanbor could establish effective internal accounting control over the parts by requiring
(1) Approval of requisitions for inventory parts by a company officer.
(2) Maintenance of inventory records for all parts included in the inventory.
(3) Physical counts of the parts on a cycle basis rather than at year end.
(4) Separation of the storekeeping function from the production and inventory recordkeeping functions.

h. Based on observations made during an audit, the independent auditor should discuss with management the effectiveness of the company's internal procedures that protect against the purchase of
(1) Required supplies provided by a vendor who offers *no* trade or cash discounts.
(2) Inventory items acquired based on an economic order quantity (EOQ) inventory management concept.
(3) New equipment that is needed but does *not* qualify for investment tax credit treatment.
(4) Supplies individually ordered, without considering possible volume discounts.

i. To avoid potential errors and irregularities a well-designed system of internal accounting control in the accounts payable area should include a separation of which of the following functions?
(1) Cash disbursements and invoice verification.
(2) Invoice verification and merchandise ordering.

(3) Physical handling of merchandise received and preparation of receiving reports.

(4) Check signing and cancellation of payment documentation.

j. Which of the following is a standard internal accounting control for cash disbursements?

(1) Checks should be signed by the controller and at least one other employee of the company.

(2) Checks should be sequentially numbered and the numerical sequence should be accounted for by the person preparing bank reconciliations.

(3) Checks and supporting documents should be marked "Paid" immediately after the check is returned with the bank statement.

(4) Checks should be sent directly to the payee by the employee who prepares documents that authorize check preparation.

k. Which of the following is an effective internal accounting control measure that encourages receiving department personnel to count and inspect all merchandise received?

(1) Quantities ordered are excluded from the receiving department copy of the purchase order.

(2) Vouchers are prepared by accounts payable department personnel only after they match item counts on the receiving report with the purchase order.

(3) Receiving department personnel are expected to match and reconcile the receiving report with the purchase order.

(4) Internal auditors periodically examine, on a surprise basis, the receiving department copies of receiving reports.

l. A good system of internal accounting control over purchases will give proper evaluation to the time for ordering merchandise. When making this evaluation the purchasing company should give primary consideration to

(1) The price differences that exist between various vendors who can supply the merchandise at the required time.

(2) The borrowing cost of money (interest) which the company must incur as a consequence of acquiring the merchandise.

(3) The trade-off between the cost of owning and storing excess merchandise and the risk of loss by *not* having merchandise on hand.

(4) The flow of funds within the company which indicates when money is available to pay for merchandise.

m. To strengthen the system of internal accounting control over the purchase of merchandise, a company's receiving department should

(1) Accept merchandise only if a purchase order or approval granted by the purchasing department is on hand.

(2) Accept and count all merchandise received from the usual company vendors.

(3) Rely on shipping documents for the preparation of receiving reports.

(4) Be responsible for the physical handling of merchandise but *not* the preparation of receiving reports.

n. A client's materials-purchasing cycle begins with requisitions from user departments and ends with the receipt of materials and the recognition of a liability. An auditor's primary objective in reviewing this cycle is to

(1) Evaluate the reliability of information generated as a result of the purchasing process.

(2) Investigate the physical handling and recording of unusual acquisitions of materials.
(3) Consider the need to be on hand for the annual physical count if this system is *not* functioning properly.
(4) Ascertain that materials said to be ordered, received, and paid for are on hand.

o. Which of the following internal accounting control procedures is effective in preventing duplicate payment of vendors' invoices?
(1) The invoices should be stamped, perforated, or otherwise effectively canceled before submission for approval of the voucher.
(2) Unused voucher forms should be prenumbered and accounted for.
(3) Canceled checks should be sent to persons other than the cashier or accounting department personnel.
(4) Properly authorized and approved vouchers with appropriate documentation should be the basis for check preparation.

p. An important purpose of the auditor's review of the client's procurement system should be to determine the effectiveness of the procedures to protect against
(1) Improper materials handling.
(2) Unauthorized persons issuing purchase orders.
(3) Mispostings of purchase returns.
(4) Excessive shrinkage or spoilage.

q. Effective internal control over the purchasing of raw materials should usually include all the following procedures *except*
(1) Obtaining third-party written quality and quantity reports prior to payment for the raw materials.
(2) Determining the need for the raw materials prior to preparing the purchase order.
(3) Systematic reporting of product changes which will affect raw materials.
(4) Obtaining financial approval prior to making a commitment.

r. Effective internal control over purchases generally can be achieved in a well-planned organizational structure with a separate purchasing department that has
(1) The ability to prepare payment vouchers based on the information on a vendor's invoice.
(2) The responsibility of reviewing purchase orders issued by user departments.
(3) The authority to make purchases of requisitioned materials and services.
(4) A direct reporting responsibility to the controller of the organization.

s. An auditor is planning the study and evaluation of internal control for purchasing and disbursement procedures. In planning this study and evaluation the auditor will be *least* influenced by
(1) The availability of a company manual describing purchasing and disbursement procedures.
(2) The scope and results of audit work by the company's internal auditor.
(3) The existence within the purchasing and disbursement area of internal control strengths that offset weaknesses.
(4) The strength or weakness of internal control in other areas, e.g., sales and accounts receivable.

t. When evaluating inventory controls with respect to segregation of duties, a CPA would be *least* likely to
(1) Inspect documents.
(2) Make inquiries.

(3) Observe procedures.
(4) Consider policy and procedure manuals.

u. The ordinary examination of financial statements is *not* primarily designed to disclose defalcations and other irregularities although their discovery may result. Normal audit procedures are more likely to detect a fraud arising from
(1) Collusion on the part of several employees.
(2) Failure to record cash receipts for services rendered.
(3) Forgeries on company checks.
(4) Theft of inventories.

v. Which of the following is an internal control procedure that would prevent a paid disbursement voucher from being presented for payment a second time?
(1) Vouchers should be prepared by individuals who are responsible for signing disbursement checks.
(2) Disbursement vouchers should be approved by at least two responsible management officials.
(3) The date on a disbursement voucher should be within a few days of the date the voucher is presented for payment.
(4) The official signing the check should compare the check with the voucher and should deface the voucher documents.

w. With respect to a small company's system of purchasing supplies, an auditor's primary concern should be to obtain satisfaction that supplies ordered and paid for have been
(1) Requested by and approved by authorized individuals who have *no* incompatible duties.
(2) Received, counted, and checked to quantities and amounts on purchase orders and invoices.
(3) Properly recorded as assets and systematically amortized over the estimated useful life of the supplies.
(4) Used in the course of business and solely for business purposes during the year under audit.

x. Which of the following is an effective internal accounting control over cash payments?
(1) Signed checks should be mailed under the supervision of the check signer.
(2) Spoiled checks that have been voided should be disposed of immediately.
(3) Checks should be prepared only by persons responsible for cash receipts and cash disbursements.
(4) A check-signing machine with two signatures should be utilized.

(AICPA adapted)

P11–2 Select the best answer for each of the following items relating to verifying the existence of inventory.

a. An auditor will usually trace the details of the test counts made during the observation of the physical inventory taking to a final inventory schedule. This audit procedure is undertaken to provide evidence that items physically present and observed by the auditor at the time of the physical inventory count are
(1) Owned by the client.
(2) *Not* obsolete.

(3) Physically present at the time of the preparation of the final inventory schedule.
(4) Included in the final inventory schedule.

b. The physical count of inventory of a retailer was higher than shown by the perpetual records. Which of the following could explain the difference?
(1) Inventory items had been counted but the tags placed on the items had *not* been taken off the items and added to the inventory accumulation sheets.
(2) Credit memos for several items returned by customers had *not* been prepared.
(3) *No* journal entry had been made on the retailer's books for several items returned to its suppliers.
(4) An item purchased "FOB shipping point" had *not* arrived at the date of the inventory count and had *not* been reflected in the perpetual records.

c. When outside firms of nonaccountants specializing in the taking of physical inventories are used to count, list, price, and subsequently compute the total dollar amount of inventory on hand at the date of the physical count, the auditor will ordinarily
(1) Consider the report of the outside inventory-taking firm to be an acceptable alternative procedure to the observation of physical inventories.
(2) Make or observe some physical counts of the inventory, recompute certain inventory calculations and test certain inventory transactions.
(3) *Not* reduce the extent of work on the physical count of inventory.
(4) Consider the reduced audit effort with respect to the physical count of inventory as a scope limitation.

d. The auditor tests the quantity of materials charged to work in process by tracing these quantities to
(1) Cost ledgers.
(2) Perpetual inventory records.
(3) Receiving reports.
(4) Material requisitions.

e. From which of the following evidence-gathering audit procedures would an auditor obtain *most* assurance concerning the existence of inventories?
(1) Observation of physical inventory counts.
(2) Written inventory representations from management.
(3) Confirmation of inventories in a public warehouse.
(4) Auditor's recomputation of inventory extensions.

f. Which one of the following procedures would *not* be appropriate for an auditor in discharging his responsibilities concerning the client's physical inventories?
(1) Confirmation of goods in the hands of public warehouses.
(2) Supervising the taking of the annual physical inventory.
(3) Carrying out physical inventory procedures at an interim date.
(4) Obtaining written representation from the client as to the existence, quality, and dollar amount of the inventory.

g. The primary objective of a CPA's observation of a client's physical inventory count is to
(1) Discover whether a client has counted a particular inventory item or group of items.
(2) Obtain direct knowledge that the inventory exists and has been properly counted.

(3) Provide an appraisal of the quality of the merchandise on hand on the day of the physical count.
(4) Allow the auditor to supervise the conduct of the count so as to obtain assurance that inventory quantities are reasonably accurate.

h. A client's physical count of inventories was lower than the inventory quantities shown in its perpetual records. This situation could be the result of the failure to record.
(1) Sales.
(2) Sales returns.
(3) Purchases.
(4) Purchase discounts.

(AICPA adapted)

P11–3 Select the best answer for each of the following items relating to the verification of cutoff for cost of sales system accounts.

a. In order to efficiently establish the correctness of the accounts payable cutoff, an auditor will be *most* likely to
(1) Coordinate cutoff tests with physical inventory observation.
(2) Compare cutoff reports with purchase orders.
(3) Compare vendors' invoices with vendors' statements.
(4) Coordinate mailing of confirmations with cutoff tests.

b. When title to merchandise in transit has passed to the audit client, the auditor engaged in the performance of a purchase cutoff will encounter the greatest difficulty in gaining assurance with respect to the
(1) Quantity.
(2) Quality.
(3) Price.
(4) Terms.

c. The audit of year-end physical inventories should include steps to verify that the client's purchases and sales cutoffs were adequate. The audit steps should be designed to detect whether merchandise included in the physical count at year end was *not* recorded as a
(1) Sale in the subsequent period.
(2) Purchase in the current period.
(3) Sale in the current period.
(4) Purchase return in the subsequent period.

d. Purchase cutoff procedures should be designed to test that merchandise is included in the inventory of the client company, if the company
(1) Has paid for the merchandise.
(2) Has physical possession of the merchandise.
(3) Holds legal title to the merchandise.
(4) Holds the shipping documents for the merchandise issued in the company's name.

e. To *best* ascertain that a company has properly included merchandise that it owns in its ending inventory, the auditor should review and test the
(1) Terms of the open purchase orders.
(2) Purchase cutoff procedures.

(3) Contractual commitments made by the purchasing department.
(4) Purchase invoices received on or around year end.

(AICPA adapted)

P11–4 Select the best answer for each of the following items relating to the verification of valuation of inventory.

a. Which of the following is the *best* audit procedure for the discovery of damaged merchandise in a client's ending inventory?
   (1) Compare the physical quantities of slow-moving items with corresponding quantities of the prior year.
   (2) Observe merchandise and raw materials during the client's physical inventory taking.
   (3) Review the management's inventory representation letter for accuracy.
   (4) Test overall fairness of inventory values by comparing the company's turnover ratio with the industry average.

b. A CPA examining inventory may appropriately apply sampling for attributes in order to estimate the
   (1) Average price of inventory items.
   (2) Percentage of slow-moving inventory items.
   (3) Dollar value of inventory.
   (4) Physical quantity of inventory items.

c. In verifying debits to perpetual inventory records of a nonmanufacturing firm, the auditor would be *most* interested in examining the purchase
   (1) Journal.
   (2) Requisitions.
   (3) Orders.
   (4) Invoices.

d. The accuracy of perpetual inventory records may be established, in part, by comparing perpetual inventory records, with
   (1) Purchase requisitions.
   (2) Receiving reports.
   (3) Purchase orders.
   (4) Vendor payments.

e. When an auditor tests a client's cost accounting system, the auditor's tests are *primarily* designed to determine that
   (1) Quantities on hand have been computed based on acceptable cost accounting techniques that reasonably approximate actual quantities on hand.
   (2) Physical inventories are in substantial agreement with book inventories.
   (3) The system is in accordance with generally accepted accounting principles and is functioning as planned.
   (4) Costs have been properly assigned to finished goods, work in process, and cost of goods sold.

f. An auditor would be *most* likely to learn of slow-moving inventory through
   (1) Inquiry of sales personnel.
   (2) Inquiry of stores personnel.
   (3) Physical observation of inventory.
   (4) Review of perpetual inventory records.

g. An inventory turnover analysis is useful to the auditor because it may detect
   (1) Inadequacies in inventory pricing.

(2) Methods of avoiding cyclical holding costs.
(3) The optimum automatic reorder points.
(4) The existence of obsolete merchandise.

h. Which of the following would detect an understatement of a purchase discount?
(1) Verify footings and crossfootings of purchases and disbursement records.
(2) Compare purchase invoice terms with disbursement records and checks.
(3) Compare approved purchase orders to receiving reports.
(4) Verify the receipt of items ordered and invoiced.

(AICPA adapted)

P11–5 Select the best answer for each of the following items.

a. Auditor confirmation of accounts payable balances at the balance sheet date may be *unnecessary* because
(1) This is a duplication of cutoff tests.
(2) Accounts payable balances at the balance sheet date may *not* be paid before the audit is completed.
(3) Correspondence with the audit client's attorney will reveal all legal action by vendors for nonpayment.
(4) There is likely to be other reliable external evidence available to support the balances.

b. Propex Corporation uses a voucher register and does *not* record invoices in a subsidiary ledger. Propex will probably benefit most from the additional cost of maintaining an accounts payable subsidiary ledger if
(1) There are usually invoices in an unmatched invoice file.
(2) Vendors' requests for confirmation of receivables often go unanswered for several months until paid invoices can be reviewed.
(3) Partial payments to vendors are continuously made in the ordinary course of business.
(4) It is difficult to reconcile vendors' monthly statements.

c. If a client is using a voucher system, the auditor who is examining accounts payable records should obtain a schedule of all unpaid vouchers at the balance sheet date and
(1) Retrace voucher register items to the source indicated in the reference column of the register.
(2) Vouch items in the voucher register and examine related canceled checks.
(3) Confirm items on the schedule of unpaid vouchers and obtain satisfaction for all confirmation exceptions.
(4) Compare the items on the schedule with open vouchers and uncanceled entries in the voucher register and account for unmatched items.

d. An auditor generally obtains from a client a formal written statement concerning the accuracy of inventory. This particular letter of representation is used by the auditor to
(1) Reduce the scope of the auditor's physical inventory work but *not* the other inventory audit work that is normally performed.
(2) Confirm in writing the valuation basis used by the client to value the inventory at the lower of cost or market.
(3) Lessen the auditor's responsibility for the fair presentation of balance sheet inventories.

(4) Remind management that the primary responsibility for the overall fairness of the financial statements rests with management and *not* with the auditor.

e. Elijah Stone was asked to perform the first audit of a wholesale business that does *not* maintain perpetual inventory records. Stone has observed the current inventory but has *not*observed the physical inventory at the previous year-end date and concludes that the opening inventory balance, which is *not* auditable, is a material factor in the determination of cost of goods sold for the current year. Stone will probably
   (1) Decline the engagement.
   (2) Express an unqualified opinion on the balance sheet and income statement except for inventory.
   (3) Express an unqualified opinion on the balance sheet and disclaim an opinion on the income statement.
   (4) Disclaim an opinion on the balance sheet and income statement.

f. An auditor obtains a magnetic tape that contains the dollar amounts of all client inventory items by style number. The information on the tape is in no particular sequence. The auditor can *best* ascertain that *no* consigned merchandise is included on the tape by using a computer program that
   (1) Statistically selects samples of all amounts.
   (2) Excludes all amounts for items with particular style numbers that indicate consigned merchandise.
   (3) Mathematically calculates the extension of each style quantity by the unit price.
   (4) Prints on paper the information that is on the magnetic tape.

g. A client's procurement system ends with the assumption of a liability and the eventual payment of the liability. Which of the following *best* describes the auditor's primary concern with respect to liabilities resulting from the procurement system?
   (1) Accounts payable are *not* materially understated.
   (2) Authority to incur liabilities is restricted to one designated person.
   (3) Acquisition of materials is *not* made from one vendor or one group of vendors.
   (4) Commitments for all purchases are made only after established competitive bidding procedures are followed.

(AICPA adapted)

P11–6 Items **a** through **e** are questions excerpted from a typical internal control questionnaire designed to evaluate internal accounting controls over processing of purchase orders and receipt of goods and services. As explained in the text, a "yes" response to any such question indicates a potential strength in the system while a "no" response indicates a potential weakness.

a. Are purchases of all goods and services made only from valid purchase requisitions transmitted by the stores department?

b. Are prenumbered purchase orders prepared and approved by the purchasing agent as to vendor, goods or services ordered, prices, or other terms?

c. Are prenumbered receiving reports prepared for all receipts of goods and goods and services?

d. Are vendor invoices compared with receiving records and purchase orders for quantity, price, and amounts back-ordered?

Required:

For each question above, list:

a. The error or irregularity that item was designed to detect.
b. The effect that the absence of the control would have on the financial statements.
c. The compliance tests that would be necessary in order to ascertain whether the control were actually being implemented if the answer to the internal control question were "yes". When sampling of documents is involved, indicate the data file from which a sample would be chosen, along with the audit procedure (e.g., vouching, tracing, recalculation, etc.) that is most appropriate (see Figure 11–10).
d. The substantive test (see Figure 11–11) that would have to be extended, if any, if that control were missing or if the client demonstrated a low level of compliance. Organize your answer according to the format specified below. The first question has been answered as an example.

Item	Error or Irregularity	Effect on Financial Statements	Compliance Test	Substantive Test
(a)	*Invalid transactions*	*Ordering goods not needed for production*	*Vouch purchase orders to purchase requisitions*	*Scrutinize inventory turnover ratio; examine inventory records for evidence of slow-moving inventory*

P11–7 Items **a** through **g** are questions excerpted from a typical internal control questionnaire for the purpose of evaluating internal accounting controls over the accounting for purchases, accounts payable, and inventory. As explained in the text, a "yes" response indicates a potential strength in the system while a "no" response indicates a potential weakness.

a. Is the preparation of initial purchase records performed by persons who do not also prepare purchase requisitions, sign checks, and otherwise handle cash?
b. Is proper documentation (in the form of purchase orders, receiving reports, purchase requisitions, and vendor invoices) required before vouchers are prepared?
c. Are supporting records (purchase orders, receiving reports, etc.) compared to vendor invoices for prices, quantities, terms, etc., before vouchers are approved for payment?
d. Are subsidiary records maintained of trade payables by persons independent of cash disbursements and purchasing functions?
e. Are recorded cash disbursements matched individually or adequately tested against initial credits in the subsidiary accounts payable records?
f. Are perpetual records maintained over quantities and unit prices for all material inventory items?

g. Are perpetual records of inventories periodically reconciled with physical counts and with general ledger account totals?

Required:

For each question above, list:

a. The error or irregularity that control attribute was designed to detect.
b. The effect that the absence of the control attribute would have on the financial statements.
c. The compliance test that would be necessary to ascertain whether the control was actually being implemented if the answer to the internal control question were "yes." When sampling of documents is involved, indicate the data file from which a sample would be selected and the audit procedure (e.g., vouching, tracing, recalculation, etc.) most appropriate for the sample (see Figure 11–10).

CHAPTER

12

AUDIT OF PAYROLL SYSTEMS AND CASH BALANCES

One of the most important elements of the cost accounting and cash disbursement systems is payroll. In this chapter we give special attention to the audit of payroll-related transactions and balances, including cash balances. The chapter can be divided into the following main subtopics:

1. Procedures followed in auditing the payroll system and its related account balances.
2. Special considerations associated with the verification of cash balances.
3. Discussion of the substantive tests to be performed in verifying cash balances.

We also include, as appendixes to the chapter, illustrations of the working papers typically used in the audit of cash.

AUDIT OF PAYROLL SYSTEMS AND RELATED ACCOUNTS

A number of accounts are associated with the payroll system. They include work in process and finished goods inventories, direct labor, indirect labor, vacation and other fringe benefits accounts, pension expense, payroll taxes, and related accrued liabilities. Payroll systems for various clients may range from simple to very complex. However, they will always include the functions of ***employment, accumulation and distribution of payroll costs***, and ***disbursement of cash.*** As is the case for other subsystems, the verification of payroll requires an evaluation of the internal accounting controls associated with the payroll system and the verification of certain of the account balances produced by the systems. Figure 12–1 shows diagrammatically how some of these balances are related.

Cash in Bank—Regular

Debit	Credit
Beginning bal. xxx	xxx (3)
xxx (1)	xxx (8)
xxx (2)	
Ending bal. xxx	

Cash in Bank—Payroll

Debit	Credit
Beginning bal. xxx	
xxx (8)	xxx (7)
Ending bal. xxx	

Salaries and Wages Expense

Debit	Credit
xxx (4)	

Accrued Salaries and Wages

Debit	Credit
xxx (7)	Beginning bal. xxx
	xxx (4)
	Ending bal. xxx

Payroll Tax Expense

Debit	Credit
xxx (5)	

Accrued Tax Expense

Debit	Credit
xxx (7)	Beginning bal. xxx
	xxx (5)
	Ending bal. xxx

Employee Benefits Expense

Debit	Credit
xxx (6)	

Accrued Employee Benefits

Debit	Credit
xxx (7)	Beginning bal. xxx
	xxx (6)
	Ending bal. xxx

(1) Cash receipts from revenue system (Figure 10–1); (2) Cash receipts from other systems; (3) Cash disbursements from cost of sales system (Figure 11–1); (4) Accrued salaries and wages (Figure 11–1); (5) Accrued payroll taxes; (6) Accrued employee benefits; (7) Cash disbursements for accrued liabilities; (8) Reimbursement of payroll bank account.

FIGURE 12–1. Flow of Transactions: Payroll System and Cash Balance

The primary objective to be met in auditing the payroll system is the verification of transaction validity. Other audit objectives include verification of existence of payroll bank accounts and the accrued liabilities related to payrolls; proper valuation for related asset, expense, and liability accounts; appropriate cutoff for charges and credits to expense and liability accounts, respectively; and verification of appropriate statement presentation for inventories, payables, and expense balances.

Verification of Transaction Validity

The payroll system typically includes a large number of transactions involving the disbursement of cash. Therefore, the auditor must give special attention to evaluating the internal control procedures within the system as a basis for the verification of transaction validity. A primary consideration in this evaluation is to determine whether the system provides assurance that employees on the client's payroll actually exist and are being paid in accordance with prescribed managerial policy. That determination requires that the auditor evaluate the client's payroll system with respect to the elements of internal control listed in Figure 5–1.

Just as with other systems previously discussed, the independent auditor will be evaluating only the *material controls* — that is, controls which, if missing, could result in a material misstatement of an item(s) in the financial statements. To isolate those controls, it is important to visualize the *exchange transactions* and related documents that result in charges and credits to various accounts in the payroll system. Figure 12–2 lists the major exchange transactions as (1) accruals of payroll, withholding taxes, and related liabilities, and (2) payment of those liabilities.

Boundary Documents. Boundary documents for accrual of wages and related employment costs are employee time cards or sheets for hourly wage personnel, and employment records for salaried personnel. Supporting documents for payroll charges include employment files, rate authorization slips, W-4 forms, and deduction slips to ensure that the employee was working for the company at the time the costs were incurred. Additional supporting documents, such as labor distribution sheets and individual payroll records, provide for a proper system of approvals, assuring that the payroll amounts were properly recorded.

Boundary exchange documents for the payment of payroll-related liabilities are cancelled checks. These, in turn, are supported by payroll records for individual employees, and a payroll voucher system that operates in the same manner as the one

Exchange Transaction	Boundary Document	Supporting Document
Accrual of payroll, withholding taxes	Employee time cards	Employment files Rate authorization
	Salaried payroll: Employment records	Employee exemption certificates (W–4) Deduction slips Labor distribution sheets Individual payroll records
Payment of accrued liabilities	Employee paychecks	Individual payroll records Summary voucher to reimburse payroll account
	Checks in payment of other accrued liabilities	Vouchers in support of disbursements

FIGURE 12–2. Exchange Transaction and Documents: Payrolls and Related Costs

described for payment of trade payables to ensure proper controls over the issuance of payroll checks. Normally, an ***imprest payroll bank account*** will be used to further reduce the probability of improper payroll disbursements. With this arrangement, a check for the total amount of the payroll, supported by a voucher, will be drawn against the general cash account to reimburse the imprest payroll cash account each time a payroll is to be met. Payroll checks will then be drawn against the imprest account.

Exchange Functions. The payroll system can be subdivided into three segments: (1) exchange functions, (2) processing functions, and (3) safeguard functions; each requiring its own specific controls. Exchange functions include hiring of employees, authorization of rates and deductions, timekeeping, preparation of payroll, the recognition of related taxes and other charges, and payment of payroll and the related liabilities.

Processing Functions. These functions include all those activities associated with recording the exchange transactions in the books of the company. A payroll accounting department is typically responsible for processing functions, including the allocation of charges associated with payroll — for example, the distributions to direct and indirect labor in a manufacturing firm. The auditor will want to test these distributions during the course of the audit. That department should also normally be held responsible for the preparation of periodic governmental reports reflecting employee earnings and deductions.

Safeguard Functions. These functions primarily involve the custody and handling of the payroll cash account. Figure 12–3 shows the exchange, processing, and safeguard functions found in a typical payroll system, along with the possible errors or irregularities, results of undetected errors, and the related control attributes for each function.

In a manually maintained system, the auditor should study the client's functions to determine the extent to which the five elements of a good internal control system (Figure 5–1) are prescribed by the client. To do this, the auditor should use either an internal control questionnaire or flowcharts (developed from the client's organization chart, procedures manuals, or inquiry of client personnel). As explained in previous chapters, the internal control questionnaire for payrolls should contain yes – no questions about the system, designed to ascertain its strengths and weaknesses. Control attributes to be included in the questionnaire are listed in Figure 12–3. The format of the questionnaire is identical to that illustrated in previous chapters and is therefore not illustrated in this chapter. Typical internal control flowcharts for a payroll system containing the attributes of good accounting control are illustrated in Figures 12–4 and 12–5. Observe from these flowcharts that appropriate *separation of responsibilities* with respect to payrolls requires that the personnel, timekeeping, accounting, and payment functions for payroll be separated. Payroll checks should be distributed by persons other than those involved in the personnel, production, or payroll accounting functions. In many instances a receptionist or someone else having no connection with payroll computations can be assigned that task. If payments are made in cash, each employee should be asked to sign a receipt at the time the payments are distributed. *Specific placement of responsibilities* requires that each of the appropriately defined duties be assigned to specific employees.

Adequate *records, forms, and authorizations* for payrolls include separate documents for authorization of personnel changes, payroll deductions, rate authorization, timekeeping, and labor distribution. A separate imprest payroll bank account should be used for making payroll disbursements, to help safeguard the assets of the system.

Testing the System for Compliance

If the auditor is satisfied that the prescribed accounting controls have the potential for preventing, detecting, or correcting material financial statement errors or irregularities, he or she must then determine the extent of compliance with those controls. As with cases cited in previous chapters, some internal accounting controls over payrolls will not be supported by documentary evidence indicating that they were performed; these controls are the proper segregation of duties and the specific placement of responsibilities. Again, these controls are tested chiefly by means of inquiry and observation.

Other accounting controls should be supported by documentary evidence showing that they were performed. These include controls over certain of the exchange and processing functions listed in Figure 12–3, such as documentation and approval of personnel changes, wage rates, withholdings and payment of wages in accordance with prescribed managerial policies. Figure 12–6 illustrates the sampling methodology for testing compliance with documented exchange and processing controls. As you examine Figure 12–6, notice that samples are drawn from data files located in each major department depicted in the systems flowcharts shown in Figures 12–4 and 12–5. In each case where sampling is appropriate, the auditor selects the evidence-gathering technique most useful in meeting the audit objective of ascertaining internal control compliance. Where *vouching* and *tracing* are appropriate, notice that some vouching and some tracing are performed for each important data population in the system. Notice also that, whenever data files (such as the payroll register, payroll journal, job or production cost records, and cancelled checks) are part of the transaction files resulting in financial statement balances, the tests performed on these files serve a dual function — to ascertain compliance with established controls and to ascertain that transactions resulting in account balances are properly recorded.

As shown in Figure 12–6, the auditor sometimes performs a surprise observation of a client's regular distribution of payroll checks to obtain satisfaction that persons listed on the payroll actually exist and are working for the company. This procedure, although effective in achieving the desired objective, is usually performed only if other controls attributes to ensure existence of paid employees are not prescribed by the client. Appendix 12–G describes in memorandum form the audit test work typically performed for payrolls.

Substantive Tests for Verification of Payroll-Related Balances

The balances that relate to the payroll system usually include wages and salaries expense, the direct labor part of work-in-process inventories, accrued wages payable, payroll tax expenses, related accrued payables, and the payroll cash account. Procedures for verifying the payroll cash account balance are the same as those used to verify

Function	Possible Errors or Irregularities
Hiring and termination of employees; authorization of pay rates, deductions	Invalid or erroneous transactions: Hiring an unauthorized employee or paying an employee the wrong amount; Recording the hiring of a fictitious employee
Timekeeping	Invalid Transactions: Erroneous or deliberately misstated time records (punching more than one time card or misstating time tickets)
Preparation of payroll and taxes	Invalid or improperly recorded transactions: Insertion of fictitious employee by person preparing payroll; using incorrect rates (regular, overtime, incentive), hours
Paying the payroll and taxes	Improperly valued transactions: Checks issued for incorrect amounts; Invalid transactions: Checks mailed or distributed to unauthorized persons; Transactions not timely recorded: Tax returns filed and paid late; Improperly recorded and summarized transactions: Inadequate control over unclaimed wages and cash disbursements for payroll

FIGURE 12–3. Exchange Processing and Safeguard Functions Requiring Specific Controls

other balances (see the last section of this chapter). Therefore we give our attention to the verification of charges and credits to other payroll-related account balances, including the allocation of charges to work-in-process inventories, in this part of the chapter. In this phase of the audit, the auditor is primarily concerned with the possibilities of overpayments and unauthorized payments.

Results of Undetected Errors	Control Attributes to Prevent, Detect, or Correct Errors or Irregularities
Misappropriation of cash through payrolls	Require a separate personnel department through which is approved job descriptions; authorization of new hirees and terminations; rate changes; deductions.
Misappropriation of cash through payrolls	Require authorization of salaried personnel through board of directors or personnel committee. Require operating departments to requisition all new hirees, terminations, and changes. Require documentation for all wage data in personnel files. The names of persons on the payroll should be traced to the personnel department records to be sure that they were employees of the company during the period.
Overpayments or misappropriation of cash through overstatement of payroll liability	Require use of timeclocks and time cards for all hourly personnel. Require departmental supervisors to approve all regular and overtime hours worked and to supervise clock punching. Control the supply of unused time cards. Require preparation of time tickets for job costing system. Require reconciliation of time tickets with time cards. Daily time reports or job time cards should be reconciled with total hours worked as shown on employee timeclock cards.
Misstatement of payroll liability	Separate the duties of payroll preparation, timekeeping, and cash disbursements. Require approval of rates and hours worked.
Misappropriation of cash	Require verification of checks issued with payroll register.
Missappropriation of cash	Require checks to be mailed without being returned to preparer.
Inefficient use of cash	Require identification for distributees of paychecks. Require timely filing and payment of payroll taxes.
Inaccuracies in recording payroll liability and cash disbursements	Require separate imprest payroll bank account, reconciled by persons independent from other payroll functions. Require follow-up for unclaimed wages, including restoration of unclaimed checks to cash along with establishment of current liability. Unclaimed payroll checks, held by the treasury department, should be periodically checked by the accounting department against their record of those checks.

FIGURE 12–3 (continued)

The primary audit objectives to be fulfilled for payroll-related account balances include verification of the following:

- Appropriate statement presentation (disclosures) for all balances.
- Valuations for all balances.

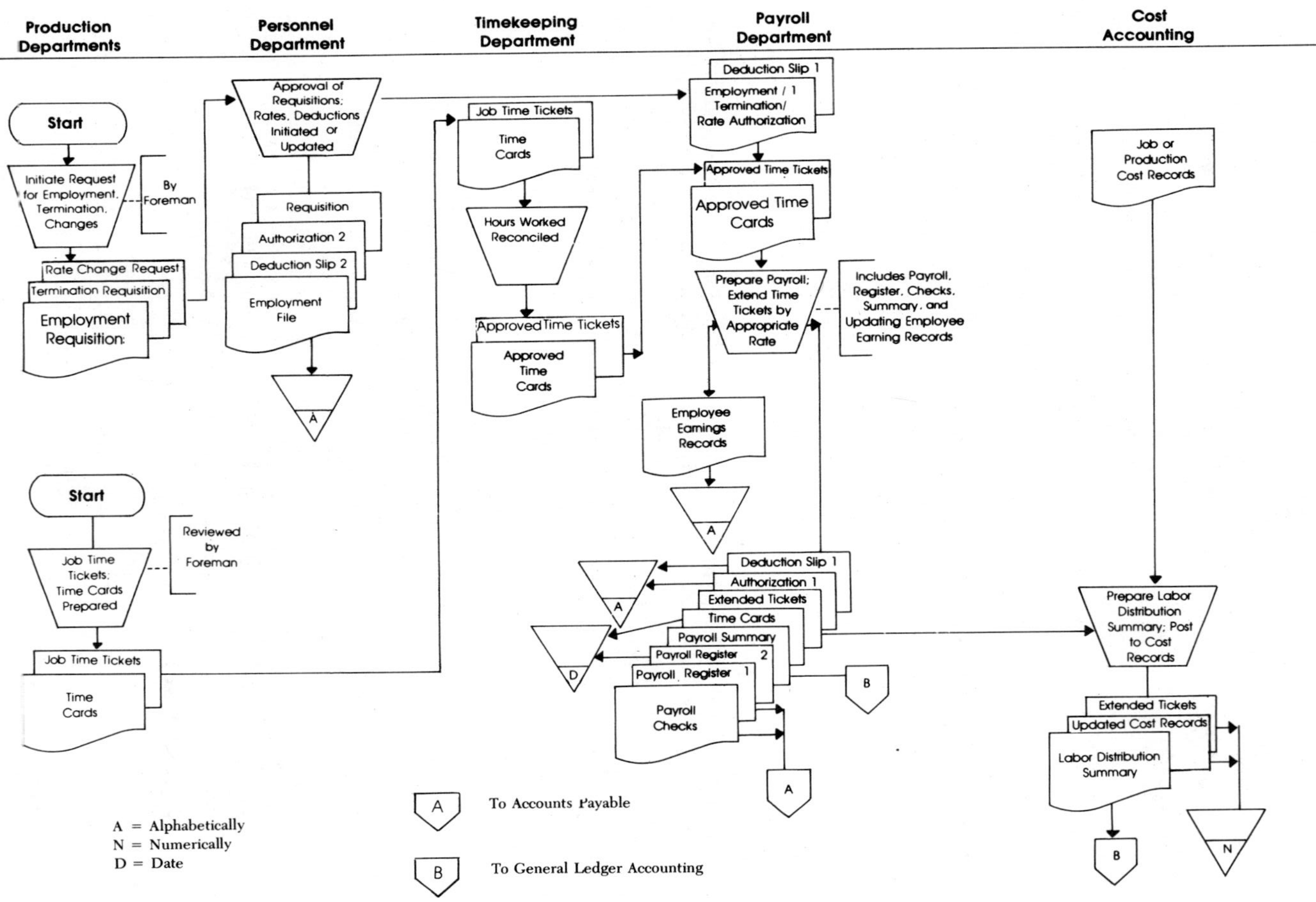

FIGURE 12–4. Employment and Payroll Cost Accumulation

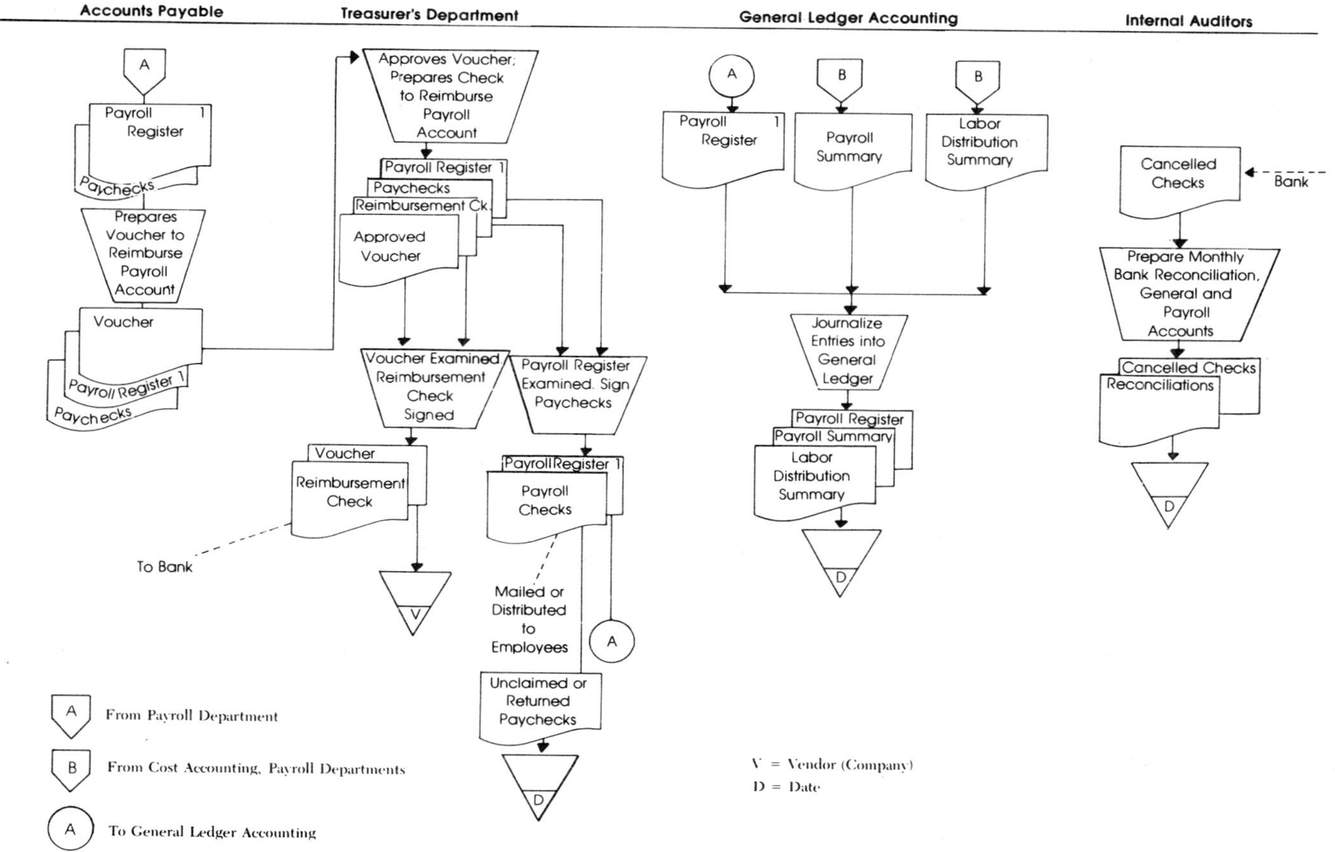

FIGURE 12–5. Cash Disbursements and General Ledger Accounting for Payrolls

Attribute of Interest	Data Field (Population)	Sample Size
New hirees, termination, rate changes, and other changes are subjected to proper approvals	Employee earnings records: new hirees, terminations, rate changes	*
Personnel being paid are both existent and authorized	Employee earnings records (names, rates)	*
Personnel actions (new hires, rate changes, terminations) are appropriately processed	Employment requisitions, terminations, rate change files	*
Payroll deductions are properly authorized by employees	Employee earnings records: deductions	*
Payroll deductions are processed correctly	Deductions slips	*
Timekeeping data about employees are adequately supported	Payroll journal (hours worked)	*
Timekeeping data about each job or department are adequately supported and in agreement with employee data	Job or production cost records	*
Regular and overtime hours worked are approved by departmental supervisors	Time cards	*
Checks issued to employees are verified to net pay per payroll register	Cancelled checks per bank statement	*
Entries in payroll register are supported by cancelled checks	Entries in payroll register	*
Identification is required of all distributees of paychecks	Cancelled checks	Use same sample as for verification of checks to payroll register
Follow-up is required for unclaimed wages	Outstanding checks from payroll bank account	Judgmental

*Determine judgmentally or statistically, according to methodology discussed in Chapter 10.

FIGURE 12–6. Transactions Testing Methodology: Payrolls System

Audit Procedure	From	To
Vouch	Employee earnings records	Authorization slips, board of directors, or personnel committee minutes
Vouch to number of hours worked as shown on approved payroll time cards	Employee earnings records	Personnel files
Trace	Employment requisition files in personnel departments	Employee earnings records
Vouch	Employee earnings records	Supporting data in employment file (W–4s, union contracts, etc.)
Trace	Deduction slips	Employee earnings records, payable journals, ledgers
Vouch	Payroll journal	Time cards
Vouch	Job or production cost records	Extended time tickets
Reconcile	Job or production cost records	Payroll summary and payroll journals
Reconcile	Time cards	Job time tickets
Vouch hours worked	Time cards	Management approval signatures
Trace	Cancelled checks	Entries in payroll register, employee earnings records
Vouch	Payroll register	Cancelled checks
Vouch	Cancelled checks	Employment files (W–4s, etc.)
Observe a surprise distribution of payroll checks†		
Trace	Outstanding check list	Subsequent entry to restore to cash and set up current liability account

†Should be performed by the auditor only if other attributes of internal control are missing.

FIGURE 12–6 (continued)

- Periodicity (cutoff) for expense and payables accounts.
- Existence for payroll-related liability accounts.

The relationship among these objectives and the procedures necessary to satisfy those objectives is shown in Figure 12–7.

Verification of *appropriate statement presentation* requires the auditor to inspect the payroll-related accounts in the financial statements for proper classification and disclosures.

Procedures for verifying the *valuation* of payroll-related account balances begin by vouching the charges and credits in the various accounts to source documents. The items to be tested should be selected from entries to the payroll general ledger accounts (salaries and wages expense, payroll tax expense, accrued payroll, etc.). Then entries should be vouched to the appropriate supporting documents (time cards, employee personnel files, etc.). The auditor should also, for one or more test periods, recalculate gross pay and deductions (FICA, withholding, and other deductions) for a sample of employees. This procedure could, for example, assist the auditor in the discovery of thefts perpetrated by the preparation of erroneous W-2 forms, which is a type of irregularity that could occur when the accounting and payroll computation functions have not been adequately separated. All footings and extensions of the payroll journal should be recalculated and traced to debit and credit postings in the labor-related expense accounts and the wages and salaries payable accounts, respectively. In auditing a computerized system, the machine readable (time cards, etc.) payroll input data for each employee in the sample should be vouched to the underlying payroll documents and data (time cards for hours worked and rates per payroll records). Net pay for each employee should also be vouched to cancelled checks.

Notice that these procedures were also described in previous sections as compliance tests. However, since they are directly balance-related, they are again mentioned here. As we have seen, these tests are often called dual-purpose tests.

Periodic net pay totals in the payroll journals should be vouched to transfers from the general bank account to the payroll bank account. The debit to the payroll bank account should then be vouched to a validated deposit slip and to the cash transfer voucher.

Valuation of charges to work-in-process inventory for labor-related costs can be verified by reconciling labor cost data per the payroll summary with total charges to labor accounts per the payroll register for one or more periods. Payroll summary totals should also be reconciled with the labor distribution summary for corresponding periods. Finally, the totals from the labor distribution summary can be traced to postings in the general ledger account. Refer to the systems flowcharts in Figures 12–4 and 12–5 for a diagrammatic picture of how this information flows into the ledger accounts. The process just described is one of following the audit trail from books of original entry to postings in the general ledger accounts. The auditor should also vouch entries in the various general ledger accounts to labor distribution and payroll summary totals, then reconcile those amounts with totals of the payroll register for selected periods. Once it has been ascertained that those payroll summaries were posted correctly, the auditor should vouch the entries in the summaries to supporting documents (such as time tickets for various jobs or departments, as shown in Figure 12–4). Also, a sample of time tickets should be selected and traced into the summaries.

AUDIT OBJECTIVES			
Verify Appropriate Statement Presentation	**Verify Appropriate Valuation**	**Verify Cutoff**	**Verify Existence of Liabilities**
1. *Inspect* payroll related accounts in the financial statements for proper classification and disclosures.	1. *Vouch* charges and credits in payroll-related general ledger accounts to payroll journal, computer input, and supporting documents 2. *Recalculate* gross pay and deductions for a sample of employees 3. *Recalculate* footings and extensions of a sample of payroll journal pages 4. *Trace* postings of payroll journal to general ledger account postings 5. *Vouch* net pay total from payroll journal to transfers from general bank account to payroll bank account 6. *Reconcile* labor costs per payroll summary to charges in labor accounts per general ledger 7. *Reconcile* payroll summary totals with labor distribution summary totals 8. *Trace* totals in labor distribution summary to posting in general ledger accounts 9. *Vouch* entries in labor distribution summary to supporting documents 10. *Analyze* payroll expense accounts 11. *Recompute* accrued salaries payable; other payroll-related accruals	1. *Recompute* accrued payables and other payroll-related accruals	1. *Recompute* salaries payable and other payroll-related accruals 2. *Compare* with recorded totals of accrued liabilities 3. *Inspect* payroll tax returns

FIGURE 12–7. Substantive Tests Transactions and Balances for Payroll-Related Accounts

Individual payroll expense accounts should be analyzed by comparing total wages in the various accounts with corresponding amounts from previous periods. Significant variations should be investigated and related to corroborative evidence. Accounts should also be scanned for unusual transactions, such as unusually large pay checks, unusually large costs, or improper classifications.

To ascertain proper ***valuation, cutoff,*** and ***existence for accrued liability accounts*** relating to payroll, the auditor should compute the client's accruals that are material in amount. For example, accrued salaries might be calculated by multiplying total gross pay for the pay period that extends through the client's year end by the fraction of that period which falls within the fiscal year. FICA taxes withheld can be recomputed for a sample of employees by multiplying the applicable rate by base wages for those employees. Withholding taxes can be recomputed for the same sample by use of appropriate payroll tax tables. Accrued payroll taxes payable can be recomputed for the final pay period as follows:

$$\left(\begin{array}{c}\text{FICA taxes withheld per}\\ \text{pay period} \times 2 + \text{withholding}\\ \text{taxes for pay period}\end{array}\right) \times \frac{\begin{array}{c}\text{days in pay period}\\ \text{prior to fiscal year end}\end{array}}{\text{days in pay period}}.$$

Unemployment tax accruals should also be recomputed using proper rates and salary bases. The recomputed accruals should then be compared with those recorded in the accounts and significant differences should be resolved. The client's payroll tax forms (940 and 941) should then be examined to ascertain whether they were filed in a timely and correct manner.

Using the Computer to Perform Payroll Audit Procedures

When records are computerized, the computer can be used to assist the auditor in performing any of the compliance or substantive procedures listed in the preceding sections, if they are repetitive or mechanical. For example, it can be used to perform a 100 percent recomputation of the gross pay, deductions, and net pay for all employees. It can also be programmed to verify the footings and extensions in payroll-related records and to trace postings of accounting summaries into the related general ledger accounts. We can also use the computer to trace related input documents to the payroll records and to print out register entries which correspond to cancelled checks. Those entries can then be used in the auditor's manual vouching procedures. The computer can also be programmed to scan the accounts for unusual transactions and to print out transactions that exceed certain limits. Such exceptions can then be discussed with the client and related to corroborative evidence, if necessary.

VERIFICATION OF CASH BALANCES

In quantitative terms, cash account balances are generally small in relation to such things as accounts receivable, inventory, and fixed assets. Nevertheless, auditors have historically, for two reasons, spent more than a proportionate amount of time in auditing cash transactions and end-of-the-period cash balances. For one thing, all business activities are oriented toward the conversion of resources to cash and the settlement of obligations in cash. Therefore, at some point in the life of the business, ***the results of all business activities will pass through cash.*** This frame of thought is evident as we refer to the "***cash back to cash***" ***cycle.*** The ***operating cycle,*** for example, is characterized as the average period elapsing between the commitment of cash to the acquisition of merchandise and the collection of receivables from the sale of the merchandise. Similarly, the time elapsing between the purchase of a fixed asset and the ultimate consumption of that asset in operations is called the ***cash to fixed assets to cash cycle.*** Therefore, because of the fact that all business activities eventually clear through cash, the verification of cash transactions over a period of many years helps us prove not only the appropriateness of cash inflows and outflows, but also the fairness of other asset and various liability accounts.

The second characteristic making the verification of cash so important to the auditor is the ***relative risk*** associated with the cash balance. Because of its universal usability and the auditor's inability, from a practical point of view, to identify specific units of cash, this resource is *more vulnerable to theft, fraud, and embezzlement* than any other resource owned by a business entity. Some types of cash receipts realized from transactions not having built-in accountability controls, such as sales of scrap, are especially vulnerable to diversion from their intended uses. Furthermore, a small difference between the amount of actual cash held by an entity and the amount shown in the cash account can be the clue leading to the discovery of much more significant irregularities in the handling of cash transactions. Consistent with this fact, the *client typically expects greater precision* in the verification of the cash balance than in the verification of other assets, such as inventory or fixed assets.

In Chapter 10, we developed the audit procedures for verifying the inflows of cash generated through revenues from the principal business activity of the client. In Chapter 11 and earlier in this chapter, we explained how the outflows of cash associated with the cost of sales cycle and payroll are verified. In later chapters, we will be dealing briefly with the verification of cash outlays for fixed assets and cash inflows and outflows relating to investments, debt capital, and owners' equity transactions. The transaction validity audit objective for exchanges involving the inflows and outflows of cash relating to those items is met in the audit of those subsystems.

It is, however, appropriate to mention here some of the general internal control characteristics and problems relating to cash. We again observe that the recordkeeping and custodial functions relating to cash should be separated. The treasurer is generally the highest ranking custodial officer. The person in that position should be responsible for opening and monitoring the bank accounts and should exercise custodial authority over all bank accounts held by the company. As we observed in Chapter 10, all cash receipts should be deposited intact and under no circumstances should payments be made from receipts. The treasurer should also have control over the check-signing process, including control over check signature machines and plates. It is also desirable to require two signatures on checks involving very large amounts, to ensure that the approval process has been performed very thoroughly on individually material disbursements.

The audit of cash, as of any other financial statement balance, begins by relating the six characteristics of an adequate system of internal control to the cash-handling and recordkeeping systems:

- ***Separation of responsibilities*** requires that custodianship, recordkeeping, and authorization functions for both cash receipts and cash disbursements should all be assigned to different employees, at the highest level within a company. This generally involves the complete separation of the controller's (recordkeeping) responsibilities from those of the treasurer (custodial officer).
- ***Assignment of responsibility*** for those functions to specific employees. For example, the chief custodial officer is generally the treasurer of the company. In that capacity, he or she has custodial responsibility for all company cash.
- ***Properly qualified personnel*** should be used in the cash-handling, recordkeeping and approval functions. This requirement extends to bonding custodial employees. Bonding not only protects against loss from embezzlement, but also minimizes the risk of employing persons in positions of trust who are of questionable integrity.
- An ***adequate records system*** should be maintained for all cash transactions by persons having no access to the asset itself.
- Appropriate provision should be made for ***physical protection*** of cash. This involves the mandatory use of checking accounts for all material cash transactions and daily deposits of cash receipts intact in the bank. Such an arrangement reduces the amount of currency and checks kept on the client's premises where they are vulnerable to misappropriation. It also involves the use of petty cash funds for small disbursements. Responsibility for such funds should be vested in specific individuals, who should keep them in a safe location pending disbursement.
- Provisions should be made for ***monitoring compliance*** with established policies and for checking custodial accountability. This will normally include preparation of monthly bank reconciliations and other monitoring activities by internal auditors.

These elements of internal control were discussed in Chapters 10 and 11. You should review them before proceeding with the rest of this chapter.

SUBSTANTIVE TESTS

The remainder of this chapter is devoted to discussion of the substantive tests (audit procedures) associated with the verification of the end-of-period cash balances. First we look at the audit objectives that should be achieved in the verification process. After that we develop the procedures the auditor should follow in meeting those objectives, including procedures designed to document the auditor's search for errors and irregularities involving cash.

Audit Objectives

Audit objectives directly related to cash balances include the *verification of existence*, *proper cutoff*, and *appropriate statement presentation*. Because of the vulnerability of cash to fraud and embezzlement, the auditor should also identify and develop auditing procedures specifically directed toward searching for errors and irregularities. Chapter 10 contained an explanation of how cash receipts, in the absence of appropriate internal controls, might be misappropriated. We also saw how cash received in the collection of receivables might be temporarily misappropriated through a *lapping procedure.* In Chapter 11, we saw how, in the absence of appropriate internal control procedures, cash could be misappropriated through the medium of false or inappropriate disbursements. Additional procedures designed to discover such errors and irregularities, plus the irregularity of *kiting*, are developed in the last part of this section.

As the auditor begins verifying the amount shown for cash in the balance sheet, he or she will first want to reconcile that amount with the underlying accounting records. This reconciliation process as well as the audit procedures followed to accomplish the audit objectives are shown in the ***cash working papers*** (see chapter appendixes). When the client has more than one cash account, a ***lead schedule*** working paper may be necessary to summarize the balances in the cash accounts. Appendixes 12–A through 12–F contain copies of the cash working papers for a typical audit client. Notice that working paper B (Appendix 12–A) contains a lead schedule, which is a summary of the details of cash balances for the JEP Manufacturing Company. The schedule shows, for example, that cash for the company totals $37,814.93 and is made up of three bank accounts — regular, mercantile, and payroll — all of which are *supported* by bank reconciliations (supporting schedules B–1, B–2, and B–3 respectively). B–1 is the only reconciliation included in the appendixes; see Appendix 12–C. The company also has a petty cash fund (B–4) and a time deposit (B–5).

If the client already has reconciled the bank and book balances, and has made appropriate adjustments to the ledger accounts, the auditor's first step in relating the statement to the accounting records is to compare the financial statement amount with the amount shown in the cash ledger account. This amount should be the same as the adjusted balance per books on the bank reconciliation. It is also important at this time to recompute (foot) both the cash receipts and cash disbursements journals and to trace the journal entries to the ledger accounts. Having completed this phase of the verification of cash, the auditor is ready to perform the auditing procedures required to meet the three audit objectives cited earlier. Figure 12–8 shows the relationships between the audit objectives and the procedures required to meet those objectives. Note that the tick marks used in the appendixes are explained in Appendix 12–B.

Verification of Existence

The cash account balance will typically include both cash on hand and cash in the bank. When the auditor considers it necessary to do so, he or she should verify the existence of cash on hand *by physical count.* This is normally done at the close of business on the last day of the fiscal period under audit. The auditor should take at least two precautions in performing the count of cash.

First of all, *the cash count should be made simultaneously with the inspection of investments and negotiable instruments.* If this arrangement is for some reason impractical, those documents must otherwise be controlled from the time the cash count is initiated until it is finished and the documents can be inspected. This requirement prevents the auditor from double-counting these assets. Without this provision, the auditor could be misled into counting cash temporarily acquired by using the nego-

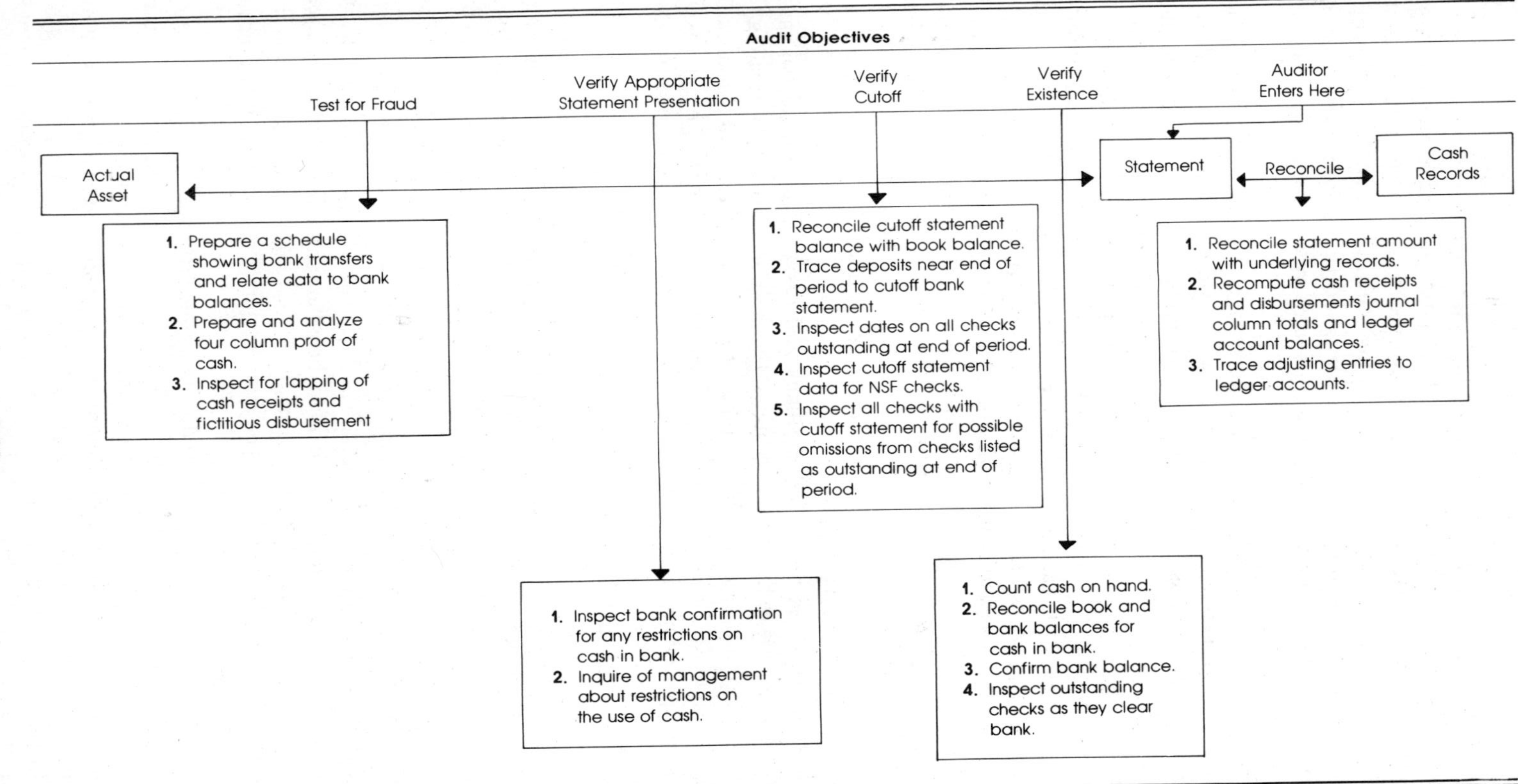
Audit Objectives
Test for Fraud
Verify Appropriate Statement Presentation
Verify Cutoff
Verify Existence
Auditor Enters Here
Actual Asset
Statement
Reconcile
Cash Records
1. Prepare a schedule showing bank transfers and relate data to bank balances.
2. Prepare and analyze four column proof of cash.
3. Inspect for lapping of cash receipts and fictitious disbursement
1. Inspect bank confirmation for any restrictions on cash in bank.
2. Inquire of management about restrictions on the use of cash.
1. Reconcile cutoff statement balance with book balance.
2. Trace deposits near end of period to cutoff bank statement.
3. Inspect dates on all checks outstanding at end of period.
4. Inspect cutoff statement data for NSF checks.
5. Inspect all checks with cutoff statement for possible omissions from checks listed as outstanding at end of period.
1. Count cash on hand.
2. Reconcile book and bank balances for cash in bank.
3. Confirm bank balance.
4. Inspect outstanding checks as they clear bank.
1. Reconcile statement amount with underlying records.
2. Recompute cash receipts and disbursements journal column totals and ledger account balances.
3. Trace adjusting entries to ledger accounts.

FIGURE 12–8. Substantive Tests of Balances for Cash

tiable instruments as collateral and later also counting the instruments themselves as investments and negotiable instruments after they have been returned to their files. Furthermore, *all cash should be controlled throughout the time of the cash count* to avoid the possibility of the auditor again being misled into counting a specified amount of cash more than once. A common way of achieving this control is to seal each container of cash immediately after it has been counted. After the count of all cash has been completed the auditor should retrace the counting cycle to verify that the individual seals were not broken after the cash in them was counted.

The second major precaution is that the *count should always be made in the presence of the custodian of each of the funds*. And he or she should be asked to sign a receipt for the return of cash after the count has been completed. This arrangement is designed to prevent the custodian from alleging that all the cash charged to his or her custody was there prior to the auditor's count but not returned after the audit. Such a claim might otherwise be made if the auditor had found a shortage in the fund.

The *cash in the bank should be confirmed* directly with the bank. In doing this the auditor should use the standard AICPA confirmation form shown in Appendix 12–D. The confirmation request must be signed by an appropriate representative of the client to allow the bank to provide the information requested by the auditor. However, the auditor should supervise the mailing of the request and arrange to have the bank's reply returned directly to the auditing firm. The balance shown on the confirmation form should be reconciled with the bank reconciliation schedule previously prepared by the client. Notice that this is done on working papers B–1 (Appendix 12–C) through cross-referencing. Also, checks shown to be outstanding as of the date of the bank reconciliation should be inspected as they clear the bank after the end of the period under audit. This procedure is illustrated in working paper B–1.

Verification of Cutoff

In Chapters 10 and 11 we described the errors that could be introduced into the financial statements by improperly cutting off cash receipts and cash disbursements. As a means of more directly verifying that these transactions have been recorded in the appropriate accounting periods, the auditor should, with appropriate authorization from the client, request a bank cutoff statement some 15 to 20 days after the end of the period under audit. That statement should include deposit slips and cancelled checks clearing the bank between the end of the fiscal period and the cutoff date. The cutoff statement should be sent directly to the auditor to prevent changes or extractions of documents by client personnel.

The auditor should reconcile the bank cutoff statement with the client's record of cash in bank. Deposits made near the end of the period should be inspected. The auditor will be particularly concerned with the dates on the outstanding checks. All should, of course, be dated prior to the end of the fiscal period. The auditor will also be concerned with the dates on which the checks have cleared the bank. If an unusually long period of time has elapsed between the date shown on a check and the date on which the check cleared the bank the auditor should raise questions as to whether the cash payment record may have been improperly cut off at the end of the fiscal period. Management should be expected to provide an explanation for the delay in clearance of the check. Kiting (which we take up in the subsection on errors and irregularities) is also detectable by examining paid checks returned with the cutoff bank statement and tracing them to cash disbursements records to see if they were recorded properly.

Charges against the account for nonsufficient funds checks (NSF) will also be of particular interest to the auditor in working with the cutoff bank statement. These are customers' checks that have been deposited but have been charged back against the client's account because the customers did not have sufficient funds to cover them. Because the NSF checks did not represent cash as of the end of the fiscal period, the auditor usually recommends adjustment for them by crediting cash and debiting a receivables account. Postdated customer checks are also receivables rather than cash. The client should follow a practice of restrictively endorsing such checks to provide proper accounting control over them.

The auditor should inspect all checks returned with the bank cutoff statement. He or she should identify the checks shown as outstanding at the end of the fiscal period and clearing with the cutoff statement to see that they have been properly listed in the end-of-period bank reconciliation. Of perhaps even greater importance is the attention that should be given to any checks dated before the end of the period under audit but omitted from the list of outstanding checks in the end-of-the-period bank reconciliation. Since this is a technique that could be used to cover a cash shortage, the auditor must secure a complete explanation of all such items. All of the above procedures are illustrated in Appendixes 12–A through 12–D. Appendix 12–E describes the audit work typically performed to ascertain proper cutoff of cash receipts and cash disbursements as of the balance sheet date.

Verification of Appropriate Statement Presentation

As you examine the bank confirmation form shown on working paper B–6 (see Appendix 12–D) you will observe that the bank is expected to disclose any restrictions on the use of cash — such as a minimum balance required under a loan agreement. The auditor should be certain that any such restrictions are appropriately disclosed in presenting cash on the audited balance sheet. It is important to recognize that cash shown in the balance sheet without any reference to restrictions is interpreted to be cash available for use at the discretion of management. The auditor should see that any adjustments or disclosures required relating to the presentation of cash in the balance sheet are appropriately reflected in the audited financial statements. It is also appropriate to observe at this point that savings account balances are appropriately reflected as current investments rather than as cash.

Searching for Errors and Irregularities

The procedures listed in the preceding paragraphs are designed to verify *whether the statement account balance for cash fairly represents the actual amount of cash held by the client*. Because cash is highly susceptible to fraud and embezzlement, the auditor must also carry through some audit procedures designed to help judge whether or not irregularities, in the form of defalcations of cash, may have occurred during the period under audit. We have already mentioned certain precautionary measures and follow-up procedures that should be performed in connection with cash receipts and cash disbursements (Chapters 10 and 11). Those are designed to determine whether or not cash receipts have been stolen or cash has been improperly extracted through the medium of the receipts and disbursements processes. We now describe procedures typically followed as the auditor tests the cash accounts for possible irregularities of different types.

The first of these checking procedures involves the ***preparation of a bank transfer schedule*** such as the one shown on working paper B–8 in Appendix 12–F. This schedule, normally incorporated into the working papers any time the client has more than one bank account, is designed to trace transfers between banks and in that way discover kiting.

Kiting occurs when an amount is withdrawn from one bank and deposited in another without the withdrawal being shown in the book record for the first bank. To implement kiting, the perpetrator makes the deposit on the last day of the fiscal period, in a bank located in a different city from the one on which the check was written. Then, the perpetrator omits the check from the disbursement record of the period under audit, thus inflating the total cash balance by the amount of the deposit. Such an action can be undertaken by upper level management as a means either of covering a theft of cash equal to the amount of the deposit or of improperly inflating the cash balance as of the balance sheet date.

Notice in Appendix 12–F that columns are provided for dates on which the cash transfer was recorded per books and per bank for both the disbursing and receiving bank accounts. A kiting situation would show *the cash receipt in the books before the balance sheet cutoff* and *the cash disbursement recorded after the balance sheet cutoff.* If the cash disbursement is not recorded, the check for the disbursing bank would not appear at all in the cash disbursements records for the period either before or after the balance sheet date. The auditor should detect the unrecorded disbursement as he or she examines the cancelled checks returned with the cutoff bank statement and traces them to the cash disbursements records of the period under audit.

The second checking procedure involves the preparation and analysis of a ***four-column proof of cash.*** An example of this schedule is shown in Figure 12–9. This working paper can be prepared in either of two ways. The more common practice is to reconcile the book balances for the beginning of the period, receipts and disbursements for the period, and the end-of-the-period cash balance with the same four elements of bank data. However, it is generally preferable to work from the unadjusted data from both records to adjusted figures for both the bank and book data. This latter refinement is the type of four-column proof reflected in Figures 12–9 and 12–10. It has at least two advantages over the more conventional one.

First, it is generally easier to think through a correction process when trying to change a previously incorrect figure to a correct one than it is to think through an adjustment of one figure to another, neither of which may be correct. Observe, as you look at Figure 12–9, that the beginning balances as well as all adjustments to those balances have to balance across the working paper. The previously cited advantage recognizes that it is, for example, easier to think through the addition of outstanding checks at the end of the period to the bank disbursements column and a simultaneous

	Balance at Beginning of Period	Receipts	Disbursements	Balance at End of Period
Balances from bank statement	$ 8,400	$21,000	$23,500	$ 5,900
Undeposited receipts at beginning of period	+1,200	−1,200		
Undeposited receipts at end of period		+1,800		+1,800
Outstanding checks at beginning of period	−2,500		−2,500	
Outstanding checks at end of period			+3,000	−3,000
Check improperly charged to account			− 800	+ 800
NSF checks charged to account		− 200	− 200	
Adjusted bank balances	$ 7,100	$21,400	$23,000	$ 5,500
Balances from books	$ 7,100	$20,200	$22,985	$ 4,315
NSF checks (see above)		− 200		− 200
Note collected by bank not recorded on books		+1,400		+1,400
Bank service charges			+ 15	− 15
Adjusted book balances	$ 7,100	$21,400	$23,000	$ 5,500

FIGURE 12–9. Four-Column Proof Schedule

subtraction from the end-of-the-period bank balance than it is to work the same data into a conventional statement that simply reconciles bank and book figures.

A second very important advantage of using the illustrated four-column proof is the fact that the adjusted cash receipts and disbursement data can be used to provide additional evidence that the sales and purchases figures are properly reflected in the financial statements. For example, sales for the period can be computed by using a modified four-element equation, stated as follows:

> End-of-period receivables balance + cash receipts from customers (adjusted cash receipts from four-column proof total less nonsales-related receipts) − receivables balance at the beginning of the period + noncash credits to accounts receivable (sales discounts allowed, sales returns and allowances, and accounts receivable written off during the period) = sales for the period.

The figure so calculated can be compared with the recorded amount for sales to provide additional evidence in support of the nominal account balance. Because the auditor will have independently verified the parts of the equation that deal with

	Balance at Beginning of Period	Receipts	Disbursements	Balance at End of Period
Balances from bank statement	$ 8,400	$20,000	$23,500	$ 4,900
Undeposited receipts at beginning of period	+1,200	−1,200		
Undeposited receipts at end of period		+1,800		+1,800
Outstanding checks at beginning of period	−2,500		−2,500	
Outstanding checks at end of period			+3,000	−3,000
Check improperly charged to account			− 800	+ 800
NSF checks charged to account		− 200	− 200	
Adjusted bank balances	$ 7,100	$20,400	$23,000	$ 4,500
Balances from books	$ 7,100	$20,200	$23,985	$ 3,315
NSF checks (see above)		− 200		− 200
Note collected by bank not recorded on books		+1,400		+1,400
Bank service charges			+ 15	− 15
Adjusted book balances	$ 7,100	$21,400	$24,000	$ 4,500

FIGURE 12–10. Four-Column Proof Schedule Disclosing Defalcation of Cash Receipts

receivables balances, this amounts to an additional independent verification of sales. This is another example of the jigsaw puzzle types of relationships that exist among the accounting data.

A similar equation can be developed for the verification of the purchases account balance independent of the amount shown in the ledger for purchases. That equation is stated as follows:

> End-of-period payables balance + cash payments to vendors (adjusted cash payments from four-column proof less nonpurchase-related payments) − payables balance at the beginning of the period + noncash charges to payables (purchase discounts allowed and purchase returns and allowances) = purchases for the period.

The four-column proof is, however, most directly useful in helping the auditor discover situations where *the book record of cash disbursements may have been deliberately overstated* to cover ***an embezzlement*** of cash receipts or where *cash* *receipts may have been deliberately understated* to cover ***a theft*** of cash through an improper cash disbursement. The first of these, for example, could occur if the person handling cash receipts had access to the cash disbursement record. In Figure 12–10, we have reproduced the source data shown in Figure 12–9 (except for the assumed theft of cash receipts in the amount of $1,000 and the overstatement of cash disbursements by the same amount to cover the theft) to show how the four-column proof schedule helps the auditor in discovering such a defalcation. You will observe that both the beginning- and end-of-period balances reconcile. Therefore, a simple bank reconciliation would not disclose the defalcation. The four-column proof of cash should always be prepared by the auditor when internal control over cash is weak.

SUMMARY

In this chapter we have described the audit procedures followed in verifying payroll-related accounts and the balances in cash accounts. We began by observing the importance of payroll transactions in accounting for cash and in creating the balances for various payroll-related accounts. The internal control procedures that should be incorporated within payroll systems and the procedures for verifying their existence were then described. We also discussed the substantive tests performed in verifying payroll-related account balances.

In the last part of the chapter we explained how cash balances are verified. Since audit procedures for verifying cash receipts and disbursements had been described previously, we focused most of our attention in the last part of this chapter on the substantive tests required to meet the audit objectives of proving existence, cutoff, and proper statement presentation for cash balances. Some attention was also given to the audit procedures that should be performed in searching for errors and irregularities in cash balances.

tactile evidence - touch

"How to create your own corporation"
paperback $25-

APPENDIX 12–A: Cash

JEP Manufacturing Co.
Cash
3-31-X1

W. P. No.	B
ACCOUNTANT	SmG
DATE	4/28/X1

#		W/P Reference		Adjusted Balance 3-31-X0 △	Balance per G/L 3-31-X1 ✓
1	Cash on Deposit - Regular	B-1		21333 51	1398 14
3	Cash on Deposit - Mercantile	B-2	*	500 00	500 00
4	Cash on Deposit - Payroll	B-3	*	1200 00	500 00
	Petty Cash	B-4	*	687 50	687 50
7	Time Deposit	B-5	*	60798 71	33843 29
				84519 72	36928 93
					A-1
	RJE ⟨D⟩			0	886 00
					37814 93
					A-1

△ Agreed to prior year auditors' W/P's

✓ Agreed to 3-31-X1 G/L

See explanation of tick marks and conclusion on Ba

* Not reproduced

APPENDIX 12–B: Tick Legend Regarding Cash

JEP Mfg. Co.
Tick Legend re: Cash
3-31-X1

W. P. No.	Ba
ACCOUNTANT	sms
DATE	5/4/X1

✓ Agreed amount to paid check returned with cutoff statement received unopened by auditors from Bank. Traced o/s checks to cutoff statement and into cash disbursements book prior to year-end. We noted that checks were properly signed and endorsed and that check cleared the bank within a reasonable period of time. Checks do appear to be o/s as of 3-31-X1

◁ Traced deposit-in-transit per bank reconciliation to deposit credited per bank cutoff statement. We noted that the time lag was reasonable.

∅ Agreed amount to 3-31-X1 Beginning Balance per bank cutoff statement.

∧ Footed

✓ Agreed amount to 3-31-X1 G/L

ℊ Confirmation sent; received.

♯ These checks had not cleared the bank as of 4-30-X1. Pass further investigation as amount is immaterial.

∠ Performed same ~~procedures~~ as in ✓ above to checks returned w/ 4-30-X1 Bank statement. Checks do appear to be o/s @ 3-31-X1.

Note: Compared receipts per cash receipts book with credits per bank statements for March 23, 19X1 through April 7, 19X1. All receipts matched appropriate credits.

Conclusion: Based upon the audit work performed, which was considered adequate to meet the objectives per the APG it appears that cash is fairly stated @ 3-31-X1.

APPENDIX 12–C: Bank Reconciliation

JEP MANUFACTURING COMPANY
Bank Statement Reconciliation
G. L. Account # ______

B-1
PBC/SMG
5/14/X1

Month Ended March 31, 19X1

General Ledger Balance Prior Month	<224,531.19>	Balance per Bank Statement as of ______	B-6 ₵ 166,642.66₵
Add Debits		Add Deposits in Transit	
		3-31-X1	258.16
Total Debits	1,115,744.57		258.16
Less Credits		Less Checks Outstanding Per List below	165,502.68
		Other	
Total Credits	889,815.24		
Balance per General Ledger	1,398.14	Balance per Reconciliation	1,399.14

B/

Checks Outstanding:*

TOTAL 165,502.68

Includes listing of checks on p. 2.

*Details omitted

APPENDIX 12–D: Standard Bank Confirmation Inquiry

STANDARD BANK CONFIRMATION INQUIRY B-6
Approved 1966 by
AMERICAN INSTITUTE OF CERTIFIED PUBLIC ACCOUNTANTS
and
BANK ADMINISTRATION INSTITUTE (FORMERLY NABAC)

ORIGINAL
To be mailed to accountant

March 31, 19X1

Your completion of the following report will be sincerely appreciated. IF THE ANSWER TO ANY ITEM IS "NONE," PLEASE SO STATE. Kindly mail it in the enclosed stamped, addressed envelope *direct* to the accountant named below.

Report from

(Bank) First Greensboro National Bank
P.O. Box 1044
Greensboro, Texas 75000

Yours truly,
JEP Manufacturing Co., Inc.
(ACCOUNT NAME PER BANK RECORDS)
By C. Paul Snelson
Authorized Signature

Bank customer should check here if confirmation of bank balances only (item 1) is desired. ☐

NOTE—If the space provided is inadequate, please enter totals hereon and attach a statement giving full details as called for by the columnar headings below.

Accountant Best and Company
Suite 4500, Byron Building
Dallas, Texas 75201

1. At the close of business on March 31, 19X1 our records showed the following balance(s) to the **credit** of the above named customer. In the event that we could readily ascertain whether there were any balances to the credit of the customer not designated in this request, the appropriate information is given below.

AMOUNT	ACCOUNT NAME	ACCOUNT NUMBER	Subject to Withdrawal by Check?	Interest Bearing? Give Rate
	JEP Manufacturing Co.			
$ 166,642.66 B-1	General Fund	00-210-5	Yes	No
21,129.18 B-3	Payroll	00-001-8	Yes	No

2. The customer was directly liable to us in respect of loans, acceptances, etc., at the close of business on that date in the total amount of $ none , as follows:

AMOUNT	DATE OF LOAN OR DISCOUNT	DUE DATE	INTEREST Rate	INTEREST Paid to	DESCRIPTION OF LIABILITY, COLLATERAL, SECURITY INTERESTS, LIENS, ENDORSERS, ETC.
$					

3. The customer was contingently liable as endorser of notes discounted and/or as guarantor at the close of business on that date in the total amount of $ none , as below:

AMOUNT	NAME OF MAKER	DATE OF NOTE	DUE DATE	REMARKS
$				

4. Other direct or contingent liabilities, open letters of credit, and relative collateral, were

none

5. Security agreements under the Uniform Commercial Code or any other agreements providing for restrictions, not noted above, were as follows (if officially recorded, indicate date and office in which filed):

none

Yours truly, (Bank) First Greensboro National Bank

Date April 30, 19X1

By Robert S Goldsboro
Authorized Signature Vice President

Additional copies of this form are available from the American Institute of CPAs, 1211 Avenue of the Americas, New York, N. Y. 10036

APPENDIX 12–E: Proper Period Cutoff on Cash

JEP Mfg. Co. Memo re: Proper Period Cutoff on Cash 3-31-X1	W. P. No.	B-7-2
	ACCOUNTANT	Smd
	DATE	5/5/X1

To determine that there was proper cutoff of all cash receipts and disbursements we performed the following procedures:

① Obtained a copy of the last check issued in FYE 19X1 (ck # 66934) and noted that all checks issued prior to that check were dated prior to 3-31-X1 and cleared the bank within a reasonable time subsequent to 3-31-X1. In addition, we examined the first 15 checks issued after 3-31-X1, noting that none of the checks had been endorsed by any bank prior to 4-1-X1.

② Examined all interbank transfers of a significant amount (see W/P B-8) noting the proper recording of all transactions.

③ Examined all deposits made 5 days before and after FYE to determine that they were properly recorded in the correct period.

No exceptions were noted in the above procedures - it appears that there was a proper cutoff of cash receipts & disbursements.

APPENDIX 12–F: Bank Transfers Schedule

JEP Mfg.
Bank Transfers Schedule
3-31-X1

W. P. No.	B-8
ACCOUNTANT	Smk
DATE	5/4/X1

All Transactions 3-23-X1 — 4/9/X1 From / To	Check #	TRANSFERRED FROM Date Per Check	Per Books	Per Bank
General A/C - Savings A/C	66727	3-23-X1	3-23-X1	3-23-X1 ∆
General A/C - Payroll A/C	66894	3-26-X1	3-26-X1	3-26-X1 ∆
General A/C - Payroll A/C	66932	3-31-X1	3-31-X1	3-31-X1 ∆
General A/C - East Texas Dist.	66934	3-31-X1	3-31-X1	3-31-X1 ∆
General A/C - Savings A/C	66946	4-6-X1	4-6-X1	4-6-X1 ∆
General A/C - Savings A/C	66982	4-9-X1	4-9-X1	4-10-X1 ∆
Savings A/C - General A/C	N/A	N/A	3-31-X1	3-31-X1 ∆
Savings A/C - General A/C	N/A	N/A	3-30-X1	3-31-X1 ∆
East Texas Dist. - General A/C	7863	3-31-X1	3-31-X1	4-3-X1 ∆

Note: The above information was obtained from a review of cash receipts and disbursements journals and bank statements.

∆ Agreed to bank statement and validated deposit slip/cancelled check.

ⓧ Not recorded - payroll account remains at a constant $500. Expense is recorded when the reimbursement check is prepared. Appears to be properly treated and is consistent w/prior years.

See conclusion on Ba

	TRANS. TO Date				
	Per Books	Per Bank		Amount	
	3-23-X1	3-23-X1 ∢		120000 00	
	3-26-X1 Ⓧ	3-26-X1 ∢		16934 37	
	3-31-X1 Ⓧ	3-31-X1 ∢		31528 57	
	3-31-X1	3-31-X1 ∢		30452 23	
	4-6-X1	4-6-X1 ∢		30000 00	
	4-9-X1	4-10-X1 ∢		B-6 P. ③ 140000 00	
	3-31-X1	3-31-X1 ∢		B-6 P. ③ 50000 00	
	3-31-X1	3-31-X1 ∢		B-6 P. ③ 190000 00	
	4-2-X1	4-2-X1 ∢		∢ˣ 886 00 B (ETDC)	

∢ˣ This deposit-in-transit has been properly removed from East Texas's Cash A/c but was Dr. to Accrued liability A/c by Sharon Spencer so that A/R could be relieved. The amount should be reclassed to Cash. See Ⓑ and RJE ⟨D⟩ on O-1.

APPENDIX 12–G: Payroll Testwork

JEP Mfg. Co.	W. P. No.	Z-4
Memo re: Payroll Testwork	ACCOUNTANT	Smd
3-31-X1	DATE	5/14/X1

All non-exempt, hourly employees are paid through a computer payroll service on a weekly basis. We reviewed these payroll procedures with Shirley Stevens, payroll clerk. The following guidelines are in effect: All employee time cards are reviewed and initialed by the appropriate foreman. All time cards are submitted to Mrs. Stevens who reviews for reasonableness. Any changes to the employee's standard pay are entered on a payroll change worksheet. All hours worked and any authorized pay changes are submitted to National Bank of Commerce (payroll service) who processes the information per JEP's master control file and prints the checks which are returned to Mrs. Stevens the following week, along with a printout of all checks, employees, employee #, and all appropriate deductions. We reviewed Mrs. Stevens's payroll and employment records noting that no employee was making more than the authorized union wage. We then selected 10 employees from throughout the year and traced their

W. P. No.
ACCOUNTANT
DATE

wage from their authorized amount per the union agreement, through their time cards, agreeing wage, employee name, no., and hours to the printout from NBC and finally agreeing the check amount per NBC to the paid check, noting date, proper employee name, employee number and endorsement. No exceptions were noted in the above procedures. Finally, we reviewed the weekly payroll for reasonableness, noting no unusual fluctuations in the period under review.

Conclusion: Based upon the audit procedures performed as outlined above, which were considered adequate to meet the objectives per the APG, it appears that payroll procedures are being adequately adhered to and that the payroll expense for the year ended 3-31-X1 is fairly stated.

QUESTIONS FOR CLASS DISCUSSION

Q12–1 What accounts are included in a typical payroll system?

Q12–2 Why should a firm use an imprest payroll bank account? Explain.

Q12–3 Which functions associated with the payroll system should be separated to provide appropriate internal control over payroll transactions? Explain.

Q12–4 What records, forms, and authorizations are typically found within the payroll system?

Q12–5 What audit procedures should be followed to determine that the personnel being paid both exist and have been authorized for employment?

Q12–6 What auditing procedures should be followed to verify that timekeeping data adequately support payroll data?

Q12–7 Under what circumstances is it important for the auditor to perform an unannounced observation of the distribution of payroll checks? Explain.

Q12–8 What procedures should the auditor follow in verifying the existence of payroll system liabilities?

Q12–9 What procedures should the auditor follow in verifying the amounts recorded in the payroll accounts?

Q12–10 How should the auditor verify the liability for accrued salaries payable? Explain.

Q12–11 For what reasons do auditors typically spend more than a proportionate amount of time in auditing cash transactions and end-of-year cash balances? Explain.

Q12–12 What is the audit risk associated with expressing an opinion regarding a firm's cash balance?

Q12–13 The treasurer of the company is generally its highest ranking custodial officer; what are her or his typical responsibilities?

Q12–14 What responsibilities should be separated in an appropriately organized system of internal control for cash?

Q12–15 What is meant by lapping?

Q12–16 What is meant by kiting?

Q12–17 What procedures should be followed when verifying the existence of cash?

Q12–18 Why does the auditor prepare a schedule showing bank transfers during the period under audit? Explain.

Q12–19 Why does the auditor prepare a four-column proof in connection with the audit of cash? Explain.

Q12–20 What are the auditor's primary concerns in determining that cash has been appropriately presented in the financial statements?

SHORT CASES

C12–1 A CPA's audit working papers contain a narrative description of a *segment* of the Croyden Factory, Inc., payroll system and an accompanying flowchart as follows:

> The internal control system with respect to the personnel department is well-functioning and is *not* included in the accompanying flowchart.
>
> At the beginning of each work week, payroll clerk No. 1 reviews the payroll department files to determine the employment status of factory employees and then prepares time cards and distributes them as each individual arrives at work. This payroll clerk, who is also responsible for custody of the signature

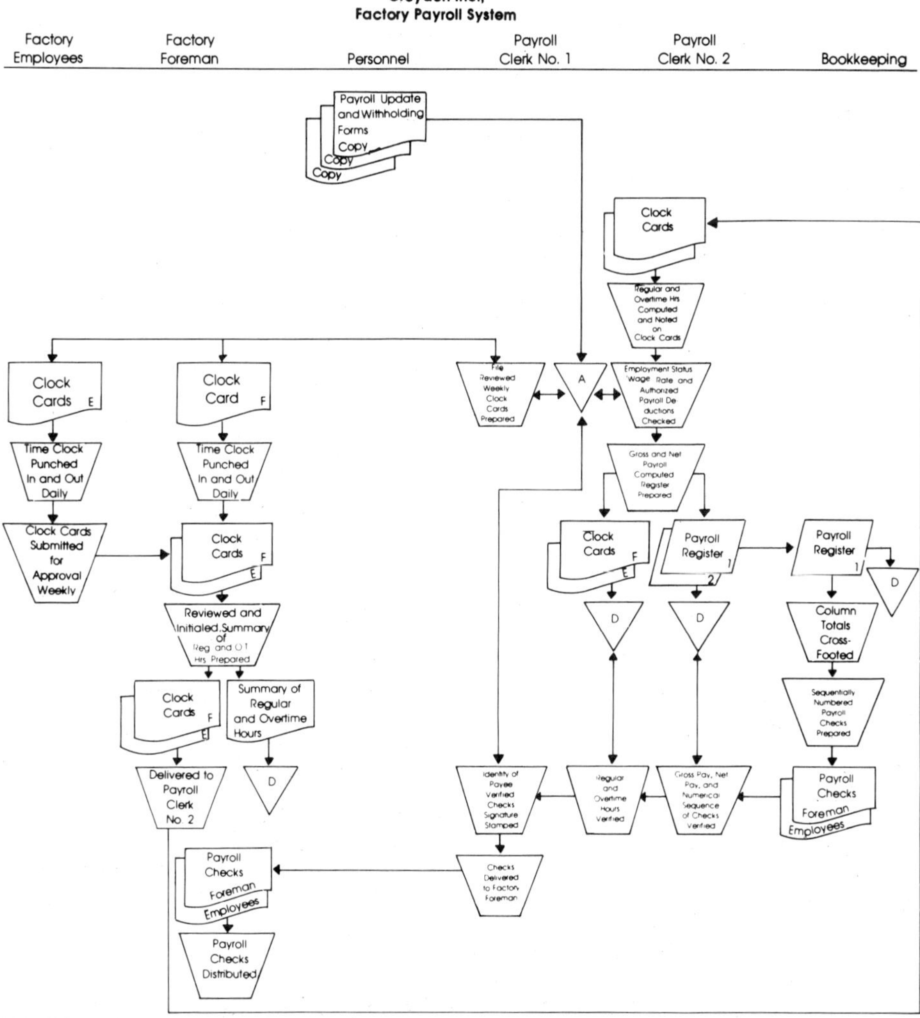

stamp machine, verifies the identity of each payee before delivering signed checks to the foreman.

At the end of each work week the foreman distributes payroll checks for the preceding work week. Concurrent with this activity, the foreman reviews the current week's employee time cards, notes the regular and overtime hours worked on a summary form, and initials the aforementioned time cards. The foreman then delivers all time cards and unclaimed payroll checks to payroll clerk No. 2.

Required:

a. On the basis of the narrative and accompanying flowchart, what are the weaknesses in the system of internal control?

b. On the basis of the narrative and accompanying flowchart, what inquiries should be made with respect to clarifying the existence of *possible additional weaknesses* in the system of internal control?

(*Note:* Do not discuss the internal control system of the personnel department.)

c. What substantive tests on payroll balances, if any, should be extended because of the weaknesses pointed out in requirements **a** and **b**?

(AICPA adapted)

C12–2 Bonnie James, who was engaged to examine the financial statement of Talbert Corporation, is about to audit payroll. Talbert uses a computer service center to process weekly payroll. James learns how the system works.

Each Monday Talbert's payroll clerk inserts data in appropriate spaces on the preprinted service center prepared input form, and sends it to the service center via messenger. The service center extracts new permanent data from the input form and updates master files. The weekly payroll data are then processed. The weekly payroll register and payroll checks are printed and delivered by messenger to Talbert on Thursday.

Part of the sample selected for audit by James includes the input form and payroll register shown on page 567.

Required:

a. Describe how James should verify the information in the preceding payroll input form.

b. Describe (but do **not** perform) the procedures that James should follow in the examination of the November 23, 19X2, payroll register.

(AICPA adapted)

C12–3 Toyco, a retail toy chain, honors two bank credit cards and makes daily deposits of credit card sales in two credit card bank accounts (Bank A and Bank B). Each day Toyco batches its credit card sales slips, bank deposit slips, and authorized sales return documents, and keypunches cards for processing by its electronic data-processing department. Each week detailed computer printouts of the general ledger credit card cash accounts are prepared. Credit card banks have been instructed to make an automatic weekly transfer of cash to Toyco's general bank account. The credit card banks charge back deposits that include sales to holders of stolen or expired cards.

Talbert Corporation
PAYROLL INPUT
Week Ending Friday, Nov. 23, 19X2

EMPLOYEE DATA — PERMANENT FILE				CURRENT WEEK'S PAYROLL DATA				
				Hours		Special Deductions		
Name	Social Security	W-4 Information	Hourly Rate	Reg	OT	Bonds	Union	Other
A. Bello	999-99-9991	M-1	10.00	35	5	18.75		
B. Cardinal	999-99-9992	M-2	10.00	35	4			
C. Dawn	999-99-9993	S-1	10.00	35	6	18.75	4.00	
D. Ellis	999-99-9994	S-1	10.00	35	2		4.00	50.00
E. Frank	999-99-9995	M-4	10.00	35	1		4.00	
F. Gillis	999-99-9996	M-4	10.00	35			4.00	
G. Huvos	999-99-9997	M-1	7.00	35	2	18.75	4.00	
H. Jones	999-99-9998	M-2	7.00	35			4.00	25.00
J. King	999-99-9999	S-1	7.00	35	4		4.00	
New Employee								
J. Siegal	999-99-9990	M-3	7.00	35				

Talbert Corporation
PAYROLL REGISTER
Nov. 23, 19X2

Employee	Social Security	Hours Reg	Hours OT	Payroll Regular	Payroll OT	Gross Payroll	Taxes Withheld FICA	Taxes Withheld Fed	Taxes Withheld State	Other Withheld	Net Pay	Check No.
A. Bello	999-99-9991	35	5	350.00	75.00	425.00	26.05	76.00	27.40	18.75	276.00	1499
B. Cardinal	999-99-9992	35	4	350.00	60.00	410.00	25.13	65.00	23.60		296.27	1500
C. Dawn	999-99-9993	35	6	350.00	90.00	440.00	26.97	100.90	28.60	22.75	260.78	1501
D. Ellis	999-99-9994	35	2	350.00	30.00	380.00	23.29	80.50	21.70	54.00	200.51	1502
E. Frank	999-99-9995	35	1	350.00	15.00	365.00	22.37	43.50	15.90	4.00	279.23	1503
F. Gillis	999-99-9996	35		350.00		350.00	21.46	41.40	15.00	4.00	268.14	1504
G. Huvos	999-99-9997	35	2	245.00	21.00	266.00	16.31	34.80	10.90	22.75	181.24	1505
H. Jones	999-99-9998	35		245.00		245.00	15.02	26.40	8.70	29.00	165.88	1506
J. King	999-99-9999	35	4	245.00	42.00	287.00	17.59	49.40	12.20	4.00	203.81	1507
J. Siegal	999-99-9990	35		245.00		245.00	15.02	23.00	7.80		199.18	1508
	Totals	350	24	3,080.00	333.00	3,413.00	209.21	540.90	171.80	159.25	2,331.84	

The auditor conducting the examination of the 19X6 Toyco financial statement has obtained the following copies of the detailed general ledger cash account printouts, a summary of the bank statements, and the manually prepared bank reconciliations, all for the week ended December 31, 19X6.

Toyco
DETAILED GENERAL LEDGER CREDIT CARD
CASH ACCOUNT PRINTOUTS
For the Week Ended December 31, 19X6

	Bank A Dr. or (Cr.)	Bank B Dr. or (Cr.)
Beginning Balance		
December 24, 19X6	$12,000	$ 4,200
Deposits		
December 27, 19X6	2,500	5,000
December 28, 19X6	3,000	7,000
December 29, 19X6	0	5,400
December 30, 19X6	1,900	4,000
December 31, 19X6	2,200	6,000
Cash Transfer		
December 27, 19X6	(10,700)	0
Chargebacks		
Expired cards	(300)	(1,600)
Invalid deposits (physically deposited in wrong account)	(1,400)	(1,000)
Redeposit of invalid deposits	1,000	1,400
Sales returns for week ending December 31, 19X6	(600)	(1,200)
Ending Balance		
December 31, 19X6	$ 9,700	$29,200

Toyco
SUMMARY OF THE BANK STATEMENTS
For the Week Ended December 31, 19X6

	Bank A	Bank B
	(Charges) or Credits	
Beginning Balance		
December 24, 19X6	$10,000	$ 0
Deposits dated		
December 24, 19X6	2,100	4,200
December 27, 19X6	2,500	5,000
December 28, 19X6	3,000	7,000
December 29, 19X6	2,000	5,500
December 30, 19X6	1,900	4,000
Cash transfers to general bank account		
December 27, 19X6	(10,700)	0
December 31, 19X6	0	(22,600)
Chargebacks		
Stolen cards	(100)	0
Expired cards	(300)	(1,600)
Invalid deposits	(1,400)	(1,000)
Bank service charges	0	(500)
Bank charge (unexplained)	(400)	0
Ending Balance		
December 31, 19X6	$ 8,600	$ 0

Toyco
BANK RECONCILIATIONS
For the Week Ended December 31, 19X6

Code No.	Bank A	Bank B
	Add or (Deduct)	
1. Balance per bank statement December 31, 19X6	$8,600	$ 0
2. Deposits in transit December 31, 19X6	2,200	6,000
3. Redeposit of invalid deposits (physically deposited in wrong account)	1,000	1,400
4. Difference in deposits of December 29, 19X6	(2,000)	(100)
5. Unexplained bank charge	400	0
6. Bank cash transfer not yet recorded	0	22,600
7. Bank Service charges	0	500
8. Chargebacks not recorded - Stolen cards	100	0
9. Sales returns recorded but not reported to the bank	(600)	(1,200)
10. Balance per general ledger December 31, 19X6	$9,700	$29,200

Required:

On the basis of a review of the December 31, 19X6, bank reconciliation and the related information available in the printouts and in the summary of bank statements, describe what procedures the auditor should perform to obtain audit satisfaction for each item on the bank reconciliations.

Assume that all amounts are material and all computations are accurate.

Organize your answer sheet as follows, using the appropriate code number for each item on the bank reconciliations:

Code No.	Procedures to Be Performed by the Auditor to Obtain Audit Satisfaction

(AICPA adapted)

C12–4 In connection with his examination of the financial statements of the Olympia Manufacturing Company, a CPA is reviewing procedures for accumulating direct labor hours. He learns that all production is by job order and that all employees are paid hourly wages, with time-and-one-half for overtime hours.

Olympia's direct labor hour input process for payroll and job-cost determination is summarized in the following flowchart:

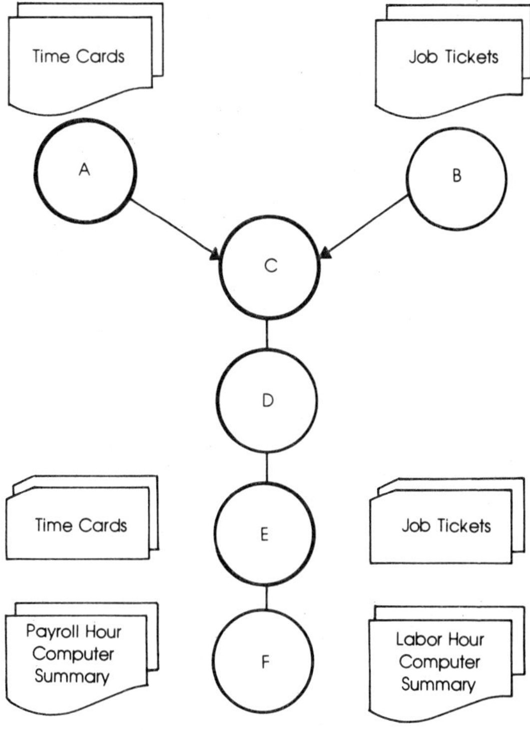

Steps A and C of the process are performed in timekeeping, step B in the factory operating departments, step D in payroll audit and control, step E in data preparation (keypunch), and step F in computer operations.

Required:

For each input processing step A through F:

a. List the possible errors or discrepancies that may occur.
b. Cite the corresponding control procedure that should be in effect for each error or discrepancy.
c. Briefly discuss the most appropriate compliance test for the control.

Note: Your discussion of Olympia's procedures should be limited to the input process for direct labor hours, as shown in steps A through F in the flowchart. Do not discuss personnel procedures for hiring, promotion, termination, and pay rate authorization. In step F do not discuss equipment, computer program, and general computer operational controls.

Organize your answer for each input-processing step as follows:

Step	Possible Errors or Discrepancies	Control Procedures	Most Appropriate Compliance Test

(AICPA adapted)

C12–5 The Wacker Company employs about 50 production workers and has the following payroll procedures:

The factory foreman interviews applicants and on the basis of the interview either hires or rejects the applicants. When the applicant is hired he prepares a W-4 form (Employee's Withholding Exemption Certificate) and gives it to the foreman. The foreman writes the hourly rate of pay for the new employee in the corner of the W-4 form and then gives the form to a payroll clerk as notice that the worker has been employed. The foreman verbally advises the payroll department of rate adjustments.

A supply of blank time cards is kept in a box near the entrance to the factory. Each worker takes a time card on Monday morning, fills in his name, and notes in pencil on the time card his daily arrival and departure times. At the end of the week the workers drop the time cards in a box near the door to the factory.

The completed time cards are taken from the box on Monday morning by a payroll clerk. Two payroll clerks divide the cards alphabetically between them, one taking the A to L section of the payroll and the other taking the M to Z section. Each clerk is fully responsible for her section of the payroll. She computes the gross pay, deductions, and net pay, posts the details to the employee's earnings records, and prepares and numbers the payroll checks. Employees are automatically removed from the payroll when they fail to turn in a time card.

The payroll checks are manually signed by the chief accountant and given to the foreman. The foreman distributes the checks to the workers in the factory and arranges for the delivery of the checks to the workers who are absent. The payroll bank account is reconciled by the chief accountant, who also prepares the various quarterly and annual payroll tax reports.

Required:

a. List the material weaknesses in the system of internal control and state the financial statement errors that are likely to result from those weaknesses.

b. For each weakness noted in **a**, suggest an internal control procedure that would improve the system.

c. For each weakness noted in **a**, list a substantive audit procedure that will have to be extended to check on it.

(AICPA adapted)

C12–6 You are engaged in auditing the financial statements of Henry Beasley, a large independent contractor. All employees are paid in cash because Beasley believes this arrangement reduces clerical expenses and is preferred by his employees.

During the audit you find in the petty cash fund approximately $200, of which $185 is stated to be unclaimed wages. Further investigation reveals that Beasley has installed the procedure of putting any unclaimed wages in the petty cash fund so that the cash can be used for disbursements. When the claimant to the wages appears, he is paid from the petty cash fund. Beasley contends that this procedure reduces the number of checks drawn to replenish the petty cash fund and centers the responsibility for all cash on hand in one person inasmuch as the petty cash custodian distributes the pay envelopes.

Required:

a. Does Beasley's system provide proper internal control of unclaimed wages? Explain fully.
b. Because Beasley insists on paying salaries in cash, what procedures would you recommend to provide better internal control over unclaimed wages?

(AICPA adapted)

C12–7 The Gibraltar Loan Company has 100 branch loan offices. Each office has a manager and four or five subordinates who are employed by the manager. Branch managers prepare the weekly payroll, including their own salaries, and pay employees from cash on hand. The employee signs the payroll sheet signifying receipt of his salary. Hours worked by hourly personnel are inserted in the payroll sheet from time cards prepared by the employees and approved by the manager.

The weekly payroll sheets are sent to the home office along with other accounting statements and reports. The home office compiles employee earnings records and prepares all federal and state salary reports from the weekly payroll sheets.

Salaries are established by home office job evaluation schedules. Salary adjustments, promotions, and transfers of full-time employees are approved by a home office salary committee based upon the recommendations of branch managers and area supervisors. Branch managers advise the salary committee of new full-time employees and terminations. Part-time and temporary employees are hired without referral to the salary committee.

Required:

a. On the basis of your review of the payroll system, how do you think funds for payroll might be diverted?
b. Prepare a payroll audit program to be used in the home office to audit the branch office payrolls of the Gibraltar Loan Company.

(AICPA adapted)

PROBLEMS

P12–1 Select the best answer for each of the following items related to general internal controls over cash.

a. Which of the following audit procedures is the *most* appropriate when internal control over cash is weak or when a client requests an investigation of cash transactions?
   (1) Proof of cash.
   (2) Bank reconciliation.

(3) Cash confirmation.
(4) Evaluate ratio of cash to current liabilities.

b. Which of the following is one of the better auditing techniques that might be used by an auditor to detect kiting between two or more banks used by the client?
(1) Review composition of authenticated deposit slips.
(2) Review subsequent bank statements received directly from the banks.
(3) Prepare a schedule of bank transfers.
(4) Prepare year-end bank reconciliations.

c. Kiting is a technique that might be used to conceal a cash shortage. The auditor can *best* detect kiting by performing which of the following procedures?
(1) Examining the details of deposits made to all bank accounts several days subsequent to the balance sheet date.
(2) Comparing cash receipts records with the details on authenticated bank deposit slips for dates subsequent to the balance sheet date.
(3) Examining paid checks returned with bank statements subsequent to the balance sheet date.
(4) Comparing year-end balances per the standard bank confirmation forms with the like balances on the client's bank reconciliations.

d. The use of fidelity bonds protects a company from embezzlement losses and also
(1) Protects employees who make unintentional errors from possible monetary damages resulting from such errors.
(2) Allows the company to substitute the fidelity bonds for various parts of internal accounting control.
(3) Reduces the company's need to obtain expensive business interruption insurance.
(4) Minimizes the possibility of employing persons with dubious records in positions of trust.

e. On the last day of the fiscal year, the cash disbursements clerk drew a company check on bank A and deposited the check in the company account at bank B to cover a previous theft of cash. The disbursement has *not* been recorded. The auditor will *best* detect this form of kiting by
(1) Comparing the detail of cash receipts as shown by the cash receipts records with the detail on the confirmed duplicate deposit tickets for three days prior to and subsequent to year end.
(2) Preparing from the cash disbursements book a summary of bank transfers for one week prior to and subsequent to year end.
(3) Examining the composition of deposits in both bank A and bank B subsequent to year end.
(4) Examining paid checks returned with the bank statement of the next accounting period after year end.

f. Internal control over cash receipts is weakened when an employee who receives customer mail receipts also
(1) Prepares initial cash receipts records.
(2) Records credits to individual accounts receivable.
(3) Prepares bank deposit slips for all mail receipts.
(4) Maintains a petty cash fund.

g. Contact with banks for the purpose of opening company bank accounts should normally be the responsibility of the corporate
(1) Board of Directors.
(2) Treasurer.

(3) Controller.
(4) Executive Committee.

h. The cashier of Safir Company covered a shortage in the cash working fund with cash obtained on December 31 from a local bank by cashing but not recording a check drawn on the Company's out-of-town bank. How would the auditor discover this manipulation?
(1) Confirming all December 31 bank balances.
(2) Counting the cash working fund at the close of business on December 31.
(3) Preparing independent bank reconciliations as of December 31.
(4) Investigating items returned with the bank cutoff statements.

i. For the purpose of proper accounting control, postdated checks remitted by customers should be
(1) Restrictively endorsed.
(2) Returned to customer.
(3) Recorded as a cash sale.
(4) Placed in the joint custody of two officers.

j. To establish illegal "slush funds," corporations may divert cash received in normal business operations. An auditor would encounter the greatest difficulty in detecting the diversion of proceeds from
(1) Scrap sales.
(2) Dividends.
(3) Purchase returns.
(4) COD sales.

k. Operating control over the check signature plate normally should be the responsibility of the
(1) Secretary.
(2) Chief accountant.
(3) Vice-president of finance.
(4) Treasurer.

l. As an in-charge auditor you are reviewing a write-up of internal control weaknesses in cash receipt and disbursement procedures. Which one of the following weaknesses, standing alone, should cause you the *least* concern?
(1) Checks are signed by only one person.
(2) Signed checks are distributed by the controller to approved payees.
(3) Treasurer fails to establish *bona fides* of names and addresses of check payees.
(4) Cash disbursements are made directly out of cash receipts.

(AICPA adapted)

P12–2 Select the best answer for each of the following items relating to the internal controls over payroll.

a. In the audit of which of the following types of profit-oriented enterprises would the auditor be most likely to place special emphasis on testing the internal controls over proper classification of payroll transactions?
(1) A manufacturing organization.
(2) A retailing organization.
(3) A wholesaling organization.
(4) A service organization.

b. A CPA reviews a client's payroll procedures. The CPA would consider internal control to be less than effective if a payroll department supervisor was assigned the responsibility for
(1) Reviewing and approving time reports for subordinate employees.
(2) Distributing payroll checks to employees.
(3) Hiring subordinate employees.
(4) Initiating requests for salary adjustments for subordinate employees.

c. For internal control purposes, which of the following individuals should preferably be responsible for the distribution of payroll checks?
(1) Bookkeeper.
(2) Payroll clerk.
(3) Cashier.
(4) Receptionist.

d. Proper internal control over the cash payroll function would mandate which of the following?
(1) The payroll clerk should fill the envelopes with cash and a computation of the net wages.
(2) Unclaimed pay envelopes should be retained by the paymaster.
(3) Each employee should be asked to sign a receipt.
(4) A separate checking account for payroll be maintained.

e. During 1979, a bookkeeper perpetrated a theft by preparing erroneous W-2 forms. The bookkeeper's FICA withheld was overstated by $500.00 and the FICA withheld from all other employees was understated. Which of the following is an audit procedure that would detect such a fraud?
(1) Multiplication of the applicable rate by the individual gross taxable earnings.
(2) Utilizing form W-4 and withholding charts to determine whether deductions authorized per pay period agree with amounts deducted per pay period.
(3) Footing and crossfooting of the payroll register, followed by tracing postings to the general ledger.
(4) Vouching cancelled checks to federal tax forms 941.

f. Effective internal control over the payroll function would include which of the following?
(1) Total time recorded on timeclock punch cards should be reconciled to job reports by employees responsible for those specific jobs.
(2) Payroll department employees should be supervised by the management of the personnel department.
(3) Payroll department employees should be responsible for maintaining employee personnel records.
(4) Total time spent on jobs should be compared with total time indicated on timeclock punch cards.

g. Which of the following individuals is the most appropriate person to be assigned the responsibility of distributing envelopes that include employee payroll checks?
(1) The company paymaster.
(2) A member of the accounting department.
(3) The internal auditor.
(4) A representative of the bank where the company payroll account is maintained.

h. A CPA reviews a client's payroll procedures. The CPA would consider internal

control to be less than effective if a payroll department supervisor was assigned the responsibility for
(1) Distributing payroll checks to employees.
(2) Reviewing and approving time reports for subordinate employees.
(3) Hiring subordinate employees.
(4) Initiating requests for salary adjustments for subordinate employees.

i. It would be appropriate for the payroll accounting department to be responsible for which of the following functions?
(1) Approval of employee time records.
(2) Maintenance of records of employment, discharges, and pay increases.
(3) Preparation of periodic governmental reports as to employees' earnings and withholding taxes.
(4) Temporary retention of unclaimed employee paychecks.

j. Effective internal accounting control over the payroll function should include procedures that segregate the duties of making salary payments to employees and
(1) Controlling unemployment insurance claims.
(2) Maintaining employee personnel records.
(3) Approving employee fringe benefits.
(4) Hiring new employees.

k. Which of the following *best* describes proper internal control over payroll?
(1) The preparation of the payroll must be under the control of the personnel department.
(2) The confidentiality of employee payroll data should be carefully protected to prevent fraud.
(3) The duties of hiring, payroll computation, and payment to employees should be segregated.
(4) The payment of cash to employees should be replaced with payment by checks.

l. Which of the following is an effective internal accounting control used to prove that production department employees are properly validating payroll time cards at a time-recording station?
(1) Time cards should be carefully inspected by those persons who distribute pay envelopes to the employees.
(2) One person should be responsible for maintaining records of employee time for which salary payment is *not* to be made.
(3) Daily reports showing time charged to jobs should be approved by the foreman and compared to the total hours worked on the employee time cards.
(4) Internal auditors should make observations of distribution of paychecks on a surprise basis.

m. Effective internal accounting control over unclaimed payroll checks that are kept by the treasury department would include accounting department procedures that require
(1) Effective cancellation and stop payment orders for checks representing unclaimed wages.
(2) Preparation of a list of unclaimed wages on a periodic basis.
(3) Accounting for all unclaimed wages in a current liability account.
(4) Periodic accounting for the actual checks representing unclaimed wages.

n. An example of an internal control weakness is to assign to a department supervisor the responsibility for

(1) Reviewing and approving time reports for subordinate employees.
(2) Initiating requests for salary adjustments for subordinate employees.
(3) Authorizing payroll checks for terminated employees.
(4) Distributing payroll checks to subordinate employees.

o. It would be appropriate for the payroll accounting department to be responsible for which of the following functions?
(1) Approval of employee time records.
(2) Maintenance of records of employment, discharges, and pay increases.
(3) Preparation of periodic governmental reports as to employees' earnings and withholding taxes.
(4) Distribution of pay checks to employees.

(AICPA adapted)

P12–3 Select the best answer for each of the following items relating to audit procedures followed with verification of cash.

Items a, b, and c are based on the following information:

Listed below are four interbank cash transfers, indicated by the numbers (1), (2), (3), and (4), of a client for late December 19X4 and early January 19X5. Your answer choice for each item of a, b, and c should be selected from this list.

	BANK ACCOUNT ONE DISBURSING DATE (MONTH/DAY)		BANK ACCOUNT TWO RECEIVING DATE (MONTH/DAY)	
	Per Bank	**Per Books**	**Per Bank**	**Per Books**
(1)	12/31	12/30	12/31	12/30
(2)	1/2	12/30	12/31	12/31
(3)	1/3	12/31	1/2	1/2
(4)	1/3	12/31	1/2	12/31

a. Which of the cash transfers indicates an error in cash cutoff at December 31, 19X4?

b. Which of the cash transfers would appear as a deposit in transit on the December 31, 19X4, bank reconciliation?

c. Which of the cash transfers would *not* appear as an outstanding check on the December 31, 19X4, bank reconciliation?

d. The auditor should ordinarily mail confirmation requests to all banks with which the client has conducted any business during the year, regardless of the year-end balance, since
(1) The confirmation form also seeks information about indebtedness to the bank.
(2) This procedure will detect kiting activities which would otherwise not be detected.
(3) The mailing of confirmation forms to all such banks is required by generally accepted auditing standards.
(4) This procedure relieves the auditor of any responsibility with respect to nondetection of forged checks.

e. With respect to contingent liabilities, the Standard Bank Confirmation Inquiry

form approved jointly by the AICPA and the Bank Administration Institute requests information regarding notes receivable
(1) Held by the bank in a custodial account.
(2) Held by the bank for collection.
(3) Collected by the bank.
(4) Discounted by the bank.

f. The auditor's count of the client's cash should be coordinated to coincide with the
(1) Study of the system of internal controls with respect to cash.
(2) Close of business on the balance sheet date.
(3) Count of marketable securities.
(4) Count of inventories.

g. The standard bank cash confirmation form requests all of the following *except*
(1) Maturity date of a direct liability.
(2) The principal amount paid on a direct liability.
(3) Description of collateral for a direct liability.
(4) The interest rate of a direct liability.

h. An internal management tool that aids in the control of the financial management function is a cash budget. The principal aim of a cash budget is to
(1) Ensure that sufficient funds are available at all times to satisfy maturing liabilities.
(2) Measure adherence to company budgetary procedures.
(3) Prevent the posting of cash receipts and disbursements to incorrect accounts.
(4) Assure that the accounting for cash receipts and disbursements is consistent from year to year.

(AICPA adapted)

P12–4 Select the best answer for each of the following items related to the audit of payroll transactions.

a. A surprise observation by an auditor of a client's regular distribution of paychecks is primarily designed to satisfy the auditor that
(1) All unclaimed payroll checks are properly returned to the cashier.
(2) The paymaster is *not* involved in the distribution of payroll checks.
(3) All employees have in their possession proper employee identification.
(4) Names on the company payroll are those of bona fide employees presently on the job.

b. In testing the payroll of a large company, the auditor wants to establish that the individuals included in a sample actually were employees of the company during the period under review. What will be the *best* source to determine this?
(1) Telephone contacts with the employees.
(2) Tracing from the payroll register to the employees' earnings records.
(3) Confirmation with the union or other independent organization.
(4) Examination of personnel department records.

c. Which of the following procedures would normally be performed by the auditor when making tests of payroll transactions?
(1) Interview employees selected in a statistical sample of payroll transactions.
(2) Trace number of hours worked as shown on payroll to time cards and time reports signed by the foreman.

(3) Confirm amounts withheld from employees' salaries with proper governmental authorities.
(4) Examine signatures on paid salary checks.

d. Which of the following is the *best* reason why an auditor should consider observing a client's distribution of regular payroll checks?
(1) Separation of payroll duties is less than adequate for effective internal control.
(2) Total payroll costs are a significant part of total operating costs.
(3) The auditor did *not* observe the distribution of the entire regular payroll during the audit in the prior year.
(4) Employee turnover is excessive.

e. If a control total were to be computed on each of the following data items, which would *best* be identified as a hash total for a payroll EDP application?
(1) Gross pay.
(2) Hours worked.
(3) Department number.
(4) Number of employees.

f. When examining payroll transactions an auditor is primarily concerned with the possibility of
(1) Overpayments and unauthorized payments.
(2) Posting of gross payroll amounts to incorrect salary expense accounts.
(3) Misfootings of employee time records.
(4) Excess withholding of amounts required to be withheld.

g. Which of the following is the *best* way for an auditor to determine that every name on a company's payroll is that of a bona fide employee presently on the job?
(1) Examine personnel records for accuracy and completeness.
(2) Examine employees' names listed on payroll tax returns for agreement with payroll accounting records.
(3) Make a surprise observation of the company's regular distribution of paychecks.
(4) Visit the working areas and confirm with employees their badge or identification numbers.

h. An auditor decides that it is important and necessary to observe a client's distribution of payroll checks on a particular audit. The client organization is so large that the auditor *cannot* conveniently observe the distribution of the entire payroll. In these circumstances, which of the following is *most* acceptable to the auditor?
(1) Observation should be limited to one or more selected departments.
(2) Observation should be made for all departments regardless of the inconvenience.
(3) Observation should be eliminated and other alternative auditing procedures should be utilized to obtain satisfaction.
(4) Observation should be limited to those departments where employees are readily available.

i. A common audit procedure in the audit of payroll transactions involves tracing selected items from the payroll journal to employee time cards that have been approved by supervisory personnel. This procedure is designed to provide evidence in support of the audit proposition that
(1) Only bona fide employees worked and their pay was properly computed.
(2) Jobs on which employees worked were charged with the appropriate labor cost.

(3) Internal controls relating to payroll disbursements are operating effectively.
(4) All employees worked the number of hours for which their pay was computed.

j. One of the auditor's objectives in observing the actual distribution of payroll checks is to determine that every name on the payroll is that of a bona fide employee. The payroll observation is an auditing procedure that is generally performed for which of the following reasons?
(1) The professional standards that are generally accepted require the auditor to perform the payroll observation.
(2) The various phases of payroll work are *not* sufficiently segregated to afford effective internal accounting control.
(3) The independent auditor uses personal judgment and decides to observe the payroll distribution on a particular audit.
(4) The standards that are generally accepted by the profession are interpreted to mean that payroll observation is expected on an audit unless circumstances dictate otherwise.

k. To check the accuracy of hours worked, an auditor would ordinarily compare clock cards with
(1) Personnel records.
(2) Shop job time tickets.
(3) Labor variance reports.
(4) Time recorded in the payroll register.

(AICPA adapted)

P12–5 Items **a** through **k** are questions excerpted from a typical internal control questionnaire for the purpose of evaluating internal accounting controls over preparation and payment of payrolls. As explained in the text, a "yes" response to such a question indicates a potential strength in the system while a "no" response indicates a potential weakness.

a. Are personnel files maintained for all employees by a separate personnel department?
b. Are new hires, terminations, and rate changes subjected to approvals by authorities in the personnel and operating departments?
c. Are personnel action forms for new hires, rate changes and terminations appropriately processed by the payroll department?
d. Are all payroll deductions based on authorization by the employees?
e. Are all payroll deductions being processed correctly?
f. Are timekeeping data used in payroll preparation adequately supported by time cards and time tickets?
g. Are all regular and overtime hours worked by employees approved by departmental supervisors?
h. Are checks issued to employees verified to net pay per the payroll register by persons who reconcile the payroll book account?
i. Are entries in the payroll register supported by cancelled checks?
j. Is proper identification required of all persons who distribute pay checks?
k. Is proper follow-up performed for all unclaimed wages by restoring such items to cash and making an equivalent entry to a current liability account?

Required:

For each question above, list

a. The error or irregularity which that control attribute was designed to detect.

b. The effect that the absence of the control attribute would have on the financial statements.

c. The compliance test necessary to ascertain whether the controls were actually being implemented if the answer to the question is "yes." When sampling of documents is involved, indicate the data file from which a sample would be chosen and the audit procedure (vouching, tracing, recalculation, etc.) which is appropriate (see Figure 12–5).

d. Whether the compliance test listed in **c** is also a substantive test of transactions. If not, indicate the substantive test (Figure 12–6) that would be extended, if any, if that control attribute were missing or if the client demonstrated a low level of compliance.

Organize your answer according to the format specified below. The first question has been answered as an example.

Item	Error or Irregularity	Effect on Financial Statements	Compliance Test	Also a Substantive Test or Substantive Test Extended
(a)	Insertion and paying fictitious employees	Misappropriation of cash	Observation	Surprise payroll observation to detect fictitious employees

P12–6 Explain the objective(s) of each of the following substantive tests performed in verifying cash balances:

a. Count cash on hand in the presence of the custodian.

b. Trace adjusting journal entries to cash accounts from journals to postings in general ledger account.

c. Trace deposits near the end of the period according to the book reconciliation to cutoff book statement and ascertain that the time lag for clearing the bank is proper.

d. Inspect book confirmation for any restrictions on cash in bank — such as time deposits, compensating balances, etc.

e. Confirm "cash per bank" on the client's bank reconciliation directly with the bank.

f. Inspect all checks clearing with the bank cutoff statement for payee, date, and amount.

g. Compare checks clearing the bank with amounts per the outstanding check list for omitted checks or errors in amounts on the outstanding checks list.

h. Prepare a schedule of interbank transfers for approximately three days before and after the balance sheet date.
i. Prepare and analyze a four-column proof of cash.

P12–7 An auditor obtains a July 10 bank statement directly from the bank.

Required:

Explain how this cutoff bank statement will be used

a. In the auditor's review of the June 30 bank reconciliation.
b. To obtain any other audit information.

(AICPA adapted)

P12–8 The following information was obtained in an audit of the cash account of Tuck Company as of December 31, 19X7. Assume that the CPA has satisfied himself as to the validity of the cash book, the bank statements, and the returned checks, except as noted.

a. The bookkeeper's bank reconciliation at November 30, 19X7.

Balance per bank statement			$ 19,400
Add deposit in transit			1,110
Total			$ 20,500
Less outstanding checks			
	#2540	$140	
	1501	750	
	1503	480	
	1504	800	
	1505	30	2,300
Balance per books			$ 18,200

b. A summary of the bank statement for December 19X7.

Balance brought forward	$ 19,400
Deposits	148,700
	$168,100
Charges	132,500
Balance, December 31, 19X7	$ 35,600

c. A summary of the cash book for December 19X7 before adjustments.

Balance brought forward	$ 18,200
Receipts	149,690
	$167,890
Disbursements	124,885
Balance, December 31, 19X7	$ 43,005

d. Included with the cancelled checks returned with the December bank statement were the following:

Number	Date of Check	Amount of Check	
#1501	November 28, 19X7	$ 75	This check was in payment of an invoice for $750 and was recorded in the cash book as $750.
#1503	November 28, 19X7	$580	This check was in payment of an invoice for $580 and was recorded in the cash book as $580.
#1523	December 5, 19X7	$150	Examination of this check revealed that it was unsigned. A discussion with the client disclosed that it had been mailed inadvertently before it was signed. The check was endorsed and deposited by the payee and processed by the bank even though it was a legal nullity. The check was recorded in the cash disbursements.
#1528	December 12, 19X7	$800	This check replaced #1504 that was returned by the payee because it was mutilated. Check #1504 was not canceled on the books.
———	December 19, 19X7	$200	This was a counter check drawn at the bank by the president of the company as a cash advance for travel expense. The president overlooked informing the bookkeeper about the check.
———	December 20, 19X7	$300	The drawer of this check was the Tucker Company.
#1535	December 20, 19X7	$350	This check had been labeled N.S.F. and returned to the payee because the bank had erroneously believed that the check was drawn by the Luck Company. Subsequently the payee was advised to redeposit the check.
#1575	January 5, 19X8	$10,000	This check was given to the payee on December 30, 19X7, as a postdated check with the understanding that it would not be deposited until January 5. The check was not recorded on the books in December.

e. The Tuck Company discounted its own 60-day note for $9,000 with the bank on December 1, 19X7. The discount rate was 6 percent. The bookkeeper recorded the proceeds as a cash receipt at the face value of the note.

f. The bookkeeper records customers' dishonored checks as a reduction of cash receipts. When the dishonored checks are redeposited they are recorded as a regular cash receipt. Two N.S.F. checks for $180 and $220 were returned by the bank during December. The $180 check was redeposited, but the $220 check was still on hand at December 31. Cancellations of Tuck Company checks are recorded by a reduction of cash disbursements.

g. December bank charges were $20. In addition a $10 service charge was made in December for the collection of a foreign draft in November. These charges were not recorded on the books.

h. Check #2540 listed in the November outstanding checks was drawn in 19X5. Since the payee cannot be located, the president of Tuck Company agreed to the CPA's suggestion that the check be written back into the accounts by a journal entry.

i. Outstanding checks at December 31, 19X7, totaled $4,000 excluding checks #2540 and #1504.

j. The cutoff bank statement disclosed that the bank had recorded a deposit of $2,400 on January 2, 19X8. The bookkeeper had recorded this deposit on the books on December 31, 19X7, and then mailed the deposit to the bank.

Required:

Prepare a four-column proof of cash of the cash receipts and cash disbursements recorded on the bank statement and on the company's books for the month of December 19X7. The reconciliation should agree with the cash figure that will appear in the company's financial statements.

(AICPA adapted)

P12–9 The Pembrook Company had poor internal control over its cash transactions. Facts about its cash position at November 30 were the following:

The cash books showed a balance of $18,901.62, which included undeposited receipts. A credit of $100 on the bank statement did not appear on the books of the company. The balance according to the bank statement was $15,550.

When the auditor received the cutoff bank statement on December 20, the following cancelled checks were enclosed: No. 62 for $116.25, No. 183 for $150.00, No. 284 for $253.25, No. 8621 for $190.71, No. 8623 for $206.80, and No. 8632 for $145.28. The only deposit was in the amount of $3,794.41 on December 7.

The cashier handles all incoming cash and makes the bank deposits personally. He also reconciles the monthly bank statement. His November 30 reconciliation is shown below.

Balance, per books, November 30		$18,901.62
Add: Outstanding checks:		
8621	$190.71	
8623	206.80	
8632	145.28	442.79
		$19,344.41
Less: Undeposited receipts		3,794.41
Balance per bank, November 30		$15,550.00
Deduct: Unrecorded credit		100.00
True cash, November 30		$15,450.00

Required:

a. You suspect that the cashier may have misappropriated some money. Prepare a schedule showing your estimate of the loss.

b. How did the cashier attempt to conceal his theft?

c. On the basis of only the information above, name two specific features of internal control that were apparently missing.

d. If the cashier's October 31 reconciliation is known to be in order and you start your audit on December 10, what specific auditing procedures could you perform to discover the theft?

(AICPA adapted)

CHAPTER

13

INVESTMENTS, INTANGIBLES, AND RELATED ACCOUNT BALANCES

We now turn our attention to the audit of the investment and intangibles subsystems and accounts. As we develop the audit procedures for verifying those accounts, we follow the same general format established in Chapter 10. This means that the chapter is divided into the following sections:

1. Development of the auditing procedures associated with the verification of accounts included in the investments subsystem.
2. Development of auditing procedures associated with the verification of intangibles and their related accounts.

We also include as appendixes illustrations of working papers typically used in the audit of investments.

INVESTMENTS

Investments typically may be included in both the current and noncurrent sections of the balance sheet. The investments included in current assets represent temporary commitments of excess cash. They are the most liquid noncash assets and may include any or all of the following items:

- Marketable equity securities of unaffiliated companies (less than 20 percent owned).
- Marketable debt securities.
- Savings accounts.
- Certificates of deposit.

Noncurrent investments are held for the long-term production of income, for incremental gains, or for the purpose of preserving operational relationships with other companies. A client's portfolio of noncurrent investments might include any or all of the following items:

- Equity or debt securities of affiliated or unaffiliated companies.
- Mortgages or notes receivable.
- Loans or advances to affiliated companies.
- Fixed assets not used in business operations.
- Cash value of life insurance policies of which the company is the beneficiary.
- Investments in partnerships or other nonstock companies.

Regardless of the nature of the investment, the audit objectives and procedures required to meet those objectives are similar. Therefore we discuss them as a group in this section. Although a company may hold other types of investments, our discussion will focus on the verification of securities and cash surrender value of officers' life insurance policies, because they are the most common forms of investments held among companies.

Clients who are not dealers or institutional investors in securities will normally have only a limited number of transactions involving the acquisitions and disposals of investments. Therefore the auditor will typically use an analysis type of working paper similar to that shown in Appendix 13–A to accumulate the audit evidence relating to these items. This involves verifying the acquisitions and disposals during the period under audit as well as the end-of-period account balances. Since the beginning-of-the-period balances will normally have been verified in the prior year's audit, we can then fit our findings into the general format of the following four-element equation:

$$\text{Beginning balance} + \text{acquisitions} - \text{disposals} = \text{ending balance.}$$

Because all four elements of this equation will have been verified independently, the fact that they "fit together" provides further evidence in support of the fairness of the end-of-period balance. Figure 13–1 presents diagrammatically the typical flows of transactions for investments.

Nevertheless, the auditor is still concerned with the verification of *transaction validity, existence, ownership, cutoff, valuation,* and *appropriate statement presentation* of year-end balances as he or she begins the examination of investments and their related accounts. As in preceding chapters, it will be helpful for you, as we examine the ways in which those objectives are achieved, to visualize them as characteristics that must be verified if the various account balances associated with investments are to be presented in accordance with GAAP.

Verification of Transaction Validity

The audit of investment accounts is directed toward verifying that acquisition, disposal, and revenue recognition transactions have been *appropriately recorded, classified* and *summarized* in the accounting records. One step in the verification process is to prove that the transactions are valid. The auditor relies heavily on the system of internal control in reaching conclusions regarding the validity of

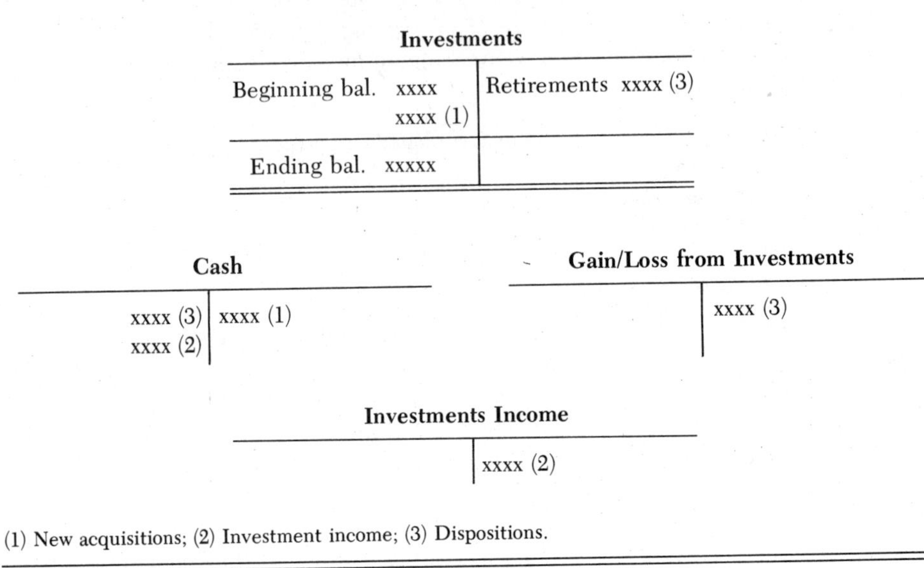

(1) New acquisitions; (2) Investment income; (3) Dispositions.

FIGURE 13–1. Flow of Transactions for Investments

investment-related transactions. Because many investments are evidenced by securities that are negotiable and thus readily convertible into cash, the internal control system is particularly important in preventing errors and irregularities in handling securities and in accounting for them. As we shall see, learning about the system of internal control involves the two classic phases:

1. Analyzing and evaluating the control practices that are supposed to be in the operation.
2. Performing compliance tests to see that the control provisions are actually being implemented.

Evaluating the System of Internal Control. The reliability of the system of internal control is evaluated by verifying the extent to which it includes the desired internal control characteristics. This involves a review and evaluation phase based on an analysis of the organization chart and the procedures manual or on an inquiry of appropriate client personnel. It also includes a compliance testing phase to see whether the provisions of those documents are actually being followed. In addition, in auditing a computerized system, the auditor will be concerned with determining whether the electronic data-processing department is properly organized and whether appropriate applications controls are in place for processing transactions.

The auditor's *preliminary review* and evaluation of internal control for investments are designed to determine the reliability of the system of internal control to produce materially correct balances. Controls upon which the auditor wishes to *rely* are those documented and evaluated in detail. In conducting the evaluation, the auditor should consider the types of errors and irregularities that could occur; he or she should then determine the accounting control procedures that would prevent or detect such errors and irregularities and then set out to discover whether the necessary procedures are prescribed by the client.

The auditor should concentrate on ***material controls*** associated with investment activities. In making the decision as to which controls are material, it is again helpful to consider the exchange transactions that produce investment account balances. Figure 13–2 lists five basic exchange transactions associated with investment accounts, as well as the boundary and supporting documents for each transaction. Since these transactions are the ones generally summarized in the financial statement accounts, controls over them are material and should be of concern to the auditor.

Satisfactory completion of the exchange transactions listed in Figure 13–2 requires controls over the performance of several functions in order to have adequate control over the acquisitions, holding, and dispositions of securities. These functions fall into three categories (see also Chapters 10 and 11):

1. *Exchange functions* (see Figure 13–3), which should incorporate controls designed to protect the securities and related revenues from misuse as they are acquired, held, and sold. These include the following:
   a. *Purchase* of securities and other investments.
   b. *Pledging* of securities as collateral for the firm's obligations.
   c. *Receipt* of interest and dividend checks as the owner of securities.
   d. *Sale* of securities and other investments.
2. *Processing functions* (see Figure 13–4), which should include controls designed to establish accountability and to provide reliable financial data. These include the following:
   a. *Recording the purchases* of investments.
   b. *Recording interest and dividend income* receipts.
   c. *Periodic adjustments of carrying values* of investments.
   d. *Recording the sales of securities* and other investments.

Exchange Transaction	Boundary Document	Supporting Document(s)
Purchase of marketable equity or debt securities	Cancelled check	Broker's advice; board of directors' minutes
Purchase of other investments	Cancelled check	Purchase agreement; board of directors' minutes
Sale of marketable equity or debt securities	Remittance advice	Broker's advice; validated deposit slip; board of directors' minutes
Sale of other investments	Remittance advice	Sales agreement; validated deposit slip; board of directors' minutes
Receipt of income from investments	Remittance advice	Dividend records of various investment services; interest contract

FIGURE 13–2. Exchange Transactions and Documents: Investments

Functions	Invalid transactions: Possible Errors or Irregularities	Possible Results of Undetected Errors	Control Attributes to Prevent, Detect, or Correct Errors or Irregularities
Purchase of securities and other investments	Investments could be acquired without the knowledge or approval of the company; Acquisition of securities for personal use with company funds	Unexpected shortages in cash from making unsound business investments	Require approval of all major investment acquisitions by board of directors or investment committee Require registered securities to be held in the name of the client or in the name of a custodian who has proper power of attorney
Pledging of securities as collateral for firm obligations	Use of company-owned securities as collateral for personal loans of custodian	Shortages in working capital Misappropriation of assets.	Require securities held as collateral to be physically segregated from other securities Require approval of such transactions by appropriate officials
Receipt of interest and dividend checks	Misappropriation of cash to personal use	Understatement of cash and income Misappropriation of cash	Require separation of recording and custodial duties associated with investments Require periodic reconciliation of records and physical assets by persons having no other recordkeeping or custodial duties
Sale of securities and other investments	Investments could be sold without the knowledge or approval of the company, and without being removed from the books	Overstatement of assets Misappropriation of cash	Require approval of all major investment disposals by board of directors or investment committee Require segregation of custodial and record-keeping functions Require periodic reconciliation of records and physical assets by persons independent of custodial functions

FIGURE 13–3. Exchange Functions Requiring Specific Controls

Functions	Possible Errors or Irregularities	Possible Results of Undetected Errors	Control Attributes to Prevent, Detect, or Correct Errors or Irregularities
Recording purchases of investment	Inaccurate or improper recording of acquisitions	Misstatement of assets	Require the accounting department to maintain an independent record of each investment or security, including serial or other identification numbers, number of shares, face amounts, dates of purchase, interest rates, etc.
			Require inspection and periodic reconciliation of purchase documents with accounting records
Recording interest and dividend income	Inaccurate or improper recording of income from investments	Misstatement of assets and income	Require proper accounting over investment income by persons independent of custodianship duties
			Require periodic reconciliation of investment income with dividend records; recalculation of interest accrued, etc., by independent persons
Recording the carrying value of investments	Improper recording of the value of assets	Misstatement of asset portfolio	Require periodic review of proper carrying value of investment portfolio by a responsible official, and adjust when necessary
Recording sale of securities and other investments	Failure to record a disposal of securities and other investments Improperly recorded disposals	Overstatement of assets	Require inspection and periodic reconciliation of securities and investments with accounting records
			Require approval of write-downs and other disposals by board of directors or investment committee
			Require proper control to be exercised over securities written down or written off

FIGURE 13–4. Processing Functions Requiring Specific Controls

3. *Safeguarding functions* (see Figure 13–5), which should include controls designed to protect the investments held and the records associated with the investment-related accounts.

Figures 13–3, 13–4, and 13–5 show examples of some of the errors and irregularities that can be introduced into the investments system if these functions are not properly controlled. After observing the problems that can be created by such errors and irregularities, we suggest certain control attributes to prevent, detect, or correct them. Logically, then, a system properly performing the exchange transaction should include the control attributes shown in Figures 13–3 through 13–5. Notice that these attributes embody the characteristics of good internal control (discussed in Chapter 5).

To document our understanding of the systems controls that are relied upon, we might use an internal control questionnaire, a systems flowchart, decision tables, narrative descriptions, or a combination of these devices. These documents are completed by reference to the organizational chart and procedures manuals, and by inquiry of client personnel. The internal control questionnaire for investments consists of a series of yes – no questions designed to assist the auditor in determining whether the control attributes listed in Figures 13–3 through 13–5 are prescribed by the client. The questionnaire is designed in such a way that a "no" answer for a particular control attribute indicates a weakness. Material weaknesses must be followed up with additional audit work, either in the form of discovery of mitigating controls or additional tests of related financial statement balances.

A typical systems flowchart for an investments system is shown in Figure 13–6. Notice from the flowchart that in handling investments and accounting for them, the appropriate ***separation of responsibilities*** requires that the elements of many of the functions listed in Figures 13–3 through 13–5 be assigned to different employees to protect the securities from misuse and to provide reliable financial data. Specifically, this requires the following:

- In processing acquisitions of securities and other investments, it is important that all acquisitions be appropriately authorized by a responsible official not having custodial or recordkeeping responsibilities for securities. Evidence of this arrangement can be produced by using an appropriate authorization and approval form to support all investment acquisitions.
- Authorization to borrow against securities should rest with a responsible official of the company having no custodial responsibilities for those securities.
- Checks received as interest and dividend income from investments should be handled by a person having no custodial responsibilities for securities and no access to the cash receipts records.
- The disposal of securities requires a separation of the authorization and approval functions from the actual conversion of securities to cash. Furthermore, the cash realized from the disposal of securities should be handled by a person having no custodial responsibilities relating to the securities and no access to the cash receipts records. The authorization to dispose of securities should be vested in a responsible official other than the person having custodial responsibility for them.
- Persons having custodial responsibility for investments should not have access to the accounting records.
- In order to properly protect the securities from theft or misuse, two persons should be required to be present to open the bank safe deposit box where the securities are kept.

Functions	Possible Errors or Irregularities	Possible Results of Undetected Errors	Control Attributes to Prevent, Detect, or Correct Errors or Irregularities
Custodianship of securities	Unauthorized personal access to assets	Unauthorized sale or use of assets as collateral	Require dual custodianship over assets held in safe deposit boxes at financial institutions; for large portfolios of assets, require independent custodian such as trust department of a bank or other fiduciary Require bonding of all custodians of investment securities Require segregation of custodianship from recordkeeping duties Require periodic reconciliation of physical assets with accounting records by independent persons

FIGURE 13–5. Safeguarding Functions Requiring Specific Controls

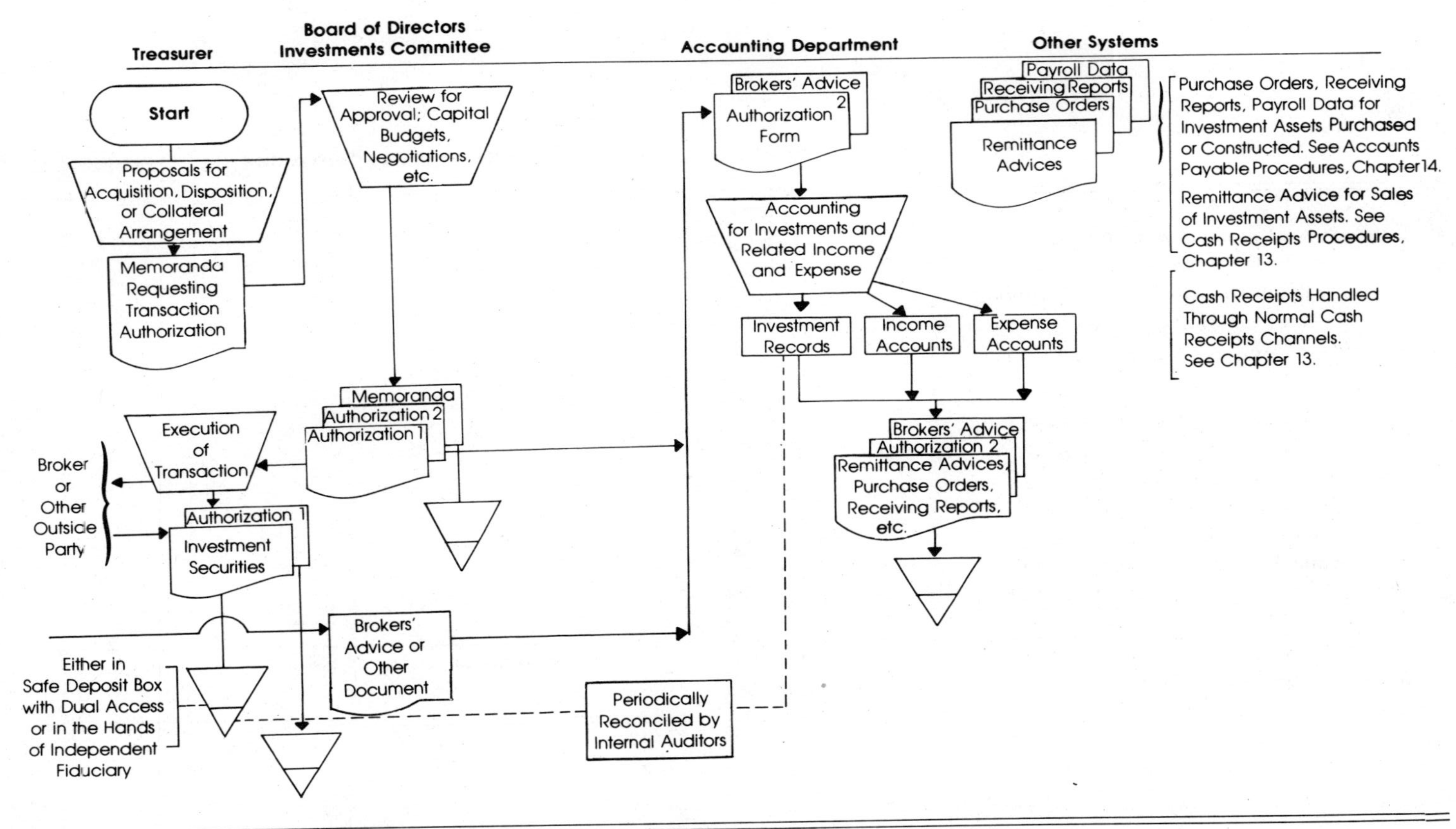

FIGURE 13–6. Flowchart for Investments

- The investments committee of the board of directors should periodically review the investment activities of the company.

As you examine the flowchart shown in Figure 13–6, you will observe that it is designed to disclose the extent to which the preceding separation of responsibilities criteria have been met.

It is also important that the responsibilities for all functions associated with the investments system be ***assigned to specific persons*** within the organization. Specifically, this requires the following:

- The person(s) given the responsibility of authorizing investment acquisitions should be specifically identified through the medium of her or his job description.
- Payments for securities acquisitions should also require authorization and approval by employees having no cash payment responsibilities. The same controls apply here as for cash payments for operations (see Chapter 11).
- The person responsible for signing checks in payment for securities should be held responsible for reviewing supporting documents prior to signing the checks (Chapter 11).
- The person charged with the responsibility of handling cash receipts from security sales, interest, and dividends should be specifically identified and should be held accountable for such funds from the point where they are received until they are deposited in the bank. The same controls apply here as for cash receipts from operations (see Chapter 10).
- Person(s) responsible for authorizing the disposal of securities should be specifically identified.

All activities associated with investment activities should be documented by an adequate system of records, forms, and authorizations. ***Supporting documents*** typically evidencing these activities include the following:

- An *authorization to buy form* that includes a specific description of the security to be purchased plus spaces for authorization signatures or initials.
- *Broker's advice forms* (invoices provided by securities brokers as evidence of purchase and sale transactions) appropriately matched with the authorizations to buy or sell securities.
- A *cash disbursement voucher* properly supported by the documents listed above and having spaces for the initials of various persons charged with checking documents, extensions, and accounting treatment of the payment (see Chapter 11).
- A *cash remittance advice form* to be used as the company's first evidence of cash received from interest, dividends, or sales of securities (see Chapter 11).
- An *authorization to sell form* having spaces for specific identification of the securities being sold plus authorization to sell signatures or initials.
- *Schedules showing reconciliation* of the periodic independent calculation of interest and dividend incomes with the amounts shown for those items in the accounting records.

The results of investment activities will normally be recorded in the cash disbursements and cash receipts journals. If a significant number of investments are held, it is also important to have *subsidiary records*, showing the individual securities held, that are periodically reconciled with the general ledger control accounts for investments. The records of a company should be organized to properly account for investment income and gains and losses from the sales of investments.

The ***qualified personnel characteristic*** requires that the persons assigned to the various responsibilities associated with investment activities have skills commensurate with those responsibilities. For example, the authorization and approval functions in the investments system should be performed by persons having appropriate training in the general area of finance. All persons having custodial responsibilities relating to securities should show evidence of trustworthiness and should be bonded.

All assets and records associated with investments should have ***appropriate protection*** from physical loss or alteration. This protection entails the following requirements:

- The firm must provide *appropriately protected storage facilities for securities* held as investments. This may take the form of a safe deposit box at a bank or other financial institution, or use of an independent firm for custodianship of securities. For example, a bank may be used as a custodial agent.
- The *records* associated with investments and investment income should be appropriately stored in a safe or vault designed to protect them from damage or alteration when they are not being used.
- All cash receipts from interest or dividends or from the disposal of securities should be promptly deposited in the bank.
- Two persons should generally be required to be present to open the bank safe deposit box where the securities are kept.

Testing the System for Compliance. All the procedures described in the preceding pages will have been identified, reviewed, and evaluated during the preliminary and detailed review phases of the audit by reference to the organization chart and procedures manual and by inquiry of client personnel. Controls upon which the auditor wishes to rely will have been documented by internal control questionnaires, systems flowcharts, and narrative descriptions. We expect management to establish *operating practices designed to promote compliance* with the established practices. Compliance with these practices should be checked periodically either by management personnel or internal auditors to see that the employees both understand and comply with the responsibilities assigned to them.

The auditor's involvement with tests of compliance is more limited in this system than in the ones previously discussed. The system and balances described to this point in the text usually involve large numbers of transactions, making it impractical to perform a 100 percent audit of the transactions comprising the balances. For the investments system, however, most clients will have only a few acquisition or sales transactions during each year, any one of which could be material to the financial position of the company. Because audit evidence for these transactions is relatively easy and inexpensive to obtain, it is *often desirable to audit all transactions* that make up an investment account balance. Therefore extensive compliance tests of documented internal controls are unnecessary. In addition, you should remember that investment transactions are processed in the same way as other transactions involving cash receipts or cash disbursements. Therefore, documented controls over these transactions should have already been tested in conjunction with the compliance tests discussed at length in Chapters 10 and 11.

Nevertheless, there are still those control attributes, such as dual custodianship over assets and adequate segregation of duties, that can and should be investigated by inquiry and observation before proceeding to substantive tests of balances. This investigation is needed because, as we have seen, the auditor has some responsibility for the discovery of errors and irregularities. Controls in the investments subsystem are designed primarily to prevent theft or misuse of securities.

Substantive Verification of Investment Account Balances

Just as was the case in the audit of other systems previously discussed, the auditor is not willing to rely completely on the system of internal control as a basis for judging that transactions have been appropriately recorded, classified, and summarized. As a result, the auditor needs to perform substantive tests of transactions and other underlying data to determine whether the account balances shown for investments fairly reflect the investment items actually owned by the client. As we describe the verification procedures for acquisitions and disposals of investments, we will, because of the relationships among the accounts, at the same time be verifying the associated debits and credits to cash (see Figure 13–1). In addition, one can use the contractual relationships reflected in debt securities and external evidence relating to dividends in verifying the interest and dividend income balances.

Audit procedures for marketable equity securities and for cash surrender value of officers' life insurance are illustrated in appendixes 13–A through 13–C. As we observed in earlier chapters, the audit objectives applicable to the investments subsystem can be identified by asking what could cause the account balances shown in the financial statements to contain amounts materially different from the GAAP defined values for investment items owned by the client. A difference, for example, would occur if the client included items in the investment account that do not really exist. Perhaps the difference is caused by the disposal of investments that were not credited to the appropriate investment account. The audit objective in proving or disproving this point can be characterized as the *verification of existence* (validity).

Closely associated with verification of existence is *verification of the ownership* of investments held by the client. In meeting this objective, the auditor is concerned with ascertaining that the investments included in the accounts belong to the client; and he or she seeks to discover the extent to which outside parties may hold claims against those investments.

The going concern convention logically requires that current marketable securities be valued at their cash realizable value. On the other hand, this same convention logically requires that long-term investments be valued at cost (amortized in certain cases) or on the equity basis. Therefore the auditor must perform the procedures required to determine that those valuation practices have been followed. In meeting the *verification of valuation* objective the auditor is concerned with ascertaining that all securities are recorded in the investment accounts at values established by generally accepted accounting principles.

Although the auditor is concerned with seeing that the acquisitions and disposals of investments as well as the income from those investments are recorded in the proper period, the *verification of cutoff* is much less important in auditing these accounts than it is in the verification of revenues and cost of sales. An error in cutoff would generally involve offsetting errors in cash and investments. Therefore, such an error would be significant only if a material gain or loss on sale were involved or if the error involved cash and noncurrent investments. For that reason, some attention should be given to verifying that transactions occurring near the end of the audit period and beginning of the following period have been recorded in the proper fiscal year.

Investments must also be properly presented in the financial statements. This includes proper classification, proper labeling, and appropriate parenthetical and footnote disclosures. It is especially important that an appropriate distinction be made between current or temporary investments and those investments which should be classified in the noncurrent assets section of the balance sheet. Furthermore, because of the valuation procedures established by GAAP, it is also necessary to distinguish between investments in marketable equity securities and other securities. Among long-term investments it is also important to disclose separately any investments held for the purpose of significantly influencing or controlling the operations of another company; they should be recorded apart from those not involving such relationships. Statements must also appropriately disclose information relating to the pledging of investments as collateral. The audit objective covering all these elements can be characterized as the verification of *appropriate statement presentation.*

We show the relationships of these audit objectives to the audit procedures that satisfy them in Figure 13–7. As we have observed before, the objective of substantive verification is to gather evidence to support the proposition that the investment accounts are fairly presented in accordance with GAAP. The number of transactions in this area is often small, but the size of transactions individually or collectively may be large. Therefore, the auditor will often determine transaction validity by verifying all acquisitions, disposals, and other changes occurring in the investment accounts during the current year. This involves *vouching* the recorded acquisitions and disposals to supporting documents — such as brokers' advices, cancelled checks, bank drafts for officers' life insurance premiums, remittance lists and advices, etc. By combining these amounts with beginning balances, which have been verified by *tracing* them to corresponding ending balances from the prior year's audit working papers, the auditor *recalculates* the ending balance for each investment account. This process is illustrated in the working papers that appear in Appendixes 13–A and 13–B.

After the recalculation of balances just described, the process of verifying the ending investment account balances and their related accounts begins. The initial step in this process is to *reconcile* the end-of-period statement account balances with the underlying accounting records. The financial statement balances should first be reconciled to the balances in the general ledger accounts. After that the investment control accounts should be reconciled with their respective subsidiary records and the account balances should be recomputed.

Verification of Existence. As shown in Appendix 13–A, the existence of securities is verified by *inspecting and listing the securities on hand.* The pertinent details of each security such as serial number, type, interest rate, face amount, number of shares, etc., should be listed. Although the auditor is not responsible for verifying the authenticity of the securities being examined, he or she should be alert for obvious forgeries. This audit procedure should be performed in the presence of the client employee(s) charged with the custodial responsibility for securities and, as observed in Chapter 12, should be carried out at the same time that cash is being counted. If it is

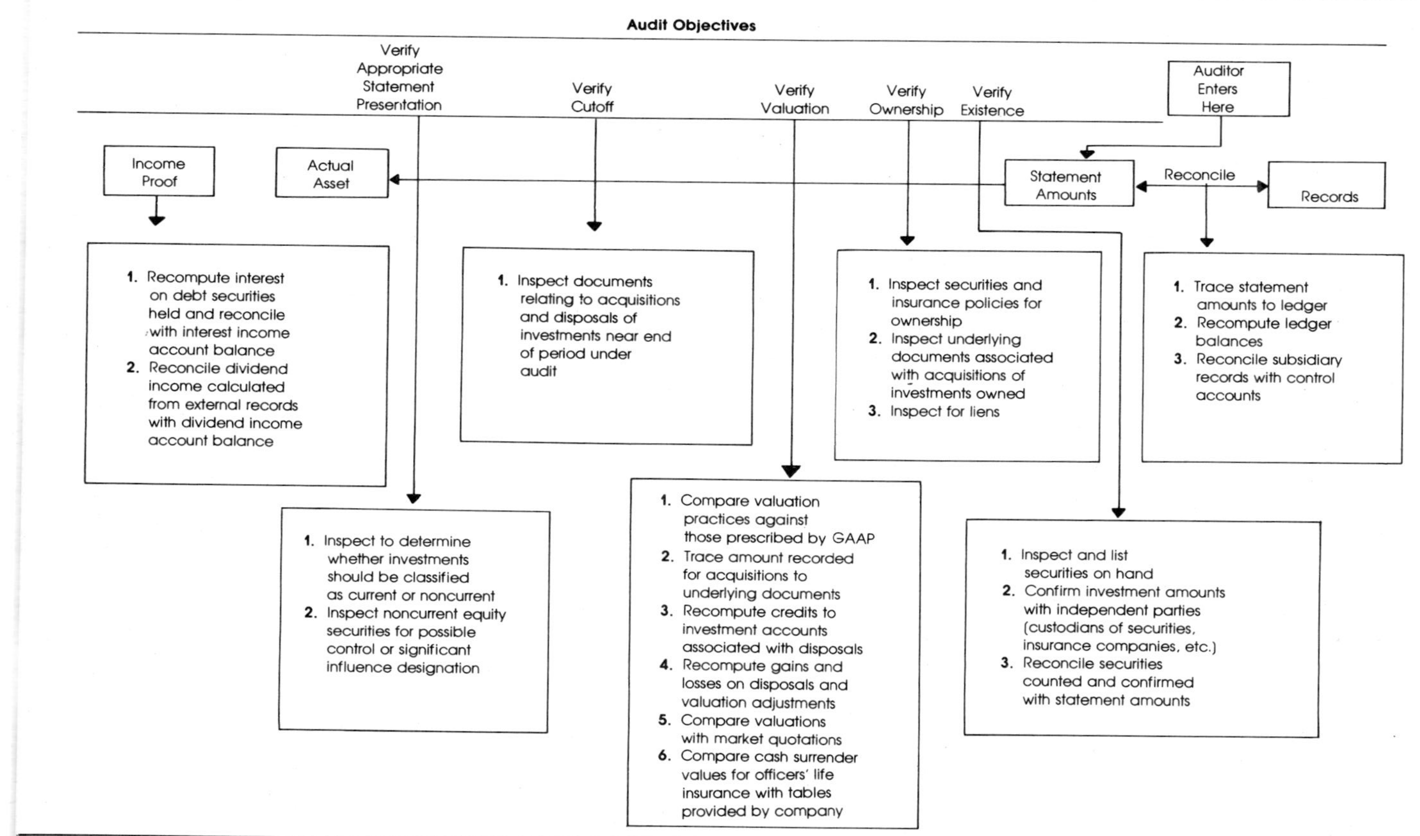

FIGURE 13–7. Flowchart for Substantive Verification of Investments

impossible to perform those procedures simultaneously, the securities storage box should be sealed at the time of the cash count and remain sealed until the securities can be inspected. The custodian of the securities should be asked to sign an acknowledgment for the return of the securities when the inspection is finished.

In instances in which investments owned by the client are held by independent custodians such as brokers or trustees, they should be confirmed with those parties. Securities in a bond sinking fund for example will generally be held by the bond trustee and should be confirmed with that party. Such confirmation requests should contain the same details as those required if the auditor had inspected and listed the securities, as discussed above. After the inspection and confirmation procedures have been completed, the list of securities verified to be in existence as of the end of the fiscal period should be reconciled with the statement balances for securities owned. The list is then used as the basic working paper on which the evidence associated with the verification of valuation, ownership, cutoff, and statement presentation is recorded. Details of insurance policies owned by the client should be confirmed with insurance companies as of the end of the audit period. As shown in Appendix 13–C, such details include policy number, name(s) of insured persons, beneficiaries, face amount, any policy loans outstanding, and selected other information.

Verification of Ownership. The ownership of investments should be verified by inspecting them for outstanding liens as the other audit procedures are performed. For securities, the auditor examines individual certificates for endorsements and inspects confirmation replies for securities held by agents and others. Also, as shown in Appendix 13–A, the broker advices, which are issued as evidence of acquisitions and disposals of securities, should be inspected to determine whether the company is the registered owner of the securities. For insurance policies, the confirmation reply from the insurance company (Appendix 13–C) gives information as to the owner of the policy in the upper right-hand portion of the form.

Verification of Valuation. The verification of valuation is a critical objective in the audit of investments. Typically, the procedures followed in verifying valuation appear on the working paper that contains the list of investments prepared at the time they were inspected and confirmed (see Appendixes 13–A and 13–B). The auditor generally begins by *comparing* the valuation practices followed with those prescribed by GAAP. He or she will also want to *vouch* the amounts recorded in the investment accounts back to the underlying documents associated with acquisitions to see that they have been properly recorded in the accounts. In meeting the valuation objective, it is also necessary to *recompute* the credits to the accounts associated with the sales of investments and to vouch details of disposition transactions to underlying documents (brokers advices, cash receipts, etc.). At this time, realized gains and losses on disposals of marketable equity securities, as well as unrealized valuation adjustments, should be *recomputed* in accordance with the provisions of FASB 12. As a last overall audit procedure, the market quotations for securities held should be compared with their recorded values. These procedures are illustrated in Appendix 13–A.

Verification of Cutoff. Transactions recording acquisitions and disposals of securities that have occurred near the end of the period should be identified and traced to the underlying documents to determine that they were recorded in the appropriate fiscal period. Here again appropriate cutoff is not as important as it is for revenues and cost of sales, but some attention should be given to it.

Verification of Appropriate Statement Presentation. Another important consideration in the audit of investments involves determining how the various investments should be disclosed in the balance sheet. For investments to be classified as a ***current asset***, they *should be readily convertible to cash;* in the normal course of operations, one can expect them to be converted to cash within a year, or within the operating cycle, whichever is longer. All other investments should be classified in the noncurrent assets section. The attitude of conservatism requires that questionable items be classified as noncurrent. A careful distinction should also be made between noncurrent investments held for the purpose of controlling or significantly influencing the operations of another company and those held only for the purpose of realizing investment income or an increment in value.

With respect to ***long-term investments***, APB 18 requires use of the *equity method of accounting* if the investment gives the client the ability to exercise significant influence over the operating and financial policies of an investee. Among other things, such as representation on the investee's board of directors, participation in management decisions, and significant intercompany transactions, APB 18 states that an investment representing 20 percent or more of the voting stock of an investee should lead to a presumption of the ability to exercise significant influence.[1] The equity method requires that the client increase the carrying value of its investment in the investee by its proportionate share of earnings and decrease it by the proportionate share of losses and dividend distributions from the investee. Therefore the auditor must be satisfied that the earnings, losses, and dividends of investee companies have been appropriately recognized. GAAP also requires that investors recognize nontemporary declines in carrying value of investments as losses.[2] That requires the auditor to determine whether such declines have occurred and, if so, whether they have been recorded.

Audited financial statements of the investee are considered sufficient evidence to enable the auditor to determine whether the equity method has been applied properly by the client. These statements may have been audited by another auditor as long as the report of the other auditor is acceptable to the auditor seeking the evidence. We discuss reliance on the work of other auditors more thoroughly in the reporting section of this text. Audited statements of investees are also considered competent (but not sufficient) evidence to assist the auditor of the investor in determining the proper carrying value of other investments. Other evidence may include market price quotations of actively traded securities of investees, as well as independent appraisals of investee asset values when securities are not actively traded.

Unaudited financial statements of the investee company can also provide some evidence as to proper application of the equity method and as to the carrying value of nonaffiliated long-term investments; but they are not considered sufficient evidence by themselves. In cases in which unaudited financial statements are used as evidence in support of significant investments, the auditor should either apply the auditing procedures deemed necessary or request the investee's independent accountant to apply those procedures. The extent of the audit procedures necessary in this case depends on the materiality of the investment in relation to the financial statements of the client investor.[3]

With respect to nonaffiliated investments in marketable equity securities, FASB 12 requires that the client's portfolio be divided into current and noncurrent components for financial reporting purposes. Each of these portfolios must then be evaluated at the lower of aggregate cost or market. Balance sheet valuation accounts should be set up for each portfolio for this purpose. Offsetting charges or credits must be made to (1) unrealized gain or loss accounts on the income statement for short-term investments, and to (2) similar accounts in owners' equity for long-term investments. The auditor should obtain evidence regarding these valuations by *comparing market quotations* with those used by the client, *recalculating* the adjustments to the valuation accounts, and *examining the journal* entries to ascertain that the client's portfolio adjustments were appropriately recorded. Appendix 13–A is organized to facilitate disclosures for marketable equity securities in accordance with FASB 12, and to illustrate the audit procedures discussed above.

As we could observe in Figure 13–7, the audit of investments requires an extension of auditing procedures beyond verifying that the statement account balances fairly reflect the values of investment assets owned. The auditor should also develop an ***independent verification of investment income.*** Typically this involves two procedures, as shown in Appendix 13–C. The first requires the auditor to *recompute* the interest or dividends that should have been earned on securities owned by the client and to verify per share amounts by reference to appropriate outside sources (Standard & Poors, Value Line Investment Survey, etc.). The second is to *reconcile* that amount with the interest or dividend income account balance. This verification for equity securities valued under the equity method will already have been accomplished by audit procedures previously described for meeting the valuation objective.

Other Types of Investments

In some instances, land, mineral deposits, or other properties may be purchased and held as investments. Such investments are held partly for the purpose of realizing an increment in value during the holding period. Therefore, such investments should be valued at their initial costs plus carrying costs, such as taxes and interest, incurred in holding them. Carrying value should then be periodically adjusted for increments or decrements in value of investments. The auditor will be concerned with analyzing such investment accounts to see that GAAP valuation practices have been followed. He or she should also document all audit procedures performed on these investments in a manner similar to that described above for investments in securities and cash surrender value of life insurance policies.

INTANGIBLES

Intangible assets are those assets whose values are primarily associated with the rights, privileges, and competitive advantages that accrue to a business owning them. They include such things as patents, limited franchises, goodwill, copyrights, etc. Such assets are usually created by a single, or by relatively few transactions. They should be recognized in the financial statements only when purchased. Because of their nature, our primary concern in evaluating the validity of transactions associated with these assets is in *determining that the client exercises appropriate control* to see that acquisitions, amortizations, and disposals are recorded in accordance with GAAP. Usually this involves auditing all of the transactions in the account balances. Therefore we need not be concerned with performing tests of compliance with internal controls. Our attention in the audit of intangibles will be directed toward the substantive verification of the asset account balances and the expenses associated with amortizing them.

As shown in Figure 13–8 we begin our audit of intangibles by reconciling the amount shown on the balance sheet with the underlying accounting records. We do this by tracing the statement amount to the ledger account and by recomputing the balance shown in the ledger account.

After the statement amount has been reconciled with the underlying accounting records, we turn our attention to the audit objectives that must be met in the verification of the account balances. These include the verification of existence, ownership, valuation, and appropriate statement presentation.

Verification of Existence

As suggested by the definition at the beginning of this section, an intangible asset exists only if it provides rights, privileges, or competitive advantages to the business. In the case of patents, copyrights, and franchises, existence will normally be evidenced by documents showing the client to have certain exclusive rights to manufacture and sell a product or the exclusive right to provide a designated service within a certain geographic area. The auditor should therefore inspect the documents, such as patent and copyright papers, that spell out these rights and privileges. In other instances the auditor may verify the validity and existence of patents by obtaining a written representation from a patent attorney.

The existence of goodwill, on the other hand, depends on the ability of a firm to realize above-normal profits. It is evidenced by an arm's-length price in excess of fair value of net tangible assets being paid in the acquisition of part or all of another business entity. Typically it is necessary to first allocate from the purchase price of the entity among tangible assets acquired amounts that are equal to the fair market values of those assets. The excess of the price paid for the business over the fair market value of tangible assets represents ***goodwill***. The auditor verifies the existence of goodwill by inspecting the documents associated with the initial outlay transaction, determining that the allocation between tangible and intangible assets is proper, and making a judgment as to whether the operating history of the client continues to show above normal earnings.

Verification of Ownership

The ownership of intangible assets is ordinarily evidenced by the supporting documents in the case of patents, copyrights, and franchises and by an arms-length

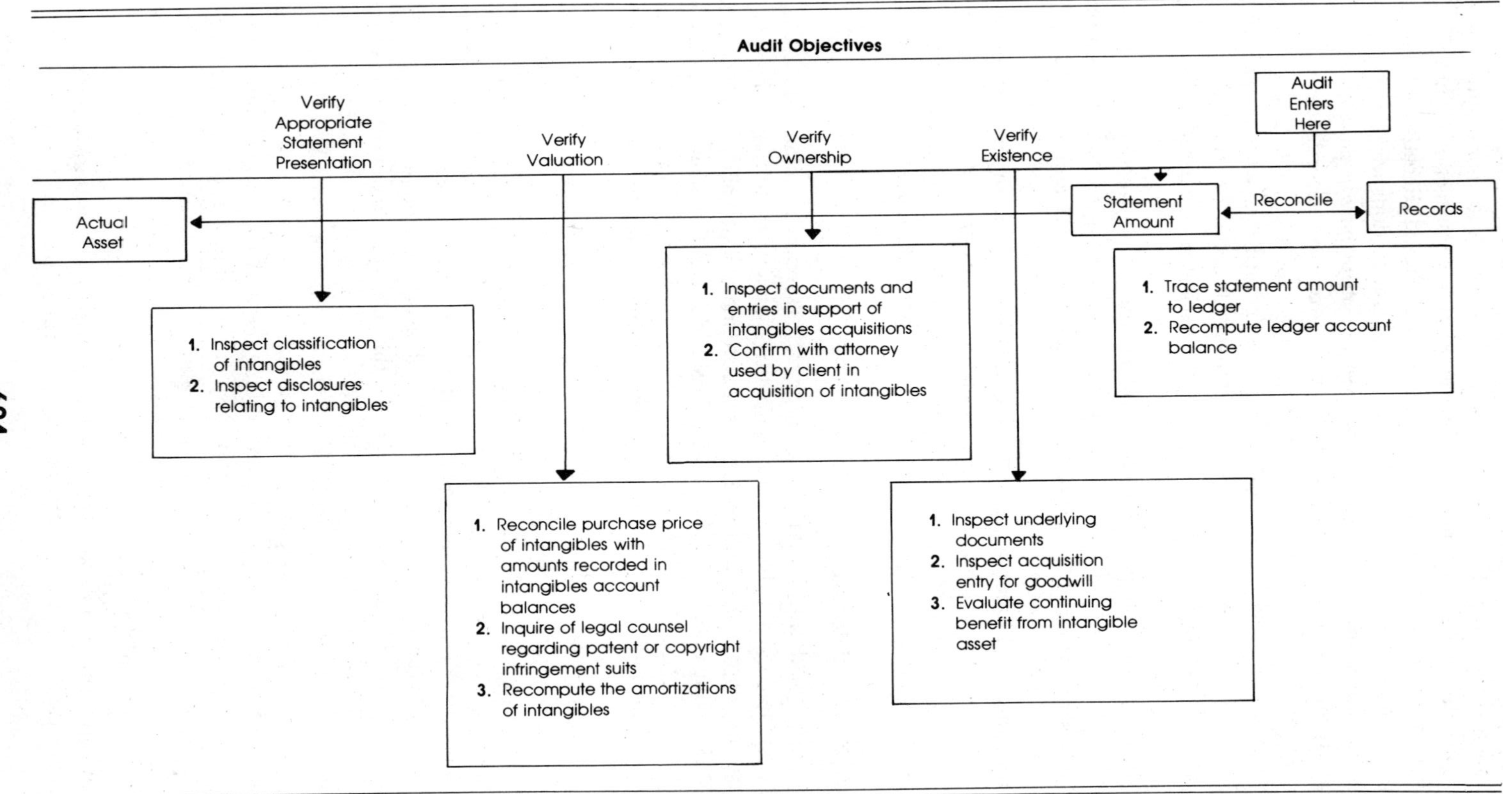

FIGURE 13–8. Flowchart for Substantive Verification of Intangibles

acquisition transaction in the case of goodwill. Therefore the auditor should inspect the documents or transactions underlying the acquisitions of intangible assets in verifying ownership. These will include not only the documents spelling out the rights and privileges but also those evidencing payments made in the acquisitions of intangibles. If the client has used an attorney in the acquisitions of intangibles, the auditor should confirm the acquisitions with that person.

Verification of Valuation

One of the important elements in the audit of intangibles is the verification of valuation. Intangibles should initially be recorded at cost and for that reason the auditor is obliged to inspect the documents supporting all intangibles acquisitions and to reconcile initial acquisition costs with amounts recorded in the accounts. *Research and development (R & D) costs* associated with the development of patents should be charged to expense in the periods incurred, in accordance with FASB 2. Whenever R & D costs have been incurred by the client, the auditor should perform extensive vouching of charges to supporting documents to ascertain whether costs were properly classified as assets or expenses in accordance with FASB 2.

Legal fees to defend the validity of patents and trademarks and to prosecute infringement suits are often the primary items charged to the patents and trademarks accounts. When patents are successfully defended, evidence exists that these intangibles are still valid assets. Therefore, legal fees are properly capitalizable in such instances. On the other hand, when infringement suits are unsuccessful, there is evidence that the patent may have lost its economic value and therefore needs to be written off. Since intangibles such as patents can lose their value through the loss of an infringement suit, the auditor must inquire of management and legal counsel regarding such legal actions during the year. *If a patent infringement suit has been lost,* the auditor should discuss with the client the need for writing off the value of the patent associated with the suit as well as expensing the legal fees associated with the suit. Likewise, goodwill has value only so long as the firm that purchased it continues to earn above-normal net income.

Amortization of intangibles is another important aspect in the valuation of those assets. Therefore, the auditor should recompute the amortization expense in verifying the valuation of intangibles. It is important that the auditor also evaluate the adequacy of amortization charges in the process of recomputing those credits to the intangible asset accounts. GAAP requires that such assets be amortized over their expected useful lives, with a maximum amortization period of 40 years.

Verification of Appropriate Statement Presentation

Intangibles should be reflected among the noncurrent assets in the balance sheet. The amortization practices followed should be disclosed either parenthetically or in a footnote to the balance sheet. Therefore, in the audit of intangibles, the auditor should *inspect* the classifications of these items and the disclosure comments associated with them.

Audit Working Paper for Intangibles

Because of the limited number of transactions typically associated with intangibles, an analysis-type workpaper will normally be prepared to accumulate the audit evidence in support of those account balances. As illustrated in Appendix 13–A for investments, this involves the basic four-element equation showing the beginning balances plus acquisitions during the year, minus disposals and amortization credits during the year to arrive at the end-of-the-year balances. The end-of-the-year audited balances are then the amounts that should be shown for each of the intangibles on the balance sheet. The amount shown in the amortization column should be reflected in the income statement as amortization of intangibles.

SUMMARY

In this chapter we have developed the auditing procedures followed in the verification of investments and intangibles. Because of the limited number of transactions affecting these accounts each year the auditor generally accumulates much of the evidence relating to them in analysis-type working papers organized around the following four-element equation:

$$\text{Beginning balance} + \text{additions} - \text{removals} = \text{ending balance.}$$

Since all transactions associated with the investment account balances during the year under audit are typically verified by the auditor, he or she is primarily concerned with evaluating the adequacy of controls procedures in preventing errors and irregularities. The auditor verifies investment income (interest and dividends) and gains and losses associated with valuation adjustments and disposals in connection with the audit of investments.

Existence and proper valuation are the primary concerns in auditing intangibles. The existence (validity) of an intangible depends on its ability to provide special benefits for the client in the form of a competitive advantage or the ability of the firm to realize above-normal profits. The auditor must judge whether those conditions exist in meeting the verification of the existence objective. Verification of valuation generally involves validating acquisition costs and recomputing amortization charges.

APPENDIX 13–A: Marketable Equity Securities

JEP Manufacturing Co.
Marketable Equity Securities
3-31-X1

W. P. No. C-1
ACCOUNTANT Client / Ch.T.
DATE 4/29/X1

Purchase Date	Description	Balance 3-31-X0	Cost: Purchases	Cost: Sales	Balance 3-31-X1
	General Motors (1000 shares) Common (Cert. # 2604)	33700 00 ∅			33700 00 ✗
	Sears Roebuck + Co. Common (4000 shares) (Cert # 4583)	80400 00 ∅			80400 00 ✗
	General Electric (1600 shares) Common (Cert # 3695)	34848 00 ∅			34848 00 ✗
	Union Carbide (1000 shares) Common (Cert # 4586)		50125 00 Ⓔ		50125 00 ✗
	IBM Common (1000 shares) (Cert # 26032)		52000 00 Ⓔ		52000 00 ✗
	ITT preferred H series (1000 shares) (Cert # 24211)		50250 00 Ⓔ		50250 00 ✗
	Xerox Common (1000 shares) (Cert # 211462)		51768 00 Ⓔ	9819 00 ⊲	41949 00 ✗
		148948 00 ^	204143 00 ^	9819 00 ^	343272 00 ^ A-1

^ Footed. * Cross-footed

✗ Inspected certificate on safe deposit box, First National Bank. Agreed total with subsidiary ledger.

⊲ Traced to cash receipts records. No exceptions noted.

∅ Details agreed to prior year audited working papers. No exceptions noted.

✓ Computation checked.

Ⓔ Examined brokers' advice. Traced to cancelled check and cash disbursements records. Examined records for evidence of transactions occuring at or near year-end cut off date. None noted.

∮ Vouched to market price per Wall Street Journal on March 31, 1981.

Ⓣ Vouched per share dividend to Value Line Investment Survey, Summary and Index. Traced dividend proceeds to cash receipts. No exceptions noted.

Net Sales Proceeds	Gain (Loss) on Sales	Dividend Income	Market Value Per Share	Market Value Total
		4265 (T)	46 3/8 ¢	46375 00
		16240 (T)	16 3/8 ¢	65500 00
		5600 (T)	55 7/8 ¢	89400 00
		2400 (T)	51 7/8 ¢	51875 00
		2600 (T)	55 1/8 ¢	55125 00
		2800 (T)	48 ¢	48000 00
7903 00 ✓	⟨1916 00⟩ ✓✗	3800 (T)	46 ¢	46000 00
7903 00 ^	⟨1916 00⟩ ^ A-3	37705 00 X-7		402275 00 * ^

Note: Ascertained that the above securities are all properly accounted for as current assets under provisions of FASB Statement No 12. In my opinion, marketable equity securities and related income are fairly presented at 3-31-X1. Cut

APPENDIX 13–B: Cash Surrender Value

JEP Mfg. Co.
Cash Surrender Value
3-31-X1

L
[initials]
5/13/X1

	Total Payment	Premium Expense	Increase in Cash Value	Cash Surrender Value
Great West Policy #1729-197 L-1 $500,000 on James E. Proctor Cash Surrender Value 3-31-X0				122000 00 Δ
Payments (1277.43 per mo.) ẋ $1000 increase in CSV w/ each payment	15329 16	3329 16	12000 00	12000 00
CSV 3-31-X1				C̸ L-1 134000 00
Great West Policy #2190 171 $300,000 on Anita Proctor Cash Surrender Value 3-31-X0				4000 00 Δ
Payments (793.49 per mo.) ẋ $400 increase in CSV w/ 1st 2 payments–$700 increase thereafter	9527 88	1727 88	7800 00	7800 00
CSV 3-31-X1				⊗ 11800 00
Gross Cash Surrender Value @ 3-31-X1				145800 00
Difference – pass				⟨500 00⟩
Balance per G/L @ 3-31-X1		5051 04 X-7		145300 00 ✓ A-1
Less: Policy Loan				C̸ L-1 ⟨76500 00⟩ A-1
Net Value 3-31-X1				68800 00 ✓ A-1

Conclusion: Based on the audit work performed, which was considered adequate to meet the objectives per the APG, it appears that the balance in CSV-Life Insurance Policies is fairly stated @ 3-31-X1.

Δ Per prior year's W/P's
✓ Agreed to 3-31-X1 G/L
C C̸ Confirmation sent - rec'd. See L-1
ẋ Examined bank draft on a test basis – no exceptions noted.
⊗ Examined table at CSV from insurance company and noted that CSV @ 3-31-X1 appeared reasonable and proper per their computation. Pass confirmation

APPENDIX 13–C: Life Insurance Confirmation

STANDARD CONFIRMATION INQUIRY
FOR LIFE INSURANCE POLICIES
Developed by
AMERICAN INSTITUTE OF CERTIFIED PUBLIC ACCOUNTANTS
LIFE OFFICE MANAGEMENT ASSOCIATION
MILLION DOLLAR ROUND TABLE

DUPLICATE
To be mailed to accountant

L-1
CWT
5/1/X1

April 2, 19X1

Dear Sirs:

Please furnish the information requested below in items 1 through 9 (and also in items 10 through 12 if any of those items are checked) for the policies identified on lines A, B and C. This information is requested as of the date indicated. IF THE ANSWER TO ANY ITEM IS "NONE," PLEASE SO STATE. The enclosed envelope is provided for the return of one copy of this form to the accountant named below.

(Ins. Co.) The Great Life Assurance Co.
c/o Mrs. Debrah Burn, Denver Policy Values
Suite 12, 16 Fifth Ave.
Denver, Colorado 80202

JEP Manufacturing Company, Inc.
(Name of owner as shown on policy contracts)

Information requested as of March 31, 19X1

(Accountant) Best and Company
Suite 4500, Bryon Building
Dallas, Texas 75201

Request authorized by

		Col. A	Col. B
A.	Policy number	1729-197	
B.	Insured James E. Proctor		
C.	Beneficiaries as shown on policies (if verification requested in item 11) Col. A— JEP Manufacturing Co Col. B—		
1.	Face amount of basic policy	$500,000 4	$
2.	Values shown as of (insert date if other than date requested)		
3.	Premiums, including prepaid premiums, are paid to (insert date)	May 21 X1	
4.	Policy surrender value (excluding dividends, additions and indebtedness adjustments)	$ 134,000 L	$ ✓
5.	Surrender value of all dividend credits, including accumulations and additions	$ NPAR	$
6.	Termination dividend currently available on surrender	$	$
7.	Other surrender values available to policyowner — a. Prepaid premium value	$	$
	b. Premium deposit funds	$	$
	c. Other	$	$
8.	Outstanding policy loans, excluding accrued interest	$76,500	$ L ✓
9.	If any loans exist, complete either "a" or "b" a. Interest accrued on policy loans	$	$
	b. 1.) Loan interest is paid to (enter date)	Jul. 21 X0	
	2.) Interest rate is (enter rate)	5 %	

The accountant will indicate by a check (✓) which if any of items 10-12 are to be answered

☐	**10.**	Is there an assignee of record? (enter Yes or No)		
☐	**11.**	Is beneficiary of record as shown in item C above? (enter Yes or No*)	*	*
☐	**12.**	Is the name of policyowner (subject to any assignment) as shown at the top of the form? (enter Yes or No) ______. If No, enter name of policyowner of record.		

*If answer to 11 is No, please give name of beneficiary or date of last beneficiary change.

Date 4-7-X1 By Diane McCarthy Title Policy Values
For the insurance company addressed

Additional copies of this form are available from the American Institute of CPA., 666 Fifth Avenue, New York, N. Y. 10019

NOTES

1. APB Opinion No. 18 (New York: AICPA, 1972).
2. AC section 5132, *Accounting for Certain Marketable Securities* (New York: AICPA, 1973).
3. Statement on Auditing Standards (SAS) 1, Section 332 (New York: AICPA, 1973).

QUESTIONS FOR CLASS DISCUSSION

Q13–1 What is the difference between current and noncurrent investments?

Q13–2 Are marketable equity securities always classified as current assets?

Q13–3 Can the noncurrent investments account include assets other than securities and notes? Explain.

Q13–4 What distinguishes noncurrent investments from plant assets? Explain.

Q13–5 What are the exchange functions associated with the investments subsystem? Describe them.

Q13–6 What safeguard controls should be present in a system of control for investments?

Q13–7 What control attributes should be present to prevent the person having custody of a company's securities from acquiring securities for personal use? Explain.

Q13–8 What control attributes are used to prevent misappropriation of cash received from interest and dividends? Explain.

Q13–9 Why should a company insist that persons having custody of securities be bonded? Is it also necessary to bond personnel handling the accounting records for investments? Explain.

Q13–10 What functions should be separated within the investments subsystem? Explain.

Q13–11 Why is it desirable to require two persons to be present to open the bank safe deposit box where securities are kept?

Q13–12 What is a broker's advice form? What functions does it serve in connection with securities transactions?

Q13–13 How does the auditor verify existence (validity) of securities included in the investment account?

Q13–14 How does the auditor verify the ownership of security held by a client?

Q13–15 How does the auditor verify the valuation of securities included in the client's investment account?

Q13–16 Under what circumstances should noncurrent investments in equity securities be valued by use of the equity method of accounting? Explain.

Q13–17 How should marketable equity securities be valued in the balance sheet?

Q13–18 Why is it important to verify independently both interest and dividend income received from investments held by the client? Explain.

Q13–19 What are intangible assets?

Q13–20 How does the auditor verify the existence (validity) of an intangible asset?

Q13–21 Under what circumstances may the intangible asset goodwill be recognized in the financial statements? Explain.

Q13–22 What is the maximum period over which intangible assets should be amortized? Explain.

Q13–23 May a firm capitalize research and development costs that produce a patent? Explain.

Q13–24 How should the costs associated with a patent infringement suit be handled in the accounting records? Explain.

SHORT CASES

C13–1 You have been engaged to examine the financial statements of the Elliott Company for the year ended December 31, 19X3. You performed a similar examination as of December 31, 19X2.

Following is the trial balance for the company as of December 31, 19X3:

	Dr. (Cr.)
Cash	$128,000
Interest receivable	47,450
Dividends receivable	1,750
6½% secured note receivable	730,000
Investments at cost:	
Bowen common stock	322,000
Investments at equity:	
Woods common stock	284,000
Land	185,000
Accounts payable	(31,000)
Interest payable	(6,500)
8% secured note payable to bank	(275,000)
Common stock	(480,000)
Paid-in capital in excess of par	(800,000)
Retained earnings	(100,500)
Dividend revenue	(3,750)
Interest revenue	(47,450)
Equity in earnings of investments carried at equity	(40,000)
Interest expense	26,000
General and administrative expense	60,000

You have obtained the following data concerning certain accounts:

a. The 6½% note receivable is due from Tysinger Corporation and is secured by a first mortgage on land sold to Tysinger by Elliott on December 21, 19X2. The note was to have been paid in 20 equal quarterly payments beginning March 31, 19X3, plus interest. Tysinger, however, is in very poor financial condition and has not made any principal or interest payments to date.

b. The Bowen common stock was purchased on September 21, 19X2, for cash in the market where it is actively traded. It is used as security for the note payable and held by the bank. Elliott's investment in Bowen represents approximately 1% of the total outstanding shares of Bowen.

c. Elliott's investment in Woods represents 40% of the outstanding common stock that is actively traded. Woods is audited by another CPA and has a December 31 year end.

d. Elliott neither purchased nor sold any stock investments during the year other than that noted above.

Required:

For the following account balances, discuss (1) the types of evidential matter you should obtain and (2) the audit procedures you should perform during your examination.

a. 6½% secured note receivable.
b. Bowen common stock.
c. Woods common stock.
d. Dividend revenue.

(AICPA adapted)

C13–2 In auditing the financial statements of Associated Milk Products, Inc., a manufacturer of ice cream and other dairy products, you find the following item on the balance sheet as of June 30, 19X6:

Cost of patents $120,000.

Referring to the ledger accounts, you note the following items regarding a patent on a soft ice cream machine acquired in 19X0:

19X0	Legal costs incurred in defining the validity of the patent	$14,000
19X1	Attorney fees for prosecuting an infringement suit	26,000
19X1	Additional legal fees in infringement suit	1,250
19X5	Improvements (unpatented) on machine	12,250

There are no credits in the account and no allowance for amortization has been set up in the books. There are three other patents issued in 19X2, 19X3, and 19X4, all of which were developed by the staff of the client. All patented machines are presently very marketable. However, they are expected to be in demand for only the next three years.

Required:

a. As auditor, what are your primary audit objectives concerning patents?
b. What audit procedures should you apply to the Associated patent account in light of the facts?
c. What audit adjustments, generally, would you recommend, if any? (Do not discuss dollar amounts.)

(AICPA adapted)

C13–3 As a result of highly profitable operations over a number of years, Western Manufacturing Corporation accumulated a substantial long-term investment portfolio. In the examination of the financial statements for the year ended December 31, the following information came to the attention of the corporation's CPA:

a. The manufacturing operations of the corporation resulted in an operating loss for the year.
b. The corporation has placed the securities making up the investment portfolio with a financial institution that will serve as custodian of the securities. Formerly the securities were kept in the corporation's safe deposit box in the local bank.

Required:

a. List the objectives of the CPA's examination of the long-term investment account. For each objective, discuss the audit procedures that would satisfy it.
b. Under what conditions would the CPA accept a confirmation of the securities on hand from the custodian in lieu of personally inspecting and counting the securities?

(AICPA adapted)

C13–4 You were engaged to examine the financial statements of Ronson Corporation for the year ended July 31, 19X9.

On May 1, 19X9, the Corporation borrowed $500,000 from First City National Bank to finance plant expansion. Due to unexpected difficulties in acquiring the building site, the construction starting was delayed until July 1, 19X9. To make use of the borrowed funds, management decided to invest in marketable equity securities. The investment was made on May 5, 19X9.

Required:

a. What are the audit objectives for short-term investments in marketable equity securities?
b. In your audit, how would you do the following:
   (1) Verify the dividend income recorded for the stocks?
   (2) Determine proper valuation for the portfolio at July 31, 19X9?
   (3) Establish the authority for the investment transaction?
   (4) Determine the validity of the purchase transaction?
   (5) Determine proper statement presentation for the investment account?

(AICPA adapted)

PROBLEMS

P13–1 Select the best answer for each of the following items.

a. In order to avoid the misappropriation of company-owned marketable securities, which of the following is the *best* course of action that can be taken by the management of a company with a large portfolio of marketable securities?
   (1) Require that one trustworthy and bonded employee be responsible for access to the safekeeping area, where securities are kept.

(2) Require that employees who enter and leave the safekeeping area sign and record in a log the exact reason for their access.
(3) Require that employees involved in the safekeeping function maintain a subsidiary control ledger for securities on a current basis.
(4) Require that the safekeeping function for securities be assigned to a bank that will act as a custodial agent.

b. Which of the following is *not* one of the auditor's primary objectives in an examination of marketable securities?
(1) To determine whether securities are authentic.
(2) To determine whether securities are the property of the client.
(3) To determine whether securities actually exist.
(4) To determine whether securities are properly classified on the balance sheet.

c. The auditor should insist that a representative of the client be present during the physical examination of securities in order to
(1) Lend authority to the auditor's directives.
(2) Detect forged securities.
(3) Coordinate the return of all securities to proper locations.
(4) Acknowledge the receipt of securities returned.

d. A company has additional temporary funds to invest. The board of directors decided to purchase marketable securities and assigned the future purchase and sale decisions to a responsible financial executive. The best person(s) to make periodic reviews of the investment activity should be
(1) The investment committee of the board of directors.
(2) The treasurer.
(3) The corporate controller
(4) The chief operating officer.

e. The auditor can *best* verify a client's bond sinking fund transactions and year-end balance by
(1) Recomputation of interest expense, interest payable, and amortization of bond discount or premium.
(2) Confirmation with individual holders of retired bonds.
(3) Confirmation with the bond trustee.
(4) Examination and count of the bonds retired during the year.

f. If the auditor discovers that the carrying amount of a client's investments is overstated because of a loss in value which is *other than a temporary decline* in market value, the auditor should insist that
(1) The approximate market value of the investments be shown on the face of the balance sheet.
(2) The investments be classified as long term for balance sheet purposes with full disclosure in the footnotes.
(3) The loss in value be recognized in the financial statements of the client.
(4) The equity section of the balance sheet separately show a charge equal to the amount of the loss.

g. In a manufacturing company, which one of the following audit procedures would give the *least* assurance of the validity of the general ledger balance of investment in stocks and bonds at the audit date?
(1) Confirmation from the broker.
(2) Inspection and count of stocks and bonds.
(3) Vouching all changes during the year to brokers' advices and statements.
(4) Examination of paid checks issued in payment of securities purchased.

h. A corporate balance sheet indicates that one of the corporate assets is a patent. An auditor will *most* likely obtain evidence regarding the continuing validity and existence of this patent by obtaining a written representation from
   (1) A patent attorney.
   (2) A regional state patent office.
   (3) The patent inventor.
   (4) The patent owner.

i. The financial management of a company should take steps to see that company investment securities are protected. Which of the following is *not* a step that is designed to protect investment securities?
   (1) Custody of securities should be assigned to persons who have the accounting responsibility for securities.
   (2) Securities should be properly controlled physically in order to prevent unauthorized usage.
   (3) Access to securities should be vested in more than one person.
   (4) Securities should be registered in the name of the owner.

j. Patentex developed a new secret formula which is of great value because it resulted in a virtual monopoly. Patentex has capitalized all research and development costs associated with this formula. Ezra Greene, CPA, who is examining this account, will probably
   (1) Confer with management regarding transfer of the amount from the balance sheet to the income statement.
   (2) Confirm that the secret formula is registered and on file with the county clerk's office.
   (3) Confer with management regarding a change in the title of the account to "goodwill."
   (4) Confer with management regarding ownership of the secret formula.

k. Which of the following material asset accounts would an auditor take exception to in the auditor's report?
   (1) Franchise fees paid.
   (2) Goodwill resulting from revaluation based on an objective appraisal by an expert.
   (3) Excess cost over the fair value of the assets of a significant subsidiary.
   (4) Research and development costs that will be billed to a customer at a subsequent date.

(AICPA adapted)

P13–2 Questions a through g below are questions from a typical internal control questionnaire designed to assist in the study of internal accounting controls over a company's portfolio of marketable equity securities. A "yes" response indicates a potential strength in the system of internal control, while a "no" response indicates a potential weakness.

a. Are all major acquisitions and disposals required to be approved by the investment committee of the board of directors?

b. Are all registered securities held in the name of the client or in the name of a custodian who has proper power of attorney?

c. Are all securities held as collateral physically segregated from other securities, and is board of director approval required for such transactions?

d. Does the company require segregation of the recordkeeping and custodial duties over investments, and is periodic reconciliation made of records and the physical assets by persons independent of both of these duties?
e. Is the accounting department required to maintain an independent record of each investment or security, including serial numbers, number of shares, face amounts, dates of purchase, interest rate, etc?
f. Is periodic review of the carrying value of the investment portfolio required by a responsible official who is independent of the day-to-day recordkeeping and custodial functions?
g. Is proper accounting required over investment income by persons independent of custodianship duties, and is periodic verification made of investment income per books with dividend and interest records of investee companies?

Required:

a. For each question **a** through **g**, indicate
   (1) The error or irregularity which that control attribute was designed to prevent, detect, or correct.
   (2) The possible financial statement effects if that control attribute were missing, resulting in a "no" response in the internal control questionnaire.
   (3) The substantive test that would be extended if there were no mitigating controls and the attribute of interest were missing, according to client response to the questionnaire. (See Figure 13–7).
b. Why do controls such as those over investments in marketable equity securities not often require tests of compliance?

P13–3 List the audit objectives for the following substantive tests of details over investments:

a. Inspect and list the securities on hand.
b. Compare valuation practices to those required by GAAP for the investment.
c. Vouch acquisitions and disposals of investments to underlying documentation.
d. Reconcile subsidiary records over investments with control account totals.
e. Confirm the details of life insurance policies on key personnel with the insurance company.
f. Confirm details of securities held with independent custodians, such as brokers or trustees.
g. Recalculate interest on debt securities held and reconcile with interest income account balance in the general ledger.

P13–4 For each of the intangible assets listed below, discuss:

a. The audit objectives that are of primary concern to the auditor.
b. The procedure(s) necessary to satisfy the objectives listed in **a**.
   (1) Patents.
   (2) Copyrights.
   (3) Goodwill.

P13–5 Swenson Manufacturing Corporation was incorporated on January 2, 19X8. The corporation's financial statements for its first year's operations were not examined by a CPA. You have been engaged to examine the financial statements for the year ended December 31, 19X9, and your examination is substantially completed.

A partial trial balance of the company's accounts is given below:

Swenson Manufacturing Corporation
TRIAL BALANCE
at December 31, 19X9

	Debit	Credit
Cash	$11,000	
Accounts receivable	$42,500	
Allowance for doubtful accounts		$ 500
Inventories	38,500	
Machinery	75,000	
Equipment	29,000	
Accumulated depreciation		10,000
Patents	85,000	
Leasehold improvements	26,000	
Prepaid expenses	10,500	
Organization expenses	29,000	
Goodwill	24,000	
Licensing agreement No. 1	50,000	
Licensing agreement No. 2	49,000	

The following information relates to accounts which may yet require adjustment:

a. Patents for Swenson's manufacturing process were purchased January 2, 19X9, at a cost of $68,000. An additional $17,000 was spent in December 19X9 to improve machinery covered by the patents and charged to the Patents account. The patents had a remaining legal term of 17 years.

b. On January 3, 19X8, Swenson purchased two licensing agreements which were then believed to have unlimited useful lives. The balance in the Licensing Agreement No. 1 account includes its purchase price of $48,000 and $2,000 in acquisition expenses. Licensing Agreement No. 2 was also purchased on January 3, 19X8 for $50,000, but it has been reduced by a credit of $1,000 for the advance collection of 19X0 revenue from the agreement.

In December 19X8 an explosion caused a permanent 60 percent reduction in the expected revenue-producing value of Licensing Agreement No. 1, and in January 19X0 a flood caused additional damage, which rendered the agreement worthless.

A study of Licensing Agreement No. 2 made by Swenson in January 19X9 revealed that its estimated remaining life expectancy was only ten years as of January 1, 19X9.

c. The balance in the Goodwill account includes $24,000 paid December 30, 19X8, for an advertising program, which, it is estimated, will assist in increasing Swenson's sales over a period of four years following the disbursement.

d. The Leasehold Improvement account includes (a) the $15,000 cost of improvements with a total estimated useful life of 12 years, which Swenson, as tenant, made to leased premises in January 19X8; (b) movable assembly line equipment costing $8,500, which was installed in the leased premises in December 19X9; and (c) real estate taxes of $2,500 paid by Swenson, which under the terms of the lease should have been paid by the landlord. Swenson paid its rent in full during 19X9. A ten-year nonrenewable lease was signed January 3, 19X8, for the leased building that Swenson used in manufacturing operations.

e. The balance in the Organization Expenses account includes preoperating cost incurred during the organizational period.

Required:

a. For each portion of information **a** through **e** listed above, state the audit procedure that would have brought the evidence to your attention. Also, name the audit objective that is being fulfilled by gathering evidence. For example:

Evidence	Audit Procedure	Audit Objective
(a) Initial cost of patents ($68,000)	Vouch cost to documentation	Valuation

b. What other audit objectives are appropriate for patents, licensing agreements, leasehold improvements, organizational expenses, and goodwill besides those listed in part **a**? For each account, list the appropriate objectives and at least one procedure that would satisfy each objective. Organize your answer as follows:

Account	Audit Objective(s)	Procedure(s)

c. On the basis of information supplied in the problem, prepare your recommended adjusting entries for these accounts.

(AICPA adapted)

P13–6 You are in charge of the audit of the financial statements of the McIver Corporation for the year ended December 31. The corporation has had the policy of investing its surplus funds in marketable securities. Its stock and bond certificates are kept in a safe deposit box in a local bank. Only the president or the treasurer of the corporation has access to the box.

You were unable to obtain access to the safe deposit box on December 31 because neither the president nor the treasurer was available. Arrangements were made for your assistant to accompany the treasurer to the bank on January 11 to examine the securities. Your assistant has never examined securities that were being kept in a safe deposit box and requires instructions. Your assistant should be able to inspect all securities on hand in an hour.

Required:

a. List the instructions you would give your assistant regarding the examination of the stock and bond certificates kept in the safe deposit box. Include in your instructions the details of the securities to be examined and the reasons for examining these details.

b. After returning from the bank, your assistant reported that the treasurer had entered the box on January 4 to remove an old photograph of the corporation's original building. The photograph was loaned to the local chamber of commerce for display purposes. List the additional audit procedures required because of the treasurer's action.

(AICPA adapted)

P13–7 During your audit of the 19X9 financial statements of Longwood, Inc., you find a new account titled "Miscellaneous Assets." Your examination reveals that in 19X9 Longwood, Inc., began investing surplus cash in marketable securities, and the corporation's bookkeeper entered all transactions she believed related to investments in this account. Information summarized from the Miscellaneous Assets account appears on page 622.

All security purchases include brokers' fees; and sales are net of brokers' fees and transfer taxes when applicable. The fair market values (net of brokers' fees and transfer taxes) for each security as of the 19X9 date of each transaction were:

Security	3/31	6/30	7/31	11/15	11/30
Compudata common	48		60	61¼	62
Standard Atomic common	26	30			
Standard Atomic preferred		16⅔	17		
Interstate Airlines bonds		102			101
Longwood, Inc., common			82		

Required:

a. For each of the transactions described above, list the evidence-gathering procedure (vouching, retracing, recalculation, confirmation, inspection, etc.) that is most appropriate, and the most appropriate and valid source document for the evidence.

b. Prepare adjusting entries, if any, that you consider appropriate.

(AICPA adapted)

P13–8 You are engaged in the examination of the accounts and records of an investment company. You find that during the year the company has purchased from a bank the mortgage notes of several individuals. Some of the notes were purchased at face value, some at a premium, and others at a small discount. The notes call for equal monthly payments to cover interest and principal.

By agreement, each mortgagor makes additional fixed monthly payments to cover

Longwood, Inc.
INFORMATION SUMMARIZED FROM
THE MISCELLANEOUS ASSETS ACCOUNT
For the Year Ended December 31, 19X9

Date 19X9		Folio	Debit	Credit
	Compudata Common Stock			
Mar. 31	Purchased 500 shares @ 48	*CD*	$24,000	
July 31	Received cash dividend of $2 per share	*CR*		$ 1,000
July 31	Sold 100 shares @ 60	*CR*		6,000
Nov. 15	Pledged 100 shares as security for $4,000 bank loan payable the following February 15	*CR*		4,000
Nov. 30	Received 150 shares by donation from stockholder whose cost in 19X1 was $10 per share	*JE*	1,500	
	Standard Atomic Common Stock			
Mar. 31	Purchased 900 shares @ 26	*CD*	23,400	
June 30	Received dividend ($.25 per share in cash and 1 share Standard Atomic preferred for each 5 shares common owned)	*CR*		225
	Standard Atomic Preferred Stock			
June 30	Received 180 shares as stock dividend on Standard Atomic common	*MEMO*		
July 31	Sold 80 shares @ 17	*CR*		1,360
	Interstate Airlines Bonds (due ten years from November 30, 19X9, with interest at 6 percent payable May 31 and November 30)			
June 30	Purchased 25 $1,000 bonds @ 102	*CD*	25,625	
Nov. 30	Received interest due	*CR*		750
Nov. 30	Accumulated amortization	*JE*		25
Nov. 30	Sold 25 bonds @ 101	*CR*		25,250
	Other			
July 31	Sold 40 shares of Longwood, Inc., treasury stock @ 82 (purchased in 19X5 at $80 per share — carried at cost)	*CR*		3,280
Dec. 29	Prepaid 19X0 rental charge on safe deposit box used for investments	*CD*	35	
	Totals		$74,560	$41,890

property taxes and insurance. The seller of the mortgage notes continues to service them, remitting monthly to your client the payments received on account of principal and interest, and retaining the payments for taxes and insurance in escrow until the tax bills and insurance bills are received for payment.

Required:

a. State the documents that should be on hand in support of your client's investment.

b. Outline the steps you would take in the audit of the transactions, covering both principal and income features. Be specific as to steps.

(AICPA adapted)

CHAPTER

14

OTHER OPERATING ASSETS AND RELATED ACCOUNTS

In this chapter, we turn our attention to audit procedures followed in the verification of other asset accounts. Our discussion covers verification of the following:

1. Fixed assets and their related accounts.
2. Prepaid expenses and their related accounts.
3. Accrued revenues and their related accounts.

We also include, as appendixes, illustrated working papers for fixed assets and prepaid expenses.

With respect to fixed assets, we give particular attention to EDP controls over records maintained by the computer and the ways in which the computer audit software can be used to assist in that phase of the audit. As we discuss the verification of prepaid expenses and accrued revenues, we concentrate our discussion mainly on the substantive tests of the balances in those accounts.

FIXED ASSETS

Fixed assets are those long-term assets having physical substance which are used in the operations of the business. They often represent the largest single component of total assets and the related income statement accounts are often material items in the determination of net income. *Buildings, land, equipment, leasehold improvements,* and *natural resources* are typical ***fixed assets.*** The fixed assets section of the balance sheet also includes ***contra accounts*** for accumulated depreciation of the various

depreciable assets. *Depreciation expense, depletion expense, lease expense, maintenance* and *repair expense,* and *gains or losses on disposals* are the income statement accounts directly associated with those balance sheet accounts. The audit procedures for the fixed assets system are designed to verify the contra accounts and income statement accounts as well as the asset accounts. They are designed to provide evidence of transaction validity, existence, ownership, proper cutoff, appropriate valuation, and appropriate statement presentation of those items.

Verification of Transaction Validity

Most fixed assets are not easily movable and thus are not as susceptible to misappropriation and fraud as are cash, receivables, and inventories. Also, except for the period during which a business is originated, it is possible that only a relatively small number of fixed asset transactions will occur within any one fiscal period. For those reasons, the auditor's approach to the study and evaluation of the system of internal control over fixed assets is different from that for current asset or current liability accounts. Nevertheless, internal control over fixed assets is still important, and the auditor depends on that system to some extent in making judgments regarding the validity of fixed asset-related transactions.

Evaluation of Prescribed Controls. The internal control system for fixed assets should be designed to ensure that the company receives *maximum efficiency* from dollars invested in the assets, and that the *assets are used effectively* in the production of goods or services. A key feature of the system in achieving those objectives is the effective use of *capital budgeting techniques* in decisions to acquire and dispose of fixed assets.

Although adequate *separation of responsibilities* is less important in handling and accounting for fixed assets than it is for current assets, the ideal arrangement calls for the fixed asset records to be maintained by someone not regularly having access to or use of movable fixed assets. Furthermore, it is important to have someone other than the custodians of those assets designated to approve all acquisitions and retirements.

Responsibility for initiating acquisitions and retirements of fixed assets should be *vested in specific individuals* (usually departmental supervisors). It is also important that the custodial responsibilities for movable fixed assets and the maintenance responsibilities for all fixed assets be assigned to specific employees.

Fixed asset records showing the following information for each fixed asset should be maintained:

- Identification number.
- Location.
- Description.
- Depreciation class (buildings, furniture and fixtures, machinery, etc.).
- Date acquired.
- Initial cost.
- Salvage value.
- Current replacement cost, when required by GAAP.
- Useful life.

- Current depreciation expense.
- Accumulated depreciation.
- Vendor information.
- Capital budget information.

Because of the volume of information contained in these files they are frequently maintained through use of the computer.

Appropriate forms should be used to support the acquisitions and retirements of fixed assets. The forms used for some of these actions, as well as for repairs and maintenance work, are often called ***work orders.*** In addition to defining the transaction, such work orders should contain spaces for authorization and approval signatures or initials. Forms used to support acquisitions of movable property and equipment include purchase orders, receiving reports, vendor invoices, and all other related documents in the vouchers or accounts payable system (discussed in Chapter 11). Forms supporting sales of property and equipment are the remittance advices from purchasers and cash receipts records (discussed in Chapter 10).

Personnel assigned the various custodial and recordkeeping responsibilities for fixed assets should be *appropriately qualified* for those assignments. For example, persons having the responsibilities for initiating and approving acquisitions and retirements should have sufficient knowledge of the specific fixed assets involved to allow them to make effective judgments regarding those actions. The persons charged with fixed asset custodial responsibilities should be skilled in the recognition of maintenance and upkeep needs.

The *proper protection of fixed assets* requires that an appropriate maintenance program be followed. Furthermore, measures should be taken to protect assets from unnecessary deterioration due to environmental exposure.

Determining Whether the Controls Are Working. The auditor, in judging whether the control system can be relied upon to ensure transaction validity of fixed asset transactions, should determine whether the control characteristics described above are included in the procedures manual and, if so, whether employees are complying with them. The preliminary review and evaluation of these controls are designed to determine the reliability of the system. Controls upon which the auditor wishes to *rely* are then documented and evaluated in detail. Compliance in this area can be verified by inquiry and by observing documents associated with fixed asset-related transactions.

The auditor has the same twofold purpose in studying and evaluating internal control over fixed assets as those set forth for all other accounts and systems:

1. To identify material controls, if any, that can be relied upon so that substantive tests on balances can be limited.
2. To communicate material control weaknesses to management.

In *determining the material controls* that should be evaluated, it is necessary to consider the significant *exchange transactions* that result in fixed asset and related account balances. These are summarized in Figure 14–1, along with related boundary and supporting documents. Observe that the *exchange functions for property and equipment* are similar to those listed in Chapters 11 and 13. Specifically, they include

Exchange Transaction	Boundary Document	Supporting Document
Purchase of property, plant, or equipment	Vendor's invoice; building contract	Acquisitions work order Purchase order Receiving report Approval of board of directors for material transactions
Sales of property, plant, or equipment	Customer remittance advice	Disposal work order Contract of sale Approval of board of directors for material transactions
Trade-in of property or equipment	Vendor invoice	Acquisition work order Disposal work order
Leasing property or equipment as lessee	Cancelled check	Accounts payable voucher Lease agreement

FIGURE 14–1. Exchange Transactions and Documents in Fixed Asset Transactions

the actions of purchasing, leasing, sales, and trade-ins of those assets. The *processing* and *safeguard functions* are also similar to those for other assets. They include the processing of transactions that record the exchanges and proper physical safeguards to protect the assets.

Figures 14–2 through 14–4 point out possible errors and irregularities that could occur in performing the various exchange, processing, and safeguard functions within this system, as well as their potential effects on the financial statements. We also show the controls that would prevent, detect, or correct those errors and irregularities. Figure 14–5 shows a typical systems flowchart for fixed assets and related accounts. Notice that the system incorporates proper assignment and separation of duties, recordkeeping, forms handling, appropriately qualified personnel, and protection of fixed assets. Just as with systems previously discussed, the auditor should follow the line of reasoning suggested in Figures 14–2 through 14–4 as he or she evaluates the system of control. Such an approach requires three steps:

1. Identification of the types of errors or irregularities that could occur.
2. Determination of the accounting control procedures that should prevent or detect such errors and irregularities.
3. Determining whether the necessary procedures are prescribed by the client.

Again the actual existence of some of these control attributes cannot be verified by sampling. They must be verified by observation and inquiry. The most readily observable of such controls is segregation of duties.

Compliance tests of documented controls take the form of sampling from fixed assets files; these are necessary only when there has been a large volume of transactions during the period. When a client has only a few material transactions, the auditor will

Functions	Possible Errors or Irregularities	Effect of Errors and Irregularities on Financial Statements	Control Attributes to Prevent, Detect, or Correct Errors and Irregularities
Purchase of property and equipment	Purchase of property and equipment that are not needed, inefficient, or ineffective	Failure to maximize profits or cash flows	Require capital budgeting techniques Segregate functions of custody of assets and approval of transactions Require review and approval of all major property and equipment purchases by board of directors
	Purchase of property and equipment for personal use	Misappropriation of cash Understatement of property and equipment	Segregate functions of custody of assets and recordkeeping Require a work order system for all property and equipment additions Require all purchases of property and equipment to go through the same approvals and vouching system as all other cash disbursements (Chapter 11).
Sales of property, plant, and equipment	Unauthorized sale or trade-in of assets	Misappropriation of cash Failure of detail records to agree with general ledger control	Segregate functions of custody of assets, recordkeeping, and approvals Require a work order system for all property and equipment sales and trade-ins
Trade-ins of property, plant, and equipment	Sale or trade-in of assets and retention of proceeds by operating personnel	Misappropriation of cash Failure of detail records to agree with general ledger control	Require all such transactions to be approved by board of directors, if material Require periodic observation of property and equipment and reconciliation of counts with fixed assets detail records Allow only designated officials to sell property and equipment Subject all sales to the same cash receipts controls as described in Chapter 10 for cash receipts from operations
Leasing property and equipment as leasee	Unauthorized or uneconomical lease agreements	Failure to maximize profits or cash flow	Require capital budgeting techniques Require use of proposals, approval and analysis techniques for leased property by qualified officials

FIGURE 14–2. Exchange Functions Requiring Specific Controls

Function	Possible Errors or Irregularities	Effect of Errors and Irregularities on Financial Statements	Control Attributes to Prevent, Detect, or Correct Errors and Irregularities
Recording purchases of property and equipment	Improperly recorded transactions: Capitalizing items that should be expensed	Overstatement of income Overstatement of assets	Require a policy on capitalization for all fixed asset purchases
	Expensing items that should be capitalized	Understatement of income Understatement of assets	Require full documentation (work orders, purchase orders, receiving reports, vendor reports) before approval of voucher
	Unauthorized transactions: Recording unauthorized or fictitious purchases	Overstatement of assets	Require periodic reconciliation of fixed asset detail records with general ledger control account by responsible official
	Erroneous transactions: Erroneous recording of purchases	Misstatement of assets Failure of detail records to agree with control accounts	
Recording sales and trade-ins of property and equipment	Erroneous recording of sales and trade-ins	Misstatement of assets Failure of detail records to agree with control accounts	Require review and double-checking of all sales transactions by supervisory personnel Require periodic reconciliation of fixed asset detail records with general ledger control account
Recording lease transactions	Improperly recorded transactions: Expensing items that should have been capitalized	Understatement of assets Misstatement of income	Require review of all lease transactions for requirements of capitalization under FASB Statement 13
Recording depreciation expenses	Inaccurate or untimely recording of transactions:	Misstatement of assets Misstatement of income	Require formal depreciation policy for all assets
	Erroneous or inaccurate records of depreciation		Require periodic review of accounting for depreciation by supervisory personnel

FIGURE 14–3. Processing Functions Requiring Specific Controls

Function	Possible Errors or Irregularities	Effect of Errors and Irregularities on Financial Statements	Control Attributes to Prevent, Detect, or Correct Errors and Irregularities
Custody of property and equipment	Undue abuse and subjection to the elements, wear and tear, etc.	Mechanical failures leading to unanticipated repairs and lower profits	Require physical protection of machinery and equipment in storage buildings, warehouses, sheds, etc.
	Carelessness leading to accidents	Losses due to casualties such as fire; lower profits	Conduct an adequate training program on equipment and building safety
			Maintain adequate fire and casualty insurance coverage

FIGURE 14–4. Safeguard Functions Requiring Specific Controls

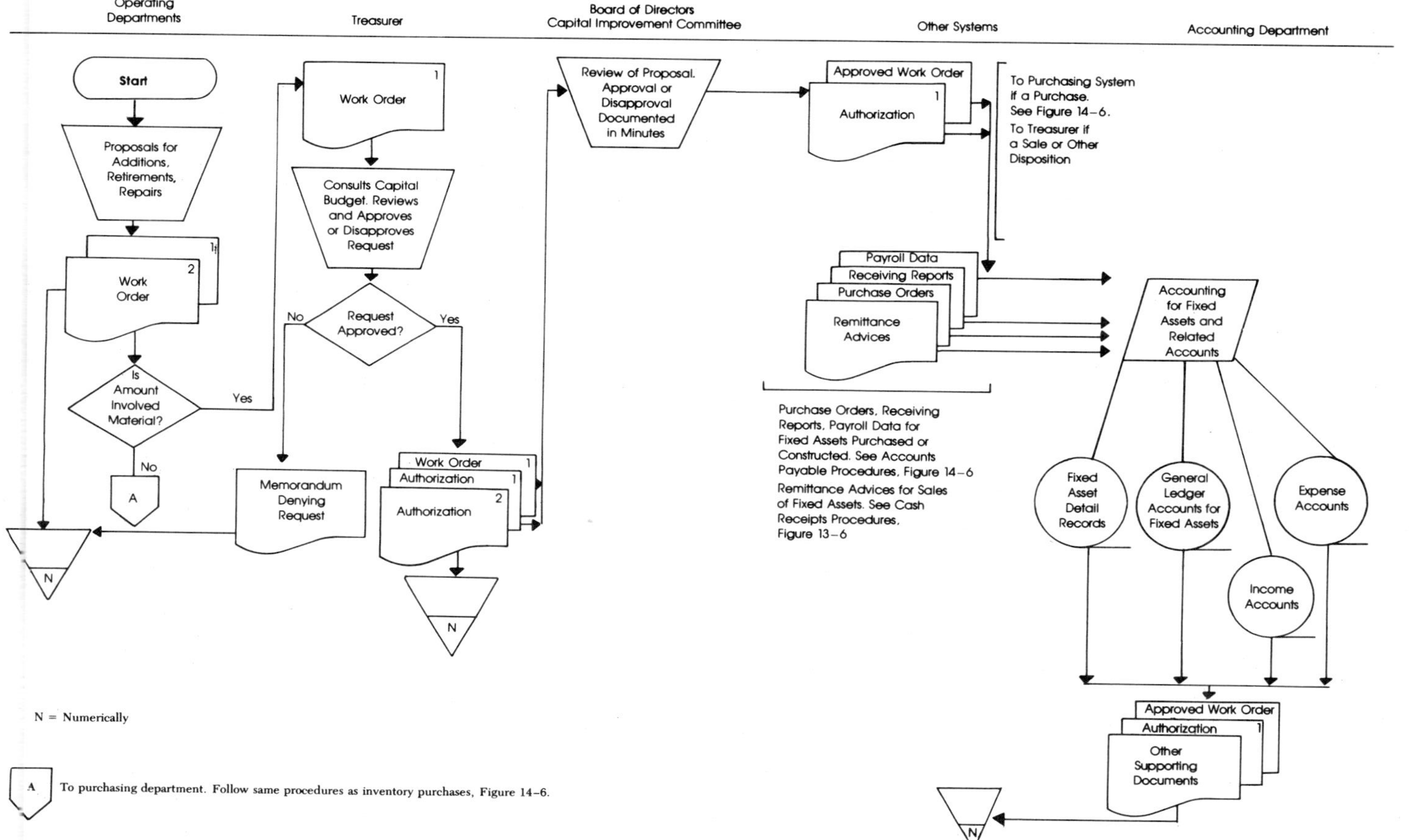

FIGURE 14–5. Flowchart for Fixed Assets and Related Accounts

generally proceed to substantive tests of the account balances after a preliminary review of internal controls. If compliance tests are performed on controls that have documentary support, the auditor determines whether the control attributes listed in Figures 14–2 through 14–4 are actually incorporated into the client's system. For example, in determining whether capital budgeting techniques were applied to all major fixed asset additions (control attribute 1 over purchases in Figure 14–2), the auditor would draw a sample from current additions to property and equipment. Then he or she would vouch the transaction to supporting documents to ascertain if those techniques had been applied. To ascertain that all material additions to property and equipment have been approved by the board of directors (control attribute 3 over purchases in Figure 14–2), the auditor could use the same sample described above, vouching approval of the additions to the minutes of the board meetings.

EDP Controls over Property and Equipment Files. When the accounting records for property and equipment are computerized to the extent that the accounts are maintained on machine readable media, some of the functions normally assigned to separate employees will be performed within the electronic data-processing department. Therefore, as we explained in Chapter 6, the evaluation of internal control requires an *analysis of the organizational structure of the electronic data-processing department* to determine the adequacy of the general controls over those activities. The auditor should also *evaluate application controls* by analyzing the input, processing, output, and file controls relating to the accounts involved. The following list describes these controls along with appropriate auditor compliance tests:

Input controls:

1. The system should include provisions designed to account for and control all property and equipment transactions data from their origin to the time they are submitted to the EDP department. Those procedures should be directed toward ensuring that *all transactions reach that department*. The auditor should read these provisions and observe client practices to ascertain that they are being carried out.
2. Within the EDP department, the firm should have an appropriate verification process designed to make sure that the person-readable transaction input data are correctly *converted to machine-readable media*. The auditor should read the client's instructions for conversion of data to machine-readable form. He or she should then select a sample of input media and ascertain that it has been subjected to proper verification techniques (keypunch or cathode ray tube verification).

Processing controls:

1. The EDP department should provide controls to ensure that all property and equipment acquisition and disposal transactions submitted to the department are processed. Typically this requires that *control totals* be developed at the point where the transactions data are received, and that these be reconciled with totals of transactions placed in process. The auditor should obtain and review client check-off sheets showing proper use of batch control totals.
2. The computer should be programmed to make *logical validity tests* on the important fields of information transmitted to the computer processing unit. Examples include code validity tests to ensure that buildings, equipment, and furniture and fixtures have been assigned the

proper estimated useful lives. The auditor might prepare and run test data to ensure that these controls are working as planned.

3. *Header and trailer* labels should be included on transaction files for fixed asset acquisitions, disposals, and depreciation expense runs and should be tested each time those files are used. Again, use of test data by the auditor is an appropriate compliance test.

Output controls:

1. *Control totals* for output should be produced by the computer. These would include batch totals for fixed asset additions, disposals, and depreciation expense. These totals should be reconciled with predetermined totals for various property and equipment transaction data by someone independent of the department originating the information. The auditor should review the client's batch control listings to ascertain that proper reconciliation procedures are being performed.
2. After processing, *error corrections and adjustments* to master files should be properly reviewed and approved prior to being incorporated in those files. The auditor should obtain and review error logs and correction reports. He or she should also observe EDP personnel review of output and should trace the distribution of this output to persons designated to receive the data.
3. Authorized and approved corrections to master files *should be followed up* to see that they are properly incorporated in the files. This procedure might be done by the internal audit staff or by the control group; and documentation of the process can be reviewed by the independent auditor.

File controls:

1. Files containing account data should be *physically protected* against fire or other types of damage. The auditor should observe the client's storage facilities to see whether such protection exists.
2. The electronic data processing or internal audit departments should make adequate provisions for *periodically checking the contents of master files* by having them printed out and reviewed against underlying data. The auditor should review the exception reports from this process and follow up with necessary tests to see that needed corrections were made.

The auditor typically documents whether all the preceding controls are operating within the system by using an application controls questionnaire similar to the one shown in Appendix 6–A.

Meeting the Other Audit Objectives

As we have observed, most clients will, as a general rule, have only a limited number of fixed asset-related transactions during each fiscal period. Therefore, after the initial audit — during which the auditor should verify the existence, ownership, cutoff, valuation, and statement presentation for all fixed tangible assets held by the client — the auditor will be concerned primarily with verifying *acquisitions and disposals during the period.* The evidence relating to those transactions is typically incorporated into an analysis type of working paper similar to the working paper shown in Appendix 14–B. As you can see, that working paper is organized around the basic four-element equation which reconciles the beginning-of-the-period balances for each of the various types of fixed assets with acquisitions, disposals, and end-of-period balances. Similar information is also shown for accumulated depreciation.

Figure 14–6 shows us that the auditor begins the *substantive verification* of fixed assets by reconciling the amounts shown on the balance sheet with the data in the underlying accounting records. Again the statement amount should be traced to the ledger account and the balance in the ledger account should be recomputed. Furthermore, the trial balance of the fixed asset subsidiary ledgers should be reconciled with their respective control accounts.

Verification of Existence. After the statement amounts have been reconciled with the underlying accounting records, the auditor will next verify the existence of the assets. In doing this, he or she will be primarily concerned with inspecting records of major assets acquired during the year. All or a sample of the fixed assets acquired should be selected from the fixed asset subsidiary ledger; the auditor should then list these items (by location, if possible) and then observe these assets in the plant. Each major fixed asset will normally be assigned a company identification equipment number when it is purchased. That number should be recorded in the accounting records and stamped or painted on the machine to specifically identify it.

The auditor may also, upon touring the plant during physical inventory observation, select a sample of fixed assets and trace them into the subsidiary ledger to ascertain that they were recorded properly. In addition, it is usually beneficial to categorize additions to tangible personal property qualifying for the investment tax credit by their estimated useful life, in order to facilitate that computation in the client's federal income tax return. Workpapers in Appendixes 14–D and 14–E illustrate this audit work for additions to the shop machinery and equipment account.

Verification of Ownership. The verification of ownership is important in the audit of fixed assets. In recent years it has become even more important because of the extensive use of leased assets. In verifying ownership, the auditor should begin by inspecting the documents underlying acquisitions and retirements during the year. He or she should also inquire about possible liens on fixed assets. Furthermore the accounting records should be inspected for evidence of rental payments which might indicate that an asset was actually leased rather than owned. In the case of land the auditor may want to inspect the public records or tax records to verify ownership. Paid real estate tax bills also provide good evidence of ownership. As a general rule, the auditor will also inspect insurance policies in the process of meeting this audit objective with the expectation that all owned assets will be insured.

As we observed in the preceding paragraph, present-day business practices often call for fixed assets to be leased on a long-term basis. FASB 13 requires that those leases, which are in substance installment purchases, should be recognized as asset acquisitions with both the fixed asset and the related obligation being shown in the balance sheet. Therefore if the client is using leased assets, it is important for the auditor to inspect and analyze all lease agreements to determine whether they should be recognized as fixed assets or treated as normal operating leases.

Verification of Cutoff. The verification of cutoff is less important for fixed asset transactions than it is for transactions involving current assets. Nevertheless, an

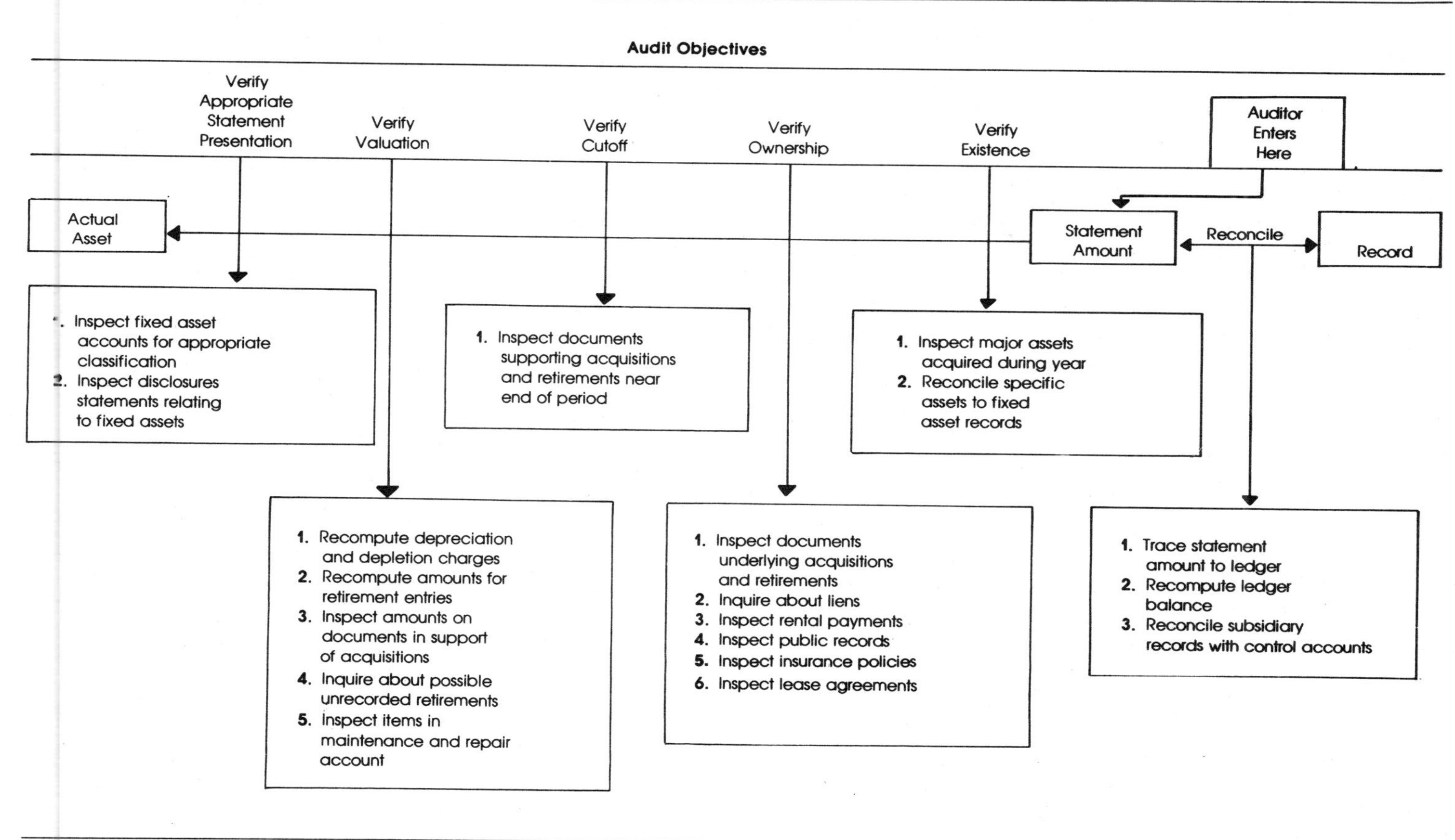
Audit Objectives
Verify Appropriate Statement Presentation
Verify Valuation
Verify Cutoff
Verify Ownership
Verify Existence
Auditor Enters Here
Actual Asset
Statement Amount
Reconcile
Record
1. Inspect fixed asset accounts for appropriate classification
2. Inspect disclosures statements relating to fixed assets
1. Inspect documents supporting acquisitions and retirements near end of period
1. Inspect major assets acquired during year
2. Reconcile specific assets to fixed asset records
1. Recompute depreciation and depletion charges
2. Recompute amounts for retirement entries
3. Inspect amounts on documents in support of acquisitions
4. Inquire about possible unrecorded retirements
5. Inspect items in maintenance and repair account
1. Inspect documents underlying acquisitions and retirements
2. Inquire about liens
3. Inspect rental payments
4. Inspect public records
5. Inspect insurance policies
6. Inspect lease agreements
1. Trace statement amount to ledger
2. Recompute ledger balance
3. Reconcile subsidiary records with control accounts

FIGURE 14–6. Flowchart for Substantive Tests of Fixed Assets

improper cutoff of a transaction involving cash and fixed assets can cause both fixed assets and current assets to be misstated. Fixed asset transactions involving the incurrence of long-term debt that are recorded in the wrong period can also cause both fixed assets and noncurrent liabilities to be misstated. In addition, depreciation can be improperly recorded or omitted from the company's records for some assets. Therefore the auditor will normally give some attention to inspecting the underlying documents relating to acquisitions and retirements occurring near the end of the year to determine whether they have been recorded in the appropriate fiscal period. Also, depreciation expense should be recalculated to ensure that it was recorded in the proper period.

Verification of Valuation. The verification of valuation is another important objective to be met in the audit of fixed assets. In meeting this audit objective, the auditor is primarily concerned with inspecting documents supporting acquisitions and retirements. Valuations assigned to assets acquired by exchange should be in accordance with the provisions of APB 29. Such transactions are also often between related parties and thus require special attention. In the case of depreciable assets, the valuation audit objective also requires verification of the valuation base for the asset and recomputation of depreciation expense. The working paper in Appendix 14–C illustrates audit work performed on accumulated depreciation and depreciation expense. This audit procedure also extends to the recomputation of depletion of wasting assets.

In *inspecting* the documents underlying fixed asset acquisitions, it is important for the auditor to verify that they have been recorded at cost. In the verification of the valuations of capitalized leases, cost is defined as the present value of lease payments. Since this procedure involves using an imputed interest rate, the auditor must evaluate the propriety of the rate used.

The auditor must be alert for items included as asset acquisitions that should have been charged to maintenance and repairs expense. He or she should inspect the documents and recompute the amounts credited to fixed assets and debited to accumulated depreciation in connection with the retirements of fixed assets. In doing that it is important for the auditor to inquire about possible unrecorded retirements, particularly if the system of control is such that retirements could be accomplished without an entry in the accounting records. That could occur, for example, if the client does not require appropriate authorization and approval actions prior to the retirement of each fixed asset. The auditor may learn of retirements of equipment by reviewing depreciation charges, analyzing debits to accumulated depreciation and reviewing insurance policy changes. Unrecorded disposals can also be discovered by reviewing the property tax files and scanning invoices for fixed asset additions. In that process the auditor is trying to determine whether assets retired are being replaced.

In verifying valuation, the auditor must also be satisfied that the client has appropriately distinguished between assets and expenses in accounting for fixed asset transactions. Maintenance and repair accounts include fixed asset-related expenditures. Therefore, it is important for the auditor to inspect the larger entries in those accounts and to vouch them to supporting documents for the purpose of discovering expenditures that should have been capitalized rather than charged to expense. In the process of making this inspection, the auditor will also be developing substantive evidence to support the balance in the maintenance and repairs expense accounts. Construction work orders issued during the year should be examined to learn of possible erroneous capitalizations of expenditures. Also, as the auditor is inspecting fixed asset acquisitions, she or he will also be concerned with determining that they should be capitalized rather than expensed. The auditor should be concerned about the possibility that assets have not been adequately maintained. The auditor relies on observations during the plant tour and conferences with the plant manager in judging whether or not provisions should be made for deferred maintenance.

Verification of Appropriate Statement Presentation. The appropriate statement presentation for fixed assets requires that they be shown in the noncurrent section of the balance sheet at their acquisition costs, offset by accumulated depreciation or depletion. Fully depreciated assets should be disclosed separately. Depletable assets may be shown net of accumulated depletion. It is also desirable to have the financial statements include a parenthetical or footnote disclosure of the method(s) of depreciation used by the client. The auditor in achieving this objective will be inspecting the fixed asset elements of the balance sheet to see that those items are appropriately presented.

Using the Computer in Auditing Fixed Assets

When fixed assets and depreciation records are maintained on machine readable media, the auditor can utilize computer audit software to perform many of the audit procedures on the systems and accounts discussed in the previous section. Both compliance and substantive tests may be performed by using the computer. *Tests of compliance* may be performed by use of test data, parallel simulation, or some of the other approaches discussed earlier in the text.

Assuming that detailed fixed asset records, including all the information specified earlier, are kept on magnetic tape files, the *substantive audit procedures* shown in Figure 14–7 can be performed by the computer with appropriate audit software.

PREPAID EXPENSES

Prepaid expenses may include such items as prepaid rent, prepaid insurance, prepaid taxes, and other deferred charges. Their inclusion among assets results more from the operation of the matching concept than from their intrinsic resale value. In most audits, the amounts shown for prepaid expenses will be relatively immaterial and therefore require only a limited amount of the auditor's attention. Also, because of the lack of significance of these items, very little attention will be given to the internal control procedures associated with them. However, because of its relationship to the audit of fixed assets and to the operating policies of the firm, some attention will generally be given to the verification of the prepaid insurance balance. Although we confine our discussion to the audit of prepaid insurance, we would find if we troubled to look into it that the audit objectives and the procedures necessary to satisfy those objectives are similar for other types of prepaid expenses.

Audit Objective	Audit Procedure
Existence	Selection of sample from detail records for observation Sorting the sample by plant location Printing sample items
Ownership; Transaction validity	Printing vendor information for use in vouching purchases to vendor invoices Printing out lease information for use in determining proper capitalization
Cutoff	Scanning and printing from vendor files for last receiving reports so that underlying documents may be examined
Valuation	Recomputation of footings for the subsidiary ledger showing cost, accumulated depreciation, and depreciation expense, and comparing the total with control accounts Scanning the file to identify fully depreciated items, and printing results so that they can be discussed with the client

FIGURE 14–7. Use of Computer Audit Software for Substantive Audit Procedures

The auditor will generally begin the audit of prepaid insurance by inspecting and listing the fire and casualty insurance policies in existence as of the end of the period being audited. In the process of listing those policies, it is important for the auditor to relate them to the specific assets covered by each of the policies to help evaluate the adequacy of the client's insurance coverage. Details of insurance policies in force will typically be confirmed with the client's insurance agent. Such details include the insuring company, policy number, type of coverage, amount of premium, and period covered by the premium. Using this information, the auditor also will generally want to recompute the amount of prepaid insurance and the premiums expired during the year as part of the verification of both insurance expense and the prepaid insurance accounts. Both of these account balances can be reconciled to premium payments for the period by using the following four-element equation:

> Beginning balance for prepaid insurance + premiums paid during the period − calculated balance for prepaid insurance at the end of the period = insurance expense for the period.

By providing this type of analysis, the auditor is in effect providing substantive evidence in verification of both prepaid insurance and insurance expense. In verifying premiums paid the auditor is also gathering substantive evidence in support of another type of credit to cash. A similar procedure can be followed in verifying the relationships between other prepaid expenses, the cash outlays for them, and their related nominal accounts. Audit work typically performed on the prepaid expense accounts is illustrated in Appendixes 14–F and 14–G.

ACCRUED REVENUES

Accrued interest receivable and accrued rent receivable are examples of accrued revenues. Generally speaking, accrued revenues will not be material enough to require a significant amount of the auditor's attention. Again, however, as part of the verification of the related income statement accounts, they may be important to the auditor as he or she seeks to establish substantive evidence by recomputing accrued revenues (revenues earned but not received as of the end of the period under audit). In performing this audit procedure the auditor will begin by inspecting the notes, bonds, or other instruments producing the revenue. Then she or he should calculate, directly from the contractual instruments under which they were issued, what the revenues earned should be for the period. The receipt of cash from debtors in payment of these receivables should be vouched to underlying support — such as cash receipts records, remittance advices, and validated bank deposit slips. The following four-element equation should then be used to provide substantive verification of the balances in the related nominal accounts:

> Calculated accrued revenues balance at end of period + revenues received during the period − accrued revenues balance at the beginning of the period = revenues earned during the period.

The recomputation procedures described above, coupled with the four-element equation, provide additional substantive verification of the notes, bonds, and other revenue-producing assets that may be held by the client. The independent determination of revenues received during the period also provides substantive evidence in support of another debit to cash.

SUMMARY

In this chapter we have discussed the audit objectives for fixed assets, prepaid expenses, and accrued revenues, along with the procedures required to meet those objectives. Because, for most clients, these accounts possess either low relative risk or have immaterial balances, the evaluation of internal accounting controls is considered less important for these items than for cash, receivables, and inventories. Instead, the auditor concentrates on performing substantive tests of additions, removals, and ending balances, which in turn are then fitted into the following four-element equation to show that the verified data "fit together."

Beginning balance + additions − reductions = ending balance.

We discussed the substantive verification of each of the elements of the above equation relating to fixed assets, prepaid expenses, and accrued revenues. We also showed how to meet the audit objectives of existence, ownership, cutoff, valuation, and appropriate statement presentation in verifying the elements of each of these subsystems. Working papers in the appendixes to this chapter illustrate how the audit procedures for fixed assets, accumulated depreciation, and prepaid expenses are documented.

APPENDIX 14–A: Auditor's Tick Mark Legend for Fixed Assets

JEP Mfg. Co.
Tick Legend re: Fixed Assets
3-31-X1

W. P. No.	Ia
ACCOUNTANT	SmG
DATE	5/5/X1

△ Agreed to prior year auditors' W/P's

✓ Agreed to 3-31-X1 G/L

∧ ⧺ Footed; Crossfooted

ƒ Recomputed by auditors - appears reasonable - no material exceptions were noted.

⊗ Depreciation method and rate appear reasonable and consistent with prior year's. Current treatment appears comparable to prior year's treatment and depreciable lives are consistent.

⧺ Agreed to paid invoice(s) noting that cost was properly recorded as a depreciable asset. Done a test basis w/o exception.

Note: Examined a listing of operating leases, noting proper classification of the leases as operating leases. No exceptions were noted.

Conclusion: Based on the audit work performed which was considered adequate to meet the objectives per the APG, it appears that the balances in Fixed Assets and related Depreciation accounts are fairly stated as of 3-31-X1.

Note: Reviewed Repairs & Maintenance expenses for the period, noting no unusual items. Amts. charged appeared reasonable & proper.

APPENDIX 14–B: Lead Schedule for Fixed Assets

JEP Manufacturing Co.
Fixed Assets
3-31-X1

W. P. No. I
ACCOUNTANT SmG
DATE 5/5/X1

A/c #	Description	W/P Reference	Adjusted Balance 3-31-X0	Additions	Retirements
131	Purchased Shop Mach. + Equip.	I-2	415943 33	23065 15	
132	Constructed Shop Mach. + Equip.	I-2	74624 82	932 01	
133	Patterns and Dies	I-4	55024 54	13769 38	
			545592 69	37766 54	
134	Truck and Auto				
135	Land				
136	Building				
137	Building Annex				
139	Office Furniture & Fixtures				
140	Building Roof				
141	Sky Point Leasehold		Details Deleted		
142	Sky Point House				
143	Sky Point Furniture & Fixtures				
144	Sky Point Caretaker's house				
145	Landscaping				
146	Computer Equipment				
147	R&D Machinery				
	Total Fixed Assets		1733767 36	106128 16	
	Less Accumulated Depreciation				
	Net Amount Per Trial Balance				

See Tick mark legend and conclusions on I a

Balance per G/L ✓ 3-31-X1	Rate / Method ⊗ △	Accumulated Depreciation: Balance 3-31-X0 △	Provision	Retirements	Balance 3-31-X1
439008 48	10%	301781 01	I-1 305332 99		332314 00
75556 83	10%				
68793 92	20%	44382 54	I-1 41555 6		48538 10
583359 23		346163 55	346885 5		380852 10
A-1					
1839895 52		687591 75	I-1 85457 99		① 773050 00 ✓
773050 20 ①					A-1
1066845 52					
A-1					

APPENDIX 14–C: Depreciation Schedule

JEP Manufacturing Co.
Depreciation Schedule
3/31/X1

W. P. No. I-1
ACCOUNTANT PBC/Smd
DATE 5/5/X1

Description	Date Acquired	Original Cost	Est. Life ⓧ (years)	Depr. Rate ⓧ (%)
Machinery and Equipment:				
Acquisitions to 4-1-X0				
(details not shown)	19X7-X8	297 234 04	10	10%
Machinery & Equipment				
Current year additions				
Machinery & Equipment	19X1	23 997 16	10	10%
		321 231 20		
Patterns and Dies:				
Acquisitions to 4-1-X0	19X7-X8	15 313 34	5	20%
Current year additions	19X1	13 769 38	5	20%
		29 082 72		
Other Property and Equipment	}	Details Deleted		
Totals		1 839 895 52		
		I		

See Tick mark legend and conclusions on Ia.

Thru 3-31-X0	Current Yr.	Remaining Cost
136572 44	2972342 ⁊	130938 18
–	80957 ⁊	2318759
13657244	3053299	15412577
	I	
573490	2704466 ⁊	687378
–	145090 ⁊	1231848
573490	415556	1919226
	I	
77305000	8545799	
I	I	

APPENDIX 14–D: Schedule for Additions to Shop Machinery and Equipment

JEP Manufacturing Co.
Additions - Shop Machinery and Equipment
3-31-X1

W. P. No. I-2
ACCOUNTANT PBC / Smd
DATE 5/5/X1

	Month Ended			Cost	
	4-30-X0			1361 23	✓✗
	5-31-X0			913 60	
	6-30-X0			704 53	
	7-31-X0			775 53	
	8-31-X0			3445 10	✓✗
	9-30-X0			227 48	
	10-31-X0			961 92	
	11-30-X0			892 55	
	12-31-X0			1108 08	✓✗
	1-31-X1			5087 90	
	2-28-X1			6580 61	✓✗
	3-31-X1			1938 63	
				23997 16	
Constructed		I	932 01		
Purchased		S	23065 15		
				23997 16	

See tick mark legend and conclusions Ia

APPENDIX 14–E: Investment Tax Credit Schedule

JEP Mfg. Co.
Investment Tax Credit
3-31-X1

W. P. No.	I-11
ACCOUNTANT	Smd
DATE	5/5/X1

Asset	Life		Amount	%	ITC Base
Machinery & Equipment	10 yrs.	I-2	23997 16	100%	23997 16
Patterns & Dies	5 yrs.	I-4	13769 38	66-67%	9179 59
Truck & Auto	4 yrs.	I-5	2041 00	33.33%	680 33
Computer Equipment	7 yrs.	I-10	3638 92	100%	3638.92
R & D Machinery	10 yrs.	I-3	12244 64	100%	12244 64
Furn. & Fixtures	10 yrs.	I-8	27696 57	100%	27696 57
Investment Credit Base					77437 21
ITC Rate (per Master Tax Guide)					10%
ITC					7743 72
					A-2

Note: The life and cost of assets were agreed to the referenced W/P. In connection with vouching the F/A additions made during the year, the assets were reviewed for inclusion in ITC computation. All examined appear to meet criteria for ITC.

APPENDIX 14–F: Lead Schedule for Prepaid Expenses

JEP Mfg. Co.
Prepaid Expenses
3-31-X1

W. P. No.	G
ACCOUNTANT	SmG
DATE	5/5/X1

A/c #	Description	W/P Reference	Adjusted Balance 3-31-X0 ⊿	Balance Per G/L 3-31-X1 ✓
	Prepaid Expenses			
123	Prepaid Insurance	G-1	26239 43	22562 42
124	Dun & Bradstreet		2153 97	2382 75 ✓ˣ
	SMU Expenses		541 66	⟨1083 28⟩
	IEEE		–	1000 00 ⓧ
	Xerox		–	1956 66 ⊿ˣ
	Total Prepd. Expenses		28935 06	26818 55
				A-1
	Deposits			
120	Workman's Comp. Deposit	G-1	5471 00	5471 00
	Houston Port Authority		–	500 00 *
	United Parcel Service	W/P N/C/N	–	50 00
122	Deposit on Returnable Containers	W/P N/C/N	290 25	290 25
	Total Deposits		5761 25	6311 25
				A-1

⊿ Agreed to prior year auditors' W/P's
✓ Agreed to 3-31-X1 G/L

ⓧ Agreed amount to check copy and invoice from the Institute of Electrical and Electronic Engineers for the prepayment on the cost of a booth at an exhibition to be held later in the year. Treatment appears proper.

⊿ˣ Amount represents the prepaid interest portion of the installment purchase agreement w/ Xerox. See PF-14-4 p. ④

✓ˣ JEP pays for D+B services 1 year in advance. The fee is on a calender year, therefore the amount prepaid appears reasonable – original cost was $3177 per paid check.
(3177 x 9/12 = $2382.75)

* Agreed amount to check copy and invoice from the Port Authority requiring a deposit on goods shipped out of the port authority. Appears reasonable + proper.

Adjustments Dr.	Adjustments Cr.	Adjusted Balance 3-31-X1			
		22562 42			
		2382 75			
A-7 <100> 1083 28 ⊕		-0-			
		1000 00			
		1956 66			
1083 28		27901 83			
		A-1			
		5471 00			
		500 00			
		50 00			
		290 25			
		6311 25			
		A-1			

Conclusion: Based on the audit work performed, which was considered adequate to meet the objectives per audit program, it appears that the balance in prepaid expenses + deposits is fairly stated @ 3-31-X1.

⊕ Adjustment made by client to correct over accrual of Jim Craver's school expenses. In the past JEP has paid for his tuition. Since SMU required the payment of 1st + last semester's tuition at beginning of the program, and since this is Mr. Craver's last semester, there is no prepaid amount, and there is no reason to accrue for any more expenses. Treatment appears proper.

APPENDIX 14–G: Prepaid Insurance Schedule

JEP Mfg. Co.
Prepaid Insurance
3-31-X1

W. P. No.	G-1
ACCOUNTANT	JB
DATE	5/5/X1

Coverage	Policy No.	Term From	Term To
Fleet Auto & Truck	540-4398-7 ∆	12-1-X0	12-1-X1
'79-Mack & Lufkin Trailer	1300 641-23 ∆	12-1-X0	12-1-X1
'79-Mack & Lufkin Trailer	CXTPF-26994 ∆	12-1-X0	12-1-X1
Blanket Crime	FBB-135607 ∆	10-6-X0	10-6-X1
Building-Fire & E.C.	8-56-59-46 ∆	6-30-X9	6-30-X2
Contents (excluding stock)	C-56-98-72 ∆	3-20-X0	6-20-X2
Business Interruption	C-56-98-71 ∆	1-30-X0	4-30-X1
Commercial Umbrella	UL-67-46-77 ∆	3-30-X0	3-30-X3
General Liability	540-4398126 ∆	12-1-X0	12-1-X1
Directors & Officers Liability	9524-84 ∆	5-20-X0	5-20-X1
Sky Point Lodge	241-795187 ∆	7-14-X0	7-14-X1
Business Travel & Commuting insurance	640 39064 ∆	3-9-X1	3-9-X2

∧ Footed

∆ Agreed amount and information on policy coverage to insurance policy from appropriate company

∆ Agreed to prior year's audited working papers

7 Recomputed insurance expense. Appears reasonable.

Issuing Company	Total Premium	Balance 3-31-X0	Payments	Expenses	Balance 3-31-X1
Intern. Ins. Co.	2693 00		2693 00	896 77	1796 23
U. S. Fire Ins. Co.	1267 00	–	1267 00	422 29	844 71
Can. Union Ins.	534 83	–	539 83	178 10	356 73
Ins. Co. of N. Amer.	636 00	–	636 00	318 00	318 00
Commonwealth	8559 52	6419 88		5478 00	941 88
" "	1963 00	1963 00		817 87	1145 13
" "	5912 08	4386 55		3863 89	492 66
Puritan Ins. Co.	13500 00	13500 00		4500 00	9000 00
N. Prince Ins. Co.	18355 00	–	18355 00	13618 74	4736 26
Nat. Union Fire	3696 00	–	3696 00	3080 00	616 00
U. S. Fire Ins. Co.	624 00	–	624 00	468 00	156 00
Fed. Ins. Co.	2680 86	–	2680 86	223 32	2457 54
		26269 43	30486 69	33864 98	22861 14
Difference - immaterial -- pass					⟨298 72⟩
					22562 42
					G

QUESTIONS FOR CLASS DISCUSSION

Q14–1 What is meant by *fixed assets*?

Q14–2 What accounts, other than tangible fixed assets, are typically verified in connection with the audit of those accounts?

Q14–3 Why is the auditor generally less concerned about the internal control procedures for the fixed assets system than for the other systems we have discussed to this point?

Q14–4 What functions associated with the acquisitions, uses, and accounting procedures for fixed assets should be separated? Explain.

Q14–5 Which exchange transactions are typically encountered within the fixed assets subsystem?

Q14–6 What control attributes should be present to reduce the probability of an improper purchase of property and equipment?

Q14–7 How do capital budgeting techniques fit into the system of control for fixed assets?

Q14–8 What errors or irregularities should be prevented by the safeguard controls for fixed assets? Explain.

Q14–9 What input controls should be present in an electronic data-processing system used to account for fixed assets? Describe them.

Q14–10 What processing controls would you expect to find when fixed assets records are maintained by an EDP system? Describe them.

Q14–11 Why does the auditor concentrate on the examination of acquisitions and disposals in verifying the existence of fixed assets? Explain.

Q14–12 What procedures are followed in verifying the ownership of fixed assets? Describe them briefly.

Q14–13 Why is it important to inspect lease agreements in verifying the ownership of fixed assets? Explain.

Q14–14 Why does the auditor analyze the items in the maintenance and repairs account during the audit of the fixed assets subsystem?

Q14–15 How does the examination of insurance policies relate to the verification of fixed assets?

Q14–16 What procedures are followed in verifying prepaid expenses? Describe.

Q14–17 How can the four-element equation be used in verifying accrued revenues and revenues earned?

SHORT CASES

C14–1 Carl Rivera, CPA, is the auditor for a manufacturing company with a balance sheet that includes the caption "Property, Plant, and Equipment." Rivera has been asked by the company's management if audit adjustments or reclassifications are required for the following material items that have been included or excluded from "Property, Plant, and Equipment."

a. A tract of land was acquired during the year. The land is the future site of the client's new headquarters, which will be constructed in the following year. Commissions were paid to the real estate agent used to acquire the land, and expenditures were made to relocate the previous owner's equipment. These commissions and expenditures were expensed and are excluded from "Property, Plant, and Equipment."
b. Clearing costs were incurred to make the land ready for construction. These costs were included in "Property, Plant, and Equipment."
c. During the land-clearing process, timber and gravel were recovered and sold. The proceeds from the sale were recorded as other income and are excluded from "Property, Plant, and Equipment."
d. A group of machines was purchased under a royalty agreement that provides royalty payments based on units of production from the machines. The cost of the machines, freight costs, unloading charges, and royalty payments were capitalized and are included in "Property, Plant, and Equipment."

Required:

a. Describe the general characteristics of assets, such as land, buildings, improvements, machinery, equipment, fixtures, etc., that should normally be classified as "Property, Plant, and Equipment," and identify audit objectives (i.e., how an auditor can obtain audit satisfaction) in connection with the examination of "Property, Plant, and Equipment." *Do not discuss specific audit procedures.*
b. Indicate whether each of items **a–d** above requires one or more audit adjustments or reclassifications, and explain why such adjustments or reclassifications are required or not required.

Organize your answer as follows:

Item No.	Is Audit Adjustment or Reclassification Required? Yes or No	Reasons Why Audit Adjustment or Reclassification Is Required or Not Required

(AICPA adapted)

C14–2 In connection with a recurring examination of the financial statements of the Louis Manufacturing Company for the year ended December 31, 19X9, you have been assigned the audit of the accounts of the manufacturing equipment, manufacturing equipment – accumulated depreciation, and repairs of manufacturing equipment. Your review of Louis's policies and procedures has disclosed the following pertinent information:

a. The manufacturing equipment account includes the net invoice price plus related freight and installation costs for all the equipment in Louis's manufacturing plant.
b. The manufacturing equipment and accumulated depreciation accounts are supported by a subsidiary ledger that shows the cost and accumulated depreciation for each piece of equipment.
c. An annual budget for capital expenditures of $1,000 or more is prepared by the budget committee and approved by the board of directors. Capital expenditures over $1,000 which are not included in this budget must be approved by the board of directors, and variations of 20 percent or more must be explained to the board. Approval by the supervisor of production is required for capital expenditures under $1,000.
d. Company employees handle installation, removal, repair, and rebuilding of the machinery. Work orders are prepared for those activities and are subject to the same budgetary control as other expenditures. Work orders are not required for external expenditures.

Required:

a. Cite the major objectives of your audit of the accounts of the manufacturing equipment, manufacturing equipment – accumulated depreciation, and repairs of manufacturing equipment. Do not include in this listing the auditing procedures designed to accomplish these objectives.
b. Prepare the portion of your audit program applicable to the review of 19X9 additions to the manufacturing equipment account.

(AICPA adapted)

C14–3 You are examining the financial statements of the Aby Company, a retail enterprise, for the year ended December 31, 19X9. The client's accounting department presented you with an analysis of the balance of $31,400 of the prepaid expenses account as of December 19X9 (see page 655).

Additional information you receive includes the following:

a. Insurance policy data:

Type	Period Covered	Premium
Fire	12/31/X8 to 12/31/X0	$1,000
Liability	6/30/X9 to 6/30/X0	9,500

b. The postage meter machine was delivered in November and the balance due was paid in January. Unused postage of $700 in the machine at December 31, 19X9 was recorded at time of purchase.
c. Bond discount represents the unamortized portion applicable to bonds maturing in 19X0.
d. The $9,600 paid and recorded for advertising was for the cost of an advertisement to be run in a monthly magazine for six months, beginning in December 19X9.

You examined an invoice received from the advertising agency and extracted the following description:

Advertising services rendered for store opened in November 19X9: $6,900

e. Aby has contracted to purchase Skyhigh Stores and has been required to accompany its offer with a check for $1,000 to be held in escrow as an indication of good faith. An examination of cancelled checks revealed the check had not been returned from the bank through January 19X0.

Aby Company
ANALYSIS OF PREPAID EXPENSES ACCOUNT
December 31, 19X9

Description	Balance as of December 31, 19X9
Unexpired Insurance:	
Fire	$ 750
Liability	4,900
Utility deposits	2,000
Loan to officer	500
Purchase of postage meter machine, one half of invoice price	400
Bond discount	3,000
Advertising of store opening	9,600
Amount due for overpayment on purchase of furniture and fixtures	675
Unsalable inventory — entered June 30, 19X9	8,300
Contributions from employees to employee welfare fund	(275)
Book value of obsolete machinery held for resale	550
Funds delivered to Skyhigh Stores with purchase offer	1,000
Total	$31,400

Required:

a. For each item in the account analysis, state the audit evidence you need to obtain to support the entry.

b. Assuming that you have examined acceptable underlying audit evidence, prepare a worksheet to show the necessary adjustments, corrections, and reclassifications of the items in the prepaid expenses account. In addition to the information shown in the account analysis, the following column headings are suggested for your worksheet:

Item	Adjustments and Reclassifications Dr. (Cr.)	AND Prepaid Expenses Adjusted Balance December 31, 19X9	Disposition of Adjustments and Reclassification: Expense Dr. (Cr.)	General Other Account Dr. (Cr.)

(AICPA adapted)

C14–4 You have assigned your assistant to the examination of the Cap Sales Company's fire insurance policies. All routine audit procedures with regard to the fire insurance register have already been completed (i.e., vouching, footing, examination of cancelled checks, computation of insurance expense and prepayment, tracing of expense charges to appropriate expense accounts, etc.). Your assistant has never examined fire insurance policies and asks for detailed instructions.

Required:

a. In addition to examining the policies for the amounts of insurance and premium and for effective and expiration dates, what other procedures should your assistant give particular attention to as he examines the policies? Give the audit objectives for each procedure. (Confine your comments to fire insurance policies covering buildings, their contents, and inventories.)

b. After reviewing your assistant's working papers, you concur in his conclusion that the insurance coverage against loss by fire is inadequate and that, if loss occurs, the company may have insufficient assets to liquidate its debts. After a discussion with you, the Cap Sales management refuses to increase the amount of insurance coverage.
   (1) What mention will you make of this condition and contingency in your short-form report? Why?
   (2) What effect will this condition and contingency have on your opinion? Give the reasons for your position.

(AICPA adapted)

PROBLEMS

P14–1 Select the best answer to each of the following items relating to internal controls within the noncurrent assets subsystem.

a. With respect to an internal control measure that will ensure accountability for fixed asset retirements, management should implement a system that includes
   (1) Continuous analysis of miscellaneous revenue to locate any cash proceeds from sale of plant assets.

(2) Periodic inquiry of plant executives by internal auditors as to whether any plant assets have been retired.
(3) Continuous utilization of serially numbered retirement work orders.
(4) Periodic observation of plant assets by the internal auditors.

b. Which of the following is an internal accounting control weakness related to factory equipment?
(1) A policy exists requiring all purchases of factory equipment to be made by the department in need of the equipment.
(2) Checks issued in payment of purchases of equipment are *not* signed by the controller.
(3) Factory equipment replacements are generally made when estimated useful lives, as indicated in depreciation schedules, have expired.
(4) Proceeds from sales of fully depreciated equipment are credited to other income.

c. Which of the following is the *most* important internal control procedure over acquisitions of property, plant, and equipment?
(1) Establishing a written company policy distinguishing between capital and revenue expenditures.
(2) Using a budget to forecast and control acquisitions and retirements.
(3) Analyzing monthly variances between authorized expenditures and actual costs.
(4) Requiring acquisitions to be made by user departments.

d. The primary purpose of internal control relating to heavy equipment is
(1) To ascertain that the equipment is properly maintained.
(2) To prevent theft of the equipment.
(3) To determine when to replace the equipment.
(4) To promote operational efficiency of the dollars invested in the equipment.

e. Which of the following policies is an internal accounting control weakness related to the acquisition of factory equipment?
(1) Acquisitions are to be made through and approved by the department in need of the equipment.
(2) Advance executive approvals are required for equipment acquisitions.
(3) Variances between authorized equipment expenditures and actual costs are to be immediately reported to management.
(4) Depreciation policies are reviewed only once a year.

f. To achieve effective internal accounting control over fixed asset additions, a company should establish procedures that require
(1) Capitalization of the cost of fixed asset additions in excess of a specific dollar amount.
(2) Performance of recurring fixed asset maintenance work solely by maintenance department employees.
(3) Classification as investments, those fixed asset additions that are *not* used in the business.
(4) Authorization and approval of major fixed asset additions.

g. An example of a transaction which may be indicative of the existence of related parties is
(1) Borrowing or lending at a rate of interest that equals the current market rate.
(2) Selling real estate at a price that is comparable to its appraised value.

(3) Making large loans with specified terms as to when or how the funds will be repaid.
(4) Exchanging property for similar property in a nonmonetary transaction.

(AICPA adapted)

P14–2 Select the best answer to the following items relating to substantive verification of plant assets and their related accounts.

a. Once the initial audit of a newly constructed industrial plant has been performed, with respect to consistency, which of the following is of *least* concern to the continuing auditor in the following year?
(1) Prior years' capitalization policy.
(2) Prior years' capitalized costs.
(3) Prior years' depreciation methods.
(4) Prior years' depreciable life.

b. An auditor would be *least* likely to use confirmations in connection with the examination of
(1) Inventories.
(2) Long-term debt.
(3) Property, plant, and equipment.
(4) Stockholders' equity.

c. The auditor is *least* likely to learn of retirements of equipment through which of the following?
(1) Review of the purchase return and allowance account.
(2) Review of depreciation.
(3) Analysis of the debits to the accumulated depreciation account.
(4) Review of insurance policy riders.

d. The auditor may conclude that depreciation charges are insufficient by noting
(1) Insured values greatly in excess of book values.
(2) Large amounts of fully depreciated assets.
(3) Continuous trade-ins of relatively new assets.
(4) Excessive recurring losses on assets retired.

e. Which of the following audit procedures would be *least* likely to lead the auditor to find unrecorded fixed asset disposals?
(1) Examination of insurance policies.
(2) Review of repairs and maintenance expense.
(3) Review of property tax files.
(4) Scanning of invoices for fixed asset additions.

f. A normal audit procedure is to analyze the current year's repairs and maintenance accounts to provide evidence in support of the audit proposition that
(1) Expenditures for fixed assets have been recorded in the proper period.
(2) Capital expenditures have been properly authorized.
(3) Noncapitalizable expenditures have been properly expensed.
(4) Expenditures for fixed assets have been capitalized.

g. Which of the following *best* describes the independent auditor's approach to obtaining satisfaction concerning depreciation expense in the income statement?
(1) Verify the mathematical accuracy of the amounts charged to income as a result of depreciation expense.
(2) Determine the method for computing depreciation expense and ascertain that it is in accordance with generally accepted accounting principles.

(3) Reconcile the amount of depreciation expense to those amounts credited to accumulated depreciation accounts.
(4) Establish the basis for depreciable assets and verify the depreciation expense.

h. Which of the following explanations might satisfy an auditor who discovers significant debits to an accumulated depreciation account?
(1) Extraordinary repairs have lengthened the life of an asset.
(2) Prior years' depreciation charges were erroneously understated.
(3) A reserve for possible loss on retirement has been recorded.
(4) An asset has been recorded at its fair value.

i. Which of the following is the *best* evidence of real estate ownership at the balance sheet date?
(1) Title insurance policy.
(2) Original deed held in the client's safe.
(3) Paid real estate tax bills.
(4) Closing statement.

j. Which of the following is a customary audit procedure for the verification of the legal ownership of real property?
(1) Examination of correspondence with the corporate counsel concerning acquisition matters.
(2) Examination of ownership documents registered and on file at a public hall of records.
(3) Examination of corporate minutes and resolutions concerning the approval to acquire property, plant, and equipment.
(4) Examination of deeds and title guaranty policies on hand.

k. An auditor determines that a client has properly capitalized a leased asset (and corresponding lease liability) as representing, in substance, an installment purchase. As part of the auditor's procedures, the auditor should
(1) Substantiate the cost of the property to the lessor and determine that this is the cost recorded by the client.
(2) Evaluate the propriety of the interest rate used in discounting the future lease payments.
(3) Determine that the leased property is being amortized over the life of the lease.
(4) Evaluate whether the total amount of lease payments represents the fair market value of the property.

l. In connection with a review of the prepaid insurance account, which of the following procedures would generally *not* be performed by the auditor?
(1) Recompute the portion of the premium that expired during the year.
(2) Prepare excerpts of insurance policies for audit working papers.
(3) Examine support for premium payments.
(4) Confirm premium rates with an independent insurance broker.

m. Tennessee Company violated company policy by erroneously capitalizing the cost of painting its warehouse. The CPA examining Tennessee's financial statements would most likely learn of this error by
(1) Discussing Tennessee's capitalization policies with its controller.
(2) Reviewing the titles and descriptions for all construction work orders issued during the year.
(3) Observing, during the physical inventory observation, that the warehouse has been painted.
(4) Examining in detail a sample of construction work orders.

n. The auditor interviews the plant manager. The auditor is most likely to rely on this interview as primary support for an audit conclusion on
(1) Capitalization vs. expensing policy.
(2) Allocation of fixed and variable costs.
(3) The necessity to record a provision for deferred maintenance costs.
(4) The adequacy of the depreciation expense.

(AICPA adapted)

P14–3 Items **a** through **j** are internal control questions designed to be used in the audit of property and equipment. A "yes" answer to such a question would indicate a potential strength in the system, while a "no" answer indicates a potential weakness.

a. Are review and approval required by responsible officials for all major property and equipment purchases and disposals?
b. Are capital budgeting techniques required before the decision is made to purchase new property and equipment?
c. Are all purchases of movable fixed assets required to be made through the same purchasing channels as all other cash disbursements?
d. Are all fixed asset disposals required to go through the same channels and cash receipts controls as sales of inventory?
e. Is a work order system required for all property and equipment purchases and sales, as well as repair and maintenance?
f. Does the company have a capitalization policy for fixed assets which allows for proper recording of assets and expenses?
g. Are periodic reconciliations made between fixed assets detail records and general ledger control accounts for fixed assets and depreciation?
h. Are all lease agreements reviewed by a responsible official prior to being recorded?
i. Is periodic review of the depreciation records performed by supervisory personnel?
j. Is the company required to maintain adequate fire and casualty insurance coverage?

Required:

For each question **a** through **j**, indicate

a. The error or irregularity, if any, which that control attribute is designed to prevent, detect, or correct.
b. The effect on the financial statements if that control attribute were missing.
c. The compliance test which would be performed if the answer to the question were "yes," indicating a potential strength in the system. If inspection of documents is appropriate, indicate the file from which the sample of documents would be selected and the file to which the sample would be vouched or traced.
d. Whether the compliance test mentioned in **c** is also a substantive test of transactions.
e. The substantive test that would need to be expanded if the answer to the question is "no," (indicating a potential weakness in the system of internal control).

Use the following format for your answer. The first item has been answered as a model.

Item	Error or Irregularity	Effect on Financial Statements	Compliance Test	Also a Substantive Test?	Expansion of Substantive Test
(a)	Invalid transaction	Misappropriation of cash and fixed assets	Inspection of documents: Vouch a sample of property and equipment additions to supporting documentation and approval per board of directors' minutes	Yes	Same as compliance test

P14–4 For each error or irregularity in property, equipment, and depreciation, name the internal control attribute that, if prescribed by the client, would prevent, detect, or correct it.

a. Repairs and maintenance expense has been inordinately high this year compared to the past three years. Analysis of the account reveals charges that should have been capitalized.
b. The purchasing agent purchased a large amount of small tools for his own use and caused the company to pay for them.
c. The depreciation expense program for computer-maintained fixed assets records does not allow for appropriate cost recovery according to the most recent Internal Revenue Service regulations.
d. The computer programmer, writing the program for fixed asset retirements, caused "net book value" to be removed from the "cost" category and failed to remove accumulated depreciation from the records for all retirements.
e. A lease that should have been capitalized was recorded as a month-to-month lease.
f. The company is still using property and equipment in everyday operations which were fully depreciated five years ago.
g. In reviewing computerized records over property and equipment, you find that a number of individual assets have been depreciated to negative carrying values (accumulated depreciation exceeds cost).
h. Printout of computer-prepared depreciation records reveals nonsensical information in important data fields.
i. Computerized fixed asset ledger detail does not agree with computer-prepared general ledger totals for property and equipment and accumulated depreciation.

P14–5 In the past, the records to be evaluated in an audit have been printed reports, listings, documents, and written papers, all of which are visible output. However, in fully computerized systems, which employ daily updating of transaction files, output and files are frequently in machine-readable forms — such as cards, tapes, or disks. Thus, they often present the auditor with an opportunity to use the computer in performing an audit.

Required:

a. List the major audit objectives for fixed assets and accumulated depreciation.
b. For each objective listed in **a**, describe one or two audit procedures that would satisfy that objective.
c. For each audit procedure discussed in **b**, describe how computer audit software can be used, if at all, to assist the auditor.

Organize your answer as follows:

Audit Objective	Audit Procedure(s)	Ways computer audit software may be used

(AICPA adapted)

P14–6 In connection with the annual examination of Johnson Corporation, a manufacturer of janitorial supplies, you have been assigned to audit the fixed assets. The company maintains a detailed property ledger for all fixed assets. You prepared an audit program for the balances of property, plant, and equipment but have yet to prepare one for accumulated depreciation and depreciation expense.

Required:

a. Prepare a separate comprehensive audit program for the accumulated depreciation and depreciation expense accounts.
b. For each procedure listed in **a** suggest ways that computer audit software can be utilized to assist in the audit, if possible.

(AICPA adapted)

P14–7 During an examination of the financial statements of Gole Inc., Elsa Robbins, CPA, requested and received a client-prepared property casualty insurance schedule which included appropriate premium information.

Required:

a. Identify the type of information, in addition to the appropriate premium information, that would ordinarily be expected to be included in a property casualty insurance schedule.
b. What are the basic audit procedures Robbins should perform in examining the client-prepared property casualty insurance schedule?

(AICPA adapted)

CHAPTER 15

CAPITAL ACQUISITION AND REPAYMENT SYSTEM

In Chapters 13 and 14, we described the audit procedures that should be performed in verifying the systems and balances for investments, intangibles, and property and equipment. This includes nominal accounts related to those assets. In this chapter we turn our attention to the verification of the accounts reflecting the acquisitions and repayments of funds used to finance the purchases of those assets. A business secures most of the resources used to acquire such assets either by incurring long-term debt or through the issuance of equity securities. We divide our discussion of the audit process for the capital acquisition and repayment system into the following subtopics:

1. The financing of business operations.
2. Evaluation of the system of internal control associated with the capital acquisition and repayment system.
3. Substantive verification procedures for long-term debt-related accounts.
4. Substantive verification procedures for equity capital-related accounts.

We have also included, as appendixes to the chapter, illustrated working papers for long-term debt and equity capital items.

FINANCING BUSINESS OPERATIONS

Financing a business through debt essentially involves a three-element cycle beginning with the issuance of the debt obligation in exchange for cash. This phase is followed by the periodic payment of interest on the obligation while it is outstanding.

Ultimately, the principal amount of the obligation will also be paid, either in installments or as a lump sum. The accounts involved in this part of the system include the following:

- Cash.
- Notes or mortgages payable.
- Installment contracts payable.
- Bonds payable.
- Interest expense.
- Accrued interest payable.

Financing through the use of equity capital primarily involves the recognition of new capital interests in exchange for cash. Periodic distributions of resources may then be made to owners, either as withdrawals or as dividends, depending on the capital structure of the business. Capital interests may also be redeemed or repurchased. Accounts involved in this part of the system include the following:

- Cash.
- Common stock.
- Preferred stock.
- Paid-in capital in excess of par or stated value.
- Donated capital.
- Unappropriated retained earnings.
- Appropriated retained earnings.
- Treasury stock.
- Dividends declared.
- Dividends payable.
- Sole proprietor's capital account.
- Partners' capital accounts.

Figure 15–1 illustrates diagrammatically the principal transactions involved in the capital acquisition and repayment system.

The capital acquisition and repayment system has four distinguishing characteristics that help shape the evidence-gathering process for the debt and equity capital accounts:

1. Typically the auditor encounters only a limited number of transactions involving these accounts in a given audit period.
2. Any given capital acquisition or repayment transaction is likely to be material in amount. As a result of that fact, the exclusion or improper recognition of a single transaction could be the source of a material error.
3. Legal or regulatory agency requirements are often associated with capital acquisition transactions. An example of such a requirement is the filing of a registration statement with the SEC before a new issue of stock or bonds can be marketed. These requirements are very important, and client records pertaining to compliance must be examined by the auditor.
4. A contractual relationship always exists between the holder of a debt security (note or bond) and the client, and the contract determines the amount of interest to be paid. In the case of equity securities, the contractual relationship for payments arises at the point of dividend declaration by the board of directors.

Because of these characteristics of capital-related transactions, the auditor will

Long-Term Debt

xxx (3)	xxx (1)
	Ending bal. xxx

Capital Stock

xxx (8)	xxx (2)
	Ending bal. xxx

Additional Paid-In Capital

xxx (8)	xxx (2)
	Ending bal. xxx

Retained Earnings

Losses xxx xxx (6)	Earnings xxx
	Ending bal. xxx

Cash

xxx (1) xxx (2)	xxx (3) xxx (5) xxx (7) xxx (8)

Interest Expense

xxx (4) xxx (5)	

Accrued Interest Payable

xxx (5)	xxx (4)
	Ending bal. xxx

Dividends Payable

xxx (7)	xxx (6)
	Ending bal. xxx

(1) Additional debt financing; (2) Additional equity financing; (3) Repayment of debt; (4) Accrual of interest; (5) Payment of interest; (6) Declaration of dividends; (7) Payment of dividends; (8) Redemptions of stock.

FIGURE 15–1. Capital Acquisition and Repayment System

generally be most concerned with verifying the substantive details of transactions producing the account balances. Also, because there are usually only a few well-documented transactions of relatively material amounts, evidence supporting details of these transactions is relatively easy to obtain.

The evidence gathered during the audit process will typically be drawn together in an analysis-type working paper which shows beginning account balances, additions, reductions, and the resulting ending account balances. Examples of such working papers are included in the appendixes to this chapter (for long-term notes payable, capital stock, paid-in capital and retained earnings).

EVALUATION OF THE SYSTEM OF INTERNAL CONTROL

Figure 15–2 depicts the exchange transactions, boundary documents, and supporting documents involved in the capital acquisition and repayment system of a corporate client. Functions over which controls should be exercised can be classified as exchange (action) functions, processing functions, and safeguard functions. Exchange functions are performed by persons who execute the various exchange transactions (1 through 8).

Exchange Transaction	Boundary Document	Supporting Document
Borrowing under note arrangements	Cash receipt	Note agreement; board of directors' approval
Borrowing under bond or other arrangements	Cash receipt	Bond indenture; registration statement; board of directors' approval; lease agreements
Payment of interest on debt obligations	Cancelled checks	Due notices for interest; note agreements; bond trustee records
Repayment of debt principal	Cancelled checks	Due notices for principal; note agreements; bond trustee records
Issuance of stock	Cash receipts	Underwriters agreement; registration statement; stock certificate stubs; board of directors' approval
Payment of dividends	Cancelled checks	Board of directors' approval
Redemption of stock	Cancelled checks	Board of directors' approval
Acquisition of treasury stock	Cancelled checks	Board of directors' approval
Sale of treasury stock	Cash receipts	Board of directors' approval

FIGURE 15–2. Exchange Transactions and Documents: Capital Acquisition and Repayment System

Processing functions involve recordkeeping responsibilities for those transactions. Safeguard functions pertain to physical custody of resources received and the issuance of obligation documents. Internal accounting control procedures within which these functions are performed should incorporate five of the six characteristics of internal control cited in Chapter 5. Figure 15–3 depicts in a flowchart how these characteristics should be embodied into the system.

Appropriate Separation of Responsibilities

The authority to borrow or approve new issues of stock should be separated from the custodial responsibilities for resources (generally cash) received in exchange for them. Notice in Figure 15–3 that the authority to borrow or to propose new equity financing generally is delegated to the corporate treasurer, but that the *board of directors must also review and approve all material transactions.* The cash-handling and obligation authorization functions should also be separated from the recordkeeping function, both for debt and equity financing transactions. The duties of maintaining owners' equity records and the handling of cash and stock certificates should be separated in a closely held corporation. In a publicly held corporation, an independent registrar or transfer agent exercises control over the issuances and transfers of stock; the corporation, in turn, holds the transfer agent accountable for the proceeds from the sale of

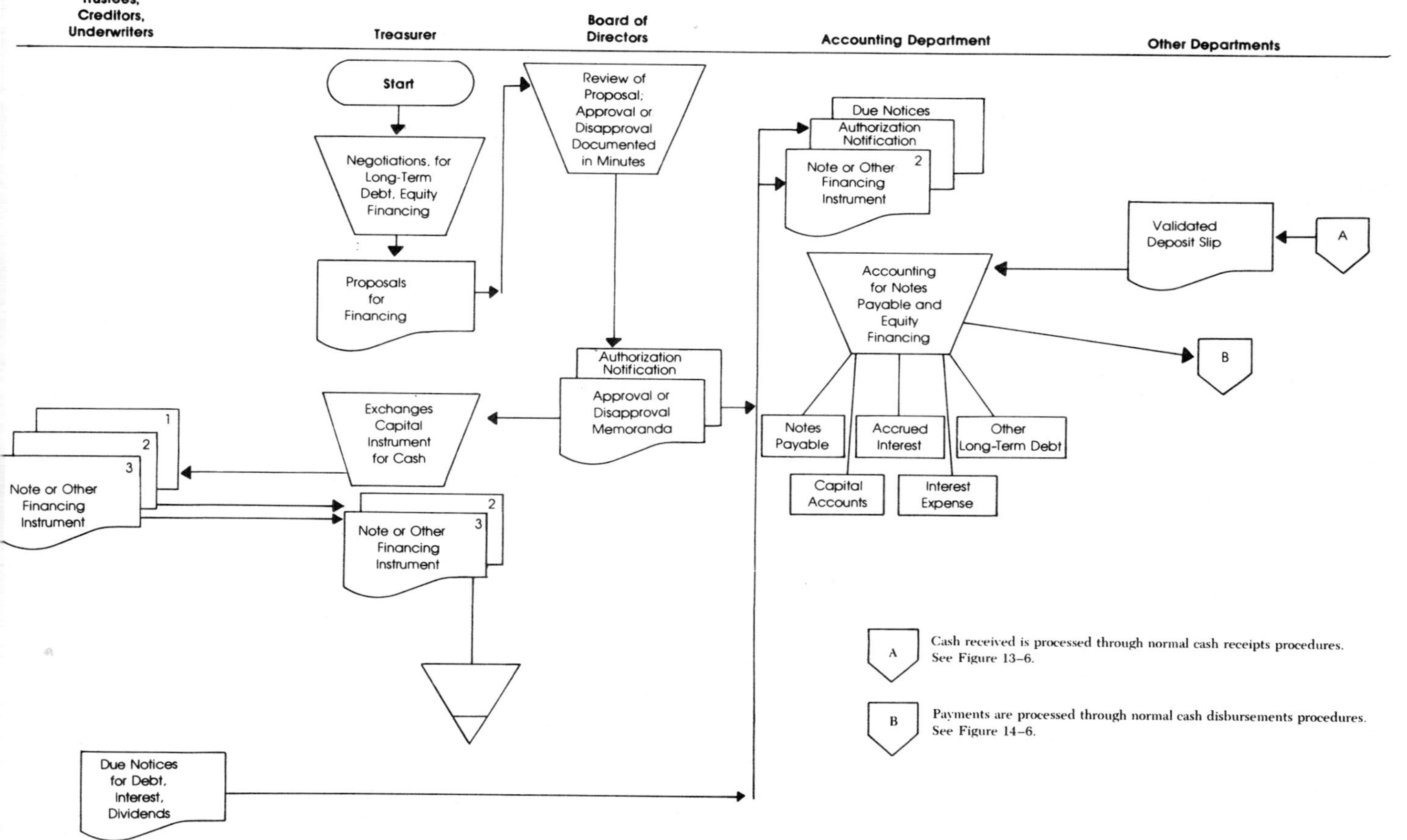

FIGURE 15–3. Flowchart for the Capital Acquisition and Repayment System

stock. Dividends must be declared by the board of directors and payments of dividends should be made on the basis of proper inspection of the stockholder records either by a company officer or by an independent registrar or transfer agent. The stockholder records should be maintained by persons having no responsibilities for the disbursement of cash.

If bond financing is used, the company may employ an independent bond trustee and an independent interest-paying agent. These parties act in a fiduciary capacity. They keep the records of bondholders, receive and distribute interest payments to registered bondholders, establish and maintain bond sinking funds, and perform various other duties in the interest of the bondholders. Notice from Figure 15–2 that the same general system of cash receipts controls applies to transactions involving debt and equity financing as those discussed in Chapter 10 for cash receipts from operations. Likewise, the same general system of cash disbursement controls applies to these transactions as to those discussed in Chapter 11 for cash disbursements for operations.

Specific Placement of Responsiblities

The authority to originate debt and equity instruments in exchange for operating resources should be specifically restricted to a limited number of upper level officers in the client's organization. The treasurer is usually one of these officers. At least two persons should be required to sign all loan agreements. Furthermore, the board of directors should be charged with the responsibility of authorizing all significant borrowing and capital stock transactions.

Records, Forms, and Authorization Procedures

An adequate system of records, forms, and authorization procedures should be maintained in support of all the exchange and processing functions. Loan amounts, interest rates, collateral, and terms of repayment should all be subject to approval, both for initial borrowings and for renewals. Many if not all equity capital transactions should be approved by the board of directors. Forms should be used to provide evidence of the formal authorization and approval of all transactions. The forms and documents for these transactions are typically nonstandardized, but are usually available for the auditor's review upon request. They might include registration statements with the SEC, bond trust indentures, underwriters' agreements for capital stock, internal memoranda, and of course, board of directors' minutes which show the actions taken by that body.

The form supporting the authorization to issue capital stock should include a description of the type of stock and the number of shares being issued, as well as spaces for authorization signatures. The basic stock certificate should require the signature of a responsible official from the firm who does not have direct access to the proceeds from the issuance of the stock. The authorization to reacquire capital stock should show the number of shares, the description of the stock, and the amount to be paid for the shares. Dividend declaration resolutions should be recorded in the minutes of the board of directors and should show the amount of the dividend per share, the date of record, and the date on which payment is to be made. A voucher system or some similar arrangement should be used to assemble the necessary supporting data for the approval of interest and dividend payments and for the retirement of debt and equity instruments.

The records underlying capital stock accounts of a corporation should be designed to make sure that the actual owners of stock are properly recognized in the corporate records or in the records of the independent registrar and transfer agent, so that the correct amounts of dividends will be paid to the stockholders owning the stock as of the dividend record date. When no transfer agent is employed, the company should maintain well-defined policies and develop appropriate documentary support for preparing and issuing stock certificates, reacquiring stock certificates, and recording capital stock transactions. This ordinarily requires a capital stock book that provides a record of the issuances and reacquisitions of capital stock over the life of the corporation and a shareholder's ledger showing the number of shares held by each individual stockholder at any point in time. When stock is redeemed, the cancelled stock certificates should be defaced to prevent reissuance and then filed with their corresponding stock issuance stubs. If an independent registrar and transfer agent is used, that party will have the responsibility of issuing stock in accordance with the authorization of the board of directors, as well as the responsibility for maintaining the stockholder records.

Appropriately qualified personnel who originate debt and equity capital instruments, receive the proceeds, and make all related payments should be *dependable and technically capable of making the judgments required in those actions.* Generally speaking, all the functions just described require some background in corporate accounting and finance.

Monitoring Compliance

The system should include provisions for monitoring compliance with established controls. Periodically, the detailed debt and equity records should be reconciled with their respective general ledger balances. This procedure should be performed by persons who have no responsibility relating to the detailed records. Interest expense on debt should also be independently calculated from the provisions of the individual note and bond agreements and reconciled with the balance in the general ledger account.

Compliance Tests

The major controls that should be compliance tested in such a system are those *relating to cash receipts* from the *issuance of securities* and *cash disbursements for payments of principal, interest, and dividends.* The errors and irregularities that can arise because of inadequate controls for these transactions, as well as the control attributes to prevent, correct, or detect them, are the same as those previously discussed for operating cash receipts and cash disbursements (Chapters 10 and 11). As mentioned previously, in auditing the capital acquisition and repayment system, we typically verify most of the transactions in our substantive tests of balances (often all of them). Hence, there is less dependence on internal controls. We shall discuss substantive tests in the sections that follow.

SUBSTANTIVE VERIFICATION PROCEDURES FOR DEBT ACCOUNTS

Debt capital is obtained most frequently through issuance of mortgage notes or bonds payable, or by use of installment contracts to acquire assets. Resources anticipated to be needed for only a short period of time may be acquired through the issuance of short-term notes. The auditing procedures used to verify such notes are essentially the same as those described in Chapter 11 for trade notes payable. Large amounts for long-term capital expenditures may be acquired through the issuance of long-term notes, generally secured by specific client assets. This type of debt capital is often referred to as ***mortgage notes payable.***

Accountants apply a substance-over-form interpretation to some building and equipment lease arrangements, causing them to be treated as installment purchases. Therefore, we may find another type of debt capital characterized as *installment contracts payable.* Corporations may also issue *bonds* in which the bond indenture becomes the contract through which that type of long-term debt capital is obtained. Because of their similarities, we shall deal with the substantive verification of these account balances as a group.

The normal starting point for verification of debt accounts is the preparation of the analysis type of working paper, showing beginning balances, additions, retirements, and ending balances for both the principal amount and accrued interest. Such a working paper is illustrated in Appendix 15–A. As you examine this working paper, notice that it follows the typical flow of transactions into and out of the notes payable account, which was illustrated in Figure 15–1.

As shown in Figure 15–4 and illustrated in the working paper, we begin our substantive verification of debt accounts by reconciling the respective liability accounts with their underlying accounting records. In doing this we trace the balances shown in the financial statements to the general ledger accounts and recompute the balances in those accounts.

Verification of Existence

In verifying the existence of debt, the auditor must, in an initial audit, inspect the documents underlying each individual debt item. These will typically include vouching authorization for new borrowing to the board of directors' minutes and obtaining copies of agreements for notes payable, installment contracts for installment contracts payable, and bond indentures for bonds payable. Pertinent data — such as the issue and maturity dates and the rates of interest — should be extracted from the bond indenture agreement. In auditing publicly held companies, the contents of the bond indenture should be confirmed with the trustee. The auditor should also ascertain that the opinion of legal counsel has been secured on the legality of the issue. Copies of these documents or confirmations should be obtained and placed in the auditor's permanent file working papers for later reference on subsequent audit engagements. The auditor should also inspect the journal entries made in recognizing debt capital obligations and trace the resources (cash, for example) received in exchange for them to the appropriate asset accounts.

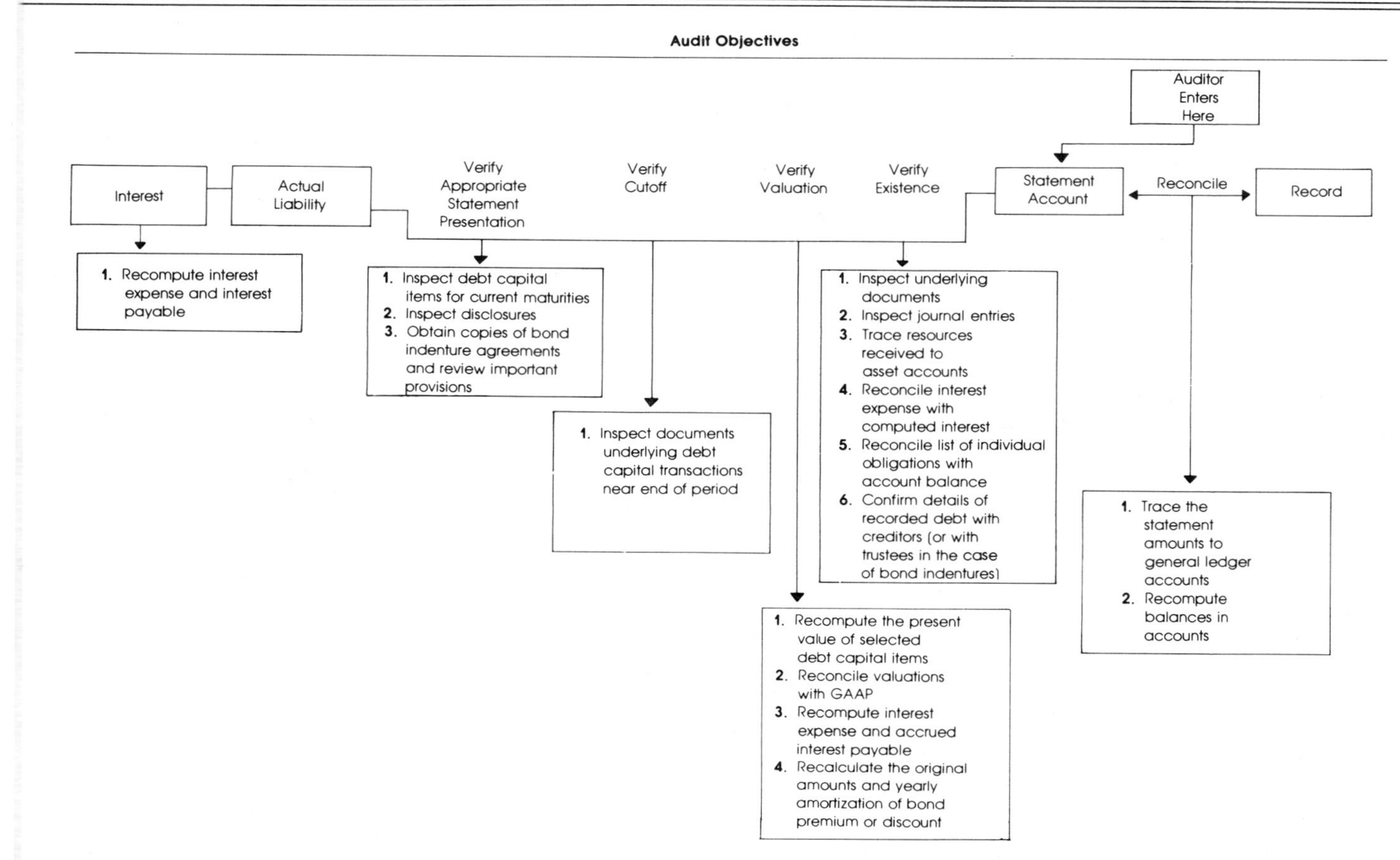

FIGURE 15–4. Flowchart for Substantive Verification of Debt Capital Accounts

In subsequent audits, only the documentation supporting changes in debt capital items occurring during the fiscal period under audit need be inspected. These items include evidence of new borrowings as well as cancelled checks issued in repayments of principal, and the payments of interest.

Because the auditor is especially concerned about unrecorded obligations, it is important to reconcile the interest expense shown in the income statement with the interest expense computed on the basis of the contractual obligations outstanding during the year. If the recorded interest expense is in excess of the computed amount, it is possible that a note payable may not have been recorded. Where the debt account balance is composed of a number of different elements, such as a number of different notes payable, it is important to reconcile the list of notes payable with the balance shown in the financial statements.

Confirmation can also play an important role in verifying the existence of recorded notes and bonds payable. For short-term notes payable, the auditor should refer to the standard bank confirmation (see Appendix 12–D). This confirmation calls for the bank to provide detailed information regarding the existence, amount, dates, interest rates, and collateral for notes payable to the bank. For long-term notes and mortgages payable, a letter of confirmation should be sent to all creditors. Appendix 15–C illustrates the long-term note payable confirmation that has been received and compared to client records with no exceptions having been noted. The confirmation should request creditors to provide all pertinent data such as issue dates, principal amounts, interest rates, terms of repayment, and collateral pledged. For bonds payable, a confirmation request should be sent to the trustee who should be asked to provide the terms of the bond indenture, plus information regarding the client's compliance with those terms during the audit period.

Verification of Valuation

Although the value to be assigned to most liabilities can be ascertained by simply examining the documents supporting the obligations, the valuations assigned to some debt items must be recomputed to determine whether they are reflected in accordance with GAAP. For example, noninterest-bearing and low-interest notes should be reflected in the financial statements at their discounted present values. The same is true for installment contracts payable. In the case of bonds, unamortized premiums should be added to the bonds payable account and any unamortized discount should be subtracted from that account in establishing the values to be assigned to those items in the balance sheet. The amortization schedules for these items and for mortgages payable should be examined. Acquisition costs associated with new mortgages should be verified by examining the related cancelled checks and closing statement.

Verification of Cutoff

Although the verification of cutoff is not as important for long-term debt items as for certain current assets and liabilities, it should still be verified. This requirement calls for the auditor to inspect duplicate copies of new note agreements as well as vouchers payable for principal and interest repayments occurring near the end of the audit period to determine whether they have been recorded in the appropriate fiscal period.

New notes should be included as liabilities in the body of the financial statements when dated on or before the balance sheet date.

Verification of Appropriate Statement Presentation

Appropriate statement presentation calls for most long-term debt items to be shown as noncurrent liabilities. Generally accepted accounting practices, however, require that current maturities of long-term debt be reflected as current liabilities unless they are to be liquidated from noncurrent assets, such as resources contained in a sinking fund account. For that reason, the auditor must inspect the outstanding debt obligations and recalculate any amounts that should be moved from noncurrent liabilities to the current liability classification in the balance sheet. Appendix 15–B illustrates the audit work done in this regard.

The auditor must also inspect disclosures relating to long-term debt accounts. These include such things as footnotes describing the terms of the debt items outstanding and the assets pledged as collateral against them. Furthermore, debt agreements frequently include restrictions on the activities of the companies, such as compensating balance provisions, restrictions on the payment of dividends, or the maintenance of a specified current ratio or balance in retained earnings. The auditor must make the necessary corroborative tests to assure that such restrictions have been adhered to and that they are appropriately disclosed in the footnotes. Such tests include confirmation of compensating balance arrangements with creditor banks, and the *recomputation* of critical ratios and amounts to assure that they are within prescribed limits.

The amount shown in the balance sheet for accrued interest payable must also be recomputed from the contractual arrangements associated with each of the debt items. This is usually done from duplicate copies of the notes. After the accrued interest payable has been recomputed it should be reconciled to the respective liability and expense account balances shown in the financial statements. Payments of interest expense are vouched to cash disbursements journals and to cancelled checks. A four-element equation including the beginning-of-period accrual balance, plus interest expense, less interest payments, and the resulting end-of-period accrual balance should be the format of the reconciliation and should be reflected in the audit working papers.

Audit of Pension Plan Accounts

A special type of audit problem exists whenever the client has adopted a pension plan for its employees. Most employee pension plans in existence today are qualified under the provisions of the Employer Retirement Income Security Act of 1974 (ERISA). Employee pension plans regulated under ERISA must satisfy a variety of criteria in order to obtain favored tax treatment for the employer and employee. Among these criteria are: (1) minimum funding levels; (2) the treatment of past service costs; (3) minimum vesting rights for participating employees; (4) minimum disclosure requirements for the employer; and (5) minimum requirements for the trustees. The auditor, in preparation for auditing an employee pension plan, should review and become familiar with all of the preceding legal requirements as well as the related income tax laws.

The auditor's main concerns in auditing a client's pension plan are to ascertain the propriety of transactions involving the plan in terms of compliance with applicable laws and regulations, and to ascertain that the provisions of the plan have been properly disclosed. A copy of the client's pension plan should be obtained and studied to identify all its pertinent features. That copy should be placed in the auditor's permanent file and retained for reference on future audits. In examining the propriety of transactions involving the pension plan, the auditor should review all material transactions involving the plan and ascertain that its provisions were carried out in compliance with ERISA. If there is currently an excess of the actuarially computed value of vested pension benefits over retirement funds and related balance sheet accruals, less prepayments and deferred charges, it should be disclosed fully in the footnotes of the financial statements and on the balance sheet as a long-term liability. In addition, if any material changes have occurred in the method of accounting for pension costs during the period, they should be evaluated by the auditor for possible effect on the audit opinion.

Amounts contributed to the plan by both the client and employees should be vouched to appropriate cash disbursements and payroll records. These may also be confirmed with the trustee of the pension plan. Entries recording pension costs should be vouched to appropriate underlying documents, such as trustee and actuarial reports. Pension plan data relating to funding levels and various other actuarially determined amounts should be confirmed with the trustee or actuary, reviewed for reasonableness, and scrutinized for compliance with applicable laws. In cases of complex actuarial computations the auditor may engage and rely on the report of an actuarial specialist to evaluate those computations.

Disclosure requirements for pension plans include: (1) a brief statement that the plan exists and identification of employee groups covered; (2) a description of the accounting and funding methods employed; (3) the current provision for pension costs; (4) the excess of any of the actuarially computed value of vested benefits over retirement funds and balance sheet accruals, less prepayments and deferred charges; and (5) the nature of any matters that might affect comparability of disclosures, such as changes in accounting methods, or significant amendments to the plan.

SUBSTANTIVE VERIFICATION PROCEDURES FOR EQUITY ACCOUNTS

The fundamental accounting equation (assets − liabilities = capital) suggests that if the auditor has appropriately verified all assets and liabilities at both the beginning and the end of the period under audit, the total equity capital balance and the net change in it during the year will have to be correct. For that reason the audit of owners' equity requires substantially less audit time than is devoted to verifying other types of account balances. However, the auditor is still concerned with verifying these items independently of the amounts that might be calculated by use of the accounting equation.

As shown in Figure 15–5, the primary objectives to be met in auditing owners' equity are verification of the existence, valuation, cutoff, and appropriate statement presentation of equity capital account balances.

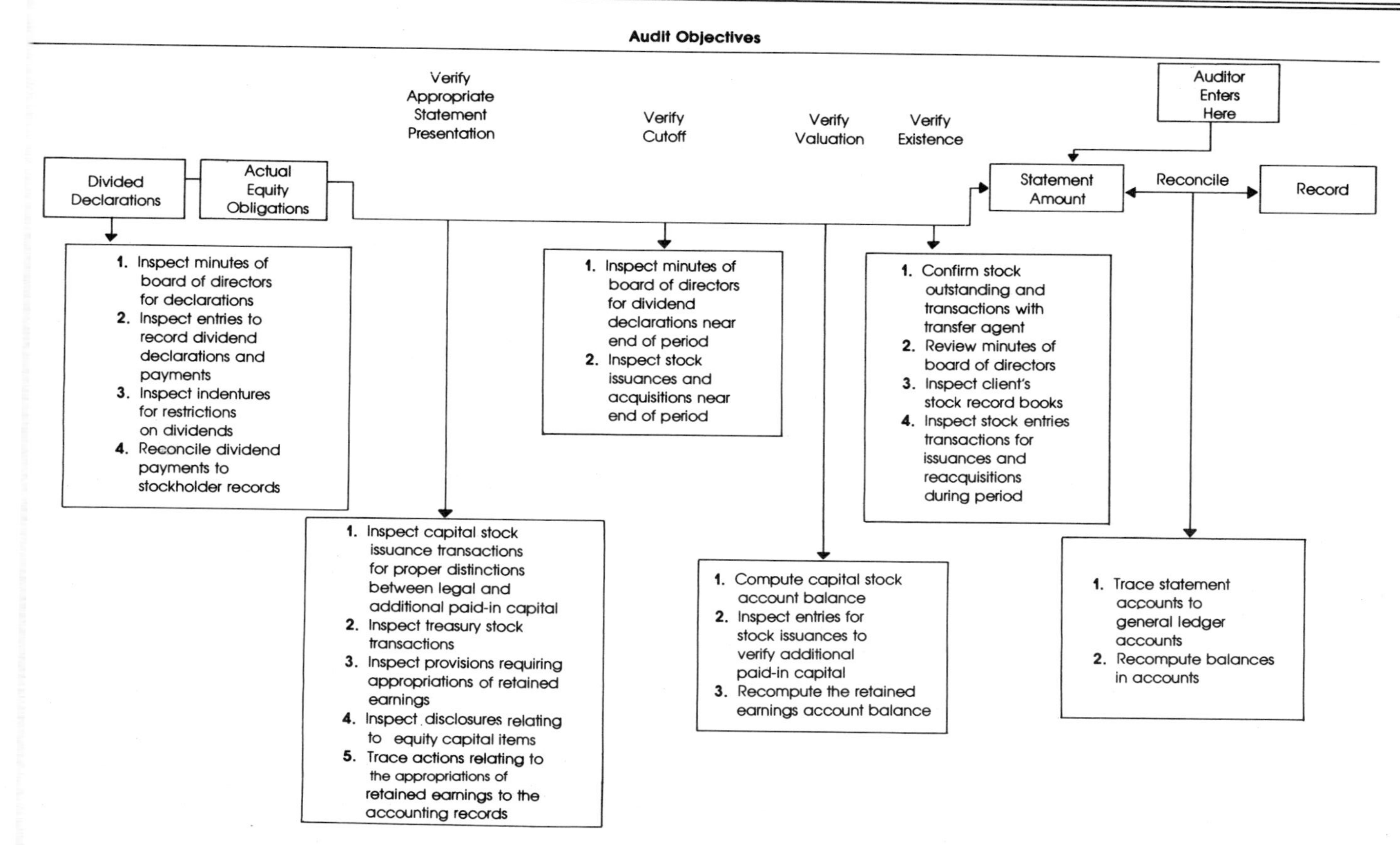

FIGURE 15–5. Flowchart for Substantive Verification of Equity Capital Accounts

Verification of Existence

The existence objective is easily satisfied when an independent registrar or transfer agent is used. In such cases the transfer agent should be asked to confirm directly to the auditor the shares of capital stock outstanding, the transactions occurring during the audit period and the values assigned to those transactions. It is also important to review the minutes of the board of directors' meetings for evidence that equity capital transactions, including declarations of dividends, new issuances of stock and repurchases of stock have been approved by that body. When an independent registrar or transfer agent is not used, it is important for the auditor to inspect the client's stock record books in the initial audit. Details of capital stock outstanding are then recorded in the auditor's permanent file working papers. In subsequent audits, the emphasis should be on *inspecting new issuances and repurchases during the period.* If new capital stock has been issued for cash or to bring about a merger with another company, the evidence supporting those transactions should also appear in the minutes of the board of directors' meetings and should be examined by the auditor. If the client holds treasury stock certificates they should always be examined and counted.

Verification of Valuation

The value assigned to each capital stock account balance is normally verified by determining the number of shares outstanding at the balance sheet date (see the procedures just outlined for determining existence) and multiplying that amount by the par or stated value of the stock. The auditor will rely either on the confirmation reply from the independent registrar or transfer agent or on an inspection of the capital stock record book to secure that information. The auditor will also need to inspect entries recording the issuance of stock to determine that the appropriate amount has been recorded in the paid-in capital in excess of par value account. Entries to record treasury stock transactions should also be examined by the auditor. The value assigned to retained earnings can be verified by recomputing the balance, using the beginning-of-period balance plus additions during the period less the deductions during the period. Entries to the retained earnings account which have not been examined in connection with the other parts of the audit should be vouched to underlying documentary support. This may be the case, for example, when prior period adjustments have been made by the client.

Verification of Cutoff

Although the problem of verifying the appropriate cutoff of equity capital transactions is not as important as verification of cutoff of current items, some attention should be given to that phase of the audit, particularly insofar as dividend obligations are concerned. In examining the retained earnings account, the auditor should inspect the minutes of the board of directors' meetings to determine the dates as of which all dividends have been declared, so that the appropriate liability can be recognized for cash dividends payable. In some instances, stock issuances or acquisitions may occur near the end of the period, in which case it will be necessary for the auditor to verify that they have been recorded in the appropriate accounting period.

Appropriate Statement Presentation

Perhaps the most important objective to be met in auditing the equity capital accounts is to verify that those accounts have been appropriately presented in the financial statements. The auditor must inspect all capital stock issuance and reacquisition transactions during the year to be sure that an appropriate distinction has been made between legal capital and paid-in capital in excess of par or stated value. Treasury stock transactions must be inspected to determine whether an appropriate distinction has been made between additional paid-in capital and noncontributed capital as those transactions were recorded.

Actions originating with the board of directors (or taken because of requirements imposed by the state or bond indenture) relating to the appropriation of retained earnings must be traced to the accounting records to be sure that an appropriate distinction is made between appropriated and unappropriated retained earnings. It is also important for the auditor to inspect disclosures relating to capital stock — such as those for stock options, stock warrants, and convertible securities — to ascertain whether such items have been appropriately disclosed in accordance with applicable APB opinions or FASB statements.

As you saw in Figure 15–5, the auditor must also verify the various transactions involving dividend declarations and payments. The procedures for meeting this audit requirement begin with an inspection of the minutes of the board of directors' meetings for the amounts and dates of dividend declarations. Each amount should then be traced to the retained earnings account. In implementing this procedure, the auditor will be particularly concerned with the possibility of discovering unrecorded dividends. It is also important in this connection to inspect long-term debt contractual agreements, such as bond indentures and preferred stock indentures, to determine whether there are restrictions on the company insofar as the payment of dividends is concerned.

The valuations assigned to dividends will be determined by the amounts per share for cash dividends and by either fair market value or the par value of the stock in the case of stock dividends. At this point it is important to recognize that the declaration of *a stock dividend creates a special stockholders' equity account rather than a liability account.* It is also important for the auditor to determine that the additional shares issued as a stock dividend conform to the authorization provided by the board of directors. The auditor should also make certain that the dividend distributions (both cash and stock) have been made to the stockholders of record as of the record date. In doing this the auditor will want to inspect a sample of recorded dividend payments by tracing the payee's name on the cancelled check to the stockholder's record as of the date of record.

An analytical schedule for each equity capital account reconciling beginning-of-period balances, additions, reductions, and end-of-period balances should be prepared to summarize the evidence gathered in the verification of those accounts. Appendix 15–D illustrates this process for capital stock, treasury stock, additional paid-in capital, and retained earnings.

As noted in Appendix 15–D, one of the primary additions to retained earnings will normally be net income for the period. The auditor should trace the credit entry in retained earnings for that item to the net income figure shown in the income statement. This procedure should be done late in the audit period, after all adjusting entries affecting net income have been recorded. In addition, the auditor should trace all audit-adjusting entries affecting retained earnings to postings in the account. Notice that this procedure has also been reflected in Appendix 15–D. Other additions to be verified in retained earnings may include prior-period adjustments, which should be verified individually.

The primary reduction to retained earnings will be the dividends declared during the period. Debit entries in the retained earnings account for that item should be vouched to board of directors' minutes. Dividends paid should be vouched to the cash disbursements records, while dividends declared but unpaid should be reconciled with the dividends payable account balance. This audit work is illustrated in Appendix 15–E. Other debits may include prior-period adjustments that should be verified individually or operating losses that should be traced to the income statement. The auditor should also inspect all debits and credits to retained earnings (other than those for net income, net losses, and dividends) to determine whether they should have been included in the income statement.

SUMMARY

Businesses finance their operations by incurring debt and by issuing equity claims against the firm. In this chapter we have explained what the auditor should do in meeting the audit objectives for these elements of the financial statements. Because of the nature of debt and equity capital transactions, all significant changes in these accounts during the audit period will normally be verified. This practice means that less reliance will be placed on the system of control to support the transaction validity objective than was the case for items in the current sections of the balance sheet. Nonetheless, the auditor must still be concerned with the adequacy of the system of internal accounting controls in preventing errors and irregularities.

In auditing both of these systems, we give special attention to the substantive verification of transactions and account balances. In that part of the audit we seek to verify the existence of the items shown in the accounts, the valuations assigned to additions to and retirements from the accounts, and the proper cutoff of transactions at the end of the audit period. Perhaps the most important audit objective to be met for the elements of both of these systems, however, is the verification that the account balances have been appropriately presented in the financial statements.

The audit evidence for each of these accounts is typically summarized in analysis types of working papers similar to those shown in the appendixes to this chapter. As you can see by studying these working papers, the audit requires analysis of the additions to and retirements from these accounts during the audit period, followed by reconciliation of those items with the related account balances at the beginning and end of the audit period.

APPENDIX 15–A: Lead Schedule for Notes Payable and Interest Expense

JEP Manufacturing Co.
Notes Payable
3-31-X1

W. P. No. M
Accountant SmG
Date 5/12/X1

A/C	Description	Balance 3-31-X0	Principal Additions	Principal Retirements	Balance 3-31-X1 ✓
206	J.E. Coletrain - 11-30-X8 Payable in 4 annual installments of $29,825 beginning 1-2-X9; Interest @ Prime rate, Payable quarterly	59650 00		29825 00 ⊗	29825 00 ɋ M-1 A-2
207	Xerox	–	7386 00 #	492 30	6893 70 C A-2
209	Prudential Insurance Co. 6-8-X3 - Payable in annual installments of $50,000 beginning on 10-1-X0 Original Amount $715,000 Interest Rate 8.70 %	400000 00		50000 00 ⊗	350000 00 ɋ M-1 A-2
205	FNB Greensboro 11¾ %	175000 00	500000 00 ⩘	675000 00 ⩘	-0- ɋ
		634650 00	507386 00	755617 30	386718 70

C ɋ Confirmations sent; received
△ Agreed to prior year working papers.
✓ Agreed to 3-31-X1 general ledger
7 Recomputed amount. Appears reasonable.
✗ Agreed amount to paid checks. No exceptions noted.
\# See copy of purchase agreement in PF-14-4
⩘ Agreed to cancelled note. Appears proper.

Current Portion/ Reclassified Balance	Interest Reasonableness Test			
	59650 X 12% X 1/4 =	1784 60		
	59650 X 13% X 1/4 =	1938 62		
	59650 X 21½% X 1/4 =	3231 96		
ma	29825 X 17% X 1/4 =	1250 10		
RJE <c> <29825 00>			8205 28 7	
-0-				
A-2				
<1477 20>	Total interest expense		2543 47	
5416 50				
A-2				
<c>	400000 X .0870 X 6/12 =	17400 00		
RJE <500000 00>	350000 X .0870 X 6/12 =	15225 00		
300000 00			32625 00 7	
A-2				
			19333 01 7 ⓧ	
305416 50	Total interest expense		60417 63	
A-2	Amortization of debt expense		1125 84	K
			61543 47	
	AJE <6>		1916 00	
			63459 47	
			A-3	

APPENDIX 15–B: Reclassification of Current Maturities

JEP Mfg. Co.
Reclassification of L-T Debt
3-31-X1

W. P. No. Ma
Accountant SmG
Date 5/12/X1

For F/S purpose, L-T Debt must be broken down into two components: that portion payable w/in one year and that portion payable in periods beyond the upcoming year. The current portion of JEP's L-T Debt is calculated as follows:

Xerox – monthly installments of #123.10	(12 x 123.10) =	1477.20 M
Prudential next payment due 10-1-X1		50000.00 Δ M
JE Coletrain next payment due 1-2-X2		29825.00 Δ M
Current portion L-T Debt		81302.20 A-2

RJE (c) A-6	Dr.	Cr.
Xerox N/P	1477.20	
Prudential N/P	50000.00	
Coletrain N/P	29825.00	
Current Portion L-T Debt		81302.20
(To reclassify current portion of Long-Term Debt.)		

Δ Per appropriate agreement

APPENDIX 15–C: Notes Payable Confirmation Received

JEP MANUFACTURING COMPANY
P.O. Box 1000
Greensboro, Texas 75401

M-1
SMG
5/12/X1

April 2, 19X1

Mrs. J. E. Coletrain
2612 S. 8th Avenue
Greensboro, Texas 75401

Dear Mrs. Coletrain:

Best and Company, Suite 4500, Byron Building, Dallas, Texas 75201, are making their usual examination of our accounts. Please confirm directly to them the amount of our indebtedness to you as of the close of business on March 31, 19X1. According to our records, our indebtedness to you on that date was as follows:

Original Balance	$119,300
Unpaid Balance at March 31, 19X1	$29,825.00
Interest Rate	Prime rate of Mercantile National Bank
Date of Note	November 3, 19X8
Date Due	
Interest paid to Date	Jan. 1, 19X1
Collateral	Unsecured

A return envelope is enclosed for your convenience.

Very truly yours,

JEP Manufacturing Co.

L. Philip Neeson

L. Philip Neeson
Financial Vice President

The above information is correct except as noted:

Elizabeth L. Coletrain
Signature

Title

4-21-X1
Date

APPENDIX 15–D: Lead Schedule for Equity Capital Accounts

JEP Manufacturing Corporation
Analysis of Equity Accounts
3-31-X1

W. P. No. U
ACCOUNTANT SmG
DATE 5/19/X1

	Preferred Stock Amount	Preferred Stock Shares	Outstanding Common Amount	Outstanding Common Shares
Balance per 3-31-X0 Financial Statements	60200.00 ∡	1204 ∡	75994.76 ∡	109664 ∡
Prior Period Adjustments:				
To reverse prior year percentage-of-completion entry				
To adjust investment in subsidiary to equity method				
To amortize excess cost of subsidiary				
To record year-end deferred tax adjustment				
Net income-statement effect of 3-31-X0 "Off-Ledger" entries				
Beginning retained earnings per general ledger, 3/31/X0				
① Preferred Stock Sinking Fund	<60200.00> ✓	<1204> ✓		
② Quarterly Dividends:				
6/30/X0, Preferred Stock (1204 shares @ .75/sh)				
8/14/X0, Preferred Stock (1204 shares @ .375/sh)				
Adjustment for tax treatment of obsolete inventory				
End-of-year adjustments:				
To reverse prior year percentage-of-completion entry (AJE <1>)				
To adjust investment in subsidiary to equity method (AJE <4>)				
To amortize excess cost of subsidiary (AJE <5>)				
To record year-end deferred tax adjustment (AJE <6>)				
To eliminate adjustment for tax treatment of obsolete inventory (AJE <3>)				
To adjust deferred taxes payable for obsolete inventory (AJE <7>)				
Net income for year	-0-	-0-	75994.76 ƒ	109664 ƒ
			A-2	

∡ Per Prior Year working papers

∡̸ Per Prior Year working papers; Certificate #13 for 1599 shares issued to JEP Manufacturing inspected; held in safe deposit box at bank. No exceptions noted.

① Per Board of Directors Minutes dated 6-9-X0. See PF-4 for copy of minutes. Authorized retirement of 1204 shares at $50/share. (1204 x 50 = 60,200)

② Vouched authorization to Board of Directors' Minutes of 6-9-X0.

✓ Vouched payment to cancelled checks. No exceptions noted.

ƒ Reviewed account; noted no activity for year.

Treasury Stock Amount	Treasury Stock Shares	Paid-in Capital		Retained Earnings
<10121 67> Δ	<1599> Δ	34638 50		228725 22 Δ
				<157280 95>
				<152354 00>
				5987 00
				72529 00
				<92704 57>
				196343 70
				<903 00> ✓
				<451 55> ✓
				1437 36
				27635 836
				187022 00
				<7903 00>
				<123599 66>
				<14370 36>
				<8054 63>
			A-3	45167 797
<10121 67> F	<1599> F	34638 50 F		273757 819
A-2		A-2		A-2

Conclusion: Based on audit work performed, which was considered adequate to meet the audit objectives for owners' equity accounts, they are fairly stated in accordance with generally accepted accounting principles @ 3-31-X1 S.A.

APPENDIX 15–E: Dividends Declared and Paid

JEP Mfg. Co.
Dividends Declared and Paid per Review of the Minutes of the Board of Directors & Exec. Committee
3-31-X1

W. P. No. Y-1
ACCOUNTANT Smg
DATE 5/21/X1

Description	Amount per share	Declaration Date	Date Paid
Board of Directors	$.75 ①	6-9-X0	7-31-X0
Board of Directors	$.375 ②	6-9-X0	3-14-X0

① For quarter ended 6-30-X0 (75 x 1204 = $903 Ⓐ)

② For ½ quarter ended 8-14-X0 - the date on which all preferred stock was retired. (.375 x 1204 = 451.55 Ⓐ)

Σ Ⓐ's = 1354.55 = (903 + 451.55)
u

QUESTIONS FOR CLASS DISCUSSION

Q15-1 How do we distinguish between capital acquisitions through the incurrence of long-term debt and capital acquisitions realized from the issuance of equity securities?

Q15-2 What are the three elements of the cycle associated with financing through the medium of debt capital?

Q15-3 What are the four distinguishing characteristics that help shape the evidence-gathering process for the capital acquisition and repayment system? Describe briefly.

Q15-4 Which responsibilities, within the capital acquisition and repayment system, should be separated to achieve appropriate internal control within the system? Explain.

Q15-5 What responsibilities should the board of directors have relating to capital acquisition transactions?

Q15-6 What are the forms and authorization procedures that should be maintained in support of the exchange and processing functions within the capital acquisition and repayment system?

Q15-7 How will the fact that a firm employs a transfer agent to handle capital stock-related transactions rather than having company employees handle such transactions affect the evidence-gathering process? Explain.

Q15-8 Which documents should be examined by the auditor in verifying the existence of long-term debt? Describe them.

Q15-9 Under what circumstances would the auditor use confirmation procedures in verifying notes and bonds payable? Explain.

Q15-10 Under what circumstances would the auditor use confirmation procedures in the verification of equity capital? Explain.

Q15-11 What procedures should the auditor follow in verifying the valuation of debt securities?

Q15-12 What is the relationship between the verification of interest expense and the verification of debt securities outstanding? Discuss.

Q15-13 Why does the audit of owners' equity typically require substantially less audit time than is required in the verification of other types of account balances?

Q15-14 What audit procedures should be performed in the verification of treasury stock held by a client?

Q15-15 How does the auditor verify the record of dividends declared during the year?

Q15-16 Do all dividend declarations create liabilities? Explain.

Q15-17 How should the workpapers used to accumulate audit evidence relating to the account balances in the capital acquisition and repayment system be organized? Explain.

Q15–18 Does the auditor use sampling procedures in verifying the account balances in the capital acquisition and repayment cycle? Explain.

SHORT CASES

C15–1 You were engaged on May 1, 19X7, by a committee of stockholders to perform a special audit as of December 31, 19X6, of the stockholders' equity of the Major Corporation, whose stock is actively traded on a stock exchange. The group of stockholders who engaged you believe that the information contained in the stockholders' equity section of the published annual report for the year ended December 31, 19X6, is not correct. If your examination confirms their suspicions, they intend to use the report in a proxy fight.

Management agrees to permit your audit but refuses to permit any direct confirmation with stockholders. To secure cooperation in the audit, the committee of stockholders has agreed to this limitation and you have been instructed to limit your audit in this respect. You have been instructed also to exclude the audit of revenue and expense accounts for the year.

Required:

a. Prepare a general audit program for the usual examination of the stockholders' equity section of a corporation's balance sheet, assuming no limitation on the scope of your examination. Exclude the audit of revenue and expense accounts.
b. Describe any special auditing procedures you would undertake in view of the limitations and other special circumstances of your examination of the Major Corporation's stockholders' equity accounts.

(AICPA adapted)

C15–2 You are a CPA engaged in an examination of the financial statements of Pate Corporation for the year ended December 31, 19X9. The financial statements and records of Pate Corporation have not been audited by a CPA in prior years.

The stockholders' equity section of Pate Corporation's balance sheet at December 31, 19X9, follows:

Stockholders' equity:	
Capital stock — 10,000 shares of \$10 par value authorized; 5,000 shares issued and outstanding	\$ 50,000
Capital contributed in excess of par value of capital stock	32,580
Retained earnings	47,320
Total stockholders' equity	\$129,900

Pate Corporation was founded in 19X1. The corporation has ten stockholders and serves as its own registrar and transfer agent. There are no capital stock subscription contracts in effect.

Required:

a. Prepare the detailed audit program for the examination of the three accounts composing the stockholders' equity section of Pate Corporation's balance sheet. (Do not include in the audit program the verification of the results of the current year's operations.)

b. After every other figure on the balance sheet has been audited, it might appear that the retained earnings figure is a balancing figure and requires no further verification. Why do you, as a CPA, verify retained earnings as you do the other figures on the balance sheet? Discuss.

(AICPA adapted)

C15–3 You were engaged to examine the financial statements of Ronlyn Corporation for the year ended June 30, 19X7.

On May 1, 19X7, the corporation borrowed $500,000 from the Second National Bank to finance plant expansion. The long-term note agreement provided for the annual payment of principal and interest over five years. The existing plant was pledged as security for the loan.

Due to unexpected difficulties in acquiring the building site, the plant expansion had not begun at June 30, 19X7. To make use of the borrowed funds, management decided to invest in stocks and bonds, and on May 16, 19X7, the $500,000 was invested in securities.

Required:

a. What are the audit objectives in the examination of long-term debt?

b. Prepare an audit program for the examination of the long-term note agreement between Ronlyn and Second National Bank.

(AICPA adapted)

C15–4 The following covenants are extracted from the indenture of a bond issue. The indenture provides that failure to comply with its terms in any respect automatically advances the due date of the loan to the date of noncompliance (the regular date is 20 years hence). Give any audit steps or reporting requirements you feel should be taken or recognized in connection with each one of the following.

a. "The debtor company shall endeavor to maintain a working capital ratio of 2 to 1 at all times, and, in any fiscal year following a failure to maintain said ratio, the company shall restrict compensation of officers to a total of $100,000. Officers for this purpose shall include chairman of the board of directors, president, all vice-presidents, secretary, and treasurer."

b. "The debtor company shall keep all property which is security for this debt insured against loss by fire to the extent of 100 percent of its actual value. Policies of insurance comprising this protection shall be filed with the trustee."

c. "The debtor company shall pay all taxes legally assessed against property which is security for this debt within the time provided by law for payment without penalty, and shall deposit receipted tax bills or equally acceptable evidence of payment of same with the trustee."

d. "A sinking fund shall be deposited with the trustee by semiannual payments of

$300,000, from which the trustee shall, in his discretion, purchase bonds of this issue."

(AICPA adapted)

C15–5 Jimmack Corporation adopted a pension plan for its employees on January 1, 19X8. Provisions of the plan were as follows:

a. The corporation shall contribute 10 percent of its net income before deducting income taxes and the contribution, but not in excess of 15 percent of the total salaries paid to the participants in the plan who are in the employ of the corporation at year end. The employees make no contribution to the plan.

b. An employee shall be eligible to participate in the plan on January 1 following completion of one full year of employment.

The following data pertain to the corporation and its employees for 19X9:

Corporate income before income taxes and contribution to pension plan: $7,325,000

Employment records:

Name	Date Employed	Date Terminated	Salary Paid in 19X9
Jimmack	12/ 8/X3	—	$179,000
Baker	2/ 1/X5	—	141,000
Cohan	2/ 8/X5	4/ 9/X9	35,000
Delman	9/15/X6	—	80,000
Jarman	9/21/X9	12/22/X9	30,000
Zibranek	5/ 6/X9	—	55,000
			$520,000

Required:

a. What are the detailed audit objectives for the corporation's liability accrual to the corporate pension plan?

b. What audit evidence needs to be obtained to satisfy the objectives listed in **a**? Include in your answer the detailed procedures needed to verify the information given above for corporate income and employment records.

c. Recalculate the corporation's contribution accrual for 19X9.

d. Based on the information provided, what deficiencies, if any, do you see in the company's accounting practices? What other information might you need to determine if the company's accounting methods comply with GAAP?

e. How might the company's accounting policies, or lack of them affect your audit opinion, considering your perceived materiality of the pension fund liability disclosures, or lack of them?

(AICPA adapted)

C15–6 The Ford Corporation leased equipment from the Nixon Company on October 1, 19X1. You have learned through conversations with the controller of Ford Corporation, your client, that the transaction was accounted for as a purchase. Terms of the lease are as follows:

a. The lease is for an eight-year period expiring September 30, 19X9.
b. Equal annual lease payments are to be made in the amount of $600,000, due October 1 of each year. The first payment was made on October 1 of 19X1.
c. The equipment has an estimated useful life of eight years with no residual value expected.
d. Ford has adopted the straight-line method of depreciation and takes a full year's depreciation in the year of purchase.
e. The rate of interest contemplated by Ford and Nixon is 10 percent. (Present value of an annuity of $1 in advance for eight periods at 10 percent is 5.868).

Required:

a. What audit evidence would you obtain with regard to the above facts? Be specific in terms of audit objectives and procedures.
b. What expense(s) should Ford record as a result of the above facts for the year ended December 31, 19X1? Show supporting computation in good form.

(AICPA adapted)

PROBLEMS

P15–1 Select the best answer for each of the following items relating to the verification of long-term debt.

a. The auditor's program for the examination of long-term debt should include steps that require the
   (1) Verification of the existence of the bond holders.
   (2) Examination of any bond trust indenture.
   (3) Inspection of the accounts payable subsidiary ledger.
   (4) Investigation of credits to the bond interest income account.
b. During an examination of a publicly held company, the auditor should obtain written confirmation regarding debenture transactions from the
   (1) Debenture holders.
   (2) Client's attorney.
   (3) Internal auditors.
   (4) Trustee.
c. Several years ago Conway, Inc., secured a conventional real estate mortgage loan. Which of the following audit procedures would be *least* likely to be performed by an auditor examining the mortgage balance?
   (1) Examine the current year's cancelled checks.
   (2) Review the mortgage amortization schedule.
   (3) Inspect public records of lien balances.
   (4) Recompute mortage interest expense.
d. Treetop Corporation acquired a building and arranged mortgage financing during the year. Verification of the related mortgage acquisition costs would be *least* likely to include an examination of the related
   (1) Deed.
   (2) Cancelled checks.
   (3) Closing statement.
   (4) Interest expense.

e. During its fiscal year, a company issued, at a discount, a substantial amount of first-mortgage bonds. When performing audit work in connection with the bond issue, the independent auditor should
   (1) Confirm the existence of the bondholders.
   (2) Review the minutes for authorization.
   (3) Trace the net cash received from the issuance to the bond payable account.
   (4) Inspect the records maintained by the bond trustee.

f. In connection with the audit of a current issue of long-term bonds payable, the auditor should
   (1) Determine whether bondholders are persons other than owners, directors, or officers of the company issuing the bond.
   (2) Calculate the effective interest rate to see if it is substantially the same as the rates for similar issues.
   (3) Decide whether the bond issue was made without violating state or local law.
   (4) Ascertain that the client has obtained the opinion of counsel on the legality of the issue.

g. During the year under audit, a company has completed a private placement of a substantial amount of bonds. Which of the following is the *most* important step in the auditor's program for the examination of bonds payable?
   (1) Confirming the amount issued with the bond trustee.
   (2) Tracing the cash received from the issue to the accounting records.
   (3) Examining the bond records maintained by the transfer agent.
   (4) Recomputing the annual interest cost and the effective yield.

h. During the course of an audit, a CPA observes that the recorded interest expense seems to be excessive in relation to the balance in the long-term debt *account*. This observation could lead the auditor to suspect that
   (1) Long-term debt is understated.
   (2) Discount on bonds payable is overstated.
   (3) Long-term debt is overstated.
   (4) Premium on bonds payable is understated.

i. A company issued bonds for cash during the year under audit. To ascertain that this transaction was properly recorded, the auditor's *best* course of action is to
   (1) Request a statement from the bond trustee as to the amount of the bonds issued and outstanding.
   (2) Confirm the results of the issuance with the underwriter or investment banker.
   (3) Trace the cash received from the issuance to the accounting records.
   (4) Verify that the net cash received is credited to an account entitled "Bonds Payable."

j. In connection with the examination of bonds payable, an auditor would expect to find in a trust indenture
   (1) The issue date and maturity date of the bond.
   (2) The names of the original subscribers to the bond issue.
   (3) The yield to maturity of the bonds issued.
   (4) The company's debt to equity ratio at the time of issuance.

(AICPA adapted)

P15–2 Select the best answer to each of the following items relating to the verification of owners' equity.

a. During the course of an audit of a medium-sized manufacturing concern, which of the following areas would you expect to require substantially less audit time than the others?
   (1) Assets.
   (2) Liabilities.
   (3) Revenues.
   (4) Owners' equity.

b. An audit program for the examination of the retained earnings account should include a step that requires verification of the
   (1) Gain or loss resulting from disposition of treasury shares.
   (2) Market value used to charge retained earnings to account for a two-for-one stock split.
   (3) Authorization for both cash and stock dividends.
   (4) Approval of the adjustment to the beginning balance as a result of a write-down of an account receivable.

c. Florida Corporation declared a 100% stock dividend during 1975. In connection with the examination of Florida's financial statements, Florida's auditor should determine that
   (1) The additional shares issued do not exceed the number of authorized but previously unissued shares.
   (2) Stockholders received their additional shares by confirming year-end holdings with them.
   (3) The stock dividend was properly recorded at fair market value.
   (4) Florida's stockholders have authorized the issuance of 100% stock dividends.

d. The auditor is concerned with establishing that dividends are paid to stockholders of the client corporation owning stock as of the
   (1) Issue date.
   (2) Declaration date.
   (3) Record date.
   (4) Payment date.

e. Which of the following is the *most* important consideration of an auditor when examining the stockholders' equity section of a client's balance sheet?
   (1) Changes in the capital stock account are verified by an independent stock transfer agent.
   (2) Stock dividends or stock splits during the year under audit were approved by the stockholders.
   (3) Stock dividends are capitalized at par or stated value on the dividend declaration date.
   (4) Entries in the capital stock account can be traced to a resolution in the minutes of the board of directors' meetings.

f. All corporate capital stock transactions should ultimately be traced to the
   (1) Minutes of the board of directors.
   (2) Cash receipts journal.
   (3) Cash disbursements journal.
   (4) Numbered stock certificates.

g. Where *no* independent stock transfer agents are employed and the corporation issues its own stocks and maintains stock records, cancelled stock certificates should
   (1) Be defaced to prevent reissuance and attached to their corresponding stubs.

(2) *Not* be defaced, but segregated from other stock certificates and retained in a cancelled certificates file.
(3) Be destroyed to prevent fraudulent reissuance.
(4) Be defaced and sent to the secretary of state.

h. If a company employs a capital stock registrar and/or transfer agent, the registrar or agent, or both, should be requested to confirm directly to the auditor the number of shares of each class of stock
(1) Surrendered and canceled during the year.
(2) Authorized at the balance sheet date.
(3) Issued and outstanding at the balance sheet date.
(4) Authorized, issued, and outstanding during the year.

i. When a company has treasury stock certificates on hand, a year-end count of the certificates by the auditor is
(1) Required when the company classifies treasury stock with other assets.
(2) Not required if treasury stock is a deduction from stockholders' equity.
(3) Required when the company had treasury stock transactions during the year.
(4) Always required.

(AICPA adapted)

P15–3 Items **a** through **e** are questions typically found in an internal control questionnaire for notes payable. A "yes" answer indicates a potential strength in the system and a "no" answer indicates a potential weakness.

a. Are subsidiary records over debt and equity securities maintained by persons who are independent of the cash receipts and disbursements function?

b. Are periodic reconciliations made between general ledger accounts over notes payable, bonds payable, and interest expense by persons who are independent of the custodianship function?

c. Are recorded amounts for debt, capital stock, and other liabilities checked or adequately tested periodically (by comparison with independent records, reference to subsequent settlements, independent computation and confirmation) by persons independent of the cash-handling and recording functions?

d. Are unissued bonds, notes capital stock, warrants, and other unissued debt securities accessible only to the custodian and to those who prepare and issue such securities?

e. Are there procedures for determining that debt and equity financing transactions are recorded at the amounts and in the accounting periods in which executed?

Required:

For each item **a** through **e** listed above, state:

a. The error or irregularity which that control was designed to prevent, detect, or correct.

b. The compliance test, if any, that would be necessary if the answer to the question were "yes," indicating a potential strength in the system.

c. The substantive audit procedure that would have to be extended if the answer to the question were "no," indicating a potential weakness in the system of internal control.

P15–4 Discuss the audit objectives for each of the following procedures over long-term debt accrued interest payable, and owners' equity accounts.

a. Recompute interest expense and accrued interest payable.
b. Confirm details of notes payable with creditors.
c. Obtain copies of bond indenture agreements and review the important details.
d. Reconcile interest expense per books with recomputed interest expense per procedure **a.**
e. Vouch new issues of capital stock to approval in minutes of board of directors.
f. Inspect client's stock record books.
g. Scan the general ledger account for retained earnings and vouch all material entries to documentary support. Investigate any unusual transactions.
h. Inspect note and stock issuances and retirements near the end of the period.
i. Recalculate the amounts and yearly amortization of bond discount or premium.

P15–5 In performing the audit of a large corporation that has a bond issue outstanding, the trust indenture is typically reviewed and a confirmation letter is obtained from the trustee.

Required:

a. What are the major audit objectives to be considered in examination of bonds payable?
b. Name at least eight matters of importance to the auditor that can be found either in the bond trust indenture or in the letter of confirmation with the trustee. For each item named, associate it with an audit objective.

(AICPA adapted)

CHAPTER 16

COMPLETING THE EVIDENCE-GATHERING PHASE OF THE AUDIT

We divide our discussion of the completion of the evidence-gathering phase of the audit into the following subtopics:

1. The search for and verification of certain estimated and contingent liabilities.
2. Post–balance sheet analytical review.
3. Review or audit of supplementary data.
4. Reconciliation of the statement of changes in financial position with the balance sheet and income statement data.
5. Review of the working papers, summarizing audit evidence, and drawing conclusions.
6. Review of subsequent events.
7. Subsequent discovery of facts existing at the audit report date.

We also include, as chapter appendixes, illustrated working papers for balance sheet and income statement items as well as adjusting and reclassifying entries.

As we have explained in each chapter of Part III, the audited account balances included in each of the financial statement subsystems should fit together like a jigsaw puzzle. When the elements of the subsystems have been verified, we are ready to fit the components into the complete financial picture. In doing so, we must first test the overall reasonableness of the data by applying certain ***analytical review procedures*** and summarizing their results: these procedures are substantive tests of the financial information, carried out by comparing various account balances and ratios over time. Financial data used in analytical review can be either balances in the financial statements or ratios calculated from those balances. The purpose of analytical review is *to identify unusual items and unexpected fluctuations*, which may indicate material misstatements in the financial data.

Because of their nature, analytical review and other procedures are typically performed near the end of the audit engagement. After finishing them, the auditor should be ready to express an overall opinion on the statements, an opinion based on the combined results of all audit evidence.

SEARCH FOR AND VERIFICATION OF ESTIMATED AND CONTINGENT LIABILITIES

Before completing the evidence-gathering phase of the audit, we must verify that estimated liabilities and contingent liabilities have been fairly presented. We give particular attention to the verification of *existence, valuation,* and appropriate *statement presentation* in this phase of the audit. In meeting those audit objectives the auditor must direct much of her or his efforts toward the discovery of omitted or understated items.

It is important to begin our discussion of this area by emphasizing the difference between an estimated liability and a contingent liability. An ***estimated liability*** is a future obligation to an outside party resulting from activities that have already occurred. It is different from other such obligations, however, in that the *precise amount of the obligation is unknown*. The estimated amount of the obligation is recorded in the accounting records and reflected in the financial statements. A ***contingent liability,*** on the other hand, is a *potential future obligation* resulting from past activities. As you can see, the word *potential* is the primary difference between the two definitions. A contingent liability is one that may or may not actually exist, depending on the future resolution of some uncertainty. The amount of a contingent liability may be either known or unknown, depending on the nature of the potential obligation.

The auditor, in distinguishing between estimated and contingent liabilities, must be guided by the provisions of FASB 5. That pronouncement states that if a potential obligation meets three criteria — that is, if (1) it exists, (2) it is both highly probable and reasonably estimatable, and (3) it is the result of events that occurred prior to the balance sheet date — it should be treated as an estimated liability rather than as a contingent liability. GAAP requires that estimated liabilities be accrued and be included in the liability section of the balance sheet, while contingent liabilities (which are considered "reasonably possible" to occur) generally are disclosed through the medium of financial statement footnotes. A point estimate or range of amount should be given, if possible; and if no estimate is possible, disclosures should indicate that fact.

Estimated Liabilities

Obligations for income taxes, product warranty agreements, and purchase commitments are typical examples of estimated liabilities. After the auditor has reconciled the statement amounts for these items with the underlying accounting records, he or she should inspect the documents (such as the tax return, the warranty agreement, or the purchase commitment contract) to verify the existence of the respective estimated liabilities. It is also important to review the minutes of the board of directors in the search for unrecorded estimated liabilities.

The *valuation* of estimated liabilities should be verified by recomputing the probable obligation from available documentation or related account balances. It is important, for example, to examine the client's tax return and the reports of internal revenue agents relating to the client's tax obligations in determining whether the estimated liability for income taxes is properly valued. The estimated liability for warranty should take into consideration the past experience of the company in establishing the percentage relationship between sales and product warranty costs. Accrued sales commissions payable should be verified against sales. Prices on purchase commitment contracts should be inspected and compared with end-of-period market quotations in determining whether an estimated liability for purchase commitments has been properly valued. The existence of open commodity futures contracts, for example, can be verified by direct confirmations with the client's commodity traders.

Estimated liabilities should be presented in the liability section of the balance sheet. They should be classified as current or noncurrent, depending on the nature of the respective obligations. Parenthetical and footnote disclosures should be added to explain uncertainties relating to the estimated liability account balances.

Contingent Liabilities

Contingent liabilities include such things as possible obligations from pending litigation, notes receivable discounted and guarantees of obligations of others, ongoing tax disputes, and open letters of credit at banks. Because of their nature, the audit procedures for verifying contingencies are not as well defined as are the procedures for verifying other elements of the financial statements. The primary auditing objective, however, is *to verify their existence*. Because they are potential liabilities, the auditing literature continues to focus attention on the discovery of undisclosed contingent obligations. The following audit procedures are designed to accomplish that objective:

- *Inquire of management* regarding their procedures for identifying, evaluating, and accounting for contingencies. A primary task of the auditor in carrying out this procedure is to let management know the different kinds of contingencies that may be associated with the client's operating environment. Obviously, this procedure will not be useful in discovering intentional failures to disclose contingencies. It will, however, be useful if management has a basic commitment to the fair presentation of the financial data.
- Closely associated with the preceding audit procedure is the requirement that the *letter of representation* from a client contain a statement that management is aware of no undisclosed contingent liabilities.
- The auditor should *analyze the legal expense account* and invoices for professional services for the period. This analysis is directed toward the discovery of possible lawsuits and tax assessments associated with legal fees paid by the client.
- The auditor should *obtain a confirmation letter* similar to the one shown in Figure 16–1 from all attorneys performing major legal services for the client during the year.[1] The precise form and content of this letter are discussed later in this section. For this purpose, the client may provide the auditor with a list of pending or threatened litigation and other claims and

CLIENT COMPANY
Anywhere, USA

January 26, 19X3

Attorney for the Client
Anywhere, USA

Gentlemen:

Our auditors, James Brown & Co., CPAs, are examining our financial statements for
the fiscal year ending 12/31/19X2. In connection with that examination, we have provided them with the attached list describing and evaluating certain contingencies to
which you have devoted substantial attention on behalf of the company in the form of
(1) legal consultation or representation. We have also provided an estimate of potential
losses where those could be provided. These contingencies are regarded by management
as material for financial reporting purposes.

We ask you to furnish to our auditors such information regarding the nature of the
litigation, the progress of each case to date, how management is responding or intends
(3) to respond to the litigation, and an evaluation of the likelihood of an unfavorable
outcome along with an estimate, if one can be made, of the amount or range of potential
loss. Please furnish our auditors any other information you consider necessary to
supplement the information already provided, including an explanation of those matters
as to which your views may differ from those stated in the attached documents. Also
please advise the auditors of any pending or threatened litigation, claims, or assess-
(4) ments you know of that have been omitted from this list. In the absence of omissions,
please state that the list provided for the auditor is complete.

We have also provided the auditors with the attached list of unasserted claims,
(2) along with our proposed responses if those claims are asserted and our judgment as
to the likelihood of an unfavorable outcome. In connection with the unasserted claims
listed in the attached document, please furnish our auditors with such explanations,
(5) if any, as you consider necessary to supplement the information included in the list,
including an explanation of those matters as to which your views may differ from those
stated in our list. It is our understanding that you are also responsible for inform-
(6) ing the management of our firm when in your judgment an unasserted claim requires
disclosure in the financial statements.

(7) We also request you to state the nature of any reasons you may have for limiting
your response to this confirmation request.

Your reply to this confirmation request should be sent directly to our auditors
in the attached, postage-paid envelope addressed to them.

Sincerely yours,

Management, Client Company

FIGURE 16–1. Typical Attorney Confirmation Letter

assessments. Alternatively, the client's lawyer may be asked to furnish the required information with respect to pending or threatened litigation.
- The auditor should *inspect letters of credit in force* as of the balance sheet date and obtain a confirmation of the used and unused portions of the balances shown in those letters.

Other procedures performed throughout the audit, although primarily for different purposes, may disclose contingent liabilities arising because of claims, litigation, or assessments. Examples of these other procedures are

- *Reading the minutes* of directors', stockholders', and other appropriate committees' meetings held during and subsequent to the period being examined; this is done to discover contingency commitments, such as guarantees of the debt of an affiliate.
- *Reading contracts, loan agreements, leases, and correspondence* from taxing or governmental agencies for evidence of these liabilities.
- *Inspecting the working papers* prepared to this point in the audit for any indication of potential contingencies. For example, the bank confirmation (illustrated in Appendix 12–D) should be inspected for potential contingent liabilities associated with notes receivable discounted or loan guarantees.

Pending or threatened litigation is among the most important of contingent liabilities. As indicated in the preceding paragraph, the auditor relies heavily on the client's legal counsel for information relating to these matters. Each attorney who has provided legal service for the client during the year should be requested to reply to a confirmation letter similar to the one shown in Figure 16–1 to secure that information. You will observe that the letter is signed by client management and asks the company's legal counsel to provide information regarding contingencies that existed as of the end of the audit period or that may have developed during the period between the balance sheet date and the date of the audit report.

The standard letter of confirmation as shown in Figure 16–1 should include the following items:

1. The client's list of material *pending or threatened litigation.*
2. The client's list of any material *unasserted claims* with which the attorney has been involved. For this purpose, an unasserted claim is a cause for legal action which someone may have against the client, but which has not been filed as of the date of the confirmation letter.
3. A request that the attorney furnish information regarding the status of each of the listed items of pending or threatened litigation. This response should provide indications as to the *probability* of an unfavorable outcome and a *range of potential loss* in the event of an unfavorable outcome.
4. A request that the attorney identify any pending or threatened legal actions of which he is aware that may not be included in the client's list.
5. A request that the lawyer comment on unasserted claims for which his views differ from management's.
6. A direct statement that the attorney is responsible for informing management when in his or her judgment there is an unasserted claim requiring disclosure in the financial statements.
7. A statement requiring the attorney to identify the nature of any reasons for limitations in response to the confirmation request.[2]

The references to each of the items listed above in the confirmation letter are identified by their respective numbers in the margin of the illustrated letter shown in

Figure 16–1. You should also observe that the letter requires that the confirmation reply be sent *directly to the auditors.*

In 1975, an agreement was reached between the American Bar Association and the American Institute of Certified Public Accountants as to the form and content of lawyers' confirmation letters. This agreement took into account the importance of maintaining the confidentiality of attorney – client communications. However, it also recognized the importance of client – auditor communications, which essentially require waiver of the attorney – client privilege with respect to the information in the confirmation letter. The letter format illustrated in Figure 16–1 is the product of this agreement. In spite of the agreement, however, auditors sometimes have difficulty securing satisfactory responses from clients' attorneys. In some cases, an unsatisfactory response consists of an inadequate reply and in other instances a refusal by the attorney to provide the information. Although reluctance to provide information can be justified by either a lack of knowledge or by what the attorney construes to be a confidential relationship between himself and his client, the auditor must have a satisfactory reply to enable the expression of an unqualified opinion on the financial statements. Therefore, if the unavailable information could directly affect the fairness of presentation of the financial statements, the auditor, in accordance with SAS 12, would have to modify her or his audit opinion to reflect the lack of available evidence. This requirement has the effect of placing pressure on the client's attorneys to cooperate with the auditor by providing contingent liability information to them.

Frequently, the auditing firm will seek a separate evaluation of a potential liability from its own legal counsel to supplement the responses of the client's attorneys. This can be particularly helpful in evaluating contingent liabilities because of the fact that the client's attorney is an *advocate of the client* and in that capacity may lose some of her or his objectivity in evaluating the potential liability associated with the pending legal action. For that reason, for example, an auditor should be concerned about the possibility of undisclosed unasserted claims if a client's attorney resigns shortly after delivering a letter indicating no significant disagreements with the client's assessment of contingent liabilities.

Inquiries in the lawyer's confirmation letter may be limited to matters that are considered individually or collectively material, provided that the client and the auditor have reached an understanding on the limits of materiality for this purpose. Likewise, the lawyer may limit her or his response to matters considered individually or collectively material, provided that the lawyer and the auditor have reached an understanding on the limits of materiality for this purpose.

ANALYTICAL REVIEW

As we have observed earlier in the text, the evidence-gathering process involves an evaluation of internal control as well as the performance of substantive tests. In turn, there are two types of substantive tests: (1) test of details, consisting of inspection, confirmation, and observation of evidence of all kinds; and (2) analytical review. The first of these has been explained in the substantive tests sections of Chapters 10 through 15. We now turn our attention to how the analytical review phase of the audit is used to gather evidential matter required by the third standard of field work.[3]

SAS 23 is the basic authoritative document relating to analytical review. It is defined there as a study of the relationships among recorded financial data. The procedures followed in implementing analytical review during this final phase of the audit depend primarily on a *comparison of the current period data with past periods' data.* For most entities, recorded data can be expected to conform to a predictable pattern over time. Deviations from this pattern may be caused by significant changes in circumstances, which need to be disclosed in the financial statements. Thus, analytical review is one means of *auditing by exception.* The implication is that any significant changes in account balances or in operating results should be explained in terms of changing circumstances existing during the audit period. Because of the periodic nature of these comparisons and because extensive tests of details have been performed on balance sheet data, final analytical review procedures tend to be *concentrated on the income statement accounts.* We may beneficially think of the analytical review procedures as being divided into three subcategories:

1. *Overall analytical review* of the general financial condition and profitability trends. The procedure used most frequently by the auditor in making an overall review of the income statement is the comparison of actual revenues and expenses with the corresponding figures for the previous year.
2. *Detailed analytical review* involving comparisons of elements of financial statement data, including operating and financial ratios.
3. *Direct tests of some account balances* or classes of transactions for reasonableness.

The basic assumption underlying the analytical review process is that the financial data and operational relationships should be consistent with those of prior periods for the client and with the client's industry. Thus the auditor should become familiar with the client's operations, the environment in which the firm operates, and the client's industry — all this for the purpose of identifying the expectations in the financial data. This means that the primary procedures followed in the analytical review will be recomputation of client-recorded amounts and comparisons using nonfinancial data, industry statistics, and analytical ratios. The most important phase of the analytical review often is the investigation of significant variations and unusual relationships. Significant deviations from expectations can usually be related to one of the following causes:

- Changes in operations, which may involve both profitability and cash flow.
- Exceptional circumstances surrounding the client's operations.
- Accounting changes.

If the auditor is unable to explain differences in terms of one of these characteristics, the possibility of errors in the financial data should be considered.

Use of Nonfinancial Data

The auditor is always looking for nonfinancial data that can be used in developing general measurements of the client's expected volume of operations. For example, in auditing the records of a hospital, the number of patient days can be multiplied by the historical average revenue per patient day to arrive at an approximation of the expected revenue from patients. In auditing a hotel or motel, the percentage of occupancy multiplied by the maximum total room revenue, if the establishment was fully occupied, can be used in estimating revenues from room rentals. In auditing a college or university, the total number of student credit hours reported by the registrar can be multiplied by the tuition rate per hour to arrive at an approximation of tuition revenue. The number of members in a country club can be multiplied by the annual dues per member to arrive at an approximation of dues revenue. Other less directly related nonfinancial measures include such things as the relationship of energy usage in a manufacturing industry to the cost of goods manufactured, or the relationship between the number of employees in a manufacturing firm and the cost of goods manufactured by the firm. In most cases where year-to-year comparisons are made, key income statement accounts such as the ones mentioned above are ***horizontally analyzed***; that is, the revenue or expense account balances for one or more prior years are compared with the respective current account balance. The auditor will typically investigate all changes exceeding a specified percentage.

A more sophisticated technique for comparing data during the analytical review involves use of ***regression analysis*** to calculate an expected account balance. This technique calls for using one or more of the financial or nonfinancial variables mentioned above as independent predictor variables in the regression equation. A computer audit software program similar to those discussed in Chapter 7 can be used to perform the regression analysis. Advantages of this technique are: (1) it provides an expected account balance based on logical relationships of business volume and other activity; (2) it automatically computes tolerances for variations from expectations; (3) it is more sensitive and, therefore, more precise, than ratio analysis; (4) it can be programmed to automatically calculate statistically valid sample sizes for additional tests of details, if needed, which corroborate the findings of the analytical review procedures. Firms that use this type of extensive analytical review rely heavily on it and, therefore, may greatly limit tests of details.[4]

Regardless of the method used to develop the auditor's expectation of the proper account balance, an important element of final analytical review is the *comparison of the recorded amount with an expected amount.* The auditor should obtain an explanation from the client for any account showing a material deviation from expectations. He or she should then follow up with corroborative tests (i.e., inspection of documents, further inquiry, etc.) to ascertain that the client's explanation is reasonable.

Use of Industry Statistics

Most industries have publications containing composite data about typical financial relationships, industry trends, etc. For example, the *Standard Periodical Directory* contains information on over 65,000 publications. Included in this directory are some 230 industrial classifications. These publications include in-depth coverage of particular industrial fields plus pertinent news and features relating to each industry. From these publications, the auditor would expect to find such things as the typical relationship of inventory to total sales or to total assets within an industry. Such relationships can be compared with parallel client data to determine whether the client fits into the normal industry pattern for those items. Because of differences in operations among individual firms, however, the auditor should be careful not to place undue emphasis on these relationships, and to weigh individual comparisons in the light of all other evidence obtained on a specified client.

Analytical Ratios

Ratios and percentage relationships are the devices most extensively used in the analytical review process. These are calculated for the year under audit and are then compared with the same ratios and percentages for prior years. We have learned that ratios and comparisons can be used during the planning stages of the audit to identify potential problem areas that might require the special attention of the auditor. However, they can also be used during the field work phase of the audit (especially in the final stages) because conclusions from the percentage relationships observed here must be consistent with conclusions derived from the auditor's tests of details. If they are not, it may be because the auditor has overlooked some critical problem that should be resolved before issuance of an audit opinion is justified. We now identify some of these ratios and relationships and explain their significance in the analytical review process:

- *Inventory turnover* (cost of units issued or sold ÷ average inventory) should be calculated for raw materials, work-in-process and finished goods and compared with the turnovers for those items in prior periods. As explained earlier in the text, this calculation and comparison is directly useful to the auditor in identifying obsolete or slow-moving merchandise. However, a significant change in turnover not explained by slow-moving merchandise can be an indication of a change in operational practices or errors in the determination of inventory. The auditor may also want to determine the average age of inventory in days (365 ÷ by the turnover figure) to gain further insight into the client's inventory situation.
- *Accounts receivable turnover* (sales on account ÷ average accounts receivable) supplemented by the average collection period for accounts receivable (365 ÷ turnover figure) can be used as a general check on the audited accounts receivable balance and on the collectibility of those accounts. Again, a significant change in this turnover figure could also be explained by a change in collections experience or possibly by an error in the accounts receivable balance.
- Accounts payable turnover (purchases on account ÷ average accounts payable) and the *average pay period* (365 ÷ turnover) can be used to help develop a general conclusion regarding the fairness of those account balances in the financial statements. These calculations, for example, can lead to the discovery of unrecorded accounts payable.
- The *gross margin percentage* (gross margin ÷ net sales) should be computed and compared with the percentages for prior years. A significant change in the percentage can be explained by one of the three reasons for deviations cited on page 702 or possibly by an error in the sales or cost of sales figures. An unexplained decrease in this percentage, for example, might suggest the possibility of unrecorded sales or overstated cost of sales.
- The auditor will want to compute the *operating margin percentage* (net operating income ÷ net sales) and compare that with prior-year percentages. If the gross margin percentage has been found to be consistent with that of prior years and the operating margin percentage has changed significantly, the auditor must seek to explain that change in terms of one of the reasons cited earlier (see page 702) or entertain the possibility that some of the operating expense items are not fairly stated.
- The *net income from continuing operations percentage* (net income from continuing opera-

tions ÷ net sales) should be computed and compared with that figure for prior years as a means of discovering possible errors in the other income or other expense elements of the income statement.

- The auditor will also want to calculate the *percentage relationship between net income from continuing operations and total assets*. That percentage should in turn be compared with the percentages for prior years. If the net operating income to sales percentage (see item 6) has been consistent with that of prior years and this percentage has changed significantly, the auditor will need to explain such a change in terms of one of the reasons for deviations cited earlier in the chapter or look for possible errors in audited balances of related assets.
- The *percentage relationship between net income from continuing operations and equity capital* should be calculated and compared with that percentage for prior periods. If the other operating percentages cited above have been consistent with those of prior periods and this one has changed significantly, the auditor will be concerned with explaining that difference. The explanation could, for example, be significant new borrowings or repayments of debt.
- *Liquidity ratios* in the form of the current ratio (current assets ÷ current liabilities) and the quick assets ratio (liquid assets ÷ current liabilities) should be calculated primarily for the purpose of determining possible errors in the classifications of current assets or current liabilities. For example, assume that a company with $100,000 in current assets and $50,000 in current liabilities (a 2 to 1 current ratio) deliberately understated current assets and current liabilities in the amount of $10,000 for checks written but not released as of the balance sheet date. Current asset would appear as $90,000 and current liabilities as $40,000 on the balance sheet. Thus the company's balance sheet shows an erroneous 2.25 to 1 current ratio. The misstatement of these ratios can be particularly important if the firm has been operating under significant net working capital constraints, such as long-term debt with restrictive covenants.
- *Solvency ratios* showing the relationships between debt and equity capital and between earnings and fixed interest charges should be calculated. Deviations from prior periods should then be explained in terms of one of the three changes cited on page 702.

In addition to relating the overall changes to the possible reasons for deviations or possible errors, the auditor must also be concerned with any *indications that the entity may be unable to continue to exist*. A probability that the entity might be forced to discontinue operations would make use of the going concern valuation convention inappropriate. SAS 34 suggests that solvency problems — such as recurring operating losses, working capital deficiencies, negative cash flows from operations, adverse key financial ratios, default on a loan, and other similar occurrences — may cause the auditor to question the continuity of the entity. Other matters — such as losses of key personnel, extensive labor problems, uneconomical long-term commitments, legal problems, loss of franchise, uninsured catastrophes, and other similar problems — may also raise questions regarding continuity.

When a client has experienced some of the problems cited above, the auditor should look for certain mitigating factors before concluding that the going concern assumption is inappropriate. SAS 34 suggests that certain asset, debt, cost, and equity factors that provide alternatives for management would tend to mitigate the conclusion that the firm would be likely to go out of existence. However, if the auditor concludes that substantial doubt remains about the entity's ability to continue to exist, he or she may find it necessary to qualify the audit report for this uncertainty. The required qualification is illustrated in Chapter 18.

REVIEW OF SUPPLEMENTARY DATA

The evidence we have gathered to this point has been designed to help the auditor determine whether he or she can express an opinion that the basic financial statements (balance sheet, income statement, statement of changes in financial position and statement of retained earnings) have been fairly stated. This is interpreted to include the parenthetical comments and footnotes associated with those statements. A typical annual report for a corporation or a 10-K report filed under the Securities Exchange Act of 1934 may include, in addition to the financial statements, a narrative report by management describing the year's operations, consolidating information, historical summaries, or projections of anticipated future trends for the company. Some of this information may be from sources outside the accounting system of the entity. The auditing profession has for some time been concerned about possible inconsistencies between the audited financial data and data outside the basic financial statements in a client's annual report.

Several recent auditing standards have addressed this issue. SAS 8 applies to information contained in annual reports, 10-K reports, and other *documents submitted to investors or creditors by the client;* it requires no audit procedures for this information. Instead, it requires the auditor merely to read the other information for inconsistencies with the information in the audited financial statements. If the auditor concludes that there is a material inconsistency, he or she should consider whether the financial statements or the auditor's report, or both, require revision. If the auditor concludes that neither the statements nor the report requires revision, the client should be requested to revise the other information. If the client declines to do so, the auditor may revise the audit report to include an explanation of the inconsistency. Of course, the more extreme option of withdrawal from the engagement and disassociation of the auditor's name with the statements is always available as well.[5]

If the supplemental data appear in an *auditor-submitted document,* as discussed in SAS 29, the auditor has the option of auditing the other information. If this option is taken, the auditor's report should be extended to express an opinion as to whether the accompanying information is fairly stated in all material respects in relation to the basic financial statements. If the other information is not audited, then the auditor's responsibility is limited to reading the accompanying information for obvious mistakes or inconsistencies with the audited information. If none are found, the auditor's disclaimer of opinion on the supplemental data should accompany the audit report on the basic financial statements.[6]

Recently the SEC, through the medium of Rule 3.17 of regulation S-X and through FASB 33, required the inclusion of current cost and price level adjusted data for inventories and property and equipment as supplementary information in published annual reports of certain larger publicly traded companies. Such data are not audited and are therefore not covered by the audit report. However, SASs 18, 27, and 28 set out the auditor's responsibilities relating to such data.

In general terms, SASs 18, 27, and 28 require that the auditor do the following:

1. *Inquire* of management regarding the methods, sources, assumptions, and judgments used to prepare the information.

2. *Read* the information and evaluate its consistency with management's responses and inquiries and other knowledge obtained during the audit.
3. Consider the *need to include representations* regarding the supplementary information in the management representation letter described later in this chapter.
4. Make any *additional inquiries* considered necessary in the circumstances.

In applying these procedures, the auditor's inquiries should be directed toward management's judgment in measuring and presenting the current cost and price level adjusted data. Accordingly, they should include these elements:

- The sources of information presented for the latest fiscal year and for the five most recent fiscal years, factors considered for selection of such sources, and appropriateness of their application in the circumstances.
- The assumptions and judgments made in calculations of constant dollars and current cost amounts.
- The need to reduce the measurements of inventory and property and equipment from (1) historical cost/constant dollar amounts or (2) current cost amounts to lower recoverable amounts and, if reduction is necessary, the reason for selecting the method used to estimate the recoverable amount and the appropriateness of the application of that method.[7]

If the results of the preceding inquiries and other procedures indicate that the client has fulfilled necessary disclosure requirements of FASB 33, the auditor need make no mention of the supplementary information in the audit report. However, if the auditor's disclosures appear to depart from the FASB guidelines, if the required information is omitted, or if the auditor is unable to complete the prescribed procedures, the auditor should expand the audit report to describe the nature of the misstatement, omission, or limitation in procedures.

STATEMENT OF CHANGES IN FINANCIAL POSITION

The auditing procedures that we have developed to this point in Part III are designed to evaluate the fairness of presentation of individual account balances presented in the income statement, balance sheet, and statement of retained earnings. These are the statements purporting to present the financial position and results of operations of the entity. Generally accepted accounting practices require the inclusion of a statement of changes in financial position with those financial statements before an auditor can render an unqualified opinion regarding financial position and results of operations.[8] Auditors' reports, since the adoption of that pronouncement, have included a specific reference to the statement of changes in financial position in the scope and opinion paragraphs. The omission of the statement of changes in financial position from the statements purporting to present financial position and results of operations is not in accordance with GAAP and therefore requires a qualification of the auditor's report.[9]

The items included in the statement of changes in financial position are *not directly traceable to the account balances* appearing in the client's records. Instead they must be *derived* from those balances by appropriately accounting for changes in the various balance sheet items between the beginning and end of the period under audit. Therefore, in determining whether the statement of changes in financial position has been fairly presented in accordance with GAAP, the auditor must recompute the elements of the statement to verify that they are presented in accordance with the provisions of APB 19. That statement allows the accountant to present the statement of changes in terms of net working capital or cash or some other definition of funds, such as quick assets. Most statements are presented in terms of inflows and outflows of net working capital with certain special interpretations designed to meet the all-financial resources concept of reporting required by APB 19.

In developing the statement of changes relating to net working capital, the accountant must calculate all changes during the year in nonworking capital balance sheet items and classify them into one or more of the following categories:

- Inflows of net working capital.
- Outflows of net working capital.
- Reciprocal changes requiring disclosure in both the sources and uses sections of the statement.
- Adjustments to the inflows and outflows of net working capital.
- Nonfund changes.

The working paper for the preparation of the statement of changes in financial position is illustrated in Appendix 16–D to this chapter.

Net Working Capital Inflows

Changes in the balance sheet accounts outside the net working capital section that are *offset by an increase to current assets or a decrease to current liabilities* are characterized as net working capital inflows and should therefore be included in the section of the statement of changes in financial position that shows the sources of net working capital. Most important of these changes will be net working capital provided by operations, which is net income adjusted for nonworking capital revenue and expense items. The net income figure, which is the first element of net working capital inflows from operations, accounts for part of the change in the retained earnings account balance during the audit period. Other examples of net working capital inflows include cash proceeds from the sale of stock, from the issuance of long-term debt, and from the sale of noncurrent assets. The auditor normally obtains evidence for these items in connection with the detailed audit tests of balances in each of these areas. Therefore at this point the only procedure necessary is to be sure that the inflow is consistent with the changes in each of those items, as documented in the audit working papers.

Outflows of Net Working Capital

Changes in the noncurrent sections of the balance sheet that are *offset by decreases in current assets or increases in current liabilities* represent outflows of net working capital and should show up in the applications (uses) of the net working capital section of the statement of changes in financial position. Such items as increases in noncurrent assets financed by cash or short-term payables, decreases in noncurrent liabilities occurring through payment of such obligations from current assets, or decreases in owner's equity through the redemption of stock or the payment of dividends — all constitute outflows of net working capital. These items, too, should be verified during the auditor's tests of details, as explained in earlier chapters. Again, the only audit procedure necessary at this point is to make sure that the outflow is consistent with the changes in those items.

Reciprocal Changes

These are changes that must be included in the statement because of the all-financial resources provision of APB 19. Acquisitions of noncurrent assets that occur through the assumption of long-term debt or the issuance of capital stock are examples of reciprocal changes: thus, the increases in noncurrent assets should be shown in the uses or applications section of the statement of changes in financial position. At the same time, however, the increase in long-term debt or capital occurring as a result of the issuance of those securities should show up in the sources of net working capital section of the statement. Also, the conversion of debt securities to common stock should be included within this provision as both a source and use in the statement. These are all considered to be *significant financing activities* and for that reason are required to be recognized within the all-financial resources concept of reporting developed in APB 19. These changes, too, should be documented by reference to the working papers covering various asset, liability, or owners' equity accounts.

Adjustments in Arriving at Net Working Capital Inflows

Earlier in this section we stated that the starting point in determining net working capital provided by operations was the net income figure, reflected as part of the change in retained earnings. That figure should be adjusted for certain revenues and expenses included in its determination — revenues that do not provide inflows and expenses that do not cause outflows of net working capital. One of the primary examples of such an adjustment is depreciation expense, which will have been subtracted from revenue in arriving at the net income for the period. Depreciation expense, however, does not represent an outflow of net working capital and should therefore be added back to net income in the statement of changes in financial position as the net income figure is adjusted to show net working capital provided by operations. On the other hand, the provision for uncollectible accounts, because ir represents an adjustment to current assets, would be an expense not requiring an outlay of funds only if the inflows and outflows of funds are shown in terms of cash.

We also subtract revenue or expense reductions included in net income that do not provide inflows of net working capital. The amortization of bond premium is an example of such an item. Since it does not produce an inflow of net working capital, it should be subtracted from net income as that figure is adjusted to show the net working capital provided by operations. The auditor should vouch depreciation and amortization to working papers for property and equipment and long-term debt, respectively, to ascertain that those amounts are correct.

Nonfund Changes

Some changes in the noncurrent sections of the balance sheet should not be recognized as inflows or outflows of funds at all. For example, the declaration and distribution of a stock dividend will decrease retained earnings and increase capital stock and perhaps additional paid-in capital. Such action should be recognized as creating *neither inflows nor outflows of net working capital.* These changes are distinguished from reciprocal changes in that they are omitted completely from the statement. Changes in accounts resulting from such actions are simply eliminated against each other. The logic supporting this treatment is that such a change *does not represent a financing or investing activity* within the definition of those items in APB 19. The auditor should, in performing the procedures discussed above, ascertain that items such as these are excluded from the statement.

SUMMARIZATION AND REVIEW PROCESS

The results of the evidence-gathering process are all contained in working papers such as those included as appendixes to the various chapters of this book. It is important to remember that, after the audit of a particular system and related account balances (including analytical review, if appropriate) has been completed, that section of the working papers should stand on its own and the auditor should be able to draw appropriate conclusions from it. For example, after the audit of the sales and accounts receivable system has been completed (including analysis of ratios and trends, as well as all compliance and substantive tests), the auditor should be able to state whether all the related accounts (sales, accounts receivable, allowance for doubtful accounts, bad debts expense, etc.) are fairly presented in accordance with GAAP. To the extent possible, all appropriate procedures applied to a system (from preliminary review of internal control through final analytical review) should be completed as a unit so that the audit work can then be subjected to a timely review by audit supervisory personnel.

The audit process almost always generates the need for certain adjusting entries that the auditor feels should be made to allow the financial statements to be fairly presented in accordance with GAAP. Such entries are typically recorded in the working trial balance and in a separate list of auditor's adjustments prepared primarily for the client. We should point out that the *client must approve these adjustments* before they can be incorporated in the financial statements. Adjusting journal entries should also be posted to the lead schedules and individual working papers so that their totals will agree with adjusted amounts for each account balance on the adjusted trial balance.

The relationships among the different elements of the working papers were depicted in Figure 3–4. The lead schedules and supporting schedules included in that figure have been presented as appendixes to various preceding chapters of the text. Illustrations of working trial balances for the balance sheet and income statement items, adjusting entries, and reclassifying journal entries are included in appendixes to this chapter. After the working trial balance has been completed, formal statements should be prepared from the adjusted data. Those are the statements on which the auditor expresses an opinion.

The working papers should also include a *letter of representation* from the client, documenting management's oral representations during the audit. This document is required by SAS 19, which suggests 20 specific matters that should be included in the letter.[10] The primary purposes of this letter are to impress upon management its responsibilities for the data included in the financial statements and to document the oral responses to auditors' inquiries from management relating to the various parts of the audit. While a management representation letter must be included as part of the audit working papers, it should not be regarded as a substitute for more direct and reliable evidence. It does, however, provide some evidence and it documents the fact that the auditor has asked management certain questions relating to the financial statements. Figure 16–2 contains an example of a typical client representation letter.[11] The letter should be dated to coincide with the date of the audit report.

After the working papers have been summarized, they will be subjected to a series of reviews. Usually, at least three reviews are conducted by separate persons, starting with the accountant in charge of the audit engagement and culminating with the review of the partner supervising the audits of the industry in which the client operates. The relationship between authority and the review processes is shown in Figure 16–3. The review process is directed toward three goals, namely:

- Evaluating performance of audit staff.
- Making sure that the audit meets the accounting firm's standard of performance.
- Counteracting any bias that may enter in to the auditor's judgment.

As the working papers move through the review process, from the initial review by the immediate supervisor of the audit staff toward final review by the partner supervising audits in the industry, it typically proceeds from a review of particulars at the lowest level to a review for general reasonableness at the partner level. For example, the supervisor will be concerned with checking such things as mathematical accuracy, the appropriate identification of various working papers, and the adequacy of the content of individual working papers. As the review process moves toward the partner level, attention must be given to the overall adequacy of the evidence, the reasonableness of the conclusions reached, and the adequacy of disclosure in the financial statements.

Because the working papers reflect the auditor's documentation of the evidence in support of the audit report, attention must ultimately be given to judging *whether the data included in the working papers make the auditor's opinion legally defensible*. It is important, for example, that the reviewers make sure that there are no unanswered questions, ambiguous conclusions, or inconsistent evaluations which would make the legal defense of the audit opinion vulnerable.

SUBSEQUENT EVENTS

The third standard of reporting states that adequate disclosures are presumed to exist in the financial statements unless otherwise stated in the audit report. This means in part that, in fulfilling the *cutoff* and *statement presentation* objectives, the auditor must be satisfied that all elements in the financial statements relate to the audit period and that all significant financial facts are disclosed. Transactions or events may occur

CLIENT COMPANY
Anywhere, USA

(Date of auditor's report)

Client's Independent Auditor
Anywhere, USA

Gentlemen:

In connection with your examination of our financial statements for the fiscal year ending 12/31/19X2, for the purpose of expressing an opinion as to whether those statements present fairly the financial position, results of operations, and changes in financial position of our company in conformity with generally accepted accounting principles, we confirm to the best of our knowledge and belief the following representations made to you during your examination:

1. We are responsible for the fair presentation in the financial statements of financial position, results of operations, and changes in financial position in accordance with generally accepted accounting principles.

2. We have made available to you all
   a. Financial records and related data.
   b. Minutes of the meetings of stockholders, directors, committees of directors, or summaries of actions of recent meetings for which minutes have not yet been prepared.

3. There have been no
   a. Irregularities involving management or employees who have significant roles in the system of internal accounting control.
   b. Irregularities involving other employees that could have a material effect on the financial statements.
   c. Communications from regulatory agencies concerning noncompliance with or deficiencies in financial reporting practices that could have a material effect on the financial statements.

4. We have no plans or intentions that may materially affect the carrying values or classifications of assets and liabilities.

5. The following have been properly recorded or disclosed in the financial statements:
   [Here will be listed the various items covered in SAS 19].

Sincerely,

Chief Executive Officer

Chief Financial Officer

FIGURE 16–2. Illustrative Client Representation Letter

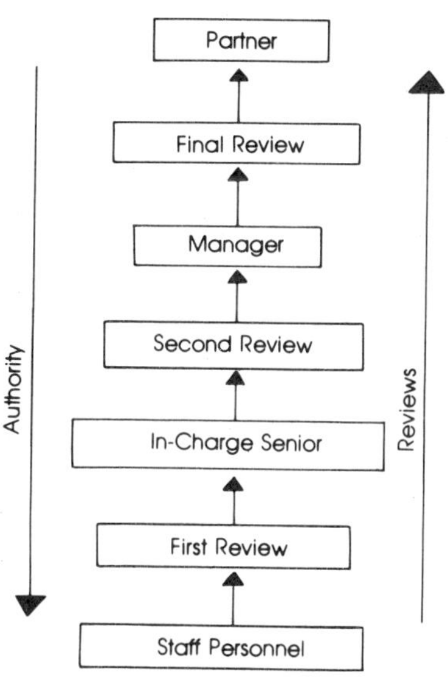

FIGURE 16–3. Relationship Between Authority and the Review Process

after the balance sheet date and before the issuance of the audit report, which, because of the hindsight they provide, affect the disclosures on the client's financial statements. We call these *subsequent events.*[12] The search for unrecorded liabilities continues through an examination of events subsequent to the balance sheet date; the discovery of an unrecorded liability is an example of a subsequent event. The auditor may need to adjust account balances or disclose the nature of the events for any of these transactions or events that have a material effect on the balances shown in the financial statements or on the interpretation of those data to meet the requirements of generally accepted accounting principles. Therefore, the auditor's formal review of subsequent events should be extended through the date of the auditor's report.

There are generally two types of subsequent events requiring the auditor's consideration. The level of disclosure that each demands depends on two things: the date of the causal event and the date of the culminating transaction.

In Figure 16–4 we relate the two types of subsequent events to the level of disclosure required for them.

The first type of subsequent event provides additional evidence with respect to conditions that existed as of the balance sheet date. By this we mean that the cause of the *change in the financial picture was present before the end of the period under audit.* Therefore the change should show up in the financial statements. When the auditor learns after the balance sheet date that a culminating transaction or event has occurred which affects the financial statements under audit, the client should be asked to *adjust the financial statements* to reflect the more recent (and more accurate) information. Examples of Type 1 subsequent events are these:

	Date of Causal Event	Date of Culminating Transaction	Level of Disclosure Necessary
Type 1	Before balance sheet date	After balance sheet date	Adjust financial statements
Type 2	After balance sheet date	After balance sheet date	Disclose in footnotes

Figure 16–4. Subsequent Events and the Auditor's Responsibilities for Disclosure

- Bankruptcy of a client's customer whose now uncollectible balance is included in accounts receivable as of the balance sheet date. Accounts receivable as of the end of the audit period should be reduced by the amount of the uncollectible account.
- Settlement of an estimated liability such as pending litigation or an income tax liability after the balance sheet date for an amount different from that shown on the balance sheet. Again, the liability account should be adjusted to show the final settlement figure.
- Payment of a claim disclosed as a contingent liability at the balance sheet date. For example, a charge to notes receivable in the cash disbursements journal during the period subsequent to the balance sheet date could reflect the settlement of an endorser's contingent liability. In that case the contingent liability should be recognized as an accrued liability.
- Discovery of an unrecorded liability.

The second type of subsequent event consists of events *whose causal and culminating factors both occurred after the balance sheet date.* If the nature of the event is of such importance that it would affect user interpretations of the financial data, the events should be disclosed in the footnotes to the financial statements. Occasionally an event such as this might be so significant that disclosure can best be accomplished by presenting pro forma statements in the footnotes. However, only narrative footnote disclosure is generally required. Type 2 subsequent events that may require disclosure (but not adjustments) in the financial statements are these:

- Sale of bond or capital stock issue.
- Purchase of a business.
- Settlement of litigation where the event giving rise to the claim occurred subsequent to the balance sheet date.
- Loss of plant or inventories as a result of casualty.
- Losses of receivables resulting from conditions such as a customer's major casualty arising subsequent to the balance sheet date.

Subsequent events of the types described in the preceding paragraphs are typically discovered by performing the following procedures during final stages of the audit fieldwork:

1. *Inspecting* the latest available interim financial statements of the client and comparing them with disclosures made in the audited financial statements.
2. *Inquiring* of officers and other persons in authority as to whether:

a. any substantial contingent liabilities or commitments existed either at the balance sheet date or at the date the inquiry is made;
b. any substantial changes were made in the capital structure of the company between the balance sheet date and the date of the audit report;
c. there has been any change in the current status of items in the financial statements that were originally accounted for on the basis of tentative or inconclusive data or any unusual adjustments that were made during the subsequent events period.

3. *Inspecting* the minutes of meetings held between the end of the audit period and the date of completion of field work.
4. *Inquiring* of client's legal counsel concerning claims, litigation, and assessments.
5. *Obtaining a client representation letter* with regard to subsequent events.

EVENTS SUBSEQUENT TO THE ISSUANCE OF FINANCIAL STATEMENTS

The procedures discussed to this point are ***overt auditing procedures,*** which must be performed before the issuance of the audit report. They are typically completed as of the date the audit field work is finished. After the audit report has been signed, the role of the auditor shifts from an active to a passive one. This means that the auditor no longer has a responsibility for actively seeking additional audit evidence after the last day of audit field work. However, he or she must still be alert for subsequent discovery of facts that existed at the date of the audit report and that would have affected the financial statements had they been known at that time.

Events Discovered Before the Issuance of the Audit Report

The responsibility for events that come to the auditor's attention after the last day of field work depends on whether the events occur (1) during the brief period after the last day of field work and before the actual issuance of the audit report or (2) after the issuance of the audit report. In the first situation there is still time to intervene in the process before the report is issued if new information comes to the auditor's attention. If such information is, in the auditor's judgment, material enough to warrant inclusion in the financial statements, it must be identified as either a Type 1 or Type 2 event. If it is a Type 1 event, the financial statements should be adjusted and the audit report will bear the same date as the original report.

If it is a Type 2 event requiring only footnote disclosure, the auditor may follow either of two courses of action. If the event is isolated, and no other events of importance have transpired since the last day of field work, the report may be dual dated. Within this arrangement, the opinion as to the newly discovered event disclosed in the footnote is dated as of the date of discovery of that event. The opinion as to the remainder of the disclosures will carry the original date. In this case, the auditor's responsibility for events occurring in the period subsequent to the end of the audit field work is limited to the event referred to in the latter footnote. On the other hand, if the auditor feels there is a strong possibility that other events may have occurred since the conclusion of field work, subsequent-events field work procedures may be performed up to the date of discovery of the new information. In this case, the entire audit report will be dated as of the date of discovery of the new information,[13] and the auditor's responsibility for events occurring in the subsequent period is extended to the date of discovery of the new information.

Subsequent Discovery of Facts Existing at Audit Report Date

After the completed financial statements and auditor's report are released to the public, the auditor *continues to have a passive responsibility* with respect to material facts existing at the audit report date, that were not disclosed because they were not known to the auditor at the time the report was issued. Responsibility for subsequent discovery of facts existing at the date of the audit report is governed by the provisions of SAS 1, Section 561.

Under this standard, the auditor has no responsibility for actively searching for erroneous or omitted financial statement disclosures after the report date. However, he or she cannot ignore material facts that come to light after that date if these facts would have had to be disclosed had they been known. Investors and other financial statement users are in possession of information the auditor now knows to be erroneous. Furthermore, they may be relying on such information to make important financial decisions regarding the client. Therefore, the auditor must take steps to correct the disclosures.[14]

Once the auditor determines that the information about erroneous or omitted facts is reliable and that it existed at the date of the audit report, he or she should request the client to make appropriate disclosures of the newly discovered facts, along with the financial statement impact, to persons who are known to be currently relying or who are likely to rely on the financial statements and audit report.[15]

If effects can be promptly determined, revised disclosures should consist of revised financial statements and audit report. When issuance of audited financial statements of a subsequent period is close at hand, revised disclosures may be made in those statements. If effects of misstatements cannot be promptly determined, the client should be asked to notify relying parties that the erroneous financial statements and audit report are not to be relied upon, and that revised financial statements and audit report will be issued upon completion of an investigation. Where annual reports or registration statements of publicly traded companies are involved, appropriate disclosure would include notification of the SEC.

If the auditor learns that client management refuses to make the appropriate disclosure of facts as described in the preceding paragraphs, he or she should undertake the following actions:

1. Notify each member of the client's board of directors of management's refusal to disclose important facts.
2. Notify the client that the audit report should no longer be associated with the financial statements.
3. Notify regulatory agencies having jurisdiction over the client that the audit report should no longer be relied upon.
4. Notify each party known by the auditor to be relying on the financial statements that the audit report should no longer be relied upon.

In all cases in which subsequent discovery of important facts existing at the audit report date arises, the auditor would be well advised to consult with legal counsel because of the possible legal implications of those events.

SUMMARY

In this chapter we have discussed the completion of the evidence-gathering phase of the audit, in which the auditor finishes field-work tests and prepares to issue the audit report. We began with a discussion of the search for and verification of estimated and contingent liabilities, including those arising from possible claims, litigation, or assessments. Then we discussed the post–balance sheet analytical review, during which the auditor forms conclusions about the relationships between findings from tests of details and the more general overview of relationships between audited account balances and the adequacy of footnotes.

The auditor's responsibilities with respect to supplementary data — such as historical summaries, statistical summaries, and other data outside the basic financial statements — were taken up next. We also discussed at some length the procedures involved in verifying the elements of the statement of changes in financial position. The review process for working papers, including procedures directed at evaluating the sufficiency and competency of evidence, was examined in this section.

In the last part of the chapter we defined subsequent events and discussed their effects on the audited financial statements and the audit report. Finally we described the auditor's reactions to the subsequent discovery of facts existing at the date of the audit report. In that section we considered the differences between the auditor's responsibilities while performing an active role in the evidence-gathering process and the passive role assumed after the audit report date.

APPENDIX 16–A: Working Trial Balance — Assets

JEP Manufacturing Co.
Working Trial Balance - Assets
3-31-X1

W. P. No.	A-1
ACCOUNTANT	SmG
DATE	4/28/X1

Assets	Adjusted Balance ∆ 3-31-X0	Balance per G/L ✓ 3-31-X1	Adjustments DR.	Adjustments CR.
Cash	84519 72	36928 93		
Marketable Securities	148948 00	343272 00		
Accounts Receivable				
Trade	535313 96	1008070 47		
Other (Details Deleted)	22739 25	9117 97		
Notes Receivable	6400 00	5400 00		
Costs + Estimated Earnings	1104937 12	—	<2> 904138 95	
Deposits	5761 25	6311 25		
Prepaid Expenses	28935 06	26818 55	<100> 1083 28	
Inventory:				
Raw Materials	591516 96	4064686 83	<103> 647417 23	<103> 4054765 90 <102> 9921 13
Work in Process	111421 90	927741 61	<103> 900577 33	<2> 706082 52 <103> 927741 61
In-Transit	24300 77	31306 01		<3> 34288 63
Obsolete		55798 89	<104> 34288 63	<104> 55798 89
Total Current Assets	2664784 09	6515452 51	2487505 42	5788598 48
Property, Plant and Equipment				
Machinery and Equipment	545592 69	583359 23		
Other (Details Deleted)	1188174 67	1256536 29		
Less: Accumulated Depreciation	⟨687592 01⟩	⟨773050 00⟩		
Net Property, Plant, & Equip.	1046175 35	1066845 52		
Investment in Subsidiary	179119 00	—	<4> 204143 00	<5> 9819 00
Cash Surrender Value of Life Ins.	125500 00	145300 00		
Less: Policy Loan	⟨76500 00⟩	⟨76500 00⟩		
Deferred Debt Expense	4827 30	3701 46		
Total Assets	3943905 74	7654799 49	2691648 42	5798417 48

∆ Agreed to prior year working papers.
✓ Agreed to 3-31-X1 general ledgers.

Adjusted Balance 3-31-X1	Reclassifications DR.	Reclassifications CR.	Reclassified Balance 3-31-X1		Working Paper Reference
36928 93	⟨D⟩ 886 00		37814 93		B
343272 00			343272 00		C-1
1008070 47			1008070 47		E
9117 97		⟨E⟩ 2155 50	6962 47		(omitted)
5400 00			5400 00		(omitted)
904138 95			904138 95		F
6311 25			6311 25		G
27901 83			27901 83		G
647417 23			647417 23		F
194494 81			194494 81		
31306 01			31306 01		
–					
3214359 45	886 00	2155 50	3213089 95		
583359 23			583359 23		I
1256536 29			1256536 29		
⟨773050 00⟩			⟨773050 00⟩		I
1066845 52			1066845 52		
194324 00			194324 00		(omitted)
145300 00			145300 00		L
⟨76500 00⟩			⟨76500 00⟩		L
3701 46			3701 46		(omitted)
4548030 43	886 00	2155 50	4546760 93		

APPENDIX 16–B: Working Trial Balance — Liabilities and Stockholders' Equities

JEP Manufacturing Co.
Working Trial Balance
Liabilities and Stockholder Equity
3-31-X1

W. P. No.	A-2
ACCOUNTANT	Smdg
DATE	4/28/X1

Liabilities	Adjusted Balance ∆ 3-31-X0	Balance Per G/L ✓ 3-31-X1	Adjustments DR.	Adjustments CR.
Current:				
Accounts Payable	500410 55	501915 83		
Intercompany Payable (Net)	–	–		
Notes Payable – Banks	175000 00	–		
Current Maturities of Long-Term				⟨105⟩ 45783 00
Accrued Expenses	232269 04	152132 31		⟨107⟩ 35302 88 ⟨108⟩ 48700 00 ⟨106⟩ 65000 00
Reserve Allowance		194324 00		
Federal Income Taxes Payable				
Current	4106 68	⟨193331 32⟩		⟨109⟩ 406376 62 ⟨6⟩ 58847 32 ⟨7⟩ 8054 63
Deferred	123599 66			
Dividends Payable – Preferred	903 00	–		
Total Current	1036288 93	655040 82		668064 75
Deferred Income	–	41778 53	⟨101⟩ 233 32 ⟨104⟩ 4603 17 ⟨3⟩ 36825 36	
Notes Payable				
Coletrain	59650 00	29825 00		
Xerox	–	6893 70		
Prudential	400000 00	350000 00		
Total Liabilities	1495938 93	1083538 05	41661 85	668064 45
Stockholders' Equity:				
Treasury Stock	⟨10121 67⟩	⟨10121 67⟩		
Preferred Stock	60200 00	–		
Common Stock	75994 76	75994 76		
Additional Paid-in Capital	34638 50	34638 50		
Retained Earnings	2287255 22	1976447 51	⟨7⟩ 8054 63 ⟨5⟩ 7903 00 ⟨6⟩ 123599 66 ⟨3⟩ 14370 36	⟨4⟩ 187022 00 ⟨1⟩ 276358 36
Current year earnings – Net		4494302 34	4042624 37	
Total Stockholders' Equity	2447966 81	6571261 44	4196552 02	463380 36
Total liabilities + Stockholder Equity	3943905 74	7654799 49	4238213 87	1131444 81

∆ Agreed to prior year's working papers.
✓ Agreed to 3-31-X1 general ledger.

Adjusted Balance 3-31-X1	Reclassifications DR.	Reclassifications CR.	Reclassified Balance 3-31-X1		Working Paper Reference
501915 83	<E> 262406 43		239509 40		N-1
		<E> 260250 93	260250 93		N-1
–			–		M
		<C> 81302 20	81302 20		Ma
346918 19		<D> 886 00	347804 19		Omitted
194324 00			194324 00		Omitted
213045 30	<F> 10316 00		202729 30		
66901 75		<F> 10316 00	77217 95		
–			–		
1323105 27	262406 43	342439 13	1403137 97		
116 68			116 68		Omitted
29825 00	<C> 29825 00		-0-		M
6893 70	<C> 1477 20		5416 50		M
350000 00	<C> 50000 00		300000 00		M
1709940 65	343708 63	342439 13	1708671 15		
<10121 67>			<10121 67>		u
–			–		
75994 76			75994 76		u
34638 50			34638 50		u
2285900 22					
			2737578 19		u
451677 77					u
2838089 78			2838089 78		
4548030 43	343708 63	342439 13	4546760 93		

APPENDIX 16–C: Working Trial Balance — Income Statement

JEP Manufacturing Co.	W. P. No.	A-3
Trial Balance -- Income Statement	ACCOUNTANT	Smds
3-31-X1	DATE	4-28-X1

	Adjusted Balance Δ 3-31-X0	Balance per Gen. Ledger 3-31-X1	Adjustments DR.	Adjustments CR.
Net Sales	6522896 05	8033080 36	<2> 22264 30 <1> 181004 49	<1> 22627 49 <2> 987150 35
Cost of Sales	4939060 41	2267916 53	<2> 706082 52 <104> 16907 09 <103> 5702429 28	<3> 16907 09 <103> 2267916 53 <1> 828578 76
Gross Profit	1583835 64	5765163 83	7628687 68	4123180 22
Selling, Administrative Expenses	969151 19	1210329 21	<106> 65000 00 <105> 45783 00 <102> 9921 13 <107> 35302 88 <108> 48700 00 <2> 60747 10	<100> 1083 28 <1> 53439 88
Motor Control Devices	40501 20	50921 52		
Operating Income	574183 25	4503913 10	7894141 79	4177703 38
Interest and Other Income	51312 78	51932 71		<101> 233 32
Equity in Earnings of Subsidiary	34668 00	—	<5> 1916 00	<4> 17121 00
Interest and Debt Expense	80887 60	61543 47		
Earnings before F.I.T.	579276 43	4494302 34	7896057 79	4195057 70
Federal Income Taxes: Current	180107 01	—	<109> 406376 62	
Federal Income Taxes: Deferred	51070 66	—		<6> 64752 34
	231177 67	—	406376 62	64752 34
Net Earnings	348098 76	4494302 34	8302434 41	4259810 04

Δ Agreed to prior year's working papers.
✓ Agreed to 3-31-X1 general ledger.

Adjusted Balance 3-31-X1	Reclassifications DR.	Reclassifications CR.	Reclassified Balance 3-31-X1		W/Paper Reference
7839589 41			7839589 41		X
5579933 04			5579933 04		X-4
2259656 37			2259656 37		
1421260 16			1421260 16		X-2
50921 52			50921 52		X-4-1
787474 69			787474 69		
52166 03			52166 03		X-7-1
15205 00			15205 00		AA-9
61543 47			61543 47		M
793302 25			793302 25		
406376 62		<F> 8054 00	398322 62		P-4
<647523 47>	<F> 8054 00		<566983 34>		P-4
341624 28	8054 00	8054 00	341624 28		
451677 97	8054 00	8054 00	451677 97		

APPENDIX 16–D: Statement of Changes in Financial Position

JEP Manufacturing Co.
Statement of Changes in Financial Position
Working Paper
3-31-X1

W. P. No. A-4
ACCOUNTANT JG
DATE 5-21-X1

	3-31-X0	3-31-X1	Change In Working Capital: Increase	Change In Working Capital: Decrease
Current Assets (Details omitted)	2501022	2869818	368796	
Long-Term Assets				
Noncurrent Receivables	1200	—		
Property & Equipment (Net)	1046176	1066846		
Investment in Subsidiary	328067	343272		
Cash Surr. Val. - Life Ins.	49000	68800		
Deferred Charges	4827	3701		
Total Assets	3930292	4352437		
Current Liabilities (Details Omitted)	1102500	1208930		106430
Long-Term Liabilities				
Notes Payable	379825	305417		
Stockholders' Equity				
Treasury Stock	‹10121›	‹10121›		
Preferred Stock	60200	—		
Common Stock	75995	75995		
Additional Paid-in Capital	34638	34638		
Retained Earnings	2287255	2737578		
Total Liabilities & Equity	3930292	4352437		
				262366
			368796	368796

Change in non-Current Accounts Debit	Change in non-Current Accounts Credit	Working Capital Source	Working Capital Use	Working Paper Reference	Explanation
				Various	
	1200	1200			
20670		85458 ①	106128 ②	I	① Depreciation ② Additions
15205		[illegible]	19121		
19800			19800	L	
	1126	1126			
				Various	
74408			74408	M	
60200			60200	U	
	450323	451678	1355	U	
262366			262366		
452649	452649	541378	541378		

APPENDIX 16–E: Adjusting Journal Entries

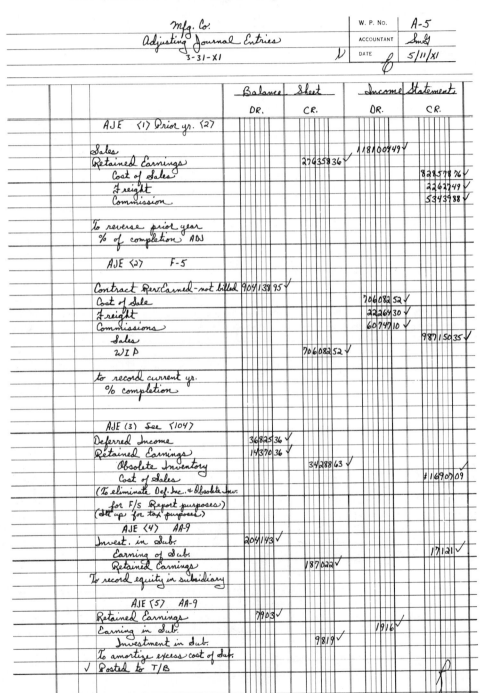

Mfg. Co.
Adjusting Journal Entries
3-31-X1

W. P. No.	A-5
ACCOUNTANT	SmG
DATE	5/11/X1

	Balance Sheet DR.	Balance Sheet CR.	Income Statement DR.	Income Statement CR.
AJE ⟨1⟩ Prior yr. ⟨2⟩				
Sales			1181004 49 ✓	
Retained Earnings		276358 36 ✓		
Cost of Sales				828578 76 ✓
Freight				22627 49 ✓
Commission				53439 88 ✓
To reverse prior year % of completion ADJ				
AJE ⟨2⟩ F-5				
Contract Rev. Earned—not billed	904138 95 ✓			
Cost of Sale			706082 52 ✓	
Freight			22264 30 ✓	
Commissions			60747 10 ✓	
Sales				987150 35 ✓
WIP		706082 52 ✓		
to record current yr. % completion				
AJE (3) See ⟨104⟩				
Deferred Income	36825 36 ✓			
Retained Earnings	14370 36 ✓			
Obsolete Inventory		34288 63 ✓		
Cost of Sales				16907 09 ✓
(To eliminate Def. Inc. & Obsolete Inv. for F/S Report purposes) (Set up for tax purposes)				
AJE ⟨4⟩ AA-9				
Invest. in Sub.	204143 ✓			
Earning of Sub.				17121 ✓
Retained Earnings		187022 ✓		
To record equity in subsidiary				
AJE ⟨5⟩ AA-9				
Retained Earnings	7903 ✓			
Earning in Sub.			1916 ✓	
Investment in Sub.		9819 ✓		
To amortize excess cost of Sub.				
✓ Posted to T/B				

Note: Other adjusting journal entries have been omitted.

APPENDIX 16–F: Reclassifying Journal Entries

JEP Mfg. Co.
Reclassifying Journal Entries
3-31-X1

W. P. No.	A-6
ACCOUNTANT	Smd
DATE	5/11/X1

			Balance Sheet		Income Statement	
			DR.	CR.	DR.	CR.
		RJE ⟨A⟩ E-4				
		Receivable from East Texas	2155 50			
		Misc. Receivables		2155 50 ②		
		(To properly reflect receivable from East Tex. for consolidating purposes)				
		RJE ⟨B⟩ N-1-2				
		Accounts Payable	262406 43 ①			
		Intercompany Pay to ET		262406 43		
		(To reclass A/P to East Tx. Dist.)				
		RJE ⟨C⟩ Ma				
		Xerox N/P	1477 20 ✓			
		Prudential N/P	50000 00 ✓			
		Caldwell N/P	29825 00 ✓			
		Current Portion L-T Debt		81302 20 ✓		
		(to reclassify the current portion of Long-Term Debt				
		RJE ⟨D⟩ O-1				
		Cash	886 00 ✓			
		Accrued Expenses		886 00 ✓		
		(To properly reflect deposit-in-transit from East Texas)				
		RJE ⟨E⟩ Net of ⟨A⟩ + ⟨B⟩				
		Accounts Payable N-1	262406 43 ① ✓			
		Intercompany Payable		260250 93 ✓		
		Misc. Receivables		2155 50 ②		
late		RJE ⟨F⟩ P-4				
		Deferred tax expense			8054 ✓	
		Current tax liability	10316 ✓			
		Current tax expense				8054 ✓
		Def. tax liability		10316 ✓		
		to properly classify current & def. FIT provision at 3-31-X1				
	✓	Posted to T/B.				

Note: Other reclassifying journal entries have been omitted.

NOTES

1. Developed from appendix to Statement on Auditing Standards (SAS) 12 (New York: AICPA, 1976), pp. 8 and 9.

2. Developed from requirements set out in SAS 12.

3. Materials in this section were developed from SAS 23 (New York: AICPA, 1978), with some direct quotations from that statement.

4. The Statistical Technique for Analytical Review (STAR) developed by Deloitte Haskins & Sells is an example of this technique.

5. SAS 8 (New York: AICPA, 1975).

6. SAS 29 (New York: AICPA, 1980).

7. SAS 28 (New York: AICPA, 1980). See also SAS 27 (1979) and SAS 18 (1977).

8. APB Opinion 19 (New York: AICPA, 1971).

9. SAS 1, Section 545.04 (New York: AICPA, 1973).

10. SAS 19, paragraph 4. (New York: AICPA, 1977).

11. Developed from illustration in SAS 19 (New York: AICPA, 1977).

12. SAS 1, Section 560.

13. Ibid., Section 530.

14. Ibid., Section 561.

15. This section does not apply to situations arising from developments or events occurring after the date of the auditor's report. Neither does it apply to ultimate resolutions or final determinations of matters that were contingent on some future event as of the date of the issuance of the report (such as litigation) or to other matters that had been adequately disclosed in the financial statements as of the report issuance date.

QUESTIONS FOR CLASS DISCUSSION

Q16–1 What is meant by the term *analytical review*?

Q16–2 What is the difference between an estimated liability and a contingent liability?

Q16–3 Why does the auditor analyze the client's legal expense account? Explain.

Q16–4 What are some procedures which, even though performed primarily for the other purposes, may disclose contingent liabilities? What liabilities would you expect to discover in performing each of those procedures?

Q16–5 What is the purpose of the attorney's confirmation letter? What items are included in that letter?

Q16–6 How should the auditor react to a failure of the client's attorney to reply to the attorney's confirmation letter? Explain.

Q16–7 What is the basic assumption underlying the analytical review process? Explain.

Q16–8 How does the auditor use nonfinancial data in the analytical review process?

Q16–9 What does the auditor do in the event that significant variations or unusual relationships are discovered in the analytical review process?

Q16–10 How are industry statistics used in the analytical review process? Explain.

Q16–11 What are the analytical ratios typically calculated during the performance of analytical review procedures? Explain how each of those ratios is used in making judgments regarding the fairness of presentation of the financial data.

Q16–12 What is the auditor's responsibility relating to supplementary data provided by management in the annual report containing audited financial statements? Explain.

Q16–13 What is the auditor's responsibility for the data on price level and current value included with the financial statements as required by FASB 33?

Q16–14 How does the audit of items appearing in the statement of changes in financial position differ from the procedures followed in auditing balance sheet and income statement accounts?

Q16–15 How should one classify the various types of items included in a statement of changes in financial position? Describe the classifications.

Q16–16 What is meant by a *reciprocal change item* in the statement of changes in financial position? Give two examples of such changes.

Q16–17 How does the treatment of the provision for uncollectible accounts in the statement of changes in financial position differ when we are using a cash-oriented rather than a working capital-oriented statement? Explain.

Q16–18 What is the general content of the letter of representation which the auditor secures from the client? What purposes does such a letter serve?

Q16–19 What steps are included in the typical public accounting firm's working paper review process? Describe them.

Q16–20 What is the auditor's responsibility relating to transactions and events occurring in the client's business between the end of the audit period and the date of the audit report? How does the auditor react to the discovery of these events?

Q16–21 What are at least two subsequent events that could occur between the end of the period under audit and the date of the audit report causing the auditor to revise items in the financial statements?

Q16–22 What three or more actions might the client take between the end of the period under audit and the date of the audit report that would require disclosure in the end-of-the-period financial statements? Justify your action in each situation.

Q16–23 How do the auditor's responsibilities relating to subsequent events change after the audit report has been issued? Explain.

Q16–24 Facts existing prior to the date of the audit report that significantly affect the audited financial statements of the client are discovered after the audit report has been issued; how should the auditor react to this situation? Explain.

SHORT CASES

C16–1 Arthur Olsen, CPA, is auditing the RCT Manufacturing Company as of February 28, 19X5. As with all engagements, one of Arthur's initial procedures is to make overall checks of the client's financial data by reviewing significant ratios and trends so that he has a better understanding of the business and can determine where to concentrate his audit efforts.

The financial statements prepared by the client with audited 19X4 figures and preliminary 19X5 figures are presented in condensed form in the accompanying table (p. 731).

Required:

a. For each year, compute the current ratio and a turnover ratio for accounts receivable. Using these ratios, identify and discuss audit procedures that should be included in Olsen's audit of (1) accounts receivable and (2) accounts payable.

b. Compute the ratios of cost of goods sold to sales, gross margin to sales, and expenses to sales; on the basis of these comparative ratios, discuss whether any further audit attention might be advisable.

(AICPA adapted)

C16–2 During the initial planning stages of the audit, a CPA may place emphasis on analytical review procedures. These procedures usually include computation of ratios, which are compared with prior years' ratios or industry-wide norms over several years.

Required:

a. Discuss at least three things that analytical review can reveal to an auditor during the initial planning phases of the audit.

b. Using the information in Chapters 4 and 16, list at least ten ratios that may be useful to the auditor during the initial planning phase of the audit. For each ratio listed, name the two (or more) accounts used in its computation.

c. What can use and comparison of client ratios with industry ratios tell the auditor?

d. When a CPA discovers that there has been a significant change in a ratio when compared to the past three or four years' ratios, he or she considers the possible reasons for such a change. Give possible reasons for the following significant changes in ratios:

   (1) The rate of inventory turnover has decreased from the prior year's rate, while gross profit has decreased.

   (2) The rate of inventory turnover has decreased from the prior year's rate, while gross profit has increased.

   (3) The number of days sales in receivables has increased while the ratio of the allowance for doubtful accounts to receivables has increased.

   (4) The number of days sales in receivables has increased while the ratio of the allowance for doubtful accounts to receivables has decreased.

RCT Manufacturing Company
CONDENSED BALANCE SHEETS
February 28, 19X5 and 19X4

Assets	**19X5**	**19X4**
Cash	$ 12,000	$ 15,000
Accounts receivable, net	93,000	50,000
Inventory	72,000	67,000
Other current assets	5,000	6,000
Plant and equipment, net of depreciation	60,000	80,000
	$242,000	$218,000

Equities		
Accounts payable	$ 38,000	$ 41,000
Federal income tax payable	30,000	14,400
Long-term liabilities	20,000	40,000
Common stock	70,000	70,000
Retained earnings	84,000	52,600
	$242,000	$218,000

RCT Manufacturing Company
CONDENSED INCOME STATEMENTS
Years Ended February 28, 19X5 and 19X4

	19X5	**19X4**
Net sales	$1,684,000	$1,250,000
Cost of goods sold	927,000	710,000
Gross margin on sales	757,000	540,000
Selling and administrative expenses	682,000	504,000
Income before federal income taxes	75,000	36,000
Income tax expense	30,000	14,400
Net income	$ 45,000	$ 21,600

Additional information: (1) The company has only an insignificant amount of cash sales. (2) The end-of-year figures are comparable to the average for each respective year.

C16–3 Marta Antonio, CPA, is conducting the 19X7 audit of the financial statements of Johnson Company and has been given the following statement of changes in financial position:

Johnson Company
STATEMENT OF CHANGES IN FINANCIAL POSITION
For the Year Ended December 31, 19X7
(Amounts in thousands)

Funds provided:	
Operations:	
Net income from operations	$46,000
Add or (deduct) items not requiring outlay of working capital in the current period:	
Depreciation	5,500
Deferred income taxes	1,500
Investment in unconsolidated subsidiary (net of cash dividends paid)	(1,700)*
From operations prior to extraordinary loss	51,300
Extraordinary loss	(13,000)
From operations after extraordinary loss	38,300
Proceeds from exercise of stock options	2,700 *
Total	$41,000

Funds Used:	
Cash dividends paid on common and preferred stock	$15,000 *
Increase in long-term investments (net of allowance)	3,000 } *
Allowance for unrealized losses on noncurrent marketable equity securities	5,000 } *
Increase in working capital	18,000
Total	$41,000

Changes in Working Capital, Increase (Decrease):	
Cash and short-term investments	$(9,000)
Accounts receivable	17,000
Inventories	18,000
Accounts payable and accrued liabilities	(7,000)
Other current assets and liabilities	(1,000)
Increase in working capital	$18,000

Antonio has completed necessary auditing procedures on the balance sheet, income statement, and statement of stockholders' equity and is satisfied that these statements are fairly presented with adequate disclosures in the statements and in the footnotes. Antonio has not yet examined the statement of changes in financial position.

Required:

a. What general steps should be followed by Antonio to examine the statement of changes in financial position of the Johnson Company? *Do not discuss the presentation or verification of any specific item on the statement.*
b. What additional specific steps should Antonio follow to verify each of the four items marked with an asterisk (*) on the statement of changes in financial position of the Johnson Company?

(AICPA adapted)

C16–4 You are examining the financial statements of Moderate Manufacturing Corporation in connection with the preparation of financial statements to be issued with an unqualified opinion. There are some strengths in internal control; but the office and bookkeeping staff comprises only three persons. You have tested a random sample of acquisition transactions in detail and found no significant exceptions.

Required:

a. Set up a detailed audit program, explaining the steps you consider necessary in connection with the following expense accounts (the total of one year's charges in each account is set forth opposite each item):

Advertising	$60,000
Rent	8,000
Salesman's commission	39,000
Insurance	4,000

b. State what documents or evidence you as an auditor would examine in the verification of each of the following.
   (1) Advertising expense, where advertising is placed through an agency.
   (2) Advertising expense, where advertising is placed directly in newspapers by the client.
   (3) Royalty expense.
   (4) Repair expense.
c. Under what circumstances would you forego analytical review of the above accounts?

(AICPA adapted)

PROBLEMS

P16–1 Select the best answer to each of the following items relating to general analytical review procedures.

a. One reason why the independent auditor makes an analytical review of the client's operations is to identify

(1) Weaknesses of a material nature in the system of internal control.
(2) Noncompliance with prescribed control procedures.
(3) Improper separation of accounting and other financial duties.
(4) Unusual transactions.

b. The auditor generally gives most emphasis to ratio and trend analysis in the examination of the statement of
(1) Retained earnings.
(2) Income.
(3) Financial position.
(4) Changes in financial position.

c. An auditor uses analytical review during the course of an audit. The most important phase of this review is the
(1) Computation of key ratios such as inventory turnover and gross profit percentages.
(2) Investigation of significant variations and unusual relationships.
(3) Comparison of client-computed statistics with industry data on a quarterly and full-year basis.
(4) Examination of the client data that generated the statistics that are analyzed.

d. Which of the following *best* describes the most important stage of an auditor's statistical analysis of significant ratios and trends?
(1) Computation of significant ratios and trends.
(2) Interpretation of significant variations and unusual relationships.
(3) Reconciliation of statistical data to the client's accounting records.
(4) Comparison of statistical data to prior-year statistics and to similar data published by governmental and private sources.

e. Which of the following is *not* a typical analytical review procedure?
(1) Study of the relationship between the financial information and relevant nonfinancial information.
(2) Comparison of the financial information with similar information regarding the industry in which the entity operates.
(3) Comparison of recorded amounts of major disbursements with appropriate invoices.
(4) Comparison of the financial information with budgeted amounts.

f. The third standard of field work states that sufficient competent evidential matter may in part be obtained through inspection, observation, inquiries, and confirmations to afford a reasonable basis for an opinion regarding the financial statements under examination. The evidential matter required by this standard may in part be obtained through
(1) Auditor working papers.
(2) Proper planning of the audit engagement.
(3) Analytical review procedures.
(4) Review of the system of internal control.

g. Analytical review procedures are
(1) Statistical tests of financial information designed to identify areas requiring intensive investigation.
(2) Analytical tests of financial information made by a computer.
(3) Substantive tests of financial information made by a study and comparison of relationships among data.
(4) Diagnostic tests of financial information which may *not* be classified as evidential matter.

h. Significant unexpected fluctuations identified by analytical review procedures will usually necessitate a (an)
   (1) Consistency qualification.
   (2) Review of internal control.
   (3) Explanation in the representation letter.
   (4) Auditor investigation.

i. Analytical review procedures may be classified as being primarily
   (1) Compliance tests.
   (2) Substantive tests.
   (3) Tests of ratios.
   (4) Detailed tests of balances.

(AICPA adapted)

P16–2 Select the best answer to each of the following items relating to analytical review of income statement account balances.

a. Which of the following is *not* a principal objective of the auditor in the examination of revenues?
   (1) To verify cash deposited during the year.
   (2) To study and evaluate internal control, with particular emphasis on the use of accrual accounting to record revenue.
   (3) To verify that earned revenue has been recorded, and recorded revenue has been earned.
   (4) To identify and interpret significant trends and variations in the amounts of various categories of revenue.

b. Auditors sometimes use comparison of ratios as audit evidence. For example, an unexplained decrease in the ratio of gross profit to sales may suggest which of the following possibilities?
   (1) Unrecorded purchases.
   (2) Unrecorded sales.
   (3) Merchandise purchases being charged to selling and general expense.
   (4) Fictitious sales.

c. Which of the following analytical review procedures should be applied to the income statement?
   (1) Select sales and expense items, and trace amounts to related supporting documents.
   (2) Ascertain that the net income amount in the statement of changes in financial position agrees with the net income amount in the income statement.
   (3) Obtain from the proper client representatives the beginning and ending inventory amounts that were used to determine costs of sales.
   (4) Compare the actual revenues and expenses with the corresponding figures of the previous year and investigate significant differences.

d. Of the following procedures, which is the *most* important for an auditor to use when making an overall review of the income statement?
   (1) Select sales and expense items, and trace amounts to related supporting documents.
   (2) Compare actual revenues and expenses with the corresponding figures of the previous year and investigate significant differences.
   (3) Obtain from the proper client representatives, inventory certificates for the beginning and ending inventory amounts (used to determine cost of sales).

(4) Ascertain that the net income amount in the statement of changes in financial position agrees with the net income amount in the income statement.

e. Which of the following ratios would be the *least* useful in reviewing the overall profitability of a manufacturing company?
   (1) Net income to net worth.
   (2) Net income to total assets.
   (3) Net income to sales.
   (4) Net income to working capital.

f. Overall analysis of income statement accounts may bring to light errors, omissions, and inconsistencies *not* disclosed in the overall analysis of balance sheet accounts. The income statement analysis can *best* be accomplished by comparing monthly
   (1) Income statement ratios to balance sheet ratios.
   (2) Revenue and expense account balances to the monthly reported net income.
   (3) Income statement ratios to published industry averages.
   (4) Revenue and expense account totals to the corresponding figures of the preceding years.

g. Which of the following situations has the *best* chance of being detected when a CPA compares 19X6 revenues and expenses with the prior year and investigates all changes exceeding a fixed percentage?
   (1) An increase in property tax rates has *not* been recognized in the company's 19X6 accrual.
   (2) The cashier began lapping accounts receivable in 19X6.
   (3) Because of worsening economic conditions, the 19X6 provision for uncollectible accounts was inadequate.
   (4) The company changed its capitalization policy for small tools in 19X6.

h. An auditor is reviewing changes in sales for two products. Sales volume (quantity) declined 10% for product A and 2% for product B. Sales prices were increased by 25% for both products. Prior-year sales were $75,000 for A and $25,000 for B. The auditor would expect this year's total sales for the two products to be approximately
   (1) $112,500.
   (2) $115,000.
   (3) $117,000.
   (4) $120,000.

(AICPA adapted)

P16–3 Select the best answer to each of the following items relating to the review of a statement of changes in financial position.

a. When reviewing a client's statement of changes in financial position, where the concept of funds is interpreted to mean cash, which of the following would the auditor expect to find under the caption "Expense not requiring outlay of funds in the current period"?
   (1) An extraordinary charge as a result of early extinguishment of debt.
   (2) Conversion of long-term debt to common stock.
   (3) Goodwill arising from acquisition of a subsidiary.
   (4) Provision for uncollectible accounts receivable.

b. When examining a client's statement of changes in financial position for audit evidence, an auditor will rely primarily upon

(1) Determination of the amount of working capital at year end.
(2) Analysis of significant ratios of prior years as compared to the current year.
(3) Cross-referencing to balances and transactions reviewed in connection with the examination of the other financial statements.
(4) The guidance provided by the APB opinion on the statement of changes in financial position.

c. Many of the Granada Corporation's convertible bondholders have converted their bonds into stock during the year under examination. The independent auditor should review the Granada Corporation's statement of changes in financial position to ascertain that it shows
(1) Only financial resources used to reduce convertible debt.
(2) Only financial resources provided by issuance of stock.
(3) Financial resources provided by the issuance of stock and used to reduce convertible debt.
(4) Nothing relating to the conversion because it does not affect net working capital.

d. Once satisfied that the balance sheet and income statement are fairly presented in accordance with generally accepted accounting principles, an auditor who is examining the statement of changes in financial position would be most concerned with details of transactions in
(1) Cash.
(2) Trade receivables.
(3) Notes payable.
(4) Dividends payable.

(AICPA adapted)

P16–4 Select the best answer to each of the following items relating to clients and client-attorney relationships.

a. As part of an audit, a CPA often requests a representation letter from his client. Which one of the following is *not* a valid purpose of such a letter?
(1) To provide audit evidence.
(2) To emphasize to the client his responsibility for the correctness of the financial statements.
(3) To satisfy himself by means of other auditing procedures when certain customary auditing procedures are not performed.
(4) To provide possible protection to the CPA against a charge of knowledge in cases where fraud is subsequently discovered to have existed in the accounts.

b. Management furnishes the independent auditor with information concerning litigation, claims, and assessments. Which of the following is the auditor's primary means of initiating action to corroborate such information?
(1) Request that client lawyers undertake a reconsideration of matters of litigation, claims, and assessments with which they were consulted during the period under examination.
(2) Request that client management send a letter of audit inquiry to those lawyers with whom management consulted concerning litigation, claims, and assessments.
(3) Request that client lawyers provide a legal opinion concerning the policies and procedures adopted by management to identify, evaluate, and account for litigation, claims, and assessments.

(4) Request that client management engage outside attorneys to suggest wording for the text of a footnote explaining the nature and probable outcome of existing litigation, claims, and assessments.

c. An auditor must obtain written client representations that normally should be signed by
   (1) The president and the chairperson of the board.
   (2) The treasurer and the internal auditor.
   (3) The chief executive officer and the chief financial officer.
   (4) The corporate counsel and the audit committee chairperson.

d. The date of the management representation letter should coincide with the
   (1) Date of the auditor's report.
   (2) Balance sheet date.
   (3) Date of the latest subsequent event referred to in the notes to the financial statements.
   (4) Date of the engagement agreement.

e. Auditors often request that the audit client send a letter of inquiry to those attorneys who have been consulted with respect to litigation, claims, or assessments. The primary reason for this request is to provide the auditor with
   (1) An estimate of the dollar amount of the probable loss.
   (2) An expert opinion as to whether a loss is possible, probable, or remote.
   (3) Information concerning the progress of cases to date.
   (4) Corroborative evidential matter.

f. A CPA has received an attorney's letter in which *no* significant disagreements with the client's assessments of contingent liabilities were noted. The resignation of the client's lawyer shortly after receipt of the letter should alert the auditor that
   (1) Undisclosed unasserted claims may have arisen.
   (2) The attorney was unable to form a conclusion with respect to the significance of litigation, claims, and assessments.
   (3) The auditor must begin a completely new examination of contingent liabilities.
   (4) An adverse opinion will be necessary.

g. A lawyer's response to a letter of audit inquiry may be limited to matters that are considered individually or collectively material to the financial statements if
   (1) The auditor has instructed the lawyer regarding the limits of materiality in financial statements.
   (2) The client and the auditor have agreed on the limits of materiality and the lawyer has been notified.
   (3) The lawyer and auditor have reached an understanding on the limits of materality for this purpose.
   (4) The lawyer's response to the inquiry explains the legal meaning of materiality limits and establishes quantitative parameters.

(AICPA adapted)

P16–5 Select the best answer to each of the following items relating to subsequent events.

a. Which event that occurred after the end of the fiscal year under audit but prior to issuance of the auditor's report would *not* require disclosure in the financial statements?
   (1) Sale of a bond or capital stock issue.
   (2) Loss of plant or inventories as a result of fire or flood.

(3) A major drop in the quoted market price of the stock of the corporation.
(4) Settlement of litigation when the event giving rise to the claim took place after the balance sheet date.

b. A client has a calendar year end. Listed below are four events that occurred after December 31. Which one of these subsequent events might result in adjustment of the December 31 financial statements?
(1) Adoption of accelerated depreciation methods.
(2) Write-off of a substantial portion of inventory as obsolete.
(3) Collection of 90% of the accounts receivable existing at December 31.
(4) Sale of a major subsidiary.

c. The auditor's formal review of subsequent events normally should be extended through the date of the
(1) Auditor's report.
(2) Next formal interim financial statements.
(3) Delivery of the audit report to the client.
(4) Mailing of the financial statements to the stockholders.

d. In connection with the annual audit, which of the following is *not* a "subsequent events" procedure?
(1) Review available interim financial statements.
(2) Read available minutes of meetings of stockholders, directors, and committees; and, as to meetings for which minutes are *not* available, inquire about matters dealt with at such meetings.
(3) Make inquiries with respect to the financial statements covered by the auditor's previously issued report if new information has become available during the current examination that might affect that report.
(4) Discuss with officers the current status of items in the financial statements that were accounted for on the basis of tentative, preliminary, or inconclusive data.

e. Which of the following material events occurring subsequent to the balance sheet date would require an adjustment to the financial statements before they could be issued?
(1) Sale of long-term debt or capital stock.
(2) Loss of a plant as a result of a flood.
(3) Major purchase of a business that is expected to double the sales volume.
(4) Settlement of litigation, in excess of the recorded liability.

f. A charge in the subsequent period to a notes receivable account from the cash disbursements journal should alert the auditor to the possibility that
(1) A contingent asset has come into existence in the subsequent period.
(2) A contingent liability has come into existence in the subsequent period.
(3) A provision for contingencies is required.
(4) A contingent liability has become a real liability and has been settled.

g. An auditor performs interim work at various times throughout the year. The auditor's subsequent events work should be extended to the date of
(1) A post-dated footnote.
(2) The next scheduled interim visit.
(3) The final billing for audit services rendered.
(4) The auditor's report.

h. The auditor learned of the following situations subsequent to the issuance of his audit report on February 6, 19X6. Each is considered important to users of the financial statements. For which one does the auditor have responsibility for appropriate disclosure of the newly discovered facts?

(1) A major lawsuit against the company, which was the basis for a "subject to" auditor's opinion, was settled on unfavorable terms on March 1, 19X6.
(2) The client undertook merger negotiations on March 16, 19X6, and concluded a tentative merger agreement on April 1, 19X6.
(3) On February 16, 19X6 a fire destroyed the principal manufacturing plant.
(4) A conflict of interest situation involving credit officers and a principal company supplier was discovered on March 3, 19X6.

i. A registration statement filed with the Securities and Exchange Commission may contain the reports of two or more independent auditors on their examinations of the financial statements for different periods. What responsibility does the auditor who has *not* examined the most recent financial statements have relative to subsequent events that may affect the financial statements on which the auditor reported?
(1) The auditor has responsibility for events up to the subsequent fiscal year end.
(2) The auditor has responsibility for events up to the date of the subsequent audit report.
(3) The auditor has responsibility for events up to the effective date of the registration statement.
(4) The auditor has no responsibility beyond the date of his original report.

j. On January 28, 19X7, a customer of Tiox Corporation suffered a total loss as a result of a major casualty. On March 1, 19X7, Tiox wrote off as uncollectible a large receivable from this customer. The auditor's report on Tiox's financial statements for the year ended December 31, 19X6, has *not* yet been issued. The write-off in the subsequent period requires
(1) Disclosure in the 19X6 financial statements.
(2) Adjustment to the 19X6 financial statements.
(3) Presentation of the 19X6 financial statements with a prior period adjustment.
(4) *No* adjustment or disclosure in the 19X6 financial statements but disclosure in the 19X7 financial statements.

k. Which of the following situations would require adjustment to or disclosure in the financial statements?
(1) A merger discussion.
(2) The application for a patent on a new production process.
(3) Discussions with a customer that could lead to a forty percent increase in the client's sales.
(4) The bankruptcy of a customer who regularly purchased thirty percent of the company's output.

l. Jeanine Harvey, CPA, is preparing an audit program for the purpose of ascertaining the occurrence of subsequent events that may require adjustment or disclosure essential to a fair presentation of the financial statements in conformity with generally accepted accounting principles. Which one of the following procedures would be *least* appropriate for this purpose?
(1) Confirm as of the completion of field work accounts receivable which have increased significantly from the year-end date.
(2) Read the minutes of the board of directors.
(3) Inquire of management concerning events that may have occurred.
(4) Obtain a lawyer's letter as of the completion of field work.

m. Subsequent events affecting the realization of assets ordinarily will require adjustment of the financial statements under examination because such events typically represent

(1) The culmination of conditions that existed at the balance sheet date.
(2) The final estimates of losses relating to casualties occurring in the subsequent events period.
(3) The discovery of new conditions occurring in the subsequent events period.
(4) The preliminary estimate of losses relating to new events that occurred subsequent to the balance sheet date.

(AICPA adapted)

P16–6 Select the best answer to each of the following items relating to the search for contingent and unrecorded liabilities.

a. When auditing contingent liabilities, which of the following procedures would be *least* effective?
   (1) Abstracting the minutes of the board of directors.
   (2) Reviewing the bank confirmation letter.
   (3) Examining customer confirmation replies.
   (4) Examining invoices for professional services.

b. A company sells a particular product only in the last month of its fiscal year. The company uses commission agents for such sales and pays them 6% of their *net sales* 30 days after the sales are made. The agents' sales were $10,000,000. Experience indicates that 10% of the sales are usually *not* collected and 2% are returned in the first month of the new year. The auditor would expect the year-end balance in the accrued commissions payable account to be
   (1) $528,000.
   (2) $540,000.
   (3) $588,000.
   (4) $600,000.

c. The audit procedures used to verify accrued liabilities differ from those employed for the verification of accounts payable because
   (1) Accrued liabilities usually pertain to services of a continuing nature while accounts payable are the result of completed transactions.
   (2) Accrued liability balances are less material than accounts payable balances.
   (3) Evidence supporting accrued liabilities is nonexistent, while evidence supporting accounts payable is readily available.
   (4) Accrued liabilities at year end will become accounts payable during the following year.

d. A company guarantees the debt of an affiliate. Which of the following *best* describes the audit procedure that would make the auditor aware of the guarantee?
   (1) Review minutes and resolutions of the board of directors.
   (2) Review prior year's working papers with respect to such guarantees.
   (3) Review the possibility of such guarantees with the chief accountant.
   (4) Review the legal letter returned by the company's outside legal counsel.

e. The auditor is *most* likely to verify accrued commissions payable in conjunction with the
   (1) Sales cutoff review.
   (2) Verification of contingent liabilities.
   (3) Review of post–balance sheet date disbursements.
   (4) Examination of trade accounts payable.

f. The *best* audit procedure for determining the existence of open commodity futures contracts at year end is the review of
   (1) Cancelled checks in the subsequent period.
   (2) Available broker trade advices.
   (3) The standard bank cash confirmation request.
   (4) Direct confirmations with the client's commodity traders.

g. When auditing a public warehouse, which of the following is the most important audit procedure with respect to disclosing unrecorded liabilities?
   (1) Confirmation of negotiable receipts with holders.
   (2) Review of outstanding receipts.
   (3) Inspection of receiving and issuing procedures.
   (4) Observation of inventory.

h. Which of the following audit procedures would be *least* effective for detecting contingent liabilities?
   (1) Abstracting the minutes of the meetings of the board of directors.
   (2) Reviewing the bank confirmation letters.
   (3) Examining confirmation letters from customers.
   (4) Confirming pending legal matters with the corporate attorney.

i. Which of the following is the *most* efficient audit procedure for the detection of unrecorded liabilities?
   (1) Compare cash disbursements in the subsequent period with the accounts payable trial balance at year end.
   (2) Confirm large accounts payable balances at the balance sheet date.
   (3) Examine purchase orders issued for several days prior to the close of the year.
   (4) Obtain a "liability certificate" from the client.

j. Which of the following is the *best* audit procedure for determining the existence of unrecorded liabilities?
   (1) Examine confirmation requests returned by creditors whose accounts appear on a subsidiary trial balance of accounts payable.
   (2) Examine a sample of cash disbursements in the period subsequent to year end.
   (3) Examine a sample of invoices a few days prior to and subsequent to year end to ascertain whether they have been properly recorded.
   (4) Examine unusual relationships between monthly accounts payable balances and recorded purchases.

k. Which of the following procedures is *least* likely to be performed before the balance sheet date?
   (1) Observation of inventory.
   (2) Review of internal control over cash disbursements.
   (3) Search for unrecorded liabilities.
   (4) Confirmation of receivables.

l. The primary reason for preparing a reconciliation between interest-bearing obligations outstanding during the year and interest expense presented in the financial statements is to
   (1) Evaluate internal control over securities.
   (2) Determine the validity of prepaid interest expense.
   (3) Ascertain the reasonableness of imputed interest.
   (4) Detect unrecorded liabilities.

(AICPA adapted)

P16–7 During an audit engagement, Rick Harper, CPA, has satisfactorily completed an examination of accounts payable and other liabilities and now plans to determine whether there are any loss contingencies arising from litigation, claims, or assessments.

Required:

What are the audit procedures that Harper should follow with respect to the existence of loss contingencies arising from litigation, claims, and assessments? Do not discuss reporting requirements.

(AICPA adapted)

P16–8 Michael Costello, CPA, is examining the financial statements of the Diannah Corporation as of and for the period ended September 30, 19X7. Costello plans to complete the field work and sign the auditor's report on November 15, 19X7. Costello's audit work is primarily designed to obtain evidence that will provide a reasonable degree of assurance that the Diannah Corporation's September 30, 19X7, financial statements present fairly the financial position, results of operations, and changes in financial position of that enterprise in accordance with generally accepted accounting principles consistently applied. Costello is concerned, however, about events and transactions of Diannah Corporation that occur after September 30, 19X7, since Costello does not have the same degree of assurance for such events as for those that occurred in the period ending September 30, 19X7.

Required:

a. Define what is commonly referred to in auditing as a "subsequent event" and describe the two general types of subsequent events that require consideration by the management of Diannah Corporation and evaluation by Costello.
b. Identify those auditing procedures that Costello should follow to obtain the necessary assurances concerning subsequent events.

(AICPA adapted)

P16–9 Saul Windek, a CPA, is nearing the completion of an examination of the financial statements of Jubilee, Inc., for the year ended December 31, 19X0. Windek is currently concerned with ascertaining the occurrence of subsequent events that may require adjustment or disclosure essential to a fair presentation in conformity with generally accepted accounting principles.

Required:

a. Briefly explain what is meant by the phrase *subsequent event.*
b. How do those subsequent events which require financial statement adjustment differ from those that require financial statement disclosure?
c. What procedures should be performed in order to ascertain the occurrence of subsequent events?

(AICPA adapted)

P16–10 Analytical review procedures are substantive tests that are extremely useful in the initial audit planning stage.

Required:

a. Explain why analytical review procedures are considered substantive tests.
b. Explain how analytical review procedures may be useful in the initial audit planning stage.
c. Identify the analytical review procedures one might expect a CPA to utilize during an examination performed in accordance with generally accepted auditing standards.

(AICPA adapted)

P16–11 In connection with his examination of the financial statements of the Time Corporation, Henry Burrell is reviewing the federal income taxes payable account.

With the approval of its board of directors, the Time Corporation made a sizable payment for advertising during the year being audited. The corporation deducted the full amount in its federal income tax return. The controller acknowledges that this deduction probably will be disallowed because it relates to political matters. He has not provided for this disallowance in his federal income tax provision and refuses to do so because he fears that this will cause the revenue agent to believe that the deduction is not valid.

Required:

a. Discuss reasons why Burrell should review federal income tax returns for prior years and the reports of internal revenue agents. What information will these reviews provide? (Do not discuss specific tax return items.)
b. What is the CPA's responsibility in the tax provision issue? Explain.

(AICPA adapted)

CHAPTER

17

AUDITS OF NONPROFIT ORGANIZATIONS

Although we have occasionally referred to some of the special problems associated with auditing nonprofit organizations in the preceding chapters, we have not dealt in a comprehensive way with the peculiarities associated with that type of audit. In this chapter we give special attention to the auditing procedures that are unique to nonprofit organizations. Our discussion will cover the following topics:

1. Major differences between generally accepted accounting practices of nonprofit organizations and those of business enterprises.
2. Internal control problems peculiar to much of the nonprofit area.
3. Special problems that may be encountered in auditing the financial statements of a nonprofit organization.

Appendixes to this chapter contain financial statement formats for selected types of nonprofit entities. These appendixes should enhance your understanding of disclosures that are unique to this area.

There are a number of different types of nonprofit entities. They include governmental entities, colleges and universities, hospitals, health and welfare organizations, and private foundations. These organizations have no equity interests that can be sold or traded and their primary operating objective is to provide a socially desirable service rather than to realize a net income from operations. Therefore they rely on taxes, contributions, or cost-based fees for operating resources. In this chapter we focus our attention on the special problems encountered in auditing the financial statements of these organizations.

Just as with profit-based organizations, the accountant may perform both audit and nonaudit services for nonprofit entities. Among the nonaudit services are: *reviews* or *compilations* of financial statements and issuance of *special reports*. The latter may be in connection with any of the following: financial statements prepared in accordance with a comprehensive basis of accounting other than generally accepted accounting principles; specified elements, accounts, or items in financial statements; compliance with aspects of contractual agreements or regulatory requirements related to audited financial statements; or financial information presented in prescribed forms or schedules that require a prescribed form of audit report. SAS 14 provides the primary source of guidance on the wording of the special reports for these entities. Just as is the case with profit organizations, if the data associated with the special report are to be audited, generally accepted auditing standards apply. If they are not to be audited, the statements on standards for accounting and review services (SSARSs) apply.

GENERALLY ACCEPTED ACCOUNTING PRACTICES

Because the operating objectives of nonprofit organizations are different from those of profit entities, their generally accepted accounting practices are, in some respects, also different. The primary operating objective for profit enterprises is to earn income for their owners. In contrast, nonprofit entities operate for the purpose of providing a service with no intention of realizing a profit from rendering those services. Also nonprofit organizations have no stockholders to whom resources may be distributed. Therefore, any excess of revenues over expenses or expenditures is simply added to the resource base of the organization to enlarge its service-rendering capability. These organizations have *no personally held ownership interests* that can be sold, transferred, or redeemed.

Because nonprofit organizations are characterized by the differences we have just seen in operating objectives and ownership characteristics, their accounting practices, too, should logically be organized to tell the "service story" rather than the profit story. Instead of emphasizing the distinction between capital and revenue items for the purpose of determining net income, many of these organizations control operations by monitoring the inflows and outflows of spendable resources. Consequently, they use appropriation control techniques and fund accounting practices in controlling operations, accounting practices which have led some of these organizations to use a ***cash*** or ***modified accrual basis*** rather than the pure accrual basis, for financial reporting purposes. We will discuss the meaning of appropriation control and fund accounting practices below. After that we will briefly describe some of the special accounts found in the financial statements of many of these organizations, as well as the literature establishing generally accepted accounting principles in the nonprofit area.

Appropriation Control

Business entities control their operations through accounting practices designed primarily to disclose the extent to which the profit objective has been achieved.

Because the service objective is substituted for the profit objective in the nonprofit area, the operations of a nonprofit organization must be controlled by monitoring the ways in which resources are used; within individual fund entities (described below) this is accomplished through a technique called *appropriation control.* It requires management to use resources within budget constraints established for each of the different types of expenditures (outflows of spendable resources).

Appropriations are reflected in a budget approved by an appropriate representative body. Governmental entities, for example, begin their operating cycle by establishing a ***line-item budget*** showing the amounts proposed to be spent for each of the various items required to carry out the entity's operations. The budget must be approved by a body of citizens (for example, the city council in the case of a city) before management is authorized to spend against it. When the budgetary provisions are approved, they are referred to as appropriations. Management can then spend against the appropriation but *must confine its spending to the amounts provided for each of the individual items.* As we shall see later, the auditor must evaluate management's compliance with budgetary provisions before expressing an opinion on the operating statement.

Fund Accounting Practices

While some resources received by nonprofit entities are available for discretionary use (within appropriation-imposed controls) by the managements of those organizations, other resources carry restrictions as to ways in which they may be used. For example, a governmental unit may, with proper approval by its voting constituency, sell bonds to secure resources for the construction of a municipal building. The accounting system of the governmental unit must then be designed to provide assurance that such funds will be used only for the intended purposes. This can best be achieved by organizing the accounting records of nonprofit organizations to maintain separate accountability, or ***separate funds,*** for each body of resources contractually or externally restricted to a specified use.

Separate fund accountability is maintained through the establishment of ***self-balancing accounting entities*** for each segment of resources restricted to a specified use. The accounting practices followed for the individual funds differ, depending on the way in which the fund is expected to operate. Funds can generally be categorized according to their purpose, as follows:

- Source and disposition funds.
- Self-sustaining funds.
- Hybrid funds.
- Other funds.

Figure 17–1 shows the funds typically used to account for the activities of four types of nonprofit entities. We will explain the use of these funds in the paragraphs that follow.

Most funds are what might be called ***source and disposition funds*** because management is primarily concerned with showing the sources from which funds were acquired and how they were used. The accounting records for these funds are designed to disclose the extent to which the inflows and outflows of spendable resources have measured up to the estimated inflows and line-by-line appropriation constraints placed on the uses of those resources. The primary accounting objective for these

Type of Fund	Colleges and Universities	Hospitals	Health and Welfare Agencies	Governmental Entities
Source and disposition	Current funds	Specific-purpose funds Plant replacement and expansion fund	Current unrestricted fund Current restricted fund Custodian funds	General fund Special revenue funds Debt service funds Capital projects funds Special assessments funds
Self-sustaining	Loan funds Endowment funds Annuity and life insurance funds	Unrestricted fund Endowment funds	Endowment funds Loan and annuity funds	Internal service funds Enterprise funds
Hybrid	Plant funds		Land, building, and equipment fund	Trust and agency funds
Other	Agency funds			

FIGURE 17–1. Funds Used in Accounting Records

funds, then, is to reflect the extent to which various externally imposed operating constraints on the acquisitions and uses of spendable resources have been met.

Because of the emphasis on fund flows, the accounting records of these funds often do not distinguish between capital and revenue items. When that is the case, the term *revenues* is used to describe all inflows and the term *expenditures* is used to describe all outflows. In such situations, because of the failure to distinguish between capital and revenue items, the accounting records should also include separate self-balancing accounting entities for long-term assets and long-term liabilities, as explained later in this section.

In contrast, ***self-sustaining funds*** operate like business entities within the overall nonprofit organization framework. These funds are called *proprietary funds* in the governmental area. Such funds follow accounting practices that are essentially the same as those followed by businesses.

We also find funds that operate as ***hybrid funds,*** incorporating some of the operating characteristics of source and disposition funds in combination with some operating characteristics of self-sustaining funds. Trust and agency funds in governmental entities fall into this category, particularly when some segment of the fund is nonexpendable.

Nonprofit organizations account for their acquisitions and uses of resources through the use of similar types of fund entities adapted to their particular operating characteristics. In Figure 17–1 we show the funds used by colleges and universities, hospitals, and health and welfare agencies, as well as those used by governmental entities.

In the governmental area, which we shall use to exemplify the fund accounting practices, we typically find five types of source and disposition funds, which include the following:

1. The *general fund,* which is the accounting entity used to account for the resources available for the general operations of the governmental unit. All financial transactions not involving the acquisitions or uses of restricted resources will be recorded in this fund.
2. *Special revenue funds,* which are used to account for the inflows and outflows of resources designated for specific operating uses. For example, if a city has a special tax levy to provide for the operation of its library system, the inflows of resources from that tax levy and the uses of the resources in operating the library system would be accounted for in a special revenue fund.
3. *Debt service funds,* which are used to account for the inflows and outflows of resources restricted to use in the repayment of long-term debt. In some instances this fund is also used to account for resources to be used in the payment of interest on that debt.
4. *Capital projects funds,* which are used to account for the acquisitions and uses of resources designated for a particular construction project, such as building a new city hall.
5. *Special assessment funds* (similar to capital project funds), which are used to account for the resources acquired and used to provide improvements that are deemed to benefit primarily particular segments of the population of a city. As an example, resources acquired and used in the construction of sidewalks in a particular residential neighborhood would probably be handled through such a fund. The residents of the neighborhood where the sidewalks will be constructed would be assessed for a major portion of the cost, with the balance being covered by contributions from general fund resources.

Governmental entities also typically have two types of self-sustaining (proprietary) funds:

1. *Internal service funds*, which are used to account for goods or services provided for the various departments of the city on a cost reimbursement basis. A vehicle maintenance center operated by the city is an example of this type of fund entity. The maintenance charges recovered by this fund from the other departments and agencies are expected to cover the total operating costs of providing those services. The accounting procedures followed by these funds are essentially the same as those for business entities.
2. *Enterprise funds*, which are used to account for operating entities created to provide services for the people of a governmental entity on a self-sustaining basis. A water utility service operated by the city is an example of an enterprise fund. Again, the accounting procedures for this type of fund should be the same as those for profit enterprises.

The presence of five types of source and disposition funds in governmental accounting records causes those entities to have to maintain account groups for long-term assets and long-term debt. These groups are called:

- The *general fixed-asset account group*, which is used to preserve a record of the costs of fixed assets acquired, offset by a balanced array of the sources from which the fixed assets were acquired.
- The *general long-term debt account group*, which lists the general long-term obligations of the city, balanced against accounts showing the amount of resources available and the amount of resources still to be provided for the retirement of those obligations.

It is important to recognize that the transactions of each fund are accounted for in a separate self-balancing accounting entity. Because of that fact, we also have ***interfund transactions***, which require accounting recognition in each of the funds involved. The records of each account group are also maintained in a separate self-balancing accounting entity. The auditor must, during the course of the audit engagement, determine whether the management of a nonprofit entity has properly complied with restrictions placed on the uses of resources before rendering an opinion on its financial statements.

Bases of Accounting

Generally accepted accounting practices require that business accounting records be maintained on the accrual basis. This requires the recognition of accrued and prepaid items, a distinction between capital and revenue items, and the recognition of depreciation on fixed assets. Because of the emphasis on controlling operations through the means of appropriation control and fund accounting techniques, many source and disposition fund entities are accounted for on the ***modified accrual basis.*** In using this method of accounting, no distinction is made between capital and revenue items and there is no accounting recognition of depreciation. Furthermore, there is typically no recognition of accrued or prepaid items. Governmental entities, for example, use the modified accrual basis in accounting for the transactions in all their source and disposition funds. The accrual basis, however, is used in accounting for the transactions of self-sustaining funds.

Official publications describing college and university accounting practices state that the accounts should be maintained on the accrual basis.[1] However, in actual practice, what the literature describes as the accrual basis does not distinguish between capital and revenue items, nor does it recognize depreciation as an element of expense in the operating statement.

The official publications defining hospital[2] and health and welfare accounting practices[3] prescribe the *full accrual basis of accounting,* including the distinction between capital and revenue items and the recognition of depreciation. Therefore the auditor should expect the same basis of accounting to be used by these entities as is used by businesses.

In December 1978 the AICPA issued its Statement of Position (SOP) 78-10, setting out accounting principles and reporting practices for certain nonprofit organizations. This statement is intended to apply to *all categories of nonprofit organizations except those that are already covered by the existing AICPA audit guides* (governmental units, colleges and universities, hospitals, and voluntary health and welfare organizations). This SOP requires that the accrual basis of accounting should be used in preparing the financial statements of these organizations to comply with GAAP. However, it does recognize the possibility that cash basis financial statements may, in some instances, not be materially different from those prepared on the accrual basis.

Special Accounts

The accounting records of nonprofit organization funds will include many of the same types of balance sheet accounts as those found in the records of business entities. However, the differences between assets and liabilities will be reflected in *fund balance accounts* rather than in capital accounts. On the other hand, funds using the modified accrual basis of accounting will use the term *revenues* to describe all inflows (capital and revenue) of liquid resources and the term *expenditures* to reflect all outflows (capital and revenue) of those resources. As a result, the term *expense* will not appear in those records. Also, because the separate fund entities have transactions with each other, we find accounts labeled *transfers from other funds, transfers to other funds, due to other funds,* and *due from other funds.* Futhermore, because of the strong emphasis on appropriation control, source and disposition funds use *encumbrance* and *reserve for encumbrance* accounts to earmark appropriated resources committed to be used to meet specified future obligations. These accounts are designed to reduce the probability of managers "overspending" their line-item appropriations. The amount still available to be spent for a particular category of expenditure can be determined by subtracting the sum of expenditures and encumbrances for the item from the appropriation for it.

Official Literature

For many years the accounting profession depended on the individual industries within the nonprofit segment of our economy to prescribe their own generally accepted accounting practices. These were reflected in the following ***industry publications:***

- Governmental Entities — *Governmental Accounting, Auditing and Financial Reporting (GAAFR).* The most recent edition of this volume was published in 1980

- Colleges and Universities — *College and University Business Administration.* The most recent edition of this volume was published in 1982.
- Hospitals — *Chart of Accounts for Hospitals.* The most recent edition of this volume was published in 1976.
- Voluntary Health and Welfare Organizations — *Standards of Accounting and Financial Reporting for Voluntary Health and Welfare Organizations.* The most recent edition of this volume was published in 1975.

The AICPA has, in recent years, published ***audit guides*** describing generally accepted accounting practices in each of the above four segments of the nonprofit organization universe. They include the following publications:

- *Audits of State and Local Governmental Units* (1975).
- *Audits of Colleges and Universities* (1973).
- *Hospital Audit Guide* (1980).
- *Audits of Voluntary Health and Welfare Organizations* (1974).

In 1978 the AICPA published Statement of Position (SOP) 78-10 entitled *Accounting and Reporting Practices for Certain Nonprofit Organizations.* The first four of these are characterized as industry audit guides and therefore reflect generally accepted accounting practices in those areas. For the most part they conform to their respective industry publications. SOP 78-10 has no real authority but reflects what the AICPA feels should be incorporated into a future audit guide for that area. A draft entitled "Audits of Certain Nonprofit Organizations" was presented to the public in exposure draft form in 1981. The important point we wish to make in connection with this section is that the *generally accepted accounting practices for all the segments of the nonprofit organization universe have been identified in these audit guides.*

INTERNAL CONTROLS

The auditor may find, for a number of reasons, that the internal controls for a nonprofit organization may be relatively weak compared with those found for most business enterprises. This observation may be particularly true for some charitable organizations.

The ***weaknesses*** in internal control can often be linked to the following operational characteristics:

- The *governing body* (board of directors, board of trustees, or similar group) will often be large and composed of volunteers who are relatively inactive in the day-by-day affairs of the organization. Furthermore, none of these people will have ownership interests in the organization that they are trying to protect. Because of these characteristics, the auditor will typically find less emphasis on accountability and control by these groups than he or she would typically expect of a corporate board of directors.
- There may be only a *limited amount of resources* that can be used to strengthen the system of internal control. Priorities in the operations of these organizations frequently place primary emphasis on implementing services and sustaining the organization rather than on improving internal control procedures.
- The *accounting function* may receive relatively little attention because of a lack of staff or because the organization places most of its emphasis on its operating activities or programs.

- The *staff of the organization* may be small, so that the desired segregation of duties is difficult to attain.
- Nonprofit organizations *do not have the normal controls provided by customers in the profit area* because many resources are contributed without the expectation of receiving specific goods or services in exchange for them. For example, a person contributing cash to a nonprofit organization will typically receive only an acknowledging receipt from the solicitor. As a result, solicitors collecting contributions for a poorly controlled charitable organization may take the cash and simply not turn in the contribution.

The auditor should look for the following ***control practices*** to be used to reduce the probability of fraud or embezzlement of charitable contribution receipts:

1. *Honesty and integrity of persons* charged with the responsibility of soliciting contributions is the most effective way of controlling door-to-door solicitations. Beyond that, however, contributors should be provided with *a duplicate receipt form* by the solicitor carrying a statement that the contribution will be independently acknowledged from the charitable organization office. The other copy of the receipt should be retained and turned in with the cash.
2. *Two volunteers or two employees* in the charitable organization's office should be involved in receiving contributions from solicitors and through the mail. Ideally these persons should perform independent counts of contributions, which should then be reconciled with copies of receipts by a responsible official.
3. A *list of contributions received*, showing each of the contributor's names, should be prepared as soon as contributions are received in the office of the organization. At this time, the office should also acknowledge the receipt of each contribution directly to the contributor. This element of control can also be achieved, to some extent, by publishing the list of contributors.
4. The *list of prospects to be solicited* by each solicitor should be prepared in duplicate. The solicitor should then send one list with the money and pledges he or she has received to the soliciting team captain and the other directly to the charitable organization.
5. *Acknowledgement forms* should be prenumbered and an operating procedure requiring periodic accountability for all numbers should be established.

In addition to looking for the controls cited above, the auditor evaluating the system of internal control for a nonprofit organization will be concerned with the same characteristics of good internal control described earlier in the text: proper segregation of duties; clearly defined lines of authority and responsibility; adequately trained employees; appropriate records, authorization, and approval procedures; appropriate provision for protection of assets; and provisions for monitoring compliance with established operating policies. Furthermore, because of the characteristic weaknesses (in the previous list) the auditor should exercise special care *not to depend as much on the system of internal control in auditing nonprofit organizations as he or she would in auditing business entities.* It is also desirable for the auditor to make some general judgments regarding the apparent honesty of employees and the general attitude toward establishing individual accountabilities within the organization.

SPECIAL AUDIT CONSIDERATIONS

In presenting the financial statements for a nonprofit organization, the management is in effect making these assertions:

- Resources and obligations reflected in the statements exist.
- Recorded changes in those items (transactions) are valid and complete.
- Restrictions relating to the rights and obligations associated with resources have been met and are appropriately reflected in the statements.
- Resources, obligations, revenues, and expenses (or expenditures) have been valued at the appropriate amounts in the financial statements, and have been allocated to the appropriate periods.
- Various financial statement components have been properly disclosed and presented in conformity with generally accepted accounting practices for the industry classification for the entity.

Notice that many of the financial statement assertions described in the preceding list for nonprofit entities are essentially the same as those for profit-seeking entities. Audit objectives for nonprofit entities are, therefore, also similar to those for profit-seeking entities and include: (1) verification of appropriate statement presentation; (2) verification of transaction validity; (3) verification of ownership; (4) verification of proper cutoff; (5) verification of proper valuation techniques, and (6) verification of existence.

However, as we have observed, the generally accepted accounting practices for many subentities (funds) in the nonprofit area are different from those for business enterprises. Therefore it is important for the auditor to recognize those differences in deciding which audit procedures will best meet the various audit objectives. Because of the natural inclination of nonprofit organizations to have less reliable systems of internal control than those found in business enterprises, *expansion of the substantive tests* of various asset and liability accounts is advisable in order to provide an appropriate level of confidence that the financial statements have been fairly presented. In addition, certain unique accounting practices for nonprofit entities may require special types of disclosures. In meeting the statement presentation objective, the auditor must be familiar with the statement formats and disclosures set forth by the various industry publications cited earlier. He or she should then take steps to see that the financial statements of the nonprofit client are organized along those lines.

Another very important difference in auditing nonprofit organization financial statements hinges on the necessity for the auditor to determine the extent to which management has adhered to the *various spending constraints* imposed on it. In this respect we must recognize that the auditor providing an unqualified opinion on nonprofit organization financial statements is in effect saying that management has adhered to the spending constraints imposed by the governing board or constituencies of the organization.

Evidence-Gathering Process

The special considerations just described and the operating characteristics of nonprofit organizations require the auditor to give special recognition to the following items in the evidence-gathering process and in meeting the reporting requirements associated with the audit of a nonprofit organization:

1. For many nonprofit organizations, the *budget* is a key element controlling the ways in which resources may be used. Therefore, in determining whether the management of the organi-

zation has effectively discharged its responsibilities to the governing board and the constituency, the auditor should review the actual results of operations and should question deviations from budgetary provisions.

2. It is often important for the auditor to identify the specific body to whom the audit report should be rendered. Many nonprofit organizations will have *audit committees* made up of board members not involved in the day-to-day activities of the organization. When this arrangement exists, the auditor should meet with that committee prior to the audit for the purpose of defining the audit scope, discussing internal control problems and other particular areas or activities that the committee believes should be stressed during the audit. After the audit has been completed, the auditor should again meet with the audit committee to discuss the results of the audit, including areas where internal controls or operating procedures might be improved.
3. Special audit attention should be given to the system of control over handling of cash receipts. Although, as we have observed earlier, the control over cash contributions may not be complete, it should be sufficient to provide reasonable assurance that contributions, if any, are not materially misstated.
4. The organization may receive *grants from outside organizations*, such as the federal government, which must be used in accordance with specified grant provisions. The auditor must be concerned with determining that the grant provisions have been met in the uses of such resources. Often, for example, the grant contract will include a stipulation that in the event funds are used improperly, the organization will be required to make refunds to the grantor equal to the misused resources. Thus an improper use of grant funds could require the recognition of a liability to the grantor. Also the auditor should be concerned with the distinction between revenue and deferred revenue in the receipt of grant funds. Often such funds should not be treated as revenues until they are committed to use for their intended purpose.
5. *Documents relating to restricted gifts* must be examined to determine that such resources are being used in accordance with the wishes of the donors. Often this requires the organization to carefully distinguish between spendable and nonspendable resources. Again it may be necessary to evaluate the distinctions that have been made between revenues and deferred revenues. Because it is sometimes difficult to determine that funds have been used in accordance with donor restrictions, the auditor may in some cases need to obtain the opinion of legal counsel in resolving this matter.
6. A major audit concern with organizations holding *pledges* is whether the pledges are, in fact, contingent assets that are not to be recognized until actual receipt, or whether they should be shown as receivables. The industry audit guides and SOP 78-10 are not all in agreement on the appropriate accounting treatment for such items. Therefore the auditor will need to refer to the pertinent publication for guidance in evaluating the client's treatment of pledges. If they are properly classified as assets, the auditor should apply the same audit procedures to them as are applied to accounts receivable in the profit area.
7. Many nonprofit organizations receive *donated services*. If these are significant, certain key ratios such as the relationship of supporting services to total contributions can be significantly different if costs are imputed for those services than they would be if costs are not imputed for them. Generally speaking, the industry pronouncements restrict the circumstances in which the value of these service contributions should be recorded, allowing them only in those situations where they can be evaluated against the costs of professional personnel and are actually used to replace such personnel.
8. Some nonprofit organizations, particularly hospitals, receive *reimbursements of costs incurred* for services provided. The auditor must be familiar with the contractual arrangements with third-party payors. In evaluating receivables from medicare, for example, the

auditor should be familiar with the provisions of the medicare audit guide published by the AICPA in 1969. This publication discusses the unusual problems inherent in auditing and reporting on statements including reimbursable costs. Cost principles incorporated into the determination of such costs must be examined to determine that they conform to the requirements of the payor agency.

9. Many nonprofit organizations solicit *members who agree to pay dues*, generally on an annual basis. Different membership levels are also provided by some organizations. The resources received in the form of membership dues would, by implication, be available for use during the membership year, which might be different from the fiscal period of the organization. Therefore the auditor must give special attention to the possible need for deferring portions of such revenue. It is also desirable to provide an overall analysis of such dues in relationship to the recognized membership of the organization as a partial proof of cash inflows.
10. We have already observed that some nonprofit organizations use the *modified accrual basis of accounting*, which does not call for the capitalization or depreciation of fixed assets. Where this is the case, the records in support of fixed assets may be inadequate. The auditor, particularly during an initial audit, may need to conduct a physical inventory and establish values for such assets. If historical costs are not known, a specialist may be needed to appraise such assets.
11. As we have observed earlier, fund accounting practices carry with them the possibilities of *interfund transactions*. Borrowing between funds, for example, is not uncommon. However, when an operating fund borrows from a restricted fund, the auditor must be particularly concerned as to whether it violates the contractual constraints associated with restricted fund resources. Furthermore, the auditor must make sure that all interfund borrowings are disclosed and have been approved by the governing board. Sometimes the collectibility of interfund loans may be in doubt. In such a situation, the auditor must make a judgment as to whether a due-from (receivable) account in a particular fund would be more appropriately listed as a transfer.
12. The audit guides and SOP 78-10 generally require or encourage the *presentation of expenditures or expenses on a functional basis*. The auditor in these situations must be satisfied that the organization's cost allocation techniques adhere to GAAP.
13. If a reporting nonprofit organization *controls another financially interrelated organization*, the financial statements of the two organizations should be either combined or consolidated. The key word in this provision is *control*. It is defined in SOP 78-10 as "the direct or indirect ability to determine the direction of management and policies through ownership, by contract or otherwise." When there is professed or readily apparent control of one organization over another, the auditor may need to insist upon access to the books and records of the legally separate organization in order to reach a satisfactory judgment regarding consolidated or combined statements.
14. Generally speaking, nonprofit organizations are not subject to income taxes. However, because of a recent new emphasis by the Internal Revenue Service on *taxing nonrelated net income* of these organizations, the auditor must give special attention to these income sources. For example, pharmacy sales to nonpatients in a hospital can be construed to be subject to income taxes. Furthermore, the auditor should examine the information tax returns filed by the nonprofit organization to see that such reporting obligations have been properly met.[5]

Reporting Requirements

If the evidence-gathering process supports the hypothesis that the financial statements of a nonprofit organization are fairly presented in accordance with the generally accepted accounting principles described in the pertinent industry audit guide or in SOP 78-10, the auditor will use the standard short-form audit report in rendering an opinion on the financial statements. Qualified or adverse opinions would also be rendered because of deviations from industry GAAP, or a violation of the principle of consistency. For most nonprofit organizations, this opinion will relate to the financial statements of the entity as a unit. However, in the governmental area, the National Council on Governmental Accounting has recommended that the scope of the annual audit should "also encompass the combining and individual financial statements of the funds and account groups."[4] This logically suggests that the opinion should make reference to the fairness of these statements in relation to the financial statements for the governmental unit.

Some nonprofit organizations may use the cash basis of accounting or modifications thereto, and in that way depart from GAAP. Still other nonprofit entities may use comprehensive bases of accounting to comply with the requirements or financial reporting provisions of a governmental regulatory agency to whose jurisdiction the entity is subject. When a comprehensive basis of accounting other than GAAP is used, the special reporting provisions of SAS 14 apply and essentially allow the auditor to express an unqualified audit opinion as long as the entity complies with one of four comprehensive bases of accounting (other than GAAP) having substantial support. In such cases, it is important for the auditor to recognize that financial statements developed from comprehensive bases of accounting other than GAAP should be properly labeled. The terms *balance sheet* and *income statement* are appropriate only for financial statements prepared in accordance with GAAP. In contrast, financial statements prepared on the cash basis of accounting might be described as statements of cash receipts and disbursements and statements of assets and liabilities arising from cash transactions. Also since such statements do not reflect the financial condition or results of operations, the basis of accounting used should be described in the footnotes to the statements. The opinion paragraph of the audit report should be worded somewhat like this:

> In our opinion the aforementioned statements present fairly the assets and liabilities of ABC Company at 12/31/X2 arising from cash transactions and the revenues collected and expenditures made by it during the year then ended, on the basis of accounting described in Note X, which basis is consistent with that of the preceding year.

The financial statements for the self-sustaining funds of governmental entities are organized and presented within essentially the same format as are the statements of business enterprises. The financial data for source and disposition funds, however, are typically presented in two statements, labeled as follows:

- Statement of revenues, expenditures, and changes in fund balances.
- Balance sheet.

In some instances, the statements of revenues and expenditures may be combined. We illustrate the general organization of source and disposition fund statements in Appendix 17–A.

Although colleges and universities place strong emphasis on fund accounting, the financial data will normally be presented through the medium of the following three financial statements, which show the combined data from various fund entity accounting records:

- Balance sheet.
- Statement of changes in fund balances.
- Statement of current funds revenues, expenditures, and other changes.

We illustrate the general format within which those statements are presented in Appendix 17–B.

As we have suggested earlier in this chapter, hospitals operate more like business enterprises than do any other nonprofit organizations. It follows logically, then, that their financial data should be presented within a format similar to that used for business entities. This includes four statements:

- Balance sheet.
- Statement of revenues and expenses.
- Statement of changes in fund balances.
- Statement of changes in financial position of unrestricted fund.

We illustrate the general organization of those statements in Appendix 17–C.

Voluntary health and welfare organizations use the accrual basis of accounting but also give much emphasis to fund accounting techniques. Their financial data reflect those influences as they are presented through the medium of three statements for the organization as a unit:

- Statement of support revenue and expenses and changes in fund balances.
- Statement of functional expenses.
- Balance sheet.

We illustrate the general format of those statements in Appendix 17–D.

SUMMARY

In this chapter we have explained some of the unique considerations associated with the audit of nonprofit organizations. We began by recognizing that for some of these organizations, generally accepted accounting practices are significantly different from the GAAP for profit entities. This difference extends to emphasis on appropriation controls over expenditures and the use of fund accounting techniques. The auditor must therefore judge whether management has complied with the constraints associated with those controls.

We also observed that the internal control systems for nonprofit organizations are often less effective than those for profit entities. Thus, the auditor normally must extend his or her substantive tests of account balances and must rely more heavily on those procedures in rendering an audit opinion.

We listed and described fourteen special audit considerations associated with the evidence-gathering process in auditing nonprofit organizations. In the last part of the chapter we described the special financial reporting formats followed for governmental source and disposition funds, colleges and universities, hospitals, and health and welfare agencies.

APPENDIX 17–A: Formats for Source and Disposition Fund Statements

STATEMENT OF REVENUES, EXPENDITURES, AND CHANGES IN FUND BALANCES

	Budget	Actual	Variances Favorable (Unfavorable)
Revenue items			
Total revenues	XXXX	XXXX	XX
Expenditure items			
Total expenditures	XXXX	XXXX	XX
Excess (deficiency) of revenues over expenditures	XXXX	XXXX	XX
Transfers			
Total transfers	XXXX	XXXX	XX
Excess (deficiency) of revenues over expenditures and transfers	XXX	XXX	XX
Fund balances—beginning of period	XXX	XXX	
Fund balances—end of period	XXX	XXX	XX

BALANCE SHEET

Assets		**Liabilities and Fund Balance**	
Asset items		Liabilities	
		Fund balance	
Total assets	XXXX	Total liabilities and fund balance	XXXX

APPENDIX 17–B: Formats for College and University Financial Statements

STATEMENT OF CHANGES IN FUND BALANCES

	Current Funds			
	Unrestricted	Restricted	Loan Funds	Endowment Funds
Fund balances — beginning of year				
Plus revenues and other additions				
Less expenditure and other deductions				
Plus (and less) transfers				
Fund balances — end of year	xxxx	xxxx	xxxx	xxxx

STATEMENT OF CHANGES IN FUND BALANCES

	Plant Funds			
	Unexpended	Renewal and Replacement	Retirement of Indebtedness	Investment in Plant
Fund balances — beginning of year				
Plus revenues and other additions				
Less expenditure and other deductions				
Plus (and less) transfers				
Fund balances — end of year	xxxx	xxxx	xxxx	xxxx

STATEMENT OF CURRENT FUNDS REVENUES, EXPENDITURES, AND OTHER CHANGES

	Unrestricted	Restricted	Total
Revenues (including revenues from auxiliary enterprises)			
Expenditures and mandatory transfers			
Auxiliary enterprises expenditures and mandatory transfers			
Other transfers, additions, and deductions			
Net increase in fund balances	xxxx	xxxx	xxxx

BALANCE SHEET

Assets		Liabilities and Fund Balances	
Current funds		Current funds	
Unrestricted		Unrestricted	
Asset items		Liabilities	
		Fund balance	
Total unrestricted	xxxx	Total unrestricted	xxxx
Restricted		Restricted	
Asset items		Liabilities	
		Fund balance	
Total restricted	xxx	Total restricted	xxx
Total current funds	xxxx	Total current funds	xxxx
Loan funds		Loan funds	
Asset items		Fund balance	
Total loan funds	xxxxx	Total loan funds	xxxxx
Endowment funds		Endowment funds	
Asset items		Fund balances	
Total endowment funds	xxxxx	Total endowment funds	xxxxx
Plant funds		Plant funds	
Unexpended assets		Liabilities	
		Unexpended fund balances	
Renewal and replacement assets		Renewal and replacement fund balances	
Assets for retirement of indebtedness		Retirement of indebtedness fund balances	
Investment in plant		Investment in plant fund balance	
Total plant funds	xxxxxx	Total plant funds	xxxxxx

APPENDIX 17–C: Formats for Hospital Financial Statements

BALANCE SHEET

Unrestricted Funds

Assets		Liabilities and Fund Balances	
Current assets		Current liabilities	
Other assets		Deferred revenue	
		Long-term debt	
		Fund balance	
Total	xxxxx	Total	xxxxx

Restricted Funds

Specific-purpose funds		Specific-purpose funds	
Asset items		Due to unrestricted funds	
		Fund balances	
Total	xxx		xxx
Endowment funds		Endowment funds	
Asset items		Fund balances	
Total	xxxx		xxxx

STATEMENT OF CHANGES IN FINANCIAL POSITION OF UNRESTRICTED FUND

Funds provided	
Various sources of net working capital	
Funds applied	
Various uses of net working capital	
Increase (or decrease) in net working capital	xxxx

SCHEDULE OF CHANGES IN INDIVIDUAL NET WORKING CAPITAL ITEMS

Changes in individual working capital items	
Increase (or decrease) in net working capital	xxxx

STATEMENT OF REVENUES AND EXPENSES

Patient service revenue	
Less allowances and uncollectible accounts	
Net patient revenue	
Other operating revenue	
Total operating revenue	
Operating expenses	
Operating expense items	
Total operating expenses	
Loss from operations	
Nonoperating revenue	
Nonoperating revenue items	
Total nonoperating revenue	
Excess of revenues over expenses	XXX

STATEMENT OF CHANGES IN FUND BALANCES

Unrestricted funds	
Balance at beginning of year	
Plus excess of revenues over expenses	
Transfers from other funds	
Less transfers to other funds	
Balance at end of year	XXXXX
Restricted funds	
Specific-purpose funds	
Balance at beginning of year	
Plus amounts received	
Less transfers to operations	
Balance at end of year	XXX
Plant replacement and expansion funds	
Balance at beginning of year	
Plus amounts received	
Less transfers to unrestricted funds	
Balance at end of year	XXXX
Endowment funds	
Balance at beginning of year	
Plus amounts received	
Gains from sale of investments	
Less losses from sale of investments	
Balance at end of year	XXXX

APPENDIX 17–D: Formats for Financial Statements of Health and Welfare Agencies

BALANCE SHEETS

CURRENT FUNDS

Unrestricted

Various asset items		Various liability items	
		Fund balance	
Total	xxxxx	Total	xxxx

Restricted

Various asset items		Fund balances	
Total	xxx		xxx

LAND, BUILDING, AND EQUIPMENT FUND

Various asset items		Mortgages payable	
		Fund balances	
Total	xxxxx		xxxxx

ENDOWMENT FUNDS

Cash and investment items		Fund balance	
Total	xxxxx	Total	xxxxx

STATEMENT OF FUNCTIONAL EXPENSES

	Program Services				
	Program 1	Program 2	Program 3	Program 4	Total
Various expense items					
Total expenses	xxxx	xxxx	xxxx	xxxx	xxxx

	Supporting Services			
	Management & General	Fund Raising	Total	Total Expense
Various expense items				
Total expenses	xxxx	xxxx	xxxx	

STATEMENT OF SUPPORT REVENUE AND EXPENSES AND CHANGES IN FUND BALANCES

	Current Funds		Land, Building, and Equipment Fund	Endow-ment Fund	Total All Funds
	Unrestricted	Restricted			
Public support and revenue					
Public support					
Revenues					
Total support and revenue					
Expenses					
Program service expenses					
Supporting expenses					
Excess (deficiency) of public support and revenues expenses	xxxx	xxxx	xxxx	xxxx	xxxx
Other changes in fund balances					
Fund balance — beginning of year					
Fund balance — end of year	xxxx	xxxx	xxxx	xxxx	xxxx

NOTES

1. National Association of College and University Business Officers, *College and University Business Administration*, 3rd ed. (Washington D.C.: National Association of College and University Business Officers, 1974), pp. 175–226.

2. American Hospital Association, *Chart of Accounts for Hospitals* (Chicago: American Hospital Association, 1976).

3. National Health Council, National Assembly of National Voluntary Health and Social Welfare Organizations, Inc., and United Way of America, *Standards of Accounting and Financial Reporting for Voluntary Health and Welfare Organizations* (New York: National Health Council, National Assembly of National Voluntary Health and Social Welfare Organizations, Inc., and United Way of America, 1975).

4. National Council on Governmental Accounting, *Governmental Accounting, Auditing, and Financial Reporting* (Chicago: Municipal Finance Officers Association, 1980), Appendix A, p. 25.

5. Summarized from professional development materials provided by Texas Society of CPAs.

QUESTIONS FOR CLASS DISCUSSION

Q17–1 What are four different types of nonprofit entities?

Q17–2 What operating characteristics distinguish nonprofit entities from business-type entities?

Q17–3 What are the primary differences between generally accepted accounting practices for business entities and generally accepted accounting practices for governmental entities? Justify the difference.

Q17–4 What do we mean by the term *appropriation control?* Why is it used in the nonprofit area?

Q17–5 How are fund accounting practices different from the accounting practices of business entities? Why are fund accounting practices followed by nonprofit entities?

Q17–6 What is the difference between source and disposition and self-sustaining funds?

Q17–7 What is the difference between the terms *expenditures* and *expenses?*

Q17–8 How do the transactions typically associated with a capital projects fund compare with those carried out through the general fund?

Q17–9 How does a special assessment fund differ from a capital projects fund?

Q17–10 How do the operations of enterprise funds differ from the operations of internal service funds?

Q17–11 What is meant by the *modified accrual basis of accounting?* Explain. In what situations is that basis of accounting in accordance with generally accepted accounting principles?

Q17–12 How do expenditure accounts differ from encumbrance accounts? Under what circumstances would the encumbrance and reserve for encumbrance accounts be used?

Q17–13 Which operating characteristics often contribute to weaknesses in the systems of internal control for nonprofit organizations?

Q17–14 What control practices should normally be associated with handling and recording the receipts of charitable contributions to reduce the probability of fraud or embezzlement? Indicate the type of fraud or embezzlement that each practice is designed to prevent.

Q17–15 How do the formats of financial statements for governmental entities compare with those of business entities?

Q17–16 How do the statement formats for college and university financial statements compare with those of business entities?

Q17–17 Of what significance is the emphasis on appropriation control by governmental units in the audits of such units?

Q17–18 Is the auditor concerned with examining the budgetary data for a governmental unit in connection with the audit of such an entity? Explain.

Q17–19 Many nonprofit organizations receive restricted gifts; what are the auditor's special responsibilities in verifying restricted gifts transactions?

Q17–20 Should pledges solicited by a nonprofit organization be shown as an asset in the organization's balance sheet? Discuss.

Q17–21 What is the significance of donated services in the audit of nonprofit organization financial statements?

Q17–22 What special concerns does an auditor have in verifying claims against third-party payors in auditing the financial statements of a hospital?

Q17–23 What is the key consideration in determining whether the financial statements of two or more financially interrelated nonprofit organizations should be combined or consolidated?

Q17–24 What wording should be used in the opinion portion of an audit report for a nonprofit organization that used the cash basis of accounting rather than the generally acceptable basis? Justify each of the different phrases used.

Q17–25 How does the financial statement format followed for hospitals compare with that used for business entities? Justify the differences.

Q17–26 What is the significance of supporting services in presenting the operating results for a health and welfare agency? Discuss.

SHORT CASES

C17–1 A friend of yours who has been operating a business for some years is commenting on the problems of preventing fraud and embezzlement. Another member of the group discussing the problem is Edgar Fallows, the chief executive officer for a large health and welfare agency. Fallows responds with a statement that the resources of his organization are even more vulnerable to fraud and embezzlement than are those of a business enterprise.

Required:

Discuss the justification for Fallows's remark.

C17–2 Laura Canavan shows you a statement of revenues and expenditures for the general fund of the city in which she lives. She, too, is an accounting student, but does not understand why the city has used the term *expenditures* rather than *expenses* to describe its outflows of resources.

Required:

Explain the difference between the two terms; justify the use of the term *expenditures* in the governmental statements.

C17–3 You are working as a staff accountant on the audit of River City's financial statements. You have been assigned to review the transactions of a capital projects fund. During the course of your examination you discover a disbursement of capital project fund resources for municipal employee salaries.

Required:

Explain the concern that you, as an auditor, would have about such a transaction.

C17–4 In examining the engagement letter for the audit of Millersville's financial statements, you discover that the senior in charge has requested the city manager to provide the audit staff with a copy of the city budget. Another staff accountant working with you states that he does not understand why the audit team would be concerned with budgetary data since the primary objective of the audit is to determine whether the financial statements are fairly presented.

Required:

Explain to your coworker why the senior has requested a copy of the city budget.

C17–5 In the audit of a governmental entity you discover a significant balance in an account called Revenues from Grants.

Required:

What special audit procedures should be applied in the verification of this account and the resources received in connection with it?

C17–6 You are auditing the financial statements of a university. During the audit you find that the university has received a significant number of gifts from its constituency.

Required:

Explain your special concerns in verifying the transactions giving recognition to those gifts.

C17–7 In auditing the financial statements of a health and welfare agency, Carol Campanelli discovers an account entitled Pledge Revenue.

Required:

Describe the special concerns that Campanelli would have as an auditor in verifying that account and its related assets accounts.

C17–8 In auditing the financial statements of a hospital, you discover a large balance in an account entitled Receivable from Medical Insurance Claims.

Required:

Explain the special concerns you would have in the examination of that account and its related nominal accounts.

C17–9 In auditing the financial statements of a university, Gunther Schmidt, the CPA, discovers that a number of fixed assets have been purchased during the period under audit. All of these have been debited to expenditure accounts rather than to the specific fixed assets accounts.

Required:

Comment on this procedure, and suggest a reasonable course of action for Schmidt to undertake in verifying these items.

C17–10 During the audit of the city of Hillsboro, you have been assigned the responsibility of examining interfund transactions. Some of these involve transfers of loans from certain restricted funds to the Hillsboro general fund.

Required:

Discuss any concerns you might have relating to such transactions.

PROBLEMS

P17–1 Select the best answer for each of the following items.

a. Governmental auditing often extends beyond examinations leading to the expression of opinion on the fairness of financial presentation and includes audits of efficiency, economy, effectiveness, and also
   (1) Accuracy.
   (2) Evaluation.
   (3) Compliance.
   (4) Internal control.

b. A nonprofit organization published a monthly magazine that had 15,000 subscribers on January 1, 19X6. The number of subscribers increased steadily throughout the year and at December 31, 19X6, there were 16,200 subscribers. The annual magazine subscription cost was $10 on January 1, 19X6, and was increased to $12 for new members on April 1, 19X6. An auditor would expect that the receipts from subscriptions for the year ended December 31, 19X6, would be approximately
   (1) $179,400.
   (2) $171,600.
   (3) $164,400.
   (4) $163,800.

c. How should charity service, contractual adjustments, and bad debts be classified in the statement of revenues and expenses for the hospital?
   (1) All three should be treated as expenses.
   (2) All three should be treated as deductions from patient service revenues.
   (3) Charity service and contractual adjustments should be treated as revenue deductions, whereas bad debts should be treated as an expense.
   (4) Charity service and bad debts should be treated as expenses, whereas contractual adjustments should be treated as a revenue deduction.
d. A university receives a cash gift in the amount of $500,000, which the donor specifies shall be used in constructing a classroom building. This gift should be recorded as
   (1) Gift revenue in the unrestricted current fund.
   (2) Gift revenue in the restricted current fund.
   (3) An increase to cash and fund balance in the plant fund.
   (4) Quasi-endowment in the endowment fund.
e. What would be the effect on the general fund balance in the current fiscal year of recording a $15,000 purchase for a new fire truck out of general fund resources, for which a $14,600 encumbrance had been recorded in the general fund in the previous fiscal year?
   (1) Reduce the general fund balance $15,000.
   (2) Reduce the general fund balance $14,600.
   (3) Reduce the general fund balance $400.
   (4) Have no effect on the general fund balance.
f. Brockton City's debt service fund (for term bonds) recorded required additions and required earnings for the current fiscal year of $15,000 and $7,000, respectively. The actual revenues and interest earnings were $16,000 and $6,500, respectively. What are the necessary entries to record the year's actual additions and earnings in the debt service fund and in the general long-term debt group, respectively?
   (1) $22,500 and $22,000.
   (2) $22,000 and $22,000.
   (3) $22,500 and $22,500.
   (4) $22,500 and no entry.

(AICPA adapted)

P17–2 At the start of your examination of the accounts of the City of Waterford, you discovered that the bookkeeper failed to keep the accounts by funds. The trial balance of the general fund for the year ended December 31, 19X2, shown on page 771, was available.

Your examination disclosed that

a. The budget for the year 19X2, not recorded on the books, estimated revenues and expenditures as follows: revenues $815,000, expenditures $775,000.
b. Outstanding purchase orders at December 31, 19X2, for operating expenses not recorded on the books totaled $2,500.
c. Included in the revenues account is a credit of $190,000, representing the value of land donated by the state as a grant-in-aid for construction of the River Bridge.

City of Waterford
GENERAL FUND TRIAL BALANCE
December 31, 19X2

	Debit	Credit
Cash	$ 207,500	
Taxes receivable — current	148,500	
Allowance for uncollectible taxes — current		$ 6,000
Appropriation expenditures	760,000	
Revenues		992,500
Donated land	190,000	
River Bridge bonds authorized — unissued	100,000	
Work in process — River Bridge	130,000	
River Bridge bonds payable		200,000
Contracts payable — River Bridge		25,000
Retained percentage — River Bridge contracts		5,000
Vouchers payable		7,500
Fund balance		300,000
Total	$1,536,000	$1,536,000

d. Interest payable in future years totals $60,000 on River Bridge bonds sold at par for $200,000.

e. Examination of the subledger containing the details of the appropriation expenditures account revealed the following items included therein:

Current operating expenses	$472,000
Additions to structures and improvements	210,000
Equipment purchases	10,000
General obligation bonds paid	50,000
Interest paid on general obligation bonds	18,000

Required:

Prepare a worksheet showing the given general fund trial balance, adjusting entries, and distributions to the proper funds or groups of accounts. The following column headings are recommended:

a. General fund trial balance — debit.
b. General fund trial balance — credit.
c. Adjustments — debit.
d. Adjustments — credit.
e. General fund — debit.
f. General fund — credit.
g. Capital projects fund.

h. General fixed assets.
i. General long-term debt.

Number all adjusting and transaction entries. Formal journal entries are not required.

(AICPA adapted)

P17–3 The current funds trial balances for Apex University is shown below.

	Current Unrestricted Funds		Current Restricted Funds	
Cash	$ 105,000		$ 60,000	
Investments	40,000		30,000	
Accounts payable		$ 55,000		$ 12,000
Tuition and fees		1,200,000		
Gifts		300,000		150,000
Auxiliary activities revenue		500,000		
Endowment income		200,000		75,000
Instructional expenditures	1,300,000			
Student aid	75,000		125,000	
Research expenditures			40,000	
Operating expenditures	600,000			
Library expenditures			10,000	
Auxiliary activities expenditures	480,000			
Fund balance		345,000		28,000
Totals	$2,600,000	$2,600,000	$265,000	$265,000

Required:

Prepare financial statements for the current funds.

P17–4 Hillcrest Blood Bank is a nonprofit organization handling all its operations through one operating fund. Its statement of cash receipts and disbursements for the year ended June 30, 19X2, is shown on page 773, and its balance sheets as of June 30, 19X1, and June 30, 19X2, appear on page 774.

Hillcrest Blood Bank
STATEMENT OF CASH RECEIPTS AND DISBURSEMENTS
For the Year Ended June 30, 19X2

Balance, July 1, 19X1			
Cash in bank			$ 2,712
Receipts			
From hospitals:			
Hillcrest Hospital	$7,702		
Good Samaritan Hospital	3,818	$11,520	
Individuals		6,675	
From other blood banks		602	
From sales of serum and supplies		2,260	
Interest on bonds		525	
Gifts and bequests		4,928	
Total receipts			26,510
Total to be accounted for			29,222
Disbursements:			
Laboratory expense:			
Serum	$3,098		
Salaries	3,392		
Supplies	3,533		
Laundry and miscellaneous	277	10,300	
Other expenses and disbursements:			
Salaries	5,774		
Dues and subscriptions	204		
Rent and utilities	1,404		
Blood testing	2,378		
Payments to other blood banks for blood given to members away from home	854		
Payments to professional blood donors	2,410		
Other expenses	1,805		
Purchase of U.S. Treasury bond	1,000	15,829	
Total disbursements			26,129
Balance, June 30, 19X2			$ 3,093

Hillcrest Blood Bank
BALANCE SHEET

	June 30, 19X1	June 30, 19X2
Assets		
Cash	$ 2,712	$ 3,093
U.S. Treasury bonds	15,000	16,000
Accounts receivable — sales of blood:		
Hospitals	1,302	1,448
Individuals	425	550
Inventories:		
Blood	480	640
Supplies and serum	250	315
Furniture and equipment, less depreciation	4,400	4,050
Total assets	$24,569	$26,096
Liabilities and Surplus		
Accounts payable — supplies	$ 325	$ 275
Fund balance	24,244	25,821
Total liabilities and fund balance	$24,569	$26,096

Required:

a. Prepare a transactions worksheet for the Hillcrest Blood Bank that develops data for an accrual-based operating statement and end-of-period balance sheet.
b. Prepare appropriate accrual-based financial statements.

(AICPA adapted)

P17–5 Assume that you are a CPA who has recently acquired a large local church as an audit client. Since this is the first audit client of its type for your firm, you feel it is necessary to instruct the audit staff as to particular problem areas often associated with the audit of charitable organizations before proceeding with the engagement. You have arranged for a conference with the audit senior to discuss the upcoming engagement.

Required:

Outline the agenda of the upcoming meeting, giving particular attention to

a. Potential internal control problems to look for and attributes of the church's system of internal controls that might prevent, detect, or correct the problems.
b. Areas of special emphasis, if any, during the substantive testing phase of the audit.
c. The audit report to be issued on financial statements of the church at the conclusion of the audit.

PART FOUR

REPORTING THE RESULTS OF THE AUDIT

CHAPTER 18

THE AUDIT REPORT

Throughout this text, we have stressed that the ultimate objective of the independent audit is the expression of an opinion regarding the presentation of the client's financial position, results of operations, and changes in financial position. To this point, we have considered how the auditor meets the general and field work standards in carrying out the evidence-gathering portion of an independent audit. Each of the audit procedures discussed in the preceding chapters is carried out with the ultimate goal of enabling the auditor to express an opinion on the financial statements. This opinion is communicated to investors and other users of financial data through the medium of the audit report. The users then rely on that report for assurance that the financial information they are receiving from the company is complete, consistent, and fairly presented within the bounds of generally accepted accounting principles.

Our primary attention in this chapter is devoted to the criteria that must be met in fulfilling the requirements of the fourth standard of reporting. Our discussion will cover the following topics:

1. Meaning of the term *association with financial statements*.
2. Examination of the auditor's standard unqualified report.
3. Possible departures from the wording reflected in the standard unqualified audit report.
4. Effect on the audit report of including segment information with the basic financial statements.
5. Reports on information accompanying the basic financial statements in auditor-submitted documents.
6. Updating and reissuing audit reports.

We have emphasized that the client controls what is presented in the financial statements and therefore has the primary responsibility for the fairness and completeness of all disclosures contained in them. Those financial statements may, if necesssary, be adjusted to reflect GAAP only with the client's permission. The audit report, on the other hand, is the property of the independent auditor. It must be written so as to communicate clearly and effectively the scope of audit activities performed, the results of those activities, and the resultant degree of assurance that the auditor can provide regarding the fairness of the financial statements. If *management declines to make essential financial disclosures*, the auditor should provide them in the audit report and should appropriately modify his or her opinion to recognize the omission.

In order to meet the requirements for clear and unambiguous communications, the accounting profession has adopted four generally accepted standards that the auditor must meet in reporting her or his findings relating to a client's financial statements. These standards were listed and discussed briefly in Chapter 2. As was stated there, the *fourth standard of reporting* is probably the most complicated and the most important of all the reporting standards. It requires that the audit report contain either an expression of opinion regarding the financial statements, taken as a whole, or an assertion that an opinion cannot be expressed and the reasons therefor. Furthermore, anytime an accountant's name is associated with financial statements, her or his report is required to contain a clear-cut indication of the character of the accountant's examination, if any, and the degree of responsibility taken regarding those statements.

ASSOCIATION WITH FINANCIAL STATEMENTS

The independent accountant is required to report on only those financial statements with which he or she is associated. It is important, therefore, that we establish what it means to be associated with financial statements. Figure 18–1 depicts the possible levels of an accountant's association with financial statements, and it serves as a graphic preview of our discussion in Chapters 18 and 19.

Observe first that we may divide all clients into two groups: public entities and nonpublic entities. For these purposes, a public entity is defined as

> any entity (a) whose securities trade in a public market either on a stock exchange (domestic or foreign) or in the over-the-counter market, including securities quoted only locally or regionally, (b) that makes a filing with a regulatory agency in preparation for the sale of any class of its securities in a public market, or (c) that is a subsidiary, corporate joint venture, or other entity controlled by an entity covered in (a) or (b).[1]

With regard to any public entity, there are generally three levels of possible association between the auditor and entity's financial statements. An accountant is

	Public Entities			Nonpublic Entities		
	(1)	(2)	(3)	(1)	(2)	(3)
Level of association	Unaudited statements	Review*	Audit	Compilation	Review	Audit
Degree of assurance given by accountant	None	Limited	Opinion	None	Limited	Opinion
Primary authoritative documents	SAS 26	SAS 36	SAS 2 SAS 15	SSARS 1	SSARS 1	SAS 2 SAS 15

*May be performed for public or nonpublic entities.

FIGURE 18–1. Levels of Auditor's Association with Financial Statements

considered ***associated*** with financial statements when he or she has consented to the use of her or his name in a report, document, or written communication (except tax returns) containing the statements. This is true *whether or not the accountant appends her or his name* to the statements.

The most remote level of association with public entities is with unaudited financial statements. The most remote level for nonpublic entities is the compilation of a client's financial statements. In this type of engagement, the accountant merely prepares unaudited financial statements from the books and records of the client. The next most remote level of association for both public and nonpublic entities involves reviews of either annual or interim financial information. A review consists largely of ***inquiry and analytical review*** procedures, which, while they are audit procedures, are not sufficient for the expression of an audit opinion. Compilations and reviews are discussed at length in Chapter 19. The closest level of association possible for the accountant for either type entity is the ***audit.*** Notice that as the level of association becomes closer, the level of assurance expected from the accountant increases — from none at the most remote level to a full expression of an opinion on the financial statement at the closest level.

Again observe that the fourth standard of reporting applies to any financial statement with which the accountant is associated. In this chapter we concentrate our discussion on reporting responsibilities for the *audit level of association (level 3) for both public and nonpublic entities* and for *unaudited financial statements (level 1) of public entities.* Reporting responsibilities for the other levels of association are discussed in Chapter 19.

Figure 18–2 is a condensed presentation of the range of reporting alternatives available to the auditor under SAS 2 and other standards. SAS 15 is closely related and covers reports on comparative financial statements. We will be discussing each of these standards, and others, relating to reports on audited and unaudited financial

UNQUALIFIED OPINION	QUALIFYING REASON	
(.06−.08)	Effects Material but Not Pervasive *	Effects Pervasive*
	1. Limitation on scope Qualifying language: "Except for" (.10–.13; .40)	1. Disclaimer (.46; .47)
	2. Failure to conform with GAAP: Qualifying language: "Except for" (.15–.19; .36)	2. Adverse (.41–.44)
	3. Lack of consistent application of GAAP Qualifying language: "Except for" or "After giving retroactive effect to" (.20; .38; Sec. 546)	3. Unchanged from qualified
	4. Material uncertainty with regard to one or more parts of financial statements. Qualifying language: "Subject to" (.21–.26; .39)	4. Disclaimer (.45, footnote 10)

Other Reasons for Disclaimer (.45−.47)

1. Unaudited financial statements (SAS 26)
2. Lack of independence (SAS 26)

Reports Requiring a Departure from Standard Wording but Not Constituting a Qualified Opinion

1. Relying on the work of other auditors (Sec. 543; .14)
2. Emphasis of a matter (.27)

Other Related Topics

Reports on comparative statements (SAS 15)
Piecemeal opinions (.48)
Reports on segment information (SAS 21)
Reporting on information accompanying the basic financial statements in auditor-submitted documents (SAS 29)

**Pervasive* means having a material impact on fair presentation of financial statements taken as a whole
Note: Numbers in parentheses are paragraph numbers of SAS 2, unless otherwise indicated.

FIGURE 18–2. Reporting Standards in a Nutshell

statements in the next section. The numbers in parentheses accompanying each type of report are paragraph numbers of SAS 2, unless otherwise indicated. We will discuss each type of report, beginning with the unqualified report and continuing through "emphasis of a matter."

THE STANDARD UNQUALIFIED SHORT-FORM REPORT

Recall that we looked at the standard unqualified audit report in Chapters 1 and 2 as we considered the ultimate goal of the independent audit. At that time we discussed the detailed contents of the report. This is the type of audit report most frequently found in corporate annual reports. The audit, we saw, may be addressed to the corporation's board of directors, the audit committee, or the shareholders. It would be helpful to review the report shown in Chapters 1 and 2 as well as other related parts of those chapters before proceeding with study of this chapter.

The audit report must always be issued on the "financial statements taken as a whole." This phrase refers to the four basic financial statements for the *current period as well as all prior years* presented for comparative purposes. However, the auditor may in some instances be asked to report on only the balance sheet, having had only limited access to information underlying all the statements. If another statement, such as a statement of changes in owner's equity, is included, the auditor may identify that statement in the scope paragraph but need not mention it in the opinion paragraph.

Typically auditors remain associated with their clients over a period of years. When they do, they become known as ***continuing auditors.*** If the annual report of a company includes comparative statements for two years, the audit report must cover both years if the auditor has performed the audits for both years. In essence, then, by issuing an unqualified audit report with comparative financial statements, the continuing auditor is issuing two separate reports:

- An unqualified audit report on the financial statements of the current year.
- An *updated* unqualified audit report on the financial statements for the preceding year if that type of report was issued in the previous year.[2]

If the prior-year statements are unaudited, they should be marked unaudited and the auditor should limit his or her opinion to the audited statements. A separate paragraph should be included, describing the responsibility assumed for the statements of the prior period.

The unqualified short-form audit report can be issued only if *all* of the following circumstances are present:

- The auditor has gathered *sufficient competent evidence* to assure that the three standards of audit field work have been met.
- Audit evidence has revealed no significant uncorrected departures from GAAP.
- There have been no significant accounting changes that affect comparability of the financial statements.
- There are no material uncertainties facing the client which cannot be estimated or satisfactorily resolved as of the audit report date.

DEPARTURES FROM THE STANDARD UNQUALIFIED AUDIT REPORT

In this section we discuss six basic reporting circumstances that require departures from the wording of the standard unqualified audit report.[3] Four of these six are related to the *absence* of one or more of the essentials in the preceding list, and they require the issuance of a ***qualified audit report.*** For example, if the scope of the audit has been restricted so that the auditor cannot obtain sufficient competent evidential matter, the audit report must be qualified. If the effects of the limitation are pervasive, an *extreme report* should be issued. As Figure 18–2 shows, extreme audit reports consist of the *disclaimer of opinion* and the *adverse opinion.*

In determining the type of report to be rendered, the auditor begins by determining whether one of the four circumstances cited above has occurred. If one of the four circumstances is present, he or she must make a judgment as to whether it would affect the decision of an informed user of the financial information. If so, it is *material* and the audit report must at least be qualified. Beyond that, however, the auditor must decide whether the circumstances of qualification produce a *pervasive* (very material) impact on fairness of presentation of the financial statements taken as a whole. If they do, a qualified opinion would no longer be appropriate: instead, an extreme opinion should be issued. As shown in Figure 18–2, the extreme audit report for the limitation of audit scope (circumstance 1) and the material uncertainty (circumstance 4) is the disclaimer of opinion. The extreme audit report for the failure of the statement to conform with GAAP (circumstance 2) is the adverse opinion.

The most commonly used determinant of pervasiveness is the relative magnitude, or dollar effect of an item, on an important financial statement variable, such as total assets or net income. For example, if the client has failed to adhere to GAAP in one or more disclosures and refuses to correct the financial statements, the auditor should, as part of completion of the evidence-gathering phase of the audit, combine the dollar effects of all adjusting entries which the client has failed to make. The aggregate error should then be compared with a judgmentally predetermined cutoff level for materiality. If the dollar effect of the errors is *material* (important enough to affect users' decisions) *but isolated* to, say, one or a relatively few elements of the financial statements taken as a whole, a qualified opinion should be issued. If, however, the effect of errors on key financial statement variables is so material (either very large or very pervasive) that it affects the fairness of presentation of the financial statements taken as a whole, an adverse opinion would be required.

Other determinants of materiality include consideration of these factors:

- *The user group.* Investors are usually more interested in items which affect income or ability to pay dividends. Creditors, on the other hand, usually are more concerned with balance sheet items, because these affect the client's ability to meet creditor claims. The auditor does not always know the primary user group but should be more sensitive to effects of disclosures on certain selected variables when he or she does know the user group.
- *Susceptibility of the item to measurement.* For example, in the case of a material uncertainty, such as potential litigation, the item in question often is not susceptible to reasonable estimation. Measurement of the dollar magnitude of the effect on the financial statements

taken as a whole is therefore not possible. In this case, the auditor should consider the *qualitative factors* of the decision, such as the relative importance of the matter to the overall disclosures in the financial statements, or even to the very existence of the entity. Also, the *likelihood of occurrence* of the item would have an effect on the type of opinion issued.

- *The nature of the item.* For example, where *fraud or irregularities* or other illegal acts have taken place, the materiality threshold for disclosure is lower than for inadvertant errors. Similarly, items involving *related parties* would be more sensitive to materiality standards than those arising from transactions among unrelated business entities.

Reports Accompanying Scope Limitations

A scope limitation occurs when, for some reason, the auditor is *unable to obtain sufficient evidence* to support one or more of the disclosures in the financial statements. Such limitations can arise because of: (1) restrictions caused by underlying conditions, or (2) restrictions imposed by the client. When a client imposes restrictions on the scope of the audit, it is generally regarded as a more serious matter than when the restrictions result from other conditions; this is because such restrictions limit the auditor's investigative independence. The AICPA encourages use of a disclaimer of opinion in such situations, although a scope-qualified opinion is also permissible if circumstances justify it. Examples of client-imposed scope restrictions are those which deny the auditor the opportunity to observe physical inventory counts or to confirm certain accounts receivable. Clients may impose such scope restrictions because they want to limit the amount of audit fees, or, in the case of receivables confirmation, to avoid annoying any of their customers who may be particularly averse to receiving confirmation requests. Other types of client-imposed restrictions are refusal to provide copies of board of directors' minutes, and refusal to provide a client representation letter. In all cases, the reasons for the restrictions should be evaluated by the auditor prior to her or his deciding whether to issue a qualified opinion or a disclaimer of opinion. However, professional standards require scope-qualified or disclaimer audit reports when clients refuse to supply such vital evidence as the representation letter. Of course, the auditor's main concern is that the client may be trying to conceal a misstatement.

In other cases, the client may have imposed no restrictions but, owing to unusual circumstances beyond the client's control, the auditor is nonetheless unable to obtain necessary evidence. For example:

- Inability to confirm accounts receivable or to perform alternative procedures because of poor customer response to confirmation requests and inadequate subsequent collection information.
- Inability to observe the physical count of inventories or to perform alternative inventory verification procedures because the client has no perpetual inventory system; this could happen if the auditor was hired only after the end of the client's fiscal year.
- Refusal of the client's attorney to furnish a lawyer's letter.

Qualifying language in a scope-restricted audit report should appear in three places. In the scope paragraph, the second sentence (referring to application of generally accepted auditing standards) should be preceded with the qualifying phrase, "except as noted below." A middle paragraph should then be inserted, containing the *facts* associated with the qualification as well as the *effects* on the financial statements of the items to which the scope limitation pertains. Finally, the first sentence of the opinion paragraph should be modified with the qualifying phrase, beginning with the words "except for."

An example follows, in which the auditor was not hired until after the client's fiscal 19X2 year end and thus was unable to observe physical inventories. Inventories in this situation are considered material but not pervasive to the financial statements taken as a whole, and alternative procedures (outlined in Chapter 11) were not possible. The qualifying language is emphasized in italics.

SCOPE PARAGRAPH:

We have examined the balance sheet of ABC Company, Inc., as of December 31, 19X2 and 19X1, and the related statements of income, retained earnings, and changes in financial position for the years then ended. *Except as explained in the following paragraph,* our examinations were conducted in accordance with generally accepted auditing standards, and accordingly included such tests of the accounting records and such other auditing procedures as we considered necessary in the circumstances.

MIDDLE PARAGRAPH:

We did not observe the taking of physical inventories as of December 31, 19X2 (stated at $X,XXX,XXX) and December 31, 19X1 (stated at $X,XXX,XXX), since those dates were prior to the time we were engaged as auditors for the company. Due to the nature of the company's records, we were unable to satisfy ourselves as to the inventory quantities by means of other auditing procedures.

OPINION PARAGRAPH:

In our opinion, *except for the effects of such adjustments, if any, as might have been determined to be necessary had we been able to observe the physical inventories,* the financial statements mentioned above present fairly the financial position of ABC Company, Inc., at December 31, 19X2, and X1, and the results of its operations and changes in its financial position for the years then ended, in conformity with generally accepted accounting principles applied on a consistent basis.

Notice that the qualifying language is "except for" in both the scope and opinion paragraphs. Notice also that both the surrounding *facts* and the *effects* of the qualification are set forth clearly in a middle paragraph. Finally, you should remember that when such an opinion is expressed, the reference in the opinion paragraph should be to the *possible effects* of potential financial statement adjustments and not to the qualification itself.

A *disclaimer of opinion* in this case would have been justified if the inventories of ABC, Inc., at December 31, 19X2 and 19X1, had been *both material and pervasive* with respect to the financial statements taken as a whole. Alternatively, there may have been more than one scope qualification, such as failure to obtain evidence regarding other accounts. Although a scope limitation pertaining to a single account may not be material and pervasive, the combined effects of scope limitations on several accounts might be. An example of a disclaimer produced by multiple pervasive scope limitations follows.

SCOPE PARAGRAPH (*Same as Above*)

MIDDLE PARAGRAPH:

We did not observe the taking of physical inventories as of December 31, 19X2 (stated at $X,XXX,XXX) and December 31, 19X1 (stated at $X,XXX,XXX) since those dates were prior to the time we were engaged as auditor for the company. Furthermore, evidence supporting the cost of property and equipment acquired prior to December 31, 19X1 is no longer available. Due to the nature of the company's records, we were unable to satisfy ourselves as to the inventory quantities or the cost of property and equipment by means of alternative procedures.

OPINION PARAGRAPH:

Since we were unable to satisfy ourselves as to inventory quantities or cost of property and equipment by application of standard or adequate alternative procedures, as noted in the preceding paragraph, the scope of our work was not sufficient to enable us to express, and accordingly we do not express, an opinion on the financial statements referred to above.

If a material and pervasive scope limitation exists with respect to one or more of the financial statements taken as a whole, but not to the others, the auditor *may split her or his opinion,* by disclaiming an opinion on the affected statements and expressing an unqualified opinion on the remainder of the statement. For example, if the auditor has been hired early in 19X1 so that only the beginning inventories as of that year (assumed material and pervasive) could not be observed or adequately audited by means of alternative procedures, the auditor could proceed as follows:

1. Explain the scope limitation in the scope and middle paragraphs, as illustrated above.
2. Disclaim an opinion on the statements of income, retained earnings, and changes in financial position for 19X1.
3. Issue an unqualified opinion on the balance sheet as of December 31, 19X1 as well as on all the financial statements for the year ended December 31, 19X2.

Reports Accompanying Statements That Contain Departures from GAAP

When the client has (1) made material disclosures that do not conform to GAAP, or (2) omitted material disclosures necessary for compliance with GAAP, *either a qualified or an adverse opinion is necessary.* This conforms to the first audit standard of reporting (which requires that the audit report shall state whether the financial statements are in conformity with GAAP) and with the third reporting standard (which provides for a presumption of adequate informative disclosures in the financial statements unless otherwise specified in the audit report). Whether a qualified or an adverse opinion is required *depends on the materiality of the departure* from GAAP.

"Materiality" for this purpose may be interpreted in much the same manner as explained in the previous section.

These types of reports are probably regarded as requiring the most serious kind of qualification, because they deal with a willful violation of GAAP by the client. The SEC will not allow clients to submit any 10-K annual reports under the Securities Exchange Act of 1934, or registration statements under the Securities Act of 1933, that contain auditor knowledge of material departures from GAAP: that disallowance is one reason why these types of reports are so rarely seen in practice. Following is an example of an audit report *qualified* because of the failure to capitalize a long-term lease obligation. Qualifying language is emphasized in italics.

> SCOPE PARAGRAPH *(Unchanged from the Unqualified Report)*
>
> MIDDLE PARAGRAPH:
>
> The Company has excluded from assets and liabilities in the accompanying balance sheet as of December 31, 19X2 certain lease obligations, which, in our opinion, should be capitalized in order to conform with generally accepted accounting principles. If these lease obligations were capitalized, property would be increased by $X,XXX,XXX; long-term debt by $X,XXX,XXX; and retained earnings by $X,XXX,XXX as of December 31, 19X2. Net income and earnings per share would be increased (decreased) by $XXX,XXX and $X.XX, respectively, for the year ended.
>
> OPINION PARAGRAPH:
>
> In our opinion, *except for the effect of not capitalizing lease obligations, as discussed in the preceding paragraph,* the financial statements present fairly the financial position of the ABC Company at December 31, 19X2 and X1, and the results of its operations and changes in its financial position for the years then ended, in conformity with generally accepted accounting principles applied on a consistent basis.

Notice that the opinion qualified for departures from GAAP contains the following characteristics:

- No change in the scope paragraph from the unqualified report — because the scope requirements of GAAS have been met.
- A middle paragraph that discloses the *fact* of the departures(s) from GAAP and the related *dollar effects* on all affected financial statement components.
- The qualifying language beginning with the phrase "*except for*" in the opinion paragraph.

One exception to the practices just cited occurs when the auditor can show that the departure from GAAP was necessary to keep the financial statements from being misleading. In such a rare situation, an unqualified opinion may be issued.

When the uncorrected departures from GAAP have an effect that is so material that a qualified opinion is not justified, an *adverse opinion* should be issued. An adverse opinion may be issued, for example, when one very material and pervasive departure from GAAP has been discovered; or when there are several uncorrected departures from GAAP, the combined effects of which are material to the financial statements taken as a whole. In the preceding example, for instance, if the effects of the failure to capitalize the lease were material to the financial statements taken as a whole, the audit report would be modified as follows:

SCOPE PARAGRAPH *(Same as Above)*

MIDDLE PARAGRAPH *(Same as Above)*

OPINION PARAGRAPH:

In our opinion, *because of the effects of the matters discussed in the preceding paragraph,* the financial statements referred to above *do not present fairly,* in conformity with generally accepted accounting principles, the financial position of the ABC Company, Inc., as of December 31, 19X2 and X1, or the results of its operations and the changes in its financial position for the years then ended.

Notice the distinctive features of the adverse opinion:

- It contains no scope paragraph modification — again, because the scope requirements of GAAS have been met.
- Like its qualified counterpart, it contains a middle paragraph disclosing the facts of the departure from GAAP and the effects on the financial statements.
- The opinion is adverse because of the material effect of the departures from GAAP on the financial statements taken as a whole.
- There is *no reference to consistency,* because that reference implies the application of GAAP. This does not, however, prevent the auditor from also qualifying as to consistency when a material adverse change in accounting principles has occurred during the year under audit.

Reports Accompanying Material Accounting Changes

The second reporting standard requires that the report shall state whether generally accepted accounting principles have been consistently applied. The purpose of the ***consistency phrase*** in the audit report is to provide assurance that comparability between financial statements has not been materially affected by an accounting change. Therefore the audit report relating to a client's first year of operations will include no reference to consistency.

If the financial statements being reported on are *comparative financial statements,* the standard consistency wording in the unqualified audit report is as follows (emphasized in italics):

. . . .in conformity with generally accepted accounting principles *applied on a consistent basis.*

If the financial statements being reported on are *single-year statements,* the consistency phrase unqualified report should read as follows:

. . . .in conformity with generally accepted accounting principles *applied on a basis consistent with that of the preceding year.*

Finally, if comparative statements for both the current year and a prior year are presented, along with the statements of one or more earlier years, *for comparative purposes only*, the consistency phrase in the unqualified audit report should read thus:

> . . . .in conformity with generally accepted accounting principles, *applied on a consistent basis and on a basis consistent with that of the preceding year.*

Accounting changes are defined in APB Opinion 20 as *changes which are made in accounting principles or methods of applying those principles, changes in reporting entities, or corrections of prior periods' errors.* These changes may occur at the clients' discretion, if it can be shown that the newly adopted accounting principle is the preferable way of reporting. Also, such changes may be mandated by the FASB or other authoritative bodies; and the client may be forced to adopt the change in order for financial statements to continue to comply with GAAP. The auditor is required to qualify the consistency statement in the audit report any time an accounting change has been made which affects comparability, regardless of whether the accounting change has been made at the discretion of the client. The auditor should also state in the qualification whether or not he or she concurs with the change. Generally accepted auditing standards differentiate between accounting changes that affect comparability and those that do not. Changes deemed to affect *comparability*, and therefore to *require qualification of the audit report*, include these:

- Changes in reporting entities (such as inclusion of subsidiary companies in consolidated financial statements of the current year) that were not included in a previous year, even though owned during that year.
- Changes in an accounting principle or in the method of applying a principle.
- Corrections of prior-period errors involving principles, such as the correction of the prior period's improper application of an inventory accounting method.[4]

Changes deemed *not to affect comparability* and therefore not requiring a consistency-qualified audit report include the following:

- Changes in accounting estimate, such as changes in the estimated lives of fixed assets for depreciation purposes.
- Error corrections that do not involve principles, such as the correction of a mathematical mistake from a prior period.
- Variations in format and presentation of the statement of changes in financial position.
- Changes arising because of substantially different transactions or events, such as the purchase or sale of product lines or services, or perhaps purchases or sales of subsidiaries.[5]

Also, an accounting change having no material effect on current period financial statements but expected to have a substantial effect in later years does not require a modification of the consistency statement. The change should, however, be disclosed in the notes to the financial statements.

According to generally accepted accounting principles, there are certain changes that require a *retroactive restatement of prior period's financial statements* in order to meet the comparability standard. APB opinion 20 lists the following as examples of circumstances requiring such restatement:

- Changes in reporting entity.
- Changes from the LIFO method of inventory costing to another method (but not a change from FIFO to LIFO).

- Changes to or from the full-cost method of accounting in the extractive industries.
- Changes in method of accounting used for long-term construction contracts.[6]

Even when the financial statements of the prior period have been retroactively restated to reflect the effects of an accounting change, the audit opinion should still be modified because of the need for restatement. An example follows — for a change from the completed-contract method to the percentage-of-completion method of accounting for long-term construction contracts. Qualifying language is once again emphasized in italics.

SCOPE PARAGRAPH *(Same as Unqualified)*

MIDDLE PARAGRAPH *(None)*

OPINION PARAGRAPH:

. . . in conformity with generally accepted accounting principles applied on a consistent basis, *after giving retroactive effect to the change (with which we concur) in the method of accounting for long-term construction contracts as described in Note 8 to the financial statements.*

The usual method of recording prior-period cumulative effects of accounting changes is to compute the cumulate net effects; to disclose those effects as a separate item in the income statement of the period of the change; and to disclose additional pro forma earnings and per share earnings for all prior-year income statements presented, giving effect to the accounting change. In that case, the auditor's opinion qualification is worded as follows:

SCOPE PARAGRAPH *(Same as Unqualified)*

MIDDLE PARAGRAPH *(None)*

OPINION PARAGRAPH:

. . . applied on a consistent basis, *except for the change (with which we concur) in the method of providing for depreciation,* as described in Note 5 to the financial statements.

There are several unique features about the *consistency-qualified audit report* that should be observed. First, it represents the least serious type of qualified audit report. Notice in Figure 18–2 that there is *no extreme case disclosure* for the accounting change. Either the change is regarded as material enough to qualify the audit report, or it is not. There is no such thing as an accounting change so material that it necessitates an adverse opinion for that reason alone. As pointed out in the last section, a change that represents a very material *departure from GAAP* requires an adverse opinion, but it is the departure from GAAP and not the accounting change that requires the adverse opinion. Usually consistency of application of GAAP is not mentioned in the adverse opinion, although there is nothing to prevent the auditor from issuing *both a consistency qualification and an adverse opinion,* in the appropriate circumstances. Furthermore, the disclosure of the accounting changes on the auditor's part is *redundant*, because the client is already obliged to report all material accounting changes and their effects in the footnotes to the financial statements.

It might appear that, since consistency is a generally accepted accounting principle, the standard unqualified audit report stating that the financial statements are fairly presented (including disclosures of the accounting change) would be sufficient. The Commission on Auditors' Responsibilities final report in 1978 recommended dropping the consistency phrase from the audit report for this reason. An exposure draft was released by the AICPA to its members in the spring of 1981 containing a revised audit report that incorporated this change. However, the exposure draft was rejected by the membership, so it appears that the consistency wording has retained its position in the auditing literature, in spite of its redundancy.

Finally, the consistency-qualified audit report is the only type of qualified report that usually *does not require a middle paragraph.* Exceptions occur only in these situations:

- Changes are made to an accounting principle that is not generally accepted.
- Accounting changes are made with which the accountant does not concur.
- It is the first examination by the auditing firm and, owing to inadequate client records, it is impracticable or impossible to determine whether GAAP have been consistently applied.

Reports Relating to Material Uncertainties

All financial statements include some disclosures that involve uncertainties. For example, there are the allowance for doubtful accounts, the allowance for depreciation, and various estimated liabilities. These items, however, are usually susceptible to estimation and can be supported by various types of audit evidence. There are other uncertainties, however, which are *not susceptible to reasonable estimation* as of the date of the audit report because their outcome is contingent on the future when one or more events occur or fail to occur. It is these types of uncertainties which require an opinion qualification. Examples of such uncertainties include the following:

- The outcome of pending or threatened litigation, the effects of which are not estimable by the client or the client's attorney.
- The resolution of a pending tax investigation involving possible claim for refund or deficiency.
- Potential recoverability of a deferred cost.
- Realizability of certain receivables, such as those from officers and directors whose financial resources are not known.
- The possibility that the company may not be able to continue as a going concern.

The appropriate type of audit opinion to be used when material uncertainties exist *depends on the materiality of the uncertainty.* Here materiality sometimes does not depend on the relative dollar amount of the uncertainty. This is because the distinguishing characteristic of the uncertainty is the fact that it cannot be estimated. Qualitative factors such as relative importance of the item and number of uncertainties facing the company must also be considered. When the company faces an uncertainty that is material but relatively isolated (not pervasive), the audit opinion should be qualified subject to the resolution of the uncertainty. Although the AICPA has stated that this type of qualifying language is usually strong enough to express the auditor's views, he or she is not precluded from expressing *a disclaimer* if it is considered more appropriate. Although no guidance is given in the auditing standard for progression from the qualified opinion to the disclaimer, we should expect that in cases involving potentially very large or multiple uncertainties that threaten the very existence of the entity, a disclaimer of opinion might be appropriate.

An example of an opinion qualified because of *a going concern uncertainty* follows:

> SCOPE PARAGRAPH *(Same as Unqualified)*
>
> MIDDLE PARAGRAPH:
>
> As shown in the financial statements, the company incurred a net loss of $456,000 during the year ended December 31, 19X2. In addition, as of December 31, 19X2, the company's current liabilities exceeded its current assets by $346,000. These factors, among others, as discussed in Note 2, indicate that the company may not be able to continue in existence. The financial statements do not include any adjustments relating to the recoverability and classification of recorded asset amounts or the amounts and classification of liabilities that might be necessary should the company be unable to continue in existence.
>
> OPINION PARAGRAPH:
>
> In our opinion, *subject to the effects on the financial statements of such adjustments, if any, as might have been required had the outcome of the uncertainty about the recoverability and classification of recorded asset amounts and classification of liabilities referred to in the preceding paragraph been known,* the financial statements referred to above present fairly the financial position of ABC Company, due at December 31, 19X2 and the results of its operation and changes in its financial position for the year then ended, in conformity with generally accepted accounting principles applied on a basis consistent with that of the preceding year.

When comparative financial statements are issued and the concern about the company's ability to remain a going concern arises in the current year, this fact will not normally affect the opinion on the statements of the prior year. Thus, the auditor should modify the report only on the financial statements of the current year.

When an uncertainty is thought to be so material and pervasive as to preclude the expression of an opinion on the financial statements taken as a whole, the *disclaimer of opinion* should read as follows, assuming the same example as above.

> SCOPE PARAGRAPH *(Same as Above)*
>
> MIDDLE PARAGRAPH *(Same as Above)*
>
> OPINION PARAGRAPH:
>
> Because it is impossible to determine the future of operational activities of the company and the effects of the material uncertainties referred to in the preceding paragraph, we are unable to express, and accordingly we do not express, an

opinion on the accompanying financial statements of the ABC Company, Inc., for the year ended December 31, 19X2.

Other Reasons for Disclaimer of an Audit Opinion

There are many reasons for disclaiming an audit opinion. Two of these, for the material and pervasive scope limitation and the material and pervasive uncertainty, were discussed above. Still other reasons for the disclaimer of audit opinion include *association with unaudited financial statements of a public entity* and *nonindependence of the auditor.*

We have stated previously in this chapter that an accountant is associated with financial statements when consent has been given to use the CPA's name in a report, document, or other written communication containing the statements, whether or not the accountant prepares the statements or appends his or her name to them. When an auditor is associated with the statements of a public entity, but *has not audited or reviewed* the statements, the following disclaimer of opinion is appropriate:

class notes

> DISCLAIMER OF OPINION *(Unaudited Financial Statements):*
>
> The accompanying balance sheet of ABC Company as of December 31, 19X2 and 19X1, and the related statements of income, retained earnings, and changes in financial position for the year then ended were not audited by us and, accordingly, we do not express an opinion on them.[7]

The above disclaimer may accompany the unaudited financial statements or it may be placed directly on them. In addition, each page of the financial statements should be clearly and conspicuously marked as unaudited. In such a case, the accountant has no responsibility to apply audit precedures beyond reading the financial statements for obvious material errors. Also, no reference should be made to any procedures applied because this might lead to misunderstanding on the part of readers. This does not, however, preclude the accountant from disclosing any departures from GAAP that are discovered during the reading of the financial statements and that the client refuses to disclose. In such cases, the above disclaimer should be modified to include the necessary disclosures and their effects on the financial data, if readily determinable. *The accountant is never justified in simply disclaiming an opinion if evidence exists that the financial statements are misleading.* If the client will not agree to a revision of the financial statements or to a modified disclaimer of opinion, the accountant should withdraw from the engagement and refuse to be associated with the financial statements.

If it becomes apparent that the accountant's name is to be included in a *client-prepared written communication* of a public entity containing financial statements that have not been audited or reviewed, the accountant should request (a) that his or her name not be included, or (b) that the financial statements be marked unaudited and be accompanied by a disclaimer of opinion. Failing that, the accountant should advise the client that consent was not given and should take other measures, such as consultation with an attorney.

When the auditor is *not independent* of the client, any auditing procedures that might be performed would not be in conformity with generally accepted auditing standards. The nonindependence disclaimer overrides all other disclaimers; and when other reasons to disclaim besides nonindependence exist, they should not be mentioned. Even when auditing procedures are performed, they should not be mentioned. In addition, each page of the financial statements should be marked as unaudited. The following disclaimer is recommended when an accountant is not independent:

> We are not independent with respect to ABC Company, Inc., and the accompanying balance sheets as of December 31, 19X2 and 19X1, and the related statements of income, retained earnings, and changes in financial position were not audited by us, and, accordingly, we do not express an opinion on them.[8]

Notice that the reason for lack of independence, as specified in Rule 101 of the Rules of Professional Conduct of the AICPA, need not be disclosed in the disclaimer for lack of independence.

Reliance on the Work of Other Auditors

Sometimes an auditor will be engaged to audit the parent company, or a subsidiary or branch of a consolidated or combined group of entities, while other accountants are auditing the other components concurrently. In such cases, the first thing an auditor should decide is whether or not he or she can serve as the ***principal auditor.*** Factors to be considered in this decision include the following:

- The materiality of the portion of the financial statements he or she has examined, compared to the materiality of the components examined by others; plus
- The extent of her or his knowledge of the overall financial statements, compared to that possessed by the other auditors; and
- The relative importance of the component that he or she is auditing to the overall financial statements of the combined group.[9]

If the auditor decides, on the basis of these and other factors, that he or she cannot serve as the principal auditor, then upon completion of the audit, the auditor should submit his or her audit report to the principal auditor. The principal auditor then relies on that report in the issuance of an opinion on the financial statements of the consolidated entity.

The principal auditor should ordinarily make inquiries of appropriate business associates concerning the professional reputation of the other auditor(s). Additionally, he or she should obtain a *representation letter* from each other auditor stating that person's independence of the client under the rules of the AICPA and, if applicable, the rules of the SEC. The principal auditor should also ascertain

- That the auditor is aware that the financial statements of the component are to be included in financial statements upon which the principal auditor is reporting, and that the report of the contributing auditor will be relied upon by the principal auditor.
- That the auditor is familiar with GAAP in the United States, or accounting practices required by the SEC, where appropriate.
- That the auditor is aware that a review will be made of matters affecting elimination of intercompany transactions and the uniformity of accounting practices among components included in the combined financial statements.

When other auditors are involved, the principal auditor must *decide whether to make reference* in the audit report to the work of the other auditor(s). Such references are generally omitted when the examination is made by an associated or correspondent firm (such as an international affiliate); or when the other auditor was retained by the principal auditor who closely supervised the work. Also, the contributing auditor might be unacknowledged if the portion of the financial statements he or she examined is immaterial to the financial statements covered by the principal auditor's report and the principal auditor takes steps to ascertain the adequacy of the other auditor's examination.

In cases of no reference, barring other circumstances, the standard unqualified audit report would be rendered by the principal auditor. All auditors must still be responsible, of course, in the event of lawsuit or action by the SEC, for the work that each did individually. The following *additional audit procedures* should be performed by the principal auditor when the decision is made not to make reference to the work of other auditors:

1. Visit the other auditors, and discuss the audit procedures followed and the results thereof.
2. Review the other auditors' programs and, perhaps, issue instructions for the other auditors to follow.
3. Review the working papers of the other auditors, including the evaluation of internal control and the audit conclusions reached.

If, on the other hand, the principal auditor decides to *make reference* to the work of the other auditors, the additional procedures in the preceding list need not be performed. Instead, the principal auditor expands the scope paragraph of the standard report to include a reference to the portion of the financial statements examined by other auditors. The language of the opinion paragraph is also modified to disclose that the principal auditor's report, insofar as it relates to the entity audited by the other auditor, is based on that auditor's report. Such a modification does not constitute a qualified audit report.

An audit report that makes reference to the work of other auditors follows. The scope paragraph is the same as unqualified for a consolidated entity except that it includes the following additions:

SCOPE PARAGRAPH:

. . . We did not examine the financial statements of XYZ Company, Inc., whose statements reflect assets and revenues constituting approximately 12 percent and 15 percent, respectively, of the related consolidated totals for 19X2 and 19X1, respectively. These statements were audited by other auditors whose reports thereon have been furnished to us. Our opinion, insofar as it relates to amounts included for XYZ Company, Inc., is based solely on the report of the other auditors.

OPINION PARAGRAPH:

In our opinion, *based upon our examination and the reports of other auditors referred to above*, the aforementioned consolidated financial statements present fairly. . . .

A less frequently applied alternative to the above presentation is to present both the report of the principal auditor and that of the other auditor, after securing permission from the other auditor to do so.

Emphasis of a Matter

In rare instances the auditor may wish to emphasize certain circumstances even though issuing an unqualified audit report. Normally, such information should be included in a separate explanatory middle paragraph of the audit report. The following are examples of items that may be so emphasized:

- The entity is a component of a larger business enterprise.
- The entity has had significant transactions with related parties.
- An unusually important subsequent event has occurred.
- An unusually important accounting matter affects the comparability of current financial statements with those of the preceding period.[10]

Piecemeal Opinions

The term ***piecemeal opinion*** was historically used to define the situation in which the auditor disclaimed an opinion or issued an adverse opinion on the financial statements taken as a whole, while expressing an unqualified opinion on specified accounts in the statements. Although such reports were once used *they are now generally considered inappropriate*, since it is feared that the piecemeal opinion on the specified accounts might tend to contradict or overshadow the disclaimer or adverse opinion on the financial statements taken as a whole.[11]

REPORTS ON SEGMENT INFORMATION

FASB Statements 14 and 21 require that publicly traded companies include certain segment information in their annual reports. This required information comprises disclosures about the company's operations in different industries, its foreign operations and export sales, and its major customers. Disclosure of segment information requires *disaggregation of certain significant financial statement components* — such as revenue, operating profit or loss, identifiable assets, depreciation, and capital expenditures.

The auditor must seek evidence that the segment information is presented in conformity with GAAP in relation to the *financial statements taken as a whole.* He or she is not required to narrow the application of the concept of materiality with respect to any errors or misstatements in the segment information, or to issue a separate opinion on the segment information. Auditing procedures for segment information should include the following procedures, where applicable:

1. Consideration of whether the entity's revenue, operating expenses, and identifiable assets are appropriately classified among industry segments and geographic areas.
2. Inquiry of management concerning methods used in deriving segment information, and judgments as to the reasonableness of those methods when evaluated against the criteria of FASB 14.

3. Inquiry as to the practices followed in accounting for sales and transfers between industry segments and between geographic areas, and tests of those transactions.
4. Tests of the disaggregation of the entity's financial statements into segment information, to verify whether it is in accordance with GAAP.
5. Inquiry as to the methods (and reasonableness thereof) of allocation of expenses between segments or geographic areas.
6. Determination of whether segment information has been consistently prepared from period to period.[12]

The audit report on the overall financial statements applies to segment information as well as all other audited information. As such, the report would not normally refer to the segment information or to audit procedures performed on the information. However, the following situations would call for an opinion qualification, if the segment information is material to the financial statements taken as a whole:

- A misstatement or omission of the segment information.
- A change in the accounting principle relating to the segment information.
- Inability to apply adequate auditing procedures to the segment information.

In such instances, the same considerations apply as those stated earlier for the various types of qualified reports.

REPORTS ON INFORMATION ACCOMPANYING THE BASIC FINANCIAL STATEMENTS IN AUDITOR-SUBMITTED DOCUMENTS

As explained in Chapter 16, the auditor may submit to the client or to others documents that contain, in addition to the basic financial statements and the auditor's standard report thereon, certain supplemental information. This is commonly referred to as a long-form audit report. SAS 29, which deals with reports on such supplemental information, states that the auditor's standard report covers the basic financial statements.[13] The ***basic financial statements*** contain the following elements:

- Balance sheet(s).
- Statement(s) of income.
- Statement(s) of retained earnings.
- Statement(s) of changes in financial position.
- Financial statement(s) prepared according to a comprehensive basis of accounting other than GAAP.
- Descriptions of accounting policies.
- Notes to financial statements.
- Other schedules identified as being a part of the basic financial statements.

Supplementary information included in the long-form report, on the other hand, is presented outside the basic financial statements and is not considered a necessary part of compliance with GAAP. It may include such things as these:

- Additional details of accounts (such as general and administrative expenses) included in the basic financial statements.
- Consolidating information.
- Historical summaries of items, such as incomes and earnings per share, extracted from the basic financial statements.
- Statistical data.
- Other material, perhaps from sources outside the accounting system of the entity.
- A description of audit procedures applied to specific items in the financial statements.

When the auditor submits a document including both the basic financial statements and supplemental data, sometimes called a ***long-form audit report,*** he or she *must*, in accordance with the fourth audit standard of reporting, *report on all information included in the document*. This means that the auditor's report must do the following:

1. State that the examination has been conducted for the purpose of forming an opinion on the basic financial statements.
2. Identify the supplemental data.
3. State that the accompanying information is presented for purposes of additional analysis and is not a required part of the basic financial statements.
5. Include either an opinion as to whether the accompanying information is fairly presented in all material respects in relation to the financial statements taken as a whole, or a disclaimer of opinion if sufficient auditing procedures were not applied to the supplemental data.

If auditing procedures have been performed on the supplementary data, the auditor's concept of materiality should again be directed toward items that are material to the financial statements taken as a whole, and not to the individual disclosures in the supplemental information. The audit report, if any, on the supplemental information may be presented separately or added to the auditor's standard report on the basic financial statements.

Where the audit report includes descriptions of additional audit procedures applied to specific elements supporting financial statement items, these procedure descriptions should not contradict or detract from the description of the scope of the examination in the standard audit report on the basic financial statements. They should also be set forth separately so as to maintain a *clear distinction between management's representations and the auditor's representations.*

Special rules in this area apply whenever the auditor reports on the following information:

- Condensed annual or interim financial statements that are derived from audited financial statements of a public entity that is required to file, at least annually, complete audited financial statements with a regulatory agency.
- Selected financial data that are derived from audited financial statements of either a public or a nonpublic entity and that are presented in a document that includes audited financial statements (or, in the case of a public entity, that incorporates audited financial statements by reference to information filed with a regulatory agency).

SAS 42 governs the specific presentation of these types of financial information under the general reporting guidelines of SAS 29. Condensed financial statements are defined for purposes of this statement as financial presentations in considerably less detail than those provided in the basic audited financial statements. Condensed financial statements may not include all of the necessary disclosures for full conformity with GAAP and should be read in conjunction with the complete financial statements in order to gain a complete picture of the client's financial position and results of operations. Therefore, if an auditor is engaged to report on condensed financial statements that are derived from audited financial statements, the report on those statements should be different from the audit report on the basic financial statements. Specifically, the report on the condensed financial statements should indicate

- That the auditor has examined and expressed an opinion on the complete financial statements.
- The date of the audit report on the complete financial statements.
- The type of opinion expressed on those statements.
- Whether, in the auditor's opinion, the information set forth in the condensed financial statements is fairly stated in all material respects in relation to the complete financial statements from which it has been derived.

If the auditor is engaged to report on selected financial data, the report should be limited to data that are derived from *audited financial statements*. This may include data calculated from amounts presented in the financial statements, such as working capital. If the financial data presented includes both data derived from the financial statements and other information (such as number of employees or square footage of buildings), the auditor's report should specifically identify the data upon which he or she is reporting. The report should indicate

- That the auditor has examined and expressed an opinion on the complete financial statements.
- The type of opinion expressed on those financial statements.
- Whether, in the auditor's opinion, the information set forth in the selected financial data is fairly stated in all material respects in relation to the complete financial statements from which it has been derived.

Sometimes a client might make a statement in a *client-prepared document* that names the auditor and also states that condensed financial statements or other financial data have been derived from audited financial statements. Such statements do not in themselves require the auditor to report on the condensed financial statements or other selected financial data, provided that these disclosures are included in a document that contains audited financial statements (or, as is the case with public entities, that incorporates such statements by reference to information filed with a regulatory agency). However, if such statements are made in a document that does *not* include (or incorporate by reference) audited financial statements, the auditor should request that neither his or her name nor reference to the work be associated with the information. Alternatively, the auditor may disclaim an opinion on the information and request that the disclaimer be included in the document. If the client does not comply with this request, the auditor should advise the client of denial of consent to association. Additionally, he or she should consider what other actions might be appropriate, such as consultation with legal counsel.

UPDATING AND REISSUING AUDIT REPORTS

When a continuing auditor issues an opinion on comparative financial statements, he or she should ***update*** the opinion issued on the previous year's financial statements. Updating the opinion of a previous year can take the form of either (1) reexpression of the opinion previously expressed; or (2) issuing a different opinion from that previously expressed. In the latter case, the auditor may decide to issue a report with an updated opinion different from a previous opinion because he or she has become aware, during the current examination, of circumstances or events that affect the prior period. For example, the auditor may have qualified her or his opinion for a material uncertainty in the prior period. If that uncertainty is resolved during the current period, the resolution should be recognized in the updated version of the report, and the opinion on the comparative financial statements should be unqualified. Other circumstances that require an updated opinion different from a previously issued opinion are these:

- Discovery of an uncertainty relating to prior-period financial statements in a subsequent period. The auditor should explain the circumstances in a middle paragraph of the current period's report and qualify or disclaim an opinion with respect to the prior year's financial statements in the updated audit report.
- Subsequent restatement of a prior period's financial statements. If the audit report of the prior period was modified because of a departure from GAAP, and the prior period's financial statements are restated in the current year to conform to GAAP, the auditor's updated report on the prior period's financial statements should indicate that they have been restated, and an unqualified opinion can now be expressed.

In an updated opinion, if an auditor expresses an opinion on prior period financial statements that is different from the one previously expressed, he or she should disclose all the reasons for the different opinion in a separate explanatory paragraph of the audit report. Also, if the updated report is other than unqualified, the auditor should include in the opinion paragraph an appropriate reference to the explanatory paragraph. The explanatory paragraph should contain the following disclosures:

- The date of the auditor's previous report.
- The type of opinion previously expressed.
- The circumstances or events that caused the auditor to express a different opinion.
- The fact that the auditor's updated opinion is different from the previous opinion on those statements.

Reissuance of an audit report involves merely the reproduction of a previously issued audit report in a subsequent period. Reissuance might occur if, for example, the client was requested by a prospective creditor to provide copies of the most recent audited financial statements in connection with a bank loan subsequent to the original issuance date of the audit report. It might also occur if a predecessor auditor were requested by a former client to reissue or to consent to the reuse of a previously issued audit report. In these situations, the auditor may presently have no revised information with respect to the financial statements covered by the previously issued audit report. Therefore, it is important that the *original report date be used* to avoid any confusion to the reader as to the date of the auditor's representations.

A predecessor auditor, before consenting to the reissuance of a report, should take steps to ascertain that the previously issued report is still appropriate. These steps include the following:

1. Reading the financial statements of the current period.
2. Comparing the financial statements of the prior period with those of the current period.
3. Obtaining a letter of representation from the successor auditor as to whether the successor auditor's examination revealed any matters that, in the successor's opinion, might have a material effect on the financial statements reported on by the predecessor auditor.

If a *successor auditor is reporting on comparative financial statements* and the *report of the predecessor is not presented,* the successor auditor's report should indicate in the scope paragraph the fact that the financial statements of the prior period were examined by other auditors (names need not be presented), along with the date of the predecessor auditor's report and the type of opinion expressed by the predecessor. The scope paragraph should also give the reasons if the predecessor's report was other than unqualified.

After the scope paragraph, the successor's report should express an opinion on the financial statements of the *current period only.* A successor auditor, in meeting the consistency standard, should adopt procedures that are practical and reasonable in the circumstances to obtain assurance that the principles employed are consistent between the current and preceding years. The successor auditor may review the predecessor's working papers and in that way reduce the scope of audit tests of opening balances. This of course must be agreed to by both the client and predecessor auditor. If the successor auditor becomes aware of information that indicates a need for revising the prior-period statements, he or she should ask the client to arrange a meeting of the three parties to resolve the matter.

SUMMARY

In this chapter we have focused on meeting the standards of reporting, with particular emphasis on the requirements imposed by the fourth standard. We began by defining *association with financial statements* as that term is interpreted in the fourth standard. We then reviewed the full spectrum of audit reports available under generally accepted auditing standards and gave examples of various types of reports. We explored the reasons for disclaimers, such as unaudited financial statements of a public entity and lack of independence.

We also discussed other departures from the wording of the standard unqualified audit report which do not constitute qualifications, such as reliance on the work of other auditors, and emphasis of certain important matters. The effects of segment information on audit reports was considered next. Finally, we discussed the requirements for reports on information accompanying the basic financial statements in auditor-submitted documents (which are also known as long-form reports).

In the next chapter we will extend our discussion of the other levels of association with financial statements and illustrate the reports that should be rendered with each type of association. Other special reporting topics will also be addressed.

NOTES

1. Statement on Auditing Standards (SAS) 26 (New York: AICPA, 1979).
2. SAS 15 (New York: AICPA, 1977).
3. Material in this section is largely derived from SAS 2 (New York: AICPA, 1974).
4. SAS 1, Section 420 (New York: AICPA, 1973).
5. Ibid.
6. APB Opinion No. 20, *Accounting Changes* (New York: AICPA, 1971).
7. SAS 26.
8. Ibid.
9. SAS 1, Section 543.
10. SAS 2, paragraph 27.
11. Ibid., paragraph 48.
12. SAS 21 (New York: AICPA, 1977).
13. Material in this section is derived from SAS 29 (New York: AICPA, 1980) and from SAS 42 (New York: AICPA, 1982).

QUESTIONS FOR CLASS DISCUSSION

Q18–1 What recourse does an auditor have when he or she discovers that the client has omitted a footnote disclosure which, in the auditor's judgment, must be included to have the financial statements be fairly presented? Explain.

Q18–2 What recourse does the auditor have if she or he discovers a material departure from generally accepted accounting practices which the client refuses to change? Discuss.

Q18–3 What is meant by the term *association with financial statements* as it relates to an accountant's reporting responsibility? Explain.

Q18–4 What levels of association may an accountant have with a client's financial statements?

Q18–5 How does an accountant disclose his or her association with unaudited financial statements? With audited financial statements? Explain.

Q18–6 To whom should the short-form audit report be addressed?

Q18–7 Does an audit report issued with comparative statements cover the statements for both years? Explain.

Q18–8 How does one distinguish between an "except for" and a "subject to" type of qualification?

Q18–9 Under what circumstances may an auditor issue a disclaimer of opinion?

Q18–10 How does the auditor determine whether to issue a qualified opinion or an adverse opinion? Explain.

Q18–11 Assume that an accountant, in preparing an unaudited financial statement, discovers a departure from generally accepted accounting principles, material enough to make the statement misleading; may the auditor issue a disclaimer opinion in this situation? Explain.

Q18–12 What is meant by a scope limitation in an audit report? Does such a limitation always require a qualification in the opinion paragraph? Explain.

Q18–13 How should the auditor react to a refusal by the client to provide a representation letter? Justify that reaction.

Q18–14 What is typically included in the middle paragraph of an audit report? Under what circumstances would a middle paragraph be included in an audit report?

Q18–15 What is the difference between a qualified opinion relating to departure from generally accepted accounting principles and qualification relating to consistency in the audit report?

Q18–16 In what situation might a client have a departure from generally accepted accounting principles and still receive an unqualified report? Explain.

Q18–17 What are three types of accounting changes that would require a report qualification for lack of consistency?

Q18–18 What five types of accounting changes do not require a consistency qualification in the audit report?

Q18–19 What accounting changes require a retroactive restatement of prior periods' financial statements? Explain.

Q18–20 How does the auditor report on accounting changes that require prior-period financial statements to be restated retroactively to give effect to the accounting change?

Q18–21 In which two situations would the auditor omit a reference to consistency in the audit report?

Q18–22 How does the auditor modify his or her audit report when material uncertainties relating to the operations of the client are discovered? Explain.

Q18–23 How does an auditor who is not independent report on his or her association with financial statements?

Q18–24 What three possible positions might a principal auditor engaged in the audit of consolidated financial statements take regarding the work of another auditor who had examined the financial statements of a subsidiary?

Q18–25 What factors should be considered in determining whether an auditor can serve as a principal auditor for a firm's consolidated financial statements?

Q18–26 How does the principal auditor associated with consolidated financial statements decide whether the work of another auditor, relating to a subsidiary's financial statement, can be accepted? Explain.

Q18–27 What steps must be taken by the principal auditor if he or she wishes to include another auditor's report with his report on consolidated financial statements? Explain.

Q18–28 What is the auditor's responsibility relating to segment information included with the financial statements to make them conform to the requirements of FASB 14?

Q18–29 What is the auditor's responsibility for supplementary information included in the long-form audit report? Explain.

Q18–30 What date should be shown as the date of issuance of the audit report?

Q18–31 How should the discovery of an event occurring between the time field work was completed and the time the audit report is delivered be handled by the auditor?

Q18–32 What is meant by the reissuance of an audit report? What date should be shown on such a reissued audit report? Explain.

Q18–33 What is meant by the term *predecessor auditor?*

Q18–34 What three steps should a predecessor auditor take before allowing his or her audit report to be reissued with the audit report of a successor auditor?

Q18–35 What steps should be taken by the successor auditor if the report of the predecessor auditor is not presented with comparative financial statements?

SHORT CASES

C18–1 Patricia Leer, CPA, has discussed various reporting considerations with three of her audit clients. The three clients presented the following situations and asked how each would affect the audit report.

a. A client has changed its concept of "funds" on its statement of changes in financial position. Both Leer and the client agree that the new concept of "funds" is a more meaningful presentation. In prior years, when Leer issued an unqualified report on the client's comparative financial statements, this statement showed the net change in working capital, whereas in the current year the statement shows net change in cash balance. The client agrees with Leer that the change is material but believes the change is obvious to readers and need not be discussed in the footnotes to the financial statements or in Leer's report. The client is issuing comparative statements but wishes only to restate the prior year's statement to conform to the current format.

b. A client has a loan agreement that restricts the amount of cash dividends that can be paid and requires the maintenance of a particular current ratio. The client is in compliance with the terms of the agreement and it is not likely that there will be a violation in the foreseeable future. The client believes there is no need to mention the restriction in the financial statements because such mention might mislead the readers.

c. During the year, a client correctly accounted for the acquisition of a majority-owned domestic subsidiary but did not properly present the minority interest in retained earnings or net income of the subsidiary in the consolidated financial statements. The client agrees with Leer that the minority interest presented in the consolidated financial statements is materially misstated but takes the position that the minority shareholders of the subsidiary should look to that subsidiary's financial statements for information concerning their interest therein.

Required:

Each of the situations above relates to *one* of the four generally accepted auditing standards of reporting.

Identify and describe the applicable generally accepted auditing standard (GAAS) of reporting in each situation and discuss how the particular client situation relates to the standard and to Leer's report.

Organize your answer sheet as follows:

Situation	Applicable GAAS of Reporting	Discussion of Relationship of Client Situation to Standard of Reporting and to Leer's Report

(AICPA adapted)

C18–2 Lando Corporation is a domestic company with two wholly owned domestic subsidiaries. Albert Michaels, CPA, has been engaged to examine the financial statements of the parent company and one of the subsidiaries and to act as the principal auditor. Ira Thomas, CPA, has examined the financial statements of the other subsidiary whose operations are material in relation to the consolidated financial statement.

The work performed by Michaels is sufficient for Michaels to serve as the principal auditor and to report as such on the financial statements. Michaels has not yet decided whether to make reference to the examination made by Thomas.

Required:

a. There are certain required audit *procedures* that Michaels should perform with respect to the examination made by Thomas, whether or not Michaels decides to make reference to Thomas in Michaels's auditor's report. What are these audit *procedures?*

b. What are the reporting requirements with which Michaels must comply if Michaels decides to name Thomas and make reference to the examination of Thomas?

(AICPA adapted)

C18–3 Tamara Rose, CPA, has satisfactorily completed the examination of the financial statements of Bale & Booster, a partnership, for the year ended December 31, 19X9. The financial statements were prepared on the basis of GAAP and include footnotes that indicate that the partnership was involved in continuing litigation of material amounts relating to alleged infringement of a competitor's patent. The amount of damages, if any, resulting from this litigation could not be determined at the time of completion of the engagement. The prior years' financial statements were not presented.

Required:

On the basis of the information presented, prepare an auditor's report that includes appropriate explanatory disclosure of significant facts.

(AICPA adapted)

C18–4 The following tentative auditor's report was drafted by a staff accountant and submitted to a partner in the accounting firm of Better & Best, CPAs:

To the Audit Committee of
American Widgets, Inc.

We have examined the consolidated balance sheets of American Widgets, Inc., and subsidiaries as of December 31, 19X2 and 19X1, and the related consolidated statements of income, retained earnings, and changes in financial position, for the years then ended. Our examinations were made in accordance with generally accepted auditing standards as we considered necessary in the circumstances. Other auditors examined the financial statements of certain subsidiaries and have furnished us with reports thereon containing no exceptions. Our opinion expressed herein, insofar as it relates to the amounts included for those subsidiaries, is based solely upon the reports of the other auditors.

As discussed in Note 4 to the financial statements, on January 8, 19X3, the company halted the production of certain medical equipment as a result of inquiries by the Food and Drug Administration, which raised questions as to the adequacy of some of the company's sterilization equipment and related procedures. Management is not in a position to evaluate the effect of this production halt and the ensuing litigation, which may have an adverse effect on the financial position of American Widgets, Inc.

As fully discussed in Note 7 to the financial statements, in 19X1 the company extended the use of the last-in, first-out (LIFO) method of accounting to include all inventories. In examining inventories, we engaged Dr. Irwin Same (Nobel Prize winner 19X0) to test check the technical requirements and specifications of certain items of equipment manufactured by the company.

In our opinion, except for the effects, if any, on the financial statements of the ultimate resolution of the matter discussed in the second preceding paragraph, the financial statements referred to above present fairly the financial position of American Widgets, Inc., as of December 31, 19X1, and the results of operations for the years then ended, in conformity with generally accepted accounting principles applied on a basis consistent with that of the preceding year.

To be signed by
Better & Best, CPAs

March 1, 19X3, except
for Note 4 as to which
the date is January 8, 19X3

Required:

Identify deficiencies in the staff accountant's tentative report which constitute departures from the generally accepted standards of reporting.

(AICPA adapted)

C18–5 Upon completion of all field work on September 23, 19X5, the following short-form report was rendered by Timothy Ross to the directors of The Rancho Corporation.

> To the Directors of
> The Rancho Corporation:
>
> We have examined the balance sheet and the related statement of income and retained earnings of The Rancho Corporation as of July 31, 19X5. In accordance with your instructions, a complete audit was conducted.
>
> In many respects, this was an unusual year for The Rancho Corporation. The weakening of the economy in the early part of the year and the strike of plant employees in the summer of 19X5 led to a decline in sales and net income. After several tests of sales records, nothing came to our attention that would indicate that sales have not been properly recorded.
>
> In our opinion, with the explanation given above, and with the exception of some minor errors that are considered immaterial, the aforementioned financial statements present fairly the financial position of The Rancho Corporation at July 31, 19X5; and the results of its operations for the year then ended, in conformity with pronouncements of the Accounting Principles Board and the Financial Accounting Standards Board applied consistently throughout the period.
>
> *Timothy Ross, CPA*
> *September 23, 19X5*

Required:

List and explain deficiencies and omissions in the auditor's report. The type of opinion (unqualified, qualified, adverse, or disclaimer) is of no consequence and need not be discussed.

Organize your answer sheet by paragraph (scope, explanatory, and opinion) of the auditor's report.

(AICPA adapted)

C18–6 The *complete set* of financial statements for The Maumee Corporation for the year ended August 31, 19X5, is presented on pages 809 and 810.

Required:

List deficiencies and omissions in The Maumee Corporation's financial statements and discuss the probable effect of the deficiency or omission on the auditor's report. Assume that The Maumee Corporation is unwilling to change the financial statements or make additional disclosures therein.

The Maumee Corporation
BALANCE SHEET
August 31, 19X5
(In Thousands of Dollars)

Assets

Cash		$ 103
Marketable securities, at cost that approximates market value		54
Trade accounts receivable (net of $65,000 allowable for doubtful accounts)		917
Inventories, at cost		775
Property, plant and equipment	$3,200	
Less: Accumulated depreciation	1,475	1,725
Prepayments and other assets		125
Total assets		$3,699

Liabilities and Stockholders' Equity

Accounts payable	$ 221
Accrued taxes	62
Bank loans and long-term debt	1,580
Total liabilities	1,863
Capital stock, $10 par value (authorized 50,000 shares, issued and outstanding 42,400 shares)	424
Paid-in capital in excess of par value	366
Retained earnings	1,046
Total stockholders' equity	1,836
Total liabilities and stockholders' equity	$3,699

The Maumee Corporation
STATEMENT OF INCOME AND RETAINED EARNINGS
For the Year Ended August 31, 19X5
(In Thousands of Dollars)

Product sales (net of $850,000 sales returns and allowances)		$10,700
Cost of goods sold		8,700
Gross profit on sales		2,000
Operating expenses:		
Selling expenses	$1,500	
General and administrative expense	940	2,440
Operating loss		(440)
Interest expense		150
Net loss		(590)
Retained earnings, September 1, 19X4		1,700
		1,110
Dividends:		
Cash — $1 per share	40	
Stock — 6% of shares outstanding	24	64
Retained earnings, August 31, 19X5		$ 1,046

Consider each deficiency or omission separately, and do *not* consider the cumulative effect of the deficiencies and omissions on the auditor's report. There are *no* arithmetical errors in the statements.

Organize your answer sheet in two columns as indicated below and write your answer in the order of appearance within the general headings of Balance Sheet, Statement of Income and Retained Earnings, and Other.

Financial Statement Deficiency or Omission	Discussion of Effect on Auditor's Report

(AICPA adapted)

C18–7 Lila Roscoe, CPA, has completed the examination of the financial statements of Excelsior Corporation as of and for the year ended December 31, 19X5. Roscoe also examined and reported on the Excelsior financial statements for the prior year. She drafted the following report for 19X5.

March 15, 19X6

We have examined the balance sheet and statements of income and retained earnings of Excelsior Corporation as of December 31, 19X5. Our examination was made in accordance with generally accepted accounting standards and accordingly included such tests of the accounting records as we considered necessary in the circumstances.

In our opinion, the above-mentioned financial statements are accurately prepared and fairly presented in accordance with generally accepted accounting principles in effect at December 31, 19X5.

Lila Roscoe, CPA
(Signed)

Other Information:

a. Excelsior is presenting comparative financial statements.
b. Excelsior does not wish to present a statement of changes in financial position for either year.
c. During 19X5 Excelsior changed its method of accounting for long-term construction contracts and properly showed the effect of the change in the current year's financial statements and restated the prior-year statements. Roscoe is satisfied with Excelsior's justification for making the change. The change is discussed in footnote number 12.
d. Roscoe was unable to perform normal accounts-receivable confirmation procedures but alternate procedures were used to satisfy her as to the validity of the receivables.
e. Excelsior Corporation is the defendant in a litigation, the outcome of which is highly uncertain. If the case is settled in favor of the plaintiff, Excelsior will be required to pay a substantial amount of cash, which might require the sale of certain fixed assets. The litigation and the possible effects have been properly disclosed in footnote number 11.
f. Excelsior issued debentures on January 31, 19X4, in the amount of $10,000,000. The funds obtained from the issuance were used to finance the expansion of plant facilities. The debenture agreement restricts the payment of future cash dividends to earnings after December 31, 19X9. Excelsior declined to disclose this essential data in the footnotes to the financial statements.

Required:

Consider all facts given and rewrite the auditor's report in acceptable and complete format incorporating any necessary departures from the standard (short-form) report.

Do not discuss the draft of Roscoe's report but identify and explain any items included in "*Other Information*" that need not be part of the auditor's report.

(AICPA adapted)

C18–8 Various types of "accounting changes" can affect the second reporting standard of the generally accepted auditing standards. This standard reads, "The report shall state whether such principles have been consistently observed in the current period in relation to the preceding period."

Assume that the following list describes changes which have a material effect on a client's financial statements for the current year.

a. A change from the completed-contract method to the percentage-of-completion method of accounting for long-term construction-type contracts.
b. A change in the estimated useful life of previously recorded fixed assets, based on newly acquired information.

c. Correction of a mathematical error in inventory pricing made in a prior period.
d. A change from prime costing to full absorption costing for inventory valuation.
e. A change from presentation of statements of individual companies to presentation of consolidated statements.
f. A change from deferring and amortizing preproduction costs to recording such costs as an expense when incurred because future benefits of the costs have become doubtful. The new accounting method was adopted in recognition of the change in estimated future benefits.
g. A change to including the employer share of FICA taxes as "Retirement benefits" on the income statement from including it with "Other taxes."
h. A change from the FIFO method of inventory pricing to the LIFO method of inventory pricing.

Required:

Identify the type of change described in each item above; state whether any modification is required in the auditor's report *as it relates to the second standard of reporting;* and state whether the prior year's financial statements should be restated when presented in comparative form with the current year's statements. Organize your answer sheet as shown below.

For example, a change from the LIFO method of inventory pricing to the FIFO method of inventory pricing would appear as shown.

Item No.	Type of Change	Should Auditor's Report Be Modified?	Should Prior Year's Statements Be Restated?
Example	An accounting change from one generally accepted accounting principle to another generally accepted accounting principle	Yes	Yes

(AICPA adapted)

C18–9 Sturdy Corporation owns and operates a large office building in a desirable section of New York City's financial center. For many years the management of Sturdy Corporation has modified the presentation of their financial statements by:

a. Showing a write-up to appraisal values in the building accounts.
b. Accounting for depreciation expense on the basis of such valuations.

Warren Wyley, a successor CPA, was asked to examine the financial statements of Sturdy Corporation, for the year ended December 31, 19X0. After completing the examination Wyley concluded that, consistent with prior years, an adverse opinion would have to be expressed because of the materiality of the apparent deviation from the historical-cost principle.

Required:

a. *Describe* in detail the form of presentation of the middle paragraph of the auditor's report on the financial statements of Sturdy Corporation for the year ended December 31, 19X0, clearly identifying the information contained in the paragraph. *Do not discuss deferred taxes.*

b. *Write a draft* of the opinion paragraph of the auditor's report on the financial statements of Sturdy Corporation for the year ended December 31, 19X0.

(AICPA adapted)

C18–10 John Darden, CPA, was asked to submit to his client, the Dundee Corporation and consolidated subsidiaries, a report that contained the following information:

a. Audited comparative consolidated balance sheets, income statement, statements of retained earnings, and statements of changes in financial position for the years 19X2 and 19X1.
b. Complete description of the company's accounting policies.
c. Consolidating information.
d. A ten-year summary of earnings and earnings per share for the consolidated entity.
e. Complete footnotes to consolidated financial statements.
f. A description of audit procedures applied to specific items in the financial statements.
g. Additional details of general and administrative expenses.

Required:

a. Label each of the preceding listed items of information with a (B) if it is part of the basic financial statements or with an (S) if it is considered supplementary information of the kind sometimes included in auditor-submitted documents (also known as "long-form reports").
b. Outline the CPA's investigative and reporting responsibility for: items in the basic financial statements and for items included in supplementary information.

C18–11 The limitations on the CPA's professional responsibilities when he is associated with unaudited financial statements are often misunderstood. The auditor can substantially reduce these misunderstandings by carefully following professional pronouncements in the course of her or his work, and by taking other appropriate measures.

Required:

The following list describes seven situations the CPA may encounter, or contentions he or she may have to deal with in the association with and preparation of unaudited financial statements. Briefly discuss the extent of the CPA's responsibilities and, if appropriate, the actions he or she should take to minimize any misunderstandings. Letter your answers to correspond with the following list.

a. The CPA was engaged by telephone to perform write-up work including the preparation of financial statements. The client believes that the CPA has been engaged to audit the financial statements and examine the records accordingly.
b. A group of businessmen who own a farm managed by an independent agent engage a CPA to prepare quarterly unaudited financial statements for them. The CPA prepares the financial statements from information given to her by the independent agent. Subsequently, the businessmen find the statements were inaccurate because their independent agent was embezzling funds. The businessmen refuse to pay the CPA's fee and blame her for allowing the situation to go

undetected, contending that she should not have relied on representations from the independent agent.

c. In comparing the trial balance with the general ledger, the CPA finds an account labeled "audit fees" in which the client has accumulated the CPA's quarterly billings for accounting services, including the preparation of quarterly unaudited financial statements.

d. Unaudited financial statements were accompanied by the following letter of transmittal from the CPA:

   "We are enclosing your company's balance sheet as of June 30, 19X4, and the related statements of income and retained earnings and changes in financial position for the six months then ended which we have reviewed."

e. To determine appropriate account classification, the CPA reviewed a number of the client's invoices. He noted in his working papers that some invoices were missing but did nothing further because he felt they did not affect the unaudited financial statements he was preparing. When the client subsequently discovered that invoices were missing, he contended that the CPA should not have ignored the missing invoices when preparing the financial statements and had a responsibility to at least inform him that they were missing.

f. The CPA has prepared a draft of unaudited financial statements from the client's records. While reviewing this draft with her client, the CPA learns that the land and building were recorded at appraisal value.

g. The CPA is engaged to review without audit the financial statements prepared by the client's controller. During this review, the CPA learns of several items which by generally accepted accounting principles would require adjustment of the statements and footnote disclosure. The controller agrees to make the recommended adjustments to the statements but says that he is not going to add the footnotes because the statements are unaudited.

(AICPA adapted)

PROBLEMS

P18–1 Select the best answer for each of the following items relating to the general organization and content of the short-form audit report.

a. If the basic financial statements are accompanied by a separate statement of changes in stockholders' equity, this statement
   (1) Should *not* be identified in the scope paragraph but should be reported separately in the opinion paragraph.
   (2) Should be excluded from both the scope and opinion paragraphs.
   (3) Should be identified in the scope paragraph of the report but need *not* be reported separately in the opinion paragraph.
   (4) Should be identified in the scope paragraph of the report and must be reported separately in the opinion paragraph.

b. The auditor's *best* course of action with respect to "other financial information" included in an annual report containing the auditor's report is to
   (1) Indicate in the auditor's report, that the "other financial information" is unaudited.

(2) Consider whether the "other financial information" is accurate by performing a limited review.
(3) Obtain written representations from management as to the material accuracy of the "other financial information."
(4) Read and consider the manner of presentation of the "other financial information."

c. Which of the following would *not* be required for the statements to be "presented fairly" in conformity with generally accepted accounting principles?
(1) That generally accepted accounting principles be followed in presenting all material items in the statements.
(2) That the generally accepted accounting principles selected from alternatives be appropriate for the circumstances of the particular company.
(3) That generally accepted accounting principles be applied on a basis consistent with those followed in the prior year.
(4) That the generally accepted accounting principles selected from alternatives reflect transactions in accordance with their substance.

d. Which of the following should be recognized in the auditor's report — whether or *not* the item is fully disclosed in the financial statements?
(1) A change in accounting estimate.
(2) Correction of an error not involving a change in accounting principle.
(3) A change from a nonaccepted accounting principle to a generally accepted one.
(4) A change in classification.

e. In which of the following instances would it be appropriate for the auditor to refer to the work of an appraiser in the auditor's report?
(1) An unqualified opinion is expressed and the auditor wishes to place emphasis on the use of a specialist.
(2) A qualified opinion is expressed because of a major uncertainty unrelated to the work of the appraiser.
(3) An adverse opinion is expressed, based on a difference of opinion between the client and the outside appraiser as to the value of certain assets.
(4) A disclaimer of opinion is expressed due to a scope limitation imposed on the auditor by the appraiser.

f. The fourth generally accepted auditing standard of reporting requires an auditor to render a report whenever an auditor's name is associated with financial statements. The overall purpose of the fourth standard of reporting is to require that reports
(1) Ensure that the auditor is independent with respect to the financial statements under examination.
(2) State that the auditor's examination of the financial statements has been conducted in accordance with generally accepted auditing standards.
(3) Indicate the character of the auditor's examination and the degree of responsibility assumed.
(4) Express whether the accounting principles used in preparing the financial statements have been applied consistently in the period under examination.

g. The fourth reporting standard requires the auditor's report to contain either an expression of opinion regarding the financial statements, taken as a whole, or an assertion to the effect that an opinion cannot be expressed. The objective of the fourth standard is to prevent

(1) The CPA from reporting on one basic financial statement and *not* the others.
(2) The CPA from expressing different opinions on each of the basic financial statements.
(3) Misinterpretations regarding the degree of responsibility the auditor is assuming.
(4) Management from reducing its final responsibility for the basic financial statements.

h. The auditor's report makes reference to the basic financial statements, which are customarily considered to be the balance sheet and the statements of
(1) Income and changes in financial position.
(2) Income, changes in retained earnings, and changes in financial position.
(3) Income, retained earnings, and changes in financial position.
(4) Income and retained earnings.

i. An investor is reading the financial statements of The Sundby Corporation and observes that the statements are accompanied by an unqualified auditor's report. From this the investor may conclude that
(1) Any disputes over significant accounting issues have been settled to the auditor's satisfaction.
(2) The auditor is satisfied that Sundby is operationally efficient.
(3) The auditor has ascertained that Sundby's financial statements have been prepared accurately.
(4) Informative disclosures in the financial statements but not necessarily in the footnotes are to be regarded as reasonably adequate.

j. A CPA's report on a client's balance sheet, income statement, and statement of changes in financial position was sent to the stockholders. The client now wishes to present only the balance sheet along with an appropriately modified auditor's report in a newspaper advertisement. The auditor may
(1) Permit the publication as requested.
(2) Permit only the publication of the originally issued auditor's report and accompanying financial statements.
(3) *Not* permit publication of a modified auditor's report.
(4) *Not* permit publication of any auditor's report in connection with a newspaper advertisement.

k. Which of the following circumstances would *not* be considered a departure from the auditor's standard report?
(1) The auditor wishes to emphasize a particular matter regarding the financial statements.
(2) The auditor's opinion is based in part on the report of another auditor.
(3) The financial statements are affected by a departure from a generally accepted accounting principle.
(4) The auditor is asked to report only on the balance sheet but has unlimited access to information underlying all the basic financial statements.

l. Generally accepted auditing standards are applicable when an auditor examines and reports on any financial statement. For reporting purposes, the independent auditor should consider each of the following types of financial presentations to be a financial statement *except* a
(1) Statement of assets and liabilities arising from cash transactions.
(2) Statement of changes in owners' equity.
(3) Statement of forecasted results of operations.
(4) Statement of operations by product line.

m. Which of the following *best* describes the objective of the fourth standard of reporting, which requires that the auditor's report shall contain either an expression of opinion regarding the financial statements, taken as a whole, or an assertion to the effect than an opinion cannot be expressed?
   (1) To protect the auditor against allegations that some portion of the financial statements includes a material misstatement.
   (2) To prevent misinterpretation of the degree of responsibility the auditor is assuming when the auditor's name is associated with the financial statements.
   (3) To prevent the reader from assuming that an auditor will detect errors or irregularities that have a material effect on the financial statements.
   (4) To protect auditors who are *not* associated with financial statements and who do *not* lend their names to the financial statements.

n. Which of the following *best* describes the reference to the expression "taken as a whole" in the fourth generally accepted auditing standard of reporting?
   (1) It applies equally to a complete set of financial statements and to each individual financial statement.
   (2) It applies only to a complete set of financial statements.
   (3) It applies equally to each item in each financial statement.
   (4) It applies equally to each material item in each financial statement.

o. When comparative financial statements are presented, the fourth standard of reporting, which refers to financial statements "taken as a whole," should be considered to apply to the financial statements of the
   (1) Periods presented plus the one preceding period.
   (2) Current period only.
   (3) Current period and those of the other periods presented.
   (4) Currant and immediately preceding period only.

p. The standard short-form auditor's report is generally considered to have a scope paragraph and an opinion paragraph. In the report the auditor refers to both generally accepted accounting principles (GAAP) and generally accepted auditing standards (GAAS). In which of the paragraphs are these terms used?
   (1) GAAP in the scope paragraph and GAAS in the opinion paragraph.
   (2) GAAS in the scope paragraph and GAAP in the opinion paragraph.
   (3) GAAS in both paragraphs and GAAP in the scope paragraph.
   (4) GAAP in both paragraphs and GAAS in the opinion paragraph.

q. The accuracy of information included in footnotes that accompany the audited financial statements of a company whose shares are traded on a stock exchange is the primary responsibility of
   (1) The stock exchange officials.
   (2) The independent auditor.
   (3) The company's management.
   (4) The Securities and Exchange Commission.

(AICPA adapted)

P18–2 Select the best answer to each of the following items relating to addressing and dating the audit report.

a. Which of the following would be an *inappropriate* addressee for an auditor's report?
   (1) The corporation whose financial statements were examined.

(2) A third party, even if the third party is a client who engaged the auditor for examination of a nonclient corporation.
(3) The president of the corporation whose financial statements were examined.
(4) The stockholders of the corporation whose financial statements were examined.

b. The auditor's report may be addressed to the company whose financial statements are being examined or to that company's
(1) Chief operating officer.
(2) President.
(3) Board of directors.
(4) Chief financial officer.

c. On February 13, 19X8, Celia Fox, CPA, met with the audit committee of the Gem Corporation to review the draft of Fox's report on the company's financial statements as of and for the year ended December 31, 19X7. On February 16, 19X8, Fox completed all remaining field work at the Gem Corporation's headquarters. On February 17, 19X8, Fox typed and signed the final version of the auditor's report. On February 18, 19X8, the final report was mailed to Gem's audit committee. What date should have been used on Fox's report?
(1) February 13, 19X8.
(2) February 16, 19X8.
(3) February 17, 19X8.
(4) February 18, 19X8.

d. With respect to issuance of an audit report that is dual dated for a subsequent event occurring after the completion of field work but before issuance of the auditor's report, the auditor's responsibility for events occurring subsequent to the completion of field work is
(1) Extended to include all events occurring until the date of the last subsequent event referred to.
(2) Limited to the specific event referred to.
(3) Limited to all events occurring through the date of issuance of the report.
(4) Extended to include all events occurring through the date of submission of the report to the client.

e. Cornelius Karr has examined the financial statements of Lurch Corporation for the year ended December 31, 19X0. Although Karr's field work was completed on February 27, 19X1, Karr's auditor's report was dated February 28, 19X1, and was received by the management of Lurch on March 5, 19X1. On April 4, 19X1, the management of Lurch asked that Karr approve inclusion of this report in their annual report to stockholders which will include unaudited financial statements for the first quarter ended March 31, 19X1. Karr approved of the inclusion of this auditor's report in the annual report to stockholders. Under the circumstances Karr is responsible for inquiring as to subsequent events occurring through
(1) February 27, 19X1.
(2) February 28, 19X1.
(3) March 31, 19X1.
(4) April 4, 19X1.

f. On August 5, 19X5, a CPA completes field work on a client's financial statements for the year ended June 30, 19X5. On August 20, 19X5, the anticipated date for delivery of the report, the CPA reads in the paper that one of the client's plants burned to the ground. The CPA calls the client to confirm the information and tells the client this subsequent event should be disclosed in the financial statements. The client agrees to add a footnote but still needs the report today. The CPA quickly revises the statements by adding a "Note G" and delivers the report on time. What date should the report bear?

(1) August 5, 19X5.
(2) August 5, 19X5, except for Note G, which is August 20, 19X5.
(3) August 20, 19X5.
(4) June 30, 19X5.

(AICPA adapted)

P18–3 Select the best answer to each of the following items relating to the audit report when the client has changed auditors.

a. Before reissuing a report that was previously issued on the financial statements of a prior period, a predecessor auditor should
   (1) Review the successor auditor's working papers.
   (2) Examine significant transactions or events since the date of previous issuance.
   (3) Obtain a signed engagement letter from the client.
   (4) Obtain a letter of representation from the successor auditor.

b. Jerry Jerome has completed an examination of the financial statements of Bold, Inc. Last year's financial statements were examined by Tom Smith, CPA. Since last year's financial statements will be presented for comparative purposes without Smith's report, Jerome's report should
   (1) State that the prior year's financial statements were examined by another auditor.
   (2) State that the prior year's financial statements were examined by Smith.
   (3) *Not* refer to the prior year's examination.
   (4) Refer to Smith's report only if the opinion was other than unqualified.

c. After performing all necessary procedures, a predecessor auditor reissues a prior-period report on financial statements at the request of the client without revising the original wording. The predecessor auditor should
   (1) Delete the date of the report
   (2) Dual-date the report.
   (3) Use the reissue date.
   (4) Use the date of the previous report.

d. If, during an audit examination, the successor auditor becomes aware of information that may indicate that financial statements reported on by the predecessor auditor may require revision, the successor auditor should
   (1) Ask the client to arrange a meeting among the three parties to discuss the information and attempt to resolve the matter.
   (2) Notify the client and the predecessor auditor of the matter and ask them to attempt to resolve it.
   (3) Notify the predecessor auditor, who may be required to revise the previously issued financial statements and auditor's report.
   (4) Ask the predecessor auditor to arrange a meeting with the client to discuss and resolve the matter.

e. Elizabeth Rusk, CPA, succeeded Fenwick Boone, CPA, as auditor of Moonlight Corporation. Boone had issued an unqualified report for the calendar year 19X5. What can Rusk do to establish the basis for expressing an opinion on the 19X6 financial statements with regard to opening balances?

(1) Rusk may review Boone's working papers and thereby reduce the scope of audit tests Rusk would otherwise have to do with respect to opening balances.
(2) Rusk must apply appropriate auditing procedures to account balances at the beginning of the period so as to be satisfied that they are properly stated and may *not* rely on the work done by Boone.
(3) Rusk may rely on the prior year's financial statements since an unqualified opinion was issued and must make reference in the auditor's report to Boone's report.
(4) Rusk may rely on the prior year's financial statements since an unqualified opinion was issued and must refer in a middle paragraph of the auditor's report to Boone's report of the prior year.

f. When financial statements of the prior year are presented together with those of the current year, the current auditor should report on the financial statements of the prior year if
(1) The current auditor has examined the statements of the prior year.
(2) The client requests the current auditor to review the financial statements of the prior year and report thereon.
(3) The prior auditor previously disclaimed an opinion on the prior-year financial statements.
(4) The statements of the prior year were unaudited.

(AICPA adapted)

P18–4 Select the best answer to each of the following items relating to audit reports on consolidated financial statements.

a. Thomas Feiner, CPA, has examined the consolidated financial statements of Kass Corporation. Ezra Jones, CPA, has examined the financial statements of the sole subsidiary material in relation to the total examined by Feiner. It would be appropriate for Feiner to serve as the principal auditor, but it is impractical for him to review the work of Jones. Assuming an unqualified opinion is expressed by Jones, one would expect Feiner to
(1) Refuse to express an opinion on the consolidated financial statements.
(2) Express an unqualified opinion on the consolidated financial statements and not refer to the work of Jones.
(3) Express an unqualified opinion on the consolidated financial statements and refer to the work of Jones.
(4) Express an "except for" opinion on the consolidated financial statements and refer to the work of Jones.

b. The principal auditor is satisfied with the independence and professional reputation of the other auditor who has audited a subsidiary but wants to indicate the division of responsibility. The principal auditor should
(1) Modify the scope paragraph of the report.
(2) Modify the scope and opinion paragraphs of the report.
(3) *Not* modify the report except for inclusion of an explanatory middle paragraph.
(4) Modify the opinion paragraph of the report.

c. Hedy Nielsen, CPA, is the principal auditor who is auditing the consolidated financial statements of her client. Nielsen plans to refer to another CPA's examination of the financial statements of a subsidiary company but does *not* wish to present the other CPA's audit report. Both Nielsen's and the other CPA's audit

reports have noted no exceptions to generally accepted accounting principles. Under these circumstances the opinion paragraph of Nielsen's consolidated audit report should express
(1) An unqualified opinion.
(2) A "subject to" opinion.
(3) An "except for" opinion.
(4) A principal opinion.

d. Kathryn Morgan, CPA, is the principal auditor for a multinational corporation. Another CPA has examined and reported on the financial statements of a significant subsidiary of the corporation. Morgan is satisfied with the independence and professional reputation of the other auditor, as well as the quality of the other auditor's examination. With respect to Morgan's report on the financial statements, taken as a whole, Morgan
(1) Must *not* refer to the examination of the other auditor.
(2) Must refer to the examination of the other auditor.
(3) May refer to the examination of the other auditor.
(4) May refer to the examination of the other auditor, in which case Morgan must include in the auditor's report on the consolidated financial statements a qualified opinion with respect to the examination of the other auditor.

e. When a principal auditor decides to make reference to the examination of another auditor, the principal auditor's report should clearly indicate the
(1) Principal auditor's qualification on the overall fairness of the financial statements, taken as a whole, "subject to" the work and report of the other auditor.
(2) Procedures that were performed by the other auditor in connection with the other auditor's examination.
(3) Division of responsibility between that portion of the financial statements covered by the examination of the principal auditor and that covered by the examination of the other auditor.
(4) Procedures that were performed by the principal auditor to obtain satisfaction as to the reasonableness of the examination of the other auditor.

f. When a principal auditor decides to make reference to the examination of another auditor, the principal auditor's report should indicate clearly the division of responsibility between the portions of the financial statements covered by each auditor. In which paragraph(s) of the report should the division of responsibility be stated?
(1) Only the opinion paragraph.
(2) Either the scope or opinion paragraph.
(3) Only the scope paragraph.
(4) Both the scope and opinion paragraphs.

g. In connection with the examination of the consolidated financial statements of Mott Industries, Hal Frazier, CPA, plans to refer to another CPA's examination of the financial statements of a subsidiary company. Under these circumstances Frazier's report must disclose
(1) The name of the other CPA and the type of report issued by the other CPA.
(2) The magnitude of the portion of the financial statements examined by the other CPA.
(3) The nature of Frazier's review of the other CPA's work.
(4) In a footnote, the portions of the financial statements covered by the examinations of both auditors.

h. Heather Halsey is the independent auditor examining the consolidated financial statements of Rex, Inc., a publicly held corporation. Jeffrey Lincoln is the independent auditor who has examined and reported on the financial statements of a wholly owned subsidiary of Rex, Inc. Halsey's *first* concern with respect to the Rex financial statements is to decide whether Halsey

(1) Can serve as the principal auditor and report as such on the consolidated financial statements of Rex, Inc.
(2) Can make reference to the work of Lincoln in Halsey's report on the consolidated financial statements.
(3) Should review the workpapers of Lincoln with respect to the examination of the subsidiary's financial statements.
(4) Should resign from the engagement since a qualified opinion is the only type that could be rendered on the consolidated financial statements.

i. A principal auditor decides to assume responsibility for the work of another CPA insofar as the other CPA's work relates to the principal auditor's expression of an opinion on the financial statements taken as a whole. The opinion of the other CPA is qualified but the subject of the qualification is *not* material in relation to the financial statements taken as a whole. In discharging the reporting obligation, the principal auditor
   (1) Must qualify his opinion.
   (2) Must make reference to the other CPA's qualified opinion and state that it is not material to the financial statements taken as a whole.
   (3) Need not make reference in the report to the qualification but must disclose, in a note to the financial statements, the subject of the qualification and its effect on financial position, results of operations, and changes in financial position.
   (4) Need not make reference in the report to the qualification.

j. In forming an opinion on the consolidated financial statements of Albom Corp., a CPA relies upon another auditor's examination of the financial statements of Henig Company, a wholly owned subsidiary. Henig's auditor expressed an unqualified opinion. In the report on Albom's consolidated financial statements, the CPA expresses an unqualified opinion and refers to the other auditor's examination. This indicates that
   (1) The CPA concludes, on the basis of a review of the other auditor's work, that the same responsibility can be assumed as though the CPA had audited Henig.
   (2) The CPA is satisfied with the other auditor's work in general but has some reservation relating to that auditor's independence or professional standing.
   (3) The CPA's review of the subsidiary's financial statements indicates a problem that may have escaped the other auditor.
   (4) The CPA is satisfied with the other auditor's independence and professional standing but is unwilling to take responsibility for his work.

k. A CPA is reporting on the consolidated financial statements of a company having a significant subsidiary that is audited by another CPA. Which of the following procedures is *unnecessary* if the first CPA plans to refer in his report to the report of the other CPA?
   (1) Obtain a representation from the other CPA that such CPA is independent under the requirements of the American Institute of Certified Public Accountants.
   (2) Ascertain through communication with the other CPA that such CPA is aware

that the financial statements of the subsidiary will be included in the consolidated financial statements.

(3) Ascertain through communication with the other CPA that a review will be made of matters affecting elimination of intercompany transactions and accounts.

(4) Visit the other CPA and discuss the audit procedures followed and results thereof.

l. Which of the following is the *least* important consideration when an auditor is deciding whether he can act as principal auditor for consolidated financial statements and utilize the work and reports of other independent auditors?

(1) Whether the portion of the financial statements he has examined is material compared with the portion examined by other auditors.

(2) Whether the components he examined are important relative to the enterprise as a whole.

(3) Whether he has examined the parent company statements.

(4) Whether he has sufficient knowledge of the overall financial statements.

m. Marina Abbot, CPA, as principal auditor for consolidated financial statements is using a qualified report of another auditor. Abbot does *not* consider the qualification material relative to the consolidated financial statements. What recognition, if any, must Abbot make in her report to the report of the other audit?

(1) She need make no reference.

(2) She must refer to the qualification of the other auditor and qualify her report similarly.

(3) She must include the other auditor's report with her report but need not qualify her report.

(4) She must include the other auditor's report with her report and give an explanation of its significance.

(AICPA adapted)

P18–5 Select the best answer for each of the following items relating to audit reports qualified because of departures from GAAP.

a. An auditor is confronted with an exception considered sufficiently material as to warrant some deviation from the standard unqualified auditor's report. If the exception relates to a departure from generally accepted accounting principles, the auditor must decide between expressing a (an)

(1) Adverse opinion and a "subject to" opinion.

(2) Adverse opinion and an "except for" opinion.

(3) Adverse opinion and a disclaimer of opinion.

(4) Disclaimer of opinion and a "subject to" opinion.

b. A company issues audited financial statements under circumstances that require the presentation of a statement of changes in financial position. If the company refuses to present a statement of changes in financial position, the independent auditor should

(1) Disclaim an opinion.

(2) Prepare a statement of changes in financial position and note in a middle paragraph of the report that this statement is auditor-prepared.

(3) Prepare a statement of changes in financial position and disclose in a footnote that this statement is auditor-prepared.
(4) Qualify his opinion with an "except for" qualification and a description of the omission in a middle paragraph of the report.

c. When financial statements are prepared on the basis of a going concern and the auditor believes that the client may *not* continue as a going concern, the auditor should issue
(1) A "subject to" opinion.
(2) An unqualified opinion with an explanatory middle paragraph.
(3) An "except for" opinion.
(4) An adverse opinion.

d. If the auditor believes that required disclosures of a significant nature are omitted from the financial statements under examination, the auditor should decide between issuing
(1) A qualified opinion or an adverse opinion.
(2) A disclaimer of opinion or a qualified opinion.
(3) An adverse opinion or a disclaimer of opinion.
(4) An unqualified opinion or a qualified opinion.

e. The auditor who intends to express a qualified opinion should disclose all the substantive reasons in a separate explanatory paragraph of the report, *except* when the opinion paragraph
(1) Makes reference to a note in the financial statements which discloses the pertinent facts.
(2) Describes a limitation on the scope of the examination.
(3) Describes an insufficiency in evidential matter.
(4) Has been modified because of a change in accounting principle.

f. When a client declines to make essential disclosures in the financial statements or in the footnotes, the independent auditor should
(1) Provide the necessary disclosures in the auditor's report and appropriately modify the opinion.
(2) Explain to the client that an adverse opinion must be issued.
(3) Issue an unqualified report and inform the stockholders of the improper disclosure in an "unaudited" footnote.
(4) Issue an opinion "subject to" the client's lack of disclosure of supplementary information as explained in a middle paragraph of the report.

g. Limitation on the scope of the auditor's examination may require the auditor to issue a qualified opinion or to disclaim an opinion. Which of the following would generally be a limitation on the scope of the auditor's examination?
(1) The unavailability of sufficient competent evidential matter.
(2) The engagement of the auditor to report on only one basic financial statement.
(3) The examination of a subsidiary's financial statements by an auditor other than the one who examines and reports on the consolidated financial statements.
(4) The engagement of the auditor after year end.

h. If an auditor wishes to issue a qualified opinion because the financial statements include a departure from generally accepted accounting principles, the auditor's report should have an explanatory paragraph referring to a footnote that discloses the principal effects of the subject matter of the qualification. The qualification should be referred to in the opinion paragraph by using language such as
(1) "With the exception of."

(2) "When read in conjunction with the footnotes."
(3) "With the foregoing explanation."
(4) "Subject to the departure explained in the footnotes."

i. A limitation on the scope of the auditor's examination sufficient to preclude an unqualified opinion will *always* result when management
(1) Engages an auditor after the year-end physical inventory count.
(2) Refuses to furnish a representation letter.
(3) Knows that direct confirmation of accounts receivable with debtors is not feasible.
(4) Engages an auditor to examine only the balance sheet.

j. In which of the following circumstances would an auditor be required to issue a qualified report with a separate explanatory paragraph?
(1) The auditor satisfactorily performed alternative accounts receivable procedures because scope limitations prevented performance of normal procedures.
(2) The financial statements reflect the effects of a change in accounting principles from one period to the next.
(3) A particular note to the financial statements discloses a company accounting method which deviates from generally accepted accounting principles.
(4) The financial statements of a significant subsidiary were examined by another auditor, and reference to the other auditor's report is to be made in the principal auditor's report.

k. An opinion as to the "fairness" of financial statement presentation in accordance with generally accepted accounting principles is based on several judgments made by the auditor. One such judgment is whether the accounting principles used
(1) Have general acceptance.
(2) Are promulgated by the AICPA Auditing Standards Executive Committee.
(3) Are the most conservative of those available for use.
(4) Emphasize the legal form of transactions.

l. Brian Keller, CPA, was about to issue an unqualified opinion on the audit of Lupton Television Broadcasting Company when he received a letter from Lupton's independent counsel. The letter stated that the Federal Communications Commission has notified Lupton that its broadcasting license will *not* be renewed because of some alleged irregularities in its broadcasting practices. Lupton *cannot* continue to operate without this license. Keller has also learned that Lupton and its independent counsel plan to take all necessary legal action to retain the license. The letter from independent counsel, however, states that a favorable outcome of any legal action is highly uncertain. Based on this information what action should Keller take?
(1) Issue a qualified opinion, subject to the outcome of the license dispute, with disclosure of the substantive reasons for the qualification in a separate explanatory paragraph of his report.
(2) Issue an unqualified opinion if full disclosure is made of the license dispute in a footnote to the financial statements.
(3) Issue an adverse opinion on the financial statements and disclose all reasons therefore.
(4) Issue a piecemeal opinion with full disclosure made of the license dispute in a footnote to the financial statements.

m. What recognition, if any, should be given to an accounting change that has *no* material effect on the financial statements in the current year but the change is reasonably certain to have substantial effect in later years?
   (1) There is no need for recognition because when the change was made it had no material effect.
   (2) The change should be disclosed in the notes to the financial statements whenever the statements of the year of change are presented, but the CPA need not recognize the change in the CPA's opinion as to consistency.
   (3) The change should be disclosed in the notes to the financial statements whenever the statements of the year of change are presented and the CPA must recognize the change in the CPA's opinion as to consistency.
   (4) The change should be recognized in the CPA's opinion as to consistency only when it is not disclosed in notes to the financial statements.

n. Under the AICPA Code of Professional Ethics, a CPA may issue an unqualified opinion on financial statements which contain a departure from generally accepted accounting principles if he can demonstrate that due to unusual circumstances the financial statements would be misleading if the departure were not made. Which of the following is an example of unusual circumstances which could justify such a departure?
   (1) New legislation.
   (2) An unusual degree of materiality.
   (3) Conflicting industry practices.
   (4) A theoretical disagreement with a standard promulgated by the Financial Accounting Standards Board.

o. An auditor's client has violated a minor requirement of its bond indenture which could result in the trustee requiring immediate payment of the principal amount due. The client refuses to seek a waiver from the bond trustee. Request for immediate payment is *not* considered likely. Under these circumstances the auditor must
   (1) Require classification of bonds payable as a current liability.
   (2) Contact the bond trustee directly.
   (3) Disclose the situation in the auditor's report.
   (4) Obtain an opinion from the company's attorney as to the likelihood of the trustee's enforcement of the requirement.

p. In determining the type of opinion to express, an auditor assesses the nature of the reporting qualifications and the materiality of their effects. Materiality will be the primary factor considered in the choice between
   (1) An "except for" opinion and an adverse opinion.
   (2) An "except for" opinion and a "subject to" opinion.
   (3) An adverse opinion and a disclaimer of opinion.
   (4) A "subject to" opinion and a piecemeal opinion.

(AICPA adapted)

P18–6 Select the best answer for each of the following items relating to the consistency phrase of the audit report.

a. The annual report of a publicly held company presents the prior year's financial statements (which are clearly marked "unaudited") in comparative form with current-year audited financial statements. The auditor's report should

(1) Express an opinion on the audited financial statements and contain a separate paragraph describing the responsibility assumed for the financial statements of the prior period.
(2) Disclaim an opinion on the unaudited financial statements, modify the consistency phrase, and express an opinion on the current year's financial statements.
(3) State that the unaudited financial statements are presented solely for comparative purposes and express an opinion only on the current year's financial statements.
(4) Express an opinion on the audited financial statements and state whether the unaudited financial statements were compiled or reviewed.

b. Which of the following consistency phrases would be contained in a continuing auditor's standard report on comparative financial statements?
(1) Applied on a consistent basis.
(2) Applied on a basis consistent with that of the preceding year.
(3) Applied consistently during interim periods.
(4) Applied consistently with previous years audited.

c. An auditor need *not* mention consistency in the audit report if
(1) The client has acquired another company through a "pooling of interests."
(2) An adverse opinion is issued.
(3) This is the first year the client has had an audit.
(4) Comparative financial statements are issued.

d. A CPA's client has changed from straight-line depreciation to sum-of-the-year's-digits depreciation. The effect on this year's income is immaterial but in the future the change, which is adequately disclosed in the notes to the financial statements, may be expected to result in materially different results. On the basis of this fact, the auditor should express
(1) An unqualified opinion.
(2) A consistency exception.
(3) A "subject to" opinion.
(4) An "except for" opinion.

e. Which of the following, when materially affecting comparability, would ordinarily be referred to by an independent auditor reporting on the statement of changes in financial position?
(1) Changing from a balanced to an unbalanced form of presentation.
(2) Changes in terminology.
(3) Changing from a cash to working capital form of presentation.
(4) Changes in the content of working capital.

f. A change from cash to working capital in a statement of changes in financial position constitutes a change which requires
(1) No disclosure in the auditor's report.
(2) That the auditor's opinion contain a "subject to" qualification as to consistency.
(3) That the auditor's opinion contain an exception as to conformity with generally accepted accounting principles.
(4) That the auditor's opinion contain an exception as to consistency in the opinion paragraph.

g. The consistency standard does *not* apply to an accounting change that results from a change in

(1) An accounting principle that is *not* generally accepted.
(2) An accounting estimate.
(3) The reporting entity.
(4) An accounting principle inseparable from a change in accounting estimate.

h. With respect to consistency, which of the following should be done by an independent auditor, one who has *not* examined a company's financial statements for the preceding year but is doing so in the current year?
(1) Report on the financial statements of the current year without referring to consistency.
(2) Consider the consistent application of principles within the year under examination but *not* between the current and preceding year.
(3) Adopt procedures, that are practicable and reasonable in the circumstances, to obtain assurance that the principles employed are consistent between the current and preceding year.
(4) Rely on the report of the prior year's auditors if such a report does *not* take exception as to consistency.

i. Which of the following four events may be expected to result in a consistency exception in the auditor's report?
(1) The declining balance method of depreciation was adopted for newly acquired assets.
(2) A revision was made in the service lives and salvage values of depreciable assets.
(3) A mathematical error in computing the year-end LIFO inventory was corrected.
(4) The provision for bad debts increased considerably over the previous year.

j. What is the objective of the reporting standard relating to consistency?
(1) To give assurance that adequate disclosure will be made so that there will be comparability of financial statements between companies in the same industry.
(2) To give assurance that the comparability of financial statements between periods has not been materially affected by changes in accounting principles.
(3) To give assurance that the comparability of financial statements between periods has *not* been materially affected by any change.
(4) To give assurance only that the same accounting principles have been applied to all similar transactions within each period presented.

k. When comparative financial statements are presented and a change in accounting principle is made in the current year, the financial statements of the prior year should be restated *except* when the change is
(1) From the completed-contract to the percentage-of-completion method of accounting for long-term construction-type contracts.
(2) From the LIFO to the FIFO method of inventory pricing.
(3) From the FIFO to the LIFO method of inventory pricing.
(4) From the "full cost" to another acceptable method of accounting used in the extractive industry.

l. Which of the following should *not* be treated as an accounting change that affects the standard of reporting relating to consistency?
(1) Change in the service lives of all assets.
(2) Change from cash basis to accrual method of accounting.
(3) Change from FIFO to LIFO inventory method.
(4) Change from straight-line to declining-balance method of depreciation.

m. Which of the following requires recognition in the auditor's opinion as to consistency?
(1) Changing the salvage value of an asset.
(2) Changing the presentation of prepaid insurance from inclusion in "other assets" to disclosing it as a separate line item.
(3) Division of the consolidated subsidiary into two subsidiaries that are both consolidated.
(4) Changing from consolidating a subsidiary to carrying it on the equity basis.

(AICPA adapted)

P18–7 Select the best answer to each of the following items relating to a disclaimer of opinion.

a. In which one of the following situations must the CPA issue a disclaimer of opinion?
(1) He owns stock in the company.
(2) Some portion of the client's financial statements does not conform to generally accepted accounting principles.
(3) He has omitted a normally required auditing procedure.
(4) Generally accepted accounting principles have not been applied on a basis consistent with that of the preceding year.

b. It is *less* likely that a disclaimer of opinion would be issued when the auditor has reservations arising from
(1) Inability to apply necessary auditing procedures.
(2) Uncertainties.
(3) Inadequate internal control.
(4) Lack of independence.

c. An auditor is unable to determine the amounts associated with certain illegal acts committed by a client. In these circumstances the auditor would *most* likely
(1) Issue either a qualified opinion or a disclaimer of opinion.
(2) Issue only an adverse opinion.
(3) Issue either a qualified opinion or an adverse opinion.
(4) Issue only a disclaimer of opinion.

d. When are an auditor's reporting responsibilities *not* met by attaching an explanation of the circumstances and a disclaimer of opinion to the client's financial statements?
(1) When he believes the financial statements are misleading.
(2) When he was unable to observe the taking of the physical inventory.
(3) When he is uncertain about the outcome of a material contingency.
(4) When he has performed insufficient auditing procedures to express an opinion.

(AICPA adapted)

P18–8 Select the best answer to each of the following items relating to miscellaneous aspects of audit reports.

a. When the report of a principal auditor makes reference to the examination made by another auditor, the other auditor may be named if express permission to do so is given and

(1) The report of the principal auditor names the other auditor in both the scope and opinion paragraphs.
(2) The principal auditor accepts responsibility for the work of the other auditor.
(3) The report of the other auditor is presented together with the report of the principal auditor.
(4) The other auditor is *not* an associate or correspondent firm whose work is done at the request of the principal auditor.

b. A CPA has completed the initial audit of a new client which has *not* previously been audited. The client has prepared an annual report with comparative financial statements of the prior year which have been marked "unaudited." What comment should the CPA make to his client or in his report relative to the prior year's financial statements?
(1) The CPA should tell his client that if the client wants to include the CPA's report on this year's financial statements in the annual report, the client can not include the comparative statements because the CPA has not audited them.
(2) The CPA must add a disclaimer of opinion on the prior year's financial statements to his report.
(3) The CPA must qualify his report to the effect that comparison with the prior-year figures may not be valid because they are unaudited.
(4) The CPA need do nothing.

c. A continuing auditor would update his opinion on prior financial statements by issuing a "subject to" opinion for the
(1) Subsequent resolution of an uncertainty in the current period.
(2) Discovery of an uncertainty in the current period.
(3) Discovery of an uncertainty in the current period that relates to the prior-period statements being reported on.
(4) Restatement of prior-period statements in conformity with generally accepted accounting principles.

d. A CPA has audited financial statements and issued an unqualified opinion on them. Subsequently the CPA was requested to compile financial statements for the same period that omit substantially all disclosures and are to be used for comparative purposes. In these circumstances the CPA may report on comparative compiled financial statements that omit such disclosures provided the
(1) Missing disclosures are immaterial in amount.
(2) Financial statements and notes appended thereto are not misleading.
(3) Accountant's report indicates the previous audit and the date of the previous report.
(4) Previous auditor's report accompanies the comparative financial statement.

e. When a contingency is resolved immediately subsequent to the issuance of a report qualified with respect to the contingency, the auditor should
(1) Insist that the client issue revised financial statements.
(2) Inform the audit committee that the report can *not* be relied upon.
(3) Take *no* action regarding the event.
(4) Inform the appropriate authorities that the report can *not* be relied upon.

f. In which of the following circumstances would an adverse opinion be appropriate?
(1) The auditor is not independent with respect to the enterprise being audited.
(2) An uncertainty prevents the issuance of an unqualified opinion.

(3) The statements are *not* in conformity with APB Opinion No. 8 regarding pension plans.
(4) A client-imposed scope limitation prevents the auditor from complying with generally accepted auditing standards.

g. In a first audit of a new company the auditor's report will
(1) Remain silent with respect to consistency.
(2) State that the accounting principles have been applied on a consistent basis.
(3) State that accounting principles have been applied consistently during the period.
(4) State that the consistency standard does *not* apply because the current year is the first year of audit.

h. A CPA is conducting the first examination of a nonpublic company's financial statements. The CPA hopes to reduce the audit work by consulting with the predecessor auditor and reviewing the predecessor's working papers. This procedure is
(1) Acceptable if the client and the predecessor auditor agree to it.
(2) Acceptable if the CPA refers in the audit report to reliance on the predecessor auditor's work.
(3) Required if the CPA is to render an unqualified opinion.
(4) Unacceptable because the CPA should bring an independent viewpoint to a new engagement.

i. When an adverse opinion is expressed, the opinion paragraph should include a direct reference to
(1) A footnote to the financial statements, which discusses the basis for the opinion.
(2) The scope paragraph that discusses the basis for the opinion rendered.
(3) A separate paragraph that discusses the basis for the opinion rendered.
(4) The consistency or lack of consistency in the application of generally accepted accounting principles.

(AICPA adapted)

P18–9 Select the best answer for each of the following items relating to long-form reports.

a. A long-form report generally includes the basic financial statement but would *not* include
(1) Exceptions or reservations to the standard (short-form) report.
(2) Details of items in basic financial statements.
(3) Statistical data.
(4) Explanatory comments.

b. Herman Ansman, CPA, has been requested by a client, Rainco Corp., to prepare a "long-form report" for this year's audit engagement. Which of the following is the *best* reason for Rainco's requesting a long-form report?
(1) To provide for a piecemeal opinion because certain items are not in accordance with generally accepted accounting principles.
(2) To provide Rainco's creditors a greater degree of assurance as to the financial soundness of the company.
(3) To provide Rainco's management with information to supplement and analyze the basic financial statements.

(4) To provide the documentation required by the Securities and Exchange Commission in anticipation of a public offering of Rainco's stock.

c. With regard to the request described in the preceding problem, what action, in issuing a long-form report, must Ansman be certain to undertake?

(1) Issue a standard short-form report on the same engagement.
(2) Include a description of the scope of the examination in more detail than the description in the usual short-form report.
(3) State the source of any statistical data and that such data have not been subjected to the same auditing procedures as the basic financial statements.
(4) Maintain a clear-cut distinction between the management's representations and the auditor's representations.

d. Which of the following best describes the difference between a long-form auditor's report and the standard short-form report?

(1) The long-form report may contain a more detailed description of the scope of the auditor's examination.
(2) The long-form report's use permits the auditor to explain exceptions or reservations in a way that does not require an opinion qualification.
(3) The auditor may make factual representations with a degree of certainty that would not be appropriate in a short-form report.
(4) The long-form report's use is limited to special situations such as cash basis statements, modified accrual basis statements, or not-for-profit organization statements.

e. Nonaccounting data included in a long-form report have been subjected to auditing procedures. The auditor's report should state this fact and should explain that the nonaccounting data are presented for analysis purposes. In addition, the auditor's report should state whether the nonaccounting data are

(1) Beyond the scope of the normal engagement and therefore *not* covered by the opinion on the financial statements.
(2) Within the framework of generally accepted auditing standards, which apply to the financial statements, taken as a whole.
(3) Audited, unaudited, or reviewed on a limited basis.
(4) Fairly stated in all material respects in relation to the basic financial statements, taken as a whole.

(AICPA adapted)

CHAPTER

19

OTHER TYPES OF REPORTS RENDERED BY ACCOUNTANTS

In this chapter we continue our discussion of reports rendered by accountants. In Chapter 18 our discussion centered around the audit report that accompanies comparative audited financial statements designed to show whether an entity's financial position, results of operations, and changes in financial position are presented in conformity with GAAP. We also discussed briefly the report that should be included with the unaudited financial statements of a public entity when the accountant has been associated with those statements. But accountants also issue many other types of reports, some of which we examine in this chapter. Such reports can be classified into the following categories:

1. Unaudited financial statements of nonpublic entities.
2. Reports on interim financial information that has been reviewed by the accountant.
3. Special reports.
4. Other reports classified according to type of service rendered.

The specific content of those reports depends primarily on the following factors: the level of association the accountant has had with the financial statements (look again at Figure 18–1); the nature of the financial data being reported on; and the type of service being performed by the accountant.

The term *association with financial statements* was defined in Chapter 18. This term should not be confused with a CPA's preparation of financial statements as an employee of a firm or as a member of an organization. Because of an employee CPA's nonindependence, any statement prepared in that capacity should be signed as an employee or organization member, and not as a CPA.

Recall that there are basically three levels of association for outside accountants providing services to both public and nonpublic entities. Besides the audit level of association, there are the *review and compilation levels for unaudited financial statements of nonpublic entities*. Similarly, there are *reviews of interim financial information* and association with *unaudited financial statements* for public entities. Each of these other levels of association requires a specific type of report.

Some special reports of accountants may be classified on the basis of the *nature of the financial data* covered by the report. Audited financial statements may, for example, be prepared in accordance with a comprehensive basis of accounting other than GAAP. If a full scope audit is not required, the accountant may be engaged to audit only specific elements or accounts of a financial statement. In other instances, the accountant may be asked to apply only selected audit procedures to certain elements or accounts of a financial statement. In other cases, the auditor may be asked to report on client compliance with contractual agreements or regulatory requirements. Finally, the auditor may be associated with financial information presented in prescribed forms or schedules, such as those required by state insurance boards.

Still other accountants' reports can better be described by relating them to *types of services* performed to produce them. Such reports include letters to underwriters; reports on internal accounting control; reports following management advisory services engagements; reports by internal auditors; and reports of governmental auditors.

Our discussion in this chapter will cover all these different types of reports.

UNAUDITED FINANCIAL STATEMENTS OF NONPUBLIC ENTITIES

Accountants are frequently asked to prepare financial statements *from a nonpublic client's accounting records* for use in obtaining credit or for other purposes. The accountant, in accepting such an engagement, may perform all the accounting work necessary to prepare the financial statements, including posting from the journals to the ledgers. Or, the accountant may prepare the client's financial statements from information in the client's ledger or trial balance. In many instances, such financial statement preparation service is provided by small public accounting firms as an end product of "write-up work."

Initially the accounting profession took the position that unless the financial statements were included in a binder carrying the accountant's name or were presented on the accountant's letterhead, the accounting firm was not deemed to have been associated with them. Some years later the profession changed its official stance to say that the accountant was deemed to be associated with financial statements if he or she prepared them, even though they were presented on plain paper. With that interpretation of association, the accountant was required to disclaim an opinion on any unaudited statements prepared for a client, regardless of whether the firm binder or letterhead was used. However, the accountant was still judged to have no responsibility for data in the statements if he or she disclaimed an opinion on them.

Gradually, as a result of some legal involvements and soul searching, the profession decided that the accountant might have some implied responsibility for disclosing errors and irregularities that come to light during the engagement if these irregularities should be obvious to a professionally trained person in the course of preparing the statements. This decision led to the requirement that accountants disclose departures from GAAP that were observed in the preparation of unaudited financial statements.

Even more recently, the AICPA has taken the position that an accountant's association with unaudited financial statements of a nonpublic entity will be construed to involve either a *compilation* or a *review* of the financial statements. The authoritative literature regarding these two relationships with the financial statements is presented in Statements on Standards for Accounting Review Services (SSARS). These statements establish the working and reporting responsibilities of the accountant in both compilation and review engagements. After we have examined each of these types of engagements, we deal with the problems of changing engagement responsibilities and the discovery of facts pertinent to the financial statements subsequent to the date of issuing the compilation or review report.

Compilation of Financial Statements

The compilation of financial statements is defined by SSARS 1 as presenting, in the form of financial statements, information that is the representation of management (owners) without undertaking to express any assurance on the statements.[1] Because the users of such financial statements should be able readily to identify the degree of responsibility, if any, the accountant is taking with respect to such statements, the accountant compiling such statements is required to present a report providing that information. That report should state these three facts:

- A compilation has been performed.
- A compilation is limited to presenting in the form of financial statements information that is the representation of management (owners).
- The financial statements have not been audited or reviewed and accordingly the accountant does not express an opinion or any other form of assurance on them.

The standard report that is appropriate for a compilation is shown in Figure 19–1. Each page of the financial statements should include a reference, such as "See Accountant's Compilation Report." The compilation report should be dated as of the date of completion of the compilation engagement.

The accompanying balance sheet of XYZ Company as of December 31, 19X2, and the related statements of income, retained earnings, and changes in financial position for the year then ended have been compiled by (us).

A compilation is limited to presenting, in the form of financial statements, information that is the representation of management (owners). We have not audited or reviewed the accompanying financial statements and accordingly do not express an opinion or any other form of assurance on them.

Date and Signature

FIGURE 19–1. Accountant's Compilation Report

The accountant may be asked to issue a compilation report on one financial statement such as the balance sheet, and not on the other related financial statements. There is no theoretical reason for the accountant not to accept such an assignment.

The acceptance of an engagement to compile financial statements carries with it certain implied *capabilities of the accountant* accepting such an appointment. The accountant is expected to have knowledge of accounting principles and practices of the industry in which the entity operates. To obtain this knowledge, publications such as AICPA industry audit guides and industry periodicals should be consulted. The accountant should also possess a general understanding of the nature of the entity's transactions, the form of its accounting records, the stated qualifications of its accounting personnel, the accounting basis on which the financial statements are to be presented, and the form and content of the financial statements. On the basis of that understanding, the accountant should consider whether it is necessary to perform other accounting services, such as assistance in adjusting the books of account or consultation on accounting matters, in the process of compiling financial statements.

The accountant is *not required to make inquiries* or perform other procedures to verify, corroborate, or review information supplied by the entity. However, if inquiries or other contacts with the client have shown the information supplied by the client to be incorrect, incomplete, or otherwise unsatisfactory, the accountant should insist on providing the additional or revised information. If the client refuses to provide the needed information, the accountant should withdraw from the compilation engagement.

In some cases, clients may ask the accountant to compile financial statements that contain only information needed to make specific decisions. In these instances, it may be impracticable to spend the time necessary to pull together substantially all the informative disclosures necessary for conformity with GAAP. Omitted disclosures might include selected footnotes or the statement of changes in financial position. Compilation standards permit the association of the CPA's name with such statements, provided that the omission of substantially all disclosures is indicated in the report and is not, to the CPA's knowledge, made with the intent to deceive users of the financial statements. The compilation report should be modified in these cases (1) to cite the election of management to omit substantially all disclosures that, if included, might influence users' conclusions, and (2) to state that the financial statements are not designed to be used by those who are not informed about the missing disclosures. However, if the client should later provide a copy of the statements to an outside party who expects full disclosures, the statements should be revised to include the appropriate footnotes and a revised compilation report.

A nonindependent accountant is not prohibited from compiling the financial statements for an entity. In such situations, the accountant's report should carry a statement informing the users of the financial statements that he or she is not independent with respect to the client company. That statement should not include the reason for lack of independence.

An accountant may also compile financial data in conformity with a comprehensive basis of accounting other than GAAP, such as the cash basis of accounting. In such cases, the accountant's compilation report should be expanded to include disclosure of the basis of accounting that was used.

Review of Financial Statements

The accountant may be asked either to review the financial statements in connection with compiling them, or to review financial statements already compiled by the client. The *purpose of a review* is to provide the accountant with a basis for giving *limited assurance* to the client as to whether material modifications need to be made to financial statements in order to make them conform to GAAP or other comprehensive bases of accounting.

The review engagement assumes the same background knowledge relating to the industry as that described for a compilation engagement. In addition, however, SSARS 1 prescribes the following *inquiry and analytical procedures* that the accountant should perform in such an engagement:

1. Inquiries should be made concerning the entity's
   a. Accounting principles and practices and the methods followed in applying them;
   b. Procedures for recording, classifying, and summarizing transactions and accumulating information for disclosure in the financial statements.

   Appendix 19–A includes a list of illustrative inquiries that may be used in meeting these two review requirements.
2. Analytical procedures, designed to identify relationships and individual items that appear to be unusual, should be performed during the reviewing process. These consist of
   a. Comparison of the financial statements with statements for comparable prior periods;
   b. Comparison of the financial statements with anticipated results such as budgets and forecasts if they are available;
   c. A study of the relationships of the elements of the financial statements that would be expected to conform to a predictable pattern based on the entity's experience. Examples are the relationships between changes in sales and changes in accounts receivable; between sales and expenses, such as commissions, which ordinarily fluctuate with sales; and between changes in property, plant, and equipment and changes in the repairs and maintenance expense accounts.
3. Inquiries should be made concerning actions taken at meetings of the stockholders, board of directors, committees of the board of directors, and other similar meetings that may affect the financial statements.
4. The accountant should read the financial statements to consider, on the basis of informa-

tion coming to his or her attention, whether the financial statements appear to conform with generally accepted accounting principles.

5. The accountant should obtain reports from other accountants, if any, who have been engaged to audit or review the financial statements of significant components of the reporting entity, such as its subsidiaries and investees.
6. Inquiry should be made of persons having responsibility for financial and accounting matters concerning the following points:
   a. Whether the financial statements have been prepared in conformity with generally accepted accounting principles consistently applied;
   b. Changes in the entity's business activities or accounting principles and practices during the year;
   c. Any matters as to which questions have arisen in the course of applying the foregoing procedures;
   d. Events subsequent to the date of the financial statements that would have a material effect on the financial statements.[2]

It is important to observe that a review of financial statements does not contemplate a study and evaluation of internal accounting control. Neither does it involve tests of accounting records, responses to inquiries by obtaining corroborating evidential matter, and certain other procedures ordinarily performed during an audit. Therefore a review does not provide assurance that the accountant will become aware of all significant matters that would be disclosed in an audit. On the other hand, a review is intended to provide greater assurance to users than the compilation. This is evidenced by the fact that a nonindependent CPA is prohibited from issuing a review report, which is in contrast to the nonindependent CPA's association with compiled financial statements. In this respect, the review engagement is more similar to an audit engagement than to a compilation. Moreover, a CPA is prohibited from issuing a review report on financial statements that omit substantially all disclosures, a requirement that is similar to audit standards. If the accountant performing the review becomes aware that information in the financial statements is incorrect, incomplete, or otherwise unsatisfactory, he or she should perform additional procedures that will allow the expression of limited assurance on the financial statements. The accountant may also wish to *obtain a representation letter*, similar to the one shown in Appendix 19–B, from the owner, manager, or executive officer.

If the review suggests no need for modifying the financial statements, a report should accompany the statements, declaring the following:

- A review was performed in accordance with standards established by the American Institute of Certified Public Accountants.
- All information included in the financial statements is the representation of management (owners) of the entity.
- A review consists primarily of inquiries of company personnel and analytical procedures applied to financial statements.
- A review is substantially less in scope than an audit, the objective of which is the expression of an opinion regarding the financial statements taken as a whole, and accordingly no such opinion is expressed.
- The accountant is not aware of any material modifications that should be made to the financial statements in order for them to be in conformity with generally accepted accounting principles other than those modifications, if any, indicated in the report.

As with a compilation, the report should be dated as of the completion of the review engagement; and each page of the financial statements should include a reference such as "See Accountant's Review Report." The standard report shown in Figure 19–2 illustrates how these reporting requirements can be met.

If for some reason the accountant is *unable to perform the inquiry and analytical procedures* considered necessary to achieve the limited assurance expressed in the preceding report, he or she *has no adequate basis for issuing a review report.* In such a situation, the accountant should consider whether the circumstances resulting in an incomplete review also preclude the issuance of a compilation report (the next-lower level of assurance). If the accountant concludes that there is reasonable justification for the limitation of review procedures, an appropriate compilation report can be issued.

An accountant may be asked to issue a *review report on one financial statement* but not on the others. This may be done if the scope of the accountant's inquiry and analytical procedures has not been restricted. The accountant may in some instances be asked to perform specific audit procedures, such as the confirmation of accounts receivable during the preparation of unaudited financial statements. Such procedures may be performed but should be considered a separate accounting service rather than a part of an audit.

Changing an Audit Engagement to a Compilation or Review Engagement

In some instances, an accountant who was initially engaged to perform an audit may be asked by the client to change the engagement to a review or compilation status. Before consenting to such a change, the accountant should consider the following:

- The reason the client gives for the request, and the implications of the restrictions on the scope of the audit whether the restrictions will be imposed by the client or by circumstances.
- The additional effort required to complete the audit.
- The estimated additional cost to complete the audit.

We have reviewed the accompanying balance sheet of XYZ Company as of December 31, 19X2, and the related statements of income, retained earnings, and changes in financial position for the year then ended in accordance with standards established by the American Institute of Certified Public Accountants. All information included in those financial statements is the representation of management (owners) of XYZ Company.

A review consists primarily of inquiries of company personnel and analytical procedures applied to financial data. It is substantially less in scope than an examination in accordance with generally accepted auditing standards, the objective of which is the expression of an opinion regarding the financial statements as a whole. Accordingly, we do not express such an opinion.

On the basis of our review, we are not aware of any material modifications that should be made to the accompanying financial statements in order for them to be in conformity with generally accepted accounting principles.

Date and Signature

FIGURE 19–2. Accountant's Review Report

An original misunderstanding of the client concerning the nature of an audit or a change of circumstances that eliminates the entity's need for audited statements (such as changes in their intended use) would ordinarily be considered reasonable bases for requesting a change in the engagement. However, in considering the implications of a restriction on the scope of the examination, the accountant should evaluate the possibility that the information affected by the scope restriction may be incorrect, incomplete, or otherwise unsatisfactory. Also, when the accountant has been prohibited by the client from corresponding with the entity's legal counsel, or when management (owners) have refused to sign a client representation letter, the accountant ordinarily would be precluded from issuing a review or compilation report on the financial statements.

If the accountant concludes on the basis of professional judgment that there is reasonable justification for changing the engagement and he or she complies with the standards applicable to the changed engagement, an appropriate review or compilation report can be issued. That report, however, should not include reference to the original engagement, or to any auditing procedures that may have been performed, or to the scope limitations that resulted from the changed engagement.

Responsibilities Subsequent to Issuance of Report

After the compilation or review report has been issued, facts may come to the accountant's attention that indicate that the information included in compiled or reviewed financial statements is erroneous or misleading. In such circumstances, the accountant should refer for guidance to SAS 1, Section 561, relating to subsequent discovery of facts existing at the audit report date. Procedures similar to those required for an audit are also required for a compilation or review engagement, after making allowances for the differences in objectives among these types of engagements.

Documentation Associated with Compilation and Review Processes

Although professional standards do not prescribe specific content for working papers, the accountant should provide supporting documentation for both compilation and review engagements. The elements of the working papers that are suggested for each of these types of engagements are shown in Figure 19–3. These include the engagement letter; various checklists showing that the accountant obtained the required knowledge of the client's business and industry; working trial balance and adjustments; summary of data in support of footnote disclosures; summaries of key discussions with the client; and other evidence in support of the work that was done.

Reports on Comparative Financial Statements

SSARS 2 gives guidance with respect to reports on comparative financial statements that have been compiled or reviewed. Treatment of this subject is complex because various combinations of present and past services may have been performed for the client. SSARS 1 requires that the report on financial statements of a particular year correspond to the *highest level of service* performed in that year. For example, when

	Compilations	Reviews
1. Engagement letter	yes	yes
2. Checklist showing accountant's knowledge of business and industry	yes	yes
3. Checklist in support of inquiries and analytical procedures	N/A	yes
4. Working trial balance, including adjustments and other data connecting the client's accounting records to the financial statements	yes	yes
5. Indication that CPA has read the compiled financial statements	yes	N/A
6. Summary of data in support of notes to financial statements	yes	yes
7. Reasons for omissions of disclosures	yes	N/A
8. Summaries of discussions of unusual matter encountered	yes	yes
9. Representation letters	optional	yes
10. Copies of reports from other accountants associated with subsidiary entities included in consolidated financial statements	yes	yes
11. Reasons for step-down from higher level engagement, if applicable	yes	yes

FIGURE 19–3. Suggested Working Paper Documentation for Compilation and Review Engagements

full-scope review services are performed, the accountant may not, because of personal preference, prepare and render a compilation report: the review services (higher level of association than compilation services) require, at a minimum, a review report. *Complexities arise when the level of service rendered varies* from higher to lower levels from one year to the next.

When the same or higher levels of service have been performed in the current as the prior year, the accountant's reporting obligation is generally to: (1) report on the current service, and (2) update the report on the financial statements of the prior period. Examples of reporting language can be found in SSARS 2, paragraphs .09 and .10. This kind of comparative reporting is appropriate in the following situations:

- Compilation in the prior year followed by compilation in the current year.
- Compilation in the prior year followed by review in the current year.
- Review in the prior year followed by review in the current year.

When the prior year's financial statements have been compiled or reviewed by another accountant, the successor accountant is not in a position to update the predecessor accountant's report. In such a case, two options are available to the successor:

1. Request the predecessor to *reissue* the previously issued compilation or review report. In that case the predecessor must decide whether this is the appropriate action to take (see SSARS 2, paragraphs 20 and 24).
2. Revise the current-period report to include a paragraph stating that the prior-period financial statements were compiled or reviewed by another accountant, and give the date and nature of the previous report along with the nature of any modification thereto.

When the current year's service is an audit, generally accepted auditing standards rather than accounting and review services standards are applicable and should be followed by the accountant.

When the *current level of service for a client is lower than a previous level* of service, the accountant is prohibited from updating a previously issued report. This prohibition exists because the accountant is not performing the requisite level of service in the current period with respect to the previous period's statements to permit the higher-level updated report. This situation occurs when there is a review in the prior year followed by a compilation in the current year or when there is an audit in the prior year followed by a review or compilation in the current year. In these circumstances, the accountant may take one of the following courses of action:

1. Reissue the report of the previous period, being careful (as in all reissuance cases) to use the *original*, and not the more recent, report date.
2. Write a separate paragraph into the current (lower level) report explaining the nature of the service rendered in the prior period, the date of the previous report, the type of service rendered in the previous period, the report issued on the previous period's financial statements, and the reasons for any modifications from standard reports. If an audit was performed in the previous year, the current (lower level) report should also state that no audit procedures were performed after the date of the previous audit report. If a review was performed in the previous year, the current year's compilation report should state that no review procedures were performed after the date of the previous review report.

When the previous-year services have been performed by a predecessor accountant, that firm may be asked to reissue its previously issued report. Alternatively, a descriptive paragraph may be added by the successor accountant to the current-period report — describing the prior-year service, type and date of report, and, when necessary, the fact that no subsequent audit or review services have been performed.

Communications Between Predecessor and Successor Accountants

SAS 7 requires successor auditors to communicate with predecessor auditors as part of the audit planning process, in order to help determine whether the successor should accept an audit engagement. Predecessor *auditors are generally obligated*, subject to the confidential client information rules of the Code of Professional Conduct (see Chapter 20) to respond to the successor's direct questions involving integrity of the client and other matters. In contrast, SSARS 4, regarding communications between predecessor and successor accountants, does *not require the successor accountant* to communicate with the predecessor. However, once this communication takes place, subject to client permission, the predecessor accountant is generally obligated to respond to the successor accountant's inquiries regarding integrity of client management. As in the case of audit engagements, communication can also take place between predecessor and successor accountants after the engagement has been accepted. The form of this communication may include questions to the predecessor regarding inadequacies in the entity's underlying financial data or areas that may have required inordinate time in the prior period. Additionally, the predecessor should, with the client's permission, provide the successor access to selected working papers of continuing accounting significance, unless a valid business reason (including unpaid fees) prevents the request from being honored.

REPORTS ON REVIEWS OF INTERIM FINANCIAL INFORMATION

Publicly held corporations typically issue interim financial information to shareholders. The period of time covered by this information may be for a quarter or a month ending on a date other than the entity's fiscal year end. Interim financial information *may be presented alone or may be included in a note to audited financial statements.* The SEC requires the inclusion of selected quarterly data with audited annual financial statements. Such data include net sales, gross profit, income before extraordinary items, and cumulative effects of changes in accounting principles. Per share data for the above income statement items must also be disclosed for each full quarter within the two most recent fiscal years and any subsequent interim period for which income statements are presented.

The independent accountant may be involved with a client's interim financial information in a variety of ways. At the lowest level, this involvement may take the form of ***informal consultation*** on matters that arise as the interim financial information is being prepared. At the other extreme, the accountant may perform an ***audit*** of the interim financial statements in accordance with generally accepted auditing standards. The most common type of involvement, however, can be characterized as a ***limited review*** of the interim financial information; SAS 36 states that "the objective of a limited review of interim financial information is to provide the accountant, based on objectively applying his knowledge of financial reporting practices to significant accounting matters of which he becomes aware through inquiries and analytical review procedures, with a basis for reporting whether material modifications should be made for such information to conform with generally accepted accounting principles."[3] It is important to recognize that a limited review, like a review of yearly information discussed in the previous section, *does not provide the basis for the expression of an audit opinion* because it does not contemplate a study and evaluation of internal accounting control, tests of accounting records, or other corroborating evidential matter obtained through inspection, observation, or confirmation.

Timeliness is a very important element in interim financial reporting. Such information must be made available to interested parties more promptly than the annual financial statements. For that reason, some expenses included in interim financial reports are estimated. Furthermore, each interim period is viewed primarily as an integral part of an annual period calling for the application of the ***annualization concept*** in presenting deferrals, accruals, and estimations.

Procedures for the Interim Review

The procedures associated with the interim review are similar to those already described for a review and compilation engagement. Specifically, they can be summarized from SAS 36 as follows:

1. *Inquiry* concerning the accounting system to obtain an understanding of the manner in which transactions were recorded, classified, and summarized in the preparation of interim financial information, and inquiry into any significant changes in the system of internal accounting control to ascertain their potential effect on the preparation of interim financial information.
2. *Analytical review* of interim financial information by reference to internal financial statements, trial balances, or other financial data to help in the identification of unusual relationships and individual items that appear to be unusual. This involves
   a. A systematic comparison of current financial information with that anticipated for the current period, that of the immediately preceding interim period, and that of the corresponding interim period of the previous fiscal year;
   b. A study of the interrelationships of the elements of the financial information that would be expected to conform to a predictable pattern based on the entity's past experience;
   c. A consideration of the types of matters that in the preceding year or quarters required accounting adjustment.
3. *Reading the minutes* of meetings of stockholders, board of directors, and committees of the board of directors to identify actions that might affect the interim financial information.
4. *Reading the interim financial information* to consider, on the basis of information coming to the accountant's attention, whether the information being reported conforms with generally accepted accounting principles.
5. *Obtaining letters from other accountants*, if any, who have been engaged to make a limited review of the interim financial information of significant segments of the reporting entity, its subsidiaries, or other significant investees.
6. *Inquiry of officers and other executives* having the responsibility for financial and accounting matters concerning
   a. Whether the interim financial information has been prepared in conformity with generally accepted accounting principles consistently applied;
   b. Changes in the entity's business activities or accounting practices;
   c. Matters as to which questions have arisen in the course of applying the foregoing procedures;
   d. Events subsequent to the date of the interim financial information that would have a material effect on the presentation of such information.

Factors Affecting the Use of the Interim Review

The extent to which these procedures should be applied varies with the nature of the engagement. SAS 36 cites the following variables that should be considered in making that judgment:

- The accountant's knowledge of the accounting and reporting practices of the entity. Since the accountant will usually have audited the firm's most recent annual financial statements, her or his knowledge of these practices will be extensive and may permit the application of limited procedures to the interim data.
- The accountant's knowledge of weaknesses in internal accounting control. This knowledge, also, should have been acquired during the audit of the most recent annual financial

statements. The accountant should then direct interim procedures towards discovering changes in the system during the interim period and differences between controls underlying the interim and annual information. Material accounting control weaknesses could prevent preparation of interim financial information in conformity with GAAP, and may thus require a scope limitation on the review procedures sufficient to preclude the issuance of a review report.

- The accountant's knowledge of changes in the nature or volume of the client's activities. Examples include business combinations; disposal of a segment of the business; or extraordinary items.
- Issuance of accounting pronouncements during the interim period. Such pronouncements may affect the client's reporting practices, and therefore need to be covered in the accountant's review procedures.
- Accounting records maintained at multiple locations. This situation may call for performing review procedures at both corporate headquarters and other locations selected by the accountant.

Reporting Requirements

Reporting requirements for reviews of interim financial information depend on whether the interim financial information is presented (1) alone or (2) in a footnote to audited financial statements.

If the information is *presented alone*, and appropriate review procedures have been performed, permission is generally given for the accountant's name to be associated with a review report. If the scope of procedures performed does not permit the completion of a review, the accountant should not permit the use of his or her name. Scope restrictions might be caused by such circumstances as timing of the review work, inadequate accounting records, or a material weakness in internal accounting control. If the client subsequently presents, in a document issued to stockholders, third parties, or the SEC, interim financial information on which the accountant has made a limited review, the accountant should request that the review report be included. If the client will not agree to the accountant's request, or if the scope of the review has been limited, the accountant should request that neither his or her name nor reference to work performed be associated with the information. Also, if the accountant concludes that the interim financial information does not conform to GAAP he or she should advise the board of directors of the respects in which the information does not conform. The report should be modified if the accountant finds disclosures to be inadequate.

The accountant's *report associated with the interim financial information presented alone* should be addressed to the company, its board of directors, or stockholders and should be dated as of the completion of the review. It should, according to SAS 36, include the following elements:

- A statement that the review of interim financial information was made in accordance with the standards for such reviews.
- An identification of the interim financial information reviewed.
- A description of the procedures for a review of interim financial information.
- A statement that a review of interim financial information is substantially less in scope than an audit and a disclaimer of opinion regarding fairness of presentation

- A statement indicating whether the accountant is aware of any material modifications that should be made to the interim information to make it conform to GAAP.

Each page of the interim financial information should be clearly marked as "unaudited." Notice that, except for identification of the type of financial statements being reviewed and the time periods covered, the elements included in the review report for interim information are the same as those included in the review report for annual financial statements of a nonpublic entity, discussed earlier.

Circumstances which require deviations from the standard report format include *departures from GAAP* and *inadequate disclosures.* Normally no modifications are required for uncertainties affecting the interim information, or the lack of consistency in application of GAAP, as long as these items are adequately disclosed in the interim information.

If interim financial information is presented with audited annual financial statements, as is usually the case for publicly traded companies reporting under SEC regulations, the interim data are ordinarily regarded as supplementary information. As such, this information will not have been subjected to the audit procedures applied to the basic financial statements. Management should therefore *clearly mark the information as unaudited.*

If the auditor has performed the review procedures discussed previously, no separate report on that information is ordinarily necessary. In addition, the auditor ordinarily need not modify the report on the audited financial statements. However, the audit report *should be expanded* to include appropriate disclosures when any of the following four circumstances exists:

- Selected quarterly *data required by SEC regulations are omitted or have not been reviewed.* The audit report in this case would include expanded disclosures of the omission or lack of review.
- Interim financial information included in the note to audited financial statements has *not been clearly marked as unaudited.* In this case, the audit report should be expanded to disclaim an opinion on the interim information.
- Interim financial information is *not presented in conformity with GAAP.* In this case the audit report would contain a separate paragraph setting out the facts and explaining the effects of any departures from GAAP.
- Interim financial information includes an indication that a review was made but *fails to include the statements that the review is substantially less in scope than an audit examination and a disclaimer of opinion.* In this case, the audit report should contain a separate paragraph disclosing those facts.

Engagement Letter and Working Papers

An *engagement letter* is recommended for reviews of interim financial information, so that the accountant and the client may avoid any misunderstanding as to the nature of the work performed or the degree of responsibility accepted by the accountant. The letter would normally include (a) a description of procedures to be performed; (b) an explanation that such procedures do not constitute an audit; and (c) a description of the form of the report to be rendered, if any.

There are no formal guidelines for *working papers* in support of reviews of interim financial information. However the accountant should logically follow the general guidelines set forth in SAS 41 (Chapter 4) in this case, which states that the working papers should be adapted to the needs of the particular engagement.

SPECIAL REPORTS

Certified public accountants are sometimes asked to

1. Perform audits of financial statements prepared in accordance with the *cash basis or some other basis of accounting that is not in accordance with GAAP.*
2. Perform audits of specified elements, accounts, or items of financial statements.
3. Perform procedures that lead to reports on compliance with aspects of contractual agreements or regulatory requirements related to audited financial statements.
4. Prepare financial information presented in prescribed forms or schedules that require a prescribed form of audit report.[4]

In addition, they may be asked to apply *selected audit procedures* not constituting a full audit to specified elements or accounts of a financial statement.

All such engagements require "special reports." SAS 14 sets out the guidelines for these special types of reports.

Audits of Financial Statements Prepared in Accordance with a Comprehensive Basis of Accounting Other than GAAP

Generally accepted auditing standards must be met for the audit examination and report anytime an opinion is to be expressed on *financial statements.* SAS 14 defines a financial statement as

> a presentation of financial data, including accompanying notes, derived from accounting records and intended to communicate an entity's economic resources or obligations at a point in time or the changes therein for a period of time in accordance with a comprehensive basis of accounting.[5]

SAS 14 also describes four types of comprehensive bases of accounting other than GAAP:

- A basis of accounting that the reporting entity uses to comply with the requirements or financial reporting provisions of *a government regulatory agency* to whose jurisdiction the entity is subject. An example is the uniform system of accounts prescribed by the Interstate Commerce Commission for railroad companies.
- A basis of accounting that the reporting entity uses or expects to use to file its income tax return for the period covered by the financial statements. This may be characterized as the *tax basis.*
- The *cash receipts and disbursements* basis of accounting, including modifications of the cash basis having substantial support, such as capitalizing fixed assets and recording depreciation on fixed assets or accruing only income taxes.
- *Any other basis* involving a definite set of criteria having substantial support and applied to all material items appearing in the financial statements. (An example of this basis of accounting is the *price-level adjusted basis of accounting.*)

Normally, fairness of presentation must be judged by the auditor in terms of compliance of the financial statements with GAAP. The use of GAAP presumes that the financial statements purport to present financial position and results of operations. However, some financial statements are not intended to present financial position and results of operations:

- Statements of assets and liabilities arising from cash transactions that do not include owners' equity accounts.
- Statements of cash receipts and disbursements.
- Summaries of operations.
- Statements of operations by product lines.

The definition of financial statements is broad enough to cover all the above examples, as well as the balance sheet, income statement, statement of retained earnings, and statement of changes in financial position. SAS 14, therefore, allows the auditor to change the guidelines against which fairness of presentation is measured from GAAP to another comprehensive basis of accounting, *as long as that basis is one of the four listed above*. This means that the auditor can render any one of the types of reports discussed earlier, ranging from an unqualified report through a disclaimer of opinion (see Figure 18–2) with financial statements presented in accordance with an acceptable comprehensive basis of accounting other than GAAP.

The auditor reporting on financial statements prepared in accordance with one of these bases of accounting should include all of the following elements in the audit report:

1. A paragraph identifying the financial statements examined and stating whether the examination was made in accordance with generally accepted auditing standards. This is basically the same as the scope paragraph of the standard audit report.
2. A paragraph that
   a. States (or preferably refers to the note to the financial statements that states) the *basis of presentation* of the financial statements on which the auditor is reporting;
   b. Refers to the note to the financial statements that describes how the basis of presentation differs from generally accepted accounting principles;
   c. States that the *financial statements are not intended to be presented in conformity with generally accepted accounting principles.*
3. A paragraph that expresses the auditor's opinion (or disclaims an opinion) on whether
   a. The financial statements are presented fairly in conformity with the basis of accounting described. If the auditor concludes that the financial statements are not presented fairly on the basis of accounting described, he or she should *disclose all the substantive reasons for that conclusion in an additional explanatory paragraph* of his or her report and should include in the opinion paragraph appropriate modifying language and a reference to the explanatory paragraph;
   b. The disclosed basis of accounting used has been applied in a manner consistent with that of the preceding period.

As you can see from the preceding discussion, the scope and opinion paragraphs generally differ from the standard short-form audit report only in referring to the comprehensive basis of accounting rather than to generally accepted accounting principles. However, such a report must include a paragraph (see item 2 of the list) that informs the reader about the basis of accounting followed, about how it differs from generally accepted accounting principles, and specifically about the fact that the financial statements are not intended to be presented in conformity with GAAP.

In some instances, the auditor is forced to consider whether the financial statements being reported on are *suitably titled*. For example, a cash basis financial statement containing asset, liability, and capital accounts is not appropriately referred to as a balance sheet. If the auditor believes that the financial statements are not suitably titled, the report should be modified to disclose that fact. For example, the cash basis financial statement purporting to be a balance sheet might be titled "Statement of Assets and Liabilities Arising from Cash Transactions."

Reports on Specified Elements of Financial Statements

In rare instances, a client may request an accountant to issue a report on specified elements, accounts, or items in a financial statement. Such reports normally fall into one of two categories:

- Reports expressing an *audit opinion* on one or more specified elements or accounts (such as an opinion regarding the fairness of presentation of trade accounts receivable); and
- Reports relating to the results of *applying agreed-upon procedures* to one or more specified elements or accounts (such as confirmation of trade accounts receivable).

An audit geared to express an opinion on specified elements or accounts requires the auditor to meet the general and field work auditing standards, plus the third and fourth reporting standards. The first and second reporting standards need not be met because they pertain to the financial statements taken as a whole, which is not a part of the scope of the audit work in engagements such as these. In auditing only the trade accounts receivable of an entity, for example, the auditor's procedures (confirmation, inspection of documents, etc.) are narrowed to a single account and the related accounts, such as sales. Therefore the auditor should not make mention of the financial statements taken as a whole in the audit report. Neither should the report be allowed to accompany the financial statements of the entity — even with a disclaimer of opinion on them. In most cases, issuing a disclaimer of opinion or an adverse opinion on the financial statements taken as a whole while expressing an opinion on a specified element or account is tantamount to expressing a *piecemeal opinion*, which is no longer permitted under generally accepted auditing standards.

Since the audit report in this instance is narrowed to a specified element or account in the financial statements, the *auditor's judgment regarding materiality should be narrowed* as well, to that element or account alone. Thus, disclosures, or lack of them, which would ordinarily not be material might become material in this context.

The report should be written so as to accomplish the following purposes:

1. Identify the specified elements, accounts, or items examined.
2. State whether the examination was made in accordance with generally accepted auditing standards and, if applicable, that it was made in conjunction with an examination of the financial statements.
3. Identify the basis on which the specified elements, accounts, or items are presented and, when applicable, any agreements specifying such basis.

4. Describe and indicate the sources of significant client interpretations relating to the provisions of a relevant agreement.
5. Indicate whether in the auditor's opinion the specified elements, accounts, or items are presented fairly on the basis indicated.
6. If applicable, indicate whether, in the auditor's opinion, the disclosed basis has been applied in a manner consistent with that of the preceding period.

Engagements to report on the results of applying agreed-upon procedures to specified elements or accounts (see SAS 35) require the auditor to meet only the general standards and the first standard of field work. These engagements may include selected audit procedures (not constituting a full audit) to specified accounts in connection with a proposed acquisition or claims of creditors. Because of their limited nature, such engagements may be accepted only if the following conditions are met:

- *The parties involved must have a clear understanding* of the specific audit procedures being performed. This may be accomplished through (1) discussions with the client; (2) review of correspondence with the named parties; (3) comparisons of the procedures to be applied with the written requirements of a supervisory agency, when applicable; or (4) distributing a draft of the report or client engagement letter to the parties involved with a request for their reply before the report is issued.
- *Distribution of the report must be restricted to the parties* involved and named in the engagement letter.

The accountant's report should indicate the specified elements or accounts to which procedures were applied as well as the intended distribution of the report. It should enumerate the procedures performed and state the accountant's finding while disclaiming an opinion on the specified elements or accounts. It should also state that the report relates only to the specified elements of the financial statements and not to the financial statements taken as a whole.

Reports on Compliance with Contractual Agreements or Regulatory Requirements

Companies may be required by contractual agreement or by regulatory agencies to furnish compliance reports prepared by independent auditors. For example, loan agreements may impose on borrowers a variety of convenants involving matters such as payment into a sinking fund, payment of interest, maintenance of current ratio, restriction of dividend payments, and use of the proceeds from the sale of property. The lenders in such a situation may request assurance from the independent auditor that the borrower has complied with the covenants of the agreement.

A report in this type of situation *generally gives negative assurance relative to the applicable convenants.* Such assurance may be given in a separate report or in one or more paragraphs of the auditor's report accompanying the financial statements. *However, it should not be given unless the auditor has examined the financial statements* to which the contractual agreement or regulatory requirements relate. In this case, a negative assurance statement could read as follows:

> In connection with our examination, nothing came to our attention that caused us to believe that the company was not in compliance with any of the terms,

covenants, provisions or conditions of. . . . However, it should be noted that our examination was not directed primarily toward obtaining knowledge of such noncompliance.[6]

Financial Information Presented in Prescribed Forms or Schedules

The accountant is often expected to use printed forms or schedules provided by the bodies with which they are to be filed that prescribe the wording of an auditor's report. *Many of these forms are not acceptable to the independent auditor* because the prescribed form of auditor's report does not conform with the applicable professional reporting standards. For example, the prescribed language may call for assertions that are not consistent with the auditor's function or responsibility. In some instances, the special report forms can be made acceptable by inserting additional wording; others can be made acceptable only by complete revision. When a printed report form calls for an independent auditor to make an assertion that cannot be justified within professional standards, the *form should be reworded or a separate report should be attached.* The reporting provisions in such instances should conform to those described earlier for reporting on financial statements that are prepared in accordance with a comprehensive basis of accounting other than generally accepted accounting principles.

OTHER REPORTS CLASSIFIED BY TYPE OF SERVICE RENDERED

Letters to Underwriters

Certified public accountants may provide still other services for clients; one of these is the audit examination of financial statements and schedules contained in registration statements filed with the Securities and Exchange Commission.

In connection with an audit examination, the public accountant is frequently asked to issue letters to underwriters (commonly called ***comfort letters***) providing additional information relating to both audited and unaudited elements of the registration statement. Such letters generally refer to one or more of the following subjects:

1. A statement as to the independence of the accountant.
2. An opinion as to whether the audited financial statements and schedules included in the registration statement comply as to form in all material respects with the applicable accounting requirements of the Securities Act of 1933 and the published rules and regulations thereunder.
3. ***Negative assurances*** as to whether unaudited financial statements and schedules included in the registration statements
   a. *Comply as to form* with the applicable accounting requirements of the Securities Act of 1933 and the published rules and regulations thereunder;
   b. Are fairly presented in conformity with generally accepted accounting principles on a *basis substantially consistent with that of the audited financial statements and schedules* included therein.

4. ***Negative assurances*** as to whether during a specified period following the date of the latest financial statements in the registration statement and prospectus, there have been *any significant changes* in capital stock or long-term debt or any significant changes in other specified financial statement items.

Each individual letter should be tailored to meet the needs of the underwriter. However, the CPA should avoid phrases such as "examined" and "made a limited review" to describe the work performed, because they might mislead the reader to infer that an audit or limited review was made of the information. In order to avoid a misunderstanding as to the purpose and intended use of the comfort letter, it should conclude with a paragraph reading somewhat as follows:

> This letter is solely for the information of, and assistance to, the underwriters in conducting and documenting their investigation of the affairs of the company in connection with the offering of the securities covered by the Registration Statement and is not to be used, circulated, quoted, or otherwise referred to within or outside the underwriting group for any other purpose, including but not limited to the registration, purchase, or sales of securities, nor is it to be filed with or referred to in whole or in part in the Registration Statement or any other document except that reference may be made to it in the underwriting agreement or in any list of closing documents pertaining to the offering of the securities covered by the Registration Statement.[7]

The comfort letter should also contain a statement saying that the accountant has not examined the financial statements of the company as of any date or for any period subsequent to dates of the last audited statements. That statement should be followed by another that the accountant is unable to, and does not, express an opinion on the unaudited data presented subsequent to the date of the last audited statement.

The addressee of the comfort letter is typically the underwriter, with a copy being sent to the client. The date of the letter is ordinarily on or shortly before the ***closing date,*** which is the date on which the issuer (client) delivers the securities to the underwriter in exchange for the proceeds of the securities offering.

Reports on Internal Accounting Control

An independent accountant may be engaged to report on an entity's system of internal control in at least four ways:

1. Expressing an *opinion* on the entity's system of internal accounting control in effect as of a specified date.
2. Reporting on the entity's system *for the restricted use of some specified party* — management, named regulatory agencies, or other specified third parties — based *solely on a study and evaluation of internal accounting control made as part of an audit* of the entity's financial statements but not sufficient for expressing an opinion on the system.
3. Reporting on all or part of an entity's system for the *restricted use of management or regulatory bodies based on the regulatory agency's prescribed criteria.* In making such a report, however, if a weakness is discovered that is outside the prescribed criteria, it should also be included in the report.
4. Making *other special-purpose reports* on all or part of an entity's system for the restricted use of management, specified regulatory agencies, or other specified third parties.[8]

The procedures required in the evidence-gathering process vary with the nature of the report. In all instances, however, the accountant will be concerned with evaluating the system and verifying that the control procedures are in compliance with the provisions of the organization chart and procedures manual.

In Chapter 5, we discussed the report on the entity's system of control based solely on the study and evaluation of internal controls made as part of a financial statement audit. There we established a requirement that the auditor communicate (preferably in writing) to management any material weaknesses in internal controls discovered during an audit examination. This type of report amounts to an extension of the auditor's traditional attest function.

We now turn our attention to the accountant's report rendered in connection with an engagement to *express an opinion* on the entity's system of internal accounting control, in which the accountant places no restrictions on the use of the report (report type 1). Such reports may be useful to regulatory agencies, management, or internal auditors but should be of little value to some other users (such as creditors). In the final analysis regulatory agencies, directors, and officers of the corporation have the responsibility of deciding whether such reports would be useful to the general public.

An internal control audit engagement should involve planning the scope of the engagement, reviewing the design of the system, testing compliance with prescribed procedures, and evaluating the results of the review and tests. The accountant should obtain from management the following written representations:

- Acknowledgement of management's responsibility for establishing and maintaining the system of internal accounting control.
- A statement that management has disclosed to the accountant all material weaknesses in the system of which it is aware, including those for which management believes the cost of corrective action may exceed the benefits.
- Descriptions of any irregularities involving managers or employees who have significant roles in the system of internal accounting control.
- A statement as to whether there are any changes subsequent to the date being reported on that would significantly affect the system of internal accounting control, including any corrective actions taken by management with regard to material weaknesses.

The accountant should also *document the work done* to express an opinion on the system of internal accounting control. The working papers should include documents prepared by the entity to describe its system of internal accounting control. Other documents should provide evidence regarding the planning, the review of the system, and the testing of compliance phases of the examination.

Upon completion of the examination, the accountant's report expressing an opinion on an entity's system of internal accounting control should contain the following elements:

- A description of the scope of the engagement.
- The date to which the opinion relates.
- A statement that the establishment and maintenance of the system is the responsibility of management.
- A brief explanation of the broad objectives and inherent limitations of internal accounting control.
- The accountant's opinion as to whether the system taken as a whole is sufficient to meet the

> broad objectives of internal accounting control insofar as those objectives pertain to the prevention or detection of errors and irregularities in amounts that would be material in relation to the financial statements.

The report should be dated as of the date of completion of field work and may be addressed to the entity whose system is being studied or to its board of directors or stockholders.[9]

Report types (3) and (4) relate to studies of internal control made as part of very limited-purpose engagements, which are relatively infrequent. As such, they are considered beyond the scope of this text and are not included in our discussion.

Reports on Management Advisory Services

Within Appendix 1–D, following Chapter 1, we presented a summary of management advisory services standards. One element of those standards gives particular attention to the responsibility of the accountant for communicating the results of a management advisory services engagement to the client. No specific report format is suggested, but the standards state that the report is expected to be a tailored, concise statement of the consultant's conclusions, recommendations, accomplishments, and the major assumptions he or she relied on — together with any limitations, reservations, or qualifications. Although the report may be presented orally, in most cases it is presented in written form. If an oral report is rendered, the practitioner should prepare a memorandum for the files documenting recommendations and other information discussed with the client.

Reports of Internal Auditors

In Appendix 1–A, we presented a summary of the standards for the professional practice of internal auditing as adopted by the Institute of Internal Auditors. One element of those standards relates to the ways in which the findings of the internal auditors should be reported to management. Although no specific format is recommended, the internal auditor is expected to report his or her findings to the appropriate level of management. A signed, written report should be issued after the internal audit examination is completed. In addition, the internal auditor should discuss conclusions and recommendations with appropriate levels of management before issuing final written reports. The general format of the internal audit report should be designed to present the purpose, scope, and results of the audit. Where appropriate, the report may contain an expression of the auditor's opinion.

Internal audit reports may include recommendations by the auditor for possible improvements in operating systems and, where appropriate, may acknowledge satisfactory performance and corrective action taken by operating departments. In addition, these reports may include documentation of the auditor's views about audit conclusions or recommendations of the internal auditor. The director of the internal auditing department should review and approve the final audit report before issuance and should decide to whom the report will be distributed.

Reports of Governmental Auditors

Governmental audit reports are prepared and published to reflect the findings of GAO auditors relating to various agencies and activities of the federal government. Because most of these audits are directed toward evaluating efficiency, effectiveness, and compliance with government regulations, the audit reports should be written so as to disclose most effectively the findings relating to those characteristics. In many respects such audits can be characterized as operational audits conducted with authorization from the U.S. Congress. Therefore, each report is typically addressed to that body or to some specific subgroup within that body.

SUMMARY

In this chapter we have discussed and illustrated various reports that accountants may render in connection with engagements other than an independent audit of financial statements. The contents of these reports depend primarily on the level of association the auditor has with the client, the nature of the financial data being reported on, and the types of services being performed. A report must be rendered in any situation where the accountant is associated with a client's financial statements. He or she is presumed to be associated with a client's financial statements anytime he or she has consented to the use of his or her name in connection with a report, document, or written communication containing the client's financial statements. Our discussion of reports on unaudited financial statements of nonpublic entities was subdivided into two categories: compilation reports and review reports. Both are defined by SSARS 1.

We then described reports rendered in connection with the review of interim financial information. Here we observed the similarity between these reports and the review report for unaudited statements of nonpublic entities.

In the last section of the chapter we described various special reports issued by public accountants performing audits of statements prepared in accordance with a basis of accounting other than GAAP and providing other services for clients. Reports on other services include letters to underwriters, reports on internal accounting control, and reports on management advisory services. We also briefly considered reports rendered by internal auditors and by the general accounting office.

APPENDIX 19–A: Review of Financial Statements — Illustrative Inquiries

The inquiries to be made in a review of financial statements are a matter of the accountant's judgment. In determining inquiries, an accountant may consider (1) the nature and materiality of the items, (2) the likelihood of misstatement, (3) knowl-

Appendix 19–A is from Statement on Standards for Accounting and Review Services (SSARS) 1 (New York: AICPA, 1978), pp. 20–23.

edge obtained during current and previous engagements, (4) the stated qualifications of the entity's accounting personnel, (5) the extent to which a particular item is affected by management's judgment, and (6) inadequacies in the entity's underlying financial data. The following list of inquiries is for illustrative purposes only. The inquiries do not necessarily apply to every engagement, nor are they meant to be all-inclusive. This list is not intended to serve as a program or checklist in the conduct of a review; rather it describes the general areas in which inquiries might be made. For example, the accountant may feel it is necessary to make several inquiries to answer one of the questions listed below, such as item 3(a).

1. *General*
   a. What are the procedures for recording, classifying, and summarizing transactions (relates to each section discussed below)?
   b. Do the general ledger control accounts agree with subsidiary records (for example, receivables, inventories, investments, property and equipment, accounts payable, accrued expenses, noncurrent liabilities)?
   c. Have accounting principles been applied on a consistent basis?
2. *Cash*
   a. Have bank balances been reconciled with book balances?
   b. Have old or unusual reconciling items between bank balances and book balances been reviewed and adjustments made where necessary?
   c. Has a proper cutoff of cash transactions been made?
   d. Are there any restrictions on the availability of cash balances?
   e. Have cash funds been counted and reconciled with control accounts?
3. *Receivables*
   a. Has an adequate allowance been made for doubtful accounts?
   b. Have receivables considered uncollectible been written off?
   c. If appropriate, has interest been reflected?
   d. Has a proper cutoff of sales transactions been made?
   e. Are there any receivables from employees and related parties?
   f. Are any receivables pledged, discounted, or factored?
   g. Have receivables been properly classified between current and noncurrent?
4. *Inventories*
   a. Have inventories been physically counted? If not, how have inventories been determined?
   b. Have general ledger control accounts been adjusted to agree with physical inventories?
   c. If physical inventories are taken at a date other than the balance sheet date, what procedures were used to record changes in inventory between the date of the physical inventory and the balance sheet date?
   d. Were consignments in or out considered in taking physical inventories?
   e. What is the basis of valuation?
   f. Does inventory cost include materials, labor, and overhead where applicable?
   g. Have write-downs for obsolescence or cost in excess of net realizable value been made?
   h. Have proper cutoffs of purchases, goods in transit, and returned goods been made?
   i. Are there any inventory encumbrances?
5. *Prepaid expenses*
   a. What is the nature of the amounts included in prepaid expenses?
   b. How are these amounts amortized?

6. *Investments, including loans, mortgages, and intercorporate investments*
   a. Have gains and losses on disposal been reflected?
   b. Has investment income been reflected?
   c. Has appropriate consideration been given to the classification of investments between current and noncurrent, and the difference between the cost and market value of investments?
   d. Have consolidation or equity accounting requirements been considered?
   e. What is the basis of valuation of marketable equity securities?
   f. Are investments unencumbered?
7. *Property and equipment*
   a. Have gains or losses on disposal of property or equipment been reflected?
   b. What are the criteria for capitalization of property and equipment? Have such criteria been applied during the fiscal period?
   c. Does the repairs and maintenance account only include items of an expense nature?
   d. Are property and equipment stated at cost?
   e. What are the depreciation methods and rates? Are they appropriate and consistent?
   f. Are there any unrecorded additions, retirements, abandonments, sales, or trade-ins?
   g. Does the entity have material lease agreements? Have they been properly reflected?
   h. Is any property or equipment mortgaged or otherwise encumbered?
8. *Other assets*
   a. What is the nature of the amounts included in other assets?
   b. Do these assets represent costs that will benefit future periods? What is the amortization policy? Is it appropriate?
   c. Have other assets been properly classified between current and noncurrent?
   d. Are any of these assets mortgaged or otherwise encumbered?
9. *Accounts and notes payable and accrued liabilities*
   a. Have all significant payables been reflected?
   b. Are all bank and other short-term liabilities properly classified?
   c. Have all significant accruals, such as payroll, interest, and provisions for pension and profit-sharing plans been reflected?
   d. Are there any collateralized liabilities?
   e. Are there any payables to employees and related parties?
10. *Long-term liabilities*
   a. What are the terms and other provisions of long-term liability agreements?
   b. Have liabilities been properly classified between current and noncurrent?
   c. Has interest expense been reflected?
   d. Has there been compliance with restrictive covenants of loan agreements?
   e. Are any long-term liabilities collateralized or subordinated?
11. *Income and other taxes*
   a. Has provision been made for current and prior-year federal income taxes payable?
   b. Have any assessments or reassessments been received? Are there tax examinations in process?
   c. Are there timing differences? If so, have deferred taxes been reflected?
   d. Has provision been made for state and local income, franchise, sales, and other taxes payable?
12. *Other liabilities, contingencies, and commitments*
   a. What is the nature of the amounts included in other liabilities?
   b. Have other liabilities been properly classified between current and noncurrent?

c. Are there any contingent liabilities, such as discounted notes, drafts, endorsements, warranties, litigation, and unsettled asserted claims? Are there any unasserted potential claims?
d. Are there any material contractual obligations for construction or purchase of real property and equipment and any commitments or options to purchase or sell company securities?

13. *Equity*
    a. What is the nature of any changes in equity accounts?
    b. What classes of capital stock have been authorized?
    c. What is the par or stated value of the various classes of stock?
    d. Do amounts of outstanding shares of capital stock agree with subsidiary records?
    e. Have capital stock preferences, if any, been disclosed?
    f. Have stock options been granted?
    g. Has the entity made any acquisitions of its own capital stock?
    h. Are there any restrictions on retained earnings or other capital?
14. *Revenue and expenses*
    a. Are revenues from the sale of major products and services recognized in the appropriate period?
    b. Are purchases and expenses recognized in the appropriate period and properly classified?
    c. Do the financial statements include discontinued operations or items that might be considered extraordinary?
15. *Other*
    a. Are there any events that occurred after the end of the fiscal period that have a significant effect on the financial statements?
    b. Have actions taken at stockholder, board of directors, or comparable meetings that affect the financial statements been reflected?
    c. Have there been any material transactions between related parties?
    d. Are there any material uncertainties? Is there any change in the status of material uncertainties previously disclosed?

APPENDIX 19–B: Illustrative Engagement Letter

(Appropriate Salutation)

This letter is to confirm our understanding of the terms and objectives of our engagement and the nature and limitations of the services we will provide.

We will perform the following services:

1. We will compile, from information you provide, the annual and interim balance sheets and related statements of income, retained earnings, and changes in financial position of XYZ Company for the year 19XX. We will not audit or review such financial statements. Our report on the annual financial statements of XYZ Company is presently expected to read as follows:

    > The accompanying balance sheet of XYZ Company as of December 31, 19XX, and the related statements of income, retained earnings, and changes in financial position for the year then ended have been compiled by us.
    >
    > A compilation is limited to presenting in the form of financial statements information that is the representation of management. We have not audited or reviewed the accompanying financial statements and, accordingly, do not express an opinion or any other form of assurance on them.

    Our report on your interim financial statements, which statements will omit substantially all disclosures, will include an additional paragraph that will read as follows:

    > Management has elected to omit substantially all of the disclosures required by generally accepted accounting principles. If the omitted disclosures were included in the financial statements, they might influence the user's conclusions about the company's financial position, results of operations, and changes in financial position. Accordingly, these financial statements are not designed for those who are not informed about such matters.

    If, for any reason, we are unable to complete the compilation of your financial statements, we will not issue a report on such statements as a result of this engagement.

2. We will also . . . [discussion of other services].

Our engagement cannot be relied upon to disclose errors, irregularities, or illegal acts, including fraud or defalcations, that may exist. However, we will inform you of any such matters that come to our attention.

Our fees for these services. . . .

We shall be pleased to discuss this letter with you at any time.

If the foregoing is in accordance with your understanding, please sign the copy of this letter in the space provided and return it to us.

Sincerely yours,

____
(Signature of accountant)

Acknowledge:
XYZ Company

____
President

____
Date

Source: Statement on Standards for Accounting and Review Services (SSARS) 1 (New York: AICPA), pp. 23–24.

NOTES

1. Statement on Standards for Accounting and Review Services (SSARS) 1 (New York: AICPA, 1979). We have summarized segments of that publication in this section of the chapter.
2. Ibid.
3. Statement on Auditing Standards (SAS) 36 (New York: AICPA, 1981).
4. SAS 14 (New York: AICPA, 1976). We have summarized segments of that publication in this section of the chapter.
5. Ibid., paragraph 2.
6. Ibid., paragraph 19.
7. Statement on Auditing Standards (SAS) 38, (New York: AICPA, 1981).
8. SAS 30, paragraph 2 (New York: AICPA, 1980).
9. Ibid., paragraphs 35 through 38.

QUESTIONS FOR CLASS DISCUSSION

Q19–1 What is meant by *other types of reports rendered by accountants?*

Q19–2 What four types of presentations are typically characterized as special reports?

Q19–3 What are five reports rendered by accountants that can best be described by relating them to the types of services performed?

Q19–4 What are the differences between an accountant's reports on unaudited financial statements of public entities and those on unaudited financial statements of non-public entities? Explain.

Q19–5 What is meant by the term "compilation of financial statements"?

Q19–6 How is a review of financial statements different from the compilation of financial statements? Explain.

Q19–7 In a compilation engagement, how should the accountant react to information supplied by the client that appears to be incomplete or otherwise unsatisfactory? Explain.

Q19–8 What analytical procedures are used in performing a review of financial statements?

Q19–9 Which inquiries should the accountant make in performing a review of financial statements?

Q19–10 What are the contents of the accountant's report on a review of the financial statements?

Q19–11 How should the accountant react to a request by the client to perform specific audit procedures on some element of the accounting records in connection with a review engagement?

Q19–12 Suppose that an audit client wants to change that engagement to an engagement to review the financial statements: how should the auditor react to such a request? Explain.

Q19–13 How do the procedures followed in reviewing interim financial information compare with those followed in a review engagement for unaudited financial statements?

Q19–14 What questions should be asked of officers and other executives during an engagement calling for the review of interim financial data? Indicate the reasons for each of the questions asked.

Q19–15 What are two ways in which the interim financial information reviewed by the accountant may be used by the client?

Q19–16 How does the typical short-form audit report compare with an audit report rendered in connection with an audit of financial statements prepared in accordance with a comprehensive basis of accounting other than GAAP?

Q19–17 What special concerns will the auditor have in writing a report on financial statements prepared by using the cash basis of accounting?

Q19–18 What are the special characteristics associated with an accountant's report on the examination of specified elements or accounts appearing in a client's financial statements? Should such a report include a disclaimer of opinion on the financial statements taken as a whole? Explain.

Q19–19 How would an auditor react to an engagement requiring that his or her report be presented on printed forms or schedules provided by regulatory bodies? Explain.

Q19–20 What is meant by a comfort letter? What is typically included in such a letter?

Q19–21 Under what four circumstances may an independent accountant be engaged to report on an entity's system of internal control?

Q19–22 What interested groups might logically find an accountant's report on internal control useful?

Q19–23 What, briefly, is the accountant's general responsibility in reporting to a client the findings on a management advisory services engagement?

Q19–24 What three elements should be included in the report of an internal auditor to the management of a corporation?

Q19–25 Can the General Accounting Office auditors be characterized as independent auditors? Discuss.

SHORT CASES

C19–1 Loretta Loman is a CPA who has examined the financial statements of the Broadwall Corporation, a publicly held company, for the year ended December 31, 19X1. Loman was asked to perform a limited review of the financial statements of Broadwall Corporation for the period ending March 31, 19X2. The engagement letter stated that a limited review does not provide a basis for the expression of an opinion.

Required:

a. Explain why Loman's limited review will not provide a basis for the expression of an opinion.

b. What are the review procedures Loman should perform, and what is the purpose of each procedure? Structure your response as follows:

Procedure	Purpose of Procedure

c. Assuming that Loman's review procedures do not reveal any material departures from generally accepted accounting principles, draft the typical report that Loman should issue.

(AICPA adapted)

C19–2 Irving Brown, CPA, received a telephone call from Leo Calhoun, the sole owner and manager of a small corporation. Calhoun asked Brown to prepare the financial statements for the corporation and told Brown that the statements were needed in two weeks for external financing purposes. Calhoun was vague when Brown inquired about the intended use of the statements. Brown was convinced that Calhoun thought Brown's work would constitute an audit. To avoid confusion Brown decided not to explain to Calhoun that the engagement would only be to prepare the financial statements. Brown, with the understanding that a substantial fee would be paid if the work were completed in two weeks, accepted the engagement and started the work at once.

During the course of the work, Brown discovered an accrued expense account labeled "professional fees" and learned that the balance in the account represented an accrual for the cost of Brown's services. Brown suggested to Calhoun's bookkeeper that the account name be changed to "fees for limited audit engagement." Brown also reviewed several invoices to determine whether accounts were being properly classified. Some of the invoices were missing. Brown listed the missing invoice numbers in the working papers with a note indicating that there should be a follow-up on the next engagement. Brown also discovered that the available records included the fixed asset values at estimated current replacement costs. Based on the records available, Brown prepared a balance sheet, income statement, and statement of stockholder's equity. In addition, Brown drafted the footnotes but decided that any mention of the replacement costs would only mislead the readers. Brown suggested to Calhoun that readers of the financial statements would be better informed if they received a separate letter from Calhoun explaining the meaning and effect of the estimated replacement costs of the fixed assets. Brown mailed the financial statements and footnotes to Calhoun with the following note included on each page: "The accompanying financial statements are submitted to you without complete audit verification."

Required:

Identify the inappropriate actions of Brown and indicate what Brown should have done to avoid each inappropriate action.

Organize your answer sheet as follows:

Inappropriate Action	What Brown Should Have Done to Avoid Inappropriate Action

(*AICPA adapted*)

C19–3 Grace Collins, CPA, has been the auditor for Murbank Enterprises, a medium-sized publicly traded company, for the past five years. Recently Murbank requested that Collins perform quarterly reviews of the company's interim financial statements. Collins has agreed to perform those reviews and to issue a quarterly report based on the review procedures.

Required:

a. What is the purpose of a limited review of interim financial information?
b. How does the nature of a limited review of interim financial information differ from an audit?
c. How does the nature of a limited review of interim financial information differ from a limited review of yearly information for nonpublic entities?
d. Describe the procedures Collins should follow in conducting her review.
e. Describe the report that Collins should render to Murbank's audit committee, based on the above circumstances.
f. How would Collins's reporting responsibility differ if, instead of being issued alone, the interim financial statements were included in footnotes to the company's annual audited financial statements?

C19–4 Middleboro Corporation, a company with which you have not previously been associated, has been having a great deal of trouble in valuing its ending finished goods inventory as of June 30, 19X2. The production and accounting branches of the company are currently in disagreement as to the exact value to place on an ending finished goods inventory. They have asked if you could perform an audit examination of the finished goods inventory account and render an opinion as to the fairness of its presentation in the company's financial statements, which they have agreed to accept as an arbitrated value for finished goods. Middleboro Corporation has not previously been audited.

Required:

a. Do generally accepted auditing standards allow such engagements? If so, under what conditions, if any, may the audit of the inventory account be performed?
b. Outline some special considerations for this audit that would not otherwise be as important (such as materiality guidelines, reporting considerations, etc.).
c. Describe the report that would be rendered in an engagement such as this.
d. How would your reporting responsibility differ if, instead of being asked to audit the finished goods inventory account, you had been asked to give your opinion regarding the company's compliance with a contractual arrangement with a vendor, an arrangement that involved finished goods inventories?

C19–5 The board of directors of Walenda Associates, a large local building supply concern in your city, has recently elected an audit committee for the first time. Up to this year the company has never been audited. The board of directors has also decided that the company does not need a financial statement audit for the current year because they are convinced that your firm's review services are sufficient to meet Walenda's immediate needs. They approach you with a request that you conduct a thorough audit of the company's system of internal controls for the past year; they theorize that a competent professional accountant like you can surely discover the system's major weaknesses and communicate them. The audit of internal controls, they feel, should improve efficiency of operations and enhance future profitability of the company — if they choose to follow your suggestions.

Required:

a. How does an engagement such as this one differ in objective from a study and evaluation of internal control conducted as part of a financial statement audit?

b. Describe how audit procedures for this engagement differ from audit procedures performed during a study and evaluation of internal control conducted as part of a financial statement audit (see SAS 30).

c. What representations should be obtained from Walenda's management in regard to the engagement described?

d. How will the report rendered by the auditor for this engagement differ from a standard report on internal control based on a study conducted as part of a financial statement audit?

PROBLEMS

P19–1 Select the best answer for each of the following items relating to reports on unaudited financial statements.

a. When an independent CPA is associated with the financial statements of a publicly held entity, but has *not* audited or reviewed such statements, the appropriate form of report to be issued must include a (an)

(1) Negative assurance.
(2) Compilation opinion.
(3) Disclaimer of opinion.
(4) Explanatory paragraph.

b. Which of the following procedures is *not* included in a review engagement of a nonpublic entity?

(1) Inquiries of management.
(2) Inquiries regarding events subsequent to the balance sheet date.
(3) Any procedures designed to identify relationships among data that appear to be unusual.
(4) A study and evaluation of internal control.

c. Which of the following would *not* be included in a CPA's report based on a review of the financial statements of a nonpublic entity?

(1) A statement that the review was in accordance with generally accepted auditing standards.
(2) A statement that all information included in the financial statements is the representation of management.
(3) A statement describing the principal procedures performed.
(4) A statement describing the auditor's conclusions based on the results of the review.

d. You are a CPA retained by the manager of a cooperative retirement village to do "write-up work." You are expected to prepare unaudited financial statements with each page marked "unaudited" and accompanied by a disclaimer of opinion stating no audit was made. In performing the work you discover that there are no invoices to support $25,000 of the manager's claimed disbursements. The manager informs you that all the disbursements are proper. What should you do?
   (1) Submit the expected statements but omit the $25,000 of unsupported disbursements.
   (2) Include the unsupported disbursements in the statements since you are not expected to make an audit.
   (3) Obtain from the manager a written statement that you informed him of the missing invoices and his assurance that the disbursements are proper.
   (4) Notify the owners that some of the claimed disbursements are unsupported and withdraw if the situation is not satisfactorily resolved.

e. Carson Jeffries, CPA, had prepared unaudited financial statements for a client, the Gold Company. Since the statements were only to be used internally by the client, Jeffries did *not* include any footnotes and so noted this in the accompanying disclaimer of opinion. Three months after the statements were issued, the Gold Company asked Jeffries if it would be all right to give a copy of the statements to its banker who had requested financial statements. How should Jeffries respond?
   (1) Jeffries should revise the statements to include appropriate footnotes and attach a revised disclaimer of opinion before they are released to the banker.
   (2) Gold may give the statements to the banker as long as Jeffries's disclaimer of opinion accompanies the statements.
   (3) Gold should retype the statements on plain paper and send them to the banker without Jeffries's report.
   (4) Gold may let the banker review the statements and take notes but should not give the banker a copy of the statements.

f. Which of the following best describes the responsibility of the CPA when he prepares unaudited financial statements for his client?
   (1) He should make a proper study and evaluation of the existing internal control as a basis for reliance thereon.
   (2) He is relieved of any responsibility to third parties.
   (3) He does not have responsibility to apply auditing procedures to the financial statements.
   (4) He has only to satisfy himself that the financial statements were prepared to conformity with generally accepted accounting principles.

g. A CPA has a financial interest in a corporation and is associated with that corporation's unaudited financial statements. Under such circumstances the CPA's report should state that the CPA is *not* independent with respect to the corporation and should include
   (1) A statement that the financial statements were unaudited and accordingly the CPA does *not* express an opinion on the financial statements.
   (2) A description of the reasons for the CPA's lack of independence and a disclaimer of opinion on the financial statements.
   (3) A statement that each page of the financial statements is "unaudited" and a qualified opinion on the financial statements.
   (4) A description of the reasons for the CPA's lack of independence and a qualified opinion on the financial statements.

h. When engaged to prepare unaudited financial statements the CPA's responsibility to detect fraud
   (1) Is limited to informing the client of any matters that come to the auditor's attention which cause the auditor to believe that an irregularity exists.
   (2) Is the same as the responsibility that exists when the CPA is engaged to perform an audit of financial statements in accordance with generally accepted auditing standards.
   (3) Arises out of the CPA's obligation to apply procedures designed to bring to light indications that a fraud or defalcation may have occurred.
   (4) Does *not* exist unless an engagement letter is prepared.

i. Which of the following must accompany unaudited financial statements prepared by a CPA?
   (1) Only a disclaimer of opinion.
   (2) Either a disclaimer of opinion or adverse opinion.
   (3) Either a disclaimer of opinion or a qualified opinion.
   (4) Either a disclaimer of opinion, adverse opinion, or qualified opinion.

j. Richard Loeb, CPA, has completed a review of the Bloto Company's unaudited financial statements and has prepared the following report to accompany them:

   > The accompanying balance sheet of the Bloto Company as of August 31, 19X5, and the related statements of income, retained earnings, and changes in financial position for the year then ended were not audited by us and accordingly we do not express an opinion on them.
   >
   > The financial statements fail to disclose that the debentures issued on July 15, 19X2, limit the payment of cash dividends to the amount of earnings after August 31, 19X3. The company's statements of income for the years 19X4 and 19X5, both of which are unaudited, show this amount to be $18,900. Generally accepted accounting principles require disclosure of matters of this nature.

   Which of the following comments best describes the appropriateness of this report?
   (1) The report is satisfactory.
   (2) The report is deficient because Loeb does not describe the scope of the review.
   (3) The report is deficient because the second paragraph gives the impression that some audit work was done.
   (4) The report is deficient because the explanatory comment in the second paragraph should precede the opinion paragraph.

k. Which of the following is the *least* important factor a CPA should consider in determining whether financial statements with which the CPA is associated may be issued as unaudited?
   (1) The restrictions a client might place on observing inventories or confirming receivables.
   (2) The intended use of the financial statements.
   (3) The procedures actually performed.
   (4) The needs of the client.

l. Sharon Reed, a partner in a local CPA firm, performs free accounting services for a private club of which Reed is treasurer. In which of the following manners should Reed issue the financial statements of the club?
   (1) On the firm's letterhead with a disclaimer for lack of independence.
   (2) On the firm's letterhead with a disclaimer for unaudited financial statements.

(3) On plain paper with no reference to Reed so that Reed will not be associated with the statements.
(4) On the club's letterhead with Reed signing as treasurer.

m. In the course of an engagement to prepare unaudited financial statements the client requests that the CPA perform normal accounts-receivable audit confirmation procedures. The CPA agrees and performs such procedures. The conformation procedures
(1) Are part of an auditing service that change the scope of the engagement to that of an audit in accordance with generally accepted auditing standards.
(2) Are part of an accounting service and are *not* performed for the purpose of conducting an audit in accordance with generally accepted auditing standards.
(3) Are *not* permitted when the purpose of the engagement is to prepare unaudited financial statements and the work to be performed is *not* in accordance with generally accepted auditing standards.
(4) Would require the CPA to render a report that indicates that the examination was conducted in accordance with generally accepted auditing standards but was limited in scope.

n. Jamal Rogers, a CPA who is *not* in public practice, works as an internal auditor for a large conglomerate. The management of the conglomerate asked Rogers to perform an examination and report on a potential acquisition. Rogers's report will be used by the management for internal purposes. Under these circumstances, how should Rogers sign the report?
(1) Jamal Rogers, CPA.
(2) Jamal Rogers, CPA (Internal Auditor).
(3) Jamal Rogers, Internal Auditor.
(4) Jamal Rogers, Internal Auditor (CPA).

(AICPA adapted)

P19–2 Select the best answer to each of the following items relating to the review of interim financial information.

a. If, as a result of a limited review of interim financial information, a CPA concludes that such information does *not* conform with generally accepted accounting principles, the CPA should
(1) Insist that the management conform the information with generally accepted accounting principles and if this is not done, resign from the engagement.
(2) Adjust the financial information so that it conforms with generally accepted accounting principles.
(3) Prepare a qualified report that makes reference to the lack of conformity with generally accepted accounting principles.
(4) Advise the board of directors of the respects in which the information does *not* conform with generally accepted accounting principles.

b. The objective of a review of the interim financial information of a publicly held company is to
(1) Provide the accountant with a basis for the expression of an opinion.
(2) Estimate the accuracy of financial statements based on limited tests of accounting records.
(3) Provide the accountant with a basis for reporting to the board of directors or stockholders.

(4) Obtain corroborating evidential matter through inspection, observation, and confirmation.

c. A report based on a limited review of interim financial statements would include all of the following elements *except*
   (1) A statement that an examination was performed in accordance with generally accepted auditing standards.
   (2) A description of the procedures performed or a reference to procedures described in an engagement letter.
   (3) A statement that a limited review would *not* necessarily disclose all matters of significance.
   (4) An identification of the interim financial information reviewed.

d. In a limited review of interim financial information, the auditor's work consists primarily of
   (1) Studying and evaluating limited amounts of documentation supporting the interim financial information.
   (2) Scanning and reviewing client-prepared internal financial statements.
   (3) Making inquiries and performing analytical procedures concerning significant accounting matters.
   (4) Confirming and verifying significant account balances at the interim date.

e. A modification of the CPA's report on a review of the interim financial statements of a publicly held company would be necessitated by which of the following?
   (1) An uncertainty.
   (2) Lack of consistency.
   (3) Reference to another accountant.
   (4) Inadequate disclosure.

(AICPA adapted)

P 19–3 Select the best answer to each of the following items relating to reports on internal control.

a. A CPA should *not* issue a report on internal control if
   (1) The report is to be sent to stockholders with unaudited interim financial statements.
   (2) The CPA has not audited the company's financial statements.
   (3) The report is to be given to creditors.
   (4) The report is to be given to prospective investors.

b. Because of the technical nature and complexity of internal accounting control and the consequent problem of understanding reports thereon, questions have been raised as to the benefits of such reports prepared by independent auditors. Which of the following groups probably would find a report on internal control *least* useful?
   (1) Regulatory agencies.
   (2) General creditors.
   (3) Management.
   (4) Internal auditors.

c. Dey, Knight, & Co., CPAs, has issued a qualified opinion on the financial statements of Adams, Inc., because of a scope limitation. Adams, Inc., requested a report on internal control which it intends to give to one of its major creditors. What effect, if any, would the qualified opinion have on the internal control report that Dey, Knight, & Co. intends to prepare based on its audit engagement?

(1) The audit scope limitation should be indicated in the report on internal control.

(2) A report on internal control cannot be issued based on a qualified opinion.

(3) The audit scope limitation has no effect but Dey, Knight, & Co. should not issue the report if it will be given to a creditor.

(4) The audit scope limitation has no effect on a report on internal control.

d. Ramirez Corp. has received a government grant and asked you, as a CPA, to prepare a report on internal control which is required by the terms of the grant. The governmental agency responsible for the grant has prepared written criteria, including a questionnaire, for such a report. During your study to prepare the report you find what you consider a material internal-control weakness in accounting for the grant. This weakness was not covered by the criteria established by the governmental agency. What action should you take in your report to the governmental agency?

(1) Include the weakness in the report even though not covered by the agency's criteria.

(2) Do not include the weakness in the report because it is outside the criteria established by the agency.

(3) Advise Ramirez Corp.'s management but do not include the weakness in the report.

(4) Include a comment in the report that you do not believe the criteria established by the agency are comprehensive but do not include the weakness in the report.

e. Paulo Greco, CPA, is preparing a report on internal control. He has already discussed the internal-control weaknesses with the appropriate client officials. During these discussions the client stated that, given its circumstances, there was no practicable corrective action which could be taken for one of the major weaknesses and therefore asked that it not be included in Greco's report. In the final analysis, Greco concurred that *no* corrective action by management is practicable. Which of the following is the most appropriate course of action for Greco to take?

(1) He must include this weakness in his report; otherwise, he will be in violation of generally accepted auditing standards.

(2) He may omit this weakness from his report without any further mention.

(3) He may omit this weakness from his report but should send a confidential memo to the board of directors pointing out the nature of the weakness and why it was omitted from his report.

(4) He may omit this weakness from his report but should clearly state that the report is restricted to material weaknesses for which corrective action by management may be practicable in the circumstances.

f. Which of the following reports is an indication of the changing role of the CPA that calls for an extension of the auditor's attest function?

(1) Report on annual comparative financial statements.

(2) Report on internal control based on an audit.

(3) Report on separate balance sheet of a holding company.

(4) Report on balance sheet and statements of income, retained earnings, and changes in financial position prepared from incomplete financial records.

g. If an auditor's report on internal control is distributed to the general public, it must contain specific language describing several matters. Which of the following *must* be included in the specific language?
   (1) The distinction between internal administrative controls and internal accounting controls.
   (2) The objective of internal accounting controls.
   (3) The various tests and procedures utilized by the auditor during the review of internal controls.
   (4) The reason(s) why management requested a report on internal controls.

(AICPA adapted)

P19–4 Select the best answer to each of the following items relating to special reports.

a. An auditor's report would be designated as a special report when it is issued in connection with which of the following?
   (1) Financial statements for an interim period which are subjected to a limited review.
   (2) Financial statements prepared in accordance with a comprehensive basis of accounting other than generally accepted accounting principles.
   (3) Financial statements that purport to be in accordance with generally accepted accounting principles but do *not* include a presentation of the statement of changes in financial position.
   (4) Financial statements that are unaudited and are prepared from a client's accounting records.

b. One example of a "special report," as defined by Statements on Auditing Standards, is a report issued in connection with
   (1) A feasibility study.
   (2) A limited review of interim financial information.
   (3) Price-level basis financial statements.
   (4) Compliance with a contractual agreement *not* related to the financial statements.

c. The term "special reports" may include all of the following *except* reports on financial statements
   (1) Of an organization that has limited the scope of the auditor's examination.
   (2) Prepared for limited purposes such as a report that relates to only certain aspects of financial statements.
   (3) Of a not-for-profit organization that follows accounting practices differing in some respects from those followed by business enterprises organized for profit.
   (4) Prepared in accordance with a cash basis of accounting.

d. In a comfort letter to underwriters, the CPA should normally avoid using which of the following terms to describe the work performed?
   (1) Examined.
   (2) Read.
   (3) Made inquiries.
   (4) Made a limited review.

e. A CPA should *not* normally refer to which one of the following subjects in a comfort letter to underwriters?
   (1) The independence of the CPA.

(2) Changes in financial statement items during a period subsequent to the date and period of the latest financial statements in the registration statement.
(3) Unaudited financial statements and schedules in the registration statement.
(4) Management's determination of line of business classifications.

f. When asked to perform an examination in order to express an opinion on one or more specified elements, accounts, or items of a financial statement, the auditor
(1) May *not* describe auditing procedures applied.
(2) Should advise the client that the opinion will result in a piecemeal opinion.
(3) May assume that the first standard of reporting with respect to generally accepted accounting principles does *not* apply.
(4) Should comply with the request only if they constitute a major portion of the financial statements on which an auditor has disclaimed an opinion based on an audit.

g. Under which of the following circumstances could an auditor consider rendering an opinion on pro forma statements that give effect to proposed transactions?
(1) When the pro forma statements include amounts based on financial projections.
(2) When the time interval between the date of the financial statements and consummation of the transactions is relatively long.
(3) When certain subsequent events have some chance of interfering with the consummation of the transactions.
(4) When the proposed transactions are subject to a definitive agreement among the parties.

h. If an auditor was engaged to discover errors or irregularities and the auditor performed extensive detail work, which of the following could the auditor be expected to detect?
(1) Mispostings of recorded transactions.
(2) Unrecorded transactions.
(3) Counterfeit signatures on paid checks.
(4) Collusive fraud.

(AICPA adapted)

P 19–5 Select the best answer to each of the following items relating to reporting on financial data prepared on a comprehensive basis other than GAAP.

a. An auditor is reporting on cash-basis financial statements. These statements are best referred to in his opinion by which one of the following descriptions?
(1) Financial position and results of operations arising from cash transactions.
(2) Assets and liabilities arising from cash transactions, and revenue collected and expenses paid.
(3) Balance sheet and income statement resulting from cash transactions.
(4) Cash balance sheet and the source and application of funds.

b. Which of the generally accepted auditing standards of reporting would *not* normally apply to special reports such as cash-basis statements?
(1) First standard.
(2) Second standard.
(3) Third standard.
(4) Fourth standard.

c. A CPA has been engaged to audit financial statements that were prepared on a cash basis. The CPA
(1) Must ascertain that there is proper disclosure of the fact that the cash basis has been used, the general nature of material items omitted, and the net effect of such omissions.
(2) May *not* be associated with such statements, which are *not* in accordance with generally accepted accounting principles.
(3) Must render a qualified report explaining the departure from generally accepted accounting principles in the opinion paragraph.
(4) Must restate the financial statements on an accrual basis and then render the standard (short-form) report.

d. An auditor was engaged to study the internal control procedures of a governmental agency, and the agency set forth the criteria for the study in questionnaire format. The auditor then performed a study based on such criteria. The auditor's report should *not*
(1) Identify the matters covered by the auditor's study.
(2) Express a conclusion, based on the agency criteria, concerning the procedures studied.
(3) Exclude any relevant condition that the auditor believes to be a material weakness although *not* covered by the criteria of the agency.
(4) Indicate whether the study included tests of compliance with procedures covered by the auditor's study.

e. Whenever special reports, filed on a printed form designed by authorities, call upon the independent auditor to make an assertion that the auditor believes is *not* justified, the auditor should
(1) Submit a short-form report with explanations.
(2) Reword the form or attach a separate report.
(3) Submit the form with questionable items clearly omitted.
(4) Withdraw from the engagement.

f. An auditor's report must state whether financial statements are presented in accordance with generally accepted accounting principles in each of the following situations *except* on an engagement involving
(1) A development-stage enterprise.
(2) A corporation in liquidation.
(3) A not-for-profit entity.
(4) A regulated company.

g. If the auditor believes that financial statements prepared on a comprehensive basis of accounting other than generally accepted accounting principles are *not* suitably titled, the auditor should
(1) Modify the auditor's report to disclose any reservations.
(2) Consider the effect of the titles on the financial statements taken as a whole.
(3) Issue a disclaimer of opinion.
(4) Add a footnote to the financial statements which explains alternative terminology.

(AICPA adapted)

CHAPTER

ETHICS UNDERLYING THE PUBLIC ACCOUNTING PROFESSION

One of the distinguishing marks of a profession is that its members, in recognition of their responsibility to the public and others, impose on themselves codes of professional ethics and are careful to establish means for observance of ethical rules. Codes of ethical conduct are characteristic of the fields of law, medicine, accounting, and many other professions. In this chapter we consider the codes of ethics that have been adopted by different professional accounting groups, with particular attention to the AICPA Code of Professional Ethics.

Our discussion of professional ethics is divided among the following topics:

1. General ethical concepts underlying our behavior as members of society.
2. Background and composition of the AICPA Code of Professional Ethics.
3. The peer review process for independent accounting firms.
4. The impact of the Securities and Exchange Commission and other regulatory bodies on the code of professional ethics for accountants.
5. Problems of enforcing the code of ethics governing the behavior of accountants.

We also include as appendixes to this chapter selected portions of the AICPA Code of Professional Ethics and the complete Code of Ethics of the Institute of Internal Auditors (IIA).

GENERAL ETHICAL CONCEPTS

Ethics may be defined as "a discipline dealing with good and evil and with moral duty."[1] By implication it involves reflective choice in establishing standards of right and wrong. The phrase *standards of right and wrong* suggests that the basic subject of ethics is the establishment of criteria for right behavior and, consequently, the identification of wrong behavior. But what is *right* and what is *wrong*? These terms would be without meaning if constraints were not established within which subsequent actions can be judged.

We establish perimeters for right and wrong behavior because of the need for order in society; also, because self-serving desires tend to influence the actions of all persons to a greater or lesser degree. There are those who would stop at nothing to fulfill their own selfish desires, even to the extent of taking another's life. Perimeters that define right and wrong behavior are often established in society through a system of statutory and common law. However, usually within these boundaries, we find that most individuals have established written or unwritten moral codes for themselves that enforce a higher standard than that imposed by law. These codes deal with the way we treat others and the way we restrain our selfish desires in deference to the rights and expectations of others; this behavior and its underlying beliefs are the essence of ***ethics.***

While it is true that each person may have a unique philosophy of what is right and what is wrong, our individual perspectives on ethics are shaped by our cultural, socioeconomic, and religious backgrounds. Many people, for instance, draw on their religious beliefs as standards for the establishment of personal ethical principles.

A good portion of the Old Testament in the Bible contains laws that form the basis of much of the moral code for the Judeo-Christian world. In addition, the Christian philosophy of life, begun by Jesus of Nazareth and promoted by his followers through the centuries, requires behavior that is opposite to that which would promote our short-term selfish interests. The Christian philosophy goes beyond even the standards of the Old Testament in promoting the spirit versus the letter of moral law. For those who accept the whole Biblical philosophy as the ultimate in good behavior, we may say that it is ethical to live within those constraints, even though the legal system does not require it. Those who espouse other beliefs may also, because of cultural, religious, or ethnic background, incorporate rules of conduct in their personal lives that require a higher standard than that imposed by law.

Regardless of the differences that may exist in the way individuals make ethical choices, the public, as well as the government and the business community, have a right to expect consistent standards of integrity and competence from members of professions whom they depend on for certain things. Codes of ethics are therefore established by professional groups as self-imposed and self-enforced constraints on behavior, and these codes provide the basis for outsiders' expectations of the conduct of the group's members. While individuals within the group might have personal ethical standards more restrictive than those imposed by the ethical code of the group, it is expected that all members of the profession will, as a minimum standard, adhere to the ethical code of the group.

Professional Responsibilities

The term ***profession*** is used to describe a group of people pursuing a learned art as a common calling *in the spirit of public service*[2] and at the same time pursuing a means of livelihood. The practices of accounting by certified public accountants and certified internal auditors have, when measured against the definition cited above, been held to be professions. Generally speaking, people engaged in professional activities, as defined above, are proud of their affiliations and, because they are professionals, regulate themselves by imposing constraints on their conduct. Realistically, the codifications of these codes of behavior serve two purposes. First, the codes set out for the members of the profession the *pattern of behavior expected of them* if they are to continue in the profession. Equally important, however, is the fact that the code of behavior *discloses to the public the self-imposed constraints* within which the profession operates; in that way the code improves the image of the profession, lends credibility to reports rendered by professionals, and in other ways helps professionals in performing service functions more effectively.

Public Accounting as a Profession

The specific code of ethics within which a professional operates is partly determined by the nature of the group's professional responsibilities. The internal auditor, for example, performs essentially a single function (auditing) and has responsibilities to one group (management of the company). The Code of Ethics of the Institute of Internal Auditors is directed, therefore, toward the professional practice of internal auditing. The certified public accountant, however, logically operates under slightly different interpretations of a single code of behavior in the performance of each of the various types of public accounting services. For example, the code of behavior expected of the certified public accountant in providing tax services or management advisory services is slightly different from the one expected of the same person performing an independent audit. As is the case in any profession, the code of ethics for the work depends ultimately on the self-imposed *constraints the public is expecting the professional to exercise in the task being performed.* In the paragraphs that follow, we examine the broad ethical concepts that define behavior expected of the accountant in the *performance of all professional services:* auditing, tax services, management consulting services (MAS), and accounting and review services. We then show how the elements of that behavior pattern provide the basis for the AICPA Code of Ethics.

As we have observed, the certified public accountant has responsibilities to both the public and clients. These responsibilities require the accountant to accept behavioral constraints that promote *independence, integrity,* and *objectivity.* Furthermore, the accountant must be willing to maintain a *confidential relationship* with each client, as well as to accept responsibility for being *professionally competent* to perform various types of engagements. If public accounting is to be accepted as a profession, the accountant has an additional responsibility to maintain *appropriate relationships with colleagues* in the profession. Beyond that, each accountant also has a responsibility for *enhancing the image of the profession.* Professional expectations require the accountant to accept a code of rules that will promote such relationships and at the same time present a favorable image to the public.

Importance of Public Confidence

The public must have confidence in the accounting profession for the accountant properly to meet his or her commitment to society. Public confidence is a response to a good image that the profession has earned in its service to the public. Thus, the code of ethical behavior imposed on the accountant serves two purposes: it not only sets out appropriate standards of behavior but, at the same time, also conveys to the public the constraints that the profession has imposed upon itself. In that way, a code of ethics helps to instill the confidence of the public in a profession.

From the foregoing observations, we can conclude that the development of a code of behavior for the professional is at least partially motivated by an attitude of "intelligent selfishness." This means that the code is to some extent accepted by the profession because it is judged, over the long run, to be the best course of action for the profession, and therefore, ultimately beneficial to individuals engaged in the profession. Stated another way, the acceptance of the constraints included in a code of ethics may reduce the short-term material benefits available to the professional, but, over the long run, the members of the profession will realize greater material and other benefits than they would without the constraints.

Regulatory Bodies Involved

Conceptually the practicing certified public accountant is subject to a number of agency-imposed codes of behavior. The CPA certificate, for example, is granted by the state in which the accountant practices. As a result, each state has a public agency generally called a State Board of Public Accountancy, which regulates public accounting practice within the state. In the process of accepting and discharging this responsibility, many state boards have issued codes of ethics setting out the behavior constraints expected of all certified public accountants in their states.

In most states, CPAs have also voluntarily created an organization called the State Society of Certified Public Accountants. These organizations have a number of operating objectives, one of which is to enhance the reputation of professional accounting within the state. In working toward that goal, each of these organizations typically carries on continuing professional education activities and generally establishes its own code of ethics for members of the society. We should note, however, that a state society code of ethics is enforceable by the state society only against those accountants who voluntarily join the organization. This may include most but not all the CPAs within a particular state.

The most comprehensive code of ethics for the accounting profession has been established by the American Institute of Certified Public Accountants. The codes imposed by the state boards and state societies generally incorporate the significant elements of the AICPA code. Again, however, because membership in the AICPA is voluntary, many accountants involved in the practice of public accounting are not members of the AICPA. Nevertheless because the AICPA is a national organization having close ties with state societies and state boards, the *AICPA Code of Ethics* more than any other code reflects the behavior patterns generally expected of professional accountants. It should be noted that when a CPA is licensed to practice accounting in a particular state, and is also a member of the AICPA and state society of CPAs, he or she is subject to three codes of professional conduct. If, with regard to a matter of ethics, a provision of one of these codes is more stringent in that provision than the others, *the CPA must always abide by the most restrictive provision.* The historical development of the AICPA Code along with its content are discussed later in this chapter.

Since the rules contained in a code of ethics require behavioral constraints that extend beyond those imposed by law, *initial penalties for the violation of any code of ethics must be assessed by the membership of the organization establishing the code rather than by the courts.* For example, violations of the rules of conduct of a state board of public accountancy are typically assessed by an ethics committee or trial board made up of professional accountants. Appeals procedures may also be applied within various professional bodies should the professional accountant disagree with the findings of the committee. Ultimately, however, conclusions of authoritative ethics bodies of the AICPA, a state society of CPAs, or a state board of public accountancy may be appealed to the Federal District Court system.

In most states the profession has looked to the state society to enforce ethical behavior of certified public accountants within the state. The American Institute of Certified Public Accountants, on the other hand, has followed a policy of influencing ethical behavior by encouraging state societies to accept the elements of the AICPA Code of Ethics. While membership in these organizations is voluntary, most CPAs value such memberships because the accountant's image, both professionally and ethically, is enhanced by them. Nevertheless, memberships are voluntary and in the final analysis the only organization through which ethical behavior can be imposed upon nonmembers is the state board of public accountancy. As a result, ethical behavior problems of certified public accountants not holding membership in the state society may be examined and appropriately acted upon by the accountant's state board (consequent to communications from the state society).

AICPA CODE OF ETHICS

The American Institute of Certified Public Accountants is the most important national organization in which practicing public accountants may hold membership. Originally organized as the American Institute of Accountants (AIA) it has been the primary professional organization for practicing certified public accountants for more than seventy-five years. One of its many services to the profession has been the development of the AICPA Code of Ethics. Because this code of ethics is national in scope and most of the other codes of ethics are derived from it, we now consider the development and present content of that code of ethics, in these steps:

1. Briefly tracing the historical background of the present code.
2. Examining the general composition of the present code of ethics.
3. Describing the rules-of-conduct portion of the code of ethics.
4. Relating the contents of the code of ethics to the general ethical responsibilities of public accountants.

Historical Background

The American Institute of Accountants adopted its first code of ethics in 1917. That code was a very simple one, having only eight "do not" rules that prohibited the accountant from

1. Describing the firm as "members of the Institute" if it is not in fact a partnership in which all partners are Institute members.
2. Expressing an opinion on financial statements containing an essential misstatement of fact or an omission of anything that would amount to an essential misstatement.
3. Allowing anyone to practice in a member's name who is not his or her partner, his or her employee, or a member of the Institute.
4. Sharing fees with the laity or accepting rebates or "kickbacks" from the laity.
5. Engaging in any activity that is incompatible or inconsistent with the member's accounting practice.
6. Expressing an opinion on financial statements that have not been examined under the supervision of the member, the member's partner or employee, a member of the Institute, or a member of a similar association abroad.
7. Attempting to influence legislation or governmental regulation affecting the accounting profession without advising the Institute.
8. Soliciting the clients or encroaching upon the business of another member of the Institute.[3]

It is interesting to observe that while many of the eight provisions included in the first code are either expressly or implicitly part of the present AICPA Code of Ethics, some of the areas of much concern sixty-five years later were not even mentioned originally. For example, we find no mention of conflicts of interest, independence, advertising, competitive bidding, contingent fees, or the confidential relationship between a member and his or her client. The apparent shift in emphasis in the code is due to the fact that the first code of ethics was consistent with the role of the public accountant prior to the present-day emphasis on the attest function. The present code recognizes the problems associated with the performance of that function.

The original code has, over the years, been revised and expanded to meet the needs of the changing environment of the audit practice. As the attest function became more important, the need for independence became more important. As a result, a rule was adopted and subsequently strengthened to require *independence in appearance as well as independence in fact* for accountants who perform audits.

In recent years, public accountants have seen the management advisory services part of their work increase significantly. The combination of this type of service with the auditing responsibility has repeatedly raised a question as to whether one auditing firm could perform both of these services for a particular client and still maintain its appearance of independence. The present position of the AICPA is that there is danger that the accountant's independence may be questioned if management accepts the proposals of the public accountant without subjecting them to critical review. The general conclusion, however, is that the performance of management advisory services does not negate the consultant's audit independence.

Of particular importance in the revision process was the restatement of the code in 1973. At that time, the code restatement committee developed a conceptual foundation for the code by presenting a philosophical essay on the concepts from which the

rules of conduct should flow, and showing why these concepts are imp
profession. That essay concluded that the conduct toward which CPAs sh
embodied in five broad ethical goals stated as ***affirmative ethical princ***
principles are as follows:

- *Independence, integrity, and objectivity.* This principle requires that a certified public accountant acting in any capacity should maintain his or her integrity and objectivity and, when engaged in the practice of auditing, should be independent of those being served.
- *Competence and technical standards.* The essay states that a certified public accountant should always observe the profession's technical standards and strive continuously to improve his or her competence and quality of services.
- *Responsibilities to clients.* This principle requires the certified public accountant to be fair and candid with clients and serve them with professional concern for their best interests consistent with his or her responsibility to the public.
- *Responsibilities to colleagues.* This principle requires the certified public accountant to adhere to standards of conduct that will promote cooperation and good relations among members of the profession.
- *Other responsibilities and practices.* This principle requires the certified public accountant to adhere to standards of conduct that will enhance the stature of the profession and its ability to serve the public.[4]

After accepting these basic principles, the code restatement committee prepared a second section, rules of conduct, designed to spell out more specifically the behavior patterns expected of accountants in the process of achieving those goals. The rules of conduct, discussed in the following pages, consist of enforceable ethical standards, the infraction of which would make a member liable to disciplinary action.

In recognition of the fact that rules are subject to interpretation, the committee added a third section, on interpretation of the rules. That section was intended to explain the application and scope of the rules. The interpretations were subdivided in accordance with the five basic concepts just described. Interpretations are not themselves enforceable, but anyone who departs from the guidelines set therein must be prepared to justify the departure in a disciplinary hearing.

Composition of the Present Code of Ethics

In 1973 the AICPA Code of Ethics was approved and published in the form described above. Between 1973 and 1977 a section entitled "Ethics Rulings" was added. This section includes ongoing questions and answers relating to specific acts that the accountant might encounter. These rulings are included in the present ethics standards, grouped according to the five basic concepts underlying ethical conduct for accountants.

Another revision of the rules of conduct was also approved in 1978. This publication included two new sections — one setting out the objectives of the American Institute of Certified Public Accountants and another describing the professional practice of certified public accountants. These two segments of the publication serve to further point up the relationship between the environment in which certified public accountants operate and the code of ethics prescribing the behavior expected of them.

Rules of Conduct

The AICPA Code of Ethics derives its authority from the bylaws of the AICPA. Those bylaws provide that a trial may, after a hearing, appropriately discipline any member found guilty of infringing on any of the provisions of the rules of conduct. Disciplinary actions may range from simple admonition to the expulsion of any member found guilty of a violation.

The rules of conduct apply to all services performed by AICPA members in the practice of public accounting (including auditing, management advisory services, tax practice, and accounting and review services) except: (1) where the wording of the code states otherwise (as in the case of Rule 101, which relates only to an audit practice) or (2) when a member is practicing outside the United States and therefore should follow the rules of the organized accounting profession in the country in which he or she is practicing. However, if by the circumstances, the accountant implies that United States practices were being followed, he or she must comply with Rules 202 and 203.[5] Members of the AICPA who are not in public practice must observe Rules 102 and 501. All the other rules relate to the practice of public accounting.

Independence, Integrity, and Objectivity

The basic concept of *independence, integrity,* and *objectivity* is presently judged to be appropriately maintained by ***Rules 101*** and ***102***.[6] Part A of Rule 101 states that a member, or a firm of which the member is a partner or shareholder, *shall not express an opinion on the financial statements of an enterprise unless he or she and the firm are independent with respect to that enterprise.* Within part A of Rule 101, independence is considered to be impaired if, *during the period of the professional engagement or at the time of expressing the opinion,* the accountant or the firm:

1. Had or was committed to acquire *any direct or material indirect financial interest* in the enterprise or was a trustee of any trust or executor of any estate if such trust or estate had (or was committed to acquire) any direct or material indirect financial interest in the enterprise. This rule generally prohibits the CPA or members of his or her immediate family (whose financial interests may be attributed to the CPA) from owning any stock or other ownership interest in audit clients during the audit engagement or at the time of expressing the audit opinion.
2. Had any joint closely held business interests with the enterprise or any officer, director, or principal stockholder thereof, if that interest was material in relation to either the member's or the accounting firm's net worth.
3. Had any loan to or from the enterprise or any officer – director or principal stockholder thereof. Exceptions are provided for secured loans made from a financial institution under normal lending procedures terms and requirements, as well as loans obtained by a member or a firm if that loan is not material to the net worth of the borrower.

Independence can be impaired under Part B of Rule 101 if, during the period previously mentioned *or during the period covered by the financial statements,* either the auditor or the auditing firm of which the member is a partner or shareholder

1. Was connected with the enterprise as a promoter, underwriter, or voting trustee, a director,

or officer, or in any capacity equivalent to that of a member of management or of an employee.
2. Was a trustee for any pension or profit-sharing trust of the enterprise.

Independence is fittingly placed as the first rule of professional ethics, because it is the very cornerstone upon which the auditing profession is built. Notice that, by prohibiting only the expression of an opinion in certain cases, Rule 101 applies uniquely to the auditing portion of an accountant's practice. As contemplated by this rule, independence is a two-pronged issue. First, the auditor must be independent in mental attitude. In this respect, independence is a state of mind known only to the auditor and cannot be judged by another. Therefore, to make the rule operational in practice, the accountant is required to maintain the *appearance of independence* to outsiders who might look upon thc accountant – client relationship. Under Rule 101, part A, specific direct and indirect *financial interests* in the client, which are considered to impair the CPA's audit independences, are defined. Under Rule 101, part B, specific *employment* or management relationships with the client are prohibited. Interpretations of Rule 101 (see Appendix 20–A) and numerous situational rulings help to make the independence rule operational by further describing these elements:

- The effect on independence of the CPA holding honorary directorships or trusteeships.
- The effect on firm independence when retired partners have relationships with the client.
- The effect on audit independence of the CPA providing concurrent accounting services for clients.
- The effect of family relationships of the CPA on audit independence.
- The meaning of the term *normal lending procedures* as used in Rule 101 (A) (3).
- The effect of actual or threatened litigation between the auditor and others upon audit independence.
- The effect on independence of financial interests in nonclients having investor or investee relationships with a member's client.

Rule 102 relates to *integrity and objectivity*. It states that a member shall not knowingly misrepresent facts and, when engaged in the practice of public accounting, including the rendering of tax and management advisory services, shall not subordinate his judgment to others. In tax practice a member is considered to be acting as an advocate of the client and may therefore resolve doubt in favor of the client as long as there is reasonable support for the position taken. It should be seen that, although an accountant who is not engaged in auditing a client is not required to adhere to the audit level of independence, this accountant still has the responsibility to maintain an impartial attitude with respect to all matters under his or her review. This rule, for example, requires an AICPA member engaged in tax practice to adhere to Statements of Responsibilities in Tax Practice, which forbid the CPA from knowingly signing an erroneous tax return. When engaged in MAS (management advisory services) work, the CPA should always refrain from assuming the role of either management or employee of the client. Of course, when audit, tax, and MAS services are all performed for the same client, the CPA should maintain audit independence with respect to the client.

Competence and Technical Standards

Adherence to the general and technical standards of the AICPA for the various areas of practice (audit, MAS, tax, and accounting and review services) is the subject of Rules 201, 202, 203, and 204.[7] ***Rule 201*** (general standard) defines four responsibilities and also contains a prohibition. Under this rule, the accountant has a responsibility for *professional competence,* for *due professional care,* for *planning and supervision,* and for *the acquisition of sufficient relevant data* to form a reasonable basis for any conclusions or recommendations associated with the engagement. The fifth general standard requires *that a member not permit his or her name to be used in conjunction with any forecasts of future transactions in a manner which may lead to the belief that the member vouches for the achievability of the forecast.* The auditor meets the first four of these standards by adherence to certain of the generally accepted auditing standards (GAAS). However, it should be noted that Rule 201 alone is broad enough to cover professional competence, due professional care, planning and supervision, and sufficient relevant data for tax, MAS, and accounting services areas of practice as well as the audit area.

With respect to forecasts, Rule 201 does not prohibit the CPA from preparing or assisting the client in preparing a forecast. In 1980 the AICPA published *Guide for a Review of a Financial Forecast* which, while not a generally accepted auditing standard, is a guide to good practice in this area. It contains the following guidelines, which are borrowed from generally accepted auditing standards and Rule 201 of the Code of Professional Ethics:

1. The review should be performed by persons having technical training and proficiency to review a financial forecast.
2. In all matters relating to the engagement, the accountant should maintain an independence of mental attitude.
3. Due professional care should be exercised in the performance of the review and the preparation of the report.
4. The work should be adequately planned and assistants, if any, are to be appropriately supervised.
5. The accountant should obtain an understanding of the forecasting process as a basis for determining the scope of the review.
6. Suitable support should be obtained to provide a reasonable basis for the accountant's report on the forecast.
7. The report should contain a statement regarding whether the accountant believes the financial forecast is presented in conformity with the applicable AICPA guidelines and has been prepared using assumptions that provide a reasonable basis for management's forecast.

When a CPA's name is associated with a forecast, he or she must make disclosures of

- The sources of the information used.
- The major assumptions used.
- The character of the work performed.
- The degree of responsibility taken by the CPA.

Rule 202 requires that a member not permit his or her name to be associated with financial statements in such a manner as to imply that he or she is acting as an independent public accountant unless he or she has complied with the *applicable* generally accepted auditing standards promulgated by the Institute. It should be noted that the ten generally accepted auditing standards apply to *all services* covered by Statements on Auditing Standards to the extent that those standards are relevant. For example, independence (the second general standard) applies to engagements covered by SAS 30, *Reporting on Internal Accounting Controls,* even though the first standard of reporting would not apply in such an engagement because it is not relevant.[8] An interpretation of this section also explains that, although generally accepted auditing standards are intended to apply primarily to audited financial statements, the fourth reporting standard is sufficiently broad in coverage to make it equally applicable to unaudited financial statements. This application was illustrated in the last chapter (see Figure 19–1).

Rule 203 requires that a member shall not express an opinion that financial statements are presented in conformity with generally accepted accounting principles if such statements contain any departure from an accounting principle promulgated by the body designated by the council to establish such principles if that departure has a material effect on the financial statements taken as a whole. An exception to that prohibition could occur only if the member can demonstrate that, due to unusual circumstances, the financial statements would otherwise have been misleading.

The Financial Accounting Standards Board (FASB) has been designated as the primary body authorized to promulgate accounting rules. Statements and interpretations of the FASB, as well as Accounting Principles Board Opinions and Accounting Research Bulletins (unless superseded by FASB action), have all been judged to contain generally accepted accounting principles whenever these statements stipulate disclosures in the basic financial statements (balance sheet, income statement, statement of retained earnings, statement of changes in financial position, and descriptions of accounting policies and related financial statement footnotes). The primary responsibility for justifying a departure from promulgated rules rests on the shoulders of the accountant. Examples of such a departure are new legislation or the evolution of a new form of business transaction not previously addressed by traditional accounting principles.

Rule 204 requires a member to *comply with other technical standards* promulgated by bodies designated by the council to establish such standards. Departures therefrom must be justified by those who do not follow them. The rule is designed to require accountants engaged in *nonauditing activities* to comply with the technical standards promulgated for those activities. Specific examples include the technical standards established for rendering management advisory services and tax services listed in Appendix A of Chapter 2. Again the rules relating to competence and adherence to standards are subject to interpretations of the AICPA. These interpretations are included in Appendix B at the end of this chapter.

Responsibilities to Clients

The *responsibilities of the accountant to clients* are spelled out in Rules 301 and 302.[9] ***Rule 301*** states that a *member shall not disclose any confidential information* obtained in the course of a professional engagement except with the consent of the client. It is important, however, to observe that this rule is not interpreted to prevent the accountant from responding to a validly issued subpoena or summons enforceable by order of a court or from responding to any inquiry made by the ethics division or trial board of the AICPA or by a duly constituted investigative or disciplinary body of a state society established under state statutes. Neither does it apply where, in the peer review process, compliance with technical standards (Rules 202 and 203) is being evaluated. However, Rule 301 does apply when, for example, a CPA is communicating with any other persons (including other CPAs) about information that has passed between the CPA and the client. As explained in Chapter 3, the confidential client information rule is important during the planning stages of the engagement with regard to communication between predecessor and successor auditors. All such communication, whether it occurs before or after the engagement has been accepted, must be with the full consent of the client, regardless of the circumstances surrounding the predecessor accountant's departure.

Rule 302 states that professional services shall not be offered or rendered under an arrangement whereby no fee will be charged unless a specified finding or result is attained or where the fee is otherwise contingent on the findings or results of such services. This is frequently referred to as the ***contingent fees rule.*** The rule should not be interpreted to preclude a member's fee from varying in relationship to the complexity of the services rendered. Furthermore, fees are not regarded as being contingent if fixed by courts or other public authorities, or in tax matters if determined by the results of the judicial or by the findings of governmental agencies. The important thing to emphasize in understanding this rule is that the *fee must not be related to the findings of the accountant.* A good rule of thumb to remember, with respect to fees, is that the fee should usually be based on number of hours spent multiplied by the rate per hour. Generally, if the fee is charged on another basis, it is subject to ethical scrutiny.

An interpretation of Rule 301 is included in Appendix 20–C.

Responsibilities to Colleagues

Prior to 1979 the Code included Rule 401 relating to encroachment upon the practice of another CPA. Under this rule, a CPA was prohibited from seeking or accepting new engagements with clients of other CPAs, or from making employment offers to employees of other CPAs without first advising the other CPAs. When the rule prohibiting direct solicitation of a specific potential client (see Rule 502) was withdrawn in 1979, however, the encroachment rule was rendered unenforceable and was, therefore, also withdrawn. It should be remembered, however, that the concept of ethical conduct with respect to responsibilities to colleagues remains part of the AICPA's code of professional conduct. This concept states that the CPA should conduct himself or herself in a manner that will promote cooperation and good relations among members of the accounting profession. The CPA should always treat fellow practitioners in the manner in which he or she would like to be treated.

Other Responsibilities and Practices

Members of the AICPA should adhere to five basic rules in meeting their other responsibilities.[10]

Rule 501. This rule requires that a member shall *not commit an act discreditable to the profession.* Examples of acts discreditable to the profession, which are outlined in Appendix 20–D, include refusal to return critical original client records and discrimination in employment practices by CPA firms. Other related actions that could cause repercussions in this area are felony convictions, disclosure of confidential information from a nonclient, and acceptance of fees based on the amount of taxes saved a potential client.

Rule 502. Rule 502 relates to advertising and other forms of solicitation. This rule has been changed significantly as a result of a judgment that prohibition of advertising would, like the rule against competitive bidding, be a violation of federal antitrust laws. This rule currently states that a member shall not seek to obtain clients by advertising or other forms of solicitation in a manner that is false, misleading, or deceptive. Interpretations (see Appendix 20–D) state that objective informational advertising is permitted. Limits on informational advertising are quite flexible and include information about the member and the firm such as the following:

- Names, addresses, telephone numbers, number of partners, shareholders or employees, office hours, foreign language competence, and date the firm was established.
- Services offered and fees for those services, including hourly rates and fixed fees.
- Educational and professional attainments, including date and place of certifications, schools attended, dates of graduation, degrees received, and memberships in professional associations.

In addition, the member is permitted to publish statements of position relating to a subject of public interest and containing the member's name. There are no restrictions as to type of advertising media, frequency of placement, size, artwork, or type style. A recent interpretation also permits rendering professional services to clients or customers of third parties who have obtained those clients or customers as the result of advertising or solicitation efforts as long as the member's actions continue to be within the bounds of the AICPA's Code of Professional Ethics. On the other hand, Rule 502 prohibits misleading, or deceptive advertising, including activities that would do the following:

- Create false or unjustified expectations of favorable results.
- Imply the ability to influence courts, tribunals, or regulatory agencies.
- Consist of self-laudatory statements which are not based on verifiable facts.
- Make comparisons with other CPAs.
- Contain testimonials or endorsements, or any other potentially misleading statements.

Self-designation as an industry expert or other expert is considered false, misleading, or deceptive advertising. However, designations as "tax consultant," "auditor," or "MAS specialist" are generally considered informational regarding the form of practice and are permitted.

Rule 503. Rule 503 prohibits a member from paying a commission to obtain a client. It also prevents members from accepting a commission for a referral to a client of products or services of others. This rule is, in some ways, similar to the contingent fee rule.

Rule 504. This rule covers *incompatible occupations.* It states that a member who is engaged in the practice of public accounting shall not *concurrently engage in any business or occupation, which would create a conflict of interest* in rendering professional services. Since the advertising rules were changed in 1978, the definition of an "incompatible occupation" under rule 504 has become less clear than before. Prior to that time, the accountant was prevented from engaging in any activity conjointly with public accounting which, through advertising efforts in the other activity, would serve as a "feeder" to the accountant's practice. Now the accountant is prohibited from engaging in conjoint activities with his public accounting which would interfere with his or her independence, integrity, or objectivity in rendering professional services. Rulings under Rule 504 have *permitted* the following activities to be performed conjointly with a public accounting practice:

- Practicing law when licensed in both professions.
- Representing a computer tax service to CPAs and other tax professionals on a fee-per-return basis.
- Serving as an officer or director of a consumer credit company.

Conjoint activities that are *questionable or prohibited* under rule 504 include the following:

- Accepting a position as a bank director where the member's clients are likely to engage in significant transactions with the bank.
- Forming a tax partnership with a non-CPA who has been asked to serve as a public member of the board of tax appeals recently established under a municipal income tax ordinance.
- Serving as a state controller.

Rule 505. Rule 505 defines the form of the organization within which a member may practice. Before 1969, all public accounting practice was carried out through the medium of *proprietorships or partnerships.* However, in response to the strong desire on the part of accountants to operate within a corporate framework, the council of the AICPA approved in 1969 a resolution allowing public accountants to render services *through a professional corporation.* Rule 505 states that a member may practice public accounting whether as an owner or employee only of a *proprietorship, a partnership, or a professional corporation* whose characteristics conform to the resolutions of the council. This rule also prohibits the use of fictitious names, specializations, and so forth.

PEER REVIEWS

The Code of Professional Ethics discussed in the preceding section governs the *behavior of accountants as individuals.* In recent years we have seen increased pressure on the accounting profession by Congress to have public accounting *firms* regulate and discipline themselves in a more effective manner. The AICPA's response to this pressure was the establishment of the Division for CPA Firms in 1978.

Division for CPA Firms

Within this division there are two sections: the SEC Practice Section and the Private Companies Practice Section. Although membership in the division is voluntary, it is expected that all firms will belong to one or both of these sections. Among the requirements for membership in both of these sections are these: (1) adherence to quality control standards established by the AICPA Quality Control Standards Committee; (2) voluntary submission of the firm to peer reviews of its accounting and auditing practice at least every three years (these are usually conducted by another firm who is a member of the division); and (3) periodic participation by all firm employees in continuing professional education (CPE) courses.[11]

Quality Control Standards

The peer review process is based on the expectation that public accounting firms should comply with specified qualitative standards of operations. *Generally accepted auditing standards* define the correct conduct of an audit engagement. *Quality control standards* define the correct conduct of the overall operations of the firm.

The elements of quality control for CPA firms, first cited in SAS 4, have now been codified into Statement on Quality Control Standards No. 1. These standards were issued by the AICPA Quality Control Standards Committee in 1979. They cover the following elements of a firm's operations:

- Independence.
- Assigning personnel to engagements.
- Consultation.
- Supervision.
- Hiring.
- Professional development.
- Advancement.
- Acceptance and continuance of clients.
- Inspection.[12]

Many of these elements are interrelated. For example, a firm's hiring policies might affect its professional development and advancement policies. Furthermore, the specific nature and extent of a firm's quality control policies and procedures depend on such factors as a firm's size and the nature of a firm's practice, its organization, and whether the cost of implementing the policies would outweigh the expected benefits. We now briefly describe the standards established for each of the elements and discuss the AICPA enforcement of them.

Independence. *Independence* has the same meaning as an operating standard for a firm as it has for the activities of the individual accountant. The significance of it as a quality control standard is that it *requires the firm to establish policies and procedures for implementation of the independence rule* of the Code of Professional Ethics (Rule 101). Such procedures might include: (1) requiring all personnel to adhere to the independence rules of the AICPA, state CPA society, state board of accountancy, and other bodies including the SEC, when applicable; (2) communicating the firm's policy with respect to independence to all personnel; (3) monitoring compliance with firm policies in the area of independence; (4) confirming, when acting as principal auditor, the independence of the other auditing firm(s).

Assignment of Personnel. Care should be taken to be sure that persons assigned to perform various audit tasks possess the technical training and proficiency required. The firm should adopt policies and procedures to make sure that these criteria are met. They may include: (1) timely identification of staff requirements for each specific engagement; (2) designation of persons to be responsible for assignment of personnel to engagements; (3) planning for a firm's total personnel needs for all audit engagements; and (4) use of time budgets and scheduling practices to establish manpower requirements and to schedule audit field work.

Consultation. Consultation services should be used when complex accounting and auditing questions arise on an engagement. Policies and procedures to implement this standard include the referral of complex or specialized technical accounting and auditing questions to designated experienced personnel within the firm. Another recourse is to refer questions to a division or group in the AICPA or state CPA society established to handle technical inquiries. This standard also implies the need for maintaining a technical reference library for staff use.

Supervision. The work of all aspects of the accounting firm's practice should be adequately supervised at all levels. Policies and procedures to implement this standard include required planning for all engagements, including assignment of personnel to engagements, development of background information on clients, and the development of an overall engagement strategy. Operating policies should also require a review process for all audit workpapers, audit reports, and financial statements, as well as the use of standard forms, checklists, and questionnaires.

Hiring. To ensure minimum standards of quality among entry-level personnel, the firm should establish recruiting policies throughout the firm to obtain well-qualified candidates. It should establish an appropriate experience requirement before an applicant can be considered for an advanced starting position. A background investigation should be required for all new personnel. Employees acquired through merger with or the acquisition of another firm should be appropriately indoctrinated into the firm's operating policies.

Professional Development. The professional development standard requires the firm to establish continuing professional education (CPE) activities in the form of *on-the-job training* and *classroom instruction* to keep employees abreast of the ever-increasing number of technical standards emerging from various authoritative groups. To implement this standard of professional development, a firm should undertake the following procedures: (1) provide instruction as needed to personnel on job assignments; (2) require personnel to attend formal CPE programs conducted by the firm, by a college or university, or by a professional organization; (3) distribute written communications regarding the firm policy on various technical issues to all firm personnel;

and (4) make copies or summaries of new technical pronouncements (FASB standards, SASs, etc.) available to all firm personnel.

Advancement. The CPA firm should establish procedures that prevent employees from advancing to higher positions within the firm before they are capable of handling the responsibilities of those positions. Each employee's moral character, intelligence, judgment, and motivation should be carefully evaluated before he or she is promoted. This requires the firm to establish qualifications deemed necessary for various levels of responsibility within the firm and to make use of evaluations by supervisors and, in some cases, subordinates. In addition, there should be partner committees to review the qualifications of individuals being considered for promotion.

Acceptance and Continuance of Clients. The CPA firm should adopt policies and procedures to give guidance in the decision of whether to accept an engagement from a prospective client and whether to continue an engagement with an existing client. Policies such as these, when followed, help to minimize the likelihood of the CPA's association with a client whose management lacks integrity. Implementing policies include such things as: (1) preengagement inquiry and review, (2) review of financial statements of prospective clients; and (3) an evaluation of the firm's ability to service the client.

Inspection. Finally, there should be a periodic *inspection of a firm's overall quality control program,* to help assure that it is working effectively. This inspection program may be accomplished internally by members of the management group of the firm; but most often it is accomplished by voluntarily submitting to a peer review, as discussed earlier.

THE SECURITIES AND EXCHANGE COMMISSION AND PROFESSIONAL ETHICS

The Securities and Exchange Commission was established in 1934 with the authority to define the content and form of financial statements and other reports submitted to it. This authority is interpreted to include the methods of accounting used to derive those statements. Over the years the SEC has delegated to the private sector (the AICPA and the FASB) the general responsibility for the establishment of accounting principles, including the ethical constraints under which public accountants are to operate. However, the Commission has seen fit to issue rules and interpretations through the medium of *Accounting Series Releases* specifying procedures and ethical interpretations to be applied to situations involving filings with the SEC.

Insofar as auditors' independence is concerned, the positions of the AICPA and SEC are slightly different in regard to two areas. First, with the exception of audit fee arrangements, the SEC interprets any business transaction between an auditor and a client as a "direct financial interest" as defined in Rule 101, Part A. Second, the SEC interprets almost any form of recordkeeping for clients (manual or EDP) as an impairment to audit independence.[18] The SEC feels that the accountant cannot objectively audit books and records that he or she has maintained for the client. Also, the renting of computer time to a client is considered by the SEC to be a business transaction with the client and therefore to adversely affect the independence of the CPA. As a result, the *SEC's interpretations of independence are generally more stringent than those of the AICPA*.

Aside from the presently existing differences of opinion cited above, it is important to recognize that over the years the SEC has, without question, had considerable influence on the general content of the AICPA Code of Professional Ethics. Generally speaking the AICPA has been inclined to amend its code toward compliance with SEC expectations for the accountant engaged in work with the SEC. As a result the present AICPA code is probably more stringent than it would have been without the influence of the SEC.

ENFORCEMENT OF ETHICAL BEHAVIOR

As we observed earlier in the chapter, a utopian or ideal situation calls for ethical behavior even without the threat of discipline. However, the necessity of maintaining public confidence has prevented the profession from risking the careers of many on the necessity of compliance by every individual. In this section we consider the disciplinary problems associated with ethical behavior as we look at the responsibility of the profession in enforcing its code of ethics. We also examine briefly the relationship of ethical violations to legal liability.

Discipline by the Profession

The AICPA has established procedures for disciplining its members and the firms holding membership in its Division for CPA Firms. Disciplinary action for individual accountants may range from a reprimand to expulsion from the Institute. Action taken by the AICPA may in turn cause the state board to act, perhaps even to suspend or revoke the member's CPA certificate or license to practice. It is also possible that an accountant's license or permit to practice will be suspended or revoked by governmental authority.

Generally speaking, if the professional ethics committee concludes that there is a violation of any of the bylaws of the Institute or any provision of the AICPA Code of Professional Ethics, or the code of ethics of the involved state society, they will report the matter to a trial board. Normally, cases are referred to the *appropriate regional trial board*, which will act on the case. The member has the right to request that the case be heard by a panel of the *national review board*, rather than by a regional trial board.

As observed earlier, the primary vehicle within the profession for the discipline of firms is the AICPA Division of CPA firms, which is divided into two sections, the SEC Practice Section and Private Companies Practice Section. Both sections require their member firms to do the following:

1. Adhere to quality control standards established by the AICPA Quality Control Standards Committee.
2. Submit to peer reviews of their accounting and auditing practice every three years or at such additional times as designated.
3. Ensure that all their professionals participate in continuing professional education.
4. Maintain minimum amounts and types of liability insurance.[14]

The executive committee of each section has the authority to impose sanctions on member firms. These can include required corrective measures, additional requirements for continuing professional education, accelerated peer review, admonishments or reprimands, monetary fines, suspension of membership, or expulsion from membership.

Ethical Responsibilities Related to Legal Liability

As we have indicated in the preceding paragraphs, ethical violations are disciplined by the profession. It is important, however, to observe that *violations of the code of ethics can lead to legal liability*. This can occur when either a client or a third party can demonstrate in the courts that a loss has been suffered because the accountant violated ethical requirements such as those relating to independence, competence, or confidential relationship with the client. Therefore the accountant may suffer not only embarrassment by the professional discipline described in the preceding paragraphs but may also suffer financially as a result of loss of clients as well as potential litigation.

SUMMARY

In this chapter we have discussed the ethics underlying the public accounting profession. We observed that a certain level of behavior, more restrictive than that prescribed by law, is expected of persons involved in professional activities. Codes of ethics are established to provide guidelines for that behavior and to enhance the image of the profession. In the long run such restrictions are also materially beneficial to the profession.

Although it is true that most ethics violations are defined in terms of the code adopted by the state society or state board, those codes are generally consistent with the provisions of the AICPA Code of Professional Ethics. Therefore considerable attention was given to the rules included in that code. Interpretations of the rules are included in appendixes at the end of the chapter.

We listed and described the quality control standards for CPA firms and explained how the peer review process is used to monitor adherence to those standards. We also dealt briefly with the ethics enforcement process for both individual CPAs and public accounting firms.

In the last part of the chapter, we explained that although ethics violations are subject to punishment only by the profession, they can also become the basis for actions involving legal liability.

APPENDIX 20–A: Selected AICPA Interpretations of Rule 101 on Independence

101-1 — Directorships

Members are often asked to lend the prestige of their name as a director of a charitable, religious, civic or other similar type of nonprofit organization whose board is large and representative of the community's leadership. An auditor who permits his name to be used in this manner would not be considered lacking in independence under Rule 101 so long as he does not perform or give advice on management functions, and the board itself is sufficiently large that a third party would conclude that his membership was honorary.

101-2 — Retired Partners and Firm Independence

A retired partner having a relationship of a type specified in Rule 101 with a client of his former firm would not be considered as impairing the firm's independence with respect to the client provided that he is no longer active in the firm, that the fees received from such client do not have a material effect on his retirement benefits and that he is not held out as being associated with his former partnership.

101-3 — Accounting Services

Members in public practice are sometimes asked to provide manual or automated bookkeeping or data processing services to clients who are of insufficient size to employ an adequate internal accounting staff. Computer systems design and programming assistance are also rendered by members either in conjunction with data processing services or as a separate engagement. Members who perform such services and who are engaged in the practice of public accounting are subject to the bylaws and Rules of Conduct.

On occasion members also rent "block time" on their computers to their clients but are not involved in the processing of transactions or maintaining the client's accounting records. In such cases the sale of block time constitutes a business rather than a professional relationship and must be considered together with all other relationships between the member and his client to determine if their aggregate impact is such as to impair the member's independence.

When a member performs manual or automated bookkeeping services, concern may arise whether the performance of such services would impair his audit independence — that the performance of such basic accounting services would cause his audit to be lacking in a review of mechanical accuracy or that the accounting judgments made by him in recording transactions may somehow be less reliable than if made by him in connection with the subsequent audit.

Members are skilled in, and well accustomed to, applying techniques to control mechanical accuracy, and the performance of the record-keeping function should have no effect on application of such techniques. With regard to accounting judgments, if third parties have confidence in a member's judgment in performing an audit, it is difficult to contend that they would have less confidence where the same judgment is applied in the process of preparing the underlying accounting records.

Nevertheless, a member performing accounting services for an audit client must meet the following requirements to retain the appearance that he is not virtually an employee and therefore lacking in independence in the eyes of a reasonable observer:

- The CPA must not have any relationship or combination of relationships with the client or any conflict of interest which would impair his integrity and objectivity.
- The client must accept the responsibility for the financial statements as his own. A small client may not have anyone in his employ to maintain accounting records and may rely on the CPA for this purpose. Nevertheless, the client must be sufficiently knowledgeable of the enterprise's activities and financial condition and the applicable accounting principles so that he can reasonably accept such responsibility, including, specifically, fairness of valuation and presentation and adequacy of disclosure. When necessary, the CPA must discuss accounting matters with the client to be sure that the client has the required degree of understanding.
- The CPA must not assume the role of employee or of management conducting the operations of an enterprise. For example, the CPA shall not consummate transactions, have custody of assets, or exercise authority on behalf of the client. The client must prepare the source documents on all transactions in sufficient detail to identify clearly the nature and amount of such transactions and maintain an accounting control over data processed by the CPA, such as control totals and document counts. The CPA should not make changes in such basic data without the concurrence of the client.
- The CPA, in making an examination of financial statements prepared from books and records which he has maintained completely or in part, must conform to generally accepted auditing standards. The fact that he has processed or maintained certain records does not eliminate the need to make sufficient audit tests.

When a client's securities become subject to regulation by the Securities and Exchange Commission or other federal or state regulatory body, responsibility for maintenance of the accounting records, including accounting classification decisions, must be assumed by accounting personnel employed by the client. The assumption of this responsibility must commence with the first fiscal year after which the client's securities qualify for such regulation.

101-4 — Effect of Family Relationships on Independence

[Partially omitted.] Relationships that arise through family bloodlines and marriage give rise to circumstances that may impair a member's independence:

- *Financial and business relationships ascribed to the member.* Independence of a member may be impaired by the financial interests and business relationships of the member's spouse, dependent children, or any relative living in a common household with or supported by the member. The financial interests or business relationships of such family, dependents, or relatives in a member's client are ascribed to the member; in such circumstances the independence of the member or his firm would be impaired under Rule 101.
- *Financial and business relationships that* may *be ascribed to the member.*

Close Kin Family relationships may also involve other circumstances in which the appearance of independence is lacking. However, it is not reasonable to assume that all kinships, per se, will impair the appearance of independence since some kinships are too remote. The following guidelines to the effect of kinship on the appearance of independence have evolved over the years:

A presumption that the appearance of independence is impaired arises from a significant financial interest, investment, or business relationship by the following close kin in a member's client: nondependent children, brothers and sisters, grandparents, parents, parents-in-law, and the respective spouses of any of the foregoing.

If the close kin's financial interest in a member's client is material in relationship to the kin's net worth, a third party could conclude that the member's objectivity is impaired with respect to the client since the kinship is so close. In addition, financial interests held by close kin may result in an indirect financial interest being ascribed to the member.

The presumption that the appearance of independence is impaired would also prevail where a close kin has an important role or responsible executive position (e.g , director, chief executive or financial officer) with a client.

Geographical separation from the close kin and infrequent contact may mitigate such impairment.

- *Financial and business relationships that are not normally ascribed to the member.*

Remote Kin. A presumption that the appearance of independence is impaired would not normally arise from the financial interests and business relationships of remote kin: uncles, aunts, cousins, nephews, nieces, other in-laws, and other kin who are not close.

The financial interests and business relationships of these remote kin are not considered either direct or indirect interests ascribed to the member. However, the presumption of no impairment with remote kin would be negated if other factors indicating a closeness exist, such as living in the same household with the member, having financial ties, or jointly participating in other business enterprises.

Summary. Members must be aware that it is impossible to enumerate all circumstances wherein the appearance of a member's independence might be questioned by third parties because of family relationships. In situations involving the assessment of relationships with both close and remote kin, members must consider whether geographical proximity, strength of personal and other business relationships, and other factors — when viewed together with financial interests in question — would lead a reasonable observer to conclude that the specified relationships pose an unacceptable threat to the member's objectivity and appearance of independence.

101-5 – Meaning of the Term *Normal Lending Procedures, Terms, and Requirements*

[Partially omitted.] Rule 101 (A) (3) prohibits loans to a member from his client except for certain specified kinds of loans from a client financial institution when made under "normal lending procedures, terms, and requirements." The member would meet the criteria prescribed by this rule if the procedures, terms, and requirements relating to his loan are reasonably comparable to those relating to other loans of a similar character committed to other borrowers during the period in which the loan to the member is committed.

101-6 — The Effect of Actual or Threatened Litigation on Independence

[Partially omitted.] Rule of Conduct 101 prohibits the expression of an opinion on financial statements of an enterprise unless a member and his firm are independent with respect to the enterprise. In some circumstances, independence may be considered to be impaired as a result of litigation or the expressed intention to commence litigation.

Litigation Between Client and Auditor. When the present management of a client company commences, or expresses an intention to commence, legal action against the auditor, the auditor and the client management may be placed in adversary positions in which the management's willingness to make complete disclosures and the auditor's objectivity may be affected by self-interest.

. . . Independence may be impaired whenever the auditor and his client company or its management are in threatened or actual positions of material adverse interests by reason of actual or intended litigation. Because of the complexity and diversity of the situations of adverse interests which may arise, however, it is difficult to prescribe precise points at which independence may be impaired. The following criteria are offered as guidelines:

1. The commencement of litigation by the present management alleging deficiencies in audit work for the client would be considered to impair independence.
2. The commencement of litigation by the auditor against the present management alleging management fraud or deceit would be considered to impair independence.
3. An expressed intention by the present management to commence litigation against the auditor alleging deficiencies in audit work for the client is considered to impair independence if the auditor concludes that there is a strong possibility that such a claim will be filed.
4. Litigation not related to audit work for the client (whether threatened or actual) for an amount not material to the member's firm or to the financial statements of the client company would not usually be considered to affect the relationship in such a way as to impair independence.

Litigation by Security Holders. The auditor may also become involved in litigation ("primary litigation") in which he and the client company or its management are defendants. Such litigation may arise, for example, when one or more stockholders bring a stockholders' derivative action or a so-called class action against the client company or its management, officers, directors, underwriters, or auditors under the securities laws. Such primary litigation in itself would not alter fundamental relationships between the client company or its management and auditor and therefore should not be deemed to have an adverse impact on the auditor's independence. These situations should be examined carefully, however, since the potential for adverse interests may exist if cross-claims are filed against the auditor alleging that he is responsible for any deficiencies or if the auditor alleges fraud or deceit by the present management as a defense.

Effects of Impairment of Independence. If the auditor believes that the circumstances would lead a reasonable person having knowledge of the facts to conclude that the actual or intended litigation poses an unacceptable threat to the auditor's independence, he should either (a) disengage himself to avoid the appearance that his self-interest would affect his objectivity, or (b) disclaim an opinion because of lack of independence as prescribed by SAS 26.

101-7 — Application of Rule 101 to Professional Personnel

The term *he and his firm* as used in the first sentence of Rule 101 means (1) all partners or shareholders in the firm and (2) all full- and part-time professional employees participating in the engagement or located in an office participating in a significant portion of the engagement.

APPENDIX 20–B: Selected AICPA Interpretations of Rules 201 and 202 Relating to Competence and Technical Standards

201-1 — Competence

A member who accepts a professional engagement implies that he has the necessary competence to complete the engagement according to professional standards, applying his knowledge and skill with reasonable care and diligence, but he does not assume a responsibility for infallibility of knowledge or judgment.

Competence in the practice of public accounting involves both the technical qualifications of the member and his staff and his ability to supervise and evaluate the quality of the work performed. Competence relates both to knowledge of the profession's standards, techniques and the technical subject matter involved, and to the capability to exercise sound judgment in applying such knowledge to each engagement.

The member may have the knowledge required to complete an engagement professionally before undertaking it. In many cases, however, additional research or consultation with others may be necessary during the course of the engagement. This does not ordinarily represent a lack of competence, but rather is a normal part of the professional conduct of an engagement.

However, if a CPA is unable to gain sufficient competence through these means, he should suggest, in fairness to his client and the public, the engagement of someone competent to perform the needed service, either independently or as an associate.

201-2 — Forecasts

Rule 201 does not prohibit a member from preparing, or assisting a client in the preparation of, forecasts of the results of future transactions. When a member's name is associated with such forecasts, there shall be the presumption that such data may be

Appendix 20–B is from *Rules of Conduct* (New York: AICPA, 1978).

used by parties other than the client. Therefore, full disclosure must be made of the sources of the information used and the major assumptions made in the preparation of the statements and analyses, the character of the work performed by the member, and the degree of the responsibility he is taking.

202-1 — Unaudited Financial Statements

Rule 202 does not preclude a member from associating himself with the unaudited financial statements of his clients. The Rule states in part that "A member shall not permit his name to be associated with financial statements in such a manner as to imply that he is acting as an independent public accountant unless he has complied with the applicable generally accepted auditing standards promulgated by the Institute."

In applying this provision to situations in which a member's name is associated with unaudited financial statements, it is necessary to recognize that the standards were specifically written to apply to audited financial statements. The fourth reporting standard, however, was made sufficiently broad to be applicable to unaudited financial statements as well.

The fourth reporting standard states in part that

> in *all* cases where an auditor's name is associated with financial statements, the report should contain a clear-cut indication of the character of the auditor's examination, *if any*, and the degree of responsibility he is taking.

203-1 — Departures from Established Accounting Principles

Rule 203 was adopted to require compliance with accounting principles promulgated by the body designated by Council to establish such principles. There is a strong presumption that adherence to officially established accounting principles would in nearly all instances result in financial statements that are not misleading.

However, in the establishment of accounting principles it is difficult to anticipate all of the circumstances to which such principles might be applied. This rule therefore recognizes that upon occasion there may be unusual circumstances where the literal application of pronouncements on accounting principles would have the effect of rendering financial statements misleading. In such cases, the proper accounting treatment is that which will render the financial statements not misleading.

The question of what constitutes unusual circumstances as referred to in Rule 203 is a matter of professional judgment involving the ability to support the position that adherence to a promulgated principle would be regarded generally by reasonable men as producing a misleading result.

Examples of events which may justify departures from a principle are new legislation or the evolution of a new form of business transaction. An unusual degree of materiality or the existence of conflicting industry practices are examples of circumstances which would not ordinarily be regarded as unusual in the context of Rule 203.

203-2 — Status of FASB Interpretations

Council is authorized under Rule 203 to designate a body to establish accounting principles and has designated the Financial Accounting Standards Board as such body.

Council also has resolved that FASB Statements of Financial Accounting Standards, together with those Accounting Research Bulletins and APB Opinions which are not superseded by action of the FASB, constitute accounting principles as contemplated in Rule 203.

In determining the existence of a departure from an accounting principle established by a Statement of Financial Accounting Standards, Accounting Research Bulletin, or APB Opinion encompassed by Rule 203, the division of professional ethics will construe such Statement, Bulletin, or Opinion in the light of any interpretation thereof issued by the FASB.

APPENDIX 20–C: Selected AICPA Interpretations of Rule 301 on Responsibilities to Clients

301-1 — Confidential Information and Technical Standards

The prohibition against disclosure of confidential information obtained in the course of a professional engagement does not apply to disclosure of such information when required to properly discharge the member's responsibility according to the profession's standards. The prohibition would not apply, for example, to disclosure, as required by Section 561 of Statement of Auditing Standards No. 1, of subsequent discovery of facts existing at the date of the auditor's report which would have affected the auditor's report had he been aware of such facts.

APPENDIX 20–D: Selected AICPA Interpretations of Rules 501, 502, and 505 on Other Responsibilities

501-1 — Client's Records and Accountant's Workpapers

[Partially omitted.] Retention of client records after a demand is made for them is an act discreditable to the profession in violation of Rule 501. The fact that the statutes of the state in which a member practices may specifically grant him a lien on all client records in his possession does not change the ethical standard that it would be a violation of the Code to retain the records to enforce payment.

A member's working papers are his property and need not be surrendered to the client. However, in some instances a member's working papers will contain data which should properly be reflected in the client's books and records but which for convenience have not been duplicated therein, with the result that the client's records are incomplete. In such instances, the portion of the working papers containing such data constitutes part of the client's records, and copies should be made available to the client upon request.

501-2 — Discrimination in Employment Practices

Discrimination based on race, color, religion, sex, age, or national origin in hiring, promotion, or salary practices is presumed to constitute an act discreditable to the profession in violation of Rule 501.

502-1 — Informational Advertising

Advertising that is informative and objective is permitted. Such advertising should be in good taste and be professionally dignified. There are no other restrictions, such as on the type of advertising media, frequency of placement, size, art work, or type style. Some examples of informative and objective content are

1. Information about the member and the member's firm, such as
   a. Names, addresses, telephone numbers, number of partners, shareholders or employees, office hours, foreign language competence, and date the firm was established.
   b. Services offered and fees for such services, including hourly rates and fixed fees.
   c. Educational and professional attainments, including date and place of certifications, schools attended, dates of graduation, degrees received, and memberships in professional associations.
2. Statements of policy or position made by a member or a member's firm related to the practice of public accounting or addressed to a subject of public interest.

502-2 — False, Misleading, or Deceptive Acts

Advertising or other forms of solicitation that are false, misleading, or deceptive are not in the public interest and are prohibited. Such activities include those that

1. Create false or unjustified expectations of favorable results.
2. Imply the ability to influence any court, tribunal, regulatory agency, or similar body official.
3. Consist of self-laudatory statements that are not based on verifiable facts.
4. Make comparisons with other CPAs.
5. Contain testimonials or endorsements.
6. Contain any other representations that would be likely to cause a reasonable person to misunderstand or be deceived.

APPENDIX 20–E: The Code of Ethics of the Institute of Internal Auditors

The Institute of Internal Auditors (IIA) Code of Ethics is shown in its entirety on page 900. Notice that, in contrast to the AICPA's code of ethics, described in the body of this chapter, it is rather brief and simple. Notice, too, that the introduction to the Code stresses the obligation of internal auditors, not to outsiders, but to the management of the client company. The Interpretation of Principles section stresses individual judgment in application of the principles of ethics contained in the Code. There are eight articles dealing with various ethical issues. The IIA Code is similar to the AICPA Code in its emphasis on professionalism and technical proficiency. The major difference

THE INSTITUTE OF INTERNAL AUDITORS, INC.

CODE OF ETHICS

INTRODUCTION: Recognizing that ethics are an important consideration in the practice of internal auditing and that the moral principles followed by members of *The Institute of Internal Auditors, Inc.*, should be formalized, the Board of Directors at its regular meeting in New Orleans on December 13, 1968, received and adopted the following resolution:

WHEREAS the members of *The Institute of Internal Auditors, Inc.*, represent the profession of internal auditing; and

WHEREAS managements rely on the profession of internal auditing to assist in the fulfillment of their management stewardship; and

WHEREAS said members must maintain high standards of conduct, honor and character in order to carry on proper and meaningful internal auditing practice;

THEREFORE BE IT RESOLVED that a Code of Ethics be now set forth, outlining the standards of professional behavior for the guidance of each member of *The Institute of Internal Auditors, Inc.*

In accordance with this resolution, the Board of Directors further approved of the principles set forth.

INTERPRETATION OF PRINCIPLES: The provisions of this Code of Ethics cover basic principles in the various disciplines of internal auditing practice. Members shall realize that individual judgment is required in the application of these principles. They have a responsibility to conduct themselves so that their good faith and integrity should not be open to question. While having due regard for the limit of their technical skills, they will promote the highest possible internal auditing standards to the end of advancing the interest of their company or organization.

ARTICLES:

I. Members shall have an obligation to exercise honesty, objectivity, and diligence in the performance of their duties and responsibilities.

II. Members, in holding the trust of their employers, shall exhibit loyalty in all matters pertaining to the affairs of the employer or to whomever they may be rendering a service. However, members shall not knowingly be a part to any illegal or improper activity.

III. Members shall refrain from entering into any activity which may be in conflict with the interest of their employers or which would prejudice their ability to carry out objectively their duties and responsibilities.

IV. Members shall not accept a fee or a gift from an employee, a client, a customer, or a business associate of their employer without the knowledge and consent of their senior management.

V. Members shall be prudent in the use of information acquired in the course of their duties. They shall not use confidential information for any personal gain nor in a manner which would be detrimental to the welfare of their employer.

VI. Members, in expressing an opinion, shall use all reasonable care to obtain sufficient factual evidence to warrant such expression. In their reporting, members shall reveal such material facts known to them, which, if not revealed, could either distort the report of the results of operations under review or conceal unlawful practice.

VII. Members shall continually strive for improvement in the proficiency and effectiveness of their service.

VIII. Members shall abide by the bylaws and uphold the objectives of *The Institute of Internal Auditors, Inc.* In the practice of their profession, they shall be ever mindful of their obligation to maintain the high standard of competence, morality, and dignity which *The Institute of Internal Auditors, Inc.*, and its members have established.

Source: Institute of Internal Auditors, Inc. Reproduced with permission.

between the two codes lies in the IIA's emphasis on responsibility to the client (employer) versus the AICPA emphasis on responsibility to the public.

The IIA Code should be studied in conjunction with the Statement of Responsibilities of Internal Auditing contained in Appendix 1–A. Note specifically that independence is a part of those responsibilities, although the degree of independence necessary for an internal auditor is not as great as that of an independent auditor. It is useful to compare this responsibility for independence with the independent auditor's responsibility under Rule 101 of the AICPA Code and with the SEC requirements for independence as expressed in the latter part of this chapter.

NOTES

1. *New Merriam-Webster Pocket Dictionary* (New York: Pocket Books, 1964), p. 168.
2. Floyd W. Windall and Robert N. Corley, *The Accounting Professional* (Englewood Cliffs, N.J.: Prentice-Hall, 1980), p. 198.
3. Thomas G. Higgins, "Professional Ethics: A Time for Reappraisal," *Journal of Accountancy* (March 1962): 29–35.
4. *Restatement of the Code of Professional Ethics* (New York: AICPA, 1972), p. 7.
5. *Rules of Conduct* (New York: AICPA, 1978), p. 4.
6. Ibid., pp. 5–6.
7. Ibid., pp. 6–7.
8. Statement on Auditing Standards (SAS) 43, paragraph 6 (New York: AICPA, 1982).
9. *Rules of Conduct*, pp. 7–8.
10. Ibid., pp. 9–10.
11. Windall and Corley, *Accounting Professional*, p. 137.
12. SAS 4, paragraphs 5 through 21 (New York: AICPA, 1974).
13. SEC Accounting Series Releases 126 and 234.
14. Windall and Corley, *Accounting Professional*, p. 137.

QUESTIONS FOR CLASS DISCUSSION

Q20–1 What does the term *ethics* mean?

Q20–2 What distinguishes a profession from a vocation?

Q20–3 Why do the members of a profession adopt a code of ethics governing their behavior? Discuss.

Q20–4 What relationship exists between a society's code of law and the code of ethics adopted by a segment of that society?

Q20–5 How does a profession's code of ethics relate to the services performed by that profession? Discuss.

Q20–6 Is a code of ethics selfishly beneficial to a profession? Explain.

Q20–7 Who is responsible for enforcing the provisions of a code of ethics?

Q20–8 A CPA is typically licensed to practice by his or her state board of public accountants; why, then, does the auditing profession give so much attention to the provisions of the AICPA Code of Ethics? Discuss.

Q20–9 What are the relationships between the five broad ethical goals underlying the AICPA Code of Professional Ethics and the practice of public accountancy?

Q20–10 Is the public accountant governed by the same ethical rules in performing all public accounting services? Discuss.

Q20–11 The first code of ethics adopted by the American Institute of Accountants contained no reference to the need for independence in the performance of public accounting services; why has that changed in later editions of the AICPA Code of Ethics?

Q20–12 What is the difference between being independent and appearing to be independent? Why is the appearance of independence important to the auditing profession?

Q20–13 How are competence and technical standards associated with the AICPA Code of Ethics?

Q20–14 What is meant by a *contingent fee*? Why are such fees not allowed under the AICPA Code of Ethics?

Q20–15 What is meant by the term *acts discreditable to the profession*?

Q20–16 What is meant by the term *incompatible occupation*? Discuss.

Q20–17 What relationship exists between quality control standards for public accounting firms and the profession's code of ethics?

Q20–18 What is meant by the term *peer review*? How does it relate to the maintenance of quality control standards?

Q20–19 What is the relationship between a public accounting firm's hiring practices and the maintenance of quality control within an accounting firm?

Q20–20 How is the participation of a firm's employees in continuing education seminars related to the maintenance of appropriate quality control standards for the firm?

Q20–21 What influence has the SEC had on the AICPA Code of Professional Ethics?

Q20–22 What is likely to happen in the event that a certified public accountant violates the profession's code of ethics?

Q20–23 What is likely to happen if a public accounting firm is found to be deficient in maintaining appropriate quality control standards?

Q20–24 What is the relationship between ethical responsibilities and potential legal liability for public accountants?

SHORT CASES

C20–1 Ben Seastrunk, a BBA graduate of a small midwestern university, recently took a job with Sleeper and Sleeper, CPAs, a local firm in his hometown of Midwest City, Nebraska. After he had worked for the firm for six months, a partner of the firm, Loc Tran, invited Seastrunk into his office for his semiannual review.

"Seastrunk, I like you," Tran told the young man. "I believe you have what it takes to succeed in this business. I want to give you a little advice, son. It's a dog-eat-dog world out there, and only the strong survive. We're adopting a more aggressive policy of client service to try to expand our share of the market for clients in this town. We're planning on developing a drastically lower first-year fee structure to attract new clients and undercut the competition. We figure that we can 'cut a few corners' on each engagement to save dollars off the fees, and next year we can increase fees above their former levels to more than make up the difference.

"In addition, I'd like to talk to your father this year about taking him on as an audit client next year. You know, that $45,000 fee he's paying Arthur Crumley would surely do a lot for our P & L. And who knows, we might even be able to work up a little bonus for you of, say, 10 percent off the top. You aren't a CPA yet, so it won't hurt you a bit professionally, and nobody in this town would dare sue me for violating the code of ethics. Besides, no one needs to know anything about this conversation except you and me. Right, son?"

Required:

a. Evaluate Tran's statements in light of the AICPA Code of Professional Ethics.

b. Were there any of Tran's statements which, while not a violation of the AICPA Code of Professional Ethics, you found personally objectionable?

c. Are lawsuits generally the recourse sought by other professionals when a CPA violates the Code of Professional Ethics of the AICPA? If not, what other recourse is available against Tran and the firm of Sleeper and Sleeper?

C20–2 Joyce Gilbert and Elissa Bradley formed a corporation called Financial Services, Inc., each woman taking 50 percent of the authorized common stock. Gilbert is a CPA and a member of the American Institute of CPAs. Bradley is a CPCU (Chartered Property Casualty Underwriter). The corporation performs auditing and tax services under Gilbert's direction and insurance services under Bradley's supervision. The opening of the corporation's office was announced by a three-inch, two-column "card" in the local newspaper.

One of the corporation's first audit clients was the Grandtime Company. Grandtime had total assets of $600,000 and total liabilities of $270,000. In the course of her examination, Gilbert found that Grandtime's building with a book value of $240,000 was pledged as security for a ten-year-term note in the amount of $200,000. The client's statement did not mention that the building was pledged as security for the ten-year-term note.

Gilbert realized that the failure to disclose the lien did not affect either the value of the assets or the amount of the liabilities; because her examination was satisfactory in all other respects, Gilbert rendered an unqualified opinion on Grandtime's financial statements. About two months after the date of her opinion, Gilbert learned that an insurance company was planning to loan Grandtime $150,000 in the form of a first-mortgage note on the building. Realizing that the insurance company was unaware of the existing lien on the building, Gilbert had Bradley notify the insurance company of the fact that Grandtime's building was pledged as security for the term note.

Shortly after the events described above, Gilbert was charged with a violation of professional ethics.

Required:

Identify and discuss the ethical implications of those acts by Gilbert that were in violation of the AICPA Code of Professional Ethics.

(AICPA adapted)

C20–3 You have been elected treasurer of your local church. The church board recently adopted a policy whereby emergency financial needs of the members could be met through an emergency benevolence fund. The church's policy is that members may designate special church offerings to be used for meeting the needs of church members who are in dire financial straits. These needs are to be screened by a special committee of which you have been appointed chairperson.

Shortly after that policy was approved, you were approached by the chairman of the church board, who has a son in a seminary supported by your denomination about 100 miles away from your city. The chairman (also the wealthiest and most influential member of the church) told you that he had decided to support his son through the church benevolence fund. His plan is to give an extra $500 per month to the church, designated for his son; and he wants you to direct that the money be so disbursed. He plans to deduct the extra $6,000 given by him to the church as part of charitable contributions on his personal tax return.

Required:

a. Would you accommodate the chairman of the church board?
b. If you decided to accommodate the chairman of the board, which provision of the AICPA's Code of Professional Conduct would you be violating, if any? Does this answer affect your response to question a?

C20–4 Alex Blum, a retired partner of your CPA firm, has just been appointed to the board of directors of Palmore Corporation, your firm's client. Blum is also an ex officio member of your firm's MAS advisory committee, which meets monthly to discuss MAS problems of the partnership's clients, some of which are competitors of Palmore Corporation. Your partnership pays Blum $200 for each advisory committee meeting attended plus a monthly retirement benefit, fixed by a retirement plan policy, of $2,000.

Required:

Discuss the effect of Blum's appointment to the board of directors of Palmore Corporation on the partnership's independence in expressing an opinion on Palmore Corporation's financial statements. Are there other matters of ethics involved in this situation?

(AICPA adapted)

C20–5 An auditor's report was appended to the financial statements of Worthmore, Inc. The statements consisted of a balance sheet as of November 30, 19X8, and statements of income, retained earnings, and changes in financial position for the year then ended. The first two paragraphs of the report contained the wording of the standard unqualified short-form report, and a third paragraph read as follows:

> The wives of two partners of our CPA firm owned a material investment in the outstanding common stock of Worthmore, Inc., during the fiscal year ended November 30, 19X8. These individuals disposed of their holdings on December 3, 19X8 in a transaction that did not result in a profit or a loss. This information is included in our audit report in order to comply with disclosure requirements of the Rules of Conduct of the American Institute of Certified Public Accountants.
>
> *Bell & Davis*
> *Certified Public Accountants*

Required:

a. Was the CPA firm of Bell & Davis independent with respect to the fiscal 19X8 audit of Worthmore, Inc.'s financial statements? Explain.
b. Do you find Bell & Davis's audit report satisfactory? Explain.
c. Assume that no members of Bell & Davis or any members of their families held any financial interests in Worthmore, Inc., during 19X8. For each of the following cases, indicate if independence would be lacking for Bell & Davis, assuming that Worthmore, Inc., is a profit-seeking enterprise. In each case, explain why independence would or would not be lacking.
   (1) Two directors of Worthmore, Inc., became partners in the CPA firm of Bell & Davis on July 1, 19X0, resigning their directorships on that date.
   (2) During 19X8 the former controller of Worthmore, now a Bell & Davis partner, was frequently called on for assistance by Worthmore. He made decisions for Worthmore's management regarding fixed asset acquisitions and the company's product marketing mix. In addition, he conducted a computer feasibility study for Worthmore.

(AICPA adapted)

C20–6 A client, without consulting its CPA, has changed its accounting so that it is not in accordance with generally accepted accounting principles. During the regular audit engagement the CPA discovers that the statements based on the accounts are so grossly misleading that they might be considered fraudulent.

Required:

a. Discuss the action to be taken by the CPA.
b. In this situation what obligation does the CPA have to outsiders if he is replaced? Discuss briefly.
c. In this situation what obligation does the CPA have to a new auditor if he is replaced? Discuss briefly.

(AICPA adapted)

C20–7 The Miller Corporation is indebted to Delores Ruiz, CPA, for unpaid fees and has offered to give her unsecured interest-bearing notes.

Required:

Decide whether the CPA's acceptance of these notes would have any bearing upon her independence in the audit engagement with the Miller Corporation. Would your conclusion be the same if Miller Corporation had offered to give Ruiz 200 shares of its common stock (after which 10,200 shares would be outstanding)? Discuss all facets of these two separate fact situations.

(AICPA adapted)

C20–8 With the approval of its board of directors, the Thames Corporation made a sizable payment for advertising during the year being audited. The corporation deducted the full amount as a business expense in its federal income tax return, but the controller acknowledges that this deduction probably will be disallowed because the advertising relates to political matters. The controller has not provided for this disallowance in his federal income tax provision and refuses to do so because he fears that such a step would cause the revenue agent to believe that the deduction is not valid.

Required:

What is the CPA's responsibility in this situation? Explain with regard to ethical responsibilities, audit responsibilities, and tax practice responsibilities.

(AICPA adapted)

C20–9 Richard Royal recently moved to Center City, Illinois, and joined a local church. Upon learning that Royal was a CPA, the church board elected Royal as church treasurer for the year 19X2. At the same time, the board asked Royal to perform the annual audit of the church for the fiscal year 19X1. Royal has agreed to perform the audit for no fee.

Required:

a. Discuss the ethical implications of Royal's acceptance of the 19X1 audit.
b. Does the fact that Royal would perform the audit for no fee have any bearing on your decision in part **a**?
c. What could Royal do, if anything, that would allow him to accept the church audit engagement within the rules of the AICPA Code of Ethics?

C20–10 Peter Hampden, a third-year member of his firm's audit staff, was debating whether he should continue working as a public accountant. During his college years, he had considered himself to be somewhat of an idealist with a strong sense of public responsibility. Over the last few years, he had increasingly found himself questioning some of the decisions of his superiors on matters which he considered involved ethical issues — the responsibility of the profession to the client and statement users, and "fair" reporting. Hampden realized these issues were difficult

Case 20–10 is by David F. Hawkins, Professor of Business Administration, Harvard University, as published in John C. Burton, ed., *Corporate Financial Reporting: Ethical and Other Problems* (New York: AICPA, 1972).

to resolve — especially those involving concepts of right and wrong as applied to auditor behavior. He also recognized that his ethical standards were changing as he grew older and that he "did not have all the answers." Therefore, before he reached his career decision, he sought the opinion of a second person.

Hampden spoke to the firm's senior partner about his problem. The partner said that Hampden's seniors had rated him "excellent and definite partner material if he continued to develop in the future as he had in the past." The senior partner was also sympathetic to Hampden's concern and suggested they spend some time together during the following week discussing it.

To facilitate their planned discussion, the senior partner suggested Hampden prepare for him thumbnail descriptions of some of the situations involving financial reporting that had troubled him over the last few years. The senior partner also suggested that Hampden outline the "ethically correct" action he would have taken if he had been the partner in charge. The following is a copy of the material Hampden submitted to his senior partner.

a. ***Disclosure of Anticipated Accounting Change.*** A client company had invited the partner in charge of their audit to discuss with their president some decisions made at a board of directors meeting at which the preliminary third quarter results and the accounting principles policies to be followed in the annual report were discussed. The publication of the third quarter results was to follow this meeting with the president. The audit partner had brought me to this meeting to expand my knowledge of how to maintain effective top management – audit relations.

At its meeting the board had decided to find out "if it is feasible" to change the depreciation accounting policy followed in their annual report to stockholders. It was anticipated that this change, if made, would permit the company to show improved earnings per share over the previous year's results. If the old depreciation policy were followed, the company would most likely show a decline in earnings.

The board had asked the president to request their auditor to review the company's accounting department's proposed adjustments to the asset accounts. Also, the president indicated that before the annual report was submitted to stockholders other accounting principle changes might be necessary "in order to put the company's accounting on a more realistic basis." If these changes were made, the president planned to discuss them with the company's auditors.

Comment. In my opinion, the auditor should have insisted that the company indicate in its third quarter report to stockholders that they were contemplating a change in accounting practices. None of the directors apparently thought this was necessary, and neither did the audit partner.

b. ***Disclosure of Tax Status of Lease Transaction.*** Our company had been requested to help a client draw up some sale and leaseback agreements that would qualify for tax and financial reporting purposes as leases and not as conditional sales. Subsequently, at the insistence of the Internal Revenue Service, the agreements were treated for tax purposes as conditional sales. The client was very disturbed by this ruling, but on the advice of the company counsel decided not to challenge it. This lawyer, who had replaced the company counsel involved in the original transaction, described the sale and lease agreement as "a classic example of the type of lease agreement involving nominal purchase options used to teach law students how not to try and fool the tax authorities."

After making his tax decision, the client discussed the financial reporting implications of the decision with the partner in charge of the audit. In the process of this discussion, the client indicated that he was very upset at the "poor advice" given by his auditors and that he preferred to continue treating the sale and leaseback as a lease for financial reporting purposes. If the lease were capitalized, the company's long-term liabilities would have increased about 17 percent.

The partner in charge of the audit later agreed with the client's treatment of the transaction as a lease. In his opinion, since the agreement had been drawn up prior to the most recent accounting pronouncement on leases, the provisions of the pronouncement did not apply. No mention of the agreement's tax status was indicated in the footnotes to the annual statements.

Comment. In my opinion, at least the lease's tax status should have been disclosed; preferably, the lease should have been capitalized. Not taking either of these actions leaves the auditor open to the criticism of (1) trying to cover up his earlier poor advice and (2) being biased in his opinion of what constitutes a full and fair presentation of financial data.

The economic substance of the lease transaction was equivalent to a sale under accounting principles. The legal and tax authorities used the same criteria as stated in accounting principles to make their decision. These criteria are similar to those presented in tax guides to distinguish between genuine leases and conditional sales disguised as leases.

c. ***Responsibility for Disclosing Control and Reporting Deficiencies.*** The founder – president of a client company raised $20 million through a public stock sale for his new company to develop, manufacture, market, and lease on a cancelable basis at an unusually low monthly rental price a revolutionary photo-copying system. To date, no major company had been able to develop the technology and production capability needed to make this kind of equipment at the low rental levels proposed by the client company. At the time of the public offering, the client company also had not developed the needed technology or production capability.

Soon after the public issue the stock's price soared to four times its offering price of $12.50. This upward movement was accompanied by optimistic articles in the financial and trade press on the company's prospects for success.

Shortly after these funds were raised, I attended a public seminar during which the client company's president discussed his technique for raising venture capital. He said:

> Raising money is very much like running for office. You have to put a campaign together. . . . The business plan you prepare must be a lie . . . but it must be a detailed and precise lie rather than a vague and general lie. . . . If you promise enough risk, loss, and catastrophe, the financier will begin to wonder whether you're hiding something from him. . . . Go public as fast as you can.

Subsequently, the company went into bankruptcy, losing some $18 million on sales of $700,000. The principal causes for failure were poor control over production costs and a decision to sell rather than lease its equipment. This decision led to the cancellation of a number of letters of intent to purchase.

Comment. In cases such as these, is it acceptable by the public's standards for the auditor simply to comment on the fairness of the financial statements and their adherence to generally accepted accounting principles? Whose standards of conduct should prevail? Those of the AICPA or some other? Who is responsible for telling the public about the poor control over production costs and the cancellation of the letters of intent? Indeed, should the public be told at all?

I have no answer to this kind of problem beyond saying that it is management's responsibility to disclose unfavorable information. If they will not, the auditor should use all of his power to see that they do. Yet, is this his function?

d. ***Responsibility of the Financial Press.*** In order to reflect better a change in their business, a client company changed from accelerated to straight-line depreciation and started capitalizing certain product development expenses. We agreed with the client that these changes were desirable.

Subsequently, a prominent financial writer used this accounting change as a perfect example of how companies change their accounting methods to boost earnings. The writer failed to mention any of the reasons presented by management in their annual report for the change in accounting.

Comment. As an individual auditor, I suspect that I cannot do much to impose more responsible standards on the press; yet, this kind of reporting disturbs me. What can be done about it? Can I as an individual auditor do anything?

e. ***Responsibilities of Financial Analysts.*** Incidentally, while I am raising questions about the way financial reporters discuss our client's financial report, I would like to discuss the implications for me as an auditor of this kind of reporting of our client's situation:

> The 10 percent stock dividend recently announced by ______ makes ______ an attractive investment at current prices.
>
> If you have not got ______ in your portfolio, now would be an appropriate time to make a purchase at the current depressed levels.
>
> At present, the company is making huge capital investments, and one can expect a return within the next two or three years. Investors should not worry about the auditors qualifying ______'s recent record profits by $1.4 million. It is only an accountant's wrangle.
>
> In any case, look at provisions in the income statement for depreciation which is up from $10.0 million to $12.5 million this year. Such a provision is no more than a way of creating reserves out of profits.

This company's earnings for the current year were about the same as the prior year. We disagreed with the company's deferred tax accounting practices. They refused to apply comprehensive tax allocation to some mining expenditures that they capitalized for book purposes but wrote off on their tax return as incurred. The stock is traded over-the-counter.

Comment. Why should auditors struggle to determine what are "fair" reporting practices while this kind of reporting persists?

Required:

If you were the senior partner, how would you respond to the cases presented to you by Hampden? Do these involve ethical issues? Accounting principle issues? Audit judgment issues? Is it desirable that the auditor behave in the manner suggested by Hampden in situations **a** and **b** above?

PROBLEMS

P20–1 Select the best answer to the following items relating to the AICPA Code of Ethics.

a. A CPA in public practice is permitted to make an offer of employment to an employee of another public accountant if the CPA
(1) Makes the offer on behalf of an audit client.
(2) Has an executive search staff that is involved in personnel placement.
(3) Informs the other public accountant prior to making the offer.
(4) Makes the offer verbally to an employee who is *not* a CPA.

b. Which of the following statements best describes why the profession of certified public accountants has deemed it essential to promulgate a code of ethics and to establish a mechanism for enforcing observance of the code:
(1) A distinguishing mark of a profession is its acceptance of responsibility to the public.
(2) A prerequisite to success is the establishment of an ethical code that stresses primarily the professional's responsibility to clients and colleagues.
(3) A requirement of most state laws calls for the profession to establish a code of ethics.
(4) An essential means of self-protection for the profession is the establishment of flexible ethical standards by the profession.

c. A CPA accepts an engagement for a professional service *without* violating the AICPA Code of Professional Ethics if the service involves
(1) The preparation of cost projections for submission to a governmental agency as an application for a rate increase, and the fee will be paid if there is a rate increase.
(2) Tax preparation, and the fee will be based on whether the CPA signs the tax return prepared.
(3) A litigatory matter, and the fee is *not* known but is to be determined by a district court.
(4) Tax return preparation, and the fee is to be based on the amount of taxes saved, if any.

d. The AICPA Code of Professional Ethics requires compliance with accounting principles promulgated by the body designated by AICPA Council to establish such principles. The pronouncements comprehended by the code include all of the following *except*
(1) Opinions issued by the Accounting Principles Board.
(2) AICPA Accounting Research Studies.
(3) Interpretations issued by the Financial Accounting Standards Board.
(4) AICPA Accounting Research Bulletins.

e. The AICPA Code of Professional Ethics recognizes that the reliance of the public, the government, and the business community on sound financial reporting imposes particular obligations on CPAs. The code derives its authority from
(1) Public laws enacted over the years.
(2) General acceptance of the code by the business community.
(3) Requirements of governmental regulatory agencies, such as the Securities and Exchange Commission.
(4) Bylaws of the American Institute of Certified Public Accountants.

f. Judith Green, a CPA not in public practice, is an employee in the internal audit department of Bigg Conglomerate Company. The management has asked Green to perform examinations of potential acquisitions and to express an opinion thereon. Bigg will use the reports for internal purposes and to show to its bankers in accordance with certain loan agreements. Your response to items **g** and **h** should be based on the AICPA Code of Professional Ethics.

How should Green sign the report?

(1) Judith Green, CPA.
(2) Judith Green, Internal Auditor.
(3) Judith Green, CPA (Internal Auditor).
(4) Judith Green, Internal Auditor (CPA).

g. If in the situation described in the preceding problem, Green performed the same examination as would have been done by the outside auditors, what difference should there be in the opinion Green would render?

(1) None.
(2) Green should not refer to generally accepted auditing standards.
(3) Green should qualify her opinion on the basis of lack of independence.
(4) Green should disclaim an opinion on the basis of lack of independence.

h. A CPA's retention of client records as a means of enforcing payment of an overdue audit fee is an action that is

(1) Considered acceptable by the AICPA Code of Professional Ethics.
(2) Ill advised since it would impair the CPA's independence with respect to the client.
(3) Considered discreditable to the profession.
(4) A violation of generally accepted auditing standards.

i. An auditor should *not* render a report on

(1) The achievability of forecasts.
(2) Client internal control.
(3) Management performance.
(4) Quarterly financial information.

j. Upon discovering irregularities in a client's tax return that the client refused to correct, a CPA withdraws from the engagement. How should the CPA respond if asked by the successor CPA why the relationship was terminated?

(1) "It was a misunderstanding."
(2) "I suggest you get the client's permission for us to discuss all matters freely."
(3) "I suggest you ask the client."
(4) "I found irregularities in the tax return which the client would not correct."

k. Which of the following actions should be avoided by a CPA?

(1) A CPA who is in public practice agrees to be the committee chairperson for a local fund-raising activity.
(2) A CPA who is an officer of a local bank arranges a loan for another CPA, who is in public practice.
(3) A CPA who is in public practice prepares a tax return for a friend without a fee and does *not* sign the return.
(4) A CPA who is retired from public practice accepts a finder's fee from a public relations company for introducing a former client to that firm.

l. A CPA who has given correct tax advice which is later affected by changes in the tax law is *required* to

(1) Notify the client upon learning of any change.
(2) Notify the client only when the CPA is actively assisting with implementing the advice or is obliged to so notify by specific agreement.
(3) Notify the Internal Revenue Service.

(4) Take no action if the client has already followed the advice unless the client asks the question again.

m. Mario Cella, CPA, is succeeding Bill Tyrone, CPA, on the audit engagement of Genesis Corporation. Cella plans to consult Tyrone and to review Tyrone's prior-year working papers. Cella may do so if

(1) Tyrone and Genesis consent.
(2) Tyrone consents.
(3) Genesis consents.
(4) Tyrone and Cella consent.

n. According to the AICPA rules of conduct, contingent fees are permitted by CPAs engaged in tax practice because

(1) This practice establishes fees commensurate with the value of the services.
(2) Attorneys in tax practice customarily set contingent fees.
(3) Determinations by taxing authorities are a matter of judicial proceedings which do not involve third parties.
(4) The consequences are based on findings of judicial proceedings or the findings of tax authorities.

o. With respect to records in a CPA's possession, rules of conduct provide that

(1) Copies of client records incorporated into audit workpapers must be returned to the client on request.
(2) Worksheets in lieu of a general ledger belong to the auditor and need *not* be furnished to the client on request.
(3) An extensive analysis of inventory prepared by the client at the auditor's request are workpapers that belong to the auditor and need *not* be furnished to the client on request.
(4) The auditor who returns copies of client records, must return the original records on request.

(AICPA adapted)

P20–2 Select the best answer for each of the following items relating to the maintenance of objectivity and integrity in performing an audit.

a. The AICPA Code of Professional Ethics states, in part, that a CPA should maintain integrity and objectivity. Objectivity in the code refers to a CPA's ability

(1) To maintain an impartial attitude on all matters that come under the CPA's review.
(2) To distinguish independently between accounting practices that are acceptable and those that are *not*.
(3) To be unyielding in all matters dealing with auditing procedures.
(4) To choose independently between alternate accounting principles and auditing standards.

b. Renée Richard, CPA, performs accounting services for Norton Corporation. Norton wishes to offer its shares to the public and asks Richard to audit the financial statements prepared for registration purposes. Richard refers Norton to Carmen Cruz, CPA, who is more competent in the area of registration statements. Cruz performs the audit of Norton's financial statements and subsequently thanks Richard for the referral by giving Richard a portion of the audit fee collected. Richard accepts the fee. Who, if anyone, has violated professional ethics?

(1) Only Richard.
(2) Both Richard and Cruz.
(3) Only Cruz.
(4) Neither Richard nor Cruz.

c. A CPA examines the financial statements of a local bank. According to the AICPA Code of Professional Ethics, the appearance of independence ordinarily would *not* be impaired if the CPA
(1) Serves on the bank's committee that approves loans.
(2) Owns several shares of the bank's common stock.
(3) Obtains a short-term loan from the bank.
(4) Uses the bank's time-sharing computer service to solve client-related problems.

d. During the course of an audit, the client's controller asks your advice on how to revise the purchase journal so as to reduce the amount of time his staff takes in posting. How should you respond?
(1) Explain that under the AICPA Code of Professional Ethics you cannot give advice on management advisory service areas at the same time you are doing an audit.
(2) Explain that under the AICPA Statement on Management Advisory Services informal advice of this type is prohibited.
(3) Respond with definite recommendations based on your audit of these records but state that you will not assume any responsibility for any changes unless your specific recommendations are followed.
(4) Respond as practicable at the moment and express the basis for your response so it will be accepted for what it is.

(AICPA adapted)

P20–3 Select the best answer to each of the following items relating to publicizing and promoting an accounting practice.

a. Inclusion of which of the following in a promotional brochure published by a CPA firm would be most likely to result in a violation of the AICPA rules of conduct?
(1) Names and addresses, telephone numbers, number of partners, office hours, foreign language competence, and date the firm was established.
(2) Services offered and fees for such services, including hourly rates and fixed fees.
(3) Educational and professional attainments, including date and place of certification, schools attended, dates of graduation, degrees received, and memberships in professional associations.
(4) Names, addresses and telephone numbers of the firm's clients, including the number of years served.

b. Below are the names of four CPA firms and pertinent facts relating to each firm. Unless otherwise indicated, the individuals named are CPAs and partners, and there are no other partners. Which firm name and related facts indicate a violation of the AICPA Code of Professional Ethics?
(1) Arthur, Barry, and Clark, CPAs (Clark died about five years ago; Arthur and Barry are continuing the firm).
(2) Davis and Edwards, CPAs (the name of Fredricks, CPA, a third active partner, is omitted from the firm name).

(3) Jones & Co., CPAs, P.C. (the firm is a professional corporation and has ten other stockholders who are all CPAs).
(4) George and Howard, CPAs (Howard died three years ago; George is continuing the firm as a sole proprietorship).

c. Abrams and Barrow, CPAs, are partners in a public accounting firm that has a large tax practice. Abrams is a member of the AICPA. Which of the following is the best firm name?
(1) Abrams & Barrow, members AICPA.
(2) Abrams & Barrow, Tax Accountants.
(3) Abrams & Barrow, P.C. (Professional Corporation).
(4) Abrams & Barrow, Certified Public Accountants.

d. Under the AICPA Code of Professional Ethics, a CPA is prohibited from performing which of the following actions?
(1) Expressing an opinion on whether a financial forecast can be achieved.
(2) Permitting the CPA's college alumni magazine to report that the CPA has opened offices as "an accountant."
(3) Making a direct uninvited solicitation of a specific potential client.
(4) Assisting a client in preparing forecasts of the results of future transactions and events.

e. A CPA who is a member of the American Institute of Certified Public Accountants wrote an article for publication in a professional journal. The AICPA Code of Professional Ethics would be violated if the CPA allowed the article to state that the CPA was
(1) A member of the American Institute of Certified Public Accountants.
(2) A professor at a school of professional accountancy.
(3) A partner in a national CPA firm.
(4) A practitioner specialized in providing tax services.

f. Which of the following is prohibited by the AICPA Code of Professional Ethics?
(1) Use of a firm name which indicates specialization.
(2) Practice of public accounting in the form of a professional corporation.
(3) Use of the partnership name for a limited period by one of the partners in a public accounting firm after the death or withdrawal of all other partners.
(4) Holding as an investment 10 of 1,000 outstanding shares in a commercial corporation which performs bookkeeping services.

(AICPA adapted)

P20–4 Select the best answer to each of the following items relating to maintenance of confidence and fees charged for accounting services.

a. The AICPA Code of Professional Ethics states that a CPA shall not disclose any confidential information obtained in the course of a professional engagement except with the consent of the client. This rule should be understood to preclude a CPA from responding to an inquiry made by
(1) The trial board of the AICPA.
(2) An investigative body of a state CPA society.
(3) A CPA-shareholder of the client corporation.
(4) An AICPA voluntary quality review body.

b. The AICPA Code of Professional Ethics states that a CPA shall *not* disclose any confidential information obtained in the course of a professional engagment except with the consent of his client. In which one of the situations given below would disclosure by a CPA be in violation of the Code?

(1) Disclosing confidential information in order to properly discharge the CPA's responsibilities in accordance with his profession's standards.
(2) Disclosing confidential information in compliance with a subpoena issued by a court.
(3) Disclosing confidential information to another accountant interested in purchasing the CPA's practice.
(4) Disclosing confidential information in a review of the CPA's professional practice by the AICPA Quality Review Committee.

c. In which of the following circumstances would a CPA be bound by ethics to refrain from disclosing any confidential information obtained during the course of a professional engagement?
(1) The CPA is issued a summons enforceable by a court order which orders the CPA to present confidential information.
(2) A major stockholder of a client company seeks accounting information from the CPA after management declined to disclose the requested information.
(3) Confidential client information is made available as part of a quality review of the CPA's practice by a review team authorized by the AICPA.
(4) An inquiry by a disciplinary body of a state CPA society requests confidential client information.

d. In which one of the following situations would a CPA be in violation of the AICPA Code of Professional Ethics in determining his fee?
(1) A fee based on whether the CPA's report on the client's financial statements results in the approval of a bank loan.
(2) A fee based on the outcome of a bankruptcy proceeding.
(3) A fee based on the nature of the service rendered and the CPA's particular expertise instead of the actual time spent on the engagement.
(4) A fee based on the fee charged by the prior auditor.

e. The AICPA Code of Professional Ethics would be violated if a CPA accepted a fee for services and the fee was
(1) Fixed by a public authority.
(2) Based on a price quotation submitted in competitive bidding.
(3) Determined, based on the results of judicial proceedings.
(4) Payable after a specified finding was attained.

(AICPA adapted)

P20–5 Select the best answer for each of the following items relating to maintenance of quality controls for an accounting firm.

a. In pursuing its quality control objectives with respect to acceptance of a client, a CPA firm is *not* likely to
(1) Make inquiries of the proposed client's legal counsel.
(2) Review financial statements of the proposed client.
(3) Make inquiries of previous auditors.
(4) Review the personnel practices of the proposed client.

b. In pursuing its quality control objectives with respect to assigning personnel to engagements, a firm of independent auditors may use policies and procedures such as

(1) Designating senior qualified personnel to provide advice on accounting or auditing questions throughout the engagement.
(2) Requiring timely identification of the staffing requirements of specific engagements so that enough qualified personnel can be made available.
(3) Establishing at entry levels a policy for recruiting that includes minimum standards of academic preparation and accomplishment.
(4) Requiring auditing personnel to have current accounting and auditing literature available for research and reference purposes throughout the engagement.

c. A basic objective of a CPA firm is to provide professional services to conform with professional standards. Reasonable assurance of achieving this basic objective is provided through
(1) Continuing professional education.
(2) A system of quality control.
(3) Compliance with generally accepted reporting standards.
(4) A system of peer review.

d. A CPA establishes quality control policies and procedures for deciding whether to accept a new client or continue to perform services for a current client. The primary purpose for establishing such policies and procedures is
(1) To enable the auditor to attest to the integrity or reliability of a client.
(2) To comply with the quality control standards established by regulatory bodies.
(3) To minimize the likelihood of association with clients whose managements lack integrity.
(4) To lessen the exposure to litigation resulting from failure to detect irregularities in client financial statements.

e. Which of the following is *not* an element of quality control that should be considered by a firm of independent auditors?
(1) Assigning personnel to engagements.
(2) Consultation with appropriate persons.
(3) Keeping records of quality control policies and procedures.
(4) Supervision.

f. In order to achieve effective quality control, a firm of independent auditors should establish policies and procedures for
(1) Determining the minimum procedures necessary for unaudited financial statements.
(2) Setting the scope of audit work.
(3) Deciding whether to accept or continue a client.
(4) Setting the scope of internal control study and evaluation.

(AICPA adapted)

P20–6 Which of the following actions, if any, would constitute a violation of the AICPA's Code of Professional Ethics with respect to advertising and solicitation. Explain your opinion for each case.

a. A CPA moves office locations and advertises the new address and telephone number in the local press.
b. A CPA publishes a monthly newsletter on financial management. The CPA firm's name is featured prominently on the front of the newsletter.

c. A CPA's client proposes to use public advertising to assure readers that his published financial facts regarding products sold are genuine. The CPA's name would be associated with the advertisement.
d. A CPA was associated with a nonaccounting partnership specializing in work relating to tax-free mergers and acquisitions. The firm advertises its expertise in handling mergers and acquisitions, both in media advertisements and on the firm's letterhead.
e. The CPA places his name and address in the yellow pages of the telephone book enclosed in a box, with the firm's logo included, and the name and telephone number in boldface type.
f. A CPA places an advertisement in the local newspaper stating his name, address, telephone number, fees for various services, and expertise in farm and ranch taxation.

P20–7 Which, if any, of the following might constitute incompatible occupations prohibited under Rule 504? Explain your answers.

a. Operation of the separate practices of actuarial services and public accounting.
b. Serving as an officer or director of a consumer credit company while practicing public accounting.
c. Serving as state comptroller while practicing public accounting.
d. Engaging in the concurrent practices of law and public accounting.
e. Engaging in the concurrent practices of public accounting and life, fire, and casualty insurance sales.
f. Forming a bookkeeping services partnership with a non-CPA.
g. Forming a tax consulting partnership with an attorney who is not a CPA.

P20–8 Janice Utmore, CPA, is approached by a prospective tax client who promises to pay Utmore "10 percent of the amount you save me in taxes from my own computation."

a. May Utmore accept the engagement on this basis?
b. Under what circumstances could Utmore have accepted the engagement for a percentage-based fee?
c. What should be the general basis for a CPA's fees under the AICPA Code of Professional Conduct?

P20–9 Each of the following cases involves possible violations of the AICPA's Code of Professional Ethics. For each situation, state whether a violation of the code has occurred and why.

a. Rudolph Ross, CPA, provides bookkeeping, tax, and auditing for one of their clients. Since Ross's firm is small, one person typically performs all of the above services.
b. Jack Pritchett, CPA, was convicted of possession of marijuana, after two marijuana cigarettes were found on his person during a raid of a local discotheque and bar.
c. Donna Eberhart, CPA, is presently employed by C. P. Smart & Co. CPAs, and seeks employment with Goode & Co. CPAs. Ms. Eberhart informs Goode & Co. that she works for another firm in the same locale but refuses to allow them to contact Smart. Goode and Co. hire Eberhart without notifying Smart.

d. Margaret Teitelbaum, CPA, belongs to Ridgecrest Country Club, membership in which involves the acquisition of a pro rata share of equity or debt securities. The club asks Teitelbaum to perform its annual audit and she accepts the engagement.

e. A brother of John Sealy, CPA, is a stockholder and one of four vice-presidents of a closely held corporation which is located in the same city as Sealy's public accounting practice. The company asks Sealy to perform the annual audit and Sealy accepts.

f. Same as **e** except that the corporation is in a city 3,000 miles away from Sealy's practice.

g. Maria Leipold, CPA, has a client Alpha Corporation, which has been unable to meet its current obligations due to severely depressed economic conditions. The corporation owes Leipold $5,200 in unpaid audit fees from the previous year. They persuade her to perform their current audit, after giving her a promissory note for her unpaid fees.

h. Arthur Anderby Co. engages in "executive search" for a client, which involves recruiting and hiring a company controller.

i. Jack Thorp, a CPA in public practice, wishes to also be a representative of a computer tax service. The computer organization provides services only to tax practitioners. Thorp uses his professional contacts to introduce possible clients to the computer service.

j. Morgan and Sons, CPAs, designates itself on its letterhead as "Members of the American Institute of Certified Public Accountants." Morgan is a member of the AICPA, but neither of his sons is a member.

CHAPTER

21 ACCOUNTANTS' LEGAL LIABILITY

In preceding chapters we have examined the profession of auditing and the relationships of the independent auditor to the various groups using the results of the audit. We developed and discussed the conceptual framework within which an audit is performed. From those sources it became clear that the independent auditor, even though engaged by the company whose records are being audited, has responsibilities to various third-party users as well as to the client. In performing independent auditing services, the auditor becomes responsible to both the client and third parties. A part of the benefits associated with an audit, therefore, springs from the liability the auditor takes for appropriately discharging those responsibilities through the attest function.

In this chapter we describe and analyze the auditor's legal liability, both to the client and to third-party users of audited data. Our discussion will cover the following topics:

1. The litigious nature of the present-day auditing environment.
2. Possible civil liability of auditors.
3. Possible criminal liability of auditors.
4. The profession's response to the perils of a litigious age.

The appendix to the chapter contains summaries of key court cases that illustrate the application of the legal concepts covered in the chapter.

As we move through this chapter, it is important to recognize not only the current legal implications associated with the independent auditor's work, but also the ways in which legal actions against accountants have influenced the profession.

THE PRESENT-DAY AUDITING ENVIRONMENT

Prior to the 1920s, the auditor had little responsibility to anyone other than the client. As a result of that fact, plus the general inclination of the public to rely less on legal action at that time, we find only a minimal number of lawsuits lodged against auditors during those years. However, with the development of the attest function throughout the past 60 years and the resultant establishment of legal liability to third parties, we have seen an increased incidence of legal actions against public accounting firms, particularly during the past two decades. The recent increase has been, to some extent, caused by changes in general attitudes: people have come to rely more heavily on legal action in *all* types of controversies.

We begin our coverage of legal liability by analyzing the current environment in which the independent auditor operates. We accomplish this by the following steps:

1. Identifying pertinent legal terminology.
2. Observing the present-day litigious climate in which auditors work.
3. Examining some of the more important reasons for present-day litigation relating to public accounting.
4. Discussing the provisions of the Foreign Corrupt Practices Act of 1977.
5. Tracing the impact of certain legal actions to their effects on accounting and auditing practices.
6. Recognizing the relationship between related party transactions and legal liability.

Pertinent Legal Terminology

The liability for violating the numerous statutes enacted to protect the investing public may be either civil or criminal. Although it is difficult to draw a precise distinction between these two types of liability, ***criminal liability*** occurs when an act, considered to be a wrong against society, is committed. As a result of such violations, the offender can be fined or imprisoned, or both. On the other hand, ***civil liability*** involves a violation of the rights of some specific party, such as the client or a third party. The penalty for a civil offense will be payment of damages. It is also important to observe that some conduct can expose the accountant to both civil and criminal liability. We elaborate on each of these terms later in the chapter.

The term ***negligence*** describes the failure to exercise the degree of care which a reasonable person would exercise under similar circumstances. The auditor is expected to exercise reasonable care in performing an audit. The ***standard of reasonable care*** for accountants is measured by the level of quality, accuracy, and completeness expected of the average accountant. Honest inaccuracies and errors of judgment do not give rise to liability for negligence so long as it can be shown that the accountant has exercised reasonable care. Negligence as a cause of liability is subdivided into ***ordinary negligence*** and ***gross negligence.*** The first of these is characterized as a *lack of reasonable care* in the performance of professional accounting tasks. Gross negligence, on the other hand, is characterized as the *lack of even minimum care* in performing professional duties, thereby indicating "reckless disregard for duty and responsibility."[1] This type of negligence can lead to a charge of constructive fraud.

Fraud is defined as an intentional act of deceit, or scienter [sī′entə(r)], designed to obtain an unjust advantage that results in injury to the rights or interests of another. ***Constructive fraud,*** however, can occur with proof of gross negligence, without a conscious intent to deceive.

Privity of contract is a legal term that defines the contractual relationship between two parties. In auditing contracts, usually made formal by the engagement letter, the parties generally possessing privity of contract are the auditor and the *client* (who, in most cases, are the persons to whom the audit report is addressed). It is important under common law to establish privity because clients who have privity of contract have certain rights of recovery against auditors which third parties do not have.

The auditor's defense in most lawsuits involves convincing the court of his or her ***due diligence*** — that is, adherence to generally accepted auditing standards (GAAS) and generally accepted accounting principles (GAAP) in performing the audit. In this phase of the defense, the attorney for the auditor will often seek ***expert testimony*** — which is generally the testimony of another CPA as to whether, in that witness's opinion, the auditor has adhered to GAAS/GAAP. In such cases three types of questions are likely to arise: ***questions of the facts*** in the situation, the ***question of the law*** governing the situation, and ***questions involving a mixture of fact and law.***[2] The expert witness can be particularly helpful in interpreting questions of fact — such as whether or not the accounting or auditing criteria have been met. It is also important to observe at this point that the Securities and Exchange Commission and the courts may impose higher standards of performance than those implied by adherence to GAAP and GAAS. Therefore expert testimony is not necessarily binding in cases involving possible violations of Securities and Exchange Commission regulations.

Civil liability cases generally involve contractual or intentional tort of fraud violations. Violations of contractual arrangements may be either expressed or implied. ***Expressed contractual violations*** occur when one of the parties to a contract fails to carry out his or her responsibilities as stated in the contract. ***Implied contractual violations,*** however, can occur when there was a failure on the part of one party to meet the obligations implied by his or her *relationship* to the activities being performed.

Intentional tort of fraud violations involve intentional injury or wrong to another party. As they relate to auditing, they require proof of the following allegations for damages to be assessed:

- It must be shown that the action was committed with *intention to mislead the users* of the data.
- There must be a *false representation* or *concealment.*
- The plaintiff must show that *he or she relied on the false statements.*
- It must be shown that the *plaintiff was injured as a consequence of reliance on the audited statements.*[3]

The burden of proof for various allegations can fall on the plaintiff (client or third party) or the auditor, depending on whether the suit is brought under common law or statutory (SEC) law, as explained later in the chapter.

Another term that has become important in recent legal actions is the ***class action lawsuit:*** this involves collective actions where the plaintiff represents a class of persons similarly situated. For example, one stockholder, suing for damages on the basis of false information included in the financial statements, may, under proper conditions, file the suit as a class action suit on behalf of all of the stockholders. The verdict in the case then would apply to all stockholders included in the class action.

Litigious Climate for Auditors

The environment in which auditors operate today is a highly litigious one. The profession has to be concerned with the number of civil suits, criminal suits, and the SEC injunctive and enforcement proceedings that have been lodged against public accountants during the 1970s. Without question, the auditor today faces risks of legal liability unknown to the public practitioner some thirty or forty years ago. Not only have more lawsuits been filed but we also have seen the courts taking a stronger position on criminal cases filed against public accountants than was the case some years ago. Furthermore, recent court cases suggest that the *definition of fairness* of presentation of the financial statements (explained in Chapter 2) is broadening to the point where courts may interpret it not to be constrained by the standard of generally accepted accounting principles (GAAP). The *Continental Vending* case in Appendix 21–A shows a good example of that trend.

The increasingly litigious nature of the environment in which accountants now operate has developed partially as a result of business failures occurring during periodic economic recessions since the late 60s. In difficult economic times it is often convenient for third parties to seek damages from the public accounting firm that audited the financial statements prior to the failures. An examination of such failures, however, discloses that many of them were caused by well-executed management fraud or poor management. Unfortunately, however, in many cases the auditing firm had *failed to exhibit an appropriate degree of objectivity or an appropriately skeptical attitude* in its examination of the financial statements. Auditors often have been *too willing to conform to the wishes of management* in the presentation of financial statements.

Recent lawsuits against auditors have involved both civil and criminal cases. They have been initiated by both clients and third parties. Suits lodged on behalf of clients have generally been based either on a ***breach of contract*** or on a ***tort action for negligence.*** The first type of case contends an alleged failure to carry out the duties created by mutual agreement of the parties involved. A tort liability on the other hand, is based on failure to carry out duties implied by the code of conduct governing the activities of accountants. Those actions are therefore closely associated with the accountants' code of ethics and GAAS. Lawsuits by clients, for example, can allege such things as ***violation of confidence*** or ***negligence associated with a failure to detect fraud.*** The first of these is a violation of the behavior expected of the accountant under the AICPA Code of Ethics. The second violates the due professional care auditing standard. It is important to observe that accountants have been held liable for damages to the client in connection *with both audited and unaudited* financial statements.

Third-party lawsuits generally seek recovery of losses alleged to have been suffered because of reliance on audited financial data. The auditor has no contract with those parties. However, as we have said before, one of the important values associated with the auditor's work is third-party reliance on the results of that work. The first case involving third-party recovery of damages in a lawsuit was the *Ultramares* v. *Touche* case.[4] It was associated with an audit performed in 1923. In that case a third-party creditor (Ultramares) sued the auditors for both negligence and fraud. The charge of negligence was ultimately disallowed because Ultramares, the plaintiff, did not have a contract with Touche. The court, however, refused to disallow the charge of fraud. At that point the case was settled out of court. The court held that Ultramares (a third party factoring company) could not recover on the basis of ordinary negligence but would have to prove gross negligence. The court continued, however, by saying that had Ultramares been named in the contract, it would have been a third-party beneficiary and would have enjoyed the same privilege of recovery as would the client. Since the *Ultramares* decision, the courts have liberalized the definition of a ***third-party beneficiary*** to include parties reasonably foreseen to be relying on the audited data. During this time we have also seen the conduct standard creating liability to third parties move from fraud toward ordinary negligence.

The *CIT Financial* case in 1955 held the accountants liable for ordinary negligence when the third-party plaintiff was the *primary beneficiary of the audit report.* More recently, however, in two cases — *Rusch Factors* (1968) and *Shatterproof Glass* (1971) — the courts held the accountant liable for ordinary negligence because they concluded that he should have foreseen the class of user and the transaction involved in the suit.

These cases and others since 1971 show that public accountants must recognize that a primary function of audits is to supply information to persons who are not clients and that they can be legally liable for failure to discharge that function appropriately. They can be held liable to third parties for gross negligence under a *common law action of deceit.* However, where the auditor's work is primarily for the benefit of an identified third party (third-party beneficiary), he or she can also be held *liable for ordinary negligence where lack of reasonable care can be shown.*[5] This trend toward holding public accountants liable for ordinary negligence could well extend to third parties suffering a loss where the accountant can be reasonably expected to foresee their dependence on the audited data.

The litigious climate and the increasing number of lawsuits facing auditors in recent years is of obvious concern to the auditing profession. It is important, however, to recognize that deviations from the ordinary, such as audits resulting in lawsuits, receive much more attention than the thousands of "clean" audits performed regularly by public accounting firms. We must also be aware that the number of independent audits being performed is expanding rapidly; so, by virtue of that fact alone, we should expect to have more lawsuits against the profession. Also, in the final analysis, we can see the litigious climate and the increased volume of lawsuits as vehicles through which the full responsibilities of the accounting profession can be more fully recognized.

Other Reasons for Litigation Against Accountants

We have already mentioned business recessions as one cause of the increased number of lawsuits being filed against accountants. The merger and acquisition movement, so evident in the sixties and early seventies, was probably another contributing factor.

Some conglomerates, for example, were created to take advantage of weaknesses in GAAP which would permit them to show improvement in the combined financial picture (such as earnings per share) without there being a real improvement in those characteristics due to operations.

There is some evidence to support the contention that the accounting profession was forced to expand rapidly during the decade of the sixties, and perhaps, as a result of that, was not fully prepared to meet its responsibilities to third parties. Ironically there may also have been a failure on the part of the accounting profession to realize the importance (as perceived by the general public) of the auditing services it had been rendering. Failure to recognize that fact could well have been a reason for assigning inappropriately prepared personnel to some audit engagements. As an example, see the *Bar Chris Construction* case in Appendix 21–A.

As a final observation we should recognize that the failure of the accounting profession to insist on more uniformity of generally accepted accounting principles in similar alternate situations was another important underlying cause of many of the lawsuits filed during that period. Cases such as the *Continental Vending* and *Bar Chris Construction* cases provide support for this contention.

Foreign Corrupt Practices Act

In 1977 a new dimension was added to the independent audit with the origination of the Foreign Corrupt Practices Act. This statute was an outgrowth of a campaign by the Securities and Exchange Commission to *prohibit payments involving the bribery of foreign officials by U. S. companies*. The Act establishes criminal penalties for offending corporations and corporate personnel. It also requires that corporations develop internal control procedures directed toward preventing such payments.

In reaction, partially, to the Foreign Corrupt Practices Act, the accounting profession adopted Statements on Auditing Standards (SAS) 16 and 17, entitled "The Independent Auditor's Responsibility for the Detection of Errors and Irregularities" and "Illegal Acts by Clients," respectively. The general contents of these statements were discussed in Chapter 2. SAS 16 makes the auditor responsible for searching for material errors and irregularities in the financial statements. However it also states that the audit cannot be relied upon as the only control against them.[6]

The most effective deterrent against errors and irregularities is a strong internal control system. Even though the auditor is required by auditing standards to study and evaluate the client's system of internal control, the primary purpose of that study and evaluation is to enable the auditor to determine the extent of substantive audit tests required for expressing an opinion on the financial statements. However, since the Foreign Corrupt Practices Act requires companies reporting under SEC jurisdiction to maintain strong controls designed to prevent such acts from occurring, this requirement surely has implications for auditors. There is still some uncertainty about the extent of those implications. Most auditors feel that they are not, on the basis of GAAS, currently required to perform the type of study and evaluation of internal controls contemplated by the Foreign Corrupt Practices Act. As pointed out in Chapter 19, SAS 30 now provides the vehicle whereby auditors can perform an audit of the client's system of internal accounting control. This type of audit is much more extensive with respect to the study and evaluation of the system of internal controls than an audit designed to enable the expression of opinion on the financial statements. Thus, there is a higher probability that material internal control weaknesses would be detected in such audits. SAS 30 stops short of saying that even such examinations can establish compliance with the Foreign Corrupt Practices Act. It does, however, state that *such examinations can help management of the company evaluate its own compliance* with the Foreign Corrupt Practices Act.

With regard to illegal acts of clients, SAS 17, while disclaiming the CPA's responsibility to *detect* illegal acts, clearly requires the auditor to react appropriately to those acts when they are determined to have occurred during the audit period.[7] Failure to do so could place the auditor in the position of being legally liable to stockholders of the offending firm for losses associated with the illegal actions.

Impact of Litigation

Stepped-up legal actions against accountants during the last several years have had a significant impact on the accounting profession. Even though the financial losses suffered by individual public accounting firms have been significant, the profession as a whole also has to be concerned with its *growing loss of credibility* as lawsuits have been filed and as judgments have been rendered on those lawsuits. Partly in response to this problem, the Commission on Auditors' Responsibilities was appointed by the AICPA in 1974 to study the role and responsibilities of auditors.[8] The report of that commission, issued in 1978, contains numerous constructive recommendations made at least partially in response to this apparent credibility loss. Those recommendations should have a far-reaching effect on the work of independent auditors in the future. Elements of those recommendations have been presented at various points throughout the text.

Other direct responses of the profession to litigation have included actions taken to make the professionalism of accountants more substantive. Minimum criteria have been established within most jurisdictions for education prior to being admitted to the profession. Most states have also enacted *continuing professional education requirements* for members of the profession. As observed in Chapter 20, quality control standards have been established for public accounting firms.[9] All of these appear to be evidence of a profession coming of age.

The ultimate outcome of these actions will depend on how far the profession is willing to go in imposing on itself the necessary cures for past failures. It has already moved in that direction by *requiring that independent audit committees be established for clients whose stock is traded on the New York Stock Exchange.* Also SAS 20 now requires the auditor to *report deficiencies in systems of internal control* of audit clients to client management.[10] Further action may well involve restricting the scope of consulting services provided to audit clients. The Securities and Exchange Commission, too, appears to have been pressing the profession toward implementation of these "cures."

One apparently undesirable result of the extensive litigation of the 1970s has been the inclination of the public accounting profession to *draw back from the idea of extending and enlarging accountants' services, such as certain management advisory services to clients.* This reaction is, of course, prompted by the fear of incurring liabilities in connection with such services. Closely related to this action is the apparent *fear of experimenting with many new ideas and concepts* that could make the work of the accountant more useful because of the liability that might be incurred in implementing them.

Another reaction of the profession has been a movement toward *recognizing the differences between the practices of large and small public accounting firms.* Firms having extensive practice before the Securities and Exchange Commission should logically, by virtue of that fact, meet higher levels of qualifications than would be expected of smaller firms not involved in that type of practice. The question of whether or not this distinction should be drawn is still being debated within the profession.

The litigious age has also caused some practitioners to feel that the profession should support statutory limitations of liability to third parties. One approach would impose the following limits on the recognition of liability:

- Liability in situations where physical injury or damage results from the auditor's work.
- Liability in situations where only gross negligence could be proved.
- Liability only when the representation of the auditor is for the primary benefit of a third party.
- Liability to only the classes of persons the auditor knows will rely on his or her representations.[11]

While these limitations might be desirable from the point of view of limiting the extent of liability of public accounting firms, they would also move the profession in the direction of taking less risk. That in turn would mean that the audit would become a less desirable product than would be the case if the present level of risk continued to be assumed.

Certain legal cases have had directly traceable effects on the auditing process. We have summarized some of those cases in the appendix at the end of this chapter. We now list those cases in chronological order and briefly state the primary effect(s) each has had in establishing the responsibilities of the accountant as an auditor and as a preparer of unaudited financial statements.

***Ultramares Corporation* v. *Touche* (1931).** This case established that an auditor may be liable to a third party when his or her duties were performed for the primary benefit of a third party named in the contract. As a result of this case, auditors began to recognize more fully their responsibilities to third-party users of audited financial statements.

The *McKesson & Robbins* Case (1940). This case pointed up the need for specifically identified auditing standards, including independent verification of certain account balances, such as accounts receivable and inventory. As a result of this case, the profession began the formal codification of auditing standards as a means of more specifically defining the auditor's responsibilities to third-party users of audited data. The ten generally accepted auditing standards, as well as procedures requiring the auditor to confirm accounts receivable and observe the taking of inventory, were established largely as a result of this case.

The *Bar Chris Construction Corporation* Case (1968). This was one of the lawsuits occurring in the litigious age of the 1960s, which demonstrated the increasingly active role of the SEC and the auditor's expanded responsibility to third parties. This case showed that the 1933 Securities Act pertaining to accountants liability could be used as a basis for suing auditing firms. It also yielded some rather specific interpretations of the principle of materiality. Furthermore, and perhaps most importantly, while stating that "accountants should not be held to a higher standard than that recognized in the profession," the findings of the case showed that the courts were willing to choose between alternate accounting principles if the court believed the application of a certain practice does not result in fair presentation of financial statements. It demonstrated the willingness of the court to apply its interpretation to fairness of presentation. Finally, the standards for subsequent events procedures contained in SAS 1 (Section 560) and SAS 37, while not existing at the time, have since been adopted and contain principles embodied in this case. SAS 37 adds to the auditor's usual responsibility for subsequent events procedures the responsibility to review and make a "reasonable investigation" of events between the date of the audit report (the end of audit field work) and the effective date of the registration statement. The additional time period for subsequent events review under SAS 37 extends for as much as several weeks after the date of the audit report. During this time, the auditor should arrange with the client to be kept advised of the progress of the registration proceedings so that his or her review of subsequent events can be completed by the effective date. In addition to the regular subsequent events procedures outlined in Section 560, the auditor should: (a) read the prospectus and other pertinent portions of the registration statement; and (b) inquire of and obtain written representations from officers and other responsible executives as to whether any material undisclosed events transpired other than those already shown in the registration statement.

***Rusch Factors, Inc.* v. *Levin* (1968).** This case held that the accountant should be liable in negligence for careless misrepresentations relied upon by actually foreseen and limited classes of persons, rather than only those persons named in the contract. It, in effect, extended the *Ultramares* concept of responsibilities to third parties beyond those specifically identified in the contract as beneficiaries of the audit.

The *Continental Vending* Case (*United States* v. *Simon*) (1969). This case has imposed on auditors a responsibility to disclose what they know about the client when there is reason to believe that a corporation is operating primarily for the benefit of a manager-stockholder rather than in the interest of all stockholders. It recognizes these differences between the natural goals that may exist for hired managers and for investors in the firm. The *Continental Vending* case demonstrated that auditors could be held criminally liable for violations of federal securities laws. Although the audit standard for related party transactions (SAS 6) did not exist at that time, that standard now embodies the principles set forth in *United States* v. *Simon*.

***1136 Tenants Corporation* v. *Max Rothenberg and Company* (1971).** This case established liability of the accountant to the client for failure to discover fraud in connection with the preparation of unaudited financial statements. It showed the need for preparing an engagement letter for write-up work specifically describing the work to be done plus the inclusion of an appropriately worded disclaimer with the financial statements. It also established the fact that the accountant has a responsibility for normal professional alertness as financial statements are prepared, even though they are unaudited.

The *Equity Funding* Case (*United States* v. *Weiner*) (1973). This case involved fraud perpetrated by top level management through collusion between officers and computer personnel. Several CPA firms had worked as auditors for Equity Funding over a period of years, but none had detected the fraud, which began in the late 1960s and continued into the early 1970s. This case demonstrated for the first time that the auditors' assumption regarding the integrity of top level management had to be reexamined. Partially as a result of this case, Statement on Auditing Standards (SAS) 4 was adopted, establishing quality control criteria for public accounting firms. One provision in that statement required that policies and procedures should be established for deciding whether to accept or continue a client in order the minimize the likelihood of association with a client whose management lacks integrity.[12] This case also has had an influence on the elements of SAS 16 relating to auditors' responsibilities to detect management fraud.

***Ernst and Ernst* v. *Hochfelder et Al.* (1976).** This case showed that proof of negligence is not sufficient evidence to prove the intent to defraud, which is required for recovery by investors under the antifraud provisions of the Securities Exchange Act of 1934. This case has been characterized by some as the turning point in court-awarded judgments to third-party groups. It showed that *knowledge* by the auditor of client fraud must be proven by the plaintiff before third parties can recover from the auditor under the criminal fraud statutes (Section 10b and its companion SEC Rule 10b-5) of the Securities Exchange Act of 1934.

***Aaron* v. *SEC* (1980).** The decision issued by the Supreme Court in this case required the SEC to establish "scienter" (intent to deceive) in certain enforcement actions seeking injunctions under federal securities laws. The decision was based on the reasoning followed in the *Ernst and Ernst* v. *Hochfelder* case.[13]

Effect of Related Party Transactions

The auditing process depends, to some extent, on the assumption that each of the parties to a business transaction will seek to maximize expected economic benefits from the transaction. This can be expected to occur if the parties to the transaction have opposite interests (deal at arm's length). In situations where this arm's-length dealing does not occur (related party transactions), improper values can be introduced into the accounting records. The *Continental Vending* case (*United States* v. *Simon*) showed the effects this kind of abuse can have.

SAS 6 defines the related parties of a company to be its "affiliates, principal owners, management and immediate members of their families, entities accounted for by the equity method, or any other party that might significantly influence or be significantly influenced by the company."[14] Although generally accepted auditing standards cannot be expected to provide assurance that all of the related party transactions will be disclosed, SAS 6 requires that special attention be given to material related party transactions to ascertain the economic substance of those transactions. Furthermore, the auditor is required to ascertain whether the client has disclosed: (a) the existence of related parties, (b) the fact that the reporting entity participated in related party transactions, and (c) the economic substance of those transactions if they were material.[15]

CIVIL LIABILITY OF AUDITORS

Most lawsuits against auditors involve claims for damages to the clients or third parties and thus represent what is described as ***civil liabilities.*** We now expand the earlier discussion on the nature of those liabilities and explain how they may be claimed under common law, under the securities acts, and in connection with the responsibility for detection of fraud.

Civil Liability Under Common Law

Common law includes a system of jurisprudence that originated in England and is based on judicial precedent rather than legislative enactments. Its principles are determined basically by the social needs of the community and therefore can change with changes in such needs. Many contracts, including contracts between an auditor and a client are governed by the contents of the contract — as interpreted within the common law system. Therefore, as observed earlier, an auditor's liability to clients may involve a *breach of contract or tort liability.* The latter is based on failure to carry out a duty created by either social policy or social policy in combination with the contract.

As explained earlier, an accountant's contractual responsibilities to the client may either be expressed or implied. For example, the expressed duties are those spelled out by the terms of the contract. On the other hand, the implied duties are those which the courts have previously determined to be a part of every contract, whether or not they are specifically included in the terms of the contract. These implied responsibilities constitute the primary source of *legal liability for negligence.* For example, the accountant has an implied contractual duty not to perform in a negligent or fraudulent manner. The client, on the other hand, has an implied contractual responsibility not to interfere with or prevent the accountant from performing the elements of the audit. As we have observed before, the test for negligence involves determining whether the accountant has exercised reasonable care under the circumstances. Within this interpretation of the law, the accountant may also be held liable for acts or omissions that amount to actual or constructive fraud. To constitute actual fraud the acts or omissions must be intentional and have the intent to deceive. Constructive fraud, on the other hand, involves acts or omissions occurring because of gross negligence without a conscious intent to deceive.

The accountant may also be held *liable to third parties* within the system of common law. Such liability generally occurs under the common law provisions of negligence and fraud. It extends to third-party beneficiaries of the audit contract. As explained earlier, these are people whom the contracting parties intended to receive primary benefits of the accountant's services. They were first defined in the *Ultramares* v. *Touche* case as any *third party named in the contract* who would stand to benefit from the contract. That definition has gradually been liberalized over the years to include parties reasonably foreseen by the auditor to be relying on the audited data (see ***Rusch*** *Factors, Inc.* v. *Levin*). Under current law, then, the accountant's liability to third parties for ordinary negligence normally extends only to those whom the accountant knew or should have known would be using the audited data.[16]

Liability to third parties for *fraud* (deceit) can exist regardless of whether the services were intended primarily for the benefit of third parties or for the benefit of the client. In such a situation, however, the third party must show that reasonable reliance was placed on the auditor's work.[17] The common law elements of deceit in general are as follows:

- A false representation of material fact made by the defendant.
- Knowledge or belief of falsity, technically described as "scienter."
- An intent that the plaintiff rely on the false representation.
- Justifiable reliance on the false representation.

Civil Liabilities Under the Security Acts

In the preceding paragraphs we have discussed the accountant's civil liability based on common law. The auditor may also be liable for such liability under the federal statutes included in the Securities Act of 1933 and the Securities Exchange Act of 1934. These statutes were enacted to provide certain protections for the investing public — judged to be necessary partly as a result of the stock market crash of 1929.

The ***Securities Act of 1933*** was designed to provide the investing public with appropriate information to allow them to evaluate the merits of new security issues. It requires companies issuing securities for public sale to file a registration statement with the Securities and Exchange Commission prior to offering such securities for sale. The registration statement includes facts concerning the securities to be issued along with audited financial statements. The act makes the accountant liable for any false statements in the registration statement or in the prospectus, which includes essentially the same financial information as that included in the registration statement.

The auditor preparing the registration statement can be held liable to any purchaser of an initial issue of securities covered by the registration statement if it contains false statements or material omissions.[18] The investor is required to prove the existence of the false statement or material omission and the fact that the security purchased was offered through the inaccurate registration statement. It is not necessary for the purchaser to prove reliance on the accountant's error unless a 12-month earnings statement has been issued for a period after the effective date of the registration statement. However, recent cases suggest that accountants may not generally be held liable unless their work was fraudulent or performed with reckless disregard for known facts.[19] Thus, the accountant must prove that he or she has exercised due diligence by showing that after reasonable investigation there was reasonable basis for presenting the data as shown in the registration statement. Upon failing to prove due diligence, the accountant may try to prove that the plaintiff's loss was caused by something other than the misleading financial statements (lack of ***causation***).

Accountants are excluded from the liability mentioned above for reports on unaudited supplementary information relating to changing prices and oil and gas reserves, both of which are disclosures required by the FASB. This exclusion has been allowed in order to facilitate experimentation with new financial information without the added hazards of liability.

The ***Securities Exchange Act of 1934*** is designed to regulate the national securities exchanges, including the securities listed on those exchanges. It requires each listed company to submit to the Securities and Exchange Commission an annual report commonly referred to as ***Form 10-K***. This report includes audited financial statements, which constitute the chief source of the accountant's liability under this act. The act imposes civil liability on any accountant who makes a material false or misleading statement in any SEC annual report.[20] For the accountant to be held liable under the 1934 act, the investor must prove a purchase or sale of the security at a price that was influenced by the false or misleading statement plus reliance on the statement as the cause of the loss. Furthermore, this act requires proof of scienter.[21] The burden of proof is on the auditor that he or she acted *in good faith with no knowledge of a misleading statement.*

Figure 21–1 is presented to help you see the circumstances in which the auditors may be held liable to clients and third parties for negligence and to summarize the auditor's legal position under both common law and statutory law. As the figure shows, the main differences between the auditor's civil liability under common and statutory law are these:

- Under common law, the rights of clients and third-party beneficiaries are more extensive than the rights of third parties. Specifically, third parties must prove gross negligence to recover from the auditor, while clients and third-party beneficiaries must prove only ordinary negligence. In contrast, under statutory law, there is no distinction between the rights of the two groups. Any purchaser of securities may sue the accountant.
- Under common law, the burden of proof for proving negligence of the auditor rests on the plaintiff (client or third party). Under statutory law, the auditor has the burden of proving that he or she was not negligent. In addition, under the Securities Act of 1933, the plaintiff need not show reliance on misleading financial statements or proximate cause unless the security was purchased after the registrant has filed an income statement covering a 12-month period beginning after the effective date of the registration statement.

Responsibility for the Detection of Fraud

In Chapter 2 we discussed at some length the auditor's responsibility for detecting fraud. As we discussed that responsibility, we observed that the ordinary audit cannot be relied on to discover all fraud, particularly if the fraud does not materially affect the financial data. However, *if the auditor is negligent* and as a result fails to discover fraud that results in losses that could have been prevented by its discovery, he or she may be held liable for damages. *Negligence can occur anytime the auditor fails to exercise due care* in the performance of the audit. The test of due care is generally based on the interpretation of the appropriate generally accepted auditing standards.

COMMON LAW		STATUTORY LAW	
		Clients and All Third Parties (Any Purchaser)	
Clients and Third-Party Beneficiaries	Third Parties	Securities Act of 1933	Securities Exchange Act of 1934
	Basis for Suit if Alleged and Proved:		
Misleading financial statements Reliance Damages (loss) Proximate cause Auditor negligence Breach of contract	Misleading financial statements Reliance Damages (loss) Proximate cause Auditor gross negligence (constructive fraud) or actual fraud	Misleading financial statements* Damages (loss)	Misleading financial statements Reliance Damages (loss) Proximate cause
	Auditor's Defense:		
Due diligence	Due diligence	Due diligence Lack of causation	Due diligence Lack of knowledge of misleading statements
	Burden of Proof for Negligence:		
Plaintiff	Plaintiff	Defendant (accountant)	Defendant (accountant)

*Reliance not necessary unless a twelve-month statement of earnings (beginning after effective date of registration statement) is issued.

FIGURE 21–1. The Auditor's Civil Liability

The determination of whether an auditor was negligent in failing to discover fraud may often be a question for the jury to decide. As we have observed, the courts have, in some instances, expected a level of performance that appears to be above that contained in the generally accepted standards.[22] Nevertheless, it is clear that when certain standard auditing procedures (normally prescribed by the profession for the discovery of the fraud) have not been met, such failures are likely to be construed as negligence.

Our discussion to this point has been primarily concerned with the responsibilities of the accountant only as they relate to audited financial statements. Engagements to prepare unaudited financial statements can, under certain conditions, create a liability for the accountant if the responsibility assumed with those statements is not clearly stated or if the accountant fails to exercise normal professional alertness in the work performed (the *1136 Tenants Corporation* case illustrates that fact). For that reason, any accountant associated with unaudited financial statements should have *written documentation in the form of an engagement letter* indicating the limitations of the responsibility undertaken in connection with the preparation of the statements. Furthermore, those statements should be accompanied by an appropriately worded *disclaimer of opinion.* Failure to do those things can place the accountant in the position of being held liable for what the courts could construe to be an inadequately performed audit.

AUDITOR'S CRIMINAL LIABILITY

Most of the lawsuits against accountants have involved the recovery of damages for alleged civil liability. Criminal liability can occur, however, when an act, considered to be a *wrong against society,* is committed. Certain willful violations of the provisions included in both the Securities Act of 1933 and the Securities Exchange Act of 1934, as well as certain violations of the Internal Revenue Code, can subject the offender to criminal penalties in the form of a fine and/or a possible prison term. In addition, states have enacted laws calling for the recognition of criminal liability for certain other activities normally involving accountants.

Willful Violation and Fraud

Generally speaking, a *crime must involve both an act and criminal intent.* The intent, however, may be implied from the facts in the case because the accused party is presumed to intend to achieve the natural and probable consequences of his or her acts. The Securities Act of 1933 states that willful violations of its provision constitute a crime:

> Any person who willfully violates any provisions of this title or the rules and regulations promulgated by the commission under authority thereof; or any person who willfully, in a registration statement filed under this title, makes any untrue statement of a material fact or omits the statement of any material facts required to be stated therein, or are necessary to make the statements therein not misleading, shall upon conviction, be fined not more than $10,000 or imprisoned not more than 5 years, or both.[23]

The key element of this provision of the act is the interpretation of the word *willfully.* The normal expectation is that the accountant will exercise "due diligence" in the performance of all tasks undertaken. Failure to do so can be construed as a willful violation of the act.

The Securities Exchange Act of 1934 calls for criminal action for false and misleading statements. Specifically, the act includes the following provision:

> Any person who willfully violates any provision of this title or any rule or regulation thereunder . . . or any person who willfully and knowingly makes or causes to be made any statement in any application, report or document required

> to be filed under this title or any rule or regulation thereunder . . . which . . . was false or misleading with respect to any material fact shall upon conviction be fined not more than $10,000 or imprisoned not more than 5 years, or both.[24]

The *Continental Vending* case, referred to earlier in this chapter and summarized in the appendix, can help us in interpreting this section of the 1934 act. That act requires accountants to disclose what they know when they have reason to believe that a corporation is being operated for the primary benefit of related party shareholders-managers rather than in the interest of all stockholders. It also makes a point of the fact that compliance with generally accepted accounting principles is not an absolute defense in a criminal case.

Liability for fraud in a statutory law exists under Section 17 of the Securities Act of 1933 and under Section 120, Rule 10b-5 of the Securities Exchange Act of 1934.

Rule 10b-5 of the Securities Exchange Act of 1934 defines liability for fraud under that act as follows:

> It shall be unlawful for any person, directly or indirectly, by the use of any means or instrumentality of interstate commerce, or of the mails, or of any facility of any national securities exchange,
>
> 1. To employ any device, scheme, or artifice to defraud,
> 2. To make any untrue statement of a material fact or to omit a material fact necessary in order to make the statements made, in light of the circumstances under which they were made, not misleading, or
> 3. To engage in any act, practice, or course of business which operates or would operate as a fraud or deceit upon any person in connection with the purchase or sale of any security.[25]

The accountant must exercise due diligence in work relating to this act in order to avoid liability. The *Ernst and Ernst* v. *Hochfelder et al.* case has been especially important in interpreting *the due diligence requirement* especially as it relates to possible fraudulent activity. Specifically, it showed that negligence alone on the part of the auditor is not sufficient evidence to prove the intent to defraud required for establishing liability under the antifraud provision of the Securities Exchange Act of 1934.

Liabilities of the Tax Practitioner

The CPA who prepares tax returns for clients should remember that individuals engaged in practice before the Internal Revenue Service (IRS) are subject to both civil and criminal penalties under the Internal Revenue Code for making false statements and for other negligent or fraudulent misconduct. Civil penalties in tax practice were imposed upon CPAs for the first time in the Tax Reform Act of 1976. The basis for liability under this act is an understatement of the federal income tax liability of the taxpayer. A final determination of the tax liability by the IRS or the courts is not a necessary condition for establishing an understatement of that liability. Where the understatement is due to the negligent or intentional disregard of the income tax rules and regulations, the penalty is $100. The penalty is assessed upon the *preparer*, and not necessarily on the employing firm. In the event of a trial, the burden of proof is upon the preparer to show that he or she was not at fault. Where it is found that understatement is *willful*, the preparer's penalty is $500. In addition, the Tax Reform Act imposes the following ***civil penalties*** on preparers for the following reasons:

- $25 for failure to furnish the client with a copy of the tax return.
- $50 for failure to retain either a copy of all returns prepared or a list of all taxpayers and their taxpayer identification numbers.
- $25 for failure to provide the preparer's tax identification number on the tax return.
- $25 for failure to sign the return.
- $500 for each taxpayer's income tax check endorsed or otherwise negotiated by the preparer.

Criminal penalties are imposed on preparers under Section 7206 of the Internal Revenue Code for aid or assistance in preparation of fraudulent tax returns. Under this section an accountant found guilty of such acts may be fined not more than $5,000, or imprisoned not more than three years, or both, in addition to costs of prosecution.

THE PROFESSION'S RESPONSE TO THE PERILS OF A LITIGIOUS AGE

Without question, the legal penalties imposed on accountants and the public disclosure of them have moved the profession to reexamine and strengthen its technical standards and to enforce compliance with them. For example, the Code of Ethics has been revised and quality control (peer) reviews of firms have been implemented. Although these changes may have to some extent been made in response to a recognized professional obligation, they obviously have been encouraged by litigation. It is clear that there is an evolving public concern for corporate accountability and the auditor should have a significant role in providing that accountability.

It is quite clear that, in fulfilling that role, the auditor must *exercise due diligence and reasonable care* in all services rendered. That includes careful adherence to generally accepted auditing standards, including their interpretations. Clients and prospective clients should be critically evaluated in making client acceptance and retention decisions. It is also important that the accountant's responsibilities in connection with any engagement be clearly established through use of some kind of documentation, such as an engagement letter.

The recommendations of the Commission on Auditors' Responsibilities, summarized in the following paragraphs, best describe what the auditor's posture should be in the present-day litigious age. It is important to note that while all of the Commission's recommendations have not been adopted to date, many of our present Statements on Auditing Standards have adopted positions similar to these recommendations. The first recommendation relates to detection of illegal or questionable acts:

> In regard to detecting illegal or questionable acts, the commission concludes that, because the auditor will frequently not be able to detect material fraud and illegal and questionable payments made by the client, each corporation should develop its own code of conduct. When that is done, the independent auditors

should be willing to provide users with assurance as to whether the company is taking effective action to implement that code of conduct. Within such an arrangement, the auditor should be expected to review the company's code of conduct and the procedures adopted to monitor compliance with it.

Since it is doubtful that auditors can detect with any regularity, willfully concealed, illegal or questionable acts involving relatively small amounts, any expression of assurance suggesting that the auditor knows such acts have not occurred, would be of no real value. However, auditors must continue to be aware of the possibility that illegal acts have occurred and should evaluate the evidence obtained in the audit which may suggest that such acts, have in fact, occurred. It is also important, however, for the auditor to be aware that illegal or questionable acts involving immaterial amounts may also raise important questions of disclosure.[26]

The auditor's recommended response to detected illegal or questionable acts is another matter. If an act, believed to be illegal or questionable, is discovered, the auditor can follow only one course of action — namely, to *bring the act to the attention of the appropriate level of authority* within the entity. This is consistent with the provision of Statement on Auditing Standards (SAS) 17.

The Commission on Auditors' Responsibilities suggests that there are at least three factors that the auditor should consider in obtaining evidence as to the circumstances of the illegal or questionable act:

- The auditor should determine *the extent to which the item might affect the financial statements* to see whether or not it would cause a material misstatement of either operations or financial position. If so, enough additional or alternative audit procedures should be performed to determine the extent and consequences of the irregularity.
- The auditor should have a responsibility for comparing *the act with the standard of corporate conduct against which the auditor was conducting the examination.* Because the auditor is not a lawyer, he or she might be confronted with acts whose conformity with policy might be unclear. This would require consultation with corporate counsel, and a procedure for implementing such consultation should be established. In all instances, however, the auditor should act within a deliberate bias toward pursuing suspicious acts.
- *The extent of public disclosure of illegal or questionable acts* that come to the attention of the auditor must be considered. Generally speaking, when a violation of a corporate policy statement is discovered, the auditor should begin by obtaining an appropriate response at the level of authority stipulated in the corporate code. An appropriate response to such action would be to stop an existing violation and the establishment of controls designed to prevent its recurrence. If the auditor failed to obtain appropriate disposition at the highest level available in the corporation — namely, the audit committee of the board of directors — the auditor should disclose the violation. If the client refuses to allow the disclosure with the financial statements, the situation should be disclosed in the auditor's report. If the client objects to such disclosure, the auditor should seriously consider withdrawal from the engagement.[27]

The Commission further suggests that if a company has adopted a corporate code of conduct, a separate report by management in the company's annual report should include a statement of that fact and that procedures have been implemented to monitor compliance with it. The auditor's report should then state that the code of conduct has been reviewed. It should also describe the review of the company's monitoring procedures and provide conclusions on those aspects that could be audited. If a legislative or regulation rule is adopted to require corporations to adopt and enforce codes of conduct and if they fail to do so, that fact should be disclosed in the report by management. If management fails to disclose that fact, the independent auditor's report should include a comment that no policy has been adopted or that the company did not establish a means to enforce its adopted policy.[28]

The Commission also proposed increased involvement of lawyers in connection with pending and foreseeable legal claims. In the current litigious climate, this becomes important in determining whether a liability should be recognized or the matter should be disclosed in a footnote in accordance with FASB 5. The Commission believes that the information, now provided by management, substantiated by assurances given by counsel to the auditor, should be presented directly to users when financial information is issued. Even this, however, would not satisfy demands for greater audit assurance regarding the compliance of corporations with laws and regulations. Such demands can be satisfied only by increasing the scope and extent of assurances provided by lawyers. Meeting those demands, however, may require some fundamental changes in the way lawyers view their relationships to clients and their role in society.[29]

SUMMARY

In this chapter we have analyzed and discussed the legal implications of the independent auditor's responsibilities that we first took up in Chapter 2. We began by defining pertinent legal terminology. Then we observed that present-day auditing activities are carried out in a highly litigious environment.

After that, we explained the relationship between the auditor's work and possible legal liability, by showing how some key cases have influenced the auditing profession. We saw how, with the development of the attest function, auditors have, to an increasing degree, been held liable to third parties. This in turn has influenced the profession toward the codification of generally accepted auditing standards (GAAS) and the establishment of various interpretations of them through the medium of Statements on Auditing Standards (SAS). Legal actions against accountants have also influenced the code of ethics and have encouraged the profession to develop quality control (peer review) standards for public accounting firms.

In the last part of the chapter we examined the posture that the accountant should assume in today's litigious world. That posture is probably best defined in selected recommendations of the Commission on Auditors' Responsibilities; these were summarized in the last section of the chapter.

APPENDIX 21–A: Summaries of Selected Court Cases Establishing Legal Liabilities of Public Accounting Firms

Ultramares Corporation v. *Touche* (1931)

This case involved a suit for damages to a third party contending misrepresentations, negligence, and fraud of the accountants. A client, Fred Stern and Company, Inc., engaged Touche, Niven and Company to prepare and certify the company's balance sheet as of December 31, 1923. The client firm was engaged in the importation and sale of rubber and required extensive borrowing to finance its operations. The balance sheet was prepared, with the auditor's report certifying that "subject to provision for federal taxes on income, their financial statement in our opinion presents a true and correct view of the financial condition of Fred Stern and Company, Inc., as of December 31, 1923." Later it was discovered that the books had been falsified by the management of the company to include receivables and other assets that were fictitious.

Ultramares Corporation, engaged in the factoring business, made loans to the Stern Company after insisting on receiving a balance sheet certified by public accountants. The plaintiff contended that the loan was made on the basis of the statement certified by Touche. Approximately a year later, the Stern Company was declared a bankrupt, as a result of which Ultramares Corporation failed to collect on a significant number of loans made to the Stern Company.

The initial verdict was in favor of the plaintiff. In the appeals trial, however, the charge of negligence was disallowed. Nevertheless, the court of appeals ordered a new trial on the charge of fraud. Before the fraud charges could be litigated, the case was settled out of court.

This case is important becuase it established, for the first time, an auditor's liability to a third party (outside the contractual relationship with the client) for damages sustained as a result of the auditor's gross negligence, or lack of even slight care. Additionally, designation of "third-party beneficiary" was first applied to a contract between the auditor and client in this case. A ***third-party beneficiary*** is defined as a party expressly named in the contract, other than the client, one who was clearly relying on the work performed by the auditor. Since Ultramares was not specifically named in the contract, the court ruled that they were not a third-party beneficiary and could not recover from the auditor for his ordinary negligence. Rather, Ultramares would have had to prove the more serious charge of gross negligence in order to recover from the auditor.

Rusch Factors, Inc. v. *Levin* (1968)

This is another case in which a plaintiff (Rusch Factors, Inc.) who provided financing for a company requested and received certified financial statements prior to granting a loan. Subsequently the borrower went into receivership and as a result, the plaintiff was unable to recover a portion of the loan made to the company. The plaintiff contended that the loss resulted from reliance on fraudulent or negligent misrepresentations in the financial statements certified by the defendent accountant (Levin).

The court in this case held that the accountant was liable, in negligence, for careless financial misrepresentations relied upon by an actually foreseen user of the financial statements. This case is important because it extends the responsibility of the accountant to third parties actually foreseen to be relying on the contract.

McKesson & Robbins Case (1940)

McKesson & Robbins was a wholesale drug company registered under the Securities Exchange Act. Price Waterhouse and Company served as its auditors. The company was supposed to have a Canadian subsidiary through which a significant part of its activities were conducted. Over several years, through massive collusion on the part of the president of the company and other key officers, fictitious documents were used to create fictitious receivables and inventory on the books of the Canadian subsidiary.

In 1940, the Securities and Exchange Commission conducted an investigation and concluded that the auditors were negligent and that the gross discrepancies reflected in the records of the company should have been discovered during the course of the audits. At the same time, however, the SEC conceded that the auditors had followed procedures considered acceptable at the time the audit was performed. Price Waterhouse and Company contended that their examination was not designed to detect fraud, particularly where collusion of the type present in this case existed.

As a direct result of this case, the accounting profession required that accounts receivable and inventory be validated in the future from external and independent sources. This was interpreted to mean confirmation of accounts receivable and observation of the inventory process. Ultimately this case was a basic, motivating force — causing the accounting profession to adopt presently existing generally accepted auditing standards (GAAS).

Fischer v. *Kletz (Yale Express* Case*)* (1967)

This case involved a class action suit against Peat, Marwick, Mitchell & Co. Shareholders in this case sought to establish liability on the auditor's part for failure to call to their attention previous audited financial statements later discovered to contain false data.

The public accountants in this case had audited the financial statement of Yale Express System for the year ended December 31, 1963. The audit report was dated March 31, 1964. Later, during 1964, Peat, Marwick, Mitchell & Co. was engaged to perform a special study of Yale's past and current operations. During this nonaudit engagement, the accountants discovered that certain figures in the annual report were substantially false and misleading. Although this information was discovered some time late in 1964, the findings were not released until May of 1965. The plaintiffs contended that this delay, in terms of silence and inaction, was a violation of the public accountant's responsibilities relating to the previously audited financial statements.

This case has at least two interesting aspects: First, it points up the problem that can occur when a public accounting firm serves a client in two capacities. In this case, Peat, Marwick, Mitchell & Co. provided independent audit services with respect to the financial statements for the year ended December 31, 1963. In 1964, they were employed by Yale Express in a management advisory capacity. It was while serving in this capacity that the errors in the audited financial statements were discovered. The court held that the nature of the services being performed at the time previous errors were discovered was irrelevant when related to the CPA's reporting responsibility. The second point of interest involves the determination of the accountant's responsibility for disclosing errors in previously audited financial statements after the audit report has been issued.

Partially as a result of this case, Section 561 ("Subsequent Discovery of Facts Existing at the Date of the Auditor's Report") was incorporated into SAS 1 in 1972. That statement requires that the auditor should, as soon as practicable after such subsequent information becomes known to him, discuss the matter with the client at an appropriate level of management. If the auditor concludes that action should be taken to prevent future reliance on the audit report, the client should be advised to make appropriate disclosure of the newly discovered facts and their impact on the financial statements to persons who are known to be currently relying or who are likely to rely on the financial statements and related auditor's report. If the client refuses to make the appropriate disclosures, it is then the responsibility of the CPA to see that the disclosures are made.

Escott et Al. v. *Bar Chris Construction Corporation et Al.* (1968)

In this case the holders of certain convertible debentures of Bar Chris Construction Corporation brought an action under Section 11 of the Securities Act of 1933, alleging that the registration statement of the company contained material false statements and material omissions. Among the defendants were the auditors of Bar Chris: Peat, Marwick, Mitchell & Co.

Bar Chris Construction Company was engaged in constructing bowling alleys. Its sales increased dramatically in the late 1950s. Its method of operation called for construction with a comparatively small down payment, the balance being paid in notes which Bar Chris subsequently discounted with factors. On at least one occasion, Bar Chris practiced a method of financing which was, in substance, a sale and leaseback arrangement. Construction operations were accounted for on the percentage-of-completion method.

In this case, a judgment was rendered in favor of third-party plaintiffs who brought action under the law covering false statements and misleading omissions in a registration statement. Among the charges and holdings of the court against the statements were these:

- The percentage-of-completion method was erroneous and misleading; and even if use of the method was appropriate, its application in this case caused misleading statements. The court held that use of the method was appropriate but that it had been misapplied.
- Inappropriate accounting for sale – leaseback arrangements. Bar Chris had sold a bowling alley to a factoring company who, in turn, had leased it back to a consolidated subsidiary of Bar Chris. This transaction was treated as a sale by Bar Chris in its consolidated financial statements. It is important to note that this sale occurred in 1960, prior to issuance of APB Opinion No. 5 in 1964. Before 1964, GAAP allowed profits to be recognized on such sales, as long as the transaction was fully disclosed. In ruling that this practice was inappropriate, the court in effect decided that GAAP did not necessarily result in fairness of presentation.

- Understatement of allowance for doubtful accounts, and overstatement of receivables by inclusion of sales to a consolidated subsidiary.
- Understatement of direct and contingent liabilities.

These misstatements resulted in an apparent overstatement of earnings and an overstatement of the current ratio. The court ruled that a sixteen percent overstatement of earnings and a fifteen percent overstatement of earnings per share was not material. Although their reason for this ruling was not explicitly stated, it has been speculated that they gave recognition to the company's already rapid growth in spite of the error and the fact that debentures (creditor claims) were being issued. Since prospective creditors normally are more interested in a company's ability to pay than its profitability, perhaps the net income error was construed to be less important than the error in current ratio. Consistent with that thought, the court did rule that the overstatement in the firm's current ratio (2.6:1 vs. 2.9:1) was material.

The defenses given by all defendants, including Peat, Marwick, Mitchell & Co. included due diligence. However, evidence showed that the audit team conducting the field work had been negligent in their audit, particularly in the S-1 review which covered subsequent events up to the effective date of the registration statement.

This case showed that the portion of the 1933 Securities Act pertaining to accountants' liability can be used as a basis for third parties' suits against auditing firms.

The judge presiding over the case asserted in his opinion that accountants should not be held to a standard higher than that recognized by their profession, and that he did not hold them to such a standard. On the contrary, the accountants' work did not come up to that standard. Consequently, they were liable to third parties for their negligence. The *Bar Chris* case demonstrates, too, that the courts are willing to choose between alternate accounting principles when they believe that the application of a certain practice does not result in fair presentation of information in financial statements. It also showed that the court is willing to make some rather specific interpretations of the principle of materiality.

United States v. *Simon (Continental Vending* Case*)* (1969)

In this case, Carl Simon, a senior partner with Lybrand Ross Brothers and Montgomery and two other members of that firm were convicted of drawing up and certifying false or misleading financial statements of Continental Vending Machine Corporation. A key element of the trial involved transactions between Continental Vending, its affiliate, Valley Commerical Corporation, and Roth, the president of Continental Vending. Roth also controlled the operations of Valley Commercial Corporation. Over a period of years, Valley Commercial Corporation became deeply indebted to Continental Vending. Further analysis showed that Valley had lent Roth an amount approximately equal to the amount owed to Continental. Roth was unable to pay but offered to secure the indebtedness with his equity in stocks, bonds, and other securities of Continental and another company if this would be acceptable. He also agreed to post as collateral a mortgage on his house and furnishings. Over a short period of time, the market value of the collateral supporting the receivable from Valley declined to the point where it was worth only $395,000. This was collateral pledged to cover receivables of approximately 3.5 million dollars. Other issues involved improperly netting receivables against payables and inadequate footnote disclosure of the substance of the entire transaction between Roth, Valley, and Continental.

In the trial, eight expert witnesses (independent accountants) testified generally that the footnote disclosure of the Valley receivable was not inconsistent with generally accepted accounting principles. The dominating issue, however, centered around the president's diversion of corporate funds to his personal benefit. It was concluded that one of the accountants knew this had been occurring and that Simon, the partner in charge of the engagement, must have had a good reason to suspect what was occurring. The court concluded that the accountants failed to discharge their responsibilities appropriately — both because of an inadequate disclosure of the situation and because of not appropriately describing the situation about the securities pledged as collateral. The accountants were also cited for failure to insist that Roth mortgage his house and furnishings as additional collateral. The government also provided additional evidence of criminal intent in the form of conflicting statements by defendants and contradictions by other witnesses.

Simon and the other two accountants were convicted and fined for their failure to make proper disclosure of the circumstances surrounding the loan to Valley.

This case clearly imposes on auditors a responsibility (with possible criminal penalties) to disclose what they know about the client when there is reason to believe that a corporation is being operated primarily for the benefit of management rather than in the interest of all stockholders. Aspects of the case can clearly be seen in SAS 6 (written in 1975), which requires disclosure of all related parties and the substance of transactions between them.

The 1136 Tenants Corporation v. *Max Rothenberg and Company* (1971)

This case involved the preparation of unaudited financial statements by the accountant for the 1136 Tenants Corporation (an apartment cooperative) which was being defrauded by its leasing agent. There was apparently a misunderstanding between the corporation and the accountant as to the nature and extent of the services to be rendered. The accountant orally agreed to write up transactions and to prepare periodic financial statements for the corporation. The fee was set at $50 per month. No letter had been written confirming the terms of the engagement. The owners apparently thought that an audit should be performed whereas the accountants understood the services to be confined to write-up work. In this particular instance, some audit procedures were followed, which apparently caused the judge to construe the services to be an audit. There were a number of missing invoices which the accountant failed to follow up but listed in his working papers. However, no independent verifications of the account balances were made. A statement to this effect was made in the transmittal letter accompanying the financial statements. The financial statements, although they referred to the transmittal letter, were not marked "unaudited."

When it was later discovered that the defalcations had been committed by the leasing agents of the 1136 Tenants Corporation, the accountants were sued by the owners for negligence in failure to discover the fraud. The court decided in favor of the owners and $237,000 in damages were awarded to the plaintiffs.

This case is important because it established liability of the accountant for failure to discover fraud in connection with the preparation of unaudited statements. It emphasizes the need for a written engagement letter and a clearly worded disclaimer in connection with this type of service.

United States v. *Weiner (Equity Funding* Case*)* (1973)

This case, like the *McKesson & Robbins* case, involved massive collusion on the part of higher management with the objective of falsifying assets and earnings. Traditionally, auditors assume the integrity of client top level management. This case clearly demonstrates that such an assumption may be inappropriate.

Equity Funding Corporation of America was engaged in investing mutual funds and money received from sales of capital stock, and in selling life insurance to stockholders. During the early 1960s, the earnings of the company grew rapidly. However, as mutual funds lost some of their glamour, the management was apparently unwilling to acknowledge the consequences of that situation. As a result, dummy customers were made up and false information was stored in computer files. A set of computer programs was used to conceal the deception. By doing this, Equity Funding secured advances from other insurance companies on a co-insurance arrangement. However, a sizable number of the policies never existed, and as a result, the insurance companies lost most of what they had advanced to Equity Funding.

Over a period of years several CPA firms worked on the audits of Equity Funding but none detected the fraud. When the facts finally became known, the case was a serious embarrassment to the accounting profession. It clearly demonstrated that an auditor's assumption regarding the honesty of top level management had to be reexamined. The most direct effect of this case was to cause the issuance of Statement on Auditing Standards 16, which includes comments relating to the auditor's responsibility for detection of management fraud.

Ernst and Ernst v. *Hochfelder et Al.* (1977)

This case involved a suit brought against Ernst and Ernst by a group who had invested in a fraudulent security scheme perpetrated by the president of the First Securities Company in Chicago, a long-time client of Ernst and Ernst. The fraud actually came to light in 1968 when the president committed suicide. The investors then filed a class action suit for damages against Ernst and Ernst. The accounting firm was accused of negligent conduct because of failure to discover the weakness in internal control which allowed the fraudulent securities scheme to be perpetrated. The investors, by bringing suit under Rule 10b-5 of the Securities Exchange Act of 1934 were implying, as many had in the past, that a public accountant's ordinary negligence constitutes an act of fraud. It is interesting to note that the court never reached the issue of whether Ernst and Ernst had been negligent. Instead it concluded that the main issue was whether the CPA could be sued for fraud (deceit or scienter) when he or she had merely been ordinarily negligent.

The court was unwilling to extend the scope of Rule 10b-5 of the Securities Exchange Act of 1934 to negligent conduct, and therefore it ruled in favor of the accounting firm. This case has been characterized by some as a turning point in the history of court-awarded judgments to third-party groups. It showed that the auditor's knowledge of client fraud must be proved by the plaintiff before damages can be recovered under the antifraud provisions of the 1934 Act.

In at least one other case since 1976 (*Aaron* v. *SEC*, 1980) the Supreme Court required the SEC to establish scienter in seeking injunctions under the 1934 Act. This decision was based on the reasoning followed in the *Hochfelder* case.

NOTES

1. National Institute of Accountants, *CPA Review Business Law* (Gainesville, Fla.: National Institute of Accountants, 1980), p. 6.

2. Denzil Y. Causey, Jr., *Duties and Liabilities of the CPA* (Austin: Bureau of Business Research, University of Texas, 1976), pp. 16–18.

3. Ibid., p. 127.

4. Ibid., p. 177.

5. National Institute of Accountants, *CPA Review Business Law*, p. 6.

6. Statement on Auditing Standards (SAS) 16, paragraph 5 (New York: AICPA, 1977).

7. SAS 17, paragraph 13 (New York: AICPA, 1977).

8. The Commission on Auditors' Responsibilities established by AICPA in 1974.

9. See Statement on Quality Control Standard 1 (New York, AICPA, 1979).

10. SAS 20, paragraph 4 (New York: AICPA, 1977).

11. Causey, *Duties and Liabilities of the CPA*, p. 192.

12. SAS 4, paragraphs 19 and 20.

13. *The Week in Review*, Deloitte Haskins & Sells, June 6, 1980.

14. SAS 6 (New York: AICPA, 1975).

15. Ibid.

16. National Institute of Accountants, *CPA Review Business Law*, p. 6.

17. Ibid., p. 7.

18. Ibid.

19. Ibid., pp. 7, 8.

20. Ibid., p. 9.

21. Ibid.

22. See *Escott et al.* v. *Bar Chris Construction Corporation et al.* case (U.S. District Court for the Southern District of New York, 283 F. Supp. 643, 1968).

23. Section 24 of Securities Act of 1933.

24. Section 32(a) of Securities Exchange Act of 1934.

25. Section 10(b) of Securities Exchange Act of 1934.

26. Commission on Auditors' Responsibilities, *Report, Conclusions and Recommendations* (New York: Commission on Auditors' Responsibilities, 1978), pp. 47–48.

27. Ibid., p. 48.

28. Ibid., p. 48–49.
29. Ibid., p. 49–50.

QUESTIONS FOR CLASS DISCUSSION

Q21–1 What is the relationship between the benefits typically associated with an audit and the liability which the auditor takes in connection with the attest function?

Q21–2 In general how have the legal actions against accountants influenced the profession?

Q21–3 What is the difference between criminal liability and civil liability? Discuss.

Q21–4 What is the meaning of the term *negligence* as it is used in legal actions against accountants?

Q21–5 What is the difference between *ordinary negligence* and *gross negligence* as those terms are used in legal actions against accountants?

Q21–6 What is the difference between *fraud* and *constructive fraud?*

Q21–7 What is meant by the term *privity of contract?* How does it relate to actions seeking to recover damages from auditors?

Q21–8 What is meant by the term *expert testimony*? How can such testimony be used in connection with legal action against an auditor?

Q21–9 What is a class action suit? Discuss.

Q21–10 What is the difference between an action based on breach of contract and one based on tort action for negligence?

Q21–11 What, briefly, is the significance of the *Ultramares* v. *Touche* case?

Q21–12 What is the possibility of a public accountant being held liable to third parties for ordinary negligence in the performance of an audit?

Q21–13 What are some of the reasons for litigation against accountants? Discuss briefly.

Q21–14 What are the general provisions of the Foreign Corrupt Practices Act?

Q21–15 Do the provisions of SAS 30 allow the auditor to establish a client's compliance with the Foreign Corrupt Practices Act? Explain.

Q21–16 How should the auditor react to illegal acts of a client which have been determined to have occurred during the audit period? Discuss.

Q21–17 How has the accounting profession responded to the growing loss of credibility that has occurred because of judgments rendered against public accounting firms? Discuss.

Q21–18 What are some of the desirable and undesirable results that have come from the extensive litigation against members of the profession during the 1970s? Discuss briefly.

Q21–19 Can you name four suggestions that have been made to establish statutory limitations governing an auditor's liability to third parties? Are these limitations desirable? Discuss.

Q21–20 How has each of the following cases affected the auditing process? (1) The *Ultramares* v. *Touche* case; (2) the *McKesson & Robbins* case; (3) the *Bar Chris Construction Corporation* case; (4) the *Continental Vending* case.

Q21–21 Can an accountant be held liable for the discovery of fraud in connection with the preparation of unaudited financial statements? Discuss. (Your discussion should include a reference to the case most pertinent to this question.)

Q21–22 How has the *Equity Funding* case affected the activities of the accounting profession?

Q21–23 What is the significance of the *Ernst and Ernst* v. *Hochfelder* case? Discuss.

Q21–24 What is a related party transaction? Why is the auditor concerned with such transactions?

Q21–25 What is the responsibility of the auditor in connection with material related party transactions?

Q21–26 What is the difference between an accountant's expressed and implied contractual responsibilities to a client?

Q21–27 What is the difference between an accountant's civil liability under common law and his or her civil liability under the Securities Acts?

Q21–28 Do auditors subject themselves to the same potential liabilities relating to materials presented in supplementary disclosures of price level data and oil and gas reserves as they do for fair presentation of data included in the conventional financial statements? Discuss.

Q21–29 What is the auditor's responsibility for detection of fraud in the performance of an independent audit?

Q21–30 What difference is there between civil liability and criminal liability actions against auditors?

Q21–31 Under what circumstances may a CPA who prepares tax returns be subject to civil penalties? To criminal penalties? Discuss.

Q21–32 What are the recommendations of the Commission on Auditors' Responsibilities as they relate to the profession's response to the perils of our litigious age?

SHORT CASES

C21–1 Diana Jackson was a junior staff member of an accounting firm. She began the audit of the Bosco Corporation, which manufactured and sold expensive watches. In the middle of the audit, she resigned her position with the firm. The accounting firm hired another person to continue the audit of Bosco. Due to the changeover and the time pressure to finish the audit, the firm violated certain generally accepted auditing standards when they did not follow adequate procedures with respect to the physical inventory. Had the proper procedures been used during the examination, they would have discovered that watches worth more than $20,000 were missing. The employee who was stealing the watches was able to steal an additional $30,000 worth before the thefts were discovered six months after the completion of the audit.

Required:

Discuss the legal problems of the accounting firm as a result of the above facts.

(AICPA adapted)

C21–2 Briefly discuss the development of the common law regarding the liability of CPAs to third parties.

(AICPA adapted)

C21–3 The CPA firm of Martinson, Brinks & Sutherland, a partnership, was the auditor for Masco Corporation, a medium-sized wholesaler. Masco leased warehouse facilities and sought financing for leasehold improvements to these facilities. Masco assured its bank that the leasehold improvements would result in a more efficient and profitable operation. Based on these assurances, the bank granted Masco a line of credit.

The loan agreement required annual audited financial statements. Masco submitted to the bank its 19X5 audited financial statements, which showed an operating profit of $75,000; leasehold improvements of $250,000; and net worth of $350,000. In reliance thereon, the bank lent Masco $200,000. The audit report that accompanied the financial statements disclaimed an opinion because the cost of the leasehold improvements could not be determined from the company's records. The part of the audit report dealing with leasehold improvements reads as follows:

> Additions to fixed assets in 19X5 were found to include principally warehouse improvements. Practically all of this work was done by company employees and the cost of materials and overhead were paid by Masco. Unfortunately, fully complete detailed cost records were not kept of these leasehold improvements and no exact determination could be made as to the actual cost of said improvements. The total amount capitalized is set forth in note 4 to the financial statements.

In late 1976 Masco went out of business, at which time it was learned that the claimed leasehold improvements were totally fictitious. The labor expenses charged as leasehold improvements proved to be operating expenses. No item of building material cost had been recorded. No independent investigation of the existence of the leasehold improvements had been made by the auditors.

If the $250,000 had not been capitalized, the income statement would have shown a substantial loss from operations and the net worth would have been correspondingly decreased.

The bank has sustained a loss on its loan to Masco of $200,000 and now seeks to recover damages from the CPA firm, alleging that the accountants negligently audited the financial statements.

Required:

Answer the following, setting forth reasons for any conclusions stated.

a. Will the disclaimer of opinion absolve the CPA firm from liability?

b. Are the individual partners of Martinson, Brinks & Sutherland, who did not take part in the audit, liable?

(AICPA adapted)

C21–4 A CPA firm has been named as a defendant in a class action by purchasers of the shares of stock of the Newly Corporation. The offering was a public offering of securities within the meaning of the Securities Act of 1933. The plaintiffs alleged that the firm was either negligent or fraudulent in connection with the preparation of the audited financial statements that accompanied the registration statement filed with the SEC. Specifically, they allege that the CPA firm either intentionally disregarded, or failed to exercise reasonable care to discover, material facts which occurred subsequent to January 31, 19X8, the date of the auditor's report. The securities were sold to the public on March 16, 19X8. The plaintiffs have subpoenaed copies of the CPA firm's working papers. The CPA firm is considering refusing to relinquish the papers, asserting that they contain privileged communication between the CPA firm and its client. The CPA firm will, of course, defend on the merits, irrespective of the question regarding the working papers.

Required:

Answer the following, setting forth reasons for any conclusions stated.

a. Can the CPA firm rightfully refuse to surrender its working papers? (See Chapter 20.)

b. Discuss the liability of the CPA firm in respect to events which occur in the period between the date of the auditor's report and the effective date of the public offering of the securities.

(AICPA adapted)

C21–5 Justin Marcall is a limited partner of Guarcross, a limited partnership, and is suing a CPA firm that was retained by the limited partnership to perform auditing and tax return preparation services. Guarcross was formed for the purpose of investing in a diversified portfolio of risk capital securities. The partnership agreement included the following provisions:

> The initial capital contribution of each limited partner shall not be less than \$250,000; no partner may withdraw any part of his interest in the partnership, except at the end of any fiscal year upon giving written notice of such intention not less than 30 days prior to the end of such year; the books and records of the partnership shall be audited as of the end of the fiscal year by a certified public accountant designated by the general partners; and proper and complete books of account shall be kept and shall be open to inspection by any of the partners or his or her accredited representative.

Marcall's claim of malpractice against the CPA firm centers on the firm's alleged failure to comment, in its audit report, on the withdrawal by the general partners of

$2,000,000 of their $2,600,000 capital investment based on back-dated notices, and the lumping together of the $2,000,000 withdrawals with $49,000 in withdrawals by limited partners so that a reader of the financial statement would not be likely to realize that the two general partners have withdrawn a major portion of their investments.

The CPA firm's contention is that its contract was made with the limited partnership, not its partners. It further contends that since the CPA firm had no privity of contract with the third-party limited partners, the limited partners have no right of action for negligence.

Required:

Answer the following, setting forth reasons for any conclusions stated.

Discuss the various theories Marcall would rely upon in order to prevail in a lawsuit against the CPA firm.

(AICPA adapted)

C21–6 Farr & Madison, CPAs, audited Glamour, Inc. Their audit was deficient in several respects:

a. Farr & Madison failed to verify properly certain receivables which later proved to be fictitious.

b. With respect to other receivables, although they made a cursory check, they did not detect many accounts that were long overdue and obviously uncollectible.

c. No physical inventory was taken of the securities claimed to be in Glamour's possession, which in fact had been sold. Both the securities and cash received from the sales were listed on the balance sheet as assets.

There is no indication that Farr & Madison actually believed that the financial statements were false. Subsequent creditors, not known to Farr & Madison, are now suing, on the basis of the deficiencies in the audit described above. Farr & Madison moved to dismiss the lawsuit against it on the basis that the firm did not have actual knowledge of falsity and therefore did not commit fraud.

Required:

Answer the following, setting forth reasons for any conclusions stated.

May the creditors recover without demonstrating Farr & Madison had actual knowledge of falsity?

(AICPA adapted)

C21–7 For the first time in the history of federal income tax law, Congress enacted legislation in 1976 that imposed civil liabilities and penalties upon individuals who are guilty of certain misconduct in connection with their preparing income tax returns for a fee. Prior provisions of the Internal Revenue Code which dealt with criminal fraud remained unchanged.

Required:

Answer the following, setting forth reasons for any conclusions stated.

What potential civil liabilities and penalties to the United States government should the practitioner be aware of in connection with the improper preparation of a federal income tax return, and what types of conduct would give rise to these liabilities and penalties?

(AICPA adapted)

C21–8 Whitlow & Company is a brokerage firm registered under the Securities Exchange Act of 1934. The Act requires such a brokerage firm to file audited financial statements with the SEC annually. Mitchell & Moss, Whitlow's CPAs, performed the annual audit for the year ended December 31, 19X9, and rendered an unqualified opinion, which was filed with the SEC along with Whitlow's financial statements. During 1979, Charles, the president of Whitlow & Company, engaged in a huge embezzlement scheme that eventually bankrupted the firm. As a result, substantial losses were suffered by customers and shareholders of Whitlow & Company, including Thaxton, who had recently purchased several shares of stock of Whitlow & Company after reviewing the company's 19X9 audit report. Mitchell & Moss' audit was deficient; if they had complied with generally accepted auditing standards, the embezzlement would have been discovered. However, Mitchell & Moss had no knowledge of the embezzlement nor could their conduct be categorized as reckless.

Required:

Answer the following, setting forth reasons for any conclusions stated.

a. What liability to Thaxton, if any, does Mitchell & Moss have under the Securities Exchange Act of 1934?
b. What theory or theories of liability, if any, are available to Whitlow & Company's customers and shareholders under the common law?

(AICPA adapted)

C21–9 The Chriswell Corporation decided to raise additional long-term capital by issuing $5 million of 8-percent subordinated debentures to the public. May, Clark & Company, CPAs, the company's auditors, were engaged to examine the June 30, 19X2 financial statements which were included in the bond registration statement.

May, Clark & Company completed its examination and submitted an unqualified auditor's report dated July 15, 19X2. The registration statement was filed and later became effective on September 1, 19X2. On August 15 one of the partners of May, Clark & Company called on Chriswell Corporation and had lunch with the financial vice-president and the controller. He questioned both officials on the company's operations since June 30 and inquired whether there had been any material changes in the company's financial position since that date. Both officers assured him that everything had proceeded normally and that the financial condition of the company had not changed materially.

Unfortunately the officers' representation was not true. On July 30, a substantial debtor of the company failed to pay the $400,000 due on its account receivable and indicated to Chriswell that it would probably be forced into bankruptcy. This receivable was shown as a collateralized loan on the June 30 financial statements. It was secured by stock of the debtor corporation, which had a value in excess of the loan at the time the financial statements were prepared but was virtually worthless at the effective date of the registration statement. This $400,000 account receivable was material to the financial condition of Chriswell Corporation, and the market price of the subordinated debentures decreased by nearly 50 percent after the foregoing facts were disclosed.

The debenture holders of Chriswell are seeking recovery of their loss against all parties connected with the debenture registration.

Required:

Is May, Clark & Company liable to the Chriswell debenture holders under Section 11 of the Securities Act of 1933? Explain.

(AICPA adapted)

C21–10 Meglow Corporation manufactured ladies' dresses and blouses. Because its cash position was deteriorating, Meglow sought a loan from Bernardi Factors. Bernardi had previously extended $25,000 credit to Meglow but refused to lend any additional money without obtaining copies of Meglow's audited financial statements.

Meglow contacted the CPA firm of Watkins, Winslow & Watkins to perform the audit. In arranging for the examination, Meglow clearly indicated that its purpose was to satisfy Bernardi Factors as to the corporation's sound financial condition and thus to obtain an additional loan of $50,000. Watkins, Winslow & Watkins accepted the engagement, performed the examination in a negligent manner, and rendered an unqualified auditor's opinion. If an adequate examination had been performed, the financial statements would have been found to be misleading.

Meglow submitted the audited financial statements to Bernardi Factors and obtained an additional loan of $35,000. Bernardi refused to lend more than that amount. After several other factors also refused, Meglow finally was able to persuade Maxwell Department Stores, one of its customers, to lend the additional $15,000. Maxwell relied upon the financial statements examined by Watkins, Winslow & Watkins.

Meglow is now in bankruptcy, and Bernardi seeks to collect from Watkins, Winslow & Watkins the $60,000 it lent to Meglow. Maxwell seeks to recover from Watkins, Winslow & Watkins the $15,000 it lent Meglow.

Required:

Under common law

a. Will Bernardi recover? Explain.
b. Will Maxwell recover? Explain.

(AICPA adapted)

C21–11 Coopers and Miselle were engaged to perform the audit of Southwest Corporation, a large, publicly traded corporation that operated coin laundries throughout the southwestern United States. Carla Williams was president and owner of about 25 percent of the stock of Southwest, and she was president and owned about 26 percent of the stock of Easy Street Finance Corporation, an unconsolidated subsidiary of Southwest, which was not audited by Coopers and Miselle. Carla Williams was a flamboyant individual who enjoyed all of the things that money can buy. Not satisfied with her $150,000 per year salary, Williams decided that she would try to "make the companies pay off" for her.

Williams caused Southwest to issue notes payable to Easy Street, who then discounted the notes at Continental Bank and remitted the proceeds to Southwest. In an unrelated series of transactions, Williams then had Southwest advance cash to Easy Street (shown as a "Note Receivable" on Southwest's financial statements) and caused Easy Street to advance the funds to herself. Williams then used the "advanced" funds to invest in the stock market.

For the fiscal years 19X0 – 19X2 the financial statements of Southwest reflected the following for the notes receivable from, and notes payable to, Easy Street:

July 30	Receivable from Easy Street	Payable to Easy Street	Net Receivable (Payable)
19X0	400,000	1,000,000	(600,000)
19X1	850,000	800,000	50,000
19X2	3,500,000	1,000,000	2,500,000

Each year, the *net amounts* were reflected in the financial statements of Southwest under "Notes Receivable." Also, in 19X1 and 19X2, the amount shown as net receivable from Easy Street on Southwest's financial statements was also shown as "notes receivable from officer" on the financial statements of Easy Street.

Coopers and Miselle allowed the notes receivable and payable to be netted against each other in the financial statements for 19X0 and 19X1, respectively, because the amounts were deemed immaterial to the financial statements, which showed $10,000,000 in assets. When the net receivable became material in 19X2, the auditors realized that they had erred in the past but decided that since the SEC had not questioned the practice in the past (as well as the fact that it would be embarrassing for the firm to admit the mistake in 19X2), the practice would be continued.

In trying to determine the collectibility of Southwest's $3.5 million receivable from Easy Street in 19X2, the auditors were faced with another dilemma: since they were not engaged as the auditors of Easy Street, they had no access to the records of that company or to those of Williams, its president. However, since the auditors knew of Williams's arrangement with the companies, they decided that they could be assured as to the collectibility of the Easy Street receivable by requesting that Williams collateralize her payable to Easy Street with stock, which would then act as collateral for the Easy Street receivable on Southwest's financial statements. Williams agreed and immediately put up $3.5 million of Southwest Corporation stock against her obligation to easy Street.

Footnote disclosure of the above series of transactions on Southwest's 10-K annual report with the SEC under the Securities Exchange Act of 1934 included the following:

a. Williams was "an officer, director, and stockholder" of Easy Street (exact relationship was not described and her name was not mentioned).

b. Collateral securing the loan from Southwest to Easy Street consisted of "certain marketable securities," the fair market value of which was approximately $3.5 million.

Required:

a. What provisions, if any, of SAS 6 (on related party transactions) have been violated by Coopers and Miselle?

b. What generally accepted accounting principles have been violated by Southwest?
c. In your opinion, can the shareholders assert civil claims against Coopers and Miselle? Explain.
d. In your opinion, can Coopers and Miselle (or partners thereof) suffer criminal liability? Explain. What additional information might be helpful to you in answering this question?

PROBLEMS

P21–1 Select the best answer for each of the following items.

a. The most significant aspect of the *Continental Vending* case was that it
   (1) Created a more general awareness of the auditor's exposure to criminal prosecution.
   (2) Extended the auditor's responsibility for financial statements of subsidiaries.
   (3) Extended the auditor's responsibility for events after the end of the audit period.
   (4) Defined the auditor's common law responsibilities to third parties.

b. In connection with a law suit, a third party attempts to gain access to the auditor's working papers. The client's defense of privileged communication will be successful only to the extent it is protected by the
   (1) Auditor's acquiescence in use of this defense.
   (2) Common law.
   (3) AICPA Code of Professional Ethics.
   (4) State law.

c. The 1136 Tenants case was important chiefly because of its emphasis upon the legal liability of the CPA when associated with
   (1) A review of interim statements.
   (2) Unaudited financial statements.
   (3) An audit resulting in a disclaimer of opinion.
   (4) Letters for underwriters.

d. Which of the following best describes a trend in litigation involving CPAs?
   (1) A CPA can not render an opinion on a company unless the CPA has audited all affiliates of that company.
   (2) A CPA may not successfully assert as a defense that the CPA had no motive to be part of a fraud.
   (3) A CPA may be exposed to criminal as well as civil liability.
   (4) A CPA is primarily responsible for a client's footnotes in an annual report filed with the SEC.

e. Which of the following is an example of a related party transaction?
   (1) An action is taken by the directors of company A to provide additional compensation for vice-presidents in charge of the principal business functions of company A.
   (2) A long-term agreement is made by company A to provide merchandise or services to company B, a long-time, friendly competitor.
   (3) A short-term loan is granted to company A by a bank that has a depositor who is a member of the board of directors of company A.
   (4) A nonmonetary exchange occurs whereby company A exchanges property for

similar property owned by company B, an unconsolidated subsidiary of company A.

(AICPA adapted)

P21–2 A CPA firm was engaged to examine the financial statements of Martin Manufacturing Corporation for the year ending December 31, 19X2. The facts revealed that Martin was in need of cash to continue its operations and agreed to sell its common stock investment in a subsidiary through a private placement. The buyers insisted the proceeds be placed in escrow because of the possibility of a major contingent tax liability that might result from a pending government claim. The payment in escrow was completed in late November 19X2. The president of Martin told the audit partner that the proceeds from the sale of the subsidiary's common stock, held in escrow, should be shown on the balance sheet as an unrestricted current account receivable. The president was of the opinion that the government's claim was groundless and that Martin needed an "uncluttered" balance sheet and a "clean" auditor's opinion to obtain additional working capital from lenders. The audit partner agreed with the president and issued an unqualified opinion on the Martin financial statements, which did not refer to the contingent liability and did not properly describe the escrow arrangement.

The government's claim proved to be valid, and pursuant to the agreement with the buyers, the purchase price of the subsidiary was reduced by $450,000. This adverse development forced Martin into bankruptcy. The CPA firm is being sued for deceit (fraud) by several of Martin's unpaid creditors who extended credit in reliance on the CPA firm's unqualified opinion on Martin's financial statements.

Required:

a. Upon what facts are the creditors of Martin claiming deceit by the CPA firm?
b. Does the fact that the creditors do not have privity of contract with the CPA firm affect their ability to recover damages?
c. List the five general elements of common law deceit.
d. Will the creditors be able to recover from the CPA firm?

(AICPA adapted)

P21–3 Risk Capital Limited, a Delaware corporation, was considering the purchase of a substantial amount of the treasury stock held by Florida Sunshine Corporation, a closely held corporation. Initial discussions with the Florida Sunshine Corporation began late in 19X1.

Wilson and Wyatt, Florida Sunshine's accountants, regularly prepared quarterly and annual unaudited financial statements. The most recently prepared financial statements were for the year ended September 20, 19X2.

On November 15, 19X2, after protracted negotiations, Risk Capital agreed to purchase 100,000 shares of no par, Class A capital stock of Florida Sunshine at $12.50 per share. However, Risk Capital insisted upon audited statements for calendar year 19X2. The contract made available to Wilson & Wyatt specifically provided:

> Risk Capital shall have the right to rescind the purchase of said stock if the audited financial statements of Florida Sunshine for calendar year 19X2 show a material adverse change in the financial condition of the corporation.

The audited financial statements furnished to Florida Sunshine by Wilson and Wyatt showed no such material adverse change. Risk Capital relied on the audited statements and purchased the treasury stock of Florida Sunshine. It was subsequently discovered that as of the balance sheet date, the audited statements were incorrect and that in fact there had been a material adverse change in the financial condition of the corporation. Florida Sunshine is insolvent and Risk Capital will lose virtually its entire investment.

Risk Capital seeks recovery against Wilson and Wyatt.

Required:

Assuming that only ordinary negligence is proven, will Risk Capital prevail

a. Under the principles set forth in *Ultramares* v. *Touche?*

b. Under the principles set forth in *Rusch Factors* v. *Levin?*

(AICPA adapted)

INDEX